JAVA™

IN A NUTSHELL

Fifth Edition

David Flanagan

O'REILLY®

Beijing • Cambridge • Farnham • Köln • Paris • Sebastopol • Taipei • Tokyo

Java™ in a Nutshell, Fifth Edition
by David Flanagan

Published by O'Reilly Media, Inc., 1005 Gravenstein Highway North, Sebastopol, CA 95472.

O'Reilly books may be purchased for educational, business, or sales promotional use. Online editions are also available for most titles (*safari.oreilly.com*). For more information, contact our corporate/institutional sales department: (800) 998-9938 or *corporate@oreilly.com*.

Editors: Debra Cameron and Mike Loukides

Production Editor: Jamie Peppard

Cover Designer: Edie Freedman

Interior Designer: David Futato

Printing History:

February 1996: First Edition.

May 1997: Second Edition.

November 1999: Third Edition.

March 2002: Fourth Edition.

March 2005: Fifth Edition.

ISBN: 0-596-00773-6

[M] [7/05]

This book is dedicated to all

who teach peace and resist violence.

Table of Contents

Part II. API Quick Reference

Preface

This book is a desktop Java™ quick reference, designed to sit faithfully by your keyboard while you program. Part I of the book is a fast-paced, "no-fluff" introduction to the Java programming language and the core APIs of the Java platform. Part II is a quick reference section that succinctly details most classes and interfaces of those core APIs. The book covers Java 1.0, 1.1, 1.2, 1.3, 1.4, and 5.0.

Changes in the Fifth Edition

The fifth edition of this book covers Java 5.0. As its incremented version number attests, this new version of Java has a lot of new features. The three most significant new language features are generic types, enumerated types, and annotations, which are covered in a new chapter of their own. Experienced Java programmers who just want to learn about these new features can jump straight to Chapter 4.

Other new language features of Java 5.0 are:

- The `for/in` statement for easily iterating through arrays and collections (this statement is sometimes called "foreach").
- Autoboxing and autounboxing conversions to automatically convert back and forth between primitive values and their corresponding wrapper objects (such as `int` values and `Integer` objects) as needed.
- Varargs methods to define and invoke methods that accept an arbitrary number of arguments.
- Covariant returns to allow a subclass to override a superclass method and narrow the return type of the method.
- The `import static` declaration to import the `static` members of a type into the namespace.

Although each of these features is new in Java 5.0, none of them is large enough to merit a chapter of its own. Coverage of these features is integrated into Chapter 2.

In addition to these language changes, Java 5.0 also includes changes to the Java platform. Important enhancements include the following:

- The `java.util` collections classes have been converted to be generic types, providing support for typesafe collections. This is covered in Chapter 4.
- The `java.util` package also includes the new `Formatter` class. This class enables C-style formatted text output with `printf()` and `format()` methods. Examples are included in Chapter 5. The `java.util.Formatter` entry in the quick reference includes a detailed table of formatting options.
- The new package `java.util.concurrent` includes important utilities for threadsafe concurrent programming. Chapter 5 provides examples.
- `java.lang` has three new subpackages:
  - `java.lang.annotation`
  - `java.lang.instrument`
  - `java.lang.management`

  These packages support Java 5.0 annotations and the instrumentation, management, and monitoring of a running Java interpreter. Although their position in the `java.lang` hierarchy marks these packages as very important, they are not commonly used. Annotation examples are provided in Chapter 4, and a simple instrumentation and management example is found in Chapter 5.
- New packages have been added to the `javax.xml` hierarchy. `javax.xml.validation` supports document validation with schemas. `javax.xml.xpath` supports the XPath query language. And `javax.xml.namespace` provides simple support for XML namespaces. Validation and XPath examples are in Chapter 5.

In a mostly futile attempt to make room for this new material, I've had to make some cuts. I've removed coverage of the packages `java.beans`, `java.beans.beancontext`, `java.security.acl`, and `org.ietf.jgss` from the quick reference. JavaBeans standards have not caught on in core Java APIs and now appear to be relevant only for Swing and related graphical APIs. As such, they are no longer relevant in this book. The `java.security.acl` package has been deprecated since Java 1.2 and I've taken this opportunity to remove it. And the `org.ietf.jgss` package is of interest to only a very narrow subset of readers.

Along with removing coverage of `java.beans` from the quick reference section, I've also cut the chapter on JavaBeans from Part I of this book. The material on JavaBeans naming conventions from that chapter remains useful, however, and has been moved into Chapter 7.

Contents of This Book

The first eight chapters of this book document the Java language, the Java platform, and the Java development tools that are supplied with Sun's Java Development Kit (JDK). The first five chapters are essential; the next three cover topics of interest to some, but not all, Java programmers.

Chapter 1: Introduction

This chapter is an overview of the Java language and the Java
explains the important features and benefits of Java. It conclu
example Java program and walks the new Java programmer through
by line.

Chapter 2: Java Syntax from the Ground Up

This chapter explains the details of the Java programming language, including some of the Java 5.0 language changes. It is a long and detailed chapter that does not assume substantial programming experience. Experienced Java programmers can use it as a language reference. Programmers with substantial experience with languages such as C and C++ should be able to pick up Java syntax quickly by reading this chapter; beginning programmers with only a modest amount of experience should be able to learn Java programming by studying this chapter carefully.

Chapter 3: Object-Oriented Programming in Java

This chapter describes how the basic Java syntax documented in Chapter 2 is used to write object-oriented programs in Java. The chapter assumes no prior experience with OO programming. It can be used as a tutorial by new programmers or as a reference by experienced Java programmers.

Chapter 4: Java 5.0 Language Features

This chapter documents the three biggest new features of Java 5.0: generic types, enumerated types, and annotations. If you read previous editions of this book, you might want to skip directly to this chapter.

Chapter 5: The Java Platform

This chapter is an overview of the essential Java APIs covered in this book. It contains numerous short examples that demonstrate how to perform common tasks with the classes and interfaces that comprise the Java platform. Programmers who are new to Java (and especially those who learn best by example) should find this a valuable chapter.

Chapter 6: Java Security

This chapter explains the Java security architecture that allows untrusted code to run in a secure environment from which it cannot do any malicious damage to the host system. It is important for all Java programmers to have at least a passing familiarity with Java security mechanisms.

Chapter 7: Programming and Documentation Conventions

This chapter documents important and widely adopted Java programming conventions, including JavaBeans naming conventions. It also explains how you can make your Java code self-documenting by including specially formatted documentation comments.

Chapter 8: Java Development Tools

Sun's JDK includes a number of useful Java development tools, most notably the Java interpreter and the Java compiler. This chapter documents those tools.

These first eight chapters teach you the Java language and get you up and running with the Java APIs. Part II of the book is a succinct but detailed API reference formatted for optimum ease of use. Please be sure to read *How to Use This Quick*

Reference in Part II; it explains how to get the most out of the quick reference section. Also, please note that the quick reference chapters are followed by one final chapter called "Class, Method, and Field Index." This special index allows you to look up the name of a type and find the package in which it is defined or to look up the name of a method or field and find the type in which it it is defined.

Related Books

O'Reilly publishes an entire series of books on Java programming, including several companion books to this one. The companion books are:

Java Examples in a Nutshell
: This book contains hundreds of complete, working examples illustrating many common Java programming tasks using the core, enterprise, and desktop APIs. *Java Examples in a Nutshell* is like Chapter 4 of this book, but greatly expanded in breadth and depth, and with all the code snippets fully fleshed out into working examples. This is a particularly valuable book for readers who learn well by experimenting with existing code.

Java Enterprise in a Nutshell
: This book is a succinct tutorial for the Java "Enterprise" APIs such as JDBC, RMI, JNDI, and CORBA. It also cover enterprise tools such as Hibernate, Struts, Ant, JUnit, and XDoclet.

J2ME in a Nutshell
: This book is a tutorial and quick reference for the graphics, networking, and database APIs of the Java 2 Micro Edition (J2ME) platform.

You can find a complete list of Java books from O'Reilly at *http://java.oreilly.com/*. Books that focus on the core Java APIs, as this one does, include:

Learning Java, by Pat Niemeyer and Jonathan Knudsen
: This book is a comprehensive tutorial introduction to Java, with an emphasis on client-side Java programming.

Java Swing, by Marc Loy, Robert Eckstein, Dave Wood, James Elliott, and Brian Cole
: This book provides excellent coverage of the Swing APIs and is a must-read for GUI developers.

Java Threads, by Scott Oaks and Henry Wong
: Java makes multithreaded programming easy, but doing it right can still be tricky. This book explains everything you need to know.

Java I/O, by Elliotte Rusty Harold
: Java's stream-based input/output architecture is a thing of beauty. This book covers it in the detail it deserves.

Java Network Programming, by Elliotte Rusty Harold
: This book documents the Java networking APIs in detail.

Java Security, by Scott Oaks
: This book explains the Java access-control mechanisms in detail and also documents the authentication mechanisms of digital signatures and message digests.

Java Cryptography, by Jonathan Knudsen
: This book provides thorough coverage of the Java Cryptography Extension, the `javax.crypto.*` packages, and cryptography in Java.

Examples Online

The examples in this book are available online and can be downloaded from the home page for the book at *http://www.oreilly.com/catalog/javanut5*. You may also want to visit this site for any important notes or errata that have been published there.

Conventions Used in This Book

We use the following formatting conventions in this book:

Italic
: Used for emphasis and to signify the first use of a term. Italic is also used for commands, email addresses, web sites, FTP sites, and file and directory names.

Bold
: Occasionally used to refer to particular keys on a computer keyboard or to portions of a user interface, such as the **Back** button or the **Options** menu.

`Constant Width`
: Used for all Java code as well as for anything that you would type literally when programming, including keywords, data types, constants, method names, variables, class names, and interface names.

`Constant Width Italic`
: Used for the names of function arguments and generally as a placeholder to indicate an item that should be replaced with an actual value in your program. Sometimes used to refer to a conceptual section or line of code as in *`statement`*.

Franklin Gothic Book Condensed
: Used for the Java class synopses in the quick reference section. This very narrow font allows us to fit a lot of information on the page without a lot of distracting line breaks. This font is also used for code entities in the descriptions in the quick reference section.

Franklin Gothic Demi Condensed
: Used for highlighting class, method, field, property, and constructor names in the quick reference section, which makes it easier to scan the class synopses.

Franklin Gothic Book Condensed Italic
: Used for method parameter names and comments in the quick reference section.

Request for Comments

Please address comments and questions concerning this book to the publisher:

O'Reilly Media, Inc.
1005 Gravenstein Highway North
Sebastopol, CA 95472
(800) 998-9938 (in the United States or Canada)
(707) 829-0515 (international or local)
(707) 829-1014 (fax)

There is a web page for this book, which lists errata, examples, and any additional information. You can access this page at:

http://www.oreilly.com/catalog/javanut5

To ask technical questions or comment on this book, send email to:

bookquestions@oreilly.com

For more information about books, conferences, Resource Centers, and the O'Reilly Network, see the O'Reilly web site at:

http://www.oreilly.com

How the Quick Reference Is Generated

For the curious reader, this section explains a bit about how the quick reference material in *Java in a Nutshell* and related books is created.

As Java has evolved, so has my system for generating Java quick reference material. The current system is part of a larger commercial documentation browser system I'm developing (visit *http://www.davidflanagan.com/Jude* for more information about it). The program works in two passes: the first pass collects and organizes the API information, and the second pass outputs that information in the form of quick reference chapters.

The first pass begins by reading the class files for all of the classes and interfaces to be documented. Almost all of the API information in the quick reference is available in these class files. The notable exception is the names of method arguments, which are not stored in class files. These argument names are obtained by parsing the Java source file for each class and interface. Where source files are not available, I obtain method argument names by parsing the API documentation generated by *javadoc*. The parsers I use to extract API information from the source files and *javadoc* files are created using the Antlr parser generator developed by Terence Parr. (See *http://www.antlr.org* for details on this very powerful programming tool.)

Once the API information has been obtained by reading class files, source files, and *javadoc* files, the program spends some time sorting and cross-referencing everything. Then it stores all the API information into a single large data file.

The second pass reads API information from that data file and outputs quick reference chapters using a custom XML doctype. Once I've generated the XML output, I hand it off to the production team at O'Reilly. In the past, these XML documents were converted to troff and formatted with GNU *groff* using a highly customized macro package. In this edition, the chapters were converted from XML to Framemaker instead, using in-house production tools.

Acknowledgments

Many people helped in the creation of this book, and I am grateful to them all. I am indebted to the many, many readers of the first four editions who wrote in with comments, suggestions, bug reports, and praise. Their many small contributions are scattered throughout the book. Also, my apologies to those who made many good suggestions that could not be incorporated into this edition.

Deb Cameron was the editor for the fifth edition. Deb edited not only the material that was new in this edition but also made the time to carefully read over the old material, giving it a much-needed updating. Deb was patient when my work on this book veered off in an unexpected direction and provided steady guidance to help get me back on track. The fourth edition was edited by Bob Eckstein, a careful editor with a great sense of humor. Paula Ferguson, a friend and colleague, was the editor of the first three editions of this book. Her careful reading and practical suggestions made the book stronger, clearer, and more useful.

As usual, I've had a crack team of technical reviewers for this edition of the book. Gilad Bracha of Sun reviewed the material on generic types. Josh Bloch, a former Sun employee who is now at Google, reviewed the material on enumerated types and annotations. Josh was also a reviewer for the third and fourth editions of the book, and his helpful input has been an invaluable resource for me. Josh's book *Effective Java Programming Guide* (Addison Wesley) is highly recommended. Neal Gafter, who, like Josh, left Sun for Google, answered many questions about annotations and generics. David Biesack of SAS, Changshin Lee of the Korean company Tmax Soft, and Tim Peierls were colleagues of mine on the JSR-201 expert group that was responsible for a number of language changes in Java 5.0. They reviewed the generics and enumerated type material. Joseph Bowbeer, Brian Goetz, and Bill Pugh were members of the JSR-166 or JSR-133 expert groups and helped me to understand threading and concurrency issues behind the `java.util.concurrency` package. Iris Garcia of Sun answered my questions about the new `java.util.Formatter` class that she authored. My sincere thanks go to each of these engineers. Any mistakes that remain in the book are, of course, my own.

The fourth edition was also reviewed by a number of engineers from Sun and elsewhere. Josh Bloch reviewed material on assertions and the Preferences API. Bob Eckstein reviewed XML material. Graham Hamilton reviewed the Logging API material. Ron Hitchens reviewed the New I/O material. Jonathan Knudsen (who is also an O'Reilly author) reviewed the JSSE and Certification Path material. Charlie Lai reviewed the JAAS material. Ram Marti reviewed the JGSS material. Philip Milne, a former Sun employee, now at Dresdner Kleinwort Wasserstein, reviewed the material on the JavaBeans persistence mechanism. Mark Reinhold reviewed the `java.nio` material. Mark deserves special thanks for having been a reviewer for the second, third, and fourth editions of this book. Andreas Sterbenz and Brad Wetmore reviewed the JSSE material.

The third edition also benefited greatly from the contributions of reviewers who are intimately familiar with the Java platform. Joshua Bloch, one of the primary authors of the Java collections framework, reviewed my descriptions of the collections classes and interfaces. Josh was also helpful in discussing the `Timer` and `TimerTask` classes of Java 1.3 with me. Mark Reinhold, creator of the `java.lang.ref` package, explained the package to me and reviewed my documentation of it. Scott Oaks reviewed my descriptions of the Java security and cryptography classes and interfaces. The documentation of the `javax.crypto` package and its subpackages was also reviewed by Jon Eaves. Finally, Chapter 1 was improved by the comments of reviewers who were *not* already familiar with the Java platform: Christina Byrne reviewed it from the standpoint of a novice programmer, and Judita Byrne of Virginia Power offered her comments as a professional COBOL programmer.

For the second edition, John Zukowski reviewed my Java 1.1 AWT quick reference material, and George Reese reviewed most of the remaining new material. The second edition was also blessed with a "dream team" of technical reviewers from Sun. John Rose, the author of the Java inner class specification, reviewed the chapter on inner classes. Mark Reinhold, author of the new character stream classes in `java.io`, reviewed my documentation of these classes. Nakul Saraiya, the designer of the Java Reflection API, reviewed my documentation of the `java.lang.reflect` package.

Mike Loukides provided high-level direction and guidance for the first edition of the book. Eric Raymond and Troy Downing reviewed that first edition—they helped spot my errors and omissions and offered good advice on making the book more useful to Java programmers.

The O'Reilly production team has done its usual fine work of creating a book out of the electronic files I submit. My thanks to them all.

As always, my thanks and love to Christie.

David Flanagan
http://www.davidflanagan.com
February 2005

I

Introducing Java

Part I is an introduction to the Java language and the Java platform. These chapters provide enough information for you to get started using Java right away.

1
Introduction

Welcome to Java. This chapter begins by explaining what Java is and describing some of the features that distinguish it from other programming languages. Next, it outlines the structure of this book, with special emphasis on what is new in Java 5.0. Finally, as a quick tutorial introduction to the language, it walks you through a simple Java program you can type, compile, and run.

What Is Java?

In discussing Java, it is important to distinguish between the Java programming language, the Java Virtual Machine, and the Java platform. The Java programming language is the language in which Java applications, applets, servlets, and components are written. When a Java program is compiled, it is converted to byte codes that are the portable machine language of a CPU architecture known as the Java Virtual Machine (also called the Java VM or JVM). The JVM can be implemented directly in hardware, but it is usually implemented in the form of a software program that interprets and executes byte codes.

The Java platform is distinct from both the Java language and Java VM. The Java platform is the predefined set of Java classes that exist on every Java installation; these classes are available for use by all Java programs. The Java platform is also sometimes referred to as the Java runtime environment or the core Java APIs (application programming interfaces). The Java platform can be extended with optional packages (formerly called standard extensions). These APIs exist in some Java installations but are not guaranteed to exist in all installations.

The Java Programming Language

The Java programming language is a state-of-the-art, object-oriented language that has a syntax similar to that of C. The language designers strove to make the Java language powerful, but, at the same time, they tried to avoid the overly complex features that have bogged down other object-oriented languages like C++. By keeping the language simple, the designers also made it easier for programmers to write robust, bug-free code. As a result of its elegant design and next-generation features, the Java language has proved popular with programmers, who typically find it a pleasure to work with Java after struggling with more difficult, less powerful languages.

Java 5.0, the latest version of the Java language,* includes a number of new language features, most notably generic types, which increase both the complexity and the power of the language. Most experienced Java programmers have welcomed the new features, despite the added complexity they bring.

The Java Virtual Machine

The Java Virtual Machine, or Java interpreter, is the crucial piece of every Java installation. By design, Java programs are portable, but they are only portable to platforms to which a Java interpreter has been ported. Sun ships VM implementations for its own Solaris operating system and for Microsoft Windows and Linux platforms. Many other vendors, including Apple and various commercial Unix vendors, provide Java interpreters for their platforms. The Java VM is not only for desktop systems, however. It has been ported to set-top boxes and handheld devices that run Windows CE and PalmOS.

Although interpreters are not typically considered high-performance systems, Java VM performance has improved dramatically since the first versions of the language. The latest releases of Java run remarkably fast. Of particular note is a VM technology called *just-in-time* (JIT) compilation whereby Java byte codes are converted on the fly into native platform machine language, boosting execution speed for code that is run repeatedly.

The Java Platform

The Java platform is just as important as the Java programming language and the Java Virtual Machine. All programs written in the Java language rely on the set of predefined classes† that comprise the Java platform. Java classes are organized into related groups known as *packages*. The Java platform defines packages for functionality such as input/output, networking, graphics, user-interface creation, security, and much more.

It is important to understand what is meant by the term platform. To a computer programmer, a platform is defined by the APIs he can rely on when writing programs. These APIs are usually defined by the operating system of the target computer. Thus, a programmer writing a program to run under Microsoft Windows must use a different set of APIs than a programmer writing the same program for a Unix-based system. In this respect, Windows and Unix are distinct platforms.

* Java 5.0 represents a significant change in version numbering for Sun. The previous version of Java is Java 1.4 so you may sometimes hear Java 5.0 informally referred to as Java 1.5.

† A *class* is a module of Java code that defines a data structure and a set of methods (also called procedures, functions, or subroutines) that operate on that data.

Java is not an operating system. Nevertheless, the Java platform provides APIs with a comparable breadth and depth to those defined by an operating system. With the Java platform, you can write applications in Java without sacrificing the advanced features available to programmers writing native applications targeted at a particular underlying operating system. An application written on the Java platform runs on any operating system that supports the Java platform. This means you do not have to create distinct Windows, Macintosh, and Unix versions of your programs, for example. A single Java program runs on all these operating systems, which explains why "Write once, run anywhere" is Sun's motto for Java.

The Java platform is not an operating system, but for programmers, it is an alternative development target and a very popular one at that. The Java platform reduces programmers' reliance on the underlying operating system, and, by allowing programs to run on top of any operating system, it increases end users' freedom to choose an operating system.

Versions of Java

As of this writing, there have been six major versions of Java. They are:

Java 1.0
: This was the first public version of Java. It contained 212 classes organized in 8 packages. It was simple and elegant but is now completely outdated.

Java 1.1
: This release of Java more than doubled the size of the Java platform to 504 classes in 23 packages. It introduced nested types (or "inner classes"), an important change to the Java language itself, and included significant performance improvements in the Java VM. This version is outdated.

Java 1.2
: This was a very significant release of Java; it tripled the size of the Java platform to 1,520 classes in 59 packages. Important additions included the Collections API for working with sets, lists, and maps of objects and the Swing API for creating graphical user interfaces. Because of the many new features included in the 1.2 release, the platform was rebranded as "the Java 2 Platform." The term "Java 2" was simply a trademark, however, and not an actual version number for the release.

Java 1.3
: This was primarily a maintenance release, focused on bug fixes, stability, and performance improvements (including the high-performance "HotSpot" virtual machine). Additions to the platform included the Java Naming and Directory Interface (JNDI) and the Java Sound APIs, which were previously available as extensions to the platform. The most interesting classes in this release were probably `java.util.Timer` and `java.lang.reflect.Proxy`. In total, Java 1.3 contains 1,842 classes in 76 packages.

Java 1.4
: This was another big release, adding important new functionality and increasing the size of the platform by 62% to 2,991 classes and interfaces in 135 packages. New features included a high-performance, low-level I/O API;

support for pattern matching with regular expressions; a logging API; a user preferences API; new Collections classes; an XML-based persistence mechanism for JavaBeans; support for XML parsing using both the DOM and SAX APIs; user authentication with the Java Authentication and Authorization Service (JAAS) API; support for secure network connections using the SSL protocol; support for cryptography; a new API for reading and writing image files; an API for network printing; a handful of new GUI components in the Swing API; and a simplified drag-and-drop architecture for Swing. In addition to these platform changes, the 1.4 release introduced an `assert` statement to the Java language.

Java 5.0

The most recent release of Java introduces a number of changes to the core language itself including generic types, enumerated types, annotations, varargs methods, autoboxing, and a new `for/in` statement. Because of the major language changes, the version number was incremented. This release would logically be known as "Java 2.0" if Sun had not already used the term "Java 2" for marketing Java 1.2.

In addition to the language changes, Java 5.0 includes a number of additions to the Java platform as well. This release includes 3562 classes and interfaces in 166 packages. Notable additions include utilities for concurrent programming, a remote management framework, and classes for the remote management and instrumentation of the Java VM itself.

See the Preface for a list of changes in this edition of the book, including pointers to coverage of the new language and platform features.

To write programs in Java, you must obtain the Java Development Kit (JDK). Sun releases a new version of the JDK for each new version of Java. Don't confuse the JDK with the Java Runtime Environment (JRE). The JRE contains everything you need to run Java programs, but it does not contain the tools you need to develop Java programs (primarily the compiler).

In addition to the Standard Edition of Java used by most Java developers and documented in this book, Sun has also released the Java 2 Platform, Enterprise Edition (or J2EE) for enterprise developers and the Java 2 Platform, Micro Edition (J2ME) for consumer electronic systems, such as handheld PDAs and cellular telephones. See *Java Enterprise in a Nutshell* and *Java Micro Edition in a Nutshell* (both by O'Reilly) for more information on these other editions.

Key Benefits of Java

Why use Java at all? Is it worth learning a new language and a new platform? This section explores some of the key benefits of Java.

Write Once, Run Anywhere

Sun identifies "Write once, run anywhere" as the core value proposition of the Java platform. Translated from business jargon, this means that the most important promise of Java technology is that you have to write your application only once—for the Java platform—and then you'll be able to run it *anywhere*.

Anywhere, that is, that supports the Java platform. Fortunately, Java support is becoming ubiquitous. It is integrated into practically all major operating systems. It is built into the popular web browsers, which places it on virtually every Internet-connected PC in the world. It is even being built into consumer electronic devices such as television set-top boxes, PDAs, and cell phones.

Security

Another key benefit of Java is its security features. Both the language and the platform were designed from the ground up with security in mind. The Java platform allows users to download untrusted code over a network and run it in a secure environment in which it cannot do any harm: untrusted code cannot infect the host system with a virus, cannot read or write files from the hard drive, and so forth. This capability alone makes the Java platform unique.

Java 1.2 took the security model a step further. It made security levels and restrictions highly configurable and extended them beyond applets. As of Java 1.2, any Java code, whether it is an applet, a servlet, a JavaBeans component, or a complete Java application, can be run with restricted permissions that prevent it from doing harm to the host system.

The security features of the Java language and platform have been subjected to intense scrutiny by security experts around the world. In the earlier days of Java, security-related bugs, some of them potentially serious, were found and promptly fixed. Because of the strong security promises Java makes, it is big news when a new security bug is found. No other mainstream platform can make security guarantees nearly as strong as those Java makes. No one can say that Java security holes will not be found in the future, but if Java's security is not yet perfect, it has been proven strong enough for practical day-to-day use and is certainly better than any of the alternatives.

Network-Centric Programming

Sun's corporate motto has always been "The network is the computer." The designers of the Java platform believed in the importance of networking and designed the Java platform to be network-centric. From a programmer's point of view, Java makes it easy to work with resources across a network and to create network-based applications using client/server or multitier architectures.

Dynamic, Extensible Programs

Java is both dynamic and extensible. Java code is organized in modular object-oriented units called *classes*. Classes are stored in separate files and are loaded into the Java interpreter only when needed. This means that an application can decide as it is running what classes it needs and can load them when it needs them. It also means that a program can dynamically extend itself by loading the classes it needs to expand its functionality.

The network-centric design of the Java platform means that a Java application can dynamically extend itself by loading new classes over a network. An application that takes advantage of these features ceases to be a monolithic block of code. Instead, it becomes an interacting collection of independent software components. Thus, Java enables a powerful new metaphor of application design and development.

Internationalization

The Java language and the Java platform were designed from the start with the rest of the world in mind. When it was created, Java was the only commonly used programming language that had internationalization features at its core rather than tacked on as an afterthought. While most programming languages use 8-bit characters that represent only the alphabets of English and Western European languages, Java uses 16-bit Unicode characters that represent the phonetic alphabets and ideographic character sets of the entire world. Java's internationalization features are not restricted to just low-level character representation, however. The features permeate the Java platform, making it easier to write internationalized programs with Java than it is with any other environment.

Performance

As described earlier, Java programs are compiled to a portable intermediate form known as byte codes, rather than to native machine-language instructions. The Java Virtual Machine runs a Java program by interpreting these portable bytecode instructions. This architecture means that Java programs are faster than programs or scripts written in purely interpreted languages, but Java programs are typically slower than C and C++ programs compiled to native machine language. Keep in mind, however, that although Java programs are compiled to byte code, not all of the Java platform is implemented with interpreted byte codes. For efficiency, computationally intensive portions of the Java platform—such as the string-manipulation methods—are implemented using native machine code.

Although early releases of Java suffered from performance problems, the speed of the Java VM has improved dramatically with each new release. The VM has been highly tuned and optimized in many significant ways. Furthermore, most current implementations include a just-in-time (JIT) compiler, which converts Java byte codes to native machine instructions on the fly. Using sophisticated JIT compilers, Java programs can execute at speeds comparable to the speeds of native C and C++ applications.

Java is a portable, interpreted language; Java programs run almost as fast as native, nonportable C and C++ programs. Performance used to be an issue that made some programmers avoid using Java. With the improvements made in Java 1.2, 1.3, 1.4, and 5.0, performance issues should no longer keep anyone away.

Programmer Efficiency and Time-to-Market

The final, and perhaps most important, reason to use Java is that programmers like it. Java is an elegant language combined with a powerful and (usually) well-designed set of APIs. Programmers enjoy programming in Java and are often amazed at how quickly they can get results with it. Because Java is a simple and elegant language with a well-designed, intuitive set of APIs, programmers write better code with fewer bugs than for other platforms, thus reducing development time.

An Example Program

Example 1-1 shows a Java program to compute factorials.* Note that the numbers at the beginning of each line are not part of the program; they are there for ease of reference when we dissect the program line-by-line.

Example 1-1. Factorial.java: a program to compute factorials

```
/**
 * This program computes the factorial of a number
 */
public class Factorial {                           // Define a class
  public static void main(String[] args) {  // The program starts here
    int input = Integer.parseInt(args[0]);  // Get the user's input
    double result = factorial(input);       // Compute the factorial
    System.out.println(result);             // Print out the result
  }                                         // The main() method ends here

  public static double factorial(int x) {   // This method computes x!
    if (x < 0)                              // Check for bad input
      return 0.0;                           // If bad, return 0
    double fact = 1.0;                      // Begin with an initial value
    while(x > 1) {                          // Loop until x equals 1
      fact = fact * x;                      // Multiply by x each time
      x = x - 1;                            // And then decrement x
    }                                       // Jump back to start of loop
    return fact;                            // Return the result
  }                                         // factorial() ends here
}                                           // The class ends here
```

Compiling and Running the Program

Before we look at how the program works, we must first discuss how to run it. In order to compile and run the program, you need a Java development kit (JDK) of some sort. Sun Microsystems created the Java language and ships a free JDK for its Solaris operating system and also for Linux and Microsoft Windows platforms.† At the time of this writing, the current version of Sun's JDK is available for download from *http://java.sun.com*. Be sure to get the JDK and not the Java Runtime Environment. The JRE enables you to run existing Java programs, but not to write and compile your own.

* The factorial of an integer is the product of the number and all positive integers less than the number. So, for example, the factorial of 4, which is also written 4!, is 4 times 3 times 2 times 1, or 24. By definition, 0! is 1.

† Other companies, such as Apple, have licensed and ported the JDK to their operating systems. In Apple's case, this arrangement leads to a delay in the latest JDK being available on that platform.

The Sun JDK is not the only Java programming environment you can use. *gcj*, for example, is a Java compiler released under the GNU general public license. A number of companies sell Java IDEs (integrated development environments), and high-quality open-source IDEs are also available. This book assumes that you are using Sun's JDK and its accompanying command-line tools. If you are using a product from some other vendor, be sure to read that vendor's documentation to learn how to compile and run a simple program, like that shown in Example 1-1.

Once you have a Java programming environment installed, the first step towards running our program is to type it in. Using your favorite text editor, enter the program as it is shown in Example 1-1.* Omit the line numbers, which are just for reference. Note that Java is a case-sensitive language, so you must type lowercase letters in lowercase and uppercase letters in uppercase. You'll notice that many of the lines of this program end with semicolons. It is a common mistake to forget these characters, but the program won't work without them, so be careful! You can omit everything from // to the end of a line: those are *comments* that are there for your benefit and are ignored by Java.

When writing Java programs, you should use a text editor that saves files in plain-text format, not a word processor that supports fonts and formatting and saves files in a proprietary format. My favorite text editor on Unix systems is *Emacs*. If you use a Windows system, you might use *Notepad* or *WordPad*, if you don't have a more specialized programmer's editor (versions of GNU Emacs, for example, are available for Windows). If you are using an IDE, it should include an appropriate text editor; read the documentation that came with the product. When you are done entering the program, save it in a file named *Factorial.java*. This is important; the program will not work if you save it by any other name.

After writing a program like this one, the next step is to compile it. With Sun's JDK, the Java compiler is known as *javac*. *javac* is a command-line tool, so you can only use it from a terminal window, such as an MS-DOS window on a Windows system or an *xterm* window on a Unix system. Compile the program by typing the following command:

```
C:\> javac Factorial.java
```

If this command prints any error messages, you probably got something wrong when you typed in the program. If it does not print any error messages, however, the compilation has succeeded, and *javac* creates a file called *Factorial.class*. This is the compiled version of the program.

Once you have compiled a Java program, you must still run it. Java programs are not compiled into native machine language, so they cannot be executed directly by the system. Instead, they are run by another program known as the Java interpreter. In Sun's JDK, the interpreter is a command-line program named, appropriately enough, *java*. To run the factorial program, type:

```
C:\> java Factorial 4
```

* I recommend that you type this example in by hand, to get a feel for the language. If you *really* don't want to, however, you can download this, and all examples in the book, from *http://www.oreilly.com/catalog/javanut5/*.

java is the command to run the Java interpreter, *Factorial* is the name of the Java program we want the interpreter to run, and *4* is the input data—the number we want the interpreter to compute the factorial of. The program prints a single line of output, telling us that the factorial of 4 is 24:

```
C:\> java Factorial 4
24.0
```

Congratulations! You've just written, compiled, and run your first Java program. Try running it again to compute the factorials of some other numbers.

Analyzing the Program

Now that you have run the factorial program, let's analyze it line by line to see what makes a Java program tick.

Comments

The first three lines of the program are a comment. Java ignores them, but they tell a human programmer what the program does. A comment begins with the characters `/*` and ends with the characters `*/`. Any amount of text, including multiple lines of text, may appear between these characters. Java also supports another type of comment, which you can see in lines 4 through 21. If the characters `//` appear in a Java program, Java ignores those characters and any other text that appears between those characters and the end of the line.

Defining a class

Line 4 is the first line of Java code. It says that we are defining a class named `Factorial`. This explains why the program had to be stored in a file named *Factorial.java*. That filename indicates that the file contains Java source code for a class named `Factorial`. The word `public` is a *modifier*; it says that the class is publicly available and that anyone may use it. The open curly-brace character (`{`) marks the beginning of the body of the class, which extends all the way to line 21, where we find the matching close curly-brace character (`}`). The program contains a number of pairs of curly braces; the lines are indented to show the nesting within these braces.

A class is the fundamental unit of program structure in Java, so it is not surprising that the first line of our program declares a class. All Java programs are classes, although some programs use many classes instead of just one. Java is an object-oriented programming language, and classes are a fundamental part of the object-oriented paradigm. Each class defines a unique kind of object. Example 1-1 is not really an object-oriented program, however, so I'm not going to go into detail about classes and objects here. That is the topic of Chapter 3. For now, all you need to understand is that a class defines a set of interacting *members*. Those members may be fields, methods, or other classes. The `Factorial` class contains two members, both of which are methods. They are described in upcoming sections.

Defining a method

Line 5 begins the definition of a *method* of our `Factorial` class. A method is a named chunk of Java code. A Java program can call, or *invoke*, a method to execute the code in it. If you have programmed in other languages, you have probably seen methods before, but they may have been called functions, procedures, or subroutines. The interesting thing about methods is that they have *parameters* and *return values*. When you call a method, you pass it some data you want it to operate on, and it returns a result to you. A method is like an algebraic function:

```
y = f(x)
```

Here, the mathematical function `f` performs some computation on the value represented by `x` and returns a value, which we represent by `y`.

To return to line 5, the `public` and `static` keywords are modifiers. `public` means the method is publicly accessible; anyone can use it. The meaning of the `static` modifier is not important here; it is explained in Chapter 3. The `void` keyword specifies the return value of the method. In this case, it specifies that this method does not have a return value.

The word `main` is the name of the method. `main` is a special name.* When you run the Java interpreter, it reads in the class you specify, then looks for a method named `main()`.† When the interpreter finds this method, it starts running the program at that method. When the `main()` method finishes, the program is done, and the Java interpreter exits. In other words, the `main()` method is the main entry point into a Java program. It is not actually sufficient for a method to be named `main()`, however. The method must be declared `public static void` exactly as shown in line 5. In fact, the only part of line 5 you can change is the word `args`, which you can replace with any word you want. You'll be using this line in all of your Java programs, so go ahead and commit it to memory now!

Following the name of the `main()` method is a list of method parameters in parentheses. This `main()` method has only a single parameter. `String[]` specifies the type of the parameter, which is an array of strings (i.e., a numbered list of strings of text). `args` specifies the name of the parameter. In the algebraic equation `f(x)`, `x` is simply a way of referring to an unknown value. `args` serves the same purpose for the `main()` method. As we'll see, the name `args` is used in the body of the method to refer to the unknown value that is passed to the method.

* All Java programs that are run directly by the Java interpreter must have a `main()` method. Programs of this sort are often called *applications*. It is possible to write programs that are not run directly by the interpreter, but are dynamically loaded into some other already running Java program. Examples are *applets*, which are programs run by a web browser, and *servlets*, which are programs run by a web server. Applets are discussed in *Java Foundation Classes in a Nutshell* (O'Reilly) while servlets are discussed in *Java Enterprise in a Nutshell* (O'Reilly). In this book, we consider only applications.

† By convention, when this book refers to a method, it follows the name of the method by a pair of parentheses. As you'll see, parentheses are an important part of method syntax, and they serve here to keep method names distinct from the names of classes, fields, variables, and so on.

As I've just explained, the main() method is a special one that is called by the Java interpreter when it starts running a Java class (program). When you invoke the Java interpreter like this:

```
C:\> java Factorial 4
```

the string "4" is passed to the main( ) method as the value of the parameter named args. More precisely, an array of strings containing only one entry, 4, is passed to main(). If we invoke the program like this:

```
C:\> java Factorial 4 3 2 1
```

then an array of four strings, 4, 3, 2, and 1, is passed to the main( ) method as the value of the parameter named args. Our program looks only at the first string in the array, so the other strings are ignored.

Finally, the last thing on line 5 is an open curly brace. This marks the beginning of the body of the main() method, which continues until the matching close curly brace on line 9. Methods are composed of *statements*, which the Java interpreter executes in sequential order. In this case, lines 6, 7, and 8 are three statements that compose the body of the main() method. Each statement ends with a semicolon to separate it from the next. This is an important part of Java syntax; beginning programmers often forget the semicolons.

Declaring a variable and parsing input

The first statement of the main() method, line 6, declares a variable and assigns a value to it. In any programming language, a *variable* is simply a symbolic name for a value. We've already seen that, in this program, the name args refers to the parameter value passed to the main() method. Method parameters are one type of variable. It is also possible for methods to declare additional "local" variables. Methods can use local variables to store and reference the intermediate values they use while performing their computations.

This is exactly what we are doing on line 6. That line begins with the words int input, which declare a variable named input and specify that the variable has the type int; that is, it is an integer. Java can work with several different types of values, including integers, real or floating-point numbers, characters (e.g., letters and digits), and strings of text. Java is a *strongly typed* language, which means that all variables must have a type specified and can refer only to values of that type. Our input variable always refers to an integer, so it cannot refer to a floating-point number or a string. Method parameters are also typed. Recall that the args parameter had a type of String[ ].

Continuing with line 6, the variable declaration int input is followed by the = character. This is the assignment operator in Java; it sets the value of a variable. When reading Java code, don't read = as "equals," but instead read it as "is assigned the value." As we'll see in Chapter 2, there is a different operator for "equals."

The value assigned to our input variable is Integer.parseInt(args[0]). This is a method invocation. This first statement of the main( ) method invokes another method whose name is Integer.parseInt( ). As you might guess, this method "parses" an integer; that is, it converts a string representation of an integer, such as 4, to the integer itself. The Integer.parseInt() method is not part of the Java language, but it is a core part of the Java API or Application Programming Interface. Every Java program can use the powerful set of classes and methods defined by this core API. The second half of this book is a quick reference that documents that core API.

When you call a method, you pass values (called *arguments*) that are assigned to the corresponding parameters defined by the method, and the method returns a value. The argument passed to Integer.parseInt() is args[0]. Recall that args is the name of the parameter for main(); it specifies an array (or list) of strings. The elements of an array are numbered sequentially, and the first one is always numbered 0. We care about only the first string in the args array, so we use the expression args[0] to refer to that string. When we invoke the program as shown earlier, line 6 takes the first string specified after the name of the class, 4, and passes it to the method named Integer.parseInt(). This method converts the string to the corresponding integer and returns the integer as its return value. Finally, this returned integer is assigned to the variable named input.

Computing the result

The statement on line 7 is a lot like the statement on line 6. It declares a variable and assigns a value to it. The value assigned to the variable is computed by invoking a method. The variable is named result, and it has a type of double. double means a double-precision floating-point number. The variable is assigned a value that is computed by the factorial() method. The factorial() method, however, is not part of the standard Java API. Instead, it is defined as part of our program by lines 11 through 19. The argument passed to factorial() is the value referred to by the input variable that was computed on line 6. We'll consider the body of the factorial() method shortly, but you can surmise from its name that this method takes an input value, computes the factorial of that value, and returns the result.

Displaying output

Line 8 simply calls a method named System.out.println(). This commonly used method is part of the core Java API; it causes the Java interpreter to print out a value. In this case, the value that it prints is the value referred to by the variable named result. This is the result of our factorial computation. If the input variable holds the value 4, the result variable holds the value 24, and this line prints out that value.

The System.out.println() method does not have a return value. There is no variable declaration or = assignment operator in this statement since there is no value to assign to anything. Another way to say this is that, like the main() method of line 5, System.out.println() is declared void.

The end of a method

Line 9 contains only a single character, }. This marks the end of the method. When the Java interpreter gets here, it is through executing the main() method, so it stops running. The end of the main() method is also the end of the *variable scope* for the input and result variables declared within main() and for the args parameter of main(). These variable and parameter names have meaning only within the main() method and cannot be used elsewhere in the program unless other parts of the program declare different variables or parameters that happen to have the same name.

Blank lines

Line 10 is a blank line. You can insert blank lines and spaces anywhere in a program, and you should use them liberally to make the program readable. A blank line appears here to separate the main() method from the factorial() method that begins on line 11. You'll notice that the program also uses whitespace to indent the various lines of code. This kind of indentation is optional; it emphasizes the structure of the program and greatly enhances the readability of the code.

Another method

Line 11 begins the definition of the factorial() method that was used by the main() method. Compare this line to line 5 to note its similarities and differences. The factorial() method has the same public and static modifiers. It takes a single integer parameter, which we call x. Unlike the main() method, which had no return value (void), factorial() returns a value of type double. The open curly brace marks the beginning of the method body, which continues past the nested braces on lines 15 and 18 to line 20, where the matching close curly brace is found. The body of the factorial() method, like the body of the main() method, is composed of statements, which are found on lines 12 through 19.

Checking for valid input

In the main() method, we saw variable declarations, assignments, and method invocations. The statement on line 12 is different. It is an if statement, which executes another statement conditionally. We saw earlier that the Java interpreter executes the three statements of the main() method one after another. It always executes them in exactly that way, in exactly that order. An if statement is a flow-control statement; it can affect the way the interpreter runs a program.

The if keyword is followed by a parenthesized expression and a statement. The Java interpreter first evaluates the expression. If it is true, the interpreter executes the statement. If the expression is false, however, the interpreter skips the statement and goes to the next one. The condition for the if statement on line 12 is x < 0. It checks whether the value passed to the factorial() method is less than zero. If it is, this expression is true, and the statement on line 13 is executed. Line 12 does not end with a semicolon because the statement on line 13 is part of the if statement. Semicolons are required only at the end of a statement.

Line 13 is a return statement. It says that the return value of the factorial() method is 0.0. return is also a flow-control statement. When the Java interpreter sees a return, it stops executing the current method and returns the specified value immediately. A return statement can stand alone, but in this case, the return statement is part of the if statement on line 12. The indentation of line 13 helps emphasize this fact. (Java ignores this indentation, but it is very helpful for humans who read Java code!) Line 13 is executed only if the expression on line 12 is `true`.

Before we move on, we should pull back a bit and talk about why lines 12 and 13 are necessary in the first place. It is an error to try to compute a factorial for a negative number, so these lines make sure that the input value `x` is valid. If it is not valid, they cause `factorial()` to return a consistent invalid result, `0.0`.

An important variable

Line 14 is another variable declaration; it declares a variable named `fact` of type `double` and assigns it an initial value of `1.0`. This variable holds the value of the factorial as we compute it in the statements that follow. In Java, variables can be declared anywhere; they are not restricted to the beginning of a method or block of code.

Looping and computing the factorial

Line 15 introduces another type of statement: the `while` loop. Like an `if` statement, a `while` statement consists of a parenthesized expression and a statement. When the Java interpreter sees a `while` statement, it evaluates the associated expression. If that expression is `true`, the interpreter executes the statement. The interpreter repeats this process, evaluating the expression and executing the statement if the expression is `true`, until the expression evaluates to `false`. The expression on line 15 is `x > 1`, so the `while` statement loops *while* the parameter `x` holds a value that is greater than 1. Another way to say this is that the loop continues *until* `x` holds a value less than or equal to 1. We can assume from this expression that if the loop is ever going to terminate, the value of `x` must somehow be modified by the statement that the loop executes.

The major difference between the `if` statement on lines 12–13 and the `while` loop on lines 15–18 is that the statement associated with the `while` loop is a *compound statement*. A compound statement is zero or more statements grouped between curly braces. The `while` keyword on line 15 is followed by an expression in parentheses and then by an open curly brace. This means that the body of the loop consists of all statements between that opening brace and the closing brace on line 18. Earlier in the chapter, I said that all Java statements end with semicolons. This rule does not apply to compound statements, however, as you can see by the lack of a semicolon at the end of line 18. The statements inside the compound statement (lines 16 and 17) do end with semicolons, of course.

The body of the `while` loop consists of the statements on line 16 and 17. Line 16 multiplies the value of `fact` by the value of `x` and stores the result back into `fact`. Line 17 is similar. It subtracts 1 from the value of `x` and stores the result back into `x`. The * character on line 16 is important: it is the multiplication *operator*. And, as you can probably guess, the - on line 17 is the subtraction operator. An operator is a key part of Java syntax: it performs a computation on one or two *operands* to produce a new value. Operands and operators combine to form *expressions*, such as `fact * x` or `x - 1`. We've seen other operators in the program. Line 15, for example, uses the greater-than operator (>) in the expression `x > 1`, which compares the value of the variable x to 1. The value of this expression is a boolean truth value—either true or false, depending on the result of the comparison.

To understand this while loop, it is helpful to think like the Java interpreter. Suppose we are trying to compute the factorial of 4. Before the loop starts, fact is 1.0, and x is 4. After the body of the loop has been executed once—after the first *iteration*—fact is 4.0, and x is 3. After the second iteration, fact is 12.0, and x is 2. After the third iteration, fact is 24.0, and x is 1. When the interpreter tests the loop condition after the third iteration, it finds that x > 1 is no longer true, so it stops running the loop, and the program resumes at line 19.

Returning the result

Line 19 is another return statement, like the one we saw on line 13. This one does not return a constant value like 0.0, but instead returns the value of the fact variable. If the value of x passed into the factorial() function is 4, then, as we saw earlier, the value of fact is 24.0, so this is the value returned. Recall that the factorial() method was invoked on line 7 of the program. When this return statement is executed, control returns to line 7, where the return value is assigned to the variable named result.

Exceptions

If you've made it all the way through the line-by-line analysis of Example 1-1, you are well on your way to understanding the basics of the Java language.* It is a simple but nontrivial program that illustrates many of the features of Java. There is one more important feature of Java programming I want to introduce, but it is one that does not appear in the program listing itself. Recall that the program computes the factorial of the number you specify on the command line. What happens if you run the program without specifying a number?

```
C:\> java Factorial
java.lang.ArrayIndexOutOfBoundsException: 0
        at Factorial.main(Factorial.java:6)
C:\>
```

And what happens if you specify a value that is not a number?

```
C:\> java Factorial ten
java.lang.NumberFormatException: ten
        at java.lang.Integer.parseInt(Integer.java)
        at java.lang.Integer.parseInt(Integer.java)
        at Factorial.main(Factorial.java:6)
C:\>
```

* If you didn't understand all the details of this factorial program, don't worry. We'll cover the details of the Java language a lot more thoroughly in subsequent chapters. However, if you feel like you didn't understand any of the line-by-line analysis, you may also find that the upcoming chapters are over your head. In that case, you should probably go elsewhere to learn the basics of the Java language and return to this book to solidify your understanding, and, of course, to use as a reference. One resource you may find useful in learning the language is Sun's online Java tutorial, available at *http://java.sun.com/docs/books/tutorial*.

In both cases, an error occurs or, in Java terminology, an *exception* is thrown. When an exception is thrown, the Java interpreter prints a message that explains what type of exception it was and where it occurred (both exceptions above occurred on line 6). In the first case, the exception is thrown because there are no strings in the args list, meaning we asked for a nonexistent string with `args[0]`. In the second case, the exception is thrown because `Integer.parseInt()` cannot convert the string "ten" to a number. We'll see more about exceptions in Chapter 2 and learn how to handle them gracefully as they occur.

2
Java Syntax from the Ground Up

This chapter is a terse but comprehensive introduction to Java syntax. It is written primarily for readers who are new to the language but have at least some previous programming experience. Determined novices with no prior programming experience may also find it useful. If you already know Java, you should find it a useful language reference. The chapter includes comparisons of Java to C and C++ for the benefit of programmers coming from those languages.

This chapter documents the syntax of Java programs by starting at the very lowest level of Java syntax and building from there, covering increasingly higher orders of structure. It covers:

- The characters used to write Java programs and the encoding of those characters.
- Literal values, identifiers, and other tokens that comprise a Java program.
- The data types that Java can manipulate.
- The operators used in Java to group individual tokens into larger expressions.
- Statements, which group expressions and other statements to form logical chunks of Java code.
- Methods (also called functions, procedures, or subroutines), which are named collections of Java statements that can be invoked by other Java code.
- Classes, which are collections of methods and fields. Classes are the central program element in Java and form the basis for object-oriented programming. Chapter 3 is devoted entirely to a discussion of classes and objects.
- Packages, which are collections of related classes.
- Java programs, which consist of one or more interacting classes that may be drawn from one or more packages.

The syntax of most programming languages is complex, and Java is no exception. In general, it is not possible to document all elements of a language without referring to other elements that have not yet been discussed. For example, it is not really possible to explain in a meaningful way the operators and statements supported by Java without referring to objects. But it is also not possible to document objects thoroughly without referring to the operators and statements of the language. The process of learning Java, or any language, is therefore an iterative one. If you are new to Java (or a Java-style programming language), you may find that you benefit greatly from working through this chapter and the next *twice*, so that you can grasp the interrelated concepts.

Java Programs from the Top Down

Before we begin our bottom-up exploration of Java syntax, let's take a moment for a top-down overview of a Java program. Java programs consist of one or more files, or *compilation units*, of Java source code. Near the end of the chapter, we describe the structure of a Java file and explain how to compile and run a Java program. Each compilation unit begins with an optional `package` declaration followed by zero or more `import` declarations. These declarations specify the namespace within which the compilation unit will define names, and the namespaces from which the compilation unit imports names. We'll see `package` and `import` again in "Packages and the Java Namespace" later in this chapter.

The optional `package` and `import` declarations are followed by zero or more reference type definitions. These are typically `class` or `interface` definitions, but in Java 5.0 and later, they can also be `enum` definitions or annotation definitions. The general features of reference types are covered later in this chapter, and detailed coverage of the various kinds of reference types is in Chapters 3 and 4.

Type definitions include members such as fields, methods, and constructors. Methods are the most important type member. Methods are blocks of Java code comprised of *statements*. Most statements include *expressions*, which are built using *operators* and values known as *primitive data types*. Finally, the keywords used to write statements, the punctuation characters that represent operators, and the literals values that appear in a program are all *tokens*, which are described next. As the name of this section implies, this chapter moves from describing the smallest units, tokens, to progressively larger units. Since the concepts build upon one another, we recommend reading this chapter sequentially.

Lexical Structure

This section explains the lexical structure of a Java program. It starts with a discussion of the Unicode character set in which Java programs are written . It then covers the tokens that comprise a Java program, explaining comments, identifiers, reserved words, literals, and so on.

The Unicode Character Set

Java programs are written using Unicode. You can use Unicode characters anywhere in a Java program, including comments and identifiers such as variable names. Unlike the 7-bit ASCII character set, which is useful only for English, and the 8-bit ISO Latin-1 character set, which is useful only for major Western European languages, the Unicode character set can represent virtually every written language in common use on the planet. 16-bit Unicode characters are typically written to files using an encoding known as UTF-8, which converts the 16-bit characters into a stream of bytes. The format is designed so that plain ASCII text (and the 7-bit characters of Latin-1) are valid UTF-8 byte streams. Thus, you can simply write plain ASCII programs, and they will work as valid Unicode.

If you do not use a Unicode-enabled text editor, or if you do not want to force other programmers who view or edit your code to use a Unicode-enabled editor, you can embed Unicode characters into your Java programs using the special Unicode escape sequence `\uxxxx`, in other words, a backslash and a lowercase u, followed by four hexadecimal characters. For example, `\u0020` is the space character, and `\u03c0` is the character π.

Unicode 3.1 and above, used in Java 5.0 and later, includes "supplementary characters" that require 21 bits to represent. 16-bit encodings of Unicode characters represent these supplementary characters using a *surrogate pair*, which is a sequence of two 16-bit characters taken from a special reserved range of the 16-bit encoding space. If you ever need to include one of these (rarely used) supplementary characters in Java source code, use two `\u` sequences to represent the surrogate pair. (Details of surrogate pair encoding are beyond the scope of this book, however.)

Case-Sensitivity and Whitespace

Java is a case-sensitive language. Its keywords are written in lowercase and must always be used that way. That is, `While` and `WHILE` are not the same as the `while` keyword. Similarly, if you declare a variable named `i` in your program, you may not refer to it as `I`.

Java ignores spaces, tabs, newlines, and other whitespace, except when it appears within quoted characters and string literals. Programmers typically use whitespace to format and indent their code for easy readability, and you will see common indentation conventions in the code examples of this book.

Comments

Comments are natural-language text intended for human readers of a program. They are ignored by the Java compiler. Java supports three types of comments. The first type is a single-line comment, which begins with the characters `//` and continues until the end of the current line. For example:

```
int i = 0;   // Initialize the loop variable
```

The second kind of comment is a multiline comment. It begins with the characters `/*` and continues, over any number of lines, until the characters `*/`. Any text between the `/*` and the `*/` is ignored by the Java compiler. Although this style of comment is typically used for multiline comments, it can also be used for single-line comments. This type of comment cannot be nested (i.e., one `/* */` comment cannot appear within another). When writing multiline comments, programmers often use extra `*` characters to make the comments stand out. Here is a typical multiline comment:

```
/*
 * First, establish a connection to the server.
 * If the connection attempt fails, quit right away.
 */
```

The third type of comment is a special case of the second. If a comment begins with /**, it is regarded as a special *doc comment*. Like regular multiline comments, doc comments end with */ and cannot be nested. When you write a Java class you expect other programmers to use, use doc comments to embed documentation about the class and each of its methods directly into the source code. A program named *javadoc* extracts these comments and processes them to create online documentation for your class. A doc comment can contain HTML tags and can use additional syntax understood by *javadoc*. For example:

```
/**
 * Upload a file to a web server.
 *
 * @param file The file to upload.
 * @return <tt>true</tt> on success,
 *         <tt>false</tt> on failure.
 * @author David Flanagan
 */
```

See Chapter 7 for more information on the doc comment syntax and Chapter 8 for more information on the *javadoc* program.

Comments may appear between any tokens of a Java program, but may not appear within a token. In particular, comments may not appear within double-quoted string literals. A comment within a string literal simply becomes a literal part of that string.

Reserved Words

The following words are reserved in Java: they are part of the syntax of the language and may not be used to name variables, classes, and so forth.

```
abstract  const     final       int        public        throw
assert    continue  finally     interface  return        throws
boolean   default   float       long       short         transient
break     do        for         native     static        true
byte      double    goto        new        strictfp      try
case      else      if          null       super         void
catch     enum      implements  package    switch        volatile
char      extends   import      private    synchronized  while
class     false     instanceof  protected  this
```

We'll meet each of these reserved words again later in this book. Some of them are the names of primitive types and others are the names of Java statements, both of which are discussed later in this chapter. Still others are used to define classes and their members (see Chapter 3).

Note that `const` and `goto` are reserved but aren't actually used in the language. `strictfp` was added in Java 1.2, `assert` was added in Java 1.4, and `enum` was added in Java 5.0.

Identifiers

An *identifier* is simply a name given to some part of a Java program, such as a class, a method within a class, or a variable declared within a method. Identifiers may be of any length and may contain letters and digits drawn from the entire Unicode character set. An identifier may not begin with a digit, however, because the compiler would then think it was a numeric literal rather than an identifier.

In general, identifiers may not contain punctuation characters. Exceptions include the ASCII underscore (_) and dollar sign (`$`) as well as other Unicode currency symbols such as £ and ¥. Currency symbols are intended for use in automatically generated source code, such as code produced by parser generators. By avoiding the use of currency symbols in your own identifiers you don't have to worry about collisions with automatically generated identifiers. Formally, the characters allowed at the beginning of and within an identifier are defined by the methods `isJavaIdentifierStart()` and `isJavaIdentifierPart()` of the class `java.lang.Character`.

The following are examples of legal identifiers:

```
i    x1    theCurrentTime    the_current_time    θ
```

Literals

Literals are values that appear directly in Java source code. They include integer and floating-point numbers, characters within single quotes, strings of characters within double quotes, and the reserved words `true`, `false` and `null`. For example, the following are all literals:

```
1    1.0    '1'    "one"    true    false    null
```

The syntax for expressing numeric, character, and string literals is detailed in "Primitive Data Types" later in this chapter.

Punctuation

Java also uses a number of punctuation characters as tokens. The Java Language Specification divides these characters (somewhat arbitrarily) into two categories, separators and operators. Separators are:

```
(  )  {  }  [  ]  <  >  :  ;  ,  .  @
```

Operators are:

```
+    -    *    /    %    &    |    ^    <<    >>    >>>
+=   -=   *=   /=   %=   &=   |=   ^=   <<=   >>=   >>>=
=    ==   !=   <    <=   >    >=
!    ~    &&   ||   ++   --   ?    :
```

We'll see separators throughout the book, and will cover each operator individually in "Expressions and Operators" later in this chapter.

Primitive Data Types

Java supports eight basic data types known as *primitive types* as secribed in Table 2-1. The primitive types include a boolean type, a character type, four integer types, and two floating-point types. The four integer types and the two floating-point types differ in the number of bits that represent them and therefore in the range of numbers they can represent. The next section summarizes these primitive data types. In addition to these primitive types, Java supports nonprimitive data types such as classes, interfaces, and arrays. These composite types are known as reference types, which are introduced in "Reference Types" later in this chapter.

Table 2-1. Java primitive data types

Type	Contains	Default	Size	Range
`boolean`	`true` or `false`	`false`	1 bit	NA
`char`	Unicode character	`\u0000`	16 bits	`\u0000` to `\uFFFF`
`byte`	Signed integer	0	8 bits	–128 to 127
`short`	Signed integer	0	16 bits	–32768 to 32767
`int`	Signed integer	0	32 bits	–2147483648 to 2147483647
`long`	Signed integer	0	64 bits	–9223372036854775808 to 9223372036854775807
`float`	IEEE 754 floating point	0.0	32 bits	±1.4E-45 to ±3.4028235E+38
`double`	IEEE 754 floating point	0.0	64 bits	±4.9E-324 to ±1.7976931348623157E+308

The boolean Type

The `boolean` type represents truth values. This type has only two possible values, representing the two boolean states: on or off, yes or no, true or false. Java reserves the words `true` and `false` to represent these two boolean values.

C and C++ programmers should note that Java is quite strict about its `boolean` type: `boolean` values can never be converted to or from other data types. In particular, a `boolean` is not an integral type, and integer values cannot be used in place of a `boolean`. In other words, you cannot take shortcuts such as the following in Java:

```
if (o) {
    while(i) {
    }
}
```

Instead, Java forces you to write cleaner code by explicitly stating the comparisons you want:

```
if (o != null) {
    while(i != 0) {
    }
}
```

The char Type

The `char` type represents Unicode characters. It surprises many experienced programmers to learn that Java `char` values are 16 bits long, but in practice this fact is totally transparent. To include a character literal in a Java program, simply place it between single quotes (apostrophes):

```
char c = 'A';
```

You can, of course, use any Unicode character as a character literal, and you can use the \u Unicode escape sequence. In addition, Java supports a number of other escape sequences that make it easy both to represent commonly used nonprinting ASCII characters such as newline and to escape certain punctuation characters that have special meaning in Java. For example:

```
char tab = '\t', apostrophe = '\'', nul = '\000', aleph='\u05D0';
```

Table 2-2 lists the escape characters that can be used in char literals. These characters can also be used in string literals, which are covered in the next section.

Table 2-2. Java escape characters

Escape sequence	Character value
\b	Backspace
\t	Horizontal tab
\n	Newline
\f	Form feed
\r	Carriage return
\"	Double quote
\'	Single quote
\\	Backslash
xxx	The Latin-1 character with the encoding *xxx*, where *xxx* is an octal (base 8) number between 000 and 377. The forms *x* and *xx* are also legal, as in '\0', but are not recommended because they can cause difficulties in string constants where the escape sequence is followed by a regular digit.
\u*xxxx*	The Unicode character with encoding *xxxx*, where *xxxx* is four hexadecimal digits. Unicode escapes can appear anywhere in a Java program, not only in character and string literals.

char values can be converted to and from the various integral types. Unlike byte, short, int, and long, however, char is an unsigned type. The Character class defines a number of useful static methods for working with characters, including isDigit(), isJavaLetter(), isLowerCase(), and toUpperCase().

The Java language and its char type were designed with Unicode in mind. The Unicode standard is evolving, however, and each new version of Java adopts the latest version of Unicode. Java 1.4 used Unicode 3.0 and Java 5.0 adopts Unicode 4.0. This is significant because Unicode 3.1 was the first release to include characters whose encodings, or *codepoints*, do not fit in 16 bits. These supplementary characters, which are mostly infrequently used Han (Chinese) ideographs, occupy 21 bits and cannot be represented in a single char value. Instead, you must use an int value to hold the codepoint of a supplementary character, or you must encode it into a so-called "surrogate pair" of two char values. Unless you commonly write programs that use Asian languages, you are unlikely to encounter any supplementary characters. If you do anticipate having to process characters that do not fit into a char, Java 5.0 has added methods to the Character, String, and related classes for working with text using int codepoints.

Strings

In addition to the char type, Java also has a data type for working with strings of text (usually simply called *strings*). The String type is a class, however, and is not one of the primitive types of the language. Because strings are so commonly used, though, Java does have a syntax for including string values literally in a program. A String literal consists of arbitrary text within double quotes. For example:

```
"Hello, world"
"'This' is a string!"
```

String literals can contain any of the escape sequences that can appear as char literals (see Table 2-2). Use the \" sequence to include a double-quote within a String literal. Since String is a reference type, string literals are described in more detail in "Object Literals" later in this chapter. Chapter 5 demonstrates some of the ways you can work with String objects in Java.

Integer Types

The integer types in Java are byte, short, int, and long. As shown in Table 2-1, these four types differ only in the number of bits and, therefore, in the range of numbers each type can represent. All integral types represent signed numbers; there is no unsigned keyword as there is in C and C++.

Literals for each of these types are written exactly as you would expect: as a string of decimal digits, optionally preceded by a minus sign.* Here are some legal integer literals:

```
0
1
123
-42000
```

Integer literals can also be expressed in hexadecimal or octal notation. A literal that begins with 0x or 0X is taken as a hexadecimal number, using the letters A to F (or a to f) as the additional digits required for base-16 numbers. Integer literals beginning with a leading 0 are taken to be octal (base-8) numbers and cannot include the digits 8 or 9. Java does not allow integer literals to be expressed in binary (base-2) notation. Legal hexadecimal and octal literals include:

```
0xff              // Decimal 255, expressed in hexadecimal
0377              // The same number, expressed in octal (base 8)
0xCAFEBABE        // A magic number used to identify Java class files
```

* Technically, the minus sign is an operator that operates on the literal, but is not part of the literal itself. Also, all integer literals are 32-bit int values unless followed by the letter L, in which case they are 64-bit long values. There is no special syntax for byte and short literals, but int literals are usually converted to these shorter types as needed. For example, in the following code

```
byte b = 123;
```

123 is a 32-bit int literal that is automatically converted (without requiring a cast) to a byte in the assignment statement.

Integer literals are 32-bit int values unless they end with the character L or l, in which case they are 64-bit long values:

```
1234        // An int value
1234L       // A long value
0xffL       // Another long value
```


Integer arithmetic in Java is modular, which means that it never produces an overflow or an underflow when you exceed the range of a given integer type. Instead, numbers just wrap around. For example:

```
byte b1 = 127, b2 = 1;        // Largest byte is 127
byte sum = (byte)(b1 + b2);   // Sum wraps to -128, which is the smallest byte
```

Neither the Java compiler nor the Java interpreter warns you in any way when this occurs. When doing integer arithmetic, you simply must ensure that the type you are using has a sufficient range for the purposes you intend. Integer division by zero and modulo by zero are illegal and cause an ArithmeticException to be thrown.

Each integer type has a corresponding wrapper class: Byte, Short, Integer, and Long. Each of these classes defines MIN_VALUE and MAX_VALUE constants that describe the range of the type. The classes also define useful static methods, such as Byte.parseByte( ) and Integer.parseInt( ), for converting strings to integer values.

Floating-Point Types

Real numbers in Java are represented by the float and double data types. As shown in Table 2-1, float is a 32-bit, single-precision floating-point value, and double is a 64-bit, double-precision floating-point value. Both types adhere to the IEEE 754-1985 standard, which specifies both the format of the numbers and the behavior of arithmetic for the numbers.

Floating-point values can be included literally in a Java program as an optional string of digits, followed by a decimal point and another string of digits. Here are some examples:

```
123.45
0.0
.01
```

Floating-point literals can also use exponential, or scientific, notation, in which a number is followed by the letter e or E (for exponent) and another number. This second number represents the power of ten by which the first number is multiplied. For example:

```
1.2345E02      // 1.2345 × 10^2, or 123.45
1e-6           // 1 × 10^-6, or 0.000001
6.02e23        // Avogadro's Number: 6.02 × 10^23
```

Floating-point literals are double values by default. To include a float value literally in a program, follow the number with f or F:

```
double d = 6.02E23;
float f = 6.02e23f;
```

Floating-point literals cannot be expressed in hexadecimal or octal notation.

Most real numbers, by their very nature, cannot be represented exactly in any finite number of bits. Thus, it is important to remember that float and double values are only approximations of the numbers they are meant to represent. A float is a 32-bit approximation, which results in at least 6 significant decimal digits, and a double is a 64-bit approximation, which results in at least 15 significant digits. In practice, these data types are suitable for most real-number computations.

In addition to representing ordinary numbers, the float and double types can also represent four special values: positive and negative infinity, zero, and NaN. The infinity values result when a floating-point computation produces a value that overflows the representable range of a float or double. When a floating-point computation underflows the representable range of a float or a double, a zero value results. The Java floating-point types make a distinction between positive zero and negative zero, depending on the direction from which the underflow occurred. In practice, positive and negative zero behave pretty much the same. Finally, the last special floating-point value is NaN, which stands for "not-a-number." The NaN value results when an illegal floating-point operation, such as 0.0/0.0, is performed. Here are examples of statements that result in these special values:

```
double inf = 1.0/0.0;             // Infinity
double neginf = -1.0/0.0;         // -Infinity
double negzero = -1.0/inf;        // Negative zero
double NaN = 0.0/0.0;             // Not-a-Number
```

Because the Java floating-point types can handle overflow to infinity and underflow to zero and have a special NaN value, floating-point arithmetic never throws exceptions, even when performing illegal operations, like dividing zero by zero or taking the square root of a negative number.

The float and double primitive types have corresponding classes, named Float and Double. Each of these classes defines the following useful constants: MIN_VALUE, MAX_VALUE, NEGATIVE_INFINITY, POSITIVE_INFINITY, and NaN.

The infinite floating-point values behave as you would expect. Adding or subtracting any finite value to or from infinity, for example, yields infinity. Negative zero behaves almost identically to positive zero, and, in fact, the == equality operator reports that negative zero is equal to positive zero. One way to distinguish negative zero from positive, or regular, zero is to divide by it. 1.0/0.0 yields positive infinity, but 1.0 divided by negative zero yields negative infinity. Finally, since NaN is not-a-number, the == operator says that it is not equal to any other number, including itself! To check whether a float or double value is NaN, you must use the Float.isNaN() and Double.isNaN() methods.

Primitive Type Conversions

Java allows conversions between integer values and floating-point values. In addition, because every character corresponds to a number in the Unicode encoding, char values can be converted to and from the integer and floating-point types. In fact, boolean is the only primitive type that cannot be converted to or from another primitive type in Java.

There are two basic types of conversions. A *widening conversion* occurs when a value of one type is converted to a wider type—one that has a larger range of legal values. Java performs widening conversions automatically when, for example, you assign an int literal to a double variable or a char literal to an int variable.

Narrowing conversions are another matter, however. A *narrowing conversion* occurs when a value is converted to a type that is not wider than it is. Narrowing conversions are not always safe: it is reasonable to convert the integer value 13 to a byte, for example, but it is not reasonable to convert 13000 to a byte since byte can hold only numbers between –128 and 127. Because you can lose data in a narrowing conversion, the Java compiler complains when you attempt any narrowing conversion, even if the value being converted would in fact fit in the narrower range of the specified type:

```
int i = 13;
byte b = i;    // The compiler does not allow this
```

The one exception to this rule is that you can assign an integer literal (an int value) to a byte or short variable if the literal falls within the range of the variable.

If you need to perform a narrowing conversion and are confident you can do so without losing data or precision, you can force Java to perform the conversion using a language construct known as a *cast*. Perform a cast by placing the name of the desired type in parentheses before the value to be converted. For example:

```
int i = 13;
byte b = (byte) i;   // Force the int to be converted to a byte
i = (int) 13.456;    // Force this double literal to the int 13
```

Casts of primitive types are most often used to convert floating-point values to integers. When you do this, the fractional part of the floating-point value is simply truncated (i.e., the floating-point value is rounded towards zero, not towards the nearest integer). The methods Math.round( ), Math.floor( ), and Math.ceil( ) perform other types of rounding.

The char type acts like an integer type in most ways, so a char value can be used anywhere an int or long value is required. Recall, however, that the char type is *unsigned*, so it behaves differently than the short type, even though both are 16 bits wide:

```
short s = (short) 0xffff; // These bits represent the number -1
char c = '\uffff';        // The same bits, representing a Unicode character
int i1 = s;               // Converting the short to an int yields -1
int i2 = c;               // Converting the char to an int yields 65535
```

Table 2-3 shows which primitive types can be converted to which other types and how the conversion is performed. The letter N in the table means that the conversion cannot be performed. The letter Y means that the conversion is a widening conversion and is therefore performed automatically and implicitly by Java. The letter C means that the conversion is a narrowing conversion and requires an explicit cast. Finally, the notation Y* means that the conversion is an automatic widening conversion, but that some of the least significant digits of the value may be lost in the conversion. This can happen when converting an int or long to a float or double. The floating-point types have a larger range than the integer types, so any int or long can be represented by a float or double. However, the floating-point types are approximations of numbers and cannot always hold as many significant digits as the integer types.

Table 2-3. Java primitive type conversions

Convert from:	Convert to: boolean	byte	short	char	int	long	float	double
boolean	–	N	N	N	N	N	N	N
byte	N	–	Y	C	Y	Y	Y	Y
short	N	C	–	C	Y	Y	Y	Y
char	N	C	C	–	Y	Y	Y	Y
int	N	C	C	C	–	Y	Y*	Y
long	N	C	C	C	C	–	Y*	Y*
float	N	C	C	C	C	C	–	Y
double	N	C	C	C	C	C	C	–

Expressions and Operators

So far in this chapter, we've learned about the primitive types that Java programs can manipulate and seen how to include primitive values as *literals* in a Java program. We've also used *variables* as symbolic names that represent, or hold, values. These literals and variables are the tokens out of which Java programs are built.

An *expression* is the next higher level of structure in a Java program. The Java interpreter *evaluates* an expression to compute its value. The very simplest expressions are called *primary expressions* and consist of literals and variables. So, for example, the following are all expressions:

```
1.7         // A floating-point literal
true        // A boolean literal
sum         // A variable
```

When the Java interpreter evaluates a literal expression, the resulting value is the literal itself. When the interpreter evaluates a variable expression, the resulting value is the value stored in the variable.

Primary expressions are not very interesting. More complex expressions are made by using *operators* to combine primary expressions. For example, the following expression uses the assignment operator to combine two primary expressions—a variable and a floating-point literal—into an assignment expression:

```
sum = 1.7
```

But operators are used not only with primary expressions; they can also be used with expressions at any level of complexity. The following are all legal expressions:

```
sum = 1 + 2 + 3*1.2 + (4 + 8)/3.0
sum/Math.sqrt(3.0 * 1.234)
(int)(sum + 33)
```

Operator Summary

The kinds of expressions you can write in a programming language depend entirely on the set of operators available to you. Table 2-4 summarizes the operators available in Java. The P and A columns of the table specify the precedence and associativity of each group of related operators, respectively. These concepts—and the operators themselves—are explained in more detail in the following sections.

Table 2-4. Java operators

P	A	Operator	Operand type(s)	Operation performed
15	L	.	object, member	object member access
		[ ]	array, int	array element access
		(*args*)	method, arglist	method invocation
		++, --	variable	post-increment, decrement
14	R	++, --	variable	pre-increment, decrement
		+, -	number	unary plus, unary minus
		~	integer	bitwise complement
		!	boolean	boolean NOT
13	R	new	class, arglist	object creation
		(*type*)	type, any	cast (type conversion)
12	L	*, /, %	number, number	multiplication, division, remainder
11	L	+, -	number, number	addition, subtraction
		+	string, any	string concatenation
10	L	<<	integer, integer	left shift
		>>	integer, integer	right shift with sign extension
		>>>	integer, integer	right shift with zero extension
9	L	<, <=	number, number	less than, less than or equal
		>, >=	number, number	greater than, greater than or equal
		instanceof	reference, type	type comparison
8	L	==	primitive, primitive	equal (have identical values)
		!=	primitive, primitive	not equal (have different values)
		==	reference, reference	equal (refer to same object)
		!=	reference, reference	not equal (refer to different objects)
7	L	&	integer, integer	bitwise AND
		&	boolean, boolean	boolean AND
6	L	^	integer, integer	bitwise XOR
		^	boolean, boolean	boolean XOR
5	L	|	integer, integer	bitwise OR
		|	boolean, boolean	boolean OR
4	L	&&	boolean, boolean	conditional AND
3	L	||	boolean, boolean	conditional OR
2	R	?:	boolean, any	conditional (ternary) operator
1	R	=	variable, any	assignment
		*=, /=, %=, +=, -=, <<=, >>=, >>>=, &=, ^=, |=	variable, any	assignment with operation

Precedence

The **P** column of Table 2-4 specifies the *precedence* of each operator. Precedence specifies the order in which operations are performed. Consider this expression:

```
a + b * c
```

The multiplication operator has higher precedence than the addition operator, so a is added to the product of b and c. Operator precedence can be thought of as a measure of how tightly operators bind to their operands. The higher the number, the more tightly they bind.

Default operator precedence can be overridden through the use of parentheses that explicitly specify the order of operations. The previous expression can be rewritten as follows to specify that the addition should be performed before the multiplication:

```
(a + b) * c
```

The default operator precedence in Java was chosen for compatibility with C; the designers of C chose this precedence so that most expressions can be written naturally without parentheses. There are only a few common Java idioms for which parentheses are required. Examples include:

```
// Class cast combined with member access
((Integer) o).intValue();

// Assignment combined with comparison
while((line = in.readLine()) != null) { ... }

// Bitwise operators combined with comparison
if ((flags & (PUBLIC | PROTECTED)) != 0) { ... }
```

Associativity

When an expression involves several operators that have the same precedence, the operator associativity governs the order in which the operations are performed. Most operators are left-to-right associative, which means that the operations are performed from left to right. The assignment and unary operators, however, have right-to-left associativity. The **A** column of Table 2-4 specifies the associativity of each operator or group of operators. The value L means left to right, and R means right to left.

The additive operators are all left-to-right associative, so the expression a+b-c is evaluated from left to right: (a+b)-c. Unary operators and assignment operators are evaluated from right to left. Consider this complex expression:

```
a = b += c = -~d
```

This is evaluated as follows:

```
a = (b += (c = -(~d)))
```

As with operator precedence, operator associativity establishes a default order of evaluation for an expression. This default order can be overridden through the use of parentheses. However, the default operator associativity in Java has been chosen to yield a natural expression syntax, and you rarely need to alter it.

Operand number and type

The fourth column of Table 2-4 specifies the number and type of the operands expected by each operator. Some operators operate on only one operand; these are called unary operators. For example, the unary minus operator changes the sign of a single number:

```
-n              // The unary minus operator
```

Most operators, however, are binary operators that operate on two operand values. The - operator actually comes in both forms:

```
a - b           // The subtraction operator is a binary operator
```

Java also defines one ternary operator, often called the conditional operator. It is like an `if` statement inside an expression. Its three operands are separated by a question mark and a colon; the second and third operands must be convertible to the same type:

```
x > y ? x : y  // Ternary expression; evaluates to the larger of x and y
```

In addition to expecting a certain number of operands, each operator also expects particular types of operands. Column four of the table lists the operand types. Some of the codes used in that column require further explanation:

number
: An integer, floating-point value, or character (i.e., any primitive type except `boolean`). In Java 5.0 and later, autounboxing (see "Boxing and Unboxing Conversions" later in this chapter) means that the wrapper classes (such as `Character`, `Integer`, and `Double`) for these types can be be used in this context as well.

integer
: A `byte`, `short`, `int`, `long`, or `char` value (`long` values are not allowed for the array access operator [ ]). With autounboxing, `Byte`, `Short`, `Integer`, `Long`, and `Character` values are also allowed.

reference
: An object or array.

variable
: A variable or anything else, such as an array element, to which a value can be assigned

Return type

Just as every operator expects its operands to be of specific types, each operator produces a value of a specific type. The arithmetic, increment and decrement, bitwise, and shift operators return a `double` if at least one of the operands is a `double`. They return a `float` if at least one of the operands is a `float`. They return a `long` if at least one of the operands is a `long`. Otherwise, they return an `int`, even if both operands are `byte`, `short`, or `char` types that are narrower than `int`.

The comparison, equality, and boolean operators always return `boolean` values. Each assignment operator returns whatever value it assigned, which is of a type compatible with the variable on the left side of the expression. The conditional operator returns the value of its second or third argument (which must both be of the same type).

Side effects

Every operator computes a value based on one or more operand values. Some operators, however, have *side effects* in addition to their basic evaluation. If an expression contains side effects, evaluating it changes the state of a Java program in such a way that evaluating the expression again may yield a different result. For example, the ++ increment operator has the side effect of incrementing a variable. The expression ++a increments the variable a and returns the newly incremented value. If this expression is evaluated again, the value will be different. The various assignment operators also have side effects. For example, the expression a*=2 can also be written as a=a*2. The value of the expression is the value of a multiplied by 2, but the expression also has the side effect of storing that value back into a. The method invocation operator () has side effects if the invoked method has side effects. Some methods, such as Math.sqrt(), simply compute and return a value without side effects of any kind. Typically, however, methods do have side effects. Finally, the new operator has the profound side effect of creating a new object.

Order of evaluation

When the Java interpreter evaluates an expression, it performs the various operations in an order specified by the parentheses in the expression, the precedence of the operators, and the associativity of the operators. Before any operation is performed, however, the interpreter first evaluates the operands of the operator. (The exceptions are the &&, ||, and ?: operators, which do not always evaluate all their operands.) The interpreter always evaluates operands in order from left to right. This matters if any of the operands are expressions that contain side effects. Consider this code, for example:

```
int a = 2;
int v = ++a + ++a * ++a;
```

Although the multiplication is performed before the addition, the operands of the + operator are evaluated first. Thus, the expression evaluates to 3+4*5, or 23.

Arithmetic Operators

Since most programs operate primarily on numbers, the most commonly used operators are often those that perform arithmetic operations. The arithmetic operators can be used with integers, floating-point numbers, and even characters (i.e., they can be used with any primitive type other than boolean). If either of the operands is a floating-point number, floating-point arithmetic is used; otherwise, integer arithmetic is used. This matters because integer arithmetic and floating-point arithmetic differ in the way division is performed and in the way underflows and overflows are handled, for example. The arithmetic operators are:

Addition (+)
: The + operator adds two numbers. As we'll see shortly, the + operator can also be used to concatenate strings. If either operand of + is a string, the other

one is converted to a string as well. Be sure to use parentheses when you want to combine addition with concatenation. For example:

```
System.out.println("Total: " + 3 + 4);    // Prints "Total: 34", not 7!
```

Subtraction (-)
When the - operator is used as a binary operator, it subtracts its second operand from its first. For example, 7-3 evaluates to 4. The - operator can also perform unary negation.

Multiplication (*)
The * operator multiplies its two operands. For example, 7*3 evaluates to 21.

Division (/)
The / operator divides its first operand by its second. If both operands are integers, the result is an integer, and any remainder is lost. If either operand is a floating-point value, however, the result is a floating-point value. When dividing two integers, division by zero throws an `ArithmeticException`. For floating-point calculations, however, division by zero simply yields an infinite result or NaN:

```
7/3          // Evaluates to 2
7/3.0f       // Evaluates to 2.333333f
7/0          // Throws an ArithmeticException
7/0.0        // Evaluates to positive infinity
0.0/0.0      // Evaluates to NaN
```

Modulo (%)
The % operator computes the first operand modulo the second operand (i.e., it returns the remainder when the first operand is divided by the second operand an integral number of times). For example, 7%3 is 1. The sign of the result is the same as the sign of the first operand. While the modulo operator is typically used with integer operands, it also works for floating-point values. For example, 4.3%2.1 evaluates to 0.1. When operating with integers, trying to compute a value modulo zero causes an `ArithmeticException`. When working with floating-point values, anything modulo 0.0 evaluates to `NaN`, as does infinity modulo anything.

Unary minus (-)
When the - operator is used as a unary operator—that is, before a single operand—it performs unary negation. In other words, it converts a positive value to an equivalently negative value, and vice versa.

String Concatenation Operator

In addition to adding numbers, the + operator (and the related += operator) also concatenates, or joins, strings. If either of the operands to + is a string, the operator converts the other operand to a string. For example:

```
System.out.println("Quotient: " + 7/3.0f); // Prints "Quotient: 2.3333333"
```

As a result, you must be careful to put any addition expressions in parentheses when combining them with string concatenation. If you do not, the addition operator is interpreted as a concatenation operator.

The Java interpreter has built-in string conversions for all primitive types. An object is converted to a string by invoking its `toString()` method. Some classes define custom `toString()` methods so that objects of that class can easily be converted to strings in this way. An array is converted to a string by invoking the built-in `toString()` method, which, unfortunately, does not return a useful string representation of the array contents.

Increment and Decrement Operators

The `++` operator increments its single operand, which must be a variable, an element of an array, or a field of an object, by one. The behavior of this operator depends on its position relative to the operand. When used before the operand, where it is known as the *pre-increment* operator, it increments the operand and evaluates to the incremented value of that operand. When used after the operand, where it is known as the *post-increment* operator, it increments its operand, but evaluates to the value of that operand before it was incremented.

For example, the following code sets both `i` and `j` to 2:

```
i = 1;
j = ++i;
```

But these lines set `i` to 2 and `j` to 1:

```
i = 1;
j = i++;
```

Similarly, the `--` operator decrements its single numeric operand, which must be a variable, an element of an array, or a field of an object, by one. Like the `++` operator, the behavior of `--` depends on its position relative to the operand. When used before the operand, it decrements the operand and returns the decremented value. When used after the operand, it decrements the operand, but returns the *undecremented* value.

The expressions `x++` and `x--` are equivalent to `x=x+1` and `x=x-1`, respectively, except that when using the increment and decrement operators, `x` is only evaluated once. If `x` is itself an expression with side effects, this makes a big difference. For example, these two expressions are not equivalent:

```
a[i++]++;             // Increments an element of an array
a[i++] = a[i++] + 1;  // Adds one to an array element and stores it in another
```

These operators, in both prefix and postfix forms, are most commonly used to increment or decrement the counter that controls a loop.

Comparison Operators

The comparison operators consist of the equality operators that test values for equality or inequality and the relational operators used with ordered types (numbers and characters) to test for greater than and less than relationships. Both types of operators yield a `boolean` result, so they are typically used with `if` statements and `while` and `for` loops to make branching and looping decisions. For example:

```
if (o != null) ...;           // The not equals operator
while(i < a.length) ...;      // The less than operator
```

Java provides the following equality operators:

Equals (==)
The == operator evaluates to true if its two operands are equal and false otherwise. With primitive operands, it tests whether the operand values themselves are identical. For operands of reference types, however, it tests whether the operands refer to the same object or array. In other words, it does not test the equality of two distinct objects or arrays. In particular, note that you cannot test two distinct strings for equality with this operator.

If == is used to compare two numeric or character operands that are not of the same type, the narrower operand is converted to the type of the wider operand before the comparison is done. For example, when comparing a short to a float, the short is first converted to a float before the comparison is performed. For floating-point numbers, the special negative zero value tests equal to the regular, positive zero value. Also, the special NaN (not-a-number) value is not equal to any other number, including itself. To test whether a floating-point value is NaN, use the Float.isNan( ) or Double.isNan( ) method.

Not equals (!=)
The != operator is exactly the opposite of the == operator. It evaluates to true if its two primitive operands have different values or if its two reference operands refer to different objects or arrays. Otherwise, it evaluates to false.

The relational operators can be used with numbers and characters, but not with boolean values, objects, or arrays because those types are not ordered. Java provides the following relational operators:

Less than (<)
Evaluates to true if the first operand is less than the second.

Less than or equal (<=)
Evaluates to true if the first operand is less than or equal to the second.

Greater than (>)
Evaluates to true if the first operand is greater than the second.

Greater than or equal (>=)
Evaluates to true if the first operand is greater than or equal to the second.

Boolean Operators

As we've just seen, the comparison operators compare their operands and yield a boolean result, which is often used in branching and looping statements. In order to make branching and looping decisions based on conditions more interesting than a single comparison, you can use the boolean (or logical) operators to combine multiple comparison expressions into a single, more complex expression. The boolean operators require their operands to be boolean values and they evaluate to boolean values. The operators are:

Conditional AND (&&)
This operator performs a boolean AND operation on its operands. It evaluates to true if and only if both its operands are true. If either or both operands are false, it evaluates to false. For example:

```
if (x < 10 && y > 3) ... // If both comparisons are true
```

This operator (and all the boolean operators except the unary ! operator) have a lower precedence than the comparison operators. Thus, it is perfectly legal to write a line of code like the one above. However, some programmers prefer to use parentheses to make the order of evaluation explicit:

```
if ((x < 10) && (y > 3)) ...
```

You should use whichever style you find easier to read.

This operator is called a conditional AND because it conditionally evaluates its second operand. If the first operand evaluates to `false`, the value of the expression is `false`, regardless of the value of the second operand. Therefore, to increase efficiency, the Java interpreter takes a shortcut and skips the second operand. Since the second operand is not guaranteed to be evaluated, you must use caution when using this operator with expressions that have side effects. On the other hand, the conditional nature of this operator allows us to write Java expressions such as the following:

```
if (data != null && i < data.length && data[i] != -1)
    ...
```

The second and third comparisons in this expression would cause errors if the first or second comparisons evaluated to `false`. Fortunately, we don't have to worry about this because of the conditional behavior of the && operator.

Conditional OR (||)
: This operator performs a boolean OR operation on its two `boolean` operands. It evaluates to `true` if either or both of its operands are `true`. If both operands are `false`, it evaluates to `false`. Like the && operator, || does not always evaluate its second operand. If the first operand evaluates to `true`, the value of the expression is `true`, regardless of the value of the second operand. Thus, the operator simply skips the second operand in that case.

Boolean NOT (!)
: This unary operator changes the `boolean` value of its operand. If applied to a `true` value, it evaluates to `false`, and if applied to a `false` value, it evaluates to `true`. It is useful in expressions like these:

```
if (!found) ...          // found is a boolean variable declared somewhere
while (!c.isEmpty()) ... // The isEmpty() method returns a boolean value
```

Because ! is a unary operator, it has a high precedence and often must be used with parentheses:

```
if (!(x > y && y > z))
```

Boolean AND (&)
: When used with `boolean` operands, the & operator behaves like the && operator, except that it always evaluates both operands, regardless of the value of the first operand. This operator is almost always used as a bitwise operator with integer operands, however, and many Java programmers would not even recognize its use with `boolean` operands as legal Java code.

Boolean OR (|)
: This operator performs a boolean OR operation on its two boolean operands. It is like the || operator, except that it always evaluates both operands, even if the first one is true. The | operator is almost always used as a bitwise operator on integer operands; its use with boolean operands is very rare.

Boolean XOR (^)
: When used with boolean operands, this operator computes the Exclusive OR (XOR) of its operands. It evaluates to true if exactly one of the two operands is true. In other words, it evaluates to false if both operands are false or if both operands are true. Unlike the && and || operators, this one must always evaluate both operands. The ^ operator is much more commonly used as a bitwise operator on integer operands. With boolean operands, this operator is equivalent to the != operator.

Bitwise and Shift Operators

The bitwise and shift operators are low-level operators that manipulate the individual bits that make up an integer value. The bitwise operators are most commonly used for testing and setting individual flag bits in a value. In order to understand their behavior, you must understand binary (base-2) numbers and the twos-complement format used to represent negative integers. You cannot use these operators with floating-point, boolean, array, or object operands. When used with boolean operands, the &, |, and ^ operators perform a different operation, as described in the previous section.

If either of the arguments to a bitwise operator is a long, the result is a long. Otherwise, the result is an int. If the left operand of a shift operator is a long, the result is a long; otherwise, the result is an int. The operators are:

Bitwise complement (~)
: The unary ~ operator is known as the bitwise complement, or bitwise NOT, operator. It inverts each bit of its single operand, converting ones to zeros and zeros to ones. For example:

```
byte b = ~12;           // ~00001100 ==> 11110011 or -13 decimal
flags = flags & ~f;     // Clear flag f in a set of flags
```

Bitwise AND (&)
: This operator combines its two integer operands by performing a boolean AND operation on their individual bits. The result has a bit set only if the corresponding bit is set in both operands. For example:

```
10 & 7                  // 00001010 & 00000111 ==> 00000010 or 2
if ((flags & f) != 0)   // Test whether flag f is set
```

When used with boolean operands, & is the infrequently used boolean AND operator described earlier.

Bitwise OR (|)
: This operator combines its two integer operands by performing a boolean OR operation on their individual bits. The result has a bit set if the corresponding bit is set in either or both of the operands. It has a zero bit only where both corresponding operand bits are zero. For example:

```
10 | 7                    // 00001010 | 00000111 ==> 00001111 or 15
flags = flags | f;        // Set flag f
```

When used with boolean operands, | is the infrequently used boolean OR operator described earlier.

Bitwise XOR (^)

This operator combines its two integer operands by performing a boolean XOR (Exclusive OR) operation on their individual bits. The result has a bit set if the corresponding bits in the two operands are different. If the corresponding operand bits are both ones or both zeros, the result bit is a zero. For example:

```
10 ^ 7               // 00001010 ^ 00000111 ==> 00001101 or 13
```

When used with boolean operands, ^ is the infrequently used boolean XOR operator.

Left shift (<<)

The << operator shifts the bits of the left operand left by the number of places specified by the right operand. High-order bits of the left operand are lost, and zero bits are shifted in from the right. Shifting an integer left by *n* places is equivalent to multiplying that number by 2*n*. For example:

```
10 << 1      // 00001010 << 1 = 00010100 = 20 = 10*2
7 << 3       // 00000111 << 3 = 00111000 = 56 = 7*8
-1 << 2      // 0xFFFFFFFF << 2 = 0xFFFFFFFC = -4 = -1*4
```

If the left operand is a long, the right operand should be between 0 and 63. Otherwise, the left operand is taken to be an int, and the right operand should be between 0 and 31.

Signed right shift (>>)

The >> operator shifts the bits of the left operand to the right by the number of places specified by the right operand. The low-order bits of the left operand are shifted away and are lost. The high-order bits shifted in are the same as the original high-order bit of the left operand. In other words, if the left operand is positive, zeros are shifted into the high-order bits. If the left operand is negative, ones are shifted in instead. This technique is known as *sign extension*; it is used to preserve the sign of the left operand. For example:

```
10 >> 1       // 00001010 >> 1 = 00000101 = 5 = 10/2
27 >> 3       // 00011011 >> 3 = 00000011 = 3 = 27/8
-50 >> 2      // 11001110 >> 2 = 11110011 = -13 != -50/4
```

If the left operand is positive and the right operand is *n*, the >> operator is the same as integer division by 2*n*.

Unsigned right shift (>>>)

This operator is like the >> operator, except that it always shifts zeros into the high-order bits of the result, regardless of the sign of the left-hand operand. This technique is called *zero extension*; it is appropriate when the left operand is being treated as an unsigned value (despite the fact that Java integer types are all signed). These are examples:

```
0xff >>> 4     // 11111111 >>> 4 = 00001111 = 15  = 255/16
-50 >>> 2      // 0xFFFFFFCE >>> 2 = 0x3FFFFFF3 = 1073741811
```

Assignment Operators

The assignment operators store, or assign, a value into some kind of variable. The left operand must evaluate to an appropriate local variable, array element, or object field. The right side can be any value of a type compatible with the variable. An assignment expression evaluates to the value that is assigned to the variable. More importantly, however, the expression has the side effect of actually performing the assignment. Unlike all other binary operators, the assignment operators are right-associative, which means that the assignments in `a=b=c` are performed right-to-left, as follows: `a=(b=c)`.

The basic assignment operator is `=`. Do not confuse it with the equality operator, `==`. In order to keep these two operators distinct, I recommend that you read `=` as "is assigned the value."

In addition to this simple assignment operator, Java also defines 11 other operators that combine assignment with the 5 arithmetic operators and the 6 bitwise and shift operators. For example, the `+=` operator reads the value of the left variable, adds the value of the right operand to it, stores the sum back into the left variable as a side effect, and returns the sum as the value of the expression. Thus, the expression `x+=2` is almost the same as `x=x+2`. The difference between these two expressions is that when you use the `+=` operator, the left operand is evaluated only once. This makes a difference when that operand has a side effect. Consider the following two expressions, which are not equivalent:

```
a[i++] += 2;
a[i++] = a[i++] + 2;
```

The general form of these combination assignment operators is:

```
var op= value
```

This is equivalent (unless there are side effects in `var`) to:

```
var = var op value
```

The available operators are:

```
+=   -=   *=   /=   %=     // Arithmetic operators plus assignment
&=   |=   ^=               // Bitwise operators plus assignment
<<=  >>=  >>>=             // Shift operators plus assignment
```

The most commonly used operators are `+=` and `-=`, although `&=` and `|=` can also be useful when working with `boolean` flags. For example:

```
i += 2;          // Increment a loop counter by 2
c -= 5;          // Decrement a counter by 5
flags |= f;      // Set a flag f in an integer set of flags
flags & ~f;      // Clear a flag f in an integer set of flags
```

The Conditional Operator

The conditional operator `?:` is a somewhat obscure ternary (three-operand) operator inherited from C. It allows you to embed a conditional within an expression. You can think of it as the operator version of the `if/else` statement. The first and second operands of the conditional operator are separated by a question mark (`?`)

while the second and third operands are separated by a colon (:). The first operand must evaluate to a boolean value. The second and third operands can be of any type, but they must be convertible to the same type.

The conditional operator starts by evaluating its first operand. If it is true, the operator evaluates its second operand and uses that as the value of the expression. On the other hand, if the first operand is false, the conditional operator evaluates and returns its third operand. The conditional operator never evaluates both its second and third operand, so be careful when using expressions with side effects with this operator. Examples of this operator are:

```
int max = (x > y) ? x : y;
String name = (name != null) ? name : "unknown";
```

Note that the ?: operator has lower precedence than all other operators except the assignment operators, so parentheses are not usually necessary around the operands of this operator. Many programmers find conditional expressions easier to read if the first operand is placed within parentheses, however. This is especially true because the conditional if statement always has its conditional expression written within parentheses.

The instanceof Operator

The instanceof operator requires an object or array value as its left operand and the name of a reference type as its right operand. It evaluates to true if the object or array is an *instance* of the specified type; it returns false otherwise. If the left operand is null, instanceof always evaluates to false. If an instanceof expression evaluates to true, it means that you can safely cast and assign the left operand to a variable of the type of the right operand.

The instanceof operator can be used only with reference types and objects, not primitive types and values. Examples of instanceof are:

```
"string" instanceof String      // True: all strings are instances of String
"" instanceof Object            // True: strings are also instances of Object
null instanceof String          // False: null is never an instance of anything

Object o = new int[] {1,2,3};
o instanceof int[]   // True: the array value is an int array
o instanceof byte[]  // False: the array value is not a byte array
o instanceof Object  // True: all arrays are instances of Object

// Use instanceof to make sure that it is safe to cast an object
if (object instanceof Point) {
   Point p = (Point) object;
}
```

Special Operators

Java has five language constructs that are sometimes considered operators and sometimes considered simply part of the basic language syntax. These "operators" were included in Table 2-4 in order to show their precedence relative to the other true operators. The use of these language constructs is detailed elsewhere in this book but is described briefly here so that you can recognize them in code examples.

Object member access (`.`)
An *object* is a collection of data and methods that operate on that data; the data fields and methods of an object are called its members. The dot (`.`) operator accesses these members. If `o` is an expression that evaluates to an object reference, and `f` is the name of a field of the object, `o.f` evaluates to the value contained in that field. If `m` is the name of a method, `o.m` refers to that method and allows it to be invoked using the `( )` operator shown later.

Array element access (`[ ]`)
An *array* is a numbered list of values. Each element of an array can be referred to by its number, or *index*. The `[ ]` operator allows you to refer to the individual elements of an array. If `a` is an array, and `i` is an expression that evaluates to an `int`, `a[i]` refers to one of the elements of `a`. Unlike other operators that work with integer values, this operator restricts array index values to be of type `int` or narrower.

Method invocation (`( )`)
A *method* is a named collection of Java code that can be run, or *invoked*, by following the name of the method with zero or more comma-separated expressions contained within parentheses. The values of these expressions are the *arguments* to the method. The method processes the arguments and optionally returns a value that becomes the value of the method invocation expression. If `o.m` is a method that expects no arguments, the method can be invoked with `o.m( )`. If the method expects three arguments, for example, it can be invoked with an expression such as `o.m(x,y,z)`. Before the Java interpreter invokes a method, it evaluates each of the arguments to be passed to the method. These expressions are guaranteed to be evaluated in order from left to right (which matters if any of the arguments have side effects).

Object creation (`new`)
In Java, objects (and arrays) are created with the `new` operator, which is followed by the type of the object to be created and a parenthesized list of arguments to be passed to the object *constructor*. A constructor is a special method that initializes a newly created object, so the object creation syntax is similar to the Java method invocation syntax. For example:

```
new ArrayList( );
new Point(1,2)
```

Type conversion or casting (`( )`)
As we've already seen, parentheses can also be used as an operator to perform narrowing type conversions, or casts. The first operand of this operator is the type to be converted to; it is placed between the parentheses. The second operand is the value to be converted; it follows the parentheses. For example:

```
(byte) 28            // An integer literal cast to a byte type
(int) (x + 3.14f)    // A floating-point sum value cast to an integer value
(String)h.get(k)     // A generic object cast to a more specific string type
```

Statements

A *statement* is a single command executed by the Java interpreter. By default, the Java interpreter runs one statement after another, in the order they are written. Many of the statements defined by Java, however, are flow-control statements, such as conditionals and loops, that alter this default order of execution in well-defined ways. Table 2-5 summarizes the statements defined by Java.

Table 2-5. Java statements

Statement	Purpose	Syntax
expression	side effects	`var = expr; expr++; method(); new Type();`
compound	group statements	`{ statements }`
empty	do nothing	`;`
labeled	name a statement	`label : statement`
variable	declare a variable	`[final] type name [= value] [, name [= value]] ...;`
`if`	conditional	`if ( expr ) statement [ else statement]`
`switch`	conditional	`switch ( expr ) { [ case expr : statements ] ... [ default: statements ] }`
`while`	loop	`while ( expr ) statement`
`do`	loop	`do statement while ( expr );`
`for`	simplified loop	`for ( init ; test ; increment ) statement`
`for/in`	collection iteration	`for ( variable : iterable ) statement` Java 5.0 and later; also called "foreach"
`break`	exit block	`break [ label ] ;`
`continue`	restart loop	`continue [ label ] ;`
`return`	end method	`return [ expr ] ;`
`synchronized`	critical section	`synchronized ( expr ) { statements }`
`throw`	throw exception	`throw expr ;`
`try`	handle exception	`try { statements } [ catch ( type name ) { statements } ] ... [ finally { statements } ]`
`assert`	verify invariant	`assert invariant [ : error] ;` Java 1.4 and later.

Expression Statements

As we saw earlier in the chapter, certain types of Java expressions have side effects. In other words, they do not simply evaluate to some value; they also change the program state in some way. Any expression with side effects can be used as a statement simply by following it with a semicolon. The legal types of expression statements are assignments, increments and decrements, method calls, and object creation. For example:

```
a = 1;                          // Assignment
x *= 2;                         // Assignment with operation
i++;                            // Post-increment
--c;                            // Pre-decrement
System.out.println("statement"); // Method invocation
```

Compound Statements

A *compound statement* is any number and kind of statements grouped together within curly braces. You can use a compound statement anywhere a statement is required by Java syntax:

```
for(int i = 0; i < 10; i++) {
   a[i]++;                    // Body of this loop is a compound statement.
   b[i]--;                    // It consists of two expression statements
}                             // within curly braces.
```


The Empty Statement

An *empty statement* in Java is written as a single semicolon. The empty statement doesn't do anything, but the syntax is occasionally useful. For example, you can use it to indicate an empty loop body in a for loop:

```
for(int i = 0; i < 10; a[i++]++)  // Increment array elements
     /* empty */;                 // Loop body is empty statement
```

Labeled Statements

A *labeled statement* is simply a statement that has been given a name by prepending an identifier and a colon to it. Labels are used by the break and continue statements. For example:

```
rowLoop: for(int r = 0; r < rows.length; r++) {        // A labeled loop
   colLoop: for(int c = 0; c < columns.length; c++) {  // Another one
     break rowLoop;                                     // Use a label
   }
}
```

Local Variable Declaration Statements

A *local variable*, often simply called a variable, is a symbolic name for a location to store a value that is defined within a method or compound statement. All variables must be declared before they can be used; this is done with a variable declaration statement. Because Java is a strongly typed language, a variable declaration specifies the type of the variable, and only values of that type can be stored in the variable.

In its simplest form, a variable declaration specifies a variable's type and name:

```
int counter;
String s;
```

A variable declaration can also include an *initializer*: an expression that specifies an initial value for the variable. For example:

```
int i = 0;
String s = readLine();
int[] data = {x+1, x+2, x+3};  // Array initializers are documented later
```

The Java compiler does not allow you to use a local variable that has not been initialized, so it is usually convenient to combine variable declaration and initialization into a single statement. The initializer expression need not be a literal value or a constant expression that can be evaluated by the compiler; it can be an arbitrarily complex expression whose value is computed when the program is run.

A single variable declaration statement can declare and initialize more than one variable, but all variables must be of the same type. Variable names and optional initializers are separated from each other with commas:

```
int i, j, k;
float x = 1.0, y = 1.0;
String question = "Really Quit?", response;
```

In Java 1.1 and later, variable declaration statements can begin with the `final` keyword. This modifier specifies that once an initial value is specified for the variable, that value is never allowed to change:

```
final String greeting = getLocalLanguageGreeting();
```

C programmers should note that Java variable declaration statements can appear anywhere in Java code; they are not restricted to the beginning of a method or block of code. Local variable declarations can also be integrated with the *initialize* portion of a `for` loop, as we'll discuss shortly.

Local variables can be used only within the method or block of code in which they are defined. This is called their *scope* or *lexical scope*:

```
void method() {              // A method definition
   int i = 0;                // Declare variable i
   while (i < 10) {          // i is in scope here
     int j = 0;              // Declare j; the scope of j begins here
     i++;                    // i is in scope here; increment it
   }                         // j is no longer in scope; can't use it anymore
   System.out.println(i);    // i is still in scope here
}                            // The scope of i ends here
```

The if/else Statement

The `if` statement is the fundamental control statement that allows Java to make decisions or, more precisely, to execute statements conditionally. The `if` statement has an associated expression and statement. If the expression evaluates to `true`, the interpreter executes the statement. If the expression evaluates to `false` the interpreter skips the statement. In Java 5.0, the expression may be of the wrapper type `Boolean` instead of the primitive type `boolean`. In this case, the wrapper object is automatically unboxed.

Here is an example `if` statement:

```
if (username == null)         // If username is null,
   username = "John Doe";     // use a default value
```

Although they look extraneous, the parentheses around the expression are a required part of the syntax for the `if` statement.

As I already mentioned, a block of statements enclosed in curly braces is itself a statement, so we can also write `if` statements that look like this:

```
if ((address == null) || (address.equals(""))) {
```

```
        address = "[undefined]";
        System.out.println("WARNING: no address specified.");
    }
```

An if statement can include an optional else keyword that is followed by a second statement. In this form of the statement, the expression is evaluated, and, if it is true, the first statement is executed. Otherwise, the second statement is executed. For example:

```
if (username != null)
   System.out.println("Hello " + username);
else {
   username = askQuestion("What is your name?");
   System.out.println("Hello " + username + ". Welcome!");
}
```

When you use nested if/else statements, some caution is required to ensure that the else clause goes with the appropriate if statement. Consider the following lines:

```
if (i == j)
   if (j == k)
     System.out.println("i equals k");
else
   System.out.println("i doesn't equal j");    // WRONG!!
```

In this example, the inner if statement forms the single statement allowed by the syntax of the outer if statement. Unfortunately, it is not clear (except from the hint given by the indentation) which if the else goes with. And in this example, the indentation hint is wrong. The rule is that an else clause like this is associated with the nearest if statement. Properly indented, this code looks like this:

```
if (i == j)
   if (j == k)
     System.out.println("i equals k");
   else
     System.out.println("i doesn't equal j");    // WRONG!!
```

This is legal code, but it is clearly not what the programmer had in mind. When working with nested if statements, you should use curly braces to make your code easier to read. Here is a better way to write the code:

```
if (i == j) {
   if (j == k)
     System.out.println("i equals k");
}
else {
   System.out.println("i doesn't equal j");
}
```

The else if clause

The if/else statement is useful for testing a condition and choosing between two statements or blocks of code to execute. But what about when you need to choose between several blocks of code? This is typically done with an else if clause, which is not really new syntax, but a common idiomatic usage of the standard if/else statement. It looks like this:

```
if (n == 1) {
    // Execute code block #1
}
else if (n == 2) {
    // Execute code block #2
}
else if (n == 3) {
    // Execute code block #3
}
else {
    // If all else fails, execute block #4
}
```

There is nothing special about this code. It is just a series of `if` statements, where each `if` is part of the else clause of the previous statement. Using the `else if` idiom is preferable to, and more legible than, writing these statements out in their fully nested form:

```
if (n == 1) {
   // Execute code block #1
}
else {
   if (n == 2) {
     // Execute code block #2
   }
   else {
     if (n == 3) {
       // Execute code block #3
     }
     else {
       // If all else fails, execute block #4
     }
   }
}
```

The switch Statement

An `if` statement causes a branch in the flow of a program's execution. You can use multiple `if` statements, as shown in the previous section, to perform a multiway branch. This is not always the best solution, however, especially when all of the branches depend on the value of a single variable. In this case, it is inefficient to repeatedly check the value of the same variable in multiple `if` statements.

A better solution is to use a `switch` statement, which is inherited from the C programming language. Although the syntax of this statement is not nearly as elegant as other parts of Java, the brute practicality of the construct makes it worthwhile. If you are not familiar with the `switch` statement itself, you may at least be familiar with the basic concept, under the name computed goto or jump table.

A `switch` statement starts with an expression whose type is an `int`, `short`, `char`, or `byte`. In Java 5.0 `Integer`, `Short`, `Character` and `Byte` wrapper types are allowed, as are enumerated types. (Enums are new in Java 5.0; see Chapter 4 for details on enumerated types and their use in `switch` statements.) This expression is followed by a block of code in curly braces that contains various entry points that correspond to possible values for the expression. For example, the following switch statement is equivalent to the repeated if and else/if statements shown in the previous section:

```
switch(n) {
   case 1:                        // Start here if n == 1
     // Execute code block #1
     break;                       // Stop here
   case 2:                        // Start here if n == 2
     // Execute code block #2
     break;                       // Stop here
   case 3:                        // Start here if n == 3
     // Execute code block #3
     break;                       // Stop here
   default:                       // If all else fails...
     // Execute code block #4
     break;                       // Stop here
}
```


As you can see from the example, the various entry points into a switch statement are labeled either with the keyword case, followed by an integer value and a colon, or with the special default keyword, followed by a colon. When a switch statement executes, the interpreter computes the value of the expression in parentheses and then looks for a case label that matches that value. If it finds one, the interpreter starts executing the block of code at the first statement following the case label. If it does not find a case label with a matching value, the interpreter starts execution at the first statement following a special-case default: label. Or, if there is no default: label, the interpreter skips the body of the switch statement altogether.

Note the use of the break keyword at the end of each case in the previous code. The break statement is described later in this chapter, but, in this case, it causes the interpreter to exit the body of the switch statement. The case clauses in a switch statement specify only the starting point of the desired code. The individual cases are not independent blocks of code, and they do not have any implicit ending point. Therefore, you must explicitly specify the end of each case with a break or related statement. In the absence of break statements, a switch statement begins executing code at the first statement after the matching case label and continues executing statements until it reaches the end of the block. On rare occasions, it is useful to write code like this that falls through from one case label to the next, but 99% of the time you should be careful to end every case and default section with a statement that causes the switch statement to stop executing. Normally you use a break statement, but return and throw also work.

A switch statement can have more than one case clause labeling the same statement. Consider the switch statement in the following method:

```
boolean parseYesOrNoResponse(char response) {
   switch(response) {
     case 'y':
     case 'Y': return true;
     case 'n':
```

```
        case 'N': return false;
        default: throw new IllegalArgumentException("Response must be Y or N");
    }
}
```

The switch statement and its case labels have some important restrictions. First, the expression associated with a switch statement must have a byte, char, short, or int value. The floating-point and boolean types are not supported, and neither is long, even though long is an integer type. Second, the value associated with each case label must be a constant value or a constant expression the compiler can evaluate. A case label cannot contain a runtime expression involving variables or method calls, for example. Third, the case label values must be within the range of the data type used for the switch expression. And finally, it is obviously not legal to have two or more case labels with the same value or more than one default label.

The while Statement

Just as the if statement is the basic control statement that allows Java to make decisions, the while statement is the basic statement that allows Java to perform repetitive actions. It has the following syntax:

```
while (expression)
   statement
```

The while statement works by first evaluating the *expression*, which must result in a boolean (or, in Java 5.0, a Boolean) value. If the value is false, the interpreter skips the *statement* associated with the loop and moves to the next statement in the program. If it is true, however, the *statement* that forms the body of the loop is executed, and the *expression* is reevaluated. Again, if the value of *expression* is false, the interpreter moves on to the next statement in the program; otherwise it executes the *statement* again. This cycle continues while the *expression* remains true (i.e., until it evaluates to false), at which point the while statement ends, and the interpreter moves on to the next statement. You can create an infinite loop with the syntax while(true).

Here is an example while loop that prints the numbers 0 to 9:

```
int count = 0;
while (count < 10) {
   System.out.println(count);
   count++;
}
```

As you can see, the variable count starts off at 0 in this example and is incremented each time the body of the loop runs. Once the loop has executed 10 times, the expression becomes false (i.e., count is no longer less than 10), the while statement finishes, and the Java interpreter can move to the next statement in the program. Most loops have a counter variable like count. The variable names i, j, and k are commonly used as loop counters, although you should use more descriptive names if it makes your code easier to understand.

The do Statement

A do loop is much like a while loop, except that the loop expression is tested at the bottom of the loop rather than at the top. This means that the body of the loop is always executed at least once. The syntax is:

```
do
   statement
while ( expression ) ;
```


Notice a couple of differences between the do loop and the more ordinary while loop. First, the do loop requires both the do keyword to mark the beginning of the loop and the while keyword to mark the end and introduce the loop condition. Also, unlike the while loop, the do loop is terminated with a semicolon. This is because the do loop ends with the loop condition rather than simply ending with a curly brace that marks the end of the loop body. The following do loop prints the same output as the while loop just discussed:

```
int count = 0;
do {
   System.out.println(count);
   count++;
} while(count < 10);
```

The do loop is much less commonly used than its while cousin because, in practice, it is unusual to encounter a situation where you are sure you always want a loop to execute at least once.

The for Statement

The for statement provides a looping construct that is often more convenient than the while and do loops. The for statement takes advantage of a common looping pattern. Most loops have a counter, or state variable of some kind, that is initialized before the loop starts, tested to determine whether to execute the loop body, and then incremented or updated somehow at the end of the loop body before the test expression is evaluated again. The initialization, test, and update steps are the three crucial manipulations of a loop variable, and the for statement makes these three steps an explicit part of the loop syntax:

```
for(initialize ; test ; update)
    statement
```

This for loop is basically equivalent to the following while loop:*

```
initialize;
while(test) {
   statement;
   update;
}
```

* As you'll see when we consider the continue statement, this while loop is not exactly equivalent to the for loop.

Placing the *initialize*, *test*, and *update* expressions at the top of a for loop makes it especially easy to understand what the loop is doing, and it prevents mistakes such as forgetting to initialize or update the loop variable. The interpreter discards the values of the *initialize* and *update* expressions, so in order to be useful, these expressions must have side effects. *initialize* is typically an assignment expression while *update* is usually an increment, decrement, or some other assignment.

The following for loop prints the numbers 0 to 9, just as the previous while and do loops have done:

```
int count;
for(count = 0 ; count < 10 ; count++)
   System.out.println(count);
```

Notice how this syntax places all the important information about the loop variable on a single line, making it very clear how the loop executes. Placing the update expression in the for statement itself also simplifies the body of the loop to a single statement; we don't even need to use curly braces to produce a statement block.

The for loop supports some additional syntax that makes it even more convenient to use. Because many loops use their loop variables only within the loop, the for loop allows the *initialize* expression to be a full variable declaration, so that the variable is scoped to the body of the loop and is not visible outside of it. For example:

```
for(int count = 0 ; count < 10 ; count++)
   System.out.println(count);
```

Furthermore, the for loop syntax does not restrict you to writing loops that use only a single variable. Both the *initialize* and *update* expressions of a for loop can use a comma to separate multiple initializations and update expressions. For example:

```
for(int i = 0, j = 10 ; i < 10 ; i++, j--)
     sum += i * j;
```

Even though all the examples so far have counted numbers, for loops are not restricted to loops that count numbers. For example, you might use a for loop to iterate through the elements of a linked list:

```
for(Node n = listHead; n != null; n = n.nextNode())
   process(n);
```

The *initialize*, *test*, and *update* expressions of a for loop are all optional; only the semicolons that separate the expressions are required. If the *test* expression is omitted, it is assumed to be true. Thus, you can write an infinite loop as for(;;).

The for/in Statement

The for/in statement is a powerful new loop that was added to the language in Java 5.0. It iterates through the elements of an array or collection or any object that implements java.lang.Iterable (we'll see more about this new interface in a moment). On each iteration it assigns an element of the array or Iterable object to the loop variable you declare and then executes the loop body, which typically uses the loop variable to operate on the element. No loop counter or Iterator object is involved; the for/in loop performs the iteration automatically, and you need not concern yourself with correct initialization or termination of the loop.

A for/in loop is written as the keyword for followed by an open parenthesis, a variable declaration (without initializer), a colon, an expression, a close parenthesis, and finally the statement (or block) that forms the body of the loop.

```
for( declaration : expression )
     statement
```

Despite its name, the for/in loop does not use the keyword in. It is common to read the colon as "in," however. Because this statement does not have a keyword of its own, it does not have an unambiguous name. You may also see it called "enhanced for" or "foreach."

For the while, do, and for loops, we've shown an example that prints ten numbers. The for/in loop can do this too, but not on its own. for/in is not a general-purpose loop like the others. It is a specialized loop that executes its body once for each element *in* an array or collection. So, in order to loop ten times (to print out ten numbers), we need an array or other collection with ten elements. Here's code we can use:

```
// These are the numbers we want to print
int[] primes = new int[] { 2, 3, 5, 7, 11, 13, 17, 19, 23, 29 };
// This is the loop that prints them
for(int n : primes)
     System.out.println(n);
```

Here are some more things you should know about the syntax of the for/in loop:

- As noted earlier, *expression* must be either an array or an object that implements the java.lang.Iterable interface. This type must be known at compile-time so that the compiler can generate appropriate looping code. For example, you can't use this loop with an array or List that you have cast to an Object.
- The type of the array or Iterable elements must be assignment-compatible with the type of the variable declared in the *declaration*. If you use an Iterable object that is not parameterized with an element type, the variable must be declared as an Object. (Parameterized types are also new in Java 5.0; they are covered in Chapter 4.)
- The *declaration* usually consists of just a type and a variable name, but it may include a final modifier and any appropriate annotations (see Chapter 4). Using final prevents the loop variable from taking on any value other than the array or collection element the loop assigns it and serves to emphasize that the array or collection cannot be altered through the loop variable.
- The loop variable of the for/in loop must be declared as part of the loop, with both a type and a variable name. You cannot use a variable declared outside the loop as you can with the for loop.

The following class further illustrates the use of the for/in statement. It relies on parameterized types, which are covered in Chapter 4, and you may want to return to this section after reading that chapter.

```
import java.util.*;

public class ForInDemo {
    public static void main(String[ ] args) {
        // This is a collection we'll iterate over below.
        Set<String> wordset = new HashSet<String>( );

        // We start with a basic loop over the elements of an array.
        // The body of the loop is executed once for each element of args[ ].
        // Each time through one element is assigned to the variable word.
        for(String word : args) {
            System.out.print(word + " ");
            wordset.add(word);
        }
        System.out.println( );

        // Now iterate through the elements of the Set.
        for(String word : wordset) System.out.print(word + " ");
    }
}
```

Iterable and iterator

To understand how the for/in loop works with collections, we need to consider two interfaces, java.lang.Iterable, introduced in Java 5.0, and java.util.Iterator, introduced in Java 1.2, but parameterized with the rest of the Collections Framework in Java 5.0.* The APIs of both interfaces are reproduced here for convenience:

```
public interface Iterator<E> {
    boolean hasNext( );
    E next( );
    void remove( );
}
```

Iterator defines a way to iterate through the elements of a collection or other data structure. It works like this: while there are more elements in the collection (hasNext( ) returns true), call next( ) to obtain the next element of the collection. Ordered collections, such as lists, typically have iterators that guarantee that they'll return elements in order. Unordered collections like Set simply guarantee that repeated calls to next( ) return all elements of the set without omissions or duplications but do not specify an ordering.

```
public interface Iterable<E> {
    java.util.Iterator<E> iterator( );
}
```

* If you are not already familiar with parameterized types, you may want to skip this section now and return to it after reading Chapter 4.

The Iterable interface was introduced to make the for/in loop work. A class implements this interface in order to advertise that it is able to provide an Iterator to anyone interested. (This can be useful in its own right, even when you are not using the for/in loop). If an object is Iterable<E>, that means that that it has an iterator() method that returns an Iterator<E>, which has a next() method that returns an object of type E. If you implement Iterable and provide an Iterator for your own classes, you'll be able to iterate over those classes with the for/in loop.

Remember that if you use the for/in loop with an Iterable<E>, the loop variable must be of type E or a superclass or interface. For example, to iterate through the elements of a List<String>, the variable must be declared String or its superclass Object, or one of its interfaces CharSequence, Comparable, or Serializable.

If you use for/in to iterate through the elements of a raw List with no type parameter, the Iterable and Iterator also have no type parameter, and the type returned by the next() method of the raw Iterator is Object. In this case, you have no choice but to declare the loop variable to be an Object.

What for/in cannot do

for/in is a specialized loop that can simplify your code and reduce the possibility of looping errors in many circumstances. It is not a general replacement for the while, for, or do loops, however, because it hides the loop counter or Iterator from you. This means that some algorithms simply cannot be expressed with a for/in loop.

Suppose you want to print the elements of an array as a comma-separated list. To do this, you need to print a comma after every element of the array except the last, or equivalently, before every element of the array except the first. With a traditional for loop, the code might look like this:

```
for(int i = 0; i < words.length; i++) {
    if (i > 0) System.out.print(", ");
    System.out.print(words[i]);
}
```

This is a very straightforward task, but you simply cannot do it with for/in. The problem is that the for/in loop doesn't give you a loop counter or any other way to tell if you're on the first iteration, the last iteration, or somewhere in between. Here are two other simple loops that can't be converted to use for/in, for the same basic reason:

```
String[] args;  // Initialized elsewhere
for(int i = 0; i < args.length; i++)
    System.out.println(i + ": " + args[i]);

// Map words to the position at which they occur.
List<String> words;  // Initialized elsewhere
Map<String,Integer> map = new HashMap<String,Integer>();
for(int i = 0, n = words.size(); i < n; i++) map.put(words.get(i), i);
```

A similar issue exists when using for/in to iterate through the elements of the collection. Just as a for/in loop over an array has no way to obtain the array index of the current element, a for/in loop over a collection has no way to obtain the

Iterator object that is being used to itemize the elements of the collection. This means, for example, that you cannot use the remove( ) method of the iterator (or any of the additional methods defined by java.util.ListIterator) as you could if you used the Iterator explicitly yourself.

Here are some other things you cannot do with for/in:

- Iterate backwards through the elements of an array or List.
- Use a single loop counter to access the same-numbered elements of two distinct arrays.
- Iterate through the elements of a List using calls to its get( ) method rather than calls to its iterator.

The break Statement

A break statement causes the Java interpreter to skip immediately to the end of a containing statement. We have already seen the break statement used with the switch statement. The break statement is most often written as simply the keyword break followed by a semicolon:

```
break;
```

When used in this form, it causes the Java interpreter to immediately exit the innermost containing while, do, for, or switch statement. For example:

```
for(int i = 0; i < data.length; i++) {  // Loop through the data array.
    if (data[i] == target) {             // When we find what we're looking for,
        index = i;                       // remember where we found it
        break;                           // and stop looking!
    }
}   // The Java interpreter goes here after executing break
```

The break statement can also be followed by the name of a containing labeled statement. When used in this form, break causes the Java interpreter to immediately exit the named block, which can be any kind of statement, not just a loop or switch. For example:

```
testfornull: if (data != null) {               // If the array is defined,
   for(int row = 0; row < numrows; row++) {    // loop through one dimension,
     for(int col = 0; col < numcols; col++) {  // then loop through the other.
       if (data[row][col] == null)             // If the array is missing data,
         break testfornull;                    // treat the array as undefined.
     }
   }
}  // Java interpreter goes here after executing break testfornull
```

The continue Statement

While a break statement exits a loop, a continue statement quits the current iteration of a loop and starts the next one. continue, in both its unlabeled and labeled forms, can be used only within a while, do, or for loop. When used without a label, continue causes the innermost loop to start a new iteration. When used with a label that is the name of a containing loop, it causes the named loop to start a new iteration. For example:

```
for(int i = 0; i < data.length; i++) {  // Loop through data.
  if (data[i] == -1)                    // If a data value is missing,
    continue;                           // skip to the next iteration.
  process(data[i]);                     // Process the data value.
}
```

while, do, and for loops differ slightly in the way that continue starts a new iteration:

- With a while loop, the Java interpreter simply returns to the top of the loop, tests the loop condition again, and, if it evaluates to true, executes the body of the loop again.
- With a do loop, the interpreter jumps to the bottom of the loop, where it tests the loop condition to decide whether to perform another iteration of the loop.
- With a for loop, the interpreter jumps to the top of the loop, where it first evaluates the *update* expression and then evaluates the *test* expression to decide whether to loop again. As you can see, the behavior of a for loop with a continue statement is different from the behavior of the "basically equivalent" while loop presented earlier; *update* gets evaluated in the for loop but not in the equivalent while loop.

The return Statement

A return statement tells the Java interpreter to stop executing the current method. If the method is declared to return a value, the return statement is followed by an expression. The value of the expression becomes the return value of the method. For example, the following method computes and returns the square of a number:

```
double square(double x) {      // A method to compute x squared
  return x * x;                // Compute and return a value
}
```

Some methods are declared void to indicate that they do not return any value. The Java interpreter runs methods like this by executing their statements one by one until it reaches the end of the method. After executing the last statement, the interpreter returns implicitly. Sometimes, however, a void method has to return explicitly before reaching the last statement. In this case, it can use the return statement by itself, without any expression. For example, the following method prints, but does not return, the square root of its argument. If the argument is a negative number, it returns without printing anything:

```
void printSquareRoot(double x) {       // A method to print square root of x
  if (x < 0) return;                   // If x is negative, return explicitly
  System.out.println(Math.sqrt(x));    // Print the square root of x
}                                      // End of method: return implicitly
```

The synchronized Statement

Java makes it easy to write multithreaded programs (see Chapter 5 for examples). When working with multiple threads, you must often take care to prevent multiple threads from modifying an object simultaneously in a way that might corrupt the object's state. Sections of code that must not be executed simultaneously are known as *critical sections*. Java provides the synchronized statement to protect these critical sections. The syntax is:

```
synchronized ( expression ) {
   statements
}
```

expression is an expression that must evaluate to an object or an array. The *statements* constitute the code of the critical section and must be enclosed in curly braces. Before executing the critical section, the Java interpreter first obtains an exclusive lock on the object or array specified by *expression*. It holds the lock until it is finished running the critical section, then releases it. While a thread holds the lock on an object, no other thread can obtain that lock. Therefore, no other thread can execute this or any other critical sections that require a lock on the same object. If a thread cannot immediately obtain the lock required to execute a critical section, it simply waits until the lock becomes available.

Note that you do not have to use the synchronized statement unless your program creates multiple threads that share data. If only one thread ever accesses a data structure, there is no need to protect it with synchronized. When you do have to use synchronized, it might be in code like the following:

```
public static void SortIntArray(int[] a) {
   // Sort the array a. This is synchronized so that some other thread
   // cannot change elements of the array while we're sorting it (at
   // least not other threads that protect their changes to the array
   // with synchronized).
   synchronized (a) {
      // Do the array sort here
   }
}
```

The synchronized keyword is also available as a modifier in Java and is more commonly used in this form than as a statement. When applied to a method, the synchronized keyword indicates that the entire method is a critical section. For a synchronized class method (a static method), Java obtains an exclusive lock on the class before executing the method. For a synchronized instance method, Java obtains an exclusive lock on the class instance. (Class and instance methods are discussed in Chapter 3.)

The throw Statement

An *exception* is a signal that indicates some sort of exceptional condition or error has occurred. To *throw* an exception is to signal an exceptional condition. To *catch* an exception is to handle it—to take whatever actions are necessary to recover from it.

In Java, the throw statement is used to throw an exception:

```
throw expression ;
```

The *expression* must evaluate to an exception object that describes the exception or error that has occurred. We'll talk more about types of exceptions shortly; for now, all you need to know is that an exception is represented by an object. Here is some example code that throws an exception:

```
public static double factorial(int x) {
  if (x < 0)
    throw new IllegalArgumentException("x must be >= 0");
  double fact;
  for(fact=1.0; x > 1; fact *= x, x--)
    /* empty */ ;          // Note use of the empty statement
  return fact;
}
```


When the Java interpreter executes a `throw` statement, it immediately stops normal program execution and starts looking for an exception handler that can catch, or handle, the exception. Exception handlers are written with the `try/catch/finally` statement, which is described in the next section. The Java interpreter first looks at the enclosing block of code to see if it has an associated exception handler. If so, it exits that block of code and starts running the exception-handling code associated with the block. After running the exception handler, the interpreter continues execution at the statement immediately following the handler code.

If the enclosing block of code does not have an appropriate exception handler, the interpreter checks the next higher enclosing block of code in the method. This continues until a handler is found. If the method does not contain an exception handler that can handle the exception thrown by the `throw` statement, the interpreter stops running the current method and returns to the caller. Now the interpreter starts looking for an exception handler in the blocks of code of the calling method. In this way, exceptions propagate up through the lexical structure of Java methods, up the call stack of the Java interpreter. If the exception is never caught, it propagates all the way up to the `main()` method of the program. If it is not handled in that method, the Java interpreter prints an error message, prints a stack trace to indicate where the exception occurred, and then exits.

Exception types

An exception in Java is an object. The type of this object is `java.lang.Throwable`, or more commonly, some subclass* of `Throwable` that more specifically describes the type of exception that occurred. `Throwable` has two standard subclasses: `java.lang.Error` and `java.lang.Exception`. Exceptions that are subclasses of `Error` generally indicate unrecoverable problems: the virtual machine has run out of memory, or a class file is corrupted and cannot be read, for example. Exceptions of this sort can be caught and handled, but it is rare to do so. Exceptions that are subclasses of `Exception`, on the other hand, indicate less severe conditions. These exceptions can be reasonably caught and handled. They include such exceptions as `java.io.EOFException`, which signals the end of a file, and `java.lang.ArrayIndexOutOfBoundsException`, which indicates that a program has tried to read past the end of an array. In this book, I use the term "excep-

* We haven't talked about subclasses yet; they are covered in detail in Chapter 3.

tion" to refer to any exception object, regardless of whether the type of that exception is Exception or Error.

Since an exception is an object, it can contain data, and its class can define methods that operate on that data. The Throwable class and all its subclasses include a String field that stores a human-readable error message that describes the exceptional condition. It's set when the exception object is created and can be read from the exception with the getMessage( ) method. Most exceptions contain only this single message, but a few add other data. The java.io.InterruptedIOException, for example, adds a field named bytesTransferred that specifies how much input or output was completed before the exceptional condition interrupted it.

The try/catch/finally Statement

The try/catch/finally statement is Java's exception-handling mechanism. The try clause of this statement establishes a block of code for exception handling. This try block is followed by zero or more catch clauses, each of which is a block of statements designed to handle a specific type of exception. The catch clauses are followed by an optional finally block that contains cleanup code guaranteed to be executed regardless of what happens in the try block. Both the catch and finally clauses are optional, but every try block must be accompanied by at least one or the other. The try, catch, and finally blocks all begin and end with curly braces. These are a required part of the syntax and cannot be omitted, even if the clause contains only a single statement.

The following code illustrates the syntax and purpose of the try/catch/finally statement:

```
try {
   // Normally this code runs from the top of the block to the bottom
   // without problems. But it can sometimes throw an exception,
   // either directly with a throw statement or indirectly by calling
   // a method that throws an exception.
}
catch (SomeException e1) {
   // This block contains statements that handle an exception object
   // of type SomeException or a subclass of that type. Statements in
   // this block can refer to that exception object by the name e1.
}
catch (AnotherException e2) {
   // This block contains statements that handle an exception object
   // of type AnotherException or a subclass of that type. Statements
   // in this block can refer to that exception object by the name e2.
}
finally {
   // This block contains statements that are always executed
   // after we leave the try clause, regardless of whether we leave it:
   //   1) normally, after reaching the bottom of the block;
   //   2) because of a break, continue, or return statement;
   //   3) with an exception that is handled by a catch clause above; or
   //   4) with an uncaught exception that has not been handled.
   // If the try clause calls System.exit(), however, the interpreter
   // exits before the finally clause can be run.
}
```

try

The try clause simply establishes a block of code that either has its exceptions handled or needs special cleanup code to be run when it terminates for any reason. The try clause by itself doesn't do anything interesting; it is the catch and finally clauses that do the exception-handling and cleanup operations.

catch

A try block can be followed by zero or more catch clauses that specify code to handle various types of exceptions. Each catch clause is declared with a single argument that specifies the type of exceptions the clause can handle and also provides a name the clause can use to refer to the exception object it is currently handling. The type and name of an exception handled by a catch clause are exactly like the type and name of an argument passed to a method, except that for a catch clause, the argument type must be Throwable or one of its subclasses.

When an exception is thrown, the Java interpreter looks for a catch clause with an argument of the same type as the exception object or a superclass of that type. The interpreter invokes the first such catch clause it finds. The code within a catch block should take whatever action is necessary to cope with the exceptional condition. If the exception is a java.io.FileNotFoundException exception, for example, you might handle it by asking the user to check his spelling and try again. It is not required to have a catch clause for every possible exception; in some cases the correct response is to allow the exception to propagate up and be caught by the invoking method. In other cases, such as a programming error signaled by NullPointerException, the correct response is probably not to catch the exception at all, but allow it to propagate and have the Java interpreter exit with a stack trace and an error message.

finally

The finally clause is generally used to clean up after the code in the try clause (e.g., close files and shut down network connections). What is useful about the finally clause is that it is guaranteed to be executed if any portion of the try block is executed, regardless of how the code in the try block completes. In fact, the only way a try clause can exit without allowing the finally clause to be executed is by invoking the System.exit( ) method, which causes the Java interpreter to stop running.

In the normal case, control reaches the end of the try block and then proceeds to the finally block, which performs any necessary cleanup. If control leaves the try block because of a return, continue, or break statement, the finally block is executed before control transfers to its new destination.

If an exception occurs in the try block and there is an associated catch block to handle the exception, control transfers first to the catch block and then to the finally block. If there is no local catch block to handle the exception, control transfers first to the finally block, and then propagates up to the nearest containing catch clause that can handle the exception.

If a finally block itself transfers control with a return, continue, break, or throw statement or by calling a method that throws an exception, the pending control transfer is abandoned, and this new transfer is processed. For example, if a finally clause throws an exception, that exception replaces any exception that was in the process of being thrown. If a finally clause issues a return statement, the method returns normally, even if an exception has been thrown and has not yet been handled.

try and finally can be used together without exceptions or any catch clauses. In this case, the finally block is simply cleanup code that is guaranteed to be executed, regardless of any break, continue, or return statements within the try clause.

In previous discussions of the for and continue statements, we've seen that a for loop cannot be naively translated into a while loop because the continue statement behaves slightly differently when used in a for loop than it does when used in a while loop. The finally clause gives us a way to write a while loop that handles the continue statement in the same way that a for loop does. Consider the following generalized for loop:

```
for( initialize ; test ; update )
    statement
```

The following while loop behaves the same, even if the statement block contains a continue statement:

```
initialize ;
while ( test ) {
   try { statement }
   finally { update ; }
}
```

Note, however, that placing the update statement within a finally block causes this while loop to respond to break statements differently than the for loop does.

The assert Statement

An assert statement is used to document and verify design assumptions in Java code. This statement was added in Java 1.4 and cannot be used with previous versions of the language. An *assertion* consists of the assert keyword followed by a boolean expression that the programmer believes should always evaluate to true. By default, assertions are not enabled, and the assert statement does not actually do anything. It is possible to enable assertions as a debugging and testing tool, however; when this is done, the assert statement evaluates the expression. If it is indeed true, assert does nothing. On the other hand, if the expression evaluates to false, the assertion fails, and the assert statement throws a java.lang.AssertionError.

The assert statement may include an optional second expression, separated from the first by a colon. When assertions are enabled and the first expression evaluates to false, the value of the second expression is taken as an error code or error message and is passed to the AssertionError( ) constructor. The full syntax of the statement is:

```
assert assertion ;
```

or:

```
assert assertion : errorcode ;
```

It is important to remember that the *assertion must* be a boolean expression, which typically means that it contains a comparison operator or invokes a boolean-valued method.

Compiling assertions

Because the assert statement was added in Java 1.4, and because assert was not a reserved word prior to Java 1.4, the introduction of this new statement can cause code that uses "assert" as an identifier to break. For this reason, the *javac* compiler does not recognize the assert statement by default. To compile Java code that uses the assert statement, you must use the command-line argument -source 1.4. For example:

```
javac -source 1.4 ClassWithAssertions.java
```

In Java 1.4, the *javac* compiler allows "assert" to be used as an identifier unless -source 1.4 is specified. If it finds assert used as an identifier, it issues an incompatibility warning to encourage you to modify your code.

In Java 5.0, the *javac* compiler recognizes the assert statement (as well as all the new Java 5.0 syntax) by default, and no special compiler arguments are required to compile code that contains assertions. If you have legacy code that still uses assert as an identifier, it will no longer compile by default in Java 5.0. If you can't fix it, you can compile it in Java 5.0 using the -source 1.3 option.

Enabling assertions

assert statements encode assumptions that should always be true. For efficiency, it does not make sense to test assertions each time code is executed. Thus, by default, assertions are disabled, and assert statements have no effect. The assertion code remains compiled in the class files, however, so it can always be enabled for testing, diagnostic, and debugging purposes. You can enable assertions, either across the board or selectively, with command-line arguments to the Java interpreter. To enable assertions in all classes except for system classes, use the -ea argument. To enable assertions in system classes, use -esa. To enable assertions within a specific class, use -ea followed by a colon and the classname:

```
java -ea:com.example.sorters.MergeSort com.example.sorters.Test
```

To enable assertions for all classes in a package and in all of its subpackages, follow the -ea argument with a colon, the package name, and three dots:

```
java -ea:com.example.sorters... com.example.sorters.Test
```

You can disable assertions in the same way, using the -da argument. For example, to enable assertions throughout a package and then disable them in a specific class or subpackage, use:

```
java -ea:com.example.sorters... -da:com.example.sorters.QuickSort
java -ea:com.example.sorters... -da:com.example.sorters.plugins...
```

If you prefer verbose command-line arguments, you can use -enableassertions and -disableassertions instead of -ea and -da and -enablesystemassertions instead of -esa.

Java 1.4 added to `java.lang.ClassLoader` methods for enabling and disabling the assertions for classes loaded through that `ClassLoader`. If you use a custom class loader in your program and want to turn on assertions, you may be interested in these methods. See `ClassLoader` in the reference section.

Using assertions

Because assertions are disabled by default and impose no performance penalty on your code, you can use them liberally to document any assumptions you make while programming. It may take some time to get used to this, but as you do, you'll find more and more uses for the `assert` statement. Suppose, for example, that you're writing a method in such a way that you know that the variable `x` is either 0 or 1. Without assertions, you might code an `if` statement that looks like this:

```
if (x == 0) {
   ...
}
else {  // x is 1
   ...
}
```

The comment in this code is an informal assertion indicating that you believe that within the body of the `else` clause, `x` will always equal 1.

Now suppose your code is later modified in such a way that `x` can take on a value other than 0 and 1. The comment and the assumption that go along with it are no longer valid, and this may cause a bug that is not immediately apparent or is difficult to localize. The solution in this situation is to convert your comment into an `assert` statement. The code becomes:

```
if (x == 0) {
   ...
}
else {
   assert x == 1 : x  // x must be 0 or 1
   ...
}
```

Now, if `x` somehow ends up holding an unexpected value, an `AssertionError` is thrown, which makes the bug immediately apparent and easy to pinpoint. Furthermore, the second expression (following the colon) in the `assert` statement includes the unexpected value of `x` as the "error message" of the `AssertionError`. This message is not intended to mean anything to an end user, but to provide enough information so that you know not just that an assertion failed but also what caused it to fail.

A similar technique is useful with `switch` statements. If you write a `switch` statement without a `default` clause, you make an assumption about the set of possible values for the `switch` expression. If you believe that no other value is possible, you can add an `assert` statement to document and validate that fact. For example:

```
switch(x) {
   case -1: return LESS;
   case 0: return EQUALS;
   case 1: return GREATER;
   default: assert false:x; // Throw AssertionError if x is not -1, 0, or 1.
}
```

Note that the form `assert false;` always fails. It is a useful "dead-end" statement when you believe that the statement can never be reached.

Another common use of the `assert` statement is to test whether the arguments passed to a method all have values that are legal for that method; this is also known as enforcing method preconditions. For example:

```
private static Object[] subArray(Object[] a, int x, int y) {
   assert x <= y : "subArray: x > y";    // Precondition: x must be <= y
   // Now go on to create and return a subarray of a...
}
```

Note that this is a private method. The programmer has used an `assert` statement to document a precondition of the `subArray()` method and state that she believes that all methods that invoke this private method do in fact honor that precondition. She can state this because she has control over all the methods that invoke `subArray()`. She can verify her belief by enabling assertions while testing the code. But once the code is tested, if assertions are left disabled, the method does not suffer the overhead of testing its arguments each time it is called. Note that the programmer did not use an `assert` statement to test that argument *a* is non-null and that the *x* and *y* arguments were legal indexes into that array. These implicit preconditions are always tested by Java at runtime, and a failure results in an unchecked `NullPointerException` or an `ArrayIndexOutOfBoundsException`, so an assertion is not required for them.

It is important to understand that the `assert` statement is not suitable for enforcing preconditions on public methods. A public method can be called from anywhere, and the programmer cannot assert in advance that it will be invoked correctly. To be robust, a public API must explicitly test its arguments and enforce its preconditions each time it is called, whether or not assertions are enabled.

A related use of the `assert` statement is to verify a class invariant. Suppose you are creating a class that represents a list of objects and allows objects to be inserted and deleted but always maintains the list in sorted order. You believe that your implementation is correct and that the insertion methods always leave the list in sorted order, but you want to test this to be sure. You might write a method that tests whether the list is actually sorted, then use an `assert` statement to invoke the method at the end of each method that modifies the list. For example:

```
public void insert(Object o) {
    ...                  // Do the insertion here
   assert isSorted();  // Assert the class invariant here
}
```

When writing code that must be threadsafe, you must obtain locks (using a `synchronized` method or statement) when required. One common use of the `assert` statement in this situation is to verify that the current thread holds the lock it requires:

```
assert Thread.holdsLock(data);
```

The `Thread.holdsLock()` method was added in Java 1.4 primarily for use with the `assert` statement.

To use assertions effectively, you must be aware of a couple of fine points. First, remember that your programs will sometimes run with assertions enabled and sometimes with assertions disabled. This means that you should be careful not to write assertion expressions that contain side effects. If you do, your code will run differently when assertions are enabled than it will when they are disabled. There are a few exceptions to this rule, of course. For example, if a method contains two `assert` statements, the first can include a side effect that affects only the second assertion. Another use of side effects in assertions is the following idiom that determines whether assertions are enabled (which is not something that your code should ever really need to do):

```
boolean assertions = false;  // Whether assertions are enabled
assert assertions = true;    // This assert never fails but has a side effect
```

Note that the expression in the `assert` statement is an assignment, not a comparison. The value of an assignment expression is always the value assigned, so this expression always evaluates to `true`, and the assertion never fails. Because this assignment expression is part of an `assert` statement, the `assertions` variable is set to `true` only if assertions are enabled.

In addition to avoiding side effects in your assertions, another rule for working with the `assert` statement is that you should never try to catch an `AssertionError` (unless you catch it at the top level simply so that you can display the error in a more user-friendly fashion). If an `AssertionError` is thrown, it indicates that one of the programmer's assumptions has not held up. This means that the code is being used outside of the parameters for which it was designed, and it cannot be expected to work correctly. In short, there is no plausible way to recover from an `AssertionError`, and you should not attempt to catch it.

Methods

A *method* is a named sequence of Java statements that can be invoked by other Java code. When a method is invoked, it is passed zero or more values known as *arguments*. The method performs some computations and, optionally, returns a value. As described in "Expressions and Operators" earlier in this chapter, a method invocation is an expression that is evaluated by the Java interpreter. Because method invocations can have side effects, however, they can also be used as expression statements. This section does not discuss method invocation, but instead describes how to define methods.

Defining Methods

You already know how to define the body of a method; it is simply an arbitrary sequence of statements enclosed within curly braces. What is more interesting about a method is its *signature*.* The signature specifies the following:

- The name of the method
- The number, order, type, and name of the parameters used by the method
- The type of the value returned by the method

* In the Java Language Specification, the term "signature" has a technical meaning that is slightly different than that used here. This book uses a less formal definition of method signature.

- The checked exceptions that the method can throw (the signature may also list unchecked exceptions, but these are not required)
- Various method modifiers that provide additional information about the method

A method signature defines everything you need to know about a method before calling it. It is the method *specification* and defines the API for the method. The reference section of this book is essentially a list of method signatures for all publicly accessible methods of all publicly accessible classes of the Java platform. In order to use the reference section of this book, you need to know how to read a method signature. And, in order to write Java programs, you need to know how to define your own methods, each of which begins with a method signature.

A method signature looks like this:

```
modifiers type  name ( paramlist ) [ throws exceptions ]
```

The signature (the method specification) is followed by the method body (the method implementation), which is simply a sequence of Java statements enclosed in curly braces. If the method is *abstract* (see Chapter 3), the implementation is omitted, and the method body is replaced with a single semicolon. In Java 5.0 and later, the signature of a *generic method* may also include type variable declarations. Generic methods and type variables are discussed in Chapter 4.

Here are some example method definitions, which begin with the signature and are followed by the method body:

```
// This method is passed an array of strings and has no return value.
// All Java programs have a main entry point with this name and signature.
public static void main(String[] args) {
     if (args.length > 0) System.out.println("Hello " + args[0]);
     else System.out.println("Hello world");
}

// This method is passed two double arguments and returns a double.
static double distanceFromOrigin(double x, double y) {
     return Math.sqrt(x*x + y*y);
}

// This method is abstract which means it has no body.
// Note that it may throw exceptions when invoked.
protected abstract String readText(File f, String encoding)
    throws FileNotFoundException, UnsupportedEncodingException;
```

modifiers is zero or more special modifier keywords, separated from each other by spaces. A method might be declared with the `public` and `static` modifiers, for example. The allowed modifiers and their meanings are described in the next section.

The *type* in a method signature specifies the return type of the method. If the method does not return a value, *type* must be `void`. If a method is declared with a non-void return type, it must include a `return` statement that returns a value of (or convertible to) the declared type.

A *constructor* is a special kind of method used to initialize newly created objects. As we'll see in Chapter 3, constructors are defined just like methods, except that their signatures do not include this *type* specification.

The *name* of a method follows the specification of its modifiers and type. Method names, like variable names, are Java identifiers and, like all Java identifiers, may contain letters in any language represented by the Unicode character set. It is legal, and often quite useful, to define more than one method with the same name, as long as each version of the method has a different parameter list. Defining multiple methods with the same name is called *method overloading*. The `System.out.println()` method we've seen so much of is an overloaded method. One method by this name prints a string and other methods by the same name print the values of the various primitive types. The Java compiler decides which method to call based on the type of the argument passed to the method.

When you are defining a method, the name of the method is always followed by the method's parameter list, which must be enclosed in parentheses. The parameter list defines zero or more arguments that are passed to the method. The parameter specifications, if there are any, each consist of a type and a name and are separated from each other by commas (if there are multiple parameters). When a method is invoked, the argument values it is passed must match the number, type, and order of the parameters specified in this method signature line. The values passed need not have exactly the same type as specified in the signature, but they must be convertible to those types without casting. C and C++ programmers should note that when a Java method expects no arguments, its parameter list is simply `()`, not `(void)`.

In Java 5.0 and later, it is possible to define and invoke methods that accept a variable number of arguments, using a syntax known colloquially as *varargs*. Varargs are covered in detail later in this chapter.

The final part of a method signature is the `throws` clause, which is used to list the *checked exceptions* that a method can throw. Checked exceptions are a category of exception classes that must be listed in the `throws` clauses of methods that can throw them. If a method uses the `throw` statement to throw a checked exception, or if it calls some other method that throws a checked exception and does not catch or handle that exception, the method must declare that it can throw that exception. If a method can throw one or more checked exceptions, it specifies this by placing the `throws` keyword after the argument list and following it by the name of the exception class or classes it can throw. If a method does not throw any exceptions, it does not use the `throws` keyword. If a method throws more than one type of exception, separate the names of the exception classes from each other with commas. More on this in a bit.

Method Modifiers

The modifiers of a method consist of zero or more modifier keywords such as `public`, `static`, or `abstract`. Here is a list of allowed modifiers and their meanings. Note that in Java 5.0 and later, annotations, such as `@Override`, `@Deprecated`, and `@SuppressWarnings`, are treated as modifiers and may be mixed in with the modifier list. Anyone can define new annotation types, so it is not possible to list all possible method annotations. See Chapter 4 for more on annotations.

`abstract`
: An `abstract` method is a specification without an implementation. The curly braces and Java statements that would normally comprise the body of the method are replaced with a single semicolon. A class that includes an `abstract` method must itself be declared `abstract`. Such a class is incomplete and cannot be instantiated (see Chapter 3).

`final`
: A `final` method may not be overridden or hidden by a subclass, which makes it amenable to compiler optimizations that are not possible for regular methods. All `private` methods are implicitly `final`, as are all methods of any class that is declared `final`.

`native`
: The `native` modifier specifies that the method implementation is written in some "native" language such as C and is provided externally to the Java program. Like `abstract` methods, `native` methods have no body: the curly braces are replaced with a semicolon.

  When Java was first released, `native` methods were sometimes used for efficiency reasons. That is almost never necessary today. Instead, native methods are used to interface Java code to existing libraries written in C or C++. Native methods are implicitly platform-dependent, and the procedure for linking the implementation with the Java class that declares the method is dependent on the implementation of the Java virtual machine. Native methods are not covered in this book.

`public`, `protected`, `private`
: These access modifiers specify whether and where a method can be used outside of the class that defines it. These very important modifiers are explained in Chapter 3.

`static`
: A method declared `static` is a *class method* associated with the class itself rather than with an instance of the class. This is explained in detail in Chapter 3.

`strictfp`
: A method declared `strictfp` must perform floating-point arithmetic using 32- or 64-bit floating point formats strictly and may not take advantage of any extended exponent bits available to the platform's floating-point hardware. The "fp" in this awkwardly named, rarely used modifier stands for "floating point."

`synchronized`
: The `synchronized` modifier makes a method threadsafe. Before a thread can invoke a `synchronized` method, it must obtain a lock on the method's class (for `static` methods) or on the relevant instance of the class (for non-`static` methods). This prevents two threads from executing the method at the same time.

  The `synchronized` modifier is an implementation detail (because methods can make themselves threadsafe in other ways) and is not formally part of the method specification or API. Good documentation specifies explicitly whether a method is threadsafe; you should not rely on the presence or absence of the synchronized keyword when working with multithreaded programs.

Declaring Checked Exceptions

In the discussion of the throw statement, we said that exceptions are Throwable objects and that exceptions fall into two main categories, specified by the Error and Exception subclasses. In addition to making a distinction between Error and Exception classes, the Java exception-handling scheme also distinguishes between checked and unchecked exceptions. Any exception object that is an Error is unchecked. Any exception object that is an Exception is checked, unless it is a subclass of java.lang.RuntimeException, in which case it is unchecked. (RuntimeException is a subclass of Exception.)

The distinction between checked and unchecked exceptions has to do with the circumstances under which the exceptions are thrown. Practically any method can throw an unchecked exception at essentially any time. There is no way to predict an OutOfMemoryError, for example, and any method that uses objects or arrays can throw a NullPointerException if it is passed an invalid null argument. Checked exceptions, on the other hand, arise only in specific, well-defined circumstances. If you try to read data from a file, for example, you must at least consider the possibility that a FileNotFoundException will be thrown if the specified file cannot be found.

Java has different rules for working with checked and unchecked exceptions. If you write a method that throws a checked exception, you must use a throws clause to declare the exception in the method signature. The reason these types of exceptions are called checked exceptions is that the Java compiler checks to make sure you have declared them in method signatures and produces a compilation error if you have not.

Even if you never throw an exception yourself, sometimes you must use a throws clause to declare an exception. If your method calls a method that can throw a checked exception, you must either include exception-handling code to handle that exception or use throws to declare that your method can also throw that exception. For example, the following method reads the first line of text from a named file. It uses methods that can throw various types of java.io.IOException objects, so it declares this fact with a throws clause:

```
public static String readFirstLine(String filename) throws IOException {
    BufferedReader in = new BufferedReader(new FileReader(filename));
    String firstline = in.readLine();
    in.close();
    return firstline;
}
```

How do you know if the method you are calling can throw a checked exception? You can look at its method signature to find out. Or, failing that, the Java compiler will tell you (by reporting a compilation error) if you've called a method whose exceptions you must handle or declare.

Variable-Length Argument Lists

In Java 5.0 and later, methods may be declared to accept, and may be invoked with, variable numbers of arguments. Such methods are commonly known as *varargs* methods. The new `System.out.printf()` method as well as the related `format()` methods of `String` and `java.util.Formatter` use varargs. The similar, but unrelated, `format()` method of `java.text.MessageFormat` has been converted to use varargs as have a number of important methods from the Reflection API of `java.lang.reflect`.

A variable-length argument list is declared by following the type of the last argument to the method with an ellipsis (`...`), indicating that this last argument can be repeated zero or more times. For example:

```
public static int max(int first, int... rest) {
     int max = first;
     for(int i: rest) {
         if (i > max) max = i;
     }
     return max;
}
```

This `max()` method is declared with two arguments. The first is just a regular `int` value. The second, however may be repeated zero or more times. All of the following are legal invocations of `max()`:

```
max(0)
max(1, 2)
max(16, 8, 4, 2, 1)
```

As you can tell from the `for/in` statement in the body of `max()`, the second argument is treated as an array of `int` values. Varargs methods are handled purely by the compiler. To the Java interpreter, the `max()` method is indistinguishable from this one:

```
public static int max(int first, int[] rest) { /* body omitted */ }
```

To convert a varargs signature to the "real" signature, simply replace `...` with `[ ]`. Remember that only one ellipsis can appear in a parameter list, and it may only appear on the last parameter in the list.

Since varargs methods are compiled into methods that expect an array of arguments, invocations of those methods are compiled to include code that creates and initializes such an array. So the call `max(1,2,3)` is compiled to this:

```
max(1, new int[] { 2, 3 })
```

If you already have method arguments stored in an array, it is perfectly legal for you to pass them to the method that way, instead of writing them out individually. You can treat any `...` argument as if it were declared as an array. The converse is not true, however: you can only use varargs method invocation syntax when the method is actually declared as a varargs method using an ellipsis.

Varargs methods interact particularly well with the new autoboxing feature of Java 5.0 (see "Boxing and Unboxing Conversions" later in this chapter). A method that has an `Object...` variable length argument list can take arguments of any reference type because all objects and arrays are subclasses of Object. Furthermore, autoboxing allows you to invoke the method using primitive values as well: the compiler boxes these up into wrapper objects as it builds the Object[ ] that is the true argument to the method. The printf( ) and format( ) methods mentioned at the beginning of this section are all declared with an Object... parameter.

One quirk arises with methods with an Object... parameter. It does not arise very often in practice, but studying the quirk will solidify your understanding of varargs. Recall that varargs methods can be invoked with an argument of array type or any number of arguments of the element type. When a method is declared with an Object... argument, you can pass an Object[ ] of arguments, or zero or more individual Object arguments. But every Object[ ] is also an Object. What do you do if you want to pass an Object[ ] as the single object argument to the method? Consider the following code that uses the printf( ) method:

```
import static java.lang.System.out;  // out now refers to System.out

// Here we invoke the varargs method with individual Object arguments.
// Note the use of autoboxing to convert primitives to wrapper objects
out.printf("%d %d %d\n", 1, 2, 3);

// This line does the same thing but passes the arguments in an array
// that has already been created:
Object[ ] args = new Object[ ] { 1, 2, 3 };
out.printf("%d %d %d\n", args);

// Now consider the following Object[ ], which we wish to pass
// as a single argument, not as an array of two arguments.
Object[ ] arg =  new Object[ ] { "hello", "world" };
// These two lines do the same thing: print "hello".  Not what we want.
out.printf("%s\n", "hello", "world");
out.printf("%s\n", arg);

// If we want arg to be treated as a single Object argument, we need to
// pass it as an the element of an array.  Here's one way:
out.printf("%s\n", new Object[ ] { arg });

// An easier way is to convince the compiler to create the array itself.
// We use a cast to say that arg is a single Object argument, not an array:
out.printf("%s\n", (Object)arg);
```

Covariant Return Types

As part of the addition of generic types, Java 5.0 now also supports *covariant returns*. This means that an overriding method may narrow the return type of the method it overrides.* The following example makes this clearer:

```
class Point2D { int x, y; }
class Point3D extends Point2D { int z; }
```

* Method overriding is *not* the same as method overloading discussed earlier in this section. Method overriding involves subclassing and is covered in Chapter 3. If you are not already familiar with these concepts, you should skip this section for now and return to it later.

```
class Event2D {
    public Point2D getLocation() { return new Point2D(); }
}

class Event3D extends Event2D {
    @Override public Point3D getLocation() { return new Point3D(); }
}
```


This code defines four classes: a two-dimensional point, a three-dimensional point, and event objects that represent an event in two-dimensional space and in three-dimensional space. Each event class has a getLocation() method. The Event2D method returns a Point2D object. Event3D subclasses Event2D and overrides getLocation(). Its version of the method sensibly returns a Point3D. Because every Point3D object is also a Point2D object, this is a perfectly reasonable thing to do. It simply wasn't allowed prior to Java 5.0.

In Java 1.4 and earlier, the return type of an overriding method must be identical to the type of the method it overrides. In order to compile under Java 1.4, the Event3D.getLocation() method would have to be modified to have a return type of Point2D. It could still return a Point3D object, of course, but the caller would have to cast the return value from Point2D to Point3D.

The @Override in the code example is an *annotation*, covered in Chapter 4. This one is a compile-time assertion that the method overrides something. The compiler would have produced a compilation error if the assertion failed.

Classes and Objects Introduced

Now that we have introduced operators, expressions, statements, and methods, we can finally talk about classes. A *class* is a named collection of fields that hold data values and methods that operate on those values. Classes are just one of five reference types supported by Java, but they are the most important type. Classes are thoroughly documented in a chapter of their own, Chapter 3. We introduce them here, however, because they are the next higher level of syntax after methods, and because the rest of this chapter requires a basic familiarity with the concept of class and the basic syntax for defining a class, instantiating it, and using the resulting *object*.

The most important thing about classes is that they define new data types. For example, you might define a class named Point to represent a data point in the two-dimensional Cartesian coordinate system. This class would define fields (each of type double) to hold the X and Y coordinates of a point and methods to manipulate and operate on the point. The Point class is a new data type.

When discussing data types, it is important to distinguish between the data type itself and the values the data type represents. char is a data type: it represents Unicode characters. But a char value represents a single specific character. A class is a data type; a class value is called an *object*. We use the name class because each class defines a type (or kind, or species, or class) of objects. The Point class is a data type that represents X,Y points, while a Point object represents a single specific X,Y point. As you might imagine, classes and their objects are closely linked. In the sections that follow, we will discuss both.

Defining a Class

Here is a possible definition of the Point class we have been discussing:

```
/** Represents a Cartesian (x,y) point */
public class Point {
     public double x, y;                         // The coordinates of the point
     public Point(double x, double y) {          // A constructor that
         this.x = x; this.y = y;                 // initializes the fields
     }

     public double distanceFromOrigin() {        // A method that operates on
         return Math.sqrt(x*x + y*y);            // the x and y fields
     }
}
```

This class definition is stored in a file named *Point.java* and compiled to a file named *Point.class*, where it is available for use by Java programs and other classes. This class definition is provided here for completeness and to provide context, but don't expect to understand all the details just yet; most of Chapter 3 is devoted to the topic of defining classes.

Keep in mind that you don't have to define every class you want to use in a Java program. The Java platform includes thousands of predefined classes that are guaranteed to be available on every computer that runs Java.

Creating an Object

Now that we have defined the Point class as a new data type, we can use the following line to declare a variable that holds a Point object:

```
Point p;
```

Declaring a variable to hold a Point object does not create the object itself, however. To actually create an object, you must use the new operator. This keyword is followed by the object's class (i.e., its type) and an optional argument list in parentheses. These arguments are passed to the constructor method for the class, which initializes internal fields in the new object:

```
// Create a Point object representing (2,-3.5).
// Declare a variable p and store a reference to the new Point object in it.
Point p = new Point(2.0, -3.5);

// Create some other objects as well
Date d = new Date();          // A Date object that represents the current time
Set words = new HashSet();  // A HashSet object to hold a set of objects
```

The new keyword is by far the most common way to create objects in Java. A few other ways are also worth mentioning. First, a couple of classes are so important that Java defines special literal syntax for creating objects of those types (as we discuss later in this section). Second, Java supports a dynamic loading mechanism that allows programs to load classes and create instances of those classes dynamically. This dynamic instantiation is done with the newInstance() methods of java.lang.Class and java.lang.reflect.Constructor. Finally, objects can also be created by deserializing them. In other words, an object that has had its state saved, or serialized, usually to a file, can be recreated using the `java.io.ObjectInputStream` class.

Using an Object

Now that we've seen how to define classes and instantiate them by creating objects, we need to look at the Java syntax that allows us to use those objects. Recall that a class defines a collection of fields and methods. Each object has its own copies of those fields and has access to those methods. We use the dot character (`.`) to access the named fields and methods of an object. For example:

```
Point p = new Point(2, 3);           // Create an object
double x = p.x;                      // Read a field of the object
p.y = p.x * p.x;                     // Set the value of a field
double d = p.distanceFromOrigin(); // Access a method of the object
```

This syntax is central to object-oriented programming in Java, so you'll see it a lot. Note, in particular, the expression `p.distanceFromOrigin()`. This tells the Java compiler to look up a method named `distanceFromOrigin()` defined by the class `Point` and use that method to perform a computation on the fields of the object `p`. We'll cover the details of this operation in Chapter 3.

Object Literals

In our discussion of primitive types, we saw that each primitive type has a literal syntax for including values of the type literally into the text of a program. Java also defines a literal syntax for a few special reference types, as described next.

String literals

The `String` class represents text as a string of characters. Since programs usually communicate with their users through the written word, the ability to manipulate strings of text is quite important in any programming language. In some languages, strings are a primitive type, on a par with integers and characters. In Java, however, strings are objects; the data type used to represent text is the `String` class.

Because strings are such a fundamental data type, Java allows you to include text literally in programs by placing it between double-quote (") characters. For example:

```
String name = "David";
System.out.println("Hello, " + name);
```

Don't confuse the double-quote characters that surround string literals with the single-quote (or apostrophe) characters that surround `char` literals. String literals can contain any of the escape sequences `char` literals can (see Table 2-2). Escape sequences are particularly useful for embedding double-quote characters within double-quoted string literals. For example:

```
String story = "\t\"How can you stand it?\" he asked sarcastically.\n";
```

String literals cannot contain comments and may consist of only a single line. Java does not support any kind of continuation-character syntax that allows two separate lines to be treated as a single line. If you need to represent a long string of text that does not fit on a single line, break it into independent string literals and use the + operator to concatenate the literals. For example:

```
String s = "This is a test of the          // This is illegal; string  literals
            emergency broadcast system";  // cannot be broken across lines.

String s = "This is a test of the " +     // Do this instead
            "emergency broadcast system";
```

This concatenation of literals is done when your program is compiled, not when it is run, so you do not need to worry about any kind of performance penalty.

Type literals

The second type that supports its own special object literal syntax is the class named `Class`. Instances of the `Class` class represent a Java data type. To include a `Class` object literally in a Java program, follow the name of any data type with `.class`. For example:

```
Class typeInt = int.class;
Class typeIntArray = int[ ].class;
Class typePoint = Point.class;
```

The null reference

The `null` keyword is a special literal value that is a reference to nothing, or an absence of a reference. The `null` value is unique because it is a member of every reference type. You can assign `null` to variables of any reference type. For example:

```
String s = null;
Point p = null;
```

Arrays

An *array* is a special kind of object that holds zero or more primitive values or references. These values are held in the *elements* of the array, which are unnamed variables referred to by their position or *index*. The type of an array is characterized by its *element type*, and all elements of the array must be of that type.

Array elements are numbered starting with zero, and valid indexes range from zero to the number of elements minus one. The array element with index 1, for example, is the *second* element in the array. The number of elements in an array is its *length*. The length of an array is specified when the array is created, and it never changes.

The element type of an array may be any valid Java type, including array types. This means that Java supports arrays of arrays, which provide a kind of multidimensional array capability. Java does not support the matrix-style multidimensional arrays found in some languages.

Array Types

Array types are reference types, just as classes are. Instances of arrays are objects, just as the instances of a class are.* Unlike classes, array types do not have to be defined. Simply place square brackets after the element type. For example, the following code declares three variables of array type:

```
byte b;                        // byte is a primitive type
byte[ ] arrayOfBytes;          // byte[ ] is an array type: array of byte
byte[ ][ ] arrayOfArrayOfBytes; // byte[ ][ ] is another type: array of byte[ ]
String[ ] points;              // String[ ] is an array of String objects
```


The length of an array is not part of the array type. It is not possible, for example, to declare a method that expects an array of exactly four int values, for example. If a method parameter is of type int[ ], a caller can pass an array with any number (including zero) of elements.

Array types are not classes, but array instances are objects. This means that arrays inherit the methods of java.lang.Object. Arrays implement the Cloneable interface and override the clone( ) method to guarantee that an array can always be cloned and that clone( ) never throws a CloneNotSupportedException. Arrays also implement Serializable so that any array can be serialized if its element type can be serialized. Finally, all arrays have a public final int field named length that specifies the number of elements in the array.

Array type widening conversions

Since arrays extend Object and implement the Cloneable and Serializable interfaces, any array type can be widened to any of these three types. But certain array types can also be widened to other array types. If the element type of an array is a reference type T, and T is assignable to a type S, the array type T[ ] is assignable to the array type S[ ]. Note that there are no widening conversions of this sort for arrays of a given primitive type. As examples, the following lines of code show legal array widening conversions:

```
String[ ] arrayOfStrings;      // Created elsewhere
int[ ][ ] arrayOfArraysOfInt;  // Created elsewhere
// String is assignable to Object, so String[ ] is assignable to Object[ ]
Object[ ] oa = arrayOfStrings;
// String implements Comparable, so a String[ ] can be considered a Comparable[ ]
Comparable[ ] ca = arrayOfStrings;
// An int[ ] is an Object, so int[ ][ ] is assignable to Object[ ]
Object[ ] oa2 = arrayOfArraysOfInt;
// All arrays are cloneable, serializable Objects
Object o = arrayOfStrings;
Cloneable c = arrayOfArraysOfInt;
Serializable s = arrayOfArraysOfInt[0];
```

* There is a terminology difficulty when discussing arrays. Unlike with classes and their instances, we use the term "array" for both the array type and the array instance. In practice, it is usually clear from context whether a type or a value is being discussed.

This ability to widen an array type to another array type means that the compile-time type of an array is not always the same as its runtime type. The compiler must usually insert runtime checks before any operation that stores a reference value into an array element to ensure that the runtime type of the value matches the runtime type of the array element. If the runtime check fails, an ArrayStoreException is thrown.

C compatibility syntax

As we've seen, an array type is written simply by placing brackets after the element type. For compatibility with C and C++, however, Java supports an alternative syntax in variable declarations: brackets may be placed after the name of the variable instead of, or in addition to, the element type. This applies to local variables, fields, and method parameters. For example:

```
// This line declares local variables of type int, int[] and int[][]
int justOne, arrayOfThem[], arrayOfArrays[][];

// These three lines declare fields of the same array type:
public String[][] aas1;   // Preferred Java syntax
public String aas2[][];   // C syntax
public String[] aas3[];   // Confusing hybrid syntax

// This method signature includes two parameters with the same type
public static double dotProduct(double[] x, double y[]) { ... }
```

This compatibility syntax is uncommon, and its use is strongly discouraged.

Creating and Initializing Arrays

To create an array value in Java, you use the new keyword, just as you do to create an object. Array types don't have constructors, but you are required to specify a length whenever you create an array. Specify the desired size of your array as a nonnegative integer between square brackets:

```
byte[] buffer = new byte[1024];  // Create a new array to hold 1024 bytes
String[] lines = new String[50]; // Create an array of 50 references to strings
```

When you create an array with this syntax, each of the array elements is automatically initialized to the same default value that is used for the fields of a class: false for boolean elements, '\u0000' for char elements, 0 for integer elements, 0.0 for floating-point elements, and null for elements of reference type.

Array creation expressions can also be used to create and initialize a multidimensional rectangular array of arrays. This syntax is somewhat more complicated and is explained later in this section.

Array initializers

To create an array and initialize its elements in a single expression, omit the array length and follow the square brackets with a comma-separated list of expressions within curly braces. The type of each expression must be assignable to the element type of the array, of course. The length of the array that is created is equal to the number of expressions. It is legal, but not necessary, to include a trailing comma following the last expression in the list. For example:

```
String[] greetings = new String[] { "Hello", "Hi", "Howdy" };
int[] smallPrimes = new int[] { 2, 3, 5, 7, 11, 13, 17, 19, };
```

Note that this syntax allows arrays to be created, initialized, and used without ever being assigned to a variable. In a sense these array creation expressions are anonymous array literals. Here are examples:

```
// Call a method, passing an anonymous array literal that contains two strings
String response = askQuestion("Do you want to quit?",
                              new String[] {"Yes", "No"});

// Call another method with an anonymous array (of anonymous objects)
double d = computeAreaOfTriangle(new Point[] { new Point(1,2),
                                               new Point(3,4),
                                               new Point(3,2) });
```

When an array initializer is part of a variable declaration, you may omit the `new` keyword and element type and list the desired array elements within curly braces:

```
String[] greetings = { "Hello", "Hi", "Howdy" };
int[] powersOfTwo = {1, 2, 4, 8, 16, 32, 64, 128};
```

The Java Virtual Machine architecture does not support any kind of efficient array initialization. In other words, array literals are created and initialized when the program is run, not when the program is compiled. Consider the following array literal:

```
int[] perfectNumbers = {6, 28};
```

This is compiled into Java byte codes that are equivalent to:

```
int[] perfectNumbers = new int[2];
perfectNumbers[0] = 6;
perfectNumbers[1] = 28;
```

If you want to initialize a large array, you should think twice before including the values literally in the program, since the Java compiler has to emit lots of Java byte codes to initialize the array. It may be more space-efficient to store your data in an external file and read it into the program at runtime.

The fact that Java does all array initialization at runtime has an important corollary, however. It means that the expressions in an array initializer may be computed at runtime and need not be compile-time constants. For example:

```
Point[] points = { circle1.getCenterPoint(), circle2.getCenterPoint() };
```

Using Arrays

Once an array has been created, you are ready to start using it. The following sections explain basic access to the elements of an array and cover common idioms of array usage such as iterating through the elements of an array and copying an array or part of an array.

Accessing array elements

The elements of an array are variables. When an array element appears in an expression, it evaluates to the value held in the element. And when an array element appears on the left-hand side of an assignment operator, a new value is stored into that element. Unlike a normal variable, however, an array element has no name, only a number. Array elements are accessed using a square bracket notation. If a is an expression that evaluates to an array reference, you index that array and refer to a specific element with `a[i]`, where `i` is an integer literal or an expression that evaluates to an `int`. For example:

```
String[] responses = new String[2];   // Create an array of two strings
responses[0] = "Yes";                 // Set the first element of the array
responses[1] = "No";                  // Set the second element of the array

// Now read these array elements
System.out.println(question + " (" + responses[0] + "/" +
                   responses[1] + " ): ");

// Both the array reference and the array index may be more complex expressions
double datum = data.getMatrix()[data.row()*data.numColumns() +  data.column()];
```

The array index expression must be of type `int`, or a type that can be widened to an `int`: `byte`, `short`, or even `char`. It is obviously not legal to index an array with a `boolean`, `float`, or `double` value. Remember that the `length` field of an array is an `int` and that arrays may not have more than `Integer.MAX_VALUE` elements. Indexing an array with an expression of type `long` generates a commpile-time error, even if the value of that expression at runtime would be within the range of an `int`.

Array bounds

Remember that the first element of an array a is `a[0]` , the second element is `a[1]` and the last is `a[a.length-1]`. If you are accustomed to a language in which the arrays are 1-based, 0-based arrays take some getting used to.

A common bug involving arrays is use of an index that is too small (a negative index) or too large (greater than or equal to the array `length`). In languages like C or C++, accessing elements before the beginning or after the end of an array yields unpredictable behavior that can vary from invocation to invocation and platform to platform. Such bugs may not always be caught, and if a failure occurs, it may be at some later time. While it is just as easy to write faulty array indexing code in Java, Java guarantees predictable results by checking every array access at runtime. If an array index is too small or too large, Java throws an `ArrayIndexOutOfBoundsException` immediately.

Iterating arrays

It is common to write loops that iterate through each of the elements of an array in order to perform some operation on it. This is typically done with a `for` loop. The following code, for example, computes the sum of an array of integers:

```
int[] primes = { 2, 3, 5, 7, 11, 13, 17, 19 };
int sumOfPrimes = 0;
```

```
for(int i = 0; i < primes.length; i++)
    sumOfPrimes += primes[i];
```

The structure of this for loop is idiomatic, and you'll see it frequently.

In Java 5.0 and later, arrays can also be iterated with the for/in loop. The summing code could be rewritten succinctly as follows:

```
for(int p : primes) sumOfPrimes += p;
```


Copying arrays

All array types implement the Cloneable interface, and any array can be copied by invoking its clone( ) method. Note that a cast is required to convert the return value to the appropriate array type, but that the clone( ) method of arrays is guaranteed not to throw CloneNotSupportedException:

```
int[] data = { 1, 2, 3 };
int[] copy = (int[]) data.clone();
```

The clone( ) method makes a shallow copy. If the element type of the array is a reference type, only the references are copied, not the referenced objects themselves. Because the copy is shallow, any array can be cloned, even if the element type is not itself Cloneable.

Sometimes you simply want to copy elements from one existing array to another existing array. The System.arraycopy( ) method is designed to do this efficiently, and you can assume that Java VM implementations performs this method using high-speed block copy operations on the underlying hardware.

arraycopy( ) is a straightforward function that is difficult to use only because it has five arguments to remember. First pass the source array from which elements are to be copied. Second, pass the index of the start element in that array. Pass the destination array and the destination index as the third and fourth arguments. Finally, as the fifth argument, specify the number of elements to be copied.

arraycopy( ) works correctly even for overlapping copies within the same array. For example, if you've "deleted" the element at index 0 from array a and want to shift the elements between indexes 1 and n down one so that they occupy indexes 0 through n-1 you could do this:

```
System.arraycopy(a, 1, a, 0, n);
```

Array utilities

The java.util.Arrays class contains a number of static utility methods for working with arrays. Most of these methods are heavily overloaded, with versions for arrays of each primitive type and another version for arrays of objects. The sort( ) and binarySearch( ) methods are particularly useful for sorting and searching arrays. The equals( ) method allows you to compare the content of two arrays. The Arrays.toString( ) method is useful when you want to convert array content to a string, such as for debugging or logging output.

As of Java 5.0, the Arrays class includes deepEquals( ), deepHashCode( ), and deepToString( ) methods that work correctly for multidimensional arrays.

Multidimensional Arrays

As we've seen, an array type is written as the element type followed by a pair of square brackets. An array of `char` is `char[ ]`, and an array of arrays of `char` is `char[ ][ ]`. When the elements of an array are themselves arrays, we say that the array is *multidimensional*. In order to work with multidimensional arrays, you need to understand a few additional details.

Imagine that you want to use a multidimensional array to represent a multiplication table:

```
int[ ][ ] products;      // A multiplication table
```

Each of the pairs of square brackets represents one dimension, so this is a two-dimensional array. To access a single `int` element of this two-dimensional array, you must specify two index values, one for each dimension. Assuming that this array was actually initialized as a multiplication table, the `int` value stored at any given element would be the product of the two indexes. That is, `products[2][4]` would be 8, and `products[3][7]` would be 21.

To create a new multidimensional array, use the `new` keyword and specify the size of both dimensions of the array. For example:

```
int[ ][ ] products = new int[10][10];
```

In some languages, an array like this would be created as a single block of 100 `int` values. Java does not work this way. This line of code does three things:

- Declares a variable named `products` to hold an array of arrays of `int`.
- Creates a 10-element array to hold 10 arrays of `int`.
- Creates 10 more arrays, each of which is a 10-element array of `int`. It assigns each of these 10 new arrays to the elements of the initial array. The default value of every `int` element of each of these 10 new arrays is 0.

To put this another way, the previous single line of code is equivalent to the following code:

```
int[ ][ ] products = new int[10][ ];    // An array to hold 10 int[ ] values
for(int i = 0; i < 10; i++)             // Loop 10 times...
    products[i] = new int[10];          // ...and create 10 arrays
```

The `new` keyword performs this additional initialization automatically for you. It works with arrays with more than two dimensions as well:

```
float[ ][ ][ ] globalTemperatureData = new float[360][180][100];
```

When using `new` with multidimensional arrays, you do not have to specify a size for all dimensions of the array, only the leftmost dimension or dimensions. For example, the following two lines are legal:

```
float[ ][ ][ ] globalTemperatureData = new float[360][ ][ ];
float[ ][ ][ ] globalTemperatureData = new float[360][180][ ];
```

The first line creates a single-dimensional array, where each element of the array can hold a `float[ ][ ]`. The second line creates a two-dimensional array, where each element of the array is a `float[ ]`. If you specify a size for only some of the dimensions of an array, however, those dimensions must be the leftmost ones. The following lines are not legal:

```
float[ ][ ][ ] globalTemperatureData = new float[360][ ][100];  // Error!
float[ ][ ][ ] globalTemperatureData = new float[ ][180][100];  // Error!
```

Like a one-dimensional array, a multidimensional array can be initialized using an array initializer. Simply use nested sets of curly braces to nest arrays within arrays. For example, we can declare, create, and initialize a 5×5 multiplication table like this:

```
int[ ][ ] products = { {0, 0, 0, 0, 0},
                       {0, 1, 2, 3, 4},
                       {0, 2, 4, 6, 8},
                       {0, 3, 6, 9, 12},
                       {0, 4, 8, 12, 16} };
```

Or, if you want to use a multidimensional array without declaring a variable, you can use the anonymous initializer syntax:

```
boolean response = bilingualQuestion(question, new String[ ][ ] {
                                                   { "Yes", "No" },
                                                   { "Oui", "Non" }});
```

When you create a multidimensional array using the new keyword, you always get a *rectangular* array: one in which all the array values for a given dimension have the same size. This is perfect for rectangular data structures, such as matrices. However, because multidimensional arrays are implemented as arrays of arrays in Java, instead of as a single rectangular block of elements, you are in no way constrained to use rectangular arrays. For example, since our multiplication table is symmetrical diagonally from top left to bottom right, we can represent the same information in a nonrectangular array with fewer elements:

```
int[ ][ ] products = { {0},
                       {0, 1},
                       {0, 2, 4},
                       {0, 3, 6, 9},
                       {0, 4, 8, 12, 16} };
```

When working with multidimensional arrays, you'll often find yourself using nested loops to create or initialize them. For example, you can create and initialize a large triangular multiplication table as follows:

```
int[ ][ ] products = new int[12][ ];          // An array of 12 arrays of int.
for(int row = 0; row < 12; row++) {           // For each element of that array,
    products[row] = new int[row+1];           // allocate an array of int.
    for(int col = 0; col < row+1; col++)      // For each element of the int[ ],
        products[row][col] = row * col;       // initialize it to the  product.
}
```

Reference Types

Now that we've covered arrays and introduced classes and objects, we can turn to a more general description of *reference types*. Classes and arrays are two of Java's five kinds of reference types. Classes were introduced earlier and are covered in complete detail, along with *interfaces*, in Chapter 3. Enumerated types and annotation types are reference types introduced in Java 5.0 (see Chapter 4).

This section does not cover specific syntax for any particular reference type, but instead explains the general behavior of reference types and illustrates how they differ from Java's primitive types. In this section, the term *object* refers to a value or instance of any reference type, including arrays.

Reference vs. Primitive Types

Reference types and objects differ substantially from primitive types and their primitive values:

- Eight primitive types are defined by the Java language. Reference types are user-defined, so there is an unlimited number of them. For example, a program might define a class named `Point` and use objects of this newly defined type to store and manipulate X,Y points in a Cartesian coordinate system. The same program might use an array of characters—of type `char[ ]`—to store text and might use an array of `Point` objects—of type `Point[ ]`—to store a sequence of points.
- Primitive types represent single values. Reference types are aggregate types that hold zero or more primitive values or objects. Our hypothetical `Point` class, for example, might hold two `double` values to represent the X and Y coordinates of the points. The `char[ ]` and `Point[ ]` array types are obviously aggregate types because they hold a sequence of primitive `char` values or `Point` objects.
- Primitive types require between one and eight bytes of memory. When a primitive value is stored in a variable or passed to a method, the computer makes a copy of the bytes that hold the value. Objects, on the other hand, may require substantially more memory. Memory to store an object is dynamically allocated on the heap when the object is created and this memory is automatically "garbage-collected" when the object is no longer needed. When an object is assigned to a variable or passed to a method, the memory that represents the object is not copied. Instead, only a reference to that memory is stored in the variable or passed to the method.

This last difference between primitive and reference types explains why reference types are so named. The sections that follow are devoted to exploring the substantial differences between types that are manipulated by value and types that are manipulated by reference.

Before moving on, however, it is worth briefly considering the nature of references. A *reference* is simply some kind of reference to an object. References are completely opaque in Java and the representation of a reference is an implementation detail of the Java interpreter. If you are a C programmer, however, you can safely imagine a reference as a pointer or a memory address. Remember, though, that Java programs cannot manipulate references in any way. Unlike pointers in C and C++, references cannot be converted to or from integers, and they cannot be incremented or decremented. C and C++ programmers should also note that Java does not support the `&` address-of operator or the `*` and `->` dereference operators. In Java, primitive types are always handled exclusively by value, and objects are always handled exclusively by reference: the `.` operator in Java is more like the `->` operator in C and C++ than it is like the `.` operator of those languages.

Copying Objects

The following code manipulates a primitive int value:

```
int x = 42;
int y = x;
```

After these lines execute, the variable y contains a copy of the value held in the variable x. Inside the Java VM, there are two independent copies of the 32-bit integer 42.

Now think about what happens if we run the same basic code but use a reference type instead of a primitive type:

```
Point p = new Point(1.0, 2.0);
Point q = p;
```

After this code runs, the variable q holds a copy of the reference held in the variable p. There is still only one copy of the Point object in the VM, but there are now two copies of the reference to that object. This has some important implications. Suppose the two previous lines of code are followed by this code:

```
System.out.println(p.x);  // Print out the X coordinate of p: 1.0
q.x = 13.0;               // Now change the X coordinate of q
System.out.println(p.x);  // Print out p.x again; this time it is 13.0
```

Since the variables p and q hold references to the same object, either variable can be used to make changes to the object, and those changes are visible through the other variable as well.

This behavior is not specific to objects; the same thing happens with arrays, as illustrated by the following code:

```
char[] greet = { 'h','e','l','l','o' };  // greet holds an array reference
char[] cuss = greet;                     // cuss holds the same reference
cuss[4] = '!';                           // Use reference to change an element
System.out.println(greet);               // Prints "hell!"
```

A similar difference in behavior between primitive types and reference types occurs when arguments are passed to methods. Consider the following method:

```
void changePrimitive(int x) {
    while(x > 0)
        System.out.println(x--);
}
```

When this method is invoked, the method is given a copy of the argument used to invoke the method in the parameter x. The code in the method uses x as a loop counter and decrements it to zero. Since x is a primitive type, the method has its own private copy of this value, so this is a perfectly reasonable thing to do.

On the other hand, consider what happens if we modify the method so that the parameter is a reference type:

```
void changeReference(Point p) {
    while(p.x > 0)
        System.out.println(p.x--);
}
```

When this method is invoked, it is passed a private copy of a reference to a Point object and can use this reference to change the Point object. Consider the following:

```
Point q = new Point(3.0, 4.5);  // A point with an X coordinate of 3
changeReference(q);             // Prints 3,2,1 and modifies the Point
System.out.println(q.x);        // The X coordinate of q is now 0!
```

When the changeReference( ) method is invoked, it is passed a copy of the reference held in variable q. Now both the variable q and the method parameter p hold references to the same object. The method can use its reference to change the contents of the object. Note, however, that it cannot change the contents of the variable q. In other words, the method can change the Point object beyond recognition, but it cannot change the fact that the variable q refers to that object.

The title of this section is "Copying Objects," but, so far, we've only seen copies of references to objects, not copies of the objects and arrays themselves. To make an actual copy of an object, you must use the special clone( ) method (inherited by all objects from java.lang.Object):

```
Point p = new Point(1,2);    // p refers to one object
Point q = (Point) p.clone(); // q refers to a copy of that object
q.y = 42;                    // Modify the copied object, but not the original

int[] data = {1,2,3,4,5};            // An array
int[] copy = (int[]) data.clone();  // A copy of the array
```

Note that a cast is necessary to coerce the return value of the clone( ) method to the correct type. There are a couple of points you should be aware of when using clone( ). First, not all objects can be cloned. Java only allows an object to be cloned if the object's class has explicitly declared itself to be cloneable by implementing the Cloneable interface. (We haven't discussed interfaces or how they are implemented yet; that is covered in Chapter 3.) The definition of Point that we showed earlier does not actually implement this interface, so our Point type, as implemented, is not cloneable. Note, however, that arrays are always cloneable. If you call the clone( ) method for a noncloneable object, it throws a CloneNotSupportedException. When you use the clone( ) method, you may want to use it within a try block to catch this exception.

The second thing you need to understand about clone( ) is that, by default, it creates a shallow copy of an object. The copied object contains copies of all the primitive values and references in the original object. In other words, any references in the object are copied, not cloned; clone( ) does not recursively make copies of the objects referred to by those references. A class may need to override this shallow copy behavior by defining its own version of the clone( ) method that explicitly performs a deeper copy where needed. To understand the shallow copy behavior of clone( ), consider cloning a two-dimensional array of arrays:

```
int[][] data = {{1,2,3}, {4,5}};          // An array of 2 references
int[][] copy = (int[][]) data.clone(); // Copy the 2 refs to a new array
copy[0][0] = 99;                         // This changes data[0][0] too!
copy[1] = new int[] {7,8,9};             // This does not change data[1]
```

If you want to make a deep copy of this multidimensional array, you have to copy each dimension explicitly:

```
int[][] data = {{1,2,3}, {4,5}};         // An array of 2 references
int[][] copy = new int[data.length][];  // A new array to hold copied arrays
for(int i = 0; i < data.length; i++)
   copy[i] = (int[]) data[i].clone();
```

Java Syntax

Comparing Objects

We've seen that primitive types and reference types differ significantly in the way they are assigned to variables, passed to methods, and copied. The types also differ in the way they are compared for equality. When used with primitive values, the equality operator (==) simply tests whether two values are identical (i.e., whether they have exactly the same bits). With reference types, however, == compares references, not actual objects. In other words, == tests whether two references refer to the same object; it does not test whether two objects have the same content. For example:

```
String letter = "o";
String s = "hello";                         // These two String objects
String t = "hell" + letter;                 // contain exactly the same text.
if (s == t) System.out.println("equal");    // But they are not equal!

byte[] a = { 1, 2, 3 };                     // An array.
byte[] b = (byte[]) a.clone();              // A copy with identical content.
if (a == b) System.out.println("equal");    // But they are not equal!
```

When working with reference types, there are two kinds of equality: equality of reference and equality of object. It is important to distinguish between these two kinds of equality. One way to do this is to use the word "identical" when talking about equality of references and the word "equal" when talking about two distinct objects that have the same content. To test two nonidentical objects for equality, pass one of them to the equals() method of the other:

```
String letter = "o";
String s = "hello";                         // These two String objects
String t = "hell" + letter;                 // contain exactly the same text.
if (s.equals(t))                            // And the equals() method
    System.out.println("equal");            // tells us so.
```

All objects inherit an equals() method (from Object), but the default implementation simply uses == to test for identity of references, not equality of content. A class that wants to allow objects to be compared for equality can define its own version of the equals() method. Our Point class does not do this, but the String class does, as indicated in the code example. You can call the equals() method on an array, but it is the same as using the == operator, because arrays always inherit the default equals() method that compares references rather than array content. You can compare arrays for equality with the convenience method java.util.Arrays.equals().

Terminology: Pass by Value

I've said that Java handles objects "by reference." Don't confuse this with the phrase "pass by reference." "Pass by reference" is a term used to describe the method-calling conventions of some programming languages. In a pass-by-reference language, values—even primitive values—are not passed directly to methods. Instead, methods are always passed references to values. Thus, if the method modifies its parameters, those modifications are visible when the method returns, even for primitive types.

Java does *not* do this; it is a "pass by value" language. However, when a reference type is involved, the value that is passed is a reference. But this is still not the same as pass-by-reference. If Java were a pass-by-reference language, when a reference type is passed to a method, it would be passed as a reference to the reference.

Memory Allocation and Garbage Collection

As we've already noted, objects are composite values that can contain a number of other values and may require a substantial amount of memory. When you use the `new` keyword to create a new object or use an object literal in your program, Java automatically creates the object for you, allocating whatever amount of memory is necessary. You don't need to do anything to make this happen.

In addition, Java also automatically reclaims that memory for reuse when it is no longer needed. It does this through a process called *garbage collection*. An object is considered garbage when no references to it are stored in any variables, the fields of any objects, or the elements of any arrays. For example:

```
Point p = new Point(1,2);              // Create an object
double d = p.distanceFromOrigin();  // Use it for something
p = new Point(2,3);                    // Create a new object
```

After the Java interpreter executes the third line, a reference to the new `Point` object has replaced the reference to the first one. No references to the first object remain, so it is garbage. At some point, the garbage collector discovers this and reclaims the memory used by the object.

C programmers, who are used to using `malloc( )` and `free( )` to manage memory, and C++ programmers, who are used to explicitly deleting their objects with `delete`, may find it a little hard to relinquish control and trust the garbage collector. Even though it seems like magic, it really works! There is a slight, but usually negligible, performance penalty due to the use of garbage collection. However, having garbage collection built into the language dramatically reduces the occurrence of memory leaks and related bugs and almost always improves programmer productivity.

Reference Type Conversions

Objects can be converted between different reference types. As with primitive types, reference type conversions can be widening conversions (allowed automatically by the compiler) or narrowing conversions that require a cast (and possibly a runtime check). In order to understand reference type conversions, you need to understand that reference types form a hierarchy, usually called the *class hierarchy*.

Every Java reference type *extends* some other type, known as its *superclass*. A type inherits the fields and methods of its superclass and then defines its own additional fields and methods. A special class named `Object` serves as the root of the class hierarchy in Java. All Java classes extend `Object` directly or indirectly. The `Object` class defines a number of special methods that are inherited (or overridden) by all objects.

The predefined `String` class and the `Point` class we discussed earlier in this chapter both extend `Object`. Thus, we can say that all `String` objects are also `Object` objects. We can also say that all `Point` objects are `Object` objects. The opposite is not true, however. We cannot say that every `Object` is a `String` because, as we've just seen, some `Object` objects are `Point` objects.

With this simple understanding of the class hierarchy, we can return to the rules of reference type conversion:

- An object cannot be converted to an unrelated type. The Java compiler does not allow you to convert a `String` to a `Point`, for example, even if you use a cast operator.
- An object can be converted to the type of its superclass or of any ancestor class. This is a widening conversion, so no cast is required. For example, a `String` value can be assigned to a variable of type `Object` or passed to a method where an `Object` parameter is expected. Note that no conversion is actually performed; the object is simply treated as if it were an instance of the superclass.
- An object can be converted to the type of a subclass, but this is a narrowing conversion and requires a cast. The Java compiler provisionally allows this kind of conversion, but the Java interpreter checks at runtime to make sure it is valid. Only cast an object to the type of a subclass if you are sure, based on the logic of your program, that the object is actually an instance of the subclass. If it is not, the interpreter throws a `ClassCastException`. For example, if we assign a `String` object to a variable of type `Object`, we can later cast the value of that variable back to type `String`:

  ```
  Object o = "string";    // Widening conversion from String to Object
  // Later in the program...
  String s = (String) o;  // Narrowing conversion from Object to String
  ```

Arrays are objects and follow some conversion rules of their own. First, any array can be converted to an `Object` value through a widening conversion. A narrowing conversion with a cast can convert such an object value back to an array. For example:

```
Object o = new int[] {1,2,3}; // Widening conversion from array to Object
// Later in the program...
int[] a = (int[]) o;          // Narrowing conversion back to array type
```

In addition to converting an array to an object, an array can be converted to another type of array if the "base types" of the two arrays are reference types that can themselves be converted. For example:

```
// Here is an array of strings.
String[] strings = new String[] { "hi", "there" };
// A widening conversion to CharSequence[] is allowed because String
// can be widened to CharSequence
CharSequence[] sequences = strings;
// The narrowing conversion back to String[] requires a cast.
strings = (String[]) sequences;
// This is an array of arrays of strings
String[][] s = new String[][] { strings };
// It cannot be converted to CharSequence[] because String[] cannot be
// converted to CharSequence: the number of dimensions don't match
sequences = s;  // This line will not compile
// s can be converted to Object or Object[], however because all array types
// (including String[] and String[][]) can be converted to Object.
Object[] objects = s;
```

Note that these array conversion rules apply only to arrays of objects and arrays of arrays. An array of primitive type cannot be converted to any other array type, even if the primitive base types can be converted:

```
// Can't convert int[] to double[] even though int can be widened to double
double[] data = new int[] {1,2,3};  // This line causes a compilation error
// This line is legal, however, since int[] can be converted to Object
Object[] objects = new int[][] {{1,2},{3,4}};
```

Boxing and Unboxing Conversions

Primitive types and reference types behave quite differently. It is sometimes useful to treat primitive values as objects, and for this reason, the Java platform includes wrapper classes for each of the primitive types. `Boolean`, `Byte`, `Short`, `Character`, `Integer`, `Long`, `Float`, and `Double` are immutable classes whose instances each hold a single primitive value. These wrapper classes are usually used when you want to store primitive values in collections such as `java.util.List`:

```
List numbers = new ArrayList();                  // Create a List collection
numbers.add(new Integer(-1));                    // Store a wrapped primitive
int i = ((Integer)numbers.get(0)).intValue(); // Extract the primitive value
```

Prior to Java 5.0, no conversions between primitive types and reference types were allowed. This code explicitly calls the `Integer()` constructor to wrap a primitive `int` in an object and explicitly calls the `intValue()` method to extract a primitive value from the wrapper object.

Java 5.0 introduces two new types of conversions known as boxing and unboxing conversions. Boxing conversions convert a primitive value to its corresponding wrapper object and unboxing conversions do the opposite. You may explicitly specify a boxing or unboxing conversion with a cast, but this is unnecessary since these conversions are automatically performed when you assign a value to a variable or pass a value to a method. Furthermore, unboxing conversions are also automatic if you use a wrapper object when a Java operator or statement expects a primitive value. Because Java 5.0 performs boxing and unboxing automatically, this new language feature is often known as *autoboxing*.

Here are some examples of automatic boxing and unboxing conversions:

```
Integer i = 0;    // int literal 0 is boxed into an Integer object
Number n = 0.0f;  // float literal is boxed into Float and widened to Number
Integer i = 1;    // this is a boxing conversion
int j = i;        // i is unboxed here
i++;              // i is unboxed, incremented, and then boxed up again
Integer k = i+2;  // i is unboxed and the sum is boxed up again
i = null;
j = i;            // unboxing here throws a NullPointerException
```

Automatic boxing and unboxing conversions make it much simple to use primitive values with collection classes. The list-of-numbers code earlier in this section can be translated as follows in Java 5.0. Note that the translation also uses generics, another new feature of Java 5.0 that is covered in Chapter 4.

```
List<Integer> numbers = new ArrayList<Integer>(); // Create a List of Integer
numbers.add(-1);                                  // Box int to Integer
int i = numbers.get(0);                           // Unbox Integer to int
```

Packages and the Java Namespace

A *package* is a named collection of classes, interfaces, and other reference types. Packages serve to group related classes and define a namespace for the classes they contain.

The core classes of the Java platform are in packages whose names begin with `java`. For example, the most fundamental classes of the language are in the package `java.lang`. Various utility classes are in `java.util`. Classes for input and output are in `java.io`, and classes for networking are in `java.net`. Some of these packages contain subpackages, such as `java.lang.reflect` and `java.util.regex`. Extensions to the Java platform that have been standardized by Sun typically have package names that begin with `javax`. Some of these extensions, such as `javax.swing` and its myriad subpackages, were later adopted into the core platform itself. Finally, the Java platform also includes several "endorsed standards," which have packages named after the standards body that created them, such as `org.w3c` and `org.omg`.

Every class has both a simple name, which is the name given to it in its definition, and a fully qualified name, which includes the name of the package of which it is a part. The `String` class, for example, is part of the `java.lang` package, so its fully qualified name is `java.lang.String`.

This section explains how to place your own classes and interfaces into a package and how to choose a package name that won't conflict with anyone else's package name. Next, it explains how to selectively import type names into the namespace so that you don't have to type the package name of every class or interface you use. Finally, the section explains a feature that is new in Java 5.0: the ability to import static members of types into the namespace so that you don't need to prefix these with a package name *or* a class name.

Package Declaration

To specify the package a class is to be part of, you use a package declaration. The `package` keyword, if it appears, must be the first token of Java code (i.e., the first thing other than comments and space) in the Java file. The keyword should be followed by the name of the desired package and a semicolon. Consider a Java file that begins with this directive:

```
package com.davidflanagan.examples;
```

All classes defined by this file are part of the package `com.davidflanagan.examples`.

If no `package` directive appears in a Java file, all classes defined in that file are part of an unnamed default package. In this case, the qualified and unqualified names of a class are the same. The possibility of naming conflicts means that you should use this default package only for very simple code or early on in the development process of a larger project.

Globally Unique Package Names

One of the important functions of packages is to partition the Java namespace and prevent name collisions between classes. It is only their package names that keep the `java.util.List` and `java.awt.List` classes distinct, for example. In order for this to work, however, package names must themselves be distinct. As the developer of Java, Sun controls all package names that begin with `java`, `javax`, and `sun`.

For the rest of us, Sun proposes a package-naming scheme, which, if followed correctly, guarantees globally unique package names. The scheme is to use your Internet domain name, with its elements reversed, as the prefix for all your package names. My web site is at *http://davidflanagan.com*, so all my Java packages begin with `com.davidflanagan`. It is up to me to decide how to partition the namespace below `com.davidflanagan`, but since I own that domain name, no other person or organization who is playing by the rules can define a package with the same name as any of mine.

Note that these package-naming rules apply primarily to API developers. If other programmers will be using classes that you develop along with unknown other classes, it is important that your package name be globally unique. On the other hand, if you are developing a Java application and will not be releasing any of the classes for reuse by others, you know the complete set of classes that your application will be deployed with and do not have to worry about unforeseen naming conflicts. In this case, you can choose a package naming scheme for your own convenience rather than for global uniqueness. One common approach is to use the application name as the main package name (it may have subpackages beneath it).

Importing Types

When referring to a class or interface in your Java code, you must, by default, use the fully qualified name of the type, including the package name. If you're writing code to manipulate a file and need to use the `File` class of the `java.io` package, you must type `java.io.File`. This rule has three exceptions:

- Types from the package java.lang are so important and so commonly used that they can always be referred to by their simple names.
- The code in a type p.T may refer to other types defined in the package p by their simple names.
- Types that have been *imported* into the namespace with an import declaration may be referred to by their simple names.

The first two exceptions are known as "automatic imports." The types from java.lang and the current package are "imported" into the namespace so that they can be used without their package name. Typing the package name of commonly used types that are not in java.lang or the current package quickly becomes tedious, and so it is also possible to explicitly import types from other packages into the namespace. This is done with the import declaration.

import declarations must appear at the start of a Java file, immediately after the package declaration, if there is one, and before any type definitions. You may use any number of import declarations in a file. An import declaration applies to all type definitions in the file (but not to any import declarations that follow it).

The import declaration has two forms. To import a single type into the namespace, follow the import keyword with the name of the type and a semicolon:

```
import java.io.File;    // Now we can type File instead of java.io.File
```

This is known as the "single type import" declaration.

The other form of import is the "on-demand type import." In this form, you specify the name of a package followed the characters .* to indicate that any type from that package may be used without its package name. Thus, if you want to use several other classes from the java.io package in addition to the File class, you can simply import the entire package:

```
import java.io.*;   // Now we can use simple names for all classes in java.io
```

This on-demand import syntax does not apply to subpackages. If I import the java.util package, I must still refer to the java.util.zip.ZipInputStream class by its fully qualified name.

Using an on-demand type import declaration is not the same as explicitly writing out a single type import declaration for every type in the package. It is more like an explicit single type import for every type in the package *that you actually use* in your code. This is the reason it's called "on demand"; types are imported as you use them.

Naming conflicts and shadowing

import declarations are invaluable to Java programming. They do expose us to the possibility of naming conflicts, however. Consider the packages java.util and java.awt. Both contain types named List. java.util.List is an important and commonly used interface. The java.awt package contains a number of important types that are commonly used in client-side applications, but java.awt.List has been superseded and is not one of these important types. It is illegal to import both `java.util.List` and `java.awt.List` in the same Java file. The following single type import declarations produce a compilation error:

```
import java.util.List;
import java.awt.List;
```

Using on-demand type imports for the two packages is legal:

```
import java.util.*;  // For collections and other utilities.
import java.awt.*;   // For fonts, colors, and graphics.
```

Difficulty arises, however, if you actually try to use the type `List`. This type can be imported "on demand" from either package, and any attempt to use `List` as an unqualified type name produces a compilation error. The workaround, in this case, is to explicitly specify the package name you want.

Because `java.util.List` is much more commonly used than `java.awt.List`, it is useful to combine the two on-demand type import declarations with a single-type import declaration that serves to disambiguate what we mean when we say `List`:

```
import java.util.*;     // For collections and other utilities.
import java.awt.*;      // For fonts, colors, and graphics.
import java.util.List; // To disambiguate from java.awt.List
```

With these `import` declarations in place, we can use `List` to mean the `java.util.List` interface. If we actually need to use the `java.awt.List` class, we can still do so as long as we include its package name. There are no other naming conflicts between `java.util` and `java.awt`, and their types will be imported "on demand" when we use them without a package name.

Importing Static Members

In Java 5.0 and later, you can import the static members of types as well as types themselves using the keywords `import static`. (Static members are explained in Chapter 3. If you are not already familiar with them, you may want to come back to this section later.) Like type import declarations, these static import declarations come in two forms: single static member import and on-demand static member import. Suppose, for example, that you are writing a text-based program that sends a lot of output to `System.out`. In this case, you might use this single static member import to save yourself typing:

```
import static java.lang.System.out;
```

With this import in place, you can then use `out.print()` instead of `System.out.print()`. Or suppose you are writing a program that uses many of the the trigonometric and other functions of the `Math` class. In a program that is clearly focused on numerical methods like this, having to repeatedly type the class name "Math" does not add clarity to your code; it just gets in the way. In this case, an on-demand static member import may be appropriate:

```
import static java.lang.Math.*
```

With this import declaration, you are free to write concise expressions like `sqrt(abs(sin(x)))` without having to prefix the name of each static method with the class name `Math`.

Another important use of import static declarations is to import the names of constants into your code. This works particularly well with enumerated types (see Chapter 4). Suppose, for example that you want to use the values of this enumerated type in code you are writing:

```
package climate.temperate;
enum Seasons { WINTER, SPRING, SUMMER, AUTUMN };
```


You could import the type climate.temperate.Seasons and then prefix the constants with the type name: Seasons.SPRING. For more concise code, you could import the enumerated values themselves:

```
import static climate.temperate.Seasons.*;
```

Using static member import declarations for constants is generally a better technique than implementing an interface that defines the constants.

Static member imports and overloaded methods

A static import declaration imports a *name*, not any one specific member with that name. Since Java allows method overloading and allows a type to have fields and methods with the same name, a single static member import declaration may actually import more than one member. Consider this code:

```
import static java.util.Arrays.sort;
```

This declaration imports the name "sort" into the namespace, not any one of the 19 sort() methods defined by java.util.Arrays. If you use the imported name sort to invoke a method, the compiler will look at the types of the method arguments to determine which method you mean.

It is even legal to import static methods with the same name from two or more different types as long as the methods all have different signatures. Here is one natural example:

```
import static java.util.Arrays.sort;
import static java.util.Collections.sort;
```

You might expect that this code would cause a syntax error. In fact, it does not because the sort() methods defined by the Collections class have different signatures than all of the sort() methods defined by the Arrays class. When you use the name "sort" in your code, the compiler looks at the types of the arguments to determine which of the 21 possible imported methods you mean.

Java File Structure

This chapter has taken us from the smallest to the largest elements of Java syntax, from individual characters and tokens to operators, expressions, statements, and methods, and on up to classes and packages. From a practical standpoint, the unit of Java program structure you will be dealing with most often is the Java file. A

Java file is the smallest unit of Java code that can be compiled by the Java compiler. A Java file consists of:

- An optional package directive
- Zero or more `import` or `import static` directives
- One or more type definitions

These elements can be interspersed with comments, of course, but they must appear in this order. This is all there is to a Java file. All Java statements (except the `package` and `import` directives, which are not true statements) must appear within methods, and all methods must appear within a type definition.

Java files have a couple of other important restrictions. First, each file can contain at most one class that is declared `public`. A `public` class is one that is designed for use by other classes in other packages. This restriction on public classes only applies to top-level classes; a class can contain any number of nested or inner classes that are declared `public`. We'll see more about the `public` modifier and nested classes in Chapter 3.

The second restriction concerns the filename of a Java file. If a Java file contains a `public` class, the name of the file must be the same as the name of the class, with the extension *.java* appended. Thus, if `Point` is defined as a `public` class, its source code must appear in a file named *Point.java*. Regardless of whether your classes are `public` or not, it is good programming practice to define only one per file and to give the file the same name as the class.

When a Java file is compiled, each of the classes it defines is compiled into a separate *class* file that contains Java byte codes to be interpreted by the Java Virtual Machine. A class file has the same name as the class it defines, with the extension *.class* appended. Thus, if the file *Point.java* defines a class named `Point`, a Java compiler compiles it to a file named *Point.class*. On most systems, class files are stored in directories that correspond to their package names. Thus, the class `com.davidflanagan.examples.Point` is defined by the class file *com/davidflanagan/examples/Point.class*.

The Java interpreter knows where the class files for the standard system classes are located and can load them as needed. When the interpreter runs a program that wants to use a class named `com.davidflanagan.examples.Point`, it knows that the code for that class is located in a directory named *com/davidflanagan/examples/* and, by default, it "looks" in the current directory for a subdirectory of that name. In order to tell the interpreter to look in locations other than the current directory, you must use the `-classpath` option when invoking the interpreter or set the `CLASSPATH` environment variable. For details, see the documentation for the Java interpreter, *java*, in Chapter 8.

Defining and Running Java Programs

A Java program consists of a set of interacting class definitions. But not every Java class or Java file defines a program. To create a program, you must define a class that has a special method with the following signature:

```
public static void main(String[ ] args)
```

This main( ) method is the main entry point for your program. It is where the Java interpreter starts running. This method is passed an array of strings and returns no value. When main( ) returns, the Java interpreter exits (unless main( ) has created separate threads, in which case the interpreter waits for all those threads to exit).

To run a Java program, you run the Java interpreter, *java*, specifying the fully qualified name of the class that contains the main( ) method. Note that you specify the name of the class, *not* the name of the class file that contains the class. Any additional arguments you specify on the command line are passed to the main( ) method as its String[ ] parameter. You may also need to specify the -classpath option (or -cp) to tell the interpreter where to look for the classes needed by the program. Consider the following command:

```
% java -classpath /usr/local/Jude com.davidflanagan.jude.Jude datafile.jude
```

java is the command to run the Java interpreter. *-classpath /usr/local/Jude* tells the interpreter where to look for *.class* files. com.davidflanagan.jude.Jude is the name of the program to run (i.e., the name of the class that defines the main( ) method). Finally, *datafile.jude* is a string that is passed to that main( ) method as the single element of an array of String objects.

There is an easier way to run programs. If a program and all its auxiliary classes (except those that are part of the Java platform) have been properly bundled in a Java archive (JAR) file, you can run the program simply by specifying the name of the JAR file:

```
% java -jar /usr/local/Jude/jude.jar datafile.jude
```

Some operating systems make JAR files automatically executable. On those systems, you can simply say:

```
% /usr/local/Jude/jude.jar datafile.jude
```

See Chapter 8 for details.

Differences Between C and Java

If you are a C or C++ programmer, you should have found much of the syntax of Java—particularly at the level of operators and statements—to be familiar. Because Java and C are so similar in some ways, it is important for C and C++ programmers to understand where the similarities end. C and Java differ in important ways, as summarized in the following list:

No preprocessor

Java does not include a preprocessor and does not define any analogs of the #define, #include, and #ifdef directives. Constant definitions are replaced with static final fields in Java. (See the java.lang.Math.PI field for an example.) Macro definitions are not available in Java, but advanced compiler technology and inlining has made them less useful. Java does not require an #include directive because Java has no header files. Java class files contain both the class API and the class implementation, and the compiler reads API information from class files as necessary. Java lacks any form of conditional compilation, but its cross-platform portability means that this feature is rarely needed.

No global variables

Java defines a very clean namespace. Packages contain classes, classes contain fields and methods, and methods contain local variables. But Java has no global variables, and thus there is no possibility of namespace collisions among those variables.

Well-defined primitive type sizes

All the primitive types in Java have well-defined sizes. In C, the size of `short`, `int`, and `long` types is platform-dependent, which hampers portability.

No pointers

Java classes and arrays are reference types, and references to objects and arrays are akin to pointers in C. Unlike C pointers, however, references in Java are entirely opaque. There is no way to convert a reference to a primitive type, and a reference cannot be incremented or decremented. There is no address-of operator like `&`, dereference operator like `*` or `->`, or `sizeof` operator. Pointers are a notorious source of bugs. Eliminating them simplifies the language and makes Java programs more robust and secure.

Garbage collection

The Java Virtual Machine performs garbage collection so that Java programmers do not have to explicitly manage the memory used by all objects and arrays. This feature eliminates another entire category of common bugs and all but eliminates memory leaks from Java programs.

No goto statement

Java doesn't support a `goto` statement. Use of `goto` except in certain well-defined circumstances is regarded as poor programming practice. Java adds exception handling and labeled `break` and `continue` statements to the flow-control statements offered by C. These are a good substitute for `goto`.

Variable declarations anywhere

C requires local variable declarations to be made at the beginning of a method or block, while Java allows them anywhere in a method or block. Many programmers prefer to keep all their variable declarations grouped together at the top of a method, however.

Forward references

The Java compiler is smarter than the C compiler in that it allows methods to be invoked before they are defined. This eliminates the need to declare functions in a header file before defining them in a program file, as is done in C.

Method overloading

Java programs can define multiple methods with the same name, as long as the methods have different parameter lists.

No struct and union types

Java doesn't support C `struct` and `union` types. A Java `class` can be thought of as an enhanced `struct`, however.

No bitfields

Java doesn't support the (infrequently used) ability of C to specify the number of individual bits occupied by fields of a `struct`.

No typedef

Java doesn't support the `typedef` keyword used in C to define aliases for type names. Java's lack of pointers makes its type-naming scheme simpler and more consistent than C's, however, so many of the common uses of `typedef` are not really necessary in Java.

No method pointers

C allows you to store the address of a function in a variable and pass this function pointer to other functions. You cannot do this with Java methods, but you can often achieve similar results by passing an object that implements a particular interface. Also, a Java method can be represented and invoked through a `java.lang.reflect.Method` object.

3
Object-Oriented Programming in Java

Now that we've covered fundamental Java syntax, we are ready to begin object-oriented programming in Java. All Java programs use objects, and the type of an object is defined by its *class* or *interface*. Every Java program is defined as a class, and nontrivial programs usually include a number of classes and interface definitions. This chapter explains how to define new classes and interfaces and how to do object-oriented programming with them.*

This is a relatively long and detailed chapter, so we begin with an overview and some definitions. A *class* is a collection of fields that hold values and methods that operate on those values. Classes are the most fundamental structural element of all Java programs. You cannot write Java code without defining a class. All Java statements appear within methods, and all methods are implemented within classes.

A class defines a new reference type, such as the `Point` type defined in Chapter 2. An *object* is an *instance* of a class. The `Point` class defines a type that is the set of all possible two-dimensional points. A `Point` object is a value of that type: it represents a single two-dimensional point.

Objects are usually created by *instantiating* a class with the `new` keyword and a constructor invocation, as shown here:

```
Point p = new Point(1.0, 2.0);
```

Constructors are covered in "Creating and Initializing Objects" later in this chapter.

* If you do not have object-oriented (OO) programming background, don't worry; this chapter does not assume any prior experience. If you do have experience with OO programming, however, be careful. The term "object-oriented" has different meanings in different languages. Don't assume that Java works the same way as your favorite OO language. This is particularly true for C++ programmers. Although Java and C++ borrow much syntax from C, the similarities between the two languages do not go far beyond the level of syntax. Don't let your experience with C++ lull you into a false familiarity with Java.

A class definition consists of a *signature* and a *body*. The class signature defines the name of the class and may also specify other important information. The body of a class is a set of *members* enclosed in curly braces. The members of a class may include fields and methods, constructors and initializers, and nested types.

Members can be *static* or nonstatic. A static member belongs to the class itself while a nonstatic member is associated with the instances of a class (see "Fields and Methods" later in this chapter).

The signature of a class may declare that the class *extends* another class. The extended class is known as the *superclass* and the extension is known as the *subclass*. A subclass *inherits* the members of its superclass and may declare new members or *override* inherited methods with new implementations.

The signature of a class may also declare that the class *implements* one or more interfaces. An *interface* is a reference type that defines method signatures but does not include method bodies to implement the methods. A class that implements an interface is required to provide bodies for the interface's methods. Instances of such a class are also instances of the interface type that it implements.

The members of a class may have *access modifiers* `public`, `protected`, or `private`, which specify their visibility and accessibility to clients and to subclasses. This allows classes to hide members that are not part of their public API. When applied to fields, this ability to hide members enables an object-oriented design technique known as *data encapsulation*.

Classes and interfaces are the most important of the five fundamental reference types defined by Java. Arrays, enumerated types (or "enums") and annotation types are the other three. Arrays are covered in Chapter 2. Enumerated types and annotation types were introduced in Java 5.0 (see Chapter 4). Enums are a specialized kind of class and annotation types are a specialized kind of interface.

Class Definition Syntax

At its simplest level, a class definition consists of the keyword `class` followed by the name of the class and a set of class members within curly braces. The `class` keyword may be preceded by modifier keywords and annotations (see Chapter 4). If the class extends another class, the class name is followed by the `extends` keyword and the name of the class being extended. If the class implements one or more interfaces then the class name or the `extends` clause is followed by the `implements` keyword and a comma-separated list of interface names. For example:

```
public class Integer extends Number implements Serializable, Comparable {
    // class members go here
}
```

Generic class declarations include additional syntax that is covered in Chapter 4.

Class declarations may include zero or more of the following modifiers:

`public`
: A `public` class is visible to classes defined outside of its package. See "Data Hiding and Encapsulation" later in this chapter.

abstract
: An abstract class is one whose implementation is incomplete and cannot be instantiated. Any class with one or more abstract methods must be declared abstract.

final
: The final modifier specifies that the class may not be extended. Declaring a class final may enable the Java VM to optimize its methods.

strictfp
: If a class is declared strictfp, all its methods behave as if they were declared strictfp. This rarely used modifier is discussed in "Methods" in Chapter 2.

A class cannot be both abstract and final. By convention, if a class has more than one modifier, they appear in the order shown.

Fields and Methods

A class can be viewed as a collection of data and code to operate on that data. The data is stored in fields, and the code is organized into methods. This section covers fields and methods, the two most important kinds of class members. Fields and methods come in two distinct types: class members (also known as static members) are associated with the class itself, while instance members are associated with individual instances of the class (i.e., with objects). This gives us four kinds of members:

- Class fields
- Class methods
- Instance fields
- Instance methods

The simple class definition for the class Circle, shown in Example 3-1, contains all four types of members.

Example 3-1. A simple class and its members

```
public class Circle {
  // A class field
  public static final double PI= 3.14159;     // A useful constant

  // A class method: just compute a value based on the arguments
  public static double radiansToDegrees(double rads) {
    return rads * 180 / PI;
  }

  // An instance field
  public double r;                  // The radius of the circle

  // Two instance methods: they operate on the instance fields of an object
  public double area() {            // Compute the area of the circle
    return PI * r * r;
  }
```

Example 3-1. A simple class and its members (continued)

```
  public double circumference() {   // Compute the circumference of the circle
    return 2 * PI * r;
  }
}
```

The following sections explain all four kinds of members. First, however, we cover field declaration syntax. (Method declaration syntax is covered in "Methods" later in this chapter.)

Field Declaration Syntax

Field declaration syntax is much like the syntax for declaring local variables (see Chapter 2) except that field definitions may also include modifiers. The simplest field declaration consists of the field type followed by the field name. The type may be preceded by zero or more modifier keywords or annotations (see Chapter 4), and the name may be followed by an equals sign and initializer expression that provides the initial value of the field. If two or more fields share the same type and modifiers, the type may be followed by a comma-separated list of field names and initializers. Here are some valid field declarations:

```
int x = 1;
private String name;
public static final DAYS_PER_WEEK = 7;
String[] daynames = new String[DAYS_PER_WEEK];
private int a = 17, b = 37, c = 53;
```

Field modifiers are comprised of zero or more of the following keywords:

`public`, `protected`, `private`
: These access modifiers specify whether and where a field can be used outside of the class that defines it. These important modifiers are covered in "Data Hiding and Encapsulation" later in this chapter. No more than one of these access modifiers may appear in any field declaration.

`static`
: If present, this modifier specifies that the field is associated with the defining class itself rather than with each instance of the class.

`final`
: This modifier specifies that once the field has been initialized, its value may never be changed. Fields that are both `static` and `final` are compile-time constants that the compiler can inline. `final` fields can also be used to create classes whose instances are immutable.

`transient`
: This modifier specifies that a field is not part of the persistent state of an object and that it need not be serialized along with the rest of the object. Serialization is covered in Chapter 5.

`volatile`
: Roughly speaking, a `volatile` field is like a `synchronized` method: safe for concurrent use by two or more threads. More accurately, `volatile` says that

the value of a field must always be read from and flushed to main memory, and that it may not be cached by a thread (in a register or CPU cache).

Class Fields

A *class field* is associated with the class in which it is defined rather than with an instance of the class. The following line declares a class field:

```
public static final double PI = 3.14159;
```

This line declares a field of type `double` named `PI` and assigns it a value of 3.14159. As you can see, a field declaration looks quite a bit like a local variable declaration. The difference, of course, is that variables are defined within methods while fields are members of classes.

The `static` modifier says that the field is a class field. Class fields are sometimes called static fields because of this `static` modifier. The `final` modifier says that the value of the field does not change. Since the field `PI` represents a constant, we declare it `final` so that it cannot be changed. It is a convention in Java (and many other languages) that constants are named with capital letters, which is why our field is named `PI`, not `pi`. Defining constants like this is a common use for class fields, meaning that the `static` and `final` modifiers are often used together. Not all class fields are constants, however. In other words, a field can be declared `static` without being declared `final`. Finally, the `public` modifier says that anyone can use the field. This is a visibility modifier, and we'll discuss it and related modifiers in more detail later in this chapter.

The key point to understand about a static field is that there is only a single copy of it. This field is associated with the class itself, not with instances of the class. If you look at the various methods of the `Circle` class, you'll see that they use this field. From inside the `Circle` class, the field can be referred to simply as `PI`. Outside the class, however, both class and field names are required to uniquely specify the field. Methods that are not part of `Circle` access this field as `Circle.PI`.

A `public` class field is essentially a global variable. The names of class fields are qualified by the unique names of the classes that contain them, however. Thus, Java does not suffer from the name collisions that can affect other languages when different modules of code define global variables with the same name.

Class Methods

As with class fields, *class methods* are declared with the `static` modifier:

```
public static double radiansToDegrees(double rads) { return rads * 180 / PI; }
```

This line declares a class method named `radiansToDegrees()`. It has a single parameter of type `double` and returns a `double` value. The body of the method is quite short; it performs a simple computation and returns the result.

Like class fields, class methods are associated with a class, rather than with an object. When invoking a class method from code that exists outside the class, you must specify both the name of the class and the method. For example:

```
// How many degrees is 2.0 radians?
double d = Circle.radiansToDegrees(2.0);
```

If you want to invoke a class method from inside the class in which it is defined, you don't have to specify the class name. However, it is often good style to specify the class name anyway, to make it clear that a class method is being invoked.

Note that the body of our `Circle.radiansToDegrees()` method uses the class field `PI`. A class method can use any class fields and class methods of its own class (or of any other class). But it cannot use any instance fields or instance methods because class methods are not associated with an instance of the class. In other words, although the `radiansToDegrees()` method is defined in the `Circle` class, it does not use any `Circle` objects. The instance fields and instance methods of the class are associated with `Circle` objects, not with the class itself. Since a class method is not associated with an instance of its class, it cannot use any instance methods or fields.

As we discussed earlier, a class field is essentially a global variable. In a similar way, a class method is a global method, or global function. Although `radiansToDegrees()` does not operate on `Circle` objects, it is defined within the `Circle` class because it is a utility method that is sometimes useful when working with circles. In many nonobject-oriented programming languages, all methods, or functions, are global. You can write complex Java programs using only class methods. This is not object-oriented programming, however, and does not take advantage of the power of the Java language. To do true object-oriented programming, we need to add instance fields and instance methods to our repertoire.

Instance Fields

Any field declared without the `static` modifier is an *instance field*:

```
public double r;     // The radius of the circle
```

Instance fields are associated with instances of the class, rather than with the class itself. Thus, every `Circle` object we create has its own copy of the `double` field `r`. In our example, `r` represents the radius of a circle. Thus, each `Circle` object can have a radius independent of all other `Circle` objects.

Inside a class definition, instance fields are referred to by name alone. You can see an example of this if you look at the method body of the `circumference()` instance method. In code outside the class, the name of an instance method must be prefixed with a reference to the object that contains it. For example, if the variable `c` holds a reference to a `Circle` object, we use the expression `c.r` to refer to the radius of that circle:

```
Circle c = new Circle(); // Create a Circle object; store a reference in c
c.r = 2.0;               // Assign a value to its instance field r
Circle d = new Circle(); // Create a different Circle object
d.r = c.r * 2;           // Make this one twice as big
```

Instance fields are key to object-oriented programming. Instance fields hold the state of an object; the values of those fields make one object distinct from another.

Instance Methods

Any method not declared with the static keyword is an instance method. An *instance method* operates on an instance of a class (an object) instead of operating on the class itself. It is with instance methods that object-oriented programming starts to get interesting. The Circle class defined in Example 3-1 contains two instance methods, area( ) and circumference(), that compute and return the area and circumference of the circle represented by a given Circle object.

To use an instance method from outside the class in which it is defined, we must prefix it with a reference to the instance that is to be operated on. For example:

```
Circle c = new Circle();   // Create a Circle object; store in variable c
c.r = 2.0;                 // Set an instance field of the object
double a = c.area();       // Invoke an instance method of the object
```

If you're new to object-oriented programming, that last line of code may look a little strange. We do not write:

```
a = area(c);
```

Instead, we write:

```
a = c.area();
```

This is why it is called object-oriented programming; the object is the focus here, not the function call. This small syntactic difference is perhaps the single most important feature of the object-oriented paradigm.

The point here is that we don't have to pass an argument to c.area(). The object we are operating on, c, is implicit in the syntax. Take a look at Example 3-1 again. You'll notice the same thing in the signature of the area( ) method: it doesn't have a parameter. Now look at the body of the area( ) method: it uses the instance field r. Because the area() method is part of the same class that defines this instance field, the method can use the unqualified name r. It is understood that this refers to the radius of whatever Circle instance invokes the method.

Another important thing to notice about the bodies of the area( ) and circumference() methods is that they both use the class field PI. We saw earlier that class methods can use only class fields and class methods, not instance fields or methods. Instance methods are not restricted in this way: they can use any member of a class, whether it is declared static or not.

How instance methods work

Consider this line of code again:

```
a = c.area();
```

What's going on here? How can a method that has no parameters know what data to operate on? In fact, the area( ) method does have a parameter. All instance methods are implemented with an implicit parameter not shown in the method signature. The implicit argument is named this; it holds a reference to the object through which the method is invoked. In our example, that object is a Circle.

The implicit this parameter is not shown in method signatures because it is usually not needed; whenever a Java method accesses the instance fields in its class, it is implicit that it is accessing fields in the object referred to by the this parameter. The same is true when an instance method invokes another instance method in the same class. I said earlier that to invoke an instance method you must prepend a reference to the object to be operated on. When an instance method is invoked within another instance method in the same class, however, you don't need to specify an object. In this case, it is implicit that the method is being invoked on the this object.

You can use the this keyword explicitly when you want to make it clear that a method is accessing its own fields and/or methods. For example, we can rewrite the area() method to use this explicitly to refer to instance fields:

```
public double area() { return Circle.PI * this.r * this.r; }
```

This code also uses the class name explicitly to refer to class field PI. In a method this simple, it is not necessary to be explicit. In more complicated cases, however, you may find that it increases the clarity of your code to use an explicit this where it is not strictly required.

In some cases, the this keyword *is* required, however. For example, when a method parameter or local variable in a method has the same name as one of the fields of the class, you must use this to refer to the field since the field name used alone refers to the method parameter or local variable. For example, we can add the following method to the Circle class:

```
public void setRadius(double r) {
  this.r = r;       // Assign the argument (r) to the field (this.r)
                    // Note that we cannot just say r = r
}
```

Finally, note that while instance methods can use the this keyword, class methods cannot. This is because class methods are not associated with objects.

Instance methods or class methods?

Instance methods are one of the key features of object-oriented programming. That doesn't mean, however, that you should shun class methods. In many cases, it is perfectly reasonable to define class methods. When working with the Circle class, for example, you might find that you often want to compute the area of a circle with a given radius but don't want to bother creating a Circle object to represent that circle. In this case, a class method is more convenient:

```
public static double area(double r) { return PI * r * r; }
```

It is perfectly legal for a class to define more than one method with the same name, as long as the methods have different parameters. Since this version of the area() method is a class method, it does not have an implicit this parameter and must have a parameter that specifies the radius of the circle. This parameter keeps it distinct from the instance method of the same name.

As another example of the choice between instance methods and class methods, consider defining a method named bigger() that examines two Circle objects and returns whichever has the larger radius. We can write bigger( ) as an instance method as follows:

```
// Compare the implicit "this" circle to the "that" circle passed
// explicitly as an argument and return the bigger one.
public Circle bigger(Circle that) {
  if (this.r > that.r) return this;
  else return that;
}
```

We can also implement bigger( ) as a class method as follows:

```
// Compare circle a to circle b and return the one with the larger radius
public static Circle bigger(Circle a, Circle b) {
  if (a.r > b.r) return a;
  else return b;
}
```

Given two Circle objects, x and y, we can use either the instance method or the class method to determine which is bigger. The invocation syntax differs significantly for the two methods, however:

```
Circle biggest = x.bigger(y);          // Instance method: also y.bigger(x)
Circle biggest = Circle.bigger(x, y);  // Static method
```

Both methods work well, and, from an object-oriented design standpoint, neither of these methods is "more correct" than the other. The instance method is more formally object-oriented, but its invocation syntax suffers from a kind of asymmetry. In a case like this, the choice between an instance method and a class method is simply a design decision. Depending on the circumstances, one or the other will likely be the more natural choice.

Case Study: System.out.println( )

Throughout this book, we've seen a method named System.out.println() used to display output to the terminal window or console. We've never explained why this method has such an long, awkward name or what those two periods are doing in it. Now that you understand class and instance fields and class and instance methods, it is easier to understand what is going on: System is a class. It has a class field named out. The field System.out refers to an object. The object System.out has an instance method named println( ). If you want to explore this in more detail, you can look up the java.lang.System class in the reference section. The class synopsis there tells you that the field out is of type java.io.PrintStream, and you can look up that class to find out about the println( ) method.

Creating and Initializing Objects

Now that we've covered fields and methods, we move on to other important members of a class. Constructors and initializers are class members whose job is to initialize the fields of a class.

Take another look at how we've been creating Circle objects:

```
Circle c = new Circle();
```

What are those parentheses doing there? They make it look like we're calling a method. In fact, that is exactly what we're doing. Every class in Java has at least one *constructor*, which is a method that has the same name as the class and whose purpose is to perform any necessary initialization for a new object. Since we didn't explicitly define a constructor for our `Circle` class in Example 3-1, Java gave us a default constructor that takes no arguments and performs no special initialization.

Here's how a constructor works. The `new` operator creates a new, but uninitialized, instance of the class. The constructor method is then called, with the new object passed implicitly (a `this` reference, as we saw earlier) as well as whatever arguments that are specified between parentheses passed explicitly. The constructor can use these arguments to do whatever initialization is necessary.

Defining a Constructor

There is some obvious initialization we could do for our circle objects, so let's define a constructor. Example 3-2 shows a new definition for `Circle` that contains a constructor that lets us specify the radius of a new `Circle` object. The constructor also uses the `this` reference to distinguish between a method parameter and an instance field of the same name.

Example 3-2. A constructor for the Circle class

```
public class Circle {
    public static final double PI = 3.14159;  // A constant
    public double r;   // An instance field that holds the radius of the circle

    // The constructor method: initialize the radius field
    public Circle(double r) { this.r = r; }

    // The instance methods: compute values based on the radius
    public double circumference() { return 2 * PI * r; }
    public double area() { return PI * r*r; }
}
```

When we relied on the default constructor supplied by the compiler, we had to write code like this to initialize the radius explicitly:

```
Circle c = new Circle();
c.r = 0.25;
```

With this new constructor, the initialization becomes part of the object creation step:

```
Circle c = new Circle(0.25);
```

Here are some important notes about naming, declaring, and writing constructors:

- The constructor name is always the same as the class name.
- Unlike all other methods, a constructor is declared without a return type, not even `void`.

- The body of a constructor should initialize the this object.
- A constructor may not return this or any other value. A constructor may include a return statement, but only one that does not include a return value.

Defining Multiple Constructors

Sometimes you want to initialize an object in a number of different ways, depending on what is most convenient in a particular circumstance. For example, we might want to initialize the radius of a circle to a specified value or a reasonable default value. Since our Circle class has only a single instance field, we can't initialize it too many ways, of course. But in more complex classes, it is often convenient to define a variety of constructors. Here's how we can define two constructors for Circle:

```
public Circle() { r = 1.0; }
public Circle(double r) { this.r = r; }
```

It is perfectly legal to define multiple constructors for a class, as long as each constructor has a different parameter list. The compiler determines which constructor you wish to use based on the number and type of arguments you supply. This is simply an example of method overloading, as we discussed in Chapter 2.

Invoking One Constructor from Another

A specialized use of the this keyword arises when a class has multiple constructors; it can be used from a constructor to invoke one of the other constructors of the same class. In other words, we can rewrite the two previous Circle constructors as follows:

```
// This is the basic constructor: initialize the radius
public Circle(double r) { this.r = r; }
// This constructor uses this() to invoke the constructor above
public Circle() { this(1.0); }
```

The this( ) syntax is a method invocation that calls one of the other constructors of the class. The particular constructor that is invoked is determined by the number and type of arguments, of course. This is a useful technique when a number of constructors share a significant amount of initialization code, as it avoids repetition of that code. This would be a more impressive example, of course, if the one-parameter version of the Circle( ) constructor did more initialization than it does.

There is an important restriction on using this(): it can appear only as the first statement in a constructor. It may, of course, be followed by any additional initialization a particular version of the constructor needs to do. The reason for this restriction involves the automatic invocation of superclass constructor methods, which we'll explore later in this chapter.

Field Defaults and Initializers

Not every field of a class requires initialization. Unlike local variables, which have no default value and cannot be used until explicitly initialized, the fields of a class are automatically initialized to the default value false, '\u0000', 0, 0.0, or null, depending on their type. These default values are guaranteed by Java and apply to both instance fields and class fields.

If the default field value is not appropriate for your field, you can explicitly provide a different initial value. For example:

```
public static final double PI = 3.14159;
public double r = 1.0;
```

Field declarations and local variable declarations have similar syntax, but there is an important difference in how their initializer expressions are handled. As described in Chapter 2, a local variable declaration is a statement that appears within a Java method; the variable initialization is performed when the statement is executed. Field declarations, however, are not part of any method, so they cannot be executed as statements are. Instead, the Java compiler generates instance-field initialization code automatically and puts it in the constructor or constructors for the class. The initialization code is inserted into a constructor in the order in which it appears in the source code, which means that a field initializer can use the initial values of any fields declared before it. Consider the following code excerpt, which shows a constructor and two instance fields of a hypothetical class:

```
public class TestClass {
  public int len = 10;
  public int[] table = new int[len];

  public TestClass() {
    for(int i = 0; i < len; i++) table[i] = i;
  }

  // The rest of the class is omitted...
}
```

In this case, the code generated for the constructor is actually equivalent to the following:

```
public TestClass() {
  len = 10;
  table = new int[len];
  for(int i = 0; i < len; i++) table[i] = i;
}
```

If a constructor begins with a this( ) call to another constructor, the field initialization code does not appear in the first constructor. Instead, the initialization is handled in the constructor invoked by the this( ) call.

So, if instance fields are initialized in constructor methods, where are class fields initialized? These fields are associated with the class, even if no instances of the class are ever created, so they need to be initialized even before a constructor is called. To support this, the Java compiler generates a class initialization method automatically for every class. Class fields are initialized in the body of this method, which is invoked exactly once before the class is first used (often when the class is first loaded by the Java VM.)* As with instance field initialization, class field initialization expressions are inserted into the class initialization method in the order in which they appear in the source code. This means that the initialization expression for a class field can use the class fields declared before it. The class initialization method is an internal method that is hidden from Java programmers. In the class file, it bears the name `<clinit>`.

Initializer blocks

So far, we've seen that objects can be initialized through the initialization expressions for their fields and by arbitrary code in their constructor methods. A class has a class initialization method, which is like a constructor, but we cannot explicitly define the body of this method as we can for a constructor. Java does allow us to write arbitrary code for the initialization of class fields, however, with a construct known as a *static initializer*. A static initializer is simply the keyword `static` followed by a block of code in curly braces. A static initializer can appear in a class definition anywhere a field or method definition can appear. For example, consider the following code that performs some nontrivial initialization for two class fields:

```
// We can draw the outline of a circle using trigonometric functions
// Trigonometry is slow, though, so we precompute a bunch of values
public class TrigCircle {
  // Here are our static lookup tables and their own simple initializers
  private static final int NUMPTS = 500;
  private static double sines[] = new double[NUMPTS];
  private static double cosines[] = new double[NUMPTS];

  // Here's a static initializer that fills in the arrays
  static {
    double x = 0.0;
    double delta_x = (Circle.PI/2)/(NUMPTS-1);
    for(int i = 0, x = 0.0; i < NUMPTS; i++, x += delta_x) {
      sines[i] = Math.sin(x);
      cosines[i] = Math.cos(x);
    }
  }
  // The rest of the class is omitted...
}
```

A class can have any number of static initializers. The body of each initializer block is incorporated into the class initialization method, along with any static field initialization expressions. A static initializer is like a class method in that it cannot use the `this` keyword or any instance fields or instance methods of the class.

* It is actually possible to write a class initializer for a class C that calls a method of another class that creates an instance of C. In this contrived recursive case, an instance of C is created before the class C is fully initialized. This situation is not common in everyday practice, however.

In Java 1.1 and later, classes are also allowed to have instance initializers. An instance initializer is like a static initializer, except that it initializes an object, not a class. A class can have any number of instance initializers, and they can appear anywhere a field or method definition can appear. The body of each instance initializer is inserted at the beginning of every constructor for the class, along with any field initialization expressions. An instance initializer looks just like a static initializer, except that it doesn't use the `static` keyword. In other words, an instance initializer is just a block of arbitrary Java code that appears within curly braces.

Instance initializers can initialize arrays or other fields that require complex initialization. They are sometimes useful because they locate the initialization code right next to the field, instead of separating into a constructor method. For example:

```
private static final int NUMPTS = 100;
private int[] data = new int[NUMPTS];
{ for(int i = 0; i < NUMPTS; i++) data[i] = i; }
```

In practice, however, this use of instance initializers is fairly rare. Instance initializers were introduced in Java 1.1 to support anonymous inner classes, which are not allowed to define constructors. (Anonymous inner classes are covered in "Nested Types" later in this chapter.)

Destroying and Finalizing Objects

Now that we've seen how new objects are created and initialized in Java, we need to study the other end of the object life cycle and examine how objects are finalized and destroyed. *Finalization* is the opposite of initialization.

In Java, the memory occupied by an object is automatically reclaimed when the object is no longer needed. This is done through a process known as *garbage collection*. Garbage collection is a technique that has been around for years in languages such as Lisp. It takes some getting used to for programmers accustomed to such languages as C and C++, in which you must call the `free()` function or the `delete` operator to reclaim memory. The fact that you don't need to remember to destroy every object you create is one of the features that makes Java a pleasant language to work with. It is also one of the features that makes programs written in Java less prone to bugs than those written in languages that don't support automatic garbage collection.

Garbage Collection

The Java interpreter knows exactly what objects and arrays it has allocated. It can also figure out which local variables refer to which objects and arrays and which objects and arrays refer to which other objects and arrays. Thus, the interpreter is able to determine when an allocated object is no longer referred to by any other active object or variable. When the interpreter finds such an object, it knows it can safely reclaim the object's memory and does so. The garbage collector can also detect and destroy cycles of objects that refer to each other, but are not referenced by any other active objects. Any such cycles are also reclaimed.

Different VM implementations handle garbage collection in different ways. It is reasonable, however, to imagine the garbage collector running as a low-priority background thread, so it does most of its work when nothing else is going on, such as during idle time while waiting for user input. The only time the garbage collector must run while something high-priority is going on (i.e., the only time it actually slows down the system) is when available memory has become dangerously low. This doesn't happen very often because the low-priority thread cleans things up in the background.

Memory Leaks in Java

The fact that Java supports garbage collection dramatically reduces the incidence of a class of bugs known as *memory leaks*. A memory leak occurs when memory is allocated and never reclaimed. At first glance, it might seem that garbage collection prevents all memory leaks because it reclaims all unused objects. A memory leak can still occur in Java, however, if a valid (but unused) reference to an unused object is left hanging around. For example, when a method runs for a long time (or forever), the local variables in that method can retain object references much longer than they are actually required. The following code illustrates:

```
public static void main(String args[]) {
  int big_array[] = new int[100000];

  // Do some computations with big_array and get a result.
  int result = compute(big_array);

  // We no longer need big_array. It will get garbage collected when there
  // are no more references to it. Since big_array is a local variable,
  // it refers to the array until this method returns. But this method
  // doesn't return. So we've got to explicitly get rid of the reference
  // ourselves, so the garbage collector knows it can reclaim the array.
  big_array = null;

  // Loop forever, handling the user's input
  for(;;) handle_input(result);
}
```

Memory leaks can also occur when you use a hash table or similar data structure to associate one object with another. Even when neither object is required anymore, the association remains in the hash table, preventing the objects from being reclaimed until the hash table itself is reclaimed. If the hash table has a substantially longer lifetime than the objects it holds, this can cause memory leaks.

The key to avoiding memory leaks is to set object references to `null` when they are no longer needed if the object that contains those references is going to continue to exist. One common source of leaks is in data structures in which an `Object` array is used to represent a collection of objects. It is common to use a separate `size` field to keep track of which elements of the array are currently valid. When removing an object from the collection, it is not sufficient to simply decrement this `size` field: you must also set the appropriate array element to `null` so that the obsolete object reference does not live on.

Object Finalization

A *finalizer* in Java is the opposite of a constructor. While a constructor method performs initialization for an object, a finalizer method can be used to perform cleanup or "finalization" for the object. Garbage collection automatically frees up the memory resources used by objects, but objects can hold other kinds of resources, such as open files and network connections. The garbage collector cannot free these resources for you, so you may occasionally want to write a finalizer method for any object that needs to perform such tasks as closing files, terminating network connections, deleting temporary files, and so on. This is particularly true for classes that use native methods: these classes may need a `native` finalizer to release native resources (including memory) that are not under the control of the Java garbage collector.

A finalizer is an instance method that takes no arguments and returns no value. There can be only one finalizer per class, and it must be named `finalize()`.* A finalizer can throw any kind of exception or error, but when a finalizer is automatically invoked by the garbage collector, any exception or error it throws is ignored and serves only to cause the finalizer method to return. Finalizer methods are typically declared `protected` (which we have not discussed yet) but can also be declared `public`. An example finalizer looks like this:

```
protected void finalize() throws Throwable {
  // Invoke the finalizer of our superclass
  // We haven't discussed superclasses or this syntax yet
  super.finalize();

  // Delete a temporary file we were using
  // If the file doesn't exist or tempfile is null, this can throw
  // an exception, but that exception is ignored.
  tempfile.delete();
}
```

Here are some important points about finalizers:

- If an object has a finalizer, the finalizer method is invoked sometime after the object becomes unused (or unreachable), but before the garbage collector reclaims the object.
- Java makes no guarantees about when garbage collection will occur or in what order objects will be collected. Therefore, Java can make no guarantees about when (or even whether) a finalizer will be invoked, in what order finalizers will be invoked, or what thread will execute finalizers.
- The Java interpreter can exit without garbage collecting all outstanding objects, so some finalizers may never be invoked. In this case, resources such as network connections are closed and reclaimed by the operating system. Note, however, that if a finalizer that deletes a file does not run, that file will not be deleted by the operating system.

* C++ programmers should note that although Java constructor methods are named like C++ constructors, Java finalization methods are not named like C++ destructor methods. As we will see, they do not behave quite like C++ destructor methods either.

To ensure that certain actions are taken before the VM exits, Java 1.1 provided the `Runtime` method `runFinalizersOnExit()`. Unfortunately, however, this method can cause deadlock and is inherently unsafe; it was deprecated in 1.2. In Java 1.3 and later, the `Runtime` method `addShutdownHook()` can safely execute arbitrary code before the Java interpreter exits.

- After a finalizer is invoked, objects are not freed right away. This is because a finalizer method can resurrect an object by storing the `this` pointer somewhere so that the object once again has references. Thus, after `finalize()` is called, the garbage collector must once again determine that the object is unreferenced before it can garbage-collect it. However, even if an object is resurrected, the finalizer method is never invoked more than once. Resurrecting an object is never a useful thing to do—just a strange quirk of object finalization.
- The `finalize()` method is an instance method, and finalizers act on instances. There is no equivalent mechanism for finalizing a class.

In practice, it is quite rare for an application-level class to require a `finalize()` method. Finalizer methods are more useful, however, when writing Java classes that interface to native platform code with `native` methods. In this case, the native implementation can allocate memory or other resources that are not under the control of the Java garbage collector and need to be reclaimed explicitly by a `native` `finalize()` method.

Furthermore, because of the uncertainty about when and whether a finalizer runs, it is best to avoid dependence on finalizers. For example, a class that includes a reference to a network socket should define a public `close()` method, which calls the `close()` method of the socket. This way, when the user of your class is done with it, she can call `close()` and be sure that the network connection is closed. You might, however, define a `finalize()` method as backup in case the user of your class forgets to call `close()` and allows an unclosed instance to be garbage-collected.

Subclasses and Inheritance

The `Circle` defined earlier is a simple class that distinguishes circle objects only by their radii. Suppose, instead, that we want to represent circles that have both a size and a position. For example, a circle of radius 1.0 centered at point 0,0 in the Cartesian plane is different from the circle of radius 1.0 centered at point 1,2. To do this, we need a new class, which we'll call `PlaneCircle`. We'd like to add the ability to represent the position of a circle without losing any of the existing functionality of the `Circle` class. This is done by defining `PlaneCircle` as a subclass of `Circle` so that `PlaneCircle` inherits the fields and methods of its superclass, `Circle`. The ability to add functionality to a class by subclassing, or extending, is central to the object-oriented programming paradigm.

Extending a Class

Example 3-3 shows how we can implement `PlaneCircle` as a subclass of the `Circle` class.

Example 3-3. Extending the Circle class

```
public class PlaneCircle extends Circle {
  // We automatically inherit the fields and methods of Circle,
  // so we only have to put the new stuff here.
  // New instance fields that store the center point of the circle
  public double cx, cy;

  // A new constructor method to initialize the new fields
  // It uses a special syntax to invoke the Circle() constructor
  public PlaneCircle(double r, double x, double y) {
    super(r);       // Invoke the constructor of the superclass, Circle()
    this.cx = x;    // Initialize the instance field cx
    this.cy = y;    // Initialize the instance field cy
  }

  // The area() and circumference() methods are inherited from Circle
  // A new instance method that checks whether a point is inside the circle
  // Note that it uses the inherited instance field r
  public boolean isInside(double x, double y) {
    double dx = x - cx, dy = y - cy;             // Distance from center
    double distance = Math.sqrt(dx*dx + dy*dy); // Pythagorean theorem
    return (distance < r);                       // Returns true or false
  }
}
```

Object-Oriented

Note the use of the keyword extends in the first line of Example 3-3. This keyword tells Java that `PlaneCircle` extends, or subclasses, `Circle`, meaning that it inherits the fields and methods of that class.* The definition of the `isInside()` method shows field inheritance; this method uses the field `r` (defined by the `Circle` class) as if it were defined right in `PlaneCircle` itself. `PlaneCircle` also inherits the methods of `Circle`. Thus, if we have a `PlaneCircle` object referenced by variable pc, we can say:

```
double ratio = pc.circumference() / pc.area();
```

This works just as if the `area( )` and `circumference()` methods were defined in `PlaneCircle` itself.

Another feature of subclassing is that every `PlaneCircle` object is also a perfectly legal `Circle` object. If pc refers to a `PlaneCircle` object, we can assign it to a `Circle` variable and forget all about its extra positioning capabilities:

```
PlaneCircle pc = new PlaneCircle(1.0, 0.0, 0.0);  // Unit circle at the origin
Circle c = pc;     // Assigned to a Circle variable without casting
```

This assignment of a `PlaneCircle` object to a `Circle` variable can be done without a cast. As we discussed in "Reference Type Conversions" in Chapter 2 a widening conversion like this is always legal. The value held in the `Circle` variable c is still a valid `PlaneCircle` object, but the compiler cannot know this for sure, so it doesn't allow us to do the opposite (narrowing) conversion without a cast:

* C++ programmers should note that extends is the Java equivalent of : in C++; both are used to indicate the superclass of a class.

```
// Narrowing conversions require a cast (and a runtime check by the VM)
PlaneCircle pc2 = (PlaneCircle) c;
boolean origininside = ((PlaneCircle) c).isInside(0.0, 0.0);
```

Final classes

When a class is declared with the final modifier, it means that it cannot be extended or subclassed. java.lang.String is an example of a final class. Declaring a class final prevents unwanted extensions to the class: if you invoke a method on a String object, you know that the method is the one defined by the String class itself, even if the String is passed to you from some unknown outside source. Because String is final, no one can create a subclass of it and change the meaning or behavior of its methods.

Declaring a class final also allows the compiler to make certain optimizations when invoking the methods of a class. We'll explore this when we talk about method overriding later in this chapter.

Superclasses, Object, and the Class Hierarchy

In our example, PlaneCircle is a subclass from Circle. We can also say that Circle is the superclass of PlaneCircle. The superclass of a class is specified in its extends clause:

```
public class PlaneCircle extends Circle { ... }
```

Every class you define has a superclass. If you do not specify the superclass with an extends clause, the superclass is the class java.lang.Object. Object is a special class for a couple of reasons:

- It is the only class in Java that does not have a superclass.
- All Java classes inherit the methods of Object.

Because every class has a superclass, classes in Java form a class hierarchy, which can be represented as a tree with Object at its root. Figure 3-1 shows a partial class hierarchy diagram that includes our Circle and PlaneCircle classes, as well as some of the standard classes from the Java API.

Subclass Constructors

Look again at the PlaneCircle() constructor method of Example 3-3:

```
public PlaneCircle(double r, double x, double y) {
  super(r);       // Invoke the constructor of the superclass, Circle()
  this.cx = x;    // Initialize the instance field cx
  this.cy = y;    // Initialize the instance field cy
}
```

This constructor explicitly initializes the cx and cy fields newly defined by PlaneCircle, but it relies on the superclass Circle() constructor to initialize the inherited fields of the class. To invoke the superclass constructor, our constructor calls super(). super is a reserved word in Java. One of its uses is to invoke the constructor method of a superclass from within the constructor method of a subclass. This use is analogous to the use of this() to invoke one constructor

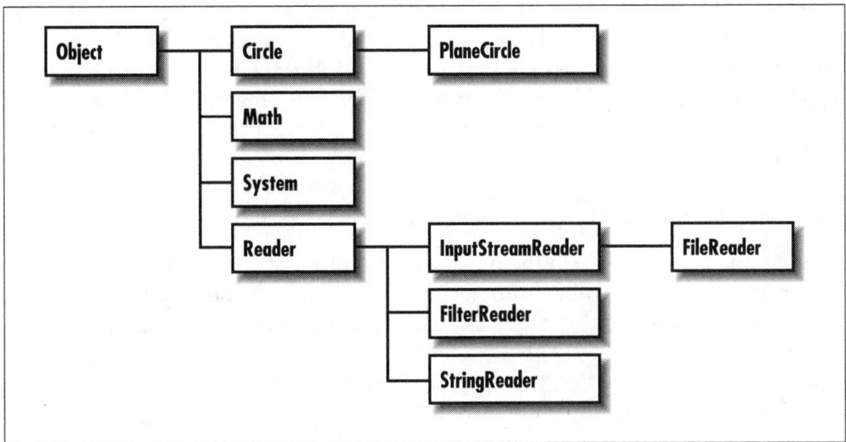

Figure 3-1. A class hierarchy diagram

method of a class from within another constructor method of the same class. Invoking a constructor using `super()` is subject to the same restrictions as is using `this()`:

- `super()` can be used in this way only within a constructor method.
- The call to the superclass constructor must appear as the first statement within the constructor method, even before local variable declarations.

The arguments passed to `super()` must match the parameters of the superclass constructor. If the superclass defines more than one constructor, `super()` can be used to invoke any one of them, depending on the arguments passed.

Constructor Chaining and the Default Constructor

Java guarantees that the constructor method of a class is called whenever an instance of that class is created. It also guarantees that the constructor is called whenever an instance of any subclass is created. In order to guarantee this second point, Java must ensure that every constructor method calls its superclass constructor method. Thus, if the first statement in a constructor does not explicitly invoke another constructor with `this()` or `super()`, Java implicitly inserts the call `super()`, that is, it calls the superclass constructor with no arguments. If the superclass does not have a constructor that takes no arguments, this implicit invocation causes a compilation error.

Consider what happens when we create a new instance of the `PlaneCircle` class. First, the `PlaneCircle` constructor is invoked. This constructor explicitly calls `super(r)` to invoke a `Circle` constructor, and that `Circle()` constructor implicitly calls `super()` to invoke the constructor of its superclass, `Object`. The body of the `Object` constructor runs first. When it returns, the body of the `Circle()` constructor runs. Finally, when the call to `super(r)` returns, the remaining statements of the `PlaneCircle()` constructor are executed.

What all this means is that constructor calls are chained; any time an object is created, a sequence of constructor methods is invoked, from subclass to superclass on up to `Object` at the root of the class hierarchy. Because a superclass constructor is always invoked as the first statement of its subclass constructor, the body of the `Object` constructor always runs first, followed by the constructor of its subclass and on down the class hierarchy to the class that is being instantiated. There is an important implication here; when a constructor is invoked, it can count on the fields of its superclass to be initialized.

The default constructor

There is one missing piece in the previous description of constructor chaining. If a constructor does not invoke a superclass constructor, Java does so implicitly. But what if a class is declared without a constructor? In this case, Java implicitly adds a constructor to the class. This default constructor does nothing but invoke the superclass constructor. For example, if we don't declare a constructor for the `PlaneCircle` class, Java implicitly inserts this constructor:

```
public PlaneCircle() { super(); }
```

If the superclass, `Circle`, doesn't declare a no-argument constructor, the `super()` call in this automatically inserted default constructor for `PlaneCircle()` causes a compilation error. In general, if a class does not define a no-argument constructor, all its subclasses must define constructors that explicitly invoke the superclass constructor with the necessary arguments.

If a class does not declare any constructors, it is given a no-argument constructor by default. Classes declared `public` are given `public` constructors. All other classes are given a default constructor that is declared without any visibility modifier: such a constructor has default visibility. (The notion of visibility is explained later in this chapter.) If you are creating a `public` class that should not be publicly instantiated, you should declare at least one non-`public` constructor to prevent the insertion of a default `public` constructor. Classes that should never be instantiated (such as `java.lang.Math` or `java.lang.System`) should define a `private` constructor. Such a constructor can never be invoked from outside of the class, but it prevents the automatic insertion of the default constructor.

Finalizer chaining?

You might assume that since Java chains constructor methods, it also automatically chains the finalizer methods for an object. In other words, you might assume that the finalizer method of a class automatically invokes the finalizer of its superclass, and so on. In fact, Java does *not* do this. When you write a `finalize()` method, you must explicitly invoke the superclass finalizer. (You should do this even if you know that the superclass does not have a finalizer because a future implementation of the superclass might add a finalizer.)

As we saw in our example finalizer earlier in the chapter, you can invoke a superclass method with a special syntax that uses the `super` keyword:

```
// Invoke the finalizer of our superclass
super.finalize();
```

We'll discuss this syntax in more detail when we consider method overriding. In practice, the need for finalizer methods, and thus finalizer chaining, rarely arises.

Hiding Superclass Fields

For the sake of example, imagine that our `PlaneCircle` class needs to know the distance between the center of the circle and the origin (0,0). We can add another instance field to hold this value:

```
public double r;
```

Adding the following line to the constructor computes the value of the field:

```
this.r = Math.sqrt(cx*cx + cy*cy);  // Pythagorean theorem
```

But wait; this new field `r` has the same name as the radius field `r` in the `Circle` superclass. When this happens, we say that the field `r` of `PlaneCircle` *hides* the field `r` of `Circle`. (This is a contrived example, of course: the new field should really be called `distanceFromOrigin`. Although you should attempt to avoid it, subclass fields do sometimes hide fields of their superclass.)

Object-Oriented

With this new definition of `PlaneCircle`, the expressions `r` and `this.r` both refer to the field of `PlaneCircle`. How, then, can we refer to the field `r` of `Circle` that holds the radius of the circle? A special syntax for this uses the `super` keyword:

```
r        // Refers to the PlaneCircle field
this.r   // Refers to the PlaneCircle field
super.r  // Refers to the Circle field
```

Another way to refer to a hidden field is to cast `this` (or any instance of the class) to the appropriate superclass and then access the field:

```
((Circle) this).r   // Refers to field r of the Circle class
```

This casting technique is particularly useful when you need to refer to a hidden field defined in a class that is not the immediate superclass. Suppose, for example, that classes `A`, `B`, and `C` all define a field named `x` and that `C` is a subclass of `B`, which is a subclass of `A`. Then, in the methods of class `C`, you can refer to these different fields as follows:

```
x                 // Field x in class C
this.x            // Field x in class C
super.x           // Field x in class B
((B)this).x       // Field x in class B
((A)this).x       // Field x in class A
super.super.x     // Illegal; does not refer to x in class A
```

You cannot refer to a hidden field `x` in the superclass of a superclass with `super.super.x`. This is not legal syntax.

Similarly, if you have an instance `c` of class `C`, you can refer to the three fields named `x` like this:

```
c.x               // Field x of class C
((B)c).x          // Field x of class B
((A)c).x          // Field x of class A
```

So far, we've been discussing instance fields. Class fields can also be hidden. You can use the same `super` syntax to refer to the hidden value of the field, but this is never necessary since you can always refer to a class field by prepending the name of the desired class. Suppose that the implementer of `PlaneCircle` decides that the

Circle.PI field does not express π to enough decimal places. She can define her own class field PI:

```
public static final double PI = 3.14159265358979323846;
```

Now, code in PlaneCircle can use this more accurate value with the expressions PI or PlaneCircle.PI. It can also refer to the old, less accurate value with the expressions super.PI and Circle.PI. Note, however, that the area() and circumference() methods inherited by PlaneCircle are defined in the Circle class, so they use the value Circle.PI, even though that value is hidden now by PlaneCircle.PI.

Overriding Superclass Methods

When a class defines an instance method using the same name, return type, and parameters as a method in its superclass, that method *overrides* the method of the superclass. When the method is invoked for an object of the class, it is the new definition of the method that is called, not the superclass's old definition. In Java 5.0 and later, the return type of the overriding method may be a subclass of return type of the overridden method instead of being exactly the same type. This is known as a *covariant return* and is described in "Covariant Return Types" in Chapter 2.

Method overriding is an important and useful technique in object-oriented programming. PlaneCircle does not override either of the methods defined by Circle, but suppose we define another subclass of Circle, named Ellipse.* In this case, it is important for Ellipse to override the area() and circumference() methods of Circle since the formulas used to compute the area and circumference of a circle do not work for ellipses.

The upcoming discussion of method overriding considers only instance methods. Class methods behave quite differently, and there isn't much to say. Like fields, class methods can be hidden by a subclass but not overridden. As noted earlier in this chapter, it is good programming style to always prefix a class method invocation with the name of the class in which it is defined. If you consider the class name part of the class method name, the two methods have different names, so nothing is actually hidden at all. It is, however, illegal for a class method to hide an instance method.

Before we go any further with the discussion of method overriding, you should understand the difference between method overriding and method overloading. As we discussed in Chapter 2, method overloading refers to the practice of defining multiple methods (in the same class) that have the same name but different parameter lists. This is very different from method overriding, so don't get them confused.

* Mathematical purists may argue that since all circles are ellipses, Ellipse should be the superclass and Circle the subclass. A pragmatic engineer might counter that circles can be represented with fewer instance fields, so Circle objects should not be burdened by inheriting unnecessary fields from Ellipse. In any case, this is a useful example here.

Overriding is not hiding

Although Java treats the fields and methods of a class analogously in many ways, method overriding is not like field hiding at all. You can refer to hidden fields simply by casting an object to an instance of the appropriate superclass, but you cannot invoke overridden instance methods with this technique. The following code illustrates this crucial difference:

```
class A {                          // Define a class named A
  int i = 1;                       // An instance field
  int f() { return i; }            // An instance method
  static char g() { return 'A'; }  // A class method
}

class B extends A {                // Define a subclass of A
  int i = 2;                       // Hides field i in class A
  int f() { return -i; }           // Overrides instance method f in class A
  static char g() { return 'B'; }  // Hides class method g() in class A
}

public class OverrideTest {
  public static void main(String args[]) {
    B b = new B();               // Creates a new object of type B
    System.out.println(b.i);     // Refers to B.i; prints 2
    System.out.println(b.f());   // Refers to B.f(); prints -2
    System.out.println(b.g());   // Refers to B.g(); prints B
    System.out.println(B.g());   // This is a better way to invoke B.g()

    A a = (A) b;                 // Casts b to an instance of class A
    System.out.println(a.i);     // Now refers to A.i; prints 1
    System.out.println(a.f());   // Still refers to B.f(); prints -2
    System.out.println(a.g());   // Refers to A.g(); prints A
    System.out.println(A.g());   // This is a better way to invoke A.g()
  }
}
```

While this difference between method overriding and field hiding may seem surprising at first, a little thought makes the purpose clear. Suppose we are manipulating a bunch of `Circle` and `Ellipse` objects. To keep track of the circles and ellipses, we store them in an array of type `Circle[]`. (We can do this because `Ellipse` is a subclass of `Circle`, so all `Ellipse` objects are legal `Circle` objects.) When we loop through the elements of this array, we don't have to know or care whether the element is actually a `Circle` or an `Ellipse`. What we do care about very much, however, is that the correct value is computed when we invoke the `area()` method of any element of the array. In other words, we don't want to use the formula for the area of a circle when the object is actually an ellipse! Seen in this context, it is not surprising at all that method overriding is handled differently by Java than is field hiding.

Dynamic method lookup

If we have a `Circle[]` array that holds `Circle` and `Ellipse` objects, how does the compiler know whether to call the `area()` method of the `Circle` class or the

Ellipse class for any given item in the array? In fact, the compiler does not know this because it cannot know it. The compiler knows that it does not know, however, and produces code that uses dynamic method lookup at runtime. When the interpreter runs the code, it looks up the appropriate area( ) method to call for each of the objects in the array. That is, when the interpreter interprets the expression o.area(), it checks the actual type of the object referred to by the variable o and then finds the area( ) method that is appropriate for that type. It does not simply use the area( ) method that is statically associated with the type of the variable o. This process of dynamic method lookup is sometimes also called virtual method invocation.*

Final methods and static method lookup

Virtual method invocation is fast, but method invocation is faster when no dynamic lookup is necessary at runtime. Fortunately, Java does not always need to use dynamic method lookup. In particular, if a method is declared with the final modifier, it means that the method definition is the final one; it cannot be overridden by any subclasses. If a method cannot be overridden, the compiler knows that there is only one version of the method, and dynamic method lookup is not necessary.† In addition, all methods of a final class are themselves implicitly final and cannot be overridden. As we'll discuss later in this chapter, private methods are not inherited by subclasses and, therefore, cannot be overridden (i.e., all private methods are implicitly final). Finally, class methods behave like fields (i.e., they can be hidden by subclasses but not overridden). Taken together, this means that all methods of a class that is declared final, as well as all methods that are final, private, or static, are invoked without dynamic method lookup. These methods are also candidates for inlining at runtime by a just-in-time compiler (JIT) or similar optimization tool.

Invoking an overridden method

We've seen the important differences between method overriding and field hiding. Nevertheless, the Java syntax for invoking an overridden method is quite similar to the syntax for accessing a hidden field: both use the super keyword. The following code illustrates:

```
class A {
  int i = 1;                  // An instance field hidden by subclass B
  int f() { return i; }       // An instance method overridden by subclass B
}

class B extends A {
  int i;                      // This field hides i in A
  int f() {                   // This method overrides f() in A
```

* C++ programmers should note that dynamic method lookup is what C++ does for virtual functions. An important difference between Java and C++ is that Java does not have a virtual keyword. In Java, methods are virtual by default.

† In this sense, the final modifier is the opposite of the virtual modifier in C++. All non-final methods in Java are virtual.

```
        i = super.i + 1;          // It can retrieve A.i like this
        return super.f() + i;    // It can invoke A.f() like this
    }
}
```

Recall that when you use super to refer to a hidden field, it is the same as casting this to the superclass type and accessing the field through that. Using super to invoke an overridden method, however, is not the same as casting this. In other words, in the previous code, the expression super.f() is not the same as ((A)this).f( ).

When the interpreter invokes an instance method with this super syntax, a modified form of dynamic method lookup is performed. The first step, as in regular dynamic method lookup, is to determine the actual class of the object through which the method is invoked. Normally, the dynamic search for an appropriate method definition would begin with this class. When a method is invoked with the super syntax, however, the search begins at the superclass of the class. If the superclass implements the method directly, that version of the method is invoked. If the superclass inherits the method, the inherited version of the method is invoked.

Object-Oriented

Note that the super keyword invokes the most immediately overridden version of a method. Suppose class A has a subclass B that has a subclass C and that all three classes define the same method f( ). The method C.f() can invoke the method B.f( ), which it overrides directly, with super.f( ). But there is no way for C.f() to invoke A.f( ) directly: super.super.f( ) is not legal Java syntax. Of course, if C.f() invokes B.f( ), it is reasonable to suppose that B.f( ) might also invoke A.f(). This kind of chaining is relatively common when working with overridden methods: it is a way of augmenting the behavior of a method without replacing the method entirely. We saw this technique in the the example finalize() method shown earlier in the chapter: that method invoked super.finalize() to run its superclass finalization method.

Don't confuse the use of super to invoke an overridden method with the super() method call used in constructor methods to invoke a superclass constructor. Although they both use the same keyword, these are two entirely different syntaxes. In particular, you can use super to invoke an overridden method anywhere in the overriding class while you can use super() only to invoke a superclass constructor as the very first statement of a constructor.

It is also important to remember that super can be used only to invoke an overridden method from within the class that overrides it. Given an Ellipse object e, there is no way for a program that uses an object (with or without the super syntax) to invoke the area() method defined by the Circle class on this object.

Data Hiding and Encapsulation

We started this chapter by describing a class as a collection of data and methods. One of the important object-oriented techniques we haven't discussed so far is hiding the data within the class and making it available only through the methods. This technique is known as *encapsulation* because it seals the data (and internal methods) safely inside the "capsule" of the class, where it can be accessed only by trusted users (i.e., the methods of the class).

Why would you want to do this? The most important reason is to hide the internal implementation details of your class. If you prevent programmers from relying on those details, you can safely modify the implementation without worrying that you will break existing code that uses the class.

Another reason for encapsulation is to protect your class against accidental or willful stupidity. A class often contains a number of interdependent fields that must be in a consistent state. If you allow a programmer (including yourself) to manipulate those fields directly, he may change one field without changing important related fields, leaving the class in an inconsistent state. If instead he has to call a method to change the field, that method can be sure to do everything necessary to keep the state consistent. Similarly, if a class defines certain methods for internal use only, hiding these methods prevents users of the class from calling them.

Here's another way to think about encapsulation: when all the data for a class is hidden, the methods define the only possible operations that can be performed on objects of that class. Once you have carefully tested and debugged your methods, you can be confident that the class will work as expected. On the other hand, if all the fields of the class can be directly manipulated, the number of possibilities you have to test becomes unmanageable.

Other reasons to hide fields and methods of a class include:

- Internal fields and methods that are visible outside the class just clutter up the API. Keeping visible fields to a minimum keeps your class tidy and therefore easier to use and understand.
- If a field or method is visible to the users of your class, you have to document it. Save yourself time and effort by hiding it instead.

Access Control

All the fields and methods of a class can always be used within the body of the class itself. Java defines access control rules that restrict members of a class from being used outside the class. In a number of examples in this chapter, you've seen the `public` modifier used in field and method declarations. This `public` keyword, along with `protected` and `private`, are *access control modifiers*; they specify the access rules for the field or method.

Access to packages

A package is always accessible to code defined within the package. Whether it is accessible to code from other packages depends on the way the package is deployed on the host system. When the class files that comprise a package are stored in a directory, for example, a user must have read access to the directory and the files within it in order to have access to the package. Package access is not part of the Java language itself. Access control is usually done at the level of classes and members of classes instead.

Access to classes

By default, top-level classes are accessible within the package in which they are defined. However, if a top-level class is declared `public`, it is accessible everywhere (or everywhere that the package itself is accessible). The reason that we've restricted these statements to top-level classes is that, as we'll see later in this chapter, classes can also be defined as members of other classes. Because these inner classes are members of a class, they obey the member access-control rules.

Access to members

The members of a class are always accessible within the body of the class. By default, members are also accessible throughout the package in which the class is defined. This implies that classes placed in the same package should trust each other with their internal implementation details. This default level of access is often called *package access*. It is only one of four possible levels of access. The other three levels of access are defined by the `public`, `protected`, and `private` modifiers. Here is some example code that uses these modifiers:


```
public class Laundromat {       // People can use this class.
  private Laundry[] dirty;      // They cannot use this internal field,
  public void wash() { ... }    // but they can use these public methods
  public void dry() { ... }     // to manipulate the internal field.
  protected int temperature;    // A subclass might want to tweak this field
}
```

These access rules apply to members of a class:

- If a member of a class is declared with the `public` modifier, it means that the member is accessible anywhere the containing class is accessible. This is the least restrictive type of access control.
- If a member of a class is declared `private`, the member is never accessible, except within the class itself. This is the most restrictive type of access control.
- If a member of a class is declared `protected`, it is accessible to all classes within the package (the same as the default package accessibility) and also accessible within the body of any subclass of the class, regardless of the package in which that subclass is defined. This is more restrictive than `public` access, but less restrictive than package access.
- If a member of a class is not declared with any of these modifiers, it has the default package access: it is accessible to code within all classes that are defined in the same package but inaccessible outside of the package.

`protected` access requires a little more elaboration. Suppose class `A` declares a `protected` field `x` and is extended by a class `B`, which is defined in a different package (this last point is important). Class `B` inherits the `protected` field `x`, and its code can access that field in the current instance of `B` or in any other instances of `B` that the code can refer to. This does not mean, however, that the code of class `B` can start reading the protected fields of arbitrary instances of `A`! If an object is an instance of `A` but is not an instance of `B`, its fields are obviously not inherited by `B`, and the code of class `B` cannot read them.

Access control and inheritance

The Java specification states that a subclass inherits all the instance fields and instance methods of its superclass accessible to it. If the subclass is defined in the same package as the superclass, it inherits all non-`private` instance fields and methods. If the subclass is defined in a different package, however, it inherits all `protected` and `public` instance fields and methods. `private` fields and methods are never inherited; neither are class fields or class methods. Finally, constructors are not inherited; they are chained, as described earlier in this chapter.

The statement that a subclass does not inherit the inaccessible fields and methods of its superclass can be a confusing one. It would seem to imply that when you create an instance of a subclass, no memory is allocated for any `private` fields defined by the superclass. This is not the intent of the statement, however. Every instance of a subclass does, in fact, include a complete instance of the superclass within it, including all inaccessible fields and methods. It is simply a matter of terminology. Because the inaccessible fields cannot be used in the subclass, we say they are not inherited. Earlier in this section we said that the members of a class are always accessible within the body of the class. If this statement is to apply to all members of the class, including inherited members, we must define "inherited members" to include only those members that are accessible. If you don't care for this definition, you can think of it this way instead:

- A class inherits *all* instance fields and instance methods (but not constructors) of its superclass.
- The body of a class can always access all the fields and methods it declares itself. It can also access the *accessible* fields and members it inherits from its superclass.

Member access summary

Table 3-1 summarizes the member access rules.

Table 3-1. Class member accessibility

	Member visibility			
Accessible to	**Public**	**Protected**	**Package**	**Private**
Defining class	Yes	Yes	Yes	Yes
Class in same package	Yes	Yes	Yes	No
Subclass in different package	Yes	Yes	No	No
Non-subclass different package	Yes	No	No	No

Here are some simple rules of thumb for using visibility modifiers:

- Use `public` only for methods and constants that form part of the public API of the class. Certain important or frequently used fields can also be `public`, but it is common practice to make fields non-`public` and encapsulate them with `public` accessor methods.
- Use `protected` for fields and methods that aren't required by most programmers using the class but that may be of interest to anyone creating a subclass

as part of a different package. Note that protected members are technically part of the exported API of a class. They should be documented and cannot be changed without potentially breaking code that relies on them.

- Use the default package visibility for fields and methods that are internal implementation details but are used by cooperating classes in the same package. You cannot take real advantage of package visibility unless you use the package directive to group your cooperating classes into a package.
- Use private for fields and methods that are used only inside the class and should be hidden everywhere else.

If you are not sure whether to use protected, package, or private accessibility, it is better to start with overly restrictive member access. You can always relax the access restrictions in future versions of your class, if necessary. Doing the reverse is not a good idea because increasing access restrictions is not a backward-compatible change and can break code that relies on access to those members.

Object-Oriented

Data Accessor Methods

In the Circle example, we declared the circle radius to be a public field. The Circle class is one in which it may well be reasonable to keep that field publicly accessible; it is a simple enough class, with no dependencies between its fields. On the other hand, our current implementation of the class allows a Circle object to have a negative radius, and circles with negative radii should simply not exist. As long as the radius is stored in a public field, however, any programmer can set the field to any value she wants, no matter how unreasonable. The only solution is to restrict the programmer's direct access to the field and define public methods that provide indirect access to the field. Providing public methods to read and write a field is not the same as making the field itself public. The crucial difference is that methods can perform error checking.

Example 3-4 shows how we might reimplement Circle to prevent circles with negative radii. This version of Circle declares the r field to be protected and defines accessor methods named getRadius() and setRadius() to read and write the field value while enforcing the restriction on negative radius values. Because the r field is protected, it is directly (and more efficiently) accessible to subclasses.

Example 3-4. The Circle class using data hiding and encapsulation

```
package shapes;           // Specify a package for the class

public class Circle {     // The class is still public
  // This is a generally useful constant, so we keep it public
  public static final double PI = 3.14159;

  protected double r;     // Radius is hidden but visible to subclasses

  // A method to enforce the restriction on the radius
  // This is an implementation detail that may be of interest to subclasses
  protected void checkRadius(double radius) {
    if (radius < 0.0)
      throw new IllegalArgumentException("radius may not be negative.");
```

Example 3-4. The Circle class using data hiding and encapsulation (continued)

```
  }

  // The constructor method
  public Circle(double r) {
    checkRadius(r);
    this.r = r;
  }

  // Public data accessor methods
  public double getRadius() { return r; }
  public void setRadius(double r) {
    checkRadius(r);
    this.r = r;
  }

  // Methods to operate on the instance field
  public double area() { return PI * r * r; }
  public double circumference() { return 2 * PI * r; }
}
```

We have defined the `Circle` class within a package named `shapes`. Since `r` is `protected`, any other classes in the `shapes` package have direct access to that field and can set it however they like. The assumption here is that all classes within the `shapes` package were written by the same author or a closely cooperating group of authors and that the classes all trust each other not to abuse their privileged level of access to each other's implementation details.

Finally, the code that enforces the restriction against negative radius values is itself placed within a `protected` method, `checkRadius()`. Although users of the `Circle` class cannot call this method, subclasses of the class can call it and even override it if they want to change the restrictions on the radius.

Note particularly the `getRadius()` and `setRadius()` methods of Example 3-4. It is a common convention in Java that data accessor methods begin with the prefixes "get" and "set." If the field being accessed is of type `boolean`, however, the `get()` method may be replaced with an equivalent method that begins with "is." For example, the accessor method for a `boolean` field named `readable` is typically called `isReadable()` instead of `getReadable()`. In the programming conventions of the JavaBeans component model (covered in Chapter 7), a hidden field with one or more data accessor methods whose names begin with "get," "is," or "set" is called a *property*. An interesting way to study a complex class is to look at the set of properties it defines. Properties are particularly common in the AWT and Swing APIs, which are covered in *Java Foundation Classes in a Nutshell* (O'Reilly).

Abstract Classes and Methods

In Example 3-4, we declared our `Circle` class to be part of a package named `shapes`. Suppose we plan to implement a number of shape classes: `Rectangle`, `Square`, `Ellipse`, `Triangle`, and so on. We can give these shape classes our two basic `area()` and `circumference()` methods. Now, to make it easy to work with an array of shapes, it would be helpful if all our shape classes had a common superclass, Shape. If we structure our class hierarchy this way, every shape object, regardless of the actual type of shape it represents, can be assigned to variables, fields, or array elements of type Shape. We want the Shape class to encapsulate whatever features all our shapes have in common (e.g., the area() and circumference( ) methods). But our generic Shape class doesn't represent any real kind of shape, so it cannot define useful implementations of the methods. Java handles this situation with *abstract methods*.

Java lets us define a method without implementing it by declaring the method with the abstract modifier. An abstract method has no body; it simply has a signature definition followed by a semicolon.* Here are the rules about abstract methods and the abstract classes that contain them:

- Any class with an abstract method is automatically abstract itself and must be declared as such.
- An abstract class cannot be instantiated.
- A subclass of an abstract class can be instantiated only if it overrides each of the abstract methods of its superclass and provides an implementation (i.e., a method body) for all of them. Such a class is often called a *concrete* subclass, to emphasize the fact that it is not abstract.
- If a subclass of an abstract class does not implement all the abstract methods it inherits, that subclass is itself abstract and must be declared as such.
- static, private, and final methods cannot be abstract since these types of methods cannot be overridden by a subclass. Similarly, a final class cannot contain any abstract methods.
- A class can be declared abstract even if it does not actually have any abstract methods. Declaring such a class abstract indicates that the implementation is somehow incomplete and is meant to serve as a superclass for one or more subclasses that complete the implementation. Such a class cannot be instantiated.

There is an important feature of the rules of abstract methods. If we define the Shape class to have abstract area() and circumference( ) methods, any subclass of Shape is required to provide implementations of these methods so that it can be instantiated. In other words, every Shape object is guaranteed to have implementations of these methods defined. Example 3-5 shows how this might work. It defines an abstract Shape class and two concrete subclasses of it.

Example 3-5. An abstract class and concrete subclasses

```
public abstract class Shape {
  public abstract double area();              // Abstract methods: note
  public abstract double circumference();     // semicolon instead of body.
}

class Circle extends Shape {
```

* An abstract method in Java is something like a pure virtual function in C++ (i.e., a virtual function that is declared = 0). In C++, a class that contains a pure virtual function is called an abstract class and cannot be instantiated. The same is true of Java classes that contain abstract methods.

Example 3-5. An abstract class and concrete subclasses (continued)

```
  public static final double PI = 3.14159265358979323846;
  protected double r;                               // Instance data
  public Circle(double r) { this.r = r; }           // Constructor
  public double getRadius() { return r; }           // Accessor
  public double area() { return PI*r*r; }           // Implementations of
  public double circumference() { return 2*PI*r; } // abstract methods.
}

class Rectangle extends Shape {
  protected double w, h;                                // Instance data
  public Rectangle(double w, double h) {                // Constructor
    this.w = w;  this.h = h;
  }
  public double getWidth() { return w; }                // Accessor method
  public double getHeight() { return h; }               // Another accessor
  public double area() { return w*h; }                  // Implementations of
  public double circumference() { return 2*(w + h); }  // abstract methods.
}
```

Each abstract method in Shape has a semicolon right after its parentheses. They have no curly braces, and no method body is defined. Using the classes defined in Example 3-5, we can now write code such as:

```
Shape[] shapes = new Shape[3];              // Create an array to hold shapes
shapes[0] = new Circle(2.0);                // Fill in the array
shapes[1] = new Rectangle(1.0, 3.0);
shapes[2] = new Rectangle(4.0, 2.0);

double total_area = 0;
for(int i = 0; i < shapes.length; i++)
    total_area += shapes[i].area();         // Compute the area of the shapes
```

Notice two important points here:

- Subclasses of Shape can be assigned to elements of an array of Shape. No cast is necessary. This is another example of a widening reference type conversion (discussed in Chapter 2).
- You can invoke the area() and circumference() methods for any Shape object, even though the Shape class does not define a body for these methods. When you do this, the method to be invoked is found using dynamic method lookup, so the area of a circle is computed using the method defined by Circle, and the area of a rectangle is computed using the method defined by Rectangle.

Important Methods of java.lang.Object

As we've noted, all classes extend, directly or indirectly, java.lang.Object. This class defines several important methods that you should consider overriding in every class you write. Example 3-6 shows a class that overrides these methods. The sections that follow the example document the default implementation of each method and explain why you might want to override it. You may also find it helpful to look up Object in the reference section for an API listing.

Some of the syntax in Example 3-6 may be unfamiliar to you. The example uses two Java 5.0 features. First, it implements a parameterized, or generic, version of the Comparable interface. Second, the example uses the @Override annotation to emphasize (and have the compiler verify) that certain methods override Object. Parameterized types and annotations are covered in Chapter 4.

Example 3-6. A class that overrides important Object methods

```
// This class represents a circle with immutable position and radius.
public class Circle implements Comparable<Circle> {
    // These fields hold the coordinates of the center and the radius.
    // They are private for data encapsulation and final for immutability
    private final int x, y, r;

    // The basic constructor: initialize the fields to specified values
    public Circle(int x, int y, int r) {
        if (r < 0) throw new IllegalArgumentException("negative radius");
        this.x = x; this.y = y; this.r = r;
    }

    // This is a "copy constructor"--a useful alternative to clone()
    public Circle(Circle original) {
        x = original.x;   // Just copy the fields from the original
        y = original.y;
        r = original.r;
    }

    // Public accessor methods for the private fields.
    // These are part of data encapsulation.
    public int getX() { return x; }
    public int getY() { return y; }
    public int getR() { return r; }

    // Return a string representation
    @Override public String toString() {
        return String.format("center=(%d,%d); radius=%d", x, y, r);
    }

    // Test for equality with another object
    @Override public boolean equals(Object o) {
        if (o == this) return true;                      // Identical references?
        if (!(o instanceof Circle)) return false; // Correct type and non-null?
        Circle that = (Circle) o;                        // Cast to our type
        if (this.x == that.x && this.y == that.y && this.r == that.r)
            return true;                                 // If all fields match
        else
            return false;                                // If fields differ
    }

    // A hash code allows an object to be used in a hash table.
    // Equal objects must have equal hash codes.  Unequal objects are allowed
```

Object-Oriented

Example 3-6. A class that overrides important Object methods (continued)

```
    // to have equal hash codes as well, but we try to avoid that.
    // We must override this method since we also override equals().
    @Override public int hashCode() {
        int result = 17;          // This hash code algorithm from the book
        result = 37*result + x;   // _Effective Java_, by Joshua Bloch
        result = 37*result + y;
        result = 37*result + r;
        return result;
    }

    // This method is defined by the Comparable interface.
    // Compare this Circle to that Circle.  Return a value < 0 if this < that.
    // Return 0 if this == that. Return a value > 0 if this > that.
    // Circles are ordered top to bottom, left to right, and then by radius
    public int compareTo(Circle that) {
        long result = that.y - this.y;  // Smaller circles have bigger y values
        if (result == 0) result = this.x - that.x;  // If same compare l-to-r
        if (result == 0) result = this.r - that.r;  // If same compare radius

        // We have to use a long value for subtraction because the differences
        // between a large positive and large negative value could overflow
        // an int. But we can't return the long, so return its sign as an int.
        return Long.signum(result);  // new in Java 5.0
    }
}
```

toString()

The purpose of the `toString( )` method is to return a textual representation of an object. The method is invoked automatically on objects during string concatenation and by methods such as `System.out.println( )`. Giving objects a textual representation can be quite helpful for debugging or logging output, and a well-crafted `toString()` method can even help with tasks such as report generation.

The version of `toString()` inherited from `Object` returns a string that includes the name of the class of the object as well as a hexadecimal representation of the `hashCode()` value of the object (discussed later in this chapter). This default implementation provides basic type and identity information for an object but is not usually very useful. The `toString( )` method in Example 3-6 instead returns a human-readable string that includes the value of each of the fields of the `Circle` class.

equals( )

The == operator tests two references to see if they refer to the same object. If you want to test whether two distinct objects are equal to one another, you must use the `equals()` method instead. Any class can define its own notion of equality by overriding `equals()`. The `Object.equals( )` method simply uses the `==` operator: this default method considers two objects equal only if they are actually the very same object.

The equals() method in Example 3-6 considers two distinct Circle objects to be equal if their fields are all equal. Note that it first does a quick identity test with == as an optimization and then checks the type of the other object with instanceof: a Circle can be equal only to another Circle, and it is not acceptable for an equals() method to throw a ClassCastException. Note that the instanceof test also rules out null arguments: instanceof always evaluates to false if its left-hand operand is null.

hashCode()

Whenever you override equals(), you must also override hashCode(). This method returns an integer for use by hash table data structures. It is critical that two objects have the same hash code if they are equal according to the equals() method. It is important (for efficient operation of hash tables) but not required that unequal objects have unequal hash codes, or at least that unequal objects are unlikely to share a hash code. This second criterion can lead to hashCode() methods that involve mildly tricky arithmetic or bit-manipulation.

Object-Oriented

The Object.hashCode() method works with the Object.equals() method and returns a hash code based on object identity rather than object equality. (If you ever need an identity-based hash code, you can access the functionality of Object.hashCode() through the static method System.identityHashCode().) When you override equals(), you must always override hashCode() to guarantee that equal objects have equal hash codes. Since the equals() method in Example 3-6 bases object equality on the values of the three fields, the hashCode() method computes its hash code based on these three fields as well. It is clear from the code that if two Circle objects have the same field values, they will have the same hash code.

Note that the hashCode() method in Example 3-6 does not simply add the three fields and return their sum. Such an implementation would be legal but not efficient because two circles with the same radius but whose X and Y coordinates were reversed would then have the same hash code. The repeated multiplication and addition steps "spread out" the range of hash codes and dramatically reduce the likelihood that two unequal Circle objects have the same code. *Effective Java Programming Guide* by Joshua Bloch (Addison Wesley) includes a helpful recipe for constructing efficient hashCode() methods like this one.

Comparable.compareTo()

Example 3-6 includes a compareTo() method. This method is defined by the java.lang.Comparable interface rather than by Object. (It actually uses the generics features of Java 5.0 and implements a parameterized version of the interface: Comparable<Circle>, but we can ignore that fact until Chapter 4.) The purpose of Comparable and its compareTo() method is to allow instances of a class to be compared to each other in the way that the <, <=, > and >= operators compare numbers. If a class implements Comparable, we can say that one instance is less than, greater than, or equal to another instance. Instances of a Comparable class can be sorted.

Since compareTo( ) is defined by an interface, the Object class does not provide any default implementation. It is up to each individual class to determine whether and how its instances should be ordered and to include a compareTo() method that implements that ordering. The ordering defined by Example 3-6 compares Circle objects as if they were words on a page. Circles are first ordered from top to bottom: circles with larger Y coordinates are less than circles with smaller Y coordinates. If two circles have the same Y coordinate, they are ordered from left to right. A circle with a smaller X coordinate is less than a circle with a larger X coordinate. Finally, if two circles have the same X and Y coordinates, they are compared by radius. The circle with the smaller radius is smaller. Notice that under this ordering, two circles are equal only if all three of their fields are equal. This means that the ordering defined by compareTo() is consistent with the equality defined by equals(). This is very desirable (but not strictly required).

The compareTo( ) method returns an int value that requires further explanation. compareTo() should return a negative number if the this object is less than the object passed to it. It should return 0 if the two objects are equal. And compareTo() should return a positive number if this is greater than the method argument.

clone()

Object defines a method named clone() whose purpose is to return an object with fields set identically to those of the current object. This is an unusual method for two reasons. First, it works only if the class implements the java.lang.Cloneable interface. Cloneable does not define any methods, so implementing it is simply a matter of listing it in the implements clause of the class signature. The other unusual feature of clone() is that it is declared protected (see "Data Hiding and Encapsulation" earlier in this chapter). This means that subclasses of Object can call and override Object.clone(), but other code cannot call it. Therefore, if you want your object to be cloneable, you must implement Cloneable and override the clone() method, making it public.

The Circle class of Example 3-6 does not implement Cloneable; instead it provides a *copy constructor* for making copies of Circle objects:

```
Circle original = new Circle(1, 2, 3);  // regular constructor
Circle copy = new Circle(original);     // copy constructor
```

It can be difficult to implement clone( ) correctly, and it is usually easier and safer to provide a copy constructor. To make the Circle class cloneable, you would add Cloneable to the implements clause and add the following method to the class body:

```
@Override public Object clone() {
    try { return super.clone(); }
    catch(CloneNotSupportedException e) { throw new AssertionError(e); }
}
```

See *Effective Java Programming Guide* by Joshua Bloch for a detailed discussion of the ins and outs of clone() and Cloneable.

Interfaces

Like a class, an *interface* defines a new reference type. Unlike classes, however, interfaces provide no implementation for the types they define. As its name implies, an interface specifies only an API: all of its methods are abstract and have no bodies. It is not possible to directly instantiate an interface and create a member of the interface type. Instead, a class must *implement* the interface to provide the necessary method bodies. Any instances of that class are members of both the type defined by the class and the type defined by the interface. Interfaces provide a limited but very powerful alternative to *multiple inheritance*.* Classes in Java can inherit members from only a single superclass, but they can implement any number of interfaces. Objects that do not share the same class or superclass may still be members of the same type by virtue of implementing the same interface.

Defining an Interface

An interface definition is much like a class definition in which all the methods are abstract and the keyword `class` has been replaced with `interface`. For example, the following code shows the definition of an interface named `Centered`. A `Shape` class, such as those defined earlier in the chapter, might implement this interface if it wants to allow the coordinates of its center to be set and queried:

```
public interface Centered {
    void setCenter(double x, double y);
    double getCenterX();
    double getCenterY();
}
```

A number of restrictions apply to the members of an interface:

- An interface contains no implementation whatsoever. All methods of an interface are implicitly `abstract` and must have a semicolon in place of a method body. The `abstract` modifier is allowed but, by convention, is usually omitted. Since static methods may not be abstract, the methods of an interface may not be declared `static`.
- An interface defines a public API. All members of an interface are implicitly `public`, and it is conventional to omit the unnecessary `public` modifier. It is an error to define a `protected` or `private` method in an interface.
- An interface may not define any instance fields. Fields are an implementation detail, and an interface is a pure specification without any implementation. The only fields allowed in an interface definition are constants that are declared both `static` and `final`.
- An interface cannot be instantiated, so it does not define a constructor.
- Interfaces may contain nested types. Any such types are implicitly `public` and `static`. See "Nested Types" later in this chapter.

* C++ supports multiple inheritance, but the ability of a class to have more than one superclass adds a lot of complexity to the language.

Extending interfaces

Interfaces may extend other interfaces, and, like a class definition, an interface definition may include an extends clause. When one interface extends another, it inherits all the abstract methods and constants of its superinterface and can define new abstract methods and constants. Unlike classes, however, the extends clause of an interface definition may include more than one superinterface. For example, here are some interfaces that extend other interfaces:

```
public interface Positionable extends Centered {
    void setUpperRightCorner(double x, double y);
    double getUpperRightX();
    double getUpperRightY();
}
public interface Transformable extends Scalable, Translatable, Rotatable {}
public interface SuperShape extends Positionable, Transformable {}
```

An interface that extends more than one interface inherits all the abstract methods and constants from each of those interfaces and can define its own additional abstract methods and constants. A class that implements such an interface must implement the abstract methods defined directly by the interface, as well as all the abstract methods inherited from all the superinterfaces.

Implementing an Interface

Just as a class uses `extends` to specify its superclass, it can use `implements` to name one or more interfaces it supports. `implements` is a Java keyword that can appear in a class declaration following the `extends` clause. `implements` should be followed by a comma-separated list of interfaces that the class implements.

When a class declares an interface in its `implements` clause, it is saying that it provides an implementation (i.e., a body) for each method of that interface. If a class implements an interface but does not provide an implementation for every interface method, it inherits those unimplemented `abstract` methods from the interface and must itself be declared `abstract`. If a class implements more than one interface, it must implement every method of each interface it implements (or be declared `abstract`).

The following code shows how we can define a `CenteredRectangle` class that extends the `Rectangle` class from earlier in the chapter and implements our `Centered` interface.

```
public class CenteredRectangle extends Rectangle implements Centered {
  // New instance fields
  private double cx, cy;

  // A constructor
  public CenteredRectangle(double cx, double cy, double w, double h) {
    super(w, h);
    this.cx = cx;
    this.cy = cy;
  }

  // We inherit all the methods of Rectangle but must
```

```
    // provide implementations of all the Centered methods.
    public void setCenter(double x, double y) { cx = x; cy = y; }
    public double getCenterX() { return cx; }
    public double getCenterY() { return cy; }
  }
```

Suppose we implement CenteredCircle and CenteredSquare just as we have implemented this CenteredRectangle class. Since each class extends Shape, instances of the classes can be treated as instances of the Shape class, as we saw earlier. Since each class implements the Centered interface, instances can also be treated as instances of that type. The following code demonstrates how objects can be members of both a class type and an interface type:

```
Shape[] shapes = new Shape[3];          // Create an array to hold shapes

// Create some centered shapes, and store them in the Shape[]
// No cast necessary: these are all widening conversions
shapes[0] = new CenteredCircle(1.0, 1.0, 1.0);
shapes[1] = new CenteredSquare(2.5, 2, 3);
shapes[2] = new CenteredRectangle(2.3, 4.5, 3, 4);

// Compute average area of the shapes and average distance from the origin
double totalArea = 0;
double totalDistance = 0;
for(int i = 0; i < shapes.length; i++) {
  totalArea += shapes[i].area();       // Compute the area of the shapes
  if (shapes[i] instanceof Centered) { // The shape is a Centered shape
    // Note the required cast from Shape to Centered (no cast would
    // be required to go from CenteredSquare to Centered, however).
    Centered c = (Centered) shapes[i]; // Assign it to a Centered variable
    double cx = c.getCenterX();        // Get coordinates of the center
    double cy = c.getCenterY();        // Compute distance from origin
    totalDistance += Math.sqrt(cx*cx + cy*cy);
  }
}
System.out.println("Average area: " + totalArea/shapes.length);
System.out.println("Average distance: " + totalDistance/shapes.length);
```

This example demonstrates that interfaces are data types in Java, just like classes. When a class implements an interface, instances of that class can be assigned to variables of the interface type. Don't interpret this example to imply that you must assign a CenteredRectangle object to a Centered variable before you can invoke the setCenter( ) method or to a Shape variable before you can invoke the area() method. CenteredRectangle defines setCenter( ) and inherits area() from its Rectangle superclass, so you can always invoke these methods.

Implementing multiple interfaces

Suppose we want shape objects that can be positioned in terms of not only their center points but also their upper-right corners. And suppose we also want shapes that can be scaled larger and smaller. Remember that although a class can extend only a single superclass, it can implement any number of interfaces. Assuming we have defined appropriate UpperRightCornered and Scalable interfaces, we can declare a class as follows:

```
public class SuperDuperSquare extends Shape
    implements Centered, UpperRightCornered, Scalable {
   // Class members omitted here
}
```

When a class implements more than one interface, it simply means that it must provide implementations for all abstract methods in all its interfaces.

Interfaces vs. Abstract Classes

When defining an abstract type (e.g., Shape) that you expect to have many subtypes (e.g., Circle, Rectangle, Square), you are often faced with a choice between interfaces and abstract classes. Since they have similar features, it is not always clear which to use.

An interface is useful because any class can implement it, even if that class extends some entirely unrelated superclass. But an interface is a pure API specification and contains no implementation. If an interface has numerous methods, it can become tedious to implement the methods over and over, especially when much of the implementation is duplicated by each implementing class.

An abstract class does not need to be entirely abstract; it can contain a partial implementation that subclasses can take advantage of. In some cases, numerous subclasses can rely on default method implementations provided by an abstract class. But a class that extends an abstract class cannot extend any other class, which can cause design difficulties in some situations.

Another important difference between interfaces and abstract classes has to do with compatibility. If you define an interface as part of a public API and then later add a new method to the interface, you break any classes that implemented the previous version of the interface. If you use an abstract class, however, you can safely add nonabstract methods to that class without requiring modifications to existing classes that extend the abstract class.

In some situations, it is clear that an interface or an abstract class is the right design choice. In other cases, a common design pattern is to use both. Define the type as a totally abstract interface, then create an abstract class that implements the interface and provides useful default implementations that subclasses can take advantage of. For example:

```
// Here is a basic interface. It represents a shape that fits inside
// of a rectangular bounding box. Any class that wants to serve as a
// RectangularShape can implement these methods from scratch.
public interface RectangularShape {
    void setSize(double width, double height);
    void setPosition(double x, double y);
    void translate(double dx, double dy);
    double area();
    boolean isInside();
}
```

```
// Here is a partial implementation of that interface. Many
// implementations may find this a useful starting point.
public abstract class AbstractRectangularShape implements RectangularShape {
    // The position and size of the shape
    protected double x, y, w, h;

    // Default implementations of some of the interface methods
    public void setSize(double width, double height) { w = width; h = height; }
    public void setPosition(double x, double y) { this.x = x; this.y = y; }
    public void translate (double dx, double dy) { x += dx; y += dy; }
}
```

Marker Interfaces

Sometimes it is useful to define an interface that is entirely empty. A class can implement this interface simply by naming it in its `implements` clause without having to implement any methods. In this case, any instances of the class become valid instances of the interface. Java code can check whether an object is an instance of the interface using the `instanceof` operator, so this technique is a useful way to provide additional information about an object.

The `java.io.Serializable` interface is a marker interface of this sort. A class implements `Serializable` interface to tell `ObjectOutputStream` that its instances may safely be serialized. `java.util.RandomAccess` is another example: `java.util.List` implementations implement this interface to advertise that they provide fast random access to the elements of the list. `ArrayList` implements `RandomAccess`, for example, while `LinkedList` does not. Algorithms that care about the performance of random-access operations can test for `RandomAccess` like this:

```
// Before sorting the elements of a long arbitrary list, we may want to make
// sure that the list allows fast random access.  If not, it may be quicker
// make a random-access copy of the list before sorting it.
// Note that this is not necessary when using java.util.Collections.sort().
List l = ...;  // Some arbitrary list we're given
if (l.size() > 2 && !(l instanceof RandomAccess))  l = new ArrayList(l);
sortListInPlace(l);
```

Interfaces and Constants

As noted earlier, constants can appear in an interface definition. Any class that implements an interface inherits the constants it defines and can use them as if they were defined directly in the class itself. Importantly, there is no need to prefix the constants with the name of the interface or provide any kind of implementation of the constants.

When a set of constants is used by more than one class, it is tempting to define the constants once in an interface and then have any classes that require the constants implement the interface. This situation might arise, for example, when client and server classes implement a network protocol whose details (such as the port number to connect to and listen on) are captured in a set of symbolic constants. As a concrete example, consider the `java.io.ObjectStreamConstants` interface, which defines constants for the object serialization protocol and is implemented by both `ObjectInputStream` and `ObjectOutputStream`.

The primary benefit of inheriting constant definitions from an interface is that it saves typing: you don't need to specify the type that defines the constants. Despite its use with `ObjectStreamConstants`, this is not a recommended technique. The use of constants is an implementation detail that is not appropriate to declare in the `implements` clause of a class signature.

A better approach is to define constants in a class and use the constants by typing the full class name and the constant name. In Java 5.0 and later, you can save typing by importing the constants from their defining class with the `import static` declaration. See "Packages and the Java Namespace" in Chapter 2 for details.

Nested Types

The classes, interfaces, and enumerated types we have seen so far in this book have all been defined as top-level classes. This means that they are direct members of packages, defined independently of other types. However, type definitions can also be nested within other type definitions. These *nested types*, commonly known as "inner classes," are a powerful and elegant feature of the Java language. A type can be nested within another type in four ways:

Static member types
: A static member type is any type defined as a `static` member of another type. A `static` method is called a class method, so, by analogy, we could call this type of nested type a "class type," but this terminology would obviously be confusing. A static member type behaves much like an ordinary top-level type, but its name is part of the namespace, rather than the package, of the containing type. Also, a static member type can access the `static` members of the class that contains it. Nested interfaces, enumerated types, and annotation types are implicitly static, whether or not the `static` keyword appears. Any type nested within an interface or annotation is also implicitly `static`. Static member types may be defined within top-level types or nested to any depth within other static member types. A static member type may not be defined within any other kind of nested type, however.

Nonstatic member classes
: A "nonstatic member type" is simply a member type that is not declared `static`. Since interfaces, enumerated types, and annotations are always implicitly static, however, we usually use the term "nonstatic member class" instead. Nonstatic member classes may be defined within other classes or enumerated types and are analogous to instance methods or fields. An instance of a nonstatic member class is always associated with an instance of the enclosing type, and the code of a nonstatic member class has access to all the fields and methods (both `static` and non-`static`) of its enclosing type. Several features of Java syntax exist specifically to work with the enclosing instance of a nonstatic member class.

Local classes

A local class is a class defined within a block of Java code. Interfaces, enumerated types, and annotation types may not be defined locally. Like a local variable, a local class is visible only within the block in which it is defined. Although local classes are not member classes, they are still defined within an enclosing class, so they share many of the features of member classes. Additionally, however, a local class can access any `final` local variables or parameters that are accessible in the scope of the block that defines the class.

Anonymous classes

An anonymous class is a kind of local class that has no name; it combines the syntax for class definition with the syntax for object instantiation. While a local class definition is a Java statement, an anonymous class definition (and instantiation) is a Java expression, so it can appear as part of a larger expression, such as method invocation. Interfaces, enumerated types, and annotation types cannot be defined anonymously.

Nested types have no universally adopted nomenclature. The term "inner class" is commonly used. Sometimes, however, inner class is used to refer to a nonstatic member class, local class, or anonymous class, but not a static member type. Although the terminology for describing nested types is not always clear, the syntax for working with them is, and it is usually clear from context which kind of nested type is being discussed.

Now we'll describe each of the four kinds of nested types in greater detail. Each section describes the features of the nested type, the restrictions on its use, and any special Java syntax used with the type. These four sections are followed by an implementation note that explains how nested types work under the hood.

Static Member Types

A *static member type* is much like a regular top-level type. For convenience, however, it is nested within the namespace of another type. Example 3-7 shows a helper interface defined as a static member of a containing class. The example also shows how this interface is used both within the class that contains it and by external classes. Note the use of its hierarchical name in the external class.

Example 3-7. Defining and using a static member interface

```
// A class that implements a stack as a linked list
public class LinkedStack {
    // This static member interface defines how objects are linked
    // The static keyword is optional: all nested interfaces are static
    public static interface Linkable {
        public Linkable getNext();
        public void setNext(Linkable node);
    }

    // The head of the list is a Linkable object
    Linkable head;

    // Method bodies omitted
```

Example 3-7. Defining and using a static member interface (continued)

```
    public void push(Linkable node) { ... }
    public Object pop() { ... }
}

// This class implements the static member interface
class LinkableInteger implements LinkedStack.Linkable {
    // Here's the node's data and constructor
    int i;
    public LinkableInteger(int i) { this.i = i; }

    // Here are the data and methods required to implement the interface
    LinkedStack.Linkable next;
    public LinkedStack.Linkable getNext() { return next; }
    public void setNext(LinkedStack.Linkable node) { next = node; }
}
```

Features of static member types

A static member type is defined as a `static` member of a containing type. Any type (class, interface, enumerated type, or annotation type) may be defined as a static member of any other type. Interfaces, enumerated types, and annotation types are implicitly static, whether or not the `static` keyword appears in their definition.

A static member type is like the other static members of a class: static fields and static methods. Like a class method, a static member type is not associated with any instance of the containing class (i.e., there is no `this` object). A static member type does, however, have access to all the `static` members (including any other static member types) of its containing type. A static member type can use any other static member without qualifying its name with the name of the containing type.

A static member type has access to all static members of its containing type, including `private` members. The reverse is true as well: the methods of the containing type have access to all members of a static member type, including the `private` members. A static member type even has access to all the members of any other static member types, including the `private` members of those types.

Top-level types can be declared with or without the `public` modifier, but they cannot use the `private` and `protected` modifiers. Static member types, however, are members and can use any access control modifiers that other members of the containing type can. These modifiers have the same meanings for static member types as they do for other members of a type. In Example 3-7, the `Linkable` interface is declared `public`, so it can be implemented by any class that is interested in being stored on a `LinkedStack`. Recall that all members of interfaces (and annotation types) are implicitly `public`, so static member types nested within interfaces or annotation types cannot be `protected` or `private`.

Restrictions on static member types

A static member type cannot have the same name as any of its enclosing classes. In addition, static member types can be defined only within top-level types and other static member types. This is actually part of a larger prohibition against static members of any sort within member, local, and anonymous classes.

Syntax for static member types

In code outside the containing class, a static member type is named by combining the name of the outer type with the name of the inner type (e.g., LinkedStack.Linkable). You can use the import directive to import a static member type:

```
import pkg.LinkedStack.Linkable;  // Import a specific nested type
import pkg.LinkedStack.*;         // Import all nested types of LinkedStack
```

In Java 5.0 and later, you can also use the import static directive to import a static member type. See "Packages and the Java Namespace" in Chapter 2 for details on import and import static. Note that importing a nested type obscures the fact that that type is closely associated with its containing type, and it is not commonly done.

Nonstatic Member Classes

A *nonstatic member class* is a class that is declared as a member of a containing class or enumerated type without the static keyword. If a static member type is analogous to a class field or class method, a nonstatic member class is analogous to an instance field or instance method. Example 3-8 shows how a member class can be defined and used. This example extends the previous LinkedStack example to allow enumeration of the elements on the stack by defining an iterator() method that returns an implementation of the java.util.Iterator interface. The implementation of this interface is defined as a member class. The example uses Java 5.0 generic type syntax in a couple of places, but this should not prevent you from understanding it. (Generics are covered in Chapter 4.)

Example 3-8. An iterator implemented as a member class

```
import java.util.Iterator;

public class LinkedStack {
    // Our static member interface
    public interface Linkable {
        public Linkable getNext();
        public void setNext(Linkable node);
    }

    // The head of the list
    private Linkable head;

    // Method bodies omitted here
    public void push(Linkable node) { ... }
    public Linkable pop() { ... }
```

Example 3-8. An iterator implemented as a member class (continued)

```
    // This method returns an Iterator object for this LinkedStack
    public Iterator<Linkable> iterator() { return new LinkedIterator(); }

    // Here is the implementation of the Iterator interface,
    // defined as a nonstatic member class.
    protected class LinkedIterator implements Iterator<Linkable> {
        Linkable current;
        // The constructor uses the private head field of the containing class
        public LinkedIterator() { current = head; }
        // The following 3 methods are defined by the Iterator interface
        public boolean hasNext() {  return current != null; }
        public Linkable next() {
            if (current == null) throw new java.util.NoSuchElementException();
            Linkable value = current;
            current = current.getNext();
            return value;
        }
        public void remove() { throw new UnsupportedOperationException(); }
    }
}
```

Notice how the `LinkedIterator` class is nested within the `LinkedStack` class. Since `LinkedIterator` is a helper class used only within `LinkedStack`, there is real elegance to having it defined so close to where it is used by the containing class.

Features of member classes

Like instance fields and instance methods, every instance of a nonstatic member class is associated with an instance of the class in which it is defined. This means that the code of a member class has access to all the instance fields and instance methods (as well as the `static` members) of the containing class, including any that are declared `private`.

This crucial feature is illustrated in Example 3-8. Here is the `LinkedStack.LinkedIterator()` constructor again:

```
public LinkedIterator() { current = head; }
```

This single line of code sets the `current` field of the inner class to the value of the `head` field of the containing class. The code works as shown, even though `head` is declared as a `private` field in the containing class.

A nonstatic member class, like any member of a class, can be assigned one of three visibility levels: `public`, `protected`, or `private`. If none of these visibility modifiers is specified, the default package visibility is used. In Example 3-8, the `LinkedIterator` class is declared `protected`, so it is inaccessible to code (in a different package) that uses the `LinkedStack` class but is accessible to any class that subclasses `LinkedStack`.

Restrictions on member classes

Member classes have three important restrictions:

- A nonstatic member class cannot have the same name as any containing class or package. This is an important rule, one not shared by fields and methods.
- Nonstatic member classes cannot contain any `static` fields, methods, or types, except for constant fields declared both `static` and `final`. `static` members are top-level constructs not associated with any particular object while every member class is associated with an instance of its enclosing class. Defining a `static` top-level member within a member class that is not at the top level would cause confusion, so it is not allowed.
- Only classes may be defined as nonstatic members. Interfaces, enumerated types, and annotation types are all implicitly static, even if the `static` keyword is omitted.

Object-Oriented

Syntax for member classes

The most important feature of a member class is that it can access the instance fields and methods in its containing object. We saw this in the `LinkedStack.LinkedIterator()` constructor of Example 3-8:

```
public LinkedIterator() { current = head; }
```

In this example, `head` is a field of the `LinkedStack` class, and we assign it to the `current` field of the `LinkedIterator` class. What if we want to make these references explicit? We could try code like this:

```
public LinkedIterator() { this.current = this.head; }
```

This code does not compile, however. `this.current` is fine; it is an explicit reference to the `current` field in the newly created `LinkedIterator` object. It is the `this.head` expression that causes the problem; it refers to a field named `head` in the `LinkedIterator` object. Since there is no such field, the compiler generates an error. To solve this problem, Java defines a special syntax for explicitly referring to the containing instance of the `this` object. Thus, if we want to be explicit in our constructor, we can use the following syntax:

```
public LinkedIterator() { this.current = LinkedStack.this.head; }
```

The general syntax is *`classname`*`.this`, where *`classname`* is the name of a containing class. Note that member classes can themselves contain member classes, nested to any depth. Since no member class can have the same name as any containing class, however, the use of the enclosing class name prepended to `this` is a perfectly general way to refer to any containing instance. This syntax is needed only when referring to a member of a containing class that is hidden by a member of the same name in the member class.

Accessing superclass members of the containing class. When a class shadows or overrides a member of its superclass, you can use the keyword `super` to refer to the hidden member. This `super` syntax can be extended to work with member classes as well. On the rare occasion when you need to refer to a shadowed field `f` or an overridden method m of a superclass of a containing class C, use the following expressions:

```
C.super.f
C.super.m()
```

Specifying the containing instance. As we've seen, every instance of a member class is associated with an instance of its containing class. Look again at our definition of the iterator() method in Example 3-8:

```
public Iterator<Linkable> iterator() { return new LinkedIterator(); }
```

When a member class constructor is invoked like this, the new instance of the member class is automatically associated with the this object. This is what you would expect to happen and exactly what you want to occur in most cases. Occasionally, however, you may want to specify the containing instance explicitly when instantiating a member class. You can do this by preceding the new operator with a reference to the containing instance. Thus, the iterator() method shown earlier is shorthand for the following:

```
public Iterator<Linkable> iterator() { return this.new LinkedIterator(); }
```

Let's pretend we didn't define an iterator() method for LinkedStack. In this case, the code to obtain an LinkedIterator object for a given LinkedStack object might look like this:

```
LinkedStack stack = new LinkedStack();    // Create an empty stack
Iterator i = stack.new LinkedIterator();  // Create an Iterator for it
```

The containing instance implicitly specifies the containing class; it is a syntax error to explicitly specify the containing class name:

```
Iterator i = stack.new LinkedStack.LinkedIterator();  // Syntax error
```

One other special piece of Java syntax specifies an enclosing instance for a member class explicitly. Before we consider it, however, let me point out that you should rarely, if ever, need to use this syntax. It is one of the pathological cases that snuck into the language along with all the elegant features of nested types.

As strange as it may seem, it is possible for a top-level class to extend a member class. This means that the subclass does not have a containing instance, but its superclass does. When the subclass constructor invokes the superclass constructor, it must specify the containing instance. It does this by prepending the containing instance and a period to the super keyword. If we had not declared our LinkedIterator class to be a protected member of LinkedStack, we could subclass it. Although it is not clear why we would want to do so, we could write code like the following:

```
// A top-level class that extends a member class
class SpecialIterator extends LinkedStack.LinkedIterator {
  // The constructor must explicitly specify a containing instance
  // when invoking the superclass constructor.
  public SpecialIterator(LinkedStack s) { s.super(); }
    // Rest of class omitted...
}
```

Scope versus inheritance

We've just noted that a top-level class can extend a member class. With the introduction of nonstatic member classes, two separate hierarchies must be considered for any class. The first is the *inheritance hierarchy*, from superclass to subclass, that defines the fields and methods a member class inherits. The second is the *containment hierarchy*, from containing class to contained class, that defines a set of fields and methods that are in the scope of (and are therefore accessible to) the member class.

The two hierarchies are entirely distinct from each other; it is important that you do not confuse them. This should not be a problem if you refrain from creating naming conflicts, where a field or method in a superclass has the same name as a field or method in a containing class. If such a naming conflict does arise, however, the inherited field or method takes precedence over the field or method of the same name in the containing class. This behavior is logical: when a class inherits a field or method, that field or method effectively becomes part of that class. Therefore, inherited fields and methods are in the scope of the class that inherits them and take precedence over fields and methods by the same name in enclosing scopes.

A good way to prevent confusion between the class hierarchy and the containment hierarchy is to avoid deep containment hierarchies. If a class is nested more than two levels deep, it is probably going to cause more confusion than it is worth. Furthermore, if a class has a deep class hierarchy (i.e., it has many ancestors), consider defining it as a top-level class rather than as a nonstatic member class.

Local Classes

A *local class* is declared locally within a block of Java code rather than as a member of a class. Only classes may be defined locally: interfaces, enumerated types and annotation types must be top-level or static member types. Typically, a local class is defined within a method, but it can also be defined within a static initializer or instance initializer of a class. Because all blocks of Java code appear within class definitions, all local classes are nested within containing classes. For this reason, local classes share many of the features of member classes. It is usually more appropriate, however, to think of them as an entirely separate kind of nested type. A local class has approximately the same relationship to a member class as a local variable has to an instance variable of a class.

The defining characteristic of a local class is that it is local to a block of code. Like a local variable, a local class is valid only within the scope defined by its enclosing block. If a member class is used only within a single method of its containing class, for example, there is usually no reason it cannot be coded as a local class rather than a member class. Example 3-9 shows how we can modify the `iterator()` method of the `LinkedStack` class so it defines `LinkedIterator` as a local class instead of a member class. By doing this, we move the definition of the class even closer to where it is used and hopefully improve the clarity of the code even further. For brevity, Example 3-9 shows only the `iterator()` method, not the entire `LinkedStack` class that contains it.

Example 3-9. Defining and using a local class

```
// This method returns an Iterator object for this LinkedStack
public Iterator<Linkable> Iterator() {
    // Here's the definition of LinkedIterator as a local class
    class LinkedIterator implements Iterator<Linkable> {
        Linkable current;

        // The constructor uses the private head field of the containing class
        public LinkedIterator() { current = head; }
        // The following 3 methods are defined by the Iterator interface
        public boolean hasNext() {  return current != null; }
        public Linkable next() {
            if (current == null) throw new java.util.NoSuchElementException();
            Linkable value = current;
            current = current.getNext();
            return value;
        }
        public void remove() { throw new UnsupportedOperationException(); }
    }

    // Create and return an instance of the class we just defined
    return new LinkedIterator();
}
```

Features of local classes

Local classes have the following interesting features:

- Like member classes, local classes are associated with a containing instance and can access any members, including `private` members, of the containing class.
- In addition to accessing fields defined by the containing class, local classes can access any local variables, method parameters, or exception parameters that are in the scope of the local method definition and are declared `final`.

Restrictions on local classes

Local classes are subject to the following restrictions:

- The name of a local class is defined only within the block that defines it; it can never be used outside that block. (Note however that instances of a local class created within the scope of the class can continue to exist outside of that scope. This situation is described in more detail later in this section.)
- Local classes cannot be declared `public`, `protected`, `private`, or `static`. These modifiers are for members of classes; they are not allowed with local variable declarations or local class declarations.
- Like member classes, and for the same reasons, local classes cannot contain `static` fields, methods, or classes. The only exception is for constants that are declared both `static` and `final`.
- Interfaces, enumerated types, and annotation types cannot be defined locally.

- A local class, like a member class, cannot have the same name as any of its enclosing classes.
- As noted earlier, a local class can use the local variables, method parameters, and even exception parameters that are in its scope but only if those variables or parameters are declared `final`. This is because the lifetime of an instance of a local class can be much longer than the execution of the method in which the class is defined. For this reason, a local class must have a private internal copy of all local variables it uses (these copies are automatically generated by the compiler). The only way to ensure that the local variable and the private copy are always the same is to insist that the local variable is `final`.

Syntax for local classes

In Java 1.0, only fields, methods, and classes could be declared `final`. The addition of local classes in Java 1.1 required a liberalization in the use of the `final` modifier. As of Java 1.1, `final` can be applied to local variables, method parameters, and even the exception parameter of a `catch` statement. The meaning of the `final` modifier remains the same in these new uses: once the local variable or parameter has been assigned a value, that value cannot be changed.

Instances of local classes, like instances of nonstatic member classes, have an enclosing instance that is implicitly passed to all constructors of the local class. Local classes can use the same `this` syntax as nonstatic member classes to refer explicitly to members of enclosing classes. Because local classes are never visible outside the blocks that define them, however, there is never a need to use the `new` and `super` syntax used by member classes to specify the enclosing instance explicitly.

Scope of a local class

In discussing nonstatic member classes, we saw that a member class can access any members inherited from superclasses and any members defined by its containing classes. The same is true for local classes, but local classes can also access `final` local variables and parameters. The following code illustrates the many fields and variables that may be accessible to a local class:

```
class A { protected char a = 'a'; }
class B { protected char b = 'b'; }

public class C extends A {
  private char c = 'c';         // Private fields visible to local class
  public static char d = 'd';
  public void createLocalObject(final char e)
  {
    final char f = 'f';
    int i = 0;                  // i not final; not usable by local class
    class Local extends B
    {
      char g = 'g';
      public void printVars()
      {
```

```
        // All of these fields and variables are accessible to this class
        System.out.println(g);  // (this.g) g is a field of this class
        System.out.println(f);  // f is a final local variable
        System.out.println(e);  // e is a final local parameter
        System.out.println(d);  // (C.this.d) d -- field of containing class
        System.out.println(c);  // (C.this.c) c -- field of containing class
        System.out.println(b);  // b is inherited by this class
        System.out.println(a);  // a is inherited by the containing class
      }
    }
    Local l = new Local();      // Create an instance of the local class
    l.printVars();              // and call its printVars() method.
  }
}
```

Local variables, lexical scoping, and closures

A local variable is defined within a block of code that defines its scope. A local variable ceases to exist outside of its scope. Java is a *lexically scoped* language, which means that its concept of scope has to do with the way the source code is written. Any code within the curly braces that define the boundaries of a block can use local variables defined in that block.*

Lexical scoping simply defines a segment of source code within which a variable can be used. It is common, however, to think of a scope as a temporal scope—to think of a local variable as existing from the time the Java interpreter begins executing the block until the time the interpreter exits the block. This is usually a reasonable way to think about local variables and their scope.

The introduction of local classes confuses the picture, however, because local classes can use local variables, and instances of a local class can have a lifetime much longer than the time it takes the interpreter to execute the block of code. In other words, if you create an instance of a local class, the instance does not automatically go away when the interpreter finishes executing the block that defines the class, as shown in the following code:

```
public class Weird {
  // A static member interface used below
  public static interface IntHolder { public int getValue(); }

  public static void main(String[] args) {
    IntHolder[] holders = new IntHolder[10];  // An array to hold 10 objects
    for(int i = 0; i < 10; i++) {             // Loop to fill the array up
      final int fi = i;                       // A final local variable
      class MyIntHolder implements IntHolder {// A local class
        public int getValue() { return fi; }  // It uses the final variable
      }
      holders[i] = new MyIntHolder();         // Instantiate the local class
    }
```

* This section covers advanced material; first-time readers may want to skip it for now and return to it later.

```
        // The local class is now out of scope, so we can't use it. But we have
        // 10 valid instances of that class in our array. The local variable
        // fi is not in our scope here, but it is still in scope for the
        // getValue() method of each of those 10 objects. So call getValue()
        // for each object and print it out. This prints the digits 0 to 9.
        for(int i = 0; i < 10; i++) System.out.println(holders[i].getValue());
    }
}
```

The behavior of the previous program is pretty surprising. To make sense of it, remember that the lexical scope of the methods of a local class has nothing to do with when the interpreter enters and exits the block of code that defines the local class. Here's another way to think about it: each instance of a local class has an automatically created private copy of each of the final local variables it uses, so, in effect, it has its own private copy of the scope that existed when it was created.

The local class `MyIntHolder` is sometimes called a *closure*. In general terms, a closure is an object that saves the state of a scope and makes that scope available later. Closures are useful in some styles of programming, and different programming languages define and implement closures in different ways. Java's closures are relatively weak (and some would argue that they are not truly closures) because they retain the state of only `final` variables.

Anonymous Classes

An *anonymous class* is a local class without a name. An anonymous class is defined and instantiated in a single succinct expression using the `new` operator. While a local class definition is a statement in a block of Java code, an anonymous class definition is an expression, which means that it can be included as part of a larger expression, such as a method call. In practice, anonymous classes are much more common than local classes. If you find yourself defining a short local class and then instantiating it exactly once, consider rewriting it using anonymous class syntax, which places the definition and use of the class in exactly the same place.

Consider Example 3-10, which shows the `LinkedIterator` class implemented as an anonymous class within the `iterator()` method of the `LinkedStack` class. Compare it with Example 3-9, which shows the same class implemented as a local class. The generic syntax in this example is covered in Chapter 4.

Example 3-10. An enumeration implemented with an anonymous class

```
public Iterator<Linkable> iterator() {
    // The anonymous class is defined as part of the return statement
    return new Iterator<Linkable>() {
        Linkable current;
        // Replace constructor with an instance initializer
        { current = head; }

        // The following 3 methods are defined by the Iterator interface
        public boolean hasNext() {  return current != null; }
        public Linkable next() {
            if (current == null) throw new java.util.NoSuchElementException();
```

Example 3-10. An enumeration implemented with an anonymous class (continued)

```
            Linkable value = current;
            current = current.getNext();
            return value;
        }
        public void remove() { throw new UnsupportedOperationException(); }
    }; // Note the required semicolon. It terminates the return statement
}
```

One common use for an anonymous class is to provide a simple implementation of an adapter class. An *adapter class* is one that defines code that is invoked by some other object. Take, for example, the `list()` method of the `java.io.File` class. This method lists the files in a directory. Before it returns the list, though, it passes the name of each file to a `FilenameFilter` object you must supply. This `FilenameFilter` object accepts or rejects each file. When you implement the `FilenameFilter` interface, you are defining an adapter class for use with the `File.list()` method. Since the body of such a class is typically quite short, it is easy to define an adapter class as an anonymous class. Here's how you can define a `FilenameFilter` class to list only those files whose names end with *.java*:

```
File f = new File("/src");      // The directory to list

// Now call the list() method with a single FilenameFilter argument
// Define and instantiate an anonymous implementation of FilenameFilter
// as part of the method invocation expression.
String[] filelist = f.list(new FilenameFilter() {
  public boolean accept(File f, String s) { return s.endsWith(".java"); }
}); // Don't forget the parenthesis and semicolon that end the method call!
```

As you can see, the syntax for defining an anonymous class and creating an instance of that class uses the `new` keyword, followed by the name of a class and a class body definition in curly braces. If the name following the `new` keyword is the name of a class, the anonymous class is a subclass of the named class. If the name following `new` specifies an interface, as in the two previous examples, the anonymous class implements that interface and extends `Object`. The syntax does not include any way to specify an `extends` clause, an `implements` clause, or a name for the class.

Because an anonymous class has no name, it is not possible to define a constructor for it within the class body. This is one of the basic restrictions on anonymous classes. Any arguments you specify between the parentheses following the superclass name in an anonymous class definition are implicitly passed to the superclass constructor. Anonymous classes are commonly used to subclass simple classes that do not take any constructor arguments, so the parentheses in the anonymous class definition syntax are often empty. In the previous examples, each anonymous class implemented an interface and extended `Object`. Since the `Object()` constructor takes no arguments, the parentheses were empty in those examples.

Features of anonymous classes

Anonymous classes allow you to define a one-shot class exactly where it is needed. Anonymous classes have all the features of local classes but use a more concise syntax that can reduce clutter in your code.

Restrictions on anonymous classes

Because an anonymous class is just a type of local class, anonymous classes and local classes share the same restrictions. An anonymous class cannot define any `static` fields, methods, or classes, except for `static final` constants. Interfaces, enumerated types, and annotation types cannot be defined anonymously. Also, like local classes, anonymous classes cannot be `public`, `private`, `protected`, or `static`.

Since an anonymous class has no name, it is not possible to define a constructor for an anonymous class. If your class requires a constructor, you must use a local class instead. However, you can often use an instance initializer as a substitute for a constructor.

The syntax for defining an anonymous class combines definition with instantiation. Using an anonymous class instead of a local class is not appropriate if you need to create more than a single instance of the class each time the containing block is executed.

Syntax for anonymous classes

We've already seen examples of the syntax for defining and instantiating an anonymous class. We can express that syntax more formally as:

```
new class-name ( [ argument-list ] ) { class-body }
```

or:

```
new interface-name () { class-body }
```

Although they are not limited to use with anonymous classes, instance initializers were introduced into the language for this purpose. As described earlier in this chapter in "Field Defaults and Initializers," an instance initializer is a block of initialization code contained within curly braces inside a class definition. The contents of all instance initializers for a class are automatically inserted into all constructors for the class, including any automatically created default constructor. An anonymous class cannot define a constructor, so it gets a default constructor. By using an instance initializer, you can get around the fact that you cannot define a constructor for an anonymous class.

When to use an anonymous class

As we've discussed, an anonymous class behaves just like a local class and is distinguished from a local class merely in the syntax used to define and instantiate it. In your own code, when you have to choose between using an anonymous class and a local class, the decision often comes down to a matter of style. You should use whichever syntax makes your code clearer. In general, you should consider using an anonymous class instead of a local class if:

- The class has a very short body.
- Only one instance of the class is needed.
- The class is used right after it is defined.
- The name of the class does not make your code any easier to understand.

Anonymous class indentation and formatting

The common indentation and formatting conventions we are familiar with for block-structured languages like Java and C begin to break down somewhat once we start placing anonymous class definitions within arbitrary expressions. Based on their experience with nested types, the engineers at Sun recommend the following formatting rules:

- The opening curly brace should not be on a line by itself; instead, it should follow the closing parenthesis of the `new` operator. Similarly, the `new` operator should, when possible, appear on the same line as the assignment or other expression of which it is a part.
- The body of the anonymous class should be indented relative to the beginning of the line that contains the `new` keyword.
- The closing curly brace of an anonymous class should not be on a line by itself either; it should be followed by whatever tokens are required by the rest of the expression. Often this is a semicolon or a closing parenthesis followed by a semicolon. This extra punctuation serves as a flag to the reader that this is not just an ordinary block of code and makes it easier to understand anonymous classes in a code listing.

How Nested Types Work

The preceding sections explained the features and behavior of the four kinds of nested types. Strictly speaking, that should be all you need to know about nested types. You may find it easier to understand nested types if you understand how they are implemented, however.

Nested types were added in Java 1.1. Despite the dramatic changes to the Java language, the introduction of nested types did not change the Java Virtual Machine or the Java class file format. As far as the Java interpreter is concerned, there is no such thing as a nested type: all classes are normal top-level classes. In order to make a nested type behave as if it is actually defined inside another class, the Java compiler ends up inserting hidden fields, methods, and constructor arguments into the classes it generates. You may want to use the *javap* disassembler to disassemble some of the class files for nested types so you can see what tricks the compiler has used to make the nested types work. (See Chapter 8 for information on *javap*.)

Static member type implementation

Recall our first `LinkedStack` example (Example 3-7), which defined a static member interface named `Linkable`. When you compile this `LinkedStack` class, the compiler actually generates two class files. The first one is *LinkedStack.class*, as expected. The second class file, however, is called *LinkedStack$Linkable.class*. The $ in this name is automatically inserted by the Java compiler. This second class file contains the implementation of the static member interface.

As we discussed earlier, a static member type can access all the `static` members of its containing class. If a static member type does this, the compiler automatically qualifies the member access expression with the name of the containing class. A static member type is even allowed to access the `private static` fields of its containing class. Since the static member type is compiled into an ordinary top-level class, however, there is no way it can directly access the `private` members of its container. Therefore, if a static member type uses a `private` member of its containing type (or vice versa), the compiler generates synthetic non-`private` access methods and converts the expressions that access the `private` members into expressions that invoke these specially generated methods. These methods are given the default package access, which is sufficient, as the member class and its containing class are guaranteed to be in the same package.

Nonstatic member class implementation

A nonstatic member class is implemented much like a static member type. It is compiled into a separate top-level class file, and the compiler performs various code manipulations to make interclass member access work correctly.

The most significant difference between a nonstatic member class and a static member type is that each instance of a nonstatic member class is associated with an instance of the enclosing class. The compiler enforces this association by defining a synthetic field named `this$0` in each member class. This field is used to hold a reference to the enclosing instance. Every nonstatic member class constructor is given an extra parameter that initializes this field. Every time a member class constructor is invoked, the compiler automatically passes a reference to the enclosing class for this extra parameter.

As we've seen, a nonstatic member class, like any member of a class, can be declared `public`, `protected`, or `private`, or given the default package visibility. Member classes are compiled to class files just like top-level classes, but top-level classes can have only public or package access. Therefore, as far as the Java interpreter is concerned, member classes can have only public or package visibility. This means that a member class declared `protected` is actually treated as a public class, and a member class declared `private` actually has package visibility. This does not mean you should never declare a member class as `protected` or `private`. Although the Java VM cannot enforce these access control modifiers, the modifiers are stored in the class file and conforming Java compilers do enforce them.

Local and anonymous class implementation

A local class is able to refer to fields and methods in its containing class for exactly the same reason that a nonstatic member class can; it is passed a hidden reference to the containing class in its constructor and saves that reference away in a `private` synthetic field added by the compiler. Also, like nonstatic member classes, local classes can use `private` fields and methods of their containing class because the compiler inserts any required accessor methods.

What makes local classes different from member classes is that they have the ability to refer to local variables in the scope that defines them. The crucial restriction on this ability, however, is that local classes can reference only local variables and parameters that are declared `final`. The reason for this restriction becomes apparent in the implementation. A local class can use local variables because the compiler automatically gives the class a `private` instance field to hold a copy of each local variable the class uses. The compiler also adds hidden parameters to each local class constructor to initialize these automatically created `private` fields. A local class does not actually access local variables but merely its own private copies of them. The only way this can work correctly is if the local variables are declared `final` so that they are guaranteed not to change. With this guarantee, the local class can be assured that its internal copies of the variables are always in sync with the real local variables.

Since anonymous classes have no names, you may wonder what the class files that represent them are named. This is an implementation detail, but Sun's Java compiler uses numbers to provide anonymous class names. If you compile the example code shown in Example 3-10, you'll find that it produces a class file for the anonymous class with a name like *LinkedStack$1.class*.

Modifier Summary

As we've seen, classes, interfaces, and their members can be declared with one or more *modifiers*—keywords such as `public`, `static`, and `final`. Table 3-2 lists the Java modifiers, explains what types of Java constructs they can modify, and explains what they do. See also "Class Definition Syntax" and "Field Declaration Syntax" earlier in this chapter, as well as "Method Modifiers" in Chapter 2.

Table 3-2. Java modifiers

Modifier	Used on	Meaning
`abstract`	Class	The class contains unimplemented methods and cannot be instantiated.
	Interface	All interfaces are `abstract`. The modifier is optional in interface declarations.
`abstract`	Method	No body is provided for the method; it is provided by a subclass. The signature is followed by a semicolon. The enclosing class must also be `abstract`.
`final`	Class	The class cannot be subclassed.
	Method	The method cannot be overridden (and is not subject to dynamic method lookup).
	Field	The field cannot have its value changed. `static final` fields are compile-time constants.
	Variable	A local variable, method parameter, or exception parameter cannot have its value changed. Useful with local classes.
`native`	Method	The method is implemented in some platform-dependent way (often in C). No body is provided; the signature is followed by a semicolon.
None (package)	Class	A non-`public` class is accessible only in its package.
	Interface	A non-`public` interface is accessible only in its package.
	Member	A member that is not `private`, `protected`, or `public` has package visibility and is accessible only within its package.
`private`	Member	The member is accessible only within the class that defines it.

Table 3-2. Java modifiers (continued)

Modifier	Used on	Meaning
`protected`	Member	The member is accessible only within the package in which it is defined and within subclasses.
`public`	Class	The class is accessible anywhere its package is.
	Interface	The interface is accessible anywhere its package is.
	Member	The member is accessible anywhere its class is.
`strictfp`	Class	All methods of the class are implicitly `strictfp`.
`strictfp`	Method	All floating-point computation done by the method must be performed in a way that strictly conforms to the IEEE 754 standard. In particular, all values, including intermediate results, must be expressed as IEEE `float` or `double` values and cannot take advantage of any extra precision or range offered by native platform floating-point formats or hardware. This modifier is rarely used.
`static`	Class	An inner class declared `static` is a top-level class, not associated with a member of the containing class.
	Method	A `static` method is a class method. It is not passed an implicit `this` object reference. It can be invoked through the class name.
	Field	A `static` field is a class field. There is only one instance of the field, regardless of the number of class instances created. It can be accessed through the class name.
	Initializer	The initializer is run when the class is loaded rather than when an instance is created.
`synchronized`	Method	The method makes nonatomic modifications to the class or instance, so care must be taken to ensure that two threads cannot modify the class or instance at the same time. For a `static` method, a lock for the class is acquired before executing the method. For a non-`static` method, a lock for the specific object instance is acquired.
`transient`	Field	The field is not part of the persistent state of the object and should not be serialized with the object. Used with object serialization; see `java.io.ObjectOutputStream`.
`volatile`	Field	The field can be accessed by unsynchronized threads, so certain optimizations must not be performed on it. This modifier can sometimes be used as an alternative to `synchronized`. This modifier is very rarely used.

Object-Oriented

C++ Features Not Found in Java

This chapter indicates similarities and differences between Java and C++ in footnotes. Java shares enough concepts and features with C++ to make it an easy language for C++ programmers to pick up. Several features of C++ have no parallel in Java, however. In general, Java does not adopt those features of C++ that make the language significantly more complicated.

C++ supports multiple inheritance of method implementations from more than one superclass at a time. While this seems like a useful feature, it actually introduces many complexities to the language. The Java language designers chose to avoid the added complexity by using interfaces instead. Thus, a class in Java can inherit method implementations only from a single superclass, but it can inherit method declarations from any number of interfaces.

C++ supports templates that allow you, for example, to implement a `Stack` class and then instantiate it as `Stack<int>` or `Stack<double>` to produce two separate types: a stack of integers and a stack of floating-point values. Java 5.0 introduces parameterized types or "generics" that provide similar functionality in a more robust fashion. Generics are covered in Chapter 4.

C++ allows you to define operators that perform arbitrary operations on instances of your classes. In effect, it allows you to extend the syntax of the language. This is a nifty feature, called operator overloading, that makes for elegant examples. In practice, however, it tends to make code quite difficult to understand. After much debate, the Java language designers decided to omit such operator overloading from the language. Note, though, that the use of the + operator for string concatenation in Java is at least reminiscent of operator overloading.

C++ allows you to define conversion functions for a class that automatically invokes an appropriate constructor method when a value is assigned to a variable of that class. This is simply a syntactic shortcut (similar to overriding the assignment operator) and is not included in Java.

In C++, objects are manipulated by value by default; you must use `&` to specify a variable or function argument automatically manipulated by reference. In Java, all objects are manipulated by reference, so there is no need for the `&` syntax.

4
Java 5.0 Language Features

This chapter covers the three most important new language features of Java 5.0. *Generics* add type-safety and expressiveness to Java programs by allowing types to be parameterized with other types. A `List` that contains `String` objects, for example, can be written as `List<String>`. Using parameterized types makes Java code clearer and allows us to remove most casts from our programs.

Enumerated types, or *enums*, are a new category of reference type, like classes and interfaces. An enumerated type defines a finite ("enumerated") set of values, and, importantly, provides type-safety: a variable of enumerated type can hold only values of that enumerated type or `null`. Here is a simple enumerated type definition:

```
public enum Seasons { WINTER, SPRING, SUMMER, AUTUMN }
```

The third Java 5.0 feature discussed in this chapter is program annotations and the annotation types that define them. An *annotation* associates arbitrary data (or metadata) with a program element such as a class, method, field, or even a method parameter or local variable. The type of data held in an annotation is defined by its *annotation type*, which, like enumerated types, is another new category of reference type. The Java 5.0 platform includes three standard annotation types used to provide additional information to the Java compiler. Annotations will probably find their greatest use with code generation tools in Java enterprise programming.

Java 5.0 also introduces a number of other important new language features that don't require a special chapter to explain. Coverage of these changes is found in sections throughout Chapter 2. They include:

- Autoboxing and unboxing conversions
- The `for/in` looping statement, sometimes called "foreach"
- Methods with variable-length argument lists, also known as *varargs* methods
- The ability to narrow the return type of a method when overriding, known as a "covariant return"
- The `import static` directive, which imports the static members of a type into the namespace

Generic Types

Generic types and methods are the defining new feature of Java 5.0. A *generic type* is defined using one or more *type variables* and has one or more methods that use a type variable as a placeholder for an argument or return type. For example, the type `java.util.List<E>` is a generic type: a list that holds elements of some type represented by the placeholder `E`. This type has a method named `add()`, declared to take an argument of type `E`, and a method named `get()`, declared to return a value of type `E`.

In order to use a generic type like this, you specify actual types for the type variable (or variables), producing a *parameterized type* such as `List<String>`.* The reason to specify this extra type information is that the compiler can provide much stronger compile-time type checking for you, increasing the type safety of your programs. This type checking prevents you from adding a `String[]`, for example, to a `List` that is intended to hold only `String` objects. Also, the additional type information enables the compiler to do some casting for you. The compiler knows that the `get()` method of a `List<String>` (for example) returns a `String` object: you are no longer required to cast a return value of type `Object` to a `String`.

The collections classes of the `java.util` package have been made generic in Java 5.0, and you will probably use them frequently in your programs. Typesafe collections are the canonical use case for generic types. Even if you never define generic types of your own and never use generic types other than the collections classes in `java.util`, the benefits of typesafe collections are so significant that they justify the complexity of this major new language feature.

We begin by exploring the basic use of generics in typesafe collections, then delve into more complex details about the use of generic types. Next we cover type parameter wildcards and bounded wildcards. After describing how to use generic types, we explain how to write your own generic types and generic methods. Our coverage of generics concludes with a tour of important generic types in the core Java API. It explores these types and their use in depth in order to provide a deeper understanding of how generics work.

Typesafe Collections

The `java.util` package includes the Java Collections Framework for working with sets and lists of objects and mappings from key objects to value objects. Collections are covered in Chapter 5. Here, we discuss the fact that in Java 5.0 the collections classes use type parameters to identify the type of the objects in the collection. This is not the case in Java 1.4 and earlier. Without generics, the use of collections requires the programmer to remember the proper element type for each collection. When you create a collection in Java 1.4, you know what type of

* Throughout this chapter, I've tried to consistently use the term "generic type" to mean a type that declares one or more type variables and the term "parameterized type" to mean a generic type that has had actual type arguments substituted for its type varaiables. In common usage, however, the distinction is not a sharp one and the terms are sometimes used interchangeably.

objects you intend to store in that collection, but the compiler cannot know this. You must be careful to add elements of the appropriate type. And when querying elements from a collection, you must write explicit casts to convert them from `Object` to their actual type. Consider the following Java 1.4 code:

```
public static void main(String[] args) {
    // This list is intended to hold only strings.
    // The compiler doesn't know that so we have to remember ourselves.
    List wordlist = new ArrayList();

    // Oops! We added a String[] instead of a String.
    // The compiler doesn't know that this is an error.
    wordlist.add(args);

    // Since List can hold arbitrary objects, the get() method returns
    // Object.  Since the list is intended to hold strings, we cast the
    // return value to String but get a ClassCastException because of
    // the error above.
    String word = (String)wordlist.get(0);
}
```


Generic types solve the type safety problem illustrated by this code. `List` and the other collection classes in `java.util` have been rewritten to be generic. As mentioned above, `List` has been redefined in terms of a type variable named `E` that represents the type of the elements of the list. The `add()` method is redefined to expect an argument of type `E` instead of `Object` and `get()` has been redefined to return `E` instead of `Object`.

In Java 5.0, when we declare a `List` variable or create an instance of an `ArrayList`, we specify the actual type we want `E` to represent by placing the actual type in angle brackets following the name of the generic type. A `List` that holds strings is a `List<String>`, for example. Note that this is much like passing an argument to a method, except that we use types rather than values and angle brackets instead of parentheses.

The elements of the `java.util` collection classes must be objects; they cannot be used with primitive values. The introduction of generics does not change this. Generics do not work with primitives: we can't declare a `Set<char>`, or a `List<int>` for example. Note, however, that the autoboxing and autounboxing features of Java 5.0 make working with a `Set<Character>` or a `List<Integer>` just as easy as working directly with `char` and `int` values. (See Chapter 2 for details on autoboxing and autounboxing).

In Java 5.0, the example above would be rewritten as follows:

```
public static void main(String[] args) {
    // This list can only hold String objects
    List<String> wordlist = new ArrayList<String>();

    // args is a String[], not String, so the compiler won't let us do this
    wordlist.add(args);  // Compilation error!

    // We can do this, though.
    // Notice the use of the new for/in looping statement
```

```
        for(String arg : args) wordlist.add(arg);

        // No cast is required.  List<String>.get() returns a String.
        String word = wordlist.get(0);
    }
```

Note that this code isn't much shorter than the nongeneric example it replaces. The cast, which uses the word String in parentheses, is replaced with the type parameter, which places the word String in angle brackets. The difference is that the type parameter has to be declared only once, but the list can be used any number of times without a cast. This would be more apparent in a longer example. But even in cases where the generic syntax is more verbose than the nongeneric syntax, it is still very much worth using generics because the extra type information allows the compiler to perform much stronger error checking on your code. Errors that would only be apparent at runtime can now be detected at compile time. Furthermore, the compilation error appears at the exact line where the type safety violation occurs. Without generics, a ClassCastException can be thrown far from the actual source of the error.

Just as methods can have any number of arguments, classes can have more than one type variable. The java.util.Map interface is an example. A Map is a mapping from key objects to value objects. The Map interface declares one type variable to represent the type of the keys and one variable to represent the type of the values. As an example, suppose you want to map from String objects to Integer objects:

```
    public static void main(String[] args) {
        // A map from strings to their position in the args[] array
        Map<String,Integer> map = new HashMap<String,Integer>();

        // Note that we use autoboxing to wrap i in an Integer object.
        for(int i=0; i < args.length; i++) map.put(args[i], i);

        // Find the array index of a word.  Note no cast is required!
        Integer position = map.get("hello");

        // We can also rely on autounboxing to convert directly to an int,
        // but this throws a NullPointerException if the key does not exist
        // in the map
        int pos = map.get("world");
    }
```

A parameterized type like List<String> is itself a type and can be used as the value of a type parameter for some other type. You might see code like this:

```
    // Look at all those nested angle brackets!
    Map<String, List<List<int[]>>> map = getWeirdMap();

    // The compiler knows all the types and we can write expressions
    // like this without casting.  We might still get NullPointerException
    // or ArrayIndexOutOfBounds at runtime, of course.
    int value = map.get(key).get(0).get(0)[0];

    // Here's how we break that expression down step by step.
    List<List<int[]>> listOfLists = map.get(key);
```

```
List<int[]> listOfIntArrays = listOfLists.get(0);
int[] array = listOfIntArrays.get(0);
int element = array[0];
```

In the code above, the get() methods of java.util.List<E> and java.util.Map<K,V> return a list or map element of type E and V respectively. Note, however, that generic types can use their variables in more sophisticated ways. Look up List<E> in the reference section of this book, and you'll find that its iterator() method is declared to return an Iterator<E>. That is, the method returns an instance of a parameterized type whose actual type parameter is the same as the actual type parameter of the list. To illustrate this concretely, here is a way to obtain the first element of a List<String> without calling get(0).

```
List<String> words = // ...initialized elsewhere...
Iterator<String> iterator = words.iterator();
String firstword = iterator.next();
```

Understanding Generic Types

This section delves deeper into the details of generic type usage, explaining the following topics:

- The consequences of using generic types *without* type parameters
- The parameterized type hierarchy
- A hole in the compile-time type safety of generic types and a patch to ensure runtime type safety
- Why arrays of parameterized types are not typesafe

Raw types and unchecked warnings

Even though the Java collection classes have been modified to take advantage of generics, you are not required to specify type parameters to use them. A generic type used without type parameters is known as a *raw type*. Existing pre-5.0 code continues to work: you simply write all the casts that you're already used to writing, and you put up with some pestering from the compiler. Consider the following code that stores objects of mixed types into a raw List:

```
List l = new ArrayList();
l.add("hello");
l.add(new Integer(123));
Object o = l.get(0);
```

This code works fine in Java 1.4. If we compile it using Java 5.0, however, *javac* compiles the code but prints this complaint:

```
Note: Test.java uses unchecked or unsafe operations.
Note: Recompile with -Xlint:unchecked for details.
```

When we recompile with the -Xlint option as suggested, we see these warnings:

```
Test.java:6: warning: [unchecked]
    unchecked call to add(E) as a member of the raw type java.util.List
        l.add("hello");
         ^
```

```
Test.java:7: warning: [unchecked]
    unchecked call to add(E) as a member of the raw type java.util.List
        l.add(new Integer(123));
         ^
```

The compiler warns us about the add( ) calls because it cannot ensure that the values being added to the list have the correct types. It is letting us know that because we've used a raw type, it cannot verify that our code is typesafe. Note that the call to get( ) is okay because it is extracting an element that is already safely in the list.

If you get unchecked warnings on files that do not use any of the new Java 5.0 features, you can simply compile them with the -source 1.4 flag, and the compiler won't complain. If you can't do that, you can ignore the warnings, suppress them with an @SuppressWarnings("unchecked") annotation (see "Annotations" later in this chapter) or upgrade your code to specify a type parameter.* The following code, for example, compiles with no warnings and still allows you to add objects of mixed types to the list:

```
List<Object> l = new ArrayList<Object>();
l.add("hello");
l.add(123);                  // autoboxing
Object o = l.get(0);
```

The parameterized type hierarchy

Parameterized types form a type hierarchy, just as normal types do. The hierarchy is based on the base type, however, and not on the type of the parameters. Here are some experiments you can try:

```
ArrayList<Integer> l = new ArrayList<Integer>();
List<Integer> m = l;                            // okay
Collection<Integer> n = l;                      // okay
ArrayList<Number> o = l;                        // error
Collection<Object> p = (Collection<Object>)l;   // error, even with cast
```

A List<Integer> is a Collection<Integer>, but it is not a List<Object>. This is nonintuitive, and it is important to understand why generics work this way. Consider this code:

```
List<Integer> li = new ArrayList<Integer>();
li.add(123);

// The line below will not compile.  But for the purposes of this
// thought-experiment, assume that it does compile and see how much
// trouble we get ourselves into.
List<Object> lo = li;

// Now we can retrieve elements of the list as Object instead of Integer
Object number = lo.get(0);

// But what about this?
```

* At the time of this writing, *javac* does not yet honor the @SuppressWarnings annotation. It is expected to do so in Java 5.1.

```
lo.add("hello world");

// If the line above is allowed then the line below throws ClassCastException
Integer i = li.get(1);  // Can't cast a String to Integer!
```

This then is the reason that a `List<Integer>` is not a `List<Object>`, even though all elements of a `List<Integer>` are in fact instances of `Object`. If the conversion to `List<Object>` were allowed, non-`Integer` objects could be added to the list.

Runtime type safety

As we've seen, a `List<X>` cannot be converted to a `List<Y>`, even when `X` *can* be converted to `Y`. A `List<X>` can be converted to a `List`, however, so that you can pass it to a legacy method that expects an argument of that type and has not been updated for generics.

This ability to convert parameterized types to nonparameterized types is essential for backward compatibility, but it does open up a hole in the type safety system that generics offer:

```
// Here's a basic parameterized list.
List<Integer> li = new ArrayList<Integer>();

// It is legal to assign a parameterized type to a nonparameterized variable
List l = li;

// This line is a bug, but it compiles and runs.
// The Java 5.0 compiler will issue an unchecked warning about it.
// If it appeared as part of a legacy class compiled with Java 1.4, however,
// then we'd never even get the warning.
l.add("hello");

// This line compiles without warning but throws ClassCastException at runtime.
// Note that the failure can occur far away from the actual bug.
Integer i = li.get(0);
```

Generics provide compile-time type safety only. If you compile all your code with the Java 5.0 compiler and do not get any unchecked warnings, these compile-time checks are enough to ensure that your code is also typesafe at runtime. But if you have unchecked warnings or are working with legacy code that manipulates your collections as raw types, you may want to take additional steps to ensure type safety at runtime. You can do this with methods like `checkedList()` and `checkedMap( )` of `java.util.Collections`. These methods enclose your collection in a wrapper collection that performs runtime type checks to ensure that only values of the correct type are added to the collection. For example, we could prevent the type safety hole shown above like this:

```
// Here's a basic parameterized list.
List<Integer> li = new ArrayList<Integer>();

// Wrap it for runtime type safety
List<Integer> cli = Collections.checkedList(li, Integer.class);

// Now widen the checked list to the raw type
```

```
List l = cli;

// This line compiles but fails at runtime with a ClassCastException.
// The exception occurs exactly where the bug is, rather than far away
l.add("hello");
```

Arrays of parameterized type

Arrays require special consideration when working with generic types. Recall that an array of type S[ ] is also of type T[], if T is a superclass (or interface) of S. Because of this, the Java interpreter must perform a runtime check every time you store an object in an array to ensure that the runtime type of the object and of the array are compatible. For example, the following code fails this runtime check and throws an ArrayStoreException:

```
String[] words = new String[10];
Object[] objs = words;
objs[0] = 1;  // 1 autoboxed to an Integer, throws ArrayStoreException
```

Although the compile-time type of objs is Object[], its runtime type is String[ ], and it is not legal to store an Integer in it.

When we work with generic types, the runtime check for array store exceptions is no longer sufficient because a check performed at runtime does not have access to the compile-time type parameter information. Consider this (hypothetical) code:

```
List<String>[] wordlists = new ArrayList<String>[10];
ArrayList<Integer> ali = new ArrayList<Integer>();
ali.add(123);
Object[] objs = wordlists;
objs[0] = ali;                       // No ArrayStoreException
String s = wordlists[0].get(0);      // ClassCastException!
```

If the code above were allowed, the runtime array store check would succeed: without compile-time type parameters, the code simply stores an ArrayList into an ArrayList[] array, which is perfectly legal. Since the compiler can't prevent you from defeating type safety in this way, it instead prevents you from creating any array of parameterized type. The scenario above can never occur because the compiler will refuse to compile the first line.

Note that this is not a blanket restriction on using arrays with generics; it is just a restriction on creating arrays of parameterized type. We'll return to this issue when we look at how to write generic methods.

Type Parameter Wildcards

Suppose we want to write a method to display the elements of a List.* Before List was a generic type, we'd just write code like this:

```
public static void printList(PrintWriter out, List list) {
```

* The three printList() methods shown in this section ignore the fact that the List implementations classes in java.util all provide working toString() methods. Notice also that the methods assume that the List implements RandomAccess and provides very poor performance on LinkedList instances.

```
    for(int i=0, n=list.size(); i < n; i++) {
        if (i > 0) out.print(", ");
        out.print(list.get(i).toString());
    }
}
```

In Java 5.0, `List` is a generic type, and, if we try to compile this method, we'll get unchecked warnings. In order to get rid of those warnings, you might be tempted to modify the method as follows:

```
public static void printList(PrintWriter out, List<Object> list) {
    for(int i=0, n=list.size(); i < n; i++) {
        if (i > 0) out.print(", ");
        out.print(list.get(i).toString());
    }
}
```

This code compiles without warnings but isn't very useful because the only lists that can be passed to it are lists explicitly declared of type `List<Object>`. Remember that `List<String>` and `List<Integer>` (for example) cannot be widened or cast to `List<Object>`. What we really want is a typesafe `printList()` method to which we can pass any `List`, regardless of how it has been parameterized. The solution is to use a wildcard as the type parameter. The method would then be written like this:

```
public static void printList(PrintWriter out, List<?> list) {
    for(int i=0, n=list.size(); i < n; i++) {
        if (i > 0) out.print(", ");
        Object o = list.get(i);
        out.print(o.toString());
    }
}
```

This version of the method compiles without warnings and can be used the way we want it to be used. The `?` wildcard represents an unknown type, and the type `List<?>` is read as "List of unknown."

As a general rule, if a type is generic and you don't know or don't care about the value of the type variable, you should always use a `?` wildcard instead of using a raw type. Raw types are allowed only for backward compatibility and should be used only in legacy code. Note, however, that you cannot use a wildcard when invoking a constructor. The following code is not legal:

```
List<?> l = new ArrayList<?>();
```

There is no sense in creating a `List` of unknown type. If you are creating it, you should know what kind of elements it will hold. You may later want to pass such a list to a method that does not care about its element type, but you need to specify an element type when you create it. If what you really want is a `List` that can hold any type of object, do this:

```
List<Object> l = new ArrayList<Object>();
```

It should be clear from the `printList()` variants above that a `List<?>` is not the same thing as a `List<Object>` and that neither is the same thing as a raw `List`. A `List<?>` has two important properties that result from the use of a wildcard. First, consider methods like get() that are declared to return a value of the same type as the type parameter. In this case, that type is unknown, so these methods return an Object. Since all we need to do with the object is invoke its toString() method, this is fine for our needs.

Second, consider List methods such as add() that are declared to accept an argument whose type is specified by the type parameter. This is the more surprising case: when the type parameter is unknown, the compiler does not let you invoke any methods that have a parameter of the unknown type because it cannot check that you are passing an appropriate value. A List<?> is effectively read-only since the compiler does not allow us to invoke methods like add( ), set(), and addAll( ).

Bounded wildcards

Let's continue now with a slightly more complex variant of our original example. Suppose that we want to write a sumList() method to compute the sum of a list of Number objects. As before, we could use a raw List, but we would give up type safety and have to deal with unchecked warnings from the compiler. Or we could use a List<Number>, but then we wouldn't be able to call the method for a List<Integer> or List<Double>, types we are more likely to use in practice. But if we use a wildcard, we don't actually get the type safety that we want because we have to trust that our method will be called with a List whose type parameter is actually Number or a subclass and not, say, a String. Here's what such a method might look like:

```
public static double sumList(List<?> list) {
    double total = 0.0;
    for(Object o : list) {
        Number n = (Number) o;  // A cast is required and may fail
        total += n.doubleValue();
    }
    return total;
}
```

To fix this method and make it truly typesafe, we need to use a *bounded wildcard* that states that the type parameter of the List is an unknown type that is either Number or a subclass of Number. The following code does just what we want:

```
public static double sumList(List<? extends Number> list) {
    double total = 0.0;
    for(Number n : list) total += n.doubleValue();
    return total;
}
```

The type List<? extends Number> could be read as "List of unknown descendant of Number." It is important to understand that, in this context, Number is considered a descendant of itself.

Note that the cast is no longer required. We don't know the type of the elements of the list, but we know that they have an "upper bound" of Number so we can extract them from the list as Number objects. The use of a for/in loop obscures the process of extracting elements from a list somewhat. The general rule is that when you use a bounded wildcard with an upper bound, methods (like the get() method of List) that return a value of the type parameter use the upper bound. So if we called list.

get() instead of using a for/in loop, we'd also get a Number. The prohibition on calling methods like list.add() that have arguments of the type parameter type still stands: if the compiler allowed us to call those methods we could add an Integer to a list that was declared to hold only Short values, for example.

It is also possible to specify a lower-bounded wildcard using the keyword super instead of extends. This technique has a different impact on what methods can be called. Lower-bounded wildcards are much less commonly used than upper-bounded wildcards, and we discuss them later in the chapter.

Writing Generic Types and Methods

Creating a simple generic type is straightforward. First, declare your type variables by enclosing a comma-separated list of their names within angle brackets after the name of the class or interface. You can use those type variables anywhere a type is required in any instance fields or methods of the class. Remember, though, that type variables exist only at compile time, so you can't use a type variable with the runtime operators instanceof and new.

We begin this section with a simple generic type, which we will subsequently refine. This code defines a Tree data structure that uses the type variable V to represent the type of the value held in each node of the tree:

```
import java.util.*;

/**
 * A tree is a data structure that holds values of type V.
 * Each tree has a single value of type V and can have any number of
 * branches, each of which is itself a Tree.
 */
public class Tree<V> {
    // The value of the tree is of type V.
    V value;

    // A Tree<V> can have branches, each of which is also a Tree<V>
    List<Tree<V>> branches = new ArrayList<Tree<V>>();

    // Here's the constructor.  Note the use of the type variable V.
    public Tree(V value) { this.value = value; }

    // These are instance methods for manipulating the node value and branches.
    // Note the use of the type variable V in the arguments or return types.
    V getValue() { return value; }
    void setValue(V value) { this.value = value; }
    int getNumBranches() { return branches.size(); }
    Tree<V> getBranch(int n) { return branches.get(n); }
    void addBranch(Tree<V> branch) { branches.add(branch); }
}
```

As you've probably noticed, the naming convention for type variables is to use a single capital letter. The use of a single letter distinguishes these variables from the names of actual types since real-world types always have longer, more descriptive names. The use of a capital letter is consistent with type naming conventions and distinguishes type variables from local variables, method parameters, and fields, which are sometimes written with a single lowercase letter. Collection classes like those in `java.util` often use the type variable `E` for "Element type." When a type variable can represent absolutely anything, `T` (for Type) and `S` are used as the most generic type variable names possible (like using `i` and `j` as loop variables).

Notice that the type variables declared by a generic type can be used only by the instance fields and methods (and nested types) of the type and not by static fields and methods. The reason, of course, is that it is instances of generic types that are parameterized. Static members are shared by all instances and parameterizations of the class, so static members do not have type parameters associated with them. Methods, including static methods, can declare and use their own type parameters, however, and each invocation of such a method can be parameterized differently. We'll cover this later in the chapter.

Type variable bounds

The type variable `V` in the declaration above of the `Tree<V>` class is unconstrained: `Tree` can be parameterized with absolutely any type. Often we want to place some constraints on the type that can be used: we might want to enforce that a type parameter implements one or more interfaces, or that it is a subclass of a specified class. This can be done by specifying a *bound* for the type variable. We've already seen upper bounds for wildcards, and upper bounds can also be specified for type variables using a similar syntax. The following code is the `Tree` example rewritten to make `Tree` objects `Serializable` and `Comparable`. In order to do this, the example uses a type variable bound to ensure that its value type is also `Serializable` and `Comparable`. Note how the addition of the `Comparable` bound on `V` enables us to write the `compareTo()` method `Tree` by guaranteeing the existence of a `compareTo()` method on `V`.*

```
import java.io.Serializable;
import java.util.*;

public class Tree<V extends Serializable & Comparable<V>>
    implements Serializable, Comparable<Tree<V>>
{
    V value;
    List<Tree<V>> branches = new ArrayList<Tree<V>>();

    public Tree(V value) { this.value = value; }

    // Instance methods
    V getValue() { return value; }
    void setValue(V value) { this.value = value; }
    int getNumBranches() { return branches.size(); }
    Tree<V> getBranch(int n) { return branches.get(n); }
```

* The bound shown here requires that the value type `V` is comparable to itself, in other words, that it implements the `Comparable` interface directly. This rules out the use of types that inherit the `Comparable` interface from a superclass. We'll consider the `Comparable` interface in much more detail at the end of this section and present an alternative there.

```
    void addBranch(Tree<V> branch) { branches.add(branch); }

    // This method is a nonrecursive implementation of Comparable<Tree<V>>
    // It only compares the value of this node and ignores branches.
    public int compareTo(Tree<V> that) {
        if (this.value == null && that.value == null) return 0;
        if (this.value == null) return -1;
        if (that.value == null) return 1;
        return this.value.compareTo(that.value);
    }

    // javac -Xlint warns us if we omit this field in a Serializable class
    private static final long serialVersionUID = 833546143621133467L;
}
```

The bounds of a type variable are expressed by following the name of the variable with the word extends and a list of types (which may themselves be parameterized, as `Comparable` is). Note that with more than one bound, as in this case, the bound types are separated with an ampersand rather than a comma. Commas are used to separate type variables and would be ambiguous if used to separate type variable bounds as well. A type variable can have any number of bounds, including any number of interfaces and at most one class.

Java 5.0

Wildcards in generic types

Earlier in the chapter we saw examples using wildcards and bounded wildcards in methods that manipulated parameterized types. They are also useful in generic types. Our current design of the `Tree` class requires the value object of every node to have exactly the same type, `V`. Perhaps this is too strict, and we should allow branches of a tree to have values that are a subtype of `V` instead of requiring `V` itself. This version of the `Tree` class (minus the `Comparable` and `Serializable` implementation) is more flexible:

```
public class Tree<V> {
    // These fields hold the value and the branches
    V value;
    List<Tree<? extends V>> branches = new ArrayList<Tree<? extends V>>();

    // Here's a constructor
    public Tree(V value) { this.value = value; }

    // These are instance methods for manipulating value and branches
    V getValue() { return value; }
    void setValue(V value) { this.value = value; }
    int getNumBranches() { return branches.size(); }
    Tree<? extends V> getBranch(int n) { return branches.get(n); }
    void addBranch(Tree<? extends V> branch) { branches.add(branch); }
}
```

The use of bounded wildcards for the branch type allow us to add a `Tree<Integer>`, for example, as a branch of a `Tree<Number>`:

```
Tree<Number> t = new Tree<Number>(0);  // Note autoboxing
t.addBranch(new Tree<Integer>(1));     // int 1 autoboxed to Integer
```

If we query the branch with the getBranch() method, the value type of the returned branch is unknown, and we must use a wildcard to express this. The next two lines are legal, but the third is not:

```
Tree<? extends Number> b = t.getBranch(0);
Tree<?> b2 = t.getBranch(0);
Tree<Number> b3 = t.getBranch(0);  // compilation error
```

When we query a branch like this, we don't know the precise type of the value, but we do still have an upper bound on the value type, so we can do this:

```
Tree<? extends Number> b = t.getBranch(0);
Number value = b.getValue();
```

What we cannot do, however, is set the value of the branch, or add a new branch to that branch. As explained earlier in the chapter, the existence of the upper bound does not change the fact that the value type is unknown. The compiler does not have enough information to allow us to safely pass a value to setValue() or a new branch (which includes a value type) to addBranch(). Both of these lines of code are illegal:

```
b.setValue(3.0); // Illegal, value type is unknown
b.addBranch(new Tree<Double>(Math.PI));
```

This example has illustrated a typical trade-off in the design of a generic type: using a bounded wildcard made the data structure more flexible but reduced our ability to safely use some of its methods. Whether or not this was a good design is probably a matter of context. In general, generic types are more difficult to design well. Fortunately, most of us will use the preexisting generic types in the java.util package much more frequently than we will have to create our own.

Generic methods

As noted earlier, the type variables of a generic type can be used only in the instance members of the type, not in the static members. Like instance methods, however, static methods can use wildcards. And although static methods cannot use the type variables of their containing class, they can declare their own type variables. When a method declares its own type variable, it is called a *generic method*.

Here is a static method that could be added to the Tree class. It is not a generic method but uses a bounded wildcard much like the sumList() method we saw earlier in the chapter:

```
/** Recursively compute the sum of the values of all nodes on the tree */
public static double sum(Tree<? extends Number> t) {
    double total = t.value.doubleValue();
    for(Tree<? extends Number> b : t.branches) total += sum(b);
    return total;
}
```

This method could also be rewritten as a generic method by declaring a type variable to express the upper bound imposed by the wildcard:

```
public static <N extends Number> double sum(Tree<N> t) {
    N value = t.value;
```

```
        double total = value.doubleValue();
        for(Tree<? extends N> b : t.branches) total += sum(b);
        return total;
    }
```

The generic version of sum() is no simpler than the wildcard version and the declaration of the type variable does not gain us anything. In a case like this, the wildcard solution is typically preferred over the generic solution. Generic methods are required where a single type variable is used to express a relationship between two parameters or between a parameter and a return value. The following method is an example:

```
    // This method returns the largest of two trees, where tree size
    // is computed by the sum() method.  The type variable ensures that
    // both trees have the same value type and that both can be passed to sum().
    public static <N extends Number> Tree<N> max(Tree<N> t, Tree<N> u) {
        double ts = sum(t);
        double us = sum(u);
        if (ts > us) return t;
        else return u;
    }
```

This method uses the type variable N to express the constraint that both arguments and the return value have the same type parameter and that that type parameter is Number or a subclass.

It could be argued that constraining both arguments to have the same value type is too restrictive and that we should be allowed to call the max() method on a Tree<Integer> and a Tree<Double>. One way to express this is to use two unrelated type variables to represent the two unrelated value types. Note, however, that we cannot use either variable in the return type of the method and must use a wildcard there:

```
    public static <N extends Number, M extends Number>
        Tree<? extends Number> max(Tree<N> t, Tree<M> u) {...}
```

Since the two type variables N and M have no relation to each other, and since each is used in only a single place in the signature, they offer no advantage over bounded wildcards. The method is better written this way:

```
    public static Tree<? extends Number> max(Tree<? extends Number> t,
                                             Tree<? extends Number> u) {...}
```

All the examples of generic methods shown here have been static methods. This is not a requirement: instance methods can declare their own type variables as well.

Invoking generic methods

When you use a generic type, you must specify the actual type parameters to be substituted for its type variables. The same is not generally true for generic methods: the compiler can almost always figure out the correct parameterization of a generic method based on the arguments you pass to the method. Consider the max() method defined above, for instance:

```
    public static <N extends Number> Tree<N> max(Tree<N> t, Tree<N> u) {...}
```

You need not specify N when you invoke this method because N is implicitly specified in the values of the method arguments *t* and *u*. In the following code, for example, the compiler determines that N is Integer:

```
Tree<Integer> x = new Tree<Integer>(1);
Tree<Integer> y = new Tree<Integer>(2);
Tree<Integer> z = Tree.max(x, y);
```

The process the compiler uses to determine the type parameters for a generic method is called *type inference*. Type inference is relatively intuitive to understand, but the actual algorithm the compiler must use is surprisingly complex and is well beyond the scope of this book. Complete details are in Chapter 15 of *The Java Language Specification, Third Edition*.

Let's look at a slightly more complex version of type inference. Consider this method:

```
public class Util {
    /** Set all elements of a to the value v; return a. */
    public static <T> T[] fill(T[] a, T v) {
        for(int i = 0; i < a.length; i++) a[i] = v;
        return a;
    }
}
```

Here are two invocations of the method:

```
Boolean[] booleans = Util.fill(new Boolean[100], Boolean.TRUE);
Object o = Util.fill(new Number[5], new Integer(42));
```

In the first invocation, the compiler can easily determine that T is Boolean. In the second invocation, the compiler determines that T is Number.

In very rare circumstances you may need to explicitly specify the type parameters for a generic method. This is sometimes necessary, for example, when a generic method expects no arguments. Consider the java.util.Collections.emptySet() method: it returns a set with no elements, but unlike the Collections.singleton() method (you can look these up in the reference section), it takes no arguments that would specify the type parameter for the returned set. You can specify the type parameter explicitly by placing it in angle brackets *before* the method name:

```
Set<String> empty = Collections.<String>emptySet();
```

Type parameters cannot be used with an unqualified method name: they must follow a dot or come after the keyword new or before the keyword this or super used in a constructor.

It turns out that if you assign the return value of Collections.emptySet() to a variable, as we did above the type inference mechanism is able to infer the type parameter based on the variable type. Although the explicit type parameter specification in the code above can be a helpful clarification, it is not necessary and the line could be rewritten as:

```
Set<String> empty = Collections.emptySet();
```

An explicit type parameter is necessary when you use the return value of the emptySet() method within a method invocation expression. For example, suppose you want to call a method named `printWords()` that expects a single argument of type `Set<String>`. If you want to pass an empty set to this method, you could use this code:

```
printWords(Collections.<String>emptySet());
```

In this case, the explicit specification of the type parameter `String` is required.

Generic methods and arrays

Earlier in the chapter we saw that the compiler does not allow you to create an array whose type is parameterized. This is not, however, a restriction on all uses of arrays with generics. Consider the `Util.fill()` method defined above, for example. Its first argument and its return value are both of type `T[]`. The body of the method does not have to create an array whose element type is `T`, so the method is perfectly legal.

If you write a method that uses varargs (see "Variable-Length Argument Lists" in Chapter 2) and a type variable, remember that invoking a varargs method performs an implicit array creation. Consider this method:

```
/** Return the largest of the specified values or null if there are none */
public static <T extends Comparable<T>> T max(T... values) { ... }
```

You can invoke this method with parameters of type `Integer` because the compiler can insert the necessary array creation code for you when you call it. But you cannot call the method if you've cast the same arguments to be type `Comparable<Integer>` because it is not legal to create an array of type `Comparable<Integer>[ ]`.

Parameterized exceptions

Exceptions are thrown and caught at runtime, and there is no way for the compiler to perform type checking to ensure that an exception of unknown origin matches type parameters specified in a `catch` clause. For this reason, `catch` clauses may not include type variables or wildcards. Since it is not possible to catch an exception at runtime with compile-time type parameters intact, you are not allowed to make any subclass of `Throwable` generic. Parameterized exceptions are simply not allowed.

You can, however, use a type variable in the `throws` clause of a method signature. Consider this code, for example:

```
public interface Command<X extends Exception> {
    public void doit(String arg) throws X;
}
```

This interface represents a "command": a block of code with a single string argument and no return value. The code may throw an exception represented by the type parameter `X`. Here is an example that uses a parameterization of this interface:

```
Command<IOException> save = new Command<IOException>() {
    public void doit(String filename) throws IOException {
        PrintWriter out = new PrintWriter(new FileWriter(filename));
        out.println("hello world");
```

```
            out.close();
        }
    };

    try { save.doit("/tmp/foo"); }
    catch(IOException e) { System.out.println(e); }
```

Generics Case Study: Comparable and Enum

The new generics features in Java 5.0 are used in the Java 5.0 APIs, most notably in `java.util` but also in `java.lang`, `java.lang.reflect`, and `java.util.concurrent`. These APIs were carefully created or reviewed by the inventors of generic types, and we can learn a lot about the good design of generic types and methods through the study of these APIs.

The generic types of `java.util` are relatively easy: for the most part they are collections classes, and type variables are used to represent the element type of the collection. Several important generic types in `java.lang` are more difficult. They are not collections, and it is not immediately apparent why they have been made generic. Studying these difficult generic types gives us a deeper understanding of how generics work and introduces some concepts that we have not yet covered in this chapter. Specifically, we'll examine the `Comparable` interface and the `Enum` class (the supertype of enumerated types, described later in this chapter) and will learn about an important but infrequently used feature of generics known as lower-bounded wildcards.

In Java 5.0, the `Comparable` interface has been made generic, with a type variable that specifies what a class is comparable to. Most classes that implement `Comparable` implement it on themselves. Consider `Integer`:

```
public final class Integer extends Number implements Comparable<Integer>
```

The raw `Comparable` interface is problematic from a type-safety standpoint. It is possible to have two `Comparable` objects that cannot be meaningfully compared to each other. Prior to Java 5.0, the nongeneric `Comparable` interface was useful but not fully satisfactory. The generic version of this interface, however, captures exactly the information we want: it tells us that a type is comparable and tells us what we can compare it to.

Now consider subclasses of comparable classes. `Integer` is `final` and cannot be subclassed, so let's look at `java.math.BigInteger` instead:

```
public class BigInteger extends Number implements Comparable<BigInteger>
```

If we implement a `BiggerInteger` subclass of `BigInteger`, it inherits the `Comparable` interface from its superclass. But note that it inherits `Comparable<BigInteger>` and not `Comparable<BiggerInteger>`. This means that `BigInteger` and `BiggerInteger` objects are mutually comparable, which is usually a good thing. `BiggerInteger` can override the `compareTo()` method of its superclass, but it is not allowed to implement a different parameterization of `Comparable`. That is, `BiggerInteger` cannot both extend `BigInteger` and implement `Comparable<BiggerInteger>`. (In general, a class is not allowed to implement two different parameterizations of the same interface: we cannot define a type that implements both Comparable<Integer> and Comparable<String>, for example.)

When you're working with comparable objects (as you do when writing sorting algorithms, for example), remember two things. First, it is not sufficient to use Comparable as a raw type: for type safety, you must also specify what it is comparable to. Second, types are not always comparable to themselves: sometimes they're comparable to one of their ancestors. To make this concrete, consider the java.util.Collections.max() method:

```
public static <T extends Comparable<? super T>> T max(Collection<? extends T> c)
```

This is a long, complex generic method signature. Let's walk through it:

- The method has a type variable T with complicated bounds that we'll return to later.
- The method returns a value of type T.
- The name of the method is max( ).
- The method's argument is a Collection. The element type of the collection is specified with a bounded wildcard. We don't know the exact type of the collection's elements, but we know that they have an upper bound of T. That is, we know that the elements of the collection are type T or a subclass of T. Any element of the collection could therefore be used as the return value of the method.

That much is relatively straightforward. We've seen upper-bounded wildcards elsewhere in this section. Now let's look again at the type variable declaration used by the max( ) method:

```
<T extends Comparable<? super T>>
```

This says first that the type T must implement Comparable. (Generics syntax uses the keyword extends for all type variable bounds, whether classes or interfaces.) This is expected since the purpose of the method is to find the "maximum" object in a collection. But look at the parameterization of the Comparable interface. This is a wildcard, but it is bounded with the keyword super instead of the keyword extends. This is a lower-bounded wildcard. ? extends T is the familiar upper bound: it means T or a subclass. ? super T is less commonly used: it means T or a superclass.

To summarize, then, the type variable declaration states "T is a type that is comparable to itself or to some superclass of itself." The Collections.min() and Collections.binarySearch( ) methods have similar signatures.

For other examples of lower-bounded wildcards (that have nothing to do with Comparable), consider the addAll(), copy( ), and fill() methods of Collections. Here is the signature for addAll():

```
public static <T> boolean addAll(Collection<? super T> c, T... a)
```

This is a varargs method that accepts any number of arguments of type T and passes them as a T[ ] named *a*. It adds all the elements of *a* to the collection *c*. The element type of the collection is unknown but has a lower bound: the elements are all of type T or a superclass of T. Whatever the type is, we are assured that the elements of the array are instances of that type, and so it is always legal to add those array elements to the collection.

Recall from our earlier discussion of upper-bounded wildcards that if you have a collection whose element type is an upper-bounded wildcard, it is effectively read-only. Consider `List<? extends Serializable>`. We know that all elements are `Serializable`, so methods like `get()` return a value of type `Serializable`. The compiler won't let us call methods like `add()` because the actual element type of the list is unknown. You can't add arbitrary serializable objects to the list because their implementing class may not be of the correct type.

Since upper-bounded wildcards result in read-only collections, you might expect lower-bounded wildcards to result in write-only collections. This isn't actually the case, however. Suppose we have a `List<? super Integer>`. The actual element type is unknown, but the only possibilities are `Integer` or its ancestors `Number` and `Object`. Whatever the actual type is, it is safe to add `Integer` objects (but not `Number` or `Object` objects) to the list. And, whatever the actual element type is, all elements of the list are instances of `Object`, so `List` methods like `get()` return `Object` in this case.

Finally, let's turn our attention to the `java.lang.Enum` class. `Enum` serves as the supertype of all enumerated types (described later). It implements the `Comparable` interface but has a confusing generic signature:

```
public class Enum<E extends Enum<E>> implements Comparable<E>, Serializable
```

At first glance, the declaration of the type variable `E` appears circular. Take a closer look though: what this signature really says is that `Enum` must be parameterized by a type that is itself an `Enum`. The reason for this seemingly circular type variable declaration becomes apparent if we look at the `implements` clause of the signature. As we've seen, `Comparable` classes are usually defined to be comparable to themselves. And subclasses of those classes are comparable to their superclass instead. `Enum`, on the other hand, implements the `Comparable` interface not for itself but for a subclass `E` of itself!

Enumerated Types

In previous chapters, we've seen the `class` keyword used to define class types, and the `interface` keyword used to define interface types. This section introduces the `enum` keyword, which is used to define an enumerated type (informally called an enum). Enumerated types are new in Java 5.0, and the features described here cannot be used (although they can be partially simulated) prior to that release.

We begin with the basics: how to define and use an enumerated type, including common programming idioms involving enumerated types and values. Next, we discuss the more advanced features of enums and show how to simulate enums prior to Java 5.0.

Enumerated Types Basics

An *enumerated type* is a reference type with a finite (usually small) set of possible values, each of which is individually listed, or enumerated. Here is a simple enumerated type defined in Java:

```
public enum DownloadStatus { CONNECTING, READING, DONE, ERROR }
```

Like class and interface, the enum keyword defines a new reference type. The single line of Java code above defines an enumerated type named DownloadStatus. The body of this type is simply a comma-separated list of the four values of the type. These values are like static final fields (which is why their names are capitalized), and you refer to them with names like DownloadStatus.CONNECTING, DownloadStatus.READING, and so on. A variable of type DownloadStatus can be assigned one of these four values or null but nothing else. The values of an enumerated type are called *enumerated values* and are sometimes also referred to as *enum constants*.

It is possible to define more complex enumerated types than the one shown here, and we describe the complete enum syntax later in this chapter. For now, however, you can define simple, but very useful, enumerated types with this basic syntax.

Enumerated types are classes

Prior to the introduction of enumerated types in Java 5.0, the DownloadStatus values would probably have been implemented as integer constants with lines like the following in a class or interface:

```
public static final int CONNECTING = 1;
public static final int READING = 2;
public static final int DONE = 3;
public static final int ERROR = 4;
```

The use of integer constants has a number of shortcomings, the most important of which is its lack of type safety. If a method expects a download status constant value, for example, no error checking prevents me from passing an illegal value. The compiler can't tell me that I've used the constant UploadStatus.DONE when I should have used DownloadStatus.DONE.

Fortunately, enumerated types in Java are not simple integer constants. The type defined by an enum keyword is actually a class and its enumerated values are instances of that class. This provides type safety: if I try to pass a DownloadStatus value to a method that expects an UploadStatus, the compiler issues an error. Enumerated types do not have a public constructor, so a program cannot create a new undefined instance of the type. If a method expects a DownloadStatus, it can be confident that it will not be passed some unknown instance of the type.

If you are accustomed to writing code using integer constants instead of true enumerated types, you have probably already made a list of pragmatic advantages of integers over objects for enumerated values. Hold your judgment, however: the sections that follow illustrate common enumerated type programming idioms and demonstrate that anything you can do with integer constants can be done elegantly, efficiently, and more safely with enums. First, however, we consider the basic features of all enumerated types.

Features of enumerated types

The following list describes the basic facts about enumerated types. These are the features of enums that you need to know to understand and use them effectively:

- Enumerated types have no public constructor. The only instances of an enumerated type are those declared by the enum.
- Enums are not `Cloneable`, so copies of the existing instances cannot be created.
- Enums implement `java.io.Serializable` so they can be serialized, but the Java serialization mechanism handles them specially to ensure that no new instances are ever created.
- Instances of an enumerated type are immutable: each enum value retains its identity. (We'll see later in this chapter that you can add your own fields and methods to an enumerated type, which means that you can create enumerated values that have mutable portions. This is not recommended, but does not affect the basic identity of each value.)
- Instances of an enumerated type are stored in `public static final` fields of the type itself. Because these fields are `final`, they cannot be overwritten with inappropriate values: you can't assign the `DownloadStatus.ERROR` value to the `DownloadStatus.DONE` field, for example.
- By convention, the values of enumerated types are written using all capital letters, just as other `static final` fields are.
- Because there is a strictly limited set of distinct enumerated values, it is always safe to compare enum values using the `==` operator instead of calling the `equals()` method.
- Enumerated types do have a working `equals()` method, however. The method uses `==` internally and is `final` so that it cannot be overridden. This working `equals()` method allows enumerated values to be used as members of collections such as `Set`, `List`, and `Map`.
- Enumerated types have a working `hashCode()` method consistent with their `equals()` method. Like `equals()`, `hashCode()` is `final`. It allows enumerated values to be used with classes like `java.util.HashMap`.
- Enumerated types implement `java.lang.Comparable`, and the `compareTo()` method orders enumerated values in the order in which they appear in the `enum` declaration.
- Enumerated types include a working `toString()` method that returns the name of the enumerated value. For example, `DownloadStatus.DONE.toString()` returns the string `"DONE"` by default. This method is not `final`, and enum types can provide a custom implementation if they choose.
- Enumerated types provide a static `valueOf()` method that does the opposite of the default `toString()` method. For example, `DownloadStatus.valueOf("DONE")` would return `DownloadStatus.DONE`.
- Enumerated types define a `final` instance method named `ordinal()` that returns an integer for each enumerated value. The ordinal of an enumerated value represents its position (starting at zero) in the list of value names in the `enum` declaration. You do not typically need to use the `ordinal()` method, but it is used by a number of enum-related facilities, as described later in the chapter.

- Each enumerated type defines a static method named `values()` that returns an array of enumerated values of that type. This array contains the complete set of values, in the order they were declared, and is useful for iterating through the complete set of possible values. Because arrays are mutable, the `values()` method always returns a newly created and initialized array.
- Enumerated types are subclasses of `java.lang.Enum`, which is new in Java 5.0. (`Enum` is not itself an enumerated type.) You cannot produce an enumerated type by manually extending the `Enum` class, and it is a compilation error to attempt this. The only way to define an enumerated type is with the `enum` keyword.
- It is not possible to extend an enumerated type. Enumerated types are effectively `final`, but the `final` keyword is neither required nor permitted in their declarations. Because enums are effectively `final`, they may not be `abstract`. (We'll return to this point later in the chapter.)
- Like classes, enumerated types may implement interfaces. (We'll see how enumerated types may define methods later in the chapter.)

Using Enumerated Types

The following sections illustrate common idioms for working with enumerated types. They demonstrate the use of the `switch` statement with enumerated types and introduce the important new `EnumSet` and `EnumMap` collections.

Java 5.0

Enums and the switch statement

In Java 1.4 and earlier, the `switch` statement works only with `int`, `short`, `char`, and `byte` values. Because enumerated types have a finite set of values, they are ideally suited for use with the `switch` statement, and this statement has been extended in Java 5.0 to support the use of enumerated types. If the compile-time type of the `switch` expression is an enumerated type, the case labels must all be unqualified names of instances of that type. The following hypothetical code shows a `switch` statement used with the `DownloadStatus` enumerated type.

```
DownloadStatus status = imageLoader.getStatus();
switch(status) {
case CONNECTING:
    imageLoader.waitForConnection();
    imageLoader.startReading();
    break;
case READING:
    break;
case DONE:
    return imageLoader.getImage();
case ERROR:
    throw new IOException(imageLoader.getError());
}
```

Note that the case labels are just the constant name: the syntax of the `switch` statement does not allow the class name `DownloadStatus` to appear here. The ability to omit the class name is very convenient since it would otherwise appear in every single case. However the *requirement* that the class name be omitted is surprising since (in the absence of an `import static` declaration) the class name *is* required in every other context.

If the `switch` expression (`status` in the code above) evaluates to `null`, a `NullPointerException` is thrown. It is not legal to use `null` as the value of a case label.

If you use the `switch` statement on an enumerated type and do not include either a `default:` label or a case label for each enumerated value, the compiler will most likely issue an `-Xlint` warning letting you know that you have not written code to handle all possible values of the enumerated type.* Even when you do write a case for each enumerated value, you may still want to include a `default:` clause; this covers the possibility that a new value is added to the enumerated type after your `switch` statement has been compiled. The following `default` clause, for example, could be added to the `switch` statement shown earlier:

```
default: throw new AssertionError("Unexpected enumerated value: " + status);
```

EnumMap

A common programming technique when using integer constants instead of true enumerated values is to use those constants as array indexes. For example, if the `DownloadStatus` values are defined as integers between 0 and 3, we can write code like this:

```
String[] statusLineMessages = new String[] {
    "Connecting...",    // CONNECTING
    "Loading...",       // READING
    "Done.",            // DONE
    "Download Failed." // ERROR
};

int status = getStatus();
String message = statusLineMessages[status];
```

In the big picture, this technique creates a mapping from enumerated integer constants to strings. We can't use Java's enumerated values as array indexes, but we can use them as keys in a `java.util.Map`. Because this is a common thing to do, Java 5.0 defines a new `java.util.EnumMap` class that is optimized for exactly this case. `EnumMap` requires an enumerated type as its key, and, relying on the fact the number of possible keys is finite, it uses an array to hold the corresponding values. This implementation means that `EnumMap` is more efficient than `HashMap`. The `EnumMap` equivalent of the code above is:

```
EnumMap<DownloadStatus,String> messages =
    new EnumMap<DownloadStatus,String>(DownloadStatus.class);
messages.put(DownloadStatus.CONNECTING, "Connecting...");
messages.put(DownloadStatus.READING,    "Loading...");
messages.put(DownloadStatus.DONE,       "Done.");
messages.put(DownloadStatus.ERROR,      "Download Failed.");

DownloadStatus status = getStatus();
String message = messages.get(status);
```

* At the time of this writing, this warning is expected to appear in Java 5.1.

Like other collection classes in Java 5.0, EnumMap is a generic type that accepts type parameters.

The use of an EnumMap to associate a value with each instance of an enumerated type is appropriate when you're working with an enum defined elsewhere. If you defined the enum value yourself, you can create the necessary associations as part of the enum definition itself. We'll see how to do this later in the chapter.

EnumSet

Another common programming idiom when using integer-based constants instead of an enumerated type is to define all the constants as powers of two so that a set of those constants can be compactly represented as bit-flags in an integer. Consider the following flags that describe options that can apply to an American-style espresso drink:

```
public static final int SHORT      = 0x01;  // 8 ounces
public static final int TALL       = 0x02;  // 12 ounces
public static final int GRANDE     = 0x04;  // 16 ounces
public static final int DOUBLE     = 0x08;  // 2 shots of espresso
public static final int SKINNY     = 0x10;  // made with nonfat milk
public static final int WITH_ROOM  = 0x20;  // leave room for cream
public static final int SPLIT_SHOT = 0x40;  // half decaffeinated
public static final int DECAF      = 0x80;  // fully decaffeinated
```

These power-of-two constants can be combined with the bitwise OR operator (|) to create a compact set of constants that is easy to work with:

```
int drinkflags = DOUBLE | SHORT | WITH_ROOM;
```

The bitwise AND operator (&) can be used to test for the presence or absence of bits:

```
boolean isBig = (drinkflags & (TALL | GRANDE)) != 0;
```

If we step back from the binary representation of these bit flags and the boolean operators that manipulate them, we can see that integer bit flags are simply compact sets of values. For reference types such as Java's enumerated values, we can use a java.util.Set instead. Since this is an important and common thing to do with enumerated values, Java 5.0 provides the special-purpose java.util.EnumSet class. Like EnumMap, EnumSet is optimized for enumerated types. It requires that its members be values of the same enumerated type and uses a compact and fast representation of the set based on bit flags that correspond to the ordinal() of each enumerated value.

The espresso drink code above could be rewritten as follows using an enum and EnumSet:

```
public enum DrinkFlags {
    SHORT, TALL, GRANDE, DOUBLE, SKINNY, WITH_ROOM, SPLIT_SHOT, DECAF
}

EnumSet<DrinkFlags> drinkflags =
    EnumSet.of(DrinkFlags.DOUBLE, DrinkFlags.SHORT, DrinkFlags.WITH_ROOM);

boolean isbig =
```

```
    drinkflags.contains(DrinkFlags.TALL) ||
    drinkflags.contains(DrinkFlags.GRANDE);
```

Note that the code above can be made as compact as the integer-based code with a simple static import:

```
// Import all static DrinkFlag enum constants
import static com.davidflanagan.coffee.DrinkFlags.*;
```

See "Packages and the Java Namespace" in Chapter 2 for details on the `import static` declaration.

`EnumSet` defines a number of useful factory methods for initializing sets of enumerated values. The `of()` method shown above is overloaded: several versions of the method take different fixed numbers of arguments. A varargs (see Chapter 2) form that can accept any number of arguments is also defined. Here are some other ways that you can use `of()` and related `EnumSet` factories:

```
// Make the following examples fit on the page better
import static com.davidflanagan.coffee.DrinkFlags.*;

// We can remove individual members or sets of members from a set.
// Start with a set that includes all enumerated values, then remove a subset:
EnumSet<DrinkFlags> fullCaffeine = EnumSet.allOf(DrinkFlags.class);
fullCaffeine.removeAll(EnumSet.of(DECAF, SPLIT_SHOT));

// Here's another technique to achieve the same result:
EnumSet<DrinkFlags> fullCaffeine =
    EnumSet.complementOf(EnumSet.of(DECAF,SPLIT_SHOT));

// Here's an empty set if you ever need one
// Note that since we don't specify a value, we must specify the element type
EnumSet<DrinkFlags> plainDrink = EnumSet.noneOf(DrinkFlags.class);

// You can also easily describe a contiguous subset of values:
EnumSet<DrinkFlags> drinkSizes = EnumSet.range(SHORT, GRANDE);

// EnumSet is Iterable, and its iterator returns values in ordinal() order,
// so it is easy to loop through the elements of an EnumSet.
for(DrinkFlag size : drinkSizes) System.out.println(size);
```

The example code shown here demonstrates the use and capabilities of the `EnumSet` class. Note, however, that an `EnumSet<DrinkFlags>` is not really an appropriate representation for the description of an espresso drink. An `EnumSet<DrinkFlags>` might be overspecified, including both `SHORT` and `GRANDE`, for example, or it might be underspecified and include no drink size at all.

At the root, the problem is that the `DrinkFlag` type is a naive translation of the integer bit flags we began this section with. A better and more complete representation is captured by the following interface, which requires one value from each of five different enumerated types and a set of values from a sixth enum. The enums are defined as *nested types* within the interface itself (see Chapter 3). This example highlights the type safety provided by enumerated types. It is not possible (as it would be with integer constants) to specify a drink strength where a drink size is required, for example.

```
public interface Espresso {
    enum Drink { LATTE, MOCHA, AMERICANO, CAPPUCCINO, ESPRESSO }
    enum Size { SHORT, TALL, GRANDE }
    enum Strength { SINGLE, DOUBLE, TRIPLE, QUAD }
    enum Milk { SKINNY, ONE_PERCENT, TWO_PERCENT, WHOLE, SOY }
    enum Caffeine { REGULAR, SPLIT_SHOT, DECAF }
    enum Flags { WITH_ROOM, EXTRA_HOT, DRY }

    Drink getDrink();
    Size getSize();
    Strength getStrength();
    Milk getMilk();
    Caffeine getCaffeine();
    java.util.Set<Flags> getFlags();
}
```

Advanced Enum Syntax

The examples shown so far have all used the simplest `enum` syntax in which the body of the enum simply consists of a comma-separated list of value names. The full `enum` syntax actually provides quite a bit more power and flexibility:

- You can define your own fields, methods, and constructors for the enumerated type.
- If you define one or more constructors, you can invoke a constructor for each enumerated value by following the value name with constructor arguments in parentheses.
- Although an `enum` may not `extend` anything, it may `implement` one or more interfaces.
- Most esoterically, individual enumerated values can have their own class bodies that override methods defined by the type.

Rather than formally specifying the syntax for each of these advanced `enum` declarations, we'll demonstrate the syntax in the examples that follow.

The class body of an enumerated type

Consider the type `Prefix`, defined below. It is an `enum` that includes a regular class body following the list of enumerated values. It defines two instance fields and accessor methods for those fields. It defines a custom constructor that initializes the instance field. Each named value of the enumerated type is followed by constructor arguments in parentheses:

```
public enum Prefix {
    // These are the values of this enumerated type.
    // Each one is followed by constructor arguments in parentheses.
    // The values are separated from each other by commas, and the
    // list of values is terminated with a semicolon to separate it from
    // the class body that follows.
    MILLI("m",    .001),
    CENTI("c",    .01),
    DECI("d",     .1),
```

```
        DECA("D",   10.0),
        HECTA("h", 100.0),
        KILO("k", 1000.0);  // Note semicolon


        // This is the constructor invoked for each value above.
        Prefix(String abbrev, double multiplier) {
            this.abbrev = abbrev;
            this.multiplier = multiplier;
        }

        // These are the private fields set by the constructor
        private String abbrev;
        private double multiplier;

        // These are accessor methods for the fields.  They are instance methods
        // of each value of the enumerated type.
        public String abbrev() { return abbrev; }
        public double multiplier() { return multiplier; }
    }
```

Note that enum syntax requires a semicolon after the last enumerated value if that value is followed by a class body. This semicolon may be omitted in the simple case where there is no class body. It is also worth noting that enum syntax allows a comma following the last enumerated value. A trailing comma looks somewhat odd but prevents syntax errors if in the future you add new enumerated values or rearrange existing ones.

Implementing an interface

An enum cannot be declared to extend a class or enumerated type. It is perfectly legal, however, for an enumerated type to implement one or more interfaces. Suppose, for example, that you defined a new enumerated type Unit with an abbrev() method like Prefix has. In this case, you might define an interface Abbrevable for any objects that have abbreviations. Your code might look like this:

```
public interface Abbrevable {
    String abbrev();
}

public enum Prefix implements Abbrevable {
    // the body of this enum type remains the same as above.
}
```

Value-specific class bodies

In addition to defining a class body for the enumerated type itself, you can also provide a class body for individual enumerated values within the type. We've seen above that we can add fields to an enumerated type and use a constructor to initialize those fields. This gives us value-specific data. The ability to define class bodies for each enumerated value means that we can write methods for each one: this gives us value-specific *behavior*. Value-specific behavior is useful when defining an enumerated type that represents an operator in an expression parser or an opcode in a virtual machine of some sort. The `Operator.ADD` constant might have a `compute()` method that behaves differently than the `Operator.SUBTRACT` constant, for example.

To define a class body for an individual enumerated value, simply follow the value name and its constructor arguments with the class body in curly braces. Individual values must still be separated from each other with commas, and the last value in the list must be separated from the type's class body with a semicolon: it can be easy to forget about this required punctuation with the presence of curly braces for class and method bodies.

Each value-specific class body you write results in the creation of an anonymous subclass of the enumerated type and makes the enumerated value a singleton instance of that anonymous subclass. (Enumerated types can not be extended, but they are not strictly `final` in the sense that `final` classes are since they can have these anonymous subclasses.) Because these subclasses are anonymous, you cannot refer to them in your code: the compile-time type of each enumerated value is the enumerated type, not the anonymous subclass specific to that value. Therefore, the only useful thing you can do in value-specific class bodies is override methods defined by the type itself. If you define a new public field or method, you will not be able to refer to or invoke it. (It is perfectly legitimate, of course, to define helper methods or fields that you invoke or use from the overriding methods.)

A common pattern is to define default behavior in a method of the type-specific class body. Then, each enumerated value that requires behavior other than the default can override that method in its value-specific class body. A very useful variant of this pattern is to declare the method in the type-specific class body `abstract` and to define a value-specific implementation of the method for every enumerated value. If the type-specific method is `abstract`, the compiler forces you to implement that method for every enumerated value in the type: it is not possible to accidentally omit an implementation. Note that even though the type-specific class body contains an `abstract` method, the enumerated type as a whole is not `abstract` (and may not be declared `abstract`) since each value-specific class body implements the method.

The following code is an excerpt from a larger example that uses an enumerated type to represent the opcodes of a simulated stack-based CPU. The `Opcode` enumerated type defines an `abstract` method `perform()`, which is then implemented by the class body of each value of the type. The type includes a constructor to illustrate the full syntax for each enumerated value: name, constructor arguments, and class body. `enum` syntax requires the enumerated values and their class bodies to appear first. The code is easiest to understand, however, if you skip past the values and read the type-specific class body first:

```
// These are the opcodes that our stack machine can execute.
public enum Opcode {
    // Push the single operand onto the stack
    PUSH(1) {
        public void perform(StackMachine machine, int[] operands) {
            machine.push(operands[0]);
        }
```

```
        },   // Remember to separate enum values with commas

        // Add the top two values on the stack and push the result
        ADD(0) {
            public void perform(StackMachine machine, int[] operands) {
                machine.push(machine.pop() + machine.pop());
            }
        },

        /* Other opcode values have been omitted for brevity */

        // Branch if Equal to Zero
        BEZ(1) {
            public void perform(StackMachine machine, int[] operands) {
                if (machine.top() == 0) machine.setPC(operands[0]);
            }
        };    // Remember the required semicolon before the class body


        // This is the constructor for the type.
        Opcode(int numOperands) { this.numOperands = numOperands; }

        int numOperands;  // how many integer operands does it expect?

        // Each opcode constant must implement this abstract method in a
        // value-specific class body to perform the operation it represents.
        public abstract void perform(StackMachine machine, int[] operands);
    }
```

When to use value-specific class bodies. Value-specific class bodies are an extremely powerful language feature when each enumerated value must perform a unique computation of some sort. Keep in mind, however, that value-specific class bodies are an advanced feature that is not commonly used and may be confusing to less experienced programmers. Before you decide to use this feature, be sure that it is necessary.

Before using value-specific class bodies, ensure that your design is neither too simple nor too complex for the feature. First, check that you do indeed require value-specific behavior and not simply value-specific data. Value-specific data can be encoded in constructor arguments as was shown in the `Prefix` example earlier. It would be unnecessary and inappropriate to rewrite that example to use value-specific versions of the `abbrev()` method, for example.

Next, think about whether an enumerated type is sufficient for your needs. If your design requires value-specific methods with complex implementations or requires more than a few methods for each value, you may find it unwieldy to code everything within a single type. Instead, consider defining your own custom type hierarchy using traditional `class` and `interface` declarations and whatever singleton instances are necessary.

If value-specific behavior is indeed required within the framework of an enumerated type, value-specific class bodies are appropriate. Whether value-specific bodies are truly elegant or simply confusing is a matter of opinion, and some programmers prefer to avoid them when possible. An alternative that appeals to some is to encode the value-specific behavior in a type-specific method that uses a switch statement to treat each value as a separate case. The compute( ) method of the following enum is an example. The simplicity of this enumerated type makes a switch statement a compelling alternative to value-specific class bodies:

```
public enum ArithmeticOperator {
    // The enumerated values
    ADD, SUBTRACT, MULTIPLY, DIVIDE;

    // Value-specific behavior using a switch statement
    public double compute(double x, double y) {
        switch(this) {
        case ADD:       return x + y;
        case SUBTRACT:  return x - y;
        case MULTIPLY:  return x * y;
        case DIVIDE:    return x / y;
        default: throw new AssertionError(this);
        }
    }

    // Test case for using this enum
    public static void main(String args[]) {
        double x = Double.parseDouble(args[0]);
        double y = Double.parseDouble(args[1]);
        for(ArithmeticOperator op : ArithmeticOperator.values())
            System.out.printf("%f %s %f = %f%n", x, op, y, op.compute(x,y));
    }
}
```

A shortcoming to the switch approach is that each time you add a new enumerated value, you must remember to add a corresponding case to the switch statement. And if there is more than one method that uses a switch statement, you'll have to maintain their switch statements in parallel. Forgetting to implement value-specific behavior using a switch statement leads to a runtime AssertionError. With a value-specific class body overriding an abstract method in the type-specific class body, the same omission leads to a compilation error and can be corrected sooner.

The performance of value-specific methods and switch statements in a type-specific method are quite similar. The overhead of virtual method invocation in one case is balanced by the overhead of the switch statement in the other. Value-specific class bodies result in the generation of additional class files, each of which has overhead in terms of storage space and loading time.

Restrictions on enum types

Java places a few restrictions on the code that can appear in an enumerated type. You won't encounter these restrictions that often in practice, but you should still be aware of them.

When you define an enumerated type, the compiler does a lot of work behind the scenes: it creates a class that extends java.lang.Enum and it generates the values()

and valueOf() methods as well as the static fields that hold the enumerated values. If you include a class body for the type, you should not include members whose names conflict with the automatically generated members or with the final methods inherited from Enum.

enum types may not be declared final. Enumerated types are effectively final, and the compiler does not allow you to extend an enum. The class file generated for an enum is not technically declared final if the enum contains value-specific class bodies, however.

Types in Java may not be both final and abstract. Since enumerated types are effectively final, they may not be declared abstract. If the type-specific class body of an enum declaration contains an abstract method, the compiler requires that each enum value have a value-specific class body that includes an implementation of that abstract method. Considered as a self-contained whole, the enumerated type defined this way is not abstract.

The constructor, instance field initializers, and instance initializer blocks of an enumerated type are subject to a sweeping but obscure restriction: they may not use the static fields of the type (including the enumerated values themselves). The reason for this is that static initialization of enumerated types (and of all types) proceeds from top to bottom. The enumerated values are static fields that appear at the top of the type and are initialized first. Since they are self-typed fields, they invoke the constructor and any other instance initializer code of the type. This means that the instance initialization code is invoked before the static initialization of the class is complete. Since the static fields have not been initialized yet, the compiler does not allow them to be used. The only exception is static fields whose values are compile-time constant expressions (such as integers and strings) that the compiler resolves.

If you define a constructor for an enumerated type, it may not use the super() keyword to invoke the superclass constructor. This is because the compiler automatically inserts hidden name and ordinal arguments into any constructor you define. If you define more than one constructor for the type, it is okay to use this() to invoke one constructor from the other. Remember that the class bodies of individual enumerated values (if you define any) are anonymous, which means that they cannot have any constructors at all.

The Typesafe Enum Pattern

For a deeper understanding of how the enum keyword works, or to be able to simulate enumerated types prior to Java 5.0, it is useful to understand the *Typesafe Enum Pattern*. This pattern is described definitively by Joshua Bloch* in his book *Effective Java Programming Language Guide* (Addison Wesley); we do not cover all the nuances here.

If you want to use the enumerated type Prefix (from earlier in the chapter) prior to Java 5.0, you could approximate it with a class like the following one. Note,

* Josh was cochair of the the JSR 201 committee that developed many of the new language features of Java 5.0. He is the creator of and the driving force behind enumerated types.

however, that instances of this class won't work with the switch statement or with the EnumSet and EnumMap classes. Also, the code shown here does not include the values() or valueOf( ) methods that the compiler generates automatically for true enum types. A class like this does not have special serialization support like an enum type does, so if you make it Serializable, you must provide a readResolve( ) method to prevent deserialization from creating multiple instances of the enumerated values.

```
public final class Prefix {
    // These are the self-typed constants
    public static final Prefix MILLI = new Prefix("m",    .001);
    public static final Prefix CENTI = new Prefix("c",    .01);
    public static final Prefix DECI  = new Prefix("d",    .1);
    public static final Prefix DECA  = new Prefix("D",   10.0);
    public static final Prefix HECTA = new Prefix("h",  100.0);
    public static final Prefix KILO  = new Prefix("k", 1000.0);

    // Keep the fields private so the instances are immutable
    private String name;
    private double multiplier;

    // The constructor is private so no instances can be created except
    // for the ones above.
    private Prefix(String name, double multiplier) {
        this.name = name;
        this.multiplier = multiplier;
    }

    // These accessor methods are public
    public String toString() { return name; }
    public double getMultiplier() { return multiplier; }
}
```

Annotations

Annotations provide a way to associate arbitrary information or *metadata* with program elements. Syntactically, annotations are used like modifiers and can be applied to the declarations of packages, types, constructors, methods, fields, parameters, and local variables. The information stored in an annotation takes the form of *name=value* pairs, whose type is specified by the *annotation type*. The annotation type is a kind of interface that also serves to provide access to the annotation through the Java Reflection API.

Annotations can be used to associate any kind of information you want with a program element. The only fundamental rule is that an annotation cannot affect the way the program runs: the code must run identically even if you add or remove annotations. Another way to say this is that the Java interpreter ignores annotations (although it does make "runtime-visible" annotations available for reflective access through the Java Reflection API). Since the Java VM ignores annotations, an annotation type is not useful unless accompanied by a tool that can do something with the information stored in annotations of that type. In this chapter we'll cover standard annotation and meta-annotation types like Override and Target. The tool that accompanies these types is the Java compiler, which must process them in certain ways (as we'll describe later in this section).

It is easy to imagine any number of other uses for annotations.* A local variable might be annotated with a type named NonNull, as an assertion that the variable would never have a null value. An associated (hypothetical) code-analysis tool could then parse the code and attempt to verify the assertion. The JDK includes a tool named *apt* (for Annotation Processing Tool) that provides a framework for annotation processing tools: it scans source code for annotations and invokes specially written annotation processor classes that you provide. See Chapter 8 for more on *apt*. Annotations will probably find their widest use in enterprise programming where they may replace tools such as *XDoclet*, which processes metadata embedded in ad-hoc javadoc comments.

This section begins with an introduction to annotation-related terminology. We then cover the standard annotation types introduced in Java 5.0, annotations supported by *javac* that you can use in your programs right away. Next, we describe the syntax for writing arbitrary annotations and briefly cover the use of the Java Reflection API for querying annotations at runtime. At this point, we move on to more esoteric material on defining new annotation types, a task that few programmers will ever need to do. This final part of the chapter also discusses meta-annotations.

Annotation Concepts and Terminology

The key concept to understand about annotations is that an annotation simply associates information or metadata with a program element. Annotations *never affect the way a Java program runs*, but they may affect things like compiler warnings or the behavior of auxiliary tools such as documentation generators, stub generators, and so forth.

The following terms are used frequently when discussing annotations. Of particular importance is the distinction between *annotation* and *annotation type*.

annotation
: An *annotation* associates arbitrary information or metadata with a Java program element. Annotations use new syntax introduced in Java 5.0 and behave like modifiers such as public or final. Each annotation has a name and zero or more members. Each member has a name and a value, and it is these *name=value* pairs that carry the annotation's information.

annotation type
: The name of an annotation as well as the names, types, and default values of its members are defined by the *annotation type*. An annotation type is essentially a Java interface with some restrictions on its members and some new syntax used in its declaration. When you query an annotation using the Java Reflection API, the returned value is an object that implements the annota-

* We won't have to imagine these uses for long. At the time of this writing, JSR 250 is making its way through the Java Community Process to define a standard set of common annotations for J2SE and J2EE.

tion type interface and allows individual annotation members to be queried. Java 5.0 includes three standard annotation types in the `java.lang` package. We'll see these annotations in "Using Standard Annotations" later in this chapter.

annotation member
: The *members* of an annotation are declared in an annotation type as no-argument methods. The method name and return type define the name and type of the member. A special `default` syntax allows the declaration of a default value for any annotation member. An annotation appearing on a program element includes *name=value* pairs that define values for all annotation members that do not have default values and may also include values that override the defaults of other members.

marker annotation
: An annotation type that defines no members is called a *marker annotation*. An annotation of this type carries information simply by its presence or absence.

meta-annotation
: A *meta-annotation* is an annotation applied to the declaration of an annotation type. Java 5.0 includes several standard meta-annotation types in the `java.lang.annotation` package. They are used to specify things like which program elements the annotation can be applied to.

target
: The *target* of an annotation is the program element that is annotated. Annotations can be applied to packages, types (classes, interfaces, enumerated types, and even annotation types), type members (methods, constructors, fields, and enumerated values), method parameters, and local variables (including loop variables and `catch` parameters). The declaration of an annotation type may include a *meta-annotation* that restricts the allowable targets for that type of annotation.

retention
: The *retention* of an annotation specifies how long the information contained in the annotation is retained. Some annotations are discarded by the compiler and appear only in source code. Others are compiled into the class file. Of those that are compiled into the class file, some are ignored by the virtual machine, and others are read by the virtual machine when the class that contains them is loaded. The declaration of an annotation type can use a *meta-annotation* to specify the retention for annotations of that type. Annotations that are loaded by the VM are *runtime-visible* and can be queried by the reflective APIs of `java.lang.reflect`.

metadata
: When discussing annotations, the term *metadata* commonly refers to the information carried by an annotation or to the annotation itself. Because this term is used in many different ways in computer programming literature, I have avoided using it in this chapter.

Using Standard Annotations

Java 5.0 defines three standard annotation types in the `java.lang` package. The following sections describe these annotation types and explain how to use them to annotate your code.

Override

`java.lang.Override` is a marker annotation type that can be used to annotate methods but no other program element. An annotation of this type serves as an assertion that the annotated method overrides a method of a superclass. If you use this annotation on a method that does not override a superclass method, the compiler issues a compilation error to alert you to this fact.

This annotation is intended to address a common category of programming errors that result when you attempt to override a superclass method but get the method name or signature wrong. In this case, you may have overloaded the method name but not actually overridden the method, and your code never gets invoked.

To use this annotation type, simply include `@Override` in the modifiers of the desired method. By convention, `@Override` comes before other modifiers. Also by convention, there is no space between the `@` character and the name `Override`, even though it is technically allowed. Note that because the `java.lang` package is always automatically imported, you never need to include the package name to use this annotation type. Here is an example in which the `@Override` annotation is used on a method that fails to correctly override the `toString()` method of its superclass.

```
@Override
public String toSting() {   // Oops.  Note the misspelling here!
    // Simply put square brackets around our superclass's output
    return "[" + super.toString() + "]";
}
```

Without the annotation, the typo might go unnoticed and we'd have a puzzling bug: why isn't the `toString()` method working correctly? But with the annotation, the compiler gives us the answer: the `toString()` method does not work as expected because it is not actually overridden.

Note that the `@Override` annotation applies only to methods that are intended to override a superclass method and not to methods that are intended to implement a method defined in an interface. The compiler already produces an error if you fail to correctly implement an interface method.

Deprecated

`java.lang.Deprecated` is a marker annotation that is similar to the `@deprecated` javadoc tag. (See Chapter 7 for details on writing Java documentation comments.) If you annotate a type or type member with `@Deprecated`, it tells the compiler that use of the annotated element is discouraged. If you use (or extend or override) a deprecated type or member from code that is not itself declared `@Deprecated`, the compiler issues a warning.

Note that the @Deprecated annotation type does not deprecate the @deprecated javadoc tag. The @Deprecated annotation is intended for the Java compiler. The javadoc tag, on the other hand, is intended for the *javadoc* tool and serves as documentation: it may include a description of why the program element has been deprecated and what it has been superseded by or replaced with.

In Java 5.0, the compiler continues to look for @deprecated javadoc tags and uses them to generate warnings as it always has. This behavior may be phased out, however, and you should begin to use the @Deprecated annotation in addition to the @deprecated javadoc tag.

Here is an example that uses both the annotation and the javadoc tag:

```
/**
 * The Sony Betamax video cassette format.
 * @deprecated No one has players for this format any more.  Use VHS instead.
 */
@Deprecated public class Betamax { ... }
```

SuppressWarnings

The @SuppressWarnings annotation is used to selectively turn off compiler warnings for classes, methods, or field and variable initializers.* In Java 5.0, Sun's *javac* compiler has a powerful -Xlint option that causes it to issue warnings about "lint" in your program—code that is legal but is likely to represent a programming error. These warnings include the "unchecked warning" that appears when you use a generic collection class without specifying a value for its type parameters, for example, or the warning that appears if a case in a switch statement does not end with a break, return, or throw and allows control to "fall through" to the next case.

Typically, when you see one of these lint warnings from the compiler, you should investigate the code that caused it. If it truly represents an error, you then correct it. If it simply represents sloppy programming, you may be able to rewrite your code so that the warning is no longer necessary. For example, if the warning tells you that you have not covered all possible cases in a switch statement on an enumerated type, you can avoid the warning by adding a defensive default case to the switch statement, even if you are sure that it will never be invoked.

On the other hand, sometimes there is nothing you can do to avoid the error. For example, if you use a generic collection class in code that must interact with nongeneric legacy code, you cannot avoid an unchecked warning. This is where @SuppressWarnings comes in: add this annotation to the nearest relevant set of modifiers (typically on method modifiers) to tell the compiler that you're aware of the issue and that it should stop pestering you about it.

Unlike Override and Deprecated, SuppressWarnings is not a marker annotation. It has a single member named value whose type is String[ ]. The value of this member is the names of the warnings to be suppressed. The SuppressWarnings annotation does not define what warning names are allowed: this is an issue for

* The *javac* compiler did not yet support the @SuppressWarnings annotation when this chapter was written. Full support is expected in Java 5.1.

compiler implementors. For the *javac* compiler, the warning names accepted by the `-Xlint` option are also legal for the `@SuppressWarnings` annotation. It is legal to specify any warning names you want: compilers ignore (but may warn about) warning names they do not recognize.

So, to suppress warnings named `unchecked` and `fallthrough`, you could use an annotation that looks like the following. Annotation syntax follows the name of the annotation type with a parenthesized, comma-separated list of *`name=value`* pairs. In this case, the `SuppressWarnings` annotation type defines only a single member, so there is only a single pair within parentheses. Since the member value is an array, curly braces are used to delimit array elements:

```
@SuppressWarnings(value={"unchecked","fallthrough"})
public void lintTrap() { /* sloppy method body omitted */ }
```

We can abbreviate this annotation somewhat. When an annotation has a single member and that member is named "value", you are allowed (and encouraged) to omit the "value=" in the annotation. So the annotation above should be rewritten as:

```
@SuppressWarnings({"unchecked","fallthrough"})
```

Hopefully you will not often have more than one unresolvable lint warning in any particular method and will need to suppress only a single named warning. In this case, another annotation abbreviation is possible. When writing an array value that contains only a single member, you are allowed to omit the curly braces. In this case we might have an annotation like this:

```
@SuppressWarnings("unchecked")
```

Annotation Syntax

In the descriptions of the standard annotation types, we've seen the syntax for writing marker annotations and the syntax for writing single-member annotations, including the shortcut allowed when the single member is named "value" and the shortcut allowed when an array-typed member has only a single array element. This section describes the complete syntax for writing annotations.

An annotation consists of the `@` character followed by the name of the annotation type (which may include a package name) followed by a parenthesized, comma-separated list of *`name=value`* pairs for each of the members defined by the annotation type. Members may appear in any order and may be omitted if the annotation type defines a default value for that member. Each *`value`* must be a literal or compile-time constant, a nested annotation, or an array.

Near the end of this chapter, we define an annotation type named `Reviews` that has a single member that is an array of `@Review` annotations. The `Review` annotation type has three members: "reviewer" is a `String`, "comment" is an optional `String` with a default value, and "grade" is a value of the nested enumerated type `Review.Grade`. Assuming that the `Reviews` and `Review` types are properly imported, an annotation using these types might look like this (note the use of nested annotations, enumerated types, and arrays in this annotation):

```
@Reviews({  // Single-value annotation, so "value=" is omitted here
   @Review(grade=Review.Grade.EXCELLENT,
```

```
                reviewer="df"),
        @Review(grade=Review.Grade.UNSATISFACTORY,
                reviewer="eg",
                comment="This method needs an @Override annotation")
    })
```

Another important rule of annotation syntax is that no program element may have more than one instance of the same annotation. It is not legal, for example, to simply place multiple `@Review` annotations on a class. This is why the `@Reviews` annotation is defined to allow an array of `@Review` annotations.

Annotation member types and values

The values of annotation members must be non-`null` compile-time constant expressions that are assignment-compatible with the declared type of the member. Allowed member types are the primitive types, `String`, `Class`, enumerated types, annotation types, and arrays of any of the above types (but not an array of arrays). For example, the expressions `2*Math.PI` and `"hello"+"world"` are legal values for members of type `double` and `String`, respectively.

Near the end of the chapter, we define an annotation type named `UncheckedExceptions` whose sole member is an array of classes that extend `RuntimeException`. An annotation of this type might look like this:

```
@UncheckedExceptions({
    IllegalArgumentException.class, StringIndexOutOfBoundsException.class
})
```

Annotation targets

Annotations are most commonly placed on type definitions (such as classes) and their members (such as methods and fields). Annotations may also appear on packages, parameters, and local variables. This section provides more information about these less common annotation targets.

A package annotation appears before the package declaration in a file named *package-info.java*. This file should not contain any type declarations ("package-info" is not a legal Java identifier, so it cannot contain any public type definitions). Instead, it should contain an optional javadoc comment, zero or more annotations, and a package declaration. For example:

```
/**
 * This package holds my custom annotation types.
 */
@com.davidflanagan.annotations.Author("David Flanagan")
package com.davidflanagan.annotations;
```

When the *package-info.java* file is compiled, it produces a class file named *package-info.class* that contains a synthetic interface declaration. This interface has no members, and its name, `package-info`, is not a legal Java identifier, so it cannot be used in Java source code. It exists simply as a placeholder for package annotations with class or runtime retention.

Note that package annotations appear outside the scope of any package or import declaration. This means that package annotations should always include the package name of the annotation type (unless the package is java.lang).

Annotations on method parameters, catch clause parameters, and local variables simply appear as part of the modifier list for those program elements. The Java class file format has no provision for storing annotations on local variables or catch clause parameters, so those annotations always have source retention. Method parameter annotations can be retained in the class file, however, and may have class or runtime retention.

Finally, note that the syntax for enumerated type definitions does not allow any modifiers to be specified for enumerated values. It does, however, allow annotations on any of the values.

Annotations and defaults

Annotations must include a value for every member that does not have a default value defined by the annotation type. Annotations may, of course, include values for other members as well.

There is one important detail to understand about how default values are handled. Default values are stored in the class file of the annotation type and are not compiled into annotations themselves. If you modify an annotation type so that the default value of one of its members changes, that change affects all annotations of that type that do not specify an explicit value for that member. Already-compiled annotations are affected, even if they are never recompiled after the change to the type.

Annotations and Reflection

The Reflection API of java.lang.reflect has been extended in Java 5.0 to support reading of runtime-visible annotations. (Remember that an annotation is only visible at runtime if its annotation type is specified to have runtime retention, that is, if the annotation is both stored in the class file and read by the Java VM when the class file is loaded.) This section briefly covers the new reflective capabilities. For full details, look up the interface java.lang.reflect.AnnotatedElement in the reference section. AnnotatedElement represents a program element that can be queried for annotations. It is implemented by java.lang.Package, java.lang.Class, and indirectly implemented by the Method, Constructor, and Field classes of java.lang.reflect. Annotations on method parameters can be queried with the getParameterAnnotations() method of the Method or Constructor class.

The following code uses the isAnnotationPresent() method of AnnotatedElement to determine whether a method is unstable by checking for an @Unstable annotation. It assumes that the Unstable annotation type, which we'll define later in the chapter, has runtime retention. Note that this code uses class literals to specify both the class to be checked and the annotation to check for:

```
import java.lang.reflect.*;

Class c = WhizzBangClass.class;
```

```
Method m = c.getMethod("whizzy", int.class, int.class);
boolean unstable = m.isAnnotationPresent(Unstable.class);
```

`isAnnotationPresent()` is useful for marker annotations. When working with annotations that have members, though, we typically want to know the value of those members. For this, we use the `getAnnotation()` method. And here we see the beauty of the Java annotation system: if the specified annotation exists, the object returned by this method implements the annotation type interface, and you can query the value of any member simply by invoking the annotation type method that defines that member. Consider the `@Reviews` annotation that appeared earlier in the chapter, for example. If the annotation type was declared with runtime retention, you could query it as follows:

```
AnnotatedElement target = WhizzBangClass.class; // the type to query
// Ask for the @Reviews annotation as an object that implements Reviews
Reviews annotation = target.getAnnotation(Reviews.class);
// Reviews has a single member named "value" that is an array of reviews
Review[] reviews = annotation.value();
// Loop through the reviews
for(Review r : reviews) {
    Review.Grade grade = r.grade();
    String reviewer = r.reviewer();
    String comment = r.comment();
    System.out.printf("%s assigned a grade of %s and comment '%s'%n",
                      reviewer, grade, comment);
}
```

Note that these reflective methods correctly resolve default annotation values for you. If an annotation does not include a value for a member with a default value, the default value is looked up within the annotation type itself.

Defining Annotation Types

An annotation type is an interface, but it is not a normal one. An annotation type differs from a normal interface in the following ways:

- An annotation type is defined with the keyword `@interface` rather than with `interface`. An `@interface` declaration implicitly extends the interface `java.lang.annotation.Annotation` and may not have an explicit `extends` clause of its own.
- The methods of an annotation type must be declared with no arguments and may not throw exceptions. These methods define annotation members: the method name becomes the member name, and the method return type becomes the member type.
- The return value of annotation methods may be a primitive type, a `String`, a `Class`, an enumerated type, another annotation type, or a single-dimensional array of one of those types.
- Any method of an annotation type may be followed by the keyword `default` and a value compatible with the return type of the method. This strange new syntax specifies the default value of the annotation member that corresponds to the method. The syntax for default values is the same as the syntax used to

specify member values when writing an annotation. null is never a legal default value.

- Annotation types and their methods may not have type parameters—annotation types and members cannot be made generic. The only valid use of generics in annotation types is for methods whose return type is Class. These methods may use a bounded wildcard to specify a constraint on the returned class.

In other ways, annotation types declared with @interface are just like regular interfaces. They may include constant definitions and static member types such as enumerated type definitions. Annotation types may also be implemented or extended just as normal interfaces are. (The classes and interfaces that result from doing this are not themselves annotation types, however: annotation types can be created only with an @interface declaration.)

We now define the annotation types used in our examples. These examples illustrate the syntax of annotation type declarations and demonstrate many of the differences between @interface and interface. We start with the simple marker annotation type Unstable. Because we used this type earlier in the chapter in a reflection example, its definition includes a meta-annotation that gives it runtime retention and makes it accessible to the reflection API. Meta-annotations are covered below.

```
package com.davidflanagan.annotations;
import java.lang.annotation.*;

/**
 * Specifies that the annotated element is unstable and its API is
 * subject to change.
 */
@Retention(RetentionPolicy.RUNTIME)
public @interface Unstable {}
```

The next annotation type defines a single member. By naming the member value, we enable a syntactic shortcut for anyone using the annotation:

```
/**
 * Specifies the author of a program element.
 */
public @interface Author {
    /** Return the name of the author */
    String value();
}
```

The next example is more complex. The Reviews annotation type has a single member, but the type of the member is complex: it is an array of Review annotations. The Review annotation type has three members, one of which has an enumerated type defined as a member of the Review type itself, and another of which has a default value. Because the Reviews annotation type is used in a reflection example, we've given it runtime retention with a meta-annotation:

```
import java.lang.annotation.*;

/**
```

```
 * An annotation of this type specifies the results of one or more
 * code reviews for the annotated element
 */
@Retention(RetentionPolicy.RUNTIME)
public @interface Reviews {
    Review[] value();
}

/**
 * An annotation of this type represents a single code review of the
 * annotated element.  Every review must specify the name of the reviewer
 * and the grade assigned to the code.  Optionally, reviews may also include
 * a comment string.
 */
public @interface Review {
    // Nested enumerated type
    public static enum Grade { EXCELLENT, SATISFACTORY, UNSATISFACTORY };

    // These methods define the annotation members
    Grade grade();                // member named "grade" with type Grade
    String reviewer();
    String comment() default "";  // Note default value here.
}
```

Finally, suppose we wanted to annotate methods to list the unchecked exceptions (but not errors) that they might throw. Our annotation type would have a single member of array type. Each element of the array would be the `Class` of an exception. In order to enforce the requirement that only unchecked exceptions are used, we use a bounded wildcard on `Class`:

```
public @interface UncheckedExceptions {
    Class<? extends RuntimeException>[] value();
}
```

Meta-Annotations

Annotation types can themselves be annotated. Java 5.0 defines four standard *meta-annotation* types that provide information about the use and meaning of other annotation types. These types and their supporting classes are in the `java.lang.annotation` package, and you can find complete details in the quick-reference section of the book.

Target

The `Target` meta-annotation type specifies the "targets" for an annotation type. That is, it specifies which program elements may have annotations of that type. If an annotation type does not have a `Target` meta-annotation, it can be used with any of the program elements described earlier. Some annotation types, however, make sense only when applied to certain program elements. `Override` is one example: it is only meaningful when applied to a method. An `@Target` meta-annotation applied to the declaration of the `Override` type makes this explicit and allows the compiler to reject an `@Override` when it appears in an inappropriate context.

The Target meta-annotation type has a single member named value. The type of this member is java.lang.annotation.ElementType[]. ElementType is an enumerated type whose enumerated values represent program elements that can be annotated.

Retention

We discussed annotation *retention* earlier in the chapter. It specifies whether an annotation is discarded by the compiler or retained in the class file, and, if it is retained in the class file, whether it is read by the VM when the class file is loaded. By default, annotations are stored in the class file but not available for runtime reflective access. The three possible retention values (source, class, and runtime) are described by the enumerated type java.lang.annotation.RetentionPolicy.

The Retention meta-annotation type has a single member named value whose type is RetentionPolicy.

Documented

Documented is a meta-annotation type used to specify that annotations of some other type should be considered part of the public API of the annotated program element and should therefore be documented by tools like *javadoc*. Documented is a marker annotation: it has no members.

Inherited

The @Inherited meta-annotation is a marker annotation that specifies that the annotated type is an inherited one. That is, if an annotation type @Inherited is used to annotate a class, the annotation applies to subclasses of that class as well.

Note that @Inherited annotation types are inherited only by subclasses of an annotated class. Classes do not inherit annotations from interfaces they implement, and methods do not inherit annotations from methods they override.

The Reflection API enforces the inheritance if the @Inherited annotation type is also annotated @Retention(RetentionPolicy.RUNTIME). If you use java.lang.reflect to query a class for an annotation of an @Inherited type, the reflection code checks the specified class and each of its ancestors until an annotation of the specified type is found or the top of the class hierarchy is reached.

5
The Java Platform

Chapters 2, 3, and 4 documented the Java programming language. This chapter switches gears and covers the Java platform—a vast collection of predefined classes available to every Java program, regardless of the underlying host system on which it is running. The classes of the Java platform are collected into related groups, known as *packages*. This chapter begins with an overview of the packages of the Java platform that are documented in this book. It then moves on to demonstrate, in the form of short examples, the most useful classes in these packages. Most of the examples are code snippets only, not full programs you can compile and run. For fully fleshed-out, real-world examples, see *Java Examples in a Nutshell* (O'Reilly). That book expands greatly on this chapter and is intended as a companion to this book.

Java Platform Overview

Table 5-1 summarizes the key packages of the Java platform that are covered in this book.

Table 5-1. Key packages of the Java platform

Package	Description
`java.io`	Classes and interfaces for input and output. Although some of the classes in this package are for working directly with files, most are for working with streams of bytes or characters.
`java.lang`	The core classes of the language, such as `String`, `Math`, `System`, `Thread`, and `Exception`.
`java.lang.annotation`	Annotation types and other supporting types for the Java 5.0 annotation feature. (See Chapter 4.)
`java.lang.instrument`	Support classes for Java virtual machine instrumentation agents, which are allowed to modify the byte code of the program the JVM is running. New in Java 5.0.
`java.lang.management`	A framework for monitoring and managing a running Java virtual machine. New in Java 5.0.

Table 5-1. Key packages of the Java platform (continued)

Package	Description
`java.lang.ref`	Classes that define weak references to objects. A weak reference is one that does not prevent the referent object from being garbage-collected.
`java.lang.reflect`	Classes and interfaces that allow Java programs to reflect on themselves by examining the constructors, methods, and fields of classes.
`java.math`	A small package that contains classes for arbitrary-precision integer and floating-point arithmetic.
`java.net`	Classes and interfaces for networking with other systems.
`java.nio`	Buffer classes for the New I/O API. Added in Java 1.4.
`java.nio.channels`	Channel and selector interfaces and classes for high-performance, nonblocking I/O.
`java.nio.charset`	Character set encoders and decoders for converting Unicode strings to and from bytes.
`java.security`	Classes and interfaces for access control and authentication. This package and its subpackages support cryptographic message digests and digital signatures.
`java.text`	Classes and interfaces for working with text in internationalized applications.
`java.util`	Various utility classes, including the powerful collections framework for working with collections of objects.
`java.util.concurrent`	Thread pools and other utility classes for concurrent programming. Subpackages support atomic variables and locks. New in Java 5.0.
`java.util.jar`	Classes for reading and writing JAR files.
`java.util.logging`	A flexible logging facility. Added in Java 1.4.
`java.util.prefs`	An API to read and write user and system preferences. Added in Java 1.4.
`java.util.regex`	Text pattern matching using regular expressions. Added in Java 1.4.
`java.util.zip`	Classes for reading and writing ZIP files.
`javax.crypto`	Classes and interfaces for encryption and decryption of data.
`javax.net`	Defines factory classes for creating sockets and server sockets. Enables the creation of socket types other than the default.
`javax.net.ssl`	Classes for encrypted network communication using the Secure Sockets Layer (SSL).
`javax.security.auth`	The top-level package for the JAAS API for authentication and authorization. Various subpackages hold most of the actual classes. Added in Java 1.4.
`javax.xml.parsers`	A high-level API for parsing XML documents using pluggable DOM and SAX parsers.
`javax.xml.transform`	A high-level API for transforming XML documents using a pluggable XSLT transformation engine and for converting XML documents between streams, DOM trees, and SAX events. Subpackages provide support for DOM, SAX and stream transformations. Added in Java 1.4.

Table 5-1 does not list all the packages in the Java platform, only the most important of those documented in this book. Java also defines numerous packages for graphics and graphical user interface programming and for distributed, or enterprise, computing. The graphics and GUI packages are `java.awt` and `javax.swing` and their many subpackages. These packages are documented in *Java Foundation Classes in a Nutshell* and *Java Swing*, both from O'Reilly. The enterprise packages of Java include `java.rmi`, `java.sql`, `javax.jndi`, `org.omg.CORBA`, `org.omg.CosNaming`, and all of their subpackages. These packages, as well as several standard extensions to the Java platform, are documented in *Java Enterprise in a Nutshell* (O'Reilly).

Text

Most programs manipulate text in one form or another, and the Java platform defines a number of important classes and interfaces for representing, formatting, and scanning text. The sections that follow provide an overview.

The String Class

Strings of text are a fundamental and commonly used data type. In Java, however, strings are not a primitive type, like `char`, `int`, and `float`. Instead, strings are represented by the `java.lang.String` class, which defines many useful methods for manipulating strings. `String` objects are *immutable*: once a `String` object has been created, there is no way to modify the string of text it represents. Thus, each method that operates on a string typically returns a new `String` object that holds the modified string.

This code shows some of the basic operations you can perform on strings:

```
// Creating strings
String s = "Now";                    // String objects have a special literal syntax
String t = s + " is the time.";  // Concatenate strings with + operator
String t1 = s + " " + 23.4;          // + converts other values to strings
t1 = String.valueOf('c');            // Get string corresponding to char value
t1 = String.valueOf(42);             // Get string version of integer or any value
t1 = object.toString();              // Convert objects to strings with toString()

// String length
int len = t.length();                // Number of characters in the string: 16

// Substrings of a string
String sub = t.substring(4);         // Returns char 4 to end: "is the time."
sub = t.substring(4, 6);             // Returns chars 4 and 5: "is"
sub = t.substring(0, 3);             // Returns chars 0 through 2: "Now"
sub = t.substring(x, y);             // Returns chars between pos x and y-1
int numchars = sub.length();         // Length of substring is always (y-x)

// Extracting characters from a string
char c = t.charAt(2);                // Get the 3rd character of t: w
char[] ca = t.toCharArray();         // Convert string to an array of characters
t.getChars(0, 3, ca, 1);             // Put 1st 3 chars of t into ca[1]-ca[3]

// Case conversion
String caps = t.toUpperCase();    // Convert to uppercase
String lower = t.toLowerCase(); // Convert to lowercase

// Comparing strings
boolean b1 = t.equals("hello");           // Returns false: strings not equal
boolean b2 = t.equalsIgnoreCase(caps);    // Case-insensitive compare: true
boolean b3 = t.startsWith("Now");         // Returns true
boolean b4 = t.endsWith("time.");         // Returns true
int r1 = s.compareTo("Pow");              // Returns < 0: s comes before "Pow"
int r2 = s.compareTo("Now");              // Returns 0: strings are equal
int r3 = s.compareTo("Mow");              // Returns > 0: s comes after "Mow"
r1 = s.compareToIgnoreCase("pow");        // Returns < 0 (Java 1.2 and later)
```

The Java Platform

```
// Searching for characters and substrings
int pos = t.indexOf('i');           // Position of first 'i': 4
pos = t.indexOf('i', pos+1);        // Position of the next 'i': 12
pos = t.indexOf('i', pos+1);        // No more 'i's in string, returns -1
pos = t.lastIndexOf('i');           // Position of last 'i' in string: 12
pos = t.lastIndexOf('i', pos-1);    // Search backwards for 'i' from char 11

pos = t.indexOf("is");              // Search for substring: returns 4
pos = t.indexOf("is", pos+1);       // Only appears once: returns -1
pos = t.lastIndexOf("the ");        // Search backwards for a string
String noun = t.substring(pos+4);   // Extract word following "the"

// Replace all instances of one character with another character
String exclaim = t.replace('.', '!');  // Works only with chars, not substrings

// Strip blank space off the beginning and end of a string
String noextraspaces = t.trim();

// Obtain unique instances of strings with intern()
String s1 = s.intern();           // Returns s1 equal to s
String s2 = "Now";                // String literals are automatically interned
boolean equals = (s1 == s2);      // Now can test for equality with ==
```

The Character Class

As you know, individual characters are represented in Java by the primitive `char` type. The Java platform also defines a `Character` class, which contains useful class methods for checking the type of a character and for converting the case of a character. For example:

```
char[] text;  // An array of characters, initialized somewhere else
int p = 0;    // Our current position in the array of characters
// Skip leading whitespace
while((p < text.length) && Character.isWhitespace(text[p])) p++;
// Capitalize the first word of text
while((p < text.length) && Character.isLetter(text[p])) {
  text[p] = Character.toUpperCase(text[p]);
  p++;
}
```

The StringBuffer Class

Since `String` objects are immutable, you cannot manipulate the characters of an instantiated `String`. If you need to do this, use a `java.lang.StringBuffer` or `java.lang.StringBuilder` instead. These two classes are identical except that `StringBuffer` has synchronized methods. `StringBuilder` was introduced in Java 5.0 and you should use it in preference to `StringBuffer` unless it might actually be manipulated by multiple threads. The following code demonstrates the `StringBuffer` API but could be easily changed to use `StringBuilder`:

```
// Create a string buffer from a string
StringBuffer b = new StringBuffer("Mow");

// Get and set individual characters of the StringBuffer
char c = b.charAt(0);         // Returns 'M': just like String.charAt()
```

```
b.setCharAt(0, 'N');          // b holds "Now": can't do that with a String!

// Append to a StringBuffer
b.append(' ');                // Append a character
b.append("is the time.");     // Append a string
b.append(23);                 // Append an integer or any other value

// Insert Strings or other values into a StringBuffer
b.insert(6, "n't");           // b now holds: "Now isn't the time.23"

// Replace a range of characters with a string (Java 1.2 and later)
b.replace(4, 9, "is");        // Back to "Now is the time.23"

// Delete characters
b.delete(16, 18);             // Delete a range: "Now is the time"
b.deleteCharAt(2);            // Delete 2nd character: "No is the time"
b.setLength(5);               // Truncate by setting the length: "No is"

// Other useful operations
b.reverse();                  // Reverse characters: "si oN"
String s = b.toString();      // Convert back to an immutable string
s = b.substring(1,2);         // Or take a substring: "i"
b.setLength(0);               // Erase buffer; now it is ready for reuse
```

The CharSequence Interface

As of Java 1.4, both the String and the StringBuffer classes implement the java.lang.CharSequence interface, which is a standard interface for querying the length of and extracting characters and subsequences from a readable sequence of characters. This interface is also implemented by the java.nio.CharBuffer interface, which is part of the New I/O API that was introduced in Java 1.4. CharSequence provides a way to perform simple operations on strings of characters regardless of the underlying implementation of those strings. For example:

```
/**
 * Return a prefix of the specified CharSequence that starts at the first
 * character of the sequence and extends up to (and includes) the first
 * occurrence of the character c in the sequence. Returns null if c is
 * not found. s may be a String, StringBuffer, or java.nio.CharBuffer.
 */
public static CharSequence prefix(CharSequence s, char c) {
  int numChars = s.length();            // How long is the sequence?
  for(int i = 0; i < numChars; i++) {   // Loop through characters in sequence
    if (s.charAt(i) == c)               // If we find c,
      return s.subSequence(0,i+1);      // then return the prefix subsequence
  }
  return null;                          // Otherwise, return null
}
```

The Appendable Interface

Appendable is a Java 5.0 interface that represents an object that can have a char or a CharSequence appended to it. Implementing classes include StringBuffer,

The Java Platform

StringBuilder, java.nio.CharBuffer, java.io.PrintStream, and java.io.Writer and all of its character output stream subclasses, including PrintWriter. Thus, the Appendable interface represents the common appendability of the text buffer classes and the text output stream classes. As we'll see below, a Formatter object can send its output to any Appendable object.

String Concatenation

The + operator concatenates two String objects or one String and one value of some other type, producing a new String object. Be aware that each time a string concatenation is performed and the result stored in a variable or passed to a method, a new String object has been created. In some circumstances, this can be inefficient and can result in poor performance. It is especially important to be careful when doing string concatenation within a loop. The following code is inefficient, for example:

```
// Inefficient: don't do this
public String join(List<String> words) {
    String sentence = "";
    // Each iteration creates a new String object and discards an old one.
    for(String word: words) sentence += word;
    return sentence;
}
```

When you find yourself writing code like this, switch to a StringBuffer or a StringBuilder and use the append() method:

```
// This is the right way to do it
public String join(List<String> words) {
    StringBuilder sentence = new StringBuilder();
    for(String word: words) sentence.append(word);
    return sentence.toString();
}
```

There is no need to be paranoid about string concatenation, however. Remember that string literals are concatenated by the compiler rather than the Java interpreter. Also, when a single expression contains multiple string concatenations, these are compiled efficiently using a StringBuilder (or StringBuffer prior to Java 5.0) and result in the creation of only a single new String object.

String Comparison

Since strings are objects rather than primitive values, they cannot, in general, be compared for equality with the == operator. == compares references and can determine if two expressions evaluate to a reference to the same string. It cannot determine if two distinct strings contain the same text. To do that, use the equals() method. In Java 5.0 you can compare the content of a string to any other CharSequence with the contentEquals() method.

Similarly, the < and > relational operators do not work with strings. To compare the order of strings, use the compareTo() method, which is defined by the Comparable<String> interface and is illustrated in the sample code above. To compare strings without taking the case of the letters into account, use compareToIgnoreCase().

Note that StringBuffer and StringBuilder do not implement Comparable and do not override the default versions of equals() and hashCode() that they inherit from Object. This means that it is not possible to compare the text held in two StringBuffer or StringBuilder objects for equality or for order.

One important, but little understood method of the String class is intern(). When passed a string s, it returns a string t that is guaranteed to have the same content as s. What's important, though, is that for any given string content, it always returns a reference to the same String object. That is, if s and t are two String objects such that s.equals(t), then:

```
s.intern() == t.intern()
```

This means that the intern() method provides a way of doing fast string comparisons using ==. Importantly, string literals are always implicitly interned by the Java VM, so if you plan to compare a string s against a number of string literals, you may want to intern s first and then do the comparison with = =.

The compareTo() and equals() methods of the String class allow you to compare strings. compareTo() bases its comparison on the character order defined by the Unicode encoding while equals() defines string equality as strict character-by-character equality. These are not always the right methods to use, however. In some languages, the character ordering imposed by the Unicode standard does not match the dictionary ordering used when alphabetizing strings. In Spanish, for example, the letters "ch" are considered a single letter that comes after "c" and before "d." When comparing human-readable strings in an internationalized application, you should use the java.text.Collator class instead:

```
import java.text.*;

// Compare two strings; results depend on where the program is run
// Return values of Collator.compare() have same meanings as String.compareTo()
Collator c = Collator.getInstance();       // Get Collator for current locale
int result = c.compare("chica", "coche"); // Use it to compare two strings
```

Supplementary Characters

Java 5.0 has adopted the Unicode 4.0 standard, which, for the first time, has defined codepoints that fall outside the 16-bit range of the char type. When working with these "supplementary characters" (which are primarily Han ideographs), you must use int values to represent the individual character. In String objects, or for any other type that represents text as a sequence of char values, these supplementary characters are represented as a series of two char values known as a *surrogate pair*.

Although readers of the English edition of this book are unlikely to ever encounter supplementary characters, you should be aware of them if you are working on programs that might be localized for use in China or another country that uses Han ideographs. To help you work with supplementary characters, the Character, String, StringBuffer, and StringBuilder classes have been extended with new methods that operate on int codepoints rather than char values. The following code illustrates some of these methods. You can find other, similar methods in the reference section and read about them in the online javadoc documentation.

```
int codepoint = 0x10001;  // This codepoint doesn't fit in a char
// Get the UTF-16 surrogate pair of chars for the codepoint
char[] surrogatePair = Character.toChars(codepoint);
// Convert the chars to a string.
String s = new String(surrogatePair);

// Print string length in characters and codepoints
System.out.println(s.length());
System.out.println(s.codePointCount(0, s.length()-1));

// Print encoding of first character, then encoding of first codepoint.
System.out.println(Integer.toHexString(s.charAt(0)));
System.out.println(Integer.toHexString(s.codePointAt(0)));

// Here's how to safely loop through a string that may contain
// supplementary characters
String tricky = s + "Testing" + s + "!";
int i = 0, n = tricky.length();
while(i < n) {
    // Get the codepoint at the current position
    int cp = tricky.codePointAt(i);
    if (cp < '\uffff') System.out.println((char) cp);
    else System.out.println("\\u" + Integer.toHexString(cp));

    // Increment the string index by one codepoint (1 or 2 chars).
    i = tricky.offsetByCodePoints(i, 1);
}
```

Formatting Text with printf() and format( )

A common task when working with text output is to combine values of various types into a single block of human-readable text. One way to accomplish this relies on the string-conversion power of Java's string concatenation operator. It results in code like this:

```
System.out.println(username + " logged in after " + numattempts +
                   "attempts. Last login at: " + lastLoginDate);
```

Java 5.0 introduces an alternative that is familiar to C programmers: a `printf( )` method. "printf" is short for "print formatted" and it combines the printing and formatting functions into one call. The `printf( )` method has been added to the `PrintWriter` and `PrintStream` output stream classes in Java 5.0. It is a varargs method that expects one or more arguments. The first argument is the "format string." It specifies the text to be printed and typically includes one or more "format specifiers," which are escape sequences beginning with character `%`. The remaining arguments to `printf( )` are values to be converted to strings and substituted into the format string in place of the format specifiers. The format specifiers constrain the types of the remaining arguments and specify exactly how they are converted to strings. The string concatenation shown above can be rewritten as follows in Java 5.0:

```
System.out.printf("%s logged in after %d attempts. Last login at: %tc%n",
                  username, numattempts, lastLoginDate);
```

The format specifier %s simply substitutes a string. %d expects the corresponding argument to be an integer and displays it as such. %tc expects a Date, Calendar, or number of milliseconds and converts that value to text representation of the full date and time. %n performs no conversion: it simply outputs the platform-specific line terminator, just as the println( ) method does.

The conversions performed by printf() are all properly localized. Times and dates are displayed with locale-appropriate punctuation, for example. And if you request that a number be displayed with a thousands separator, you'll get locale-specific punctuation there, too (a comma in England and a period in France, for example).

In addition to the basic printf( ) method, PrintWriter and PrintStream also define a synonymous method named format(): it takes exactly the same arguments and behaves in exactly the same way. The String class also has a format() method in Java 5.0. This static String.format() method behaves like PrintWriter.format( ) except that instead of printing the formatted string to a stream, it simply returns it:

```
// Format a string, converting a double value to text using two decimal
// places and a thousands separator.
double balance = getBalance();
String msg = String.format("Account balance: $%,.2f", balance);
```

The java.util.Formatter class is the general-purpose formatter class behind the printf() and format( ) utility methods. It can format text to any Appendable object or to a named file. The following code uses a Formatter object to write a file:

```
public static void writeFile(String filename, String[] lines)
    throws IOException
{
    Formatter out = new Formatter(filename);  // format to a named file
    for(int i = 0; i < lines.length; i++) {
        // Write a line of the file
        out.format("%d: %s%n", i, lines[i]);
        // Check for exceptions
        IOException e = out.ioException();
        if (e != null) throw e;
    }
    out.close();
}
```

When you concatenate an object to a string, the object is converted to a string by calling its toString() method. This is what the Formatter class does by default as well. Classes that want more precise control over their formatting can implement the java.util.Formattable interface in addition to implementing toString().

We'll see additional examples of formatting with printf( ) when we cover the APIs for working with numbers, dates, and times. See java.util.Formatter for a complete list of available format specifiers and options.

Logging

Simple terminal-based programs can send their output and error messages to the console with System.out.println() or System.out.print( ). Server programs that run unattended for long periods need a different solution for output: the hardware they run on may not have a display terminal attached, and, if it does, there is unlikely to be anyone looking at it. Programs like this need *logging* functionality in which output messages are sent to a file for later analysis or through a network socket for remote monitoring. Java 1.4 provides a logging API in the `java.util.logging` package.

Typically, the application developer uses a `Logger` object associated with the class or package of the application to generate log messages at any of seven severity levels (see `java.util.logging.Level`). These messages may report errors and warnings or provide informational messages about interesting events in the application's life cycle. They can include debugging information or even trace the execution of important methods within the program.

The system administrator or end user of the application is responsible for setting up a logging configuration file that specifies where log messages are directed (the console, a file, a network socket, or a combination of these), how they are formatted (as plain text or XML documents), and at what severity threshold they are logged (log messages with a severity below the specified threshold are discarded with very little overhead and should not significantly impact the performance of the application). The logging level severity threshold can be configured independently so that `Logger` objects associated with different classes or packages can be "tuned in" or "tuned out." Because of this end-user configurability, you should feel free to use logging output liberally in your program. In normal operation, most log messages will be discarded efficiently and automatically. During program development, or when diagnosing a problem in a deployed application, however, the log messages can prove very valuable.

For most applications, using the Logging API is quite simple. Obtain a named `Logger` object whenever necessary by calling the static `Logger.getLogger()` method, passing the class or package name of the application as the logger name. Then, use one of the many `Logger` instance methods to generate log messages. The easiest methods to use have names that correspond to severity levels, such as `severe()`, `warning()`, and `info()`. Here is some sample code:

```
import java.util.logging.*;

// Get a Logger object named after the current package
Logger logger = Logger.getLogger("com.davidflanagan.servers.pop");
logger.info("Starting server.");       // Log an informational message
ServerSocket ss;                       // Do some stuff
try { ss = new ServerSocket(110); }
catch(Exception e) {                   // Log exceptions
  logger.log(Level.SEVERE, "Can't bind port 110", e); // Complex log message
  logger.warning("Exiting");                          // Simple warning
  return;
}
logger.fine("got server socket"); // Fine-detail (low-severity) debug message
```

Pattern Matching with Regular Expressions

In Java 1.4 and later, you can perform textual pattern matching with regular expressions. Regular expression support is provided by the `Pattern` and `Matcher` classes of the java.util.regex package, but the String class defines a number of convenient methods that allow you to use regular expressions even more simply. Regular expressions use a fairly complex grammar to describe patterns of characters. The Java implementation uses the same regex syntax as the Perl 5 programming language. See the java.util.regex.Pattern class in the reference section for a summary of this syntax or consult a good Perl programming book for further details. For a complete tutorial on Perl-style regular expressions, see *Mastering Regular Expressions* (O'Reilly).

The simplest String method that accepts a regular expression argument is matches( ); it returns true if the string matches the pattern defined by the specified regular expression:

```
// This string is a regular expression that describes the pattern of a typical
// sentence. In Perl-style regular expression syntax, it specifies
// a string that begins with a capital letter and ends with a period,
// a question mark, or an exclamation point.
String pattern = "^[A-Z].*[\\.?!]$";
String s = "Java is fun!";
s.matches(pattern);  // The string matches the pattern, so this returns true.
```

The matches( ) method returns true only if the entire string is a match for the specified pattern. Perl programmers should note that this differs from Perl's behavior, in which a match means only that some portion of the string matches the pattern. To determine if a string or any substring matches a pattern, simply alter the regular expression to allow arbitrary characters before and after the desired pattern. In the following code, the regular expression characters .* match any number of arbitrary characters:

The Java Platform

```
s.matches(".*\\bJava\\b.*"); // True if s contains the word "Java" anywhere
                             // The b specifies a word boundary
```

If you are already familiar with Perl's regular expression syntax, you know that it relies on the liberal use of backslashes to escape certain characters. In Perl, regular expressions are language primitives and their syntax is part of the language itself. In Java, however, regular expressions are described using strings and are typically embedded in programs using string literals. The syntax for Java string literals also uses the backslash as an escape character, so to include a single backslash in the regular expression, you must use two backslashes. Thus, in Java programming, you will often see double backslashes in regular expressions.

In addition to matching, regular expressions can be used for search-and-replace operations. The replaceFirst( ) and replaceAll( ) methods search a string for the first substring or all substrings that match a given pattern and replace the string or strings with the specified replacement text, returning a new string that contains the replacements. For example, you could use this code to ensure that the word "Java" is correctly capitalized in a string s:

```
s.replaceAll("(?i)\\bjava\\b",// Pattern: the word "java", case-insensitive
             "Java");          // The replacement string, correctly capitalized
```

The replacement string passed to replaceAll() and replaceFirst( ) need not be a simple literal string; it may also include references to text that matched parenthesized subexpressions within the pattern. These references take the form of a dollar sign followed by the number of the subexpression. (If you are not familiar with parenthesized subexpressions within a regular expression, see java.util.regex.Pattern in the reference section.) For example, to search for words such as JavaBean, JavaScript, JavaOS, and JavaVM (but not Java or Javanese) and to replace the Java prefix with the letter J without altering the suffix, you could use code such as:

```
s.replaceAll("\\bJava([A-Z]\\w+)",  // The pattern
             "J$1");                // J followed by the suffix that matched the
                                    // subexpression in parentheses: [A-Z]\\w+
```

The other String method that uses regular expressions is split(), which returns an array of the substrings of a string, separated by delimiters that match the specified pattern. To obtain an array of words in a string separated by any number of spaces, tabs, or newlines, do this:

```
String sentence = "This is a\n\ttwo-line sentence";
String[] words = sentence.split("[ \t\n\r]+");
```

An optional second argument specifies the maximum number of entries in the returned array.

The matches(), replaceFirst(), replaceAll(), and split() methods are suitable for when you use a regular expression only once. If you want to use a regular expression for multiple matches, you should explicitly use the Pattern and Matcher classes of the java.util.regex package. First, create a Pattern object to represent your regular expression with the static Pattern.compile() method. (Another reason to use the Pattern class explicitly instead of the String convenience methods is that Pattern.compile() allows you to specify flags such as Pattern.CASE_INSENSITIVE that globally alter the way the pattern matching is done.) Note that the compile() method can throw a PatternSyntaxException if you pass it an invalid regular expression string. (This exception is also thrown by the various String convenience methods.) The Pattern class defines split() methods that are similar to the String.split() methods. For all other matching, however, you must create a Matcher object with the matcher() method and specify the text to be matched against:

```
import java.util.regex.*;

Pattern javaword = Pattern.compile("\\bJava(\\w*)", Pattern.CASE_INSENSITIVE);
Matcher m = javaword.matcher(sentence);
boolean match = m.matches();  // True if text matches pattern exactly
```

Once you have a Matcher object, you can compare the string to the pattern in various ways. One of the more sophisticated ways is to find all substrings that match the pattern:

```
String text = "Java is fun; JavaScript is funny.";
m.reset(text);  // Start matching against a new string
// Loop to find all matches of the string and print details of each match
while(m.find()) {
  System.out.println("Found '" + m.group(0) + "' at position " + m.start(0));
  if (m.start(1) < m.end(1)) System.out.println("Suffix is " + m.group(1));
}
```

The Matcher class has been enhanced in several ways in Java 5.0. The most important of these is the ability to save the results of the most recent match in a MatchResult object. The previous algorithm that finds all matches in a string could be rewritten in Java 5.0 as follows:

```
import java.util.regex.*;
import java.util.*;

public class FindAll {
    public static void main(String[] args) {
        Pattern pattern = Pattern.compile(args[0]);
        String text = args[1];

        List<MatchResult> results = findAll(pattern, text);
        for(MatchResult r : results) {
            System.out.printf("Found '%s' at (%d,%d)%n",
                              r.group(), r.start(), r.end());
        }
    }

    public static List<MatchResult> findAll(Pattern pattern, CharSequence text)
    {
        List<MatchResult> results = new ArrayList<MatchResult>();
        Matcher m = pattern.matcher(text);
        while(m.find()) results.add(m.toMatchResult());
        return results;
    }
}
```

Tokenizing Text

java.util.Scanner is a general purpose text tokenizer, added in Java 5.0 to complement the java.util.Formatter class described earlier in this chapter. Scanner takes full advantage of Java regular expressions and can take its input text from a string, file, stream, or any object that implements the java.lang.Readable interface. Readable is also new in Java 5.0 and is the opposite of the Appendable interface.

A Scanner can break its input text into tokens separated by whitespace or any desired delimiter character or regular expression. It implements the Iterator<String> interface, which allows for simple looping through the returned tokens. Scanner also defines a variety of convenience methods for parsing tokens as boolean, integer, or floating-point values, with locale-sensitive number parsing. It has skip( ) methods for skipping input text that matches a specified pattern and also has methods for searching ahead in the input text for text that matches a specified pattern.

Here's how you could use a Scanner to break a String into space-separated words:

```
public static List<String> getTokens(String line) {
    List<String> result = new ArrayList<String>();
    for(Scanner s = Scanner.create(line); s.hasNext(); )
        result.add(s.next());
    return result;
}
```

Here's how you might use a Scanner to break a file into lines:

```
public static void printLines(File f) throws IOException {
    Scanner s = Scanner.create(f);
    // Use a regex to specify line terminators as the token delimiter
    s.useDelimiter("\r\n|\n|\r");
    while(s.hasNext()) System.out.println(s.next());
}
```

The following method uses Scanner to parse an input line in the form `x + y = z`. It demonstrates the ability of a Scanner to scan numbers. Note that Scanner does not just parse Java-style integer literals: it supports thousands separators and does so in a locale-sensitive way—for example, it would parse the integer 1,234 for an American user and 1.234 for a French user. This code also demonstrates the `skip()` method and shows that a Scanner can scan text directly from an InputStream.

```
public static boolean parseSum() {
    System.out.print("enter sum> "); // Prompt the user for input
    System.out.flush();          // Make sure prompt is visible immediately

    try {
        // Read and parse the user's input from the console
        Scanner s = Scanner.create(System.in);
        s.useDelimiter("");     // Don't require spaces between tokens
        int x = s.nextInt();    // Parse an integer
        s.skip("\\s*\\+\\s*"); // Skip optional space and literal +
        int y = s.nextInt();    // Parse another integer
        s.skip("\\s*=\\s*");    // Skip optional space and literal =
        int z = s.nextInt();    // Parse a third integer

        return x + y == z;
    }
    catch(InputMismatchException e) { // pattern does not match
        throw new IllegalArgumentException("syntax error");
    }
    catch(NoSuchElementException e) { // no more input available
        throw new IllegalArgumentException("syntax error");
    }
}
```

StringTokenizer

A number of other Java classes operate on strings and characters. One notable class is `java.util.StringTokenizer`, which you can use to break a string of text into its component words:

```
String s = "Now is the time";
java.util.StringTokenizer st = new java.util.StringTokenizer(s);
while(st.hasMoreTokens()) {
  System.out.println(st.nextToken());
}
```

You can even use this class to tokenize words that are delimited by characters other than spaces:

```
String s = "a:b:c:d";
java.util.StringTokenizer st = new java.util.StringTokenizer(s, ":");
```

`java.io.StreamTokenizer` is another tokenizing class. It has a more complicated API and has more powerful features than `StringTokenizer`.

Numbers and Math

Java provides the `byte`, `short`, `int`, `long`, `float`, and `double` primitive types for representing numbers. The `java.lang` package includes the corresponding `Byte`, `Short`, `Integer`, `Long`, `Float`, and `Double` classes, each of which is a subclass of `Number`. These classes can be useful as object wrappers around their primitive types, and they also define some useful constants:

```
// Integral range constants: Integer, Long, and Character also define these
Byte.MIN_VALUE      // The smallest (most negative) byte value
Byte.MAX_VALUE      // The largest byte value
Short.MIN_VALUE     // The most negative short value
Short.MAX_VALUE     // The largest short value

// Floating-point range constants: Double also defines these
Float.MIN_VALUE     // Smallest (closest to zero) positive float value
Float.MAX_VALUE     // Largest positive float value

// Other useful constants
Math.PI             // 3.14159265358979323846
Math.E              // 2.7182818284590452354
```


Mathematical Functions

The `Math` class defines a number of methods that provide trigonometric, logarithmic, exponential, and rounding operations, among others. This class is primarily useful with floating-point values. For the trigonometric functions, angles are expressed in radians. The logarithm and exponentiation functions are base *e*, not base 10. Here are some examples:

```
double d = Math.toRadians(27);       // Convert 27 degrees to radians
d = Math.cos(d);                     // Take the cosine
d = Math.sqrt(d);                    // Take the square root
d = Math.log(d);                     // Take the natural logarithm
d = Math.exp(d);                     // Do the inverse: e to the power d
d = Math.pow(10, d);                 // Raise 10 to this power
d = Math.atan(d);                    // Compute the arc tangent
d = Math.toDegrees(d);               // Convert back to degrees
double up = Math.ceil(d);            // Round to ceiling
double down = Math.floor(d);         // Round to floor
long nearest = Math.round(d);        // Round to nearest
```

In Java 5.0, several new functions have been added to the `Math` class, including the following:

```
double d = 27;
d = Math.cbrt(d);       // cube root
d = Math.log10(d);      // base-10 logarithm
d = Math.sinh(d);       // hyperbolic sine.  Also cosh() and tanh()
d = Math.hypot(3, 4);  // Hypotenuse
```

Random Numbers

The `Math` class also defines a rudimentary method for generating pseudo-random numbers, but the `java.util.Random` class is more flexible. If you need *very* random pseudo-random numbers, you can use the `java.security.SecureRandom` class:

```
// A simple random number
double r = Math.random();     // Returns d such that: 0.0 <= d < 1.0

// Create a new Random object, seeding with the current time
java.util.Random generator = new java.util.Random(System.currentTimeMillis());
double d = generator.nextDouble();   // 0.0 <= d < 1.0
float f = generator.nextFloat();     // 0.0 <= f < 1.0
long l = generator.nextLong();       // Chosen from the entire range of long
int i = generator.nextInt();         // Chosen from the entire range of int
i = generator.nextInt(limit);        // 0 <= i < limit (Java 1.2 and later)
boolean b = generator.nextBoolean(); // true or false (Java 1.2 and later)
d = generator.nextGaussian();        // Mean value: 0.0; std. deviation: 1.0
byte[] randomBytes = new byte[128];
generator.nextBytes(randomBytes);    // Fill in array with random bytes

// For cryptographic strength random numbers, use the SecureRandom subclass
java.security.SecureRandom generator2 = new java.security.SecureRandom();
// Have the generator generate its own 16-byte seed; takes a *long* time
generator2.setSeed(generator2.generateSeed(16)); // Extra random 16-byte seed
// Then use SecureRandom like any other Random object
generator2.nextBytes(randomBytes);   // Generate more random bytes
```

Big Numbers

The `java.math` package contains the `BigInteger` and `BigDecimal` classes. These classes allow you to work with arbitrary-size and arbitrary-precision integers and floating-point values. For example:

```
import java.math.*;

// Compute the factorial of 1000
BigInteger total = BigInteger.valueOf(1);
for(int i = 2; i <= 1000; i++)
  total = total.multiply(BigInteger.valueOf(i));
System.out.println(total.toString());
```

In Java 1.4, BigInteger has a method to randomly generate large prime numbers, which is useful in many cryptographic applications:

```
BigInteger prime =
  BigInteger.probablePrime(1024,         // 1024 bits long
                           generator2); // Source of randomness. From above.
```

The BigDecimal class has been overhauled in Java 5.0 and is much more usable in this release. In addition to its utility for representing very large or very precise floating point numbers, it is also useful for financial calculations because it relies on a decimal representation of fractions rather than a binary representation. float and double values cannot precisely represent a number as simple as 0.1, and this can cause rounding errors that are often unacceptable when representing monetary values. BigDecimal and its associated MathContext and RoundingMode types provide a solution. For example:

```
// Compute monthly interest payments on a loan
public static BigDecimal monthlyPayment(int amount, // amount of loan
                                        int years,  // term in years
                                        double apr) // annual interest %
{
    // Convert the loan amount to a BigDecimal
    BigDecimal principal = new BigDecimal(amount);

    // Convert term of loan in years to number of monthly payments
    int payments=years*12;

    // Convert interest from annual percent to a monthly decimal
    BigDecimal interest = BigDecimal.valueOf(apr);
    interest = interest.divide(new BigDecimal(100));     // as fraction
    interest = interest.divide(new BigDecimal(12));      // monthly

    // The monthly payment computation
    BigDecimal x = interest.add(BigDecimal.ONE).pow(payments);
    BigDecimal y = principal.multiply(interest).multiply(x);
    BigDecimal monthly = y.divide(x.subtract(BigDecimal.ONE),
                                  MathContext.DECIMAL64);  // note context

    // Convert to two decimal places
    monthly = monthly.setScale(2, RoundingMode.HALF_EVEN);

    return monthly;
}
```

Converting Numbers from and to Strings

A Java program that operates on numbers must get its input values from somewhere. Often, such a program reads a textual representation of a number and must convert it to a numeric representation. The various Number subclasses define useful conversion methods:

```
String s = "-42";
byte b = Byte.parseByte(s);             // s as a byte
short sh = Short.parseShort(s);         // s as a short
```

```
int i = Integer.parseInt(s);            // s as an int
long l = Long.parseLong(s);             // s as a long
float f = Float.parseFloat(s);          // s as a float (Java 1.2 and later)
f = Float.valueOf(s).floatValue();      // s as a float (prior to Java 1.2)
double d = Double.parseDouble(s);       // s as a double (Java 1.2 and later)
d = Double.valueOf(s).doubleValue();    // s as a double (prior to Java 1.2)

// The integer conversion routines handle numbers in other bases
byte b = Byte.parseByte("1011", 2);       // 1011 in binary is 11 in decimal
short sh = Short.parseShort("ff", 16);    // ff in base 16 is 255 in decimal

// The valueOf() method can handle arbitrary bases between 2 and 36
int i = Integer.valueOf("egg", 17).intValue();    // Base 17!

// The decode() method handles octal, decimal, or hexadecimal, depending
// on the numeric prefix of the string
short sh = Short.decode("0377").byteValue();    // Leading 0 means base 8
int i = Integer.decode("0xff").shortValue();    // Leading 0x means base 16
long l = Long.decode("255").intValue();         // Other numbers mean base 10

// Integer class can convert numbers to strings
String decimal = Integer.toString(42);
String binary = Integer.toBinaryString(42);
String octal = Integer.toOctalString(42);
String hex = Integer.toHexString(42);
String base36 = Integer.toString(42, 36);
```

Formatting Numbers

The printf() and format( ) methods of Java 5.0 described earlier in this chapter work well for formatting numbers. The %d format specifier is for formatting integers in decimal format:

```
// Format int, long and BigInteger to the string "1 10 100"
String s = String.format("%d %d %d", 1, 10L, BigInteger.TEN.pow(2));
// Add thousands separators
s = String.format("%,d", Integer.MAX_VALUE); // "2,147,483,647"
// Output value right-justified in a field 8 characters wide
s = String.format("%8d", 123);                // "     123"
// Pad on the left with zeros to make 5 digits total
s = String.format("%05d", 123);               // "00123"
```

Floating-point numbers can be formatted using %f, %e, or %g format specifiers, which differ in whether and when exponential notation is used:

```
double x = 1.234E9; // (1.234 billion)
// returns "1234000000.000000 1.234000e+09 1.234000e+09 1234.000000"
s = String.format("%f %e %g %g", x, x, x, x/1e6);
```

You'll notice that the numbers above are all formatted with six digits following the decimal point. This default can be altered by specifying a *precision* in the format string:

```
// display a BigDecimal with 2 significant digits
s = String.format("%.2f", new BigDecimal("1.234"));  // "1.23"
```

Other flags can be applied to floating-point conversions as well. The following code formats a column of numbers right-justified within a field 10 characters wide. Each number has two digits following the decimal place and includes thousands separators when necessary. Negative values are formatted in parentheses, a common formatting convention in accounting.

```
// A column of 4 numbers. %n is newline.
s = String.format("%(,10.2f%n%(,10.2f%n%(,10.2f%n%(,10.2f%n",
                  BigDecimal.TEN,                      //      10.00
                  BigDecimal.TEN.movePointRight(3),    //  10,000.00
                  BigDecimal.TEN.movePointLeft(3),     //       0.01
                  BigDecimal.TEN.negate());            //    (10.00)
```

See java.util.Formatter in the reference section for complete details on supported format specifiers and formatting options.

Prior to Java 5.0, numbers can be formatted using the java.text.NumberFormat class:

```
import java.text.*;

// Use NumberFormat to format and parse numbers for the current locale
NumberFormat nf = NumberFormat.getNumberInstance();  // Get a NumberFormat
System.out.println(nf.format(9876543.21)); // Format number for current locale
try {
  Number n = nf.parse("1.234.567,89");      // Parse strings according to locale
} catch (ParseException e) { /* Handle exception */ }

// Monetary values are sometimes formatted differently than other numbers
NumberFormat moneyFmt = NumberFormat.getCurrencyInstance();
System.out.println(moneyFmt.format(1234.56)); // Prints $1,234.56 in U.S.
```


Dates and Times

Java allows dates and times to be represented and manipulated in three forms: as long values or as java.util.Date or java.util.Calendar objects. Java 5.0 introduces the enumerated type java.util.concurrent.TimeUnit. The values of this type represent time granularities or units: seconds, milliseconds, microseconds, and nanoseconds. They have useful convenience methods but do not themselves represent a time value.

Milliseconds and Nanoseconds

At the lowest level, dates and times are represented as a long value that holds the positive or negative number of milliseconds since midnight on January 1, 1970. This special date and time is known as the epoch and is measured in Greenwich Mean Time (GMT) or Universal Time (UTC). To query the current time in this millisecond representation, use System.currentTimeMillis()

```
long now = System.currentTimeMillis();
```

In Java 5.0 and later, you can use System.nanoTime() to query time in nanoseconds. This method returns a long number of nanoseconds long. Unlike currentTimeMillis( ), the nanoTime() does not return a time relative to any defined epoch. nanoTime() is good for measuring relative or elapsed time (as long as the elapsed time is not more than 292 years) but is not suitable for absolute time:

```
long start = System.nanoTime();
doSomething();
long end = System.nanoTime();
long elapsedNanoSeconds = end - start;
```

The Date Class

java.util.Date is an object wrapper around a long that holds a number of milliseconds since the epoch. Using a Date object instead of a long allows simple conversion to a nonlocalized string with the toString method. Date objects can be compared for equality with the equals( ) method and they can be compared for order with the compareTo() method or the before( ) and after() methods.

The no-argument version of the Date( ) constructor creates a Date that represents the current time. You can also pass a long number of milliseconds to create a Date that represents some other time. getTime( ) returns the millisecond representation of the Date. Date is a mutable class, so you can also pass a number of milliseconds to setTime( ).

Date has a number of methods for querying and setting the year, month, day, hour, minute, and second. All of these methods have been deprecated, however, in favor of the Calendar class, described next.

The Calendar Class

The java.util.Calendar class is a properly localized version of Date. It is simply a wrapper around a long number of milliseconds but can represent that instant in time according to the calendar of the current locale (usually a Gregorian calendar) and the time zone of the current locale. Furthermore, it has methods for querying, setting, and doing arithmetic on the various fields of the date and time.

The code below shows common uses of the Calendar class. Note that the set( ), get(), and add( ) methods all take an initial argument that specifies what field of the date or time is being set, queried, or added to. Fields such as year, day of month, day of week, hour, minute, and second are defined by integer constants in the class. Other integer constants define values for the months and weekdays of the Gregorian calendar. The month constant UNDECIMBER represents a 13th month used in lunar calendars.

```
// Get a Calendar for current locale and time zone
Calendar cal = Calendar.getInstance();

// Figure out what day of the year today is
cal.setTimeInMillis(System.currentTimeMillis()); // Set to the current time
int dayOfYear = cal.get(Calendar.DAY_OF_YEAR);  // What day of the year is it?

// What day of the week does the leap day in the year 2008 occur on?
cal.set(2008, Calendar.FEBRUARY, 29);              // Set year, month, day fields
int dayOfWeek = cal.get(Calendar.DAY_OF_WEEK);   // Query a different field
```

```
// What day of the month is the 3rd Thursday of May, 2005?
cal.set(Calendar.YEAR, 2005);                      // Set the year
cal.set(Calendar.MONTH, Calendar.MAY);             // Set the month
cal.set(Calendar.DAY_OF_WEEK,Calendar.THURSDAY); // Set the day of week
cal.set(Calendar.DAY_OF_WEEK_IN_MONTH, 3);         // Set the week
int dayOfMonth = cal.get(Calendar.DAY_OF_MONTH); // Query the day in month

// Get a Date object that represents three months from now
cal.setTimeInMillis(System.currentTimeMillis()); // Current time
cal.add(Calendar.MONTH, 3);                        // Add 3 months
Date expiration = cal.getTime();                   // Retrieve result as a Date
long millis = cal.getTimeInMillis();               // or get it as a long
```

Formatting Dates and Times

The toString() method of Date produces a textual representation of a date and time but does no localization and allows no customization of which fields (day, month and year or hours and minutes, for example) are to be displayed. The toString() method should be used only to produce a machine-readable timestamp, not a human-readable string.

Like numbers, dates and times can be converted to strings using the String.format() method and the related java.util.Formatter class of Java 5.0. Format strings for displaying dates and times are all two-character sequences that begin with the letter t. The second letter of each sequence specifies the field or set of fields of the date or time to display. For example %tR displays the hours and minutes fields using 24-hour time, and %tD displays the month, day, and year fields separated by slashes. String.format() can format a date or time specified as a long, a Date, or a Calendar:

```
// current hours and minutes
long now = System.currentTimeMillis();
String s = String.format("%tR", now);          // "15:12"

// Current month/day/year
Date d = new Date(now);
s = String.format("%tD", d);                   // "07/13/04"

// Hours and minutes using 12-hour clock
Calendar c = Calendar.getInstance();
c.setTime(d);
s = String.format("%tl:%tM %tp", now, d, c); // "3:12 pm"
```

Prior to Java 5.0 and its Formatter class, you can format dates and times using the java.text.DateFormat class, which automatically handles locale-specific conventions for date and time formatting. DateFormat even works correctly in locales that use a calendar other than the common era (Gregorian) calendar in use throughout much of the world:

```
import java.util.Date;
import java.text.*;

// Display today's date using a default format for the current locale
DateFormat defaultDate = DateFormat.getDateInstance();
System.out.println(defaultDate.format(new Date()));
```

```
// Display the current time using a short time format for the current locale
DateFormat shortTime = DateFormat.getTimeInstance(DateFormat.SHORT);
System.out.println(shortTime.format(new Date()));

// Display date and time using a long format for both
DateFormat longTimestamp =
  DateFormat.getDateTimeInstance(DateFormat.FULL, DateFormat.FULL);
System.out.println(longTimestamp.format(new Date()));

// Use SimpleDateFormat to define your own formatting template
// See java.text.SimpleDateFormat for the template syntax
DateFormat myformat = new SimpleDateFormat("yyyy.MM.dd");
System.out.println(myformat.format(new Date()));
try {   // DateFormat can parse dates too
  Date leapday = myformat.parse("2000.02.29");
}
catch (ParseException e) { /* Handle parsing exception */ }
```

Arrays

The `java.lang.System` class defines an `arraycopy()` method that is useful for copying specified elements in one array to a specified position in a second array. The second array must be the same type as the first, and it can even be the same array:

```
char[] text = "Now is the time".toCharArray();
char[] copy = new char[100];
// Copy 10 characters from element 4 of text into copy, starting at copy[0]
System.arraycopy(text, 4, copy, 0, 10);

// Move some of the text to later elements, making room for insertions
System.arraycopy(copy, 3, copy, 6, 7);
```

In Java 1.2 and later, the `java.util.Arrays` class defines useful array-manipulation methods, including methods for sorting and searching arrays:

```
import java.util.Arrays;

int[] intarray = new int[] { 10, 5, 7, -3 }; // An array of integers
Arrays.sort(intarray);                       // Sort it in place
int pos = Arrays.binarySearch(intarray, 7);  // Value 7 is found at index 2
pos = Arrays.binarySearch(intarray, 12);     // Not found: negative return value

// Arrays of objects can be sorted and searched too
String[] strarray = new String[] { "now", "is", "the", "time" };
Arrays.sort(strarray);   // sorted to: { "is", "now", "the", "time" }

// Arrays.equals() compares all elements of two arrays
String[] clone = (String[]) strarray.clone();
boolean b1 = Arrays.equals(strarray, clone);  // Yes, they're equal

// Arrays.fill() initializes array elements
byte[] data = new byte[100];             // An empty array; elements set to 0
Arrays.fill(data, (byte) -1);            // Set them all to -1
Arrays.fill(data, 5, 10, (byte) -2);     // Set elements 5, 6, 7, 8, 9 to -2
```

Arrays can be treated and manipulated as objects in Java. Given an arbitrary object o, you can use code such as the following to find out if the object is an array and, if so, what type of array it is:

```
Class type = o.getClass();
if (type.isArray()) {
  Class elementType = type.getComponentType();
}
```

Collections

The Java Collections Framework is a set of important utility classes and interfaces in the java.util package for working with collections of objects. The Collections Framework defines two fundamental types of collections. A Collection is a group of objects while a Map is a set of mappings, or associations, between objects. A Set is a type of Collection with no duplicates, and a List is a Collection in which the elements are ordered. SortedSet and SortedMap are specialized sets and maps that maintain their elements in a sorted order. Collection, Set, List, Map, SortedSet, and SortedMap are all interfaces, but the java.util package also defines various concrete implementations, such as lists based on arrays and linked lists, and maps and sets based on hashtables or binary trees. Other important interfaces are Iterator and ListIterator, which allow you to loop through the objects in a collection. The Collections Framework was added in Java 1.2, but prior to that release you can use Vector and Hashtable, which are approximately the same as ArrayList and HashMap.

In Java 1.4, the Collections API added the RandomAccess marker interface, which is implemented by List implementations that support efficient random access (i.e., it is implemented by ArrayList and Vector but not by LinkedList). Java 1.4 also introduced LinkedHashMap and LinkedHashSet, which are hashtable-based maps and sets that preserve the insertion order of elements. Finally, IdentityHashMap is a hashtable-based Map implementation that uses the == operator to compare key objects rather than using the equals() method to compare them.

The Collections Framework has been overhauled in Java 5.0 to use generics (see Chapter 4). Java 5.0 also adds EnumSet and EnumMap classes that are specialized for working with enumerated values (see Chapter 4) and the java.lang.Iterable interface used by the new for/in looping statement. Finally, Java 5.0 adds the Queue interface. Most of the interesting Queue implementations are BlockingQueue implementations in java.util.concurrent.

The Collection Interface

Collection<E> is a parameterized interface that represents a generic group of objects of type E. The group may or may not allow duplicate elements and may or may not impose an ordering on the elements. Methods are defined for adding and removing objects from the group, testing an object for membership in the group, and iterating through all elements in the group. Additional methods return the elements of the group as an array and return the size of the collection.

The Java Collections Framework does not provide any implementations of Collection, but this interface is still very important because it defines the features common to all Set, List, and Queue implementations. The following code illustrates the operations you can perform on Collection objects:

```
// Create some collections to work with.
Collection<String> c = new HashSet<String>();  // An empty set
// We'll see these utility methods later
Collection<String> d = Arrays.asList("one", "two");    // immutable
Collection<String> e = Collections.singleton("three"); // immutable

// Add elements to a collection. These methods return true if the collection
// changes, which is useful with Sets that don't allow duplicates.
c.add("zero");            // Add a single element
c.addAll(d);              // Add a collection of elements

// Copy a collection: most implementations have a copy constructor
Collection<String> copy = new ArrayList<String>(c);

// Remove elements from a collection.
// All but clear() return true if the collection changes.
c.remove("zero");         // Remove a single element
c.removeAll(e);           // Remove a collection of elements
c.retainAll(d);           // Remove all elements that are not in e
c.clear();                // Remove all elements from the collection

// Querying collection size
boolean b = c.isEmpty(); // Collection is now empty
int s = c.size();         // Collection size is now 0.

// Restore collection from the copy we made
c.addAll(copy);

// Test membership in the collection.  Membership is based on the equals()
// method, not the == operator.
b = c.contains("zero");  // true
b = c.containsAll(d);    // true

// Iterate through collection elements with a while loop.
// Some implementations (such as lists) guarantee an order of iteration
// Others make no guarantees.
Iterator<String> iterator = c.iterator();
while(iterator.hasNext()) System.out.println(iterator.next());

// Iteration with a for loop
for(Iterator<String> i = c.iterator(); i.hasNext(); )
    System.out.println(i.next());

// Java 5.0 iteration using a for/in loop
for(String word : c) System.out.println(word);

// Most Collection implementations have a useful toString() method
System.out.println(c);   // As an alternative to the iterations above
```

```
// Obtain an array of collection elements.  If the iterator guarantees
// an order, this array has the same order. The array is a copy, not a
// reference to an internal data structure.
Object[] elements = c.toArray();

// If we want the elements in a String[], we must pass one in
String[] strings = c.toArray(new String[c.size()]);

// Or we can pass an empty String[] just to specify the type and
// the toArray() method will allocate an array for us
strings = c.toArray(new String[0]);
```

Remember that you can use any of the methods shown above with any Set, List, or Queue. These subinterfaces may impose membership restrictions or ordering constraints on the elements of the collection but still provide the same basic methods. Methods such as add( ), remove(), clear( ), and retainAll() that alter the collection are optional, and read-only implementations may throw UnsupportedOperationException.

Collection, Map, and their subinterfaces do *not* extend the Cloneable or Serializable interfaces. All of the collection and map implementation classes provided in the Java Collections Framework, however, do implement these interfaces.

Some collection implementations place restrictions on the elements that they can contain. An implementation might prohibit null as an element, for example. And EnumSet restricts membership to the values of a specified enumerated type. Attempting to add a prohibited element to a collection always throws an unchecked exception such as NullPointerException or ClassCastException. Checking whether a collection contains a prohibited element may also throw such an exception, or it may simply return false.

The Set Interface

A *set* is a collection of objects that does not allow duplicates: it may not contain two references to the same object, two references to null, or references to two objects a and b such that a.equals(b). Most general-purpose Set implementations impose no ordering on the elements of the set, but ordered sets are not prohibited (see SortedSet and LinkedHashSet). Sets are further distinguished from ordered collections like lists by the general expectation that they have an efficient contains( ) method that runs in constant or logarithmic time.

Set defines no additional methods beyond those defined by Collection but places additional restrictions on those methods. The add( ) and addAll() methods of a Set are required to enforce the no-duplicates rules: they may not add an element to the Set if the set already contains that element. Recall that the add() and addAll( ) methods defined by the Collection interface return true if the call resulted in a change to the collection and false if it did not. This return value is relevant for Set objects because the no-duplicates restriction means that adding an element does not always result in a change to the set.

Table 5-2 lists the implementations of the Set interface and summarizes their internal representation, ordering characteristics, member restrictions, and the performance of the basic add( ), remove( ), and contains() operations as well as iteration performance. You can read more about each class in the reference section. Note that CopyOnWriteArraySet is in the java.util.concurrent package; all the other implementations are part of java.util. Also note that java.util.BitSet is not a Set implementation. This legacy class is useful as a compact and efficient list of boolean values but is not part of the Java Collections Framework.

Table 5-2. Set Implementations

Class	Internal representation	Element order	Member restrictions	Basic operations	Iteration performance	Notes
HashSet	hashtable	none	none	O(1)	O(capacity)	Best general-purpose implementation.
LinkedHashSet	linked hashtable	insertion order	none	O(1)	O(n)	Preserves insertion order.
EnumSet	bit fields	enum declaration	enum values	O(1)	O(n)	Holds non-null enum values only.
TreeSet	red-black tree	sorted ascending	comparable	O(log(n))	O(n)	Comparable elements or Comparator.
CopyOnWrite ArraySet	array	insertion order	none	O(n)	O(n)	Threadsafe without synchronized methods.

The TreeSet implementation uses a red-black tree data structure to maintain a set that is iterated in ascending order according to the natural ordering of Comparable objects or according to an ordering specified by a Comparator object. TreeSet actually implements the SortedSet interface, which is a subinterface of Set.

SortedSet offers several interesting methods that take advantage of its sorted nature. The following code illustrates:

```
public static void testSortedSet(String[] args) {
    // Create a SortedSet
    SortedSet<String> s = new TreeSet<String>(Arrays.asList(args));

    // Iterate set: elements are automatically sorted
    for(String word : s) System.out.println(word);

    // Special elements
    String first = s.first();  // First element
    String last = s.last();    // Last element
    // Subrange views of the set
    SortedSet<String> tail = s.tailSet(first+'\0'); // all elements but first
    SortedSet<String> head = s.headSet(last);       // all elements but last
    SortedSet<String> middle = s.subSet(first+'\0', // all but ends
                                        last);
}
```

The List Interface

A List is an ordered collection of objects. Each element of a list has a position in the list, and the List interface defines methods to query or set the element at a particular position, or *index*. In this respect a List is like an array whose size changes as needed to accommodate the number of elements it contains. Unlike sets, lists allow duplicate elements.

In addition to its index-based get( ) and set() methods, the List interface defines methods to add or remove an element at a particular index and also defines methods to return the index of the first or last occurrence of a particular value in the list. The add( ) and remove() methods inherited from Collection are defined to append to the list and to remove the first occurrence of the specified value from the list. The inherited addAll() appends all elements in the specified collection to the end of the list, and another version inserts the elements at a specified index. The retainAll() and removeAll( ) methods behave as they do for any Collection, retaining or removing multiple occurrences of the same value, if needed.

The List interface does not define methods that operate on a range of list indexes. Instead it defines a single subList method that returns a List object that represents just the specified range of the original list. The sublist is backed by the parent list, and any changes made to the sublist are immediately visible in the parent list. Examples of subList( ) and the other basic List manipulation methods are below.

```
// Create lists to work with
List<String> l = new ArrayList<String>(Arrays.asList(args));
List<String> words = Arrays.asList("hello", "world");

// Querying and setting elements by index
String first = l.get(0);             // First element of list
String last = l.get(l.size()-1);     // Last element of list
l.set(0, last);                      // The last shall be first

// Adding and inserting elements.  add() can append or insert
l.add(first);        // Append the first word at end of list
l.add(0, first);     // Insert first word at the start of the list again
l.addAll(words);     // Append a collection at the end of the list
l.addAll(1, words); // Insert collection after first word

// Sublists: backed by the original list
List<String> sub = l.subList(1,3);  // second and third elements
sub.set(0, "hi");                   // modifies 2nd element of l
// Sublists can restrict operations to a subrange of backing list
String s = Collections.min(l.subList(0,4));
Collections.sort(l.subList(0,4));
// Independent copies of a sublist don't affect the parent list.
List<String> subcopy = new ArrayList<String>(l.subList(1,3));

// Searching lists
int p = l.indexOf(last);  // Where does the last word appear?
p = l.lastIndexOf(last);  // Search backward

// Print the index of all occurrences of last in l.  Note subList()
```

The Java Platform

```
int n = l.size();
p = 0;
do {
    // Get a view of the list that includes only the elements we
    // haven't searched yet.
    List<String> list = l.subList(p, n);
    int q = list.indexOf(last);
    if (q == -1) break;
    System.out.printf("Found '%s' at index %d%n", last, p+q);
    p += q+1;
} while(p < n);

// Removing elements from a list
l.remove(last);         // Remove first occurrence of the element
l.remove(0);            // Remove element at specified index
l.subList(0,2).clear(); // Remove a range of elements using subList()
l.retainAll(words);     // Remove all but elements in words
l.removeAll(words);     // Remove all occurrences of elements in words
l.clear();              // Remove everything
```

A general expectation of List implementations is that they can be efficiently iterated, typically in time proportional to the size of the list. Lists do not all provide efficient random-access to the elements at any index, however. Sequential-access lists, such as the LinkedList class, provide efficient insertion and deletion operations at the expense of random access performance. In Java 1.4 and later, implementations that provide efficient random access implement the RandomAccess marker interface, and you can test for this interface with instanceof if you need to ensure efficient list manipulations:

```
List<?> l = ...;  // Arbitrary list we're passed to manipulate
// Ensure we can do efficient random access.  If not, use a copy constructor
// to make a random-access copy of the list before manipulating it.
if (!(l instanceof RandomAccess)) l = new ArrayList<?>(l);
```

The Iterator returned by the iterator() method of a List iterates the list elements in the order that they occur in the list. List implements Iterable, and lists can be iterated with a for/in loop just as any other collection can.

To iterate just a portion of a list, you can use the subList( ) method to create a sublist view:

```
List<String> words = ...;  // Get a list to iterate

// Iterate just all elements of the list but the first
for(String word : words.subList(1, words.size()))
    System.out.println(word);
```

In addition to normal iteration, lists also provide enhanced bidirectional iteration using a ListIterator object returned by the listIterator() method. To iterate backward through a List, for example, start with a ListIterator with its cursor positioned after the end of the list:

```
ListIterator<String> li = words.listIterator(words.size());
while(li.hasPrevious()) {
    System.out.println(li.previous());
}
```

Table 5-3 summarizes the five general-purpose `List` implementations in the Java platform. `Vector` and `Stack` are legacy implementations left over from Java 1.0. `CopyOnWriteArrayList` is a new in Java 5.0 and is part of the `java.util.concurrent` package.

Table 5-3. List implementations

Class	Representation	Random access	Notes
ArrayList	array	yes	Best all-around implementation.
LinkedList	double-linked list	no	Efficient insertion and deletion.
CopyOnWriteArrayList	array	yes	Threadsafe; fast traversal, slow modification.
Vector	array	yes	Legacy class; synchronized method.
Stack	array	yes	Extends `Vector`; adds `push()`, `pop()`, `peek()`.

The Map Interface

A *map* is a set of *key* objects and a mapping from each member of that set to a *value* object. The `Map` interface defines an API for defining and querying mappings. `Map` is part of the Java Collections Framework, but it does not extend the `Collection` interface, so a `Map` is a little-c collection, not a big-C `Collection`. `Map` is a parameterized type with two type variables. Type variable `K` represents the type of keys held by the map, and type variable `V` represents the type of the values that the keys are mapped to. A mapping from `String` keys to `Integer` values, for example, can be represented with a `Map<String,Integer>`.

The most important `Map` methods are `put()`, which defines a key/value pair in the map, `get()`, which queries the value associated with a specified key, and `remove()`, which removes the specified key and its associated value from the map. The general performance expectation for `Map` implementations is that these three basic methods are quite efficient: they should usually run in constant time and certainly no worse than in logarithmic time.

An important feature of `Map` is its support for "collection views." Although a `Map` is not a `Collection`, its keys can be viewed as a `Set`, its values can be viewed as a `Collection`, and its mappings can be viewed as a `Set` of `Map.Entry` objects. (`Map.Entry` is a nested interface defined within `Map`: it simply represents a single key/value pair.)

The sample code below shows the `get()`, `put()`, `remove()`, and other methods of a `Map` and also demonstrates some common uses of the collection views of a `Map`:

```
// Create maps to work with
Map<String,Integer> m = new HashMap<String,Integer>();  // New, empty map
// Immutable Map containing a single key-value pair
Map<String,Integer> singleton = Collections.singletonMap("testing", -1);
// Note this rarely-used syntax to explicitly specify the parameter
// types of the generic emptyMap() method.  The returned map is immutable
Map<String,Integer> empty = Collections.<String,Integer>emptyMap();

// Populate the map using the put() method to define mappings from array
// elements to the index at which each element appears
```

```
String[] words = { "this", "is", "a", "test" };
for(int i = 0; i < words.length; i++)
    m.put(words[i], i);  // Note autoboxing of int to Integer

// Each key must map to a single value. But keys may map to the same value
for(int i = 0; i < words.length; i++)
    m.put(words[i].toUpperCase(), i);

// The putAll() method copies mappings from another Map
m.putAll(singleton);

// Query the mappings with the get() method
for(int i = 0; i < words.length; i++)
    if (m.get(words[i]) != i) throw new AssertionError();

// Key and value membership testing
m.containsKey(words[0]);        // true
m.containsValue(words.length);  // false

// Map keys, values, and entries can be viewed as collections
Set<String> keys = m.keySet();
Collection<Integer> values = m.values();
Set<Map.Entry<String,Integer>> entries = m.entrySet();

// The Map and its collection views typically have useful toString() methods
System.out.printf("Map: %s%nKeys: %s%nValues: %s%nEntries: %s%n",
                  m, keys, values, entries);

// These collections can be iterated.
// Most maps have an undefined iteration order (but see SortedMap)
for(String key : m.keySet()) System.out.println(key);
for(Integer value: m.values()) System.out.println(value);

// The Map.Entry<K,V> type represents a single key/value pair in a map
for(Map.Entry<String,Integer> pair : m.entrySet()) {
    // Print out mappings
    System.out.printf("'%s' ==> %d%n", pair.getKey(), pair.getValue());
    // And increment the value of each Entry
    pair.setValue(pair.getValue() + 1);
}

// Removing mappings
m.put("testing", null);   // Mapping to null can "erase" a mapping:
m.get("testing");         // Returns null
m.containsKey("testing"); // Returns true: mapping still exists
m.remove("testing");      // Deletes the mapping altogether
m.get("testing");         // Still returns null
m.containsKey("testing"); // Now returns false.

// Deletions may also be made via the collection views of a map.
// Additions to the map may not be made this way, however.
m.keySet().remove(words[0]);  // Same as m.remove(words[0]);
m.values().remove(2);         // Remove one mapping to the value 2
m.values().removeAll(Collections.singleton(4)); // Remove all mappings to 4
m.values().retainAll(Arrays.asList(2, 3));      // Keep only mappings to 2 & 3
```

```
// Deletions can also be done via iterators
Iterator<Map.Entry<String,Integer>> iter = m.entrySet().iterator();
while(iter.hasNext()) {
    Map.Entry<String,Integer> e = iter.next();
    if (e.getValue() == 2) iter.remove();
}

// Find values that appear in both of two maps.  In general, addAll() and
// retainAll() with keySet() and values() allow union and intersection
Set<Integer> v = new HashSet<Integer>(m.values());
v.retainAll(singleton.values());

// Miscellaneous methods
m.clear();                 // Deletes all mappings
m.size();                  // Returns number of mappings: currently 0
m.isEmpty();               // Returns true
m.equals(empty);           // true: Maps implementations override equals
```

The Map interface includes a variety of general-purpose and special-purpose implementations, which are summarized in Table 5-4. As always, complete details are in the reference section. All classes in Table 5-4 are in the java.util package except ConcurrentHashMap, which is part of java.util.concurrent.

Table 5-4. Map implementations

Class	Representation	Since	null keys	null values	Notes
HashMap	hashtable	1.2	yes	yes	General-purpose implementation.
Concurrent-HashMap	hashtable	5.0	no	no	General-purpose threadsafe implementation; see ConcurrentMap interface.
EnumMap	array	5.0	no	yes	Keys are instances of an enum.
LinkedHashMap	hashtable plus list	1.4	yes	yes	Preserves insertion or access order.
TreeMap	red-black tree	1.2	no	yes	Sorts by key value. Operations are O(log(n)). See SortedMap.
Identity-HashMap	hashtable	1.4	yes	yes	Compares with = = instead of equals( ).
WeakHashMap	hashtable	1.2	yes	yes	Doesn't prevent garbage collection of keys.
Hashtable	hashtable	1.0	no	no	Legacy class; synchronized methods.
Properties	hashtable	1.0	no	no	Extends Hashtable with String methods.

The ConcurrentHashMap class of the java.util.concurrent package implements the ConcurrentMap interface of the same package. ConcurrentMap extends Map and defines some additional atomic operations that are important in multithreaded programming. For example, the putIfAbsent() method is like put( ) but adds the key/value pair to the map only if the key is not already mapped.

TreeMap implements the SortedMap interface, which extends Map to add methods that take advantage of the sorted nature of the map. SortedMap is quite similar to the SortedSet interface. The firstKey() and lastKey( ) methods return the first and last keys in the keySet(). And headMap(), tailMap( ), and subMap() return a restricted range of the original map.

The Queue and BlockingQueue Interfaces

A *queue* is an ordered collection of elements with methods for extracting elements, in order, from the *head* of the queue. Queue implementations are commonly based on insertion order as in first-in, first-out (FIFO) queues or last in, first-out queues (LIFO queues are also known as stacks). Other orderings are possible, however: a *priority queue* orders its elements according to an external Comparator object, or according to the natural ordering of Comparable elements. Unlike a Set, Queue implementations typically allow duplicate elements. Unlike List, the Queue interface does not define methods for manipulating queue elements at arbitrary positions. Only the element at the head of the queue is available for examination. It is common for Queue implementations to have a fixed capacity: when a queue is full, it is not possible to add more elements. Similarly, when a queue is empty, it is not possible to remove any more elements. Because full and empty conditions are a normal part of many queue-based algorithms, the Queue interface defines methods that signal these conditions with return values rather than by throwing exceptions. Specifically, the peek() and poll( ) methods return null to indicate that the queue is empty. For this reason, most Queue implementations do not allow null elements.

A *blocking queue* is a type of queue that defines blocking put( ) and take() methods. The put( ) method adds an element to the queue, waiting, if necessary, until there is space in the queue for the element. And the take( ) method removes an element from the head of the queue, waiting, if necessary, until there is an element to remove. Blocking queues are an important part of many multithreaded algorithms, and the BlockingQueue interface (which extends Queue) is defined as part of the java.util.concurrent package. Queue, BlockingQueue, and their implementations are new in Java 5.0. See "Blocking Queues" later in this chapter for a list of BlockingQueue implementations.

Queues are not nearly as commonly used as sets, lists, and maps, except perhaps in certain multithreaded programming styles. In lieu of example code here, we'll try to clarify the confusing array of queue insertion and removal operations:

- Adding elements to queues

  add()
  : This Collection method simply adds an element in the normal way. In bounded queues, this method may throw an exception if the queue is full.

  offer()
  : This Queue method is like add( ) but returns false instead of throwing an exception if the element cannot be added because a bounded queue is full.

    BlockingQueue defines a timeout version of offer( ) that waits up to a specified amount of time for space to become available in a full queue. Like the basic version of the method, it returns true if the element was inserted and false otherwise.

put()
: This BlockingQueue method blocks: if the element cannot be inserted because the queue is full, put() waits until some other thread removes an element from the queue, and space becomes available for the new element.

- Removing elements from queues

remove()
: In addition to the Collection.remove() method, which removes a specified element from the queue, the Queue interface defines a no-argument version of remove() that removes and returns the element at the head of the queue. If the queue is empty, this method throws a NoSuchElementException.

poll()
: This Queue method removes and returns the element at the head of the queue, like remove() does but returns null if the queue is empty instead of throwing an exception.

  BlockingQueue defines a timeout version of poll() that waits up to a specified amount of time for an element to be added to an empty queue.

take()
: This BlockingQueue method removes and returns the element at the head of the queue. If the queue is empty, it blocks until some other thread adds an element to the queue.

drainTo()
: This BlockingQueue method removes all available elements from the queue and adds them to a specified Collection. It does not block to wait for elements to be added to the queue. A variant of the method accepts a maximum number of elements to drain.

- Querying the element at the head, without removing it from the queue

element()
: This Queue method returns the element at the head of the queue but does not remove that element from the queue. If the queue is empty, it throws NoSuchElementException.

peek()
: This Queue method is like element() but returns null if the queue is empty.

The LinkedList class has been retrofitted, in Java 5.0, to implement Queue. It provides unbounded FIFO (first in, first out) ordering, and insertion and removal operations require constant time. LinkedList allows null elements, although their use is discouraged when the list is being used as a queue.

The only other Queue implementation in the java.util package is PriorityQueue, which orders its elements according to a Comparator or orders Comparable elements according to the order defined by their compareTo() methods. The head of a PriorityQueue is always the the smallest element according to the defined ordering.

The java.util.concurrent package contains a number of BlockingQueue implementations; they are described later in the chapter. This package also contains ConcurrentLinkedQueue, an efficient threadsafe Queue implementation that does not suffer the overhead of synchronized methods.

Collection Wrappers

The java.util.Collections class is home to quite a few static utility methods designed for use with collections. One important group of these methods are the collection *wrapper* methods: they return a special-purpose collection wrapped around a collection you specify. The purpose of the wrapper collection is to wrap additional functionality around a collection that does not provide it itself. Wrappers exist to provide thread-safety, write-protection and runtime type checking. Wrapper collections are always *backed by* the original collection, which means that the methods of the wrapper simply dispatch to the equivalent methods of the wrapped collection. This means that changes made to the collection through the wrapper are visible through the wrapped collection and vice versa.

The first set of wrapper methods provides threadsafe wrappers around collections. Except for the legacy classes Vector and Hashtable, the collection implementations in java.util do not have synchronized methods and are not protected against concurrent access by multiple threads. If you need threadsafe collections, create them with code like this:

```
List<String> list = Collections.synchronizedList(new ArrayList<String>());
Set<Integer> set = Collections.synchronizedSet(new HashSet<Integer>());
Map<String,Integer> map =
    Collections.synchronizedMap(new HashMap<String,Integer>());
```

A second set of wrapper methods provides collection objects through which the underlying collection cannot be modified. They return a read-only view of a collection: any attempt to change the content of the collection results in an UnsupportedOperationException. These wrappers are useful when you must pass a collection to a method that must not be allowed to modify or mutate the content of the collection in any way:

```
List<Integer> primes = new ArrayList<Integer>();
List<Integer> readonly = Collections.unmodifiableList(primes);
// We can modify the list through primes
primes.addAll(Arrays.asList(2, 3, 5, 7, 11, 13, 17, 19));
// But we can't modify through the read-only wrapper
readonly.add(23);  // UnsupportedOperationException
```

The final set of wrapper methods provides runtime type checking of any values added to the collection. They were added in Java 5.0 to complement the compile-time type safety provided by generics. These wrappers are helpful when working with legacy code that has not been converted to use generics. If you have a SortedSet<String>, for example, and must pass it to a method that expects a Set, you can use a checked wrapper to ensure that that method cannot add anything to the set that is not a String:

```
SortedSet<String> words = new TreeSet<String>(); // A set
SortedSet<String> checkedWords =                 // A checked set
   Collections.checkedSortedSet(words, String.class);
addWordsFromFile(checkedWords, filename);        // Passed to legacy method
```

Special-Case Collections

In addition to its wrapper methods, the java.util.Collections class also defines utility methods for creating immutable collection instances that contain a single element and other methods for creating empty collections. singleton(), singletonList(), and singletonMap() return immutable Set, List, and Map objects that contain a single specified object or a single key/value pair. These methods are useful, for example, when you need to pass a single object to a method that expects a collection.

The Collections class also includes methods that return empty collections. If you are writing a method that returns a collection, it is usually best to handle the no-values-to-return case by returning an empty collection instead of a special-case value like null:

```
Set<Integer> si = Collections.emptySet();
List<String> ss = Collections.emptyList();
Map<String,Integer> m = Collections.emptyMap();
```

Finally, nCopies() returns an immutable List that contains a specified number of copies of a single specified object:

```
List<Integer> tenzeros = Collections.nCopies(10, 0);
```

Converting to and from Arrays

Arrays of objects and collections serve similar purposes. It is possible to convert from one to the other:

```
String[] a ={ "this", "is", "a", "test" };  // An array
List<String> l = Arrays.asList(a);          // View array as an ungrowable list
List<String> m = new ArrayList<String>(l);  // Make a growable copy of the view

// In Java 5.0, asList() is a varargs method so we can do this, too:
Set<Character> abc = new HashSet<Character>(Arrays.asList('a', 'b', 'c'));

// Collection defines the toArray() method.  The no-args version creates
// an Object[] array, copies collection elements to it and returns it
Object[] members = set.toArray();         // Get set elements as an array
Object[] items = list.toArray();          // Get list elements as an array
Object[] keys = map.keySet().toArray();   // Get map key objects as an array
Object[] values = map.values().toArray(); // Get map value objects as an array

// If you want the return value to be something other than Object[], pass
// in an array of the appropriate type.  If the array is not big enough,
// another one of the same type will be allocated.  If the array is too big,
// the collection elements copied to it will be null-terminated
String[] c = l.toArray(new String[0]);
```

Collections Utility Methods

Just as the java.util.Arrays class defined methods to operate on arrays, the java.util.Collections class defines methods to operate on collections. Most notable are methods to sort and search the elements of collections:

```
Collections.sort(list);
int pos = Collections.binarySearch(list, "key"); // list must be sorted first
```

Here are some other interesting Collections methods:

```
Collections.copy(list1, list2); // Copy list2 into list1, overwriting list1
Collections.fill(list, o);      // Fill list with Object o
Collections.max(c);             // Find the largest element in Collection c
Collections.min(c);             // Find the smallest element in Collection c

Collections.reverse(list);      // Reverse list
Collections.shuffle(list);      // Mix up list
```

Implementing Collections

The Java Collections Framework provides abstract classes that make it simple to implement common types of collections. The following code extends AbstractList to define a QuadraticSequence, a list implementation that computes list values on demand rather than actually storing them in memory anywhere. See also AbstractSet, AbstractMap, AbstractQueue, and AbstractSequentialList.

```
import java.util.*;

/** An immutable List<Double> representing the sequence ax^2 + bx + c */
public class QuadraticSequence extends AbstractList<Double> {
    final int size;
    final double a, b, c;

    QuadraticSequence(double a, double b, double c, int size) {
        this.a = a; this.b = b; this.c = c; this.size = size;
    }

    @Override public int size() { return size; }

    @Override public Double get(int index) {
        if (index<0 || index>=size) throw new ArrayIndexOutOfBoundsException();
        return a*index*index + b*index + c;
    }
}
```

Threads and Concurrency

The Java platform has supported multithreaded or *concurrent* programming with the Thread class and Runnable interface since Java 1.0. Java 5.0 bolsters that support with a comprehensive set of new utilities for concurrent programming.

Creating, Running, and Manipulating Threads

Java makes it easy to define and work with multiple threads of execution within a program. java.lang.Thread is the fundamental thread class in the Java API. There are two ways to define a thread. One is to subclass Thread, override the run() method and then instantiate your Thread subclass. The other is to define a class that implements the Runnable method (i.e., define a run() method) and then pass an instance of this Runnable object to the Thread() constructor. In either case, the result is a Thread object, where the run() method is the body of the thread. When you call the start() method of the Thread object, the interpreter creates a new thread to execute the run() method. This new thread continues to run until the run( ) method exits. Meanwhile, the original thread continues running itself, starting with the statement following the start() method. The following code demonstrates:

```
final List list; // Some long unsorted list of objects; initialized elsewhere

/** A Thread class for sorting a List in the background */
class BackgroundSorter extends Thread {
  List l;
  public BackgroundSorter(List l) { this.l = l; }    // Constructor
  public void run() { Collections.sort(l); }         // Thread body
}

// Create a BackgroundSorter thread
Thread sorter = new BackgroundSorter(list);
// Start it running; the new thread runs the run() method above while
// the original thread continues with whatever statement comes next.
sorter.start();

// Here's another way to define a similar thread
Thread t = new Thread(new Runnable() {          // Create a new thread
  public void run() { Collections.sort(list); } // to sort the list of objects.
});
t.start();                                      // Start it running
```

Thread lifecycle

A thread can be in one of six states. In Java 5.0, these states are represented by the Thread.State enumerated type, and the state of a thread can be queried with the getState( ) method. A listing of the Thread.State constants provides a good overview of the lifecycle of a thread:

NEW
: The Thread has been created but its start( ) method has not yet been called. All threads start in this state.

RUNNABLE
: The thread is running or is available to run when the operating system schedules it.

BLOCKED
: The thread is not running because it is waiting to acquire a lock so that it can enter a synchronized method or block. We'll see more about synchronized methods and blocks later in this section.

WAITING
: The thread is not running because it has called Object.wait() or Thread.join( ).

TIMED_WAITING
: The thread is not running because it has called Thread.sleep() or has called Object.wait( ) or Thread.join() with a timeout value.

TERMINATED
: The thread has completed execution. Its run( ) method has exited normally or by throwing an exception.

Thread priorities

Threads can run at different priority levels. A thread at a given priority level does not typically run unless no higher-priority threads are waiting to run. Here is some code you can use when working with thread priorities:

```
// Set a thread t to lower-than-normal priority
t.setPriority(Thread.NORM_PRIORITY-1);

// Set a thread to lower priority than the current thread
t.setPriority(Thread.currentThread().getPriority() - 1);

// Threads that don't pause for I/O should explicitly yield the CPU
// to give other threads with the same priority a chance to run.
Thread t = new Thread(new Runnable() {
  public void run() {
    for(int i = 0; i < data.length; i++) {  // Loop through a bunch of data
      process(data[i]);                     // Process it
      if ((i % 10) == 0)                    // But after every 10 iterations,
        Thread.yield();                     // pause to let other threads run.
    }
  }
});
```

Handling uncaught exceptions

A thread terminates normally when it reaches the end of its `run()` method or when it executes a `return` statement in that method. A thread can also terminate by throwing an exception, however. When a thread exits in this way, the default behavior is to print the name of the thread, the type of the exception, the exception message, and a stack trace. In Java 5.0, you can install a custom handler for uncaught exceptions in a thread. For example:

```
// This thread just throws an exception
Thread t = new Thread() {
        public void run() {throw new UnsupportedOperationException();}
    };

// Giving threads a name helps with debugging
t.setName("My Broken Thread");

// Here's a handler for the error.
t.setUncaughtExceptionHandler(new Thread.UncaughtExceptionHandler() {
        public void uncaughtException(Thread t, Throwable e) {
            System.err.printf("Exception in thread %d '%s':" +
                              "%s at line %d of %s%n",
                              t.getId(),    // Thread id
                              t.getName(),  // Thread name
                              e.toString(), // Exception name and message
                              e.getStackTrace()[0].getLineNumber(), // line #
                              e.getStackTrace()[0].getFileName());  // filename
        }
    });
```

Making a Thread Sleep

Often, threads are used to perform some kind of repetitive task at a fixed interval. This is particularly true when doing graphical programming that involves animation or similar effects. The key to doing this is making a thread *sleep*, or stop running, for a specified amount of time. This is done with the static `Thread.sleep()` method, or, in Java 5.0, with utility methods of enumerated constants of the `TimeUnit` class:

```
import static java.util.concurrent.TimeUnit.SECONDS;  // utility class

public class Clock extends Thread {
    // This field is volatile because two different threads may access it
    volatile boolean keepRunning = true;

    public Clock() {      // The constructor
        setDaemon(true); // Daemon thread: interpreter can exit while it runs
    }

    public void run() {        // The body of the thread
        while(keepRunning) {   // This thread runs until asked to stop
            long now = System.currentTimeMillis();    // Get current time
            System.out.printf("%tr%n", now);          // Print it out
            try { Thread.sleep(1000); }               // Wait 1000 milliseconds
            catch (InterruptedException e) { return; }// Quit on interrupt
        }
    }

    // Ask the thread to stop running.  An alternative to interrupt().
    public void pleaseStop() { keepRunning = false; }

    // This method demonstrates how to use the Clock class
    public static void main(String[] args) {
        Clock c = new Clock();                     // Create a Clock thread
        c.start();                                 // Start it
        try {  SECONDS.sleep(10); }                // Wait 10 seconds
        catch(InterruptedException ignore) {}  // Ignore interrupts
        // Now stop the clock thread.  We could also use c.interrupt()
        c.pleaseStop();
    }
}
```

Notice the `pleaseStop()` method in this example: it is designed to stop the clock thread in a controlled way. The example is coded so that it can also be stopped by calling the `interrupt()` method it inherits from `Thread`. The `Thread` class defines a `stop()` method, but it is deprecated.

Running and Scheduling Tasks

Java provides a number of ways to run tasks asynchronously or to schedule them for future execution without having to explicitly create `Thread` objects. The following sections illustrate the `Timer` class added in Java 1.3 and the executors framework of the Java 5.0 `java.util.concurrent` package.

Scheduling tasks with Timer

Added in Java 1.3, the java.util.Timer and java.util.TimerTask classes make it easy to run repetitive tasks. Here is some code that behaves much like the Clock class shown earlier:

```
import java.util.*;

// Define the time-display task
TimerTask displayTime = new TimerTask() {
  public void run() { System.out.printf("%tr%n", System.currentTimeMillis()); }
};
// Create a timer object to run the task (and possibly others)
Timer timer = new Timer();
// Now schedule that task to be run every 1,000 milliseconds, starting now
timer.schedule(displayTime, 0, 1000);

// To stop the time-display task
displayTime.cancel();
```

The Executor interface

In Java 5.0, the java.util.concurrent package includes the Executor interface. An Executor is an object that can execute a Runnable object. A user of an Executor often does not need to be aware of just how the Executor accomplishes this: it just needs to know that the Runnable will, at some point, run. Executor implementations can be created to use a number of different threading strategies, as the following code makes clear. (Note that this example also demonstrates the use of a BlockingQueue.)

```
import java.util.concurrent.*;

/** Execute a Runnable in the current thread. */
class CurrentThreadExecutor implements Executor {
    public void execute(Runnable r) { r.run(); }
}

/** Execute each Runnable using a newly created thread */
class NewThreadExecutor implements Executor {
    public void execute(Runnable r) { new Thread(r).start(); }
}

/**
 * Queue up the Runnables and execute them in order using a single thread
 * created for that purpose.
 */
class SingleThreadExecutor extends Thread implements Executor {
    BlockingQueue<Runnable> q = new LinkedBlockingQueue<Runnable>();

    public void execute(Runnable r) {
        // Don't execute the Runnable here; just put it on the queue.
        // Our queue is effectively unbounded, so this should never block.
        // Since it never blocks, it should never throw InterruptedException.
        try { q.put(r); }
```

```
        catch(InterruptedException never) { throw new AssertionError(never); }
    }

    // This is the body of the thread that actually executes the Runnables
    public void run() {
        for(;;) {                       // Loop forever
            try {
                Runnable r = q.take();  // Get next Runnable, or wait
                r.run();                // Run it!
            }
            catch(InterruptedException e) {
                // If interrupted, stop executing queued Runnables.
                return;
            }
        }
    }
}
```

These sample implementations help demonstrate how an Executor works and how it separates the notion of executing a task from the scheduling policy and threading details of the implementation. It is rarely necessary to actually implement your own Executor, however, since java.util.concurrent provides the flexible and powerful ThreadPoolExecutor class. This class is typically used via one of the static factory methods in the Executors class:

```
Executor oneThread = Executors.newSingleThreadExecutor(); // pool size of 1
Executor fixedPool = Executors.newFixedThreadPool(10); // 10 threads in pool
Executor unboundedPool = Executors.newCachedThreadPool(); // as many as needed
```

In addition to these convenient factory methods, you can also explicitly create a ThreadPoolExecutor if you want to specify a minimum and maximum size for the thread pool or want to specify the queue type (bounded, unbounded, priority-sorted, or synchronized, for example) to use for tasks that cannot immediately be run by a thread.

ExecutorService

If you've looked at the signature for ThreadPoolExecutor or for the Executors factory methods cited above, you'll see that it is an ExecutorService. The ExecutorService interface extends Executor and adds the ability to execute Callable objects. Callable is something like a Runnable. Instead of encapsulating arbitrary code in a run() method, however, a Callable puts that code in a call() method. call( ) differs from run() in two important ways: it returns a result, and it is allowed to throw exceptions.

Because call() returns a result, the Callable interface takes the result type as a parameter. A time-consuming chunk of code that computes a large prime number, for example, could be wrapped in a Callable<BigInteger>:

```
import java.util.concurrent.*;
import java.math.BigInteger;
import java.util.Random;
import java.security.SecureRandom;
```

```
/** This is a Callable implementation for computing big primes. */
public class RandomPrimeSearch implements Callable<BigInteger> {
    static Random prng = new SecureRandom();  // self-seeding
    int n;
    public RandomPrimeSearch(int bitsize) { n = bitsize; }
    public BigInteger call() { return BigInteger.probablePrime(n, prng); }
}
```

You can invoke the call( ) method of any Callable object directly, of course, but to execute it using an ExecutorService, you pass it to the submit() method. Because ExecutorService implementations typically run tasks asynchronously, the submit() method cannot simply return the result of the call( ) method. Instead, submit() returns a Future object. A Future is simply the promise of a result sometime in the future. It is parameterized with the type of the result, as shown in this code snippet:

```
// Try to compute two primes at the same time
ExecutorService threadpool = Executors.newFixedThreadPool(2);
Future<BigInteger> p = threadpool.submit(new RandomPrimeSearch(512));
Future<BigInteger> q = threadpool.submit(new RandomPrimeSearch(512));
```

Once you have a Future object, what can you do with it? You can call isDone() to see if the Callable has finished running. You can call cancel() to cancel execution of the Callable and can call isCancelled() to see if the Callable was canceled before it completed. But most of the time, you simply call get( ) to get the result of the call( ) method. get() blocks, if necessary, to wait for the call( ) method to complete. Here is code you might use with the Future objects shown above:

```
BigInteger product = p.get().multiply(q.get());
```

Note that the get() method may throw an ExecutionException. Recall that Callable.call( ) can throw any kind of exception. If this happens, the Future wraps that exception in an ExecutionException and throws it from get(). Note that the Future.isDone() method considers a Callable to be "done," even if the call( ) method terminated abnormally with an exception.

ScheduledExecutorService

ScheduledExecutorService is an extension of ExecutorService that adds Timer-like scheduling capabilities. It allows you to schedule a Runnable or Callable to be executed once after a specified time delay or to schedule a Runnable for repeated execution. In each case, the result of scheduling a task for future execution is a ScheduledFuture object. This is simply a Future that also implements the Delay interface and provides a getDelay( ) method that can be used to query the remaining time before execution of the task.

The easiest way to obtain a ScheduledExecutorService is with factory methods of the Executors class. The following code uses a ScheduledExecutorService to repeatedly perform an action and also to cancel the repeated action after a fixed interval.

```
/**
 * Print random ASCII characters at a rate of cps characters per second
 * for a total of totalSeconds seconds.
```

```
     */
    public static void spew(int cps, int totalSeconds) {
        final Random rng = new Random(System.currentTimeMillis());
        final ScheduledExecutorService executor =
            Executors.newSingleThreadScheduledExecutor();
        final ScheduledFuture<?> spewer =
            executor.scheduleAtFixedRate(new Runnable() {
                    public void run() {
                        System.out.print((char)(rng.nextInt('~' - ' ') + ' '));
                        System.out.flush();
                    }
                },
                                                0, 1000000/cps, TimeUnit.MICROSECONDS);
        executor.schedule(new Runnable() {
                public void run() {
                    spewer.cancel(false);
                    executor.shutdown();
                    System.out.println();
                }
            },
                          totalSeconds, TimeUnit.SECONDS);
    }
```

Exclusion and Locks

When using multiple threads, you must be very careful if you allow more than one thread to access the same data structure. Consider what would happen if one thread was trying to loop through the elements of a `List` while another thread was sorting those elements. Preventing this kind of unwanted concurrency is one of the central problems of multithreaded computing. The basic technique for preventing two threads from accessing the same object at the same time is to require a thread to obtain a lock on the object before the thread can modify it. While any one thread holds the lock, another thread that requests the lock has to wait until the first thread is done and releases the lock. Every Java object has the fundamental ability to provide such a locking capability.

The easiest way to keep objects threadsafe is to declare all sensitive methods `synchronized`. A thread must obtain a lock on an object before it can execute any of its `synchronized` methods, which means that no other thread can execute any other `synchronized` method at the same time. (If a `static` method is declared `synchronized`, the thread must obtain a lock on the class, and this works in the same manner.) To do finer-grained locking, you can specify `synchronized` blocks of code that hold a lock on a specified object for a short time:

```
// This method swaps two array elements in a synchronized block
public static void swap(Object[] array, int index1, int index2) {
  synchronized(array) {
    Object tmp = array[index1];
    array[index1] = array[index2];
    array[index2] = tmp;
  }
}

// The Collection, Set, List, and Map implementations in java.util do
```

```
// not have synchronized methods (except for the legacy implementations
// Vector and Hashtable). When working with multiple threads, you can
// obtain synchronized wrapper objects.
List synclist = Collections.synchronizedList(list);
Map syncmap = Collections.synchronizedMap(map);
```

The java.util.concurrent.locks package

Note that when you use the synchronized modifier or statement, the lock you acquire is block-scoped, and is automatically released when the thread exits the method or block. The `java.util.concurrent.locks` package in Java 5.0 provides an alternative: a `Lock` object that you explicitly lock and unlock. `Lock` objects are not automatically block-scoped and you must be careful to use `try/finally` constructs to ensure that locks are always released. On the other hand, `Lock` enables algorithms that are simply not possible with block-scoped locks, such as the following "hand-over-hand" linked list traversal:

```
import java.util.concurrent.locks.*;  // New in Java 5.0

/**
 * A partial implementation of a linked list of values of type E.
 * It demonstrates hand-over-hand locking with Lock
 */
public class LinkList<E> {
    E value;                // The value of this node of the list
    LinkList<E> rest;       // The rest of the list
    Lock lock;              // A lock for this node

    public LinkList(E value) {  // Constructor for a list
        this.value = value;          // Node value
        rest = null;                 // This is the only node in the list
        lock = new ReentrantLock();  // We can lock this node
    }

    /**
     * Append a node to the end of the list, traversing the list using
     * hand-over-hand locking. This method is threadsafe: multiple threads
     * may traverse different portions of the list at the same time.
     **/
    public void append(E value) {
        LinkList<E> node = this;  // Start at this node
        node.lock.lock();         // Lock it.

        // Loop 'till we find the last node in the list
        while(node.rest != null) {
            LinkList<E> next = node.rest;

            // This is the hand-over-hand part.  Lock the next node and then
            // unlock the current node.  We use a try/finally construct so
            // that the current node is unlocked even if the lock on the
            // next node fails with an exception.
            try { next.lock.lock(); }  // lock the next node
            finally { node.lock.unlock(); } // unlock the current node
            node = next;
```

```
        }

        // At this point, node is the final node in the list, and we have
        // a lock on it.  Use a try/finally to ensure that we unlock it.
        try {
            node.rest = new LinkList<E>(value); // Append new node
        }
        finally { node.lock.unlock(); }
    }
}
```

Deadlock

When you are using locking to prevent threads from accessing the same data at the same time, you must be careful to avoid *deadlock*, which occurs when two threads end up waiting for each other to release a lock they need. Since neither can proceed, neither one can release the lock it holds, and they both stop running. The following code is prone to deadlock. Whether or not a deadlock actually occurs may vary from system to system and from execution to execution.

```
// When two threads try to lock two objects, deadlock can occur unless
// they always request the locks in the same order.
final Object resource1 = new Object();   // Here are two objects to lock
final Object resource2 = new Object();
Thread t1 = new Thread(new Runnable() {  // Locks resource1 then resource2
  public void run() {
    synchronized(resource1) {
      synchronized(resource2) { compute(); }
    }
  }
});

Thread t2 = new Thread(new Runnable() {  // Locks resource2 then resource1
  public void run() {
    synchronized(resource2) {
      synchronized(resource1) { compute(); }
    }
  }
});

t1.start();  // Locks resource1
t2.start();  // Locks resource2 and now neither thread can progress!
```

Coordinating Threads

It is common in multithreaded programming to require one thread to wait for another thread to take some action. The Java platform provides a number of ways to coordinate threads, including methods built into the `Object` and `Thread` classes, as well as "synchronizer" utility classes introduced in Java 5.0.

wait( ) and notify()

Sometimes a thread needs to stop running and wait until some kind of event occurs, at which point it is told to continue running. This is done with the `wait()` and `notify( )` methods. These aren't methods of the `Thread` class, however; they are methods of `Object`. Just as every Java object has a lock associated with it, every object can maintain a list of waiting threads. When a thread calls the `wait()` method of an object, any locks the thread holds are temporarily released, and the thread is added to the list of waiting threads for that object and stops running. When another thread calls the `notifyAll( )` method of the same object, the object wakes up the waiting threads and allows them to continue running:

```
import java.util.*;

/**
 * A queue. One thread calls push() to put an object on the queue.
 * Another calls pop() to get an object off the queue. If there is no
 * data, pop() waits until there is some, using wait()/notify().
 * wait() and notify() must be used within a synchronized method or
 * block. In Java 5.0, use a java.util.concurrent.BlockingQueue instead.
 */
public class WaitingQueue<E> {
    LinkedList<E> q = new LinkedList<E>();  // Where objects are stored
    public synchronized void push(E o) {
        q.add(o);          // Append the object to the end of the list
        this.notifyAll(); // Tell waiting threads that data is ready
    }
    public synchronized E pop() {
        while(q.size() == 0) {
            try { this.wait(); }
            catch (InterruptedException ignore) {}
        }
        return q.remove(0);
    }
}
```

Note that such a class is not necessary in Java 5.0 because `java.util.concurrent` defines the `BlockingQueue` interface and general-purpose implementations such as `ArrayBlockingQueue`.

Waiting on a Condition

Java 5.0 provides an alternative to the `wait()` and `notifyAll( )` methods of `Object`. `java.util.concurrent.locks` defines a `Condition` object with `await()` and `signalAll()` methods. `Condition` objects are always associated with `Lock` objects and are used in much the same way as the locking and waiting capability built into each Java object. The primary benefit is that it is possible to have more than one `Condition` for each `Lock`, something that is not possible with `Object`-based locking and waiting.

Waiting for a thread to finish

Sometimes one thread needs to stop and wait for another thread to complete. You can accomplish this with the join() method:

```
List list;  // A long list of objects to be sorted; initialized elsewhere

// Define a thread to sort the list: lower its priority, so it runs only
// when the current thread is waiting for I/O and then start it running.
Thread sorter = new BackgroundSorter(list);              // Defined earlier
sorter.setPriority(Thread.currentThread.getPriority()-1); // Lower priority
sorter.start();                                           // Start sorting

// Meanwhile, in this original thread, read data from a file
byte[] data = readData();  // Method defined elsewhere

// Before we can proceed, we need the list to be fully sorted, so
// we must wait for the sorter thread to exit, if it hasn't already.
try { sorter.join(); } catch(InterruptedException e) {}
```

Synchronizer utilities

java.util.concurrent includes four "synchronizer" classes that help to synchronize the state of a concurrent program by making threads wait until certain conditions hold:

Semaphore
: The Semaphore class models semaphores, a traditional concurrent programming construct. Conceptually, a semaphore represents one or more "permits." A thread that needs a permit calls acquire( ) and then calls release() when done with it. acquire() blocks if no permits are available, suspending the thread until another thread releases a permit.

CountDownLatch
: A *latch* is conceptually any variable or concurrency construct that has two possible states and transitions from its initial state to its final state only once. Once the transition occurs, it remains in that final state forever. CountDownLatch is a concurrency utility that can exist in two states, closed and open. In its initial closed state, any threads that call the await( ) method block and cannot proceed until it transitions to its latched open state. Once this transition occurs, all waiting threads proceed, and any threads that call await() in the future will not block at all. The transition from closed to open occurs when a specified number of calls to countDown( ) have occurred.

Exchanger
: An Exchanger is a utility that allows two threads to *rendezvous* and exchange values. The first thread to call the exchange( ) method blocks until a second thread calls the same method. When this happens, the argument passed to the exchange() method by the first thread becomes the return value of the method for the second thread and vice-versa. When the two exchange() invocations return, both threads are free to continue running concurrently. Exchanger is a generic type and uses its type parameter to specify the type of values to be exchanged.

`CyclicBarrier`
: A `CyclicBarrier` is a utility that enables a group of N threads to wait for each other to reach a synchronization point. The number of threads is specified when the `CyclicBarrier` is first created. Threads call the `await()` method to block until the last thread calls `await()`, at which point all threads resume again. Unlike a `CountDownLatch`, a `CyclicBarrier` resets its count and is ready for immediate reuse. `CyclicBarrier` is useful in parallel algorithms in which a computation is decomposed into parts, and each part is handled by a separate thread. In such algorithms, the threads must typically rendezvous so that their partial solutions can be merged into a complete solution. To facilitate this, the `CyclicBarrier` constructor allows you to specify a `Runnable` object to be executed by the last thread that calls `await()` before any of the other threads are woken up and allowed to resume. This `Runnable` can provide the coordination required to assemble a solution from the threads computations or to assign a new computation to each of the threads.

Thread Interruption

In the examples illustrating the `sleep()`, `join()`, and `wait()` methods, you may have noticed that calls to each of these methods are wrapped in a `try` statement that catches an `InterruptedException`. This is necessary because the `interrupt()` method allows one thread to interrupt the execution of another. The outcome of an interrupt depends on how you handle the `InterruptedException`. The response that is usually preferred is for an interrupted thread to stop running. On the other hand, if you simply catch and ignore the `InterruptedException`, an interrupt simply stops a thread from blocking.

If the `interrupt()` method is called on a thread that is not blocked, the thread continues running, but its "interrupt status" is set to indicate that an interrupt has been requested. A thread can test its own interrupt status by calling the static `Thread.interrupted()` method, which returns `true` if the thread has been interrupted and, as a side effect, clears the interrupt status. One thread can test the interrupt status of another thread with the instance method `isInterrupted()`, which queries the status but does not clear it.

If a thread calls `sleep()`, `join()`, or `wait()` while its interrupt status is set, it does not block but immediately throws an `InterruptedException` (the interrupt status is cleared as a side effect of throwing the exception). Similarly, if the `interrupt()` method is called on a thread that is already blocked in a call to `sleep()`, `join()`, or `wait()`, that thread stops blocking by throwing an `InterruptedException`.

One of the most common times that threads block is while doing input/output; a thread often has to pause and wait for data to become available from the filesystem or from the network. (The `java.io`, `java.net`, and `java.nio` APIs for performing I/O operations are discussed later in this chapter.) Unfortunately, the `interrupt()` method does not wake up a thread blocked in an I/O method of the `java.io` package. This is one of the shortcomings of `java.io` that is cured by the New I/O API in `java.nio`. If a thread is interrupted while blocked in an I/O operation on any channel that implements `java.nio.channels.InterruptibleChannel`, the channel is closed, the thread's interrupt status is set, and the thread wakes up by throwing a `java.nio.channels.ClosedByInterruptException`. The same thing happens if a thread tries to call a blocking I/O method while its interrupt status is set. Similarly, if a thread is interrupted while it is blocked in the `select( )` method of a `java.nio.channels.Selector` (or if it calls `select( )` while its interrupt status is set), `select( )` will stop blocking (or will never start) and will return immediately. No exception is thrown in this case; the interrupted thread simply wakes up, and the `select()` call returns.

Blocking Queues

As noted in "The Queue and BlockingQueue Interfaces" earlier in this chapter, a *queue* is a collection in which elements are inserted at the "tail" and removed at the "head." The `Queue` interface and various implementations were added to `java.util` as part of Java 5.0. `java.util.concurrent` extends the `Queue` interface: `BlockingQueue` defines `put()` and `take( )` methods that allow you to add and remove elements of the queue, blocking if necessary until the queue has room, or until there is an element to be removed. The use of blocking queues is a common pattern in multithreaded programming: one thread produces objects and places them on a queue for consumption by another thread which removes them from the queue.

`java.util.concurrent` provides five implementations of `BlockingQueue`:

`ArrayBlockingQueue`
: This implementation is based on an array, and, like all arrays, has a fixed capacity established when it is created. At the cost of reduced throughput, this queue can operate in a "fair" mode in which threads blocking to `put()` or `take( )` an element are served in the order in which they arrived.

`LinkedBlockingQueue`
: This implementation is based on a linked-list data structure. It may have a maximum size specified, but, by default, it is essentially unbounded.

`PriorityBlockingQueue`
: This unbounded queue does not implement FIFO (first-in, first-out) ordering. Instead, it orders its elements based on a specified `Comparator` object, or based on their natural ordering if they are `Comparable` objects and no `Comparator` is specified. The element returned by `take()` is the smallest element according to the `Comparator` or `Comparable` ordering. See also `java.util.PriorityQueue` for a nonblocking version.

`DelayQueue`
: A `DelayQueue` is like a `PriorityBlockingQueue` for elements that implement the `Delayed` interface. `Delayed` is `Comparable` and orders elements by how long they are delayed. But `DelayQueue` is more than just an unbounded queue that sorts its elements. It also restricts `take( )` and related methods so that elements cannot be removed from the queue until their delay has elapsed.

`SynchronousQueue`
: This class implements the degenerate case of a `BlockingQueue` with a capacity of zero. A call to `put()` blocks until some other thread calls `take( )`, and a call to `take( )` blocks until some other thread calls `put()`.

Atomic Variables

The java.util.concurrent.atomic package contains utility classes that permit *atomic* operations on fields without locking. An atomic operation is one that is indivisible: no other thread can observe an atomic variable in the middle of an atomic operation on it. These utility classes define get() and set( ) accessor methods that have the properties of volatile fields but also define compound operations such as compare-and-set and get-and-increment that behave atomically. The code below demonstrates the use of AtomicInteger and contrasts it with the use of a traditional synchronized method:

```
// The count1(), count2() and count3() methods are all threadsafe.  Two
// threads can call these methods at the same time, and they will never
// see the same return value.
public class Counters {
    // A counter using a synchronized method and locking
    int count1 = 0;
    public synchronized int count1() { return count1++; }

    // A counter using an atomic increment on an AtomicInteger
    AtomicInteger count2 = new AtomicInteger(0);
    public int count2() { return count2.getAndIncrement(); }

    // An optimistic counter using compareAndSet()
    AtomicInteger count3 = new AtomicInteger(0);
    public int count3() {
        // Get the counter value with get() and set it with compareAndSet().
        // If compareAndSet() returns false, try again until we get
        // through the loop without interference.
        int result;
        do {
            result = count3.get();
        } while(!count3.compareAndSet(result, result+1));
        return result;
    }
}
```

Files and Directories

The java.io.File class represents a file or a directory and defines a number of important methods for manipulating files and directories. Note, however, that none of these methods allow you to read the contents of a file; that is the job of java.io.FileInputStream, which is just one of the many types of I/O streams used in Java and discussed in the next section. Here are some things you can do with File:

```
import java.io.*;
import java.util.*;

// Get the name of the user's home directory and represent it with a File
File homedir = new File(System.getProperty("user.home"));
// Create a File object to represent a file in that directory
File f = new File(homedir, ".configfile");
```

```
// Find out how big a file is and when it was last modified
long filelength = f.length();
Date lastModified = new java.util.Date(f.lastModified());

// If the file exists, is not a directory, and is readable,
// move it into a newly created directory.
if (f.exists() && f.isFile() && f.canRead()) {       // Check config file
  File configdir = new File(homedir, ".configdir"); // A new config directory
  configdir.mkdir();                                 // Create that directory
  f.renameTo(new File(configdir, ".config"));       // Move the file into it
}

// List all files in the home directory
String[] allfiles = homedir.list();

// List all files that have a ".java" suffix
String[] sourcecode = homedir.list(new FilenameFilter() {
  public boolean accept(File d, String name) { return name.endsWith(".java"); }
});
```

The File class gained some important additional functionality as of Java 1.2:

```
// List all filesystem root directories; on Windows, this gives us
// File objects for all drive letters (Java 1.2 and later).
File[] rootdirs = File.listRoots();

// Atomically, create a lock file, then delete it (Java 1.2 and later)
File lock = new File(configdir, ".lock");
if (lock.createNewFile()) {
  // We successfully created the file.  Now arrange to delete it on exit
  lock.deleteOnExit();

  // Now run the application secure in the knowledge that no one else
  // is running it at the same time
  ...
}
else {
  // We didn't create the file; someone else has a lock
  System.err.println("Can't create lock file; exiting.");
  System.exit(1);
}

// Create a temporary file to use during processing (Java 1.2 and later)
File temp = File.createTempFile("app", ".tmp");  // Filename prefix and suffix
// Do something with the temp file
  ...
// And delete it when we're done
temp.delete();
```

RandomAccessFile

The java.io package also defines a RandomAccessFile class that allows you to read binary data from arbitrary locations in a file. This can be useful in certain situations, but most applications read files sequentially, using the stream classes described in the next section. Here is a short example of using RandomAccessFile:

```
// Open a file for read/write ("rw") access
File datafile = new File(configdir, "datafile");
RandomAccessFile f = new RandomAccessFile(datafile, "rw");
f.seek(100);                    // Move to byte 100 of the file
byte[] data = new byte[100];    // Create a buffer to hold data
f.read(data);                   // Read 100 bytes from the file
int i = f.readInt();            // Read a 4-byte integer from the file
f.seek(100);                    // Move back to byte 100
f.writeInt(i);                  // Write the integer first
f.write(data);                  // Then write the 100 bytes
f.close();                      // Close file when done with it
```

Input/Output with java.io

The java.io package defines a large number of classes for reading and writing streaming, or sequential, data. The InputStream and OutputStream classes are for reading and writing streams of bytes while the Reader and Writer classes are for reading and writing streams of characters. Streams can be nested, meaning you might read characters from a FilterReader object that reads and processes characters from an underlying Reader stream. This underlying Reader stream might read bytes from an InputStream and convert them to characters.

Reading Console Input

You can perform a number of common operations with streams. One is to read lines of input the user types at the console:

```
import java.io.*;

BufferedReader console = new BufferedReader(new InputStreamReader(System.in));
System.out.print("What is your name: ");
String name = null;
try {
  name = console.readLine();
}
catch (IOException e) { name = "<" + e + ">"; }  // This should never happen
System.out.println("Hello " + name);
```

Reading Lines from a Text File

Reading lines of text from a file is a similar operation. The following code reads an entire text file and quits when it reaches the end:

```
String filename = System.getProperty("user.home") + File.separator + ".cshrc";
try {
  BufferedReader in = new BufferedReader(new FileReader(filename));
  String line;
  while((line = in.readLine()) != null) {  // Read line, check for end-of-file
    System.out.println(line);              // Print the line
  }
```

```
  in.close();    // Always close a stream when you are done with it
}
catch (IOException e) {
  // Handle FileNotFoundException, etc. here
}
```

Writing Text to a File

Throughout this book, you've seen the use of the `System.out.println()` method to display text on the console. `System.out` simply refers to an output stream. You can print text to any output stream using similar techniques. The following code shows how to output text to a file:

```
try {
  File f = new File(homedir, ".config");
  PrintWriter out = new PrintWriter(new FileWriter(f));
  out.println("## Automatically generated config file. DO NOT EDIT!");
  out.close(); // We're done writing
}
catch (IOException e) { /* Handle exceptions */ }
```

Reading a Binary File

Not all files contain text, however. The following lines of code treat a file as a stream of bytes and read the bytes into a large array:

```
try {
  File f;                             // File to read; initialized elsewhere
  int filesize = (int) f.length();    // Figure out the file size
  byte[] data = new byte[filesize];   // Create an array that is big enough
  // Create a stream to read the file
  DataInputStream in = new DataInputStream(new FileInputStream(f));
  in.readFully(data);  // Read file contents into array
  in.close();
}
catch (IOException e) { /* Handle exceptions */ }
```

Compressing Data

Various other packages of the Java platform define specialized stream classes that operate on streaming data in some useful way. The following code shows how to use stream classes from `java.util.zip` to compute a checksum of data and then compress the data while writing it to a file:

```
import java.io.*;
import java.util.zip.*;

try {
  File f;                           // File to write to; initialized elsewhere
  byte[] data;                      // Data to write; initialized elsewhere
  Checksum check = new Adler32(); // An object to compute a simple checksum

  // Create a stream that writes bytes to the file f
  FileOutputStream fos = new FileOutputStream(f);
```

```
    // Create a stream that compresses bytes and writes them to fos
    GZIPOutputStream gzos = new GZIPOutputStream(fos);
    // Create a stream that computes a checksum on the bytes it writes to gzos
    CheckedOutputStream cos = new CheckedOutputStream(gzos, check);

    cos.write(data);              // Now write the data to the nested streams
    cos.close();                  // Close down the nested chain of streams
    long sum = check.getValue(); // Obtain the computed checksum
  }
  catch (IOException e) { /* Handle exceptions */ }
```

Reading ZIP Files

The java.util.zip package also contains a ZipFile class that gives you random access to the entries of a ZIP archive and allows you to read those entries through a stream:

```
import java.io.*;
import java.util.zip.*;

String filename;   // File to read; initialized elsewhere
String entryname;  // Entry to read from the ZIP file; initialized elsewhere
ZipFile zipfile = new ZipFile(filename);         // Open the ZIP file
ZipEntry entry = zipfile.getEntry(entryname);    // Get one entry
InputStream in = zipfile.getInputStream(entry); // A stream to read the entry
BufferedInputStream bis = new BufferedInputStream(in); // Improves efficiency
// Now read bytes from bis...
// Print out contents of the ZIP file
for(java.util.Enumeration e = zipfile.entries(); e.hasMoreElements();) {
  ZipEntry zipentry = (ZipEntry) e.nextElement();
  System.out.println(zipentry.getName());
}
```

Computing Message Digests

If you need to compute a cryptographic-strength checksum (also known as a message digest), use one of the stream classes of the java.security package. For example:

```
import java.io.*;
import java.security.*;
import java.util.*;


File f;           // File to read and compute digest on; initialized elsewhere
List text = new ArrayList();  // We'll store the lines of text here

// Get an object that can compute an SHA message digest
MessageDigest digester = MessageDigest.getInstance("SHA");
// A stream to read bytes from the file f
FileInputStream fis = new FileInputStream(f);
// A stream that reads bytes from fis and computes an SHA message digest
DigestInputStream dis = new DigestInputStream(fis, digester);
// A stream that reads bytes from dis and converts them to characters
```

```
InputStreamReader isr = new InputStreamReader(dis);
// A stream that can read a line at a time
BufferedReader br = new BufferedReader(isr);
// Now read lines from the stream
for(String line; (line = br.readLine()) != null; text.add(line)) ;
// Close the streams
br.close();
// Get the message digest
byte[] digest = digester.digest();
```

Streaming Data to and from Arrays

So far, we've used a variety of stream classes to manipulate streaming data, but the data itself ultimately comes from a file or is written to the console. The java.io package defines other stream classes that can read data from and write data to arrays of bytes or strings of text:

```
import java.io.*;

// Set up a stream that uses a byte array as its destination
ByteArrayOutputStream baos = new ByteArrayOutputStream();
DataOutputStream out = new DataOutputStream(baos);
out.writeUTF("hello");          // Write some string data out as bytes
out.writeDouble(Math.PI);       // Write a floating-point value out as bytes
byte[] data = baos.toByteArray(); // Get the array of bytes we've written
out.close();                      // Close the streams

// Set up a stream to read characters from a string
Reader in = new StringReader("Now is the time!");
// Read characters from it until we reach the end
int c;
while((c = in.read()) != -1) System.out.print((char) c);
```

Other classes that operate this way include ByteArrayInputStream, StringWriter, CharArrayReader, and CharArrayWriter.

Thread Communication with Pipes

PipedInputStream and PipedOutputStream and their character-based counterparts, PipedReader and PipedWriter, are another interesting set of streams defined by java.io. These streams are used in pairs by two threads that want to communicate. One thread writes bytes to a PipedOutputStream or characters to a PipedWriter, and another thread reads bytes or characters from the corresponding PipedInputStream or PipedReader:

```
// A pair of connected piped I/O streams forms a pipe. One thread writes
// bytes to the PipedOutputStream, and another thread reads them from the
// corresponding PipedInputStream. Or use PipedWriter/PipedReader for chars.
final PipedOutputStream writeEndOfPipe = new PipedOutputStream();
final PipedInputStream readEndOfPipe = new PipedInputStream(writeEndOfPipe);

// This thread reads bytes from the pipe and discards them
Thread devnull = new Thread(new Runnable() {
  public void run() {
```

The Java Platform

```
      try { while(readEndOfPipe.read() != -1); }
      catch (IOException e) {}  // ignore it
    }
  });
  devnull.start();
```

Networking with java.net

The java.net package defines a number of classes that make writing networked applications surprisingly easy. Various examples follow.

Networking with the URL Class

The easiest networking class to use is URL, which represents a uniform resource locator. Different Java implementations may support different sets of URL protocols, but, at a minimum, you can rely on support for the http://, ftp://, and file:// protocols. As of Java 1.4, secure HTTP is also supported with the https:// protocol. Here are some ways you can use the URL class:

```
import java.net.*;
import java.io.*;

// Create some URL objects
URL url=null, url2=null, url3=null;
try {
  url = new URL("http://www.oreilly.com");          // An absolute URL
  url2 = new URL(url, "catalog/books/javanut4/"); // A relative URL
  url3 = new URL("http:", "www.oreilly.com", "index.html");
} catch (MalformedURLException e) { /* Ignore this exception */ }

// Read the content of a URL from an input stream
InputStream in = url.openStream();

// For more control over the reading process, get a URLConnection object
URLConnection conn = url.openConnection();

// Now get some information about the URL
String type = conn.getContentType();
String encoding = conn.getContentEncoding();
java.util.Date lastModified = new java.util.Date(conn.getLastModified());
int len = conn.getContentLength();

// If necessary, read the contents of the URL using this stream
InputStream in = conn.getInputStream();
```

Working with Sockets

Sometimes you need more control over your networked application than is possible with the URL class. In this case, you can use a Socket to communicate directly with a server. For example:

```
import java.net.*;
import java.io.*;
```

```
// Here's a simple client program that connects to a web server,
// requests a document and reads the document from the server.
String hostname = "java.oreilly.com";  // The server to connect to
int port = 80;                         // Standard port for HTTP
String filename = "/index.html";       // The file to read from the server
Socket s = new Socket(hostname, port); // Connect to the server

// Get I/O streams we can use to talk to the server
InputStream sin = s.getInputStream();
BufferedReader fromServer = new BufferedReader(new InputStreamReader(sin));
OutputStream sout = s.getOutputStream();
PrintWriter toServer = new PrintWriter(new OutputStreamWriter(sout));

// Request the file from the server, using the HTTP protocol
toServer.print("GET " + filename + " HTTP/1.0\r\n\r\n");
toServer.flush();

// Now read the server's response, assume it is a text file, and print it out
for(String l = null; (l = fromServer.readLine()) != null; )
  System.out.println(l);

// Close everything down when we're done
toServer.close();
fromServer.close();
s.close();
```

Secure Sockets with SSL

In Java 1.4, the Java Secure Socket Extension, or JSSE, was added to the core Java platform in the packages javax.net and javax.net.ssl.* This API enables encrypted network communication over sockets that use the SSL (Secure Sockets Layer, also known as TLS) protocol. SSL is widely used on the Internet: it is the basis for secure web communication using the https:// protocol. In Java 1.4 and later, you can use https:// with the URL class as previously shown to securely download documents from web servers that support SSL.

Like all Java security APIs, JSSE is highly configurable and gives low-level control over all details of setting up and communicating over an SSL socket. The javax.net and javax.net.ssl packages are fairly complex, but in practice, you need only a few classes to securely communicate with a server. The following program is a variant on the preceding code that uses HTTPS instead of HTTP to securely transfer the contents of the requested URL:

```
import java.io.*;
import java.net.*;
import javax.net.ssl.*;
import java.security.cert.*;

/**
```

* An earlier version of JSSE using different package names is available as a separate download for use with Java 1.2 and Java 1.3. See *http://java.sun.com/products/jsse/*.

```
 * Get a document from a web server using HTTPS. Usage:
 *   java HttpsDownload <hostname> <filename>
 **/
public class HttpsDownload {
    public static void main(String[] args) throws IOException {
        // Get a SocketFactory object for creating SSL sockets
        SSLSocketFactory factory =
            (SSLSocketFactory) SSLSocketFactory.getDefault();

        // Use the factory to create a secure socket connected to the
        // HTTPS port of the specified web server.
        SSLSocket sslsock=(SSLSocket)factory.createSocket(args[0], // Hostname
                                                          443); // HTTPS port

        // Get the certificate presented by the web server
        SSLSession session = sslsock.getSession();
        X509Certificate cert;
        try { cert = (X509Certificate)session.getPeerCertificates()[0]; }
        catch(SSLPeerUnverifiedException e) { // If no or invalid certificate
            System.err.println(session.getPeerHost() +
                               " did not present a valid certificate.");
            return;
        }

        // Display details about the certificate
        System.out.println(session.getPeerHost() +
                           " has presented a certificate belonging to:");
        System.out.println("\t[" + cert.getSubjectDN().getName() + "]");
        System.out.println("The certificate bears the valid signature of:");
        System.out.println("\t[" + cert.getIssuerDN().getName() + "]");

        // If the user does not trust the certificate, abort
        System.out.print("Do you trust this certificate (y/n)? ");
        System.out.flush();
        BufferedReader console =
            new BufferedReader(new InputStreamReader(System.in));
        if (Character.toLowerCase(console.readLine().charAt(0)) != 'y') return;

        // Now use the secure socket just as you would use a regular socket
        // First, send a regular HTTP request over the SSL socket
        PrintWriter out = new PrintWriter(sslsock.getOutputStream());
        out.print("GET " + args[1] + " HTTP/1.0\r\n\r\n");
        out.flush();

        // Next, read the server's response and print it to the console
        BufferedReader in =
         new BufferedReader(new InputStreamReader(sslsock.getInputStream()));
        String line;
        while((line = in.readLine()) != null) System.out.println(line);

        // Finally, close the socket
        sslsock.close();
    }
}
```

Servers

A client application uses a Socket to communicate with a server. The server does the same thing: it uses a Socket object to communicate with each of its clients. However, the server has an additional task in that it must be able to recognize and accept client connection requests. This is done with the ServerSocket class. The following code shows how you might use a ServerSocket. The code implements a simple HTTP server that responds to all requests by sending back (or mirroring) the exact contents of the HTTP request. A dummy server like this is useful when debugging HTTP clients:

```
import java.io.*;
import java.net.*;

public class HttpMirror {
  public static void main(String[] args) {
    try {
      int port = Integer.parseInt(args[0]);       // The port to listen on
      ServerSocket ss = new ServerSocket(port);   // Create a socket to listen
      for(;;) {                                   // Loop forever
        Socket client = ss.accept();              // Wait for a connection
        ClientThread t = new ClientThread(client);// A thread to handle it
        t.start();                                // Start the thread running
      }                                           // Loop again
    }
    catch (Exception e) {
      System.err.println(e.getMessage());
      System.err.println("Usage: java HttpMirror <port>;");
    }
  }

  static class ClientThread extends Thread {
    Socket client;
    ClientThread(Socket client) { this.client = client; }
    public void run() {
      try {
        // Get streams to talk to the client
        BufferedReader in =
          new BufferedReader(new InputStreamReader(client.getInputStream()));
        PrintWriter out =
          new PrintWriter(new OutputStreamWriter(client.getOutputStream()));

        // Send an HTTP response header to the client
        out.print("HTTP/1.0 200\r\nContent-Type: text/plain\r\n\r\n");

        // Read the HTTP request from the client and send it right back
        // Stop when we read the blank line from the client that marks
        // the end of the request and its headers.
        String line;
        while((line = in.readLine()) != null) {
          if (line.length() == 0) break;
          out.println(line);
        }
```

```
          out.close();
          in.close();
          client.close();
        }
        catch (IOException e) { /* Ignore exceptions */ }
      }
    }
  }
```

This server code could be modified using JSSE to support SSL connections. Making a server secure is more complex than making a client secure, however, because a server must have a certificate it can present to the client. Therefore, server-side JSSE is not demonstrated here.

Datagrams

Both `URL` and `Socket` perform networking on top of a stream-based network connection. Setting up and maintaining a stream across a network takes work at the network level, however. Sometimes you need a low-level way to speed a packet of data across a network, but you don't care about maintaining a stream. If, in addition, you don't need a guarantee that your data will get there or that the packets of data will arrive in the order you sent them, you may be interested in the `DatagramSocket` and `DatagramPacket` classes:

```
import java.net.*;

// Send a message to another computer via a datagram
try {
  String hostname = "host.example.com";     // The computer to send the data to
  InetAddress address =                     // Convert the DNS hostname
    InetAddress.getByName(hostname);        // to a lower-level IP address.
  int port = 1234;                          // The port to connect to
  String message = "The eagle has landed.";  // The message to send
  byte[] data = message.getBytes();          // Convert string to bytes
  DatagramSocket s = new DatagramSocket();   // Socket to send message with
  DatagramPacket p =                         // Create the packet to send
    new DatagramPacket(data, data.length, address, port);
  s.send(p);                                 // Now send it!
  s.close();                                 // Always close sockets when done
}
catch (UnknownHostException e) {}  // Thrown by InetAddress.getByName()
catch (SocketException e) {}       // Thrown by new DatagramSocket()
catch (java.io.IOException e) {}   // Thrown by DatagramSocket.send()

// Here's how the other computer can receive the datagram
try {
  byte[] buffer = new byte[4096];                   // Buffer to hold data

  DatagramSocket s = new DatagramSocket(1234); // Socket that receives it
                                                    // through
  DatagramPacket p =
    new DatagramPacket(buffer, buffer.length); // The packet that receives it
  s.receive(p);                                     // Wait for a packet to arrive
  String msg =                                      // Convert the bytes from the
```

```
        new String(buffer, 0, p.getLength());        // packet back to a string.
      s.close();                                     // Always close the socket
    }
    catch (SocketException e) {}        // Thrown by new DatagramSocket()
    catch (java.io.IOException e) {}    // Thrown by DatagramSocket.receive()
```

Testing the Reachability of a Host

In Java 5.0 the InetAddress class has an isReachable( ) method that attempts to determine whether the host is reachable. The following code uses it in a naive Java implementation of the Unix *ping* utility:

```
import java.io.IOException;
import java.net.InetAddress;
import java.net.UnknownHostException;

public class Ping {
    public static void main(String[] args) throws IOException {
        try {
            String hostname = args[0];
            int timeout = (args.length > 1)?Integer.parseInt(args[1]):2000;
            InetAddress[] addresses = InetAddress.getAllByName(hostname);
            for(InetAddress address : addresses) {
                if (address.isReachable(timeout))
                    System.out.printf("%s is reachable%n", address);
                else
                    System.out.printf("%s could not be contacted%n", address);
            }
        }
        catch (UnknownHostException e) {
            System.out.printf("Unknown host: %s%n", args[0]);
        }
        catch(IOException e) { System.out.printf("Network error: %s%n", e); }
        catch (Exception e) {
            // ArrayIndexOutOfBoundsException or NumberFormatException
            System.out.println("Usage: java Ping <hostname> [timeout in ms]");
        }
    }
}
```

I/O and Networking with java.nio

Java 1.4 introduced an entirely new API for high-performance, nonblocking I/O and networking. This API consists primarily of three new packages. java.nio defines Buffer classes that are used to store sequences of bytes or other primitive values. java.nio.channels defines *channels* through which data can be transferred between a buffer and a data source or sink, such as a file or a network socket. This package also contains important classes used for nonblocking I/O. Finally, the java.nio.charset package contains classes for efficiently converting buffers of bytes into buffers of characters. The sections that follow contain examples of using all three of these packages as well as examples of specific I/O tasks with the New I/O API.

Basic Buffer Operations

The java.nio package includes an abstract Buffer class, which defines generic operations on buffers. This package also defines type-specific subclasses such as ByteBuffer, CharBuffer, and IntBuffer. (See Buffer and ByteBuffer in the reference section for details on these classes and their various methods.) The following code illustrates typical sequences of buffer operations on a ByteBuffer. The other type-specific buffer classes have similar methods.

```
import java.nio.*;

// Buffers don't have public constructors. They are allocated instead.
ByteBuffer b = ByteBuffer.allocate(4096);  // Create a buffer for 4,096 bytes
// Or do this to try to get an efficient buffer from the low-level OS
ByteBuffer buf2 = ByteBuffer.allocateDirect(65536);
// Here's another way to get a buffer: by "wrapping" an array
byte[] data;  // Assume this array is created and initialized elsewhere
ByteBuffer buf3 = ByteBuffer.wrap(data); // Create buffer that uses the array
// It is also possible to create a "view buffer" to view bytes as other types
buf3.order(ByteOrder.BIG_ENDIAN);   // Specify the byte order for the buffer
IntBuffer ib = buf3.asIntBuffer();  // View those bytes as integers

// Now store some data in the buffer
b.put(data);        // Copy bytes from array to buffer at current position
b.put((byte)42);    // Store another byte at the new current position
b.put(0, (byte)9); // Overwrite first byte in buffer. Don't change position.
b.order(ByteOrder.BIG_ENDIAN);  // Set the byte order of the buffer
b.putChar('x');        // Store the two bytes of a Unicode character in buffer
b.putInt(0xcafebabe); // Store four bytes of an int into the buffer

// Here are methods for querying basic numbers about a buffer
int capacity = b.capacity();  // How many bytes can the buffer hold? (4,096)
int position = b.position();  // Where will the next byte be written or read?
// A buffer's limit specifies how many bytes of the buffer can be used.
// When writing into a buffer, this should be the capacity. When reading data
// from a buffer, it should be the number of bytes that were previously
// written.
int limit = b.limit();          // How many should be used?
int remaining = b.remaining(); // How many left? Return limit-position.
boolean more=b.hasRemaining(); // Test if there is still room in the buffer

// The position and limit can also be set with methods of the same name
// Suppose you want to read the bytes you've written into the buffer
b.limit(b.position());          // Set limit to current position
b.position(0);                  // Set limit to 0; start reading at beginning

// Instead of the two previous calls, you usually use a convenience method
b.flip();   // Set limit to position and position to 0; prepare for reading
b.rewind(); // Set position to 0; don't change limit; prepare for rereading
b.clear();  // Set position to 0 and limit to capacity; prepare for writing

// Assuming you've called flip(), you can start reading bytes from the buffer
buf2.put(b);         // Read all bytes from b and put them into buf2
b.rewind();          // Rewind b for rereading from the beginning
```

```
byte b0 = b.get();  // Read first byte; increment buffer position
byte b1 = b.get();  // Read second byte; increment buffer position
byte[] fourbytes = new byte[4];
b.get(fourbytes);   // Read next four bytes, add 4 to buffer position
byte b9 = b.get(9); // Read 10th byte, without changing current position
int i = b.getInt(); // Read next four bytes as an integer; add 4 to position

// Discard bytes you've already read; shift the remaining ones to the
// beginning of the buffer; set position to new limit and limit to capacity,
// preparing the buffer for writing more bytes into it.
b.compact();
```

You may notice that many buffer methods return the object on which they operate. This is done so that method calls can be "chained" in code, as follows:

```
ByteBuffer bb=ByteBuffer.allocate(32).order(ByteOrder.BIG_ENDIAN).putInt(1234);
```

Many methods throughout `java.nio` and its subpackages return the current object to enable this kind of method chaining. Note that the use of this kind of chaining is a stylistic choice (which I have avoided in this chapter) and does not have any significant impact on efficiency.

`ByteBuffer` is the most important of the buffer classes. However, another commonly used class is `CharBuffer`. `CharBuffer` objects can be created by wrapping a string and can also be converted to strings. `CharBuffer` implements the new `java.lang.CharSequence` interface, which means that it can be used like a `String` or `StringBuffer` in certain applications (e.g., for regular expression pattern matching).

```
// Create a read-only CharBuffer from a string
CharBuffer cb = CharBuffer.wrap("This string is the data for the CharBuffer");
String s = cb.toString();  // Convert to a String with toString() method
System.out.println(cb);    // or rely on an implicit call to toString().
char c = cb.charAt(0);     // Use CharSequence methods to get characters
char d = cb.get(1);        // or use a CharBuffer absolute read.
// A relative read that reads the char and increments the current position
// Note that only the characters between the position and limit are used when
// a CharBuffer is converted to a String or used as a CharSequence.
char e = cb.get();
```

Bytes in a `ByteBuffer` are commonly converted to characters in a `CharBuffer` and vice versa. We'll see how to do this when we consider the `java.nio.charset` package.

Basic Channel Operations

Buffers are not all that useful on their own—there isn't much point in storing bytes into a buffer only to read them out again. Instead, buffers are typically used with channels: your program stores bytes into a buffer, then passes the buffer to a channel, which reads the bytes out of the buffer and writes them to a file, network socket, or some other destination. Or, in the reverse, your program passes a buffer to a channel, which reads bytes from a file, socket, or other source and stores those bytes into the buffer, where they can then be retrieved by your program. The `java.nio.channels` package defines several channel classes that represent files, sockets, datagrams, and pipes. (We'll see examples of these concrete classes later in this chapter.) The following code, however, is based on the capabilities of the various channel interfaces defined by `java.nio.channels` and should work with any `Channel` object:

```
Channel c;  // Object that implements Channel interface; initialized elsewhere
if (c.isOpen()) c.close();  // These are the only methods defined by Channel

// The read() and write() methods are defined by the
// ReadableByteChannel and WritableByteChannel interfaces.
ReadableByteChannel source;      // Initialized elsewhere
WritableByteChannel destination; // Initialized elsewhere
ByteBuffer buffer = ByteBuffer.allocateDirect(16384); // Low-level 16 KB buffer

// Here is the basic loop to use when reading bytes from a source channel and
// writing them to a destination channel until there are no more bytes to read
// from the source and no more buffered bytes to write to the destination.
while(source.read(buffer) != -1 || buffer.position() > 0) {
  // Flip buffer: set limit to position and position to 0. This prepares
  // the buffer for reading (which is done by a channel *write* operation).
  buffer.flip();
  // Write some or all of the bytes in the buffer to the destination
  destination.write(buffer);
  // Discard the bytes that were written, copying the remaining ones to
  // the start of the buffer. Set position to limit and limit to capacity,
  // preparing the buffer for writing (done by a channel *read* operation).
  buffer.compact();
}

// Don't forget to close the channels
source.close();
destination.close();
```

In addition to the `ReadableByteChannel` and `WritableByteChannel` interfaces illustrated in the preceding code, `java.nio.channels` defines several other channel interfaces. `ByteChannel` simply extends the readable and writable interfaces without adding any new methods. It is a useful shorthand for channels that support both reading and writing. `GatheringByteChannel` is an extension of `WritableByteChannel` that defines `write()` methods that *gather* bytes from more than one buffer and write them out. Similarly, `ScatteringByteChannel` is an extension of `ReadableByteChannel` that defines `read()` methods that read bytes from the channel and *scatter* or distribute them into more than one buffer. The gathering and scattering `write()` and `read()` methods can be useful when working with network protocols that use fixed-size headers that you want to store in a buffer separate from the rest of the transferred data.

One confusing point to be aware of is that a channel read operation involves writing (or putting) bytes into a buffer, and a channel write operation involves reading (or getting) bytes from a buffer. Thus, when I say that the `flip()` method prepares a buffer for reading, I mean that it prepares a buffer for use in a channel `write()` operation! The reverse is true for the buffer's `compact()` method.

Encoding and Decoding Text with Charsets

A `java.nio.charset.Charset` object represents a character set plus an encoding for that character set. `Charset` and its associated classes, `CharsetEncoder` and `CharsetDecoder`, define methods for encoding strings of characters into sequences of bytes and decoding sequences of bytes into strings of characters. Since these classes are part of the New I/O API, they use the `ByteBuffer` and `CharBuffer` classes:

```
// The simplest case. Use Charset convenience routines to convert.
Charset charset = Charset.forName("ISO-8859-1"); // Get Latin-1 Charset
CharBuffer cb = CharBuffer.wrap("Hello World");  // Characters to encode
// Encode the characters and store the bytes in a newly allocated ByteBuffer
ByteBuffer bb = charset.encode(cb);
// Decode these bytes into a newly allocated CharBuffer and print them out
System.out.println(charset.decode(bb));
```

Note the use of the ISO-8859-1 (a.k.a. Latin-1) charset in this example. This 8-bit charset is suitable for most Western European languages, including English. Programmers who work only with English may also use the 7-bit US-ASCII charset. The `Charset` class does not do encoding and decoding itself, and the previous convenience routines create `CharsetEncoder` and `CharsetDecoder` classes internally. If you plan to encode or decode multiple times, it is more efficient to create these objects yourself:

```
Charset charset = Charset.forName("US-ASCII");    // Get the charset
CharsetEncoder encoder = charset.newEncoder();    // Create an encoder from it
CharBuffer cb = CharBuffer.wrap("Hello World!"); // Get a CharBuffer
WritableByteChannel destination;                  // Initialized elsewhere
destination.write(encoder.encode(cb));            // Encode chars and write
```

The preceding `CharsetEncoder.encode( )` method must allocate a new `ByteBuffer` each time it is called. For maximum efficiency, you can call lower-level methods to do the encoding and decoding into an existing buffer:

```
ReadableByteChannel source;                       // Initialized elsewhere
Charset charset = Charset.forName("ISO-8859-1"); // Get the charset
CharsetDecoder decoder = charset.newDecoder();    // Create a decoder from it
ByteBuffer bb = ByteBuffer.allocateDirect(2048); // Buffer to hold bytes
CharBuffer cb = CharBuffer.allocate(2048);        // Buffer to hold characters

while(source.read(bb) != -1) {  // Read bytes from the channel until EOF
  bb.flip();                    // Flip byte buffer to prepare for decoding
  decoder.decode(bb, cb, true); // Decode bytes into characters
  cb.flip();                    // Flip char buffer to prepare for printing
  System.out.print(cb);         // Print the characters
  cb.clear();                   // Clear char buffer to prepare for decoding
  bb.clear();                   // Prepare byte buffer for next channel read
}
source.close();                 // Done with the channel, so close it
System.out.flush();             // Make sure all output characters appear
```

The preceding code relies on the fact that ISO-8859-1 is an 8-bit encoding charset and that there is one-to-one mapping between characters and bytes. For more complex charsets, such as the UTF-8 encoding of Unicode or the EUC-JP charset used with Japanese text; however, this does not hold, and more than one byte is required for some (or all) characters. When this is the case, there is no guarantee that all bytes in a buffer can be decoded at once (the end of the buffer may contain a partial character). Also, since a single character may encode to more than one byte, it can be tricky to know how many bytes a given string will encode into. The following code shows a loop you can use to decode bytes in a more general way:

```
ReadableByteChannel source;                       // Initialized elsewhere
Charset charset = Charset.forName("UTF-8");       // A Unicode encoding
CharsetDecoder decoder = charset.newDecoder();    // Create a decoder from it
ByteBuffer bb = ByteBuffer.allocateDirect(2048); // Buffer to hold bytes
CharBuffer cb = CharBuffer.allocate(2048);        // Buffer to hold characters

// Tell the decoder to ignore errors that might result from bad bytes
decoder.onMalformedInput(CodingErrorAction.IGNORE);
decoder.onUnmappableCharacter(CodingErrorAction.IGNORE);

decoder.reset();                       // Reset decoder if it has been used before
while(source.read(bb) != -1) {        // Read bytes from the channel until EOF
  bb.flip();                           // Flip byte buffer to prepare for decoding
  decoder.decode(bb, cb, false); // Decode bytes into characters
  cb.flip();                           // Flip char buffer to prepare for printing
  System.out.print(cb);                // Print the characters
  cb.clear();                          // Clear the character buffer
  bb.compact();                        // Discard already decoded bytes
}
source.close();                        // Done with the channel, so close it

// At this point, there may still be some bytes in the buffer to decode
bb.flip();                             // Prepare for decoding
decoder.decode(bb, cb, true);          // Pass true to indicate this is the last call
decoder.flush(cb);                     // Output any final characters
cb.flip();                             // Flip char buffer
System.out.print(cb);                  // Print the final characters
```

Working with Files

FileChannel is a concrete Channel class that performs file I/O and implements ReadableByteChannel and WritableByteChannel (although its read() method works only if the underlying file is open for reading, and its write( ) method works only if the file is open for writing). Obtain a FileChannel object by using the java.io package to create a FileInputStream, a FileOutputStream, or a RandomAccessFile and then call the getChannel() method (added in Java 1.4) of that object. As an example, you can use two FileChannel objects to copy a file:

```
String filename = "test";   // The name of the file to copy
// Create streams to read the original and write the copy
FileInputStream fin = new FileInputStream(filename);
FileOutputStream fout = new FileOutputStream(filename + ".copy");
// Use the streams to create corresponding channel objects
FileChannel in = fin.getChannel();
FileChannel out = fout.getChannel();
// Allocate a low-level 8KB buffer for the copy
```

```
ByteBuffer buffer = ByteBuffer.allocateDirect(8192);
while(in.read(buffer) != -1 || buffer.position() > 0) {
  buffer.flip();       // Prepare to read from the buffer and write to the file
  out.write(buffer);   // Write some or all buffer contents
  buffer.compact();    // Discard all bytes that were written and prepare to
}                      // read more from the file and store them in the buffer.
in.close();            // Always close channels and streams when done with them
out.close();
fin.close();           // Note that closing a FileChannel does not
fout.close();          // automatically close the underlying stream.
```

`FileChannel` has special `transferTo()` and `transferFrom()` methods that make it particularly easy (and on many operating systems, particularly efficient) to transfer a specified number of bytes from a `FileChannel` to some other specified channel, or from some other channel to a `FileChannel`. These methods allow us to simplify the preceding file-copying code to the following:

```
FileChannel in, out;               // Assume these are initialized as in the
                                   // preceding example.
long numbytes = in.size();         // Number of bytes in original file
in.transferTo(0, numbytes, out);   // Transfer that amount to output channel
```

This code could be equally well-written using `transferFrom()` instead of `transferTo()` (note that these two methods expect their arguments in different orders):

```
long numbytes = in.size();
out.transferFrom(in, 0, numbytes);
```

`FileChannel` has other capabilities that are not shared by other channel classes. One of the most important is the ability to "memory map" a file or a portion of a file, i.e., to obtain a `MappedByteBuffer` (a subclass of `ByteBuffer`) that represents the contents of the file and allows you to read (and optionally write) file contents simply by reading from and writing to the buffer. Memory mapping a file is a somewhat expensive operation, so this technique is usually efficient only when you are working with a large file to which you need repeated access. Memory mapping offers you yet another way to perform the same file-copy operation shown previously:

```
long filesize = in.size();
ByteBuffer bb = in.map(FileChannel.MapMode.READ_ONLY, 0, filesize);
while(bb.hasRemaining()) out.write(bb);
```

The channel interfaces defined by `java.nio.channels` include `ByteChannel` but not `CharChannel`. The channel API is low-level and provides methods for reading bytes only. All of the previous examples have treated files as binary files. It is possible to use the `CharsetEncoder` and `CharsetDecoder` classes introduced earlier to convert between bytes and characters, but when you want to work with text files, the `Reader` and `Writer` classes of the `java.io` package are usually much easier to use than `CharBuffer`. Fortunately, the `Channels` class defines convenience methods that bridge between the old and new APIs. Here is code that wraps a `Reader` and a `Writer` object around input and output channels, reads lines of Latin-1 text from

The Java Platform

the input channel, and writes them back out to the output channel, with the encoding changed to UTF-8:

```
ReadableByteChannel in;      // Assume these are initialized elsewhere
WritableByteChannel out;
// Create a Reader and Writer from a FileChannel and charset name
BufferedReader reader=new BufferedReader(Channels.newReader(in, "ISO-8859-1"));
PrintWriter writer = new PrintWriter(Channels.newWriter(out, "UTF-8"));
String line;
while((line = reader.readLine()) != null) writer.println(line);
reader.close();
writer.close();
```

Unlike the FileInputStream and FileOutputStream classes, the FileChannel class allows random access to the contents of the file. The zero-argument position() method returns the *file pointer* (the position of the next byte to be read), and the one-argument position( ) method allows you to set this pointer to any value you want. This allows you to skip around in a file in the way that the java.io. RandomAccessFile does. Here is an example:

```
// Suppose you have a file that has data records scattered throughout, and the
// last 1,024 bytes of the file are an index that provides the position of
// those records. Here is code that reads the index of the file, looks up the
// position of the first record within the file and then reads that record.
FileChannel in = new FileInputStream("test.data").getChannel(); // The channel
ByteBuffer index = ByteBuffer.allocate(1024);    // A buffer to hold the index
long size = in.size();                           // The size of the file
in.position(size - 1024);                        // Position at start of index
in.read(index);                                  // Read the index
int record0Position = index.getInt(0);           // Get first index entry
in.position(record0Position);                    // Position file at that point
ByteBuffer record0 = ByteBuffer.allocate(128);   // Get buffer to hold data
in.read(record0);                                // Finally, read the record
```

The final feature of FileChannel that we'll consider here is its ability to lock a file or a portion of a file against all concurrent access (an exclusive lock) or against concurrent writes (a shared lock). (Note that some operating systems strictly enforce all locks while others provide only an advisory locking facility that requires programs to cooperate and to attempt to acquire a lock before reading or writing portions of a shared file.) In the previous random-access example, suppose we wanted to ensure that no other program was modifying the record data while we read it. We could acquire a shared lock on that portion of the file with the following code:

```
FileLock lock = in.lock(record0Position, // Start of locked region
                        128,     // Length of locked region
                        true);   // Shared lock: prevent concurrent updates
                                 // but allow concurrent reads.
in.position(record0Position);    // Move to start of index
in.read(record0);                // Read the index data
lock.release();                  // You're done with the lock, so release it
```

Client-Side Networking

The New I/O API includes networking capabilities as well as file-access capabilities. To communicate over the network, you can use the SocketChannel class. Create a SocketChannel with the static open() method, then read and write bytes from and to it as you would with any other channel object. The following code uses SocketChannel to send an HTTP request to a web server and saves the server's response (including all of the HTTP headers) to a file. Note the use of java.net.InetSocketAddress, a subclass of java.net.SocketAddress, to tell the SocketChannel what to connect to. These classes were also introduced as part of the New I/O API.

```
import java.io.*;
import java.net.*;
import java.nio.*;
import java.nio.channels.*;
import java.nio.charset.*;

// Create a SocketChannel connected to the web server at www.oreilly.com
SocketChannel socket =
  SocketChannel.open(new InetSocketAddress("www.oreilly.com",80));
// A charset for encoding the HTTP request
Charset charset = Charset.forName("ISO-8859-1");
// Send an HTTP request to the server. Start with a string, wrap it to
// a CharBuffer, encode it to a ByteBuffer, then write it to the socket.
socket.write(charset.encode(CharBuffer.wrap("GET / HTTP/1.0\r\n\r\n")));
// Create a FileChannel to save the server's response to
FileOutputStream out = new FileOutputStream("oreilly.html");
FileChannel file = out.getChannel();
// Get a buffer for holding bytes while transferring from socket to file
ByteBuffer buffer = ByteBuffer.allocateDirect(8192);
// Now loop until all bytes are read from the socket and written to the file
while(socket.read(buffer) != -1 || buffer.position() > 0) {  // Are we done?
  buffer.flip();       // Prepare to read bytes from buffer and write to file
  file.write(buffer);  // Write some or all bytes to the file
  buffer.compact();    // Discard those that were written
}
socket.close();        // Close the socket channel
file.close();          // Close the file channel
out.close();           // Close the underlying file
```

Another way to create a SocketChannel is with the no-argument version of open(), which creates an unconnected channel. This allows you to call the socket() method to obtain the underlying socket, configure the socket as desired, and connect to the desired host with the connect method. For example:

```
SocketChannel sc = SocketChannel.open();  // Open an unconnected socket channel
Socket s = sc.socket();                   // Get underlying java.net.Socket
s.setSoTimeout(3000);                     // Time out after three seconds
// Now connect the socket channel to the desired host and port
sc.connect(new InetSocketAddress("www.davidflanagan.com", 80));

ByteBuffer buffer = ByteBuffer.allocate(8192);  // Create a buffer
try { sc.read(buffer); }                        // Try to read from socket
catch(SocketTimeoutException e) {               // Catch timeouts here
```

```
        System.out.println("The remote computer is not responding.");
        sc.close();
    }
```

In addition to the SocketChannel class, the java.nio.channels package defines a DatagramChannel for networking with datagrams instead of sockets. DatagramChannel is not demonstrated here, but you can read about it in the reference section.

One of the most powerful features of the New I/O API is that channels such as SocketChannel and DatagramChannel can be used in nonblocking mode. We'll see examples of this in later sections.

Server-Side Networking

The java.net package defines a Socket class for communication between a client and a server and defines a ServerSocket class used by the server to listen for and accept connections from clients. The java.nio.channels package is analogous: it defines a SocketChannel class for data transfer and a ServerSocketChannel class for accepting connections. ServerSocketChannel is an unusual channel because it does not implement ReadableByteChannel or WritableByteChannel. Instead of read() and write() methods, it has an accept() method for accepting client connections and obtaining a SocketChannel through which it communicates with the client. Here is the code for a simple, single-threaded server that listens for connections on port 8000 and reports the current time to any client that connects:

```
import java.nio.*;
import java.nio.channels.*;
import java.nio.charset.*;

public class DateServer {
    public static void main(String[] args) throws java.io.IOException {
        // Get a CharsetEncoder for encoding the text sent to the client
        CharsetEncoder encoder = Charset.forName("US-ASCII").newEncoder();

        // Create a new ServerSocketChannel and bind it to port 8000
        // Note that this must be done using the underlying ServerSocket
        ServerSocketChannel server = ServerSocketChannel.open();
        server.socket().bind(new java.net.InetSocketAddress(8000));

        for(;;) {  // This server runs forever
            // Wait for a client to connect
            SocketChannel client = server.accept();
            // Get the current date and time as a string
            String response = new java.util.Date().toString() + "\r\n";
            // Wrap, encode, and send the string to the client
            client.write(encoder.encode(CharBuffer.wrap(response)));
            // Disconnect from the client
            client.close();
        }
    }
}
```

Nonblocking I/O

The preceding DateServer class is a simple network server. Because it does not maintain a connection with any client, it never needs to communicate with more than one at a time, and there is never more than one SocketChannel in use. More realistic servers must be able to communicate with more than one client at a time. The java.io and java.net APIs allow only blocking I/O, so servers written using these APIs must use a separate thread for each client. For large-scale servers with many clients, this approach does not scale well. To solve this problem, the New I/O API allows most channels (but not FileChannel) to be used in nonblocking mode and allows a single thread to manage all pending connections. This is done with a Selector object, which keeps track of a set of registered channels and can block until one or more of those channels is ready for I/O, as the following code illustrates. This is a longer example than most in this chapter, but it is a complete working server class that manages a ServerSocketChannel and any number of SocketChannel connections to clients through a single Selector object.

```
import java.io.*;
import java.net.*;
import java.nio.*;
import java.nio.channels.*;
import java.nio.charset.*;
import java.util.*;           // For Set and Iterator

public class NonBlockingServer {
    public static void main(String[] args) throws IOException {

        // Get the character encoders and decoders you'll need
        Charset charset = Charset.forName("ISO-8859-1");
        CharsetEncoder encoder = charset.newEncoder();
        CharsetDecoder decoder = charset.newDecoder();

        // Allocate a buffer for communicating with clients
        ByteBuffer buffer = ByteBuffer.allocate(512);

        // All of the channels in this code will be in nonblocking mode.
        // So create a Selector object that will block while monitoring
        // all of the channels and stop blocking only when one or more
        // of the channels is ready for I/O of some sort.
        Selector selector = Selector.open();

        // Create a new ServerSocketChannel and bind it to port 8000
        // Note that this must be done using the underlying ServerSocket
        ServerSocketChannel server = ServerSocketChannel.open();
        server.socket().bind(new java.net.InetSocketAddress(8000));
        // Put the ServerSocketChannel into nonblocking mode
        server.configureBlocking(false);
        // Now register it with the Selector (note that register() is called
        // on the channel, not on the selector object, however).
        // The SelectionKey represents the registration of this channel with
        // this Selector.
        SelectionKey serverkey = server.register(selector,
                                                 SelectionKey.OP_ACCEPT);
```

```
for(;;) {  // The main server loop. The server runs forever.
    // This call blocks until there is activity on one of the
    // registered channels. This is the key method in nonblocking
    // I/O.
    selector.select();

    // Get a java.util.Set containing the SelectionKey objects for
    // all channels that are ready for I/O.
    Set keys = selector.selectedKeys();

    // Use a java.util.Iterator to loop through the selected keys
    for(Iterator i = keys.iterator(); i.hasNext(); ) {
        // Get the next SelectionKey in the set and remove it
        // from the set. It must be removed explicitly, or it will
        // be returned again by the next call to select().
        SelectionKey key = (SelectionKey) i.next();
        i.remove();

        // Check whether this key is the SelectionKey obtained when
        // you registered the ServerSocketChannel.
        if (key == serverkey) {
            // Activity on the ServerSocketChannel means a client
            // is trying to connect to the server.
            if (key.isAcceptable()) {
                // Accept the client connection and obtain a
                // SocketChannel to communicate with the client.
                SocketChannel client = server.accept();
                // Put the client channel in nonblocking mode
                client.configureBlocking(false);
                // Now register it with the Selector object,
                // telling it that you'd like to know when
                // there is data to be read from this channel.
                SelectionKey clientkey =
                    client.register(selector, SelectionKey.OP_READ);
                // Attach some client state to the key. You'll
                // use this state when you talk to the client.
                clientkey.attach(new Integer(0));
            }
        }
        else {
            // If the key obtained from the Set of keys is not the
            // ServerSocketChannel key, then it must be a key
            // representing one of the client connections.
            // Get the channel from the key.
            SocketChannel client = (SocketChannel) key.channel();

            // If you are here, there should be data to read from
            // the channel, but double-check.
            if (!key.isReadable()) continue;

            // Now read bytes from the client. Assume that all the
            // client's bytes are in one read operation.
            int bytesread = client.read(buffer);
```

```
                // If read() returns -1, it indicates end-of-stream,
                // which means the client has disconnected, so
                // deregister the selection key and close the channel.
                if (bytesread == -1) {
                    key.cancel();
                    client.close();
                    continue;
                }

                // Otherwise, decode the bytes to a request string
                buffer.flip();
                String request = decoder.decode(buffer).toString();
                buffer.clear();
                // Now reply to the client based on the request string
                if (request.trim().equals("quit")) {
                    // If the request was "quit", send a final message
                    // Close the channel and deregister the
                    // SelectionKey
                    client.write(encoder.encode(CharBuffer.wrap("Bye.")));
                    key.cancel();
                    client.close();
                }
                else {
                    // Otherwise, send a response string comprised of
                    // the sequence number of this request plus an
                    // uppercase version of the request string. Note
                    // that you keep track of the sequence number by
                    // "attaching" an Integer object to the
                    // SelectionKey and incrementing it each time.

                    // Get sequence number from SelectionKey
                    int num = ((Integer)key.attachment()).intValue();
                    // For response string
                    String response = num + ": " +
                        request.toUpperCase();
                    // Wrap, encode, and write the response string
                    client.write(encoder.encode(CharBuffer.wrap(response)));
                    // Attach an incremented sequence nubmer to the key
                    key.attach(new Integer(num+1));
                }
            }
        }
    }
}
}
```

Nonblocking I/O is most useful for writing network servers. It is also useful in clients that have more than one network connection pending at the same time. For example, consider a web browser downloading a web page and the images referenced by that page at the same time. One other interesting use of nonblocking I/O is to perform nonblocking socket connection operations. The idea is that you can ask a `SocketChannel` to establish a connection to a remote host and then go do other stuff (such as build a GUI, for example) while the underlying OS is setting up the connection across the network. Later, you do a `select()` call to block until the connection has been established, if it hasn't been already. The code for a nonblocking connect looks like this:

```
// Create a new, unconnected SocketChannel. Put it in nonblocking
// mode, register it with a new Selector, and then tell it to connect.
// The connect call will return instead of waiting for the network
// connect to be fully established.
Selector selector = Selector.open();
SocketChannel channel = SocketChannel.open();
channel.configureBlocking(false);
channel.register(selector, SelectionKey.OP_CONNECT);
channel.connect(new InetSocketAddress(hostname, port));

// Now go do other stuff while the connection is set up
// For example, you can create a GUI here

// Now block if necessary until the SocketChannel is ready to connect.
// Since you've registered only one channel with this selector, you
// don't need to examine the key set; you know which channel is ready.
while(selector.select() == 0) /* empty loop */;

// This call is necessary to finish the nonblocking connections
channel.finishConnect();

// Finally, close the selector, which deregisters the channel from it
selector.close();
```

XML

Java 1.4 and Java 5.0 have added powerful XML processing features to the Java platform:

`org.xml.sax`
: This package and its two subpackages define the de facto standard SAX API (SAX stands for Simple API for XML). SAX is an event-driven, XML-parsing API: a SAX parser invokes methods of a specified `ContentHandler` object (as well as some other related handler objects) as it parses an XML document. The structure and content of the document are fully described by the method calls. This is a streaming API that does not build any permanent representation of the document. It is up to the `ContentHandler` implementation to store any state or perform any actions that are appropriate. This package includes classes for the SAX 2 API and deprecated classes for SAX 1.

`org.w3c.dom`
: This package defines interfaces that represent an XML document in tree form. The Document Object Model (DOM) is a recommendation (essentially a standard) of the World Wide Web Consortium (W3C). A DOM parser reads an XML document and converts it into a tree of nodes that represent the full content of the document. Once the tree representation of the document is created, a program can examine and manipulate it however it wants.

Java 1.4 includes the core module of the Level 2 DOM, and Java 5.0 includes the core, events, and load/save modules of the Level 3 DOM.

`javax.xml.parsers`
: This package provides high-level interfaces for instantiating SAX and DOM parsers for parsing XML documents.

`javax.xml.transform`
: This package and its subpackages define a Java API for transforming XML document content and representation using the XSLT standard.

`javax.xml.validation`
: This Java 5.0 package provides support for validating an XML document against a schema. Implementations are required to support the W3C XML Schema standard and may also support other schema types as well.

`javax.xml.xpath`
: This package, also new in Java 5.0, supports the evaluation of XPath for selecting nodes in an XML document.

Examples using each of these packages are presented in the following sections.

Parsing XML with SAX

The first step in parsing an XML document with SAX is to obtain a SAX parser. If you have a SAX parser implementation of your own, you can simply instantiate the appropriate parser class. It is usually simpler, however, to use the `javax.xml.parsers` package to instantiate whatever SAX parser is provided by the Java implementation. The code looks like this:

```
import javax.xml.parsers.*;

// Obtain a factory object for creating SAX parsers
SAXParserFactory parserFactory = SAXParserFactory.newInstance();

// Configure the factory object to specify attributes of the parsers it creates
parserFactory.setValidating(true);
parserFactory.setNamespaceAware(true);

// Now create a SAXParser object
SAXParser parser = parserFactory.newSAXParser();   // May throw exceptions
```

The `SAXParser` class is a simple wrapper around the `org.xml.sax.XMLReader` class. Once you have obtained one, as shown in the previous code, you can parse a document by simply calling one of the various `parse()` methods. Some of these methods use the deprecated SAX 1 `HandlerBase` class, and others use the current SAX 2 `org.xml.sax.helpers.DefaultHandler` class. The `DefaultHandler` class provides an empty implementation of all the methods of the `ContentHandler`, `ErrorHandler`, `DTDHandler`, and `EntityResolver` interfaces. These are all the methods that the SAX parser can call while parsing an XML document. By subclassing `DefaultHandler` and defining the methods you care about, you can perform whatever actions are necessary in response to the method calls generated by the parser. The following code shows a method that uses SAX to parse an XML file and determine the number of XML elements that appear in a document as well as the number of characters of plain text (possibly excluding "ignorable whitespace") that appear within those elements:

```
import java.io.*;
import javax.xml.parsers.*;
import org.xml.sax.*;
import org.xml.sax.helpers.*;

public class SAXCount {
    public static void main(String[] args)
        throws SAXException,IOException, ParserConfigurationException
    {
        // Create a parser factory and use it to create a parser
        SAXParserFactory parserFactory = SAXParserFactory.newInstance();
        SAXParser parser = parserFactory.newSAXParser();
        // This is the name of the file you're parsing
        String filename = args[0];
        // Instantiate a DefaultHandler subclass to do your counting for you
        CountHandler handler = new CountHandler();
        // Start the parser. It reads the file and calls methods of the handler.
        parser.parse(new File(filename), handler);
        // When you're done, report the results stored by your handler object
        System.out.println(filename + " contains " + handler.numElements +
                           " elements and " + handler.numChars +
                           " other characters ");
    }

    // This inner class extends DefaultHandler to count elements and text in
    // the XML file and saves the results in public fields. There are many
    // other DefaultHandler methods you could override, but you need only
    // these.
    public static class CountHandler extends DefaultHandler {
        public int numElements = 0, numChars = 0;  // Save counts here
        // This method is invoked when the parser encounters the opening tag
        // of any XML element. Ignore the arguments but count the element.
        public void startElement(String uri, String localname, String qname,
                                 Attributes attributes) {
            numElements++;
        }

        // This method is called for any plain text within an element
        // Simply count the number of characters in that text
        public void characters(char[] text, int start, int length) {
            numChars += length;
        }
    }
}
```

Parsing XML with DOM

The DOM API is much different from the SAX API. While SAX is an efficient way to scan an XML document, it is not well-suited for programs that want to modify documents. Instead of converting an XML document into a series of method calls, a DOM parser converts the document into an `org.w3c.dom.Document` object, which is a tree of `org.w3c.dom.Node` objects. The conversion of the complete XML document to tree form allows random access to the entire document but can consume substantial amounts of memory.

In the DOM API, each node in the document tree implements the `Node` interface and a type-specific subinterface. (The most common types of node in a DOM document are `Element` and `Text` nodes.) When the parser is done parsing the document, your program can examine and manipulate that tree using the various methods of `Node` and its subinterfaces. The following code uses JAXP to obtain a DOM parser (which, in JAXP parlance, is called a `DocumentBuilder`). It then parses an XML file and builds a document tree from it. Next, it examines the `Document` tree to search for `<sect1>` elements and prints the contents of the `<title>` of each.

```
import java.io.*;
import javax.xml.parsers.*;
import org.w3c.dom.*;

public class GetSectionTitles {
    public static void main(String[] args)
        throws IOException, ParserConfigurationException,
               org.xml.sax.SAXException
    {
        // Create a factory object for creating DOM parsers and configure it
        DocumentBuilderFactory factory = DocumentBuilderFactory.newInstance();
        factory.setIgnoringComments(true); // We want to ignore comments
        factory.setCoalescing(true);       // Convert CDATA to Text nodes
        factory.setNamespaceAware(false);  // No namespaces: this is default
        factory.setValidating(false);      // Don't validate DTD: also default

        // Now use the factory to create a DOM parser, a.k.a. DocumentBuilder
        DocumentBuilder parser = factory.newDocumentBuilder();

        // Parse the file and build a Document tree to represent its content
        Document document = parser.parse(new File(args[0]));

        // Ask the document for a list of all <sect1> elements it contains
        NodeList sections = document.getElementsByTagName("sect1");
        // Loop through those <sect1> elements one at a time
        int numSections = sections.getLength();
        for(int i = 0; i < numSections; i++) {
            Element section = (Element)sections.item(i);  // A <sect1>
            // The first Element child of each <sect1> should be a <title>
            // element, but there may be some whitespace Text nodes first, so
            // loop through the children until you find the first element
            // child.
            Node title = section.getFirstChild();
            while(title != null && title.getNodeType() != Node.ELEMENT_NODE)
                title = title.getNextSibling();
            // Print the text contained in the Text node child of this element
            if (title != null)
                System.out.println(title.getFirstChild().getNodeValue());
        }
    }
}
```

Transforming XML Documents

The javax.xml.transform package defines a TransformerFactory class for creating Transformer objects. A Transformer can transform a document from its Source representation into a new Result representation and optionally apply an XSLT transformation to the document content in the process. Three subpackages define concrete implementations of the Source and Result interfaces, which allow documents to be transformed among three representations:

javax.xml.transform.stream
: Represents documents as streams of XML text.

javax.xml.transform.dom
: Represents documents as DOM Document trees.

javax.xml.transform.sax
: Represents documents as sequences of SAX method calls.

The following code shows one use of these packages to transform the representation of a document from a DOM Document tree into a stream of XML text. An interesting feature of this code is that it does not create the Document tree by parsing a file; instead, it builds it up from scratch.

```
import javax.xml.transform.*;
import javax.xml.transform.dom.*;
import javax.xml.transform.stream.*;
import javax.xml.parsers.*;
import org.w3c.dom.*;

public class DOMToStream {
    public static void main(String[] args)
        throws ParserConfigurationException,
               TransformerConfigurationException,
               TransformerException
    {
        // Create a DocumentBuilderFactory and a DocumentBuilder
        DocumentBuilderFactory dbf = DocumentBuilderFactory.newInstance();
        DocumentBuilder db = dbf.newDocumentBuilder();
        // Instead of parsing an XML document, however, just create an empty
        // document that you can build up yourself.
        Document document = db.newDocument();

        // Now build a document tree using DOM methods
        Element book = document.createElement("book"); // Create new element
        book.setAttribute("id", "javanut4");           // Give it an attribute
        document.appendChild(book);                    // Add to the document
        for(int i = 1; i <= 3; i++) {                  // Add more elements
            Element chapter = document.createElement("chapter");
            Element title = document.createElement("title");
            title.appendChild(document.createTextNode("Chapter " + i));
            chapter.appendChild(title);
            chapter.appendChild(document.createElement("para"));
            book.appendChild(chapter);
        }
```

```
        // Now create a TransformerFactory and use it to create a Transformer
        // object to transform our DOM document into a stream of XML text.
        // No arguments to newTransformer() means no XSLT stylesheet
        TransformerFactory tf = TransformerFactory.newInstance();
        Transformer transformer = tf.newTransformer();

        // Create the Source and Result objects for the transformation
        DOMSource source = new DOMSource(document);          // DOM document
        StreamResult result = new StreamResult(System.out);  // to XML text

        // Finally, do the transformation
        transformer.transform(source, result);
    }
}
```

The most interesting uses of `javax.xml.transform` involve XSLT stylesheets. XSLT is a complex but powerful XML grammar that describes how XML document content should be converted to another form (e.g., XML, HTML, or plain text). A tutorial on XSLT stylesheets is beyond the scope of this book, but the following code (which contains only six key lines) shows how you can apply such a stylesheet (which is an XML document itself) to another XML document and write the resulting document to a stream:

```
import java.io.*;
import javax.xml.transform.*;
import javax.xml.transform.stream.*;
import javax.xml.parsers.*;
import org.w3c.dom.*;

public class Transform {
    public static void main(String[] args)
        throws TransformerConfigurationException,
               TransformerException
    {
        // Get Source and Result objects for input, stylesheet, and output
        StreamSource input = new StreamSource(new File(args[0]));
        StreamSource stylesheet = new StreamSource(new File(args[1]));
        StreamResult output = new StreamResult(new File(args[2]));

        // Create a transformer and perform the transformation
        TransformerFactory tf = TransformerFactory.newInstance();
        Transformer transformer = tf.newTransformer(stylesheet);
        transformer.transform(input, output);
    }
}
```


Validating XML Documents

The `javax.xml.validation` package allows you to validate XML documents against a schema. SAX and DOM parsers obtained from the `javax.xml.parsers` package can perform validation against a DTD during the parsing process, but this package separates validation from parsing and also provides general support for arbitrary schema types. All implementations must support W3C XML Schema and are allowed to support other schema types, such as RELAX NG.

To use this package, begin with a SchemaFactory instance—a parser for a specific type of schema. Use this parser to parse a schema file into a Schema object. Obtain a Validator from the Schema, and then use the Validator to validate your XML document. The document is specified as a SAXSource or DOMSource object. You may recall these classes from the subpackages of javax.xml.transform.

If the document is valid, the validate( ) method of the Validator object returns normally. If it is not valid, validate( ) throws a SAXException. You can install an org.xml.sax.ErrorHandler object for the Validator to provide some control over the kinds of validation errors that cause exceptions.

```
import javax.xml.XMLConstants;
import javax.xml.validation.*;
import javax.xml.transform.sax.SAXSource;
import org.xml.sax.*;
import java.io.*;

public class Validate {
    public static void main(String[] args) throws IOException {
        File documentFile = new File(args[0]);  // 1st arg is document
        File schemaFile = new File(args[1]);    // 2nd arg is schema

        // Get a parser to parse W3C schemas.  Note use of javax.xml package
        // This package contains just one class of constants.
        SchemaFactory factory =
            SchemaFactory.newInstance(XMLConstants.W3C_XML_SCHEMA_NS_URI);

        // Now parse the schema file to create a Schema object
        Schema schema = null;
        try { schema = factory.newSchema(schemaFile); }
        catch(SAXException e) { fail(e); }

        // Get a Validator object from the Schema.
        Validator validator = schema.newValidator();

        // Get a SAXSource object for the document
        // We could use a DOMSource here as well
        SAXSource source =
            new SAXSource(new InputSource(new FileReader(documentFile)));

        // Now validate the document
        try { validator.validate(source); }
        catch(SAXException e) { fail(e); }

        System.err.println("Document is valid");
    }

    static void fail(SAXException e) {
        if (e instanceof SAXParseException) {
            SAXParseException spe = (SAXParseException) e;
            System.err.printf("%s:%d:%d: %s%n",
                              spe.getSystemId(), spe.getLineNumber(),
                              spe.getColumnNumber(), spe.getMessage());
        }
        else {
```

```
            System.err.println(e.getMessage());
        }
        System.exit(1);
    }
}
```

Evaluating XPath Expressions

XPath is a language for referring to specific nodes in an XML document. For example, the XPath expression "//section/title/text()" refers to the text inside of a `<title>` element inside a `<section>` element at any depth within the document. A full description of the XPath language is beyond the scope of this book. The `javax.xml.xpath` package, new in Java 5.0, provides a way to find all nodes in a document that match an `XPath` expression.

```
import javax.xml.xpath.*;
import javax.xml.parsers.*;
import org.w3c.dom.*;

public class XPathEvaluator {
    public static void main(String[] args)
        throws ParserConfigurationException, XPathExpressionException,
               org.xml.sax.SAXException, java.io.IOException
    {
        String documentName = args[0];
        String expression = args[1];

        // Parse the document to a DOM tree
        // XPath can also be used with a SAX InputSource
        DocumentBuilder parser =
            DocumentBuilderFactory.newInstance().newDocumentBuilder();
        Document doc = parser.parse(new java.io.File(documentName));

        // Get an XPath object to evaluate the expression
        XPath xpath = XPathFactory.newInstance().newXPath();

        System.out.println(xpath.evaluate(expression, doc));

        // Or evaluate the expression to obtain a DOM NodeList of all matching
        // nodes.  Then loop through each of the resulting nodes
        NodeList nodes = (NodeList)xpath.evaluate(expression, doc,
                                                  XPathConstants.NODESET);
        for(int i = 0, n = nodes.getLength(); i < n; i++) {
            Node node = nodes.item(i);
            System.out.println(node);
        }
    }
}
```

Types, Reflection, and Dynamic Loading

The `java.lang.Class` class represents data types in Java and, along with the classes in the `java.lang.reflect` package, gives Java programs the capability of introspec-

The Java Platform

tion (or self-reflection); a Java class can look at itself, or any other class, and determine its superclass, what methods it defines, and so on.

Class Objects

You can obtain a Class object in Java in several ways:

```
// Obtain the Class of an arbitrary object o
Class c = o.getClass();

// Obtain a Class object for primitive types with various predefined constants
c = Void.TYPE;          // The special "no-return-value" type
c = Byte.TYPE;          // Class object that represents a byte
c = Integer.TYPE;       // Class object that represents an int
c = Double.TYPE;        // etc; see also Short, Character, Long, Float

// Express a class literal as a type name followed by ".class"
c = int.class;          // Same as Integer.TYPE
c = String.class;       // Same as "dummystring".getClass()
c = byte[].class;       // Type of byte arrays
c = Class[][].class;    // Type of array of arrays of Class objects
```

Reflecting on a Class

Once you have a Class object, you can perform some interesting reflective operations with it:

```
import java.lang.reflect.*;

Object o;                   // Some unknown object to investigate
Class c = o.getClass();     // Get its type

// If it is an array, figure out its base type
while (c.isArray()) c = c.getComponentType();

// If c is not a primitive type, print its class hierarchy
if (!c.isPrimitive()) {
  for(Class s = c; s != null; s = s.getSuperclass())
    System.out.println(s.getName() + " extends");
}

// Try to create a new instance of c; this requires a no-arg constructor
Object newobj = null;
try { newobj = c.newInstance(); }
catch (Exception e) {
  // Handle InstantiationException, IllegalAccessException
}

// See if the class has a method named setText that takes a single String
// If so, call it with a string argument
try {
    Method m = c.getMethod("setText", new Class[] { String.class });
    m.invoke(newobj, new Object[] { "My Label" });
} catch(Exception e) { /* Handle exceptions here */ }
```

```
// These are varargs methods in Java 5.0 so the syntax is much cleaner.
// Look for and invoke a method named "put" that takes two Object arguments
try {
    Method m = c.getMethod("add", Object.class, Object.class);
    m.invoke(newobj, "key", "value");
} catch(Exception e) { System.out.println(e); }

// In Java 5.0 we can use reflection on enumerated types and constants
Class<Thread.State> ts = Thread.State.class;  // Thread.State type
if (ts.isEnum()) {  // If it is an enumerated type
    Thread.State[] constants = ts.getEnumConstants(); // get its constants
}
try {
    Field f = ts.getField("RUNNABLE");       // Get the field named "RUNNABLE"
    System.out.println(f.isEnumConstant());  // Is it an enumerated constant?
}
catch(Exception e) { System.out.println(e); }

// The VM discards generic type information at runtime, but it is stored
// in the class file for the compiler and is accessible through reflection
try {
    Class map = Class.forName("java.util.Map");

    TypeVariable<?>[] typevars = map.getTypeParameters();
    for(TypeVariable<?> typevar : typevars) {
        System.out.print(typevar.getName());
        Type[] bounds = typevar.getBounds();
        if (bounds.length > 0) System.out.print(" extends ");
        for(int i = 0; i < bounds.length; i++) {
            if (i > 0) System.out.print(" & ");
            System.out.print(bounds[i]);
        }
        System.out.println();
    }
}
catch(Exception e) { System.out.println(e); }

// In Java 5.0, reflection can also be used on annotation types and to
// determine the values of runtime visible annotations
Class<?> a = Override.class;  // an annotation class
if (a.isAnnotation()) {       // is this an annotation type?
    // Look for some meta-annotations
    java.lang.annotation.Retention retention =
        a.getAnnotation(java.lang.annotation.Retention.class);
    if (retention != null)
        System.out.printf("Retention: %s%n", retention.value());
}
```

Dynamic Class Loading

`Class` also provides a simple mechanism for dynamic class loading in Java. For more complete control over dynamic class loading, however, you should use a `java.lang.ClassLoader` object, typically a `java.net.URLClassLoader`. This technique is useful, for example, when you want to load a class that is named in a configuration file instead of being hardcoded into your program:

```
// Dynamically load a class specified by name in a config file
String classname =                         // Look up the name of the class
    config.getProperty("filterclass",      // The property name
                    "com.davidflanagan.filters.Default"); // A default

try {
  Class c = Class.forName(classname);     // Dynamically load the class
  Object o = c.newInstance();             // Dynamically instantiate it
} catch (Exception e) { /* Handle exceptions */ }
```

The preceding code works only if the class to be loaded is in the class path. If this is not the case, you can create a custom ClassLoader object to load a class from a path (or URL) you specify yourself:

```
import java.net.*;
String classdir = config.getProperty("filterDirectory"); // Look up class path
try {
  ClassLoader loader = new URLClassLoader(new URL[] { new URL(classdir) });
  Class c = loader.loadClass(classname);
}
catch (Exception e) { /* Handle exceptions */ }
```

Dynamic Proxies

The Proxy class and InvocationHandler interface to the java.lang.reflect package were added to Java 1.3. Proxy is a powerful but infrequently used class that allows you to dynamically create a new class or instance that implements a specified interface or set of interfaces. It also dispatches invocations of the interface methods to an InvocationHandler object.

Object Persistence

The Java platform provides two mechanisms for object persistence: the ability to save object state so that the object can later be recreated. Both mechanisms involve serialization; the second is aimed particularly at JavaBeans.

Serialization

One of the most important features of the java.io package is the ability to *serialize* objects: to convert an object into a stream of bytes that can later be deserialized back into a copy of the original object. The following code shows how to use serialization to save an object to a file and later read it back:

```
Object o;  // The object we are serializing; it must implement Serializable
File f;    // The file we are saving it to

try {
  // Serialize the object
  ObjectOutputStream oos = new ObjectOutputStream(new FileOutputStream(f));
  oos.writeObject(o);
```

```
    oos.close();

    // Read the object back in
    ObjectInputStream ois = new ObjectInputStream(new FileInputStream(f));
    Object copy = ois.readObject();
    ois.close();
  }
  catch (IOException e) { /* Handle input/output exceptions */ }
  catch (ClassNotFoundException cnfe) { /* readObject() can throw this */ }
```

The previous example serializes to a file, but remember, you can write serialized objects to any type of stream. Thus, you can write an object to a byte array, then read it back from the byte array, creating a deep copy of the object. You can write the object's bytes to a compression stream or even write the bytes to a stream connected across a network to another program!

JavaBeans Persistence

Java 1.4 introduced a serialization mechanism intended for use with JavaBeans components. `java.io` serialization works by saving the state of the internal fields of an object. `java.beans` persistence, on the other hand, works by saving a bean's state as a sequence of calls to the public methods defined by the class. Since it is based on the public API rather than on the internal state, the JavaBeans persistence mechanism allows interoperability between different implementations of the same API, handles version skew more robustly, and is suitable for longer-term storage of serialized objects.

A bean and any descendant beans or other objects that are serialized with `java.beans.XMLEncoder` can be deserialized with `java.beans.XMLDecoder`. These classes write to and read from specified streams, but they are not stream classes themselves. Here is how you might encode a bean:

```
// Create a JavaBean, and set some properties on it
javax.swing.JFrame bean = new javax.swing.JFrame("PersistBean");
bean.setSize(300, 300);
// Now save its encoded form to the file bean.xml
BufferedOutputStream out =                   // Create an output stream
    new BufferedOutputStream(new FileOutputStream("bean.xml"));
XMLEncoder encoder = new XMLEncoder(out);    // Create encoder for stream
encoder.writeObject(bean);                   // Encode the bean
encoder.close();                             // Close encoder and stream
```

Here is the corresponding code to decode the bean from its serialized form:

```
BufferedInputStream in =                     // Create input stream
    new BufferedInputStream(new FileInputStream("bean.xml"));
XMLDecoder decoder = new XMLDecoder(in);     // Create decoder for stream
Object b = decoder.readObject();             // Decode a bean
decoder.close();                             // Close decoder and stream
bean = (javax.swing.JFrame) b;               // Cast bean to proper type
bean.setVisible(true);                       // Start using it
```

Security

The java.security package defines quite a few classes related to the Java access-control architecture, which is discussed in more detail in Chapter 6. These classes allow Java programs to run untrusted code in a restricted environment from which it can do no harm. While these are important classes, you rarely need to use them. The more interesting classes are the ones used for message digests and digital signatures; they are demonstrated in the sections that follow.

Message Digests

A *message digest* is a value, also known as cryptographic checksum or secure hash, that is computed over a sequence of bytes. The length of the digest is typically much smaller than the length of the data for which it is computed, but any change, no matter how small, in the input bytes produces a change in the digest. When transmitting data (a message), you can transmit a message digest along with it. The recipient of the message can then recompute the message digest on the received data and, by comparing the computed digest to the received digest, determine whether the message or the digest was corrupted or tampered with during transmission. We saw a way to compute a message digest earlier in the chapter when we discussed streams. A similar technique can be used to compute a message digest for nonstreaming binary data:

```
import java.security.*;

// Obtain an object to compute message digests using the "Secure Hash
// Algorithm"; this method can throw a NoSuchAlgorithmException.
MessageDigest md = MessageDigest.getInstance("SHA");

byte[] data, data1, data2, secret;  // Some byte arrays initialized elsewhere

// Create a digest for a single array of bytes
byte[] digest = md.digest(data);

// Create a digest for several chunks of data
md.reset();             // Optional: automatically called by digest()
md.update(data1);       // Process the first chunk of data
md.update(data2);       // Process the second chunk of data
digest = md.digest();   // Compute the digest

// Create a keyed digest that can be verified if you know the secret bytes
md.update(data);              // The data to be transmitted with the digest
digest = md.digest(secret);   // Add the secret bytes and compute the digest

// Verify a digest like this
byte[] receivedData, receivedDigest;  // The data and the digest we received
byte[] verifyDigest = md.digest(receivedData);  // Digest the received data
// Compare computed digest to the received digest
boolean verified =  java.util.Arrays.equals(receivedDigest, verifyDigest);
```

Digital Signatures

A *digital signature* combines a message-digest algorithm with public-key cryptography. The sender of a message, Alice, can compute a digest for a message and then encrypt that digest with her private key. She then sends the message and the encrypted digest to a recipient, Bob. Bob knows Alice's public key (it is public, after all), so he can use it to decrypt the digest and verify that the message has not been tampered with. In performing this verification, Bob also learns that the digest was encrypted with Alice's private key since he was able to decrypt the digest successfully using Alice's public key. As Alice is the only one who knows her private key, the message must have come from Alice. A digital signature is called such because, like a pen-and-paper signature, it serves to authenticate the origin of a document or message. Unlike a pen-and-paper signature, however, a digital signature is very difficult, if not impossible, to forge, and it cannot simply be cut and pasted onto another document.

Java makes creating digital signatures easy. In order to create a digital signature, however, you need a `java.security.PrivateKey` object. Assuming that a keystore exists on your system (see the *keytool* documentation in Chapter 8), you can get one with code like the following:

```
// Here is some basic data we need
File homedir = new File(System.getProperty("user.home"));
File keyfile = new File(homedir, ".keystore"); // Or read from config file
String filepass = "KeyStore password"          // Password for entire file
String signer = "david";                       // Read from config file
String password = "No one can guess this!";    // Better to prompt for this
PrivateKey key;  // This is the key we want to look up from the keystore

try {
  // Obtain a KeyStore object and then load data into it
  KeyStore keystore = KeyStore.getInstance(KeyStore.getDefaultType());
  keystore.load(new BufferedInputStream(new FileInputStream(keyfile)),
                filepass.toCharArray());
  // Now ask for the desired key
  key = (PrivateKey) keystore.getKey(signer, password.toCharArray());
}
catch (Exception e) { /* Handle various exception types here */ }
```

Once you have a `PrivateKey` object, you can create a digital signature with a `java.security.Signature` object:

```
PrivateKey key;               // Initialized as shown previously
byte[] data;                  // The data to be signed
Signature s =                 // Obtain object to create and verify signatures
  Signature.getInstance("SHA1withDSA");  // Can throw a
                                         // NoSuchAlgorithmException
s.initSign(key);               // Initialize it; can throw an InvalidKeyException
s.update(data);                // Data to sign; can throw a SignatureException
/* s.update(data2); */         // Call multiple times to specify all data
byte[] signature = s.sign(); // Compute signature
```

A `Signature` object can verify a digital signature:

```
byte[] data;        // The signed data; initialized elsewhere
byte[] signature;   // The signature to be verified; initialized elsewhere
```

```
String signername;  // Who created the signature; initialized elsewhere
KeyStore keystore;  // Where certificates stored; initialize as shown earlier

// Look for a public-key certificate for the signer
java.security.cert.Certificate cert = keystore.getCertificate(signername);
PublicKey publickey = cert.getPublicKey();  // Get the public key from it

Signature s = Signature.getInstance("SHA1withDSA"); // Or some other algorithm
s.initVerify(publickey);                           // Setup for verification
s.update(data);                                    // Specify signed data
boolean verified = s.verify(signature);            // Verify signature data
```

Signed Objects

The `java.security.SignedObject` class is a convenient utility for wrapping a digital signature around an object. The `SignedObject` can then be serialized and transmitted to a recipient, who can deserialize it and use the `verify( )` method to verify the signature:

```
Serializable o;  // The object to be signed; must be Serializable
PrivateKey k;    // The key to sign with; initialized elsewhere
Signature s = Signature.getInstance("SHA1withDSA"); // Signature "engine"
SignedObject so = new SignedObject(o, k, s);        // Create the SignedObject

// The SignedObject encapsulates the object o; it can now be serialized
// and transmitted to a recipient.

// Here's how the recipient verifies the SignedObject
SignedObject so;           // The deserialized SignedObject
Object o;                  // The original object to extract from it
PublicKey pk;              // The key to verify with
Signature s = Signature.getInstance("SHA1withDSA"); // Verification "engine"
if (so.verify(pk,s))       // If the signature is valid,
  o = so.getObject();      // retrieve the encapsulated object.
```

Cryptography

The `java.security` package includes cryptography-based classes, but it does not contain classes for actual encryption and decryption. That is the job of the `javax.crypto` package. This package supports symmetric-key cryptography, in which the same key is used for both encryption and decryption and must be known by both the sender and the receiver of encrypted data.

Secret Keys

The `SecretKey` interface represents an encryption key; the first step of any cryptographic operation is to obtain an appropriate `SecretKey`. Unfortunately, the *keytool* program supplied with the JDK cannot generate and store secret keys, so a program must handle these tasks itself. Here is some code that shows various ways to work with `SecretKey` objects:

```
import javax.crypto.*;
import javax.crypto.spec.*;
```

```
// Generate encryption keys with a KeyGenerator object
KeyGenerator desGen = KeyGenerator.getInstance("DES");       // DES algorithm
SecretKey desKey = desGen.generateKey();                     // Generate a key
KeyGenerator desEdeGen = KeyGenerator.getInstance("DESede"); // Triple DES
SecretKey desEdeKey = desEdeGen.generateKey();               // Generate a key

// SecretKey is an opaque representation of a key. Use SecretKeyFactory to
// convert to a transparent representation that can be manipulated: saved
// to a file, securely transmitted to a receiving party, etc.
SecretKeyFactory desFactory = SecretKeyFactory.getInstance("DES");
DESKeySpec desSpec = (DESKeySpec)
  desFactory.getKeySpec(desKey, javax.crypto.spec.DESKeySpec.class);
byte[] rawDesKey = desSpec.getKey();
// Do the same for a DESede key
SecretKeyFactory desEdeFactory = SecretKeyFactory.getInstance("DESede");
DESedeKeySpec desEdeSpec = (DESedeKeySpec)
  desEdeFactory.getKeySpec(desEdeKey, javax.crypto.spec.DESedeKeySpec.class);
byte[] rawDesEdeKey = desEdeSpec.getKey();

// Convert the raw bytes of a key back to a SecretKey object
DESedeKeySpec keyspec = new DESedeKeySpec(rawDesEdeKey);
SecretKey k = desEdeFactory.generateSecret(keyspec);

// For DES and DESede keys, there is an even easier way to create keys
// SecretKeySpec implements SecretKey, so use it to represent these keys
byte[] desKeyData = new byte[8];        // Read 8 bytes of data from a file
byte[] tripleDesKeyData = new byte[24]; // Read 24 bytes of data from a file
SecretKey myDesKey = new SecretKeySpec(desKeyData, "DES");
SecretKey myTripleDesKey = new SecretKeySpec(tripleDesKeyData, "DESede");
```


Encryption and Decryption with Cipher

Once you have obtained an appropriate SecretKey object, the central class for encryption and decryption is Cipher. Use it like this:

```
SecretKey key;      // Obtain a SecretKey as shown earlier
byte[] plaintext;  // The data to encrypt; initialized elsewhere

// Obtain an object to perform encryption or decryption
Cipher cipher = Cipher.getInstance("DESede");  // Triple-DES encryption
// Initialize the cipher object for encryption
cipher.init(Cipher.ENCRYPT_MODE, key);
// Now encrypt data
byte[] ciphertext = cipher.doFinal(plaintext);

// If we had multiple chunks of data to encrypt, we can do this
cipher.update(message1);
cipher.update(message2);
byte[] ciphertext = cipher.doFinal();

// We simply reverse things to decrypt
cipher.init(Cipher.DECRYPT_MODE, key);
byte[] decryptedMessage = cipher.doFinal(ciphertext);
```

```
// To decrypt multiple chunks of data
byte[] decrypted1 = cipher.update(ciphertext1);
byte[] decrypted2 = cipher.update(ciphertext2);
byte[] decrypted3 = cipher.doFinal(ciphertext3);
```

Encrypting and Decrypting Streams

The Cipher class can also be used with CipherInputStream or CipherOutputStream to encrypt or decrypt while reading or writing streaming data:

```
byte[] data;                             // The data to encrypt
SecretKey key;                           // Initialize as shown earlier
Cipher c = Cipher.getInstance("DESede"); // The object to perform encryption
c.init(Cipher.ENCRYPT_MODE, key);        // Initialize it

// Create a stream to write bytes to a file
FileOutputStream fos = new FileOutputStream("encrypted.data");

// Create a stream that encrypts bytes before sending them to that stream
// See also CipherInputStream to encrypt or decrypt while reading bytes
CipherOutputStream cos = new CipherOutputStream(fos, c);

cos.write(data);                  // Encrypt and write the data to the file
cos.close();                      // Always remember to close streams
java.util.Arrays.fill(data, (byte)0); // Erase the unencrypted data
```

Encrypted Objects

Finally, the javax.crypto.SealedObject class provides an especially easy way to perform encryption. This class serializes a specified object and encrypts the resulting stream of bytes. The SealedObject can then be serialized itself and transmitted to a recipient. The recipient can retrieve the original object only if she knows the required SecretKey:

```
Serializable o;           // The object to be encrypted; must be Serializable
SecretKey key;                                // The key to encrypt it with
Cipher c = Cipher.getInstance("Blowfish");    // Object to perform encryption
c.init(Cipher.ENCRYPT_MODE, key);             // Initialize it with the key
SealedObject so = new SealedObject(o, c);     // Create the sealed object

// Object so is a wrapper around an encrypted form of the original object o;
// it can now be serialized and transmitted to another party.
// Here's how the recipient decrypts the original object
Object original = so.getObject(key);          // Must use the same SecretKey
```

Miscellaneous Platform Features

The following sections detail important but miscellaneous features of the Java platform, including properties, preferences, processes, and management and instrumentation.

Properties

java.util.Properties is a subclass of java.util.Hashtable, a legacy collections class that predates the Collections API introduced in Java 1.2. A Properties object maintains a mapping between string keys and string values and defines methods that allow the mappings to be written to and read from a simple text file or (in Java 5.0) an XML file. This makes the Properties class ideal for configuration and user preference files. The Properties class is also used for the system properties returned by System.getProperty( ):

```
import java.util.*;
import java.io.*;

// Note: many of these system properties calls throw a security exception if
// called from untrusted code such as applets.
String homedir = System.getProperty("user.home"); // Get a system property
Properties sysprops = System.getProperties();     // Get all system properties

// Print the names of all defined system properties
for(Enumeration e = sysprops.propertyNames(); e.hasMoreElements();)
  System.out.println(e.nextElement());

sysprops.list(System.out); // Here's an even easier way to list the properties

// Read properties from a configuration file
Properties options = new Properties();              // Empty properties list
File configfile = new File(homedir, ".config");     // The configuration file
try {
  options.load(new FileInputStream(configfile));    // Load props from the file
} catch (IOException e) { /* Handle exception here */ }

// Query a property ("color"), specifying a default ("gray") if undefined
String color = options.getProperty("color", "gray");

// Set a property named "color" to the value "green"
options.setProperty("color", "green");

// Store the contents of the Properties object back into a file
try {
  options.store(new FileOutputStream(configfile),   // Output stream
                "MyApp Config File");               // File header comment text
} catch (IOException e) { /* Handle exception */ }

// In Java 5.0 properties can be written to or read from XML files
try {
  options.storeToXML(new FileOutputStream(configfile),  // Output stream
                     "MyApp Config File");              // Comment text
  options.loadFromXML(new FileInputStream(configfile)); // Read it back in
}
catch(IOException e) { /* Handle exception */ }
catch(InvalidPropertiesFormatException e) { /* malformed input */ }
```

Preferences

Java 1.4 introduced the Preferences API, which is specifically tailored for working with user and systemwide preferences and is more useful than Properties for this purpose. The Preferences API is defined by the java.util.prefs package. The key class in that package is Preferences. You can obtain a Preferences object that contains user-specific preferences with the static method Preferences.userNodeForPackage() and obtain a Preferences object that contains systemwide preferences with Preferences.systemNodeForPackage(). Both methods take a java.lang.Class object as their sole argument and return a Preferences object shared by all classes in that package. (This means that the preference names you use must be unique within the package.) Once you have a Preferences object, use the get( ) method to query the string value of a named preference, or use other type-specific methods such as getInt( ), getBoolean(), and getByteArray(). Note that to query preference values, a default value must be passed for all methods. This default value is returned if no preference with the specified name has been registered or if the file or database that holds the preference data cannot be accessed. A typical use of Preferences is the following:

```
package com.davidflanagan.editor;
import java.util.prefs.Preferences;

public class TextEditor {
  // Fields to be initialized from preference values
  public int width;              // Screen width in columns
  public String dictionary;      // Dictionary name for spell checking

  public void initPrefs() {
    // Get Preferences objects for user and system preferences for this package
    Preferences userprefs = Preferences.userNodeForPackage(TextEditor.class);
    Preferences sysprefs = Preferences.systemNodeForPackage(TextEditor.class);

    // Look up preference values. Note that you always pass a default value.
    width = userprefs.getInt("width", 80);
    // Look up a user preference using a system preference as the default
    dictionary = userprefs.get("dictionary",
                               sysprefs.get("dictionary",
                                            "default_dictionary"));
  }
}
```

In addition to the get( ) methods for querying preference values, there are corresponding put( ) methods for setting the values of named preferences:

```
// User has indicated a new preference, so store it
userprefs.putBoolean("autosave", false);
```

If your application wants to be notified of user or system preference changes while the application is in progress, it may register a PreferenceChangeListener with addPreferenceChangeListener(). A Preferences object can export the names and values of its preferences as an XML file and can read preferences from such an XML file. (See importPreferences( ), exportNode(), and exportSubtree( ) in java.util.pref.Preferences in the reference section.) Preferences objects exist in a hierarchy that typically corresponds to the hierarchy of package names. Methods for navigating this hierarchy exist but are not typically used by ordinary applications.

Processes

Earlier in the chapter, we saw how easy it is to create and manipulate multiple threads of execution running within the same Java interpreter. Java also has a java.lang.Process class that represents an operating system process running externally to the interpreter. A Java program can communicate with an external process using streams in the same way that it might communicate with a server running on some other computer on the network. Using a Process is always platform-dependent and is rarely portable, but it is sometimes a useful thing to do:

```
// Maximize portability by looking up the name of the command to execute
// in a configuration file.
java.util.Properties config;
String cmd = config.getProperty("sysloadcmd");
if (cmd != null) {
  // Execute the command; Process p represents the running command
  Process p = Runtime.getRuntime().exec(cmd);         // Start the command
  InputStream pin = p.getInputStream();               // Read bytes from it
  InputStreamReader cin = new InputStreamReader(pin); // Convert them to chars
  BufferedReader in = new BufferedReader(cin);        // Read lines of chars
  String load = in.readLine();                        // Get the command output
  in.close();                                         // Close the stream
}
```

The Java Platform

In Java 5.0 the java.lang.ProcessBuilder class provides a more flexible way to launch new processes than the Runtime.exec() method. ProcessBuilder allows control of environment variables through a Map and makes it simple to set the working directory. It also has an option to automatically redirect the standard error stream of the processes it launches to the standard output stream, which makes it much easier to read all output of a Process.

```
import java.util.Map;
import java.io.*

public class JavaShell {
    public static void main(String[] args) {
        // We use this to start commands
        ProcessBuilder launcher = new ProcessBuilder();
        // Our inherited environment vars.  We may modify these below
        Map<String,String> environment = launcher.environment();
        // Our processes will merge error stream with standard output stream
        launcher.redirectErrorStream(true);
        // Where we read the user's input from
        BufferedReader console =
            new BufferedReader(new InputStreamReader(System.in));

        while(true) {
            try {
```

```
                System.out.print("> ");               // display prompt
                System.out.flush();                   // force it to show
                String command = console.readLine();  // Read input

                if (command.equals("exit")) return;   // Exit command

                else if (command.startsWith("cd ")) { // change directory
                    launcher.directory(new File(command.substring(3)));
                }

                else if (command.startsWith("set ")) {// set environment var
                    command = command.substring(4);
                    int pos = command.indexOf('=');
                    String name = command.substring(0,pos).trim();
                    String var = command.substring(pos+1).trim();
                    environment.put(name, var);
                }

                else { // Otherwise it is a process to launch
                    // Break command into individual tokens
                    String[] words = command.split(" ");
                    launcher.command(words);       // Set the command
                    Process p = launcher.start(); // And launch a new process

                    // Now read and display output from the process
                    // until there is no more output to read
                    BufferedReader output = new BufferedReader(
                            new InputStreamReader(p.getInputStream()));
                    String line;
                    while((line = output.readLine()) != null)
                        System.out.println(line);

                    // The process should be done now, but wait to be sure.
                    p.waitFor();
                }
            }
            catch(Exception e) {
                System.out.println(e);
            }
        }
    }
}
```

Management and Instrumentation

Java 5.0 includes the powerful JMX API for remote monitoring and management of running applications. The full `javax.management` API is beyond the scope of this book. The reference section does cover the `java.lang.management` package, however: this package is an application of JMX for the monitoring and management of the Java virtual machine itself. `java.lang.instrument` is another Java 5.0 package: it allows the definition of "agents" that can be used to instrument the running JVM. In VMs that support it, `java.lang.instrument` can be used to redefine class files as they are loaded to add profiling or coverage testing code, for example. Class redefinition is beyond the scope of this chapter, but the following code uses the new instrumentation and management features of Java 5.0 to determine resource usages of a Java program. The example also demonstrates the `Runtime.addShutdownHook()` method, which registers code to be run when the VM starts shutting down.

```
import java.lang.instrument.*;
import java.lang.management.*;
import java.util.List;
import java.io.*;

public class ResourceUsageAgent {
    // A Java agent class defines a premain() method to run before main()
    public static void premain(final String args, final Instrumentation inst) {
       // This agent simply registers a shutdown hook to run when the VM exits
        Runtime.getRuntime().addShutdownHook(new Thread() {
                public void run() {
                    // This code runs when the VM exits
                    try {
                        // Decide where to send our output
                        PrintWriter out;
                        if (args != null && args.length() > 0)
                            out = new PrintWriter(new FileWriter(args));
                        else
                            out = new PrintWriter(System.err);

                        // Use java.lang.management to query peak thread usage
                        ThreadMXBean tb = ManagementFactory.getThreadMXBean();
                        out.printf("Current thread count: %d%n",
                                   tb.getThreadCount());
                        out.printf("Peak thread count: %d%n",
                                   tb.getPeakThreadCount());

                        // Use java.lang.management to query peak memory usage
                        List<MemoryPoolMXBean> pools =
                            ManagementFactory.getMemoryPoolMXBeans();
                        for(MemoryPoolMXBean pool: pools) {
                            MemoryUsage peak = pool.getPeakUsage();
                            out.printf("Peak %s memory used: %,d%n",
                                       pool.getName(), peak.getUsed());
                            out.printf("Peak %s memory reserved: %,d%n",
                                       pool.getName(), peak.getCommitted());
                        }

                        // Use the Instrumentation object passed to premain()
                        // to get a list of all classes that have been loaded
                        Class[] loaded = inst.getAllLoadedClasses();
                        out.println("Loaded classes:");
                        for(Class c : loaded) out.println(c.getName());

                        out.close();  // close and flush the output stream
                    }
                    catch(Throwable t) {
                        // Exceptions in shutdown hooks are ignored so
```

The Java Platform

```
                        // we've got to print this out explicitly
                        System.err.println("Exception in agent: " + t);
                    }
                }
            });
    }
}
```

To monitor the resource usage of a Java program with this agent, you first must compile the class normally. You then store the generated class files in a JAR file with a manifest that specifies the class that contains the `premain()` method. Create a manifest file that contains this line:

```
Premain-Class: ResourceUsageAgent
```

Create the JAR file with a command like this:

```
% jar cmf manifest agent.jar ResourceUsageAgent*.class
```

Finally, to use the agent, specify the JAR file and the agent arguments with the `-javaagent` flag to the Java interpreter:

```
% java -javaagent:agent.jar=/tmp/usage.info my.java.Program
```

6 Java Security

Java programs can dynamically load Java classes from a variety of sources, including untrusted sources, such as web sites reached across an insecure network. The ability to create and work with such mobile code is one of the great strengths and features of Java. To make it work successfully, however, Java puts great emphasis on a security architecture that allows untrusted code to run safely, without fear of damage to the host system.

The need for a security system in Java is most acutely demonstrated by applets—miniature Java applications designed to be embedded in web pages.* When a user visits a web page (with a Java-enabled web browser) that contains an applet, the web browser downloads the Java class files that define that applet and runs them. In the absence of a security system, an applet could wreak havoc on the user's system by deleting files, installing a virus, stealing confidential information, and so on. Somewhat more subtly, an applet could take advantage of the user's system to forge email, generate spam, or launch hacking attempts on other systems.

Java's main line of defense against such malicious code is *access control*: untrusted code is simply not given access to certain sensitive portions of the core Java API. For example, an untrusted applet is not typically allowed to read, write, or delete files on the host system or connect over the network to any computer other than the web server from which it was downloaded. This chapter describes the Java access control architecture and a few other facets of the Java security system.

* Applets are documented in *Java Foundation Classes in a Nutshell* (O'Reilly) and are not covered in this book. Still, they serve as good examples here.

Security Risks

Java has been designed from the ground up with security in mind; this gives it a great advantage over many other existing systems and platforms. Nevertheless, no system can guarantee 100% security, and Java is no exception.

The Java security architecture was designed by security experts and has been studied and probed by many other security experts. The consensus is that the architecture itself is strong and robust, theoretically without any security holes (at least none that have been discovered yet). The implementation of the security architecture is another matter, however, and there is a long history of security flaws being found and patched in particular implementations of Java. For example, in April 1999, a flaw was found in Sun's implementation of the class verifier in Java 1.1. Patches for Java 1.1.6 and 1.1.7 were issued and the problem was fixed in Java 1.1.8. In August 1999, a severe flaw was found in Microsoft's Java Virtual Machine. Microsoft fixed the problem, and no longer distributes their VM with the latest versions of their web browser.

In all likelihood, security flaws will continue to be discovered (and patched) in Java VM implementations. Despite this, Java remains perhaps the most secure platform currently available. There have been few, if any, reported instances of malicious Java code exploiting security holes "in the wild." For practical purposes, the Java platform appears to be adequately secure, especially when contrasted with some of the insecure and virus-ridden alternatives.

Java VM Security and Class File Verification

The lowest level of the Java security architecture involves the design of the Java Virtual Machine and the byte codes it executes. The Java VM does not allow any kind of direct access to individual memory addresses of the underlying system, which prevents Java code from interfering with the native hardware and operating system. These intentional restrictions on the VM are reflected in the Java language itself, which does not support pointers or pointer arithmetic. The language does not allow an integer to be cast to an object reference or vice versa, and there is no way whatsoever to obtain an object's address in memory. Without capabilities like these, malicious code simply cannot gain a foothold.

In addition to the secure design of the Virtual Machine instruction set, the VM goes through a process known as *byte-code verification* whenever it loads an untrusted class. This process ensures that the byte codes of a class (and their operands) are all valid; that the code never underflows or overflows the VM stack; that local variables are not used before they are initialized; that field, method, and class access control modifiers are respected; and so on. The verification step is designed to prevent the VM from executing byte codes that might crash it or put it into an undefined and untested state where it might be vulnerable to other attacks by malicious code. Byte-code verification is a defense against malicious handcrafted Java byte codes and untrusted Java compilers that might output invalid byte codes.

Authentication and Cryptography

The `java.security` package (and its subpackages) provides classes and interfaces for *authentication*. As described in Chapter 5, this piece of the security architecture allows Java code to create and verify message digests and digital signatures. These technologies can ensure that any data (such as a Java class file) is authentic: that it originates from the person who claims to have originated it and has not been accidentally or maliciously modified in transit.

The Java Cryptography Extension, or JCE, consists of the `javax.crypto` package and its subpackages. These packages define classes for encryption and decryption of data. This is an important security-related feature for many applications, but is not directly relevant to the basic problem of preventing untrusted code from damaging the host system, so it is not discussed in this chapter.

Access Control

As we noted at the beginning of this chapter, the heart of the Java security architecture is access control: untrusted code simply must not be granted access to the sensitive parts of the Java API that would allow it to do malicious things. As we'll discuss in the following sections, the Java access control model evolved significantly between Java 1.0 and Java 1.2. Since then, the access control model has been relatively stable; it has not changed significantly since Java 1.2. The next sections provide a brief history of the evolution of Java security as it developed from Java 1.0 to Java 1.2, which marked the last major changes to the security model.

Java 1.0: The Sandbox

In this first release of Java, all Java code installed locally on the system is trusted implicitly. All code downloaded over the network, however, is untrusted and run in a restricted environment playfully called "the sandbox." The access control policies of the sandbox are defined by the currently installed `java.lang.SecurityManager` object. When system code is about to perform a restricted operation, such as reading a file from the local filesystem, it first calls an appropriate method (such as `checkRead()`) of the currently installed `SecurityManager` object. If untrusted code is running, the `SecurityManager` throws a `SecurityException` that prevents the restricted operation from taking place.

The most common user of the `SecurityManager` class is a Java-enabled web browser, which installs a `SecurityManager` object to allow applets to run without damaging the host system. The precise details of the security policy are an implementation detail of the web browser, of course, but applets are typically restricted in the following ways:

- An applet cannot read, write, rename, or delete files. It cannot query the length or modification date of a file or even check whether a given file exists. Similarly, an applet cannot create, list, or delete a directory.
- An applet cannot connect to or accept a connection from any computer other than the one it was downloaded from. It cannot use any privileged ports (i.e., ports below and including port 1024).

- An applet cannot perform system-level functions, such as loading a native library, spawning a new process, or exiting the Java interpreter. An applet cannot manipulate any threads or thread groups, except for those it creates itself. In Java 1.1 and later, applets cannot use the Java Reflection API to obtain information about the nonpublic members of classes, except for classes that were downloaded with the applet.
- An applet cannot access certain graphics- and GUI-related facilities. It cannot initiate a print job or access the system clipboard or event queue. In addition, all windows created by an applet typically display a prominent visual indicator that they are "insecure" to prevent an applet from spoofing the appearance of some other application.
- An applet cannot read certain system properties, notably the `user.home` and `user.dir` properties, that specify the user's home directory and current working directory.
- An applet cannot circumvent these security restrictions by registering a new `SecurityManager` object.

How the sandbox works

Suppose that an applet (or some other untrusted code running in the sandbox) attempts to read the contents of the file */etc/passwd* by passing this filename to the `FileInputStream()` constructor. The programmers who wrote the `FileInputStream` class were aware that the class provides access to a system resource (a file), so use of the class should therefore be subject to access control. For this reason, they coded the `FileInputStream( )` constructor to use the `SecurityManager` class.

Every time `FileInputStream( )` is called, it checks to see if a `SecurityManager` object has been installed. If so, the constructor calls the `checkRead()` method of that `SecurityManager` object, passing the filename (*/etc/passwd*, in this case) as the sole argument. The `checkRead()` method has no return value; it either returns normally or throws a `SecurityException`. If the method returns, the `FileInputStream()` constructor simply proceeds with whatever initialization is necessary and returns. Otherwise, it allows the `SecurityException` to propagate to the caller. When this happens, no `FileInputStream` object is created, and the applet does not gain access to the */etc/passwd* file.

Java 1.1: Digitally Signed Classes

Java 1.1 retained the sandbox model of Java 1.0 but added the `java.security` package and its digital signature capabilities. With these capabilities, Java classes can be digitally signed and verified. Thus, web browsers and other Java installations can be configured to trust downloaded code that bears a valid digital signature of a trusted entity. Such code is treated as if it were installed locally, so it is given full access to the Java APIs. In this release, the *javakey* program manages keys and digitally signs JAR files of Java code. Although Java 1.1 added the important ability to trust digitally signed code that would otherwise be untrusted, it sticks to the basic sandbox model: trusted code gets full access and untrusted code gets totally restricted access.

Java 1.2: Permissions and Policies

Java 1.2 introduced substantial access control features into the Java security architecture. These features are implemented by classes in the `java.security` package. The `Policy` class is one of the most important: it defines a Java security policy. A `Policy` object maps `CodeSource` objects to associated sets of `Permission` objects. A `CodeSource` object represents the source of a piece of Java code, which includes both the URL of the class file (and can be a local file) and a list of entities that have applied their digital signatures to the class file. The `Permission` objects associated with a `CodeSource` in the `Policy` define the permissions that are granted to code from a given source. Various Java APIs include subclasses of `Permission` that represent different types of permissions. These include `java.lang.RuntimePermission`, `java.io.FilePermission`, and `java.net.SocketPermission`, for example.

Under this access control model, the `SecurityManager` class continues to be the central class; access control requests are still made by invoking methods of a `SecurityManager`. However, the default `SecurityManager` implementation delegates most of those requests to an `AccessController` class that makes access decisions based on the `Permission` and `Policy` architecture.

The Java 1.2 access control architecture has several important features:

- Code from different sources can be given different sets of permissions. In other words, the architecture supports fine-grained levels of trust. Even locally installed code can be treated as untrusted or partially untrusted. Under this architecture, only system classes and standard extensions run as fully trusted.
- It is no longer necessary to define a custom subclass of `SecurityManager` to define a security policy. Policies can be configured by a system administrator by editing a text file or using the *policytool* program, described in Chapter 8.
- The architecture is not limited to a fixed set of access control methods in the `SecurityManager` class. `Permission` subclasses can be defined easily to govern access to system resources (which might be exposed, for example, by standard extensions that include native code).

How policies and permissions work

Let's return to the example of an applet that attempts to create a `FileInputStream` to read the file */etc/passwd*. In Java 1.2 and later, the `FileInputStream()` constructor behaves exactly the same as it does in Java 1.0 and Java 1.1: it looks to see if a `SecurityManager` is installed and, if so, calls its `checkRead()` method, passing the name of the file to be read.

What changed as of Java 1.2 is the default behavior of the `checkRead()` method. Unless a program has replaced the default security manager with one of its own, the default implementation creates a `FilePermission` object to represent the access being requested. This `FilePermission` object has a *target* of "/etc/passwd" and an *action* of "read." The `checkRead()` method passes this `FilePermission` object to the static `checkPermission()` method of the `java.security.AccessController` class.

It is the `AccessController` and its `checkPermission( )` method that do the real work of access control as of Java 1.2. The method determines the `CodeSource` of each calling method and uses the current `Policy` object to determine the `Permission` objects associated with it. With this information, the `AccessController` can determine whether read access to the */etc/passwd* file should be allowed.

The `Permission` class represents both the permissions granted by a `Policy` and the permissions requested by a method like the `FileInputStream()` constructor. When requesting a permission, Java typically uses a `FilePermission` (or other `Permission` subclass) with a very specific target, like "/etc/passwd". When granting a permission, however, a `Policy` commonly uses a `FilePermission` object with a wildcard target, such as "/etc/*", to represent many files. One of the key features of a `Permission` subclass such as `FilePermission` is that it defines an `implies()` method that can determine whether permission to read "/etc/*" implies permission to read "/etc/passwd".

Security for Everyone

Programmers, system administrators, and end users all have different security concerns and, thus, different roles to play in the Java security architecture.

Security for System Programmers

System programmers are the people who define new Java APIs that allow access to sensitive system resources. These programmers are typically working with native methods that have unprotected access to the system. They need to use the Java access control architecture to prevent untrusted code from executing those native methods. To do this, system programmers must carefully insert `SecurityManager` calls at appropriate places in their code. A system programmer may choose to use an existing `Permission` subclass to govern access to the system resources exposed by her API, or she may decide to define a specialized subclass of `Permission`.

The system programmer carries a tremendous security burden: if she does not perform appropriate access control checks in her code, she compromises the security of the entire Java platform. The details are complex and are beyond the scope of this book. Fortunately, however, system programming that involves native methods is rare in Java; almost all of us are application programmers who can simply rely on the existing APIs.

Security for Application Programmers

Programmers who use the core Java APIs and standard extensions but do not define new extensions or write native methods can simply rely on the security efforts of the system programmers who created those APIs. In other words, most of us Java programmers can simply use the Java APIs and need not worry about introducing security holes into the Java platform.

In fact, application programmers rarely have to use the access control architecture. If you are writing Java code that may be run as untrusted code, you should be aware of the restrictions placed on untrusted code by typical security policies.

Keep in mind that some methods (such as methods that read or write files) can throw `SecurityException` objects, but don't feel you must write your code to catch these exceptions. Often, the appropriate response to a `SecurityException` is to allow it to propagate uncaught so that it terminates the application.

Sometimes, as an application programmer, you want to write an application (such as an applet viewer) that can load untrusted classes and run them subject to access control checks. To do this in Java 1.2 and later, you must first install a security manager:

```
System.setSecurityManager(new SecurityManager());
```

You then use `java.net.URLClassLoader` to load the untrusted classes. `URLClassLoader` assigns a default set of safe permissions to the classes it loads, but in some cases you may want to modify the permissions granted to the loaded code through the `Policy` and `PermissionCollection` classes.

Security for System Administrators

In Java 1.2 and later, system administrators are responsible for defining the default security policy for the computers at their site. The default policy is stored in the file *lib/security/java.policy* in the Java installation. A system administrator can edit this text file by hand or use the *policytool* program from Sun to edit the file graphically. *policytool* is the preferred way to define policies, so the syntax of the underlying policy file is not documented in this book.

The default *java.policy* file defines a policy that is much like the policy of Java 1.0 and Java 1.1: system classes and installed extensions are fully trusted, while all other code is untrusted and only allowed a few simple permissions. While this default policy is adequate for many purposes, it may not be appropriate for all sites. For example, at some organizations, it may be appropriate to grant extra permissions to code downloaded from a secure intranet.

In order to define effective security policies, a system administrator must understand the various `Permission` subclasses of the Java platform, the target and action names they support, and the security implications of granting any particular permission. These topics are explained well in a document titled "Permissions in the Java 2 Standard Edition Development Kit (JDK)," which is available online at *http://java.sun.com/j2se/1.5.0/docs/guide/security/permissions.html*.

Security for End Users

Most end users do not have to think about security at all: their Java programs should simply run in a secure way with no intervention from them. Some sophisticated end users may want to define their own security policies, however. An end user can do this by running *policytool* himself to define personal policy files that augment the system policy. The default personal policy is stored in a file named *.java.policy* in the user's home directory. By default, Java loads this policy file and uses it to augment the system policy file.

In Java 1.2 and later, a user can specify an additional policy file to use when starting up the Java interpreter. To do so, you use the -D option to define the java.security.policy property. For example:

```
C:\> java -Djava.security.policy=policyfile UntrustedApp
```

This line runs the class UntrustedApp after augmenting the default system and user policies with the policy specified in the file or URL *policyfile*. To replace the system and user policies instead of augmenting them, use a double equals sign in the property specification:

```
C:\> java -Djava.security.policy==policyfile UntrustedApp
```

Note, however, that specifying a policy file is useful only if there is a SecurityManager installed. If a user doesn't trust an application, he presumably doesn't trust that application to voluntarily install its own security manager. In this case, he can define the java.security.manager system property:

```
C:\> java -Djava.security.manager -Djava.security.policy=policyfile \
UntrustedApp
```

The value of this property does not matter; simply defining it is enough to tell the Java interpreter to automatically install a default SecurityManager object that subjects an application to the access control policies described in the system, user, and java.security.policy policy files.

Permission Classes

Table 6-1 lists some important Permission subclasses defined by the core Java platform and summarizes the permissions they represent. See the reference section for more information on the individual classes. See *http://java.sun.com/j2se/1.5.0/docs/guide/security/permissions.html* for a complete list and detailed description of these permissions classes, along with their target and action names and a list of methods and the permissions they require (this document is part of the standard documentation bundle that can be downloaded along with the JDK).

Table 6-1. Java permission classes

Permission class	Description
java.security.AllPermission	An instance of this special permission class implies all other permissions.
javax.sound.sampled.AudioPermission	Controls the ability to play and record sound.
javax.security.auth.AuthPermission	Controls access to authentication methods in javax.security.auth and its subpackages.
java.awt.AWTPermission	Controls access to sensitive methods in java.awt and its subpackages.
java.io.FilePermission	Governs access to the filesystem.
java.util.logging.LoggingPermission	Controls the ability of a program to modify the logging configuration.
java.net.NetPermission	Governs access to networking-related resources such as stream handlers and HTTP authentication. See also java.net.SocketPermission.

Table 6-1. Java permission classes (continued)

Permission class	Description
`java.util.PropertyPermission`	Governs access to system properties.
`java.lang.reflect.ReflectPermission`	Governs access through the `java.lang.reflect` package to classes and class members that would normally be inaccessible.
`java.lang.RuntimePermission`	Governs access to a number of methods and resources. Many of the controlled methods are defined by `java.lang.System` and `java.lang.Runtime`.
`java.security.SecurityPermission`	Governs access to various security-related methods.
`java.io.SerializablePermission`	Governs access to serialization-related methods.
`java.net.SocketPermission`	Governs access to the network.
`java.sql.SQLPermission`	Governs the ability to specify logging streams in the `java.sql` JDBC API.

7

Programming and Documentation Conventions

This chapter explains a number of important and useful Java programming and documentation conventions. It covers:

- General naming and capitalization conventions
- Portability tips and conventions
- Javadoc documentation comment syntax and conventions
- JavaBeans conventions

None of the conventions described here are mandatory. Following them, however, will make your code easier to read and maintain, portable, and self-documenting.

Naming and Capitalization Conventions

The following widely adopted naming conventions apply to packages, reference types, methods, fields, and constants in Java. Because these conventions are almost universally followed and because they affect the public API of the classes you define, they should be followed carefully:

Packages
: Ensure that your publicly visible package names are unique by prefixing them with the inverted name of your Internet domain (e.g., `com.davidflanagan.utils`). All package names should be lowercase. Packages of code used internally by applications distributed in self-contained JAR files are not publicly visible and need not follow this convention. It is common in this case to use the application name as the package name or as a package prefix.

Reference types
: A type name should begin with a capital letter and be written in mixed case (e.g., `String`). If a class name consists of more than one word, each word should begin with a capital letter (e.g., `StringBuffer`). If a type name, or one

of the words of a type name, is an acronym, the acronym can be written in all capital letters (e.g., `URL`, `HTMLParser`).

Since classes and enumerated types are designed to represent objects, you should choose class names that are nouns (e.g., `Thread`, `Teapot`, `FormatConverter`).

When an interface is used to provide additional information about the classes that implement it, it is common to choose an interface name that is an adjective (e.g., `Runnable`, `Cloneable`, `Serializable`). Annotation types are also commonly named in this way. When an interface works more like an abstract superclass, use a name that is a noun (e.g., `Document`, `FileNameMap`, `Collection`).

Methods

A method name always begins with a lowercase letter. If the name contains more than one word, every word after the first begins with a capital letter (e.g., `insert()`, `insertObject()`, `insertObjectAt()`). Method names are typically chosen so that the first word is a verb. Method names can be as long as is necessary to make their purpose clear, but choose succinct names where possible.

Fields and constants

Nonconstant field names follow the same capitalization conventions as method names. If a field is a `static final` constant, it should be written in uppercase. If the name of a constant includes more than one word, the words should be separated with underscores (e.g., `MAX_VALUE`). A field name should be chosen to best describe the purpose of the field or the value it holds.

The constants defined by `enum` types are also typically written in all capital letters. Because other programming languages use lowercase or mixed case for enumerated values, however, this convention is not as strong as the convention for capital letters in the `static final` fields of classes and interfaces.

Parameters

Method parameters follow the same capitalization conventions as nonconstant fields. The names of method parameters appear in the documentation for a method, so you should choose names that make the purpose of the parameters as clear as possible. Try to keep parameter names to a single word and use them consistently. For example, if a `WidgetProcessor` class defines many methods that accept a `Widget` object as the first parameter, name this parameter `widget` or even `w` in each method.

Local variables

Local variable names are an implementation detail and never visible outside your class. Nevertheless, choosing good names makes your code easier to read, understand, and maintain. Variables are typically named following the same conventions as methods and fields.

In addition to the conventions for specific types of names, there are conventions regarding the characters you should use in your names. Java allows the $ character in any identifier, but, by convention, its use is reserved for synthetic names generated by source-code processors. (It is used by the Java compiler, for example, to make inner classes work.) Also, Java allows names to use any alphanumeric characters from the entire Unicode character set. While this can be convenient for non-English-speaking programmers, the use of Unicode characters should typically be restricted to local variables, private methods and fields, and other names that are not part of the public API of a class.

Portability Conventions and Pure Java Rules

Sun's motto, or core value proposition, for Java is "Write once, run anywhere." Java makes it easy to write portable programs, but Java programs do not automatically run successfully on any Java platform. The following tips help to avoid portability problems. Portability rules like those listed here were the focus of Sun's now-defunct "100% Pure Java" certification program and branding campaign.

Native methods
: Portable Java code can use any methods in the core Java APIs, including methods implemented as `native` methods. However, portable code must not define its own native methods. By their very nature, native methods must be ported to each new platform, so they directly subvert the "Write once, run anywhere" promise of Java.

The `Runtime.exec()` *method*
: Calling the `Runtime.exec()` method to spawn a process and execute an external command on the native system is rarely allowed in portable code. This is because the native OS command to be executed is never guaranteed to exist or behave the same way on all platforms. The only time it is legal to use `Runtime.exec()` is when the user is allowed to specify the command to run, either by typing the command at runtime or by specifying the command in a configuration file or preferences dialog box.

The `System.getenv()` *method*
: Using `System.getenv()` is nonportable. The method was deprecated but has been reintroduced in Java 5.0.

Undocumented classes
: Portable Java code must use only classes and interfaces that are a documented part of the Java platform. Most Java implementations ship with additional undocumented public classes that are part of the implementation but not part of the Java platform specification. Nothing prevents a program from using and relying on these undocumented classes, but doing so is not portable because the classes are not guaranteed to exist in all Java implementations or on all platforms.

The `java.awt.peer` *package*
: The interfaces in the `java.awt.peer` package are part of the Java platform but are documented for use by AWT implementors only. Applications that use these interfaces directly are not portable.

Implementation-specific features
: Portable code must not rely on features specific to a single implementation. For example, Microsoft distributed a version of the Java runtime system that

included a number of additional methods that were not part of the Java platform as defined by Sun. Any program that depends on such extensions is obviously not portable to other platforms. Microsoft's proprietary extension of the Java platform resulted in legal action between Sun and Microsoft and ultimately caused Microsoft to discontinue ongoing support for Java.

Implementation-specific bugs
: Just as portable code must not depend on implementation-specific features, it must not depend on implementation-specific bugs. If a class or method behaves differently than the specification says it should, a portable program cannot rely on this behavior, which may be different on different platforms, and ultimately may be fixed.

Implementation-specific behavior
: Sometimes different platforms and different implementations present different behaviors, all of which are legal according to the Java specification. Portable code must not depend on any one specific behavior. For example, the Java specification does not indicate whether threads of equal priority share the CPU or if one long-running thread can starve another thread at the same priority. If an application assumes one behavior or the other, it may not run properly on all platforms.

Standard extensions
: Portable code can rely on standard extensions to the Java platform, but, if it does so, it should clearly specify which extensions it uses and exit cleanly with an appropriate error message when run on a system that does not have the extensions installed.

Complete programs
: Any portable Java program must be complete and self-contained: it must supply all the classes it uses, except core platform and standard extension classes.

Defining system classes
: Portable Java code never defines classes in any of the system or standard extension packages. Doing so violates the protection boundaries of those packages and exposes package-visible implementation details.

Hardcoded filenames
: A portable program contains no hardcoded file or directory names. This is because different platforms have significantly different filesystem organizations and use different directory separator characters. If you need to work with a file or directory, have the user specify the filename, or at least the base directory beneath which the file can be found. This specification can be done at runtime, in a configuration file, or as a command-line argument to the program. When concatenating a file or directory name to a directory name, use the `File()` constructor or the `File.separator` constant.

Line separators
: Different systems use different characters or sequences of characters as line separators. Do not hardcode `\n`, `\r`, or `\r\n` as the line separator in your program. Instead, use the `println()` method of `PrintStream` or `PrintWriter`, which automatically terminates a line with the line separator appropriate for

the platform, or use the value of the `line.separator` system property. In Java 5.0 and later, you can also use the "%n" format string to `printf()` and `format()` methods of `java.util.Formatter` and related classes.

Java Documentation Comments

Most ordinary comments within Java code explain the implementation details of that code. By contrast, the Java language specification defines a special type of comment known as a *doc comment* that serves to document the API of your code. A doc comment is an ordinary multiline comment that begins with `/**` (instead of the usual `/*`) and ends with `*/`. A doc comment appears immediately before a type or member definition and contains documentation for that type or member. The documentation can include simple HTML formatting tags and other special keywords that provide additional information. Doc comments are ignored by the compiler, but they can be extracted and automatically turned into online HTML documentation by the *javadoc* program. (See Chapter 8 for more information about *javadoc*.) Here is an example class that contains appropriate doc comments:

```
/**
 * This immutable class represents <i>complex numbers</i>.
 *
 * @author David Flanagan
 * @version 1.0
 */
public class Complex {
    /**
     * Holds the real part of this complex number.
     * @see #y
     */
    protected double x;

    /**
     * Holds the imaginary part of this complex number.
     * @see #x
     */
    protected double y;

    /**
     * Creates a new Complex object that represents the complex number x+yi.
     * @param x The real part of the complex number.
     * @param y The imaginary part of the complex number.
     */
    public Complex(double x, double y) {
        this.x = x;
        this.y = y;
    }

    /**
     * Adds two Complex objects and produces a third object that represents
     * their sum.
     * @param c1 A Complex object
     * @param c2 Another Complex object
```

```
         * @return  A new Complex object that represents the sum of
         *          <code>c1</code> and <code>c2</code>.
         * @exception java.lang.NullPointerException
         *              If either argument is <code>null</code>.
         */
        public static Complex add(Complex c1, Complex c2) {
            return new Complex(c1.x + c2.x, c1.y + c2.y);
        }
    }
```

Structure of a Doc Comment

The body of a doc comment should begin with a one-sentence summary of the type or member being documented. This sentence may be displayed by itself as summary documentation, so it should be written to stand on its own. The initial sentence may be followed by any number of other sentences and paragraphs that describe the class, interface, method, or field in full detail.

After the descriptive paragraphs, a doc comment can contain any number of other paragraphs, each of which begins with a special doc-comment tag, such as `@author`, `@param`, or `@returns`. These tagged paragraphs provide specific information about the class, interface, method, or field that the *javadoc* program displays in a standard way. The full set of doc-comment tags is listed in the next section.

The descriptive material in a doc comment can contain simple HTML markup tags, such as such as `<i>` for emphasis, `<code>` for class, method, and field names, and `<pre>` for multiline code examples. It can also contain `<p>` tags to break the description into separate paragraphs and `<ul>`, `<li>`, and related tags to display bulleted lists and similar structures. Remember, however, that the material you write is embedded within a larger, more complex HTML document. For this reason, doc comments should not contain major structural HTML tags, such as `<h2>` or `<hr>`, that might interfere with the structure of the larger document.

Avoid the use of the `<a>` tag to include hyperlinks or cross-references in your doc comments. Instead, use the special `{@link}` doc-comment tag, which, unlike the other doc-comment tags, can appear anywhere within a doc comment. As described in the next section, the `{@link}` tag allows you to specify hyperlinks to other classes, interfaces, methods, and fields without knowing the HTML-structuring conventions and filenames used by *javadoc*.

If you want to include an image in a doc comment, place the image file in a *doc-files* subdirectory of the source code directory. Give the image the same name as the class, with an integer suffix. For example, the second image that appears in the doc comment for a class named `Circle` can be included with this HTML tag:

```
<img src="doc-files/Circle-2.gif">
```

Because the lines of a doc comment are embedded within a Java comment, any leading spaces and asterisks (*) are stripped from each line of the comment before processing. Thus, you don't need to worry about the asterisks appearing in the generated documentation or about the indentation of the comment affecting the indentation of code examples included within the comment with a `<pre>` tag.

Doc-Comment Tags

javadoc recognizes a number of special tags, each of which begins with an `@` character. These doc-comment tags allow you to encode specific information into your comments in a standardized way, and they allow *javadoc* to choose the appropriate output format for that information. For example, the `@param` tag lets you specify the name and meaning of a single parameter for a method. *javadoc* can extract this information and display it using an HTML `<dl>` list, an HTML `<table>`, or however it sees fit.

The following doc-comment tags are recognized by *javadoc*; a doc comment should typically use these tags in the order listed here:

`@author` *name*

Adds an "Author:" entry that contains the specified name. This tag should be used for every class or interface definition but must not be used for individual methods and fields. If a class has multiple authors, use multiple `@author` tags on adjacent lines. For example:

```
@author David Flanagan
@author Paula Ferguson
```

List the authors in chronological order, with the original author first. If the author is unknown, you can use "unascribed." *javadoc* does not output authorship information unless the `-author` command-line argument is specified.

`@version` *text*

Inserts a "Version:" entry that contains the specified text. For example:

```
@version 1.32, 08/26/04
```

This tag should be included in every class and interface doc comment but cannot be used for individual methods and fields. This tag is often used in conjunction with the automated version-numbering capabilities of a version control system, such as SCCS, RCS, or CVS. *javadoc* does not output version information in its generated documentation unless the `-version` command-line argument is specified.

`@param` *parameter-name description*

Adds the specified parameter and its description to the "Parameters:" section of the current method. The doc comment for a method or constructor must contain one `@param` tag for each parameter the method expects. These tags should appear in the same order as the parameters specified by the method. The tag can be used only in doc comments for methods and constructors. You are encouraged to use phrases and sentence fragments where possible to keep the descriptions brief. However, if a parameter requires detailed documentation, the description can wrap onto multiple lines and include as much text as necessary. For readability in source-code form, consider using spaces to align the descriptions with each other. For example:

```
@param o      the object to insert
@param index  the position to insert it at
```

`@return` *`description`*

Inserts a "Returns:" section that contains the specified description. This tag should appear in every doc comment for a method, unless the method returns `void` or is a constructor. The description can be as long as necessary, but consider using a sentence fragment to keep it short. For example:

```
@return <code>true</code> if the insertion is successful, or
        <code>false</code> if the list already contains the specified object.
```

`@exception` *`full-classname description`*

Adds a "Throws:" entry that contains the specified exception name and description. A doc comment for a method or constructor should contain an `@exception` tag for every checked exception that appears in its `throws` clause. For example:

```
@exception java.io.FileNotFoundException
           If the specified file could not be found
```

The `@exception` tag can optionally be used to document unchecked exceptions (i.e., subclasses of `RuntimeException`) the method may throw, when these are exceptions that a user of the method may reasonably want to catch. If a method can throw more than one exception, use multiple `@exception` tags on adjacent lines and list the exceptions in alphabetical order. The description can be as short or as long as necessary to describe the significance of the exception. This tag can be used only for method and constructor comments. The `@throws` tag is a synonym for `@exception`.

`@throws` *`full-classname description`*

This tag is a synonym for `@exception`.

`@see` *`reference`*

Adds a "See Also:" entry that contains the specified reference. This tag can appear in any kind of doc comment. The syntax for the *`reference`* is explained in "Cross-References in Doc Comments" later in this chapter.

`@deprecated` *`explanation`*

This tag specifies that the following type or member has been deprecated and that its use should be avoided. *javadoc* adds a prominent "Deprecated" entry to the documentation and includes the specified *`explanation`* text. This text should specify when the class or member was deprecated and, if possible, suggest a replacement class or member and include a link to it. For example:

```
@deprecated As of Version 3.0, this method is replaced
            by {@link #setColor}.
```

Although the Java compiler ignores all comments, it does take note of the `@deprecated` tag in doc comments. When this tag appears, the compiler notes the deprecation in the class file it produces. This allows it to issue warnings for other classes that rely on the deprecated feature.

`@since` *`version`*

Specifies when the type or member was added to the API. This tag should be followed by a version number or other version specification. For example:

```
@since JNUT 3.0
```

Every doc comment for a type should include an `@since` tag, and any members added after the initial release of the type should have `@since` tags in their doc comments.

`@serial` *description*
: Technically, the way a class is serialized is part of its public API. If you write a class that you expect to be serialized, you should document its serialization format using `@serial` and the related tags listed below. `@serial` should appear in the doc comment for any field that is part of the serialized state of a `Serializable` class. For classes that use the default serialization mechanism, this means all fields that are not declared `transient`, including fields declared `private`. The *description* should be a brief description of the field and of its purpose within a serialized object.

  As of Java 1.4, you can also use the `@serial` tag at the class and package level to specify whether a "serialized form page" should be generated for the class or package. The syntax is:

```
@serial include
@serial exclude
```

`@serialField` *name type description*
: A `Serializable` class can define its serialized format by declaring an array of `ObjectStreamField` objects in a field named `serialPersistentFields`. For such a class, the doc comment for `serialPersistentFields` should include an `@serialField` tag for each element of the array. Each tag specifies the name, type, and description for a particular field in the serialized state of the class.

`@serialData` *description*
: A `Serializable` class can define a `writeObject()` method to write data other than that written by the default serialization mechanism. An `Externalizable` class defines a `writeExternal()` method responsible for writing the complete state of an object to the serialization stream. The `@serialData` tag should be used in the doc comments for these `writeObject()` and `writeExternal()` methods, and the *description* should document the serialization format used by the method.

Inline Doc Comment Tags

In addition to the preceding tags, *javadoc* also supports several *inline tags* that may appear anywhere that HTML text appears in a doc comment. Because these tags appear directly within the flow of HTML text, they require the use of curly braces as delimiters to separate the tagged text from the HTML text. Supported inline tags include the following:

`{@link` *reference*`}`
: In Java 1.2 and later, the `{@link}` tag is like the `@see` tag except that instead of placing a link to the specified *reference* in a special "See Also:" section, it inserts the link inline. An `{@link}` tag can appear anywhere that HTML text appears in a doc comment. In other words, it can appear in the initial description of the class, interface, method, or field and in the descriptions associated with the `@param`, `@returns`, `@exception`, and `@deprecated` tags. The *reference*

for the {@link} tag uses the syntax described next in "Cross-References in Doc Comments." For example:

```
@param regexp The regular expression to search for. This string
              argument must follow the syntax rules described for
              {@link java.util.regex.Pattern}.
```

{@linkplain *reference*}
: In Java 1.4 and later, the {@linkplain} tag is just like the {@link} tag, except that the text of the link is formatted using the normal font rather than the code font used by the {@link} tag. This is most useful when *reference* contains both a *feature* to link to and a *label* that specifies alternate text to be displayed in the link. See "Cross-References in Doc Comments" for a discussion of the *feature* and *label* portions of the *reference* argument.

{@inheritDoc}
: When a method overrides a method in a superclass or implements a method in an interface, you can omit a doc comment, and *javadoc* automatically inherits the documentation from the overridden or implemented method. As of Java 1.4, however, the {@inheritDoc} tag allows you to inherit the text of individual tags. This tag also allows you to inherit and augment the descriptive text of the comment. To inherit individual tags, use it like this:

```
@param index @{inheritDoc}
@return @{inheritDoc}
```

To inherit the entire doc comment, including your own text before and after it, use the tag like this:

```
This method overrides {@link java.langObject#toString}, documented as follows:
<P>{@inheritDoc}
<P>This overridden version of the method returns a string of the form...
```

{@docRoot}
: This inline tag takes no parameters and is replaced with a reference to the root directory of the generated documentation. It is useful in hyperlinks that refer to an external file, such as an image or a copyright statement:

```
<img src="{@docroot}/images/logo.gif">
This is <a href="{@docRoot}/legal.html">Copyrighted</a> material.
```

{@docRoot} was introduced in Java 1.3.

{@literal *text*}
: This inline tag displays *text* literally, escaping any HTML in it and ignoring any javadoc tags it may contain. It does not retain whitespace formatting but is useful when used within a <pre> tag. {@literal} is available in Java 5.0 and later.

{@code *text*}
: This tag is like the {@literal} tag, but displays the literal *text* in code font. Equivalent to:

```
<code>{@literal text}</code>
```

{@code} is available in Java 5.0 and later.

`{@value}`
: The `{@value}` tag, with no arguments, is used inline in doc comments for `static final` fields and is replaced with the constant value of that field. This tag was introduced in Java 1.4 and is used only for constant fields.

`{@value` *`reference`*`}`
: This variant of the `{@value}` tag includes a *`reference`* to a `static final` field and is replaced with the constant value of that field. Although the no-argument version of the `{@value}` tag was introduced in Java 1.4, this version is available only in Java 5.0 and later. See "Cross-References in Doc Comments" for the syntax of the reference.

Cross-References in Doc Comments

The `@see` tag and the inline tags `{@link}`, `{@linkplain}` and `{@value}` all encode a cross-reference to some other source of documentation, typically to the documentation comment for some other type or member.

`reference` can take three different forms. If it begins with a quote character, it is taken to be the name of a book or some other printed resource and is displayed as is. If *`reference`* begins with a < character, it is taken to be an arbitrary HTML hyperlink that uses the `<a>` tag and the hyperlink is inserted into the output documentation as is. This form of the `@see` tag can insert links to other online documents, such as a programmer's guide or user's manual.

If *`reference`* is not a quoted string or a hyperlink, it is expected to have the following form:

```
feature label
```

In this case, *javadoc* outputs the text specified by *`label`* and encodes it as a hyperlink to the specified *`feature`*. If *`label`* is omitted (as it usually is), *javadoc* uses the name of the specified *`feature`* instead.

`feature` can refer to a package, type, or type member, using one of the following forms:

`pkgname`
: A reference to the named package. For example:

```
@see java.lang.reflect
```

`pkgname.typename`
: A reference to a class, interface, enumerated type, or annotation type specified with its full package name. For example:

```
@see java.util.List
```

`typename`
: A reference to a type specified without its package name. For example:

```
@see List
```

javadoc resolves this reference by searching the current package and the list of imported classes for a class with this name.

typename#methodname
A reference to a named method or constructor within the specified type. For example:

```
@see java.io.InputStream#reset
@see InputStream#close
```

If the type is specified without its package name, it is resolved as described for *typename*. This syntax is ambiguous if the method is overloaded or the class defines a field by the same name.

typename#methodname(paramtypes)
A reference to a method or constructor with the type of its parameters explicitly specified. This is useful when cross-referencing an overloaded method. For example:

```
@see InputStream#read(byte[], int, int)
```

#methodname
A reference to a nonoverloaded method or constructor in the current class or interface or one of the containing classes, superclasses, or superinterfaces of the current class or interface. Use this concise form to refer to other methods in the same class. For example:

```
@see #setBackgroundColor
```

#methodname(paramtypes)
A reference to a method or constructor in the current class or interface or one of its superclasses or containing classes. This form works with overloaded methods because it lists the types of the method parameters explicitly. For example:

```
@see #setPosition(int, int)
```

typename#fieldname
A reference to a named field within the specified class. For example:

```
@see java.io.BufferedInputStream#buf
```

If the type is specified without its package name, it is resolved as described for *typename*.

#fieldname
A reference to a field in the current type or one of the containing classes, superclasses, or superinterfaces of the current type. For example:

```
@see #x
```


Doc Comments for Packages

Documentation comments for classes, interfaces, methods, constructors, and fields appear in Java source code immediately before the definitions of the features they document. *javadoc* can also read and display summary documentation for packages. Since a package is defined in a directory, not in a single file of source code, *javadoc* looks for the package documentation in a file named *package.html* in the directory that contains the source code for the classes of the package.

The *package.html* file should contain simple HTML documentation for the package. It can also contain `@see`, `@link`, `@deprecated`, and `@since` tags. Since *package.html* is not a file of Java source code, the documentation it contains should be HTML and should *not* be a Java comment (i.e., it should not be enclosed within `/**` and `*/` characters). Finally, any `@see` and `@link` tags that appear in *package.html* must use fully qualified class names.

In addition to defining a *package.html* file for each package, you can also provide high-level documentation for a group of packages by defining an *overview.html* file in the source tree for those packages. When *javadoc* is run over that source tree, it uses *overview.html* as the highest level overview it displays.

JavaBeans Conventions

JavaBeans is a framework for defining reusable modular software components. The JavaBeans specification includes the following definition of a bean: "a reusable software component that can be manipulated visually in a builder tool." As you can see, this is a rather loose definition; beans can take a variety of forms. The most common use of beans is for graphical user interface components, such as components of the `java.awt` and `javax.swing` packages, which are documented in *Java Foundation Classes in a Nutshell* and *Java Swing*, both from O'Reilly. Although all beans can be manipulated visually, this does not mean every bean has its own visual representation. For example, the `javax.sql.RowSet` class (documented in O'Reilly's *Java Enterprise in a Nutshell*) is a JavaBeans component that represents the data resulting from a database query. There are no limits on the simplicity or complexity of a JavaBeans component. The simplest beans are typically basic graphical interface components, such as a `java.awt.Button` object. But even complex systems, such as an embeddable spreadsheet application, can function as individual beans.

The JavaBeans component model consists of the `java.beans`, the `java.beans.beancontext` packages, and a number of important naming and API conventions to which conforming beans and bean-manipulation tools must adhere. These conventions are not part of the JavaBeans API itself but are in many ways more important to bean developers than the API itself. The conventions are sometimes referred to as *design patterns*; they specify such things as method names and signatures for property accessor methods defined by a bean. If the class you are writing is not intended to be a bean, suitable for visual manipulation in a builder tool, you don't need to follow these conventions. The JavaBeans conventions are widely used and well-understood, however, and you can improve the usability and reusabilty of your code by following the relevant ones. This is particularly true of the property accessor method naming conventions.

We cover the conventions themselves later in this section. First, however, an overview of the JavaBeans model is in order.

Bean Basics

Any object that conforms to certain basic rules can be a bean; there is no `Bean` class that all beans are required to subclass. Many beans are GUI components, but it is also quite possible, and often useful, to write "invisible" beans that do not have an onscreen appearance. (A bean having no onscreen appearance in a finished application does not mean it cannot be visually manipulated by a beanbox tool, however.)

A bean is characterized by the properties, events, and methods it exports. It is these properties, events, and methods that an application designer manipulates in a beanbox tool. A *property* is a piece of the bean's internal state that can be programmatically set and/or queried, usually through a standard pair of get and set accessor methods.

A bean communicates with the application in which it is embedded as well as with other beans by generating *events*. The JavaBeans API uses the same event model that AWT and Swing components use. The model is based on the `java.util.EventObject` class and the `java.util.EventListener` interface; it is described in detail in *Java Foundation Classes in a Nutshell* (O'Reilly). In brief, the event model works like this:

- A bean defines an event if it provides `add` and `remove` methods for registering and deregistering listener objects for that event.
- An application that wants to be notified when an event of that type occurs uses these methods to register an event listener object of the appropriate type.
- When the event occurs, the bean notifies all registered listeners by passing an event object that describes the event to a method defined by the event listener interface.

A *unicast event* is a rare kind of event for which there can be only a single registered listener object. The `add` registration method for a unicast event throws a `TooManyListenersException` if an attempt is made to register more than a single listener.

The *methods* exported by a bean are simply any public methods defined by the bean, excluding those methods that get and set property values and register and remove event listeners.

In addition to the regular sort of properties described earlier, the JavaBeans API also supports several specialized property subtypes. An *indexed property* is a property that has an array value, as well as getter and setter methods that access both individual elements of the array and the entire array. A *bound property* is one that sends a `PropertyChangeEvent` to any interested `PropertyChangeListener` objects whenever the value of the property changes. A *constrained property* is one that can have any changes vetoed by any interested listener. When the value of a constrained property of a bean changes, the bean must send out a `PropertyChangeEvent` to the list of interested `VetoableChangeListener` objects. If any of these objects throws a `PropertyVetoException`, the property value is not changed, and the `PropertyVetoException` is propagated back to the property setter method.

Bean Classes

A bean class itself must adhere to the following conventions:

Class name
: There are no restrictions on the class name of a bean.

Superclass
: A bean can extend any other class. Beans are often AWT or Swing components, but there are no restrictions.

Instantiation

A bean should provide a no-parameter constructor so bean manipulation tools can easily instantiate the bean.

Properties

A bean defines a property *p* of type *T* if it has accessor methods that follow these patterns (if *T* is `boolean`, a special form of getter method is allowed):

Getter

`public T getP()`

Boolean getter

`public boolean isP()`

Setter

`public void setP(T)`

Exceptions

Property accessor methods can throw any type of checked or unchecked exceptions.

Indexed Properties

An indexed property is a property of array type that provides accessor methods that get and set the entire array as well as methods that get and set individual elements of the array. A bean defines an indexed property *p* of type `T[]` if it defines the following accessor methods:

Array getter

`public T[] getP()`

Element getter

`public T getP(int)`

Array setter

`public void setP(T[])`

Element setter

`public void setP(int,T)`

Exceptions

Indexed property accessor methods can throw any type of checked or unchecked exceptions. They should throw an `ArrayIndexOutOfBoundsException` if the supplied index is out of bounds.

Bound Properties

A bound property is one that generates a `PropertyChangeEvent` when its value changes. Here are the conventions for a bound property:

Accessor methods

The getter and setter methods for a bound property follow the same conventions as a regular property.

Listener registration

A bean that defines one or more bound properties must define a pair of methods for the registration of listeners that are notified when any bound property value changes. The methods must have these signatures:

```
public void addPropertyChangeListener(PropertyChangeListener)
public void removePropertyChangeListener(PropertyChangeListener)
```

Named property listener registration

A bean can optionally provide additional methods that allow event listeners to be registered for changes to a single bound property value. These methods are passed the name of a property and have the following signatures:

```
public void addPropertyChangeListener(String, PropertyChangeListener)
public void removePropertyChangeListener(String, PropertyChangeListener)
```

Per-property listener registration

A bean can optionally provide additional event listener registration methods that are specific to a single property. For a property *p*, these methods have the following signatures:

```
public void addPListener(PropertyChangeListener)
public void removePListener(PropertyChangeListener)
```

Methods of this type allow a beanbox to distinguish a bound property from an unbound property.

Notification

When the value of a bound property changes, the bean should update its internal state to reflect the change and then pass a `PropertyChangeEvent` to the `propertyChange()` method of every `PropertyChangeListener` object registered for the bean or the specific bound property.

Support

`java.beans.PropertyChangeSupport` is a helpful class for implementing bound properties.

Constrained Properties

A constrained property is one for which any changes can be vetoed by registered listeners. Most constrained properties are also bound properties. Here are the conventions for a constrained property:

Getter

The getter method for a constrained property is the same as the getter method for a regular property.

Setter

The setter method of a constrained property throws a `PropertyVetoException` if the property change is vetoed. For a property *p* of type *T*, the signature looks like this:

```
public void setP(T) throws PropertyVetoException
```

Listener registration

A bean that defines one or more constrained properties must define a pair of methods for the registration of listeners that are notified when any constrained property value changes. The methods must have these signatures:

```
public void addVetoableChangeListener(VetoableChangeListener)
public void removeVetoableChangeListener(VetoableChangeListener)
```

Named property listener registration
A bean can optionally provide additional methods that allow event listeners to be registered for changes to a single constrained property value. These methods are passed the name of a property and have the following signatures:

```
public void addVetoableChangeListener(String, VetoableChangeListener)
public void removeVetoableChangeListener(String, VetoableChangeListener)
```

Per-property listener registration
A bean can optionally provide additional listener registration methods that are specific to a single constrained property. For a property *p*, these methods have the following signatures:

```
public void addPListener(VetoableChangeListener)
public void removePListener(VetoableChangeListener)
```

Notification
When the setter method of a constrained property is invoked, the bean must generate a `PropertyChangeEvent` that describes the requested change and pass that event to the `vetoableChange()` method of every `VetoableChangeListener` object registered for the bean or the specific constrained property. If any listener vetoes the change by throwing a `PropertyVetoException`, the bean must send out another `PropertyChangeEvent` to revert the property to its original value. It should then throw a `PropertyVetoException` itself. If, on the other hand, the property change is not vetoed, the bean should update its internal state to reflect the change. If the constrained property is also a bound property, the bean should notify `PropertyChangeListener` objects at this point.

Support
`java.beans.VetoableChangeSupport` is a helpful class for implementing constrained properties.

Events

In addition to `PropertyChangeEvent` events generated when bound and constrained properties are changed, a bean can generate other types of events. An event named *E* should follow these conventions:

Event class
The event class should directly or indirectly extend `java.util.EventObject` and should be named *E*`Event`.

Listener interface
The event must be associated with an event listener interface that extends `java.util.EventListener` and is named *E*`Listener`.

Listener methods
The event listener interface can define any number of methods that take a single argument of type *E*`Event` and return `void`.

Listener registration

The bean must define a pair of methods for registering event listeners that want to be notified when an *E* event occurs. The methods should have the following signatures:

```
public void addEListener(EListener)
public void removeEListener(EListener)
```

Unicast events

A unicast event allows only one listener object to be registered at a single time. If *E* is a unicast event, the listener registration method should have this signature:

```
public void addEListener(EListener) throws TooManyListenersException
```

Java Conventions

8

Java Development Tools

Sun's implementation of Java includes a number of tools for Java developers. Chief among these are the Java interpreter and the Java compiler, of course, but there are a number of others as well. This chapter documents most tools shipped with the JDK. Notable omissions are the RMI and IDL tools that are specific to enterprise programming and which are documented in *Java Enterprise in a Nutshell* (O'Reilly).

The tools documented here are part of Sun's development kit; they are implementation details and not part of the Java specification itself. If you are using a Java development environment other than Sun's JDK, you should consult your vendor's tool documentation.

Some examples in this chapter use Unix conventions for file and path separators. If Windows is your development platform, change forward slashes in filenames to backward slashes, and colons in path specifications to semicolons.

apt

Annotation Processing Tool

Synopsis

```
apt [options] sourcefiles
```

Description

apt reads and parses the specified *`sourcefiles`*. Any annotations it finds are passed to appropriate annotation processor factory objects, which can use the annotations to produce auxiliary source or resource files based on annotation content. *apt* next compiles *`sourcefiles`* and generated files.

Annotation processor classes and factory classes are defined with the `com.sun.mirror.apt` API and other subpackages of `com.sun.mirror`.

Options

apt shares several options with *javac*. If a command-line argument begins with `@`, *apt* treats it as a file and reads options and source files from that specified file. See *javac* for more on this.

`-Aname=value`
: Passes the `name=value` pair as an argument to annotation processors.

`-cp path`

`-classpath path`
: Sets the classpath. See *javac*.

`-d dir`
: The directory under which to place class files. See *javac*.

`-factory classname`
: Explicitly specifies the class name of the annotation processor factory to use.

`-factorypath path`
: A path to search for annotation processor factories instead of searching the classpath.

`-help`
: Prints usage information and exits.

`-nocompile`
: Tells *apt* not to compile the `sourcefiles` or any generated files.

`-print`
: Simply parses the specified `sourcefiles` and prints a synopsis of the types they define. Does not process annotations or compile any files.

`-s dir`
: Specifies the root directory beneath which generated source files will be stored.

`-source version`
: Specifies what version of the language to accept. See *javac*.

`-version`
: Prints *apt* version information.

`-X`
: Displays information about nonstandard options.

See also *javac*, Chapter 4

---

extcheck

JAR Version Conflict Utility

Synopsis

```
extcheck [-verbose] jarfile
```

Description

extcheck checks to see if the extension contained in the specified `jarfile` (or a newer version of that extension) has already been installed on the system. It does this by reading the `Specification-Title` and `Specification-Version` manifest attributes from the specified `jarfile` and from all of the JAR files found in the system extensions directory.

Java Tools

extcheck is designed for use in automated installation scripts. Without the -verbose option, it does not print the results of its check. Instead, it sets its exit code to 0 if the specified extension does not conflict with any installed extensions and can be safely installed. It sets its exit code to a nonzero value if an extension with the same name is already installed and has a specification version number equal to or greater than the version of the specified file.

Options

`-verbose`
: Lists the installed extensions as they are checked and displays the results of the check.

See also

jar

---

jarsigner

JAR Signing and Verification Tool

Synopsis

```
jarsigner [options] jarfile signer
jarsigner -verify jarfile
```

Description

jarsigner adds a digital signature to the specified `jarfile`, or, if the -verify option is specified, it verifies the digital signature or signatures already attached to the JAR file. The specified `signer` is a case-insensitive nickname or alias for the entity whose signature is to be used. The specified `signer` name is used to look up the private key that generates the signature.

When you apply your digital signature to a JAR file, you are implicitly vouching for the contents of the archive. You are offering your personal word that the JAR file contains only nonmalicious code, files that do not violate copyright laws, and so forth. When you verify a digitally signed JAR file, you can determine who the signer or signers of the file are and (if the verification succeeds) that the contents of the JAR file have not been changed, corrupted, or tampered with since the signature or signatures were applied. Verifying a digital signature is entirely different from deciding whether or not you trust the person or organization whose signature you verified.

jarsigner and the related *keytool* program replace the *javakey* program of Java 1.1.

Options

jarsigner defines a number of options, many of which specify how a private key is to be found for the specified `signer`. Most of these options are unnecessary when using the -verify option to verify a signed JAR file:

`-certs`
: If this option is specified along with either the -verify or -verbose option, it causes *jarsigner* to display details of the public key certificates associated with the signed JAR file.

`-J`*`javaoption`*
: Passes the specified `javaoption` directly to the Java interpreter.

`-keypass` *`password`*
: Specifies the password that encrypts the private key of the specified *`signer`*. If this option is not specified, *jarsigner* prompts you for the password.

`-keystore` *`url`*
: A *keystore* is a file that contains keys and certificates. This option specifies the filename or URL of the keystore in which the private and public key certificates of the specified *`signer`* are looked up. The default is the file named *.keystore* in the user's home directory (the value of the system property `user.home`). This is also the default location of the keystore managed by *keytool*.

`-sigfile` *`basename`*
: Specifies the base names of the *.SF* and *.DSA* files added to the *META-INF/* directory of the JAR file. If you leave this option unspecified, the base filename is chosen based on the *`signer`* name.

`-signedjar` *`outputfile`*
: Specifies the name for the signed JAR file created by *jarsigner*. If this option is not specified, *jarsigner* overwrites the *`jarfile`* specified on the command line.

`-storepass` *`password`*
: Specifies the password that verifies the integrity of the keystore (but does not encrypt the private key). If this option is omitted, *jarsigner* prompts you for the password.

`-storetype` *`type`*
: Specifies the type of keystore specified by the `-keystore` option. The default is the system-default keystore type, which on most systems is the Java Keystore type, known as `JKS`. If you have the Java Cryptography Extension installed, you may want to use a `JCEKS` keystore instead.

`-verbose`
: Displays extra information about the signing or verification process.

`-verify`
: Specifies that *jarsigner* should verify the specified JAR file rather than sign it.

See also *jar*, *keytool*, *javakey*

---

jar

Java Archive Tool

Synopsis

```
jar c|t|u|x[f][m][M][0][v] [jar-file] [manifest] [-C directory] [input-files]
jar i [jar-file]
```

Description

jar is a tool that can create and manipulate Java Archive (JAR) files. A JAR file is a ZIP file that contains Java class files, auxiliary resource files required by those classes, and optional meta-information. This meta-information includes a manifest file that lists the contents of the JAR archive and provides auxiliary information about each file.

The *jar* command can create JAR files, list the contents of JAR files, and extract files from a JAR archive. In Java 1.2 and later, it can also add files to an existing archive or update the manifest file of an archive. In Java 1.3 and later, *jar* can also add an index entry to a JAR file.

The syntax of the *jar* command is reminiscent of the Unix *tar* (tape archive) command. Most options to *jar* are specified as a block of concatenated letters passed as a single argument rather than as individual command-line arguments. The first letter of the first argument specifies what action *jar* is to perform; it is required. Other letters are optional. The various file arguments depend on which letters are specified.

As in *javac*, any command-line argument that begins with @ is taken to be the name of a file that contains options or filenames.

Command options

The first letter of the first option to *jar* specifies the basic operation *jar* is to perform. The available options are:

`c`
: Creates a new JAR archive. A list of input files and/or directories must be specified as the final arguments to *jar*. The newly created JAR file has a *META-INF/MANIFEST.MF* file as its first entry. This automatically created manifest lists the contents of the JAR file and contains a message digest for each file.

`i`
: Indexes the contents of this JAR file as well as the contents of all JAR files it refers to in the `Class-Path` manifest attribute. The resulting index is stored in the JAR file as *META-INF/INDEX.LIST* and can be used by a Java interpreter or applet viewer to optimize its class and resource lookup algorithm and avoid downloading unnecessary JAR files. This `i` option must be followed by the name of the JAR file to be indexed. No other options are allowed. Java 1.3 and later.

`t`
: Lists the contents of a JAR archive.

`u`
: Updates the contents of a JAR archive. Any files listed on the command line are added to the archive. When used with the `m` option, this adds the specified manifest information to the JAR file. Java 1.2 and later.

`x`
: Extracts the contents of a JAR archive. The files and directories specified on the command line are extracted and created in the current working directory. If no file or directory names are specified, all the files and directories in the JAR file are extracted.

Modifier options

Each of the four command specifier letters can be followed by additional letters that provide further detail about the operation to be performed:

`f`
: Indicates that *jar* is to operate on a JAR file whose name is specified on the command line. If this option is not present, *jar* reads a JAR file from standard input and/or writes a JAR file to standard output. If the `f` option is present, the command line must contain the name of the JAR file to operate on.

`m`
: When *jar* creates or updates a JAR file, it automatically creates (or updates) a manifest file named *META-INF/MANIFEST.MF* in the JAR archive. This default manifest simply lists the contents of the JAR file. Many JAR files require additional information to be specified in the manifest; the `m` option tells the *jar* command that a manifest template is specified on the command line. *jar* reads this manifest file and stores all the information it contains into the *META-INF/MANIFEST.MF* file it creates. This `m` option should be used only with the `c` or `u` commands, not with the `t` or `x` commands.

`M`
: Used with the `c` and `u` commands to tell *jar* not to create a default manifest file.

`v`
: Tells *jar* to produce verbose output.

`0`
: Used with the `c` and `u` commands to tell *jar* to store files in the JAR archive without compressing them. Note that this option is the digit zero, not the letter O.

Files

The first option to *jar* consists of an initial command letter and various option letters. This first option is followed by a list of files:

jar-file
: If the first option contains the letter `f`, that option must be followed by the name of the JAR file to create or manipulate.

manifest-file
: If the first option contains the letter `m`, that option must be followed by the name of the file that contains manifest information. If the first option contains both the letters `f` and `m`, the JAR and manifest files should be listed in the same order the `f` and `m` options appear. *jar* automatically creates a manifest for the JAR file it creates unless the `M` option is specified. The *manifest-file* specified with the `m` option should contain additional manifest entries to be placed in the manifest in addition to the automatically generated entries.

files
: The list of one or more files and/or directories to be inserted into or extracted from the JAR archive.

Additional options

In addition to all the options listed previously, *jar* also supports the following:

`-C` *dir*
: Used within the list of files to process; it tells *jar* to change to the specified *dir* while processing the subsequent files and directories. The subsequent file and directory names are interpreted relative to *dir* and are inserted into the JAR archive without *dir* as a prefix. Any number of `-C` options can be used; each remains in effect until the next is encountered. The directory specified by a `-C` option is interpreted relative to the current working directory, not the directory specified by the previous `-C` option. Java 1.2 and later.

`-J`*javaopt*
: Passes the option *javaopt* to the Java interpreter.

Examples

The *jar* command has a confusing array of options, but, in most cases, its use is quite simple. To create a simple JAR file that contains all the class files in the current directory and all files in a subdirectory called *images*, you can type:

```
% jar cf my.jar *.class images
```

To verbosely list the contents of a JAR archive:

```
% jar tvf your.jar
```

To extract the manifest file from a JAR file for examination or editing:

```
% jar xf the.jar META-INF/MANIFEST.MF
```

To update the manifest of a JAR file:

```
% jar ufm my.jar manifest.template
```

See also *jarsigner*

java

Synopsis

```
java [ interpreter-options ] classname [ program-arguments ]
java [ interpreter-options ] -jar jarfile [ program-arguments ]
```

Description

java is the Java byte-code interpreter; it runs Java programs. The program to be run is the class specified by `classname`. This must be a fully qualified name: it must include the package name of the class but not the *.class* file extension. For example:

```
% java david.games.Checkers
% java Test
```

The specified class must define a `main()` method with exactly the following signature:

```
public static void main(String[] args)
```

This method serves as the program entry point: the interpreter begins execution here.

In Java 1.2 and later, a program can be packaged in an executable JAR file. To run a program packaged in this fashion, use the `-jar` option to specify the JAR file. The manifest of an executable JAR file must contain a `Main-Class` attribute that specifies which class within the JAR file contains the `main()` method at which the interpreter is to begin execution.

Any command-line options that precede the name of the class or JAR file to execute are options to the Java interpreter itself. Any options that follow the class name or JAR filename are options to the program; they are ignored by the Java interpreter and passed as an array of strings to the `main()` method of the program.

The Java interpreter runs until the `main()` method exits, and any threads (except for threads marked as daemon threads) created by the program have also exited.

Interpreter versions

The *java* program is the basic version of the Java interpreter. In addition to this program, however, there are several other versions of the Java interpreter. Each of these versions is similar to *java* but has a specialized function. This list includes all the interpreter versions, including those that are no longer in use.

java
: This is the basic version of the Java interpreter; it is usually the correct one to use.

javaw
: This version of the interpreter is included only on Windows platforms. Use *javaw* when you want to run a Java program (from a script, for example) without forcing a console window to appear.

Client or Server VM
: Sun's "HotSpot" virtual machine comes in two versions: one is tuned for use with short-lived client applications and one is for use with long-running server code. As of Java 1.4, you can select the server version of the VM with the `-server` option. You can specify the client VM (which is the default) with the `-client` option. In Java 5.0, the interpreter automatically enters server mode if it detects that it is running on "server-class" hardware (typically a computer with multiple CPUs).

Legacy interpreter versions

oldjava

This version of the interpreter was included in Java 1.2 and Java 1.3 for compatibility with the Java 1.1 interpreter. It loaded classes using the Java 1.1 class-loading scheme. Very few Java applications needed to use this version of the interpreter, and it was removed in Java 1.4.

oldjavaw

In Java 1.2 and 1.3, this version of the interpreter, included only on Windows platforms, combined the features of *oldjava* and *javaw*.

java_g

In Java 1.0 and Java 1.1, *java_g* was a debugging version of the Java interpreter. It included a few specialized command-line options. Windows platforms also had a *javaw_g* program. *java_g* is not included in Java 1.2 or later versions.

Classic VM

In Java 1.3, you could use the `-classic` option to specify that you wanted to use the "Classic VM" (essentially the same as the Java 1.2 VM) instead of the HotSpot VM (which uses incremental compilation). This option was removed in Java 1.4.

Just-in-time compiler

In Java 1.2 and Java 1.3 when you specified the `-classic` option, the Java interpreter used a just-in-time compiler (if one were available for your platform). A JIT converts Java byte codes to native machine instructions at runtime and significantly speeds up the execution of a typical Java program. If you do not want to use the JIT, you can disable it by setting the `JAVA_COMPILER` environment variable to "NONE" or the `java.compiler` system property to "NONE" using the `-D` option:

```
% setenv JAVA_COMPILER NONE                    // Unix csh syntax
% java -Djava.compiler=NONE MyProgram
```

If you want to use a different JIT compiler implementation, set the environment variable or system property to the name of the desired implementation. This environment variable and property are no longer used as of Java 1.4, which uses the HotSpot VM, which includes efficient JIT technology.

Threading systems

On Solaris and related Unix platforms, you had a choice of the type of threads used by the Java 1.2 interpreter and the "Classic VM" of Java 1.3. To use native OS threads, you could specify `-native`. To use nonnative, or green, threads (the default), you could specify `-green`. In Java 1.3, the default "Client VM" used native threads. Specifying `-green` or `-native` in Java 1.3 implicitly specified `-classic` as well. These options are no longer supported (or necessary) as of Java 1.4.

Common options

The following options are the most commonly used.

`-classpath` *path*

Specifies the directories and JAR files *java* searches when trying to load a class. In Java 1.2 and later, this option specifies only the location of application classes. In Java 1.0 and 1.1, and with the *oldjava* interpreter, this option specified the location of system classes, extension classes, and application classes.

`-cp`

A synonym for `-classpath`. Java 1.2 and later.

`-Dpropertyname=value`
: Defines *propertyname* to equal *value* in the system properties list. Your Java program can then look up the specified value by its property name. You can specify any number of `-D` options. For example:

```
% java -Dawt.button.color=gray -Dmy.class.pointsize=14 my.class
```

`-fullversion`
: Prints the full Java version string, including build number, and exits. Compare with `-version`.

`-help, -?`
: Prints a usage message and exits. See also `-X`.

`-jar jarfile`
: Runs the specified executable *jarfile*. The manifest of the specified *jarfile* must contain a `Main-Class` attribute that identifies the class with the `main()` method at which program execution is to begin. Java 1.2 and later.

`-showversion`
: Works like the `-version` option, except that the interpreter continues running after printing the version information. Java 1.3 and later.

`-version`
: Prints the version of the Java interpreter and exits.

`-X`
: Displays usage information for the nonstandard interpreter options (those beginning with `-X`) and exits. See also `-help`. Java 1.2 and later.

`-Xbootclasspath:path`
: Specifies a search path consisting of directories, ZIP files, and JAR files the *java* interpreter should use to look up system classes. Use of this option is very rare. Java 1.2 and later.

`-Xbootclasspath/a:path`
: Appends the specified *path* to the system classpath. Java 1.3 and later.

`-Xbootclasspath/p:path`
: Prepends the specified *path* to the system boot classpath. Java 1.3 and later.

Assertion options

The following options specify whether and where assertions are tested. These options were added in Java 1.4.

`-disableassertions[:where]`
: Disables assertions. It is new in Java 1.4 and can be abbreviated `-da`. Used alone, it disables all assertions (except those in the system classes), which is the default. To disable assertions in a single class, follow the option with a colon and the fully qualified class name. To disable assertions in an entire package (and all of its subpackages), follow this option with a colon, the name of the package, and three dots. See also `-enableassertions` and `-disablesystemassertions`.

`-da[:where]`
: Disables assertions. See `-disableassertions`.

`-disablesystemassertions`
: Disables assertions in all system classes (which is the default). It can be abbreviated `-dsa` and takes no options.

`-dsa`
: An abbreviation for `-disablesystemassertions`.

`-enableassertions[:`*`where`*`]`
: Enables assertions. This option can be abbreviated `-ea`. Used alone, it enables all assertions (except in system classes). To enable assertions in a single class, follow the option with a colon and the full class name. To enable assertions in an entire package (and its subpackages), follow the option with a colon, the package name, and three dots. See also `-disableassertions` and `-enablesystemassertions`.

`-ea[:`*`where`*`]`
: Enables assertions. An abbreviation for `-enableassertions`.

`-enablesystemassertions`
: Enables assertions in all system classes. May be abbreviated `-esa`.

`-esa`
: An abbreviation for `-enablesystemassertions`.

Performance tuning options

The following options select which version of the VM is to be run and fine-tune its memory allocation, garbage collection, and incremental compilation. Options beginning with `-X` are nonstandard and may change from release to release.

`-classic`
: Runs the "Classic VM" instead of the default high-performance "Client VM." Java 1.3 only.

`-client`
: Optimizes the incremental compilation of the HotSpot VM for typical client-side applications. This option typically defers some compilation to favor quicker application launch times. Java 1.4 and later. See also the `-server` option.

`-d32`
: Runs in 32-bit mode. This option is valid in Java 1.4 and later but is currently implemented only for Solaris platforms.

`-d64`
: Runs in 64-bit mode. This option is valid in Java 1.4 and later but is currently implemented only for Solaris platforms.

`-green`
: Selects nonnative, or green, threads on operating systems such as Solaris and Linux that support multiple styles of threading. This is the default in Java 1.2. In Java 1.3, using this option also selects the `-classic` option. See also `-native`. Java 1.2 and 1.3 only.

`-native`
: Selects native threads, instead of the default green threads, on operating systems such as Solaris that support multiple styles of threading. Using native threads can be advantageous in some circumstances, such as when running on a multi-CPU computer. In Java 1.3, the default HotSpot virtual machine uses native threads. Java 1.2 and 1.3 only.

`-server`
: Optimizes the incremental compilation of the VM for server-class applications. In general, this option results in slower startup time but better subsequent performance. Java 1.4 and later. In Java 5.0 and later, many VMs automatically select this option if they are running on "server-class" hardware such as a dual-processor machine. See also `-client`.

`-Xbatch`
: Tells the HotSpot VM to perform all just-in-time compilation in the foreground, regardless of the time required for compilation. Without this option, the VM compiles methods in the background while interpreting them in the foreground. Java 1.3 and later.

`-Xincgc`
: Uses incremental garbage collection. In this mode, the garbage collector runs continuously in the background, and a running program is rarely, if ever, subject to noticeable pauses while garbage collection occurs. Using this option typically results in a 10% decrease in overall performance, however. Java 1.3 and later.

`-Xint`
: Tells the HotSpot VM to operate in interpreted mode only, without performing any just-in-time compilation. Java 1.3 and later.

`-Xmixed`
: Tells the HotSpot VM to perform just-in-time compilation on frequently used methods ("hotspots") and execute other methods in interpreted mode. This is the default behavior. Contrast with `-Xbatch` and `-Xint`. Java 1.3 and later.

`-Xms` *`initmem`*`[k|m]`
: Specifies how much memory is allocated for the heap when the interpreter starts up. By default, *`initmem`* is specified in bytes. You can specify it in kilobytes by appending the letter `k` or in megabytes by appending the letter `m`. The default is 2 MB. For large or memory-intensive applications (such as the Java compiler), you can improve runtime performance by starting the interpreter with a larger amount of memory. You must specify an initial heap size of at least 1 MB. Java 1.2 and later. Prior to Java 1.2, use `-ms`.

`-Xmx`*`maxmem`*`[k|m]`
: Specifies the maximum heap size the interpreter uses for dynamically allocated objects and arrays. *`maxmem`* is specified in bytes by default. You can specify *`maxmem`* in kilobytes by appending the letter `k` and in megabytes by appending the letter `m`. The default is 64 MB. You cannot specify a heap size less than 2 MB. Java 1.2 and later. Prior to Java 1.2, use `-mx`.

`-Xnoclassgc`
: Does not garbage-collect classes. Java 1.2 and later. In Java 1.1, use `-noclassgc`.

`-Xss`*`size`*`[k|m]`
: Sets the thread stack size in bytes, kilobytes, or megabytes. Java 1.3 and later.

Instrumentation options

The following options support debugging, profiling, and other VM instrumentation. Options beginning with `-X` are nonstandard and may change from release to release.

`-agentlib:`*`agent[=options]`*
: New in Java 5.0, this option specifies a JVMTI agent, and options for it, to be started along with the interpeter. JVMTI is the Java Virtual Machine Tool Interface, and it is slated to supercede the JVMDI and JVMPI (debugging and profiling interfaces) in a future release. This means that the general `-agentlib` option will replace tool-specific options such as `-Xdebug` and `-Xrunhprof`. Examples:

```
% java -agentlib:hprof=help
% java -agentlib:jdwp=help
```

`-agentpath:`*`path-to-agent[=options]`*
: Like `-agentlib`, but with an explicitly specified path to the agent library. Java 5.0 and later.

`-debug`
: Causes *java* to start up in a way that allows the *jdb* debugger to attach itself to the interpreter session. In Java 1.2 and later, this option has been replaced with `-Xdebug`.

`-javaagent:`*`jarfile[=options]`*
: Load a Java-language instrumentation agent when the interpreter starts. The specified *jarfile* must have a manifest that includes an `Agent-Class` attribute. This attribute must name a class that includes the agent's `premain()` method. Any *`options`* will be passed to this `premain()` method along with a `java.lang.instrument.Instrumentation` object. See `java.lang.instrument` for further detail.

`-verbose`, `-verbose:class`
: Prints a message each time *java* loads a class. In Java 1.2 and later, you can use `-verbose:class` as a synonym.

`-verbose:gc`
: Prints a message when garbage collection occurs. Java 1.2 and later. Prior to Java 1.2, use `-verbosegc`.

`-verbose:jni`
: Prints a message when native methods are called. Java 1.2 and later.

`-Xcheck:jni`
: Performs additional validity checks when using Java Native Interface functions. Java 1.2 and later.

`-Xdebug`
: Starts the interpreter in a way that allows a debugger to communicate with it. Java 1.2 and later. Prior to Java 1.2, use `-debug`. Deprecated in Java 5.0 in favor of the `-agentlib` option.

`-Xfuture`
: Strictly checks the format of all class files loaded. Without this option, *java* performs the same checks that were performed in Java 1.1. Java 1.2 and later.

`-Xloggc:`*`filename`*
: Logs garbage collection events with timestamps to the named file.

`-Xprof`
: Prints profiling output to standard output. Java 1.3 and later. In Java 1.2, or when using the `-classic` option, use `-Xrunhprof`. Prior to Java 1.2, use `-prof`.

`-Xrunhprof:`*`suboptions`*
: Turns on CPU, heap, or monitor profiling. *`suboptions`* is a comma-separated list of `name=value` pairs. Use `-Xrunhprof:help` for a list of supported options and values. Java 1.2 and later. Deprecated in Java 5.0 in favor of the `-agentlib` option.

Advanced options

The Java interpreter also supports quite a few advanced configuration options that begin with `-XX`. These options are release and platform-dependent, and Sun's documentation describes them as "not recommended for casual use." If you want to fine-tune the threading, memory allocation, garbage collection, signal-handling, or just-in-time compilation performance of a production application, however, you may be interested in them. See *http://java.sun.com/docs/hotspot/*.

Loading classes

The Java interpreter knows where to find the system classes that comprise the Java platform. In Java 1.2 and later, it also knows where to find the class files for all extensions installed in the system extensions directory. However, the interpreter must be told where to find the nonsystem classes that comprise the application to be run.

Class files are stored in a directory that corresponds to their package name. For example, the class `com.davidflanagan.utils.Util` is stored in a file *com/davidflanagan/utils/Util.class*. By default, the interpreter uses the current working directory as the root and looks for all classes in and beneath this directory.

The interpreter can also search for classes within ZIP and JAR files. To tell the interpreter where to look for classes, you specify a *classpath*: a list of directories and ZIP and JAR archives. When looking for a class, the interpreter searches each of the specified locations in the order in which they are specified.

The easiest way to specify a classpath is to set the `CLASSPATH` environment variable, which works much like the `PATH` variable used by a Unix shell or a Windows command-interpreter path. To specify a classpath in Unix, you might type a command like this:

```
% setenv CLASSPATH .:~/myclasses:/usr/lib/javautils.jar:/usr/lib/javaapps
```

On a Windows system, you might use a command like the following:

```
C:\> set CLASSPATH=.;c:\myclasses;c:\javatools\classes.zip;d:\javaapps
```

Note that Unix and Windows use different characters to separate directory and path components.

You can also specify a classpath with the `-classpath` or `-cp` options to the Java interpreter. A path specified with one of these options overrides any path specified by the `CLASSPATH` environment variable. In Java 1.2 and later, the `-classpath` option specifies only the search path for application and user classes. Prior to Java 1.2, or when using the *oldjava* interpreter, this option specified the search path for all classes, including system classes and extension classes.

See also *javac*, *jdb*

javac

The Java Compiler

Synopsis

```
javac [ options ] files
```

Description

javac is the Java compiler; it compiles Java source code (in *.java* files) into Java byte codes (in *.class* files). The Java compiler is itself written in Java.

javac can be passed any number of Java source files, whose names must all end with the *.java* extension. *javac* produces a separate *.class* class file for each class defined in the source files. Each source file can contain any number of classes, although only one can be a `public` top-level class. The name of the source file (minus the *.java* extension) must match the name of the `public` class it contains.

In Java 1.2 and later, if a filename specified on the command line begins with the character `@`, that file is taken not as a Java source file but as a list of compiler options and

Java source files. Thus, if you keep a list of Java source files for a particular project in a file named *project.list*, you can compile all those files at once with the command:

```
% javac @project.list
```

To compile a source file, *javac* must be able to find definitions of all classes used in the source file. It looks for definitions in both source-file and class-file form, automatically compiling any source files that have no corresponding class files or that have been modified since they were most recently compiled.

Common options

The most commonly used compilation options include the following:

`-classpath` *`path`*
: Specifies the path *javac* uses to look up classes referenced in the specified source code. This option overrides any path specified by the `CLASSPATH` environment variable. The *`path`* specified is an ordered list of directories, ZIP files, and JAR archives, separated by colons on Unix systems or semicolons on Windows systems. If the `-sourcepath` option is not set, this option also specifies the search path for source files.

`-d` *`directory`*
: Specifies the directory in which (or beneath which) class files should be stored. By default, *javac* stores the *.class* files it generates in the same directory as the *.java* files those classes were defined in. If the `-d` option is specified, however, the specified *`directory`* is treated as the root of the class hierarchy, and *.class* files are placed in this directory or the appropriate subdirectory below it, depending on the package name of the class. Thus, the following command:

```
% javac -d /java/classes Checkers.java
```

places the file *Checkers.class* in the directory */java/classes* if the *Checkers.java* file has no `package` statement. On the other hand, if the source file specifies that it is in a package:

```
package com.davidflanagan.games;
```

the *.class* file is stored in */java/classes/com/davidflanagan/games*. When the `-d` option is specified, *javac* automatically creates any directories it needs to store its class files in the appropriate place.

`-encoding` *`encoding-name`*
: Specifies the name of the character encoding used by the source files if it differs from the default platform encoding.

`-g`
: Tells *javac* to add line number, source file, and local variable information to the output class files, for use by debuggers. By default, *javac* generates only the line numbers.

`-g:none`
: Tells *javac* to include no debugging information in the output class files. Java 1.2 and later.

`-g:`*`keyword-list`*
: Tells *javac* to output the types of debugging information specified by the comma-separated *`keyword-list`*. The valid keywords are: `source`, which specifies source-file information; `lines`, which specifies line number information; and `vars`, which specifies local variable debugging information. Java 1.2 and later.

`-help`
: Prints a list of options. See also `-X`.

`-J`*`javaoption`*
: Passes the argument *`javaoption`* directly through to the Java interpreter. For example: `-J-Xmx32m`. *`javaoption`* should not contain spaces; if multiple arguments must be passed to the interpreter, use multiple `-J` options. Java 1.1 and later.

`-source` *`release-number`*
: Specifies the version of Java the code is written in. Legal values of *release-number* are 5, 1.5, 1.4, and 1.3. The options 5 and 1.5 are synonyms and are the default: the compiler accepts all Java 5.0 language features. Use `-source 1.4` to have the compiler ignore Java 5.0 language features such as the `enum` keyword. Use `-source 1.3` to have the compiler ignore the `assert` keyword that was introduced in Java 1.4. This option is available in Java 1.4 and later.

`-sourcepath` *`path`*
: Specifies the list of directories, ZIP files, and JAR archives that *javac* searches when looking for source files. The files found in this source path are compiled if no corresponding class files are found or if the source files are newer than the class files. By default, source files are searched for in the same places class files are searched for. Java 1.2 and later.

`-verbose`
: Tells the compiler to display messages about what it is doing. In particular, it causes *javac* to list all the source files it compiles, including files that did not appear on the command line.

`-X`
: Tells the *javac* compiler to display usage information for its nonstandard options (all of which begin with `-X`). Java 1.2 and later.

Warning options

The following options control the generation of warning messages by *javac*:

`-deprecation`
: Tells *javac* to issue a warning for every use of a deprecated API. By default, *javac* issues only a single warning for each source file that uses deprecated APIs. Java 1.1 and later. In Java 5.0, this is a synonym for `-Xlint:deprecation`.

`-nowarn`
: Tells *javac* not to print warning messages. Errors are still reported as usual.

`-Xlint`
: Enables all recommended warnings about program "lint." At the time of this writing, all the warnings detailed below are recommended.

`-Xlint:`*`warnings`*
: Enables or disables a comma-separated list of named warning types. At the time of this writing, the available warning types are the following. A named warning can be suppressed by preceding it with a minus sign:

  `all`
  : Enables all lint warnings.

  `deprecation`
  : Warns about the use of deprecated APIs. See also `-deprecation`.

fallthrough
: Warns when a case in a switch statement "falls through" to the next case. See also -Xswitchcheck.

finally
: Warns when a finally clause cannot complete normally.

path
: Warns if any path directories specified elsewhere on the command line are nonexistent.

serial
: Warns about Serializable classes that do not have a serialVersionUID field.

unchecked
: Provides detailed warnings about each unchecked use of a generic type.

-Xmaxerrors *num*
: Don't print more than *num* errors.

-Xmaxwarns *num*
: Don't print more than *num* warnings.

-Xstdout *filename*
: Tells *javac* to send warning and error messages to the specified file instead of writing them to the console. Java 1.4 and later.

-Xswitchcheck
: Warns about case clauses in switch statements that "fall through." In Java 5.0, use -Xlint:fallthrough.

Cross-compilation options

The following options are useful when using *javac* to compile class files intended to run under a different version of Java:

-bootclasspath *path*
: Specifies the search path *javac* uses to look up system classes. This option does not specify the system classes used to run the compiler itself, only the system classes read by the compiler. Java 1.2 and later.

-endorseddirs *path*
: Overrides the directories to search for endorsed standards JAR files.

-extdirs *path*
: Specifies a list of directories to search for standard extension JAR files. Java 1.2 and later.

-target *version*
: Specifies the class file format version to use for the generated class files. *version* may be 1.1, 1.2, 1.3, 1.4, 1.5, or 5. The options 1.5 and 5 are synonyms and are the default in Java 5.0, unless -source 1.4 is specified, in which case -target 1.4 is the default. Use of this flag sets the class file version number so that the resulting class file cannot be run by VMs from previous releases.

-Xbootclasspath:*path*
: An alternative to -bootclasspath

-Xbootclasspath/a:*path*
: Appends the specified *path* to the bootclasspath. Java 1.3 and later.

-Xbootclasspath/p:*path*
: Prefixes the bootclasspath with the specified *path*.

Environment

CLASSPATH
: Specifies an ordered list (colon-separated on Unix, semicolon-separated on Windows systems) of directories, ZIP files, and JAR archives in which *javac* should look for user class files and source files. This variable is overridden by the `-classpath` option.

See also *java*, *jdb*

javadoc

The Java Documentation Generator

Synopsis

```
javadoc [ options ] @list package... sourcefiles...
```

Description

javadoc generates API documentation for any number of packages and classes you specify. The *javadoc* command line can list any number of package names and any number of Java source files. For convenience, when working with a large number of command-line options, or a large number of package or class names, you can place them all in an auxiliary file and specify the name of that file on the command line, preceded by an `@` character.

javadoc uses the *javac* compiler to process all the specified Java source files and all the Java source files in all the specified packages. It uses the information it gleans from this processing to generate detailed API documentation. Most importantly, the generated documentation includes the contents of all documentation comments included in the source files. See Chapter 7 for information about writing doc comments in your own Java code.

When you specify a Java source file for *javadoc* to process, you must specify the name of the file that contains the source, including a complete path to the file. It is more common, however, to use *javadoc* to create documentation for entire packages of classes. When you specify a package for *javadoc* to process, you specify the package name, not the directory that contains the source code for the package. In this case, you may need to specify the `-sourcepath` option so that *javadoc* can find your package source code correctly if it is not stored in a location already listed in your default classpath.

javadoc creates HTML documentation by default, but you can customize its behavior by defining a doclet class that generates documentation in whatever format you desire. You can write your own doclets using the doclet API defined by the `com.sun.javadoc` package. Documentation for this package is included in the standard documentation bundle for Java 1.2 and later.

javadoc gained significant new functionality in Java 1.2. Here we document Java 1.2 and later versions of the program and do not distinguish these features from those in previous versions.

Options

javadoc defines a large number of options. Some are standard options that are always recognized by *javadoc*. Other options are defined by the doclet that produces the documentation. The options for the standard HTML doclet are included in the following list:

`-1.1`
: Simulates the output style and directory structure of the Java 1.1 version of *javadoc*. This option existed in Java 1.2 and 1.3 and was removed in Java 1.4.

`-author`
: Includes authorship information specified with `@author` in the generated documentation. Default doclet only.

`-bootclasspath`
: Specifies the location of an alternate set of system classes. This can be useful when cross-compiling. See *javac* for more information on this option.

`-bottom` *`text`*
: Displays *`text`* at the bottom of each generated HTML file. *`text`* can contain HTML tags. See also `-footer`. Default doclet only.

`-breakiterator`
: Uses the `java.text.BreakIterator` algorithm for determining the end of the summary sentence in doc comments. Default doclet only.

`-charset` *`encoding`*
: Specifies the character encoding for the output. This depends on the encoding used in the documentation comments of your source code, of course. The *`encoding`* value is used in a `<meta>` tag in the HTML output. Default doclet only.

`-classpath` *`path`*
: Specifies a path *javadoc* uses to look up both class files and, if you do not specify the `-sourcepath` option, source files. Because *javadoc* uses the *javac* compiler, it needs to be able to locate class files for all classes referenced by the packages being documented. See *java* and *javac* for more information about this option and the default value provided by the `CLASSPATH` environment variable.

`-d` *`directory`*
: Specifies the directory in and beneath which *javadoc* should store the HTML files it generates. If this option is omitted, the current directory is used. Default doclet only.

`-docencoding` *`encoding`*
: Specifies the encoding to be used for output HTML documents. The name of the encoding specified here may not exactly match the name of the charset specified with the `-charset` option. Default doclet only.

`-docfilessubdirs`
: Recursively copies any subdirectories of a *doc-files* directory instead of simply copying the files contained directly within *doc-files*. Default doclet only.

`-doclet` *`classname`*
: Specifies the name of the doclet class to use to generate the documentation. If this option is not specified, *javadoc* generates documentation using the default HTML doclet.

`-docletpath` *`classpath`*
: Specifies a path from which the class specified by the `-doclet` tag can be loaded if it is not available from the default classpath.

-doctitle *text*
: Provides a title to display at the top of the documentation overview file. This file is often the first thing readers see when they browse the generated documentation. The title can contain HTML tags. Default doclet only.

-encoding *encoding-name*
: Specifies the character encoding of the input source files and the documentation comments they contain. This can be different from the desired output encoding specified by -docencoding. The default is the platform default encoding.

-exclude *packages*
: Excludes the named packages from the set of packages defined by a -subpackages option. *packages* is a colon-separated list of package names. Default doclet only.

-excludedocfilessubdir *dirs*
: Excludes specified subdirectories of a *doc-files* directory when -docfilessubdirs is specified. This is useful for excluding version control directories, for example. *dirs* is a colon-separated list of directory names relative to the *doc-files* directory. Default doclet only.

-extdirs *dirlist*
: Specifies a list of directories to search for standard extensions. Only necessary when cross-compiling with -bootclasspath. See *javac* for details.

-footer *text*
: Specifies text to be displayed near the bottom of each file to the right of the navigation bar. *text* can contain HTML tags. See also -bottom and -header. Default doclet only.

-group *title packagelist*
: *javadoc* generates a top-level overview page that lists all packages in the generated document. By default, these packages are listed in alphabetical order in a single table. You can break them into groups of related packages with this option, however. The *title* specifies the title of the package group, such as "Core Packages." The *packagelist* is a colon-separated list of package names, each of which can include a trailing * character as a wildcard. The *javadoc* command line can contain any number of -group options. For example:

```
% javadoc -group "AWT Packages" java.awt* \
-group "Swing Packages" javax.accessibility:javax.swing*
```

-header *text*
: Specifies text to be displayed near the top of file, to the right of the upper navigation bar. *text* can contain HTML tags. See also -footer, -doctitle, and -windowtitle. Default doclet only.

-help
: Displays a usage message for *javadoc*.

-helpfile *file*
: Specifies the name of an HTML file that contains help for using the generated documentation. *javadoc* includes links to this help file in all files it generates. If this option is not specified, *javadoc* creates a default help file. Default doclet only.

-J*javaoption*
: Passes the argument *javaoption* directly through to the Java interpreter. When processing a large number of packages, you may need to use this option to increase the amount of memory *javadoc* is allowed to use. For example:

```
% javadoc -J-Xmx64m
```

Note that because `-J` options are passed directly to the Java interpreter before *javadoc* starts up, they cannot be included in an external file specified on the command line with the `@list` syntax.

`-keywords`
: Tells *javadoc* to include type and member names in <Meta> tag keyword lists. Default doclet only.

`-link` *`url`*
: Specifies an absolute or relative URL of the top-level directory of another *javadoc*-generated document. *javadoc* uses this URL as the base URL for links from the current document to packages, classes, methods, and fields that are not documented in the current document. For example, when using *javadoc* to produce documentation for your own packages, you can use this option to link your documentation to the *javadoc* documentation for the core Java APIs. Default doclet only.

  The directory specified by *`url`* must contain a file named *package-list*, and *javadoc* must be able to read this file at runtime. This file is automatically generated by a previous run of *javadoc*; it contains a list of all packages documented at the *`url`*.

  More than one `-link` option can be specified, although this does not work properly in early releases of Java 1.2. If no `-link` option is specified, references in the generated documentation to classes and members that are external to the documentation are not hyperlinked.

`-linkoffline` *`url packagelist`*
: Similar to the `-link` option, except that the *`packagelist`* file is explicitly specified on the command line. This is useful when the directory specified by *`url`* does not have a *package-list* file or when that file is not available when *javadoc* is run. Default doclet only.

`-linksource`
: Creates an HTML version of each source file read and includes links to it from the documentation pages. Default doclet only.

`-locale` *`language_country_variant`*
: Specifies the locale to use for generated documentation. This is used to look up a resource file that contains localized messages and text for the output files.

`-nocomment`
: Ignores all doc comments and generates documentation that includes only raw API information without any accompanying prose. Default doclet only.

`-nodeprecated`
: Tells *javadoc* to omit documentation for deprecated features. This option implies `-nodeprecatedlist`. Default doclet only.

`-nodeprecatedlist`
: Tells *javadoc* not to generate the *deprecated-list.html* file and not to output a link to it on the navigation bar. Default doclet only.

`-nohelp`
: Tells *javadoc* not to generate a help file or a link to it in the navigation bar. Default doclet only.

`-noindex`
: Tells *javadoc* not to generate index files. Default doclet only.

-nonavbar
: Tells *javadoc* to omit the navigation bars from the top and bottom of every file. Also omits the text specified by -header and -footer. This is useful when generating documentation to be printed. Default doclet only.

-noqualifier *packages* | all
: *javadoc* omits package names in its generated documentation for classes in the same package being documented. This option tells it to additionally omit package names for classes in the specified packages, or, if the all keyword is used, in all packages. *packages* is a colon-separated list of package names, which may include the * wildcard to indicate subpackages. For example, -noqualifier java.io:java.nio.* would exclude package names for all classes in the java.io package and in java.nio and its subpackages. Default doclet only.

-nosince
: Ignores @since tags in doc comments. Default doclet only.

-notimestamp
: Don't output timestamps in HTML comments. Default doclet only.

-notree
: Tells *javadoc* not to generate the *tree.html* class hierarchy diagram or a link to it in the navigation bar. Default doclet only.

-overview *filename*
: Reads an overview doc comment from *filename* and uses that comment in the overview page. This file does not contain Java source code, so the doc comment should not actually appear between /** and */ delimiters.

-package
: Includes package-visible classes and members in the output, as well as public and protected classes and members.

-private
: Includes all classes and members, including private and package-visible classes and members, in the generated documentation.

-protected
: Includes public and protected classes and members in the generated output. This is the default.

-public
: Includes only public classes and members in the generated output. Omits protected, private, and package-visible classes and members.

-quiet
: Suppresses output except warnings and error messages.

-serialwarn
: Issues warnings about serializable classes that do not adequately document their serialization format with @serial and related doc-comment tags. Default doclet only.

-source *release*
: Specifies the *release* of Java for which the source files were written. See the -source option of *javac*. Legal values are 5, 1.5, 1.4, and 1.3. The options 1.5 and 5 are synonyms and are the default.

`-sourcepath` *`path`*
: Specifies a search path for source files, typically set to a single root directory. *javadoc* uses this path when looking for the Java source files that implement a specified package.

`-splitindex`
: Generates multiple index files, one for each letter of the alphabet. Use this option when documenting large amounts of code. Otherwise, the single index file generated by *javadoc* will be too large to be useful. Default doclet only.

`-stylesheetfile` *`file`*
: Specifies a file to use as a CSS stylesheet for the generated HTML. *javadoc* inserts appropriate links to this file in the generated documentation. Default doclet only.

`-subpackages` *`packages`*
: Specifies that *javadoc* should process the specified packages and all of their subpackages. *`packages`* is a colon-separated list of package names or package name prefixes. Using this option is often easier than explicitly listing all desired package names. For example:

```
-subpackages java:javax
```

See also `-exclude`. Default doclet only.

`-tag` *`tagname`*`:`*`where`*`:`*`header-text`*
: Specifies that *javadoc* should handle a doc-comment tag named *tagname* by outputting the text *`header-text`* followed by whatever text follows the tag. This enables the use of simple custom tags (with the same syntax as `@return` and `@author`) in doc comments. *`where`* is a string of characters that specifies the types of doc comments in which this custom tag is allowed. The characters and their meanings are `a` (all: valid everywhere), `p` (packages), `t` (types: classes and interfaces), `c` (constructors), `m` (methods), and `f` (fields).

A secondary purpose of the `-tag` option is to specify the order in which tags are processed and in which their output appears. You can include the names of standard tags after the `-tag` option to specify this ordering. Custom tags and taglets can be included within this list of standard `-tag` options. Default doclet only.

`-taglet` *`classname`*
: Specifies the classname of a "taglet" class to process a custom tag. Writing taglets is not covered here. `-taglet` tags may be interspersed with `-tag` tags to specify the order in which tags should be processed and output. Default doclet only.

`-tagletpath` *`classpath`*
: Specifies a colon-separated list of JAR files or directories that form the classpath to be searched for taglet classes. Default doclet only.

`-use`
: Generates and inserts links to an additional file for each class and package that lists the uses of the class or package.

`-verbose`
: Displays additional messages while processing source files.

`-version`
: Includes information from `@version` tags in the generated output. This option does *not* tell *javadoc* to print its own version number. Default doclet only.

-windowtitle *text*

Specifies *text* to be output in the <Title> tag of each generated file. This title typically appears as the title of the web browser window and in history and bookmark lists. *text* should not contain HTML tags. See also -doctitle and -header. Default doclet only.

Environment

CLASSPATH

This environment variable specifies the default classpath *javadoc* uses to find the class files and source files. It is overridden by the -classpath and -sourcepath options. See *java* and *javac* for further discussion of the classpath.

See also *java*, *javac*

javah

Native Method C Stub Generator

Synopsis

```
javah [ options ] classnames
```

Description

javah generates C header and source files (*.h* and *.c* files) that are used when implementing Java native methods in C. The preferred native method interface changed between Java 1.0 and Java 1.1. In Java 1.1 and earlier, *javah* generated files for old-style native methods. In Java 1.1, the -jni option specified that *javah* should generate new-style files. In Java 1.2 and later, this option is the default.

This section describes only how to use *javah*. A full description of how to implement Java native methods in C is beyond the scope of this book.

Options

-bootclasspath

Specifies the path to search for system classes. See *javac* for further discussion. Java 1.2 and later.

-classpath *path*

Specifies the path *javah* uses to look up the classes named on the command line. This option overrides any path specified by the CLASSPATH environment variable. Prior to Java 1.2, this option can specify the location of the system classes and extensions. In Java 1.2 and later, it specifies only the location of application classes. See -bootclasspath. See also *java* for further discussion of the classpath.

-d *directory*

Specifies the directory into which *javah* stores the files it generates. By default, it stores them in the current directory. This option cannot be used with -o.

-force

Causes *javah* to always write output files, even if they contain no useful content.

-help

Causes *javah* to display a simple usage message and exit.

-J*javaopt*

Passes the option *javaopt* to the Java interpreter.

`-jni`
: Specifies that *javah* should output header files for use with the Java Native Interface (JNI) rather than the old JDK 1.0 native interface. This option is the default in Java 1.2 and later. See also `-old`. Java 1.1 and later.

`-o` *`outputfile`*
: Combines all output into a single file, *`outputfile`*, instead of creating separate files for each specified class.

`-old`
: Outputs files for Java 1.0-style native methods. Prior to Java 1.2, this was the default. See also `-jni`. Java 1.2 and later.

`-stubs`
: Generates *.c* stub files for the class or classes instead of header files. This option is only for the Java 1.0 native methods interface. See `-old`.

`-trace`
: Specifies that *javah* should include tracing output commands in the stub files it generates. In Java 1.2 and later, this option is obsolete and has been removed. In its place, you can use the `-verbose:jni` option of the Java interpreter.

`-v`, `-verbose`
: Specifies verbose mode. Causes *javah* to print messages about what it is doing. In Java 1.2 and later, `-verbose` is a synonym.

`-version`
: Causes *javah* to display its version number.

Environment

`CLASSPATH`
: Specifies the default classpath *javah* searches to find the specified classes. See *java* for a further discussion of the classpath.

See also *java*, *javac*

---

javap

The Java Class Disassembler

Synopsis

`javap [ `*`options`*` ] `*`classnames`*

Description

javap reads the class files specified by the class names on the command line and prints a human-readable version of the API defined by those classes. *javap* can also disassemble the specified classes, displaying the Java VM byte codes for the methods they contain.

Options

`-b`
: Enables backward compatibility with the output of the Java 1.1 version of *javap*. This option exists for programs that depend on the precise output format of *javap*. Java 1.2 and later.

`-bootclasspath` *path*
: Specifies the search path for the system classes. See *javac* for information about this rarely used option. Java 1.2 and later.

`-c`
: Displays the code (i.e., Java VM byte codes) for each method of each specified class. This option always disassembles all methods, regardless of their visibility level.

`-classpath` *path*
: Specifies the path *javap* uses to look up the classes named on the command line. This option overrides the path specified by the `CLASSPATH` environment variable. Prior to Java 1.2, this argument specifies the path for all system classes, extensions, and application classes. In Java 1.2 and later, it specifies only the application classpath. See also `-bootclasspath` and `-extdirs`. See *java* and *javac* for more information on the classpath.

`-extdirs` *dirs*
: Specifies one or more directories that should be searched for extension classes. See *javac* for information about this rarely used option. Java 1.2 and later.

`-J`*javaopt*
: Pass the option *javaopt* to the Java interpreter.

`-l`
: Displays tables of line numbers and local variables, if available in the class files. This option is typically useful only when used with `-c`. The *javac* compiler does not include local variable information in its class files by default. See `-g` and related options to *javac*.

`-help`
: Prints a usage message and exits.

`-J`*javaoption*
: Passes the specified *javaoption* directly to the Java interpreter.

`-package`
: Displays package-visible, `protected`, and `public` class members, but not `private` members. This is the default.

`-private`
: Displays all class members, including `private` members.

`-protected`
: Displays only `protected` and `public` members.

`-public`
: Displays only `public` members of the specified classes.

`-s`
: Outputs the class member declarations using the internal VM type and method signature format instead of the more readable source-code format.

`-verbose`
: Specifies verbose mode. Outputs additional information (in the form of Java comments) about each member of each specified class.

Environment

`CLASSPATH`
: Specifies the default search path for application classes. The `-classpath` option overrides this environment variable. See *java* for a discussion of the classpath.

See also

java, *javac*

---

javaws

Java Web Start launcher

Synopsis

```
javaws
javaws [ options ] url
```

Description

javaws is the command-line interface to the Java Web Start network application launcher. When started without a *`url`*, *javaws* displays a graphical cache viewer which allows cached applications to be launched and Java Web Start to be configured.

If the URL of a JNLP (Java Network Launching Protocol) is specified on the command line, *javaws* launches the specified application.

Options

`-association`
: Allows the creation of file associations during a `-silent -import`.

`-codebase` *`url`*
: Overrides the codebase in the JNLP file with the specified *`url`*.

`-import`
: Imports the specified application to the user cache but does not run it.

`-offline`
: Runs in offline mode.

`-online`
: Starts in online mode. This is the default behavior.

`-shortcut`
: Allows desktop shortcuts to be created during a `-silent -import`.

`-silent`
: When used with `-import`, this option prevents a GUI window from appearing.

`-system`
: Uses the system cache.

`-uninstall`
: Removes the application identified by *`url`* from the user's cache and exits.

`-updateVersions`
: Updates the *javaws* configuration file (such as after upgrading to a newer version of Java).

`-userConfig` *`name [value]`*
: Sets the deployment property *`name`* or, if *`value`* is specified, sets it to the specified value.

`-viewer`
: Launches the cache viewer application. This is the default behavior if *javaws* is invoked with no arguments.

`-wait`
: Does not exit until the launched application exits.

`-Xclearcache`
: Clears the user's cache and exits.

`-Xnosplash`
: Does not display the Java Web Start splash screen.

jconsole — Graphical Java Process Monitor

Synopsis

```
jconsole [ options ]
jconsole [ options ] pid
jconsole [ options ] host:port
```

Description

jconsole is a graphical interface to the memory, thread, class loading, and other monitoring tools provided by the `java.lang.management` package. It can monitor one or more local or remote Java processes. Processes can be monitored only if started with special system properties set. To allow a Java VM to be monitored locally, start it with:

```
% jconsole -Dcom.sun.management.jmxremote=true
```

To allow a Java VM to be monitored remotely, start it with:

```
% jconsole -Dcom.sun.management.jmxremote.port=port
```

where *port* is the remote port to which *jconsole* will connect.

You may start *jconsole* with no local or remote process specified and use its Connection menu to establish connections. This is the only way to connect *jconsole* to more than one Java process.

To connect *jconsole* to a local process when it starts up, simply list the process id on the command line. See *jps* to determine process ids.

To connect *jconsole* to a remote process when it starts up, specify the hostname and port number on the command line. The port should be the same as that specified by the `com.sun.management.jmxremote.port` system property of the target process.

Options

`-help`
: Display a usage message.

`-interval=`*n*
: Set the update interval to *n* seconds. The default is 4.

`-version`
: Display the *jconsole* version and exit.

See also *jps*, *jstat*

jdb

Synopsis

```
jdb [ options ] class [ program options ]
jdb connect options
```

Description

jdb is a debugger for Java classes. It is text-based, command-line-oriented, and has a command syntax like that of the Unix *dbx* or *gdb* debuggers used with C and C++ programs.

jdb is written in Java, so it runs within a Java interpreter. When *jdb* is invoked with the name of a Java class, it starts another copy of the *java* interpreter, using any interpreter options specified on the command line. The new interpreter is started with special options that enable it to communicate with *jdb*. The new interpreter loads the specified class file and then stops and waits for debugging commands before executing the first byte code.

jdb can also debug a program that is already running in another Java interpreter. Doing so requires that special options be passed to both the *java* interpreter and to *jdb*. See the `-attach` option below.

jdb expression syntax

jdb debugging commands such as `print`, `dump`, and `suspend` allow you to refer to classes, objects, methods, fields, and threads in the program being debugged. You can refer to classes by name, with or without their package names. You can also refer to `static` class members by name. You can refer to individual objects by object ID, which is an eight-digit hexadecimal integer. Or, when the classes you are debugging contain local variable information, you can often use local variable names to refer to objects. You can use normal Java syntax to refer to the fields of an object and the elements of an array; you can also use this syntax to write quite complex expressions. As of Java 1.3, *jdb* even supports method invocation using standard Java syntax.

Options

When invoking *jdb* with a specified class file, any of the *java* interpreter options can be specified. See the *java* reference page for an explanation of these options. In addition, *jdb* supports the following options:

`-attach` *[host:]port*

Specifies that *jdb* should connect to the Java VM that is already running on the specified host (or the local host, if unspecified) and listening for debugging connections on the specified port. Java 1.3 and later.

In order to use *jdb* to connect to a running VM in this way, the VM must have been started with special command-line options. In Java 1.3 and 1.4, use these options:

```
% java -Xdebug -Xrunjdwp:transport=dt_socket,address=8000,server=y,suspend=n
```

In Java 5.0, use these options instead:

```
% java -agentlib:jdwp=transport=dt_socket,address=8000,server=y,suspend=n
```

The Java debugging architecture allows a complex set of interpreter-to-debugger connection options, and *java* and *jdb* provide a complex set of options and suboptions to enable it. A detailed description of those options is beyond the scope of this book.

Java Tools

-connect *connector:args*
: This option provides the most general and flexible method for connecting *jdb* to the process to be debugged. Specify the name of a *connector* (a Java class) followed by a colon and a comma-separated list of arguments in name=value form. Java 1.4 and later. See -listconnectors for available connectors and their arguments.

-help
: Displays a usage message listing supported options.

-launch
: Starts the specified application when *jdb* starts. This avoids the need to explicitly use the run command to start it. Java 1.3 and later.

-listconnectors
: List available connection methods. Each connector is a Java class and a list of arguments. Java 5.0 and later. See the -connect option.

-listen *port*
: Listens on the specified *port* for a Java VM to connect to the debugger. To make this work, the VM must be with options like these:

```
% java -agentlib:jdwp=transport=dt_socket,address=8000,server=n,suspend=y
```

Java 1.4 and later.

-listenany
: Like the -listen option but *jdb* picks a port to listen on and prints out the port number for use when launching the Java process to debug. Java 1.4 and later.

-sourcepath *path*
: Specifies the locations *jdb* searches when attempting to find source files that correspond to the class files being debugged. If unspecified, *jdb* uses the classpath by default. Java 1.3 and later.

-tclient
: Tells *jdb* to invoke the client version of the Java interpreter.

-tserver
: Tells *jdb* to invoke the server version of the Java interpreter.

-version
: Displays the *jdb* version number and exits.

Commands

jdb understands the following debugging commands. Use the help command for more.

? *or* help
: Lists all supported commands, with a short explanation of each.

!!
: A shorthand command that is replaced with the text of the last command entered. It can be followed with additional text to append to that command.

catch *[exception-class]*
: Causes a breakpoint whenever the specified exception is thrown. If no exception is specified, the command lists the exceptions currently being caught. Use ignore to stop these breakpoints from occurring.

classes
: Lists all classes that have been loaded.

`clear`
: Lists all currently set breakpoints.

`clear` *`class.method[(param-type...)]`*
: Clears the breakpoint set in the specified method of the specified class.

`clear` *`[ class:line ]`*
: Removes the breakpoint set at the specified line of the specified class.

`cont`
: Resumes execution. This command should be used when the current thread is stopped at a breakpoint.

`down` *`[ n ]`*
: Moves down *n* frames in the call stack of the current thread. If *n* is not specified, moves down one frame.

`dump` *`id...`*
: Prints the value of all fields of the specified object or objects. If you specify the name of a class, `dump` displays all class (static) methods and variables of the class and also displays the superclass and list of implemented interfaces. Objects and classes can be specified by name or by their eight-digit hexadecimal ID numbers. Threads can also be specified with the shorthand `t@`*`thread-number`*.

`exit` *or* `quit`
: Quits *jdb*.

`gc`
: Runs the garbage collector to force unused objects to be reclaimed.

`ignore` *`exception-class`*
: Does not treat the specified exception as a breakpoint. This command turns off a `catch` command. This command does not cause the Java interpreter to ignore exceptions; it merely tells *jdb* to ignore them.

`list` *`[ line-number ]`*
: Lists the specified line of source code as well as several lines that appear before and after it. If no line number is specified, uses the line number of the current stack frame of the current thread. The lines listed are from the source file of the current stack frame of the current thread. Use the use command to tell *jdb* where to find source files.

`list` *`method`*
: Displays the source code of the specified method.

`load` *`classname`*
: Loads the specified class into *jdb*.

`locals`
: Displays a list of local variables for the current stack frame. Java code must be compiled with the -g option in order to contain local variable information.

`methods` *`class`*
: Lists all methods of the specified class. Use `dump` to list the instance variables of an object or the class (static) variables of a class.

`print` *`id...`*
: Prints the value of the specified item or items. Each item can be a class, object, field, or local variable, and can be specified by name or by eight-digit hexadecimal ID number. You can also refer to threads with the special syntax `t@`*`thread-number`*. The `print` command displays an object's value by invoking its `toString()` method.

Java Tools

`next`
: Executes the current line of source code, including any method calls it makes. See also `step`.

`resume` *[thread-id...]*
: Resumes execution of the specified thread or threads. If no threads are specified, all suspended threads are resumed. See also `suspend`.

`run` *[class] [args]*
: Runs the `main()` method of the specified class, passing the specified arguments to it. If no class or arguments are specified, uses the class and arguments specified on the *jdb* command line.

`step`
: Runs the current line of the current thread and stops again. If the line invokes a method, steps into that method and stops. See also `next`.

`stepi`
: Executes a single Java VM instruction.

`step up`
: Runs until the current method returns to its caller and stops again.

`stop`
: Lists current breakpoints.

`stop at` *class:line*
: Sets a breakpoint at the specified line of the specified class. Program execution stops when it reaches this line. Use `clear` to remove a breakpoint.

`stop in` *class.method[(param-type...)]*
: Sets a breakpoint at the beginning of the specified method of the specified class. Program execution stops when it enters the method. Use `clear` to remove a breakpoint.

`suspend` *[thread-id...]*
: Suspends the specified thread or threads. If no threads are specified, suspends all running threads. Use `resume` to restart them.

`thread` *thread-id*
: Sets the current thread to the specified thread number. This thread is used implicitly by a number of other *jdb* commands.

`threadgroup` *name*
: Sets the current thread group.

`threadgroups`
: Lists all thread groups running in the Java interpreter session being debugged.

`threads` *[threadgroup]*
: Lists all threads in the named thread group. If no thread group is specified, lists all threads in the current thread group (specified by `threadgroup`).

`up` *[n]*
: Moves up *n* frames in the call stack of the current thread. If `n` is not specified, moves up one frame.

`use` *[source-file-path]*
: Sets the path used by *jdb* to look up source files for the classes being debugged. If no path is specified, displays the current source path.

where *[thread-id]* *[all]*
: Displays a stack trace for the specified thread. If no thread is specified, displays a stack trace for the current thread. If `all` is specified, displays a stack trace for all threads.

wherei *[thread-idx]*
: Displays a stack trace for the specified or current thread, including detailed program counter information.

Environment

CLASSPATH
: Specifies an ordered list (colon-separated on Unix, semicolon-separated on Windows systems) of directories, ZIP files, and JAR archives in which *jdb* should look for class definitions. When a path is specified with this environment variable, *jdb* always implicitly appends the location of the system classes to the end of the path. If this environment variable is not specified, the default path is the current directory and the system classes. This variable is overridden by the `-classpath` option.

See also *java*

---

jinfo

Display configuration of a Java process

Synopsis

```
jinfo [ options ] pid                            // info on local process
jinfo [ options ] executable core                // info from core file
jinfo [ options ] [process-name@]hostname        // info from remote process
```

Description

jinfo prints the system properties and JVM command-line options for a running Java process or core file. *jinfo* can be started in one of three ways:

- Specify the process id of a Java process running locally to obtain configuration information about it. See *jps* to list local processes.
- To obtain post-mortem configuration information from a core file, specify the java executable that produced the core file and the core file itself on the command line.
- To obtain configuration information about a Java process running remotely, specify the name of the remote host, optionally prefixed by a remote process name. *jsadebugd* must be running on the remote host.

In Java 5.0, *jinfo* is experimental, unsupported, and not available on all platforms.

Options

These options are mutually exclusive; only one may be specified.

-flags
: Prints only JVM flags, not system properties.

-help, -h
: Prints a help message.

-sysprops
: Prints only system properties, not JVM flags.

See also *jps*, *jsadebugd*

jmap

Display memory usage

Synopsis

```
jmap [ options ] pid                          // local process
jmap [ options ] executable core               // core file
jmap [ options ] [process-name@]hostname       // remote process
```

Description

jmap prints memory usage information for a local or remote Java process or a Java core file. Depending on the option it is invoked with, *jmap* displays one of four memory usage reports. See the Options section for details. *jmap* can be started in three ways:

- Specify the process id of a Java process running locally to obtain configuration information about it. See *jps* to list local processes.
- To obtain post-mortem configuration information from a core file, specify the java executable that produced the core file and the core file itself on the command line.
- To obtain configuration information about a Java process running remotely, specify the name of the remote host, optionally prefixed by a remote process name and @ sign. *jsadebugd* must be running on the remote host.

In Java 5.0, *jmap* is experimental, unsupported, and not available on all platforms.

Options

When invoked with no options, *jmap* prints a memory map of the shared objects or libraries loaded by the VM. Other reports can be produced by using the options below. These options are mutually exclusive; only one may be specified.

`-heap`
: Displays a summary of heap memory usage.

`-help, -h`
: Prints a help message.

`-histo`
: Displays a histogram of heap usage by class.

`-permstat`
: Displays memory used by loaded classes, grouped by class loader.

See also *jps*, *jsadebugd*

jps

List Java processes

Synopsis

```
jps [ options ] [ hostname[:port ] ]
```

Description

jps lists the Java processes running on the local host or on the specified remote host. If a remote host is specified, it must be running the *jstatd* daemon. For each Java process, it displays a process id and names the class or JAR file that the process is executing. Process ids are used by a number of other Java tools, such as *jconsole*, *jstat*, and *jmap*.

Options

The options below alter the default *jps* display. The single-letter options, except for `-q`, may be combined into a single command-line argument, such as `-lmv`:

`-help`
: Displays a usage message.

`-l`
: Lists the full package name of the main class or the full path of the JAR file running in each Java process.

`-m`
: Lists the arguments passed to `main()` method of each Java process.

`-q`
: Lists only Java process identifiers, without application name or any additional information.

`-v`
: Lists arguments passed to the Java interpreter for each Java process.

`-V`
: Lists arguments passed to the interpreter through a flags file such as *.hotspotrc*.

See also *jstatd*

jsadebugd

Daemon process for remote debugging

Synopsis

```
jsadebugd pid [ process-name ]                  // running process
jsadebugd executable core [ process-name ]  // core file
```

Description

jsadebugd is a server process that allows remote invocations of *jinfo*, *jmap*, and *jstack* on a local Java process or core file. Invoke *jsadebugd* by specifying either the process id of a running Java process or an executable file and core file pair on the command line. If more than one *jsadebugd* server will run on the same host at the same time, follow these arguments with an identifying process name that remote clients can use to identify the desired process.

jsadebugd starts the *rmiregistry* server.

In Java 5.0, *jsadebugd* is experimental, unsupported, and not available on all platforms.

See also *jinfo*, *jmap*, *jstack*

jstack

Display stack traces for a Java process

Synopsis

```
jstack [ options ] pid                          // local process
jstack [ options ] executable core              // core file
jstack [ options ] [process-name@]hostname      // remote process
```

Description

jstack prints stack traces for each of the Java threads running in the specified Java process. *jstack* can be started in three ways:

- Specify the process id of a Java process running locally to obtain configuration information about it. See *jps* to list local processes.
- To obtain post-mortem configuration information from a core file, specify the Java executable that produced the core file and the core file itself on the command line.
- To obtain configuration information about a Java process running remotely, specify the name of the remote host, optionally prefixed by a remote process name and @ sign. *jsadebugd* must be running on the remote host.

In Java 5.0, *jstack* is experimental, unsupported, and not available on all platforms.

Options

`-help, -h`
: Prints a help message.

`-m`
: Displays stack traces in "mixed mode," that is, displays both Java and native method stack frames. Without this option, the default is to display Java stack frames only.

See also *jps*, *jsadebugd*

---

jstat

Java VM statistics

Synopsis

```
jstat [ options ] pid [ interval[s|ms] [ count ]]
jstat [ options ] pid@hostname[:port] [ interval[s|ms] [ count ]]
```

Description

jstat probes a running JVM once or repeatedly and displays statistics about its class loading, just-in-time compilation, memory, or garbage collection performance. The type of information to be displayed is specified by `options`. A local process to be probed is specified by its process id, as returned, for example, by *jps*. A remote Java process may be probed by specifying the remote process id, the remote host name, and the port number on which the remote host's *rmiregistry* server is running (if other than the default of 1099). The remote host must also be running the *jstatd* server.

By default, *jstat* probes the specified Java VM once. You may also specify a probe interval, in milliseconds or seconds, to have it probe repeatedly. If you do this, you may additionally specify a total number of probes it should conduct.

jconsole can report many of the same statistics that *jstat* does but displays them in graphical rather than tabular form. In Java 5.0, *jinfo* is experimental, unsupported, and not available on all platforms.

Options

`-help`
: Displays a help message.

`-options`
: Displays a list of report types that *jstat* can display. You must use one of the listed options each time you run *jstat*.

`-version`
: Displays the *jstat* version information and exits.

`-h` *n*
: When *jstat* probes the Java process repeatedly, this option specifies how often it should repeat the table headers in its output. This option must follow one of the report type options below.

`-t`
: Adds a Timestamp column to the report generated by *jstat*. The column displays elapsed time (in seconds) since the target Java process was started.

The following options specify the type of statistics to be reported by *jstat*. Unless you run *jstat* with `-help`, `-options` or `-version`, you must specify exactly one of these options, and it must be the first option on the command line. Most of the options produce detailed reports of garbage collection minutiae. Consult Sun's tool documentation (part of the JDK documentation bundle) for the interpretation of these reports.

`-class`
: Reports the number of classes loaded and their size in kilobytes.

`-compiler`
: Reports the amount of just-in-time compilation that has been performed, and how long it has taken.

`-gc`
: Reports heap garbage collection statistics.

`-gccapacity`
: Reports capacity information of the garbage collector's various memory pools.

`-gccause`
: Like the `-gcutil` report but includes information about the cause of the most recent garbage collection.

`-gcnew`
: Reports information on the "new generation" memory pools of the garbage collector.

`-gcnewcapacity`
: Reports capacity information for the garbage collector's "new generation" memory pools.

`-gcold`
: Reports information on the old generation and permanent memory pools of the garbage collector.

`-gcoldcapacity`
: Reports capacity information for the garbage collector's old generation memory pools.

`-gcpermcapacity`
: Reports capacity information for the garbage collector's permanent generation.

`-gcutil`
: Reports garbage collection summaries.

`-printcompilation`
: Reports additional information about just-in-time compilation, including the method names of compiled methods.

See also *jconsole*, *jps*, *jstatd*

jstatd

jstat daemon

Synopsis

```
jstatd options
```

Description

jstatd is a server that provides information about local Java processes to the *jps* and *jstat* programs running on remote hosts.

jstatd uses RMI and requires special security permissions to run successfully. To start *jstatd*, create the following file and name it *jstatd.policy*:

```
grant codebase "file:${java.home}../lib/tools.jar {
    permission java.security.AllPermission
}
```

This policy grants all permissions to any class loaded from the JDK's *tools.jar* JAR file. To launch *jstatd* with this policy, use this command line:

```
% jstatd -J-Djava.security.policy=jstat.policy
```

If an existing *rmiregistry* server is running, *jstatd* uses it. Otherwise, it creates its own RMI registry.

Options

`-n` *`rminame`*
: Binds the *jstatd* remote object to the name *rminame* in the RMI registry. The default name is "JStatRemoteHost", which is what *jps* and *jstat* look for. Use of this option requires *`rminame`* to be used in remote *jps* and *jstat* invocations.

`-nr`
: Tells `jstatd` that not to start an internal RMI registry if none are already running.

`-p` *`port`*
: Looks for an existing RMI registry on *`port`*, or starts one on that port if no existing registry is found.

See also *jps*, *jstat*

keytool

Key and Certificate Management Tool

Synopsis

```
keytool command options
```

Description

keytool manages and manipulates a *keystore*, a repository for public and private keys and public key certificates. *keytool* defines various commands for generating keys, importing data into the keystore, and exporting and displaying keystore data. Keys and certificates are stored in a keystore using a case-insensitive name or *alias*. *keytool* uses this alias to refer to a key or certificate.

The first option to *keytool* always specifies the basic command to be performed. Subsequent options provide details about how the command is to be performed. Only the command must be specified. If a command requires an option that does not have a default value, *keytool* prompts you interactively for the value.

Commands

`-certreq`
: Generates a certificate signing request in PKCS#10 format for the specified alias. The request is written to the specified file or to the standard output stream. The request should be sent to a certificate authority (CA), which authenticates the requestor and sends back a signed certificate authenticating the requestor's public key. This signed certificate can then be imported into the keystore with the `-import` command. This command uses the following options: `-alias`, `-file`, `-keypass`, `-keystore`, `-sigalg`, `-storepass`, `-storetype`, and `-v`.

`-delete`
: Deletes a specified alias from a specified keystore. This command uses the following options: `-alias`, `-keystore`, `-storepass`, `-storetype`, and `-v`.

`-export`
: Writes the certificate associated with the specified alias to the specified file or to standard output. This command uses the following options: `-alias`, `-file`, `-keystore`, `-rfc`, `-storepass`, `-storetype`, and `-v`.

`-genkey`
: Generates a public/private key pair and a self-signed X.509 certificate for the public key. Self-signed certificates are not often useful by themselves, so this command is often followed by `-certreq`. This command uses the following options: `-alias`, `-dname`, `-keyalg`, `-keypass`, `-keysize`, `-keystore`, `-sigalg`, `-storepass`, `-storetype`, `-v`, and `-validity`.

`-help`
: Lists all available *keytool* commands and their options. This command is not used with any other options.

`-identitydb`
: Reads keys and certificates from a legacy identity database managed with the deprecated *javakey* program and stores them into a keystore so that they can be manipulated by *keytool*. The identity database is read from the specified file or from standard input if no file is specified. The keys and certificates are written into the specified keystore file, which is automatically created if it does not exist yet. This command uses the following options: `-file`, `-keystore`, `-storepass`, `-storetype`, and `-v`.

`-import`
: Reads a certificate or PKCS#7-formatted certificate chain from a specified file or from standard input and stores it as a trusted certificate in the keystore with the specified alias. This command uses the following options: `-alias`, `-file`, `-keypass`, `-keystore`, `-noprompt`, `-storepass`, `-storetype`, `-trustcacerts`, and `-v`.

Java Tools

-keyclone
: Duplicates the keystore entry of a specified alias and stores it in the keystore under a new alias. This command uses the following options: -alias, -dest, -keypass, -keystore, -new, -storepass, -storetype, and -v.

-keypasswd
: Changes the password that encrypts the private key associated with a specified alias. This command uses the following options: -alias, -keypass, -new, -storetype, and -v.

-list
: Displays (on standard output) the fingerprint of the certificate associated with the specified alias. With the -v option, prints certificate details in human-readable format. With -rfc, prints certificate contents in a machine-readable, printable-encoding format. This command uses the following options: -alias, -keystore, -rfc, -storepass, -storetype, and -v.

-printcert
: Displays the contents of a certificate read from the specified file or from standard input. Unlike most *keytool* commands, this one does not use a keystore. This command uses the following options: -file and -v.

-selfcert
: Creates a self-signed certificate for the public key associated with the specified alias and uses it to replace any certificate or certificate chain already associated with that alias. This command uses the following options: -alias, -dname, -keypass, -keystore, -sigalg, -storepass, -storetype, -v, and -validity.

-storepasswd
: Changes the password that protects the integrity of the keystore as a whole. The new password must be at least six characters long. This command uses the following options: -keystore, -new, -storepass, -storetype, and -v.

Options

The various *keytool* commands can be passed various options from the following list. Many of these options have reasonable default values. *keytool* interactively prompts for any unspecified options that do not have defaults:

-alias *name*
: Specifies the alias to be manipulated in the keystore. The default is "mykey".

-dest *newalias*
: Specifies the new alias name (the destination alias) for the -keyclone command. If not specified, *keytool* prompts for a value.

-dname *X.500-distinguished-name*
: Specifies the X.500 distinguished name to appear on the certificate generated by -selfcert or -genkey. A distinguished name is a highly qualified name intended to be globally unique. For example:

```
CN=David Flanagan, OU=Editorial, O=OReilly, L=Cambridge, S=Massachusetts,
C=US
```

The -genkey command of *keytool* prompts for a distinguished name if none is specified. The -selfcert command uses the distinguished name of the current certificate if no replacement name is specified.

`-file` *`file`*
: Specifies the input or output file for many of the *keytool* commands. If left unspecified, *keytool* reads from the standard input or writes to the standard output.

`-keyalg` *`algorithm-name`*
: Used with `-genkey` to specify what type of cryptographic keys to generate. In the default Java implementation shipped from Sun, the only supported algorithm is "DSA"; this is the default if this option is omitted.

`-keypass` *`password`*
: Specifies the password that encrypts a private key in the keystore. If this option is unspecified, *keytool* first tries the `-storepass` password. If that does not work, it prompts for the appropriate password.

`-keysize` *`size`*
: Used with the `-genkey` command to specify the length in bits of the generated keys. If unspecified, the default is 1024.

`-keystore` *`filename`*
: Specifies the location of the keystore file. If unspecified, a file named *.keystore* in the user's home directory is used.

`-new` *`new-password-or-alias`*
: Used with the `-keyclone` command to specify the new alias name and with `-keypasswd` and `-storepasswd` to specify the new password. If unspecified, *keytool* prompts for the value of this option.

`-noprompt`
: Used with the `-import` command to disable interactive prompting of the user when a chain of trust cannot be established for an imported certificate. If this option is not specified, the `-import` command prompts the user.

`-rfc`
: Used with the `-list` and `-export` commands to specify that certificate output should be in the printable encoding format specified by RFC 1421. If this option is specified, `-export` outputs the certificate in binary format, and `-list` lists only the certificate fingerprint. This option cannot be combined with `-v` in the `-list` command.

`-sigalg` *`algorithm-name`*
: Specifies a digital signature algorithm that signs a certificate. If omitted, the default for this option depends on the type of underlying public key. If it is a DSA key, the default algorithm is "SHA1withDSA". If the key is an RSA key, the default signature algorithm is "MD5withRSA".

`-storepass` *`password`*
: Specifies a password that protects the integrity of the entire keystore file. This password also serves as a default password for any private keys that do not have their own `-keypass` specified. If `-storepass` is not specified, *keytool* prompts for it. The password must be at least six characters long.

`-storetype` *`type`*
: Specifies the type of the keystore to be used. If this option is not specified, the default is taken from the system security properties file. Often, the default is "JKS"—Sun's Java Keystore type.

`-trustcacerts`
: Used with the `-import` command to specify that the self-signed certificate authority certificates contained in the keystore in the *jre/lib/security/cacerts* file should be considered trusted. If this option is omitted, *keytool* ignores that file.

`-v`
: Specifies verbose mode, if present, and makes many *keytool* commands produce additional output.

`-validity` *`time`*
: Used with the `-genkey` and `-selfcert` commands to specify the period of validity (in days) of the generated certificate. If unspecified, the default is 90 days.

See also *jarsigner*, *policytool*

native2ascii

Convert text to ASCII with Unicode escapes

Synopsis

```
native2ascii [ options ] [ inputfile [ outputfile ]]
```

Description

native2ascii is a simple program that reads a text file (usually of Java source code) encoded using a local encoding and converts it to a Latin-1-plus-ASCII-encoded-Unicode form allowed by the Java Language Specification. This is helpful when you must edit a file of Java code but do not have an editor that can handle the encoding of the file.

The *`inputfile`* and *`outputfile`* are optional. If unspecified, standard input and standard output are used, making *native2ascii* suitable for use in pipes.

Options

`-encoding` *`encoding-name`*
: Specifies the encoding used by source files. If this option is not specified, the encoding is taken from the `file.encoding` system property.

`-reverse`
: Specifies that the conversion should be done in reverse—from encoded `\uxxxx` characters to characters in the native encoding.

See also `java.io.InputStreamReader`, `java.io.OutputStreamWriter`

pack200

Compress a JAR file

Synopsis

```
pack200 [options] outputfile jarfile
```

Description

pack200 tightly compresses a JAR file using the compression algorithm defined by JSR 200 and the standard gzip compression algorithm. Notice that the output file is specified on the command line before the input JAR file.

Basic options

All *pack200* options exist in both a long form that begins with a double dash and a single-letter form that begins with a single dash. When the option requires a value, the value should be separated from the long form of the option with an equals sign and no space or should immediately follow the short form with no intervening space or punctuation.

`--config-file=`*`file`*`, -f`*`file`*
: Reads options from the specified configuration file. *`file`* should be a `java.util.Properties` file in `name=value` format. Supported property names are the same as the long-form option names listed here, with with hyphens converted to periods.

`--effort=`*`value`*`, -E`*`value`*
: Specifies how hard to try to pack the JAR file. *`value`* must be a digit between 0 and 9. 0 means no compression at all and simply produces a copy of the input JAR file. The default is 5.

`--help, -h`
: Displays a help message and exits.

`--log-file=`*`file`*`, -l`*`file`*
: Log output to *`file`*.

`--no-gzip, -g`
: Tells *pack200* not to apply gzip compression to the packed JAR file. Use this option if you want to apply a different compression filter, such as *bzip2*. The default is `--gzip`.

`--no-keep-file-order, -o`
: Allows *pack200* to reorder the elements of the JAR file. `--keep-file-order` is the default.

`--quiet, -q`
: Suppresses output messages.

`--pass-file=`*`file`*`, -P`*`file`*
: Passes the specified *`file`* without compression. If *`file`* ends with a `/`, all files in the directory are passed through without packing. This option may be specified multiple times.

`--repack, -r`
: Packs the specified JAR file, and then immediately unpacks it. In this case, the *`outputfile`* specified on the command line should be the name of a JAR file. It is important to do a pack/unpack cycle on a JAR file before signing it with *jarsigner* because the pack/unpack cycle reorders some internal elements of a class file and invalidates any digital signatures or checksums in the JAR file manifest.

`--strip-debug, -G`
: Permanently strips debugging attributes from the Java class files instead of compressing them. This makes it harder to debug the resulting JAR file.

`--verbose, -v`
: Displays more output messages.

`--version, -V`
: Displays version number and exits.

Advanced packing options

The following options provide fine control over the compression performed by *pack200*.

`--deflate-hint=`*`value`*, `-H`*`value`*
: Specifies whether *pack200* should preserve the deflation status of each entry in the input JAR file. The default *`value`* is `keep`, which preserves the status. A *`value`* of `true` places a hint in the packed archive that the unpacker should deflate all entries after unpacking them. A *`value`* of `true` places a hint in the packed archive that the unpacker should store each entry in the JAR file without deflation. Using a value of `true` or `false` reduces the packed file size slightly because deflation hints do not need to be stored for each entry.

`--modification-time=`*`value`*, `-m`*`value`*
: With the default *`value`* of `keep`, *pack200* transmits the modification time of each entry in the JAR file. If you specify `latest` instead, only the most recent modification time is transmitted, and is applied to all entries when they are unpacked.

`--segment-limit=`*`n`*, `-S`*`n`*
: Sets a target segment size of *`n`*. Pack200 files may be divided into separately packed segments in order to reduce the amount of memory required by the unpacker. This option sets the approximate size of each segment. The default value is one million bytes. The value `-1` produces a single large segment, and the value 0 produces a single segment for each class file. Larger segment sizes result in better compression ratios, but require additional memory to unpack.

`--unknown-attribute=`*`action`*, `-U`*`action`*
: Specifies how *pack200* should handle unknown class file attributes. The default *`action`* is `pass`, which specifies that the entire class file will be transmitted with no compression. An *`action`* of `error` specifies that *pack200* should produce an error message. An *action* of `strip` says that the attribute should be stripped from the class file.

`--class-attribute=`*`name=action`*, `-C`*`name=action`*,

`--code-attribute=`*`name=action`*, `-D`*`name=action`*,

`--field-attribute=`*`name=action`*, `-F`*`name=action`*,

`--method-attribute=`*`name=action`*, `-M`*`name=action`*,
: These four options specify how *pack200* should handle specific named class, field, method, and code attributes in a class file. The name of the attribute is specified by *`name`*. The *`action`* may be any of the `pass`, `strip`, and `error` values supported by the `--unknown-attribute` option. The *`action`* may also be a "layout string" that specifies how the attribute should be packed. See the Pack200 specification for details on the layout language. These options may be repeated to specify handling for more than one attribute.

See also *unpack200*

---

policytool
Policy File Creation and Management Tool

Synopsis

```
policytool
```

Description

policytool displays a Swing user interface that makes it easy to edit security policy configuration files. The Java security architecture is based on policy files, which specify sets of permissions to be granted to code from various sources. By default, the Java security policy is defined by a system policy file stored in the *jre/lib/security/java.policy* file and a user policy file stored in the *.java.policy* file in the user's home directory. System administrators and users can edit these files with a text editor, but the syntax of the file is somewhat complex, so it is usually easier to use *policytool* to define and edit security policies.

Selecting the policy file to edit

When *policytool* starts up, it opens the *.java.policy* file in the user's home directory by default. Use the New, Open, and Save commands in the File menu to create a new policy file, open an existing file, and save an edited file, respectively.

Editing the policy file

The main *policytool* window displays a list of the entries contained in the policy file. Each entry specifies a code source and the permissions that are to be granted to code from that source. The window also contains buttons that allow you to add a new entry, edit an existing entry, or delete an entry from the policy file. If you add or edit an entry, *policytool* opens a new window that displays the details of that policy entry.

With the addition of the JAAS API to the core Java platform in Java 1.4, *policytool* allows the specification of a `Principal` to whom a set of permissions is granted.

Every policy file has an associated keystore from which it obtains the certificates it needs when verifying the digital signatures of Java code. You can usually rely on the default keystore, but if you need to specify the keystore explicitly for a policy file, use the Change Keystore command in the Edit menu of the main *policytool* window.

Adding or editing a policy entry

The policy entry editor window displays the code source for the policy entry and a list of permissions associated with that code source. It also contains buttons that allow you to add a new permission, delete a permission, or edit an existing permission.

When defining a new policy entry, the first step is to specify the code source. A code source is defined by a URL from which the code is downloaded and/or a list of digital signatures that must appear on the code. Specify one or both of these values by typing in a URL and/or a comma-separated list of aliases. These aliases identify trusted certificates in the keystore associated with the policy file.

After you have defined the code source for a policy entry, you must define the permissions to be granted to code from that source. Use the Add Permission and Edit Permission buttons to add and edit permissions. These buttons bring up yet another *policytool* window.

Defining a permission

To define a permission in the permission editor window, first select the desired permission type from the Permission pulldown menu, then select an appropriate target value from the Target Name menu. The choices in this menu are customized depending on the permission type you selected. Some types of permissions, such as `FilePermission`, do not have a fixed set of possible targets, and you usually have to type in the target you want. For example, you might type "/tmp" to specify the directory */tmp*, "/tmp/*" to specify all the files in that directory, or "/tmp/-" to specify all the files in the directory, and, recursively, any subdirectories. See the documentation of the individual `Permission` classes for a description of the targets they support.

Depending on the type of permission you select, you may also have to select one or more action values from the Actions menu. When you have selected a permission and appropriate target and action values, click the Okay button to dismiss the window.

See also *jarsigner*, *keytool*

serialver

Class Version Number Generator

Synopsis

```
serialver [ -classpath path ] classnames...
serialver [ -classpath path ] -show
```

Description

serialver displays the version number of a class or classes. This version number is used for the purposes of serialization: the version number must change each time the serialization format of the class changes.

If the specified class declares a `long serialVersionUID` constant, the value of that field is displayed. Otherwise, a unique version number is computed by applying the Secure Hash Algorithm (SHA) to the API defined by the class. This program is primarily useful for computing an initial unique version number for a class, which is then declared as a constant in the class. The output of *serialver* is a line of legal Java code, suitable for pasting into a class definition.

Options

`-classpath` *path*

Specifies the search path for classes.

`-show`

When the `-show` option is specified, *serialver* displays a simple graphical interface that allows the user to type in a single class name at a time and obtain its serialization UID. When using `-show`, no class names can be specified on the command line.

Environment

`CLASSPATH`

serialver is written in Java, so it is sensitive to the `CLASSPATH` environment variable in the same way the *java* interpreter is. The specified classes are looked up relative to this classpath.

See also `java.io.ObjectStreamClass`

unpack200

Unpack a JAR file

Synopsis

```
unpack200 [options] packedfile jarfile
```

Description

unpack200 unpacks a JAR file that has been compressed, or *packed*, by the *pack200* tool, and optionally additionally compressed with *gzip*. Specify the name of the packed file and the name of the JAR file to unpack it to on the command line.

Because *unpack200* is used as part of the Java installation process, it is a native application that can run on a system without a Java interpreter.

Options

All `unpack200` options exist in both a long form that begins with a double dash and a single-letter form that begins with a single dash. When the option requires a value, the value should be separated from the long form of the option with an equals sign and no space or should immediately follow the short form with no intervening space or punctuation.

`--deflate-hint=`*`value`* `-H`*`value`*
: Specifies whether *unpack200* should compress individual entries in the resulting JAR file. *`value`* must be `true`, `false`, or `keep`. The default is `keep`, which specifies that each JAR entry should have the same compression that it had in the original JAR file.

`--help, -h`
: Displays a help message and exits.

`--log-file=`*`file`*`, -l`*`file`*
: Logs output to *`file`*.

`--quiet, -q`
: Suppresses output messages.

`--remove-pack-file, -r`
: Deletes the packed file after unpacking it.

`--verbose, -v`
: Displays more output messages.

`--version, -V`
: Displays version number and exits.

See also *jar*, *pack200*

Java Tools

API Quick Reference

Part II provides quick-reference material for the essential APIs of the Java platform. Please read the following section, *How to Use This Quick Reference*, to learn how to get the most out of this material.

How to Use This Quick Reference

The quick-reference section that follows packs a lot of information into a small space. This introduction explains how to get the most out of that information. It describes how the quick reference is organized and how to read the individual quick-reference entries.

Finding a Quick-Reference Entry

The quick reference is organized into chapters, each of which documents a single package of the Java platform or a group of related packages. Packages are listed alphabetically within and between chapters, so you never really need to know which chapter documents which package: you can simply search alphabetically, as you might do in a dictionary. The documentation for each package begins with a quick-reference entry for the package itself. This entry includes a short overview of the package and a listing of the classes and interfaces included in the package. In this listing of package contents, package members are first grouped by general category (interfaces, eumerated types, classes and exceptions, for example). Within each category, they are grouped by class hierarchy, with indentation to indicate the level of the hierarchy. Finally, classes and interfaces at the same hierarchy level are listed alphabetically.

Each package overview is followed by individual quick-reference entries, in alphabetical order, for the types defined in the package. The overall organization of the quick-reference is therefore alphabetical by the fully-qualified name of the type. To look up a quick-reference entry for a particular type, you must also know the name of the package that defines that type. Use the dictionary-style headers on the upper corner of each page to help you quickly find the package and class you need.

Usually, the package name of a type is obvious from its context, and you should have no trouble looking up the quick-reference entry you want. Occasionally, you may need to look up a type for which you do not already know the package. In this case, refer to the *Class, Method, and Field Index*. This index allows you to look up a class by class name and find out what package it is part of.

Reading a Quick-Reference Entry

The quick-reference entries for classes and interfaces contain quite a bit of information. The sections that follow describe the structure of a quick-reference entry, explaining what information is available, where it is found, and what it means. While reading the descriptions that follow, you may find it helpful to flip through the reference section itself to find examples of the features being described.

Class Name, Package Name, Availability, and Flags

Each quick-reference entry begins with a four-part title that specifies the name, package name, and availability of the class, and may also specify various additional flags that describe the class. The class name appears in bold at the upper left of the title. The package name appears, in smaller print, in the lower left, below the class name.

The upper-right portion of the title indicates the availability of the class; it specifies the earliest release that contained the class. If a class was introduced in Java 1.1, for example, this portion of the title reads "Java 1.1". The availability section of the title is also used to indicate whether a class has been deprecated, and, if so, in what release. For example, it might read "Java 1.1; Deprecated in Java 1.2".

In the lower-right corner of the title you may find a list of flags that describe the class. Java 5.0 annotations and meta-annotations are listed here, as are the following flags:

annotation
: The type is an annotation type.

appendable
: The class implements `java.lang.Appendable`.

checked
: The class is a checked exception, meaning that it extends `java.lang.Exception`, but not `java.lang.RuntimeException`. In other words, it must be declared in the `throws` clause of any method that may throw it.

cloneable
: The class, or a superclass, implements `java.lang.Cloneable`.

closeable
: The class implements `java.io.Closeable`.

collection
: The class, or a superclass, implements `java.util.Collection` or `java.util.Map`.

comparable
: The class, or a superclass, implements `java.lang.Comparable`.

enum
: The type is an enumerated type.

error

The class extends `java.lang.Error`.

flushable

The class implements `java.io.Flushable`.

readable

The class implements `java.lang.Readable`.

runnable

The class, or a superclass, implements `java.lang.Runnable`.

serializable

The class, or a superclass, implements `java.io.Serializable`.

unchecked

The class is an unchecked exception, meaning that it extends `java.lang.RuntimeException` and therefore does not need to be declared in the `throws` clause of a method that may throw it.

Description

The title of each quick-reference entry is followed by a short description of the most important features of the class or interface. This description is typically about two paragraphs long.

Hierarchy

If a class or interface has a nontrivial class hierarchy, the "Description" section is followed by a figure that illustrates the hierarchy and helps you understand the class in the context of that hierarchy. The name of each class or interface in the diagram appears in a box; classes and enumerated types appear in rectangles (except for abstract classes, which appear in skewed rectangles or parallelograms). Interfaces and annotation types appear in rounded rectangles, in which the corners have been replaced by arcs. The current class—the one that is the subject of the diagram—appears in a box that is bolder than the others. The boxes are connected by lines: solid lines indicate an "extends" relationship, and dotted lines indicate an "implements" relationship. The superclass-to-subclass hierarchy reads from left to right in the top row (or only row) of boxes in the figure. Interfaces are usually positioned beneath the classes that implement them, although in simple cases an interface is sometimes positioned on the same line as the class that implements it, resulting in a more compact figure. Note that the hierarchy figure shows only the superclasses of a class. If a class has subclasses, those are listed in the cross-reference section at the end of the quick-reference entry for the class.

Synopsis

The most important part of every quick-reference entry is the synopsis, which follows the title and description. The synopsis for a type looks a lot like the source code for the type, except that the method bodies are omitted and some additional annotations are added. If you know Java syntax, you know how to read the synopsis.

The first line of the synopsis contains information about the class itself. It begins with a list of modifiers, such as `public`, `abstract`, and `final`. These modifiers are followed by the `class`, `interface`, `enum`, or `@interface` keyword and then by the name of the class. The class name may be followed by type variables, an `extends` clause that specifies the superclass, and an `implements` clause that specifies any interfaces the class implements.

The class definition line is followed by a list of the fields, methods, and nested types that the class defines. Once again, if you understand basic Java syntax, you should have no trouble making sense of these lines. The listing for each member includes the modifiers, type, and name of the member. For methods, the synopsis also includes the type and name of each method parameter and an optional `throws` clause that lists the exceptions the method can throw. The member names are in boldface, so it is easy to scan the list of members looking for the one you want. The names of method parameters are in italics to indicate that they are not to be used literally. The member listings are printed on alternating gray and white backgrounds to keep them visually separate.

Member availability and flags

Each member listing is a single line that defines the API for that member. These listings use Java syntax, so their meaning is immediately clear to any Java programmer. There is some auxiliary information associated with each member synopsis that requires explanation, however.

Recall that each quick-reference entry begins with a title section that includes the release in which the class was first defined. When a member is introduced into a class after the initial release of the class, the version in which the member was introduced appears, in small print, to the left of the member synopsis. For example, if a class was first introduced in Java 1.1, but had a new method added in Java 1.2 the title contains the string "1.1", and the listing for the new member is preceded by the number "1.2". Furthermore, if a member has been deprecated, that fact is indicated with a hash mark (#) to the left of the member synopsis.

The area to the right of the member synopsis is used to display a variety of flags that provide additional information about the member. Some of these flags indicate additional specification details that do not appear in the member API itself. Other flags contain implementation-specific information. This information can be quite useful in understanding the class and in debugging your code, but be aware that it may differ between implementations. The implementation-specific flags displayed in this book are based on Sun's Linux implementation of Java.

The following flags may be displayed to the right of a member synopsis:

native
: An implementation-specific flag that indicates that a method is implemented in native code. Although `native` is a Java keyword and can appear in method

signatures, it is part of the method implementation, not part of its specification. Therefore, this information is included with the member flags, rather than as part of the member listing. This flag is useful as a hint about the expected performance of a method.

synchronized
An implementation-specific flag that indicates that a method implementation is declared `synchronized`, meaning that it obtains a lock on the object or class before executing. Like the `native` keyword, the `synchronized` keyword is part of the method implementation, not part of the specification, so it appears as a flag, not in the method synopsis itself. This flag is a useful hint that the method is probably implemented in a threadsafe manner.

Whether or not a method is thread-safe is part of the method specification, and this information *should* appear (although it often does not) in the method documentation. There are a number of different ways to make a method threadsafe, however, and declaring the method with the `synchronized` keyword is only one possible implementation. In other words, a method that does not bear the `synchronized` flag can still be threadsafe.

Overrides:
This flag indicates that a method overrides a method in one of its superclasses. The flag is followed by the name of the superclass that the method overrides. This is a specification detail, not an implementation detail. As we'll see in the next section, overriding methods are usually grouped together in their own section of the class synopsis. The `Overrides:` flag is only used when an overriding method is not grouped in that way.

Implements:
This flag indicates that a method implements a method in an interface. The flag is followed by the name of the interface that is implemented. This is a specification detail, not an implementation detail. As we'll see in the next section, methods that implement an interface are usually grouped into a special section of the class synopsis. The `Implements:` flag is only used for methods that are not grouped in this way.

empty
This flag indicates that the implementation of the method has an empty body. This can be a hint to the programmer that the method may need to be overridden in a subclass.

constant
An implementation-specific flag that indicates that a method has a trivial implementation. Only methods with a `void` return type can be truly empty. Any method declared to return a value must have at least a `return` statement. The `constant` flag indicates that the method implementation is empty except for a `return` statement that returns a constant value. Such a method might have a body like `return null;` or `return false;`. Like the `empty` flag, this flag may indicate that a method needs to be overridden.

default:
This flag is used with property accessor methods that read the value of a property (i.e., methods whose names begins with get and take no argu-

ments). The flag is followed by the default value of the property. Strictly speaking, default property values are a specification detail. In practice, however, these defaults are not always documented, and care should be taken, because the default values may change between implementations.

Not all property accessors have a default: flag. A default value is determined by dynamically loading the class in question, instantiating it using a no-argument constructor, and then calling the method to find out what it returns. This technique can be used only on classes that can be dynamically loaded and instantiated and that have no-argument constructors, so default values are shown for those classes only. Furthermore, note that when a class is instantiated using a different constructor, the default values for its properties may be different.

= For `static final` fields, this flag is followed by the constant value of the field. Only constants of primitive and `String` types and constants with the value `null` are displayed. Some constant values are specification details, while others are implementation details. The reason that symbolic constants are defined, however, is so you can write code that does not rely directly upon the constant value. Use this flag to help you understand the class, but do not rely upon the constant values in your own programs.

Functional grouping of members

Within a class synopsis, the members are not listed in strict alphabetical order. Instead, they are broken down into functional groups and listed alphabetically within each group. Constructors, methods, fields, and inner classes are all listed separately. Instance methods are kept separate from static (class) methods. Constants are separated from non-constant fields. Public members are listed separately from protected members. Grouping members by category breaks a class down into smaller, more comprehensible segments, making the class easier to understand. This grouping also makes it easier for you to find a desired member.

Functional groups are separated from each other in a class synopsis with Java comments, such as `// Public Constructors`, `// Inner Classes`, and `// Methods Implementing DataInput`. The various functional categories are as follows (in the order in which they appear in a class synopsis):

Constructors
Displays the constructors for the class. Public constructors and protected constructors are displayed separately in subgroupings. If a class defines no constructor at all, the Java compiler adds a default no-argument constructor that is displayed here. If a class defines only private constructors, it cannot be instantiated, so a special, empty grouping entitled "No Constructor" indicates this fact. Constructors are listed first because the first thing you do with most classes is instantiate them by calling a constructor.

Constants
Displays all of the constants (i.e., fields that are declared `static` and `final`) defined by the class. Public and protected constants are displayed in separate subgroups. Constants are listed here, near the top of the class synopsis,

because constant values are often used throughout the class as legal values for method parameters and return values.

Inner classes
: Groups all of the inner classes and interfaces defined by the class or interface. For each inner class, there is a single-line synopsis. Each inner class also has its own quick-reference entry that includes a full class synopsis for the inner class. Like constants, inner classes are listed near the top of the class synopsis because they are often used by a number of other members of the class.

Static methods
: Lists the static methods (class methods) of the class, broken down into subgroups for public static methods and protected static methods.

Event listener registration methods
: Lists the public instance methods that register and deregister event listener objects with the class. The names of these methods begin with the words "add" and "remove" and end in "Listener". These methods are always passed a `java.util.EventListener` object. The methods are typically defined in pairs, so the pairs are listed together. The methods are listed alphabetically by event name rather than by method name.

Public instance methods
: Contains all of the public instance methods that are not grouped elsewhere.

Implementing methods
: Groups the methods that implement the same interface. There is one subgroup for each interface implemented by the class. Methods that are defined by the same interface are almost always related to each other, so this is a useful functional grouping of methods. If a class is modified so that it implements an interface after its initial release, the methods of that interface will be grouped here, but will also appear in the "Public Instance methods" section.

Overriding methods
: Groups the methods that override methods of a superclass broken down into subgroups by superclass. This is typically a useful grouping, because it helps to make it clear how a class modifies the default behavior of its superclasses. In practice, it is also often true that methods that override the same superclass are functionally related to each other.

Protected instance methods
: Contains all of the protected instance methods that are not grouped elsewhere.

Fields
: Lists all the nonconstant fields of the class, breaking them down into subgroups for public and protected static fields and public and protected instance fields. Many classes do not define any publicly accessible fields. For those that do, many object-oriented programmers prefer not to use those fields directly, but instead to use accessor methods when such methods are available.

Deprecated members
: Deprecated methods and deprecated fields are grouped at the very bottom of the class synopsis. Use of these members is strongly discouraged.

Cross-References

The synopsis section of a quick-reference entry is followed by a number of optional cross-reference sections that indicate other, related classes and methods that may be of interest. These sections are the following:

Subclasses
: This section lists the subclasses of this class, if there are any.

Implementations
: This section lists classes that implement this interface.

Passed To
: This section lists all of the methods and constructors that are passed an object of this type as an argument. This is useful when you have an object of a given type and want to figure out what you can do with it. Methods defined by this type itself are not included in the list.

Returned By
: This section lists all of the methods (but not constructors) that return an object of this type. This is useful when you know that you want to work with an object of this type, but don't know how to obtain one. Methods of this type itself are excluded.

Thrown By
: For checked exception classes, this section lists all of the methods and constructors that throw exceptions of this type. This material helps you figure out when a given exception or error may be thrown. Note, however, that this section is based on the exception types listed in the `throws` clauses of methods and constructors. Subclasses of `RuntimeException` and `Error` do not have to be listed in `throws` clauses, so it is not possible to generate a complete cross-reference of methods that throw these types of unchecked exceptions.

Type Of
: This section lists all of the fields and constants that are of this type, which can help you figure out how to obtain an object of this type. If the type defines self-typed fields or constants, they are not included on this list.

A Note About Class Names

Throughout the quick reference, you'll notice that classes are sometimes referred to by class name alone and at other times referred to by class name and package name. If package names were always used, the class synopses would become long and hard to read. On the other hand, if package names were never used, it would sometimes be difficult to know what class was being referred to. The rules for including or omitting the package name are complex. They can be summarized approximately as follows, however:

- If the class name alone is ambiguous, the package name is always used. The name `Annotation` is ambiguous, for example, because it can refer to either `java.lang.annotation.Annotation` or `java.text.Annotation`.
- If the class is part of the `java.lang` package or is a very commonly used class, such as `java.io.Serializable`, the package name is omitted.
- If the class being referred to is part of the current package (and has a quick-reference entry in the current chapter), the package name is omitted.

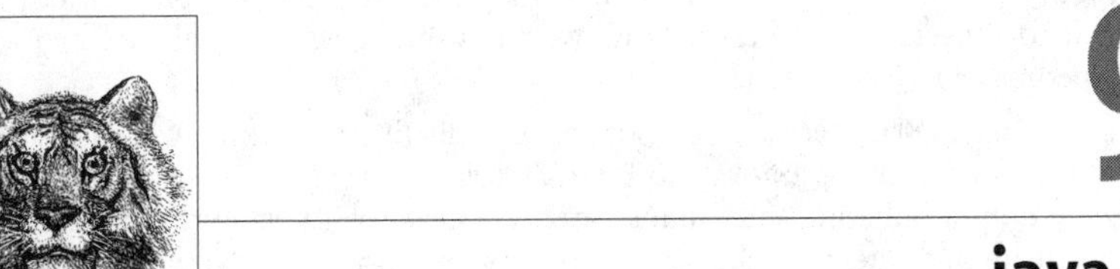

9
java.io

Package java.io **Java 1.0**

The java.io package is large, but most of the classes it contains fall into a well-structured hierarchy. Most of the package consists of byte streams—subclasses of InputStream or OutputStream and character streams—subclasses of Reader or Writer. Each of these stream subtypes has a specific purpose, and, despite its size, java.io is a straightforward package to understand and to use. In Java 1.4, the java.io package was complemented by a "New I/O API" defined in the java.nio package and its subpackages. The java.nio package is totally new, although it included some compatibility with the classes in this package. It was designed for high-performance I/O, particularly for use in servers and has a lower-level API than this package does. The I/O facilities of java.io are still quite adequate for most of the I/O required by typical client-side applications.

Before we consider the stream classes that comprise the bulk of this package, let's examine the important nonstream classes. File represents a file or directory name in a system-independent way and provides methods for listing directories, querying file attributes, and renaming and deleting files. FilenameFilter is an interface that defines a method that accepts or rejects specified filenames. It is used by File to specify what types of files should be included in directory listings. RandomAccessFile allows you to read from or write to arbitrary locations of a file. Often, though, you'll prefer sequential access to a file and should use one of the stream classes.

InputStream and OutputStream are abstract classes that define methods for reading and writing bytes. Their subclasses allow bytes to be read from and written to a variety of sources and sinks. FileInputStream and FileOutputStream read from and write to files. ByteArrayInputStream and ByteArrayOutputStream read from and write to an array of bytes in memory. PipedInputStream reads bytes from a PipedOutputStream, and PipedOutputStream writes bytes to a PipedInputStream. These classes work together to implement a *pipe* for communication between threads.

FilterInputStream and FilterOutputStream are special; they filter input and output bytes. When you create a FilterInputStream, you specify an InputStream for it to filter. When you call the read() method of a FilterInputStream, it calls the read() method of its InputStream, processes the bytes it reads, and returns the filtered bytes. Similarly, when you create a FilterOutputStream, you specify an OutputStream to be filtered. Calling the write() method of a FilterOutputStream causes it to process your bytes in some way and then pass those filtered bytes to the write() method of its OutputStream.

FilterInputStream and FilterOutputStream do not perform any filtering themselves; this is done by their subclasses. BufferedInputStream and BufferedOutputStream are filtered streams that provide input and output buffering and can increase I/O efficiency. DataInputStream reads raw bytes from a stream and interprets them in various binary formats. It has various methods to read primitive Java data types in their standard binary formats. DataOutputStream allows you to write Java primitive data types in binary format. The ObjectInputStream and ObjectOutputStream classes are special. These byte-stream classes are used for serializing and deserializing the internal state of objects for storage or interprocess communication.

The byte streams just described are complemented by an analogous set of character input and output streams. Reader is the superclass of all character input streams, and Writer is the superclass of all character output streams. Most of the Reader and Writer streams have obvious byte-stream analogs. BufferedReader is a commonly used stream; it provides buffering for efficiency and also has a readLine() method to read a line of text at a time. PrintWriter is another very common stream; its methods allow output of a textual representation of any primitive Java type or of any object (via the object's toString() method).

Java 5.0 adds the Closeable and Flushable interfaces to identify types that have close() and flush() methods. All streams have a close() method and implement the Closeable interface. And all byte and character output streams have a flush() method and implement Flushable. In a related change, all character output streams (and the byte stream PrintStream) implement the (new in Java 5.0) interface java.lang.Appendable, making them suitable for use with the java.util.Formatter class. Similarly, all character input streams implement the java.lang.Readable interface, making them suitable for use with the java.util.Scanner class. Finally, both PrintStream and PrintWriter have been enhanced in two ways for Java 5.0. Both now include constructors for creating a stream that writes directly to a file. And both include formatted-text output methods printf() and format(). See java.util.Formatter for details.

Interfaces

public interface **Closeable**;
public interface **DataInput**;
public interface **DataOutput**;
public interface **Externalizable** extends Serializable;
public interface **FileFilter**;
public interface **FilenameFilter**;
public interface **Flushable**;
public interface **ObjectInput** extends DataInput;
public interface **ObjectInputValidation**;
public interface **ObjectOutput** extends DataOutput;
public interface **ObjectStreamConstants**;
public interface **Serializable**;

Classes

public class **File** implements Serializable, Comparable<File>;
public final class **FileDescriptor**;
public final class **FilePermission** extends java.security.Permission implements Serializable;
public abstract class **InputStream** implements Closeable;
  public class **ByteArrayInputStream** extends InputStream;
  public class **FileInputStream** extends InputStream;

public class **FilterInputStream** extends InputStream;
public class **BufferedInputStream** extends FilterInputStream;
public class **DataInputStream** extends FilterInputStream implements DataInput;
public class **LineNumberInputStream** extends FilterInputStream;
public class **PushbackInputStream** extends FilterInputStream;
public class **ObjectInputStream** extends InputStream implements ObjectInput, ObjectStreamConstants;
public class **PipedInputStream** extends InputStream;
public class **SequenceInputStream** extends InputStream;
public class **StringBufferInputStream** extends InputStream;
public abstract static class **ObjectInputStream.GetField**;
public abstract static class **ObjectOutputStream.PutField**;
public class **ObjectStreamClass** implements Serializable;
public class **ObjectStreamField** implements Comparable<Object>;
public abstract class **OutputStream** implements Closeable, Flushable;
public class **ByteArrayOutputStream** extends OutputStream;
public class **FileOutputStream** extends OutputStream;
public class **FilterOutputStream** extends OutputStream;
public class **BufferedOutputStream** extends FilterOutputStream;
public class **DataOutputStream** extends FilterOutputStream implements DataOutput;
public class **PrintStream** extends FilterOutputStream implements Appendable, Closeable;
public class **ObjectOutputStream** extends OutputStream implements ObjectOutput, ObjectStreamConstants;
public class **PipedOutputStream** extends OutputStream;
public class **RandomAccessFile** implements Closeable, DataInput, DataOutput;
public abstract class **Reader** implements Closeable, Readable;
public class **BufferedReader** extends Reader;
public class **LineNumberReader** extends BufferedReader;
public class **CharArrayReader** extends Reader;
public abstract class **FilterReader** extends Reader;
public class **PushbackReader** extends FilterReader;
public class **InputStreamReader** extends Reader;
public class **FileReader** extends InputStreamReader;
public class **PipedReader** extends Reader;
public class **StringReader** extends Reader;
public final class **SerializablePermission** extends java.security.BasicPermission;
public class **StreamTokenizer**;
public abstract class **Writer** implements Appendable, Closeable, Flushable;
public class **BufferedWriter** extends Writer;
public class **CharArrayWriter** extends Writer;
public abstract class **FilterWriter** extends Writer;
public class **OutputStreamWriter** extends Writer;
public class **FileWriter** extends OutputStreamWriter;
public class **PipedWriter** extends Writer;
public class **PrintWriter** extends Writer;
public class **StringWriter** extends Writer;

Exceptions

public class **IOException** extends Exception;
public class **CharConversionException** extends IOException;
public class **EOFException** extends IOException;
public class **FileNotFoundException** extends IOException;
public class **InterruptedIOException** extends IOException;
public abstract class **ObjectStreamException** extends IOException;
public class **InvalidClassException** extends ObjectStreamException;

```
        public class InvalidObjectException extends ObjectStreamException;
        public class NotActiveException extends ObjectStreamException;
        public class NotSerializableException extends ObjectStreamException;
        public class OptionalDataException extends ObjectStreamException;
        public class StreamCorruptedException extends ObjectStreamException;
        public class WriteAbortedException extends ObjectStreamException;
    public class SyncFailedException extends IOException;
    public class UnsupportedEncodingException extends IOException;
    public class UTFDataFormatException extends IOException;
```

BufferedInputStream — Java 1.0

java.io — closeable

This class is a FilterInputStream that provides input data buffering; efficiency is increased by reading in a large amount of data and storing it in an internal buffer. When data is requested, it is usually available from the buffer. Thus, most calls to read data do not actually have to read data from a disk, network, or other slow source. Create a BufferedInputStream by specifying the InputStream that is to be buffered in the call to the constructor. See also BufferedReader.

Object — InputStream — FilterInputStream — BufferedInputStream
Closeable

```
public class BufferedInputStream extends FilterInputStream {
// Public Constructors
    public BufferedInputStream(InputStream in);
    public BufferedInputStream(InputStream in, int size);
// Public Methods Overriding FilterInputStream
    public int available() throws IOException;                       synchronized
1.2 public void close() throws IOException;
    public void mark(int readlimit);                                 synchronized
    public boolean markSupported();                                  constant
    public int read() throws IOException;                            synchronized
    public int read(byte[] b, int off, int len) throws IOException;  synchronized
    public void reset() throws IOException;                          synchronized
    public long skip(long n) throws IOException;                     synchronized
// Protected Instance Fields
    protected volatile byte[] buf;
    protected int count;
    protected int marklimit;
    protected int markpos;
    protected int pos;
}
```

BufferedOutputStream — Java 1.0

java.io — closeable flushable

This class is a FilterOutputStream that provides output data buffering; output efficiency is increased by storing values to be written in a buffer and actually writing them out only when the buffer fills up or when the flush() method is called. Create a BufferedOutputStream by specifying the OutputStream that is to be buffered in the call to the constructor. See also BufferedWriter.

Object — OutputStream — FilterOutputStream — BufferedOutputStream
Closeable Flushable

```
public class BufferedOutputStream extends FilterOutputStream {
// Public Constructors
    public BufferedOutputStream(OutputStream out);
    public BufferedOutputStream(OutputStream out, int size);
// Public Methods Overriding FilterOutputStream
    public void flush() throws IOException;                                synchronized
    public void write(int b) throws IOException;                           synchronized
    public void write(byte[] b, int off, int len) throws IOException;      synchronized
// Protected Instance Fields
    protected byte[] buf;
    protected int count;
}
```

BufferedReader — Java 1.1

java.io — readable closeable

This class applies buffering to a character input stream, thereby improving the efficiency of character input. You create a **BufferedReader** by specifying some other character input stream from which it is to buffer input. (You can also specify a buffer size at this time, although the default size is usually fine.) Typically, you use this sort of buffering with a **FileReader** or **InputStreamReader**. **BufferedReader** defines the standard set of **Reader** methods and provides a **readLine()** method that reads a line of text (not including the line terminator) and returns it as a **String**. **BufferedReader** is the character-stream analog of **BufferedInputStream**. It also provides a replacement for the deprecated **readLine()** method of **DataInputStream**, which did not properly convert bytes into characters.

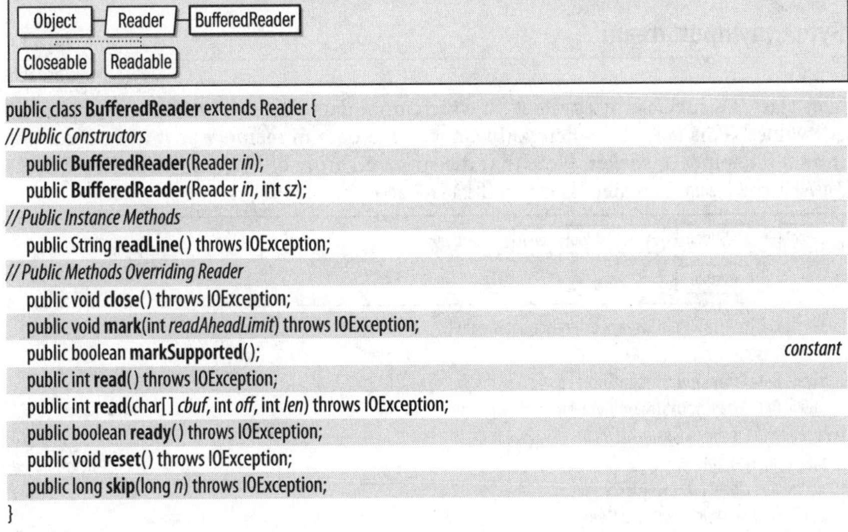


```
public class BufferedReader extends Reader {
// Public Constructors
    public BufferedReader(Reader in);
    public BufferedReader(Reader in, int sz);
// Public Instance Methods
    public String readLine() throws IOException;
// Public Methods Overriding Reader
    public void close() throws IOException;
    public void mark(int readAheadLimit) throws IOException;
    public boolean markSupported();                                        constant
    public int read() throws IOException;
    public int read(char[] cbuf, int off, int len) throws IOException;
    public boolean ready() throws IOException;
    public void reset() throws IOException;
    public long skip(long n) throws IOException;
}
```

Subclasses LineNumberReader

BufferedWriter — Java 1.1

java.io — appendable closeable flushable

This class applies buffering to a character output stream, improving output efficiency by coalescing many small write requests into a single larger request. You create a BufferedWriter by specifying some other character output stream to which it sends its buffered and coalesced output. (You can also specify a buffer size at this time, although the default size is usually satisfactory.) Typically, you use this sort of buffering with a FileWriter or OutputStreamWriter. BufferedWriter defines the standard write(), flush(), and close() methods all output streams define, but it adds a newLine() method that outputs the platform-dependent line separator (usually a newline character, a carriage-return character, or both) to the stream. BufferedWriter is the character-stream analog of BufferedOutputStream.

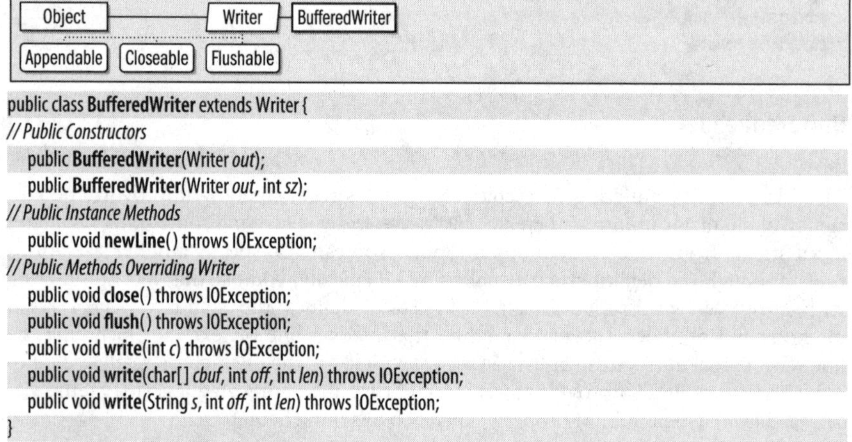


```
public class BufferedWriter extends Writer {
// Public Constructors
   public BufferedWriter(Writer out);
   public BufferedWriter(Writer out, int sz);
// Public Instance Methods
   public void newLine() throws IOException;
// Public Methods Overriding Writer
   public void close() throws IOException;
   public void flush() throws IOException;
   public void write(int c) throws IOException;
   public void write(char[] cbuf, int off, int len) throws IOException;
   public void write(String s, int off, int len) throws IOException;
}
```

ByteArrayInputStream — Java 1.0

java.io — closeable

This class is a subclass of InputStream in which input data comes from a specified array of byte values. This is useful when you want to read data in memory as if it were coming from a file, pipe, or socket. Note that the specified array of bytes is not copied when a ByteArrayInputStream is created. See also CharArrayReader.

Object — InputStream — ByteArrayInputStream
Closeable

```
public class ByteArrayInputStream extends InputStream {
// Public Constructors
   public ByteArrayInputStream(byte[] buf);
   public ByteArrayInputStream(byte[] buf, int offset, int length);
// Public Methods Overriding InputStream
   public int available();                                        synchronized
1.2 public void close() throws IOException;                        empty
1.1 public void mark(int readAheadLimit);
1.1 public boolean markSupported();                                constant
   public int read();                                              synchronized
   public int read(byte[] b, int off, int len);                    synchronized
   public void reset();                                            synchronized
```

```
    public long skip(long n);                                         synchronized
// Protected Instance Fields
    protected byte[] buf;
    protected int count;
1.1 protected int mark;
    protected int pos;
}
```

ByteArrayOutputStream Java 1.0

java.io closeable flushable

This class is a subclass of **OutputStream** in which output data is stored in an internal **byte** array. The internal array grows as necessary and can be retrieved with **toByteArray()** or **toString()**. The **reset()** method discards any data currently stored in the internal array and stores data from the beginning again. See also **CharArrayWriter**.

Object ─ OutputStream ─ ByteArrayOutputStream
Closeable, Flushable

```
public class ByteArrayOutputStream extends OutputStream {
// Public Constructors
    public ByteArrayOutputStream();
    public ByteArrayOutputStream(int size);
// Public Instance Methods
    public void reset();                                              synchronized
    public int size();
    public byte[] toByteArray();                                      synchronized
1.1 public String toString(String enc) throws UnsupportedEncodingException;
    public void writeTo(OutputStream out) throws IOException;         synchronized
// Public Methods Overriding OutputStream
1.2 public void close() throws IOException;                           empty
    public void write(int b);                                         synchronized
    public void write(byte[] b, int off, int len);                    synchronized
// Public Methods Overriding Object
    public String toString();
// Protected Instance Fields
    protected byte[] buf;
    protected int count;
// Deprecated Public Methods
#   public String toString(int hibyte);
}
```

CharArrayReader Java 1.1

java.io readable closeable

This class is a character input stream that uses a character array as the source of the characters it returns. You create a **CharArrayReader** by specifying the character array (or portion of an array) it is to read from. **CharArrayReader** defines the usual **Reader** methods and supports the **mark()** and **reset()** methods. Note that the character array you pass to the **CharArrayReader()** constructor is not copied. This means that changes you make to the elements of the array after you create the input stream affect the values read from the array. **CharArrayReader** is the character-array analog of **ByteArrayInputStream** and is similar to **StringReader**.

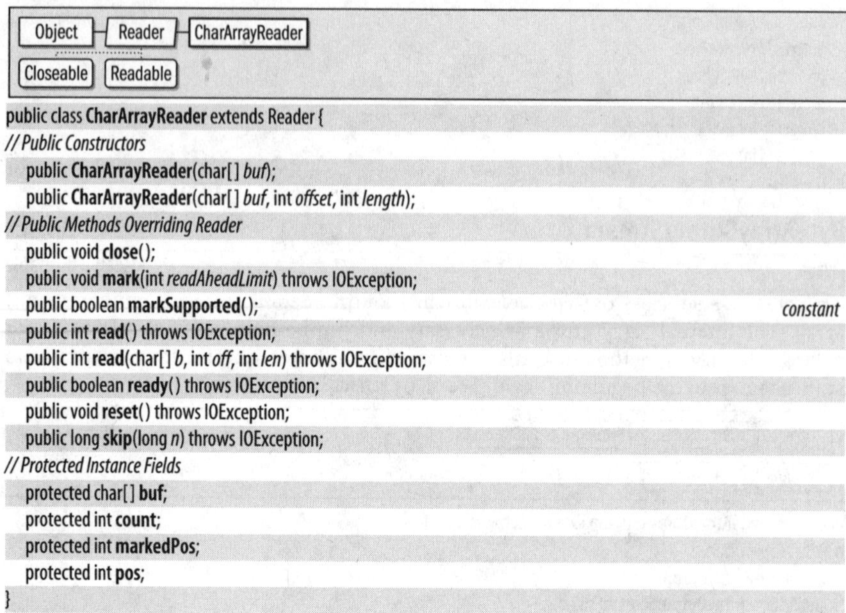


```
public class CharArrayReader extends Reader {
// Public Constructors
   public CharArrayReader(char[ ] buf);
   public CharArrayReader(char[ ] buf, int offset, int length);
// Public Methods Overriding Reader
   public void close( );
   public void mark(int readAheadLimit) throws IOException;
   public boolean markSupported( );                                    constant
   public int read( ) throws IOException;
   public int read(char[ ] b, int off, int len) throws IOException;
   public boolean ready( ) throws IOException;
   public void reset( ) throws IOException;
   public long skip(long n) throws IOException;
// Protected Instance Fields
   protected char[ ] buf;
   protected int count;
   protected int markedPos;
   protected int pos;
}
```

CharArrayWriter **Java 1.1**

java.io *appendable closeable flushable*

This class is a character output stream that uses an internal character array as the destination of characters written to it. When you create a CharArrayWriter, you may optionally specify an initial size for the character array, but you do not specify the character array itself; this array is managed internally by the CharArrayWriter and grows as necessary to accommodate all the characters written to it. The toString() and toCharArray() methods return a copy of all characters written to the stream, as a string and an array of characters, respectively. CharArrayWriter defines the standard write(), flush(), and close() methods all Writer subclasses define. It also defines a few other useful methods. size() returns the number of characters that have been written to the stream. reset() resets the stream to its initial state, with an empty character array; this is more efficient than creating a new CharArrayWriter. Finally, writeTo() writes the contents of the internal character array to some other specified character stream. CharArrayWriter is the character-stream analog of ByteArrayOutputStream and is quite similar to StringWriter.

Object — Writer — CharArrayWriter
Appendable | Closeable | Flushable

```
public class CharArrayWriter extends Writer {
// Public Constructors
   public CharArrayWriter( );
   public CharArrayWriter(int initialSize);
// Public Instance Methods
5.0 public CharArrayWriter append(CharSequence csq);
5.0 public CharArrayWriter append(char c);
5.0 public CharArrayWriter append(CharSequence csq, int start, int end);
   public void reset( );
   public int size( );
```

```
    public char[] toCharArray();
    public void writeTo(Writer out) throws IOException;
// Public Methods Overriding Writer
    public void close();                                              empty
    public void flush();                                              empty
    public void write(int c);
    public void write(char[] c, int off, int len);
    public void write(String str, int off, int len);
// Public Methods Overriding Object
    public String toString();
// Protected Instance Fields
    protected char[] buf;
    protected int count;
}
```

CharConversionException — Java 1.1

java.io — serializable checked

Signals an error when converting bytes to characters or vice versa.

Object — Throwable — Exception — IOException — CharConversionException; Throwable ⋯ Serializable

```
public class CharConversionException extends IOException {
// Public Constructors
    public CharConversionException();
    public CharConversionException(String s);
}
```

Closeable — Java 5.0

java.io — closeable

This interface defines a close() method and is implemented by closeable objects such as java.io streams and java.nio channels. This interface was added in Java 5.0 to enable java.util.Formatter to distinguish java.lang.Appendable objects that need to be closed (such as streams) from those that do not (such as StringBuilder objects). See also Flushable.

```
public interface Closeable {
// Public Instance Methods
    void close() throws IOException;
}
```

Implementations InputStream, OutputStream, PrintStream, RandomAccessFile, Reader, Writer, java.nio.channels.Channel, java.util.Formatter

DataInput — Java 1.0

java.io

This interface defines the methods required for streams that can read Java primitive data types in a machine-independent binary format. It is implemented by DataInputStream and RandomAccessFile. See DataInputStream for more information on the methods.

```
public interface DataInput {
// Public Instance Methods
    boolean readBoolean() throws IOException;
```

```
    byte readByte() throws IOException;
    char readChar() throws IOException;
    double readDouble() throws IOException;
    float readFloat() throws IOException;
    void readFully(byte[] b) throws IOException;
    void readFully(byte[] b, int off, int len) throws IOException;
    int readInt() throws IOException;
    String readLine() throws IOException;
    long readLong() throws IOException;
    short readShort() throws IOException;
    int readUnsignedByte() throws IOException;
    int readUnsignedShort() throws IOException;
    String readUTF() throws IOException;
    int skipBytes(int n) throws IOException;
}
```

Implementations DataInputStream, ObjectInput, RandomAccessFile

Passed To DataInputStream.readUTF()

DataInputStream — Java 1.0

java.io — closeable

This class is a type of **FilterInputStream** that allows you to read binary representations of Java primitive data types in a portable way. Create a **DataInputStream** by specifying the **InputStream** that is to be filtered in the call to the constructor. **DataInputStream** reads only primitive Java types; use **ObjectInputStream** to read object values.

Many of the methods read and return a single Java primitive type, in binary format, from the stream. **readUnsignedByte()** and **readUnsignedShort()** read unsigned values and return them as **int** values, since unsigned **byte** and **short** types are not supported in Java. **read()** reads data into an array of bytes, blocking until at least some data is available. By contrast, **readFully()** reads data into an array of bytes, but blocks until all requested data becomes available. **skipBytes()** blocks until the specified number of bytes have been read and discarded. **readLine()** reads characters from the stream until it encounters a newline, a carriage return, or a newline/carriage return pair. The returned string is not terminated with a newline or carriage return. This method is deprecated as of Java 1.1; see **BufferedReader** for an alternative. **readUTF()** reads a string of Unicode text encoded in a slightly modified version of the UTF-8 transformation format. UTF-8 is an ASCII-compatible encoding of Unicode characters that is often used for the transmission and storage of Unicode text. This class uses a modified UTF-8 encoding that never contains embedded null characters.

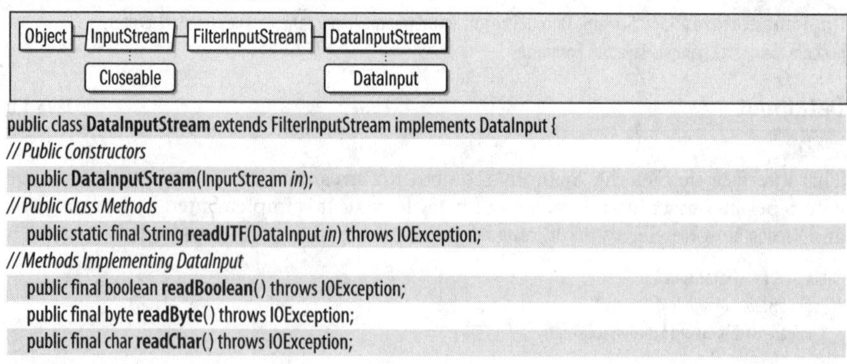


```
public class DataInputStream extends FilterInputStream implements DataInput {
// Public Constructors
    public DataInputStream(InputStream in);
// Public Class Methods
    public static final String readUTF(DataInput in) throws IOException;
// Methods Implementing DataInput
    public final boolean readBoolean() throws IOException;
    public final byte readByte() throws IOException;
    public final char readChar() throws IOException;
```

```
    public final double readDouble() throws IOException;
    public final float readFloat() throws IOException;
    public final void readFully(byte[] b) throws IOException;
    public final void readFully(byte[] b, int off, int len) throws IOException;
    public final int readInt() throws IOException;
    public final long readLong() throws IOException;
    public final short readShort() throws IOException;
    public final int readUnsignedByte() throws IOException;
    public final int readUnsignedShort() throws IOException;
    public final String readUTF() throws IOException;
    public final int skipBytes(int n) throws IOException;
// Public Methods Overriding FilterInputStream
    public final int read(byte[] b) throws IOException;
    public final int read(byte[] b, int off, int len) throws IOException;
// Deprecated Public Methods
#   public final String readLine() throws IOException;                    Implements:DataInput
}
```

DataOutput **Java 1.0**

java.io

This interface defines the methods required for streams that can write Java primitive data types in a machine-independent binary format. It is implemented by DataOutputStream and RandomAccessFile. See DataOutputStream for more information on the methods.

```
public interface DataOutput {
// Public Instance Methods
    void write(byte[] b) throws IOException;
    void write(int b) throws IOException;
    void write(byte[] b, int off, int len) throws IOException;
    void writeBoolean(boolean v) throws IOException;
    void writeByte(int v) throws IOException;
    void writeBytes(String s) throws IOException;
    void writeChar(int v) throws IOException;
    void writeChars(String s) throws IOException;
    void writeDouble(double v) throws IOException;
    void writeFloat(float v) throws IOException;
    void writeInt(int v) throws IOException;
    void writeLong(long v) throws IOException;
    void writeShort(int v) throws IOException;
    void writeUTF(String str) throws IOException;
}
```

Implementations DataOutputStream, ObjectOutput, RandomAccessFile

DataOutputStream **Java 1.0**

java.io closeable flushable

This class is a subclass of FilterOutputStream that allows you to write Java primitive data types in a portable binary format. Create a DataOutputStream by specifying the OutputStream that is to be filtered in the call to the constructor. DataOutputStream has methods that output only primitive types; use ObjectOutputStream to output object values.

Many of this class's methods write a single Java primitive type, in binary format, to the output stream. write() writes a single byte, an array, or a subarray of bytes. flush() forces any buffered data to be output. size() returns the number of bytes written so far.

writeUTF() outputs a Java string of Unicode characters using a slightly modified version of the UTF-8 transformation format. UTF-8 is an ASCII-compatible encoding of Unicode characters that is often used for the transmission and storage of Unicode text. Except for the writeUTF() method, this class is used for binary output of data. Textual output should be done with PrintWriter (or PrintStream in Java 1.0).

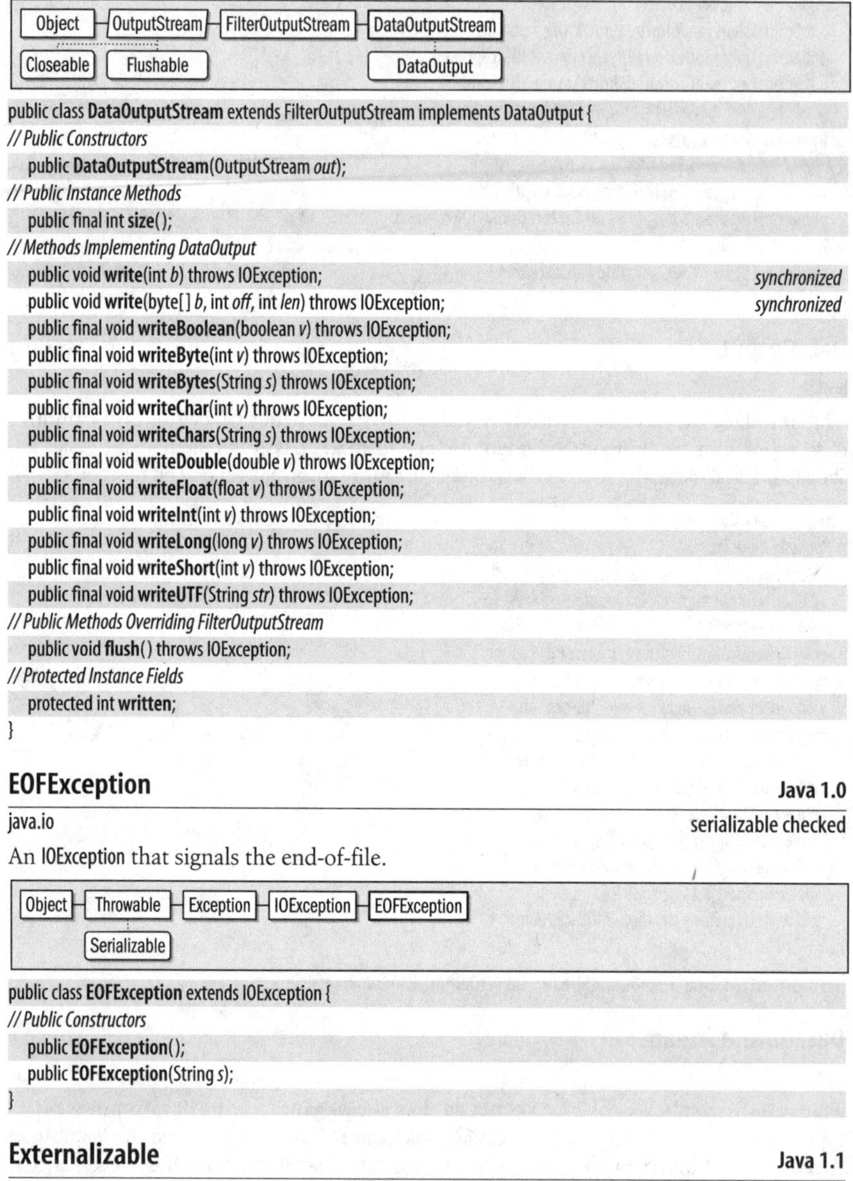


```
public class DataOutputStream extends FilterOutputStream implements DataOutput {
// Public Constructors
   public DataOutputStream(OutputStream out);
// Public Instance Methods
   public final int size();
// Methods Implementing DataOutput
   public void write(int b) throws IOException;                                synchronized
   public void write(byte[] b, int off, int len) throws IOException;           synchronized
   public final void writeBoolean(boolean v) throws IOException;
   public final void writeByte(int v) throws IOException;
   public final void writeBytes(String s) throws IOException;
   public final void writeChar(int v) throws IOException;
   public final void writeChars(String s) throws IOException;
   public final void writeDouble(double v) throws IOException;
   public final void writeFloat(float v) throws IOException;
   public final void writeInt(int v) throws IOException;
   public final void writeLong(long v) throws IOException;
   public final void writeShort(int v) throws IOException;
   public final void writeUTF(String str) throws IOException;
// Public Methods Overriding FilterOutputStream
   public void flush() throws IOException;
// Protected Instance Fields
   protected int written;
}
```

EOFException — Java 1.0

java.io — serializable checked

An IOException that signals the end-of-file.


```
public class EOFException extends IOException {
// Public Constructors
   public EOFException();
   public EOFException(String s);
}
```

Externalizable — Java 1.1

java.io — serializable

This interface defines the methods that must be implemented by an object that wants complete control over the way it is serialized. The writeExternal() and readExternal() methods should be implemented to write and read object data in some arbitrary format, using the methods of the DataOutput and DataInput interfaces. Externalizable objects must serialize their own fields and are also responsible for serializing the fields of their superclasses. Most objects do not need to define a custom output format and can use the Serializable interface instead of Externalizable for serialization.

Serializable ··· Externalizable

```
public interface Externalizable extends Serializable {
// Public Instance Methods
   void readExternal(ObjectInput in) throws IOException, ClassNotFoundException;
   void writeExternal(ObjectOutput out) throws IOException;
}
```

File

Java 1.0

java.io

serializable comparable

This class supports a platform-independent definition of file and directory names. It also provides methods to list the files in a directory; check the existence, readability, writability, type, size, and modification time of files and directories; make new directories; rename files and directories; delete files and directories; and create and delete temporary and lock files. The constants defined by this class are the platform-dependent directory and path-separator characters, available as a String and a char.

getName() returns the name of the File with any directory names omitted. getPath() returns the full name of the file, including the directory name. getParent() and getParentFile() return the directory that contains the File; the only difference between the two methods is that one returns a String, while the other returns a File. isAbsolute() tests whether the File is an absolute specification. If not, getAbsolutePath() returns an absolute filename created by appending the relative filename to the current working directory. getAbsoluteFile() returns the equivalent absolute File object. getCanonicalPath() and getCanonicalFile() are similar methods: they return an absolute filename or File object that has been converted to its system-dependent canonical form. This can be useful when comparing two File objects to see if they refer to the same file or directory. In Java 1.4 and later, the toURI() method returns a java.net.URI object that uses a file: scheme to name this file. This file-to-URI transformation can be reversed by passing a file: URI object to the File() constructor.

exists(), canWrite(), canRead(), isFile(), isDirectory(), and isHidden() perform the obvious tests on the specified File. length() returns the length of the file. lastModified() returns the modification time of the file (which should be used for comparison with other file times only and not interpreted as any particular time format). setLastModified() allows the modification time to be set; setReadOnly() makes a file or directory read-only.

list() returns the names of all entries in a directory that are not rejected by an optional FilenameFilter. listFiles() returns an array of File objects that represent all entries in a directory not rejected by an optional FilenameFilter or FileFilter. listRoots() returns an array of File objects representing all root directories on the system. Unix systems typically have only one root, /. Windows systems have a different root for each drive letter: *c:*, *d:*, and *e:*, for example.

mkdir() creates a directory, and mkdirs() creates all the directories in a File specification. renameTo() renames a file or directory; delete() deletes a file or directory. Prior to Java 1.2, the File class doesn't provide any way to create a file; that task is accomplished typically with FileOutputStream. Two special-purpose file creation methods have were added in Java 1.2. The static createTempFile() method returns a File object that refers to a newly created empty file with a unique name that begins with the specified prefix (which must be at least three characters long) and ends with the specified suffix. One version of this method creates the file in a specified directory, and the other creates it in the system temporary directory. Applications can use temporary files for any purpose without worrying about overwriting files belonging to other applications. The other file-creation method of Java 1.2 is `createNewFile()`. This instance method attempts to create a new, empty file with the name specified by the `File` object. If it succeeds, it returns `true`. However, if the file already exists, it returns `false`. `createNewFile()` works atomically and is therefore useful for file locking and other mutual-exclusion schemes. When working with `createTempFile()` or `createNewFile()`, consider using `deleteOnExit()` to request that the files be deleted when the Java VM exits normally.

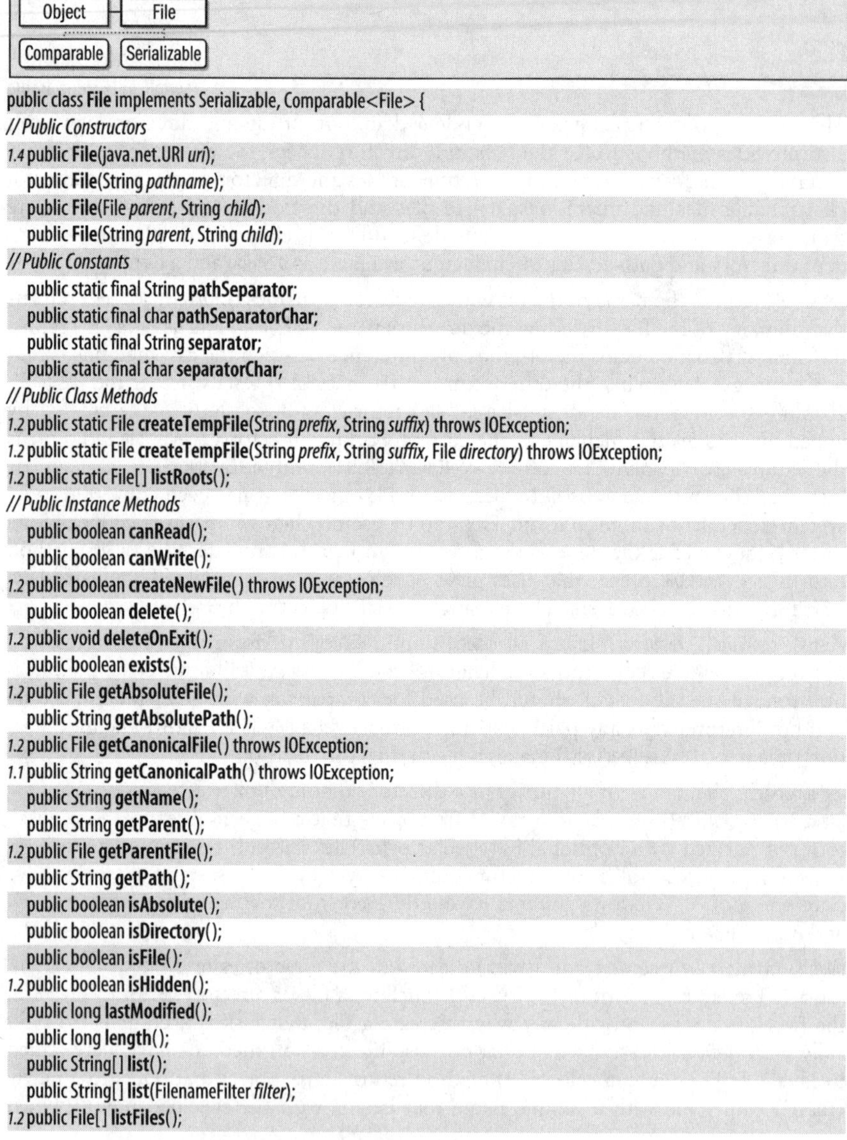


```
public class File implements Serializable, Comparable<File> {
// Public Constructors
1.4 public File(java.net.URI uri);
    public File(String pathname);
    public File(File parent, String child);
    public File(String parent, String child);
// Public Constants
    public static final String pathSeparator;
    public static final char pathSeparatorChar;
    public static final String separator;
    public static final char separatorChar;
// Public Class Methods
1.2 public static File createTempFile(String prefix, String suffix) throws IOException;
1.2 public static File createTempFile(String prefix, String suffix, File directory) throws IOException;
1.2 public static File[] listRoots();
// Public Instance Methods
    public boolean canRead();
    public boolean canWrite();
1.2 public boolean createNewFile() throws IOException;
    public boolean delete();
1.2 public void deleteOnExit();
    public boolean exists();
1.2 public File getAbsoluteFile();
    public String getAbsolutePath();
1.2 public File getCanonicalFile() throws IOException;
1.1 public String getCanonicalPath() throws IOException;
    public String getName();
    public String getParent();
1.2 public File getParentFile();
    public String getPath();
    public boolean isAbsolute();
    public boolean isDirectory();
    public boolean isFile();
1.2 public boolean isHidden();
    public long lastModified();
    public long length();
    public String[] list();
    public String[] list(FilenameFilter filter);
1.2 public File[] listFiles();
```

```
1.2 public File[] listFiles(FilenameFilter filter);
1.2 public File[] listFiles(FileFilter filter);
    public boolean mkdir();
    public boolean mkdirs();
    public boolean renameTo(File dest);
1.2 public boolean setLastModified(long time);
1.2 public boolean setReadOnly();
1.4 public java.net.URI toURI();
1.2 public java.net.URL toURL() throws java.net.MalformedURLException;
// Methods Implementing Comparable
1.2 public int compareTo(File pathname);
// Public Methods Overriding Object
    public boolean equals(Object obj);
    public int hashCode();
    public String toString();
}
```

Passed To Too many methods to list.

Returned By ProcessBuilder.directory()

FileDescriptor — Java 1.0

java.io

This class is a platform-independent representation of a low-level handle to an open file or socket. The static in, out, and err variables are FileDescriptor objects that represent the standard input, output, and error streams, respectively. There is no public constructor method to create a FileDescriptor object. You can obtain one with the getFD() method of FileInputStream, FileOutputStream, or RandomAccessFile.

```
public final class FileDescriptor {
// Public Constructors
    public FileDescriptor();
// Public Constants
    public static final FileDescriptor err;
    public static final FileDescriptor in;
    public static final FileDescriptor out;
// Public Instance Methods
1.1 public void sync() throws SyncFailedException;                    native
    public boolean valid();
}
```

Passed To FileInputStream.FileInputStream(), FileOutputStream.FileOutputStream(), FileReader.FileReader(), FileWriter.FileWriter(), SecurityManager.{checkRead(), checkWrite()}

Returned By FileInputStream.getFD(), FileOutputStream.getFD(), RandomAccessFile.getFD(), java.net.DatagramSocketImpl.getFileDescriptor(), java.net.SocketImpl.getFileDescriptor()

Type Of java.net.DatagramSocketImpl.fd, java.net.SocketImpl.fd

FileFilter — Java 1.2

java.io

This interface, added in Java 1.2, defines an accept() method that filters a list of files. You can list the contents of a directory by calling the listFiles() method of the File object that represents the desired directory. If you want a filtered listing, such as a listing of files but not subdirectories or a listing of files whose names end in *.class*, you can pass a FileFilter object to listFiles(). For each entry in the directory, a File object is passed to the accept() method. If accept() returns true, that File is included in the return value of listFiles(). If accept() returns false, that entry is not included in the listing. Use FilenameFilter if compatibility with previous releases of Java is required or if you prefer to filter filenames (i.e., String objects) rather than File objects.

```
public interface FileFilter {
// Public Instance Methods
   boolean accept(File pathname);
}
```

Passed To File.listFiles()

FileInputStream — Java 1.0

java.io — closeable

This class is a subclass of InputStream that reads bytes from a file specified by name or by a File or FileDescriptor object. read() reads a byte or array of bytes from the file. It returns –1 when the end-of-file has been reached. To read binary data, you typically use this class in conjunction with a BufferedInputStream and DataInputStream. To read text, you typically use it with an InputStreamReader and BufferedReader. Call close() to close the file when input is no longer needed.

In Java 1.4 and later, use getChannel() to obtain a FileChannel object for reading from the underlying file using the New I/O API of java.nio and its subpackages.

Object — InputStream — FileInputStream
Closeable

```
public class FileInputStream extends InputStream {
// Public Constructors
   public FileInputStream(String name) throws FileNotFoundException;
   public FileInputStream(File file) throws FileNotFoundException;
   public FileInputStream(FileDescriptor fdObj);
// Public Instance Methods
1.4 public java.nio.channels.FileChannel getChannel();
   public final FileDescriptor getFD() throws IOException;
// Public Methods Overriding InputStream
   public int available() throws IOException;                    native
   public void close() throws IOException;
   public int read() throws IOException;                         native
   public int read(byte[] b) throws IOException;
   public int read(byte[] b, int off, int len) throws IOException;
   public long skip(long n) throws IOException;                  native
// Protected Methods Overriding Object
   protected void finalize() throws IOException;
}
```

FilenameFilter — Java 1.0

java.io

This interface defines the accept() method that must be implemented by any object that filters filenames (i.e., selects a subset of filenames from a list of filenames). There are no standard FilenameFilter classes implemented by Java, but objects that implement this interface are used by the java.awt.FileDialog object and the File.list() method. A typical FilenameFilter object might check that the specified File represents a file (not a directory), is readable (and possibly writable as well), and that its name ends with some desired extension.

```
public interface FilenameFilter {
// Public Instance Methods
   boolean accept(File dir, String name);
}
```

Passed To File.{list(), listFiles()}

FileNotFoundException — Java 1.0

java.io — serializable checked

An IOException that signals that a specified file cannot be found.

Object — Throwable — Exception — IOException — FileNotFoundException; Throwable implements Serializable

```
public class FileNotFoundException extends IOException {
// Public Constructors
   public FileNotFoundException();
   public FileNotFoundException(String s);
}
```

Thrown By Too many methods to list.

FileOutputStream — Java 1.0

java.io — closeable flushable

This class is a subclass of OutputStream that writes data to a file specified by name or by a File or FileDescriptor object. If the specified file already exists, a FileOutputStream can be configured to overwrite or append to the existing file. write() writes a byte or array of bytes to the file. To write binary data, you typically use this class in conjunction with a BufferedOutputStream and a DataOutputStream. To write text, you typically use it with a PrintWriter, BufferedWriter and an OutputStreamWriter (or you use the convenience class FileWriter). Use close() to close a FileOutputStream when no further output will be written to it.

In Java 1.4 and later, use getChannel() to obtain a FileChannel object for writing to the underlying file using the New I/O API of java.nio and its subpackages.

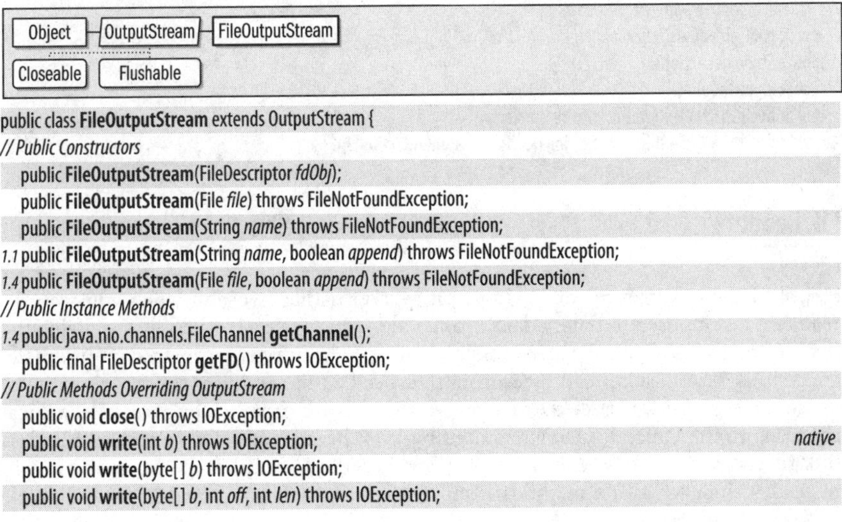


```
public class FileOutputStream extends OutputStream {
// Public Constructors
    public FileOutputStream(FileDescriptor fdObj);
    public FileOutputStream(File file) throws FileNotFoundException;
    public FileOutputStream(String name) throws FileNotFoundException;
1.1 public FileOutputStream(String name, boolean append) throws FileNotFoundException;
1.4 public FileOutputStream(File file, boolean append) throws FileNotFoundException;
// Public Instance Methods
1.4 public java.nio.channels.FileChannel getChannel();
    public final FileDescriptor getFD() throws IOException;
// Public Methods Overriding OutputStream
    public void close() throws IOException;
    public void write(int b) throws IOException;                                native
    public void write(byte[] b) throws IOException;
    public void write(byte[] b, int off, int len) throws IOException;
```

```
// Protected Methods Overriding Object
   protected void finalize() throws IOException;
}
```

FilePermission

Java 1.2

java.io

serializable permission

This class is a java.security.Permission that governs access to the local filesystem. A FilePermission has a name, or target, which specifies what file or files it pertains to, and a comma-separated list of actions that may be performed on the file or files. The supported actions are read, write, delete, and execute. Read and write permission are required by any methods that read or write a file. Delete permission is required by File.delete(), and execute permission is required by Runtime.exec().

The name of a FilePermission may be as simple as a file or directory name. FilePermission also supports the use of certain wildcards, however, to specify a permission that applies to more than one file. If the name of the FilePermission is a directory name followed by /* (* on Windows platforms), it specifies all files in the named directory. If the name is a directory name followed by /- (\- on Windows), it specifies all files in the directory, and, recursively, all files in all subdirectories. A * alone specifies all files in the current directory, and a - alone specifies all files in or beneath the current directory. Finally, the special name <<ALL FILES>> matches all files anywhere in the filesystem.

Applications do not need to use this class directly. Programmers writing system-level code and system administrators configuring security policies may need to use it, however. Be very careful when granting any type of FilePermission. Restricting access (especially write access) to files is one of the cornerstones of the Java security model with regard to untrusted code.

Object — Permission — FilePermission
Guard, Serializable — Serializable

```
public final class FilePermission extends java.security.Permission implements Serializable {
// Public Constructors
   public FilePermission(String path, String actions);
// Public Methods Overriding Permission
   public boolean equals(Object obj);
   public String getActions();
   public int hashCode();
   public boolean implies(java.security.Permission p);
   public java.security.PermissionCollection newPermissionCollection();
}
```

FileReader

Java 1.1

java.io

readable closeable

FileReader is a convenience subclass of InputStreamReader that is useful when you want to read text (as opposed to binary data) from a file. You create a FileReader by specifying the file to be read in any of three possible forms. The FileReader constructor internally creates a FileInputStream to read bytes from the specified file and uses the functionality of its superclass, InputStreamReader, to convert those bytes from characters in the local encoding to the Unicode characters used by Java. Because FileReader is a trivial subclass of InputStreamReader, it does not define any read() methods or other methods of its own. Instead, it inherits all its methods from its superclass. If you want to read Unicode characters from a file that uses some encoding other than the default encoding for the locale, you must explicitly create your own **InputStreamReader** to perform the byte-to-character conversion.

Object — Reader — InputStreamReader — FileReader
Closeable Readable

```
public class FileReader extends InputStreamReader {
// Public Constructors
   public FileReader(FileDescriptor fd);
   public FileReader(File file) throws FileNotFoundException;
   public FileReader(String fileName) throws FileNotFoundException;
}
```

FileWriter **Java 1.1**

java.io **appendable closeable flushable**

FileWriter is a convenience subclass of **OutputStreamWriter** that is useful when you want to write text (as opposed to binary data) to a file. You create a **FileWriter** by specifying the file to be written to and, optionally, whether the data should be appended to the end of an existing file instead of overwriting that file. The **FileWriter** class creates an internal **FileOutputStream** to write bytes to the specified file and uses the functionality of its superclass, **OutputStreamWriter**, to convert the Unicode characters written to the stream into bytes using the default encoding of the default locale. (If you want to use an encoding other than the default, you cannot use **FileWriter**; in that case you must create your own **OutputStreamWriter** and **FileOutputStream**.) Because **FileWriter** is a trivial subclass of **OutputStreamWriter**, it does not define any methods of its own, but simply inherits them from its superclass.

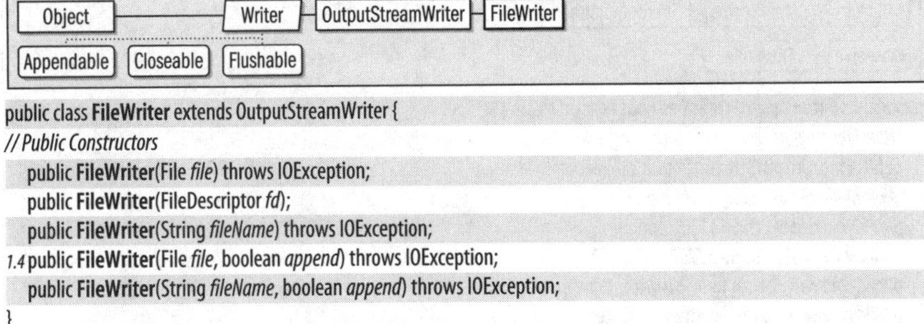


```
public class FileWriter extends OutputStreamWriter {
// Public Constructors
   public FileWriter(File file) throws IOException;
   public FileWriter(FileDescriptor fd);
   public FileWriter(String fileName) throws IOException;
1.4 public FileWriter(File file, boolean append) throws IOException;
   public FileWriter(String fileName, boolean append) throws IOException;
}
```

FilterInputStream **Java 1.0**

java.io **closeable**

This class provides method definitions required to filter data obtained from the **InputStream** specified when the **FilterInputStream** is created. It must be subclassed to perform some sort of filtering operation and cannot be instantiated directly. See the subclasses **BufferedInputStream**, **DataInputStream**, and **PushbackInputStream**.

Object — InputStream — FilterInputStream
Closeable

```
public class FilterInputStream extends InputStream {
// Protected Constructors
```

```
    protected FilterInputStream(InputStream in);
// Public Methods Overriding InputStream
    public int available() throws IOException;
    public void close() throws IOException;
    public void mark(int readlimit);                                    synchronized
    public boolean markSupported();
    public int read() throws IOException;
    public int read(byte[] b) throws IOException;
    public int read(byte[] b, int off, int len) throws IOException;
    public void reset() throws IOException;                             synchronized
    public long skip(long n) throws IOException;
// Protected Instance Fields
    protected volatile InputStream in;
}
```

Subclasses

BufferedInputStream, DataInputStream, LineNumberInputStream, PushbackInputStream, java.security.DigestInputStream, java.util.zip.CheckedInputStream, java.util.zip.InflaterInputStream, javax.crypto.CipherInputStream

FilterOutputStream — Java 1.0

java.io — closeable flushable

This class provides method definitions required to filter the data to be written to the OutputStream specified when the FilterOutputStream is created. It must be subclassed to perform some sort of filtering operation and may not be instantiated directly. See the subclasses BufferedOutputStream and DataOutputStream.

Object — OutputStream — FilterOutputStream
Closeable, Flushable

```
public class FilterOutputStream extends OutputStream {
// Public Constructors
    public FilterOutputStream(OutputStream out);
// Public Methods Overriding OutputStream
    public void close() throws IOException;
    public void flush() throws IOException;
    public void write(int b) throws IOException;
    public void write(byte[] b) throws IOException;
    public void write(byte[] b, int off, int len) throws IOException;
// Protected Instance Fields
    protected OutputStream out;
}
```

Subclasses

BufferedOutputStream, DataOutputStream, PrintStream, java.security.DigestOutputStream, java.util.zip.CheckedOutputStream, java.util.zip.DeflaterOutputStream, javax.crypto.CipherOutputStream

FilterReader — Java 1.1

java.io — readable closeable

This abstract class is intended to act as a superclass for character input streams that read data from some other character input stream, filter it in some way, and then return the filtered data when a **read()** method is called. **FilterReader** is declared **abstract** so that it cannot be instantiated. But none of its methods are themselves abstract: they all simply call the requested operation on the input stream passed to the **FilterReader()** constructor. If you were allowed to instantiate a **FilterReader**, you'd find that it is a null filter (i.e., it simply reads characters from the specified input stream and returns them without any kind of filtering).

Because **FilterReader** implements a null filter, it is an ideal superclass for classes that want to implement simple filters but do not want to override all the methods of **Reader**. In order to create your own filtered character input stream, you should subclass **FilterReader** and override both its **read()** methods to perform the desired filtering operation. Note that you can implement one of the **read()** methods in terms of the other, and thus only implement the filtration once. Recall that the other **read()** methods defined by **Reader** are implemented in terms of these methods, so you do not need to override those. In some cases, you may need to override other methods of **FilterReader** and provide methods or constructors that are specific to your subclass. **FilterReader** is the character-stream analog to **FilterInputStream**.

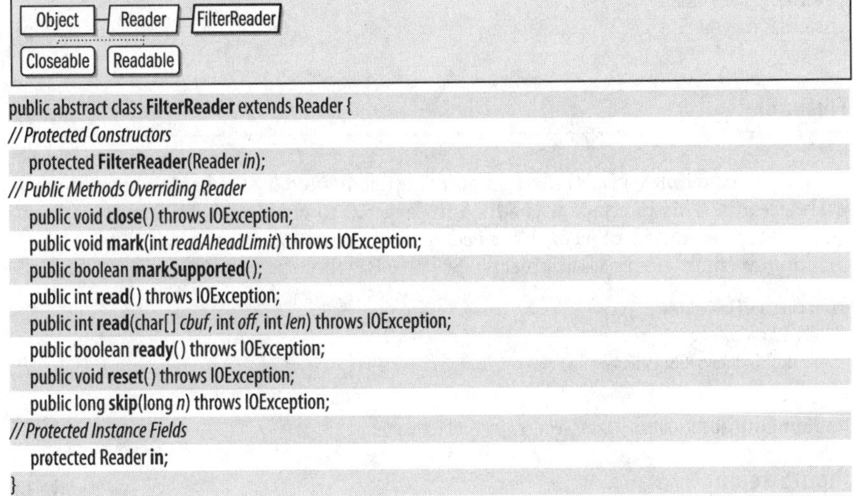


```
public abstract class FilterReader extends Reader {
// Protected Constructors
   protected FilterReader(Reader in);
// Public Methods Overriding Reader
   public void close() throws IOException;
   public void mark(int readAheadLimit) throws IOException;
   public boolean markSupported();
   public int read() throws IOException;
   public int read(char[] cbuf, int off, int len) throws IOException;
   public boolean ready() throws IOException;
   public void reset() throws IOException;
   public long skip(long n) throws IOException;
// Protected Instance Fields
   protected Reader in;
}
```

Subclasses PushbackReader

FilterWriter — Java 1.1

java.io — appendable closeable flushable

This abstract class is intended to act as a superclass for character output streams that filter the data written to them before writing it to some other character output stream. **FilterWriter** is declared **abstract** so that it cannot be instantiated. But none of its methods are themselves abstract: they all simply invoke the corresponding method on the output stream that was passed to the **FilterWriter** constructor. If you were allowed to instantiate a **FilterWriter** object, you'd find that it acts as a null filter (i.e., it simply passes the characters written to it along, without any filtration).

Because **FilterWriter** implements a null filter, it is an ideal superclass for classes that want to implement simple filters without having to override all of the methods of **Writer**. In order to create your own filtered character output stream, you should subclass **FilterWriter** and override all its **write()** methods to perform the desired filtering operation. Note that you can implement two of the write() methods in terms of the third and thus implement your filtering algorithm only once. In some cases, you may want to override other Writer methods and add other methods or constructors that are specific to your subclass. FilterWriter is the character-stream analog of FilterOutputStream.

Object — Writer — FilterWriter
Appendable Closeable Flushable

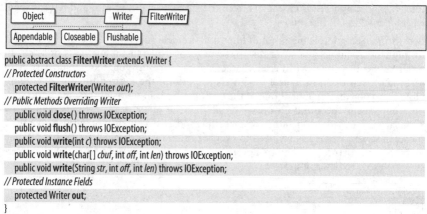

```
public abstract class FilterWriter extends Writer {
// Protected Constructors
   protected FilterWriter(Writer out);
// Public Methods Overriding Writer
   public void close() throws IOException;
   public void flush() throws IOException;
   public void write(int c) throws IOException;
   public void write(char[] cbuf, int off, int len) throws IOException;
   public void write(String str, int off, int len) throws IOException;
// Protected Instance Fields
   protected Writer out;
}
```

Flushable — Java 5.0

java.io — flushable

This interface defines a flush() method and is implemented by flushable objects such as java.io streams. This interface was added in Java 5.0 to enable java.util.Formatter to distinguish java.lang.Appendable objects that need to be flushed (such as streams) from those that do not (such as StringBuilder objects). See also Closeable.

```
public interface Flushable {
// Public Instance Methods
   void flush() throws IOException;
}
```

Implementations OutputStream, Writer, java.util.Formatter

InputStream — Java 1.0

java.io — closeable

This abstract class is the superclass of all input streams. It defines the basic input methods all input stream classes provide. read() reads a single byte or an array (or subarray) of bytes. It returns the bytes read, the number of bytes read, or –1 if the end-of-file has been reached. skip() skips a specified number of bytes of input. available() returns the number of bytes that can be read without blocking. close() closes the input stream and frees up any system resources associated with it. The stream should not be used after close() has been called.

If markSupported() returns true for a given InputStream, that stream supports mark() and reset() methods. mark() marks the current position in the input stream so that reset() can return to that position (as long as no more than the specified number of bytes have been read between the calls to mark() and reset()). See also Reader.

Object — InputStream ··· Closeable

```
public abstract class InputStream implements Closeable {
// Public Constructors
   public InputStream();
// Public Instance Methods
   public int available() throws IOException;                                         constant
   public void close() throws IOException;                          Implements:Closeable empty
   public void mark(int readlimit);                                      synchronized empty
   public boolean markSupported();                                                    constant
   public abstract int read() throws IOException;
   public int read(byte[] b) throws IOException;
   public int read(byte[] b, int off, int len) throws IOException;
   public void reset() throws IOException;                                        synchronized
   public long skip(long n) throws IOException;
// Methods Implementing Closeable
   public void close() throws IOException;                                               empty
}
```

Subclasses ByteArrayInputStream, FileInputStream, FilterInputStream, ObjectInputStream, PipedInputStream, SequenceInputStream, StringBufferInputStream

Passed To Too many methods to list.

Returned By Too many methods to list.

Type Of FilterInputStream.in, System.in

InputStreamReader — Java 1.1

java.io — readable closeable

This class is a character input stream that uses a byte input stream as its data source. It reads bytes from a specified InputStream and translates them into Unicode characters according to a particular platform- and locale-dependent character encoding. This is an important internationalization feature in Java 1.1 and later. InputStreamReader supports the standard Reader methods. It also has a getEncoding() method that returns the name of the encoding being used to convert bytes to characters.

When you create an InputStreamReader, you specify an InputStream from which the InputStreamReader is to read bytes and, optionally, the name of the character encoding used by those bytes. If you do not specify an encoding name, the InputStreamReader uses the default encoding for the default locale, which is usually the correct thing to do. In Java 1.4 and later, this class uses the charset conversion facilities of the java.nio.charset package and allows you to explicitly specify the Charset or CharsetDecoder to be used. Prior to Java 1.4, the class allows you to specify only the name of the desired charset encoding.

Object — Reader — InputStreamReader
Closeable, Readable

```
public class InputStreamReader extends Reader {
// Public Constructors
   public InputStreamReader(InputStream in);
   public InputStreamReader(InputStream in, String charsetName) throws UnsupportedEncodingException;
1.4 public InputStreamReader(InputStream in, java.nio.charset.Charset cs);
1.4 public InputStreamReader(InputStream in, java.nio.charset.CharsetDecoder dec);
// Public Instance Methods
   public String getEncoding();
// Public Methods Overriding Reader
```

```
    public void close() throws IOException;
    public int read() throws IOException;
    public int read(char[] cbuf, int offset, int length) throws IOException;
    public boolean ready() throws IOException;
}
```

Subclasses FileReader

InterruptedIOException **Java 1.0**

java.io **serializable checked**

An IOException that signals that an input or output operation was interrupted. The bytesTransferred field contains the number of bytes read or written before the operation was interrupted.

Object — Throwable — Exception — IOException — InterruptedIOException
Serializable

```
public class InterruptedIOException extends IOException {
// Public Constructors
    public InterruptedIOException();
    public InterruptedIOException(String s);
// Public Instance Fields
    public int bytesTransferred;
}
```

Subclasses java.net.SocketTimeoutException

InvalidClassException **Java 1.1**

java.io **serializable checked**

Signals that the serialization mechanism has encountered one of several possible problems with the class of an object that is being serialized or deserialized. The classname field should contain the name of the class in question, and the getMessage() method is overridden to return this class name with the message.

Object — Throwable — Exception — IOException — ObjectStreamException — InvalidClassException
Serializable

```
public class InvalidClassException extends ObjectStreamException {
// Public Constructors
    public InvalidClassException(String reason);
    public InvalidClassException(String cname, String reason);
// Public Methods Overriding Throwable
    public String getMessage();
// Public Instance Fields
    public String classname;
}
```

InvalidObjectException **Java 1.1**

java.io **serializable checked**

This exception should be thrown by the validateObject() method of an object that implements the ObjectInputValidation interface when a deserialized object fails an input validation test for any reason.

Object — Throwable — Exception — IOException — ObjectStreamException — InvalidObjectException
Serializable

```
public class InvalidObjectException extends ObjectStreamException {
// Public Constructors
    public InvalidObjectException(String reason);
}
```

Thrown By ObjectInputStream.registerValidation(), ObjectInputValidation.validateObject(), java.text.AttributedCharacterIterator.Attribute.readResolve(), java.text.DateFormat.Field.readResolve(), java.text.MessageFormat.Field.readResolve(), java.text.NumberFormat.Field.readResolve()

IOException — Java 1.0

java.io — serializable checked

Signals that an exceptional condition has occurred during input or output. This class has several more specific subclasses. See EOFException, FileNotFoundException, InterruptedIOException, and UTFDataFormatException.

Object — Throwable — Exception — IOException
Serializable

```
public class IOException extends Exception {
// Public Constructors
    public IOException();
    public IOException(String s);
}
```

Subclasses CharConversionException, EOFException, FileNotFoundException, InterruptedIOException, ObjectStreamException, SyncFailedException, UnsupportedEncodingException, UTFDataFormatException, java.net.HttpRetryException, java.net.MalformedURLException, java.net.ProtocolException, java.net.SocketException, java.net.UnknownHostException, java.net.UnknownServiceException, java.nio.channels.ClosedChannelException, java.nio.channels.FileLockInterruptionException, java.nio.charset.CharacterCodingException, java.util.InvalidPropertiesFormatException, java.util.zip.ZipException, javax.net.ssl.SSLException

Passed To java.net.ProxySelector.connectFailed()

Returned By java.util.Formatter.ioException(), java.util.Scanner.ioException()

Thrown By Too many methods to list.

LineNumberInputStream — Java 1.0; Deprecated in 1.1

java.io — @Deprecated closeable

This class is a FilterInputStream that keeps track of the number of lines of data that have been read. getLineNumber() returns the current line number; setLineNumber() sets the line number of the current line. Subsequent lines are numbered starting from that number. This class is deprecated as of Java 1.1 because it does not properly convert bytes to characters. Use LineNumberReader instead.

Object — InputStream — FilterInputStream — LineNumberInputStream
Closeable

```
public class LineNumberInputStream extends FilterInputStream {
// Public Constructors
    public LineNumberInputStream(InputStream in);
// Public Instance Methods
    public int getLineNumber();
    public void setLineNumber(int lineNumber);
// Public Methods Overriding FilterInputStream
    public int available() throws IOException;
    public void mark(int readlimit);
    public int read() throws IOException;
    public int read(byte[] b, int off, int len) throws IOException;
    public void reset() throws IOException;
    public long skip(long n) throws IOException;
}
```

LineNumberReader **Java 1.1**

java.io **readable closeable**

This class is a character input stream that keeps track of the number of lines of text that have been read from it. It supports the usual Reader methods and also the readLine() method introduced by its superclass. In addition to these methods, you can call getLineNumber() to query the number of lines set so far. You can also call setLineNumber() to set the line number for the current line. Subsequent lines are numbered sequentially from this specified starting point. This class is a character-stream analog to LineNumberInputStream, which has been deprecated as of Java 1.1.

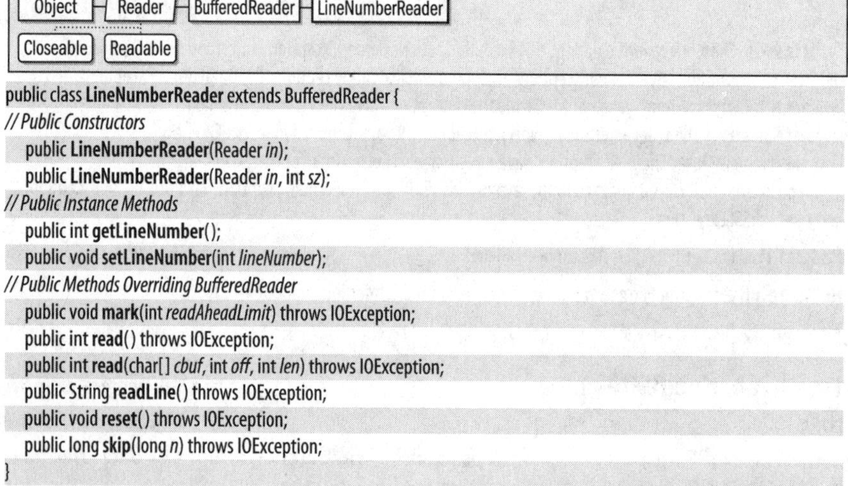


```
public class LineNumberReader extends BufferedReader {
// Public Constructors
    public LineNumberReader(Reader in);
    public LineNumberReader(Reader in, int sz);
// Public Instance Methods
    public int getLineNumber();
    public void setLineNumber(int lineNumber);
// Public Methods Overriding BufferedReader
    public void mark(int readAheadLimit) throws IOException;
    public int read() throws IOException;
    public int read(char[] cbuf, int off, int len) throws IOException;
    public String readLine() throws IOException;
    public void reset() throws IOException;
    public long skip(long n) throws IOException;
}
```

NotActiveException **Java 1.1**

java.io **serializable checked**

This exception is thrown in several circumstances. It indicates that the invoked method was not invoked at the right time or in the correct context. Typically, it means that an ObjectOutputStream or ObjectInputStream is not currently active and therefore the requested operation cannot be performed.

Object — Throwable — Exception — IOException — ObjectStreamException — NotActiveException
Serializable

```
public class NotActiveException extends ObjectStreamException {
// Public Constructors
   public NotActiveException();
   public NotActiveException(String reason);
}
```

Thrown By ObjectInputStream.registerValidation()

NotSerializableException — Java 1.1

java.io — serializable checked

Signals that an object cannot be serialized. It is thrown when serialization is attempted on an instance of a class that does not implement the Serializable interface. Note that it is also thrown when an attempt is made to serialize a Serializable object that refers to (or contains) an object that is not Serializable. A subclass of a class that is Serializable can prevent itself from being serialized by throwing this exception from its writeObject() and/or readObject() methods.

Object — Throwable — Exception — IOException — ObjectStreamException — NotSerializableException
Serializable

```
public class NotSerializableException extends ObjectStreamException {
// Public Constructors
   public NotSerializableException();
   public NotSerializableException(String classname);
}
```

ObjectInput — Java 1.1

java.io

This interface extends the DataInput interface and adds methods for deserializing objects and reading bytes and arrays of bytes.

DataInput ··· ObjectInput

```
public interface ObjectInput extends DataInput {
// Public Instance Methods
   int available() throws IOException;
   void close() throws IOException;
   int read() throws IOException;
   int read(byte[] b) throws IOException;
   int read(byte[] b, int off, int len) throws IOException;
   Object readObject() throws ClassNotFoundException, IOException;
   long skip(long n) throws IOException;
}
```

Implementations ObjectInputStream

Passed To Externalizable.readExternal()

ObjectInputStream **Java 1.1**

java.io **closeable**

ObjectInputStream deserializes objects, arrays, and other values from a stream that was previously created with an ObjectOutputStream. The readObject() method deserializes objects and arrays (which should then be cast to the appropriate type); various other methods read primitive data values from the stream. Note that only objects that implement the Serializable or Externalizable interface can be serialized and deserialized.

A class may implement its own private readObject(ObjectInputStream) method to customize the way it is deserialized. If you define such a method, there are several ObjectInputStream methods you can use to help deserialize the object. defaultReadObject() is the easiest. It reads the content of the object just as an ObjectInputStream would normally do. If you wrote additional data before or after the default object contents, you should read that data before or after calling defaultReadObject(). When working with multiple versions or implementations of a class, you may have to deserialize a set of fields that do not match the fields of your class. In this case, give your class a static field named serialPersistentFields whose value is an array of ObjectStreamField objects that describe the fields to be deserialized. If you do this, your readObject() method can call readFields() to read the specified fields from the stream and return them in a ObjectInputStream.GetField object. See ObjectStreamField and ObjectInputStream.GetField for more details. Finally, you can call registerValidation() from a custom readObject() method. This method registers an ObjectInputValidation object (typically the object being deserialized) to be notified when a complete tree of objects has been deserialized, and the original call to the readObject() method of the ObjectInputStream is about to return to its caller.

The remaining methods include miscellaneous stream-manipulation methods and several protected methods for use by subclasses that want to customize the deserialization behavior of ObjectInputStream.

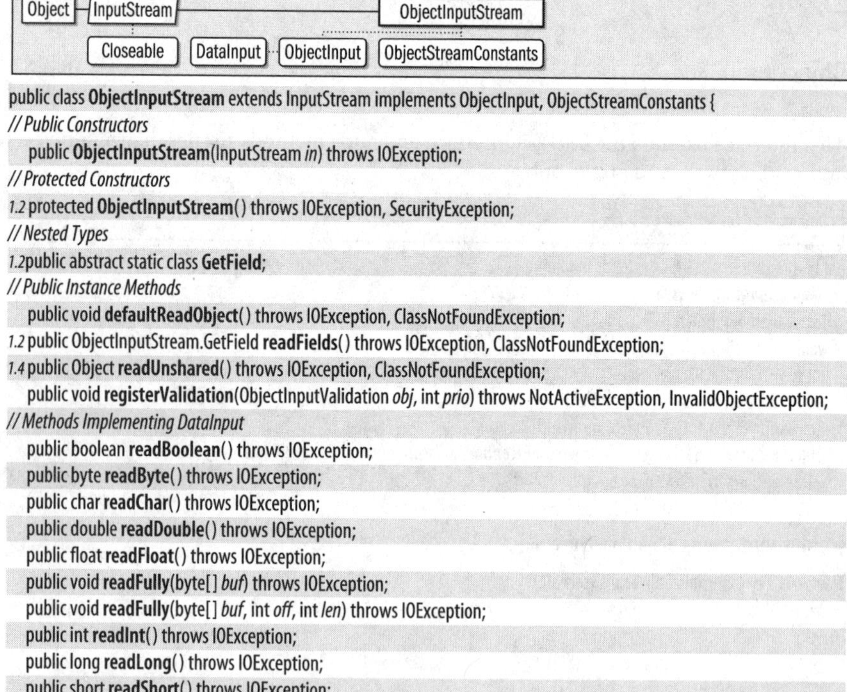


```
public class ObjectInputStream extends InputStream implements ObjectInput, ObjectStreamConstants {
// Public Constructors
    public ObjectInputStream(InputStream in) throws IOException;
// Protected Constructors
1.2 protected ObjectInputStream() throws IOException, SecurityException;
// Nested Types
1.2public abstract static class GetField;
// Public Instance Methods
    public void defaultReadObject() throws IOException, ClassNotFoundException;
1.2 public ObjectInputStream.GetField readFields() throws IOException, ClassNotFoundException;
1.4 public Object readUnshared() throws IOException, ClassNotFoundException;
    public void registerValidation(ObjectInputValidation obj, int prio) throws NotActiveException, InvalidObjectException;
// Methods Implementing DataInput
    public boolean readBoolean() throws IOException;
    public byte readByte() throws IOException;
    public char readChar() throws IOException;
    public double readDouble() throws IOException;
    public float readFloat() throws IOException;
    public void readFully(byte[] buf) throws IOException;
    public void readFully(byte[] buf, int off, int len) throws IOException;
    public int readInt() throws IOException;
    public long readLong() throws IOException;
    public short readShort() throws IOException;
```

```
    public int readUnsignedByte() throws IOException;
    public int readUnsignedShort() throws IOException;
    public String readUTF() throws IOException;
    public int skipBytes(int len) throws IOException;
// Methods Implementing ObjectInput
    public int available() throws IOException;
    public void close() throws IOException;
    public int read() throws IOException;
    public int read(byte[] buf, int off, int len) throws IOException;
    public final Object readObject() throws IOException, ClassNotFoundException;
// Protected Instance Methods
    protected boolean enableResolveObject(boolean enable) throws SecurityException;
1.3 protected ObjectStreamClass readClassDescriptor() throws IOException, ClassNotFoundException;
1.2 protected Object readObjectOverride() throws IOException, ClassNotFoundException;         constant
    protected void readStreamHeader() throws IOException, StreamCorruptedException;
    protected Class<?> resolveClass(ObjectStreamClass desc) throws IOException, ClassNotFoundException;
    protected Object resolveObject(Object obj) throws IOException;
1.3 protected Class<?> resolveProxyClass(String[] interfaces) throws IOException, ClassNotFoundException;
// Deprecated Public Methods
#   public String readLine() throws IOException;                          Implements:DataInput
}
```

ObjectInputStream.GetField — Java 1.2

java.io

This class holds the values of named fields read by an **ObjectInputStream**. It gives the programmer precise control over the deserialization process and is typically used when implementing an object with a set of fields that do not match the set of fields (and the serialization stream format) of the original implementation of the object. This class allows the implementation of a class to change without breaking serialization compatibility.

In order to use the **GetField** class, your class must implement a private **readObject()** method that is responsible for custom deserialization. Typically, when using the **GetField** class, you have also specified an array of **ObjectStreamField** objects as the value of a private static field named **serialPersistentFields**. This array specifies the names and types of all fields expected to be found when reading from a serialization stream. If there is no **serialPersistentField** field, the array of **ObjectStreamField** objects is created from the actual fields (excluding **static** and **transient** fields) of the class.

Within the **readObject()** method of your class, call the **readFields()** method of **ObjectInputStream()**. This method reads the values of all fields from the stream and stores them in an **ObjectInputStream.GetField** object that it returns. This **GetField** object is essentially a mapping from field names to field values, and you can extract the values of whatever fields you need in order to restore the proper state of the object being deserialized. The various **get()** methods return the values of named fields of specified types. Each method takes a default value as an argument, in case no value for the named field was present in the serialization stream. (This can happen when deserializing an object written by an earlier version of the class, for example.) Use the **defaulted()** method to determine whether the **GetField** object contains a value for the named field. If this method returns **true**, the named field had no value in the stream, so the **get()** method of the **GetField** object has to return the specified default value. The **getObjectStreamClass()** method of a **GetField** object returns the **ObjectStreamClass** object for the object being deserialized. This **ObjectStreamClass** can obtain the array of **ObjectStreamField** objects for the class.

See also ObjectOutputStream.PutField

```
public abstract static class ObjectInputStream.GetField {
// Public Constructors
   public GetField();
// Public Instance Methods
   public abstract boolean defaulted(String name) throws IOException;
   public abstract boolean get(String name, boolean val) throws IOException;
   public abstract byte get(String name, byte val) throws IOException;
   public abstract char get(String name, char val) throws IOException;
   public abstract short get(String name, short val) throws IOException;
   public abstract int get(String name, int val) throws IOException;
   public abstract long get(String name, long val) throws IOException;
   public abstract float get(String name, float val) throws IOException;
   public abstract double get(String name, double val) throws IOException;
   public abstract Object get(String name, Object val) throws IOException;
   public abstract ObjectStreamClass getObjectStreamClass();
}
```

Returned By ObjectInputStream.readFields()

ObjectInputValidation — Java 1.1

java.io

A class implements this interface and defines the validateObject() method in order to validate itself when it and all the objects it depends on have been completely deserialized from an ObjectInputStream. The validateObject() method is only invoked, however, if the object is passed to ObjectInputStream.registerValidation(); this must be done from the readObject() method of the object. Note that if an object is deserialized as part of a larger object graph, its validateObject() method is not invoked until the entire graph is read, and the original call to ObjectInputStream.readObject() is about to return. validateObject() should throw an InvalidObjectException if the object fails validation. This stops object serialization, and the original call to ObjectInputStream.readObject() terminates with the InvalidObjectException exception.

```
public interface ObjectInputValidation {
// Public Instance Methods
   void validateObject() throws InvalidObjectException;
}
```

Passed To ObjectInputStream.registerValidation()

ObjectOutput — Java 1.1

java.io

This interface extends the DataOutput interface and adds methods for serializing objects and writing bytes and arrays of bytes.

DataOutput ··· ObjectOutput

```
public interface ObjectOutput extends DataOutput {
// Public Instance Methods
   void close() throws IOException;
   void flush() throws IOException;
   void write(byte[] b) throws IOException;
   void write(int b) throws IOException;
   void write(byte[] b, int off, int len) throws IOException;
   void writeObject(Object obj) throws IOException;
}
```

Implementations ObjectOutputStream

Passed To Externalizable.writeExternal(), ObjectOutputStream.PutField.write()

ObjectOutputStream **Java 1.1**

java.io **closeable flushable**

The ObjectOutputStream serializes objects, arrays, and other values to a stream. The writeObject() method serializes an object or array, and various other methods write primitive data values to the stream. Note that only objects that implement the Serializable or Externalizable interface can be serialized.

A class that wants to customize the way instances are serialized should declare a private writeObject(ObjectOutputStream) method. This method is invoked when an object is being serialized and can use several additional methods of ObjectOutputStream. defaultWriteObject() performs the same serialization that would happen if no writeObject() method existed. An object can call this method to serialize itself and then use other methods of ObjectOutputStream to write additional data to the serialization stream. The class must define a matching readObject() method to read that additional data, of course. When working with multiple versions or implementations of a class, you may have to serialize a set of fields that do not precisely match the fields of your class. In this case, give your class a static field named serialPersistentFields whose value is an array of ObjectStreamField objects that describe the fields to be serialized. In your writeObject() method, call putFields() to obtain an ObjectOutputStream.PutField object. Store field names and values into this object, and then call writeFields() to write them out to the serialization stream. See ObjectStreamField and ObjectOutputStream.PutField for further details.

The remaining methods of ObjectOutputStream are miscellaneous stream-manipulation methods and protected methods for use by subclasses that want to customize its serialization behavior.

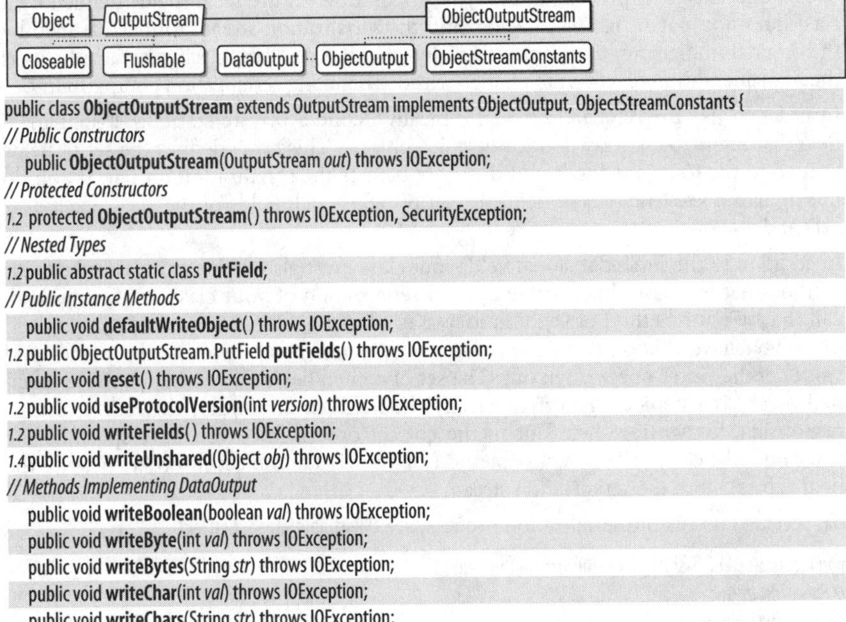


```
public class ObjectOutputStream extends OutputStream implements ObjectOutput, ObjectStreamConstants {
// Public Constructors
    public ObjectOutputStream(OutputStream out) throws IOException;
// Protected Constructors
1.2 protected ObjectOutputStream() throws IOException, SecurityException;
// Nested Types
1.2 public abstract static class PutField;
// Public Instance Methods
    public void defaultWriteObject() throws IOException;
1.2 public ObjectOutputStream.PutField putFields() throws IOException;
    public void reset() throws IOException;
1.2 public void useProtocolVersion(int version) throws IOException;
1.2 public void writeFields() throws IOException;
1.4 public void writeUnshared(Object obj) throws IOException;
// Methods Implementing DataOutput
    public void writeBoolean(boolean val) throws IOException;
    public void writeByte(int val) throws IOException;
    public void writeBytes(String str) throws IOException;
    public void writeChar(int val) throws IOException;
    public void writeChars(String str) throws IOException;
```

```
    public void writeDouble(double val) throws IOException;
    public void writeFloat(float val) throws IOException;
    public void writeInt(int val) throws IOException;
    public void writeLong(long val) throws IOException;
    public void writeShort(int val) throws IOException;
    public void writeUTF(String str) throws IOException;
// Methods Implementing ObjectOutput
    public void close() throws IOException;
    public void flush() throws IOException;
    public void write(int val) throws IOException;
    public void write(byte[] buf) throws IOException;
    public void write(byte[] buf, int off, int len) throws IOException;
    public final void writeObject(Object obj) throws IOException;
// Protected Instance Methods
    protected void annotateClass(Class<?> cl) throws IOException;                     empty
1.3 protected void annotateProxyClass(Class<?> cl) throws IOException;                empty
    protected void drain() throws IOException;
    protected boolean enableReplaceObject(boolean enable) throws SecurityException;
    protected Object replaceObject(Object obj) throws IOException;
1.3 protected void writeClassDescriptor(ObjectStreamClass desc) throws IOException;
1.2 protected void writeObjectOverride(Object obj) throws IOException;                empty
    protected void writeStreamHeader() throws IOException;
}
```

ObjectOutputStream.PutField — Java 1.2

java.io

This class holds values of named fields and allows them to be written to an ObjectOutputStream during the process of object serialization. It gives the programmer precise control over the serialization process and is typically used when the set of fields defined by a class does not match the set of fields (and the serialization stream format) defined by the original implementation of the class. In other words, ObjectOutputStream.PutField allows the implementation of a class to change without breaking serialization compatibility.

In order to use the PutField class, you typically define a private static serialPersistentFields field that refers to an array of ObjectStreamField objects. This array defines the set of fields written to the ObjectOutputStream and therefore defines the serialization format. If you do not declare a serialPersistentFields field, the set of fields is all fields of the class, excluding static and transient fields.

In addition to the serialPersistentFields field, your class must also define a private writeObject() method that is responsible for the custom serialization of your class. In this method, call the putFields() method of ObjectOutputStream to obtain an ObjectOutputStream.PutField object. Once you have this object, use its various put() methods to specify the names and values of the field to be written out. The set of named fields should match those specified by serialPersistentFields. You may specify the fields in any order; the PutField class is responsible for writing them out in the correct order. Once you have specified the values of all fields, call the write() method of your PutField object in order to write the field values out to the serialization stream.

To reverse this custom serialization process, see ObjectInputStream.GetField.

```
public abstract static class ObjectOutputStream.PutField {
// Public Constructors
    public PutField();
```

```
// Public Instance Methods
    public abstract void put(String name, long val);
    public abstract void put(String name, int val);
    public abstract void put(String name, float val);
    public abstract void put(String name, Object val);
    public abstract void put(String name, double val);
    public abstract void put(String name, byte val);
    public abstract void put(String name, boolean val);
    public abstract void put(String name, short val);
    public abstract void put(String name, char val);
// Deprecated Public Methods
#   public abstract void write(ObjectOutput out) throws IOException;
}
```

Returned By ObjectOutputStream.putFields()

ObjectStreamClass

Java 1.1

java.io

serializable

This class represents a class that is being serialized. An ObjectStreamClass object contains the name of a class, its unique version identifier, and the name and type of the fields that constitute the serialization format for the class. getSerialVersionUID() returns a unique version identifier for the class. It returns either the value of the private serialVersionUID field of the class or a computed value that is based upon the public API of the class. In Java 1.2 and later, getFields() returns an array of ObjectStreamField objects that represent the names and types of the fields of the class to be serialized. getField() returns a single ObjectStreamField object that represents a single named field. By default, these methods use all the fields of a class except those that are static or transient. However, this default set of fields can be overridden by declaring a private serialPersistentFields field in the class. The value of this field should be the desired array of ObjectStreamField objects.

ObjectStreamClass class does not have a constructor; you should use the static lookup() method to obtain an ObjectStreamClass object for a given Class object. The forClass() instance method performs the opposite operation; it returns the Class object that corresponds to a given ObjectStreamClass. Most applications never need to use this class.

Object — ObjectStreamClass ··· Serializable

```
public class ObjectStreamClass implements Serializable {
// No Constructor
// Public Constants
1.2 public static final ObjectStreamField[] NO_FIELDS;
// Public Class Methods
    public static ObjectStreamClass lookup(Class<?> cl);
// Public Instance Methods
    public Class<?> forClass();
1.2 public ObjectStreamField getField(String name);
1.2 public ObjectStreamField[] getFields();
    public String getName();
    public long getSerialVersionUID();
// Public Methods Overriding Object
    public String toString();
}
```

Passed To ObjectInputStream.resolveClass(), ObjectOutputStream.writeClassDescriptor()

Returned By ObjectInputStream.readClassDescriptor(), ObjectInputStream.GetField.getObjectStreamClass()

ObjectStreamConstants

Java 1.2

java.io

This interface defines various constants used by the Java object-serialization mechanism. Two important constants are PROTOCOL_VERSION_1 and PROTOCOL_VERSION_2, which specify the version of the serialization protocol to use. In Java 1.2, you can pass either of these values to the useProtocolVersion() method of an ObjectOutputStream. By default, Java 1.2 uses Version 2 of the protocol, and Java 1.1 uses Version 1 when serializing objects. Java 1.2 can deserialize objects written using either version of the protocol, as can Java 1.1.7 and later. If you want to serialize an object so that it can be read by versions of Java prior to Java 1.1.7, use PROTOCOL_VERSION_1.

The other constants defined by this interface are low-level values used by the serialization protocol. You do not need to use them unless you are reimplementing the serialization mechanism yourself.

```
public interface ObjectStreamConstants {
// Public Constants
    public static final int baseWireHandle;                                    =8257536
    public static final int PROTOCOL_VERSION_1;                                      =1
    public static final int PROTOCOL_VERSION_2;                                      =2
    public static final byte SC_BLOCK_DATA;                                          =8
5.0 public static final byte SC_ENUM;                                               =16
    public static final byte SC_EXTERNALIZABLE;                                      =4
    public static final byte SC_SERIALIZABLE;                                        =2
    public static final byte SC_WRITE_METHOD;                                        =1
    public static final short STREAM_MAGIC;                                     =-21267
    public static final short STREAM_VERSION;                                        =5
    public static final SerializablePermission SUBCLASS_IMPLEMENTATION_PERMISSION;
    public static final SerializablePermission SUBSTITUTION_PERMISSION;
    public static final byte TC_ARRAY;                                             =117
    public static final byte TC_BASE;                                              =112
    public static final byte TC_BLOCKDATA;                                         =119
    public static final byte TC_BLOCKDATALONG;                                     =122
    public static final byte TC_CLASS;                                             =118
    public static final byte TC_CLASSDESC;                                         =114
    public static final byte TC_ENDBLOCKDATA;                                      =120
5.0 public static final byte TC_ENUM;                                              =126
    public static final byte TC_EXCEPTION;                                         =123
1.3 public static final byte TC_LONGSTRING;                                        =124
    public static final byte TC_MAX;                                               =126
    public static final byte TC_NULL;                                              =112
    public static final byte TC_OBJECT;                                            =115
1.3 public static final byte TC_PROXYCLASSDESC;                                    =125
    public static final byte TC_REFERENCE;                                         =113
    public static final byte TC_RESET;                                             =121
    public static final byte TC_STRING;                                            =116
}
```

Implementations ObjectInputStream, ObjectOutputStream

ObjectStreamException

Java 1.1

java.io

serializable checked

This class is the superclass of a number of more specific exception types that may be raised in the process of serializing and deserializing objects with the ObjectOutputStream and ObjectInputStream classes.

Object — Throwable — Exception — IOException — ObjectStreamException
Serializable

```
public abstract class ObjectStreamException extends IOException {
// Protected Constructors
   protected ObjectStreamException();
   protected ObjectStreamException(String classname);
}
```

Subclasses InvalidClassException, InvalidObjectException, NotActiveException, NotSerializableException, OptionalDataException, StreamCorruptedException, WriteAbortedException

Thrown By java.security.KeyRep.readResolve(), java.security.cert.Certificate.writeReplace(), java.security.cert.Certificate.CertificateRep.readResolve(), java.security.cert.CertPath.writeReplace(), java.security.cert.CertPath.CertPathRep.readResolve()

ObjectStreamField

Java 1.2

java.io

comparable

This class represents a named field of a specified type (i.e., a specified Class). When a class serializes itself by writing a set of fields that are different from the fields it uses in its own implementation, it defines the set of fields to be written with an array of ObjectStreamField objects. This array should be the value of a private static field named serialPersistentFields. The methods of this class are used internally by the serialization mechanism and are not typically used elsewhere. See also ObjectOutputStream.PutField and ObjectInputStream.GetField.

Object — ObjectStreamField ··· Comparable

```
public class ObjectStreamField implements Comparable<Object> {
// Public Constructors
   public ObjectStreamField(String name, Class<?> type);
1.4 public ObjectStreamField(String name, Class<?> type, boolean unshared);
// Public Instance Methods
   public String getName();
   public int getOffset();
   public Class<?> getType();
   public char getTypeCode();
   public String getTypeString();
   public boolean isPrimitive();
1.4 public boolean isUnshared();
// Methods Implementing Comparable
   public int compareTo(Object obj);
// Public Methods Overriding Object
   public String toString();
// Protected Instance Methods
   protected void setOffset(int offset);
}
```

Returned By ObjectStreamClass.{getField(), getFields()}

Type Of ObjectStreamClass.NO_FIELDS

OptionalDataException **Java 1.1**

java.io **serializable checked**

Thrown by the readObject() method of an ObjectInputStream when it encounters primitive type data where it expects object data. Despite the exception name, this data is not optional, and object deserialization is stopped.

Object — Throwable — Exception — IOException — ObjectStreamException — OptionalDataException
Serializable

```
public class OptionalDataException extends ObjectStreamException {
// No Constructor
// Public Instance Fields
   public boolean eof;
   public int length;
}
```

OutputStream **Java 1.0**

java.io **closeable flushable**

This abstract class is the superclass of all output streams. It defines the basic output methods all output stream classes provide. write() writes a single byte or an array (or subarray) of bytes. flush() forces any buffered output to be written. close() closes the stream and frees up any system resources associated with it. The stream may not be used once close() has been called. See also Writer.

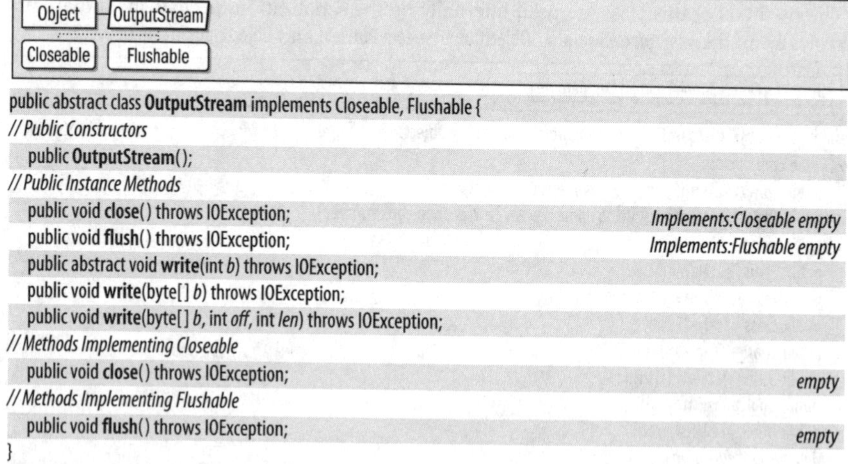


```
public abstract class OutputStream implements Closeable, Flushable {
// Public Constructors
   public OutputStream();
// Public Instance Methods
   public void close() throws IOException;                        Implements:Closeable empty
   public void flush() throws IOException;                        Implements:Flushable empty
   public abstract void write(int b) throws IOException;
   public void write(byte[] b) throws IOException;
   public void write(byte[] b, int off, int len) throws IOException;
// Methods Implementing Closeable
   public void close() throws IOException;                        empty
// Methods Implementing Flushable
   public void flush() throws IOException;                        empty
}
```

Subclasses ByteArrayOutputStream, FileOutputStream, FilterOutputStream, ObjectOutputStream, PipedOutputStream

Passed To Too many methods to list.

Returned By Process.getOutputStream(), Runtime.getLocalizedOutputStream(), java.net.CacheRequest.getBody(), java.net.Socket.getOutputStream(), java.net.SocketImpl.getOutputStream(), java.net.URLConnection.getOutputStream(), java.nio.channels.Channels.newOutputStream(), javax.xml.transform.stream.StreamResult.getOutputStream()

Type Of FilterOutputStream.out

OutputStreamWriter — Java 1.1

java.io — appendable closeable flushable

This class is a character output stream that uses a byte output stream as the destination for its data. When characters are written to an OutputStreamWriter, it translates them into bytes according to a particular locale- and/or platform-specific character encoding and writes those bytes to the specified OutputStream. This is a very important internationalization feature in Java 1.1 and later. OutputStreamWriter supports the usual Writer methods. It also has a getEncoding() method that returns the name of the encoding being used to convert characters to bytes.

When you create an OutputStreamWriter, specify the OutputStream to which it writes bytes and, optionally, the name of the character encoding that should be used to convert characters to bytes. If you do not specify an encoding name, the OutputStreamWriter uses the default encoding of the default locale, which is usually the correct thing to do. In Java 1.4 and later, this class uses the charset conversion facilities of the java.nio.charset package and allows you to explicitly specify the Charset or CharsetEncoder to be used. Prior to Java 1.4, the class allows you to specify only the name of the desired charset encoding.

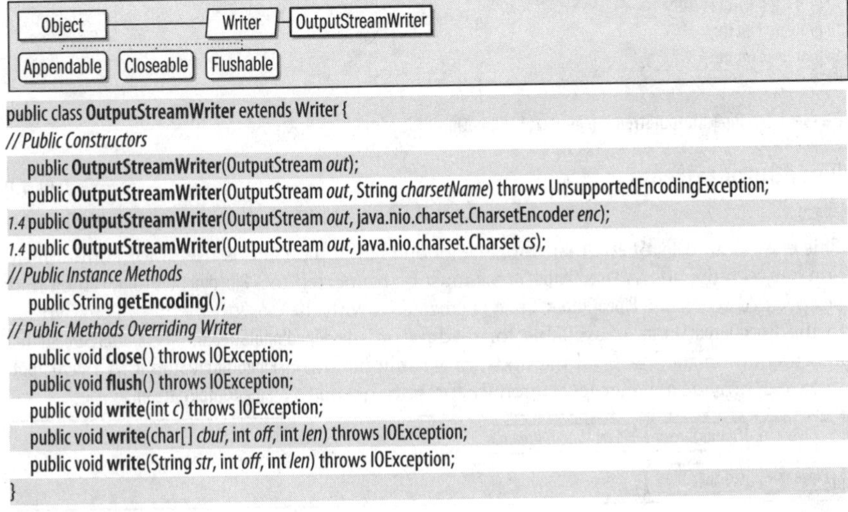


```
public class OutputStreamWriter extends Writer {
// Public Constructors
    public OutputStreamWriter(OutputStream out);
    public OutputStreamWriter(OutputStream out, String charsetName) throws UnsupportedEncodingException;
1.4 public OutputStreamWriter(OutputStream out, java.nio.charset.CharsetEncoder enc);
1.4 public OutputStreamWriter(OutputStream out, java.nio.charset.Charset cs);
// Public Instance Methods
    public String getEncoding();
// Public Methods Overriding Writer
    public void close() throws IOException;
    public void flush() throws IOException;
    public void write(int c) throws IOException;
    public void write(char[] cbuf, int off, int len) throws IOException;
    public void write(String str, int off, int len) throws IOException;
}
```

Subclasses FileWriter

PipedInputStream — Java 1.0

java.io — closeable

This class is an InputStream that implements one half of a pipe and is useful for communication between threads. A PipedInputStream must be connected to a PipedOutputStream object, which may be specified when the PipedInputStream is created or with the connect() method. Data read from a PipedInputStream object is received from the PipedOutputStream to which it is connected. See InputStream for information on the low-level methods for reading data from a PipedInputStream. A FilterInputStream can provide a higher-level interface for reading data from a PipedInputStream.

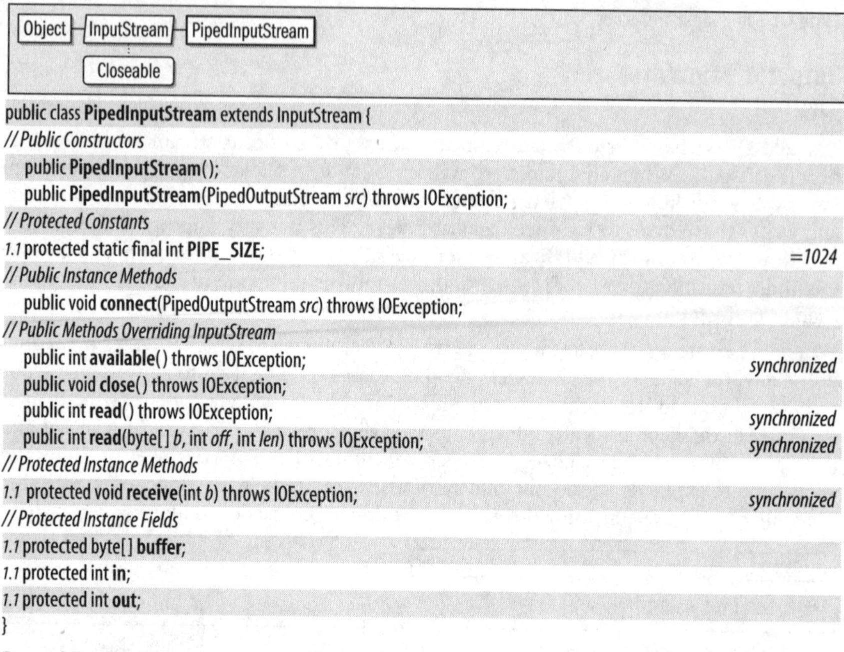


```
public class PipedInputStream extends InputStream {
// Public Constructors
   public PipedInputStream();
   public PipedInputStream(PipedOutputStream src) throws IOException;
// Protected Constants
1.1 protected static final int PIPE_SIZE;                                    =1024
// Public Instance Methods
   public void connect(PipedOutputStream src) throws IOException;
// Public Methods Overriding InputStream
   public int available() throws IOException;                          synchronized
   public void close() throws IOException;
   public int read() throws IOException;                               synchronized
   public int read(byte[] b, int off, int len) throws IOException;     synchronized
// Protected Instance Methods
1.1 protected void receive(int b) throws IOException;                  synchronized
// Protected Instance Fields
1.1 protected byte[] buffer;
1.1 protected int in;
1.1 protected int out;
}
```

Passed To PipedOutputStream.{connect(), PipedOutputStream()}

PipedOutputStream **Java 1.0**

java.io closeable flushable

This class is an OutputStream that implements one half a pipe and is useful for communication between threads. A PipedOutputStream must be connected to a PipedInputStream, which may be specified when the PipedOutputStream is created or with the connect() method. Data written to the PipedOutputStream is available for reading on the PipedInputStream. See OutputStream for information on the low-level methods for writing data to a PipedOutputStream. A FilterOutputStream can provide a higher-level interface for writing data to a PipedOutputStream.

Object — OutputStream — PipedOutputStream
Closeable, Flushable

```
public class PipedOutputStream extends OutputStream {
// Public Constructors
   public PipedOutputStream();
   public PipedOutputStream(PipedInputStream snk) throws IOException;
// Public Instance Methods
   public void connect(PipedInputStream snk) throws IOException;       synchronized
// Public Methods Overriding OutputStream
   public void close() throws IOException;
   public void flush() throws IOException;                             synchronized
   public void write(int b) throws IOException;
   public void write(byte[] b, int off, int len) throws IOException;
}
```

Passed To PipedInputStream.{connect(), PipedInputStream()}

PipedReader — Java 1.1

java.io — readable closeable

PipedReader is a character input stream that reads characters from a PipedWriter character output stream to which it is connected. PipedReader implements one half of a pipe and is useful for communication between two threads of an application. A PipedReader cannot be used until it is connected to a PipedWriter object, which may be passed to the PipedReader() constructor or to the connect() method. PipedReader inherits most of the methods of its superclass. See Reader for more information. PipedReader is the character-stream analog of PipedInputStream.

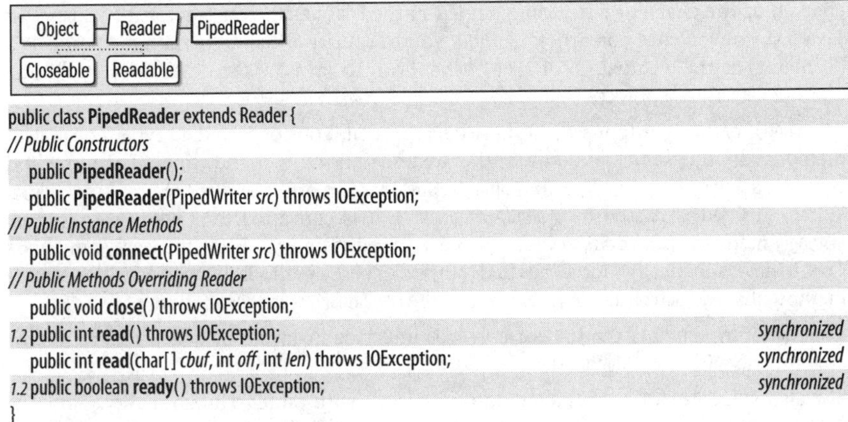


```
public class PipedReader extends Reader {
// Public Constructors
    public PipedReader();
    public PipedReader(PipedWriter src) throws IOException;
// Public Instance Methods
    public void connect(PipedWriter src) throws IOException;
// Public Methods Overriding Reader
    public void close() throws IOException;
1.2 public int read() throws IOException;                                   synchronized
    public int read(char[] cbuf, int off, int len) throws IOException;      synchronized
1.2 public boolean ready() throws IOException;                              synchronized
}
```

Passed To PipedWriter.{connect(), PipedWriter()}

PipedWriter — Java 1.1

java.io — appendable closeable flushable

PipedWriter is a character output stream that writes characters to the PipedReader character input stream to which it is connected. PipedWriter implements one half of a pipe and is useful for communication between two threads of an application. A PipedWriter cannot be used until it is connected to a PipedReader object, which may be passed to the PipedWriter() constructor or to the connect() method. PipedWriter inherits most of the methods of its superclass. See Writer for more information. PipedWriter is the character-stream analog of PipedOutputStream.

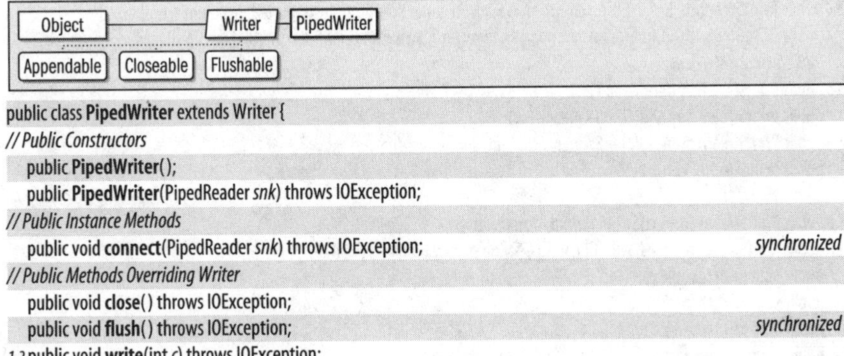


```
public class PipedWriter extends Writer {
// Public Constructors
    public PipedWriter();
    public PipedWriter(PipedReader snk) throws IOException;
// Public Instance Methods
    public void connect(PipedReader snk) throws IOException;                synchronized
// Public Methods Overriding Writer
    public void close() throws IOException;
    public void flush() throws IOException;                                 synchronized
1.2 public void write(int c) throws IOException;
```

```
   public void write(char[] cbuf, int off, int len) throws IOException;
}
```

Passed To PipedReader.{connect(), PipedReader()}

PrintStream **Java 1.0**

java.io **appendable closeable flushable**

This class is a byte output stream that implements a number of methods for displaying textual representations of Java primitive data types. System.out and System.err are PrintStream objects. PrintStream converts characters to bytes using the platform's default charset, or the charset or encoding named in the PrintStream() constructor invocation. In Java 5.0, convenience constructors allow you to specify a file (either as a file name or a File object) as the destination of a PrintStream. Prior to Java 5.0 the destination had to be another OutputStream object.

The print() methods output standard textual representations of each data type. The println() methods do the same and follow the representations with newlines. Each method converts a Java primitive type to a String representation and outputs the resulting string. When an Object is passed to a print() or println(), it is converted to a String by calling its toString() method. In Java 5.0, you can also use the printf() methods (or the format() methods that behave identically) for formatted output. These methods behave like the format() method of a java.util.Formatter object that uses the PrintStream as its destination.

This class implements the java.lang.Appendable interface in Java 5.0, which makes it suitable for use with a java.util.Formatter.

See also PrintWriter for a character output stream with similar functionality. And see DataOutputStream for a byte output stream that outputs binary, rather than textual, representations of Java's primitive types.

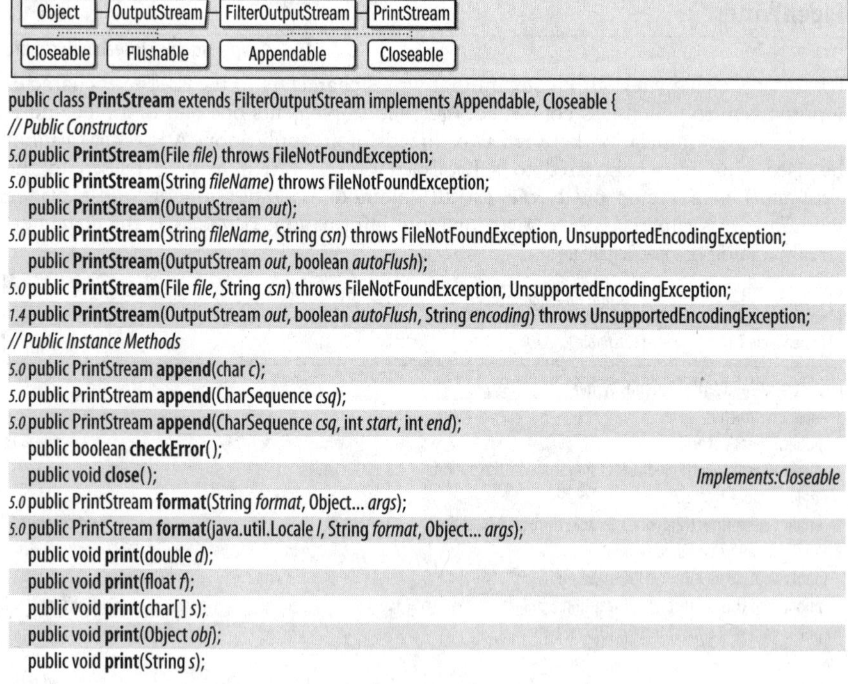


```
public class PrintStream extends FilterOutputStream implements Appendable, Closeable {
// Public Constructors
5.0 public PrintStream(File file) throws FileNotFoundException;
5.0 public PrintStream(String fileName) throws FileNotFoundException;
    public PrintStream(OutputStream out);
5.0 public PrintStream(String fileName, String csn) throws FileNotFoundException, UnsupportedEncodingException;
    public PrintStream(OutputStream out, boolean autoFlush);
5.0 public PrintStream(File file, String csn) throws FileNotFoundException, UnsupportedEncodingException;
1.4 public PrintStream(OutputStream out, boolean autoFlush, String encoding) throws UnsupportedEncodingException;
// Public Instance Methods
5.0 public PrintStream append(char c);
5.0 public PrintStream append(CharSequence csq);
5.0 public PrintStream append(CharSequence csq, int start, int end);
    public boolean checkError();
    public void close();                                              Implements:Closeable
5.0 public PrintStream format(String format, Object... args);
5.0 public PrintStream format(java.util.Locale l, String format, Object... args);
    public void print(double d);
    public void print(float f);
    public void print(char[] s);
    public void print(Object obj);
    public void print(String s);
```

```
    public void print(long l);
    public void print(boolean b);
    public void print(char c);
    public void print(int i);
5.0 public PrintStream printf(String format, Object... args);
5.0 public PrintStream printf(java.util.Locale l, String format, Object... args);
    public void println();
    public void println(char[] x);
    public void println(double x);
    public void println(Object x);
    public void println(String x);
    public void println(float x);
    public void println(char x);
    public void println(boolean x);
    public void println(long x);
    public void println(int x);
// Methods Implementing Closeable
    public void close();
// Public Methods Overriding FilterOutputStream
    public void flush();
    public void write(int b);
    public void write(byte[] buf, int off, int len);
// Protected Instance Methods
1.1 protected void setError();
}
```

Passed To System.{setErr(), setOut()}, Throwable.printStackTrace(), java.util.Formatter.Formatter(), java.util.Properties.list(), javax.xml.transform.TransformerException.printStackTrace(), javax.xml.xpath.XPathException.printStackTrace()

Type Of System.{err, out}

PrintWriter — Java 1.1

java.io — appendable closeable flushable

This class is a character output stream that implements a number of print() and println() methods that output textual representations of primitive values and objects. When you create a PrintWriter object, you specify a character or byte output stream that it should write its characters to and, optionally, whether the PrintWriter stream should be automatically flushed whenever println() is called. If you specify a byte output stream as the destination, the PrintWriter() constructor automatically creates the necessary OutputStreamWriter object to convert characters to bytes using the default encoding. In Java 5.0, convenience constructors allow you to specify a file (either as a file name or a File object) as the destination. You may optionally specify the name of a charset to use for character-to-byte conversion when writing to the file.

PrintWriter implements the normal write(), flush(), and close() methods all Writer subclasses define. It is more common to use the higher-level print() and println() methods, each of which converts its argument to a string before outputting it. println() can also terminate the line (and optionally flush the buffer) after printing its argument. In Java 5.0, you can also use the printf() methods (or the format() methods that behave identically) for formatted output. These methods behave like the format() method of a java.util.Formatter object that uses the PrintWriter as its destination.

The methods of PrintWriter never throw exceptions. Instead, when errors occur, they set an internal flag you can check by calling checkError(). checkError() first flushes the internal stream and then returns true if any exception has occurred while writing values to that stream. Once an error has occurred on a PrintWriter object, all subsequent calls to checkError() return true; there is no way to reset the error flag.

PrintWriter is the character stream analog to PrintStream, which it supersedes. You can usually easily replace any PrintStream objects in a program with PrintWriter objects. This is particularly important for internationalized programs. The only valid remaining use for the PrintStream class is for the System.out and System.err standard output streams. See PrintStream for details.

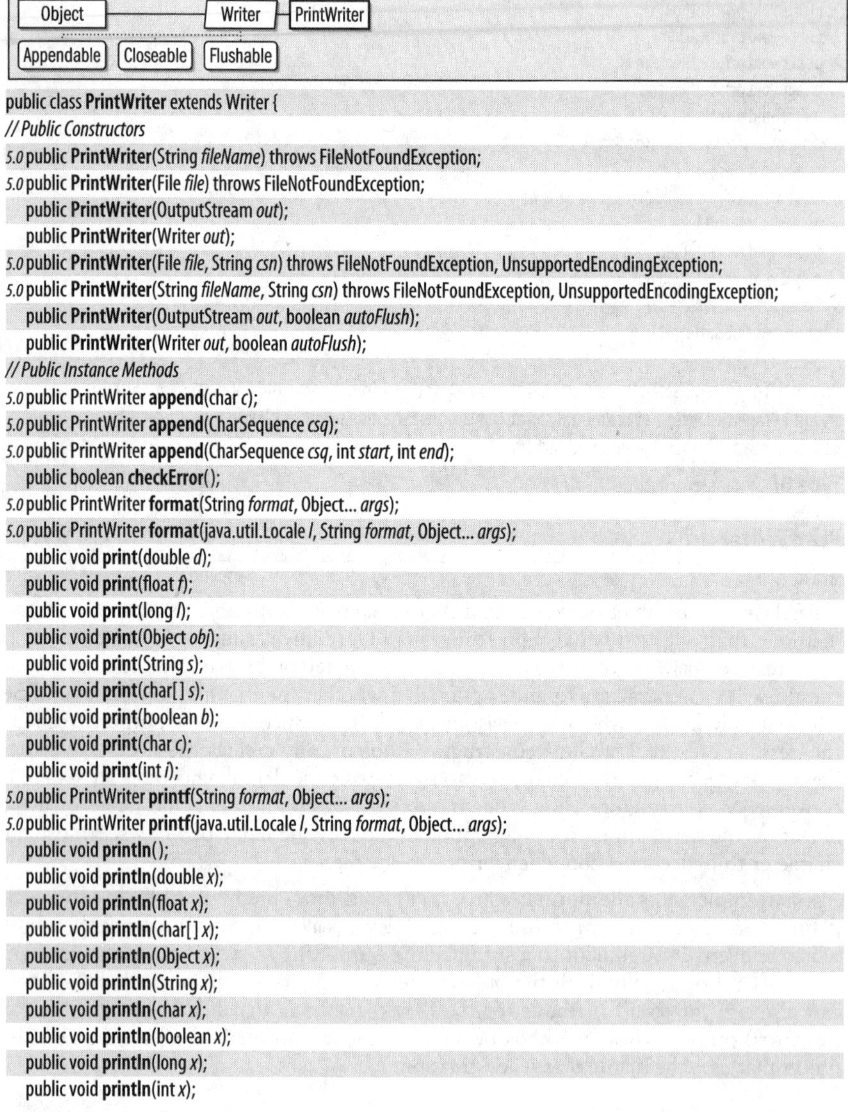


```
public class PrintWriter extends Writer {
// Public Constructors
5.0 public PrintWriter(String fileName) throws FileNotFoundException;
5.0 public PrintWriter(File file) throws FileNotFoundException;
    public PrintWriter(OutputStream out);
    public PrintWriter(Writer out);
5.0 public PrintWriter(File file, String csn) throws FileNotFoundException, UnsupportedEncodingException;
5.0 public PrintWriter(String fileName, String csn) throws FileNotFoundException, UnsupportedEncodingException;
    public PrintWriter(OutputStream out, boolean autoFlush);
    public PrintWriter(Writer out, boolean autoFlush);
// Public Instance Methods
5.0 public PrintWriter append(char c);
5.0 public PrintWriter append(CharSequence csq);
5.0 public PrintWriter append(CharSequence csq, int start, int end);
    public boolean checkError();
5.0 public PrintWriter format(String format, Object... args);
5.0 public PrintWriter format(java.util.Locale l, String format, Object... args);
    public void print(double d);
    public void print(float f);
    public void print(long l);
    public void print(Object obj);
    public void print(String s);
    public void print(char[] s);
    public void print(boolean b);
    public void print(char c);
    public void print(int i);
5.0 public PrintWriter printf(String format, Object... args);
5.0 public PrintWriter printf(java.util.Locale l, String format, Object... args);
    public void println();
    public void println(double x);
    public void println(float x);
    public void println(char[] x);
    public void println(Object x);
    public void println(String x);
    public void println(char x);
    public void println(boolean x);
    public void println(long x);
    public void println(int x);
```

```
// Public Methods Overriding Writer
   public void close();
   public void flush();
   public void write(String s);
   public void write(char[] buf);
   public void write(int c);
   public void write(String s, int off, int len);
   public void write(char[] buf, int off, int len);
// Protected Instance Methods
   protected void setError();
// Protected Instance Fields
1.2 protected Writer out;
}
```

Passed To Throwable.printStackTrace(), java.util.Properties.list(), javax.xml.transform.TransformerException.printStackTrace(), javax.xml.xpath.XPathException.printStackTrace()

PushbackInputStream **Java 1.0**

java.io closeable

This class is a FilterInputStream that implements a one-byte pushback buffer or, as of Java 1.1, a pushback buffer of a specified length. The unread() methods push bytes back into the stream; these bytes are the first ones read by the next call to a read() method. This class is sometimes useful when writing parsers. See also PushbackReader.

Object — InputStream — FilterInputStream — PushbackInputStream
Closeable

```
public class PushbackInputStream extends FilterInputStream {
// Public Constructors
   public PushbackInputStream(InputStream in);
1.1 public PushbackInputStream(InputStream in, int size);
// Public Instance Methods
   public void unread(int b) throws IOException;
1.1 public void unread(byte[] b) throws IOException;
1.1 public void unread(byte[] b, int off, int len) throws IOException;
// Public Methods Overriding FilterInputStream
   public int available() throws IOException;
1.2 public void close() throws IOException;                 synchronized
5.0 public void mark(int readlimit);                         synchronized empty
   public boolean markSupported();                           constant
   public int read() throws IOException;
   public int read(byte[] b, int off, int len) throws IOException;
5.0 public void reset() throws IOException;                 synchronized
1.2 public long skip(long n) throws IOException;
// Protected Instance Fields
1.1 protected byte[] buf;
1.1 protected int pos;
}
```

PushbackReader **Java 1.1**

java.io *readable closeable*

This class is a character input stream that uses another input stream as its input source and adds the ability to push characters back onto the stream. This feature is often useful when writing parsers. When you create a PushbackReader stream, you specify the stream to be read from and, optionally, the size of the pushback buffer (i.e., the number of characters that may be pushed back onto the stream or unread). If you do not specify a size for this buffer, the default size is one character. PushbackReader inherits or overrides all standard Reader methods and adds three unread() methods that push a single character, an array of characters, or a portion of an array of characters back onto the stream. This class is the character stream analog of PushbackInputStream.

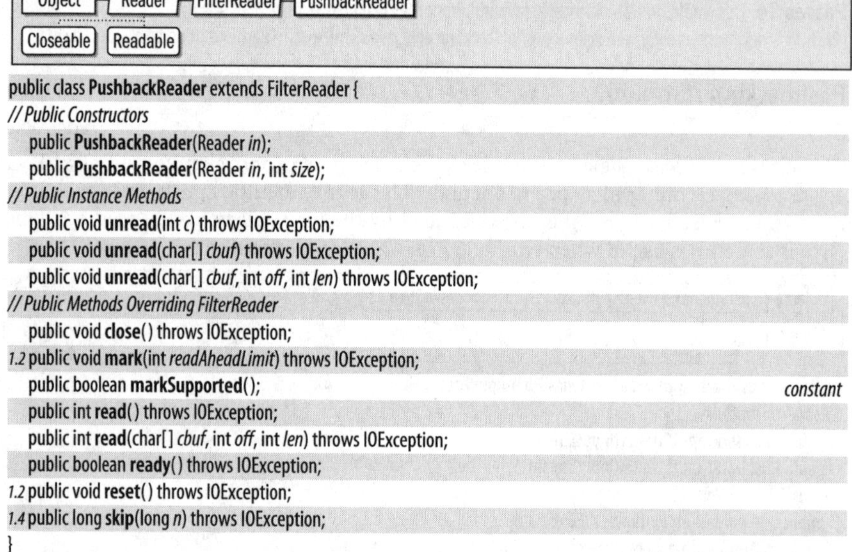


```
public class PushbackReader extends FilterReader {
// Public Constructors
   public PushbackReader(Reader in);
   public PushbackReader(Reader in, int size);
// Public Instance Methods
   public void unread(int c) throws IOException;
   public void unread(char[] cbuf) throws IOException;
   public void unread(char[] cbuf, int off, int len) throws IOException;
// Public Methods Overriding FilterReader
   public void close() throws IOException;
1.2 public void mark(int readAheadLimit) throws IOException;
   public boolean markSupported();                                    constant
   public int read() throws IOException;
   public int read(char[] cbuf, int off, int len) throws IOException;
   public boolean ready() throws IOException;
1.2 public void reset() throws IOException;
1.4 public long skip(long n) throws IOException;
}
```

RandomAccessFile **Java 1.0**

java.io *closeable*

This class allows you to read and write arbitrary bytes, text, and primitive Java data types from or to any specified location in a file. Because this class provides random, rather than sequential, access to files, it is neither a subclass of InputStream nor of OutputStream, but provides an entirely independent method for reading and writing data from or to files. RandomAccessFile implements the same interfaces as DataInputStream and DataOutputStream, and thus defines the same methods for reading and writing data as those classes do.

The seek() method provides random access to the file; it is used to select the position in the file where data should be read or written. The various read and write methods update this file position so that a sequence of read or write operations can be performed on a contiguous portion of the file without having to call the seek() method before each read or write.

The *mode* argument to the constructor methods should be "r" for a file that is to be read-only or "rw" for a file that is to be written (and perhaps read as well). In Java 1.4 and later, two other values for the *mode* argument are allowed as well. A mode of "rwd" opens the file for reading and writing, and requires that (if the file resides on a local filesystem) every update to the file content be written synchronously to the underlying file. The "rws" mode is similar, but requires synchronous updates to both the file's content and its metadata (which includes things such as file access times). Using "rws" mode may require that the file metadata be modified every time the file is read.

In Java 1.4 and later, use the getChannel() method to obtain a FileChannel object that you can use to access the file using the New I/O API of java.nio and its subpackages. If the RandomAccessFile was opened with a mode of "r", the FileChannel allows only reading. Otherwise, it allows both reading and writing.

Object — RandomAccessFile

Closeable | DataInput | DataOutput

```
public class RandomAccessFile implements Closeable, DataInput, DataOutput {
// Public Constructors
   public RandomAccessFile(File file, String mode) throws FileNotFoundException;
   public RandomAccessFile(String name, String mode) throws FileNotFoundException;
// Public Instance Methods
   public void close() throws IOException;                                Implements:Closeable
1.4 public final java.nio.channels.FileChannel getChannel();
   public final FileDescriptor getFD() throws IOException;
   public long getFilePointer() throws IOException;                                 native
   public long length() throws IOException;                                         native
   public int read() throws IOException;                                            native
   public int read(byte[] b) throws IOException;
   public int read(byte[] b, int off, int len) throws IOException;
   public void seek(long pos) throws IOException;                                   native
1.2 public void setLength(long newLength) throws IOException;                       native
// Methods Implementing Closeable
   public void close() throws IOException;
// Methods Implementing DataInput
   public final boolean readBoolean() throws IOException;
   public final byte readByte() throws IOException;
   public final char readChar() throws IOException;
   public final double readDouble() throws IOException;
   public final float readFloat() throws IOException;
   public final void readFully(byte[] b) throws IOException;
   public final void readFully(byte[] b, int off, int len) throws IOException;
   public final int readInt() throws IOException;
   public final String readLine() throws IOException;
   public final long readLong() throws IOException;
   public final short readShort() throws IOException;
   public final int readUnsignedByte() throws IOException;
   public final int readUnsignedShort() throws IOException;
   public final String readUTF() throws IOException;
   public int skipBytes(int n) throws IOException;
// Methods Implementing DataOutput
   public void write(int b) throws IOException;                                     native
   public void write(byte[] b) throws IOException;
   public void write(byte[] b, int off, int len) throws IOException;
   public final void writeBoolean(boolean v) throws IOException;
   public final void writeByte(int v) throws IOException;
   public final void writeBytes(String s) throws IOException;
```

```
    public final void writeChar(int v) throws IOException;
    public final void writeChars(String s) throws IOException;
    public final void writeDouble(double v) throws IOException;
    public final void writeFloat(float v) throws IOException;
    public final void writeInt(int v) throws IOException;
    public final void writeLong(long v) throws IOException;
    public final void writeShort(int v) throws IOException;
    public final void writeUTF(String str) throws IOException;
}
```

Reader **Java 1.1**

java.io **readable closeable**

This abstract class is the superclass of all character input streams. It is an analog to InputStream, which is the superclass of all byte input streams. Reader defines the basic methods that all character output streams provide. read() returns a single character or an array (or subarray) of characters, blocking if necessary; it returns –1 if the end of the stream has been reached. ready() returns true if there are characters available for reading. If ready() returns true, the next call to read() is guaranteed not to block. close() closes the character input stream. skip() skips a specified number of characters in the input stream. If markSupported() returns true, mark() marks a position in the stream and, if necessary, creates a look-ahead buffer of the specified size. Future calls to reset() restore the stream to the marked position if they occur within the specified look-ahead limit. Note that not all stream types support this mark-and-reset functionality. To create a subclass of Reader, you need only implement the three-argument version of read() and the close() method. Most subclasses implement additional methods, however.

Object — Reader
Closeable Readable

```
public abstract class Reader implements Closeable, Readable {
// Protected Constructors
    protected Reader();
    protected Reader(Object lock);
// Public Instance Methods
    public abstract void close() throws IOException;                    Implements:Closeable
    public void mark(int readAheadLimit) throws IOException;
    public boolean markSupported();                                     constant
    public int read() throws IOException;
    public int read(char[] cbuf) throws IOException;
    public abstract int read(char[] cbuf, int off, int len) throws IOException;
    public boolean ready() throws IOException;                          constant
    public void reset() throws IOException;
    public long skip(long n) throws IOException;
// Methods Implementing Closeable
    public abstract void close() throws IOException;
// Methods Implementing Readable
5.0 public int read(java.nio.CharBuffer target) throws IOException;
// Protected Instance Fields
    protected Object lock;
}
```

Subclasses BufferedReader, CharArrayReader, FilterReader, InputStreamReader, PipedReader, StringReader

Passed To BufferedReader.BufferedReader(), FilterReader.FilterReader(), LineNumberReader.LineNumberReader(), PushbackReader.PushbackReader(), StreamTokenizer.StreamTokenizer(), javax.xml.transform.stream.StreamSource.{setReader(), StreamSource()}, org.xml.sax.InputSource.{InputSource(), setCharacterStream()}

Returned By java.nio.channels.Channels.newReader(), javax.xml.transform.stream.StreamSource.getReader(), org.xml.sax.InputSource.getCharacterStream()

Type Of FilterReader.in

SequenceInputStream — Java 1.0

java.io — closeable

This class provides a way of seamlessly concatenating the data from two or more input streams. It provides an InputStream interface to a sequence of InputStream objects. Data is read from the streams in the order in which the streams are specified. When the end of one stream is reached, data is automatically read from the next stream. This class might be useful, for example, when implementing an include file facility for a parser.

Object — InputStream — SequenceInputStream
Closeable

```
public class SequenceInputStream extends InputStream {
// Public Constructors
   public SequenceInputStream(java.util.Enumeration<? extends InputStream> e);
   public SequenceInputStream(InputStream s1, InputStream s2);
// Public Methods Overriding InputStream
1.1 public int available() throws IOException;
   public void close() throws IOException;
   public int read() throws IOException;
   public int read(byte[] b, int off, int len) throws IOException;
}
```

Serializable — Java 1.1

java.io — serializable

The Serializable interface defines no methods or constants. A class should implement this interface simply to indicate that it allows itself to be serialized and deserialized with ObjectOutputStream.writeObject() and ObjectInputStream.readObject().

Objects that need special handling during serialization or deserialization may implement one or both of the following methods; note, however, that these methods are not part of the Serializable interface):

```
private void writeObject(java.io.ObjectOutputStream out) throws IOException;
private void readObject(java.io.ObjectInputStream in) throws IOException, ClassNotFoundException;
```

Typically, the writeObject() method performs any necessary cleanup or preparation for serialization, invokes the defaultWriteObject() method of the ObjectOutputStream to serialize the nontransient fields of the class, and optionally writes any additional data that is required. Similarly, the readObject() method typically invokes the defaultReadObject() method of the ObjectInputStream, reads any additional data written by the corresponding writeObject() method, and performs any extra initialization required by the object. The readObject() method may also register an ObjectInputValidation object to validate the object once it is completely deserialized.

```
public interface Serializable {
}
```

Implementations Too many classes to list.

Passed To java.security.SignedObject.SignedObject(), javax.crypto.SealedObject.SealedObject()

SerializablePermission Java 1.2

java.io serializable permission

This class is a java.security.Permission that governs the use of certain sensitive features of serialization. SerializablePermission objects have a name, or target, but do not have an action list. The name "enableSubclassImplementation" represents permission to serialize and deserialize objects using subclasses of ObjectOutputStream and ObjectInputStream. This capability is protected by a permission because malicious code can define object stream subclasses that incorrectly serialize and deserialize objects.

The only other name supported by SerializablePermission is "enableSubstitution," which represents permission for one object to be substituted for another during serialization or deserialization. Permission of this type is required by the ObjectOutputStream.enableReplaceObject() and ObjectInputStream.enableResolveObject() methods.

Applications never need to use this class. Programmers writing system-level code may use it, and system administrators configuring security policies should be familiar with it.

Object — Permission — BasicPermission — SerializablePermission
Guard, Serializable (Permission); Serializable (BasicPermission)

```
public final class SerializablePermission extends java.security.BasicPermission {
// Public Constructors
   public SerializablePermission(String name);
   public SerializablePermission(String name, String actions);
}
```

Type Of ObjectStreamConstants.{SUBCLASS_IMPLEMENTATION_PERMISSION, SUBSTITUTION_PERMISSION}

StreamCorruptedException Java 1.1

java.io serializable checked

Signals that the data stream being read by an ObjectInputStream has been corrupted and does not contain valid serialized object data.

Object — Throwable — Exception — IOException — ObjectStreamException — StreamCorruptedException
Serializable (Throwable)

```
public class StreamCorruptedException extends ObjectStreamException {
// Public Constructors
   public StreamCorruptedException();
   public StreamCorruptedException(String reason);
}
```

Thrown By ObjectInputStream.readStreamHeader()

StreamTokenizer Java 1.0

java.io

This class performs lexical analysis of a specified input stream and breaks the input into tokens. It can be extremely useful when writing simple parsers. nextToken() returns the next token in the stream; this is either one of the constants defined by the class (which represent end-of-file, end-of-line, a parsed floating-point number, and a parsed word) or a character value. pushBack() pushes the token back onto the stream, so that it is returned by the next call to nextToken(). The public variables sval and nval contain the string and numeric values (if applicable) of the most recently read token. They are applicable when the returned token is TT_WORD or TT_NUMBER. lineno() returns the current line number.

The remaining methods allow you to specify how tokens are recognized. wordChars() specifies a range of characters that should be treated as parts of words. whitespaceChars() specifies a range of characters that serve to delimit tokens. ordinaryChars() and ordinaryChar() specify characters that are never part of tokens and should be returned as-is. resetSyntax() makes all characters ordinary. eolIsSignificant() specifies whether end-of-line is significant. If so, the TT_EOL constant is returned for end-of-lines; otherwise, they are treated as whitespace. commentChar() specifies a character that begins a comment that lasts until the end of the line. No characters in the comment are returned. slashStarComments() and slashSlashComments() specify whether the StreamTokenizer should recognize C- and C++-style comments. If so, no part of the comment is returned as a token. quoteChar() specifies a character used to delimit strings. When a string token is parsed, the quote character is returned as the token value, and the body of the string is stored in the sval variable. lowerCaseMode() specifies whether TT_WORD tokens should be converted to all lowercase characters before being stored in sval. parseNumbers() specifies that the StreamTokenizer should recognize and return double-precision floating-point number tokens.

```
public class StreamTokenizer {
// Public Constructors
#  public StreamTokenizer(InputStream is);
1.1 public StreamTokenizer(Reader r);
// Public Constants
   public static final int TT_EOF;                                    =-1
   public static final int TT_EOL;                                    =10
   public static final int TT_NUMBER;                                 =-2
   public static final int TT_WORD;                                   =-3
// Public Instance Methods
   public void commentChar(int ch);
   public void eolIsSignificant(boolean flag);
   public int lineno();
   public void lowerCaseMode(boolean fl);
   public int nextToken() throws IOException;
   public void ordinaryChar(int ch);
   public void ordinaryChars(int low, int hi);
   public void parseNumbers();
   public void pushBack();
   public void quoteChar(int ch);
   public void resetSyntax();
   public void slashSlashComments(boolean flag);
   public void slashStarComments(boolean flag);
   public void whitespaceChars(int low, int hi);
   public void wordChars(int low, int hi);
// Public Methods Overriding Object
   public String toString();
// Public Instance Fields
   public double nval;
   public String sval;
   public int ttype;
}
```

StringBufferInputStream

Java 1.0; Deprecated in 1.1

java.io @Deprecated closeable

This class is a subclass of **InputStream** in which input bytes come from the characters of a specified **String** object. This class does not correctly convert the characters of a **StringBuffer** into bytes and is deprecated as of Java 1.1. Use **StringReader** instead to convert characters into bytes or use **ByteArrayInputStream** to read bytes from an array of bytes.

Object — InputStream — StringBufferInputStream
Closeable

```
public class StringBufferInputStream extends InputStream {
// Public Constructors
   public StringBufferInputStream(String s);
// Public Methods Overriding InputStream
   public int available();                                    synchronized
   public int read();                                         synchronized
   public int read(byte[] b, int off, int len);               synchronized
   public void reset();                                       synchronized
   public long skip(long n);                                  synchronized
// Protected Instance Fields
   protected String buffer;
   protected int count;
   protected int pos;
}
```

StringReader

Java 1.1

java.io readable closeable

This class is a character input stream that uses a **String** object as the source of the characters it returns. When you create a **StringReader**, you must specify the **String** to read from. **StringReader** defines the normal **Reader** methods and supports **mark()** and **reset()**. If **reset()** is called before **mark()** has been called, the stream is reset to the beginning of the specified string. **StringReader** is a character stream analog to **StringBufferInputStream**, which is deprecated as of Java 1.1. **StringReader** is also similar to **CharArrayReader**.

Object — Reader — StringReader
Closeable   Readable

```
public class StringReader extends Reader {
// Public Constructors
   public StringReader(String s);
// Public Methods Overriding Reader
   public void close();
   public void mark(int readAheadLimit) throws IOException;
   public boolean markSupported();                            constant
   public int read() throws IOException;
   public int read(char[] cbuf, int off, int len) throws IOException;
   public boolean ready() throws IOException;
   public void reset() throws IOException;
   public long skip(long ns) throws IOException;
}
```

StringWriter — Java 1.1

java.io — appendable closeable flushable

This class is a character output stream that uses an internal StringBuffer object as the destination of the characters written to the stream. When you create a StringWriter, you may optionally specify an initial size for the StringBuffer, but you do not specify the StringBuffer itself; it is managed internally by the StringWriter and grows as necessary to accommodate the characters written to it. StringWriter defines the standard write(), flush(), and close() methods all Writer subclasses define, as well as two methods to obtain the characters that have been written to the stream's internal buffer. toString() returns the contents of the internal buffer as a String, and getBuffer() returns the buffer itself. Note that getBuffer() returns a reference to the actual internal buffer, not a copy of it, so any changes you make to the buffer are reflected in subsequent calls to toString(). StringWriter is quite similar to CharArrayWriter, but does not have a byte-stream analog.

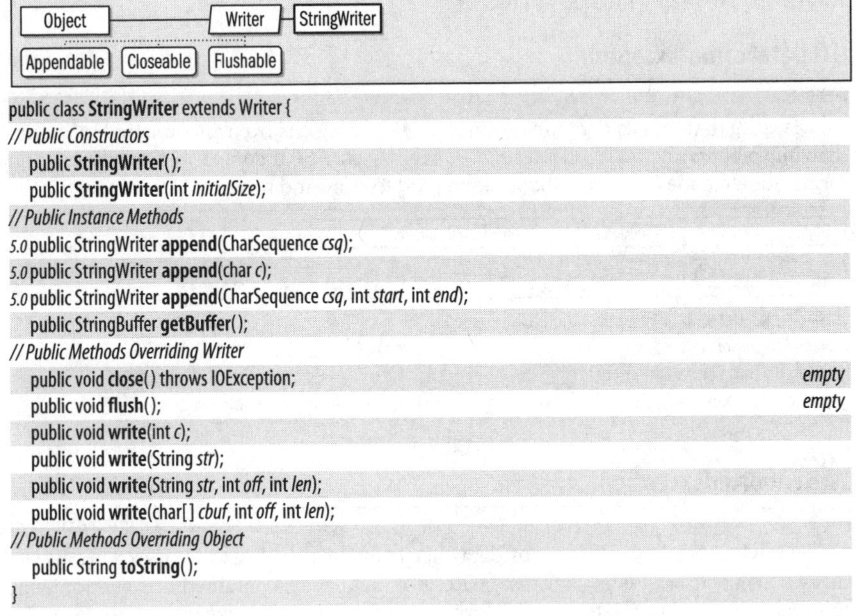


```
public class StringWriter extends Writer {
// Public Constructors
   public StringWriter();
   public StringWriter(int initialSize);
// Public Instance Methods
5.0 public StringWriter append(CharSequence csq);
5.0 public StringWriter append(char c);
5.0 public StringWriter append(CharSequence csq, int start, int end);
   public StringBuffer getBuffer();
// Public Methods Overriding Writer
   public void close() throws IOException;                          empty
   public void flush();                                             empty
   public void write(int c);
   public void write(String str);
   public void write(String str, int off, int len);
   public void write(char[] cbuf, int off, int len);
// Public Methods Overriding Object
   public String toString();
}
```

SyncFailedException — Java 1.1

java.io — serializable checked

Signals that a call to FileDescriptor.sync() did not complete successfully.

Object — Throwable — Exception — IOException — SyncFailedException

Serializable

```
public class SyncFailedException extends IOException {
// Public Constructors
   public SyncFailedException(String desc);
}
```

Thrown By FileDescriptor.sync()

UnsupportedEncodingException Java 1.1

java.io serializable checked

Signals that a requested character encoding is not supported by the current Java Virtual Machine.

Object ─ Throwable ─ Exception ─ IOException ─ UnsupportedEncodingException
Serializable

```
public class UnsupportedEncodingException extends IOException {
// Public Constructors
   public UnsupportedEncodingException();
   public UnsupportedEncodingException(String s);
}
```

Thrown By Too many methods to list.

UTFDataFormatException Java 1.0

java.io serializable checked

An IOException that signals that a malformed UTF-8 string has been encountered by a class that implements the DataInput interface. UTF-8 is an ASCII-compatible transformation format for Unicode characters that is often used to store and transmit Unicode text.

Object ─ Throwable ─ Exception ─ IOException ─ UTFDataFormatException
Serializable

```
public class UTFDataFormatException extends IOException {
// Public Constructors
   public UTFDataFormatException();
   public UTFDataFormatException(String s);
}
```

WriteAbortedException Java 1.1

java.io serializable checked

Thrown when reading a stream of data that is incomplete because an exception was thrown while it was being written. The detail field may contain the exception that terminated the output stream. In Java 1.4 and later, this exception can also be obtained with the standard Throwable getCause() method. The getMessage() method has been overridden to include the message of this detail exception, if any.

Object ─ Throwable ─ Exception ─ IOException ─ ObjectStreamException ─ WriteAbortedException
Serializable

```
public class WriteAbortedException extends ObjectStreamException {
// Public Constructors
   public WriteAbortedException(String s, Exception ex);
// Public Methods Overriding Throwable
1.4 public Throwable getCause();
   public String getMessage();
// Public Instance Fields
   public Exception detail;
}
```

Writer **Java 1.1**

java.io **appendable closeable flushable**

This abstract class is the superclass of all character output streams. It is an analog to OutputStream, which is the superclass of all byte output streams. Writer defines the basic write(), flush(), and close() methods all character output streams provide. The five versions of the write() method write a single character, a character array or subarray, or a string or substring to the destination of the stream. The most general version of this method—the one that writes a specified portion of a character array—is abstract and must be implemented by all subclasses. By default, the other write() methods are implemented in terms of this abstract one. The flush() method is another abstract method all subclasses must implement. It should force any output buffered by the stream to be written to its destination. If that destination is itself a character or byte output stream, it should invoke the flush() method of the destination stream as well. The close() method is also abstract. A subclass must implement this method so that it flushes and then closes the current stream and also closes whatever destination stream it is connected to. Once the stream is closed, any future calls to write() or flush() should throw an IOException.

In Java 5.0, this class has been modified to implement the Closeable and Flushable interfaces. It has also changed to implement java.lang.Appendable, which means that any Writer object can be used as the destination for a java.util.Formatter.

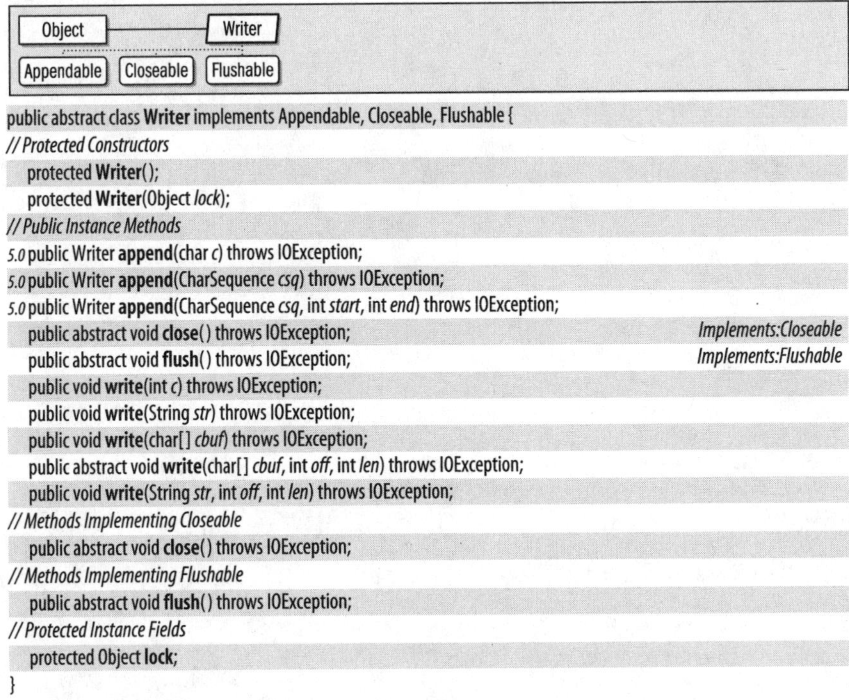


```
public abstract class Writer implements Appendable, Closeable, Flushable {
// Protected Constructors
   protected Writer();
   protected Writer(Object lock);
// Public Instance Methods
5.0 public Writer append(char c) throws IOException;
5.0 public Writer append(CharSequence csq) throws IOException;
5.0 public Writer append(CharSequence csq, int start, int end) throws IOException;
   public abstract void close() throws IOException;                    Implements:Closeable
   public abstract void flush() throws IOException;                    Implements:Flushable
   public void write(int c) throws IOException;
   public void write(String str) throws IOException;
   public void write(char[] cbuf) throws IOException;
   public abstract void write(char[] cbuf, int off, int len) throws IOException;
   public void write(String str, int off, int len) throws IOException;
// Methods Implementing Closeable
   public abstract void close() throws IOException;
// Methods Implementing Flushable
   public abstract void flush() throws IOException;
// Protected Instance Fields
   protected Object lock;
}
```

Subclasses BufferedWriter, CharArrayWriter, FilterWriter, OutputStreamWriter, PipedWriter, PrintWriter, StringWriter

Passed To BufferedWriter.BufferedWriter(), CharArrayWriter.writeTo(), FilterWriter.FilterWriter(), PrintWriter.PrintWriter(), javax.xml.transform.stream.StreamResult.{setWriter(), StreamResult()}

Returned By CharArrayWriter.append(), PrintWriter.append(), StringWriter.append(), java.nio.channels.Channels.newWriter(), javax.xml.transform.stream.StreamResult.getWriter()

Type Of FilterWriter.out, PrintWriter.out

10

java.lang and Subpackages

This chapter covers the java.lang package which defines the core classes and interfaces that are indispensable to the Java platform and the Java programming language. It also covers more specialized subpackages:

java.lang.annotation
: Defines the Annotation interface that all annotation types extend, and also defines meta-annotation types and related enumerated types. Added in Java 5.0.

java.lang.instrument
: Provides support for Java-based "agents" that can instrument a Java program by transforming class files as they are loaded. Added in Java 5.0.

java.lang.management
: Defines "management bean" interfaces for remote monitoring and management of a running Java interpreter.

java.lang.ref
: Defines "reference" classes that are used to refer to objects without preventing the garbage collector from reclaiming those objects.

java.lang.reflect
: Allows Java programs to examine the members of arbitrary classes, invoking methods, and querying and setting the value of fields.

Package java.lang — Java 1.0

The java.lang package contains the classes that are most central to the Java language. Object is the ultimate superclass of all Java classes and is therefore at the top of all class hierarchies. Class is a class that describes a Java class. There is one Class object for each class that is loaded into Java.

Boolean, Character, Byte, Short, Integer, Long, Float, and Double are immutable class wrappers around each of the primitive Java data types. These classes are useful when you need to manipulate primitive types as objects. They also contain useful conversion and utility methods. Void is a related class that defines a representation for the void method return type, but that defines no methods. String and StringBuffer are objects that represent strings. String is an immutable type, while StringBuffer can have its string changed in place. In Java 5.0, StringBuilder is like StringBuffer but without synchronized methods, which makes it the preferred choice in most applications. String, StringBuffer and StringBuilder implement the Java 1.4 interface CharSequence which allows instances of these classes to be manipulated through a simple shared API.

String and the various primitive type wrapper classes all implement the Comparable interface which defines an ordering for instances of those classes and enables sorting and searching algorithms (such as those of java.util.Arrays and java.util.Collections, for example). Cloneable is an important marker interface that specifies that the Object.clone() method is allowed to make copies of an object.

The Math class (and, in Java 1.3, the StrictMath class) defines static methods for various floating-point mathematical functions.

The Thread class provides support for multiple threads of control running within the same Java interpreter. The Runnable interface is implemented by objects that have a run() method that can serve as the body of a thread.

System provides low-level system methods. Runtime provides similar low-level methods, including an exec() method that, along with the Process class, defines a platform-dependent API for running external processes. Java 5.0 allows Process objects to be created more easily with the ProcessBuilder class.

Throwable is the root class of the exception and error hierarchy. Throwable objects are used with the Java throw and catch statements. java.lang defines quite a few subclasses of Throwable. Exception and Error are the superclasses of all exceptions and errors. RuntimeException defines a special class or "unchecked exceptions" that do not need to be declared in a method's throws clause. The Throwable class was overhauled in Java 1.4, adding the ability to "chain" exceptions, and the ability to obtain the stack trace of an exception as an array of StackTraceElement objects.

Java 5.0 adds three important interfaces to this package. Iterable marks types that have an iterator() method and enables iteration with the for/in looping statement introduced in Java 5.0. The Appendable interface is implemented by classes (such as StringBuilder and character output streams) that can have characters appended to them. Implementing this interface enables formatted text output with a java.util.Formatter. The Readable interface is implemented by classes (such as character input streams) that can sequentially copy characters into a buffer. It enables interaction with a java.util.Scanner.

Also new in Java 5.0 is Enum, which serves as the superclass of all enumerated types declared with the new enum keyword. Deprecated, Override, and SuppressWarnings are annotation types that provide metadata for the compiler.

Interfaces

public interface **Appendable**;
public interface **CharSequence**;
public interface **Cloneable**;
public interface **Comparable**<T>;
public interface **Iterable**<T>;
public interface **Readable**;
public interface **Runnable**;
public interface **Thread.UncaughtExceptionHandler**;

Enumerated Types

public enum **Thread.State**;

Annotation Types

public @interface **Deprecated**;
public @interface **Override**;
public @interface **SuppressWarnings**;

Classes

public class **Object**;
abstract class **AbstractStringBuilder** implements Appendable, CharSequence;
public final class **StringBuffer** extends AbstractStringBuilder implements CharSequence, Serializable;
public final class **StringBuilder** extends AbstractStringBuilder implements CharSequence, Serializable;
public final class **Boolean** implements Serializable, Comparable<Boolean>;
public final class **Character** implements Serializable, Comparable<Character>;
public static class **Character.Subset**;
public static final class **Character.UnicodeBlock** extends Character.Subset;
public final class **Class**<T> implements Serializable, java.lang.reflect.GenericDeclaration, java.lang.reflect.Type, java.lang.reflect.AnnotatedElement;
public abstract class **ClassLoader**;
public final class **Compiler**;
public abstract class **Enum**<E extends Enum<E>> implements Comparable<E>, Serializable;
public final class **Math**;
public abstract class **Number** implements Serializable;
public final class **Byte** extends Number implements Comparable<Byte>;
public final class **Double** extends Number implements Comparable<Double>;
public final class **Float** extends Number implements Comparable<Float>;
public final class **Integer** extends Number implements Comparable<Integer>;
public final class **Long** extends Number implements Comparable<Long>;
public final class **Short** extends Number implements Comparable<Short>;
public class **Package** implements java.lang.reflect.AnnotatedElement;
public abstract class **Process**;
public final class **ProcessBuilder**;
public class **Runtime**;
public class **SecurityManager**;
public final class **StackTraceElement** implements Serializable;
public final class **StrictMath**;
public final class **String** implements Serializable, Comparable<String>, CharSequence;
public final class **System**;
public class **Thread** implements Runnable;
public class **ThreadGroup** implements Thread.UncaughtExceptionHandler;
public class **ThreadLocal**<T>;
public class **InheritableThreadLocal**<T> extends ThreadLocal<T>;
public class **Throwable** implements Serializable;
public final class **Void**;
public final class **RuntimePermission** extends java.security.BasicPermission;

Exceptions

public class **Exception** extends Throwable;
public class **ClassNotFoundException** extends Exception;
public class **CloneNotSupportedException** extends Exception;
public class **IllegalAccessException** extends Exception;

public class **InstantiationException** extends Exception;
public class **InterruptedException** extends Exception;
public class **NoSuchFieldException** extends Exception;
public class **NoSuchMethodException** extends Exception;
public class **RuntimeException** extends Exception;
public class **ArithmeticException** extends RuntimeException;
public class **ArrayStoreException** extends RuntimeException;
public class **ClassCastException** extends RuntimeException;
public class **EnumConstantNotPresentException** extends RuntimeException;
public class **IllegalArgumentException** extends RuntimeException;
public class **IllegalThreadStateException** extends IllegalArgumentException;
public class **NumberFormatException** extends IllegalArgumentException;
public class **IllegalMonitorStateException** extends RuntimeException;
public class **IllegalStateException** extends RuntimeException;
public class **IndexOutOfBoundsException** extends RuntimeException;
public class **ArrayIndexOutOfBoundsException** extends IndexOutOfBoundsException;
public class **StringIndexOutOfBoundsException** extends IndexOutOfBoundsException;
public class **NegativeArraySizeException** extends RuntimeException;
public class **NullPointerException** extends RuntimeException;
public class **SecurityException** extends RuntimeException;
public class **TypeNotPresentException** extends RuntimeException;
public class **UnsupportedOperationException** extends RuntimeException;

Errors

public class **Error** extends Throwable;
public class **AssertionError** extends Error;
public class **LinkageError** extends Error;
public class **ClassCircularityError** extends LinkageError;
public class **ClassFormatError** extends LinkageError;
public class **UnsupportedClassVersionError** extends ClassFormatError;
public class **ExceptionInInitializerError** extends LinkageError;
public class **IncompatibleClassChangeError** extends LinkageError;
public class **AbstractMethodError** extends IncompatibleClassChangeError;
public class **IllegalAccessError** extends IncompatibleClassChangeError;
public class **InstantiationError** extends IncompatibleClassChangeError;
public class **NoSuchFieldError** extends IncompatibleClassChangeError;
public class **NoSuchMethodError** extends IncompatibleClassChangeError;
public class **NoClassDefFoundError** extends LinkageError;
public class **UnsatisfiedLinkError** extends LinkageError;
public class **VerifyError** extends LinkageError;
public class **ThreadDeath** extends Error;
public abstract class **VirtualMachineError** extends Error;
public class **InternalError** extends VirtualMachineError;
public class **OutOfMemoryError** extends VirtualMachineError;
public class **StackOverflowError** extends VirtualMachineError;
public class **UnknownError** extends VirtualMachineError;

AbstractMethodError **Java 1.0**

java.lang serializable error

Signals an attempt to invoke an abstract method.

Object — Throwable — Error — LinkageError — IncompatibleClassChangeError — AbstractMethodError
Serializable

```
public class AbstractMethodError extends IncompatibleClassChangeError {
// Public Constructors
    public AbstractMethodError();
    public AbstractMethodError(String s);
}
```

AbstractStringBuilder **Java 5.0**

java.lang appendable

This package-private class is the abstract superclass of StringBuffer and StringBuilder. Because this class is not public, you may not use it directly. It is included in this quick-reference to fully document the shared API of its two subclasses.

Note that many of the methods of this class are declared to return an AbstractStringBuilder object. StringBuilder and StringBuffer() override those methods and narrow the return type to StringBuilder or StringBuffer. (This is an example of "covariant returns," which are allowed in Java 5.0 and later.)

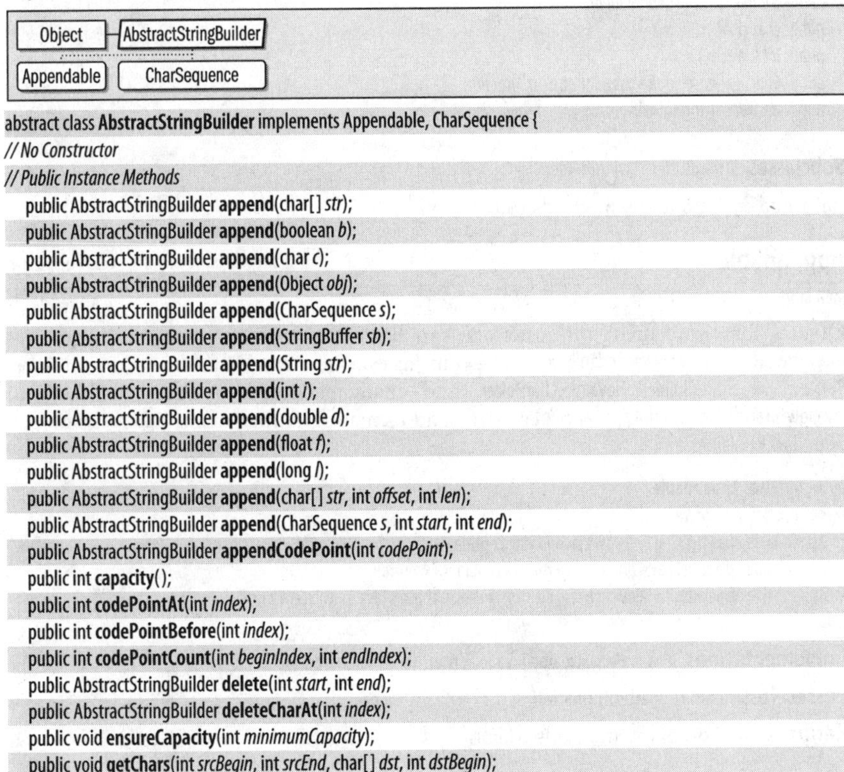


```
abstract class AbstractStringBuilder implements Appendable, CharSequence {
// No Constructor
// Public Instance Methods
    public AbstractStringBuilder append(char[] str);
    public AbstractStringBuilder append(boolean b);
    public AbstractStringBuilder append(char c);
    public AbstractStringBuilder append(Object obj);
    public AbstractStringBuilder append(CharSequence s);
    public AbstractStringBuilder append(StringBuffer sb);
    public AbstractStringBuilder append(String str);
    public AbstractStringBuilder append(int i);
    public AbstractStringBuilder append(double d);
    public AbstractStringBuilder append(float f);
    public AbstractStringBuilder append(long l);
    public AbstractStringBuilder append(char[] str, int offset, int len);
    public AbstractStringBuilder append(CharSequence s, int start, int end);
    public AbstractStringBuilder appendCodePoint(int codePoint);
    public int capacity();
    public int codePointAt(int index);
    public int codePointBefore(int index);
    public int codePointCount(int beginIndex, int endIndex);
    public AbstractStringBuilder delete(int start, int end);
    public AbstractStringBuilder deleteCharAt(int index);
    public void ensureCapacity(int minimumCapacity);
    public void getChars(int srcBegin, int srcEnd, char[] dst, int dstBegin);
```

```
    public int indexOf(String str);
    public int indexOf(String str, int fromIndex);
    public AbstractStringBuilder insert(int offset, char c);
    public AbstractStringBuilder insert(int offset, boolean b);
    public AbstractStringBuilder insert(int dstOffset, CharSequence s);
    public AbstractStringBuilder insert(int offset, int i);
    public AbstractStringBuilder insert(int offset, double d);
    public AbstractStringBuilder insert(int offset, float f);
    public AbstractStringBuilder insert(int offset, long l);
    public AbstractStringBuilder insert(int offset, char[] str);
    public AbstractStringBuilder insert(int offset, Object obj);
    public AbstractStringBuilder insert(int offset, String str);
    public AbstractStringBuilder insert(int index, char[] str, int offset, int len);
    public AbstractStringBuilder insert(int dstOffset, CharSequence s, int start, int end);
    public int lastIndexOf(String str);
    public int lastIndexOf(String str, int fromIndex);
    public int offsetByCodePoints(int index, int codePointOffset);
    public AbstractStringBuilder replace(int start, int end, String str);
    public AbstractStringBuilder reverse();
    public void setCharAt(int index, char ch);
    public void setLength(int newLength);
    public String substring(int start);
    public String substring(int start, int end);
    public void trimToSize();
// Methods Implementing CharSequence
    public char charAt(int index);
    public int length();
    public CharSequence subSequence(int start, int end);
    public abstract String toString();
}
```

Subclasses StringBuffer, StringBuilder

Returned By Too many methods to list.

Appendable Java 5.0

java.lang appendable

Objects that implement this interface can have characters or character sequences appended to them. Appendable was added in Java 5.0 as a simple unifying API for StringBuffer and StringBuilder, java.nio.CharBuffer, and character output stream subclasses of java.io.Writer. The java.util.Formatter class can send formatted output to any Appendable object. See also Readable.

```
public interface Appendable {
// Public Instance Methods
    Appendable append(char c) throws java.io.IOException;
    Appendable append(CharSequence csq) throws java.io.IOException;
    Appendable append(CharSequence csq, int start, int end) throws java.io.IOException;
}
```

Implementations java.io.PrintStream, java.io.Writer, java.nio.CharBuffer

Passed To java.util.Formatter.Formatter()

Returned By Too many methods to list.

ArithmeticException | Java 1.0

java.lang | serializable unchecked

A RuntimeException that signals an exceptional arithmetic condition, such as integer division by zero.

Object ─ Throwable ─ Exception ─ RuntimeException ─ ArithmeticException
Serializable

```
public class ArithmeticException extends RuntimeException {
// Public Constructors
    public ArithmeticException();
    public ArithmeticException(String s);
}
```

ArrayIndexOutOfBoundsException | Java 1.0

java.lang | serializable unchecked

Signals that an array index less than zero or greater than or equal to the array size has been used.

Object ─ Throwable ─ Exception ─ RuntimeException ─ IndexOutOfBoundsException ─ ArrayIndexOutOfBoundsException
Serializable

```
public class ArrayIndexOutOfBoundsException extends IndexOutOfBoundsException {
// Public Constructors
    public ArrayIndexOutOfBoundsException();
    public ArrayIndexOutOfBoundsException(String s);
    public ArrayIndexOutOfBoundsException(int index);
}
```

Thrown By Too many methods to list.

ArrayStoreException | Java 1.0

java.lang | serializable unchecked

Signals an attempt to store the wrong type of object into an array.

Object ─ Throwable ─ Exception ─ RuntimeException ─ ArrayStoreException
Serializable

```
public class ArrayStoreException extends RuntimeException {
// Public Constructors
    public ArrayStoreException();
    public ArrayStoreException(String s);
}
```

AssertionError | Java 1.4

java.lang | serializable error

An instance of this class is thrown if when an assertion fails. This happens when assertions are enabled, and the expression following an assert statement does not evaluate to true. If an assertion fails, and the assert statement has a second expression separated from the first by a colon, then the second expression is evaluated and the resulting value is passed to the AssertionError() constructor, where it is converted to a string and used as the error message.

Object — Throwable — Error — AssertionError
Serializable

```
public class AssertionError extends Error {
// Public Constructors
    public AssertionError();
    public AssertionError(long detailMessage);
    public AssertionError(float detailMessage);
    public AssertionError(double detailMessage);
    public AssertionError(int detailMessage);
    public AssertionError(Object detailMessage);
    public AssertionError(boolean detailMessage);
    public AssertionError(char detailMessage);
}
```

Boolean **Java 1.0**

java.lang serializable comparable

This class provides an immutable object wrapper around the **boolean** primitive type. Note that the **TRUE** and **FALSE** constants are **Boolean** objects; they are not the same as the **true** and **false boolean** values. As of Java 1.1, this class defines a **Class** constant that represents the **boolean** type. **booleanValue()** returns the **boolean** value of a **Boolean** object. The class method **getBoolean()** retrieves the **boolean** value of a named property from the system property list. The static method **valueOf()** parses a string and returns the **Boolean** object it represents. Java 1.4 added two static methods that convert primitive **boolean** values to **Boolean** and **String** objects. In Java 5.0, the **parseBoolean()** method behaves like **valueOf()** but returns a primitive **boolean** value instead of a **Boolean** object.

Prior to Java 5.0, this class does not implement the **Comparable** interface.

Object — Boolean
Comparable Serializable

```
public final class Boolean implements Serializable, Comparable<Boolean> {
// Public Constructors
    public Boolean(String s);
    public Boolean(boolean value);
// Public Constants
    public static final Boolean FALSE;
    public static final Boolean TRUE;
1.1 public static final Class<Boolean> TYPE;
// Public Class Methods
    public static boolean getBoolean(String name);
5.0 public static boolean parseBoolean(String s);
1.4 public static String toString(boolean b);
1.4 public static Boolean valueOf(boolean b);
    public static Boolean valueOf(String s);
// Public Instance Methods
    public boolean booleanValue();
// Methods Implementing Comparable
5.0 public int compareTo(Boolean b);
// Public Methods Overriding Object
    public boolean equals(Object obj);
```

```
    public int hashCode();
    public String toString();
}
```

Byte

Java 1.1

java.lang serializable comparable

This class provides an immutable object wrapper around the **byte** primitive type. It defines useful constants for the minimum and maximum values that can be stored by the **byte** type and a **Class** object constant that represents the **byte** type. It also provides various methods for converting **Byte** values to and from strings and other numeric types.

Most of the static methods of this class can convert a **String** to a **Byte** object or a **byte** value: the four **parseByte()** and **valueOf()** methods parse a number from the specified string using an optionally specified radix and return it in one of these two forms. The **decode()** method parses a byte specified in base 10, base 8, or base 16 and returns it as a **Byte**. If the string begins with "0x" or "#", it is interpreted as a hexadecimal number. If it begins with "0", it is interpreted as an octal number. Otherwise, it is interpreted as a decimal number.

Note that this class has two **toString()** methods. One is static and converts a **byte** primitive value to a string; the other is the usual **toString()** method that converts a **Byte** object to a string. Most of the remaining methods convert a **Byte** to various primitive numeric types.

Object — Number — Byte
Serializable Comparable

```
public final class Byte extends Number implements Comparable<Byte> {
// Public Constructors
    public Byte(byte value);
    public Byte(String s) throws NumberFormatException;
// Public Constants
    public static final byte MAX_VALUE;                                  =127
    public static final byte MIN_VALUE;                                  =-128
5.0 public static final int SIZE;                                        =8
    public static final Class<Byte> TYPE;
// Public Class Methods
    public static Byte decode(String nm) throws NumberFormatException;
    public static byte parseByte(String s) throws NumberFormatException;
    public static byte parseByte(String s, int radix) throws NumberFormatException;
    public static String toString(byte b);
    public static Byte valueOf(String s) throws NumberFormatException;
5.0 public static Byte valueOf(byte b);
    public static Byte valueOf(String s, int radix) throws NumberFormatException;
// Methods Implementing Comparable
1.2 public int compareTo(Byte anotherByte);
// Public Methods Overriding Number
    public byte byteValue();
    public double doubleValue();
    public float floatValue(); yu
    public int intValue();
    public long longValue();
    public short shortValue();
// Public Methods Overriding Object
```

```
    public boolean equals(Object obj);
    public int hashCode();
    public String toString();
}
```

Character Java 1.0

java.lang serializable comparable

This class provides an immutable object wrapper around the primitive char data type. charValue() returns the char value of a Character object. The compareTo() method implements the Comparable interface so that Character objects can be ordered and sorted. The static methods are the most interesting thing about this class, however: they categorize char values based on the categories defined by the Unicode standard. (Some of the methods are only useful if you have a detailed understanding of that standard.) Static methods beginning with "is" test whether a character is in a given category. isDigit(), isLetter(), isWhitespace(), isUpperCase() and isLowerCase() are some of the most useful. Note that these methods work for any Unicode character, not just with the familiar Latin letters and Arabic numbers of the ASCII character set. getType() returns a constant that identifies the category of a character. getDirectionality() returns a separate DIRECTIONALITY_ constant that specifies the "directionality category" of a character.

In addition to testing the category of a character, this class also defines static methods for converting characters. toUpperCase() returns the uppercase equivalent of the specified character (or returns the character itself if the character is uppercase or has no uppercase equivalent). toLowerCase() converts instead to lowercase. digit() returns the integer equivalent of a given character in a given radix (or base; for example, use 16 for hexadecimal). It works with any Unicode digit character, and also (for sufficiently large radix values) the ASCII letters a-z and A-Z. forDigit() returns the ASCII character that corresponds to the specified value (0-35) for the specified radix. getNumericValue() is similar, but also works with any Unicode character including those, such as Roman numerals, that represent numbers but are not decimal digits. Finally, the static toString() method returns a String of length 1 that contains the specified char value.

Java 5.0 introduces many new methods to this class to accommodate Unicode supplementary characters that use 21 bits and do not fit in a single char value. The two representations for these supplementary characters are as an int codepoint in the range 0 through 0x10ffff, or as a sequence of two char values known as a "surrogate pair." The first char of such a pair should fall in the "high surrogate" range and the second char should fall in the "low surrogate" range. toChars() converts an int codepoint into one or two char values. toCodePoint(), codePointAt(), and codePointBefore() convert one or two char values into the corresponding int value. codePointCount() returns the number of characters in a char array or CharSequence, counting surrogate pairs as a single supplementary character. offsetByCodePoints() tells you how many char indexes to advance in a run of text if you want to skip over the specified number of code points. Finally, the various character type testing and case conversion methods such as isWhitespace() and toUpperCase() are available in new versions that take an int codepoint argument instead of a single char argument.

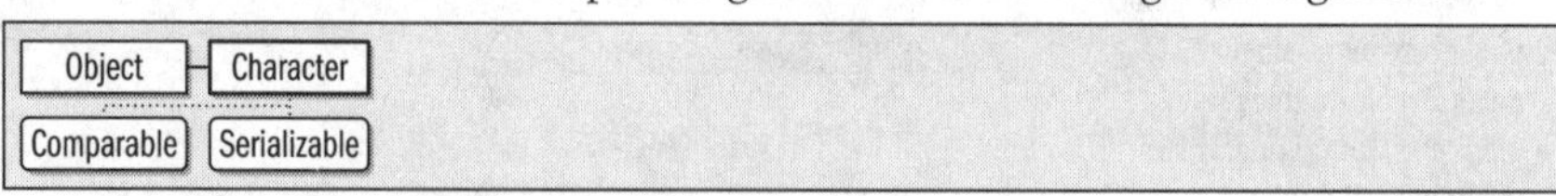


```
public final class Character implements Serializable, Comparable<Character> {
// Public Constructors
    public Character(char value);
```

```
// Public Constants
1.1 public static final byte COMBINING_SPACING_MARK;                         =8
1.1 public static final byte CONNECTOR_PUNCTUATION;                          =23
1.1 public static final byte CONTROL;                                        =15
1.1 public static final byte CURRENCY_SYMBOL;                                =26
1.1 public static final byte DASH_PUNCTUATION;                               =20
1.1 public static final byte DECIMAL_DIGIT_NUMBER;                           =9
1.4 public static final byte DIRECTIONALITY_ARABIC_NUMBER;                   =6
1.4 public static final byte DIRECTIONALITY_BOUNDARY_NEUTRAL;                =9
1.4 public static final byte DIRECTIONALITY_COMMON_NUMBER_SEPARATOR;         =7
1.4 public static final byte DIRECTIONALITY_EUROPEAN_NUMBER;                 =3
1.4 public static final byte DIRECTIONALITY_EUROPEAN_NUMBER_SEPARATOR;       =4
1.4 public static final byte DIRECTIONALITY_EUROPEAN_NUMBER_TERMINATOR;      =5
1.4 public static final byte DIRECTIONALITY_LEFT_TO_RIGHT;                   =0
1.4 public static final byte DIRECTIONALITY_LEFT_TO_RIGHT_EMBEDDING;         =14
1.4 public static final byte DIRECTIONALITY_LEFT_TO_RIGHT_OVERRIDE;          =15
1.4 public static final byte DIRECTIONALITY_NONSPACING_MARK;                 =8
1.4 public static final byte DIRECTIONALITY_OTHER_NEUTRALS;                  =13
1.4 public static final byte DIRECTIONALITY_PARAGRAPH_SEPARATOR;             =10
1.4 public static final byte DIRECTIONALITY_POP_DIRECTIONAL_FORMAT;          =18
1.4 public static final byte DIRECTIONALITY_RIGHT_TO_LEFT;                   =1
1.4 public static final byte DIRECTIONALITY_RIGHT_TO_LEFT_ARABIC;            =2
1.4 public static final byte DIRECTIONALITY_RIGHT_TO_LEFT_EMBEDDING;         =16
1.4 public static final byte DIRECTIONALITY_RIGHT_TO_LEFT_OVERRIDE;          =17
1.4 public static final byte DIRECTIONALITY_SEGMENT_SEPARATOR;               =11
1.4 public static final byte DIRECTIONALITY_UNDEFINED;                       =-1
1.4 public static final byte DIRECTIONALITY_WHITESPACE;                      =12
1.1 public static final byte ENCLOSING_MARK;                                 =7
1.1 public static final byte END_PUNCTUATION;                                =22
1.4 public static final byte FINAL_QUOTE_PUNCTUATION;                        =30
1.1 public static final byte FORMAT;                                         =16
1.4 public static final byte INITIAL_QUOTE_PUNCTUATION;                      =29
1.1 public static final byte LETTER_NUMBER;                                  =10
1.1 public static final byte LINE_SEPARATOR;                                 =13
1.1 public static final byte LOWERCASE_LETTER;                               =2
1.1 public static final byte MATH_SYMBOL;                                    =25
5.0 public static final int MAX_CODE_POINT;                                  =1114111
5.0 public static final char MAX_HIGH_SURROGATE;                             = \uDBFF
5.0 public static final char MAX_LOW_SURROGATE;                              = \uDFFF
    public static final int MAX_RADIX;                                       =36
5.0 public static final char MAX_SURROGATE;                                  = \uDFFF
    public static final char MAX_VALUE;                                      = \uFFFF
5.0 public static final int MIN_CODE_POINT;                                  =0
5.0 public static final char MIN_HIGH_SURROGATE;                             = \uD800
5.0 public static final char MIN_LOW_SURROGATE;                              = \uDC00
    public static final int MIN_RADIX;                                       =2
5.0 public static final int MIN_SUPPLEMENTARY_CODE_POINT;                    =65536
5.0 public static final char MIN_SURROGATE;                                  = \uD800
    public static final char MIN_VALUE;                                      = \0
1.1 public static final byte MODIFIER_LETTER;                                =4
1.1 public static final byte MODIFIER_SYMBOL;                                =27
1.1 public static final byte NON_SPACING_MARK;                               =6
1.1 public static final byte OTHER_LETTER;                                   =5
```

```
1.1 public static final byte OTHER_NUMBER;                                          =11
1.1 public static final byte OTHER_PUNCTUATION;                                     =24
1.1 public static final byte OTHER_SYMBOL;                                          =28
1.1 public static final byte PARAGRAPH_SEPARATOR;                                   =14
1.1 public static final byte PRIVATE_USE;                                           =18
5.0 public static final int SIZE;                                                   =16
1.1 public static final byte SPACE_SEPARATOR;                                       =12
1.1 public static final byte START_PUNCTUATION;                                     =21
1.1 public static final byte SURROGATE;                                             =19
1.1 public static final byte TITLECASE_LETTER;                                      =3
1.1 public static final Class<Character> TYPE;
1.1 public static final byte UNASSIGNED;                                            =0
1.1 public static final byte UPPERCASE_LETTER;                                      =1
// Nested Types
1.2 public static class Subset;
1.2 public static final class UnicodeBlock extends Character.Subset;
// Public Class Methods
5.0 public static int charCount(int codePoint);
5.0 public static int codePointAt(char[] a, int index);
5.0 public static int codePointAt(CharSequence seq, int index);
5.0 public static int codePointAt(char[] a, int index, int limit);
5.0 public static int codePointBefore(CharSequence seq, int index);
5.0 public static int codePointBefore(char[] a, int index);
5.0 public static int codePointBefore(char[] a, int index, int start);
5.0 public static int codePointCount(char[] a, int offset, int count);
5.0 public static int codePointCount(CharSequence seq, int beginIndex, int endIndex);
5.0 public static int digit(int codePoint, int radix);
    public static int digit(char ch, int radix);
    public static char forDigit(int digit, int radix);
1.4 public static byte getDirectionality(char ch);
5.0 public static byte getDirectionality(int codePoint);
1.1 public static int getNumericValue(char ch);
5.0 public static int getNumericValue(int codePoint);
1.1 public static int getType(char ch);
5.0 public static int getType(int codePoint);
5.0 public static boolean isDefined(int codePoint);
    public static boolean isDefined(char ch);
5.0 public static boolean isDigit(int codePoint);
    public static boolean isDigit(char ch);
5.0 public static boolean isHighSurrogate(char ch);
5.0 public static boolean isIdentifierIgnorable(int codePoint);
1.1 public static boolean isIdentifierIgnorable(char ch);
1.1 public static boolean isISOControl(char ch);
5.0 public static boolean isISOControl(int codePoint);
1.1 public static boolean isJavaIdentifierPart(char ch);
5.0 public static boolean isJavaIdentifierPart(int codePoint);
1.1 public static boolean isJavaIdentifierStart(char ch);
5.0 public static boolean isJavaIdentifierStart(int codePoint);
    public static boolean isLetter(char ch);
5.0 public static boolean isLetter(int codePoint);
    public static boolean isLetterOrDigit(char ch);
5.0 public static boolean isLetterOrDigit(int codePoint);
5.0 public static boolean isLowerCase(int codePoint);
```

```
    public static boolean isLowerCase(char ch);
5.0 public static boolean isLowSurrogate(char ch);
5.0 public static boolean isMirrored(int codePoint);
1.4 public static boolean isMirrored(char ch);
5.0 public static boolean isSpaceChar(int codePoint);
1.1 public static boolean isSpaceChar(char ch);
5.0 public static boolean isSupplementaryCodePoint(int codePoint);
5.0 public static boolean isSurrogatePair(char high, char low);
    public static boolean isTitleCase(char ch);
5.0 public static boolean isTitleCase(int codePoint);
1.1 public static boolean isUnicodeIdentifierPart(char ch);
5.0 public static boolean isUnicodeIdentifierPart(int codePoint);
5.0 public static boolean isUnicodeIdentifierStart(int codePoint);
1.1 public static boolean isUnicodeIdentifierStart(char ch);
    public static boolean isUpperCase(char ch);
5.0 public static boolean isUpperCase(int codePoint);
5.0 public static boolean isValidCodePoint(int codePoint);
5.0 public static boolean isWhitespace(int codePoint);
1.1 public static boolean isWhitespace(char ch);
5.0 public static int offsetByCodePoints(CharSequence seq, int index, int codePointOffset);
5.0 public static int offsetByCodePoints(char[] a, int start, int count, int index, int codePointOffset);
5.0 public static char reverseBytes(char ch);
5.0 public static char[] toChars(int codePoint);
5.0 public static int toChars(int codePoint, char[] dst, int dstIndex);
5.0 public static int toCodePoint(char high, char low);
    public static char toLowerCase(char ch);
5.0 public static int toLowerCase(int codePoint);
1.4 public static String toString(char c);
    public static char toTitleCase(char ch);
5.0 public static int toTitleCase(int codePoint);
    public static char toUpperCase(char ch);
5.0 public static int toUpperCase(int codePoint);
5.0 public static Character valueOf(char c);
// Public Instance Methods
    public char charValue();
// Methods Implementing Comparable
1.2 public int compareTo(Character anotherCharacter);
// Public Methods Overriding Object
    public boolean equals(Object obj);
    public int hashCode();
    public String toString();
// Deprecated Public Methods
#   public static boolean isJavaLetter(char ch);
#   public static boolean isJavaLetterOrDigit(char ch);
#   public static boolean isSpace(char ch);
}
```

Character.Subset — Java 1.2

java.lang

This class represents a named subset of the Unicode character set. The toString() method returns the name of the subset. This is a base class intended for further subclassing. Note, in particular, that it does not provide a way to list the members of the subset, nor a way to test for membership in the subset. See Character.UnicodeBlock.

```
public static class Character.Subset {
// Protected Constructors
    protected Subset(String name);
// Public Methods Overriding Object
    public final boolean equals(Object obj);
    public final int hashCode();
    public final String toString();
}
```

Subclasses Character.UnicodeBlock

Character.UnicodeBlock **Java 1.2**

java.lang

This subclass of Character.Subset defines a number of constants that represent named subsets of the Unicode character set. The subsets and their names are the character blocks defined by the Unicode specification (see *http://www.unicode.org/*). Java 1.4 and 5.0 both update this class to a new version of the Unicode standard and define a number of new block constants. The static method of() takes a character or int codepoint and returns the Character.UnicodeBlock to which it belongs, or null if it is not part of any defined block. When presented with an unknown Unicode character, this method provides a useful way to determine what alphabet it belongs to. In Java 5.0, the forName() factory method allows lookup of a UnicodeBlock by name.

```
public static final class Character.UnicodeBlock extends Character.Subset {
// No Constructor
// Public Constants
5.0 public static final Character.UnicodeBlock AEGEAN_NUMBERS;
    public static final Character.UnicodeBlock ALPHABETIC_PRESENTATION_FORMS;
    public static final Character.UnicodeBlock ARABIC;
    public static final Character.UnicodeBlock ARABIC_PRESENTATION_FORMS_A;
    public static final Character.UnicodeBlock ARABIC_PRESENTATION_FORMS_B;
    public static final Character.UnicodeBlock ARMENIAN;
    public static final Character.UnicodeBlock ARROWS;
    public static final Character.UnicodeBlock BASIC_LATIN;
    public static final Character.UnicodeBlock BENGALI;
    public static final Character.UnicodeBlock BLOCK_ELEMENTS;
    public static final Character.UnicodeBlock BOPOMOFO;
1.4 public static final Character.UnicodeBlock BOPOMOFO_EXTENDED;
    public static final Character.UnicodeBlock BOX_DRAWING;
1.4 public static final Character.UnicodeBlock BRAILLE_PATTERNS;
5.0 public static final Character.UnicodeBlock BUHID;
5.0 public static final Character.UnicodeBlock BYZANTINE_MUSICAL_SYMBOLS;
1.4 public static final Character.UnicodeBlock CHEROKEE;
    public static final Character.UnicodeBlock CJK_COMPATIBILITY;
    public static final Character.UnicodeBlock CJK_COMPATIBILITY_FORMS;
    public static final Character.UnicodeBlock CJK_COMPATIBILITY_IDEOGRAPHS;
5.0 public static final Character.UnicodeBlock CJK_COMPATIBILITY_IDEOGRAPHS_SUPPLEMENT;
1.4 public static final Character.UnicodeBlock CJK_RADICALS_SUPPLEMENT;
    public static final Character.UnicodeBlock CJK_SYMBOLS_AND_PUNCTUATION;
    public static final Character.UnicodeBlock CJK_UNIFIED_IDEOGRAPHS;
1.4 public static final Character.UnicodeBlock CJK_UNIFIED_IDEOGRAPHS_EXTENSION_A;
5.0 public static final Character.UnicodeBlock CJK_UNIFIED_IDEOGRAPHS_EXTENSION_B;
    public static final Character.UnicodeBlock COMBINING_DIACRITICAL_MARKS;
```

```
    public static final Character.UnicodeBlock COMBINING_HALF_MARKS;
    public static final Character.UnicodeBlock COMBINING_MARKS_FOR_SYMBOLS;
    public static final Character.UnicodeBlock CONTROL_PICTURES;
    public static final Character.UnicodeBlock CURRENCY_SYMBOLS;
5.0 public static final Character.UnicodeBlock CYPRIOT_SYLLABARY;
    public static final Character.UnicodeBlock CYRILLIC;
5.0 public static final Character.UnicodeBlock CYRILLIC_SUPPLEMENTARY;
5.0 public static final Character.UnicodeBlock DESERET;
    public static final Character.UnicodeBlock DEVANAGARI;
    public static final Character.UnicodeBlock DINGBATS;
    public static final Character.UnicodeBlock ENCLOSED_ALPHANUMERICS;
    public static final Character.UnicodeBlock ENCLOSED_CJK_LETTERS_AND_MONTHS;
1.4 public static final Character.UnicodeBlock ETHIOPIC;
    public static final Character.UnicodeBlock GENERAL_PUNCTUATION;
    public static final Character.UnicodeBlock GEOMETRIC_SHAPES;
    public static final Character.UnicodeBlock GEORGIAN;
5.0 public static final Character.UnicodeBlock GOTHIC;
    public static final Character.UnicodeBlock GREEK;
    public static final Character.UnicodeBlock GREEK_EXTENDED;
    public static final Character.UnicodeBlock GUJARATI;
    public static final Character.UnicodeBlock GURMUKHI;
    public static final Character.UnicodeBlock HALFWIDTH_AND_FULLWIDTH_FORMS;
    public static final Character.UnicodeBlock HANGUL_COMPATIBILITY_JAMO;
    public static final Character.UnicodeBlock HANGUL_JAMO;
    public static final Character.UnicodeBlock HANGUL_SYLLABLES;
5.0 public static final Character.UnicodeBlock HANUNOO;
    public static final Character.UnicodeBlock HEBREW;
5.0 public static final Character.UnicodeBlock HIGH_PRIVATE_USE_SURROGATES;
5.0 public static final Character.UnicodeBlock HIGH_SURROGATES;
    public static final Character.UnicodeBlock HIRAGANA;
1.4 public static final Character.UnicodeBlock IDEOGRAPHIC_DESCRIPTION_CHARACTERS;
    public static final Character.UnicodeBlock IPA_EXTENSIONS;
    public static final Character.UnicodeBlock KANBUN;
1.4 public static final Character.UnicodeBlock KANGXI_RADICALS;
    public static final Character.UnicodeBlock KANNADA;
    public static final Character.UnicodeBlock KATAKANA;
5.0 public static final Character.UnicodeBlock KATAKANA_PHONETIC_EXTENSIONS;
1.4 public static final Character.UnicodeBlock KHMER;
5.0 public static final Character.UnicodeBlock KHMER_SYMBOLS;
    public static final Character.UnicodeBlock LAO;
    public static final Character.UnicodeBlock LATIN_1_SUPPLEMENT;
    public static final Character.UnicodeBlock LATIN_EXTENDED_A;
    public static final Character.UnicodeBlock LATIN_EXTENDED_ADDITIONAL;
    public static final Character.UnicodeBlock LATIN_EXTENDED_B;
    public static final Character.UnicodeBlock LETTERLIKE_SYMBOLS;
5.0 public static final Character.UnicodeBlock LIMBU;
5.0 public static final Character.UnicodeBlock LINEAR_B_IDEOGRAMS;
5.0 public static final Character.UnicodeBlock LINEAR_B_SYLLABARY;
5.0 public static final Character.UnicodeBlock LOW_SURROGATES;
    public static final Character.UnicodeBlock MALAYALAM;
5.0 public static final Character.UnicodeBlock MATHEMATICAL_ALPHANUMERIC_SYMBOLS;
    public static final Character.UnicodeBlock MATHEMATICAL_OPERATORS;
5.0 public static final Character.UnicodeBlock MISCELLANEOUS_MATHEMATICAL_SYMBOLS_A;
5.0 public static final Character.UnicodeBlock MISCELLANEOUS_MATHEMATICAL_SYMBOLS_B;
```

```
    public static final Character.UnicodeBlock MISCELLANEOUS_SYMBOLS;
5.0 public static final Character.UnicodeBlock MISCELLANEOUS_SYMBOLS_AND_ARROWS;
    public static final Character.UnicodeBlock MISCELLANEOUS_TECHNICAL;
1.4 public static final Character.UnicodeBlock MONGOLIAN;
5.0 public static final Character.UnicodeBlock MUSICAL_SYMBOLS;
1.4 public static final Character.UnicodeBlock MYANMAR;
    public static final Character.UnicodeBlock NUMBER_FORMS;
1.4 public static final Character.UnicodeBlock OGHAM;
5.0 public static final Character.UnicodeBlock OLD_ITALIC;
    public static final Character.UnicodeBlock OPTICAL_CHARACTER_RECOGNITION;
    public static final Character.UnicodeBlock ORIYA;
5.0 public static final Character.UnicodeBlock OSMANYA;
5.0 public static final Character.UnicodeBlock PHONETIC_EXTENSIONS;
    public static final Character.UnicodeBlock PRIVATE_USE_AREA;
1.4 public static final Character.UnicodeBlock RUNIC;
5.0 public static final Character.UnicodeBlock SHAVIAN;
1.4 public static final Character.UnicodeBlock SINHALA;
    public static final Character.UnicodeBlock SMALL_FORM_VARIANTS;
    public static final Character.UnicodeBlock SPACING_MODIFIER_LETTERS;
    public static final Character.UnicodeBlock SPECIALS;
    public static final Character.UnicodeBlock SUPERSCRIPTS_AND_SUBSCRIPTS;
5.0 public static final Character.UnicodeBlock SUPPLEMENTAL_ARROWS_A;
5.0 public static final Character.UnicodeBlock SUPPLEMENTAL_ARROWS_B;
5.0 public static final Character.UnicodeBlock SUPPLEMENTAL_MATHEMATICAL_OPERATORS;
5.0 public static final Character.UnicodeBlock SUPPLEMENTARY_PRIVATE_USE_AREA_A;
5.0 public static final Character.UnicodeBlock SUPPLEMENTARY_PRIVATE_USE_AREA_B;
1.4 public static final Character.UnicodeBlock SYRIAC;
5.0 public static final Character.UnicodeBlock TAGALOG;
5.0 public static final Character.UnicodeBlock TAGBANWA;
5.0 public static final Character.UnicodeBlock TAGS;
5.0 public static final Character.UnicodeBlock TAI_LE;
5.0 public static final Character.UnicodeBlock TAI_XUAN_JING_SYMBOLS;
    public static final Character.UnicodeBlock TAMIL;
    public static final Character.UnicodeBlock TELUGU;
1.4 public static final Character.UnicodeBlock THAANA;
    public static final Character.UnicodeBlock THAI;
    public static final Character.UnicodeBlock TIBETAN;
5.0 public static final Character.UnicodeBlock UGARITIC;
1.4 public static final Character.UnicodeBlock UNIFIED_CANADIAN_ABORIGINAL_SYLLABICS;
5.0 public static final Character.UnicodeBlock VARIATION_SELECTORS;
5.0 public static final Character.UnicodeBlock VARIATION_SELECTORS_SUPPLEMENT;
1.4 public static final Character.UnicodeBlock YI_RADICALS;
1.4 public static final Character.UnicodeBlock YI_SYLLABLES;
5.0 public static final Character.UnicodeBlock YIJING_HEXAGRAM_SYMBOLS;
// Public Class Methods
5.0 public static final Character.UnicodeBlock forName(String blockName);
5.0 public static Character.UnicodeBlock of(int codePoint);
    public static Character.UnicodeBlock of(char c);
// Deprecated Public Fields
#   public static final Character.UnicodeBlock SURROGATES_AREA;
}
```

CharSequence Java 1.4

java.lang

This interface defines a simple API for read-only access to sequences of characters. In the core platform it is implemented by the String, StringBuffer and java.nio.CharBuffer classes. charAt() returns the character at a specified position in the sequence. length() returns the number of characters in the sequence. subSequence() returns a CharSequence that consists of the characters starting at, and including, the specified *start* index, and continuing up to, but not including the specified *end* index. Finally, toString() returns a String version of the sequence.

Note that CharSequence implementations do not typically have interoperable equals() or hashCode() methods, and it is not usually possible to compare two CharSequence objects or use multiple sequences in a set or hashtable unless they are instances of the same implementing class.

```
public interface CharSequence {
// Public Instance Methods
    char charAt(int index);
    int length();
    CharSequence subSequence(int start, int end);
    String toString();
}
```

Implementations String, StringBuffer, StringBuilder, java.nio.CharBuffer

Passed To Too many methods to list.

Returned By String.subSequence(), StringBuffer.subSequence(), java.nio.CharBuffer.subSequence()

Class<T> Java 1.0

java.lang serializable

This class represents a Java type. There is one Class object for each class that is loaded into the Java Virtual Machine, and, as of Java 1.1, there are special Class objects that represent the Java primitive types. The TYPE constants defined by Boolean, Integer, and the other primitive wrapper classes hold these special Class objects. Array types are also represented by Class objects in Java 1.1.

There is no constructor for this class. You can obtain a Class object by calling the getClass() method of any instance of the desired class. In Java 1.1 and later, you can also refer to a Class object by appending .class to the name of a class. Finally, and most interestingly, a class can be dynamically loaded by passing its fully qualified name (i.e., package name plus class name) to the static Class.forName() method. This method loads the named class (if it is not already loaded) into the Java interpreter and returns a Class object for it. Classes can also be loaded with a ClassLoader object.

The newInstance() method creates an instance of a given class; this allows you to create instances of dynamically loaded classes for which you cannot use the new keyword. Note that this method works only when the target class has a no-argument constructor. See newInstance() in java.lang.reflect.Constructor for a more powerful way to instantiate dynamically loaded classes. In Java 5.0, Class is a generic type and the type variable *T* specifies the type that is returned by the newInstance() method.

getName() returns the name of the class. getSuperclass() returns its superclass. isInterface() tests whether the Class object represents an interface, and getInterfaces() returns an array of the interfaces that this class implements. In Java 1.2 and later, getPackage() returns a Package object that represents the package containing the class. getProtectionDomain()

returns the java.security.ProtectionDomain to which this class belongs. The various other get() and is() methods return other information about the represented class; they form part of the Java Reflection API, along with the classes in java.lang.reflect.

Java 5.0 adds a number of methods to support the new language features it defines. isAnnotation() tests whether a type is an annotation type. Class implements java.lang.reflect.AnnotatedElement in Java 5.0 and the getAnnotation() and related methods allow the retrieval of annotations (with runtime retention) on the class. isEnum() tests whether a Class object represents an enumerated type and getEnumConstants() returns an array of the constants defined by an enumerated type. getTypeParameters() returns the type variables declared by a generic type. getGenericSuperclass() and getGenericInterfaces() are the generic variants of the getSuperclass() and getInterfaces() methods, returning the generic type information that appears in the extends and implements clause of the class declaration. See java.lang.reflect.Type for more information.

Java 5.0 also adds methods that are useful for reflection on inner classes. isMemberClass(), isLocalClass(), and isAnonymousClass() determine whether a Class represents one of these kinds of nested types. getEnclosingClass(), getEnclosingMethod(), and getEnclosingConstructor() return the type, method, or constructor that an inner class is nested within. Finally, getSimpleName() returns the name of a type as it would appear in Java source code. This is typically more useful than the Java VM formatted names returned by getName().

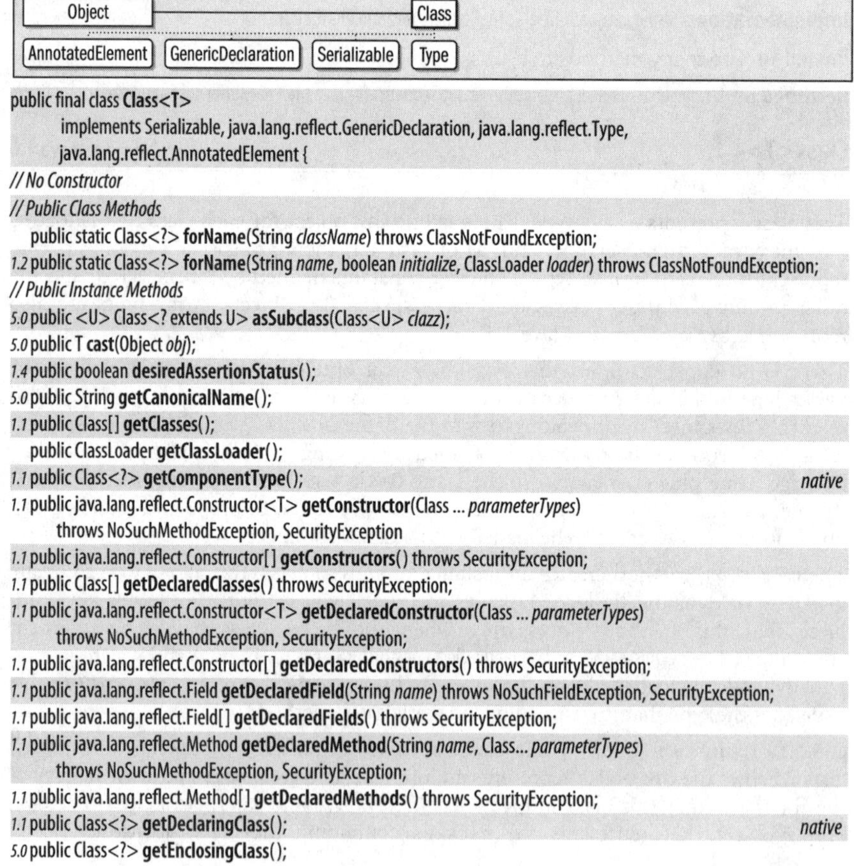


```
public final class Class<T>
        implements Serializable, java.lang.reflect.GenericDeclaration, java.lang.reflect.Type,
        java.lang.reflect.AnnotatedElement {
// No Constructor
// Public Class Methods
    public static Class<?> forName(String className) throws ClassNotFoundException;
1.2 public static Class<?> forName(String name, boolean initialize, ClassLoader loader) throws ClassNotFoundException;
// Public Instance Methods
5.0 public <U> Class<? extends U> asSubclass(Class<U> clazz);
5.0 public T cast(Object obj);
1.4 public boolean desiredAssertionStatus();
5.0 public String getCanonicalName();
1.1 public Class[] getClasses();
    public ClassLoader getClassLoader();
1.1 public Class<?> getComponentType();                                    native
1.1 public java.lang.reflect.Constructor<T> getConstructor(Class ... parameterTypes)
        throws NoSuchMethodException, SecurityException
1.1 public java.lang.reflect.Constructor[] getConstructors() throws SecurityException;
1.1 public Class[] getDeclaredClasses() throws SecurityException;
1.1 public java.lang.reflect.Constructor<T> getDeclaredConstructor(Class ... parameterTypes)
        throws NoSuchMethodException, SecurityException;
1.1 public java.lang.reflect.Constructor[] getDeclaredConstructors() throws SecurityException;
1.1 public java.lang.reflect.Field getDeclaredField(String name) throws NoSuchFieldException, SecurityException;
1.1 public java.lang.reflect.Field[] getDeclaredFields() throws SecurityException;
1.1 public java.lang.reflect.Method getDeclaredMethod(String name, Class... parameterTypes)
        throws NoSuchMethodException, SecurityException;
1.1 public java.lang.reflect.Method[] getDeclaredMethods() throws SecurityException;
1.1 public Class<?> getDeclaringClass();                                   native
5.0 public Class<?> getEnclosingClass();
```

```
5.0 public java.lang.reflect.Constructor<?> getEnclosingConstructor();
5.0 public java.lang.reflect.Method getEnclosingMethod();
5.0 public T[] getEnumConstants();
1.1 public java.lang.reflect.Field getField(String name) throws NoSuchFieldException, SecurityException;
1.1 public java.lang.reflect.Field[] getFields() throws SecurityException;
5.0 public java.lang.reflect.Type[] getGenericInterfaces();
5.0 public java.lang.reflect.Type getGenericSuperclass();
    public Class[] getInterfaces();                                                    native
1.1 public java.lang.reflect.Method getMethod(String name, Class... parameterTypes)
        throws NoSuchMethodException, SecurityException;
1.1 public java.lang.reflect.Method[] getMethods() throws SecurityException;
1.1 public int getModifiers();                                                         native
    public String getName();
1.2 public Package getPackage();
1.2 public java.security.ProtectionDomain getProtectionDomain();
1.1 public java.net.URL getResource(String name);
1.1 public java.io.InputStream getResourceAsStream(String name);
1.1 public Object[] getSigners();                                                      native
5.0 public String getSimpleName();
    public Class<? super T> getSuperclass();                                           native
5.0 public boolean isAnnotation();
5.0 public boolean isAnonymousClass();
1.1 public boolean isArray();                                                          native
1.1 public boolean isAssignableFrom(Class<?> cls);                                     native
5.0 public boolean isEnum();
1.1 public boolean isInstance(Object obj);                                             native
    public boolean isInterface();                                                      native
5.0 public boolean isLocalClass();
5.0 public boolean isMemberClass();
1.1 public boolean isPrimitive();                                                      native
5.0 public boolean isSynthetic();
    public T newInstance() throws InstantiationException, IllegalAccessException;
// Methods Implementing AnnotatedElement
5.0 public <A extends java.lang.annotation.Annotation> A getAnnotation(Class<A> annotationClass);
5.0 public java.lang.annotation.Annotation[] getAnnotations();
5.0 public java.lang.annotation.Annotation[] getDeclaredAnnotations();
5.0 public boolean isAnnotationPresent(Class<? extends java.lang.annotation.Annotation> annotationClass);
// Methods Implementing GenericDeclaration
5.0 public java.lang.reflect.TypeVariable<Class<T>>[] getTypeParameters();
// Public Methods Overriding Object
    public String toString();
}
```

Passed To Too many methods to list.

Returned By Too many methods to list.

Type Of Boolean.TYPE, Byte.TYPE, Character.TYPE, Double.TYPE, Float.TYPE, Integer.TYPE, Long.TYPE, Short.TYPE, Void.TYPE

ClassCastException — Java 1.0

java.lang — serializable unchecked

Signals an invalid cast of an object to a type of which it is not an instance.

Object ─ Throwable ─ Exception ─ RuntimeException ─ ClassCastException
Serializable

```
public class ClassCastException extends RuntimeException {
// Public Constructors
   public ClassCastException();
   public ClassCastException(String s);
}
```

Thrown By org.xml.sax.helpers.ParserFactory.makeParser()

ClassCircularityError

Java 1.0

java.lang

serializable error

Signals that a circular dependency has been detected while performing initialization for a class.

Object ─ Throwable ─ Error ─ LinkageError ─ ClassCircularityError
Serializable

```
public class ClassCircularityError extends LinkageError {
// Public Constructors
   public ClassCircularityError();
   public ClassCircularityError(String s);
}
```

ClassFormatError

Java 1.0

java.lang

serializable error

Signals an error in the binary format of a class file.

Object ─ Throwable ─ Error ─ LinkageError ─ ClassFormatError
Serializable

```
public class ClassFormatError extends LinkageError {
// Public Constructors
   public ClassFormatError();
   public ClassFormatError(String s);
}
```

Subclasses UnsupportedClassVersionError, java.lang.reflect.GenericSignatureFormatError

Thrown By ClassLoader.defineClass()

ClassLoader

Java 1.0

java.lang

This class is the abstract superclass of objects that know how to load Java classes into a Java VM. Given a ClassLoader object, you can dynamically load a class by calling the public loadClass() method, specifying the full name of the desired class. You can obtain a resource associated with a class by calling getResource(), getResources(), and getResourceAsStream(). Many applications do not need to use ClassLoader directly; these applications use the Class.forName() and Class.getResource() methods to dynamically load classes and resources using the ClassLoader object that loaded the application itself.

In order to load classes over the network or from any source other than the class path, you must use a custom ClassLoader object that knows how to obtain data from that source. A java.net.URLClassLoader is suitable for this purpose for almost all applications. Only rarely should an application need to define a ClassLoader subclass of its own. When this is necessary, the subclass should typically extend java.security.SecureClassLoader and override the findClass() method. This method must find the bytes that comprise the named class, then pass them to the defineClass() method and return the resulting Class object. In Java 1.2 and later, the findClass() method must also define the Package object associated with the class, if it has not already been defined. It can use getPackage() and definePackage() for this purpose. Custom subclasses of ClassLoader should also override findResource() and findResources() to enable the public getResource() and getResources() methods.

In Java 1.4 and later you can specify whether the classes loaded through a ClassLoader should have assertions (assert statements) enabled. setDefaultAssertionStatus() enables or disables assertions for all loaded classes. setPackageAssertionStatus() and setClassAssertionStatus() allow you to override the default assertion status for a named package or a named class. Finally, clearAssertionStatus() sets the default status to false and discards the assertions status for any named packages and classes.

```
public abstract class ClassLoader {
// Protected Constructors
    protected ClassLoader();
1.2 protected ClassLoader(ClassLoader parent);
// Public Class Methods
1.2 public static ClassLoader getSystemClassLoader();
1.1 public static java.net.URL getSystemResource(String name);
1.1 public static java.io.InputStream getSystemResourceAsStream(String name);
1.2 public static java.util.Enumeration<java.net.URL> getSystemResources(String name) throws java.io.IOException;
// Public Instance Methods
1.4 public void clearAssertionStatus();                                                    synchronized
1.2 public final ClassLoader getParent();
1.1 public java.net.URL getResource(String name);
1.1 public java.io.InputStream getResourceAsStream(String name);
1.2 public java.util.Enumeration<java.net.URL> getResources(String name) throws java.io.IOException;
1.1 public Class<?> loadClass(String name) throws ClassNotFoundException;
1.4 public void setClassAssertionStatus(String className, boolean enabled);                 synchronized
1.4 public void setDefaultAssertionStatus(boolean enabled);                                 synchronized
1.4 public void setPackageAssertionStatus(String packageName, boolean enabled);             synchronized
// Protected Instance Methods
5.0 protected final Class<?> defineClass(String name, java.nio.ByteBuffer b,
                                         java.security.ProtectionDomain protectionDomain)
        throws ClassFormatError;
1.1 protected final Class<?> defineClass(String name, byte[] b, int off, int len) throws ClassFormatError;
1.2 protected final Class<?> defineClass(String name, byte[] b, int off, int len,
                                         java.security.ProtectionDomain protectionDomain)
        throws ClassFormatError;
1.2 protected Package definePackage(String name, String specTitle, String specVersion, String specVendor, String implTitle,
                                   String implVersion, String implVendor, java.net.URL sealBase)
        throws IllegalArgumentException;
1.2 protected Class<?> findClass(String name) throws ClassNotFoundException;
1.2 protected String findLibrary(String libname);                                         constant
1.1 protected final Class<?> findLoadedClass(String name);
1.2 protected java.net.URL findResource(String name);                                      constant
1.2 protected java.util.Enumeration<java.net.URL> findResources(String name) throws java.io.IOException;
```

```
    protected final Class<?> findSystemClass(String name) throws ClassNotFoundException;
1.2 protected Package getPackage(String name);
1.2 protected Package[] getPackages();
    protected Class<?> loadClass(String name, boolean resolve) throws ClassNotFoundException;      synchronized
    protected final void resolveClass(Class<?> c);
1.1 protected final void setSigners(Class<?> c, Object[] signers);
// Deprecated Protected Methods
#   protected final Class<?> defineClass(byte[] b, int off, int len) throws ClassFormatError;
}
```

Subclasses java.security.SecureClassLoader

Passed To Class.forName(), Thread.setContextClassLoader(), java.lang.instrument.ClassFileTransformer.transform(), java.lang.instrument.Instrumentation.getInitiatedClasses(), java.lang.reflect.Proxy.{getProxyClass(), newProxyInstance()}, java.net.URLClassLoader.{newInstance(), URLClassLoader()}, java.security.ProtectionDomain.ProtectionDomain(), java.security.SecureClassLoader.SecureClassLoader(), java.util.ResourceBundle.getBundle()

Returned By Class.getClassLoader(), SecurityManager.currentClassLoader(), Thread.getContextClassLoader(), java.security.ProtectionDomain.getClassLoader()

ClassNotFoundException **Java 1.0**

java.lang — serializable checked

Signals that a class to be loaded cannot be found. If an exception of this type was caused by some underlying exception, you can query that lower-level exeption with getException() or with the newer, more general getCause().

Object — Throwable — Exception — ClassNotFoundException
Serializable

```
public class ClassNotFoundException extends Exception {
// Public Constructors
    public ClassNotFoundException();
    public ClassNotFoundException(String s);
1.2 public ClassNotFoundException(String s, Throwable ex);
// Public Instance Methods
1.2 public Throwable getException();                                                default:null
// Public Methods Overriding Throwable
1.4 public Throwable getCause();                                                    default:null
}
```

Thrown By Too many methods to list.

Cloneable **Java 1.0**

java.lang — cloneable

This interface defines no methods or variables, but indicates that the class that implements it may be cloned (i.e., copied) by calling the Object method clone(). Calling clone() for an object that does not implement this interface (and does not override clone() with its own implementation) causes a CloneNotSupportedException to be thrown.

```
public interface Cloneable {
}
```

Implementations Too many classes to list.

CloneNotSupportedException — Java 1.0

java.lang — serializable checked

Signals that the **clone()** method has been called for an object of a class that does not implement the **Cloneable** interface.

Object → Throwable → Exception → CloneNotSupportedException (Throwable implements Serializable)

```
public class CloneNotSupportedException extends Exception {
// Public Constructors
   public CloneNotSupportedException();
   public CloneNotSupportedException(String s);
}
```

Thrown By Enum.clone(), Object.clone(), java.security.MessageDigest.clone(), java.security.MessageDigestSpi.clone(), java.security.Signature.clone(), java.security.SignatureSpi.clone(), java.util.AbstractMap.clone(), java.util.EnumMap.clone(), java.util.EnumSet.clone(), javax.crypto.Mac.clone(), javax.crypto.MacSpi.clone()

Comparable<T> — Java 1.2

java.lang — comparable

This interface defines a single method, **compareTo()**, that is responsible for comparing one object to another and determining their relative order, according to some natural ordering for that class of objects. Any general-purpose class that represents a value that can be sorted or ordered should implement this interface. Any class that does implement this interface can make use of various powerful methods such as **java.util.Collections.sort()** and **java.util.Arrays.binarySearch()**. Many of the key classes in the Java API implement this interface. In Java 5.0, this interface has been made generic. The type variable *T* represents the type of the object that is passed to the **compareTo()** method.

The **compareTo()** method compares this object to the object passed as an argument. It should assume that the supplied object is of the appropriate type; if it is not, it should throw a **ClassCastException**. If this object is less than the supplied object or should appear before the supplied object in a sorted list, **compareTo()** should return a negative number. If this object is greater than the supplied object or should come after the supplied object in a sorted list, **compareTo()** should return a positive integer. If the two objects are equivalent, and their relative order in a sorted list does not matter, **compareTo()** should return 0. If **compareTo()** returns 0 for two objects, the **equals()** method should typically return **true**. If this is not the case, the **Comparable** objects are not suitable for use in **java.util.TreeSet** and **java.util.TreeMap** classes.

See **java.util.Comparator** for a way to define an ordering for objects that do not implement **Comparable** or to define an ordering other than the natural ordering defined by a **Comparable** class.

```
public interface Comparable<T> {
// Public Instance Methods
   int compareTo(T o);
}
```

Implementations Too many classes to list.

Compiler **Java 1.0**

java.lang

The static methods of this class provide an interface to the just-in-time (JIT) byte-code-to-native code compiler in use by the Java interpreter. If no JIT compiler is in use by the VM, these methods do nothing. **compileClass()** asks the JIT compiler to compile the specified class. **compileClasses()** asks the JIT compiler to compile all classes that match the specified name. These methods return **true** if the compilation was successful, or **false** if it failed or if there is no JIT compiler on the system. **enable()** and **disable()** turn just-in-time compilation on and off. **command()** asks the JIT compiler to perform some compiler-specific operation; this is a hook for vendor extensions. No standard operations have been defined.

```
public final class Compiler {
// No Constructor
// Public Class Methods
   public static Object command(Object any);                        native
   public static boolean compileClass(Class<?> clazz);              native
   public static boolean compileClasses(String string);             native
   public static void disable();                                    native
   public static void enable();                                     native
}
```

Deprecated **Java 5.0**

java.lang — @Documented @Retention(RUNTIME) annotation

This annotation type marks the annotated program element as deprecated. The Java compiler issues a warning if the annotated element is used or overrided in code that is not itself **@Deprecated**.

In Java 5.0, the **@Deprecated** annotation works in the same way as the **@deprecated** javadoc tag. In future releases of Java, the compiler may ignore **@deprecated** javadoc tag and rely only on the **@Deprecated** annotation.

This annotation type has source retention and does not have an **@Target** meta-annotation, which means it may be applied to any program element. **Deprecated** has an **@Documented** meta-annotation, meaning that the presence of an **@Deprecated** annotation should be a documented part of the annotated element's API.

Annotation ··· Deprecated

```
public @interface Deprecated {
}
```

Double **Java 1.0**

java.lang — serializable comparable

This class provides an immutable object wrapper around the **double** primitive data type. **doubleValue()** returns the primitive **double** value of a **Double** object, and there are other methods (which override **Number** methods and whose names all end in "Value") for returning a the wrapped **double** value as a variety of other primitive types.

This class also provides some useful constants and static methods for testing **double** values. **MIN_VALUE** and **MAX_VALUE** are the smallest (closest to zero) and largest representable **double** values. **POSITIVE_INFINITY** and **NEGATIVE_INFINITY** are the **double** representations of infinity and negative infinity, and **NaN** is special **double** "not a number" value. **isInfinite()** in class and instance method forms tests whether a **double** or a **Double** has an infinite value. Similarly, **isNaN()** tests whether a **double** or **Double** is not-a-number; this is a comparison that cannot be done directly because the **NaN** constant never tests equal to any other value, including itself.

The static **parseDouble()** method converts a **String** to a **double**. The static **valueOf()** converts a **String** to a **Double**, and is basically equivalent to the **Double()** constructor that takes a **String** argument. The static and instance **toString()** methods perform the opposite conversion: they convert a **double** or a **Double** to a **String**. See also **java.text.NumberFormat** for more flexible number parsing and formatting.

The **compareTo()** method makes **Double** object **Comparable** which is useful for ordering and sorting. The static **compare()** method is similar (its return values have the same meaning as those of **Comparable.compareTo()**) but works on primitive values rather than objects and is useful when ordering and sorting arrays of **double** values.

doubleToLongBits(), **doubleToRawBits()** and **longBitsToDouble()** allow you to manipulate the bit representation (defined by IEEE 754) of a **double** directly (which is not something that most applications ever need to do).

Object — Number — Double

Serializable, Comparable

```
public final class Double extends Number implements Comparable<Double> {
// Public Constructors
   public Double(String s) throws NumberFormatException;
   public Double(double value);
// Public Constants
   public static final double MAX_VALUE;                                   =1.7976931348623157E308
   public static final double MIN_VALUE;                                   =4.9E-324
   public static final double NaN;                                         =NaN
   public static final double NEGATIVE_INFINITY;                           =-Infinity
   public static final double POSITIVE_INFINITY;                           =Infinity
5.0 public static final int SIZE;                                          =64
1.1 public static final Class<Double> TYPE;
// Public Class Methods
1.4 public static int compare(double d1, double d2);
   public static long doubleToLongBits(double value);                      native
1.3 public static long doubleToRawLongBits(double value);                  native
   public static boolean isInfinite(double v);
   public static boolean isNaN(double v);
   public static double longBitsToDouble(long bits);                       native
1.2 public static double parseDouble(String s) throws NumberFormatException;
5.0 public static String toHexString(double d);
   public static String toString(double d);
   public static Double valueOf(String s) throws NumberFormatException;
5.0 public static Double valueOf(double d);
// Public Instance Methods
   public boolean isInfinite();
   public boolean isNaN();
// Methods Implementing Comparable
1.2 public int compareTo(Double anotherDouble);
// Public Methods Overriding Number
1.1 public byte byteValue();
   public double doubleValue();
```

```
   public float floatValue();
   public int intValue();
   public long longValue();
1.1 public short shortValue();
// Public Methods Overriding Object
   public boolean equals(Object obj);
   public int hashCode();
   public String toString();
}
```

Enum<E extends Enum<E>> Java 5.0

java.lang serializable comparable

This class is the common superclass of all enumerated types. It is not itself an enum type, however, and a Java compiler does not allow other classes to extend it. Subclasses of Enum may be only created with enum declarations. Enum is a generic type, and the type variable *E* represents the concrete enumerated type that actually extends Enum. This type variable exists so that Enum can implement Comparable<E>.

Every enumerated constant has a name (the name it was declared with) and an ordinal value—the first constant in an enum declaration has an ordinal of 0, the second has an ordinal of 1, and so on. The final methods name() and ordinal() return these values. Most users of enumerated constants will use toString() instead of name(). The implementation of toString() defined by Enum returns the same value as name(). The toString() method is not final, however, and it can be overridden in enum declarations.

Enum implements a number of Object and Comparable methods and makes its implementations final so that they are inherited by all enum types and may not be overridden. equals() compares enumerated constants with the == operator, and hashCode() returns the System.identityHashCode() value. In order to make this identity-based equals() implementation work, Enum overrides the protected clone() method to throw CloneNotSupportedException, preventing additional copies of enumerated values from being created. Finally, the compareTo() method of the Comparable interface is defined to compare enumerated values based on their ordinal() value.

getDeclaringClass() returns the Class object that represents the enum type of which the constant is a part. It is like the getClass() method inherited from Object, but the return values of these two methods will be different for enumerated constants that have value-specific class bodies, since those constants are instances of an anonymous subclass of the enum type.

The static valueOf() method is passed the type and name of an enumerated constant and returns the object that represents that constant (or throws an IllegalArgumentException).

Object — Enum
Comparable | Serializable

```
public abstract class Enum<E extends Enum<E>> implements Comparable<E>, Serializable {
// Protected Constructors
   protected Enum(String name, int ordinal);
// Public Class Methods
   public static <T extends Enum<T>> T valueOf(Class<T> enumType, String name);
// Public Instance Methods
   public final Class<E> getDeclaringClass();
   public final String name();
```

```
    public final int ordinal();
// Methods Implementing Comparable
    public final int compareTo(E o);
// Public Methods Overriding Object
    public final boolean equals(Object other);
    public final int hashCode();
    public String toString();
// Protected Methods Overriding Object
    protected final Object clone() throws CloneNotSupportedException;
}
```

Subclasses Thread.State, java.lang.annotation.ElementType, java.lang.annotation.RetentionPolicy, java.lang.management.MemoryType, java.math.RoundingMode, java.net.Authenticator.RequestorType, java.net.Proxy.Type, java.security.KeyRep.Type, java.util.Formatter.BigDecimalLayoutForm, java.util.concurrent.TimeUnit, javax.net.ssl.SSLEngineResult.HandshakeStatus, javax.net.ssl.SSLEngineResult.Status

Passed To Too many methods to list.

EnumConstantNotPresentException — Java 5.0

java.lang — serializable unchecked

This unchecked exception is thrown when Java code attempts to use an enum constant that no longer exists. This can happen only if the enumerated constant was removed from its enumerated type after the referencing code was compiled. The methods of the exception provide the Class of the enumerated type and the name of the nonexistent constant.

Object — Throwable — Exception — RuntimeException — EnumConstantNotPresentException
Serializable

```
public class EnumConstantNotPresentException extends RuntimeException {
// Public Constructors
    public EnumConstantNotPresentException(Class<? extends Enum> enumType, String constantName);
// Public Instance Methods
    public String constantName();
    public Class<? extends Enum> enumType();
}
```

Error — Java 1.0

java.lang — serializable error

This class forms the root of the error hierarchy in Java. Subclasses of Error, unlike subclasses of Exception, should not be caught and generally cause termination of the program. Subclasses of Error need not be declared in the throws clause of a method definition. This class inherits methods from Throwable but declares none of its own. Each of its constructors simply invokes the corresponding Throwable() constructor. See Throwable for details.

```
public class Error extends Throwable {
// Public Constructors
    public Error();
1.4 public Error(Throwable cause);
```

```
  public Error(String message);
1.4 public Error(String message, Throwable cause);
}
```

Subclasses AssertionError, LinkageError, ThreadDeath, VirtualMachineError, java.lang.annotation.AnnotationFormatError, java.nio.charset.CoderMalfunctionError, javax.xml.parsers.FactoryConfigurationError, javax.xml.transform.TransformerFactoryConfigurationError

Exception — Java 1.0

java.lang — serializable checked

This class forms the root of the exception hierarchy in Java. An Exception signals an abnormal condition that must be specially handled to prevent program termination. Exceptions may be caught and handled. An exception that is not a subclass of RuntimeException must be declared in the throws clause of any method that can throw it. This class inherits methods from Throwable but declares none of its own. Each of its constructors simply invokes the corresponding Throwable() constructor. See Throwable for details.

Object — Throwable — Exception
Serializable

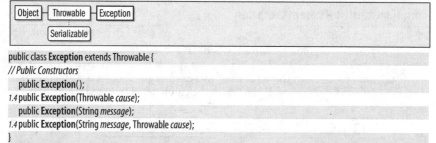

```
public class Exception extends Throwable {
// Public Constructors
  public Exception();
1.4 public Exception(Throwable cause);
  public Exception(String message);
1.4 public Exception(String message, Throwable cause);
}
```

Subclasses Too many classes to list.

Passed To java.io.WriteAbortedException.WriteAbortedException(), java.nio.charset.CoderMalfunctionError.CoderMalfunctionError(), java.security.PrivilegedActionException.PrivilegedActionException(), java.util.logging.ErrorManager.error(), java.util.logging.Handler.reportError(), javax.xml.parsers.FactoryConfigurationError.FactoryConfigurationError(), javax.xml.transform.TransformerFactoryConfigurationError.TransformerFactoryConfigurationError(), org.xml.sax.SAXException.SAXException(), org.xml.sax.SAXParseException.SAXParseException()

Returned By java.security.PrivilegedActionException.getException(), javax.xml.parsers.FactoryConfigurationError.getException(), javax.xml.transform.TransformerFactoryConfigurationError.getException(), org.xml.sax.SAXException.getException()

Thrown By java.security.PrivilegedExceptionAction.run(), java.util.concurrent.Callable.call()

Type Of java.io.WriteAbortedException.detail

ExceptionInInitializerError — Java 1.1

java.lang — serializable error

This error is thrown by the Java Virtual Machine when an exception occurs in the static initializer of a class. You can use the getException() method to obtain the Throwable object that was thrown from the initializer. In Java 1.4 and later, getException() has been superseded by the more general getCause() method of the Throwable class.

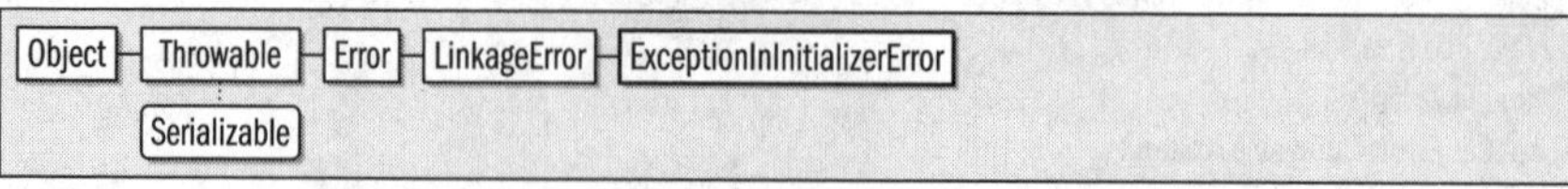

```
public class ExceptionInInitializerError extends LinkageError {
// Public Constructors
   public ExceptionInInitializerError();
   public ExceptionInInitializerError(String s);
   public ExceptionInInitializerError(Throwable thrown);
// Public Instance Methods
   public Throwable getException();                                   default:null
// Public Methods Overriding Throwable
1.4 public Throwable getCause();                                      default:null
}
```


Float

Java 1.0

java.lang

serializable comparable

This class provides an immutable object wrapper around a primitive **float** value. **floatValue()** returns the primitive **float** value of a **Float** object, and there are methods for returning the value of a **Float** as a variety of other primitive types. This class is very similar to **Double**, and defines the same set of useful methods and constants as that class does. See **Double** for details.

Object — Number — Float

Serializable Comparable

```
public final class Float extends Number implements Comparable<Float> {
// Public Constructors
   public Float(double value);
   public Float(String s) throws NumberFormatException;
   public Float(float value);
// Public Constants
   public static final float MAX_VALUE;                               =3.4028235E38
   public static final float MIN_VALUE;                               =1.4E-45
   public static final float NaN;                                     =NaN
   public static final float NEGATIVE_INFINITY;                       =-Infinity
   public static final float POSITIVE_INFINITY;                       =Infinity
5.0 public static final int SIZE;                                     =32
1.1 public static final Class<Float> TYPE;
// Public Class Methods
1.4 public static int compare(float f1, float f2);
   public static int floatToIntBits(float value);                     native
1.3 public static int floatToRawIntBits(float value);                 native
   public static float intBitsToFloat(int bits);                      native
   public static boolean isInfinite(float v);
   public static boolean isNaN(float v);
1.2 public static float parseFloat(String s) throws NumberFormatException;
5.0 public static String toHexString(float f);
   public static String toString(float f);
   public static Float valueOf(String s) throws NumberFormatException;
5.0 public static Float valueOf(float f);
// Public Instance Methods
   public boolean isInfinite();
   public boolean isNaN();
// Methods Implementing Comparable
1.2 public int compareTo(Float anotherFloat);
// Public Methods Overriding Number
```

```
1.1 public byte byteValue();
    public double doubleValue();
    public float floatValue();
    public int intValue();
    public long longValue();
1.1 public short shortValue();
// Public Methods Overriding Object
    public boolean equals(Object obj);
    public int hashCode();
    public String toString();
}
```

IllegalAccessError **Java 1.0**

java.lang **serializable error**

Signals an attempted use of a class, method, or field that is not accessible.

Object — Throwable — Error — LinkageError — IncompatibleClassChangeError — IllegalAccessError
Throwable ⋮ Serializable

```
public class IllegalAccessError extends IncompatibleClassChangeError {
// Public Constructors
    public IllegalAccessError();
    public IllegalAccessError(String s);
}
```

IllegalAccessException **Java 1.0**

java.lang **serializable checked**

Signals that a class or initializer is not accessible. Thrown by Class.newInstance().

Object — Throwable — Exception — IllegalAccessException
Throwable ⋮ Serializable

```
public class IllegalAccessException extends Exception {
// Public Constructors
    public IllegalAccessException();
    public IllegalAccessException(String s);
}
```

Thrown By Too many methods to list.

IllegalArgumentException **Java 1.0**

java.lang **serializable unchecked**

Signals an illegal argument to a method. See subclasses IllegalThreadStateException and NumberFormatException.

Object — Throwable — Exception — RuntimeException — IllegalArgumentException
Throwable ⋮ Serializable

```
public class IllegalArgumentException extends RuntimeException {
// Public Constructors
    public IllegalArgumentException();
5.0 public IllegalArgumentException(Throwable cause);
```

```
  public IllegalArgumentException(String s);
5.0 public IllegalArgumentException(String message, Throwable cause);
}
```

Subclasses IllegalThreadStateException, NumberFormatException, java.nio.channels.IllegalSelectorException, java.nio.channels.UnresolvedAddressException, java.nio.channels.UnsupportedAddressTypeException, java.nio.charset.IllegalCharsetNameException, java.nio.charset.UnsupportedCharsetException, java.security.InvalidParameterException, java.util.IllegalFormatException, java.util.regex.PatternSyntaxException

Thrown By Too many methods to list.

IllegalMonitorStateException — Java 1.0

java.lang — serializable unchecked

Signals an illegal monitor state. It is thrown by the Object notify() and wait() methods used for thread synchronization.

Object — Throwable — Exception — RuntimeException — IllegalMonitorStateException
Serializable

```
public class IllegalMonitorStateException extends RuntimeException {
// Public Constructors
  public IllegalMonitorStateException();
  public IllegalMonitorStateException(String s);
}
```

IllegalStateException — Java 1.1

java.lang — serializable unchecked

Signals that a method has been invoked on an object that is not in an appropriate state to perform the requested operation.

Object — Throwable — Exception — RuntimeException — IllegalStateException
Serializable

```
public class IllegalStateException extends RuntimeException {
// Public Constructors
  public IllegalStateException();
5.0 public IllegalStateException(Throwable cause);
  public IllegalStateException(String s);
5.0 public IllegalStateException(String message, Throwable cause);
}
```

Subclasses java.nio.InvalidMarkException, java.nio.channels.AlreadyConnectedException, java.nio.channels.CancelledKeyException, java.nio.channels.ClosedSelectorException, java.nio.channels.ConnectionPendingException, java.nio.channels.IllegalBlockingModeException, java.nio.channels.NoConnectionPendingException, java.nio.channels.NonReadableChannelException, java.nio.channels.NonWritableChannelException, java.nio.channels.NotYetBoundException, java.nio.channels.NotYetConnectedException, java.nio.channels.OverlappingFileLockException, java.util.FormatterClosedException, java.util.concurrent.CancellationException

Thrown By Too many methods to list.

IllegalThreadStateException Java 1.0

java.lang serializable unchecked

Signals that a thread is not in the appropriate state for an attempted operation to succeed.

Object ─ Throwable ─ Exception ─ RuntimeException ─ IllegalArgumentException ─ IllegalThreadStateException
Serializable

```
public class IllegalThreadStateException extends IllegalArgumentException {
// Public Constructors
   public IllegalThreadStateException();
   public IllegalThreadStateException(String s);
}
```

IncompatibleClassChangeError Java 1.0

java.lang serializable error

This is the superclass of a group of related error types. It signals an illegal use of a legal class.

Object ─ Throwable ─ Error ─ LinkageError ─ IncompatibleClassChangeError
Serializable

```
public class IncompatibleClassChangeError extends LinkageError {
// Public Constructors
   public IncompatibleClassChangeError();
   public IncompatibleClassChangeError(String s);
}
```

Subclasses AbstractMethodError, IllegalAccessError, InstantiationError, NoSuchFieldError, NoSuchMethodError

IndexOutOfBoundsException Java 1.0

java.lang serializable unchecked

Signals that an index is out of bounds. See the subclasses ArrayIndexOutOfBoundsException and StringIndexOutOfBoundsException.

Object ─ Throwable ─ Exception ─ RuntimeException ─ IndexOutOfBoundsException
Serializable

```
public class IndexOutOfBoundsException extends RuntimeException {
// Public Constructors
   public IndexOutOfBoundsException();
   public IndexOutOfBoundsException(String s);
}
```

Subclasses ArrayIndexOutOfBoundsException, StringIndexOutOfBoundsException

InheritableThreadLocal<T> Java 1.2

java.lang

This class holds a thread-local value that is inherited by child threads. See ThreadLocal for a discussion of thread-local values. Note that the inheritance referred to in the name of this class is not from superclass to subclass; it is inheritance from parent thread to child thread. Like its superclass, this class has been made generic in Java 5.0. The type variable *T* represents the type of the referenced object.

This class is best understood by example. Suppose that an application has defined an InheritableThreadLocal object and that a certain thread (the parent thread) has a thread-local value stored in that object. Whenever that thread creates a new thread (a child thread), the InheritableThreadLocal object is automatically updated so that the new child thread has the same value associated with it as the parent thread. Note that the value associated with the child thread is independent from the value associated with the parent thread. If the child thread subsequently alters its value by calling the set() method of the InheritableThreadLocal, the value associated with the parent thread does not change.

By default, a child thread inherits a parent's values unmodified. By overriding the childValue() method, however, you can create a subclass of InheritableThreadLocal in which the child thread inherits some arbitrary function of the parent thread's value.

Object — ThreadLocal — InheritableThreadLocal

```
public class InheritableThreadLocal<T> extends ThreadLocal<T> {
// Public Constructors
   public InheritableThreadLocal();
// Protected Instance Methods
   protected T childValue(T parentValue);
}
```

InstantiationError — Java 1.0

java.lang — serializable error

Signals an attempt to instantiate an interface or abstract class.

Object — Throwable — Error — LinkageError — IncompatibleClassChangeError — InstantiationError
(Throwable implements Serializable)

```
public class InstantiationError extends IncompatibleClassChangeError {
// Public Constructors
   public InstantiationError();
   public InstantiationError(String s);
}
```

InstantiationException — Java 1.0

java.lang — serializable checked

Signals an attempt to instantiate an interface or an abstract class.

Object — Throwable — Exception — InstantiationException
(Throwable implements Serializable)

```
public class InstantiationException extends Exception {
// Public Constructors
   public InstantiationException();
   public InstantiationException(String s);
}
```

Thrown By Class.newInstance(), java.lang.reflect.Constructor.newInstance(), org.xml.sax.helpers.ParserFactory.makeParser()

Integer **Java 1.0**

java.lang **serializable comparable**

This class provides an immutable object wrapper around the int primitive data type. This class also contains useful minimum and maximum constants and useful conversion methods. parseInt() and valueOf() convert a string to an int or to an Integer, respectively. Each can take a radix argument to specify the base the value is represented in. decode() also converts a String to an Integer. It assumes a hexadecimal number if the string begins with "0X" or "0x", or an octal number if the string begins with "0". Otherwise, a decimal number is assumed. toString() converts in the other direction, and the static version takes a radix argument. toBinaryString(), toOctalString(), and toHexString() convert an int to a string using base 2, base 8, and base 16. These methods treat the integer as an unsigned value. Other routines return the value of an Integer as various primitive types, and, finally, the getInteger() methods return the integer value of a named property from the system property list, or the specified default value.

Java 5.0 adds a number of static methods that operate on the bits of an int value. rotateLeft() and rotateRight() shift the bits the specified distance in the specified direction, with bits shifted off one end being shifted in on the other end. signum() returns the sign of the integer as -1, 0, or 1. highestOneBit(), numberOfTrailingZeros(), bitCount() and related methods can be useful if you use an int value as a set of bits and want to iterate through the ones bits in the set.

Object — Number — Integer
Serializable (Number), Comparable (Integer)

```
public final class Integer extends Number implements Comparable<Integer> {
// Public Constructors
    public Integer(int value);
    public Integer(String s) throws NumberFormatException;
// Public Constants
    public static final int MAX_VALUE;                          =2147483647
    public static final int MIN_VALUE;                          =-2147483648
5.0 public static final int SIZE;                               =32
1.1 public static final Class<Integer> TYPE;
// Public Class Methods
5.0 public static int bitCount(int i);
1.1 public static Integer decode(String nm) throws NumberFormatException;
    public static Integer getInteger(String nm);
    public static Integer getInteger(String nm, int val);
    public static Integer getInteger(String nm, Integer val);
5.0 public static int highestOneBit(int i);
5.0 public static int lowestOneBit(int i);
5.0 public static int numberOfLeadingZeros(int i);
5.0 public static int numberOfTrailingZeros(int i);
    public static int parseInt(String s) throws NumberFormatException;
    public static int parseInt(String s, int radix) throws NumberFormatException;
5.0 public static int reverse(int i);
5.0 public static int reverseBytes(int i);
5.0 public static int rotateLeft(int i, int distance);
5.0 public static int rotateRight(int i, int distance);
5.0 public static int signum(int i);
    public static String toBinaryString(int i);
    public static String toHexString(int i);
```

```
    public static String toOctalString(int i);
    public static String toString(int i);
    public static String toString(int i, int radix);
5.0 public static Integer valueOf(int i);
    public static Integer valueOf(String s) throws NumberFormatException;
    public static Integer valueOf(String s, int radix) throws NumberFormatException;
// Methods Implementing Comparable
1.2 public int compareTo(Integer anotherInteger);
// Public Methods Overriding Number
1.1 public byte byteValue();
    public double doubleValue();
    public float floatValue();
    public int intValue();
    public long longValue();
1.1 public short shortValue();
// Public Methods Overriding Object
    public boolean equals(Object obj);
    public int hashCode();
    public String toString();
}
```


InternalError — Java 1.0

java.lang — serializable error

Signals an internal error in the Java interpreter.

Object — Throwable — Error — VirtualMachineError — InternalError
Serializable

```
public class InternalError extends VirtualMachineError {
// Public Constructors
    public InternalError();
    public InternalError(String s);
}
```

InterruptedException — Java 1.0

java.lang — serializable checked

Signals that the thread has been interrupted.

Object — Throwable — Exception — InterruptedException
Serializable

```
public class InterruptedException extends Exception {
// Public Constructors
    public InterruptedException();
    public InterruptedException(String s);
}
```

Thrown By Too many methods to list.

Iterable<T> — Java 5.0

java.lang

This interface defines a single method for returning a java.util.Iterator object. Iterable was added in Java 5.0 to support the for/in loop, which is also new in Java 5.0. The Collection,

List, Set, and Queue collection interfaces of java.util extend this interface, making all collections other than maps Iterable. You can implement this interface in your own classes if you want to allow them to be iterated with the for/in loop.

The type variable T specifies the type parameter of the returned Iterator object, which, in turn, specifies the element type of the collection being iterated over.

```
public interface Iterable<T> {
// Public Instance Methods
   java.util.Iterator<T> iterator();
}
```

Implementations java.util.Collection

LinkageError — Java 1.0

java.lang — serializable error

The superclass of a group of errors that signal problems linking a class or resolving dependencies between classes.

Object — Throwable — Error — LinkageError
Throwable ⋮ Serializable

```
public class LinkageError extends Error {
// Public Constructors
   public LinkageError();
   public LinkageError(String s);
}
```

Subclasses ClassCircularityError, ClassFormatError, ExceptionInInitializerError, IncompatibleClassChangeError, NoClassDefFoundError, UnsatisfiedLinkError, VerifyError

Long — Java 1.0

java.lang — serializable comparable

This class provides an immutable object wrapper around the long primitive data type. This class also contains useful minimum and maximum constants and useful conversion methods. parseLong() and valueOf() convert a string to a long or to a Long, respectively. Each can take a radix argument to specify the base the value is represented in. toString() converts in the other direction and may also take a radix argument. toBinaryString(), toOctalString(), and toHexString() convert a long to a string using base 2, base 8, and base 16. These methods treat the long as an unsigned value. Other routines return the value of a Long as various primitive types, and, finally, the getLong() methods return the long value of a named property or the value of the specified default.

Java 5.0 adds a number of static methods that operate on the bits of a long value. Except for their argument type and return type, they are the same as the Integer methods of the same name.

Object — Number — Long
Number ⋮ Serializable; Long ⋮ Comparable

```
public final class Long extends Number implements Comparable<Long> {
// Public Constructors
   public Long(long value);
   public Long(String s) throws NumberFormatException;
```

```
// Public Constants
   public static final long MAX_VALUE;                                    =9223372036854775807
   public static final long MIN_VALUE;                                   =-9223372036854775808
5.0 public static final int SIZE;                                                        =64
1.1 public static final Class<Long> TYPE;
// Public Class Methods
5.0 public static int bitCount(long i);
1.2 public static Long decode(String nm) throws NumberFormatException;
   public static Long getLong(String nm);
   public static Long getLong(String nm, Long val);
   public static Long getLong(String nm, long val);
5.0 public static long highestOneBit(long i);
5.0 public static long lowestOneBit(long i);
5.0 public static int numberOfLeadingZeros(long i);
5.0 public static int numberOfTrailingZeros(long i);
   public static long parseLong(String s) throws NumberFormatException;
   public static long parseLong(String s, int radix) throws NumberFormatException;
5.0 public static long reverse(long i);
5.0 public static long reverseBytes(long i);
5.0 public static long rotateLeft(long i, int distance);
5.0 public static long rotateRight(long i, int distance);
5.0 public static int signum(long i);
   public static String toBinaryString(long i);
   public static String toHexString(long i);
   public static String toOctalString(long i);
   public static String toString(long i);
   public static String toString(long i, int radix);
5.0 public static Long valueOf(long l);
   public static Long valueOf(String s) throws NumberFormatException;
   public static Long valueOf(String s, int radix) throws NumberFormatException;
// Methods Implementing Comparable
1.2 public int compareTo(Long anotherLong);
// Public Methods Overriding Number
1.1 public byte byteValue();
   public double doubleValue();
   public float floatValue();
   public int intValue();
   public long longValue();
1.1 public short shortValue();
// Public Methods Overriding Object
   public boolean equals(Object obj);
   public int hashCode();
   public String toString();
}
```

Math — Java 1.0

java.lang

This class defines constants for the mathematical values *e* and π and defines static methods for floating-point trigonometry, exponentiation, and other operations. It is the equivalent of the C *<math.h>* functions. It also contains methods for computing minimum and maximum values and for generating pseudorandom numbers.

Most methods of Math operate on float and double floating-point values. Remember that these values are only approximations of actual real numbers. To allow implementations to take full advantage of the floating-point capabilities of a native platform, the methods of Math are not required to return exactly the same values on all platforms. In other words, the results returned by different implementations may differ slightly in the least-significant bits. As of Java 1.3, applications that require strict platform-independence of results should use StrictMath instead.

Java 5.0 adds several methods including log10() to compute the base-ten logarithm, cbrt() to compute the cube root of a number, and signum() to compute the sign of a number as well as sinh(), cosh(), and tanh() hyperbolic trigonometric functions.

```
public final class Math {
// No Constructor
// Public Constants
    public static final double E;                                    =2.718281828459045
    public static final double PI;                                   =3.141592653589793
// Public Class Methods
    public static int abs(int a);
    public static long abs(long a);
    public static float abs(float a);
    public static double abs(double a);
    public static double acos(double a);
    public static double asin(double a);
    public static double atan(double a);
    public static double atan2(double y, double x);
5.0 public static double cbrt(double a);
    public static double ceil(double a);
    public static double cos(double a);
5.0 public static double cosh(double x);
    public static double exp(double a);
5.0 public static double expm1(double x);
    public static double floor(double a);
5.0 public static double hypot(double x, double y);
    public static double IEEEremainder(double f1, double f2);
    public static double log(double a);
5.0 public static double log10(double a);
5.0 public static double log1p(double x);
    public static int max(int a, int b);
    public static long max(long a, long b);
    public static float max(float a, float b);
    public static double max(double a, double b);
    public static int min(int a, int b);
    public static long min(long a, long b);
    public static float min(float a, float b);
    public static double min(double a, double b);
    public static double pow(double a, double b);
    public static double random();
    public static double rint(double a);
    public static int round(float a);
    public static long round(double a);
5.0 public static float signum(float f);
5.0 public static double signum(double d);
    public static double sin(double a);
```

```
5.0 public static double sinh(double x);
    public static double sqrt(double a);
    public static double tan(double a);
5.0 public static double tanh(double x);
1.2 public static double toDegrees(double angrad);
1.2 public static double toRadians(double angdeg);
5.0 public static float ulp(float f);
5.0 public static double ulp(double d);
}
```


NegativeArraySizeException — Java 1.0

java.lang — serializable unchecked

Signals an attempt to allocate an array with fewer than zero elements.

Object ─ Throwable ─ Exception ─ RuntimeException ─ NegativeArraySizeException
Throwable ⋮ Serializable

```
public class NegativeArraySizeException extends RuntimeException {
// Public Constructors
    public NegativeArraySizeException();
    public NegativeArraySizeException(String s);
}
```

Thrown By java.lang.reflect.Array.newInstance()

NoClassDefFoundError — Java 1.0

java.lang — serializable error

Signals that the definition of a specified class cannot be found.

Object ─ Throwable ─ Error ─ LinkageError ─ NoClassDefFoundError
Throwable ⋮ Serializable

```
public class NoClassDefFoundError extends LinkageError {
// Public Constructors
    public NoClassDefFoundError();
    public NoClassDefFoundError(String s);
}
```

NoSuchFieldError — Java 1.0

java.lang — serializable error

Signals that a specified field cannot be found.

Object ─ Throwable ─ Error ─ LinkageError ─ IncompatibleClassChangeError ─ NoSuchFieldError
Throwable ⋮ Serializable

```
public class NoSuchFieldError extends IncompatibleClassChangeError {
// Public Constructors
    public NoSuchFieldError();
    public NoSuchFieldError(String s);
}
```

NoSuchFieldException

Java 1.1

java.lang — serializable checked

This exception signals that the specified field does not exist in the specified class.

Object — Throwable — Exception — NoSuchFieldException
Serializable

```
public class NoSuchFieldException extends Exception {
// Public Constructors
   public NoSuchFieldException();
   public NoSuchFieldException(String s);
}
```

Thrown By Class.{getDeclaredField(), getField()}

NoSuchMethodError

Java 1.0

java.lang — serializable error

Signals that a specified method cannot be found.

Object — Throwable — Error — LinkageError — IncompatibleClassChangeError — NoSuchMethodError
Serializable

```
public class NoSuchMethodError extends IncompatibleClassChangeError {
// Public Constructors
   public NoSuchMethodError();
   public NoSuchMethodError(String s);
}
```

NoSuchMethodException

Java 1.0

java.lang — serializable checked

Signals that the specified method does not exist in the specified class.

Object — Throwable — Exception — NoSuchMethodException
Serializable

```
public class NoSuchMethodException extends Exception {
// Public Constructors
   public NoSuchMethodException();
   public NoSuchMethodException(String s);
}
```

Thrown By Class.{getConstructor(), getDeclaredConstructor(), getDeclaredMethod(), getMethod()}

NullPointerException

Java 1.0

java.lang — serializable unchecked

Signals an attempt to access a field or invoke a method of a null object.

Object — Throwable — Exception — RuntimeException — NullPointerException
Serializable

```
public class NullPointerException extends RuntimeException {
// Public Constructors
   public NullPointerException();
   public NullPointerException(String s);
}
```

Thrown By org.xml.sax.helpers.ParserFactory.makeParser()

Number   Java 1.0

java.lang   serializable

This is an abstract class that is the superclass of Byte, Short, Integer, Long, Float, and Double. It defines the conversion functions those types implement.

Object ─ Number ··· Serializable

```
public abstract class Number implements Serializable {
// Public Constructors
   public Number();
// Public Instance Methods
1.1 public byte byteValue();
   public abstract double doubleValue();
   public abstract float floatValue();
   public abstract int intValue();
   public abstract long longValue();
1.1 public short shortValue();
}
```

Subclasses Byte, Double, Float, Integer, Long, Short, java.math.BigDecimal, java.math.BigInteger, java.util.concurrent.atomic.AtomicInteger, java.util.concurrent.atomic.AtomicLong

Returned By java.text.ChoiceFormat.parse(), java.text.DecimalFormat.parse(), java.text.NumberFormat.parse(), javax.xml.datatype.Duration.getField()

NumberFormatException   Java 1.0

java.lang   serializable unchecked

Signals an illegal number format.

Object ─ Throwable ─ Exception ─ RuntimeException ─ IllegalArgumentException ─ NumberFormatException
Serializable

```
public class NumberFormatException extends IllegalArgumentException {
// Public Constructors
   public NumberFormatException();
   public NumberFormatException(String s);
}
```

Thrown By Too many methods to list.

Object   Java 1.0

java.lang

This is the root class in Java. All classes are subclasses of Object, and thus all objects can invoke the public and protected methods of this class. For classes that implement the Cloneable interface, clone() makes a byte-for-byte copy of an Object. getClass() returns the Class object associated with any Object, and the notify(), notifyAll(), and wait() methods are used for thread synchronization on a given Object.

A number of these **Object** methods should be overridden by subclasses of **Object**. For example, a subclass should provide its own definition of the **toString()** method so that it can be used with the string concatenation operator and with the **PrintWriter.println()** methods. Defining the **toString()** method for all objects also helps with debugging.

The default implementation of the **equals()** method simply uses the == operator to test whether this object reference and the specified object reference refer to the same object. Many subclasses override this method to compare the individual fields of two distinct objects (i.e., they override the method to test for the equivalence of distinct objects rather than the equality of object references). Some classes, particularly those that override **equals()**, may also want to override the **hashCode()** method to provide an appropriate hashcode to be used when storing instances in a **Hashtable** data structure.

A class that allocates system resources other than memory (such as file descriptors or windowing system graphic contexts) should override the **finalize()** method to release these resources when the object is no longer referred to and is about to be garbage-collected.

```
public class Object {
// Public Constructors
   public Object();                                                              empty
// Public Instance Methods
   public boolean equals(Object obj);
   public final Class<? extends Object> getClass();                              native
   public int hashCode();                                                        native
   public final void notify();                                                   native
   public final void notifyAll();                                                native
   public String toString();
   public final void wait() throws InterruptedException;
   public final void wait(long timeout) throws InterruptedException;             native
   public final void wait(long timeout, int nanos) throws InterruptedException;
// Protected Instance Methods
   protected Object clone() throws CloneNotSupportedException;                   native
   protected void finalize() throws Throwable;                                   empty
}
```

Subclasses Too many classes to list.

Passed To Too many methods to list.

Returned By Too many methods to list.

Type Of java.io.Reader.lock, java.io.Writer.lock, java.util.EventObject.source, java.util.Vector.elementData, java.util.prefs.AbstractPreferences.lock

OutOfMemoryError — Java 1.0

java.lang — serializable error

Signals that the interpreter has run out of memory (and that garbage collection is unable to free any memory).

Object → Throwable → Error → VirtualMachineError → OutOfMemoryError; Throwable implements Serializable

```
public class OutOfMemoryError extends VirtualMachineError {
// Public Constructors
   public OutOfMemoryError();
   public OutOfMemoryError(String s);
}
```

Override Java 5.0

java.lang @Target(METHOD) @Retention(SOURCE) annotation

An annotation of this type may be applied to methods and indicates that the programmer intends for the method to override a method from a superclass. In effect, it is an assertion for the compiler to verify. If a method annotated @Override does not, in fact, override another method (perhaps because the method name was misspelled or an argument was incorrectly typed), the compiler issues an error. This annotation type has source retention.

Annotation ··· Override

```
public @interface Override {
}
```

Package Java 1.2

java.lang

This class represents a Java package. You can obtain the Package object for a given Class by calling the getPackage() method of the Class object. The static Package.getPackage() method returns a Package object for the named package, if any such package has been loaded by the current class loader. Similarly, the static Package.getPackages() returns all Package objects that have been loaded by the current class loader. Note that a Package object is not defined unless at least one class has been loaded from that package. Although you can obtain the Package of a given Class, you cannot obtain an array of Class objects contained in a specified Package.

If the classes that comprise a package are contained in a JAR file that has the appropriate attributes set in its manifest file, the Package object allows you to query the title, vendor, and version of both the package specification and the package implementation; all six values are strings. The specification version string has a special format. It consists of one or more integers, separated from each other by periods. Each integer can have leading zeros, but is not considered an octal digit. Increasing numbers indicate later versions. The isCompatibleWith() method calls getSpecificationVersion() to obtain the specification version and compares it with the version string supplied as an argument. If the package-specification version is the same as or greater than the specified string, isCompatibleWith() returns true. This allows you to test whether the version of a package (typically a standard extension) is new enough for the purposes of your application.

Packages may be sealed, which means that all classes in the package must come from the same JAR file. If a package is sealed, the no-argument version of isSealed() returns true. The one-argument version of isSealed() returns true if the specified URL represents the JAR file from which the package is loaded.

Object — Package ··· AnnotatedElement

```
public class Package implements java.lang.reflect.AnnotatedElement {
// No Constructor
// Public Class Methods
   public static Package getPackage(String name);
   public static Package[] getPackages();
// Public Instance Methods
   public String getImplementationTitle();
   public String getImplementationVendor();
```

```
    public String getImplementationVersion();
    public String getName();
    public String getSpecificationTitle();
    public String getSpecificationVendor();
    public String getSpecificationVersion();
    public boolean isCompatibleWith(String desired) throws NumberFormatException;
    public boolean isSealed();
    public boolean isSealed(java.net.URL url);
// Methods Implementing AnnotatedElement
5.0 public <A extends java.lang.annotation.Annotation> A getAnnotation(Class<A> annotationClass);
5.0 public java.lang.annotation.Annotation[] getAnnotations();
5.0 public java.lang.annotation.Annotation[] getDeclaredAnnotations();
5.0 public boolean isAnnotationPresent(Class<? extends java.lang.annotation.Annotation> annotationClass);
// Public Methods Overriding Object
    public int hashCode();
    public String toString();
}
```

Returned By Class.getPackage(), ClassLoader.{definePackage(), getPackage(), getPackages()}, java.net.URLClassLoader.definePackage()

Process **Java 1.0**

java.lang

This class describes a process that is running externally to the Java interpreter. Note that a Process is very different from a Thread; the Process class is abstract and cannot be instantiated. Call one of the Runtime.exec() methods to start a process and return a corresponding Process object.

waitFor() blocks until the process exits. exitValue() returns the exit code of the process. destroy() kills the process. getErrorStream() returns an InputStream from which you can read any bytes the process sends to its standard error stream. getInputStream() returns an InputStream from which you can read any bytes the process sends to its standard output stream. getOutputStream() returns an OutputStream you can use to send bytes to the standard input stream of the process.

```
public abstract class Process {
// Public Constructors
    public Process();
// Public Instance Methods
    public abstract void destroy();
    public abstract int exitValue();
    public abstract java.io.InputStream getErrorStream();
    public abstract java.io.InputStream getInputStream();
    public abstract java.io.OutputStream getOutputStream();
    public abstract int waitFor() throws InterruptedException;
}
```

Returned By ProcessBuilder.start(), Runtime.exec()

ProcessBuilder **Java 5.0**

java.lang

This class launches operating system processes, producing Process objects. Specify the operating system command when you invoke the ProcessBuilder() constructor or with the command() method. Commands are specified with one or more strings, typically the filename of the executable to run followed by the command-line arguments for the executable. Specify these strings in a List, a String[], or, most conveniently, using a variable-length argument list of strings.

Before launching the command you have specified, you can configure the ProcessBuilder. Query the current working directory with the no-argument version of directory() and set it with the one-argument version of the method. Query the mapping of environment variables to values with the environment() method. You can alter the mappings in the returned Map to specify the environment you want the child process to run in. Pass true to redirectErrorStream() if you would like both the standard output and the standard error stream of the child process to be merged into a single stream that you can obtain with Process.getInputStream(). If you do so, you do not have to arrange to read two separate input streams to get the output of the process.

Once you have specified a command and configured your ProcessBuilder as desired, call the start() method to launch the process. You then use methods of the returned Process to provide input to the process, read output from the process, or wait for the process to exit. start() may throw an IOException. This may occur, for example, if the executable filename you have specified does not exist. The command() and directory() methods do not perform error checking on the values you provide them; these checks are performed by the start() method, so it is also possible for start() to throw exceptions based on bad input to the configuration methods.

Note that a ProcessBuilder can be reused: once you have established a working directory and environment variables, you can change the command() and launch multiple processes with repeated calls to start().

```
public final class ProcessBuilder {
// Public Constructors
   public ProcessBuilder(java.util.List<String> command);
   public ProcessBuilder(String... command);
// Public Instance Methods
   public java.util.List<String> command();
   public ProcessBuilder command(String... command);
   public ProcessBuilder command(java.util.List<String> command);
   public java.io.File directory();
   public ProcessBuilder directory(java.io.File directory);
   public java.util.Map<String,String> environment();
   public boolean redirectErrorStream();
   public ProcessBuilder redirectErrorStream(boolean redirectErrorStream);
   public Process start() throws java.io.IOException;
}
```

Readable — Java 5.0

java.lang — readable

Objects that implement this interface can serve as a source of characters and can transfer one or more at a time to a java.nio.CharBuffer. Readable was added in Java 5.0 as a simple unifying API for java.nio.CharBuffer and character input stream subclasses of java.io.Reader. The java.util.Scanner class can parse input from any Readable object. See also Appendable.

```
public interface Readable {
// Public Instance Methods
   int read(java.nio.CharBuffer cb) throws java.io.IOException;
}
```

Implementations java.io.Reader, java.nio.CharBuffer

Passed To java.util.Scanner.Scanner()

Runnable Java 1.0

java.lang runnable

This interface specifies the run() method that is required to use with the Thread class. Any class that implements this interface can provide the body of a thread. See Thread for more information.

```
public interface Runnable {
// Public Instance Methods
   void run();
}
```

Implementations Thread, java.util.TimerTask, java.util.concurrent.FutureTask

Passed To Too many methods to list.

Returned By javax.net.ssl.SSLEngine.getDelegatedTask()

Runtime Java 1.0

java.lang

This class encapsulates a number of platform-dependent system functions. The static method getRuntime() returns the Runtime object for the current platform; this object can perform system functions in a platform-independent way.

exit() causes the Java interpreter to exit and return a specified return code. This method is usually invoked through System.exit(). In Java 1.3, addShutdownHook() registers an unstarted Thread object that is run when the virtual machine shuts down, either through a call to exit() or through a user interrupt (a CTRL-C, for example). The purpose of a shutdown hook is to perform necessary cleanup, such as shutting down network connections, deleting temporary files, and so on. Any number of hooks can be registered with addShutdownHook(). Before the interpreter exits, it starts all registered shutdown-hook threads and lets them run concurrently. Any hooks you write should perform their cleanup operation and exit promptly so they do not delay the shutdown process. To remove a shutdown hook before it is run, call removeShutdownHook(). To force an immediate exit that does not invoke the shutdown hooks, call halt().

exec() starts a new process running externally to the interpreter. Note that any processes run outside of Java may be system-dependent.

freeMemory() returns the approximate amount of free memory. totalMemory() returns the total amount of memory available to the Java interpreter. gc() forces the garbage collector to run synchronously, which may free up more memory. Similarly, runFinalization() forces the finalize() methods of unreferenced objects to be run immediately. This may free up system resources those objects were holding.

load() loads a dynamic library with a fully specified pathname. loadLibrary() loads a dynamic library with only the library name specified; it looks in platform-dependent locations for the specified library. These libraries generally contain native code definitions for native methods.

traceInstructions() and traceMethodCalls() enable and disable tracing by the interpreter. These methods are used for debugging or profiling an application. It is not specified how the VM emits the trace information, and VMs are not even required to support this feature.

Note that some of the Runtime methods are more commonly called via the static methods of the System class.

```
public class Runtime {
// No Constructor
// Public Class Methods
   public static Runtime getRuntime();
// Public Instance Methods
1.3 public void addShutdownHook(Thread hook);
1.4 public int availableProcessors();                                  native
   public Process exec(String[] cmdarray) throws java.io.IOException;
   public Process exec(String command) throws java.io.IOException;
   public Process exec(String command, String[] envp) throws java.io.IOException;
   public Process exec(String[] cmdarray, String[] envp) throws java.io.IOException;
1.3 public Process exec(String[] cmdarray, String[] envp, java.io.File dir) throws java.io.IOException;
1.3 public Process exec(String command, String[] envp, java.io.File dir) throws java.io.IOException;
   public void exit(int status);
   public long freeMemory();                                           native
   public void gc();                                                   native
1.3 public void halt(int status);
   public void load(String filename);
   public void loadLibrary(String libname);
1.4 public long maxMemory();                                           native
1.3 public boolean removeShutdownHook(Thread hook);
   public void runFinalization();
   public long totalMemory();                                          native
   public void traceInstructions(boolean on);                          native
   public void traceMethodCalls(boolean on);                           native
// Deprecated Public Methods
#  public java.io.InputStream getLocalizedInputStream(java.io.InputStream in);
#  public java.io.OutputStream getLocalizedOutputStream(java.io.OutputStream out);
1.1# public static void runFinalizersOnExit(boolean value);
}
```

RuntimeException — Java 1.0

java.lang — serializable unchecked

This exception type is not used directly, but serves as a superclass of a group of runtime exceptions that need not be declared in the throws clause of a method definition. These exceptions need not be declared because they are runtime conditions that can generally occur in any Java method. Thus, declaring them would be unduly burdensome, and Java does not require it.

This class inherits methods from Throwable but declares none of its own. Each of the RuntimeException constructors simply invokes the corresponding Exception() and Throwable() constructor. See Throwable for details.

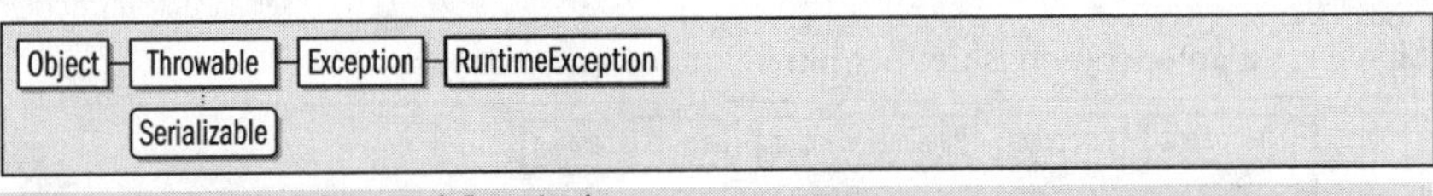


```
public class RuntimeException extends Exception {
// Public Constructors
   public RuntimeException();
1.4 public RuntimeException(Throwable cause);
```

```
    public RuntimeException(String message);
1.4 public RuntimeException(String message, Throwable cause);
}
```

Subclasses Too many classes to list.

RuntimePermission Java 1.2

java.lang serializable permission

This class is a java.security.Permission that represents access to various important system facilities. A RuntimePermission has a name, or target, that represents the facility for which permission is being sought or granted. The name "exitVM" represents permission to call System.exit(), and the name "accessClassInPackage.java.lang" represents permission to read classes from the java.lang package. The name of a RuntimePermission may use a ".*" suffix as a wildcard. For example, the name "accessClassInPackage.java.*" represents permission to read classes from any package whose name begins with "java.". RuntimePermission does not use action list strings as some Permission classes do; the name of the permission alone is enough.

The following are supported RuntimePermssion names:

accessClassInPackage.*package*	getProtectionDomain	setFactory
accessDeclaredMembers	loadLibrary.*library_name*	setIO
createClassLoader	modifyThread	setSecurityManager
createSecurityManager	modifyThreadGroup	stopThread
defineClassInPackage.*package*	queuePrintJob	writeFileDescriptor
exitVM	readFileDescriptor	
getClassLoader	set-ContextClassLoader	

System administrators configuring security policies should be familiar with these permission names, the operations they govern access to, and with the risks inherent in granting any of them. Although system programmers may need to work with this class, application programmers should never need to use RuntimePermssion directly.

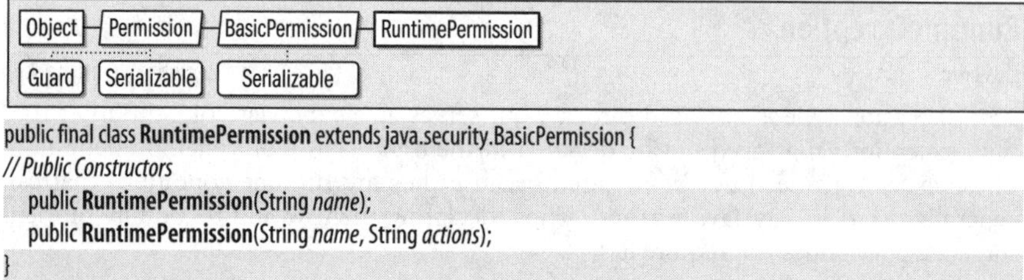


```
public final class RuntimePermission extends java.security.BasicPermission {
// Public Constructors
    public RuntimePermission(String name);
    public RuntimePermission(String name, String actions);
}
```

SecurityException Java 1.0

java.lang serializable unchecked

Signals that an operation is not permitted for security reasons.

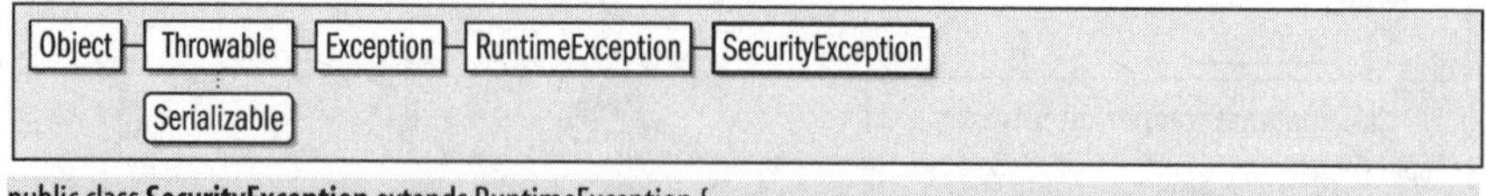


```
public class SecurityException extends RuntimeException {
// Public Constructors
    public SecurityException();
```

```
5.0 public SecurityException(Throwable cause);
    public SecurityException(String s);
5.0 public SecurityException(String message, Throwable cause);
}
```

Subclasses java.security.AccessControlException

Thrown By Too many methods to list.

SecurityManager — Java 1.0

java.lang

This class defines the methods necessary to implement a security policy for the safe execution of untrusted code. Before performing potentially sensitive operations, Java calls methods of the SecurityManager object currently in effect to determine whether the operations are permitted. These methods throw a SecurityException if the operation is not permitted. Typical applications do not need to use or subclass SecurityManager. It is typically used only by web browsers, applet viewers, and other programs that need to run untrusted code in a controlled environment.

Prior to Java 1.2, this class is abstract, and the default implementation of each check() method throws a SecurityException unconditionally. The Java security mechanism has been overhauled as of Java 1.2. As part of the overhaul, this class is no longer abstract and its methods have useful default implementations, so there is rarely a need to subclass it. checkPermission() operates by invoking the checkPermission() method of the system java.security.AccessController object. In Java 1.2 and later, all other check() methods of SecurityManager are now implemented on top of checkPermission().

```
public class SecurityManager {
// Public Constructors
    public SecurityManager();
// Public Instance Methods
    public void checkAccept(String host, int port);
    public void checkAccess(ThreadGroup g);
    public void checkAccess(Thread t);
1.1 public void checkAwtEventQueueAccess();
    public void checkConnect(String host, int port);
    public void checkConnect(String host, int port, Object context);
    public void checkCreateClassLoader();
    public void checkDelete(String file);
    public void checkExec(String cmd);
    public void checkExit(int status);
    public void checkLink(String lib);
    public void checkListen(int port);
1.1 public void checkMemberAccess(Class<?> clazz, int which);
1.1 public void checkMulticast(java.net.InetAddress maddr);
    public void checkPackageAccess(String pkg);
    public void checkPackageDefinition(String pkg);
1.2 public void checkPermission(java.security.Permission perm);
1.2 public void checkPermission(java.security.Permission perm, Object context);
1.1 public void checkPrintJobAccess();
    public void checkPropertiesAccess();
    public void checkPropertyAccess(String key);
    public void checkRead(String file);
    public void checkRead(java.io.FileDescriptor fd);
```

```
    public void checkRead(String file, Object context);
1.1 public void checkSecurityAccess(String target);
    public void checkSetFactory();
1.1 public void checkSystemClipboardAccess();
    public boolean checkTopLevelWindow(Object window);
    public void checkWrite(java.io.FileDescriptor fd);
    public void checkWrite(String file);
    public Object getSecurityContext();                    default:AccessControlContext
1.1 public ThreadGroup getThreadGroup();
// Protected Instance Methods
    protected Class[] getClassContext();                   native
// Deprecated Public Methods
1.1# public void checkMulticast(java.net.InetAddress maddr, byte ttl);
#   public boolean getInCheck();                           default:false
// Deprecated Protected Methods
#   protected int classDepth(String name);                 native
#   protected int classLoaderDepth();
#   protected ClassLoader currentClassLoader();
1.1# protected Class<?> currentLoadedClass();
#   protected boolean inClass(String name);
#   protected boolean inClassLoader();
// Deprecated Protected Fields
#   protected boolean inCheck;
}
```

Passed To System.setSecurityManager()

Returned By System.getSecurityManager()

Short **Java 1.1**

java.lang **serializable comparable**

This class provides an object wrapper around the short primitive type. It defines useful constants for the minimum and maximum values that can be stored by the short type, and also a Class object constant that represents the short type. It also provides various methods for converting Short values to and from strings and other numeric types.

Most of the static methods of this class can convert a String to a Short object or a short value; the four parseShort() and valueOf() methods parse a number from the specified string using an optionally specified radix and return it in one of these two forms. The decode() method parses a number specified in base 10, base 8, or base 16 and returns it as a Short. If the string begins with "0x" or "#", it is interpreted as a hexadecimal number; if it begins with "0", it is interpreted as an octal number. Otherwise, it is interpreted as a decimal number.

Note that this class has two different toString() methods. One is static and converts a short primitive value to a string. The other is the usual toString() method that converts a Short object to a string. Most of the remaining methods convert a Short to various primitive numeric types.

```
public final class Short extends Number implements Comparable<Short> {
// Public Constructors
```

```
    public Short(short value);
    public Short(String s) throws NumberFormatException;
// Public Constants
    public static final short MAX_VALUE;                                  =32767
    public static final short MIN_VALUE;                                  =-32768
5.0 public static final int SIZE;                                         =16
    public static final Class<Short> TYPE;
// Public Class Methods
    public static Short decode(String nm) throws NumberFormatException;
    public static short parseShort(String s) throws NumberFormatException;
    public static short parseShort(String s, int radix) throws NumberFormatException;
5.0 public static short reverseBytes(short i);
    public static String toString(short s);
    public static Short valueOf(String s) throws NumberFormatException;
5.0 public static Short valueOf(short s);
    public static Short valueOf(String s, int radix) throws NumberFormatException;
// Methods Implementing Comparable
1.2 public int compareTo(Short anotherShort);
// Public Methods Overriding Number
    public byte byteValue();
    public double doubleValue();
    public float floatValue();
    public int intValue();
    public long longValue();
    public short shortValue();
// Public Methods Overriding Object
    public boolean equals(Object obj);
    public int hashCode();
    public String toString();
}
```


StackOverflowError — Java 1.0

java.lang — serializable error

Signals that a stack overflow has occurred within the Java interpreter.

Object ─ Throwable ─ Error ─ VirtualMachineError ─ StackOverflowError
Serializable

```
public class StackOverflowError extends VirtualMachineError {
// Public Constructors
    public StackOverflowError();
    public StackOverflowError(String s);
}
```

StackTraceElement — Java 1.4

java.lang — serializable

Instances of this class are returned in an array by Throwable.getStackTrace(). Each instance represents one frame in the stack trace associated with an exception or error. getClassName() and getMethodName() return the name of the class (including package name) and method that contain the point of execution that the stack frame represents. If the class file contains sufficient information, getFileName() and getLineNumber() return the source file and line number associated with the frame. getFileName() returns null and getLineNumber() returns a negative value if source or line number information is not available. isNativeMethod() returns true if the named method is a native method (and therefore does not have a meaningful source file or line number).

Object ─ StackTraceElement ··· Serializable

```
public final class StackTraceElement implements Serializable {
// Public Constructors
5.0 public StackTraceElement(String declaringClass, String methodName, String fileName, int lineNumber);
// Public Instance Methods
   public String getClassName();
   public String getFileName();
   public int getLineNumber();
   public String getMethodName();
   public boolean isNativeMethod();
// Public Methods Overriding Object
   public boolean equals(Object obj);
   public int hashCode();
   public String toString();
}
```

Passed To Throwable.setStackTrace()

Returned By Thread.getStackTrace(), Throwable.getStackTrace(), java.lang.management.ThreadInfo.getStackTrace()

StrictMath **Java 1.3**

java.lang

This class is identical to the Math class, but additionally requires that its methods strictly adhere to the behavior of certain published algorithms. The methods of StrictMath are intended to operate identically on all platforms, and must produce exactly the same result (down to the very least significant bit) as certain well-known standard algorithms. When strict platform-independence of floating-point results is not required, use the Math class for better performance.

```
public final class StrictMath {
// No Constructor
// Public Constants
   public static final double E;                                   =2.718281828459045
   public static final double PI;                                  =3.141592653589793
// Public Class Methods
   public static int abs(int a);
   public static long abs(long a);
   public static float abs(float a);
   public static double abs(double a);
   public static double acos(double a);                            native
   public static double asin(double a);                            native
   public static double atan(double a);                            native
   public static double atan2(double y, double x);                 native
5.0 public static double cbrt(double a);                           native
   public static double ceil(double a);                            native
   public static double cos(double a);                             native
5.0 public static double cosh(double x);                           native
```

```
    public static double exp(double a);                                native
5.0 public static double expm1(double x);                              native
    public static double floor(double a);                              native
5.0 public static double hypot(double x, double y);                    native
    public static double IEEEremainder(double f1, double f2);          native
    public static double log(double a);                                native
5.0 public static double log10(double a);                              native
5.0 public static double log1p(double x);                              native
    public static int max(int a, int b);
    public static long max(long a, long b);
    public static float max(float a, float b);
    public static double max(double a, double b);
    public static int min(int a, int b);
    public static long min(long a, long b);
    public static float min(float a, float b);
    public static double min(double a, double b);
    public static double pow(double a, double b);                      native
    public static double random();
    public static double rint(double a);
    public static int round(float a);
    public static long round(double a);
5.0 public static float signum(float f);
5.0 public static double signum(double d);
    public static double sin(double a);                                native
5.0 public static double sinh(double x);                               native
    public static double sqrt(double a);                               native
    public static double tan(double a);                                native
5.0 public static double tanh(double x);                               native
    public static double toDegrees(double angrad);                     strictfp
    public static double toRadians(double angdeg);                     strictfp
5.0 public static float ulp(float f);
5.0 public static double ulp(double d);
}
```

String — Java 1.0

java.lang — serializable comparable

The String class represents a read-only string of characters. A String object is created by the Java compiler whenever it encounters a string in double quotes; this method of creation is typically simpler than using a constructor. The static valueOf() factory methods create new String objects that hold the textual representation of various Java primitive types. There are also valueOf() methods, copyValueOf() methods and String() constructors for creating a String object that holds a copy of the text contained in another String, StringBuffer, StringBuilder, or a char or int array. You can also use the String() constructor to create a String object from an array of bytes. If you do this, you may explicitly specify the name of the charset (or character encoding) to be used to decode the bytes into characters, or you can rely on the default charset for your platform. (See java.nio.charset.Charset for more on charset names.)

In Java 5.0, the static format() methods provide another useful way to create String objects that hold formatted text. These utility methods create and use a new java.util.Formatter object and behave like the sprintf() function in the C programming language.

length() returns the number of characters in a string. charAt() extracts a character from a string. You can use these two methods to iterate through the characters of a string.

You can obtain a char array that holds the characters of a string with toCharArray(), or use getChars() to copy just a selected region of the string into an existing array. Use getBytes() if you want to obtain an array of bytes that contains the encoded form of the characters in a string, using either the platform's default encoding or a named encoding.

This class defines many methods for comparing strings and substrings. equals() returns true if two String objects contain the same text, and equalsIgnoreCase() returns true if two strings are equal when uppercase and lowercase differences are ignored. As of Java 1.4, the contentEquals() method compares a string to a specified StringBuffer object, returning true if they contain the same text. startsWith() and endsWith() return true if a string starts with the specified prefix string or ends with the specified suffix string. A two-argument version of startsWith() allows you to specify a position within this string at which the prefix comparison is to be done. The regionMatches() method is a generalized version of this startsWith() method. It returns true if the specified region of the specified string matches the characters that begin at a specified position within this string. The five-argument version of this method allows you to perform this comparison ignoring the case of the characters being compared. The final string comparison method is matches(), which, as described below, compares a string to a regular expression pattern.

compareTo() is another string comparison method, but it is used for comparing the order of two strings, rather than simply comparing them for equality. compareTo() implements the Comparable interface and enables sorting of lists and arrays of String objects. See Comparable for more information. compareToIgnoreCase() is like compareTo() but ignores the case of the two strings when doing the comparison. The CASE_INSENSITIVE_ORDER constant is a Comparator for sorting strings in a way that ignores the case of their characters. (The java.util.Comparator interface is similar to the Comparable interface but allows the definition of object orderings that are different from the default ordering defined by Comparable.) The compareTo() and compareToIgnoreCase() methods and the CASE_INSENSITIVE_ORDER Comparator object order strings based only on the numeric ordering of the Unicode encoding of their characters. This is not always the preferred "alphabetical ordering" in some languages. See java.text.Collator for a more general technique for collating strings.

indexOf() and lastIndexOf() search forward and backward in a string for a specified character or substring. They return the position of the match, or -1 if there is no match. The one argument versions of these methods start at the beginning or end of the string, and the two-argument versions start searching from a specified character position.

Java 5.0 adds new comparison methods that work with any CharSequence. A new version of contentEquals() enables the comparison of a string with any CharSequence, including StringBuilder objects. The contains() method returns true if the string contains any sequence of characters equal to the specified CharSequence.

substring() returns a string that consists of the characters from (and including) the specified start position to (but not including) the specified end position. A one-argument version returns all characters from (and including) the specified start position to the end of the string. As of Java 1.4, the String class implements the CharSequence interface and defines the subSequence() method, which works just like the two-argument version of substring() but returns the specified characters as a CharSequence rather than as a String.

Several methods return new strings that contain modified versions of the text held by the original string (the original string remains unchanged). replace() creates a new string with all occurrences of one character replaced by another. Java 5.0 adds a generalized version of replace() that replaces all occurrences of one CharSequence with another. More general methods, replaceAll() and replaceFirst(), use regular expression pattern matching; they are described later in this section. toUpperCase() and toLowerCase() return a new string in which all characters are converted to upper- or lowercase respectively. These case-conversion methods take an optional Locale argument to perform locale-specific case conversion. trim() is a utility method that returns a new string in which all leading and trailing whitespace has been removed. concat() returns the new string formed by concatenating or appending the specified string to this string. String concatenation is more commonly done, however, with the + operator.

Note that String objects are immutable; there is no setCharAt() method to change the contents. The methods that return a String do not modify the string they are invoked on but instead return a new String object that holds a modified copy of the text of the original. Use a StringBuffer if you want to manipulate the contents of a string or call toCharArray() or getChars() to convert a string to an array of char values.

Java 1.4 introduced support for pattern matching with regular expressions. matches() returns true if this string exactly matches the pattern specified by the regular expression argument. replaceAll() and replaceFirst() create a new string in which all occurrences or the first occurrence of a substring that matches the specified regular expression is replaced with the specified replacement string. The split() methods return an array of substrings of this string, formed by splitting this string at positions that match the specified regular expression. These regular expression methods are all convenience methods that simply call methods of the same name in the java.util.regex package. See the Pattern and Matcher classes in that package for further details.

Many programs use strings as commonly as they use Java primitive values. Because the String type is an object rather than a primitive value, however, you cannot in general use the == operator to compare two strings for equality. Instead, even though strings are immutable, you must use the more expensive equals() method. For programs that perform a lot of string comparison, the intern() provides a way to speed up those comparisons. The String class maintains a set of String objects that includes all double-quoted string literals and all compile-time constant strings defined in a Java program. The set is guaranteed not to contain duplicates, and the set is used to ensure that duplicate String objects are not created unnecessarily. The intern() method looks up a string in or adds a new string to this set of unique strings. It searches the set for a string that contains exactly the same characters as the string you invoked the method on. If such a string is found, intern() returns it. If no matching string is found, the string you invoked intern() on is itself stored in the set ("interned") and becomes the return value of the method. What this means is that you can safely compare any strings returned by the intern() method using the == and != operators instead of equals(). You can also successfully compare any string returned by intern() to any string constant with == and !=.

In Java 5.0, Unicode supplementary characters may be represented as a single int codepoint value or as a sequence of two char values known as a "surrogate pair." See Character for more on supplementary characters and methods for working with them. String methods for working with supplementary characters, such as codePointAt(), codePointCount(), and offsetByCodePoints(), are similar to those defined by Character.

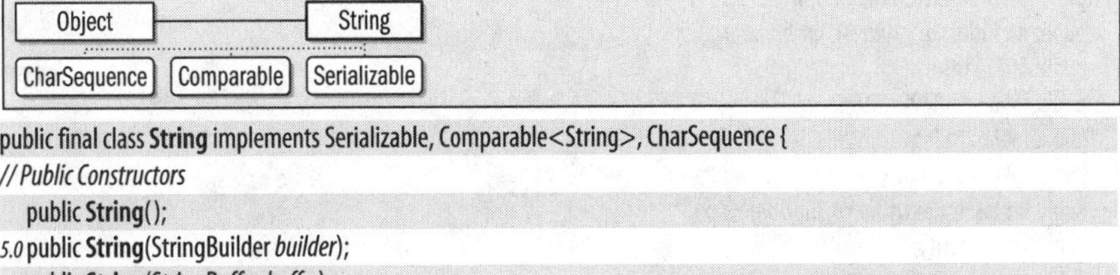


```
public final class String implements Serializable, Comparable<String>, CharSequence {
// Public Constructors
     public String();
5.0  public String(StringBuilder builder);
     public String(StringBuffer buffer);
```

```
    public String(char[] value);
    public String(String original);
1.1 public String(byte[] bytes);
1.1 public String(byte[] bytes, String charsetName) throws java.io.UnsupportedEncodingException;
#   public String(byte[] ascii, int hibyte);
    public String(char[] value, int offset, int count);
1.1 public String(byte[] bytes, int offset, int length);
5.0 public String(int[] codePoints, int offset, int count);
#   public String(byte[] ascii, int hibyte, int offset, int count);
1.1 public String(byte[] bytes, int offset, int length, String charsetName) throws java.io.UnsupportedEncodingException;
// Public Constants
1.2 public static final java.util.Comparator<String> CASE_INSENSITIVE_ORDER;
// Public Class Methods
    public static String copyValueOf(char[] data);
    public static String copyValueOf(char[] data, int offset, int count);
5.0 public static String format(String format, Object... args);
5.0 public static String format(java.util.Locale l, String format, Object... args);
    public static String valueOf(float f);
    public static String valueOf(long l);
    public static String valueOf(Object obj);
    public static String valueOf(double d);
    public static String valueOf(boolean b);
    public static String valueOf(char[] data);
    public static String valueOf(int i);
    public static String valueOf(char c);
    public static String valueOf(char[] data, int offset, int count);
// Public Instance Methods
    public char charAt(int index);                                Implements:CharSequence
5.0 public int codePointAt(int index);
5.0 public int codePointBefore(int index);
5.0 public int codePointCount(int beginIndex, int endIndex);
    public int compareTo(String anotherString);                   Implements:Comparable
1.2 public int compareToIgnoreCase(String str);
    public String concat(String str);
5.0 public boolean contains(CharSequence s);
1.4 public boolean contentEquals(StringBuffer sb);
5.0 public boolean contentEquals(CharSequence cs);
    public boolean endsWith(String suffix);
    public boolean equalsIgnoreCase(String anotherString);
1.1 public byte[] getBytes();
1.1 public byte[] getBytes(String charsetName) throws java.io.UnsupportedEncodingException;
    public void getChars(int srcBegin, int srcEnd, char[] dst, int dstBegin);
    public int indexOf(int ch);
    public int indexOf(String str);
    public int indexOf(int ch, int fromIndex);
    public int indexOf(String str, int fromIndex);
    public String intern();                                        native
    public int lastIndexOf(String str);
    public int lastIndexOf(int ch);
    public int lastIndexOf(String str, int fromIndex);
    public int lastIndexOf(int ch, int fromIndex);
    public int length();                                           Implements:CharSequence
1.4 public boolean matches(String regex);
```

```
5.0 public int offsetByCodePoints(int index, int codePointOffset);
    public boolean regionMatches(int toffset, String other, int ooffset, int len);
    public boolean regionMatches(boolean ignoreCase, int toffset, String other, int ooffset, int len);
    public String replace(char oldChar, char newChar);
5.0 public String replace(CharSequence target, CharSequence replacement);
1.4 public String replaceAll(String regex, String replacement);
1.4 public String replaceFirst(String regex, String replacement);
1.4 public String[] split(String regex);
1.4 public String[] split(String regex, int limit);
    public boolean startsWith(String prefix);
    public boolean startsWith(String prefix, int toffset);
    public String substring(int beginIndex);
    public String substring(int beginIndex, int endIndex);
    public char[] toCharArray();
    public String toLowerCase();
1.1 public String toLowerCase(java.util.Locale locale);
    public String toString();                                   Implements:CharSequence
    public String toUpperCase();
1.1 public String toUpperCase(java.util.Locale locale);
    public String trim();
// Methods Implementing CharSequence
    public char charAt(int index);
    public int length();
1.4 public CharSequence subSequence(int beginIndex, int endIndex);
    public String toString();
// Methods Implementing Comparable
    public int compareTo(String anotherString);
// Public Methods Overriding Object
    public boolean equals(Object anObject);
    public int hashCode();
// Deprecated Public Methods
#   public void getBytes(int srcBegin, int srcEnd, byte[] dst, int dstBegin);
}
```

Passed To Too many methods to list.

Returned By Too many methods to list.

Type Of Too many fields to list.

StringBuffer — Java 1.0

java.lang — serializable appendable

This class represents a mutable string of characters that can grow or shrink as necessary. Its mutability makes it suitable for processing text in place, which is not possible with the immutable String class. Its resizability and the various methods it implements make it easier to use than a char[]. Create a StringBuffer with the StringBuffer() constructor. You may pass a String that contains the initial text for the buffer to this constructor, but if you do not, the buffer will start out empty. You may also specify the initial capacity for the buffer if you can estimate the number of characters the buffer will eventually hold.

The methods of this class are synchronized, which makes StringBuffer objects suitable for use by multiple threads. In Java 5.0 and later, when working with a single thread, StringBuilder is preferred over this class because it does not have the overhead of synchronized methods. StringBuilder implements the same methods as StringBuffer and can be used in the same way.

Query the character stored at a given index with charAt() and set or delete that character with setCharAt() or deleteCharAt(). Use length() to return the length of the buffer, and use setLength() to set the length of the buffer, truncating it or filling it with null characters ('\u0000') as necessary. capacity() returns the number of characters a StringBuffer can hold before its internal buffer needs to be reallocated. If you expect a StringBuffer to grow substantially and can approximate its eventual size, you can use ensureCapacity() to preallocate sufficient internal storage.

Use the various append() methods to append text to the end of the buffer. Use insert() to insert text at a specified position within the buffer. Note that in addition to strings, primitive values, character arrays, and arbitrary objects may be passed to append() and insert(). These values are converted to strings before they are appended or inserted. Use delete() to delete a range of characters from the buffer and use replace() to replace a range of characters with a specified String.

Use substring() to convert a portion of a StringBuffer to a String. The two versions of this method work just like the same-named methods of String. Call toString() to obtain the contents of a StringBuffer as a String object. Or use getChars() to extract the specified range of characters from the StringBuffer and store them into the specified character array starting at the specified index of that array.

As of Java 1.4, StringBuffer implements CharSequence and so also defines a subSequence() method that is like substring() but returns its value as a CharSequence. Java 1.4 also added indexOf() and lastIndexOf() methods that search forward or backward (from the optionally specified index) in a StringBuffer for a sequence of characters that matches the specified String. These methods return the index of the matching string or -1 if no match was found. See also the similarly named methods of String after which these methods are modeled.

In Java 5.0, this class has a new constructor and new methods for working with CharSequence objects. It implements the Appendable interface for use with java.util.Formatter and includes new methods for working with 21-bit Unicode characters as int codepoints.

String concatenation in Java is performed with the + operator and is implemented, prior to Java 5.0, using the append() method of a StringBuffer. In Java 5.0 and later, StringBuilder is used instead. After a string is processed in a StringBuffer object, it can be efficiently converted to a String object for subsequent use. The StringBuffer.toString() method is typically implemented so that it does not copy the internal array of characters. Instead, it shares that array with the new String object, making a new copy for itself only if and when further modifications are made to the StringBuffer object.

Object	AbstractStringBuilder		StringBuffer
Appendable	CharSequence	CharSequence	Serializable

```
public final class StringBuffer extends AbstractStringBuilder implements CharSequence, Serializable {
// Public Constructors
   public StringBuffer();
   public StringBuffer(String str);
   public StringBuffer(int capacity);
5.0 public StringBuffer(CharSequence seq);
// Public Instance Methods
   public StringBuffer append(String str);                                  synchronized
1.4 public StringBuffer append(StringBuffer sb);                            synchronized
5.0 public StringBuffer append(CharSequence s);
   public StringBuffer append(Object obj);                                  synchronized
   public StringBuffer append(char[] str);                                  synchronized
```

```
    public StringBuffer append(long lng);                                           synchronized
    public StringBuffer append(float f);                                            synchronized
    public StringBuffer append(double d);                                           synchronized
    public StringBuffer append(boolean b);                                          synchronized
    public StringBuffer append(char c);                                             synchronized
    public StringBuffer append(int i);                                              synchronized
    public StringBuffer append(char[] str, int offset, int len);                    synchronized
5.0 public StringBuffer append(CharSequence s, int start, int end);                 synchronized
5.0 public StringBuffer appendCodePoint(int codePoint);                             synchronized
    public char charAt(int index);                         Implements:CharSequence synchronized
1.2 public StringBuffer delete(int start, int end);                                 synchronized
1.2 public StringBuffer deleteCharAt(int index);                                    synchronized
    public StringBuffer insert(int offset, char c);                                 synchronized
    public StringBuffer insert(int offset, boolean b);
    public StringBuffer insert(int offset, long l);
    public StringBuffer insert(int offset, int i);
    public StringBuffer insert(int offset, String str);                             synchronized
    public StringBuffer insert(int offset, Object obj);                             synchronized
5.0 public StringBuffer insert(int dstOffset, CharSequence s);
    public StringBuffer insert(int offset, char[] str);                             synchronized
    public StringBuffer insert(int offset, double d);
    public StringBuffer insert(int offset, float f);
1.2 public StringBuffer insert(int index, char[] str, int offset, int len);         synchronized
5.0 public StringBuffer insert(int dstOffset, CharSequence s, int start, int end);  synchronized
    public int length();                                   Implements:CharSequence synchronized
1.2 public StringBuffer replace(int start, int end, String str);                    synchronized
    public StringBuffer reverse();                                                  synchronized
    public String toString();                              Implements:CharSequence synchronized
// Methods Implementing CharSequence
    public char charAt(int index);                                                  synchronized
    public int length();                                                            synchronized
1.4 public CharSequence subSequence(int start, int end);                            synchronized
    public String toString();                                                       synchronized
// Public Methods Overriding AbstractStringBuilder
    public int capacity();                                                          synchronized
5.0 public int codePointAt(int index);                                              synchronized
5.0 public int codePointBefore(int index);                                          synchronized
5.0 public int codePointCount(int beginIndex, int endIndex);                        synchronized
    public void ensureCapacity(int minimumCapacity);                                synchronized
    public void getChars(int srcBegin, int srcEnd, char[] dst, int dstBegin);       synchronized
1.4 public int indexOf(String str);
1.4 public int indexOf(String str, int fromIndex);                                  synchronized
1.4 public int lastIndexOf(String str);
1.4 public int lastIndexOf(String str, int fromIndex);                              synchronized
5.0 public int offsetByCodePoints(int index, int codePointOffset);                  synchronized
    public void setCharAt(int index, char ch);                                      synchronized
    public void setLength(int newLength);                                           synchronized
1.2 public String substring(int start);                                             synchronized
1.2 public String substring(int start, int end);                                    synchronized
5.0 public void trimToSize();                                                       synchronized
}
```

Passed To Too many methods to list.

Returned By Too many methods to list.

StringBuilder

Java 5.0

java.lang

serializable appendable

This class defines the same methods as **StringBuffer** but does not declare those methods **synchronized**, which can result in better performance in the common case in which only a single thread is using the object. **StringBuilder** is a drop-in replacement for **StringBuffer** and should be used in preference to **StringBuffer** except where thread safety is required. See **StringBuffer** for an overview of the methods shared by these two classes.

Object — AbstractStringBuilder — StringBuilder

Appendable | CharSequence | CharSequence | Serializable

```
public final class StringBuilder extends AbstractStringBuilder implements CharSequence, Serializable {
// Public Constructors
   public StringBuilder();
   public StringBuilder(int capacity);
   public StringBuilder(String str);
   public StringBuilder(CharSequence seq);
// Public Instance Methods
   public StringBuilder append(long lng);
   public StringBuilder append(float f);
   public StringBuilder append(double d);
   public StringBuilder append(int i);
   public StringBuilder append(String str);
   public StringBuilder append(StringBuffer sb);
   public StringBuilder append(CharSequence s);
   public StringBuilder append(Object obj);
   public StringBuilder append(char c);
   public StringBuilder append(boolean b);
   public StringBuilder append(char[] str);
   public StringBuilder append(CharSequence s, int start, int end);
   public StringBuilder append(char[] str, int offset, int len);
   public StringBuilder appendCodePoint(int codePoint);
   public StringBuilder delete(int start, int end);
   public StringBuilder deleteCharAt(int index);
   public StringBuilder insert(int offset, boolean b);
   public StringBuilder insert(int offset, char c);
   public StringBuilder insert(int offset, int i);
   public StringBuilder insert(int dstOffset, CharSequence s);
   public StringBuilder insert(int offset, Object obj);
   public StringBuilder insert(int offset, String str);
   public StringBuilder insert(int offset, char[] str);
   public StringBuilder insert(int offset, double d);
   public StringBuilder insert(int offset, long l);
   public StringBuilder insert(int offset, float f);
   public StringBuilder insert(int index, char[] str, int offset, int len);
   public StringBuilder insert(int dstOffset, CharSequence s, int start, int end);
   public StringBuilder replace(int start, int end, String str);
   public StringBuilder reverse();
// Methods Implementing CharSequence
   public String toString();
// Public Methods Overriding AbstractStringBuilder
   public int indexOf(String str);
```

```
    public int indexOf(String str, int fromIndex);
    public int lastIndexOf(String str);
    public int lastIndexOf(String str, int fromIndex);
}
```

Passed To String.String()

StringIndexOutOfBoundsException — Java 1.0

java.lang — serializable unchecked

Signals that the index used to access a character of a String or StringBuffer is less than zero or is too large.

Object — Throwable — Exception — RuntimeException — IndexOutOfBoundsException — StringIndexOutOfBoundsException

Serializable

```
public class StringIndexOutOfBoundsException extends IndexOutOfBoundsException {
// Public Constructors
    public StringIndexOutOfBoundsException();
    public StringIndexOutOfBoundsException(int index);
    public StringIndexOutOfBoundsException(String s);
}
```

SuppressWarnings — Java 5.0

java.lang — @Target({TYPE, FIELD, METHOD, PARAMETER, CONSTRUCTOR, LOCAL_VARIABLE}) @Retention(SOURCE) annotation

An annotation of this type tells the Java compiler not to generate specified kinds of warning messages for code within the annotated program element. Annotations of this type have source retention and may be applied to any program element except packages and other annotation types. An @SuppressWarnings annotation has an array of String objects as its value. These strings specify the names of the warnings to be suppressed. The available warnings (and their names) depend on the compiler implementation, and compilers will ignore warning names they do not support. Compiler vendors are expected to cooperate in defining at least a core set of common warning names. In Java 5.0, the @SuppressWarnings warning names supported by the *javac* compiler are the same as the warning flags that can be specfied with the -Xlint compiler flag.

Annotation ··· SuppressWarnings

```
public @interface SuppressWarnings {
// Public Instance Methods
    String[] value();
}
```

System — Java 1.0

java.lang

This class defines a platform-independent interface to system facilities, including system properties and system input and output streams. All methods and variables of this class are static, and the class cannot be instantiated. Because the methods defined by this class are low-level system methods, most require special permissions and cannot be executed by untrusted code.

getProperty() looks up a named property on the system properties list, returning the optionally specified default value if no property definition is found. getProperties() returns the entire properties list. setProperties() sets a Properties object on the properties list. In Java 1.2 and later, setProperty() sets the value of a system property. In Java 5.0, you can clear a property setting with clearProperty(). The following table lists system properties that are always defined. Untrusted code may be unable to read some or all of these properties. Additional properties can be defined using the -D option when invoking the Java interpreter.

Property name	Description
file.separator	Platform directory separator character
path.separator	Platform path separator character
line.separator	Platform line separator character(s)
user.name	Current user s account name
user.home	Home directory of current user
user.dir	The current working directory
java.class.path	Where classes are loaded from
java.class.version	Version of the Java class file format
java.compiler	The name of the just-in-time compiler
java.ext.dirs	Path to directories that hold extensions
java.home	The directory Java is installed in
java.io.tmpdir	The directory that temporary files are written to
java.library.path	Directories to search for native libraries
java.specification.version	Version of the Java API specification
java.specification.vendor	Vendor of the Java API specification
java.specification.name	Name of the Java API specification
java.version	Version of the Java API implementation
java.vendor	Vendor of this Java API implementation
java.vendor.url	URL of the vendor of this Java API implementation
java.vm.specification.version	Version of the Java VM specification
java.vm.specification.vendor	Vendor of the Java VM specification
java.vm.specification.name	Name of the Java VM specification
java.vm.version	Version of the Java VM implementation
java.vm.vendor	Vendor of the Java VM implementation
java.vm.name	Name of the Java VM implementation
os.name	Name of the host operating system
os.arch	Host operating system architecture
os.version	Version of the host operating system

The in, out, and err fields hold the standard input, output, and error streams for the system. These fields are frequently used in calls such as System.out.println(). In Java 1.1, setIn(), setOut(), and setErr() allow these streams to be redirected.

System also defines various other useful static methods. exit() causes the Java VM to exit. arraycopy() efficiently copies an array or a portion of an array into a destination array. currentTimeMillis() returns the current time in milliseconds since midnight GMT, January 1, 1970 GMT. In Java 5.0, nanoTime() returns a time in nanoseconds. Unlike currentTimeMillis()

this time is not relative to any fixed point and so is useful only for elapsed time computations.

getenv() returns the value of a platform-dependent environment variable, or (in Java 5.0) returns a Map of all environment variables. The one-argument version of getenv() was previously deprecated but has been restored in Java 5.0.

identityHashCode() computes the hashcode for an object in the same way that the default Object.hashCode() method does. It does this regardless of whether or how the hashCode() method has been overridden.

In Java 5.0, inheritedChannel() returns a java.nio.channels.Channel object that represents a network connection passed to the Java process by the invoking process. This allows Java programs to be used with the Unix *inetd* daemon, for example.

load() and loadLibrary() can read libraries of native code into the system. mapLibraryName() converts a system-independent library name into a system-dependent library filename. Finally, getSecurityManager() and setSecurityManager() get and set the system SecurityManager object responsible for the system security policy.

See also Runtime, which defines several other methods that provide low-level access to system facilities.

```
public final class System {
// No Constructor
// Public Constants
   public static final java.io.PrintStream err;
   public static final java.io.InputStream in;
   public static final java.io.PrintStream out;
// Public Class Methods
   public static void arraycopy(Object src, int srcPos, Object dest, int destPos, int length);     native
5.0 public static String clearProperty(String key);
   public static long currentTimeMillis();                                                      native
   public static void exit(int status);
   public static void gc();
5.0 public static java.util.Map<String,String> getenv();
   public static String getenv(String name);
   public static java.util.Properties getProperties();
   public static String getProperty(String key);
   public static String getProperty(String key, String def);
   public static SecurityManager getSecurityManager();
1.1 public static int identityHashCode(Object x);                                               native
5.0 public static java.nio.channels.Channel inheritedChannel() throws java.io.IOException;
   public static void load(String filename);
   public static void loadLibrary(String libname);
1.2 public static String mapLibraryName(String libname);                                        native
5.0 public static long nanoTime();                                                              native
   public static void runFinalization();
1.1 public static void setErr(java.io.PrintStream err);
1.1 public static void setIn(java.io.InputStream in);
1.1 public static void setOut(java.io.PrintStream out);
   public static void setProperties(java.util.Properties props);
1.2 public static String setProperty(String key, String value);
   public static void setSecurityManager(SecurityManager s);
// Deprecated Public Methods
1.1# public static void runFinalizersOnExit(boolean value);
}
```

Thread

Java 1.0

java.lang

runnable

This class encapsulates all information about a single thread of control running on the Java interpreter. To create a thread, you must either pass a Runnable object (i.e., an object that implements the Runnable interface by defining a run() method) to the Thread constructor or subclass Thread so that it defines its own run() method. The run() method of the Thread or of the specified Runnable object is the body of the thread. It begins executing when the start() method of the Thread object is called. The thread runs until the run() method returns. isAlive() returns true if a thread has been started, and the run() method has not yet exited.

The static methods of this class operate on the currently running thread. currentThread() returns the Thread object of the currently running code. sleep() makes the current thread stop for a specified amount of time. yield() makes the current thread give up control to any other threads of equal priority that are waiting to run. holdsLock() tests whether the current thread holds a lock (through a synchronized method or statement) on the specified object; this Java 1.4 method is often useful with an assert statement.

The instance methods may be called by one thread to operate on a different thread. checkAccess() checks whether the running thread has permission to modify a Thread object and throws a SecurityException if it does not. join() waits for a thread to die. interrupt() wakes up a waiting or sleeping thread (with an InterruptedException) or sets an interrupted flag on a nonsleeping thread. A thread can test its own interrupted flag with the static interrupted() method or can test the flag of another thread with isInterrupted(). Calling interrupted() implicitly clears the interrupted flag, but calling isInterrupted() does not. Methods related to sleep() and interrupt() are the wait() and notify() methods defined by the Object class. Calling wait() causes the current thread to block until the object's notify() method is called by another thread.

setName() sets the name of a thread, which is purely optional. setPriority() sets the priority of the thread. Higher priority threads run before lower priority threads. Java does not specify what happens to multiple threads of equal priority; some systems perform time-slicing and share the CPU between such threads. On other systems, one compute-bound thread that does not call yield() may starve another thread of the same priority. setDaemon() sets a boolean flag that specifies whether this thread is a daemon or not. The Java VM keeps running as long as at least one nondaemon thread is running. Call getThreadGroup() to obtain the ThreadGroup of which a thread is part. In Java 1.2 and later, use setContextClassLoader() to specify the ClassLoader to be used to load any classes required by the thread.

suspend(), resume(), and stop() suspend, resume, and stop a given thread, respectively, but all three methods are deprecated because they are inherently unsafe and can cause deadlock. If a thread must be stoppable, have it periodically check a flag and exit if the flag is set.

In Java 1.4 and later, the four-argument Thread() constructor allows you to specify the "stack size" parameter for the thread. Typically, larger stack sizes allow threads to recurse more deeply before running out of stack space. Smaller stack sizes reduce the fixed per-thread memory requirements and may allow more threads to exist concurrently. The meaning of this argument is implementation dependent, and implementations may even ignore it.

Java 5.0 adds important new features to this class. getId() returns a unique long identifier for the thread. getState() returns the state of the thread as an enumerated constant of type Thread.State. Thread.UncaughtExceptionHandler defines an API for handling exceptions that cause the run() method of the thread to exit. Register a handler of this type with setUncaughtExceptionHandler() or register a default handler with the static methods setDefaultUncaughtExceptionHandler(). Obtain a snapshot of a thread's current stack trace with getStackTrace(). This returns an array of StackTraceElement objects: the first element of the array is the most recent method invocation and the last element is the least recent. The static getAllStackTraces() returns stack traces for all running threads (the traces may be obtained at different times for different threads).

Object — Thread ··· Runnable

```
public class Thread implements Runnable {
// Public Constructors
    public Thread();
    public Thread(String name);
    public Thread(Runnable target);
    public Thread(Runnable target, String name);
    public Thread(ThreadGroup group, String name);
    public Thread(ThreadGroup group, Runnable target);
    public Thread(ThreadGroup group, Runnable target, String name);
1.4 public Thread(ThreadGroup group, Runnable target, String name, long stackSize);
// Public Constants
    public static final int MAX_PRIORITY;                                          =10
    public static final int MIN_PRIORITY;                                          =1
    public static final int NORM_PRIORITY;                                         =5
// Nested Types
5.0 public enum State;
5.0 public interface UncaughtExceptionHandler;
// Public Class Methods
    public static int activeCount();
    public static Thread currentThread();                                          native
    public static void dumpStack();
    public static int enumerate(Thread[] tarray);
5.0 public static java.util.Map<Thread,StackTraceElement[]> getAllStackTraces();
5.0 public static Thread.UncaughtExceptionHandler getDefaultUncaughtExceptionHandler();
1.4 public static boolean holdsLock(Object obj);                                   native
    public static boolean interrupted();
5.0 public static void setDefaultUncaughtExceptionHandler(Thread.UncaughtExceptionHandler eh);
    public static void sleep(long millis) throws InterruptedException;             native
    public static void sleep(long millis, int nanos) throws InterruptedException;
    public static void yield();                                                    native
// Public Instance Methods
    public final void checkAccess();
1.2 public ClassLoader getContextClassLoader();
5.0 public long getId();                                                           default:7
    public final String getName();                                                 default:"Thread-0"
    public final int getPriority();                                                default:5
5.0 public StackTraceElement[] getStackTrace();
5.0 public Thread.State getState();
    public final ThreadGroup getThreadGroup();
5.0 public Thread.UncaughtExceptionHandler getUncaughtExceptionHandler();          default:ThreadGroup
    public void interrupt();
    public final boolean isAlive();                                                native default:false
    public final boolean isDaemon();                                               default:false
    public boolean isInterrupted();                                                default:false
```

```
    public final void join() throws InterruptedException;
    public final void join(long millis) throws InterruptedException;                synchronized
    public final void join(long millis, int nanos) throws InterruptedException;     synchronized
1.2 public void setContextClassLoader(ClassLoader cl);
    public final void setDaemon(boolean on);
    public final void setName(String name);
    public final void setPriority(int newPriority);
5.0 public void setUncaughtExceptionHandler(Thread.UncaughtExceptionHandler eh);
    public void start();                                                             synchronized
// Methods Implementing Runnable
    public void run();
// Public Methods Overriding Object
    public String toString();
// Deprecated Public Methods
#   public int countStackFrames();                                                   native
#   public void destroy();
#   public final void resume();
#   public final void stop();
#   public final void stop(Throwable obj);                                           synchronized
#   public final void suspend();
}
```

Passed To Runtime.{addShutdownHook(), removeShutdownHook()}, SecurityManager.checkAccess(), Thread.UncaughtExceptionHandler.uncaughtException(), ThreadGroup.{enumerate(), uncaughtException()}, java.util.concurrent.ThreadPoolExecutor.beforeExecute(), java.util.concurrent.TimeUnit.timedJoin(), java.util.concurrent.locks.AbstractQueuedSynchronizer.isQueued(), java.util.concurrent.locks.LockSupport.unpark(), java.util.concurrent.locks.ReentrantLock.hasQueuedThread(), java.util.concurrent.locks.ReentrantReadWriteLock.hasQueuedThread()

Returned By java.util.concurrent.ThreadFactory.newThread(), java.util.concurrent.locks.AbstractQueuedSynchronizer.getFirstQueuedThread(), java.util.concurrent.locks.ReentrantLock.getOwner(), java.util.concurrent.locks.ReentrantReadWriteLock.getOwner()

Thread.State — Java 5.0

java.lang — serializable comparable enum

This enumerated type defines the possible states of a thread. Call the getState() method of a Thread object to obtain one of the enumerated constants defined here. A NEW thread has not been started yet, and a TERMINATED thread has exited. A BLOCKED thread is waiting to enter a synchronized method or block. A WAITING thread is waiting in Object.wait(), Thread.join(), or a similar method. A TIMED_WAITING thread is waiting but is subject to a timeout, such as in Thread.sleep() or the timed versions of Object.wait() and Thread.join(). Finally, a thread that has been started and has not yet exited and is not blocked or waiting is RUNNABLE. This does not mean that the operating system is currently running it or that it is even making any forward progress, but that it is at least available to run when the operating system gives it the CPU.

```
public enum Thread.State {
// Enumerated Constants
    NEW,
    RUNNABLE,
    BLOCKED,
    WAITING,
```

```
    TIMED_WAITING,
    TERMINATED;
// Public Class Methods
    public static Thread.State valueOf(String name);
    public static final Thread.State[] values();
}
```

Returned By Thread.getState(), java.lang.management.ThreadInfo.getThreadState()

Thread.UncaughtExceptionHandler **Java 5.0**

java.lang

This interface defines a handler to be invoked when a thread throws an exception that remains uncaught. When this happens, the uncaughtException() method of the registered handler is invoked with the Thread object that threw the exception and the Throwable exception object as arguments. The handler is run by the thread that received the exception, and that thread will exit as soon as the handler exits. If uncaughtException() itself throws an exception, that exception will be ignored.

An object that implements this interface may be registered for a Thread with the setUncaughtExceptionHandler() method. A default UncaughtExceptionHandler may be registered with the static method Thread.setDefaultUncaughtExceptionHandler(). If no handler or default handler is registered, the uncaughtException() method of the containing ThreadGroup is used instead.

```
public interface Thread.UncaughtExceptionHandler {
// Public Instance Methods
    void uncaughtException(Thread t, Throwable e);
}
```

Implementations ThreadGroup

Passed To Thread.{setDefaultUncaughtExceptionHandler(), setUncaughtExceptionHandler()}

Returned By Thread.{getDefaultUncaughtExceptionHandler(), getUncaughtExceptionHandler()}

ThreadDeath **Java 1.0**

java.lang **serializable error**

Signals that a thread should terminate. This error is thrown in a thread when the Thread.stop() method is called for that thread. This is an unusual Error type that simply causes a thread to be terminated, but does not print an error message or cause the interpreter to exit. You can catch ThreadDeath errors to do any necessary cleanup for a thread, but if you do, you must rethrow the error so that the thread actually terminates.

Object — Throwable — Error — ThreadDeath
Serializable

```
public class ThreadDeath extends Error {
// Public Constructors
    public ThreadDeath();
}
```

ThreadGroup **Java 1.0**

java.lang

This class represents a group of threads and allows that group to be manipulated as a whole. A ThreadGroup can contain Thread objects, as well as other child ThreadGroup objects. All

ThreadGroup objects are created as children of some other ThreadGroup, and thus there is a parent/child hierarchy of ThreadGroup objects. Use getParent() to obtain the parent ThreadGroup, and use activeCount(), activeGroupCount(), and the various enumerate() methods to list the child Thread and ThreadGroup objects. Most applications can simply rely on the default system thread group. System-level code and applications such as servers that need to create a large number of threads may find it convenient to create their own ThreadGroup objects, however.

interrupt() interrupts all threads in the group at once. setMaxPriority() specifies the maximum priority any thread in the group can have. checkAccess() checks whether the calling thread has permission to modify the given thread group. The method throws a SecurityException if the current thread does not have access. uncaughtException() contains the code that is run when a thread terminates because of an uncaught exception or error. You can customize this method by subclassing ThreadGroup.

Object — ThreadGroup ··· Thread.UncaughtExceptionHandler

```
public class ThreadGroup implements Thread.UncaughtExceptionHandler {
// Public Constructors
   public ThreadGroup(String name);
   public ThreadGroup(ThreadGroup parent, String name);
// Public Instance Methods
   public int activeCount();
   public int activeGroupCount();
   public final void checkAccess();
   public final void destroy();
   public int enumerate(ThreadGroup[] list);
   public int enumerate(Thread[] list);
   public int enumerate(Thread[] list, boolean recurse);
   public int enumerate(ThreadGroup[] list, boolean recurse);
   public final int getMaxPriority();
   public final String getName();
   public final ThreadGroup getParent();
1.2 public final void interrupt();
   public final boolean isDaemon();
1.1 public boolean isDestroyed();                                    synchronized
   public void list();
   public final boolean parentOf(ThreadGroup g);
   public final void setDaemon(boolean daemon);
   public final void setMaxPriority(int pri);
   public void uncaughtException(Thread t, Throwable e);     Implements:Thread.UncaughtExceptionHandler
// Methods Implementing Thread.UncaughtExceptionHandler
   public void uncaughtException(Thread t, Throwable e);
// Public Methods Overriding Object
   public String toString();
// Deprecated Public Methods
1.1# public boolean allowThreadSuspension(boolean b);
#  public final void resume();
#  public final void stop();
#  public final void suspend();
}
```

Passed To SecurityManager.checkAccess(), Thread.Thread()

Returned By SecurityManager.getThreadGroup(), Thread.getThreadGroup()

ThreadLocal<T> Java 1.2

java.lang

This class provides a convenient way to create thread-local variables. When you declare a static field in a class, there is only one value for that field, shared by all objects of the class. When you declare a nonstatic instance field in a class, every object of the class has its own separate copy of that variable. ThreadLocal provides an option between these two extremes. If you declare a static field to hold a ThreadLocal object, that ThreadLocal holds a different value for each thread. Objects running in the same thread see the same value when they call the get() method of the ThreadLocal object. Objects running in different threads obtain different values from get(), however.

In Java 5.0, this class has been made generic and the type variable *T* represents the type of the object referenced by this ThreadLocal.

The set() method sets the value held by the ThreadLocal object for the currently running thread. get() returns the value held for the currently running thread. Note that there is no way to obtain the value of the ThreadLocal object for any thread other than the one that calls get(). To understand the ThreadLocal class, you may find it helpful to think of a ThreadLocal object as a hashtable or java.util.Map that maps from Thread objects to arbitrary values. Calling set() creates an association between the current Thread (Thread.currentThread()) and the specified value. Calling get() first looks up the current thread, then uses the hashtable to look up the value associated with that current thread.

If a thread calls get() for the first time without having first called set() to establish a thread-local value, get() calls the protected initialValue() method to obtain the initial value to return. The default implementation of initialValue() simply returns null, but subclasses can override this if they desire.

See also InheritableThreadLocal, which allows thread-local values to be inherited from parent threads by child threads.

```
public class ThreadLocal<T> {
// Public Constructors
    public ThreadLocal();
// Public Instance Methods
    public T get();
5.0 public void remove();
    public void set(T value);
// Protected Instance Methods
    protected T initialValue();                                    constant
}
```

Subclasses InheritableThreadLocal

Throwable Java 1.0

java.lang serializable

This is the root class of the Java exception and error hierarchy. All exceptions and errors are subclasses of Throwable. The getMessage() method retrieves any error message associated with the exception or error. The default implemenation of getLocalizedMessage() simply calls getMessage(), but subclasses may override this method to return an error message that has been localized for the default locale.

It is often the case that an Exception or Error is generated as a direct result of some other exception or error, perhaps one thrown by a lower-level API. As of Java 1.4 and later, all Throwable objects may have a "cause" which specifies the Throwable that caused this one. If there is a cause, pass it to the Throwable() constructor, or to the initCause() method. When you catch a Throwable object, you can obtain the Throwable that caused it, if any, with getCause().

Every Throwable object has information about the execution stack associated with it. This information is initialized when the Throwable object is created. If the object will be thrown somewhere other than where it was created, or if it caught and will be rethrown, you can use fillInStackTrace() to capture the current execution stack before throwing it. printStackTrace() prints a textual representation of the stack to the specified PrintWriter, PrintStream, or to the System.err stream. In Java 1.4, you can also obtain this information with getStackTrace() which returns an array of StackTraceElement objects describing the execution stack.

Object — Throwable ··· Serializable

```
public class Throwable implements Serializable {
// Public Constructors
    public Throwable();
    public Throwable(String message);
1.4 public Throwable(Throwable cause);
1.4 public Throwable(String message, Throwable cause);
// Public Instance Methods
    public Throwable fillInStackTrace();                                  native synchronized
1.4 public Throwable getCause();                                                 default:null
1.1 public String getLocalizedMessage();                                         default:null
    public String getMessage();                                                  default:null
1.4 public StackTraceElement[] getStackTrace();
1.4 public Throwable initCause(Throwable cause);                                  synchronized
    public void printStackTrace();
    public void printStackTrace(java.io.PrintStream s);
1.1 public void printStackTrace(java.io.PrintWriter s);
1.4 public void setStackTrace(StackTraceElement[] stackTrace);
// Public Methods Overriding Object
    public String toString();
}
```

Subclasses Error, Exception

Passed To Too many methods to list.

Returned By java.io.WriteAbortedException.getCause(), ClassNotFoundException.{getCause(), getException()}, ExceptionInInitializerError.{getCause(), getException()}, java.lang.reflect.InvocationTargetException.{getCause(), getTargetException()}, java.lang.reflect.UndeclaredThrowableException.{getCause(), getUndeclaredThrowable()}, java.security.PrivilegedActionException.getCause(), java.util.logging.LogRecord.getThrown(), javax.xml.transform.TransformerException.{getCause(), getException(), initCause()}, javax.xml.xpath.XPathException.getCause()

Thrown By Object.finalize(), java.lang.reflect.InvocationHandler.invoke()

TypeNotPresentException — Java 5.0

java.lang — serializable unchecked

This unchecked exception signals that a class file associated with a java.lang.reflect.Type could not be found. It typically results when a class depends on a type that has changed or been removed and indicates version skew that requires recompilation or code refactoring. This is essentially the generic type version of ClassNotFoundException.

Object — Throwable — Exception — RuntimeException — TypeNotPresentException
Serializable

```
public class TypeNotPresentException extends RuntimeException {
// Public Constructors
   public TypeNotPresentException(String typeName, Throwable cause);
// Public Instance Methods
   public String typeName();
}
```


UnknownError **Java 1.0**

java.lang **serializable error**

Signals that an unknown error has occurred at the level of the Java Virtual Machine.

Object — Throwable — Error — VirtualMachineError — UnknownError
Serializable

```
public class UnknownError extends VirtualMachineError {
// Public Constructors
   public UnknownError();
   public UnknownError(String s);
}
```

UnsatisfiedLinkError **Java 1.0**

java.lang **serializable error**

Signals that Java cannot satisfy all the links in a class that it has loaded.

Object — Throwable — Error — LinkageError — UnsatisfiedLinkError
Serializable

```
public class UnsatisfiedLinkError extends LinkageError {
// Public Constructors
   public UnsatisfiedLinkError();
   public UnsatisfiedLinkError(String s);
}
```

UnsupportedClassVersionError **Java 1.2**

java.lang **serializable error**

Every Java class file contains a version number that specifies the version of the class file format. This error is thrown when the Java Virtual Machine attempts to read a class file with a version number it does not support.

Object — Throwable — Error — LinkageError — ClassFormatError — UnsupportedClassVersionError
Serializable

```
public class UnsupportedClassVersionError extends ClassFormatError {
// Public Constructors
   public UnsupportedClassVersionError();
   public UnsupportedClassVersionError(String s);
}
```

UnsupportedOperationException — Java 1.2

java.lang — serializable unchecked

Signals that a method you have called is not supported, and its implementation does not do anything (except throw this exception). This exception is used most often by the Java collection framework of **java.util**. Immutable or unmodifiable collections throw this exception when a modification method, such as **add()** or **delete()**, is called.

Object — Throwable — Exception — RuntimeException — UnsupportedOperationException
Serializable

```
public class UnsupportedOperationException extends RuntimeException {
// Public Constructors
   public UnsupportedOperationException();
5.0 public UnsupportedOperationException(Throwable cause);
   public UnsupportedOperationException(String message);
5.0 public UnsupportedOperationException(String message, Throwable cause);
}
```

Subclasses java.nio.ReadOnlyBufferException

VerifyError — Java 1.0

java.lang — serializable error

Signals that a class has not passed the byte-code verification procedures.

Object — Throwable — Error — LinkageError — VerifyError
Serializable

```
public class VerifyError extends LinkageError {
// Public Constructors
   public VerifyError();
   public VerifyError(String s);
}
```

VirtualMachineError — Java 1.0

java.lang — serializable error

An abstract error type that serves as superclass for a group of errors related to the Java Virtual Machine. See **InternalError**, **UnknownError**, **OutOfMemoryError**, and **StackOverflowError**.

Object — Throwable — Error — VirtualMachineError
Serializable

```
public abstract class VirtualMachineError extends Error {
// Public Constructors
   public VirtualMachineError();
   public VirtualMachineError(String s);
}
```

Subclasses InternalError, OutOfMemoryError, StackOverflowError, UnknownError

Void Java 1.1

java.lang

The Void class cannot be instantiated and serves merely as a placeholder for its static TYPE field, which is a Class object constant that represents the void type.

```
public final class Void {
// No Constructor
// Public Constants
   public static final Class<Void> TYPE;
}
```


Package java.lang.annotation Java 5.0

This package defines the framework for annotations. It includes the base Annotation interface that all annotation types extend, meta-annotation types, their associated enumerated types, and exception and error classes related to annotations. The most important members of this package are the meta-annotation types: Documented, Inherited, Retention, and Target.

Interfaces

```
public interface Annotation;
```

Enumerated Types

```
public enum ElementType;
public enum RetentionPolicy;
```

Annotation Types

```
public @interface Documented;
public @interface Inherited;
public @interface Retention;
public @interface Target;
```

Exceptions

```
public class AnnotationTypeMismatchException extends RuntimeException;
public class IncompleteAnnotationException extends RuntimeException;
```

Errors

```
public class AnnotationFormatError extends Error;
```

Annotation Java 5.0

java.lang.annotation

A type declared with the @interface syntax is an annotation type that implicitly extends this interface. Note that the Annotation interface is not itself an annotation type. Furthermore, if you define an interface (rather than an @interface) that explicitly extends Annotation, the result is not an annotation type either. The only way to define an annotation type is with an @interface definition. When an annotation is queried with the java.lang.reflect.AnnotatedElement API, the object returned implements this interface as well as the interface defined by the specific annotation type.

This interface defines the annotationType() method, which returns the Class of the annotation type for any annotation object. It also includes the equals() and hashCode() methods of Object to require an implementation to compare annotations by the values of their members rather than simply by using ==. Finally, Annotation also overrides the toString() method to require implementations to provide some meaningful string representation of an annotation. The format of the returned string is not specified, but you can expect implementations to produce a string using a syntax similar to that used to encode annotations in Java source code.

```
public interface Annotation {
// Public Instance Methods
    Class<? extends java.lang.annotation.Annotation> annotationType();
    boolean equals(Object obj);
    int hashCode();
    String toString();
}
```

Implementations Deprecated, Override, SuppressWarnings, Documented, Inherited, Retention, Target

Returned By Too many methods to list.

AnnotationFormatError — Java 5.0

java.lang.annotation — serializable error

An error of this type indicates that a class file includes a malformed annotation.

Object — Throwable — Error — AnnotationFormatError
Serializable

```
public class AnnotationFormatError extends Error {
// Public Constructors
    public AnnotationFormatError(Throwable cause);
    public AnnotationFormatError(String message);
    public AnnotationFormatError(String message, Throwable cause);
}
```

AnnotationTypeMismatchException — Java 5.0

java.lang.annotation — serializable unchecked

An exception of this type indicates version skew in an annotation type. It occurs when the Java VM attempts to read an annotation from a class file and discovers that the type of an annotation member has changed since the class file (and the annotation it contains) was compiled.

Object — Throwable — Exception — RuntimeException — AnnotationTypeMismatchException
Serializable

```
public class AnnotationTypeMismatchException extends RuntimeException {
// Public Constructors
    public AnnotationTypeMismatchException(java.lang.reflect.Method element, String foundType);
// Public Instance Methods
    public java.lang.reflect.Method element();
    public String foundType();
}
```

Documented Java 5.0

java.lang.annotation @Documented @Retention(RUNTIME) @Target(ANNOTATION_TYPE) annotation

A meta-annotation of this type indicates that the annotated type should be documented by Javadoc and similar documentation tools. If an annotation type is an @Documented annotation, then the presence of an annotation of that type is part of the public API of the annotated program element. java.lang.Deprecated is an @Documented annotation type, for example, and so are each of the meta-annotation types in this package.

It is recommended that any annotation type that is @Documented should also have runtime @Retention so that the presence of the annotation can be queried via reflection.

Annotation ··· Documented

```
public @interface Documented {
}
```

ElementType Java 5.0

java.lang.annotation serializable comparable enum

The constants declared by this enumerated type represent the types of program elements that can be annotated. The value of an @Target annotation is an array of ElementType constants. Most of the constants have obvious meanings, but some require additional explanation. TYPE represents a class, interface, enumerated type, or annotation type. ANNOTATION_TYPE represents only annotation types and is used for meta-annotations. FIELD includes enumerated constants, and PARAMETER includes both method parameters and catch clause parameters. Note that the METHOD and CONSTRUCTOR are distinct constants.

Object — Enum — ElementType
Comparable Serializable

```
public enum ElementType {
// Enumerated Constants
   TYPE,
   FIELD,
   METHOD,
   PARAMETER,
   CONSTRUCTOR,
   LOCAL_VARIABLE,
   ANNOTATION_TYPE,
   PACKAGE;
// Public Class Methods
   public static ElementType valueOf(String name);
   public static final ElementType[] values();
}
```

Returned By Target.value()

IncompleteAnnotationException Java 5.0

java.lang.annotation serializable unchecked

An exception of this type indicates version skew in an annotation type. It occurs when the Java VM attempts to read an annotation from a class file and discovers that the annotation type has added a new member since the class file was compiled. This means that the annotation compiled into the class file is incomplete since it does not define a value for all members of the annotation type. Note that this exception does not occur if a new member with a default clause is added to the annotation type.

Object — Throwable — Exception — RuntimeException — IncompleteAnnotationException
Serializable

```
public class IncompleteAnnotationException extends RuntimeException {
// Public Constructors
    public IncompleteAnnotationException(Class<? extends java.lang.annotation.Annotation> annotationType,
        String elementName);
// Public Instance Methods
    public Class<? extends java.lang.annotation.Annotation> annotationType();
    public String elementName();
}
```

Inherited — Java 5.0

java.lang.annotation @Documented @Retention(RUNTIME) @Target(ANNOTATION_TYPE) annotation

When an annotation type that has an @Inherited meta-annotation is applied to a class, that annotation should be inherited by subclasses and descendants of the annotated class. The inheritance is only for classes and their subclasses. If an @Inherited annotation type is applied to a method or program element other than a class, no inheritance applies. If the @Inherited annotation type also has runtime Retention, reflective access to the annotation through java.lang.reflect.AnnotatedElement manages the inheritance of the annotation.

Annotation — Inherited

```
public @interface Inherited {
}
```

Retention — Java 5.0

java.lang.annotation @Documented @Retention(RUNTIME) @Target(ANNOTATION_TYPE) annotation

A meta-annotation of this type specifies how long the annotated annotation type should be retained. The value() of this annotation type is one of the three RetentionPolicy enumerated constants. See RetentionPolicy for details. If an annotation type does not have an @Retention meta-annotation, its default retention is RetentionPolicy.CLASS.

Annotation — Retention

```
public @interface Retention {
// Public Instance Methods
    RetentionPolicy value();
}
```

RetentionPolicy — Java 5.0

java.lang.annotation serializable comparable enum

The constants declared by the enumerated type specify the possible retention values for an @Retention meta-annotation. Annotations with SOURCE retention appear in Java source code only and are discarded by the compiler. Annotations with CLASS retention are compiled into the class file and are visible to tools that read class files but are not loaded by the Java VM at runtime. (This is the default retention for annotation types that do not have an @Retention meta-annotation.) Finally, annotations with RUNTIME retention are stored in the class file and loaded by the Java interpreter at runtime. These annotations are available for reflective access through java.lang.reflect.AnnotatedElement.

Object — Enum — RetentionPolicy
Comparable, Serializable

```
public enum RetentionPolicy {
// Enumerated Constants
   SOURCE,
   CLASS,
   RUNTIME;
// Public Class Methods
   public static RetentionPolicy valueOf(String name);
   public static final RetentionPolicy[] values();
}
```

Returned By Retention.value()

Target **Java 5.0**

java.lang.annotation @Documented @Retention(RUNTIME) @Target(ANNOTATION_TYPE) annotation

A meta-annotation of this type specifies what program elements the annotated annotation type can be applied to. The value() of a Target annotation is an array of ElementType enumerated constants. See ElementType for details on the allowed values. If an annotation type does not have an @Target meta-annotation, it can be applied to any program element.

Annotation ··· Target

```
public @interface Target {
// Public Instance Methods
   ElementType[] value();
}
```

Package java.lang.instrument **Java 5.0**

This package defines the API for instrumenting a Java VM by transforming class files to add profiling support, code coverage testing, or other features.

The -javaagent command-line option to the Java interpreter provides a hook for running the premain() method of a Java instrumentation *agent*. An Instrumentation object passed to the premain() method provides an entry point into this package, and methods of Instrumentation allow loaded classes to be redefined and ClassFileTransformer objects to be registered for classes not yet loaded.

Interfaces

```
public interface ClassFileTransformer;
public interface Instrumentation;
```

Classes

```
public final class ClassDefinition;
```

Exceptions

```
public class IllegalClassFormatException extends Exception;
public class UnmodifiableClassException extends Exception;
```

ClassDefinition Java 5.0

java.lang.instrument

This class is a simple wrapper around a Class object and an array of bytes that represents a class file for that class. An array of ClassDefinition objects is passed to the redefineClasses() method of the Instrumentation class. Class redefinitions are allowed to change method implementations, but not the members or inheritance of a class or the signature of the methods.

```
public final class ClassDefinition {
// Public Constructors
   public ClassDefinition(Class<?> theClass, byte[] theClassFile);
// Public Instance Methods
   public Class<?> getDefinitionClass();
   public byte[] getDefinitionClassFile();
}
```

Passed To Instrumentation.redefineClasses()

ClassFileTransformer Java 5.0

java.lang.instrument

A ClassFileTransformer registered through an Instrumentation object is offered a chance to transform every class that is subsequently loaded or redefined. The final argument to transform() is a byte array that contains the raw bytes of the class file (or bytes returned by a previously invoked ClassFileTransformer). If the transform() method wishes to transform the class, it should return the transformed bytes in a newly allocated array. The array passed to transform() should not be modified. If the transform() method does not wish to transform a given class, it should return null.

```
public interface ClassFileTransformer {
// Public Instance Methods
   byte[] transform(ClassLoader loader, String className, Class<?> classBeingRedefined,
                    java.security.ProtectionDomain protectionDomain, byte[] classfileBuffer)
      throws IllegalClassFormatException;
}
```

Passed To Instrumentation.{addTransformer(), removeTransformer()}

IllegalClassFormatException Java 5.0

java.lang.instrument serializable checked

A ClassFileTransformer should throw an exception of this type from its transform() method if it believes that the class file bytes it has been passed are malformed (this could happen, for example, if a defective ClassFileTransformer had previously transformed a valid class file).

Object — Throwable — Exception — IllegalClassFormatException
Serializable

```
public class IllegalClassFormatException extends Exception {
// Public Constructors
   public IllegalClassFormatException();
   public IllegalClassFormatException(String s);
}
```

Thrown By ClassFileTransformer.transform()

Instrumentation — Java 5.0

java.lang.instrument

This interface is the main entry point to the java.lang.instrument API. A Java instrumentation agent specified on the Java interpreter command line with the -javaagent argument must be a class that defines the following method:

```
public static void premain(String args, Instrumentation instr)
```

The Java interpreter invokes the premain() method during startup before calling the main() method of the program. Any arguments specified with the -javaagent command line are passed in the first premain() argument, and an Instrumentation object is passed as the second argument.

The most powerful feature of the Instrumentation object is the ability to register ClassFileTransformer objects to augment or rewrite the byte code of Java class files as they are loaded into the interpreter. If isRedefineClassesSupported() returns true, you can also redefine already-loaded classes on the fly with redefineClasses().

getAllLoadedClasses() returns an array of all classes loaded into the VM, and getInitiatedClasses() returns an array of classes loaded by a specified ClassLoader. getObjectSize() returns an implementation-specific approximation of the amount of memory required by a specified object.

```
public interface Instrumentation {
// Public Instance Methods
   void addTransformer(ClassFileTransformer transformer);
   Class[] getAllLoadedClasses();
   Class[] getInitiatedClasses(ClassLoader loader);
   long getObjectSize(Object objectToSize);
   boolean isRedefineClassesSupported();
   void redefineClasses(ClassDefinition[] definitions) throws ClassNotFoundException, UnmodifiableClassException;
   boolean removeTransformer(ClassFileTransformer transformer);
}
```

UnmodifiableClassException — Java 5.0

java.lang.instrument — serializable checked

An exception of this type is thrown from Instrumentation.redefineClasses() if a requested redefinition cannot be performed. This might occur, for example, if the redefinition attempts to add or remove members from the class.

Object — Throwable — Exception — UnmodifiableClassException
Serializable

```
public class UnmodifiableClassException extends Exception {
// Public Constructors
```

```
    public UnmodifiableClassException();
    public UnmodifiableClassException(String s);
}
```

Thrown By Instrumentation.redefineClasses()

Package java.lang.management — Java 5.0

This package defines "management bean" or "MXBean" interfaces for managing and monitoring a running Java virtual machine. It relies on the JMX API of the javax.management package, which is not covered in this book. ManagementFactory is the main entry point to this API; it defines static factory methods for obtaining instances of the various management bean interfaces. These instances can then be queried for specific information about the Java VM. The *jconsole* tool shipped with the Java 5.0 JDK demonstrates the capabilites of this package.

Interfaces

```
public interface ClassLoadingMXBean;
public interface CompilationMXBean;
public interface GarbageCollectorMXBean extends MemoryManagerMXBean;
public interface MemoryManagerMXBean;
public interface MemoryMXBean;
public interface MemoryPoolMXBean;
public interface OperatingSystemMXBean;
public interface RuntimeMXBean;
public interface ThreadMXBean;
```

Enumerated Types

```
public enum MemoryType;
```

Classes

```
public class ManagementFactory;
public final class ManagementPermission extends java.security.BasicPermission;
public class MemoryNotificationInfo;
public class MemoryUsage;
public class ThreadInfo;
```

ClassLoadingMXBean — Java 5.0

java.lang.management

This MXBean interface defines methods for determining how many classes are currently loaded in the Java VM, how many have ever been loaded, and how many have ever been unloaded. The setVerbose() method turns verbose class loading output from the VM on or off.

```
public interface ClassLoadingMXBean {
// Public Instance Methods
    int getLoadedClassCount();
    long getTotalLoadedClassCount();
    long getUnloadedClassCount();
    boolean isVerbose();
    void setVerbose(boolean value);
}
```

Returned By ManagementFactory.getClassLoadingMXBean()

CompilationMXBean Java 5.0

java.lang.management

This MXBean interface defines methods for querying the just-in-time compiler of the Java virtual machine. getName() returns an identifying name for the compiler. If the implementation tracks compilation time, getTotalCompilationTime() returns the approximate total compilation time in milliseconds.


```
public interface CompilationMXBean {
// Public Instance Methods
   String getName();
   long getTotalCompilationTime();
   boolean isCompilationTimeMonitoringSupported();
}
```

Returned By ManagementFactory.getCompilationMXBean()

GarbageCollectorMXBean Java 5.0

java.lang.management

This MXBean interface allows monitoring of the number of garbage collections that have occurred and the approximate time they consumed in milliseconds. The methods return -1 to indicate that the garbage collector does not maintain those statistics. Note that VM implementations commonly have more than one garbage collector and use different collection strategies for new objects and old objects. Note also that this is a subinterface of MemoryManagerMXBean.

MemoryManagerMXBean → GarbageCollectorMXBean

```
public interface GarbageCollectorMXBean extends MemoryManagerMXBean {
// Public Instance Methods
   long getCollectionCount();
   long getCollectionTime();
}
```

ManagementFactory Java 5.0

java.lang.management

This class provides the main entry point into the java.lang.management API. The static factory methods provide a convenient way to obtain instances of the various MXBean interfaces for the currently running Java virtual machine. The returned instances can then be queried to monitor memory usage, class loading, and other details of virtual machine performance.

To obtain an MXBean for a Java virtual machine running in another process, use the newPlatformMXBeanProxy() method, specifying a javax.management.MBeanServerConnection as well as the name and type of the desired MXBean. The constant fields of this class define the names of the available beans. Note that the javax.management package is beyond the scope of this quick reference.

```
public class ManagementFactory {
// No Constructor
// Public Constants
   public static final String CLASS_LOADING_MXBEAN_NAME;          ="java.lang:type=ClassLoading"
```

```
    public static final String COMPILATION_MXBEAN_NAME;                    ="java.lang:type=Compilation"
    public static final String GARBAGE_COLLECTOR_MXBEAN_DOMAIN_TYPE;       ="java.lang:type=GarbageCollector"
    public static final String MEMORY_MANAGER_MXBEAN_DOMAIN_TYPE;          ="java.lang:type=MemoryManager"
    public static final String MEMORY_MXBEAN_NAME;                         ="java.lang:type=Memory"
    public static final String MEMORY_POOL_MXBEAN_DOMAIN_TYPE;             ="java.lang:type=MemoryPool"
    public static final String OPERATING_SYSTEM_MXBEAN_NAME;               ="java.lang:type=OperatingSystem"
    public static final String RUNTIME_MXBEAN_NAME;                        ="java.lang:type=Runtime"
    public static final String THREAD_MXBEAN_NAME;                         ="java.lang:type=Threading"
// Public Class Methods
    public static ClassLoadingMXBean getClassLoadingMXBean();
    public static CompilationMXBean getCompilationMXBean();
    public static java.util.List<GarbageCollectorMXBean> getGarbageCollectorMXBeans();
    public static java.util.List<MemoryManagerMXBean> getMemoryManagerMXBeans();
    public static MemoryMXBean getMemoryMXBean();
    public static java.util.List<MemoryPoolMXBean> getMemoryPoolMXBeans();
    public static OperatingSystemMXBean getOperatingSystemMXBean();
    public static javax.management.MBeanServer getPlatformMBeanServer();           synchronized
    public static RuntimeMXBean getRuntimeMXBean();
    public static ThreadMXBean getThreadMXBean();
    public static <T> T newPlatformMXBeanProxy(javax.management.MBeanServerConnection connection,
        String mxbeanName, Class<T> mxbeanInterface)
        throws java.io.IOException;
}
```

ManagementPermission — Java 5.0

java.lang.management — serializable permission

This java.security.Permission subclass governs access to the Java VM monitoring and management capabilities of this package. The two defined targets for this permission are control, which grants permission to manage the VM, and monitor, which grants permission to monitor VM state. Fine-grained control over individual MXBeans is not supported.

Object — Permission — BasicPermission — ManagementPermission
Guard, Serializable (Object); Serializable (BasicPermission)

```
public final class ManagementPermission extends java.security.BasicPermission {
// Public Constructors
    public ManagementPermission(String name);
    public ManagementPermission(String name, String actions) throws IllegalArgumentException;
}
```

MemoryManagerMXBean — Java 5.0

java.lang.management

This MXBean interface allows monitoring of a single memory manager (such as a garbage collector) in a Java VM. A VM implementation typically has more than one memory manager, and the ManagementFactory method getMemoryManagerMXBeans() returns a List of objects of this type. Some or all of the objects in the returned list will also implement the GarbageCollectorMXBean subinterface.

Each memory manager may manage one or more memory pools, and getMemoryPoolNames() returns the names of these pools. See also ManagementFactory.getMemoryPoolMXBeans() and MemoryPoolMXBean.

```
public interface MemoryManagerMXBean {
// Public Instance Methods
   String[] getMemoryPoolNames();
   String getName();
   boolean isValid();
}
```

Implementations GarbageCollectorMXBean

MemoryMXBean — Java 5.0

java.lang.management

This MXBean interface allows monitoring of current memory usage information for heap memory (allocated objects) and nonheap memory (loaded classes and libraries). It also allows the garbage collector to be explicitly invoked and verbose garbage-collection related output to be turned on or off.

See MemoryUsage for details on how memory usage information is returned. See also MemoryPoolMXBean for a way to obtain both current and peak memory usage for individual memory pools.

```
public interface MemoryMXBean {
// Public Instance Methods
   void gc();
   MemoryUsage getHeapMemoryUsage();
   MemoryUsage getNonHeapMemoryUsage();
   int getObjectPendingFinalizationCount();
   boolean isVerbose();
   void setVerbose(boolean value);
}
```

Returned By ManagementFactory.getMemoryMXBean()

MemoryNotificationInfo — Java 5.0

java.lang.management

This class holds information about memory usage in a given memory pool and is generated when that usage crosses a threshold specified by a MemoryPoolMXBean. Use the from() method to construct a MemoryNotificationInfo object from the user data of a javax.management.Notification object. Notifications and the javax.management package are beyond the scope of this book.

```
public class MemoryNotificationInfo {
// Public Constructors
   public MemoryNotificationInfo(String poolName, MemoryUsage usage, long count);
// Public Constants
   public static final String MEMORY_COLLECTION_THRESHOLD_EXCEEDED;
                                  ="java.management.memory.collection.threshold.exceeded"
   public static final String MEMORY_THRESHOLD_EXCEEDED;      ="java.management.memory.threshold.exceeded"
// Public Class Methods
   public static MemoryNotificationInfo from(javax.management.openmbean.CompositeData cd);
// Public Instance Methods
   public long getCount();
   public String getPoolName();
   public MemoryUsage getUsage();
}
```

MemoryPoolMXBean — Java 5.0

java.lang.management

This MXBean interface allows monitoring of the current and peak memory usage for a single memory pool. Typical Java VM implementations segregate garbage-collected heap memory into two or more memory pools based on the age of the objects. Obtain a List of MemoryPoolMXBean instances with ManagementFactory.getMemoryPoolMXBeans(). getName() and getType() return the name and type of each pool. getUsage() and getPeakUsage() return the current and peak memory usage for the pool in the form of a MemoryUsage object.

If isUsageThresholdSupported() returns true, you can use setUsageThreshold() to define a memory usage threshold. The MemoryPoolMXBean then keeps track of threshold crossings and issues notifications through the javax.management.NotificationEmitter API. You can register a javax.management.NotificationListener to receive these notifications. (Note that the javax.management package is not covered in this book.) Use setCollectionUsageThreshold() instead to receive notifications when memory usage exceeds a specified threshold after a garbage collection pass.

```
public interface MemoryPoolMXBean {
// Public Instance Methods
   MemoryUsage getCollectionUsage();
   long getCollectionUsageThreshold();
   long getCollectionUsageThresholdCount();
   String[] getMemoryManagerNames();
   String getName();
   MemoryUsage getPeakUsage();
   MemoryType getType();
   MemoryUsage getUsage();
   long getUsageThreshold();
   long getUsageThresholdCount();
   boolean isCollectionUsageThresholdExceeded();
   boolean isCollectionUsageThresholdSupported();
   boolean isUsageThresholdExceeded();
   boolean isUsageThresholdSupported();
   boolean isValid();
   void resetPeakUsage();
   void setCollectionUsageThreshold(long threhsold);
   void setUsageThreshold(long threshold);
}
```

MemoryType — Java 5.0

java.lang.management — serializable comparable enum

The constants defined by this enumerated type define the type of a memory pool as either heap or nonheap memory. See MemoryPoolMXBean.getType().

```
public enum MemoryType {
// Enumerated Constants
   HEAP,
   NON_HEAP;
```

```
// Public Class Methods
    public static MemoryType valueOf(String name);
    public static final MemoryType[] values();
// Public Methods Overriding Enum
    public String toString();
}
```

Returned By MemoryPoolMXBean.getType()

MemoryUsage Java 5.0

java.lang.management

A MemoryUsage object represents a snapshot of memory usage for a specified type or pool of memory. Memory usage is measured as four long values, each of which represents a number of bytes. getInit() returns the initial amount of memory that the Java VM requests from the operating system. getUsed() returns the actual number of bytes used. getCommitted() returns the number of bytes that the operating system has committed to the Java VM for this pool. These bytes may not all be in use, but they are not available to other processes running on the system. getMax() returns the maximum amount of memory that the Java VM requests for this pool. getMax() returns -1 if there is no defined maximum value.

```
public class MemoryUsage {
// Public Constructors
    public MemoryUsage(long init, long used, long committed, long max);
// Public Class Methods
    public static MemoryUsage from(javax.management.openmbean.CompositeData cd);
// Public Instance Methods
    public long getCommitted();
    public long getInit();
    public long getMax();
    public long getUsed();
// Public Methods Overriding Object
    public String toString();
}
```

Passed To MemoryNotificationInfo.MemoryNotificationInfo()

Returned By MemoryMXBean.{getHeapMemoryUsage(), getNonHeapMemoryUsage()}, MemoryNotificationInfo.getUsage(), MemoryPoolMXBean.{getCollectionUsage(), getPeakUsage(), getUsage()}

OperatingSystemMXBean Java 5.0

java.lang.management

This MXBean interface allows queries of the operating system name, version, and CPU architecture as well as the number of available CPUs.

```
public interface OperatingSystemMXBean {
// Public Instance Methods
    String getArch();
    int getAvailableProcessors();
    String getName();
    String getVersion();
}
```

Returned By ManagementFactory.getOperatingSystemMXBean()

RuntimeMXBean **Java 5.0**

java.lang.management

This MXBean interface provides access to the runtime configuration of the Java virtual machine, including system properties, command-line arguments, class path, virtual machine vendor and version, and so on. getUptime() returns the uptime of the virtual machine in milliseconds.

```
public interface RuntimeMXBean {
// Public Instance Methods
   String getBootClassPath();
   String getClassPath();
   java.util.List<String> getInputArguments();
   String getLibraryPath();
   String getManagementSpecVersion();
   String getName();
   String getSpecName();
   String getSpecVendor();
   String getSpecVersion();
   long getStartTime();
   java.util.Map<String,String> getSystemProperties();
   long getUptime();
   String getVmName();
   String getVmVendor();
   String getVmVersion();
   boolean isBootClassPathSupported();
}
```

Returned By ManagementFactory.getRuntimeMXBean()

ThreadInfo **Java 5.0**

java.lang.management

This class represents information about a thread from a ThreadMXBean. Some information, such as thread name, id, state, and stack trace are also available through the java.lang.Thread object. Other more useful information includes the object upon which a thread is waiting and the owner of the lock that the thread is trying to acquire. If ThreadMXBean indicates that thread contention monitoring is supported and enabled, the ThreadInfo methods getBlockedCount() and getBlockedTime() return the number of times the thread has blocked or waited and the amount of time it has spent in the blocked and waiting states.

```
public class ThreadInfo {
// No Constructor
// Public Class Methods
   public static ThreadInfo from(javax.management.openmbean.CompositeData cd);
// Public Instance Methods
   public long getBlockedCount();
   public long getBlockedTime();
   public String getLockName();
   public long getLockOwnerId();
   public String getLockOwnerName();
   public StackTraceElement[] getStackTrace();
   public long getThreadId();
   public String getThreadName();
   public Thread.State getThreadState();
```

```
    public long getWaitedCount();
    public long getWaitedTime();
    public boolean isInNative();
    public boolean isSuspended();
// Public Methods Overriding Object
    public String toString();
}
```

Returned By ThreadMXBean.getThreadInfo()

ThreadMXBean — Java 5.0

java.lang.management

This MXBean interface allows monitoring of thread usage in a Java VM. A number of methods, such as getThreadCount() and getPeakThreadCount(), return information about all running threads. Other methods return information about individual threads. Threads are identified by their thread id, which is a long integer. getAllThreadIds() returns all ids as an array of long. Complete information, including stack trace, about a thread or set of threads can be obtained with the getThreadInfo() methods, which return ThreadInfo objects.

If isThreadCpuTimeSupported() returns true, you can enable thread timing with setThreadCpuTimeEnabled() and query the runtime of a specific thread with getThreadCpuTime() and getThreadUserTime(). The values returned by these methods are measured in nanoseconds.

One of the potentially most useful methods of this interface is findMonitorDeadlockedThreads(). It looks for cycles of threads that are deadlocked waiting to lock objects whose locks are held by other threads in the cycle.

```
public interface ThreadMXBean {
// Public Instance Methods
    long[] findMonitorDeadlockedThreads();
    long[] getAllThreadIds();
    long getCurrentThreadCpuTime();
    long getCurrentThreadUserTime();
    int getDaemonThreadCount();
    int getPeakThreadCount();
    int getThreadCount();
    long getThreadCpuTime(long id);
    ThreadInfo getThreadInfo(long id);
    ThreadInfo[] getThreadInfo(long[] ids);
    ThreadInfo[] getThreadInfo(long[] ids, int maxDepth);
    ThreadInfo getThreadInfo(long id, int maxDepth);
    long getThreadUserTime(long id);
    long getTotalStartedThreadCount();
    boolean isCurrentThreadCpuTimeSupported();
    boolean isThreadContentionMonitoringEnabled();
    boolean isThreadContentionMonitoringSupported();
    boolean isThreadCpuTimeEnabled();
    boolean isThreadCpuTimeSupported();
    void resetPeakThreadCount();
    void setThreadContentionMonitoringEnabled(boolean enable);
    void setThreadCpuTimeEnabled(boolean enable);
}
```

Returned By

ManagementFactory.getThreadMXBean()

Package java.lang.ref **Java 1.2**

The java.lang.ref package defines classes that allow Java programs to interact with the Java garbage collector. A Reference represents an indirect reference to an arbitrary object, known as the *referent*. SoftReference, WeakReference, and PhantomReference are three concrete subclasses of Reference that interact with the garbage collector in different ways, as explained in the individual class descriptions that follow. ReferenceQueue represents a linked list of Reference objects. Any Reference object may have a ReferenceQueue associated with it. A Reference object is *enqueued* on its ReferenceQueue at some point after the garbage collector determines that the referent object has become appropriately unreachable. (The exact level of unreachability depends on the type of Reference being used.) An application can monitor a ReferenceQueue to determine when referent objects enter a new reachability status.

Using the mechanisms defined in this package, you can implement a cache that grows and shrinks in size according to the amount of available system memory. Or, you can implement a hashtable that associates auxiliary information with arbitrary objects, but does not prevent those objects from being garbage-collected if they are otherwise unused. The mechanisms provided by this package are low-level ones, however, and typical applications do not use java.lang.ref directly. Instead, they rely on higher-level utilities built on top of the package. See java.util.WeakHashMap for one example.

In Java 5.0, the classes in this package have all been made into generic types. The type variable *T* represents the type of the object that is referred to.

Classes

```
public abstract class Reference<T>;
    public class PhantomReference<T> extends Reference<T>;
    public class SoftReference<T> extends Reference<T>;
    public class WeakReference<T> extends Reference<T>;
public class ReferenceQueue<T>;
```

PhantomReference<T> **Java 1.2**

java.lang.ref

This class represents a reference to an object that does not prevent the referent object from being finalized by the garbage collector. When (or at some point after) the garbage collector determines that there are no more hard (direct) references to the referent object, that there are no SoftReference or WeakReference objects that refer to the referent, and that the referent has been finalized, it enqueues the PhantomReference object on the ReferenceQueue specified when the PhantomReference was created. This serves as notification that the object has been finalized and provides one last opportunity for any required cleanup code to be run.

To prevent a PhantomReference object from resurrecting its referent object, its get() method always returns null, both before and after the PhantomReference is enqueued. Nevertheless, a PhantomReference is not automatically cleared when it is enqueued, so when you remove a PhantomReference from a ReferenceQueue, you must call its clear() method or allow the PhantomReference object itself to be garbage-collected.

This class provides a more flexible mechanism for object cleanup than the finalize() method does. Note that in order to take advantage of it, it is necessary to subclass PhantomReference and define a method to perform the desired cleanup. Furthermore, since the get() method of a PhantomReference always returns null, such a subclass must also store whatever data is required for the cleanup operation.

Object — Reference — PhantomReference

```
public class PhantomReference<T> extends Reference<T> {
// Public Constructors
   public PhantomReference(T referent, ReferenceQueue<? super T> q);
// Public Methods Overriding Reference
   public T get();                                              constant
}
```


Reference<T> Java 1.2

java.lang.ref

This abstract class represents some type of indirect reference to a referent. get() returns the referent if the reference has not been explicitly cleared by the clear() method or implicitly cleared by the garbage collector. There are three concrete subclasses of Reference. The garbage collector handles these subclasses differently and clears their references under different circumstances.

Each of the subclasses of Reference defines a constructor that allows a ReferenceQueue to be associated with the Reference object. The garbage collector places Reference objects onto their associated ReferenceQueue objects to provide notification about the state of the referent object. isEnqueued() tests whether a Reference has been placed on the associated queue, and enqueue() explicitly places it on the queue. enqueue() returns false if the Reference object does not have an associated ReferenceQueue, or if it has already been enqueued.

```
public abstract class Reference<T> {
// No Constructor
// Public Instance Methods
   public void clear();
   public boolean enqueue();
   public T get();
   public boolean isEnqueued();
}
```

Subclasses PhantomReference, SoftReference, WeakReference

Returned By ReferenceQueue.{poll(), remove()}

ReferenceQueue<T> Java 1.2

java.lang.ref

This class represents a queue (or linked list) of Reference objects that have been enqueued because the garbage collector has determined that the referent objects to which they refer are no longer adequately reachable. It serves as a notification system for object-reachability changes. Use poll() to return the first Reference object on the queue; the method returns null if the queue is empty. Use remove() to return the first element on the queue, or, if the queue is empty, to wait for a Reference object to be enqueued. You can create as many ReferenceQueue objects as needed. Specify a

ReferenceQueue for a Reference object by passing it to the SoftReference(), WeakReference(), or PhantomReference() constructor.

A ReferenceQueue is required to use PhantomReference objects. It is optional with SoftReference and WeakReference objects; for these classes, the get() method returns null if the referent object is no longer adequately reachable.

```
public class ReferenceQueue<T> {
// Public Constructors
   public ReferenceQueue();
// Public Instance Methods
   public Reference<? extends T> poll();
   public Reference<? extends T> remove() throws InterruptedException;
   public Reference<? extends T> remove(long timeout) throws IllegalArgumentException, InterruptedException;
}
```

Passed To PhantomReference.PhantomReference(), SoftReference.SoftReference(), WeakReference.WeakReference()

SoftReference<T> Java 1.2

java.lang.ref

This class represents a soft reference to an object. A SoftReference is not cleared while there are any remaining hard (direct) references to the referent. Once the referent is no longer in use (i.e., there are no remaining hard references to it), the garbage collector may clear the SoftReference to the referent at any time. However, the garbage collector does not clear a SoftReference until it determines that system memory is running low. In particular, the Java VM never throws an OutOfMemoryError without first clearing all soft references and reclaiming the memory of the referents. The VM may (but is not required to) clear soft references according to a least-recently-used ordering.

If a SoftReference has an associated ReferenceQueue, the garbage collector enqueues the SoftReference at some time after it clears the reference.

SoftReference is particularly useful for implementing object-caching systems that do not have a fixed size, but grow and shrink as available memory allows.

Object — Reference — SoftReference

```
public class SoftReference<T> extends Reference<T> {
// Public Constructors
   public SoftReference(T referent);
   public SoftReference(T referent, ReferenceQueue<? super T> q);
// Public Methods Overriding Reference
   public T get();
}
```

WeakReference<T> Java 1.2

java.lang.ref

This class refers to an object in a way that does not prevent that referent object from being finalized and reclaimed by the garbage collector. When the garbage collector determines that there are no more hard (direct) references to the object, and that there are no SoftReference objects that refer to the object, it clears the WeakReference and marks the referent object for finalization. At some point after this, it also enqueues the

WeakReference on its associated ReferenceQueue, if there is one, in order to provide notification that the referent has been reclaimed.

WeakReference is used by java.util.WeakHashMap to implement a hashtable that does not prevent the hashtable key object from being garbage-collected. WeakHashMap is useful when you want to associate auxiliary information with an object but do not want to prevent the object from being reclaimed.

Object — Reference — WeakReference

```
public class WeakReference<T> extends Reference<T> {
// Public Constructors
   public WeakReference(T referent);
   public WeakReference(T referent, ReferenceQueue<? super T> q);
}
```


Package java.lang.reflect — Java 1.1

The java.lang.reflect package contains the classes and interfaces that, along with java.lang.Class, comprise the Java Reflection API.

The Constructor, Field, and Method classes represent the constructors, fields, and methods of a class. Because these types all represent members of a class, they each implement the Member interface, which defines a simple set of methods that can be invoked for any class member. These classes allow information about the class members to be obtained, methods and constructors to be invoked, and fields to be queried and set.

Class member modifiers are represented as integers that specify a number of bit flags. The Modifier class defines static methods that help interpret the meanings of these flags. The Array class defines static methods for creating arrays and reading and writing array elements.

As of Java 1.3, the Proxy class allows the dynamic creation of new Java classes that implement a specified set of interfaces. When an interface method is invoked on an instance of such a proxy class, the invocation is delegated to an InvocationHandler object.

There have been a number of changes to this package to support the new language features of Java 5.0. The most important changes are support for querying the generic signature of classes, methods, constructors, and fields. Class, Method and Constructor implement the new GenericDeclaration interface, which provides access to the TypeVariable declarations of generic classes, methods, and constructors. In general, the package has been modified to add new generic versions of methods like Field.getType() and Method.getParameterTypes(). Instead of returning Class objects, the new generic methods, like Field.getGenericType() and Method.getGenericParameterTypes(), return Type objects. The Type interface is new in Java 5.0, and represents any kind of generic or nongeneric type. Class implements Type, so a Type object may simply be an ordinary Class. Type is also the super-interface for four other new interfaces: ParameterizedType, TypeVariable, WildcardType and GenericArrayType. A Type object that is not a Class should be an instance of one of these other interfaces, representing a generic type of some sort.

Support for reflection on annotations is provided by the AnnotatedElement interface which is implemented by Class, Package, Method, Constructor and Field. Method and Constructor also have new getParameterAnnotations() for querying annotations on method parameters. Other, more minor changes in Java 5.0 include the isEnumConstant() method of Field and the isVarArgs() method of Method and Constructor.

Interfaces

```
public interface AnnotatedElement;
public interface GenericArrayType extends Type;
public interface GenericDeclaration;
public interface InvocationHandler;
public interface Member;
public interface ParameterizedType extends Type;
public interface Type;
public interface TypeVariable<D extends GenericDeclaration> extends Type;
public interface WildcardType extends Type;
```

Classes

```
public class AccessibleObject implements AnnotatedElement;
    public final class Constructor<T> extends AccessibleObject implements GenericDeclaration, Member;
    public final class Field extends AccessibleObject implements Member;
    public final class Method extends AccessibleObject implements GenericDeclaration, Member;
public final class Array;
public class Modifier;
public class Proxy implements Serializable;
public final class ReflectPermission extends java.security.BasicPermission;
```

Exceptions

```
public class InvocationTargetException extends Exception;
public class MalformedParameterizedTypeException extends RuntimeException;
public class UndeclaredThrowableException extends RuntimeException;
```

Errors

```
public class GenericSignatureFormatError extends ClassFormatError;
```

AccessibleObject — Java 1.2

java.lang.reflect

This class is the superclass of the Method, Constructor, and Field classes; its methods provide a mechanism for trusted applications to work with private, protected, and default visibility members that would otherwise not be accessible through the Reflection API. This class is new as of Java 1.2; in Java 1.1, the Method, Constructor, and Field classes extended Object directly.

To use the java.lang.reflect package to access a member to which your code would not normally have access, pass true to the setAccessible() method. If your code has an appropriate ReflectPermission (such as "suppressAccessChecks"), this allows access to the member as if it were declared public. The static version of setAccessible() is a convenience method that sets the accessible flag for an array of members but performs only a single security check.

Object — AccessibleObject ··· AnnotatedElement

```
public class AccessibleObject implements AnnotatedElement {
// Protected Constructors
    protected AccessibleObject();
// Public Class Methods
    public static void setAccessible(AccessibleObject[] array, boolean flag) throws SecurityException;
// Public Instance Methods
```

```
  public boolean isAccessible();
  public void setAccessible(boolean flag) throws SecurityException;
// Methods Implementing AnnotatedElement
5.0 public <T extends java.lang.annotation.Annotation> T getAnnotation(Class<T> annotationClass);
5.0 public java.lang.annotation.Annotation[] getAnnotations();
5.0 public java.lang.annotation.Annotation[] getDeclaredAnnotations();
5.0 public boolean isAnnotationPresent(Class<? extends java.lang.annotation.Annotation> annotationClass);
}
```

Subclasses Constructor, Field, Method

AnnotatedElement — Java 5.0

java.lang.reflect

This interface is implemented by the classes representing program elements that can be annotated in Java 5.0: java.lang.Class, java.lang.Package, Method, Constructor, and Field. The methods of this interface allow you to test for the presence of a specific annotation, query an annotation object of a specific type, or query all annotations present on an annotated element. getDeclaredAnnotations() differs from getAnnotations() in that it does not include inherited annotations. (See the java.lang.annotation.Inherited meta-annotation.) If no annotations are present, getAnnotations() and getDeclaredAnnotations() return an array of length zero rather than null. It is safe to modify the arrays returned by these methods.

See also the getParameterAnnotations() methods of Method and Constructor, which provide access to annotations on method parameters.

```
public interface AnnotatedElement {
// Public Instance Methods
  <T extends java.lang.annotation.Annotation> T getAnnotation(Class<T> annotationType);
  java.lang.annotation.Annotation[] getAnnotations();
  java.lang.annotation.Annotation[] getDeclaredAnnotations();
  boolean isAnnotationPresent(Class<? extends java.lang.annotation.Annotation> annotationType);
}
```

Implementations Class, Package, AccessibleObject

Array — Java 1.1

java.lang.reflect

This class contains methods that allow you to set and query the values of array elements, to determine the length of an array, and to create new instances of arrays. Note that the Array class can manipulate only array values, not array types; Java data types, including array types, are represented by java.lang.Class. Since the Array class represents a Java value, unlike the Field, Method, and Constructor classes, which represent class members, the Array class is significantly different (despite some surface similarities) from those other classes in this package. Most notably, all the methods of Array are static and apply to all array values, not just a specific field, method, or constructor.

The get() method returns the value of the specified element of the specified array as an Object. If the array elements are of a primitive type, the value is converted to a wrapper object before being returned. You can also use getInt() and related methods to query array elements and return them as specific primitive types. The set() method and its primitive type variants perform the opposite operation. Also, the getLength() method returns the length of the array.

The **newInstance()** methods create new arrays. One version of this method is passed the number of elements in the array and the type of those elements. The other version of this method creates multidimensional arrays. Besides specifying the component type of the array, it is passed an array of numbers. The length of this array specifies the number of dimensions for the array to be created, and the values of each of the array elements specify the size of each dimension of the created array.

```
public final class Array {
// No Constructor
// Public Class Methods
   public static Object get(Object array, int index)                                                      native
       throws IllegalArgumentException, ArrayIndexOutOfBoundsException;
   public static boolean getBoolean(Object array, int index)                                              native
       throws IllegalArgumentException, ArrayIndexOutOfBoundsException;
   public static byte getByte(Object array, int index)                                                    native
       throws IllegalArgumentException, ArrayIndexOutOfBoundsException;
   public static char getChar(Object array, int index)                                                    native
       throws IllegalArgumentException, ArrayIndexOutOfBoundsException;
   public static double getDouble(Object array, int index)                                                native
       throws IllegalArgumentException, ArrayIndexOutOfBoundsException;
   public static float getFloat(Object array, int index)                                                  native
       throws IllegalArgumentException, ArrayIndexOutOfBoundsException;
   public static int getInt(Object array, int index)                                                      native
       throws IllegalArgumentException, ArrayIndexOutOfBoundsException;
   public static int getLength(Object array) throws IllegalArgumentException;                             native
   public static long getLong(Object array, int index)                                                    native
       throws IllegalArgumentException, ArrayIndexOutOfBoundsException;
   public static short getShort(Object array, int index)                                                  native
       throws IllegalArgumentException, ArrayIndexOutOfBoundsException;
   public static Object newInstance(Class<?> componentType, int length) throws NegativeArraySizeException;
   public static Object newInstance(Class<?> componentType, int[] dimensions)
       throws IllegalArgumentException, NegativeArraySizeException;
   public static void set(Object array, int index, Object value)                                          native
       throws IllegalArgumentException, ArrayIndexOutOfBoundsException;
   public static void setBoolean(Object array, int index, boolean z)                                      native
       throws IllegalArgumentException, ArrayIndexOutOfBoundsException;
   public static void setByte(Object array, int index, byte b)                                            native
       throws IllegalArgumentException, ArrayIndexOutOfBoundsException;
   public static void setChar(Object array, int index, char c)                                            native
       throws IllegalArgumentException, ArrayIndexOutOfBoundsException;
   public static void setDouble(Object array, int index, double d)                                        native
       throws IllegalArgumentException, ArrayIndexOutOfBoundsException;
   public static void setFloat(Object array, int index, float f)                                          native
       throws IllegalArgumentException, ArrayIndexOutOfBoundsException;
   public static void setInt(Object array, int index, int i)                                              native
       throws IllegalArgumentException, ArrayIndexOutOfBoundsException;
   public static void setLong(Object array, int index, long l)                                            native
       throws IllegalArgumentException, ArrayIndexOutOfBoundsException;
   public static void setShort(Object array, int index, short s)                                          native
       throws IllegalArgumentException, ArrayIndexOutOfBoundsException;
}
```

Constructor<T> Java 1.1

java.lang.reflect

This class represents a constructor method of a class. Instances of Constructor are obtained by calling getConstructor() and related methods of java.lang.Class. Constructor implements the Member interface, so you can use the methods of that interface to obtain the constructor name, modifiers, and declaring class. In addition, getParameterTypes() and getExceptionTypes() also return important information about the represented constructor.

In addition to these methods that return information about the constructor, the newInstance() method allows the constructor to be invoked with an array of arguments in order to create a new instance of the class that declares the constructor. If any of the arguments to the constructor are of primitive types, they must be converted to their corresponding wrapper object types to be passed to newInstance(). If the constructor causes an exception, the Throwable object it throws is wrapped within the InvocationTargetException that is thrown by newInstance(). Note that newInstance() is much more useful than the newInstance() method of java.lang.Class because it can pass arguments to the constructor.

Constructor has been modified in Java 5.0 to support generics, annotations, and varargs. The changes are the same as the Java 5.0 changes to the Method class. Additionally, Constructor has been made a generic type in Java 5.0. The type variable *T* represents the type that the constructor constructs, and is used as the return type of the newInstance() method.

Object — AccessibleObject — Constructor

AnnotatedElement | GenericDeclaration | Member

```
public final class Constructor<T> extends AccessibleObject implements GenericDeclaration, Member {
// No Constructor
// Public Instance Methods
    public Class<?>[] getExceptionTypes();
5.0 public Type[] getGenericExceptionTypes();
5.0 public Type[] getGenericParameterTypes();
5.0 public java.lang.annotation.Annotation[][] getParameterAnnotations();
    public Class<?>[] getParameterTypes();
5.0 public boolean isVarArgs();
    public T newInstance(Object... initargs)
        throws InstantiationException, IllegalAccessException, IllegalArgumentException, InvocationTargetException;
5.0 public String toGenericString();
// Methods Implementing GenericDeclaration
5.0 public TypeVariable<Constructor<T>>[] getTypeParameters();
// Methods Implementing Member
    public Class<T> getDeclaringClass();
    public int getModifiers();
    public String getName();
5.0 public boolean isSynthetic();
// Public Methods Overriding AccessibleObject
5.0 public <T extends java.lang.annotation.Annotation> T getAnnotation(Class<T> annotationClass);
5.0 public java.lang.annotation.Annotation[] getDeclaredAnnotations();
// Public Methods Overriding Object
    public boolean equals(Object obj);
    public int hashCode();
    public String toString();
}
```

Returned By Class.{getConstructor(), getConstructors(), getDeclaredConstructor(), getDeclaredConstructors(), getEnclosingConstructor()}

Field Java 1.1

java.lang.reflect

This class represents a field of a class. Instances of Field are obtained by calling the getField() and related methods of java.lang.Class. Field implements the Member interface, so once you have obtained a Field object, you can use getName(), getModifiers(), and getDeclaringClass() to determine the name, modifiers, and class of the field. Additionally, getType() returns the type of the field.

The set() method sets the value of the represented field for a specified object. (If the represented field is static, no object need be specified, of course.) If the field is of a primitive type, its value can be specified using a wrapper object of type Boolean, Integer, and so on, or it can be set using the setBoolean(), setInt(), and related methods. Similarly, the get() method queries the value of the represented field for a specified object and returns the field value as an Object. Various other methods query the field value and return it as various primitive types.

In Java 5.0, Field implements AnnotatedElement to support reflection on field annotations. The new getGenericType() method supports reflection on the generic type of fields, and isEnumConstant() supports fields of enum types.

Object — AccessibleObject — Field
AnnotatedElement Member

```
public final class Field extends AccessibleObject implements Member {
// No Constructor
// Public Instance Methods
    public Object get(Object obj) throws IllegalArgumentException, IllegalAccessException;
    public boolean getBoolean(Object obj) throws IllegalArgumentException, IllegalAccessException;
    public byte getByte(Object obj) throws IllegalArgumentException, IllegalAccessException;
    public char getChar(Object obj) throws IllegalArgumentException, IllegalAccessException;
    public double getDouble(Object obj) throws IllegalArgumentException, IllegalAccessException;
    public float getFloat(Object obj) throws IllegalArgumentException, IllegalAccessException;
5.0 public Type getGenericType();
    public int getInt(Object obj) throws IllegalArgumentException, IllegalAccessException;
    public long getLong(Object obj) throws IllegalArgumentException, IllegalAccessException;
    public short getShort(Object obj) throws IllegalArgumentException, IllegalAccessException;
    public Class<?> getType();
5.0 public boolean isEnumConstant();
    public void set(Object obj, Object value) throws IllegalArgumentException, IllegalAccessException;
    public void setBoolean(Object obj, boolean z) throws IllegalArgumentException, IllegalAccessException;
    public void setByte(Object obj, byte b) throws IllegalArgumentException, IllegalAccessException;
    public void setChar(Object obj, char c) throws IllegalArgumentException, IllegalAccessException;
    public void setDouble(Object obj, double d) throws IllegalArgumentException, IllegalAccessException;
    public void setFloat(Object obj, float f) throws IllegalArgumentException, IllegalAccessException;
    public void setInt(Object obj, int i) throws IllegalArgumentException, IllegalAccessException;
    public void setLong(Object obj, long l) throws IllegalArgumentException, IllegalAccessException;
    public void setShort(Object obj, short s) throws IllegalArgumentException, IllegalAccessException;
5.0 public String toGenericString();
// Methods Implementing Member
    public Class<?> getDeclaringClass();
    public int getModifiers();
    public String getName();
5.0 public boolean isSynthetic();
```

```
// Public Methods Overriding AccessibleObject
5.0 public <T extends java.lang.annotation.Annotation> T getAnnotation(Class<T> annotationClass);
5.0 public java.lang.annotation.Annotation[] getDeclaredAnnotations();
// Public Methods Overriding Object
   public boolean equals(Object obj);
   public int hashCode();
   public String toString();
}
```

Returned By Class.{getDeclaredField(), getDeclaredFields(), getField(), getFields()}

GenericArrayType — Java 5.0

java.lang.reflect

This interface extends Type and represents a one-dimensional array of some element Type. Note that in the case of multidimensional arrays, the Type returned by getGenericComponentType() is itself a GenericArrayType.

Type ··· GenericArrayType

```
public interface GenericArrayType extends Type {
// Public Instance Methods
   Type getGenericComponentType();
}
```

GenericDeclaration — Java 5.0

java.lang.reflect

This interface is implemented by the classes that represent program elements that can be made generic: java.lang.Class as well as Method and Constructor. It provides access to the type variables declared by the generic type, method, or constructor. getTypeParameters() never returns null: if there are no declared type variables, it returns a zero-length array.

```
public interface GenericDeclaration {
// Public Instance Methods
   TypeVariable<?>[] getTypeParameters();
}
```

Implementations Class, Constructor, Method

Returned By TypeVariable.getGenericDeclaration()

GenericSignatureFormatError — Java 5.0

java.lang.reflect — serializable error

An error of this type is thrown if the Java interpreter tries to load a class file that contains malformed generic signature information.

Object — Throwable — Error — LinkageError — ClassFormatError — GenericSignatureFormatError
Serializable

```
public class GenericSignatureFormatError extends ClassFormatError {
// Public Constructors
   public GenericSignatureFormatError();
}
```

InvocationHandler Java 1.3

java.lang.reflect

This interface defines a single invoke() method that is called whenever a method is invoked on a dynamically created Proxy object. Every Proxy object has an associated InvocationHandler object that is specified when the Proxy is instantiated. All method invocations on the proxy object are translated into calls to the invoke() method of the InvocationHandler.

The first argument to invoke() is the Proxy object through which the method was invoked. The second argument is a Method object that represents the method that was invoked. Call the getDeclaringClass() method of this Method object to determine the interface in which the method was declared. This may be a superinterface of one of the specified interfaces or even java.lang.Object when the method invoked is toString(), hashCode(), or one of the other Object methods. The third argument to invoke() is the array of method arguments. Any primitive type arguments are wrapped in their corresponding object wrappers (e.g., Boolean, Integer, Double).

The value returned by invoke() becomes the return value of the proxy object method invocation and must be of an appropriate type. If the proxy object method returns a primitive type, invoke() should return an instance of the corresponding wrapper class. invoke() can throw any unchecked (i.e., runtime) exceptions or any checked exceptions declared by the proxy object method. If invoke() throws a checked exception that is not declared by the proxy object, that exception is wrapped within an unchecked UndeclaredThrowableException that is thrown in its place.

```
public interface InvocationHandler {
// Public Instance Methods
   Object invoke(Object proxy, Method method, Object[] args) throws Throwable;
}
```

Passed To java.lang.reflect.Proxy.{newProxyInstance(), Proxy()}

Returned By java.lang.reflect.Proxy.getInvocationHandler()

Type Of java.lang.reflect.Proxy.h

InvocationTargetException Java 1.1

java.lang.reflect serializable checked

An object of this class is thrown by Method.invoke() and Constructor.newInstance() when an exception is thrown by the method or constructor invoked through those methods. The InvocationTargetException class serves as a wrapper around the object that was thrown; that object can be retrieved with the getTargetException() method. In Java 1.4 and later, all exceptions can be "chained" in this way, and getTargetException() is superseded by the more general getCause() method.

Object — Throwable — Exception — InvocationTargetException
Throwable ⋮ Serializable

```
public class InvocationTargetException extends Exception {
// Public Constructors
   public InvocationTargetException(Throwable target);
   public InvocationTargetException(Throwable target, String s);
// Protected Constructors
   protected InvocationTargetException();
```

```
// Public Instance Methods
    public Throwable getTargetException();
// Public Methods Overriding Throwable
1.4 public Throwable getCause();
}
```

Thrown By Constructor.newInstance(), Method.invoke()

MalformedParameterizedTypeException — Java 5.0

java.lang.reflect — serializable unchecked

An exception of this type is thrown during reflection if the generic type information contained in a class file is syntactically correct but semantically wrong. An example would be if the number of type parameters in a ParameterizedType differs from the number of type variables declared by the generic type. See also GenericSignatureFormatError. Although this type is not an Error, it does indicate a malformed class file and should not arise in common practice.

Object — Throwable — Exception — RuntimeException — MalformedParameterizedTypeException
Serializable

```
public class MalformedParameterizedTypeException extends RuntimeException {
// Public Constructors
    public MalformedParameterizedTypeException();
}
```

Member — Java 1.1

java.lang.reflect

This interface defines the methods shared by all members (fields, methods, and constructors) of a class. getName() returns the name of the member, getModifiers() returns its modifiers, and getDeclaringClass() returns the Class object that represents the class of which the member is a part. isSynthetic() returns true if the member is one that does not appear in the source code but was introduced by the compiler.

```
public interface Member {
// Public Constants
    public static final int DECLARED;                    =1
    public static final int PUBLIC;                      =0
// Public Instance Methods
    Class getDeclaringClass();
    int getModifiers();
    String getName();
5.0 boolean isSynthetic();
}
```

Implementations Constructor, Field, Method

Method — Java 1.1

java.lang.reflect

This class represents a method. Instances of Method are obtained by calling the getMethod() and related methods of java.lang.Class. Method implements the Member interface, so you can use the methods of that interface to obtain the method name, modifiers, and declaring class. In addition, getReturnType(), getParameterTypes(), and getExceptionTypes() also return important information about the represented method.

Perhaps most importantly, the **invoke()** method allows the method represented by the **Method** object to be invoked with a specified array of argument values. If any of the arguments are of primitive types, they must be converted to their corresponding wrapper object types in order to be passed to **invoke()**. If the represented method is an instance method (i.e., if it is not **static**), the instance on which it should be invoked must also be passed to **invoke()**. The return value of the represented method is returned by **invoke()**. If the return value is a primitive value, it is first converted to the corresponding wrapper type. If the invoked method causes an exception, the **Throwable** object it throws is wrapped within the **InvocationTargetException** that is thrown by **invoke()**.

In Java 5.0, **Method** implements **GenericDeclaration** to support reflection on the type variables defined by generic methods and **AnnotatedElement** to support reflection on method annotations. Additionally, **getParameterAnnotations()** supports reflection on method parameter annotations. The new methods **getGenericReturnType()**, **getGenericParameterTypes()**, and **getGenericExceptionTypes()** support reflection on generic method signatures. Finally, the new **isVarArgs()** method returns true if the method was declared using Java 5.0 varargs syntax.


```
public final class Method extends AccessibleObject implements GenericDeclaration, Member {
// No Constructor
// Public Instance Methods
5.0 public Object getDefaultValue();
    public Class<?>[] getExceptionTypes();
5.0 public Type[] getGenericExceptionTypes();
5.0 public Type[] getGenericParameterTypes();
5.0 public Type getGenericReturnType();
5.0 public java.lang.annotation.Annotation[][] getParameterAnnotations();
    public Class<?>[] getParameterTypes();
    public Class<?> getReturnType();
    public Object invoke(Object obj, Object... args)
        throws IllegalAccessException, IllegalArgumentException, InvocationTargetException;
5.0 public boolean isBridge();
5.0 public boolean isVarArgs();
5.0 public String toGenericString();
// Methods Implementing GenericDeclaration
5.0 public TypeVariable<Method>[] getTypeParameters();
// Methods Implementing Member
    public Class<?> getDeclaringClass();
    public int getModifiers();
    public String getName();
5.0 public boolean isSynthetic();
// Public Methods Overriding AccessibleObject
5.0 public <T extends java.lang.annotation.Annotation> T getAnnotation(Class<T> annotationClass);
5.0 public java.lang.annotation.Annotation[] getDeclaredAnnotations();
// Public Methods Overriding Object
    public boolean equals(Object obj);
    public int hashCode();
    public String toString();
}
```

Passed To java.lang.annotation.AnnotationTypeMismatchException.AnnotationTypeMismatchException(), InvocationHandler.invoke()

Returned By Class.{getDeclaredMethod(), getDeclaredMethods(), getEnclosingMethod(), getMethod(), getMethods()}, java.lang.annotation.AnnotationTypeMismatchException.element()

Modifier **Java 1.1**

java.lang.reflect

This class defines a number of constants and static methods that can interpret the integer values returned by the getModifiers() methods of the Field, Method, and Constructor classes. The isPublic(), isAbstract(), and related methods return true if the modifier value includes the specified modifier; otherwise, they return false. The constants defined by this class specify the various bit flags used in the modifiers value. You can use these constants to test for modifiers if you want to perform your own boolean algebra.


```
public class Modifier {
// Public Constructors
   public Modifier();
// Public Constants
   public static final int ABSTRACT;                           =1024
   public static final int FINAL;                              =16
   public static final int INTERFACE;                          =512
   public static final int NATIVE;                             =256
   public static final int PRIVATE;                            =2
   public static final int PROTECTED;                          =4
   public static final int PUBLIC;                             =1
   public static final int STATIC;                             =8
1.2 public static final int STRICT;                            =2048
   public static final int SYNCHRONIZED;                       =32
   public static final int TRANSIENT;                          =128
   public static final int VOLATILE;                           =64
// Public Class Methods
   public static boolean isAbstract(int mod);
   public static boolean isFinal(int mod);
   public static boolean isInterface(int mod);
   public static boolean isNative(int mod);
   public static boolean isPrivate(int mod);
   public static boolean isProtected(int mod);
   public static boolean isPublic(int mod);
   public static boolean isStatic(int mod);
1.2 public static boolean isStrict(int mod);
   public static boolean isSynchronized(int mod);
   public static boolean isTransient(int mod);
   public static boolean isVolatile(int mod);
   public static String toString(int mod);
}
```

ParameterizedType **Java 5.0**

java.lang.reflect

This subinterface of Type represents a parameterized type. getRawType() returns the base type that has been parameterized. getActualTypeArguments() returns the type parameters as a Type[]. Note that these parameters may themselves be ParameterizedType objects. getOwnerType() is used with parameterized types that are also nested types: it returns the generic type of the containing type.

Type ··· ParameterizedType

```
public interface ParameterizedType extends Type {
// Public Instance Methods
   Type[] getActualTypeArguments();
   Type getOwnerType();
   Type getRawType();
}
```

Proxy

Java 1.3

java.lang.reflect — serializable

This class defines a simple but powerful API for dynamically generating a *proxy class*. A proxy class implements a specified list of interfaces and delegates invocations of the methods defined by those interfaces to a separate invocation handler object.

The static getProxyClass() method dynamically creates a new Class object that implements each of the interfaces specified in the supplied Class[] array. The newly created class is defined in the context of the specified ClassLoader. The Class returned by getProxyClass() is a subclass of Proxy. Every class that is dynamically generated by getProxyClass() has a single public constructor, which expects a single argument of type InvocationHandler. You can create an instance of the dynamic proxy class by using the Constructor class to invoke this constructor. Or, more simply, you can combine the call to getProxyClass() with the constructor call by calling the static newProxyInstance() method, which both defines and instantiates a proxy class.

Every instance of a dynamic proxy class has an associated InvocationHandler object. All method calls made on a proxy class are translated into calls to the invoke() method of this InvocationHandler object, which can handle the call in any way it sees fit. The static getInvocationHandler() method returns the InvocationHandler object for a given proxy object. The static isProxyClass() method returns true if a specified Class object is a dynamically generated proxy class.

Object — Proxy ··· Serializable

```
public class Proxy implements Serializable {
// Protected Constructors
   protected Proxy(InvocationHandler h);
// Public Class Methods
   public static InvocationHandler getInvocationHandler(Object proxy) throws IllegalArgumentException;
   public static Class<?> getProxyClass(ClassLoader loader, Class<?> ... interfaces) throws IllegalArgumentException;
   public static boolean isProxyClass(Class<?> cl);
   public static Object newProxyInstance(ClassLoader loader, Class<?>[] interfaces, InvocationHandler h)
      throws IllegalArgumentException;
// Protected Instance Fields
   protected InvocationHandler h;
}
```

ReflectPermission

Java 1.2

java.lang.reflect — serializable permission

This class is a java.security.Permission that governs access to private, protected, and default-visibility methods, constructors, and fields through the Java Reflection API. In Java 1.2, the only defined name, or target, for ReflectPermission is “suppressAccessChecks”. This permission is required to call the setAccessible() method of AccessibleObject. Unlike some Permission subclasses, ReflectPermission does not use a list of actions. See also AccessibleObject.

System administrators configuring security policies should be familiar with this class, but application programmers should never need to use it directly.

Object — Permission — BasicPermission — ReflectPermission
Guard | Serializable | Serializable

```
public final class ReflectPermission extends java.security.BasicPermission {
// Public Constructors
   public ReflectPermission(String name);
   public ReflectPermission(String name, String actions);
}
```


Type — Java 5.0

java.lang.reflect

This interface has no members but is implemented or extended by any type that represents a generic or nongeneric type. java.lang.Class implements this interface. Type is also extended by four interfaces that represent four specific kinds of generic types: ParameterizedType, TypeVariable, WildcardType, and GenericArrayType.

```
public interface Type {
}
```

Implementations Class, GenericArrayType, ParameterizedType, TypeVariable, WildcardType

Returned By Class.{getGenericInterfaces(), getGenericSuperclass()}, Constructor.{getGenericExceptionTypes(), getGenericParameterTypes()}, Field.getGenericType(), GenericArrayType.getGenericComponentType(), Method.{getGenericExceptionTypes(), getGenericParameterTypes(), getGenericReturnType()}, ParameterizedType.{getActualTypeArguments(), getOwnerType(), getRawType()}, TypeVariable.getBounds(), WildcardType.{getLowerBounds(), getUpperBounds()}

TypeVariable<D extends GenericDeclaration> — Java 5.0

java.lang.reflect

This interface extends Type and represents the generic type represented by a type variable. getName() returns the name of the type variable, as it was declared in Java source code. getBounds() returns an array of Type objects that serve as the upper bounds for the variable. The returned array is never empty: if the type variable has no bounds declared, the single element of the array is Object.class. The getGenericDeclaration() method returns the Class, Method, or Constructor that declared this type variable (each of these classes implements the GenericDeclaration interface). Note that TypeVariable is itself a generic type and is parameterized with the kind of GenericDeclaration that declared the variable.

Type ·· TypeVariable

```
public interface TypeVariable<D extends GenericDeclaration> extends Type {
// Public Instance Methods
   Type[] getBounds();
   D getGenericDeclaration();
   String getName();
}
```

Returned By Class.getTypeParameters(), Constructor.getTypeParameters(), GenericDeclaration.getTypeParameters(), Method.getTypeParameters()

UndeclaredThrowableException Java 1.3

java.lang.reflect serializable unchecked

Thrown by a method of a Proxy object if the invoke() method of the proxy's InvocationHandler throws a checked exception not declared by the original method. This class serves as an unchecked exception wrapper around the checked exception. Use getUndeclaredThrowable() to obtain the checked exception thrown by invoke(). In Java 1.4 and later, all exceptions can be "chained" in this way, and getUndeclaredThrowable() is superseded by the more general getCause() method.

Object — Throwable — Exception — RuntimeException — UndeclaredThrowableException

Serializable

```
public class UndeclaredThrowableException extends RuntimeException {
// Public Constructors
   public UndeclaredThrowableException(Throwable undeclaredThrowable);
   public UndeclaredThrowableException(Throwable undeclaredThrowable, String s);
// Public Instance Methods
   public Throwable getUndeclaredThrowable();
// Public Methods Overriding Throwable
1.4 public Throwable getCause();
}
```

WildcardType Java 5.0

java.lang.reflect

This interface extends Type and represents a generic type declared with a bounded or unbounded wildcard. getUpperBounds() returns the upper bounds of the wildcard. The returned array always includes at least one element. If no upper bound is declared, Object.class is the implicit upper bound. getLowerBounds() returns the lower bounds of the wildcard. If no lower bound is declared, this method returns an empty array.

Type — WildcardType

```
public interface WildcardType extends Type {
// Public Instance Methods
   Type[] getLowerBounds();
   Type[] getUpperBounds();
}
```

11 java.math

Package java.math — Java 1.1

The java.math package contains the BigInteger class for arbitrary-precision integer arithmetic, which is useful for cryptography. It also contains the BigDecimal class for arbitrary precision decimal floating-point arithmetic, which is useful for financial applications that need to be careful about rounding errors. The BigDecimal class is greatly enhanced in Java 5.0 and is accompanied by the new types MathContext and RoundingMode.

Enumerated Types

public enum **RoundingMode**;

Classes

public class **BigDecimal** extends Number implements Comparable<BigDecimal>;
public class **BigInteger** extends Number implements Comparable<BigInteger>;
public final class **MathContext** implements Serializable;

BigDecimal — Java 1.1

java.math — serializable comparable

This subclass of java.lang.Number represents a floating-point number of arbitrary size and precision. Because it uses a decimal rather than binary floating-point representation, it is not subject to the rounding errors that the float and double types are. This makes BigDecimal well-suited to financial and similar applications.

BigDecimal provides add(), subtract(), multiply(), and divide() methods to support basic arithmetic. In Java 5.0, this class has been expanded to define many more methods, including pow() for exponentiation. Many of the new methods use a MathContext to specify the desired precision of the result and the RoundingMode to be used to achieve that precision.

BigDecimal extends Number and implements the Comparable interface. The compareTo() method compares the value of two BigDecimal objects and returns –1, 0, or 1 to indicate the result of the comparison. Use this method in place of the <, <=, >, and >= operators that you'd use with float and double values.

A **BigDecimal** object is represented as an integer of arbitrary size and an integer scale that specifies the number of decimal places in the value. When working with **BigDecimal** values, you can explicitly specify the precision (i.e., the number of decimal places) you are interested in. Also, whenever a **BigDecimal** method can discard precision (e.g., in a division operation), you are required to specify what sort of rounding should be performed on the digit to the left of the discarded digit or digits. The eight constants defined by this class specify the available rounding modes. In Java 5.0, however, the preferred way to specify a rounding mode is with the enumerated type **RoundingMode**.

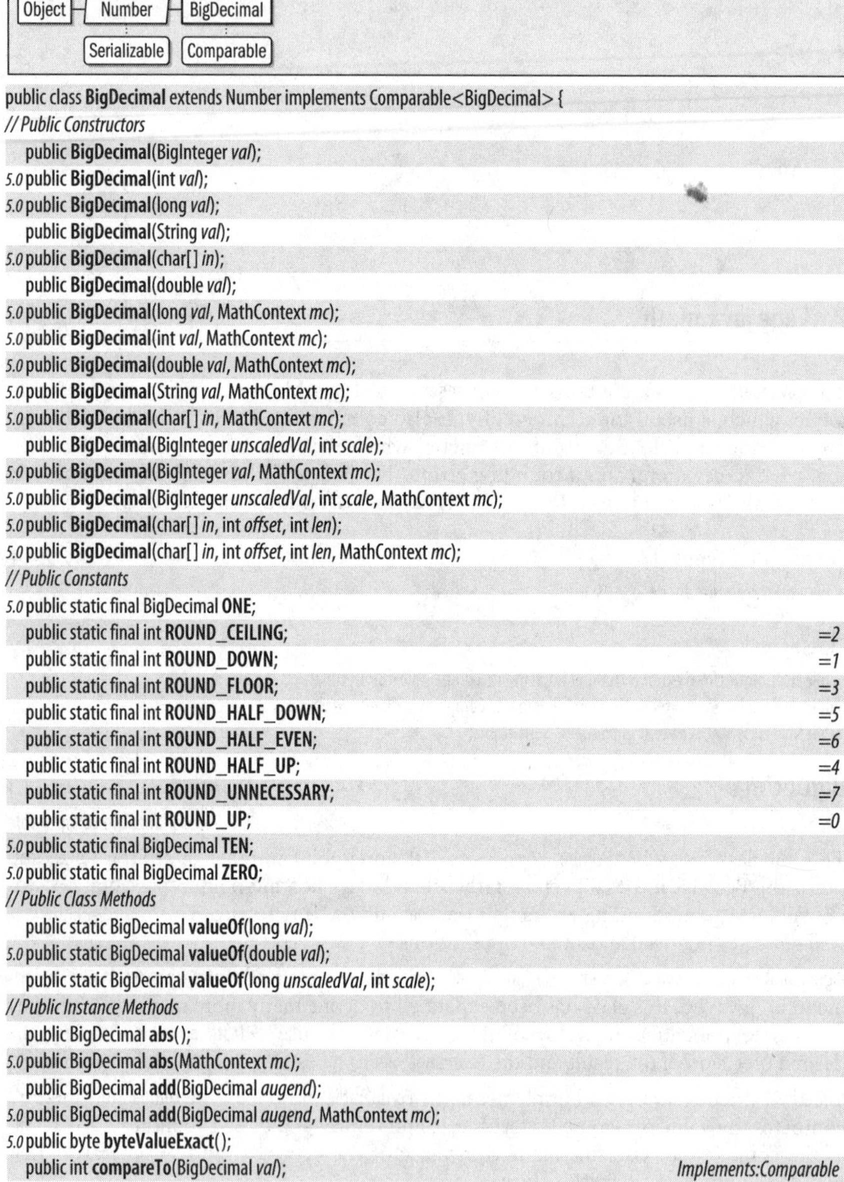


```
public class BigDecimal extends Number implements Comparable<BigDecimal> {
// Public Constructors
    public BigDecimal(BigInteger val);
5.0 public BigDecimal(int val);
5.0 public BigDecimal(long val);
    public BigDecimal(String val);
5.0 public BigDecimal(char[] in);
    public BigDecimal(double val);
5.0 public BigDecimal(long val, MathContext mc);
5.0 public BigDecimal(int val, MathContext mc);
5.0 public BigDecimal(double val, MathContext mc);
5.0 public BigDecimal(String val, MathContext mc);
5.0 public BigDecimal(char[] in, MathContext mc);
    public BigDecimal(BigInteger unscaledVal, int scale);
5.0 public BigDecimal(BigInteger val, MathContext mc);
5.0 public BigDecimal(BigInteger unscaledVal, int scale, MathContext mc);
5.0 public BigDecimal(char[] in, int offset, int len);
5.0 public BigDecimal(char[] in, int offset, int len, MathContext mc);
// Public Constants
5.0 public static final BigDecimal ONE;
    public static final int ROUND_CEILING;                        =2
    public static final int ROUND_DOWN;                           =1
    public static final int ROUND_FLOOR;                          =3
    public static final int ROUND_HALF_DOWN;                      =5
    public static final int ROUND_HALF_EVEN;                      =6
    public static final int ROUND_HALF_UP;                        =4
    public static final int ROUND_UNNECESSARY;                    =7
    public static final int ROUND_UP;                             =0
5.0 public static final BigDecimal TEN;
5.0 public static final BigDecimal ZERO;
// Public Class Methods
    public static BigDecimal valueOf(long val);
5.0 public static BigDecimal valueOf(double val);
    public static BigDecimal valueOf(long unscaledVal, int scale);
// Public Instance Methods
    public BigDecimal abs();
5.0 public BigDecimal abs(MathContext mc);
    public BigDecimal add(BigDecimal augend);
5.0 public BigDecimal add(BigDecimal augend, MathContext mc);
5.0 public byte byteValueExact();
    public int compareTo(BigDecimal val);              Implements:Comparable
```

```
5.0 public BigDecimal divide(BigDecimal divisor);
    public BigDecimal divide(BigDecimal divisor, int roundingMode);
5.0 public BigDecimal divide(BigDecimal divisor, RoundingMode roundingMode);
5.0 public BigDecimal divide(BigDecimal divisor, MathContext mc);
    public BigDecimal divide(BigDecimal divisor, int scale, int roundingMode);
5.0 public BigDecimal divide(BigDecimal divisor, int scale, RoundingMode roundingMode);
5.0 public BigDecimal[] divideAndRemainder(BigDecimal divisor);
5.0 public BigDecimal[] divideAndRemainder(BigDecimal divisor, MathContext mc);
5.0 public BigDecimal divideToIntegralValue(BigDecimal divisor);
5.0 public BigDecimal divideToIntegralValue(BigDecimal divisor, MathContext mc);
5.0 public int intValueExact();
5.0 public long longValueExact();
    public BigDecimal max(BigDecimal val);
    public BigDecimal min(BigDecimal val);
    public BigDecimal movePointLeft(int n);
    public BigDecimal movePointRight(int n);
    public BigDecimal multiply(BigDecimal multiplicand);
5.0 public BigDecimal multiply(BigDecimal multiplicand, MathContext mc);
    public BigDecimal negate();
5.0 public BigDecimal negate(MathContext mc);
5.0 public BigDecimal plus();
5.0 public BigDecimal plus(MathContext mc);
5.0 public BigDecimal pow(int n);
5.0 public BigDecimal pow(int n, MathContext mc);
5.0 public int precision();
5.0 public BigDecimal remainder(BigDecimal divisor);
5.0 public BigDecimal remainder(BigDecimal divisor, MathContext mc);
5.0 public BigDecimal round(MathContext mc);
    public int scale();
5.0 public BigDecimal scaleByPowerOfTen(int n);
    public BigDecimal setScale(int newScale);
    public BigDecimal setScale(int newScale, int roundingMode);
5.0 public BigDecimal setScale(int newScale, RoundingMode roundingMode);
5.0 public short shortValueExact();
    public int signum();
5.0 public BigDecimal stripTrailingZeros();
    public BigDecimal subtract(BigDecimal subtrahend);
5.0 public BigDecimal subtract(BigDecimal subtrahend, MathContext mc);
    public BigInteger toBigInteger();
5.0 public BigInteger toBigIntegerExact();
5.0 public String toEngineeringString();
5.0 public String toPlainString();
5.0 public BigDecimal ulp();
1.2 public BigInteger unscaledValue();
// Methods Implementing Comparable
    public int compareTo(BigDecimal val);
// Public Methods Overriding Number
    public double doubleValue();
    public float floatValue();
    public int intValue();
    public long longValue();
// Public Methods Overriding Object
    public boolean equals(Object x);
```

java.math

```
   public int hashCode();
   public String toString();
}
```

Passed To javax.xml.datatype.DatatypeFactory.{newDuration(), newXMLGregorianCalendar(), newXMLGregorianCalendarTime()}, javax.xml.datatype.Duration.multiply(), javax.xml.datatype.XMLGregorianCalendar.{setFractionalSecond(), setTime()}

Returned By java.util.Scanner.nextBigDecimal(), javax.xml.datatype.XMLGregorianCalendar.getFractionalSecond()

BigInteger **Java 1.1**

java.math **serializable comparable**

This subclass of java.lang.Number represents integers that can be arbitrarily large (i.e., integers that are not limited to the 64 bits available with the long data type). BigInteger defines methods that duplicate the functionality of the standard Java arithmetic and bit-manipulation operators. The compareTo() method compares two BigInteger objects and returns –1, 0, or 1 to indicate the result of the comparison. The gcd(), modPow(), modInverse(), and isProbablePrime() methods perform advanced operations and are used primarily in cryptographic and related algorithms.

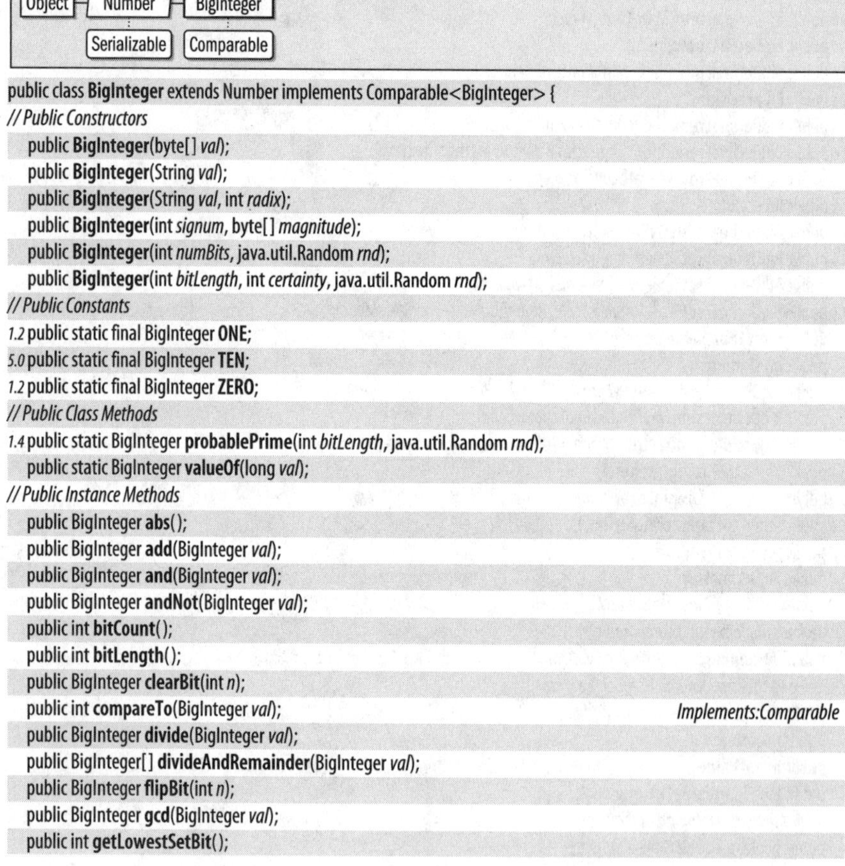


```
public class BigInteger extends Number implements Comparable<BigInteger> {
// Public Constructors
   public BigInteger(byte[] val);
   public BigInteger(String val);
   public BigInteger(String val, int radix);
   public BigInteger(int signum, byte[] magnitude);
   public BigInteger(int numBits, java.util.Random rnd);
   public BigInteger(int bitLength, int certainty, java.util.Random rnd);
// Public Constants
1.2 public static final BigInteger ONE;
5.0 public static final BigInteger TEN;
1.2 public static final BigInteger ZERO;
// Public Class Methods
1.4 public static BigInteger probablePrime(int bitLength, java.util.Random rnd);
   public static BigInteger valueOf(long val);
// Public Instance Methods
   public BigInteger abs();
   public BigInteger add(BigInteger val);
   public BigInteger and(BigInteger val);
   public BigInteger andNot(BigInteger val);
   public int bitCount();
   public int bitLength();
   public BigInteger clearBit(int n);
   public int compareTo(BigInteger val);                    Implements:Comparable
   public BigInteger divide(BigInteger val);
   public BigInteger[] divideAndRemainder(BigInteger val);
   public BigInteger flipBit(int n);
   public BigInteger gcd(BigInteger val);
   public int getLowestSetBit();
```

```
    public boolean isProbablePrime(int certainty);
    public BigInteger max(BigInteger val);
    public BigInteger min(BigInteger val);
    public BigInteger mod(BigInteger m);
    public BigInteger modInverse(BigInteger m);
    public BigInteger modPow(BigInteger exponent, BigInteger m);
    public BigInteger multiply(BigInteger val);
    public BigInteger negate();
5.0 public BigInteger nextProbablePrime();
    public BigInteger not();
    public BigInteger or(BigInteger val);
    public BigInteger pow(int exponent);
    public BigInteger remainder(BigInteger val);
    public BigInteger setBit(int n);
    public BigInteger shiftLeft(int n);
    public BigInteger shiftRight(int n);
    public int signum();
    public BigInteger subtract(BigInteger val);
    public boolean testBit(int n);
    public byte[] toByteArray();
    public String toString(int radix);
    public BigInteger xor(BigInteger val);
// Methods Implementing Comparable
    public int compareTo(BigInteger val);
// Public Methods Overriding Number
    public double doubleValue();
    public float floatValue();
    public int intValue();
    public long longValue();
// Public Methods Overriding Object
    public boolean equals(Object x);
    public int hashCode();
    public String toString();
}
```

Passed To Too many methods to list.

Returned By Too many methods to list.

Type Of java.security.spec.RSAKeyGenParameterSpec.{F0, F4}

MathContext — Java 5.0

java.math — serializable

This simple class represents a precision (number of significant digits) and a RoundingMode to be used in BigDecimal arithmetic. The constants are predefined MathContext objects that can be used to select unlimited precision arithmetic or to select specific operating modes that match decimal floating-point modes defined by the IEEE 754R standard.

Object — MathContext ··· Serializable

```
public final class MathContext implements Serializable {
// Public Constructors
    public MathContext(int setPrecision);
    public MathContext(String val);
    public MathContext(int setPrecision, RoundingMode setRoundingMode);
```

```
// Public Constants
   public static final MathContext DECIMAL128;
   public static final MathContext DECIMAL32;
   public static final MathContext DECIMAL64;
   public static final MathContext UNLIMITED;
// Public Instance Methods
   public int getPrecision();
   public RoundingMode getRoundingMode();
// Public Methods Overriding Object
   public boolean equals(Object x);
   public int hashCode();
   public String toString();
}
```

Passed To Too many methods to list.

RoundingMode **Java 5.0**

java.math **serializable comparable enum**

The constants defined by this enumerated type represent possible ways of rounding numbers. UP and DOWN specify rounding away from zero or toward zero. CEILING and FLOOR represent rounding toward positive infinity and negative infinity. HALF_UP, HALF_DOWN, and HALF_EVEN all round toward the nearest value and differ only in what they do when two values are equidistant. In this case, they round up, down, or to the "even" neighbor. UNNECESSARY is a special rounding mode that serves as an assertion that an arithmetic operation will have an exact result and that rounding is not needed. If this assertion fails—that is, if the operation does require rounding—an ArithmeticException is thrown.

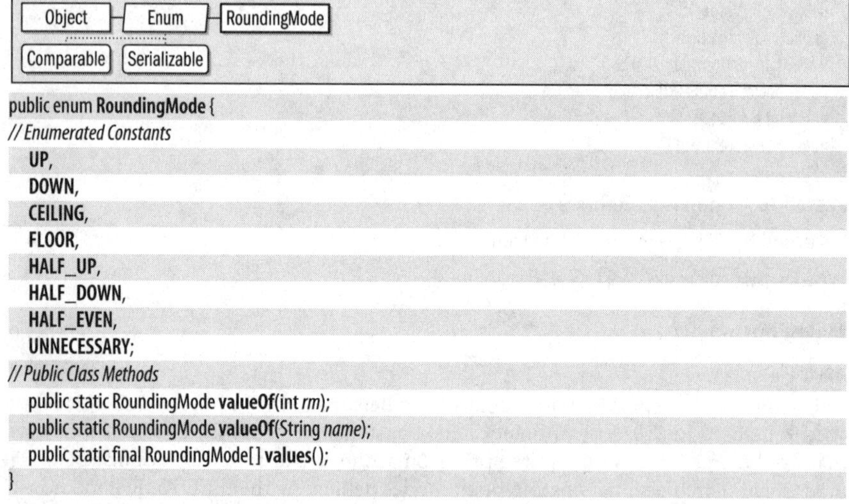


```
public enum RoundingMode {
// Enumerated Constants
   UP,
   DOWN,
   CEILING,
   FLOOR,
   HALF_UP,
   HALF_DOWN,
   HALF_EVEN,
   UNNECESSARY;
// Public Class Methods
   public static RoundingMode valueOf(int rm);
   public static RoundingMode valueOf(String name);
   public static final RoundingMode[] values();
}
```

Passed To BigDecimal.{divide(), setScale()}, MathContext.MathContext()

Returned By MathContext.getRoundingMode()

12
java.net

Package java.net

Java 1.0

The java.net package provides a powerful and flexible infrastructure for networking. This introduction describes the most commonly used classes in brief. Note that as of Java 1.4, the New I/O API of java.nio and java.nio.channels can be used for high-performance nonblocking networking. See also the javax.net.ssl package for classes for secure networking using SSL.

The URL class represents an Internet uniform resource locator (URL). It provides a very simple interface to networking: the object referred to by the URL can be downloaded with a single call, or streams may be opened to read from or write to the object. At a slightly more complex level, a URLConnection object can be obtained from a given URL object. The URLConnection class provides additional methods that allow you to work with URLs in more sophisticated ways. Java 1.4 introduced the URI class; it provides a powerful API for manipulating URI and URL strings but does not have any networking capabilities itself. Java 5.0 defines APIs for defining and registering cache, cookie, and proxy handlers to be used by built-in protocol handlers when network resources are requested through the URL class. See RequestCache, CookieHandler, ProxySelector, and Proxy.

If you want to do more than simply download an object referenced by a URL, you can do your own networking with the Socket class. This class allows you to connect to a specified port on a specified Internet host and read and write data using the InputStream and OutputStream classes of the java.io package. If you want to implement a server to accept connections from clients, you can use the related ServerSocket class. Both Socket and ServerSocket use the InetAddress address class, which represents an Internet address. Added in Java 1.4, Inet4Address and Inet6Address are subclasses that represent the addresses used by version 4 and version 6 of the IP protocol. Java 1.4 also introduced the SocketAddress class as a high-level representation of a network address that is not tied to a specific networking protocol. An IP-specific InetSocketAddress subclass encapsulates an InetAddress and a port number.

The java.net package allows you to do low-level networking with DatagramPacket objects, which may be sent and received over the network through a DatagramSocket object. MulticastSocket extends DatagramSocket to support multicast networking.

Interfaces

public interface **ContentHandlerFactory**;
public interface **DatagramSocketImplFactory**;
public interface **FileNameMap**;
public interface **SocketImplFactory**;
public interface **SocketOptions**;
public interface **URLStreamHandlerFactory**;

Enumerated Types

public enum **Authenticator.RequestorType**;
public enum **Proxy.Type**;

Classes

public abstract class **Authenticator**;
public abstract class **CacheRequest**;
public abstract class **CacheResponse**;
    public abstract class **SecureCacheResponse** extends CacheResponse;
public abstract class **ContentHandler**;
public abstract class **CookieHandler**;
public final class **DatagramPacket**;
public class **DatagramSocket**;
    public class **MulticastSocket** extends DatagramSocket;
public abstract class **DatagramSocketImpl** implements SocketOptions;
public class **InetAddress** implements Serializable;
    public final class **Inet4Address** extends InetAddress;
    public final class **Inet6Address** extends InetAddress;
public final class **NetPermission** extends java.security.BasicPermission;
public final class **NetworkInterface**;
public final class **PasswordAuthentication**;
public class **Proxy**;
public abstract class **ProxySelector**;
public abstract class **ResponseCache**;
public class **ServerSocket**;
public class **Socket**;
public abstract class **SocketAddress** implements Serializable;
    public class **InetSocketAddress** extends SocketAddress;
public abstract class **SocketImpl** implements SocketOptions;
public final class **SocketPermission** extends java.security.Permission implements Serializable;
public final class **URI** implements Comparable<URI>, Serializable;
public final class **URL** implements Serializable;
public class **URLClassLoader** extends java.security.SecureClassLoader;
public abstract class **URLConnection**;
    public abstract class **HttpURLConnection** extends URLConnection;
    public abstract class **JarURLConnection** extends URLConnection;
public class **URLDecoder**;
public class **URLEncoder**;
public abstract class **URLStreamHandler**;

Exceptions

```
public class HttpRetryException extends java.io.IOException;
public class MalformedURLException extends java.io.IOException;
public class ProtocolException extends java.io.IOException;
public class SocketException extends java.io.IOException;
    public class BindException extends SocketException;
    public class ConnectException extends SocketException;
    public class NoRouteToHostException extends SocketException;
    public class PortUnreachableException extends SocketException;
public class SocketTimeoutException extends java.io.InterruptedIOException;
public class UnknownHostException extends java.io.IOException;
public class UnknownServiceException extends java.io.IOException;
public class URISyntaxException extends Exception;
```

Authenticator — Java 1.2

java.net

This abstract class defines a customizable mechanism for requesting and performing password authentication when required in URL-based networking. The static setDefault() method establishes the systemwide Authenticator. An Authenticator implementation can obtain the required authentication information from the user however it wants (e.g., through a text- or a GUI-based interface). setDefault() can be called only once; subsequent calls are ignored. Calling setDefault() requires an appropriate NetPermission.

When an application or the Java runtime system requires password authentication (to read the contents of a specified URL, for example), it calls the static requestPasswordAuthentication() method, passing arguments that specify the host and port for which the password is required and a prompt that may be displayed to the user. This method looks up the default Authenticator for the system and calls its getPasswordAuthentication() method. Calling requestPasswordAuthentication() requires an appropriate NetPermission.

Authenticator is an abstract class; its default implementation of getPasswordAuthentication() always returns null. To create an Authenticator, you must override this method so that it prompts the user to enter a username and password and returns that information in the form of a PasswordAuthentication object. Your implementation of getPasswordAuthentication() may call the various getRequesting() methods to find out who is requesting the password and what the recommended user prompt is. Java 1.4 added a version of the static requestPasswordAuthentication() method that allows specification of the requesting hostname. A corresponding getRequestingHost() instance method was also added.

Java 5.0 adds yet another version of requestPasswordAuthentication(), and corresponding methods to query the URL that requires the password and the RequestorType of the request. RequestorType is a nested enum type that specifies whether the request comes from an HTTP server or a proxy server.

```
public abstract class Authenticator {
// Public Constructors
    public Authenticator();
// Nested Types
5.0 public enum RequestorType;
// Public Class Methods
    public static PasswordAuthentication requestPasswordAuthentication(InetAddress addr, int port, String protocol,
                                                                        String prompt, String scheme);
```

```
1.4 public static PasswordAuthentication requestPasswordAuthentication(String host, InetAddress addr, int port,
                                                    String protocol, String prompt, String scheme);
5.0 public static PasswordAuthentication requestPasswordAuthentication(String host, InetAddress addr, int port,
                                                    String protocol, String prompt, String scheme,
                                                    URL url, Authenticator.RequestorType reqType);
    public static void setDefault(Authenticator a);                                      synchronized
// Protected Instance Methods
    protected PasswordAuthentication getPasswordAuthentication();                        constant
1.4 protected final String getRequestingHost();
    protected final int getRequestingPort();
    protected final String getRequestingPrompt();
    protected final String getRequestingProtocol();
    protected final String getRequestingScheme();
    protected final InetAddress getRequestingSite();
5.0 protected URL getRequestingURL();
5.0 protected Authenticator.RequestorType getRequestorType();
}
```

Authenticator.RequestorType — Java 5.0

java.net — serializable comparable enum

The constants defined by this enumerated type specify whether an authentication request comes from an HTTP origin server or a proxy server.

```
public enum Authenticator.RequestorType {
// Enumerated Constants
    PROXY,
    SERVER;
// Public Class Methods
    public static Authenticator.RequestorType valueOf(String name);
    public static final Authenticator.RequestorType[] values();
}
```

Passed To Authenticator.requestPasswordAuthentication()

Returned By Authenticator.getRequestorType()

BindException — Java 1.1

java.net — serializable checked

Signals that a socket cannot be bound to a local address and port. This often means that the port is already in use.

Object — Throwable — Exception — IOException — SocketException — BindException
Serializable

```
public class BindException extends SocketException {
// Public Constructors
    public BindException();
    public BindException(String msg);
}
```

CacheRequest

Java 5.0

java.net

When a URLStreamHandler reads a network resource, it should call the put() method of the currently installed ResponseCache, if there is one. If the cache wants to save a local copy of the resource, it will return a CacheRequest object to the URLStreamHandler. The handler should then write the resource to the OutputStream returned by the getBody() method.

See also CacheResponse. This class is used by the implementors of URLStreamHandler, not by casual users of the java.net package.

```
public abstract class CacheRequest {
// Public Constructors
   public CacheRequest();
// Public Instance Methods
   public abstract void abort();
   public abstract java.io.OutputStream getBody() throws java.io.IOException;
}
```

Returned By ResponseCache.put()

CacheResponse

Java 5.0

java.net

If a ResponseCache holds a local copy of a network resource, it returns a CacheResponse object from the ResponseCache.get() method. The resource can then be read from the java.io.InputStream returned by getBody(). The protocol response headers are available in the form of java.util.Map from getHeaders().

See also SecureCacheResponse and CacheRequest. Note that this class is intended for use in URLStreamHandler implementations, not by casual users of the java.net package.

```
public abstract class CacheResponse {
// Public Constructors
   public CacheResponse();
// Public Instance Methods
   public abstract java.io.InputStream getBody() throws java.io.IOException;
   public abstract java.util.Map<String,java.util.List<String>> getHeaders() throws java.io.IOException;
}
```

Subclasses SecureCacheResponse

Returned By ResponseCache.get()

ConnectException

Java 1.1

java.net serializable checked

Signals that a socket cannot be connected to a remote address and port. This means that the remote host can be reached, but is not responding, perhaps because there is no process on that host that is listening on the specified port.

Object — Throwable — Exception — IOException — SocketException — ConnectException
Serializable

```
public class ConnectException extends SocketException {
// Public Constructors
   public ConnectException();
   public ConnectException(String msg);
}
```

ContentHandler Java 1.0

java.net

This abstract class defines a method that reads data from a URLConnection and returns an object that represents that data. Each subclass that implements this method is responsible for handling a different type of content (i.e., a different MIME type). Applications never create ContentHandler objects directly; they are created, when necessary, by the registered ContentHandlerFactory object. Applications should also never call ContentHandler methods directly; they should call URL.getContent() or URLConnection.getContent() instead. You need to subclass ContentHandler only if you are writing a web browser or similar application that needs to parse and understand some new content type.

```
public abstract class ContentHandler {
// Public Constructors
   public ContentHandler();
// Public Instance Methods
   public abstract Object getContent(URLConnection urlc) throws java.io.IOException;
1.3 public Object getContent(URLConnection urlc, Class[] classes) throws java.io.IOException;
}
```

Returned By ContentHandlerFactory.createContentHandler()

ContentHandlerFactory Java 1.0

java.net

This interface defines a method that creates and returns an appropriate ContentHandler object for a specified MIME type. A systemwide ContentHandlerFactory interface may be specified using the URLConnection.setContentHandlerFactory() method. Normal applications never need to use or implement this interface.

```
public interface ContentHandlerFactory {
// Public Instance Methods
   java.net.ContentHandler createContentHandler(String mimetype);
}
```

Passed To URLConnection.setContentHandlerFactory()

CookieHandler Java 5.0

java.net

This abstract class defines an API to be implemented by an application that wants to manage HTTP cookies for networking done via the URL class. Install an implementation of this class with the setDefault() method. The default HTTP protocol handler uses getDefault() to obtain the CookieHandler implementation. The protocol handler then calls get() when it wants the CookieHandler to copy cookie values into HTTP request headers and calls put() when it wants the CookieHandler to read a set of response headers and store the cookies they contain.

This class is intended to be subclassed by advanced users of the package; it is not intended for casual users.

```
public abstract class CookieHandler {
// Public Constructors
   public CookieHandler();
// Public Class Methods
   public static CookieHandler getDefault();                     synchronized
```

```
    public static void setDefault(CookieHandler cHandler);                    synchronized
// Public Instance Methods
    public abstract java.util.Map<String,java.util.List<String>>
        get(URI uri, java.util.Map<String,java.util.List<String>> requestHeaders)
        throws java.io.IOException;
    public abstract void put(URI uri, java.util.Map<String,java.util.List<String>> responseHeaders)
        throws java.io.IOException;
}
```

DatagramPacket

Java 1.0

java.net

This class implements a packet of data that may be sent or received over the network through a DatagramSocket. Create a DatagramPacket to be sent over the network with one of the consructor methods that includes a network address. Create a DatagramPacket into which data can be received using one of the constructors that does not include a network address argument. The receive() method of DatagramSocket waits for data and stores it in a DatagramPacket created in this way. The contents and sender of a received packet can be queried with the DatagramPacket instance methods.

New constructors and methods were added to this class in Java 1.4 to support the SocketAddress abstraction of a network address.

```
public final class DatagramPacket {
// Public Constructors
    public DatagramPacket(byte[] buf, int length);
1.4 public DatagramPacket(byte[] buf, int length, SocketAddress address) throws SocketException;
1.2 public DatagramPacket(byte[] buf, int offset, int length);
    public DatagramPacket(byte[] buf, int length, InetAddress address, int port);
1.4 public DatagramPacket(byte[] buf, int offset, int length, SocketAddress address) throws SocketException;
1.2 public DatagramPacket(byte[] buf, int offset, int length, InetAddress address, int port);
// Public Instance Methods
    public InetAddress getAddress();                                          synchronized
    public byte[] getData();                                                  synchronized
    public int getLength();                                                   synchronized
1.2 public int getOffset();                                                   synchronized
    public int getPort();                                                     synchronized
1.4 public SocketAddress getSocketAddress();                                  synchronized
1.1 public void setAddress(InetAddress iaddr);                                synchronized
1.1 public void setData(byte[] buf);                                          synchronized
1.2 public void setData(byte[] buf, int offset, int length);                  synchronized
1.1 public void setLength(int length);                                        synchronized
1.1 public void setPort(int iport);                                           synchronized
1.4 public void setSocketAddress(SocketAddress address);                      synchronized
}
```

Passed To DatagramSocket.{receive(), send()}, DatagramSocketImpl.{peekData(), receive(), send()}, MulticastSocket.send()

DatagramSocket

Java 1.0

java.net

This class defines a socket that can receive and send unreliable datagram packets over the network using the UDP protocol. A *datagram* is a very low-level networking interface: it is simply an array of bytes sent over the network. A datagram does not implement any kind of stream-based communication protocol, and there is no connection established between the sender and the receiver. Datagram packets are called unreliable because the protocol does not make any attempt to ensure they arrive or to resend them if they don't. Thus, packets sent through a DatagramSocket are not guaranteed to arrive in the order sent or even to arrive at all. On the other hand, this low-overhead protocol makes datagram transmission very fast. See Socket and URL for higher-level interfaces to networking. This class was introduced in Java 1.0, and was enhanced in Java 1.4 to allow local and remote addresses to be specified using the protocol-independent SocketAddress class.

send() sends a DatagramPacket through the socket. The packet must contain the destination address to which it should be sent. receive() waits for data to arrive at the socket and stores it, along with the address of the sender, in the specified DatagramPacket. close() closes the socket and frees the local port for reuse. Once close() has been called, the DatagramSocket should not be used again, except to call the isClosed() method which returns true if the socket has been closed.

Each time a packet is sent or received, the system must perform a security check to ensure that the calling code has permission to send data to or receive data from the specified host. In Java 1.2 and later, if you are sending multiple packets to or receiving multiple packets from a single host, use connect() to specify the host with which you are communicating. This causes the security check to be done a single time, but does not allow the socket to communicate with any other host until disconnect() is called. Use getRemoteSocketAddress() or getInetAddress() and getPort() to obtain the network address, if any, that the socket is connected to. Use isConnected() to determine if the socket is currently connected in this way.

By default, a DatagramSocket sends data through a local address assigned by the system. If desired, however, you can *bind* the socket to a specified local address. Do this by using one of the constructors other than the no-arg constructor. Or, bind the DatagramSocket to a local SocketAddress with the bind() method. You can determine whether a DatagramSocket is bound with isBound(), and you can obtain the local address of the socket with getLocalSocketAddress() or with getLocalAddress() and getLocalPort().

This class defines a number of get/set method pairs for setting and querying a variety of "socket options" for datagram transmission. setSoTimeout() specifies the number of milliseconds that receive() waits for a packet to arrive before throwing an InterruptedIOException. Specify 0 milliseconds to wait forever. setSendBufferSize() and setReceiveBufferSize() set hints as to the underlying size of the networking buffers. setBroadcast(), setReuseAddress(), and setTrafficClass() set more complex socket options; use of these options requires a sophisticated understanding of low-level network protocols, and an explaination of them is beyond the scope of this reference.

In Java 1.4 and later, getChannel() returns a java.nio.channels.DatagramChannel associated with this DatagramSocket. Sockets created with one of the DatagramSocket() constructors always return null from this method. getChannel() only returns a useful value for sockets that were created by and belong to a DatagramChannel.

```
public class DatagramSocket {
// Public Constructors
    public DatagramSocket() throws SocketException;
1.4 public DatagramSocket(SocketAddress bindaddr) throws SocketException;
    public DatagramSocket(int port) throws SocketException;
1.1 public DatagramSocket(int port, InetAddress laddr) throws SocketException;
// Protected Constructors
```

```
1.4 publicprotected DatagramSocket(DatagramSocketImpl impl);
// Public Class Methods
1.3 public static void setDatagramSocketImplFactory(DatagramSocketImplFactory fac)              synchronized
        throws java.io.IOException;
// Public Instance Methods
1.4 public void bind(SocketAddress addr) throws SocketException;                                synchronized
    public void close();
1.4 public void connect(SocketAddress addr) throws SocketException;
1.2 public void connect(InetAddress address, int port);
1.2 public void disconnect();
1.4 public boolean getBroadcast() throws SocketException;                        synchronized default:true
1.4 public java.nio.channels.DatagramChannel getChannel();                          constant default:null
1.2 public InetAddress getInetAddress();                                                      default:null
1.1 public InetAddress getLocalAddress();                                             default:Inet4Address
    public int getLocalPort();                                                               default:32777
1.4 public SocketAddress getLocalSocketAddress();                                default:InetSocketAddress
1.2 public int getPort();                                                                       default:-1
1.2 public int getReceiveBufferSize() throws SocketException;                   synchronized default:32767
1.4 public SocketAddress getRemoteSocketAddress();                                            default:null
1.4 public boolean getReuseAddress() throws SocketException;                    synchronized default:false
1.2 public int getSendBufferSize() throws SocketException;                      synchronized default:32767
1.1 public int getSoTimeout() throws SocketException;                               synchronized default:0
1.4 public int getTrafficClass() throws SocketException;                            synchronized default:0
1.4 public boolean isBound();                                                                 default:true
1.4 public boolean isClosed();                                                               default:false
1.4 public boolean isConnected();                                                            default:false
    public void receive(DatagramPacket p) throws java.io.IOException;                         synchronized
    public void send(DatagramPacket p) throws java.io.IOException;
1.4 public void setBroadcast(boolean on) throws SocketException;                              synchronized
1.2 public void setReceiveBufferSize(int size) throws SocketException;                        synchronized
1.4 public void setReuseAddress(boolean on) throws SocketException;                           synchronized
1.2 public void setSendBufferSize(int size) throws SocketException;                           synchronized
1.1 public void setSoTimeout(int timeout) throws SocketException;                             synchronized
1.4 public void setTrafficClass(int tc) throws SocketException;                               synchronized
}
```

Subclasses MulticastSocket

Returned By java.nio.channels.DatagramChannel.socket()

DatagramSocketImpl — Java 1.1

java.net

This abstract class defines the methods necessary to implement communication through datagram and multicast sockets. System programmers may create subclasses of this class when they need to implement datagram or multicast sockets in a nonstandard network environment, such as behind a firewall or on a network that uses a nonstandard transport protocol. Normal applications never need to use or subclass this class.

Object — DatagramSocketImpl ··· SocketOptions

```
public abstract class DatagramSocketImpl implements SocketOptions {
// Public Constructors
    public DatagramSocketImpl();
```

```
// Protected Instance Methods
   protected abstract void bind(int lport, InetAddress laddr) throws SocketException;
   protected abstract void close();
1.4 protected void connect(InetAddress address, int port) throws SocketException;          empty
   protected abstract void create() throws SocketException;
1.4 protected void disconnect();                                                            empty
   protected java.io.FileDescriptor getFileDescriptor();
   protected int getLocalPort();
1.2 protected abstract int getTimeToLive() throws java.io.IOException;
   protected abstract void join(InetAddress inetaddr) throws java.io.IOException;
1.4 protected abstract void joinGroup(SocketAddress mcastaddr, NetworkInterface netIf) throws java.io.IOException;
   protected abstract void leave(InetAddress inetaddr) throws java.io.IOException;
1.4 protected abstract void leaveGroup(SocketAddress mcastaddr, NetworkInterface netIf) throws java.io.IOException;
   protected abstract int peek(InetAddress i) throws java.io.IOException;
1.4 protected abstract int peekData(DatagramPacket p) throws java.io.IOException;
   protected abstract void receive(DatagramPacket p) throws java.io.IOException;
   protected abstract void send(DatagramPacket p) throws java.io.IOException;
1.2 protected abstract void setTimeToLive(int ttl) throws java.io.IOException;
// Protected Instance Fields
   protected java.io.FileDescriptor fd;
   protected int localPort;
// Deprecated Protected Methods
#  protected abstract byte getTTL() throws java.io.IOException;
#  protected abstract void setTTL(byte ttl) throws java.io.IOException;
}
```

Passed To DatagramSocket.DatagramSocket()

Returned By DatagramSocketImplFactory.createDatagramSocketImpl()

DatagramSocketImplFactory — Java 1.3

java.net

This interface defines a method that creates DatagramSocketImpl objects. You can register an instance of this factory interface with the static setDatagramSocketImplFactory() method of DatagramSocket. Application-level code never needs to use or implement this interface.

```
public interface DatagramSocketImplFactory {
// Public Instance Methods
   DatagramSocketImpl createDatagramSocketImpl();
}
```

Passed To DatagramSocket.setDatagramSocketImplFactory()

FileNameMap — Java 1.1

java.net

This interface defines a single method that is called to obtain the MIME type of a file based on the name of the file. The fileNameMap field of the URLConnection class refers to an object that implements this interface. The filename-to-file-type map it implements is used by the static URLConnection.guessContentTypeFromName() method.

```
public interface FileNameMap {
// Public Instance Methods
   String getContentTypeFor(String fileName);
}
```

Passed To URLConnection.setFileNameMap()

Returned By URLConnection.getFileNameMap()

HttpRetryException — Java 5.0

java.net — serializable checked

An exception of this type is thrown when an HTTP request needs to be retried (due to a server redirect or authentication request, for example) but the protocol handler cannot automatically retry it because the HttpURLConnection has been placed in streaming mode. (See the setFixedLengthStreamingMode() and setChunkedStreamingMode() methods of HttpURLConnection.) The methods of the exception provide details about how the request should be retried.

Object — Throwable — Exception — IOException — HttpRetryException
Serializable

```
public class HttpRetryException extends java.io.IOException {
// Public Constructors
    public HttpRetryException(String detail, int code);
    public HttpRetryException(String detail, int code, String location);
// Public Instance Methods
    public String getLocation();
    public String getReason();
    public int responseCode();
}
```

HttpURLConnection — Java 1.1

java.net

This class is a specialization of URLConnection. An instance of this class is returned when the openConnection() method is called for a URL object that uses the HTTP protocol. The many constants defined by this class are the status codes returned by HTTP servers. setRequestMethod() specifies what kind of HTTP request is made. The contents of this request must be sent through the OutputStream returned by the getOutputStream() method of the superclass. Once an HTTP request has been sent, getResponseCode() returns the HTTP server's response code as an integer, and getResponseMessage() returns the server's response message. The disconnect() method closes the connection. The static setFollowRedirects() specifies whether URL connections that use the HTTP protocol should automatically follow redirect responses sent by HTTP servers. In order to successfully use this class, you need to understand the details of the HTTP protocol.

Object — URLConnection — HttpURLConnection

```
public abstract class HttpURLConnection extends URLConnection {
// Protected Constructors
    protected HttpURLConnection(URL u);
// Public Constants
    public static final int HTTP_ACCEPTED;                    =202
    public static final int HTTP_BAD_GATEWAY;                 =502
    public static final int HTTP_BAD_METHOD;                  =405
    public static final int HTTP_BAD_REQUEST;                 =400
    public static final int HTTP_CLIENT_TIMEOUT;              =408
    public static final int HTTP_CONFLICT;                    =409
    public static final int HTTP_CREATED;                     =201
    public static final int HTTP_ENTITY_TOO_LARGE;            =413
```

```
   public static final int HTTP_FORBIDDEN;                                    =403
   public static final int HTTP_GATEWAY_TIMEOUT;                              =504
   public static final int HTTP_GONE;                                         =410
   public static final int HTTP_INTERNAL_ERROR;                               =500
   public static final int HTTP_LENGTH_REQUIRED;                              =411
   public static final int HTTP_MOVED_PERM;                                   =301
   public static final int HTTP_MOVED_TEMP;                                   =302
   public static final int HTTP_MULT_CHOICE;                                  =300
   public static final int HTTP_NO_CONTENT;                                   =204
   public static final int HTTP_NOT_ACCEPTABLE;                               =406
   public static final int HTTP_NOT_AUTHORITATIVE;                            =203
   public static final int HTTP_NOT_FOUND;                                    =404
1.3 public static final int HTTP_NOT_IMPLEMENTED;                             =501
   public static final int HTTP_NOT_MODIFIED;                                 =304
   public static final int HTTP_OK;                                           =200
   public static final int HTTP_PARTIAL;                                      =206
   public static final int HTTP_PAYMENT_REQUIRED;                             =402
   public static final int HTTP_PRECON_FAILED;                                =412
   public static final int HTTP_PROXY_AUTH;                                   =407
   public static final int HTTP_REQ_TOO_LONG;                                 =414
   public static final int HTTP_RESET;                                        =205
   public static final int HTTP_SEE_OTHER;                                    =303
   public static final int HTTP_UNAUTHORIZED;                                 =401
   public static final int HTTP_UNAVAILABLE;                                  =503
   public static final int HTTP_UNSUPPORTED_TYPE;                             =415
   public static final int HTTP_USE_PROXY;                                    =305
   public static final int HTTP_VERSION;                                      =505
// Public Class Methods
   public static boolean getFollowRedirects();
   public static void setFollowRedirects(boolean set);
// Public Instance Methods
   public abstract void disconnect();
1.2 public java.io.InputStream getErrorStream();                              constant
1.3 public boolean getInstanceFollowRedirects();
   public String getRequestMethod();
   public int getResponseCode() throws java.io.IOException;
   public String getResponseMessage() throws java.io.IOException;
5.0 public void setChunkedStreamingMode(int chunklen);
5.0 public void setFixedLengthStreamingMode(int contentLength);
1.3 public void setInstanceFollowRedirects(boolean followRedirects);
   public void setRequestMethod(String method) throws ProtocolException;
   public abstract boolean usingProxy();
// Public Methods Overriding URLConnection
1.4 public String getHeaderField(int n);                                      constant
1.3 public long getHeaderFieldDate(String name, long Default);
1.4 public String getHeaderFieldKey(int n);                                   constant
1.2 public java.security.Permission getPermission() throws java.io.IOException;
// Protected Instance Fields
5.0 protected int chunkLength;
5.0 protected int fixedContentLength;
1.3 protected boolean instanceFollowRedirects;
   protected String method;
   protected int responseCode;
   protected String responseMessage;
```

```
// Deprecated Public Fields
#  public static final int HTTP_SERVER_ERROR;                                  =500
}
```

Subclasses javax.net.ssl.HttpsURLConnection

Inet4Address — Java 1.4

java.net — serializable

Inet4Address implements methods defined by its superclass to make them specific to IPv4 (Internet Protocol version 4) internet addresses. Inet4Address does not have a constructor. Create instances with the static methods of InetAddress, which return instances of Inet4Address or Inet6Address as appropriate.

```
Object ─ InetAddress ─ Inet4Address
             ⋮
        Serializable
```

```
public final class Inet4Address extends InetAddress {
// No Constructor
// Public Methods Overriding InetAddress
   public boolean equals(Object obj);
   public byte[] getAddress();
   public String getHostAddress();
   public int hashCode();
   public boolean isAnyLocalAddress();
   public boolean isLinkLocalAddress();
   public boolean isLoopbackAddress();
   public boolean isMCGlobal();
   public boolean isMCLinkLocal();
   public boolean isMCNodeLocal();                                           constant
   public boolean isMCOrgLocal();
   public boolean isMCSiteLocal();
   public boolean isMulticastAddress();
   public boolean isSiteLocalAddress();
}
```

Inet6Address — Java 1.4

java.net — serializable

Inet6Address implements methods defined by its superclass to make them specific to IPv6 (Internet Protocol version 6) internet addresses. See RFC 2373 for complete details about internet addresses of this type. Inet6Address does not have a constructor. Create instances with the static methods of InetAddress, which return instances of Inet4Address or Inet6Address as appropriate. In Java 5.0, you can also use the getByAddress() factory methods of this class directly.

```
Object ─ InetAddress ─ Inet6Address
             ⋮
        Serializable
```

```
public final class Inet6Address extends InetAddress {
// No Constructor
// Public Class Methods
5.0 public static Inet6Address getByAddress(String host, byte[] addr, NetworkInterface nif) throws UnknownHostException;
5.0 public static Inet6Address getByAddress(String host, byte[] addr, int scope_id) throws UnknownHostException;
```

```
// Public Instance Methods
5.0 public NetworkInterface getScopedInterface();
5.0 public int getScopeId();
    public boolean isIPv4CompatibleAddress();
// Public Methods Overriding InetAddress
    public boolean equals(Object obj);
    public byte[] getAddress();
    public String getHostAddress();
    public int hashCode();
    public boolean isAnyLocalAddress();
    public boolean isLinkLocalAddress();
    public boolean isLoopbackAddress();
    public boolean isMCGlobal();
    public boolean isMCLinkLocal();
    public boolean isMCNodeLocal();
    public boolean isMCOrgLocal();
    public boolean isMCSiteLocal();
    public boolean isMulticastAddress();
    public boolean isSiteLocalAddress();
}
```

InetAddress — Java 1.0

java.net — serializable

This class represents an Internet Protocol (IP) address. The class does not have a public constructor but instead supports static factory methods for obtaining InetAddress objects. getLocalHost() returns the InetAddress of the local computer. getByName() returns the InetAddress of a host specified by name. getAllByName() returns an array of InetAddress objects that represents all the available addresses for a host specified by name. getByAddress() returns an InetAddress that represents the IP address defined by the specified array of bytes.

Once you have obtained an InetAddress object, its instance methods provide various sorts of information about it. Two of the most important are getHostName(), which returns the hostname, and getAddress(), which returns the IP address as an array of bytes, with the highest-order byte as the first element of the array. getHostAddress() returns the IP address formatted as a string rather than as an array of bytes. The various methods whose names begin with "is" determine whether the address falls into any of the named categories. The "isMC" methods are all related to multicast addresses.

This class was originally defined in Java 1.0, but many of its methods were added in Java 1.4. Java 1.4 also defined two subclasses, Inet4Address and Inet6Address representing IPv4 and IPv6 (version 4 and version 6) addresses. Java 5.0 adds isReachable() for testing whether the address describes a reachable (and responsive) host.

Object — InetAddress ··· Serializable

```
public class InetAddress implements Serializable {
// No Constructor
// Public Class Methods
    public static InetAddress[] getAllByName(String host) throws UnknownHostException;
1.4 public static InetAddress getByAddress(byte[] addr) throws UnknownHostException;
1.4 public static InetAddress getByAddress(String host, byte[] addr) throws UnknownHostException;
    public static InetAddress getByName(String host) throws UnknownHostException;
    public static InetAddress getLocalHost() throws UnknownHostException;
// Public Instance Methods
    public byte[] getAddress();                                          constant
```

```
1.4 public String getCanonicalHostName();
    public String getHostAddress();                                              constant
    public String getHostName();
1.4 public boolean isAnyLocalAddress();                                          constant
1.4 public boolean isLinkLocalAddress();                                         constant
1.4 public boolean isLoopbackAddress();                                          constant
1.4 public boolean isMCGlobal();                                                 constant
1.4 public boolean isMCLinkLocal();                                              constant
1.4 public boolean isMCNodeLocal();                                              constant
1.4 public boolean isMCOrgLocal();                                               constant
1.4 public boolean isMCSiteLocal();                                              constant
1.1 public boolean isMulticastAddress();                                         constant
5.0 public boolean isReachable(int timeout) throws java.io.IOException;
5.0 public boolean isReachable(NetworkInterface netif, int ttl, int timeout) throws java.io.IOException;
1.4 public boolean isSiteLocalAddress();                                         constant
// Public Methods Overriding Object
    public boolean equals(Object obj);                                           constant
    public int hashCode();                                                       constant
    public String toString();
}
```

Subclasses Inet4Address, Inet6Address

Passed To Too many methods to list.

Returned By Authenticator.getRequestingSite(), DatagramPacket.getAddress(), DatagramSocket.{getInetAddress(), getLocalAddress()}, InetSocketAddress.getAddress(), MulticastSocket.getInterface(), ServerSocket.getInetAddress(), Socket.{getInetAddress(), getLocalAddress()}, SocketImpl.getInetAddress(), URLStreamHandler.getHostAddress(), javax.security.auth.kerberos.KerberosTicket.getClientAddresses()

Type Of SocketImpl.address

InetSocketAddress — Java 1.4

java.net — serializable

InetSocketAddress represents an the combination of an IP (Internet Protocol) address and a port number. The constructors allow you to specify the IP address as an InetAddress or as a hostname, and they also allow you to omit the IP address, in which case the wildcard address is used (this is useful for server sockets).

Object — SocketAddress — InetSocketAddress
Serializable

```
public class InetSocketAddress extends SocketAddress {
// Public Constructors
    public InetSocketAddress(int port);
    public InetSocketAddress(InetAddress addr, int port);
    public InetSocketAddress(String hostname, int port);
// Public Class Methods
5.0 public static InetSocketAddress createUnresolved(String host, int port);
// Public Instance Methods
    public final InetAddress getAddress();
    public final String getHostName();
    public final int getPort();
    public final boolean isUnresolved();
```

```
// Public Methods Overriding Object
   public final boolean equals(Object obj);
   public final int hashCode();
   public String toString();
}
```

JarURLConnection

Java 1.2

java.net

This class is a specialized URLConnection that represents a connection to a jar: URL. A jar: URL is a compound URL that includes the URL of a JAR archive and, optionally, a reference to a file or directory within the JAR archive. The jar: URL syntax uses the ! character to separate the pathname of the JAR archive from the filename within the JAR archive. Note that a jar: URL contains a subprotocol that specifies the protocol that retrieves the JAR file itself. For example:

```
jar:http://my.jar.com/my.jar!/                          // The whole archive
jar:file:/usr/java/lib/my.jar!/com/jar/                 // A directory of the archive
jar:ftp://ftp.jar.com/pub/my.jar!/com/jar/Jar.class     // A file in the archive
```

To obtain a JarURLConnection, define a URL object for a jar: URL, open a connection to it with openConnection(), and cast the returned URLConnection object to a JarURLConnection. The various methods defined by JarURLConnection allow you to read the manifest file of the JAR archive and look up attributes from that manifest for the archive as a whole or for individual entries in the archive. These methods make use of various classes from the java.util.jar package.

Object — URLConnection — JarURLConnection

```
public abstract class JarURLConnection extends URLConnection {
// Protected Constructors
   protected JarURLConnection(URL url) throws MalformedURLException;
// Public Instance Methods
   public java.util.jar.Attributes getAttributes() throws java.io.IOException;
   public java.security.cert.Certificate[] getCertificates() throws java.io.IOException;
   public String getEntryName();
   public java.util.jar.JarEntry getJarEntry() throws java.io.IOException;
   public abstract java.util.jar.JarFile getJarFile() throws java.io.IOException;
   public URL getJarFileURL();
   public java.util.jar.Attributes getMainAttributes() throws java.io.IOException;
   public java.util.jar.Manifest getManifest() throws java.io.IOException;
// Protected Instance Fields
   protected URLConnection jarFileURLConnection;
}
```

MalformedURLException

Java 1.0

java.net — serializable checked

Signals that an unparseable URL specification has been passed to a method.

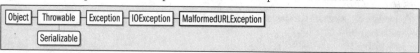

Object — Throwable — Exception — IOException — MalformedURLException
Serializable

```
public class MalformedURLException extends java.io.IOException {
// Public Constructors
```

```
public MalformedURLException();
public MalformedURLException(String msg);
}
```

Thrown By java.io.File.toURL(), JarURLConnection.JarURLConnection(), URI.toURL(), URL.URL()

MulticastSocket **Java 1.1**

java.net

This subclass of DatagramSocket can send and receive multicast UDP packets. It extends DatagramSocket by adding joinGroup() and leaveGroup() methods to join and leave multicast groups. You do not have to join a group to send a packet to a multicast address, but you must join the group to receive packets sent to that address. Note that the use of a MulticastSocket is governed by a security manager.

Use setTimeToLive() to set a time-to-live value for any packets sent through a MulticastSocket. This constrains the number of network hops a packet can take and controls the scope of a multicast. Use setInterface() or setNetworkInterface() to specify the InetAddress or the NetworkInterface that outgoing multicast packets should use: this is useful for servers or other computers that have more than one internet address or network interface. setLoopbackMode() specifies whether a multicast packets sent through this socket should be send back to this socket or not. This method should really be named "setLoopbackModeDisabled()": passing an argument of true requests (but does not require) that the system disable loopback packets.

Object — DatagramSocket — MulticastSocket

```
public class MulticastSocket extends DatagramSocket {
// Public Constructors
    public MulticastSocket() throws java.io.IOException;
1.4 public MulticastSocket(SocketAddress bindaddr) throws java.io.IOException;
    public MulticastSocket(int port) throws java.io.IOException;
// Public Instance Methods
    public InetAddress getInterface() throws SocketException;                                default:Inet4Address
1.4 public boolean getLoopbackMode() throws SocketException;                                 default:false
1.4 public NetworkInterface getNetworkInterface() throws SocketException;
1.2 public int getTimeToLive() throws java.io.IOException;                                   default:1
    public void joinGroup(InetAddress mcastaddr) throws java.io.IOException;
1.4 public void joinGroup(SocketAddress mcastaddr, NetworkInterface netIf) throws java.io.IOException;
    public void leaveGroup(InetAddress mcastaddr) throws java.io.IOException;
1.4 public void leaveGroup(SocketAddress mcastaddr, NetworkInterface netIf) throws java.io.IOException;
    public void setInterface(InetAddress inf) throws SocketException;
1.4 public void setLoopbackMode(boolean disable) throws SocketException;
1.4 public void setNetworkInterface(NetworkInterface netIf) throws SocketException;
1.2 public void setTimeToLive(int ttl) throws java.io.IOException;
// Deprecated Public Methods
#   public byte getTTL() throws java.io.IOException;                                         default:1
#   public void send(DatagramPacket p, byte ttl) throws java.io.IOException;
#   public void setTTL(byte ttl) throws java.io.IOException;
}
```

NetPermission Java 1.2

java.net serializable permission

This class is a java.security.Permission that represents various permissions required for Java's URL-based networking system. See also SocketPermission, which represents permissions to perform lower-level networking operations. A NetPermission is defined solely by its name; no actions list is required or supported. As of Java 1.2, there are three NetPermission targets defined: "setDefaultAuthenticator" is required to call Authenticator.setDefault(); "requestPasswordAuthentication" to call Authenticator.requestPasswordAuthentication(); and "specifyStreamHandler" to explicitly pass a URLStreamHandler object to the URL() constructor. The target "*" is a wildcard that represents all defined NetPermission targets.

System administrators configuring security policies must be familiar with this class and the permissions it represents. System programmers may use this class, but application programmers never need to use it explicitly.

Object — Permission — BasicPermission — NetPermission
Guard, Serializable (Permission); Serializable (BasicPermission)

```
public final class NetPermission extends java.security.BasicPermission {
// Public Constructors
   public NetPermission(String name);
   public NetPermission(String name, String actions);
}
```

NetworkInterface Java 1.4

java.net

Instances of this class represent a network interface on the local machine. getName() and getDisplayName() return the name of the interface, and getInetAddresses() returns a java.util.Enumeration of the internet addresses for the interface. Obtain a NetworkInterface object with one of the static methods defined by this class. getNetworkInterfaces() returns an enumeration of all interfaces for the local host. This class is typically only used in advanced networking applications.

```
public final class NetworkInterface {
// No Constructor
// Public Class Methods
   public static NetworkInterface getByInetAddress(InetAddress addr) throws SocketException;
   public static NetworkInterface getByName(String name) throws SocketException;
   public static java.util.Enumeration<NetworkInterface> getNetworkInterfaces() throws SocketException;
// Public Instance Methods
   public String getDisplayName();
   public java.util.Enumeration<InetAddress> getInetAddresses();
   public String getName();
// Public Methods Overriding Object
   public boolean equals(Object obj);
   public int hashCode();
   public String toString();
}
```

Passed To DatagramSocketImpl.{joinGroup(), leaveGroup()}, Inet6Address.getByAddress(), InetAddress.isReachable(), MulticastSocket.{joinGroup(), leaveGroup(), setNetworkInterface()}

Returned By Inet6Address.getScopedInterface(), MulticastSocket.getNetworkInterface()

NoRouteToHostException — Java 1.1

java.net — serializable checked

This exception signals that a socket cannot be connected to a remote host because the host cannot be contacted. Typically, this means that some link in the network between the local machine and the remote host is down or that the host is behind a firewall.

Object — Throwable — Exception — IOException — SocketException — NoRouteToHostException

Serializable

```
public class NoRouteToHostException extends SocketException {
// Public Constructors
   public NoRouteToHostException();
   public NoRouteToHostException(String msg);
}
```

PasswordAuthentication — Java 1.2

java.net

This simple immutable class encapsulates a username and a password. The password is stored as a character array rather than as a String object so that the caller can erase the contents of the array after use for increased security. Note that the PasswordAuthentication() constructor clones the specified password character array, but getPassword() returns a reference to the object's internal array.

Application programmers defining an Authenticator object for their application need to create and return a PasswordAuthentication object from the getPasswordAuthentication() method of that object. System programmers writing URLStreamHandler implementations or otherwise interacting with a network server that requests password authentication may obtain a PasswordAutentication object representing the user's name and password by calling the static Authenticator.requestPasswordAuthentication() method.

```
public final class PasswordAuthentication {
// Public Constructors
   public PasswordAuthentication(String userName, char[] password);
// Public Instance Methods
   public char[] getPassword();
   public String getUserName();
}
```

Returned By Authenticator.{getPasswordAuthentication(), requestPasswordAuthentication()}

PortUnreachableException — Java 1.4

java.net — serializable checked

An exception of this type may be thrown by a send() or receive() call on a DatagramSocket if the connect() method of that socket has been called, and if the connection attempt resulted in an ICMP "port unreachable" message.

Object — Throwable — Exception — IOException — SocketException — PortUnreachableException

Serializable

```
public class PortUnreachableException extends SocketException {
// Public Constructors
   public PortUnreachableException();
```

```
    public PortUnreachableException(String msg);
}
```

ProtocolException

Java 1.0

java.net

serializable checked

Signals a protocol error in the Socket class.


```
public class ProtocolException extends java.io.IOException {
// Public Constructors
    public ProtocolException();
    public ProtocolException(String host);
}
```

Thrown By HttpURLConnection.setRequestMethod()

Proxy

Java 5.0

java.net

An instance of this class represents a set of proxy server settings: a network address and a proxy server type. The NO_PROXY constant represents a Proxy.Type.DIRECT connection. Proxy objects may be passed to the Socket() constructor or to the URL.openConnection() method to connect through a specific proxy server. The ProxySelector class provides a way to automate the selection of proxy servers based on requested URLs.

```
public class Proxy {
// Public Constructors
    public Proxy(Proxy.Type type, SocketAddress sa);
// Public Constants
    public static final java.net.Proxy NO_PROXY;
// Nested Types
    public enum Type;
// Public Instance Methods
    public SocketAddress address();
    public Proxy.Type type();
// Public Methods Overriding Object
    public final boolean equals(Object obj);
    public final int hashCode();
    public String toString();
}
```

Passed To Socket.Socket(), URL.openConnection(), URLStreamHandler.openConnection()

Proxy.Type

Java 5.0

java.net

serializable comparable enum

The constants of this enumerated type represent a type of proxy server. DIRECT indicates a direct, nonproxied connection. HTTP represents a proxy server that understands high-level protocols such as HTTP or FTP. And SOCKS represents a low-level SOCKS proxy server.

```
public enum Proxy.Type {
// Enumerated Constants
    DIRECT,
    HTTP,
```

```
    SOCKS;
// Public Class Methods
    public static Proxy.Type valueOf(String name);
    public static final Proxy.Type[] values();
}
```

Passed To java.net.Proxy.Proxy()

Returned By java.net.Proxy.type()

ProxySelector Java 5.0

java.net

An implementation of this abstract class can be used to automatically select one or more Proxy objects to use to connect to a specified URL. Install an implementation of this class with the setDefault() method. URLConnection implementations use the installed ProxySelector, if there is one, and call select() to obtain a list of suitable Proxy objects for the connection. If a URLConnection cannot contact the proxy server specified in a Proxy object, it calls the connectFailed() method to notify the ProxySelector object of the failure.

This class is intended to be implemented by advanced users of java.net and is not for casual use.

```
public abstract class ProxySelector {
// Public Constructors
    public ProxySelector();
// Public Class Methods
    public static ProxySelector getDefault();
    public static void setDefault(ProxySelector ps);
// Public Instance Methods
    public abstract void connectFailed(URI uri, SocketAddress sa, java.io.IOException ioe);
    public abstract java.util.List<java.net.Proxy> select(URI uri);
}
```

ResponseCache Java 5.0

java.net

This abstract class defines an API for low-level caching of network resources retrieved through the URL and URLConnection classes. This class is intended for use by URLStreamHandler implementations, not by casual users of the java.net package. Clients that wish to enable local caching should register a ResponseCache implementation with setDefault() and enable caching with URLConnection.setDefaultUseCaches().

The static getDefault() and setDefault() methods query and set a ResponseCache for the system. If there is a ResponseCache installed, protocol handlers should call put() to offer a network resource to the cache. If the cache is interested, it returns a CacheRequest object into which the URLStreamHandler can write its data. A URLStreamHandler that wants to query the cache should call get(). If the ResponseCache holds a cached copy of the requested resource, it returns a CacheResponse from which the URLStreamHandler can read the resource.

```
public abstract class ResponseCache {
// Public Constructors
    public ResponseCache();
// Public Class Methods
    public static ResponseCache getDefault();                              synchronized
    public static void setDefault(ResponseCache responseCache);            synchronized
```

```
// Public Instance Methods
    public abstract CacheResponse get(URI uri, String rqstMethod, java.util.Map<String,java.util.List<String>> rqstHeaders)
        throws java.io.IOException;
    public abstract CacheRequest put(URI uri, URLConnection conn) throws java.io.IOException;
}
```

SecureCacheResponse — Java 5.0

java.net

This subclass of CacheResponse represents a cached network resource that was retreived through a secure protocol such as HTTPS. Its methods return certificates and other details about the secure transfer. See also ResponseCache. This class is not intended for casual users of the java.net package.

Object — CacheResponse — SecureCacheResponse

```
public abstract class SecureCacheResponse extends CacheResponse {
// Public Constructors
    public SecureCacheResponse();
// Public Instance Methods
    public abstract String getCipherSuite();
    public abstract java.util.List<java.security.cert.Certificate> getLocalCertificateChain();
    public abstract java.security.Principal getLocalPrincipal();
    public abstract java.security.Principal getPeerPrincipal() throws javax.net.ssl.SSLPeerUnverifiedException;
    public abstract java.util.List<java.security.cert.Certificate> getServerCertificateChain()
        throws javax.net.ssl.SSLPeerUnverifiedException;
}
```

ServerSocket — Java 1.0

java.net

This class is used by servers to listen for connection requests from clients. Before you can use a ServerSocket, it must be *bound* to the local network address that it is to listen on. All of the ServerSocket() constructors except for the no-argument constructor create a server socket and bind it to the specified local port, optionally specifying a "connection backlog" value: this is the number of client connection attempts that may be queued up before subsequent connection attempts are rejected.

In Java 1.4 and later, the no-argument ServerSocket() constructor allows you to create an unbound socket. Doing this allows you to bind the socket using the bind() method which uses a SocketAddress object rather than a port number. It also allows you to call setReuseAddress(), which is only useful when done before the socket is bound. Call isBound() to determine whether a server socket has been bound. If it has, use getLocalSocketAddress() or getLocalPort() and getInetAddress() to obtain the local address it is bound to.

Once a ServerSocket has been bound, you can call the accept() method to listen on the specified port and block until the client requests a connection on the port. When this happens, accept() accepts the connection, creating and returning a Socket the server can use to communicate with the client. A typical server starts a new thread to handle the communication with the client and calls accept() again to listen for another connection.

ServerSocket defines several methods for setting socket options that affect the socket's behavior. setSoTimeout() specifies the number of milliseconds that accept() should block before throwing an InterruptedIOException. A value of 0 means that it should block forever. setReceiveBufferSize() is an advanced option that suggests the desired size for the internal receive buffer of the Socket objects returned by accept(). This is only a hint, and may be ignored by the system. setReuseAddress() is another advanced option; it specifies that a bind() operation should succeed even if the local bind address is still nominally in use by a socket that is in the process of shutting down.

Like all sockets, a ServerSocket should be closed with the close() method when it is no longer needed. Once closed, a ServerSocket should not be used, except to call the isClosed() method which returns true if it has been closed.

The getChannel() method is a link between this ServerSocket class and the New I/O java.nio.channels.ServerSocketChannel class. It returns the ServerSocketChannel associated with this ServerSocket if there is one. Note, however, that this method always returns null for sockets created with any of the ServerSocket() constructors. If you create a ServerSocketChannel object, and obtain a ServerSocket from it, however, then the getChannel() method provides a way to link back to the parent channel.

```
public class ServerSocket {
// Public Constructors
1.4 public ServerSocket() throws java.io.IOException;
    public ServerSocket(int port) throws java.io.IOException;
    public ServerSocket(int port, int backlog) throws java.io.IOException;
1.1 public ServerSocket(int port, int backlog, InetAddress bindAddr) throws java.io.IOException;
// Public Class Methods
    public static void setSocketFactory(SocketImplFactory fac) throws java.io.IOException;    synchronized
// Public Instance Methods
    public Socket accept() throws java.io.IOException;
1.4 public void bind(SocketAddress endpoint) throws java.io.IOException;
1.4 public void bind(SocketAddress endpoint, int backlog) throws java.io.IOException;
    public void close() throws java.io.IOException;
1.4 public java.nio.channels.ServerSocketChannel getChannel();    constant default:null
    public InetAddress getInetAddress();    default:null
    public int getLocalPort();    default:-1
1.4 public SocketAddress getLocalSocketAddress();    default:null
1.4 public int getReceiveBufferSize() throws SocketException;    synchronized default:43690
1.4 public boolean getReuseAddress() throws SocketException;    default:true
1.1 public int getSoTimeout() throws java.io.IOException;    synchronized default:0
1.4 public boolean isBound();    default:false
1.4 public boolean isClosed();    default:false
5.0 public void setPerformancePreferences(int connectionTime, int latency, int bandwidth);    empty
1.4 public void setReceiveBufferSize(int size) throws SocketException;    synchronized
1.4 public void setReuseAddress(boolean on) throws SocketException;
1.1 public void setSoTimeout(int timeout) throws SocketException;    synchronized
// Public Methods Overriding Object
    public String toString();
// Protected Instance Methods
1.1 protected final void implAccept(Socket s) throws java.io.IOException;
}
```

Subclasses javax.net.ssl.SSLServerSocket

Returned By java.nio.channels.ServerSocketChannel.socket(), javax.net.ServerSocketFactory.createServerSocket()

Socket **Java 1.0**

java.net

This class implements a socket for stream-based communication over the network. See URL for a higher-level interface to networking and DatagramSocket for a lower-level interface.

Before you can use a socket for communication, it must be *bound* to a local address and *connected* to a remote address. Binding and connection are done automatically for you when you call any of the Socket() constructors except the no-argument constructor. These constructors allow you to specify either the name or the InetAddress of the computer to connect to, and also require you to specify the port number to connect to. Two of these constructors also allow you to specify the local InetAddress and port number to bind the socket to. Most applications do not need to specify a local address, and can simply use one of the two-argument versions of Socket() and can allow the constructor to choose an ephemeral local port to bind the socket to.

The no-argument Socket() constructor is different from the others: it creates an unbound and unconnected socket. In Java 1.4 and later, you can explicitly call bind() and connect() to bind and connect the socket. It can be useful to do this when you want to set a socket option (described below) that must be set before binding or connection. bind() uses a SocketAddress object to describe the local address to bind to, and connect() uses a SocketAddress to specify the remote address to connect to. There is also a version of connect() that takes a timeout value in milliseconds: if the connection attempt takes longer than the specified amount of time, connect() throws an IOException. (See ServerSocket for a description of how to write server code that accepts socket connection requests from client code.) Java 5.0 includes a constructor that takes a Proxy object as its sole argument. Like the no-argument constructor, this creates an unbound and unconnected socket. When you attempt to connect it, the connection will be made through the specified Proxy.

Use isBound() and isConnected() to determine whether a Socket is bound and connected. Use getInetAddress() and getPort() to determine the IP address and port number that the socket is connected to. Or, in Java 1.4 and later, use getRemoteSocketAddress() to obtain the remote address as a SocketAddress object. Similarly, use getLocalAddress() and getLocalPort() or use getLocalSocketAddress() to find out what address a socket is bound to.

Once you have a Socket object that is bound and connected, use getInputStream() and getOutputStream() to obtain InputStream and OutputStream objects you can use to communicate with the remote host. You can use these streams just as you would use similar streams for file input and output. When you are done with a Socket, use close() to close it. Once a socket has been closed, it is not possible to call connect() again to reuse it, and you should not call any of its methods except isClosed(). Because networking code can throw many exceptions, it is common practice to close() a socket in the finally clause of a try/catch statement to ensure that the socket always gets closed. Note, however, that the close() method itself can throw an IOException, and you may need to put it in its own try block. In Java 1.3 and later shutdownInput() and shutdownOutput() allow you to close the input and output communication channels individually without closing the entire socket. In Java 1.4 and later, isInputShutdown() and isOutputShutdown() allow you to test for this.

The Socket class defines a number of methods that allow you to set (and query) "socket options" that affect the low-level networking behavior of the socket. setSendBufferSize() and setReceiveBufferSize() provide hints to the underlying networking system about what buffer size is best to use with this socket. setSoTimeout() specifies the number of milliseconds a read() call on the input stream returned by getInputStream() waits for data before throwing an InterruptedIOException. The default value of 0 specifies that the stream blocks indefinitely. setSoLinger() specifies what to do when a socket is closed while there is still data waiting to be transmitted. If lingering is turned on, the close() call blocks for up to the specified number of seconds while attempting to transmit the remaining data. Calling setTcpNoDelay() with an argument of true causes data to be sent through the socket as soon as it is available, instead of waiting for the TCP packet to become more full before sending it. In Java 1.3, use setKeepAlive() to enable or disable the periodic exchange of control messages across an idle socket connection. The keepalive protocol enables a client to determine if its server has crashed without closing the socket and vice versa. In Java 1.4, pass true to setOOBInline() if you want to receive "out of band" data sent to this socket "inline" on the input stream of the socket (by default such data is simply discarded). This can be used to receive bytes sent with sendUrgentData(). Java 1.4 also adds setReuseAddress() which you can use before binding the socket to specify that the socket should be allowed to bind to a port that is still nominally in use by another socket that is in the process of shutting down. setTrafficClass() is also new in Java 1.4; it sets the "traffic class" field for the socket, and requires an understanding of the low-level details of the IP protocol.

The getChannel() method is a link between this Socket class and the New I/O java.nio.channels.SocketChannel class. It returns the SocketChannel associated with this Socket if there is one. Note, however, that this method always returns null for sockets created with any of the Socket() constructors. If you create a SocketChannel object, and obtain a Socket from it, then the getChannel() method provides a way to link back to the parent channel.


```
public class Socket {
// Public Constructors
1.1 public Socket();
5.0 public Socket(java.net.Proxy proxy);
    public Socket(String host, int port) throws UnknownHostException, java.io.IOException;
    public Socket(InetAddress address, int port) throws java.io.IOException;
#   public Socket(String host, int port, boolean stream) throws java.io.IOException;
#   public Socket(InetAddress host, int port, boolean stream) throws java.io.IOException;
1.1 public Socket(String host, int port, InetAddress localAddr, int localPort) throws java.io.IOException;
1.1 public Socket(InetAddress address, int port, InetAddress localAddr, int localPort) throws java.io.IOException;
// Protected Constructors
1.1 protected Socket(SocketImpl impl) throws SocketException;
// Public Class Methods
    public static void setSocketImplFactory(SocketImplFactory fac) throws java.io.IOException;     synchronized
// Public Instance Methods
1.4 public void bind(SocketAddress bindpoint) throws java.io.IOException;
    public void close() throws java.io.IOException;                                                 synchronized
1.4 public void connect(SocketAddress endpoint) throws java.io.IOException;
1.4 public void connect(SocketAddress endpoint, int timeout) throws java.io.IOException;
1.4 public java.nio.channels.SocketChannel getChannel();                                   constant default:null
    public InetAddress getInetAddress();                                                             default:null
    public java.io.InputStream getInputStream() throws java.io.IOException;
1.3 public boolean getKeepAlive() throws SocketException;                                           default:false
1.1 public InetAddress getLocalAddress();                                                    default:Inet4Address
    public int getLocalPort();                                                                         default:-1
1.4 public SocketAddress getLocalSocketAddress();                                                    default:null
1.4 public boolean getOOBInline() throws SocketException;                                           default:false
    public java.io.OutputStream getOutputStream() throws java.io.IOException;
    public int getPort();                                                                               default:0
1.2 public int getReceiveBufferSize() throws SocketException;                       synchronized default:43690
```

```
1.4 public SocketAddress getRemoteSocketAddress();                                   default:null
1.4 public boolean getReuseAddress() throws SocketException;                         default:false
1.2 public int getSendBufferSize() throws SocketException;             synchronized default:8192
1.1 public int getSoLinger() throws SocketException;                                 default:-1
1.1 public int getSoTimeout() throws SocketException;                     synchronized default:0
1.1 public boolean getTcpNoDelay() throws SocketException;                           default:false
1.4 public int getTrafficClass() throws SocketException;                             default:0
1.4 public boolean isBound();                                                        default:false
1.4 public boolean isClosed();                                                       default:false
1.4 public boolean isConnected();                                                    default:false
1.4 public boolean isInputShutdown();                                                default:false
1.4 public boolean isOutputShutdown();                                               default:false
1.4 public void sendUrgentData(int data) throws java.io.IOException;
1.3 public void setKeepAlive(boolean on) throws SocketException;
1.4 public void setOOBInline(boolean on) throws SocketException;
5.0 public void setPerformancePreferences(int connectionTime, int latency, int bandwidth);   empty
1.2 public void setReceiveBufferSize(int size) throws SocketException;               synchronized
1.4 public void setReuseAddress(boolean on) throws SocketException;
1.2 public void setSendBufferSize(int size) throws SocketException;                  synchronized
1.1 public void setSoLinger(boolean on, int linger) throws SocketException;
1.1 public void setSoTimeout(int timeout) throws SocketException;                    synchronized
1.1 public void setTcpNoDelay(boolean on) throws SocketException;
1.4 public void setTrafficClass(int tc) throws SocketException;
1.3 public void shutdownInput() throws java.io.IOException;
1.3 public void shutdownOutput() throws java.io.IOException;
// Public Methods Overriding Object
   public String toString();
}
```

Subclasses javax.net.ssl.SSLSocket

Passed To ServerSocket.implAccept(), javax.net.ssl.SSLSocketFactory.createSocket(), javax.net.ssl.X509KeyManager.{chooseClientAlias(), chooseServerAlias()}

Returned By ServerSocket.accept(), java.nio.channels.SocketChannel.socket(), javax.net.SocketFactory.createSocket(), javax.net.ssl.SSLSocketFactory.createSocket()

SocketAddress — Java 1.4

java.net — serializable

Instances of this abstract class are opaque representations of network socket addresses. The only concrete subclass in the core Java platform is InetSocketAddress which represents an internet address and port number. See InetSocketAddress.

Object — SocketAddress ··· Serializable

```
public abstract class SocketAddress implements Serializable {
// Public Constructors
   public SocketAddress();
}
```

Subclasses InetSocketAddress

Passed To Too many methods to list.

Returned By DatagramPacket.getSocketAddress(), DatagramSocket.{getLocalSocketAddress(), getRemoteSocketAddress()}, java.net.Proxy.address(), ServerSocket.getLocalSocketAddress(), Socket.{getLocalSocketAddress(), getRemoteSocketAddress()}, java.nio.channels.DatagramChannel.receive()

SocketException **Java 1.0**

java.net serializable checked

Signals an exceptional condition while using a socket.

Object — Throwable — Exception — IOException — SocketException
Serializable

```
public class SocketException extends java.io.IOException {
// Public Constructors
   public SocketException();
   public SocketException(String msg);
}
```

Subclasses BindException, ConnectException, NoRouteToHostException, PortUnreachableException

Thrown By Too many methods to list.

SocketImpl **Java 1.0**

java.net

This abstract class defines the methods necessary to implement communication through sockets. Different subclasses of this class may provide different implementations suitable in different environments (such as behind firewalls). These socket implementations are used by the Socket and ServerSocket classes. Normal applications never need to use or subclass this class.

Object — SocketImpl ··· SocketOptions

```
public abstract class SocketImpl implements SocketOptions {
// Public Constructors
   public SocketImpl();
// Public Methods Overriding Object
   public String toString();
// Protected Instance Methods
   protected abstract void accept(SocketImpl s) throws java.io.IOException;
   protected abstract int available() throws java.io.IOException;
   protected abstract void bind(InetAddress host, int port) throws java.io.IOException;
   protected abstract void close() throws java.io.IOException;
   protected abstract void connect(String host, int port) throws java.io.IOException;
   protected abstract void connect(InetAddress address, int port) throws java.io.IOException;
1.4 protected abstract void connect(SocketAddress address, int timeout) throws java.io.IOException;
   protected abstract void create(boolean stream) throws java.io.IOException;
   protected java.io.FileDescriptor getFileDescriptor();
   protected InetAddress getInetAddress();
   protected abstract java.io.InputStream getInputStream() throws java.io.IOException;
   protected int getLocalPort();
   protected abstract java.io.OutputStream getOutputStream() throws java.io.IOException;
   protected int getPort();
   protected abstract void listen(int backlog) throws java.io.IOException;
1.4 protected abstract void sendUrgentData(int data) throws java.io.IOException;
5.0 protected void setPerformancePreferences(int connectionTime, int latency, int bandwidth);     empty
```

```
1.3 protected void shutdownInput() throws java.io.IOException;
1.3 protected void shutdownOutput() throws java.io.IOException;
1.4 protected boolean supportsUrgentData();                    constant
// Protected Instance Fields
    protected InetAddress address;
    protected java.io.FileDescriptor fd;
    protected int localport;
    protected int port;
}
```

Passed To Socket.Socket()

Returned By SocketImplFactory.createSocketImpl()

SocketImplFactory — Java 1.0

java.net

This interface defines a method that creates SocketImpl objects. SocketImplFactory objects may be registered to create SocketImpl objects for the Socket and ServerSocket classes. Normal applications never need to use or implement this interface.

```
public interface SocketImplFactory {
// Public Instance Methods
    SocketImpl createSocketImpl();
}
```

Passed To ServerSocket.setSocketFactory(), Socket.setSocketImplFactory()

SocketOptions — Java 1.2

java.net

This interface defines constants that represent low-level BSD Unix-style socket options and methods that set and query the value of those options. In Java 1.2, SocketImpl and DatagramSocketImpl implement this interface. Any custom socket implementations you define should also provide meaningful implementations for the getOption() and setOption() methods. Your implementation may support options other than those defined here. Only custom socket implementations need to use this interface. All other code can use methods defined by Socket, ServerSocket, DatagramSocket, and MulticastSocket to set specific socket options for those socket types.

```
public interface SocketOptions {
// Public Constants
    public static final int IP_MULTICAST_IF;                   =16
1.4 public static final int IP_MULTICAST_IF2;                  =31
1.4 public static final int IP_MULTICAST_LOOP;                 =18
1.4 public static final int IP_TOS;                            =3
    public static final int SO_BINDADDR;                       =15
1.4 public static final int SO_BROADCAST;                      =32
1.3 public static final int SO_KEEPALIVE;                      =8
    public static final int SO_LINGER;                         =128
1.4 public static final int SO_OOBINLINE;                      =4099
    public static final int SO_RCVBUF;                         =4098
    public static final int SO_REUSEADDR;                      =4
    public static final int SO_SNDBUF;                         =4097
    public static final int SO_TIMEOUT;                        =4102
    public static final int TCP_NODELAY;                       =1
```

```
// Public Instance Methods
    Object getOption(int optID) throws SocketException;
    void setOption(int optID, Object value) throws SocketException;
}
```

Implementations DatagramSocketImpl, SocketImpl

SocketPermission **Java 1.2**

java.net *serializable permission*

This class is a java.security.Permission that governs all networking operations performed with sockets. Like all permissions, a SocketPermission consists of a name, or target, and a list of actions that may be performed on that target. The target of a SocketPermission is the host and, optionally, the port or ports for which permission is being granted or requested. The target consists of a hostname optionally followed by a colon and a port specification. The host may be a DNS domain name, a numerical IP address, or the string "localhost". If you specify a host domain name, you may use * as a wildcard as the leftmost portion of the hostname. The port specification, if present, must be a single port number or a range of port numbers in the form n1-n2. If n1 is omitted, it is taken to be 0, and if n2 is omitted, it is taken to be 65535. If no port is specified, the socket permission applies to all ports of the specified host. Here are some legal SocketPermission targets:

```
java.sun.com:80
*.sun.com:1024-2000
*:1024-
localhost:-1023
```

In addition to a target, each SocketPermission must have a comma-separated list of actions, which specify the operations that may be performed on the specified host(s) and port(s). The available actions are "connect", "accept", "listen", and "resolve". "connect" represents permission to connect to the specified target. "accept" indicates permission to accept connections from the specified target. "listen" represents permission to listen on the specified ports for connection requests. This action is only valid when used for ports on "localhost". Finally, the "resolve" action indicates permission to use the DNS name service to resolve domain names into IP addresses. This action is required for and implied by all other actions.

System administrators configuring security policies must be familiar with this class and understand the risks of granting the various permissions it represents. System programmers writing new low-level networking libraries or connecting to native code that performs networking may need to use this class. Application programmers, however, should never need to use it directly.

Object — Permission — SocketPermission
Guard, Serializable (Permission); Serializable (SocketPermission)

```
public final class SocketPermission extends java.security.Permission implements Serializable {
// Public Constructors
    public SocketPermission(String host, String action);
// Public Methods Overriding Permission
    public boolean equals(Object obj);
    public String getActions();
    public int hashCode();
    public boolean implies(java.security.Permission p);
    public java.security.PermissionCollection newPermissionCollection();
}
```

SocketTimeoutException Java 1.4

java.net serializable checked

Signals that a timeout value was exceeded for a socket read or accept operation. See the setSoTimeout() method of Socket.

Object → Throwable → Exception → IOException → InterruptedIOException → SocketTimeoutException; Throwable ⋯ Serializable

```
public class SocketTimeoutException extends java.io.InterruptedIOException {
// Public Constructors
   public SocketTimeoutException();
   public SocketTimeoutException(String msg);
}
```

UnknownHostException Java 1.0

java.net serializable checked

Signals that the name of a specified host could not be resolved.

Object → Throwable → Exception → IOException → UnknownHostException; Throwable ⋯ Serializable

```
public class UnknownHostException extends java.io.IOException {
// Public Constructors
   public UnknownHostException();
   public UnknownHostException(String host);
}
```

Thrown By Inet6Address.getByAddress(), InetAddress.{getAllByName(), getByAddress(), getByName(), getLocalHost()}, Socket.Socket(), javax.net.SocketFactory.createSocket(), javax.net.ssl.SSLSocket.SSLSocket()

UnknownServiceException Java 1.0

java.net serializable checked

Signals an attempt to use an unsupported service of a network connection.

Object → Throwable → Exception → IOException → UnknownServiceException; Throwable ⋯ Serializable

```
public class UnknownServiceException extends java.io.IOException {
// Public Constructors
   public UnknownServiceException();
   public UnknownServiceException(String msg);
}
```

URI Java 1.4

java.net serializable comparable

The URI class is an immutable representation of a Uniform Resource Identifier or URI. A URI is a generalization of the URLs or Uniform Resource Locators used on the world wide web. The URI supports parsing and textual manipulation of URI strings, but does not have any direct networking capabilities the way that the URL class does. The advantages of the URI class over the URL class are that it provides more general facilities for parsing and manipulating URLs than the URL class, that it can can represent relative URIs which do not include a scheme (or protocol), and that it can manipulate URIs that include unsupported or even unknown schemes.

Obtain a URI with one of the constructors, which allow a URI to be parsed from a single string, or allow the specification of the individual components of a URI. These constructors can throw URISyntaxException, which is a checked exception. When using hard-coded URIs (rather than URIs based on user input) you may prefer to use the static create() method which does not throw any checked exceptions.

Once you have created a URI, object you can use the various get methods to query the various portions of the URI. The getRaw() methods are like the get() methods except that they do not decode hexadecimal escape sequences of the form %xx that appear in the URI. normalize() returns a new URI object that has "." and unnecessary ".." sequences removed from its path component. resolve() interprets its URI (or string) argument relative to this URI and returns the result. relativize() performs the reverse operation. It returns a new URI which represents the same resource as the specified URI argument, but which is relative to this URI. Finally, the toURL() method converts an absolute URI object to the equivalent URL. Since the URI class provides superior textual manipulation capabilities for URLs, it can be useful to use the URI class to resolve relative URLs (for example) and then convert those URI objects to URL objects when they are ready for networking.

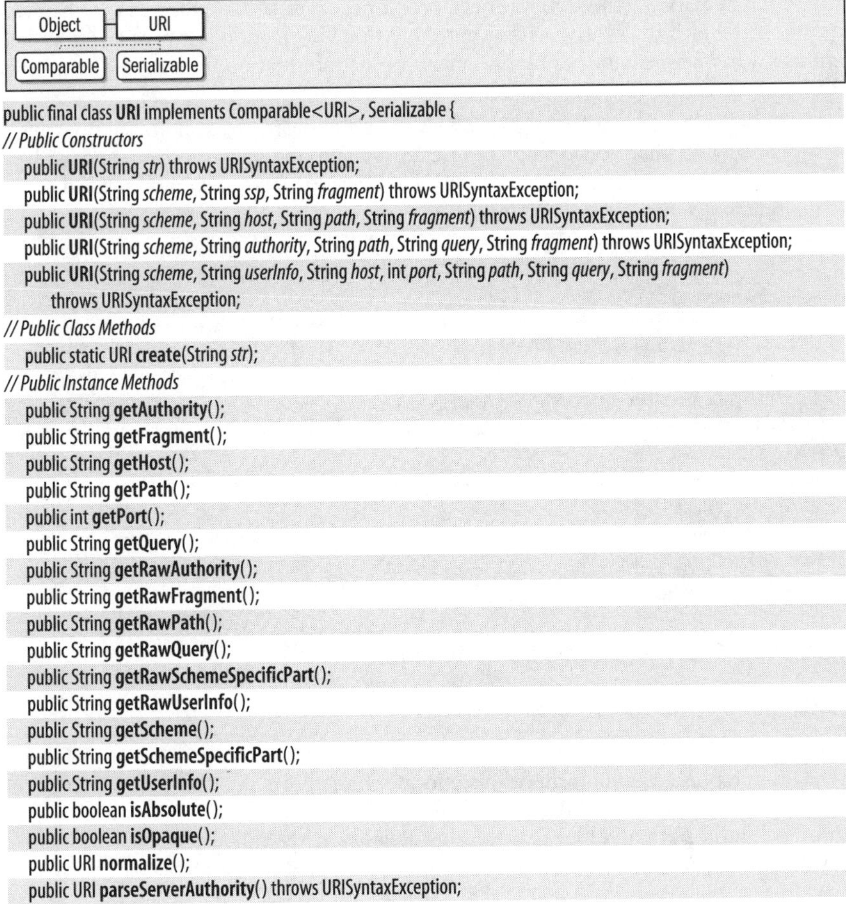


```
public final class URI implements Comparable<URI>, Serializable {
// Public Constructors
   public URI(String str) throws URISyntaxException;
   public URI(String scheme, String ssp, String fragment) throws URISyntaxException;
   public URI(String scheme, String host, String path, String fragment) throws URISyntaxException;
   public URI(String scheme, String authority, String path, String query, String fragment) throws URISyntaxException;
   public URI(String scheme, String userInfo, String host, int port, String path, String query, String fragment)
       throws URISyntaxException;
// Public Class Methods
   public static URI create(String str);
// Public Instance Methods
   public String getAuthority();
   public String getFragment();
   public String getHost();
   public String getPath();
   public int getPort();
   public String getQuery();
   public String getRawAuthority();
   public String getRawFragment();
   public String getRawPath();
   public String getRawQuery();
   public String getRawSchemeSpecificPart();
   public String getRawUserInfo();
   public String getScheme();
   public String getSchemeSpecificPart();
   public String getUserInfo();
   public boolean isAbsolute();
   public boolean isOpaque();
   public URI normalize();
   public URI parseServerAuthority() throws URISyntaxException;
```

```
    public URI relativize(URI uri);
    public URI resolve(URI uri);
    public URI resolve(String str);
    public String toASCIIString();
    public URL toURL() throws MalformedURLException;
// Methods Implementing Comparable
5.0 public int compareTo(URI that);
// Public Methods Overriding Object
    public boolean equals(Object ob);
    public int hashCode();
    public String toString();
}
```

Passed To java.io.File.File(), CookieHandler.{get(), put()}, ProxySelector.{connectFailed(), select()}, ResponseCache.{get(), put()}

Returned By java.io.File.toURI(), URL.toURI()

URISyntaxException **Java 1.4**

java.net **serializable checked**

Signals that a string could not be parsed as a valid URI. getInput() returns the string that could not be parsed. getReason() returns an error message. getIndex() returns the character position at which the syntax error occurred, if that information is available. getMessage() returns a human-readable string that includes the information from each of the other three methods.

This is a checked exception thrown by all the URI() constructors. If you are parsing a hard-coded URI that you do not believe to contain any syntax errors, and wish to avoid the checked exception, you can use the URI.create() factory method instead of the one-argument version of the URI() constructor.

Object — Throwable — Exception — URISyntaxException
Serializable

```
public class URISyntaxException extends Exception {
// Public Constructors
    public URISyntaxException(String input, String reason);
    public URISyntaxException(String input, String reason, int index);
// Public Instance Methods
    public int getIndex();
    public String getInput();
    public String getReason();
// Public Methods Overriding Throwable
    public String getMessage();
}
```

Thrown By URI.{parseServerAuthority(), URI()}, URL.toURI()

URL **Java 1.0**

java.net **serializable**

This class represents a uniform resource locator and allows the data referred to by the URL to be downloaded. A URL can be specified as a single string or with separate protocol, host, port, and file specifications. Relative URLs can also be specified with a String and the URL object to which it is relative. getFile(), getHost(), getProtocol() and related methods return the various portions of the URL specified by a URL object. sameFile() determines whether a URL object refers to the same file as this one. getDefaultPort() returns the default port number for the protocol of the URL object; it may differ from the number returned by getPort(). Use openConnection() to obtain a URLConnection object with which you can download the content of the URL. In Java 5.0, you can explicitly specify a Proxy object through which the connection should be opened. For simple cases, however, the URL class defines shortcut methods that create and invoke methods on a URLConnection internally. getContent() downloads the URL data and parses it into an appropriate Java object (such as a string or image) if an appropriate ContentHandler can be found. In Java 1.3 and later, you can pass an array of Class objects that specify the type of objects that you are willing to accept as the return value of this method. If you wish to parse the URL content yourself, call openStream() to obtain an InputStream from which you can read the data.

Object — URL ··· Serializable

```
public final class URL implements Serializable {
// Public Constructors
    public URL(String spec) throws MalformedURLException;
    public URL(URL context, String spec) throws MalformedURLException;
1.2 public URL(URL context, String spec, URLStreamHandler handler) throws MalformedURLException;
    public URL(String protocol, String host, String file) throws MalformedURLException;
    public URL(String protocol, String host, int port, String file) throws MalformedURLException;
1.2 public URL(String protocol, String host, int port, String file, URLStreamHandler handler) throws MalformedURLException;
// Public Class Methods
    public static void setURLStreamHandlerFactory(URLStreamHandlerFactory fac);
// Public Instance Methods
1.3 public String getAuthority();
    public final Object getContent() throws java.io.IOException;
1.3 public final Object getContent(Class[] classes) throws java.io.IOException;
1.4 public int getDefaultPort();
    public String getFile();
    public String getHost();
1.3 public String getPath();
    public int getPort();
    public String getProtocol();
1.3 public String getQuery();
    public String getRef();
1.3 public String getUserInfo();
    public URLConnection openConnection() throws java.io.IOException;
5.0 public URLConnection openConnection(java.net.Proxy proxy) throws java.io.IOException;
    public final java.io.InputStream openStream() throws java.io.IOException;
    public boolean sameFile(URL other);
    public String toExternalForm();
5.0 public URI toURI() throws URISyntaxException;
// Public Methods Overriding Object
    public boolean equals(Object obj);
    public int hashCode();                                              synchronized
    public String toString();
// Protected Instance Methods
    protected void set(String protocol, String host, int port, String file, String ref);
```

```
1.3 protected void set(String protocol, String host, int port, String authority, String userInfo, String path, String query,
                     String ref);
}
```

Passed To Too many methods to list.

Returned By java.io.File.toURL(), Class.getResource(), ClassLoader.{findResource(), getResource(), getSystemResource()}, Authenticator.getRequestingURL(), JarURLConnection.getJarFileURL(), URI.toURL(), URLClassLoader.{findResource(), getURLs()}, URLConnection.getURL(), java.security.CodeSource.getLocation()

Type Of URLConnection.url

URLClassLoader — Java 1.2

java.net

This ClassLoader provides a useful way to load untrusted Java code from a search path of arbitrary URLs, where each URL represents a directory or JAR file to search. Use the inherited loadClass() method to load a named class with a URLClassLoader. Classes loaded by a URLClassLoader have whatever permissions are granted to their java.security.CodeSource by the system java.security.Policy, plus they have one additional permission that allows the class loader to read any resource files associated with the class. If the class is loaded from a local file: URL that represents a directory, the class is given permission to read all files and directories below that directory. If the class is loaded from a local file: URL that represents a JAR file, the class is given permission to read that JAR file. If the class is loaded from a URL that represents a resource on another host, that class is given permission to connect to and accept network connections from that host. Note, however, that loaded classes are not granted this additional permission if the code that created the URLClassLoader in the first place would not have had that permission.

You can obtain a URLClassLoader by calling one of the URLClassLoader() constructors or one of the static newInstance() methods. If you call newInstance(), the loadClass() method of the returned URLClassLoader performs an additional check to ensure that the caller has permission to access the specified package.

Object — ClassLoader — SecureClassLoader — URLClassLoader

```
public class URLClassLoader extends java.security.SecureClassLoader {
// Public Constructors
   public URLClassLoader(URL[] urls);
   public URLClassLoader(URL[] urls, ClassLoader parent);
   public URLClassLoader(URL[] urls, ClassLoader parent, URLStreamHandlerFactory factory);
// Public Class Methods
   public static URLClassLoader newInstance(URL[] urls);
   public static URLClassLoader newInstance(URL[] urls, ClassLoader parent);
// Public Instance Methods
   public URL[] getURLs();
// Protected Methods Overriding SecureClassLoader
   protected java.security.PermissionCollection getPermissions(java.security.CodeSource codesource);
// Public Methods Overriding ClassLoader
   public URL findResource(String name);
   public java.util.Enumeration<URL> findResources(String name) throws java.io.IOException;
// Protected Methods Overriding ClassLoader
   protected Class<?> findClass(String name) throws ClassNotFoundException;
// Protected Instance Methods
   protected void addURL(URL url);
   protected Package definePackage(String name, java.util.jar.Manifest man, URL url) throws IllegalArgumentException;
}
```

URLConnection Java 1.0

java.net

This abstract class defines a network connection to an object specified by a URL. URL.openConnection() returns a URLConnection instance. You should use a URLConnection object when you want more control over the downloading of data than is available through the simpler URL methods. connect() actually establishes the network connection. Some methods must be called before the connection is made, and others depend on being connected. The methods that depend on being connected call connect() themselves if no connection exists yet, so you never need to call this method explicitly. The getContent() methods are just like the same-named methods of the URL class: they download the data referred to by the URL and parse it into an appropriate type of object (such as a string or an image). In Java 1.3 and later, there is a version of getContent() that allows you to specify the types of parsed objects that you are willing to accept by passing an array of Class objects. If you prefer to parse the URL content yourself instead of calling getContent(), you can call getInputStream() (and getOutputStream() if the URL protocol supports writing) to obtain a stream through which you can read (or write) data from (or to) the resource identified by the URL.

Before a connection is established, you may want to set request fields (such as HTTP request headers) to refine the URL request. Use setRequestProperty() to set a new value for a named header. In Java 1.4 and later, you can use addRequestProperty() to add a new comma-separated item to an existing header. Java 1.4 also added getRequestProperties(), a method that returns the current set of request properties in the form of an unmodifiable Map object that maps request header names to List objects that contain the string value or values for the named header.

Once a connection has been established, there are a number of methods you can call to obtain information from the "response headers" of the URL. getContentLength(), getContentType(), getContentEncoding(), getExpiration(), getDate(), and getLastModified() return the appropriate information about the object referred to by the URL, if that information can be determined (e.g., from HTTP header fields). getHeaderField() returns an HTTP header field specified by name or by number. getHeaderFieldInt() and getHeaderFieldDate() return the value of a named header field parsed as an integer or a date. In Java 1.4 and later, getHeaderFields() returns an unmodifiable Map object that maps response header names to an unmodifiable List that contains the string value or values for the named header.

There are a number of options you can specify to control how the URLConnection behaves. These options are set with the various set() methods and may be queried with corresponding get() methods. The options must be set before the connect() method is called. setDoInput() and setDoOutput() allow you to specify whether you are using the URLConnection for input and/or output (input-only by default). setAllowUserInteraction() specifies whether user interaction (such as typing a password) is allowed during the data transfer (false by default). setDefaultAllowUserInteraction() is a class method that allows you to change the default value for user interaction. setUseCaches() allows you to specify whether a cached version of the URL can be used. You can set this to false to force a URL to be reloaded. setDefaultUseCaches() sets the default value for setUseCaches(). setIfModifiedSince() allows you to specify that a URL should not be fetched unless it has been modified since a specified time (if it is possible to determine its modification date). In Java 5.0 and later, you can specify how long a URLConnection should wait while connecting or reading data with setConnectTimeout() and setReadTimeout().

```
public abstract class URLConnection {
// Protected Constructors
    protected URLConnection(URL url);
// Public Class Methods
    public static boolean getDefaultAllowUserInteraction();
1.1 public static FileNameMap getFileNameMap();                                                    synchronized
    public static String guessContentTypeFromName(String fname);
    public static String guessContentTypeFromStream(java.io.InputStream is) throws java.io.IOException;
    public static void setContentHandlerFactory(ContentHandlerFactory fac);                        synchronized
    public static void setDefaultAllowUserInteraction(boolean defaultallowuserinteraction);
1.1 public static void setFileNameMap(FileNameMap map);
// Public Instance Methods
1.4 public void addRequestProperty(String key, String value);
    public abstract void connect() throws java.io.IOException;
    public boolean getAllowUserInteraction();
5.0 public int getConnectTimeout();
    public Object getContent() throws java.io.IOException;
1.3 public Object getContent(Class[] classes) throws java.io.IOException;
    public String getContentEncoding();
    public int getContentLength();
    public String getContentType();
    public long getDate();
    public boolean getDefaultUseCaches();
    public boolean getDoInput();
    public boolean getDoOutput();
    public long getExpiration();
    public String getHeaderField(int n);                                                           constant
    public String getHeaderField(String name);                                                     constant
    public long getHeaderFieldDate(String name, long Default);
    public int getHeaderFieldInt(String name, int Default);
    public String getHeaderFieldKey(int n);                                                        constant
1.4 public java.util.Map<String,java.util.List<String>> getHeaderFields();
    public long getIfModifiedSince();
    public java.io.InputStream getInputStream() throws java.io.IOException;
    public long getLastModified();
    public java.io.OutputStream getOutputStream() throws java.io.IOException;
1.2 public java.security.Permission getPermission() throws java.io.IOException;
5.0 public int getReadTimeout();
1.4 public java.util.Map<String,java.util.List<String>> getRequestProperties();
    public String getRequestProperty(String key);
    public URL getURL();
    public boolean getUseCaches();
    public void setAllowUserInteraction(boolean allowuserinteraction);
5.0 public void setConnectTimeout(int timeout);
    public void setDefaultUseCaches(boolean defaultusecaches);
    public void setDoInput(boolean doinput);
    public void setDoOutput(boolean dooutput);
    public void setIfModifiedSince(long ifmodifiedsince);
5.0 public void setReadTimeout(int timeout);
    public void setRequestProperty(String key, String value);
    public void setUseCaches(boolean usecaches);
// Public Methods Overriding Object
    public String toString();
```

```
// Protected Instance Fields
   protected boolean allowUserInteraction;
   protected boolean connected;
   protected boolean doInput;
   protected boolean doOutput;
   protected long ifModifiedSince;
   protected URL url;
   protected boolean useCaches;
// Deprecated Public Methods
#  public static String getDefaultRequestProperty(String key);                          constant
#  public static void setDefaultRequestProperty(String key, String value);                  empty
}
```

Subclasses HttpURLConnection, JarURLConnection

Passed To java.net.ContentHandler.getContent(), ResponseCache.put()

Returned By URL.openConnection(), URLStreamHandler.openConnection()

Type Of JarURLConnection.jarFileURLConnection

URLDecoder — Java 1.2

java.net

This class defines a static decode() method that reverses the encoding performed by URLEncoder.encode(). It decodes 8-bit text with the MIME type "x-www-form-urlencoded", which is a standard encoding used by web browsers to submit form contents to CGI scripts and other server-side programs.

```
public class URLDecoder {
// Public Constructors
   public URLDecoder();
// Public Class Methods
1.4 public static String decode(String s, String enc) throws java.io.UnsupportedEncodingException;
// Deprecated Public Methods
#  public static String decode(String s);
}
```

URLEncoder — Java 1.0

java.net

This class defines a single static method that converts a string to its URL-encoded form. That is, spaces are converted to +, and nonalphanumeric characters other than underscore are output as two hexadecimal digits following a percent sign. Note that this technique works only for 8-bit characters. This method canonicalizes a URL specification so that it uses only characters from an extremely portable subset of ASCII that can be correctly handled by computers around the world.

```
public class URLEncoder {
// No Constructor
// Public Class Methods
1.4 public static String encode(String s, String enc) throws java.io.UnsupportedEncodingException;
// Deprecated Public Methods
#  public static String encode(String s);
}
```

13

java.nio and Subpackages

This chapter documents the New I/O API defined by the java.nio package and its subpackages. It covers:

java.nio
: Defines the Buffer class and type-specific subclasses, most notably the ByteBuffer class that is heavily used for I/O in the java.nio.channels class.

java.nio.channels
: Defines the Channel abstraction for high-performance I/O, and implements channels for file and network I/O. Also allows nonblocking I/O with the Selector class.

java.nio.channels.spi
: The service provider interface for channel and selector implementations.

java.nio.charset
: Defines classes for encoding sequences of characters into bytes and decoding sequences of bytes into characters, according to the encoding rules of a named charset.

java.nio.charset.spi
: The service provider interface for charset implementations.

Package java.nio — Java 1.4

This package defines buffer classes that are fundamental to the java.nio API. See Buffer for an overview of buffers, and see ByteBuffer (the most important of the buffer classes) for full documentation of byte buffers. The other type-specific buffer classes are close analogs to ByteBuffer and are documented in terms of that class. See the java.nio.channels package for classes that perform I/O operations on buffers.

Classes

public abstract class **Buffer**;
  public abstract class **ByteBuffer** extends Buffer implements Comparable<ByteBuffer>;
    public abstract class **MappedByteBuffer** extends ByteBuffer;
  public abstract class **CharBuffer** extends Buffer
    implements Comparable<CharBuffer>, Appendable, CharSequence, Readable;
  public abstract class **DoubleBuffer** extends Buffer implements Comparable<DoubleBuffer>;
  public abstract class **FloatBuffer** extends Buffer implements Comparable<FloatBuffer>;
  public abstract class **IntBuffer** extends Buffer implements Comparable<IntBuffer>;
  public abstract class **LongBuffer** extends Buffer implements Comparable<LongBuffer>;
  public abstract class **ShortBuffer** extends Buffer implements Comparable<ShortBuffer>;
public final class **ByteOrder**;

Exceptions

public class **BufferOverflowException** extends RuntimeException;
public class **BufferUnderflowException** extends RuntimeException;
public class **InvalidMarkException** extends IllegalStateException;
public class **ReadOnlyBufferException** extends UnsupportedOperationException;

Buffer — Java 1.4

java.nio

This class is the abstract superclass of all buffer classes in the java.nio API. A *buffer* is a linear (finite) sequence of prmitive values. The java.nio package defines a Buffer subclass for each primitive type in Java except for boolean. Buffer itself defines the common, type-independent features of all buffers. Buffer and its subclasses are intended for use by a single thread at a time, and contain no synchronization code to make them thread-safe.

The purpose of a buffer is to store data, and buffer classes must define methods for reading data from a buffer and writing data into a buffer. Because each Buffer subclass stores data of a different primitive type, however, the get() and put() methods that read and write data must be defined by each of the individual subclasses. See ByteBuffer (the most important subclass) for documentation of these methods; all the other subclasses define similar methods which differ only in the datatype of the values being read or written.

Each buffer has four numbers associated with it:

capacity
: A buffer's capacity is its maximum size; it can hold this many values. The capacity is specified when a buffer is created, and may not be changed; it can be queried with the capacity() method.

limit
: A buffer's limit is its current size, or the index of the first element that does not contain valid data. Data cannot be read from or written into a buffer beyond the limit. When data is being written into a buffer, the limit is usually the same as the capacity. When data is being read from a buffer, the limit may be less than the capacity, and indicates the amount of valid data contained in the buffer. Two limit() methods exist: one to query a buffer's limit, and one to set it.

position
: A buffer's position is the index of the element in the buffer at which data is being read or written. It is used and updated by the relative get() and put() methods defined by ByteBuffer and the other Buffer subclasses. Two position() methods exist to query and set the current position of the buffer. A buffer's position is always

greater than or equal to zero and always less than or equal to the buffer's limit. The remaining() method returns the number of elements between the position and the limit and hasRemaining() returns true if this number is greater than zero.

mark
: A buffer's mark is a temporarily saved position. Call mark() to set the mark to the current position. Call reset() to restore the buffer's position to the marked position.

Buffer defines several methods that perform important operations on a buffer:

clear()
: This method does not actually clear the contents of the buffer, but it sets the position to zero, sets the limit to the capacity, and discards any saved mark. This prepares the buffer to have new data written into it.

flip()
: This method sets the limit to the position, sets the position to zero, and discards any saved mark. After data has been written into a buffer, this method "flips" the purpose of the buffer and prepares it for reading.

rewind()
: This method sets the position to zero and discards any saved mark. It does not alter the limit, and can be used to restart a read operation at the beginning of the buffer.

Buffer objects may be read-only, in which case any attempt to store data in the buffer results in a ReadonlyBufferException. The isReadOnly() method returns true if a buffer is read-only.

```
public abstract class Buffer {
// No Constructor
// Public Instance Methods
   public final int capacity();
   public final Buffer clear(); omu
   public final Buffer flip();
   public final boolean hasRemaining();
   public abstract boolean isReadOnly();
   public final int limit();
   public final Buffer limit(int newLimit);
   public final Buffer mark();
   public final int position();
   public final Buffer position(int newPosition);
   public final int remaining();
   public final Buffer reset();
   public final Buffer rewind();
}
```

Subclasses ByteBuffer, CharBuffer, DoubleBuffer, FloatBuffer, IntBuffer, LongBuffer, ShortBuffer

BufferOverflowException — Java 1.4

java.nio — serializable unchecked

Signals that a relative put() operation on a buffer could not complete because the number of elements to write exceeds the number of remaining elements between the position and its limit.

Object — Throwable — Exception — RuntimeException — BufferOverflowException
Serializable

```
public class BufferOverflowException extends RuntimeException {
// Public Constructors
   public BufferOverflowException();
}
```

BufferUnderflowException Java 1.4

java.nio serializable unchecked

Signals that a relative get() operation on a buffer could not complete because the number of elements to read exceeds the number of remaining elements between the buffer's position and its limit.

Object — Throwable — Exception — RuntimeException — BufferUnderflowException
Serializable

```
public class BufferUnderflowException extends RuntimeException {
// Public Constructors
   public BufferUnderflowException();
}
```

ByteBuffer Java 1.4

java.nio comparable

ByteBuffer holds a sequence of bytes for use in an I/O operation. ByteBuffer is an abstract class, so you cannot instantiate one by calling a constructor. Instead, you must use allocate(), allocateDirect(), or wrap().

allocate() returns a ByteBuffer with the specified capacity. The position of this new buffer is zero, and its limit is set to its capacity. allocateDirect() is like allocate() except that it attempts to allocate a buffer that the underlying operating system can use "directly." Such direct buffers" may be substantially more efficient for low-level I/O operations than normal buffers, but may also have significantly larger allocation costs.

If you have already allocated an array of bytes, you can use the wrap() method to create a ByteBuffer that uses the byte array as its storage. In the one-argument version of wrap() you specify only the array; the buffer capacity and limit are set to the array length, and the position is set to zero. In the other form of wrap() you specify the array, as well as an offset and length that specify a portion of that array. The capacity of the resulting ByteBuffer is again set to the total array length, but its position is set to the specified offset, and its limit is set to the offset plus length.

Once you have obtained a ByteBuffer, you can use the various get() and put() methods to read data from it or write data into it. Several versions of these methods exist to read and write single bytes or arrays of bytes. The single-byte methods come in two forms. Relative get() and put() methods query or set the byte at the current position and then increment the position. The absolute forms of the methods take an additional arguement that specifies the buffer element that is to be read or written and do not affect the buffer position. Two other relative forms of the get() method exist to read as sequence of bytes (starting at and incrementing the buffer's position) into a specified byte array or a specified sub-array. These methods throw a BufferUnderflowException if there are not enough bytes left in the buffer. Two relative forms of the put() method copy bytes from a specified array or sub-array into the buffer (starting at and incrementing the buffer's position). They throw a BufferOverflowException if there is not enough room left in the buffer to hold the bytes. One final form of the put() method transfers all the remaining bytes from one ByteBuffer into this buffer, incrementing the positions of both buffers.

In addition to the get() and put() methods, ByteBuffer also defines another operation that affect the buffer's content. compact() discards any bytes before the buffer position, and copies all bytes between the position and limit to the beginning of the buffer. The position is then set to the new limit, and the limit is set to the capacity. This method compacts a buffer by discarding elements that have already been read, and then prepares the buffer for appending new elements to those that remain.

All Buffer subclasses, such as CharBuffer, IntBuffer and FloatBuffer have analogous methods which are just like these get() and put() methods except that they operate on different data types. ByteBuffer is unique among Buffer subclasses in that it has additional methods for reading and writing values of other primitive types from and into the byte buffer. These methods have names like getInt() and putChar(), and there are methods for all primitive types except byte and boolean. Each method reads or writes a single primitive value. Like the get() and put() methods, they come in relative and absolute variations: the relative methods start with the byte at the buffer's position, and increment the position by the appropriate number of bytes (two bytes for a char, four bytes for an int, eight bytes for a double, etc.). The absolute methods take an buffer index (it is a byte index and is not multiplied by the size of the primitive value) as an argument and do not modify the buffer position. The encoding of multi-byte primitive values into a byte buffer can be done most-significant byte to least-significant byte ("big-endian byte order") or the reverse ("little-endian byte order"). The byte order used by these primitive-type get and put methods is specified by a ByteOrder object. The byte order for a ByteBuffer can be queried and set with the two forms of the order() method. The default byte order for all newly-created ByteBuffer objects is ByteOrder.BIG_ENDIAN.

Other methods that are unique to ByteBuffer() are a set of methods that allow a buffer of bytes to be viewed as a buffer of other primitive types. asCharBuffer(), asIntBuffer() and related methods return "view buffers" that allow the bytes between the position and the limit of the underlying ByteBuffer to be viewed as a sequence of characters, integers, or other primitive values. The returned buffers have position, limit, and mark values that are independent of those of the underlying buffer. The initial position of the returned buffer is zero, and the limit and capacity are the number of bytes between the position and limit of the original buffer divided by the size in bytes of the relevant primitive type (two for char and short, four for int and float, and eight for long and double). Note that the returned view buffer is a view of the bytes between the position and limit of the byte buffer. Subsequent changes to the position and limit of the byte buffer do not change the size of the view buffer, but changes to the bytes themselves to change the values that are viewed through the view buffer. View buffers use the byte ordering that was current in the byte buffer when they were created; subsequent changes to the byte order of the byte buffer do not affect the view buffer. If the underlying byte buffer is direct, then the returned buffer is also direct; this is important because ByteBuffer is the only buffer class with an allocateDirect() method.

ByteBuffer defines some additional methods, which, like the get() and put() methods have analogs in all Buffer subclasses. duplicate() returns a new buffer that shares the content with this one. The two buffers have independent position, limit, and mark values, although the duplicate buffer starts off with the same values as the original buffer. The duplicate buffer is direct if the original is direct and is read-only if the original is read-only. The buffers share content, and content changes made to either buffer are visible through the other. asReadOnlyBuffer() is like duplicate() except that the returned buffer is read-only, and all of its put() and related methods throw a ReadOnlyBufferException. slice() is also somewhat like duplicate() except the returned buffer represents only the content between the current position and limit. The returned buffer has a position of zero, a limit and capacity equal to the number of remaining elements in this buffer, and an undefined mark. isDirect() is a simple method that returns true if a buffer is a direct buffer and false otherwise. If this buffer has a backing array and is not a read-only buffer (e.g., if it was created with the allocate() or wrap() methods) then hasArray() returns true, array() returns the backing array, and arrayOffset() returns the offset within that array of the first element of the buffer. If hasArray() returns false, then array() and arrayOffset() may throw an UnsupportedOperationException or a ReadOnlyBufferException.

Finally, ByteBuffer and other Buffer subclasses override several standard object methods. The equals() methods compares the elements between the position and limit of two buffers and returns true only if there are the same number and have the same value. Note that elements before the position of the buffer are not considered. The hashCode() method is implemented to match the equals() method: the hashcode is based only upon the elements between the position and limit of the buffer. This means that the hashcode changes if either the contents or position of the buffer changes. This means that instances of ByteBuffer and other Buffer subclasses are not usually useful as keys for hashtables or java.util.Map objects. toString() returns a string summary of the buffer, but the precise contents of the string are unspecified. ByteBuffer and each of the other Buffer subclasses also implement the Comparable interface and define a compareTo() method that performs an element-by-element comparison operation on the buffer elements between the position and the limit of the buffer.

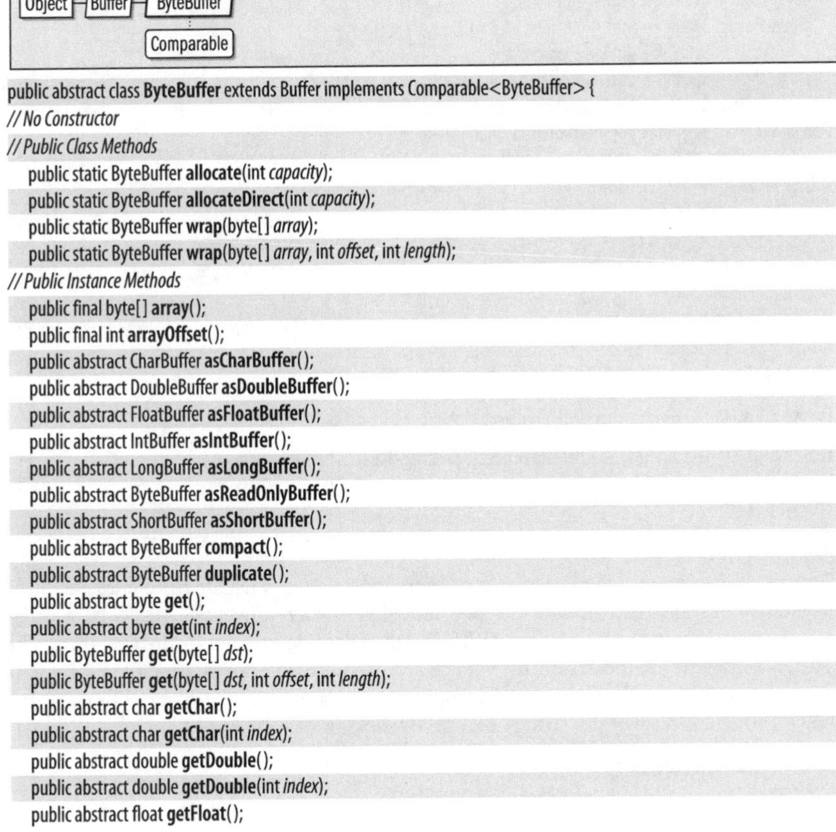


```
public abstract class ByteBuffer extends Buffer implements Comparable<ByteBuffer> {
// No Constructor
// Public Class Methods
   public static ByteBuffer allocate(int capacity);
   public static ByteBuffer allocateDirect(int capacity);
   public static ByteBuffer wrap(byte[] array);
   public static ByteBuffer wrap(byte[] array, int offset, int length);
// Public Instance Methods
   public final byte[] array();
   public final int arrayOffset();
   public abstract CharBuffer asCharBuffer();
   public abstract DoubleBuffer asDoubleBuffer();
   public abstract FloatBuffer asFloatBuffer();
   public abstract IntBuffer asIntBuffer();
   public abstract LongBuffer asLongBuffer();
   public abstract ByteBuffer asReadOnlyBuffer();
   public abstract ShortBuffer asShortBuffer();
   public abstract ByteBuffer compact();
   public abstract ByteBuffer duplicate();
   public abstract byte get();
   public abstract byte get(int index);
   public ByteBuffer get(byte[] dst);
   public ByteBuffer get(byte[] dst, int offset, int length);
   public abstract char getChar();
   public abstract char getChar(int index);
   public abstract double getDouble();
   public abstract double getDouble(int index);
   public abstract float getFloat();
```

```
    public abstract float getFloat(int index);
    public abstract int getInt();
    public abstract int getInt(int index);
    public abstract long getLong();
    public abstract long getLong(int index);
    public abstract short getShort();
    public abstract short getShort(int index);
    public final boolean hasArray();
    public abstract boolean isDirect();
    public final ByteOrder order();
    public final ByteBuffer order(ByteOrder bo);
    public ByteBuffer put(ByteBuffer src);
    public abstract ByteBuffer put(byte b);
    public final ByteBuffer put(byte[] src);
    public abstract ByteBuffer put(int index, byte b);
    public ByteBuffer put(byte[] src, int offset, int length);
    public abstract ByteBuffer putChar(char value);
    public abstract ByteBuffer putChar(int index, char value);
    public abstract ByteBuffer putDouble(double value);
    public abstract ByteBuffer putDouble(int index, double value);
    public abstract ByteBuffer putFloat(float value);
    public abstract ByteBuffer putFloat(int index, float value);
    public abstract ByteBuffer putInt(int value);
    public abstract ByteBuffer putInt(int index, int value);
    public abstract ByteBuffer putLong(long value);
    public abstract ByteBuffer putLong(int index, long value);
    public abstract ByteBuffer putShort(short value);
    public abstract ByteBuffer putShort(int index, short value);
    public abstract ByteBuffer slice();
// Methods Implementing Comparable
5.0 public int compareTo(ByteBuffer that);
// Public Methods Overriding Object
    public boolean equals(Object ob);
    public int hashCode();
    public String toString();
}
```

Subclasses MappedByteBuffer

Passed To Too many methods to list.

Returned By java.nio.charset.Charset.encode(), java.nio.charset.CharsetEncoder.encode()

ByteOrder **Java 1.4**

java.nio

This class is a type-safe enumeration of byte orders, and is used by the ByteBuffer class. The two constant fields define the two legal byte order values: BIG_ENDIAN byte order means most-significant-byte first. LITTLE_ENDIAN means least-significant-byte first. The static nativeOrder() method returns whichever of these two constants represents the native byte order of the underlying operating system and hardware. Finally, the toString() method returns the string "BIG_ENDIAN" or "LITTLE_ENDIAN".

```
public final class ByteOrder {
// No Constructor
// Public Constants
```

```
    public static final ByteOrder BIG_ENDIAN;
    public static final ByteOrder LITTLE_ENDIAN;
// Public Class Methods
    public static ByteOrder nativeOrder();
// Public Methods Overriding Object
    public String toString();
}
```

Passed To ByteBuffer.order()

Returned By ByteBuffer.order(), CharBuffer.order(), DoubleBuffer.order(), FloatBuffer.order(), IntBuffer.order(), LongBuffer.order(), ShortBuffer.order()

CharBuffer Java 1.4

java.nio comparable appendable readable

CharBuffer holds a sequence of Unicode character values for use in an I/O operation. Most of the methods of this class are directly analogous to methods defined by ByteBuffer except that they use char and char[] argument and return values instead of byte and byte[] values. See ByteBuffer for details.

In addition to the ByteBuffer analogs, this class also implements the java.lang.CharSequence interface so that it can be used with java.util.regex regular expression operations or anywhere else a CharSequence is expected. In Java 5.0, CharBuffer adds the append() and read() methods of the java.lang.Appendable and java.lang.Readable interfaces, making CharBuffer objects suitable for use with the Formatter and Scanner classes of java.util.

Note that CharBuffer is an abstract class and does not defined a constructor. There are three ways to obtain a CharBuffer:

- By calling the static allocate() method. Note that there is no allocateDirect() method as there is for ByteBuffer.
- By calling one of the static wrap() methods to create a CharBuffer that uses the specified char array or CharSequence for its content. Note that wrapping a CharSequence results in a read-only CharBuffer.
- By calling the asCharBuffer() method of a ByteBuffer to obtain a CharBuffer "view" of the underlying bytes. If the underlying ByteBuffer is direct, then the CharBuffer view will also be direct.

Note that this class holds a sequence of 16-bit Unicode characters, and does not represent text in any other encoding. Classes in the java.nio.charset package can be used to encode a CharBuffer of Unicode characters into a ByteBuffer, or decode the bytes in a ByteBuffer into a CharBuffer of Unicode text. Java 5.0 supports Unicode supplementary characters that do not fit in 16 bits. See java.lang.Character for details. Note that CharBuffer does not include any utility methods for working with int codepoints or surrogate pairs.

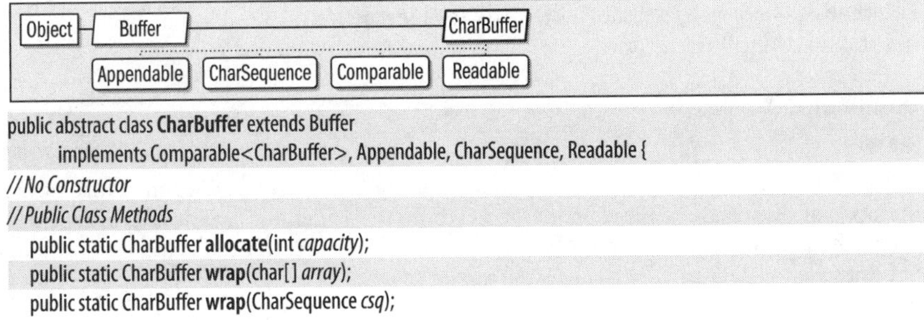


```
public abstract class CharBuffer extends Buffer
        implements Comparable<CharBuffer>, Appendable, CharSequence, Readable {
// No Constructor
// Public Class Methods
    public static CharBuffer allocate(int capacity);
    public static CharBuffer wrap(char[] array);
    public static CharBuffer wrap(CharSequence csq);
```

```
    public static CharBuffer wrap(char[] array, int offset, int length);
    public static CharBuffer wrap(CharSequence csq, int start, int end);
// Public Instance Methods
5.0 public CharBuffer append(char c);
5.0 public CharBuffer append(CharSequence csq);
5.0 public CharBuffer append(CharSequence csq, int start, int end);
    public final char[] array();
    public final int arrayOffset();
    public abstract CharBuffer asReadOnlyBuffer();
    public abstract CharBuffer compact();
    public abstract CharBuffer duplicate();
    public abstract char get();
    public abstract char get(int index);
    public CharBuffer get(char[] dst);
    public CharBuffer get(char[] dst, int offset, int length);
    public final boolean hasArray();
    public abstract boolean isDirect();
    public abstract ByteOrder order();
    public final CharBuffer put(char[] src);
    public CharBuffer put(CharBuffer src);
    public final CharBuffer put(String src);
    public abstract CharBuffer put(char c);
    public abstract CharBuffer put(int index, char c);
    public CharBuffer put(String src, int start, int end);
    public CharBuffer put(char[] src, int offset, int length);
    public abstract CharBuffer slice();
// Methods Implementing CharSequence
    public final char charAt(int index);
    public final int length();
    public abstract CharSequence subSequence(int start, int end);
    public String toString();
// Methods Implementing Comparable
5.0 public int compareTo(CharBuffer that);
// Methods Implementing Readable
5.0 public int read(CharBuffer target) throws java.io.IOException;
// Public Methods Overriding Object
    public boolean equals(Object ob);
    public int hashCode();
}
```

Passed To java.io.Reader.read(), Readable.read(), java.nio.charset.Charset.encode(), java.nio.charset.CharsetDecoder.{decode(), decodeLoop(), flush(), implFlush()}, java.nio.charset.CharsetEncoder.{encode(), encodeLoop()}

Returned By ByteBuffer.asCharBuffer(), java.nio.charset.Charset.decode(), java.nio.charset.CharsetDecoder.decode()

DoubleBuffer

Java 1.4

java.nio

comparable

DoubleBuffer holds a sequence of double values for use in an I/O operation. Most of the methods of this class are directly analogous to methods defined by ByteBuffer except that they use double and double[] argument and return values instead of byte and byte[] values. See ByteBuffer for details.

DoubleBuffer is abstract and has no constructor. Create one by calling the static allocate() or wrap() methods, which are also analogs of ByteBuffer methods. Or, create a "view" DoubleBuffer by calling the asDoubleBuffer() method of an underlying ByteBuffer.

Object — Buffer — DoubleBuffer
Comparable

```
public abstract class DoubleBuffer extends Buffer implements Comparable<DoubleBuffer> {
// No Constructor
// Public Class Methods
    public static DoubleBuffer allocate(int capacity);
    public static DoubleBuffer wrap(double[] array);
    public static DoubleBuffer wrap(double[] array, int offset, int length);
// Public Instance Methods
    public final double[] array();
    public final int arrayOffset();
    public abstract DoubleBuffer asReadOnlyBuffer();
    public abstract DoubleBuffer compact();
    public abstract DoubleBuffer duplicate();
    public abstract double get();
    public abstract double get(int index);
    public DoubleBuffer get(double[] dst);
    public DoubleBuffer get(double[] dst, int offset, int length);
    public final boolean hasArray();
    public abstract boolean isDirect();
    public abstract ByteOrder order();
    public DoubleBuffer put(DoubleBuffer src);
    public abstract DoubleBuffer put(double d);
    public final DoubleBuffer put(double[] src);
    public abstract DoubleBuffer put(int index, double d);
    public DoubleBuffer put(double[] src, int offset, int length);
    public abstract DoubleBuffer slice();
// Methods Implementing Comparable
5.0 public int compareTo(DoubleBuffer that);
// Public Methods Overriding Object
    public boolean equals(Object ob);
    public int hashCode();
    public String toString();
}
```

Returned By ByteBuffer.asDoubleBuffer()

FloatBuffer

Java 1.4

java.nio

comparable

FloatBuffer holds a sequence of float values for use in an I/O operation. Most of the methods of this class are directly analogous to methods defined by ByteBuffer except that they use float and float[] argument and return values instead of byte and byte[] values. See ByteBuffer for details.

FloatBuffer is abstract and has no constructor. Create one by calling the static allocate() or wrap() methods, which are also analogs of ByteBuffer methods. Or, create a "view" FloatBuffer by calling the asFloatBuffer() method of an underlying ByteBuffer.

Object — Buffer — FloatBuffer
Comparable

```
public abstract class FloatBuffer extends Buffer implements Comparable<FloatBuffer> {
// No Constructor
// Public Class Methods
   public static FloatBuffer allocate(int capacity);
   public static FloatBuffer wrap(float[] array);
   public static FloatBuffer wrap(float[] array, int offset, int length);
// Public Instance Methods
   public final float[] array();
   public final int arrayOffset();
   public abstract FloatBuffer asReadOnlyBuffer();
   public abstract FloatBuffer compact();
   public abstract FloatBuffer duplicate();
   public abstract float get();
   public abstract float get(int index);
   public FloatBuffer get(float[] dst);
   public FloatBuffer get(float[] dst, int offset, int length);
   public final boolean hasArray();
   public abstract boolean isDirect();
   public abstract ByteOrder order();
   public FloatBuffer put(FloatBuffer src);
   public abstract FloatBuffer put(float f);
   public final FloatBuffer put(float[] src);
   public abstract FloatBuffer put(int index, float f);
   public FloatBuffer put(float[] src, int offset, int length);
   public abstract FloatBuffer slice();
// Methods Implementing Comparable
5.0 public int compareTo(FloatBuffer that);
// Public Methods Overriding Object
   public boolean equals(Object ob);
   public int hashCode();
   public String toString();
}
```

Returned By ByteBuffer.asFloatBuffer()

IntBuffer **Java 1.4**

java.nio comparable

IntBuffer holds a sequence of int values for use in an I/O operation. Most of the methods of this class are directly analogous to methods defined by ByteBuffer except that they use int and int[] argument and return values instead of byte and byte[] values. See ByteBuffer for details.

IntBuffer is abstract and has no constructor. Create one by calling the static allocate() or wrap() methods, which are also analogs of ByteBuffer methods. Or, create a "view" IntBuffer by calling the asIntBuffer() method of an underlying ByteBuffer.

```
public abstract class IntBuffer extends Buffer implements Comparable<IntBuffer> {
// No Constructor
// Public Class Methods
   public static IntBuffer allocate(int capacity);
   public static IntBuffer wrap(int[] array);
   public static IntBuffer wrap(int[] array, int offset, int length);
// Public Instance Methods
   public final int[] array();
   public final int arrayOffset();
   public abstract IntBuffer asReadOnlyBuffer();
   public abstract IntBuffer compact();
   public abstract IntBuffer duplicate();
   public abstract int get();
   public abstract int get(int index);
   public IntBuffer get(int[] dst);
   public IntBuffer get(int[] dst, int offset, int length);
   public final boolean hasArray();
   public abstract boolean isDirect();
   public abstract ByteOrder order();
   public IntBuffer put(IntBuffer src);
   public abstract IntBuffer put(int i);
   public final IntBuffer put(int[] src);
   public abstract IntBuffer put(int index, int i);
   public IntBuffer put(int[] src, int offset, int length);
   public abstract IntBuffer slice();
// Methods Implementing Comparable
5.0 public int compareTo(IntBuffer that);
// Public Methods Overriding Object
   public boolean equals(Object ob);
   public int hashCode();
   public String toString();
}
```

Returned By ByteBuffer.asIntBuffer()

InvalidMarkException — Java 1.4

java.nio — serializable unchecked

Signals that a buffer's position cannot be reset() because there is no mark defined.

Object — Throwable — Exception — RuntimeException — IllegalStateException — InvalidMarkException
Serializable

```
public class InvalidMarkException extends IllegalStateException {
// Public Constructors
   public InvalidMarkException();
}
```

LongBuffer — Java 1.4

java.nio — comparable

LongBuffer holds a sequence of long values for use in an I/O operation. Most of the methods of this class are directly analogous to methods defined by ByteBuffer except that they use long and long[] argument and return values instead of byte and byte[] values. See ByteBuffer for details.

LongBuffer is abstract and has no constructor. Create one by calling the static allocate() or wrap() methods, which are also analogs of ByteBuffer methods. Or, create a "view" LongBuffer by calling the asLongBuffer() method of an underlying ByteBuffer.

Object — Buffer — LongBuffer
Comparable

```
public abstract class LongBuffer extends Buffer implements Comparable<LongBuffer> {
// No Constructor
// Public Class Methods
   public static LongBuffer allocate(int capacity);
   public static LongBuffer wrap(long[] array);
   public static LongBuffer wrap(long[] array, int offset, int length);
// Public Instance Methods
   public final long[] array();
   public final int arrayOffset();
   public abstract LongBuffer asReadOnlyBuffer();
   public abstract LongBuffer compact();
   public abstract LongBuffer duplicate();
   public abstract long get();
   public abstract long get(int index);
   public LongBuffer get(long[] dst);
   public LongBuffer get(long[] dst, int offset, int length);
   public final boolean hasArray();
   public abstract boolean isDirect();
   public abstract ByteOrder order();
   public LongBuffer put(LongBuffer src);
   public abstract LongBuffer put(long l);
   public final LongBuffer put(long[] src);
   public abstract LongBuffer put(int index, long l);
   public LongBuffer put(long[] src, int offset, int length);
   public abstract LongBuffer slice();
// Methods Implementing Comparable
5.0 public int compareTo(LongBuffer that);
// Public Methods Overriding Object
   public boolean equals(Object ob);
   public int hashCode();
   public String toString();
}
```

Returned By ByteBuffer.asLongBuffer()

MappedByteBuffer **Java 1.4**

java.nio **comparable**

This class is a ByteBuffer that represents a memory-mapped portion of a file. Create a MappedByteBuffer by calling the map() method of a java.nio.channels.FileChannel. All MappedByteBuffer buffers are direct buffers.

isLoaded() returns a hint as to whether the contents of the buffer are currently in primary memory (as opposed to resident on disk). If it returns true, then operations on the buffer will probably execute very quickly. The load() method requests (but does not require) that the operating system load the buffer contents into primary memory. It is not guaranteed to succeed. For buffers that are mapped in read/write mode, the force() method outputs any changes that have been made to the buffer contents to the underlying file. If the file is on a local device, then it is guaranteed to be updated before force() returns. No such guarantees can be made for mapped network files.

Note that the underlying file of a MappedByteBuffer may be shared, which means that the contents of such a buffer can change asynchronously if the contents of the file are modified by another thread or another process (such asynchronous changes to the underlying file may or may not be visible through the buffer; this is a platform-dependent, and should not be relied on). Furthermore, if another thread or process truncates the file, some or all of the elements of the buffer may no longer map to any content of the file. An attempt to read or write such an inaccesible element of the buffer will cause an implementation-defined exception, either immediately or at some later time.

Object — Buffer — ByteBuffer — MappedByteBuffer
Comparable

```
public abstract class MappedByteBuffer extends ByteBuffer {
// No Constructor
// Public Instance Methods
   public final MappedByteBuffer force();
   public final boolean isLoaded();
   public final MappedByteBuffer load();
}
```

Returned By java.nio.channels.FileChannel.map()

ReadOnlyBufferException — Java 1.4

java.nio — serializable unchecked

Signals that a buffer is read-only and that its put() or compact() methods are not allowed to modify the buffer contents.

Object — Throwable — Exception — RuntimeException — UnsupportedOperationException — ReadOnlyBufferException
Serializable

```
public class ReadOnlyBufferException extends UnsupportedOperationException {
// Public Constructors
   public ReadOnlyBufferException();
}
```

ShortBuffer — Java 1.4

java.nio — comparable

ShortBuffer holds a sequence of short values for use in an I/O operation. Most of the methods of this class are directly analogous to methods defined by ByteBuffer except that they use short and short[] argument and return values instead of byte and byte[] values. See ByteBuffer for details.

ShortBuffer is abstract and has no constructor. Create one by calling the static allocate() or wrap() methods, which are also analogs of ByteBuffer methods. Or, create a "view" ShortBuffer by calling the asShortBuffer() method of an underlying ByteBuffer.

Object ─ Buffer ─ ShortBuffer
Comparable

```
public abstract class ShortBuffer extends Buffer implements Comparable<ShortBuffer> {
// No Constructor
// Public Class Methods
   public static ShortBuffer allocate(int capacity);
   public static ShortBuffer wrap(short[] array);
   public static ShortBuffer wrap(short[] array, int offset, int length);
// Public Instance Methods
   public final short[] array();
   public final int arrayOffset();
   public abstract ShortBuffer asReadOnlyBuffer();
   public abstract ShortBuffer compact();
   public abstract ShortBuffer duplicate();
   public abstract short get();
   public abstract short get(int index);
   public ShortBuffer get(short[] dst);
   public ShortBuffer get(short[] dst, int offset, int length);
   public final boolean hasArray();
   public abstract boolean isDirect();
   public abstract ByteOrder order();
   public ShortBuffer put(ShortBuffer src);
   public abstract ShortBuffer put(short s);
   public final ShortBuffer put(short[] src);
   public abstract ShortBuffer put(int index, short s);
   public ShortBuffer put(short[] src, int offset, int length);
   public abstract ShortBuffer slice();
// Methods Implementing Comparable
5.0 public int compareTo(ShortBuffer that);
// Public Methods Overriding Object
   public boolean equals(Object ob);
   public int hashCode();
   public String toString();
}
```

Returned By ByteBuffer.asShortBuffer()

Package java.nio.channels — Java 1.4

This package is at the heart of the NIO API. A *channel* is a communication channel for transferring bytes from or to a java.nio.ByteBuffer. Channels serve a similar purpose to the InputStream and OutputStream classes of the java.io package, but are completely unrelated to those classes, and provide important features not available with the java.io API. The Channels class defines methods that bridge the java.io and java.nio.channels APIs, by returning channels based on streams and streams based on channels.

The Channel interface simply defines methods for testing whether a channel is open and for closing a channel. The other interfaces in the package extend Channel and define read() and write() methods for reading bytes from the channel into one or more byte buffers and for writing bytes from one or more byte buffers to the channel.

The FileChannel class defines an channel-based API for reading and writing from files (and also provides other important file functionality such as file locking and memory mapping that is not available through the java.io package). SocketChannel, ServerSocketChannel, and DatagramChannel are channels for communication over a network, and Pipe defines two inner classes that use the channel abstraction for communication between threads.

The network and pipe channels are all subclasses of the SelectableChannel class, and may be put into nonblocking mode, in which calls to read() and write() return immediately, even if the channel is not ready for reading or writing. nonblocking IO and networking is not possible using the stream abstraction of the java.io and java.net packages, and is perhaps the most important new feature of the java.nio API. The Selector class is crucial to the efficient use of nonblocking channels: it allows a program to register interested in I/O operations on several different channels at once. A call to the select() method of a Selector will block until one of those channels becomes ready for I/O, and will then wake up. This technique is important for writing scalable high-performance network servers. See Selector and SelectionKey for details.

Finally, this package allows for very fine-grained error handling by defining a large number of exception classes, several of which may be thrown by only a single method within the java.nio API.

Interfaces

public interface **ByteChannel** extends ReadableByteChannel, WritableByteChannel;
public interface **Channel** extends java.io.Closeable;
public interface **GatheringByteChannel** extends WritableByteChannel;
public interface **InterruptibleChannel** extends Channel;
public interface **ReadableByteChannel** extends Channel;
public interface **ScatteringByteChannel** extends ReadableByteChannel;
public interface **WritableByteChannel** extends Channel;

Classes

public final class **Channels**;
public abstract class **DatagramChannel** extends java.nio.channels.spi.AbstractSelectableChannel
    implements ByteChannel, GatheringByteChannel, ScatteringByteChannel;
public abstract class **FileChannel** extends java.nio.channels.spi.AbstractInterruptibleChannel
    implements ByteChannel, GatheringByteChannel, ScatteringByteChannel;
public static class **FileChannel.MapMode**;
public abstract class **FileLock**;
public abstract class **Pipe**;
public abstract static class **Pipe.SinkChannel** extends java.nio.channels.spi.AbstractSelectableChannel
    implements GatheringByteChannel, WritableByteChannel;
public abstract static class **Pipe.SourceChannel** extends java.nio.channels.spi.AbstractSelectableChannel
    implements ReadableByteChannel, ScatteringByteChannel;
public abstract class **SelectableChannel** extends java.nio.channels.spi.AbstractInterruptibleChannel
    implements Channel;
public abstract class **SelectionKey**;
public abstract class **Selector**;
public abstract class **ServerSocketChannel** extends java.nio.channels.spi.AbstractSelectableChannel;
public abstract class **SocketChannel** extends java.nio.channels.spi.AbstractSelectableChannel
    implements ByteChannel, GatheringByteChannel, ScatteringByteChannel;

Exceptions

```
public class AlreadyConnectedException extends IllegalStateException;
public class CancelledKeyException extends IllegalStateException;
public class ClosedChannelException extends java.io.IOException;
    public class AsynchronousCloseException extends ClosedChannelException;
        public class ClosedByInterruptException extends AsynchronousCloseException;
public class ClosedSelectorException extends IllegalStateException;
public class ConnectionPendingException extends IllegalStateException;
public class FileLockInterruptionException extends java.io.IOException;
public class IllegalBlockingModeException extends IllegalStateException;
public class IllegalSelectorException extends IllegalArgumentException;
public class NoConnectionPendingException extends IllegalStateException;
public class NonReadableChannelException extends IllegalStateException;
public class NonWritableChannelException extends IllegalStateException;
public class NotYetBoundException extends IllegalStateException;
public class NotYetConnectedException extends IllegalStateException;
public class OverlappingFileLockException extends IllegalStateException;
public class UnresolvedAddressException extends IllegalArgumentException;
public class UnsupportedAddressTypeException extends IllegalArgumentException;
```

AlreadyConnectedException — Java 1.4

java.nio.channels — serializable unchecked

Thrown by a call to connect() on a SocketChannel that is already connected.

Object — Throwable — Exception — RuntimeException — IllegalStateException — AlreadyConnectedException
Serializable

```
public class AlreadyConnectedException extends IllegalStateException {
// Public Constructors
    public AlreadyConnectedException();
}
```

AsynchronousCloseException — Java 1.4

java.nio.channels — serializable checked

Signals the termination of a blocked I/O operation because another thread closed the channel asynchronously. See also ClosedByInterruptException.

Object — Throwable — Exception — IOException — ClosedChannelException — AsynchronousCloseException
Serializable

```
public class AsynchronousCloseException extends ClosedChannelException {
// Public Constructors
    public AsynchronousCloseException();
}
```

Subclasses ClosedByInterruptException

Thrown By java.nio.channels.spi.AbstractInterruptibleChannel.end()

ByteChannel — Java 1.4

java.nio.channels — closeable

This interface extends ReadableByteChannel and WritableByteChannel but adds no methods or constants of its own. It exists simply as a convience that to unify the two interfaces.

```
public interface ByteChannel extends ReadableByteChannelWritableByteChannel {
}
```

Implementations DatagramChannel, FileChannel, SocketChannel

CancelledKeyException — Java 1.4

java.nio.channels — serializable unchecked

Signals an attempt to use a SelectionKey whose cancel() method has previously been called.

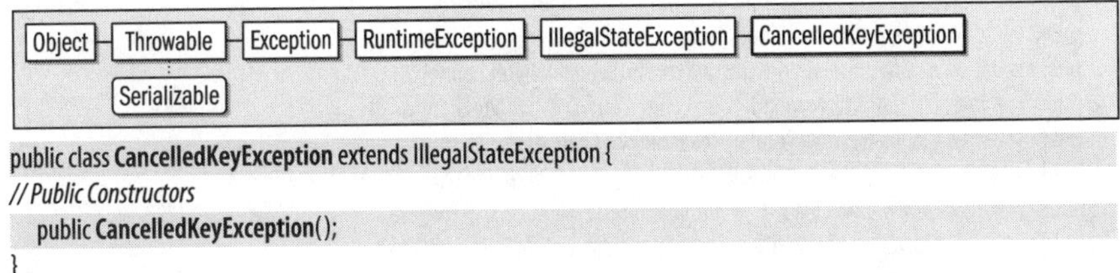


```
public class CancelledKeyException extends IllegalStateException {
// Public Constructors
   public CancelledKeyException();
}
```

Channel — Java 1.4

java.nio.channels — closeable

This interface defines a communication channel for input and output. The Channel interface is a high-level generic interface which is extended by more specific interfaces, such as ReadableByteChannel and WritableByteChannel. Channel defines only two methods: isOpen() determines whether a channel is open, and close() closes a channel. Channels are open when they are first created. Once closed, a channel remains closed forever, and no further I/O operations may take place through it.

Many channel implementations are interruptible and asynchonously closeable, and implement the InterruptibleChannel interface to advertise this fact. See InterruptibleChannel for details.

```
public interface Channel extends java.io.Closeable {
// Public Instance Methods
   void close() throws java.io.IOException;
   boolean isOpen();
}
```

Implementations InterruptibleChannel, ReadableByteChannel, SelectableChannel, WritableByteChannel, java.nio.channels.spi.AbstractInterruptibleChannel

Returned By System.inheritedChannel(), java.nio.channels.spi.SelectorProvider.inheritedChannel()

Channels

Java 1.4

java.nio.channels

This class defines static methods that provide a bridge between the byte stream and character stream classes of the java.io package and the channel classes of java.nio.channels. Channels is never intended to be instantiated: it serves solely as a placeholder for static methods. These methods create byte channels based on java.io byte streams, and create java.io byte streams based on byte channels. Note that the channel objects returned by the newChannel() methods may not implement InterruptibleChannel, and so may not be asynchonously closeable and interruptible like other channel classes in this package. Channels also defines methods to create character streams (java.io.Reader and java.io.Writer) based on the combination of a byte channel and a character encoding. The encoding may be specified by charset name, or with a CharsetDecoder or CharsetEncoder (see java.nio.charset).

```
public final class Channels {
// No Constructor
// Public Class Methods
   public static ReadableByteChannel newChannel(java.io.InputStream in);
   public static WritableByteChannel newChannel(java.io.OutputStream out);
   public static java.io.InputStream newInputStream(ReadableByteChannel ch);
   public static java.io.OutputStream newOutputStream(WritableByteChannel ch);
   public static java.io.Reader newReader(ReadableByteChannel ch, String csName);
   public static java.io.Reader newReader(ReadableByteChannel ch, java.nio.charset.CharsetDecoder dec,
                                          int minBufferCap);
   public static java.io.Writer newWriter(WritableByteChannel ch, String csName);
   public static java.io.Writer newWriter(WritableByteChannel ch, java.nio.charset.CharsetEncoder enc, int minBufferCap);
}
```

ClosedByInterruptException

Java 1.4

java.nio.channels — serializable checked

An exception of this type is thrown by a thread blocked in an I/O operation on a channel when another thread calls its interrupt() method. This exception is a subclass of AsynchronousCloseException and the channel will be closed as a side-effect of the thread interruption.

Throwable — Exception — IOException — ClosedChannelException — AsynchronousCloseException — ClosedByInterruptException

Serializable

```
public class ClosedByInterruptException extends AsynchronousCloseException {
// Public Constructors
   public ClosedByInterruptException();
}
```

ClosedChannelException

Java 1.4

java.nio.channels — serializable checked

Signals an attempt to perform I/O on a channel that has been closed with the close() method, or that is closed for a particular type of I/O operation (a SocketChannel, for example, may have its read and write halves shut down independently.) Channels may be closed asynchronously, and threads blocking to complete an I/O operation will throw a subclass of this exception type. See AsynchronousCloseException and ClosedByInterruptException.

Object ─ Throwable ─ Exception ─ IOException ─ ClosedChannelException
Serializable

```
public class ClosedChannelException extends java.io.IOException {
// Public Constructors
   public ClosedChannelException();
}
```

Subclasses AsynchronousCloseException

Thrown By SelectableChannel.register(), java.nio.channels.spi.AbstractSelectableChannel.register()

ClosedSelectorException Java 1.4

java.nio.channels serializable unchecked

Signals an attempt to use a Selector object whose close() method has been called.

Object ─ Throwable ─ Exception ─ RuntimeException ─ IllegalStateException ─ ClosedSelectorException
Serializable

```
public class ClosedSelectorException extends IllegalStateException {
// Public Constructors
   public ClosedSelectorException();
}
```

ConnectionPendingException Java 1.4

java.nio.channels serializable unchecked

Signals a call to the connect() method of a SocketChannel when there is already a connection pending for that channel. See SocketChannel.isConnectionPending().

Object ─ Throwable ─ Exception ─ RuntimeException ─ IllegalStateException ─ ConnectionPendingException
Serializable

```
public class ConnectionPendingException extends IllegalStateException {
// Public Constructors
   public ConnectionPendingException();
}
```

DatagramChannel Java 1.4

java.nio.channels closeable

This class implements a communication channel based on network datagrams. Obtain a DatagramChannel by calling the static open() method. Call socket() to obtain the java.net.DatagramSocket object on which the channel is based if you need to set any socket options to control low-level networking details.

The send() method sends the remaining bytes of the specified ByteBuffer to the host and port specified in the java.net.SocketAddress in the form of a datagram. receive() does the opposite: it receives a datagram, stores its content into the specified buffer (discarding any bytes that do not fit) and then returns a SocketAddress that specifies the sender of the datagram (or returns null if the channel was in nonblocking mode and no datagram was waiting).

The send() and receive() methods typically perform security checks on each invocation to see if the application has permissions to communicate with the remote host. If your application will use a DatagramChannel to exchange datagrams with a single remote host and port, use the connect() method to connect to a specified SocketAddress. The connect() method performs the required security checks once and allows future communication with the specified address without the overhead. Once a DatagramChannel is connected, you can use the standard read() and write() methods defined by the ReadableByteChannel, WritableByteChannel, GatheringByteChannel and ScatteringByteChannel interfaces. Like the receive() method, the read() methods silently discard any received bytes that do not fit in the specified ByteBuffer. The read() and write() methods throw a NotYetConnected exception if connect() has not been called.

DatagramChannel is a SelectableChannel; its validOps() method specifies that read and write operations may be selected. DatagramChannel objects are thread-safe. Read and write operations may proceed concurrently, but the class ensures that only one thread may read and one thread write at a time.

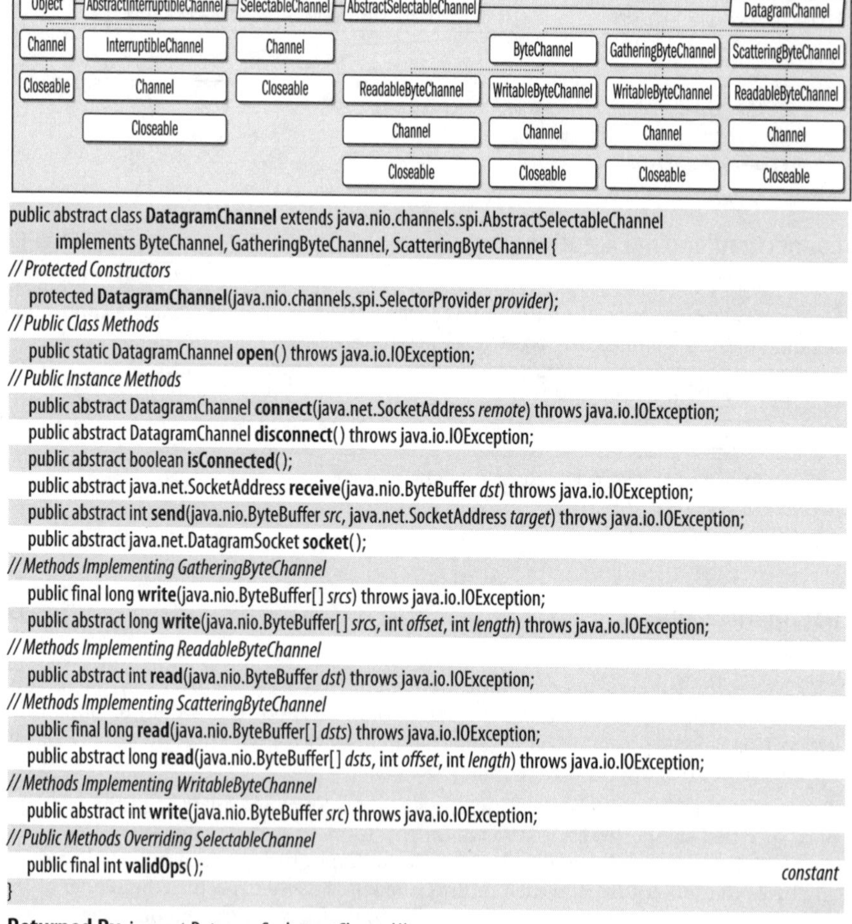


```
public abstract class DatagramChannel extends java.nio.channels.spi.AbstractSelectableChannel
        implements ByteChannel, GatheringByteChannel, ScatteringByteChannel {
// Protected Constructors
    protected DatagramChannel(java.nio.channels.spi.SelectorProvider provider);
// Public Class Methods
    public static DatagramChannel open() throws java.io.IOException;
// Public Instance Methods
    public abstract DatagramChannel connect(java.net.SocketAddress remote) throws java.io.IOException;
    public abstract DatagramChannel disconnect() throws java.io.IOException;
    public abstract boolean isConnected();
    public abstract java.net.SocketAddress receive(java.nio.ByteBuffer dst) throws java.io.IOException;
    public abstract int send(java.nio.ByteBuffer src, java.net.SocketAddress target) throws java.io.IOException;
    public abstract java.net.DatagramSocket socket();
// Methods Implementing GatheringByteChannel
    public final long write(java.nio.ByteBuffer[] srcs) throws java.io.IOException;
    public abstract long write(java.nio.ByteBuffer[] srcs, int offset, int length) throws java.io.IOException;
// Methods Implementing ReadableByteChannel
    public abstract int read(java.nio.ByteBuffer dst) throws java.io.IOException;
// Methods Implementing ScatteringByteChannel
    public final long read(java.nio.ByteBuffer[] dsts) throws java.io.IOException;
    public abstract long read(java.nio.ByteBuffer[] dsts, int offset, int length) throws java.io.IOException;
// Methods Implementing WritableByteChannel
    public abstract int write(java.nio.ByteBuffer src) throws java.io.IOException;
// Public Methods Overriding SelectableChannel
    public final int validOps();                                                          constant
}
```

Returned By java.net.DatagramSocket.getChannel(), java.nio.channels.spi.SelectorProvider.openDatagramChannel()

FileChannel Java 1.4

java.nio.channels closeable

This class implements a communication channel for efficiently reading and and writing files. It implements the standard read() and write() methods of the ReadableByteChannel, WritableByteChannel, GatheringByteChannel and ScatteringByteChannel methods. In addition, however, FileChannel provides methods for: random-access to the file, efficient transfer of bytes between the file and another channel, file locking, memory mapping, querying and setting the file size and forcing buffered updates to be written to disk. These important features are described in further detail below. Note that since file operations do not typically block for extended periods the way network operations can, FileChannel does not subclass SelectableChannel (it is the only channel class that does not) and cannot be used with Selector objects.

FileChannel has no public constructor and no static factory methods. To obtain a FileChannel, first create a FileInputStream, FileOutputStream, or RandomAccessFile object (see the java.io package) and then call the getChannel() method of that object. If you use a FileInputStream, the resulting channel will allow reading but not writing, and if you use a FileOutputStream, the channel will allow writing but not reading. If you obtain a FileChannel from a RandomAccessFile, then the channel will allow reading, or both reading and writing, depending on the *mode* argument to the RandomAccessFile constructor.

A FileChannel has a *position* or file pointer that specifies the current point in the file. You can set or query the file position with two methods, both of which share the name position(). The position of a FileChannel and of the stream or RandomAccessFile from which it is derived are always the same: changing the position of the channel changes the position of the stream, and vice versa. The initial position of a FileChannel is the position of the stream or RandomAccessFile when the getChannel() method was called. If you create a FileChannel from a FileOutputStream that was opened in append mode, then any output to the channel always occurs at the end of the file, and sets the file position to the end end of the file.

Once you have a FileChannel object, you can use the standard read() and write() methods defined by the various channel interfaces. In addition to updating the buffer position as they read and write bytes, these methods also update the file position to or from which those bytes are written or read. These standard read() methods return the number of bytes actually read, and return -1 if there are no bytes left in the file to read. The write() methods enlarge the file if they write past the current end-of-file.

FileChannel also defines position-independent read() and write() methods that take a file position as an explicit argument: they read or write starting at that position of the file, and although they update the position of the ByteBuffer, they do not update the file position of the FileChannel. If the specified position is past the end-of-file, the read() method does not read any bytes and returns -1, and the write() method enlarges the file, leaving any bytes between the old end-of-file and the specified position undefined.

It is common to read bytes from a FileChannel and then immediately write them out to some other channel (such as a SocketChannel: think of a web server, for example), or to read bytes from a channel and immediately write them to a FileChannel (consider an FTP client). FileChannel provides two methods, transferTo() and transferFrom() that do this very efficiently, without the need for a temporary ByteBuffer. transferTo() reads up to the specified number of bytes starting at the specified location from this FileChannel and writes them to the specified channel. It does not alter the file position of the FileChannel, and it returns the number of bytes actually transferred. transferFrom() does the reverse: it reads up to the specified number of available bytes from the specified channel, and writes them to this FileChannel at the specified location, without altering the file position of this channel, and returns the actual number of bytes transferred. For both methods, if the destination or source channel is a FileChannel itself, then the file position of that channel is updated.

The size() method returns the size (in bytes) of the underlying file. truncate() reduces the file size to the specified value, discarding any file content that exceeds that size. If the specified size is greater than or equal to the current file size, the file is unchanged. If the file position is greater than the new size of the file, it the position is changed to the new size.

Use the force() method to force any buffered modifications to the file to be written to the underlying storage device. If the file resides on a local device, (as opposed to a network filesystem, for example) then force() guarantees that any changes to the file made since the channel was opened or since a previous call to force() will have been written to the device. The argument to this method is a hint as to whether file meta-data (such as last modification time) is to be forced out in addition to file content. If this argument is true, the system will force content and meta-data. If false, the system may omit updates to meta-data. Note that force() is only required to output change made directly through the FileChannel. File updates made through a MappedByteBuffer returned by the map() method (described below)y should be forced out with the force() method of MappedByteBuffer.

FileChannel defines two blocking lock() and two nonblocking tryLock() methods for locking a file or a region of a file against concurrent access by another program. (These methods are not suitable for preventing concurrent access to a file by two threads within the same Java virtual machine.) The no-argument versions of these methods attempt to acquire an exclusive lock on the entire file. The three-argument versions of the methods attempt to lock a specified region of the file, and may acquire shared locks in addition to exclusive locks. (A shared lock prevents any other process from acquiring an exclusive lock, but does not prevent other shared locks: typically, you acquire a shared lock when reading a file that should not be concurrently updated, and acquire an exclusive lock before writing file content to ensure that no one else is trying to read it at the same time.) The tryLock() methods return a FileLock object, or null if there was already a conflicting lock on the file. The lock() methods block if there is already a conflicting lock and never return null. See FileLock for more information about locks. The FileChannel file locking mechanism uses whatever locking capability is provided by the underlying platform. Some operating systems enforce file locking: if one process holds a lock, other processes are prevented by the operating system from accessing the file. Other operating systems merely prevent other processes from acquiring a conflicting lock: in this case, successful file locking requires the cooperation of all processes. Some operating systems do not support shared locks: on these systems an exclusive lock is returned even when a shared lock is requested.

The map() method returns a MappedByteBuffer that represents the specified region of the file. File contents can be read directly from the buffer, and (if the mapping is done in read/write mode) bytes placed in the buffer will be written to the file. The mapping represented by a MappedByteBuffer remains valid until the buffer is garbage collected; the buffer continues to function even if the FileChannel from which it was created is closed. File mappings can be done in three different modes which specify whether bytes can be written into the buffer and what happens when this is done. See FileChannel.MapMode for a description of the three modes.

The map() method relies on the memory-mapping facilities provided by the underlying operating system. This means that a number of details may vary from implementation to implementation. In particular, it is not specified whether changes to the underlying file made after the call to map() are visible through the MappedByteBuffer. Using a mapped file is typically more efficient that an unmapped file only when the file is a large one.

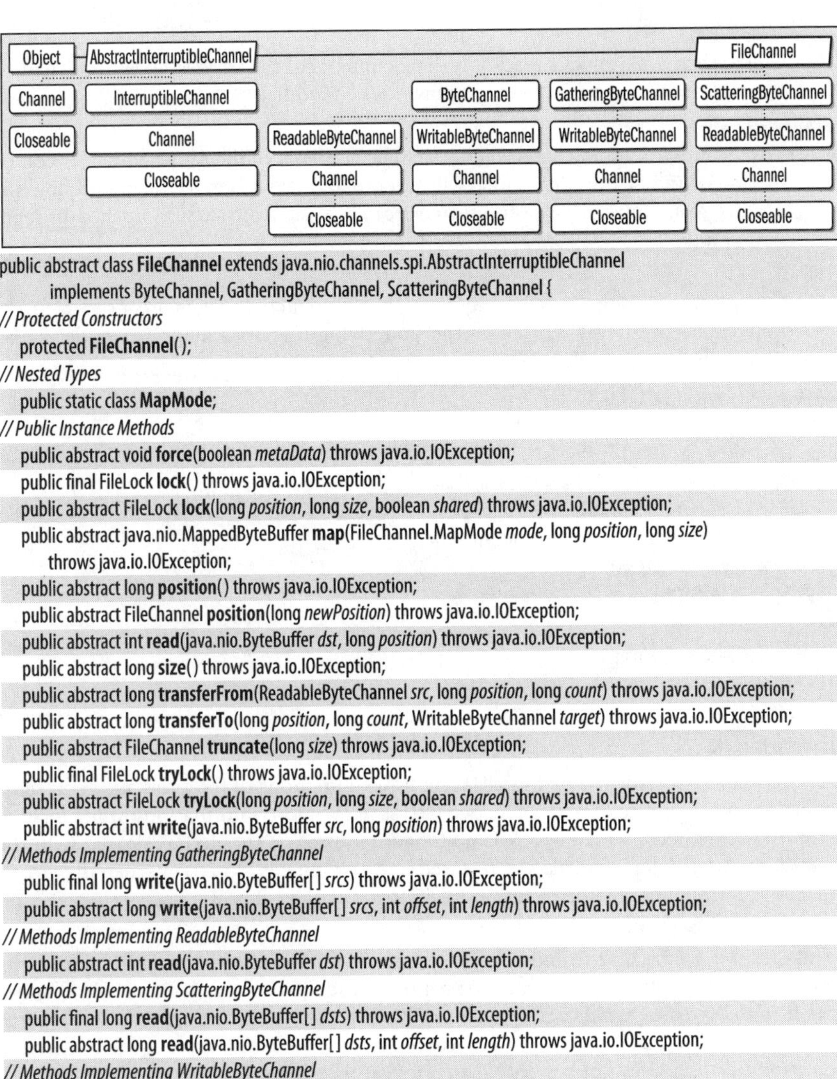


```
public abstract class FileChannel extends java.nio.channels.spi.AbstractInterruptibleChannel
        implements ByteChannel, GatheringByteChannel, ScatteringByteChannel {
// Protected Constructors
    protected FileChannel();
// Nested Types
    public static class MapMode;
// Public Instance Methods
    public abstract void force(boolean metaData) throws java.io.IOException;
    public final FileLock lock() throws java.io.IOException;
    public abstract FileLock lock(long position, long size, boolean shared) throws java.io.IOException;
    public abstract java.nio.MappedByteBuffer map(FileChannel.MapMode mode, long position, long size)
        throws java.io.IOException;
    public abstract long position() throws java.io.IOException;
    public abstract FileChannel position(long newPosition) throws java.io.IOException;
    public abstract int read(java.nio.ByteBuffer dst, long position) throws java.io.IOException;
    public abstract long size() throws java.io.IOException;
    public abstract long transferFrom(ReadableByteChannel src, long position, long count) throws java.io.IOException;
    public abstract long transferTo(long position, long count, WritableByteChannel target) throws java.io.IOException;
    public abstract FileChannel truncate(long size) throws java.io.IOException;
    public final FileLock tryLock() throws java.io.IOException;
    public abstract FileLock tryLock(long position, long size, boolean shared) throws java.io.IOException;
    public abstract int write(java.nio.ByteBuffer src, long position) throws java.io.IOException;
// Methods Implementing GatheringByteChannel
    public final long write(java.nio.ByteBuffer[] srcs) throws java.io.IOException;
    public abstract long write(java.nio.ByteBuffer[] srcs, int offset, int length) throws java.io.IOException;
// Methods Implementing ReadableByteChannel
    public abstract int read(java.nio.ByteBuffer dst) throws java.io.IOException;
// Methods Implementing ScatteringByteChannel
    public final long read(java.nio.ByteBuffer[] dsts) throws java.io.IOException;
    public abstract long read(java.nio.ByteBuffer[] dsts, int offset, int length) throws java.io.IOException;
// Methods Implementing WritableByteChannel
    public abstract int write(java.nio.ByteBuffer src) throws java.io.IOException;
}
```

Passed To FileLock.FileLock()

Returned By java.io.FileInputStream.getChannel(), java.io.FileOutputStream.getChannel(), java.io.RandomAccessFile.getChannel(), FileLock.channel()

FileChannel.MapMode **Java 1.4**

java.nio.channels

This class defines three constants that define the legal values of the *mode* argument to the map() method of the FileChannel class. The constants and their meanings are the following:

READ_ONLY
: The memory mapping is read-only. The contents of the MappedByteBuffer returned by the map() method may be read but may not be modified.

READ_WRITE
: The memory mapping is bidirectional: The contents of the returned buffer can be modified, and any modifications will (eventually) be written to the underlying file. The FileChannel must have been created from a java.io.RandomAccessFile opened in read/write mode.

PRIVATE
: The returned buffer may be modified, but any such changes are private to the buffer, and are never written to the underlying file. This mapping mode is also known as "copy-on-write."

```
public static class FileChannel.MapMode {
// No Constructor
// Public Constants
   public static final FileChannel.MapMode PRIVATE;
   public static final FileChannel.MapMode READ_ONLY;
   public static final FileChannel.MapMode READ_WRITE;
// Public Methods Overriding Object
   public String toString();
}
```

Passed To FileChannel.map()

FileLock **Java 1.4**

java.nio.channels

A FileLock object is returned by the lock() and tryLock() methods of FileChannel and represents a lock on a file or a region of a file. See FileChannel for more information on file locking with those methods. When a lock is no longer required, it should be released with the release() method. A lock will also be released if the channel is closed, or when the virtual machine terminates. isValid() returns true if the lock has not yet been released, and returns false if it has been released.

The channel(), position(), size() and isShared() methods return basic information about the lock: the FileChannel that was locked, the region of the file that was locked, and whether the lock is shared or exclusive. If the entire file is locked, then the size() method returns a value (Long.MAX_VALUE) that is much greater than the actual file size. If the underlying operating system does not support shared locks, then isShared() may return false even if a shared lock was requested. overlaps() is a convenience method that returns true if the position and size of this lock overlap the specified position and size.

```
public abstract class FileLock {
// Protected Constructors
   protected FileLock(FileChannel channel, long position, long size, boolean shared);
// Public Instance Methods
   public final FileChannel channel();
   public final boolean isShared();
   public abstract boolean isValid();
   public final boolean overlaps(long position, long size);
   public final long position();
   public abstract void release() throws java.io.IOException;
   public final long size();
```

```
// Public Methods Overriding Object
   public final String toString();
}
```

Returned By FileChannel.{lock(), tryLock()}

FileLockInterruptionException — Java 1.4

java.nio.channels — serializable checked

Signals that the interrupt() method of a thread blocked waiting to acquire a file lock was called. See FileChannel.lock().

Object ─ Throwable ─ Exception ─ IOException ─ FileLockInterruptionException
Serializable

```
public class FileLockInterruptionException extends java.io.IOException {
// Public Constructors
   public FileLockInterruptionException();
}
```

GatheringByteChannel — Java 1.4

java.nio.channels — closeable

This interface extends WritableByteChannel and adds two additional write() methods that can "gather" bytes from one or more buffers and write them out to the channel. These methods are passed an array of ByteBuffer objects, and, optionally, an offset and length that define the relevant sub-array to be used. The write() method attempts to write all the remaining bytes from all the specified buffers (in the order in which they appear in the buffer array) to the channel. The return value of the method is the number of bytes actually written. See WritableByteChannel for a discussion of exceptions and thread-safety that apply to these write() methods as well.

Closeable ··· Channel ··· WritableByteChannel ··· GatheringByteChannel

```
public interface GatheringByteChannel extends WritableByteChannel {
// Public Instance Methods
   long write(java.nio.ByteBuffer[] srcs) throws java.io.IOException;
   long write(java.nio.ByteBuffer[] srcs, int offset, int length) throws java.io.IOException;
}
```

Implementations DatagramChannel, FileChannel, Pipe.SinkChannel, SocketChannel

IllegalBlockingModeException — Java 1.4

java.nio.channels — serializable unchecked

Signals an attempt to use a channel in the wrong blocking mode. An exception of this type is thrown by SelectableChannel.register() if the channel is not in nonblocking mode.

Object ─ Throwable ─ Exception ─ RuntimeException ─ IllegalStateException ─ IllegalBlockingModeException
Serializable

```
public class IllegalBlockingModeException extends IllegalStateException {
// Public Constructors
   public IllegalBlockingModeException();
}
```

IllegalSelectorException Java 1.4

java.nio.channels serializable unchecked

Signals an attempt to register a SelectableChannel with a Selector when the channel and the selector were not created by the same java.nio.channels.spi.SelectorProvider.

Object → Throwable → Exception → RuntimeException → IllegalArgumentException → IllegalSelectorException
(Throwable implements Serializable)

```
public class IllegalSelectorException extends IllegalArgumentException {
// Public Constructors
   public IllegalSelectorException();
}
```

InterruptibleChannel Java 1.4

java.nio.channels closeable

Channels that implement this marker interface have two important properties that are relevant to multithreaded programs: they are *asynchonously closeable* and *interruptible*. When the close() method of an InterruptibleChannel is called, any other thread that is blocked waiting for an I/O operation to complete on that channel will stop blocking and receive an AsynchronousCloseException. Furthermore, if a thread is blocked waiting for an I/O operation to complete on an InterruptibleChannel, then another thread may call the interrupt() method of the blocked thread. This causes the interrupt status of the blocked thread to be set and causes the thread to wake up and receive an ClosedByInterruptException (a subclass of AsynchronousCloseException). As the name of this interrupt implies, the channel that the thread was blocked on is closed as a side-effect of the thread interruption. There is no way to interrupt a blocked thread without closing the channel upon which it is blocked. This ability to interrupt a blocked thread is particularly noteworthy because it has never worked reliably with the older java.io API.

All the concrete channel implementations that are part of this package implement InterruptibleChannel. Note, however, that methods such as Channels.newChannel() may return channel objects that are not interruptible. You can use the instanceof to determine whether an unknown channel object implements this interface.

Closeable ··· Channel ··· InterruptibleChannel

```
public interface InterruptibleChannel extends Channel {
// Public Instance Methods
   void close() throws java.io.IOException;
}
```

Implementations java.nio.channels.spi.AbstractInterruptibleChannel

NoConnectionPendingException Java 1.4

java.nio.channels serializable unchecked

Signals that SocketChannel.finishConnect() was called without a previous call to SocketChannel.connect().

Object → Throwable → Exception → RuntimeException → IllegalStateException → NoConnectionPendingException
(Throwable implements Serializable)

```
public class NoConnectionPendingException extends IllegalStateException {
// Public Constructors
    public NoConnectionPendingException();
}
```

NonReadableChannelException — Java 1.4

java.nio.channels — serializable unchecked

Signals a call to the read() method of a readable channel that is not open for reading, such as a FileChannel created from a FileOutputStream.

Object — Throwable — Exception — RuntimeException — IllegalStateException — NonReadableChannelException
Throwable : Serializable

```
public class NonReadableChannelException extends IllegalStateException {
// Public Constructors
    public NonReadableChannelException();
}
```

NonWritableChannelException — Java 1.4

java.nio.channels — serializable unchecked

Signal a call to a write() method of a writable channel that is not open for writing, such as a FileChannel created from a FileInputStream.

Object — Throwable — Exception — RuntimeException — IllegalStateException — NonWritableChannelException
Throwable : Serializable

```
public class NonWritableChannelException extends IllegalStateException {
// Public Constructors
    public NonWritableChannelException();
}
```

NotYetBoundException — Java 1.4

java.nio.channels — serializable unchecked

Signals a call to ServerSocketChannel.accept() before the underlying server socket has been bound to a local port. Call socket().bind() to bind the java.net.ServerSocket that underlies the ServerSocketChannel.

Object — Throwable — Exception — RuntimeException — IllegalStateException — NotYetBoundException
Throwable : Serializable

```
public class NotYetBoundException extends IllegalStateException {
// Public Constructors
    public NotYetBoundException();
}
```

NotYetConnectedException — Java 1.4

java.nio.channels — serializable unchecked

Signals an attempt to read() or write() on a SocketChannel that is not yet connected to a remote host. See SocketChannel.connect().

Object ─ Throwable ─ Exception ─ RuntimeException ─ IllegalStateException ─ NotYetConnectedException
Serializable

```
public class NotYetConnectedException extends IllegalStateException {
// Public Constructors
   public NotYetConnectedException();
}
```

OverlappingFileLockException   Java 1.4

java.nio.channels   serializable unchecked

This exception is thrown by the lock() and tryLock() methods of FileChannel if the requested lock region overlaps a file lock that is already held by some thread in this JVM, or if there is already a thread in this JVM waiting to lock an overlapping region of the same file. The FileChannel file locking mechanism is designed to lock files against concurrent access by two separate processes. Two threads within the same JVM should not attempt to acquire a lock on overlapping regions of the same file, and any attempt to do so causes an exception of this type to be thrown.

Object ─ Throwable ─ Exception ─ RuntimeException ─ IllegalStateException ─ OverlappingFileLockException
Serializable

```
public class OverlappingFileLockException extends IllegalStateException {
// Public Constructors
   public OverlappingFileLockException();
}
```

Pipe   Java 1.4

java.nio.channels

A pipe is an abstraction that allows the one-way transfer of bytes from one thread to another. A pipe has a "read end" and a "write end" which are represented by objects that implement the ReadableByteChannel and WritableByteChannel interfaces. Create a new pipe with the static Pipe.open() method. Call the sink() method to obtain the Pipe.SinkChannel object that represents the write end of the pipe, and call the source() method to obtain the Pipe.SourceChannel object that represents the read end of the pipe.

Programmers familiar with Unix-style pipes may find the names and return values of the sink() and source() methods confusing. A Unix pipe is an interprocess communication mechanism that is tied to two specific processes, one of which is a source of bytes and one of which is a destination, or sink, for those bytes. With this conceptual model of a pipe, you would expect the source to obtain the channel it writes to with the source() method and the sink to obtain the channel it reads from with the sink() method.

This Pipe class is not a Unix-style pipe, however. While it can be used for communication between two threads, the ends of the pipe are not tied to those threads, and there need not be a single source thread and a single sink thread. Therefore, in the Pipe API it is the pipe itself that serves as the source and the sink of bytes: bytes are read from the source end of the pipe, and are written to the sink end.

```
public abstract class Pipe {
// Protected Constructors
   protected Pipe();
// Nested Types
```

```
    public abstract static class SinkChannel extends java.nio.channels.spi.AbstractSelectableChannel
        implements GatheringByteChannel, WritableByteChannel;
    public abstract static class SourceChannel extends java.nio.channels.spi.AbstractSelectableChannel
        implements ReadableByteChannel, ScatteringByteChannel;
// Public Class Methods
    public static Pipe open() throws java.io.IOException;
// Public Instance Methods
    public abstract Pipe.SinkChannel sink();
    public abstract Pipe.SourceChannel source();
}
```

Returned By java.nio.channels.spi.SelectorProvider.openPipe()

Pipe.SinkChannel — Java 1.4

java.nio.channels — closeable

This public inner class is represents the write end of a pipe. Bytes written to a Pipe.SinkChannel become available on the corresponding Pipe.SourceChannel of the pipe. Obtain a Pipe.SinkChannel by creating a Pipe object with Pipe.open() and then calling the sink() method of that object. See also the containing Pipe class.

Pipe.SinkChannel implements WritableByteChannel and GatheringByteChannel and defines the write() methods of those interfaces. This class subclasses SelectableChannel, so that it can be used with a Selector. It overrides the abstract validOps() method of SelectableChannel to return SelectionKey.OP_WRITE, but defines no new methods of its own.

```
public abstract static class Pipe.SinkChannel extends java.nio.channels.spi.AbstractSelectableChannel
        implements GatheringByteChannel, WritableByteChannel {
// Protected Constructors
    protected SinkChannel(java.nio.channels.spi.SelectorProvider provider);
// Public Methods Overriding SelectableChannel
    public final int validOps();                                              constant
}
```

Returned By Pipe.sink()

Pipe.SourceChannel — Java 1.4

java.nio.channels — closeable

This public inner class is represents the read end of a pipe. Bytes that are written to the corresponding write end of the pipe (see Pipe.SinkChannel) become available for reading through this channel. Obtain a Pipe.SourceChannel by creating a Pipe object with Pipe.open() and then calling the source() method of that object. See also the containing Pipe class.

Pipe.SourceChannel implements ReadableByteChannel and ScatteringByteChannel and defines the read() methods of those interfaces. This class subclasses SelectableChannel, so that it can be used with a Selector. It overrides the abstract validOps() method of SelectableChannel to return SelectionKey.OP_READ, but defines no new methods of its own.

```
public abstract static class Pipe.SourceChannel extends java.nio.channels.spi.AbstractSelectableChannel
        implements ReadableByteChannel, ScatteringByteChannel {
// Protected Constructors
    protected SourceChannel(java.nio.channels.spi.SelectorProvider provider);
// Public Methods Overriding SelectableChannel
    public final int validOps();                                              constant
}
```

Returned By Pipe.source()

ReadableByteChannel

Java 1.4

java.nio.channels

closeable

This subinterface of Channel defines a single key read() method which reads bytes from the channel and stores them in the specified ByteBuffer, updating the buffer position as it does so. read() attempts to read as many bytes as will fit in the specified buffer, (see Buffer.remaining()) but may read fewer than this. If the channel is a nonblocking channel, for example, the read() will return immediately, even if there are no bytes available to be read. read() returns the number of bytes actually read (which may be zero in the nonblocking case), or returns -1 if there are no more bytes to be read in the channel (if, for example, the end of a file has been reached, or the other end of a socket has been closed.)

read() is declared to throw an IOException. More specifically, it may throw a ClosedChannelException if the channel is closed. If the channel is closed asynchronously, or if a blocked thread is interrupted, the read() method may terminate with an AsynchronousCloseException or a ClosedByInterruptException. read() may also throw an unchecked NonReadableChannelException if it is called on a channel that was not opened or configured to allow reading.

ReadableByteChannel implementations are required to be thread-safe: only one thread may perform a read operation on a channel at a time. If a read operation is in progress, then any call to read() will block until the in-progress operation completes. Some channel implementations may allow read and write operations to proceed concurrently, but none will allow two read operations to proceed at the same time.

Closeable ··· Channel ··· ReadableByteChannel

```
public interface ReadableByteChannel extends Channel {
// Public Instance Methods
    int read(java.nio.ByteBuffer dst) throws java.io.IOException;
}
```

Implementations ByteChannel, Pipe.SourceChannel, ScatteringByteChannel

Passed To Channels.{newInputStream(), newReader()}, FileChannel.transferFrom(), java.util.Scanner.Scanner()

Returned By Channels.newChannel()

ScatteringByteChannel

Java 1.4

java.nio.channels

closeable

This interface extends ReadableByteChannel and adds two additional read() methods that read bytes for a channel and "scatter" them to an array (or subarray) of buffers. These methods are passed an array of ByteBuffer objects, and, optionally, an offset and length that define the region of the array to be used. The read() method attempts to read enough bytes from the channel to fill each of the specified buffers in the order in which they appear in the buffer array (the "scattering" process is actually much more orderly and linear than the name implies). The return value of the method is the number of bytes actually read, which may be different than the sum of the remaining bytes in the buffers. See ReadableByteChannel for a discussion of exceptions and thread-safety that apply to these read() methods as well.

Closeable ··· Channel ··· ReadableByteChannel ··· ScatteringByteChannel

```
public interface ScatteringByteChannel extends ReadableByteChannel {
// Public Instance Methods
```

```
    long read(java.nio.ByteBuffer[] dsts) throws java.io.IOException;
    long read(java.nio.ByteBuffer[] dsts, int offset, int length) throws java.io.IOException;
}
```

Implementations DatagramChannel, FileChannel, Pipe.SourceChannel, SocketChannel

SelectableChannel — Java 1.4

java.nio.channels — closeable

This abstract class defines the API for channels that can be used with a Selector object to allow a thread to block while waiting for activity on any of a group of channels. All channel classes in the java.nio.channels package except for FileChannel are subclasses of SelectableChannel.

A selectable channel may only be registered with a Selector if it is nonblocking, so this class defines the configureBlocking() method. Pass false to this method to put a channel into nonblocking mode, or pass true to make calls to its read() and/or write() methods block. Use isBlocking() to determine the current blocking mode of a selectable channel.

Register a SelectableChannel with a Selector by calling the register() method of the channel (not of the selector). There are two versions of this method: both take a Selector object and a bitmask that specifies the set of channel operations that are to be "selected" on that channel. (see SelectionKey for the constants that can be OR-ed together to form this bitmask). Both methods return a SelectionKey object that represents the registration of the channel with the selector. One version of the register() method also takes an arbitrary object argument which serves as an "attachment" to the SelectionKey and allows you to associate arbitrary data with it. The validOps() method returns a bitmask that specifies the set of operations that a particular channel object allows to be selected. The bitmask passed to register() may only contain bits that are set in this validOps() value.

Note that SelectableChannel does not define a deregister() method. Instead, to remove a channel from the set of channels being monitored by a Selector, you must call the cancel() method of the SelectionKey returned by register().

Call isRegistered() to determine whether a SelectableChannel is registered with any Selector. (Note that a single channel may be registered with more than one Selector.) If you did not keep track of the SelectionKey returned by a call to register(), you can query it with the keyFor() method.

See Selector and SelectionKey for further details on multiplexing selectable channels.

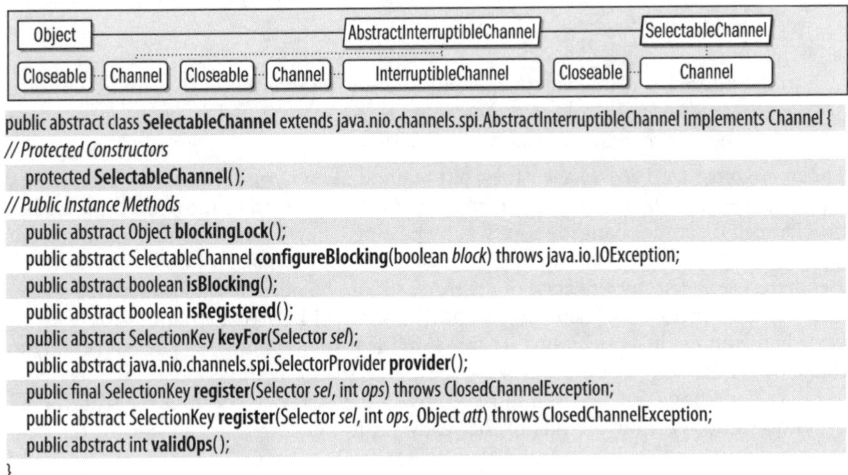


```
public abstract class SelectableChannel extends java.nio.channels.spi.AbstractInterruptibleChannel implements Channel {
// Protected Constructors
    protected SelectableChannel();
// Public Instance Methods
    public abstract Object blockingLock();
    public abstract SelectableChannel configureBlocking(boolean block) throws java.io.IOException;
    public abstract boolean isBlocking();
    public abstract boolean isRegistered();
    public abstract SelectionKey keyFor(Selector sel);
    public abstract java.nio.channels.spi.SelectorProvider provider();
    public final SelectionKey register(Selector sel, int ops) throws ClosedChannelException;
    public abstract SelectionKey register(Selector sel, int ops, Object att) throws ClosedChannelException;
    public abstract int validOps();
}
```

Subclasses java.nio.channels.spi.AbstractSelectableChannel

Returned By SelectionKey.channel(), java.nio.channels.spi.AbstractSelectableChannel.configureBlocking()

SelectionKey **Java 1.4**

java.nio.channels

A SelectionKey represents the registration of a SelectableChannel with a Selector, and serves to identify a selected channel and the operations that are ready to be performed on that channel. After a call to the select() method of a selector, the selectedKeys() method of the selector returns a Set of SelectionKey objects to identify the channel or channels that are ready for reading, for writing, or for another operation.

Create a SelectionKey by passing a Selector object to the register() method of a SelectableChannel. The channel() and selector() methods of the returned SelectionKey return the SelectableChannel and Selector objects associated with that key.

When you no longer wish the channel to be registered with the selector, call the cancel() method of the SelectionKey. isValid() determines whether a SelectionKey is still "valid"--it returns true unless the cancel() method has been called, the channel has been closed or the selector has been closed.

The main purpose of a SelectionKey is to hold the "interest set" of channel operations that the selector should monitor for the channel, and also the "ready set" of operations that the selector has determined are ready to proceed on the channel. Both sets are represented as integer bitmasks (not java.util.Set objects) formed by OR-ing together any of the OP_ constants defined by this class. Those constants are the following:

OP_READ
: In the interest set, this bit specifies an interest in read operations. In the ready set, this bit specifies that the channel has bytes available for reading, has reached the end-of-stream, has been remotely closed, or that an error has occurred.

OP_WRITE
: In the interest set, this bit specifies an interest in write operations. In the ready set, this bit specifies that the channel is ready to have bytes written, or has been closed, or that an error has occurred.

OP_CONNECT
: In the interest set, this bit specifies an interest in socket connection operations. In the ready set, it indicates that a socket channel is ready to connect, or that an error has occurred.

OP_ACCEPT
: In the interest set, this bit specifies an interest in server socket accept operations. In the ready set, it indicates that a server socket channel is ready to accept a connection or that an error has occurred.

The no-argument version of the interestOps() method allows you to query the interest set. The inital value of the interest set the bitmask that was passed to the register() method of the channel. It can be changed, however, by passing a new bitmask to the one-argument version of interestOps(). (Note that the same method name is used to both query and set the interest set.) The current state of the ready set can be queried with readyOps(). You can also use the convenience methods isReadable(), isWritable() isConnectable() and isAcceptable() to test whether individual operation bits are set in the ready set bitmask. There is no way to explicitly set the state of the ready set--each call to select() method updates the ready set for you. Note, however, that you must remove a SelectionKey object from the Set returned by Selector.selectedKeys() for the bits of the ready set to be cleared at the start of the next selection operation. If you never remove the SelectionKey from the set of selected keys, the Selector assumes that none of the I/O readyness conditions represented by the ready set have been handled yet, and leaves their bits set.

Use attach() to associate an arbitrary object with a SelectionKey, and call attachment() to query that object. This ability to associate data with a selection key is often useful when using a Selector with multiple channels: it can provide the context necessary to process a SelectionKey that has been selected.

```
public abstract class SelectionKey {
// Protected Constructors
   protected SelectionKey();
// Public Constants
   public static final int OP_ACCEPT;                                    =16
   public static final int OP_CONNECT;                                    =8
   public static final int OP_READ;                                       =1
   public static final int OP_WRITE;                                      =4
// Public Instance Methods
   public final Object attach(Object ob);
   public final Object attachment();
   public abstract void cancel();
   public abstract SelectableChannel channel();
   public abstract int interestOps();
   public abstract SelectionKey interestOps(int ops);
   public final boolean isAcceptable();
   public final boolean isConnectable();
   public final boolean isReadable();
   public abstract boolean isValid();
   public final boolean isWritable();
   public abstract int readyOps();
   public abstract Selector selector();
}
```

Subclasses java.nio.channels.spi.AbstractSelectionKey

Returned By SelectableChannel.{keyFor(), register()}, java.nio.channels.spi.AbstractSelectableChannel.{keyFor(), register()}, java.nio.channels.spi.AbstractSelector.register()

Selector — Java 1.4

java.nio.channels

A Selector is an object that monitors multiple nonblocking SelectableChannel objects and (after blocking if necessary) "selects" the channel that is (or the channels that are) ready for I/O. Create a new Selector with the static open() method. Next register the channels that it is to monitor: a channel is registered by passing the Selector to the register() method of the channel (register() is defined by the abstract SelectableChannel class). In addition to the Selector you must also pass a bitmask that specifies which I/O operations (reading, writing, connecting, and accepting) that the Selector is to monitor for that channel. Each call to this register() method returns a SelectionKey object. (The SelectionKey class also defines the constants that are used to form the bitmask of I/O operations.) Note that before a SelectableChannel can be registered, it must be in nonblocking mode, which can be accomplished with the configureBlocking() method of SelectableChannel.

Once the channels are registered with the Selector, call select() to block until one or more of the channels is ready for I/O. One version of select() takes a timeout value and returns if the specified number of milliseconds elapses without any channels becoming ready for I/O. These methods also return if any of the channels is closed, if an error occurs on any channel, if the wakeup() method of the Selector is called, or if the interrupt() method of the blocked thread is called. There is also a selectNow() method which is like select() except that it does not block: it simply polls each of the channels and determines which have become ready for I/O. The return value of selectNow() and of both select() methods is the number of channels ready for I/O. It is possible for this return value to be zero.

The select() and selectNow() methods returns the number of channels that are ready for I/O; they do not return the channels themselves. To obtain this information, you must call the selectedKeys() method, which returns a java.util.Set containing SelectionKey objects. After calling select() and selectedKeys(), applications typically obtain a java.util.Iterator for the Set and use it to loop through the SelectionKey objects that represent the channels that are ready for I/O. Use the channel() method of the SelectionKey to determine which channel is ready, and call readyOps(), isReadable(), isWritable() or related methods of the SelectionKey to determine what kind of I/O operation is ready on the channel. SelectionKey objects remain in the selectedKeys() set until explicitly removed, so after performing the I/O operation for a given SelectionKey, you should remove that key from the Set returned by selectedKeys() (use the remove() method of the Set of its Iterator).

In addition to the selectedKeys() method, Selector also defines a keys() method, which also returns a Set of SelectionKey objects. This set represents the complete set of channels that are being monitored by the Selector and may not be modified, except by closing the channel or deregistring the channel by calling the cancel() method of the associated SelectionKey. Cancelled keys are removed from the keys() set on the next call to select() or selectNow().

Call wakeup() to cause another thread blocked in a call to select() to wake up and return immediately. If wakeup() is called but no thread is currently blocked in a select() call, then the next call to select() or selectNow() will return immediately.

When a Selector object is no longer needed, close it by calling close(). If any thread is blocked in a select() call, it will return immediately as if wakeup() had been called. After calling close(), you should not call any other methods of a Selector. isOpen() returns true if a Selector is still open, and returns false if it has been closed.

The Selector class is thread-safe. Note, however, that the Set object returnd by selectedKeys() is not: it should be used by only one thread at a time.

```
public abstract class Selector {
// Protected Constructors
   protected Selector();
// Public Class Methods
   public static Selector open() throws java.io.IOException;
// Public Instance Methods
   public abstract void close() throws java.io.IOException;
   public abstract boolean isOpen();
   public abstract java.util.Set<SelectionKey> keys();
   public abstract java.nio.channels.spi.SelectorProvider provider();
   public abstract int select() throws java.io.IOException;
   public abstract int select(long timeout) throws java.io.IOException;
   public abstract java.util.Set<SelectionKey> selectedKeys();
   public abstract int selectNow() throws java.io.IOException;
   public abstract Selector wakeup();
}
```

Subclasses java.nio.channels.spi.AbstractSelector

Passed To SelectableChannel.{keyFor(), register()}, java.nio.channels.spi.AbstractSelectableChannel.{keyFor(), register()}

Returned By SelectionKey.selector()

ServerSocketChannel

Java 1.4

java.nio.channels

closeable

This class is the java.nio version of java.net.ServerSocket. It is a selectable channel that can be used by servers to accept connections from clients. Unlike other channel classes in this package, this class cannot be used for reading or writing bytes: it does not implement any of the ByteChannel interfaces, and exists only to accept and establish connections with clients, not to communicate with those clients. ServerSocketChannel differs from java.net.ServerSocket in two important ways: it can put into nonblocking mode and used with a Selector, and its accept() method returns a SocketChannel rather than a Socket, so that communication with the client whose connection was just accepted can be done using the java.nio APIs.

Create a new ServerSocketChannel with the static open() method. Next, call socket() to obtain the associated ServerSocket object, and use its bind() method to bind the server socket to a specific port on the local host. You can also call any other ServerSocket methods to configure other socket options at this point.

To accept a new connection through this ServerSocketChannel, simply call accept(). If the channel is in blocking mode, this method will block until a client connects, and will then return a SocketChannel that is connected to the client. In nonblocking mode, (see the inherited configureBlocking() method) accept() returns a SocketChannel only if there is a client currently waiting to connect, and otherwise immediately returns null. To be notified when a client is waiting to connect, use the inherited register() method to register nonblocking a ServerSocketChannel with a Selector and specify an interest in accept operations with the SelectionKey.OP_ACCEPT constant. See Selector and SelectionKey for further details.

Note that the SocketChannel object returned by the accept() method is always in nonblocking mode, regardless of the blocking mode of the ServerSocketChannel.

ServerSocketChannel is thread-safe; only one thread may call the accept() method at a time. When a ServerSocketChannel is no longer required, close it with the inherited close() method.

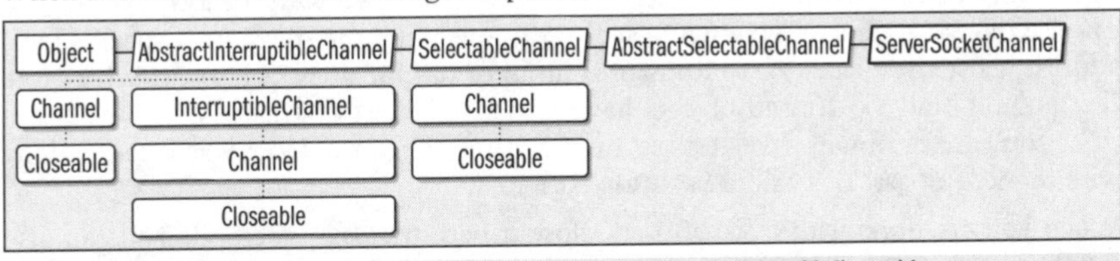


```
public abstract class ServerSocketChannel extends java.nio.channels.spi.AbstractSelectableChannel {
// Protected Constructors
   protected ServerSocketChannel(java.nio.channels.spi.SelectorProvider provider);
// Public Class Methods
   public static ServerSocketChannel open() throws java.io.IOException;
// Public Instance Methods
   public abstract SocketChannel accept() throws java.io.IOException;
   public abstract java.net.ServerSocket socket();
// Public Methods Overriding SelectableChannel
```

```
    public final int validOps();
}
```

Returned By java.net.ServerSocket.getChannel(), java.nio.channels.spi.SelectorProvider.openServerSocketChannel()

SocketChannel **Java 1.4**

java.nio.channels closeable

This class is a channel for communicating over a java.net.Socket. It implements ReadableByteChannel and WriteableByteChannel as well as GatheringByteChannel and ScatteringByteChannel. It is a subclass of SelectableChannel and can be used with a Selector.

Create a new SocketChannel with one of the static open() methods. The no-argument version of open() creates a new SocketChannel but does not connect it to a remote host. The other version of open() opens a new channel and connects it to the specified java.net.SocketAddress. If you create an unconnected socket, you can explictly connect it with the connect() method. The main reason to open the channel and connect to the remote host in separate steps is if you want to do a nonblocking connect. To do this, first put the channel into nonblocking mode with the inherited configureBlocking() method. Then, call connect(): it will return immediately, without waiting for the connection to be established. Then register the channel with a Selector specifying that you are interested in SelectionKey.OP_CONNECT operations. When you are notified that your channel is ready to connect (see Selector and SelectionKey for details) simply call the nonblocking finishConnect() method to complete the connection. isConnected() returns true once a connection is established, and false otherwise. isConnectionPending() returns true if connect() has been called in blocking mode and has not yet returned, or if connect() has been called in nonblocking mode, but finishConnect() has not been called yet.

Once you have opened and connected a SocketChannel, you can read and write bytes to it with the various read() and write() methods. SocketChannel is thread-safe: read and write operations may proceed concurrently, but SocketChannel will not allow more than one read operation and more than one write operation to proceed at the same time. If you place a SocketChannel into nonblocking mode, you can register it with a Selector using the SelectionKey constants OP_READ and OP_WRITE, to have the Selector tell you when the channel is ready for reading or writing.

The socket() method returns the java.net.Socket that is associated with the SocketChannel. You can use this Socket object to configure socket options, bind the socket to a specific local address, close the socket, or shutdown its input or output sides. See java.net.Socket. Note that although all SocketChannel objects have associated Socket objects, the reverse is not true: you cannot obtain a SocketChannel from a Socket unless the Socket was created along with the SocketChannel by a call to SocketChannel.open().

When you are done with a SocketChannel, close it with the close() method. You can also independently shut down the read and write portions of the channel with socket().shutdownInput() and socket().shutdownOutput(). When the input is shut down, any future reads (and any blocked read operation) will return -1 to indicate that the end-of-stream has been reached. When the output is shut down, any future writes throw a ClosedChannelException, and any write operation that was blocked at the time of shut down throws a AsynchronousCloseException.

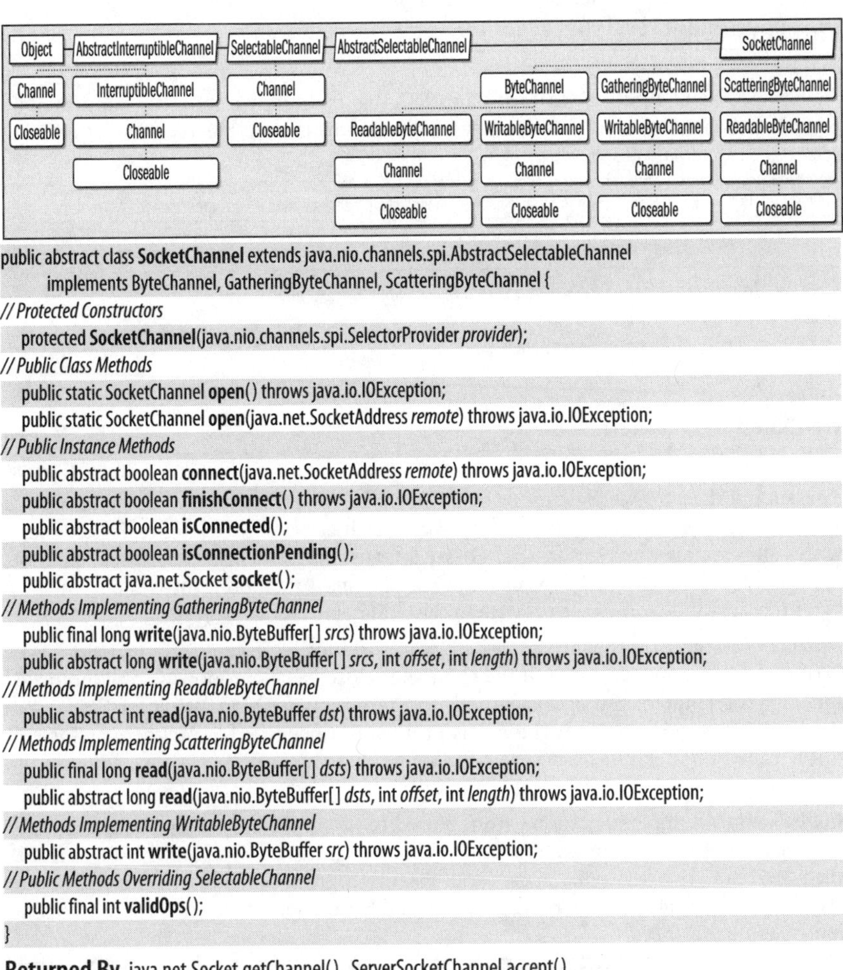


```
public abstract class SocketChannel extends java.nio.channels.spi.AbstractSelectableChannel
        implements ByteChannel, GatheringByteChannel, ScatteringByteChannel {
// Protected Constructors
    protected SocketChannel(java.nio.channels.spi.SelectorProvider provider);
// Public Class Methods
    public static SocketChannel open() throws java.io.IOException;
    public static SocketChannel open(java.net.SocketAddress remote) throws java.io.IOException;
// Public Instance Methods
    public abstract boolean connect(java.net.SocketAddress remote) throws java.io.IOException;
    public abstract boolean finishConnect() throws java.io.IOException;
    public abstract boolean isConnected();
    public abstract boolean isConnectionPending();
    public abstract java.net.Socket socket();
// Methods Implementing GatheringByteChannel
    public final long write(java.nio.ByteBuffer[] srcs) throws java.io.IOException;
    public abstract long write(java.nio.ByteBuffer[] srcs, int offset, int length) throws java.io.IOException;
// Methods Implementing ReadableByteChannel
    public abstract int read(java.nio.ByteBuffer dst) throws java.io.IOException;
// Methods Implementing ScatteringByteChannel
    public final long read(java.nio.ByteBuffer[] dsts) throws java.io.IOException;
    public abstract long read(java.nio.ByteBuffer[] dsts, int offset, int length) throws java.io.IOException;
// Methods Implementing WritableByteChannel
    public abstract int write(java.nio.ByteBuffer src) throws java.io.IOException;
// Public Methods Overriding SelectableChannel
    public final int validOps();
}
```

Returned By java.net.Socket.getChannel(), ServerSocketChannel.accept(), java.nio.channels.spi.SelectorProvider.openSocketChannel()

UnresolvedAddressException **Java 1.4**

java.nio.channels **serializable unchecked**

Signals the use of a java.net.SocketAddress that could not be resolved: for example a java.net.InetSocketAddress that contains an unknown hostname.

Object — Throwable — Exception — RuntimeException — IllegalArgumentException — UnresolvedAddressException
Serializable

```
public class UnresolvedAddressException extends IllegalArgumentException {
// Public Constructors
    public UnresolvedAddressException();
}
```

UnsupportedAddressTypeException Java 1.4

java.nio.channels serializable unchecked

Signals the use of a java.net.SocketAddress subclass that is unknown to or not supported by the implementation. It is safe to assume that addresses of the type java.net.InetSocketAddress are universally supported.

Object — Throwable — Exception — RuntimeException — IllegalArgumentException — UnsupportedAddressTypeException
Serializable

```
public class UnsupportedAddressTypeException extends IllegalArgumentException {
// Public Constructors
   public UnsupportedAddressTypeException();
}
```

WritableByteChannel Java 1.4

java.nio.channels closeable

This subinterface of Channel defines a single key write() method which writes bytes from a specified ByteBuffer (updating the buffer position as it goes) to the channel. If possible, it writes all remaining bytes in the buffer (see Buffer.remaining()). This is not always possible (with nonblocking channels, for example) so the write() method returns the number of bytes that it was actually able to write to the channel.

write() is declared to throw an IOException. More specifically, it may throw a ClosedChannelException if the channel is closed. If the channel is closed asynchronously, or if a blocked thread is interrupted, the write() method may terminate with an AsynchronousCloseException or a ClosedByInterruptException. write() may also throw an unchecked NonWritableChannelException if it is called on a channel (such as a FileChannel) that was not opened or configured to allow writing.

WritableByteChannel implementations are required to be thread-safe: only one thread may perform a write operation on a channel at a time. If a write operation is in progress, then any call to write() will block until the in-progress operation completes. Some channel implementations may allow read and write operations to proceed concurrently; some may not.

Closeable ··· Channel ··· WritableByteChannel

```
public interface WritableByteChannel extends Channel {
// Public Instance Methods
   int write(java.nio.ByteBuffer src) throws java.io.IOException;
}
```

Implementations ByteChannel, GatheringByteChannel, Pipe.SinkChannel

Passed To Channels.{newOutputStream(), newWriter()}, FileChannel.transferTo()

Returned By Channels.newChannel()

Package java.nio.channels.spi Java 1.4

This package defines four classes that are used by implementors of channels and selector classes of java.nio.channels. It also defines the SelectorProvider class which allows a custom implementation of channels and selectors to be specified for use instead of the default implementation. Application programmers should never need to use this package, except in rare circumstances to explicitly install a SelectionProvider implementation with the SelectionProvider.provider() method.

Classes

```
public abstract class AbstractInterruptibleChannel
                    implements java.nio.channels.Channel, java.nio.channels.InterruptibleChannel;
public abstract class AbstractSelectableChannel extends java.nio.channels.SelectableChannel;
public abstract class AbstractSelectionKey extends java.nio.channels.SelectionKey;
public abstract class AbstractSelector extends java.nio.channels.Selector;
public abstract class SelectorProvider;
```

AbstractInterruptibleChannel — Java 1.4

java.nio.channels.spi — closeable

This class exists as a convenience for implementors of new Channel classes. Application programmers should never need to subclass or use it.

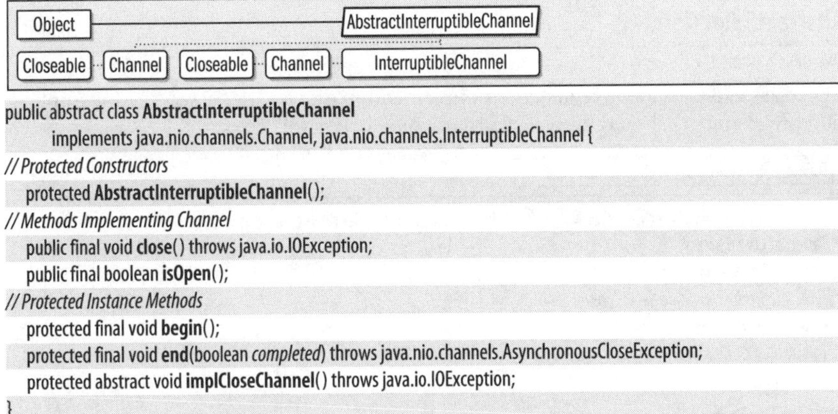


```
public abstract class AbstractInterruptibleChannel
        implements java.nio.channels.Channel, java.nio.channels.InterruptibleChannel {
// Protected Constructors
    protected AbstractInterruptibleChannel();
// Methods Implementing Channel
    public final void close() throws java.io.IOException;
    public final boolean isOpen();
// Protected Instance Methods
    protected final void begin();
    protected final void end(boolean completed) throws java.nio.channels.AsynchronousCloseException;
    protected abstract void implCloseChannel() throws java.io.IOException;
}
```

Subclasses java.nio.channels.FileChannel, java.nio.channels.SelectableChannel

AbstractSelectableChannel — Java 1.4

java.nio.channels.spi — closeable

This class exists as a convenience for implementors of new selectable channel classes: it defines common methods of SelectableChannel in terms of protected methods whose names begin with impl. Application programmers should never need to use or subclass this class.

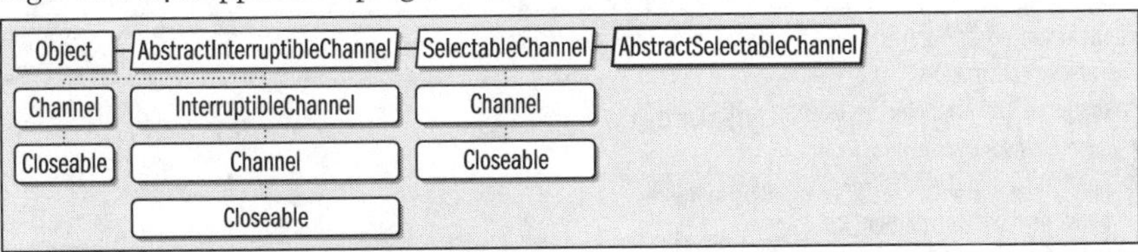


```
public abstract class AbstractSelectableChannel extends java.nio.channels.SelectableChannel {
// Protected Constructors
    protected AbstractSelectableChannel(SelectorProvider provider);
// Public Methods Overriding SelectableChannel
    public final Object blockingLock();
    public final java.nio.channels.SelectableChannel configureBlocking(boolean block) throws java.io.IOException;
```

```
    public final boolean isBlocking();
    public final boolean isRegistered();
    public final java.nio.channels.SelectionKey keyFor(java.nio.channels.Selector sel);
    public final SelectorProvider provider();
    public final java.nio.channels.SelectionKey register(java.nio.channels.Selector sel, int ops, Object att)
        throws java.nio.channels.ClosedChannelException;
// Protected Methods Overriding AbstractInterruptibleChannel
    protected final void implCloseChannel() throws java.io.IOException;
// Protected Instance Methods
    protected abstract void implCloseSelectableChannel() throws java.io.IOException;
    protected abstract void implConfigureBlocking(boolean block) throws java.io.IOException;
}
```

Subclasses java.nio.channels.DatagramChannel, java.nio.channels.Pipe.SinkChannel, java.nio.channels.Pipe.SourceChannel, java.nio.channels.ServerSocketChannel, java.nio.channels.SocketChannel

Passed To AbstractSelector.register()

AbstractSelectionKey — Java 1.4

java.nio.channels.spi

This class exists as a convenience for implementors of new SelectionKey classes. Application programmers should never need to use or subclass this class.

Object — SelectionKey — AbstractSelectionKey

```
public abstract class AbstractSelectionKey extends java.nio.channels.SelectionKey {
// Protected Constructors
    protected AbstractSelectionKey();
// Public Methods Overriding SelectionKey
    public final void cancel();
    public final boolean isValid();
}
```

Passed To AbstractSelector.deregister()

AbstractSelector — Java 1.4

java.nio.channels.spi

This class exists as a convenience for implementors of new Selector classes. Application programmers should never need to use or subclass this class.

Object — Selector — AbstractSelector

```
public abstract class AbstractSelector extends java.nio.channels.Selector {
// Protected Constructors
    protected AbstractSelector(SelectorProvider provider);
// Public Methods Overriding Selector
    public final void close() throws java.io.IOException;
    public final boolean isOpen();
    public final SelectorProvider provider();
// Protected Instance Methods
    protected final void begin();
    protected final java.util.Set<java.nio.channels.SelectionKey> cancelledKeys();
    protected final void deregister(AbstractSelectionKey key);
    protected final void end();
```

```
    protected abstract void implCloseSelector() throws java.io.IOException;
    protected abstract java.nio.channels.SelectionKey register(AbstractSelectableChannel ch, int ops, Object att);
}
```

Returned By SelectorProvider.openSelector()

SelectorProvider **Java 1.4**

java.nio.channels.spi

This class is the central service-provider class for the channels and selectors of the java.nio.channels API. A concrete subclass of SelectorProvider implements factory methods that return open socket channels, server socket channels, datagram channels, pipes (with their two internal channels) and Selector objects. There is one default SelectorProvider object per JVM: this object can be obtained with the static SelectorProvider.provider() method.

You can specify a custom SelectorProvider implementation by setting its class name as the value of the system property java.nio.channels.spi.SelectorProvider. Or, you can put the class name in a file named *META-INF/services/java.nio.channels.spi.SelectorProvider*, in your application's JAR file. The provider() method first looks for the system property, then looks for the JAR file entry. If it finds neither, it instantiates the implementation's default SelectorProvider.

Applications are not required to use the default SelectorProvider exclusively. It is legal to instantiate other SelectorProvider objects and explictly invoke their open() methods to create channels in that way.

```
public abstract class SelectorProvider {
// Protected Constructors
    protected SelectorProvider();
// Public Class Methods
    public static SelectorProvider provider();
// Public Instance Methods
5.0 public java.nio.channels.Channel inheritedChannel() throws java.io.IOException;                constant
    public abstract java.nio.channels.DatagramChannel openDatagramChannel() throws java.io.IOException;
    public abstract java.nio.channels.Pipe openPipe() throws java.io.IOException;
    public abstract AbstractSelector openSelector() throws java.io.IOException;
    public abstract java.nio.channels.ServerSocketChannel openServerSocketChannel() throws java.io.IOException;
    public abstract java.nio.channels.SocketChannel openSocketChannel() throws java.io.IOException;
}
```

Passed To java.nio.channels.DatagramChannel.DatagramChannel(), java.nio.channels.Pipe.SinkChannel.SinkChannel(), java.nio.channels.Pipe.SourceChannel.SourceChannel(), java.nio.channels.ServerSocketChannel.ServerSocketChannel(), java.nio.channels.SocketChannel.SocketChannel(), AbstractSelectableChannel.AbstractSelectableChannel(), AbstractSelector.AbstractSelector()

Returned By java.nio.channels.SelectableChannel.provider(), java.nio.channels.Selector.provider(), AbstractSelectableChannel.provider(), AbstractSelector.provider()

Package java.nio.charset **Java 1.4**

This package contains classes that represent character sets or encodings, and defines methods that encode characters into bytes and decode bytes into characters. The key class is Charset, and you can obtain a Charset object for a named character encoding with the static forName() method. Charset defines encode() and decode() convenience methods, but for full control over the encoding and decoding process, you can also obtain a CharsetEncoder or CharsetDecoder object from the Charset.

The Java platform has had a character encoding and decoding facility since Java 1.1, and defines a number of classes and methods that perform character encoding or decoding. Some of these classes and methods are specified to use the default charset for the locale; others take the name of a charset as a method or constructor argument. See, for example, the String(), java.io.InputStreamReader() and java.io.OutputStreamWriter() constructors. In Java 1.4, the java.nio.charset package defines a public API to the character encoding and decoding facility and allows applications to work with it explicitly. Most applications will not have to do this, however, and can simply continue to rely on the default charset, or can continue to supply charset names where needed. Even applications that use the java.nio.channels package can avoid explicit character encoding and decoding by passing the name of a desired charset to the newReader() and newWriter() methods of java.nio.channels.Channels.

Classes

```
public abstract class Charset implements Comparable<Charset>;
public abstract class CharsetDecoder;
public abstract class CharsetEncoder;
public class CoderResult;
public class CodingErrorAction;
```

Exceptions

```
public class CharacterCodingException extends java.io.IOException;
    public class MalformedInputException extends CharacterCodingException;
    public class UnmappableCharacterException extends CharacterCodingException;
public class IllegalCharsetNameException extends IllegalArgumentException;
public class UnsupportedCharsetException extends IllegalArgumentException;
```

Errors

```
public class CoderMalfunctionError extends Error;
```

CharacterCodingException — Java 1.4

java.nio.charset — serializable checked

Signals a problem encoding or decoding characters or bytes. This is a generic superclass for more-specific exception types. Note that the one-argument versions of CharsetEncoder.encode() and CharsetDecoder.decode() may throw an exception of this type, but that the three-argument versions of the same method instead report encoding problems through their CoderResult return value. Note also that the encode() and decode() convenience methods of Charset do not throw this exception because they specify that malformed input and unmappable characters or bytes should be replaced. (See CodingErrorAction.)

Object — Throwable — Exception — IOException — CharacterCodingException; Throwable ⋯ Serializable

```
public class CharacterCodingException extends java.io.IOException {
// Public Constructors
    public CharacterCodingException();
}
```

Subclasses MalformedInputException, UnmappableCharacterException

Thrown By CharsetDecoder.decode(), CharsetEncoder.encode(), CoderResult.throwException()

Charset **Java 1.4**

java.nio.charset comparable

A Charset represents a character set or encoding. Each Charset has a cannonical name, returned by name(), and a set of aliases, returned by aliases(). You can look up a Charset by name or alias with the static Charset.forName() method, which throws an UnsupportedCharsetException if the named charset is not installed on the system. In Java 5.0, you can obtain the default Charset used by the Java VM with the static defaultCharset() method. Check whether a charset specified by name or alias is supported with the static isSupported(). Obtain the complete set of installed charsets with availableCharsets() which returns a sorted map from canonical names to Charset objects. Note that charset names are not case-sensitive, and you can use any capitialization for charset names you pass to isSupported() and forName(). Note that there are a number of classes and methods in the Java platform that specify charsets by name rather than by Charset object. See, for example, java.io.InputStreamReader, java.io.OutputStreamWriter, String.getBytes(), and java.nio.channels.Channels.newWriter(). When working with classes and methods such as these, there is no need to use a Charset object.

All implementations of Java are required to support at least the following 6 charsets:

Canonical name	Description
US-ASCII	seven-bit ASCII
ISO-8859-1	The 8-bit superset of ASCII which includes the characters used in most Western-European languages. Also known as ISO-LATIN-1.
UTF-8	An 8-bit encoding of Unicode characters that is compatible with US-ASCII.
UTF-16BE	A 16-bit encoding of Unicode characters, using big-endian byte order.
UTF-16LE	A 16-bit encoding of Unicode characters, using little-endian byte order.
UTF-16	A 16-bit encoding of Unicode characters, with byte order specified by a byte order mark character. Assumes big-endian when decoding if there is no byte order mark. Encodes using big-endian byte order and outputs an appropriate byte order mark.

Once you have obtained a Charset with forName() or availableCharsets(), you can use the encode() method to encode a String or CharBuffer of text into a ByteBuffer, or you can use the decode() method to convert the bytes in a ByteBuffer into characters in a CharBuffer. These convenience methods create a new CharsetEncoder or CharsetDecoder, specify that malformed input or unmappable characters or bytes should be replaced with the default replacement string or bytes, and then invoke the encode() or decode() method of the encoder or decoder. For full control over the encoding and decoding process, you may prefer to obtain your own CharsetEncoder or CharsetDecoder object with newEncoder() or newDecoder(). See CharsetDecoder for details.

Instead of using a Charset, CharsetEncoder, or CharsetDecoder directly, you may also pass an encoder or decoder to the static methods of java.nio.channels.Channels to obtain a java.io.Reader or java.io.Writer that you can use to read or write characters from or to a byte-oriented Channel.

Note that not all Charset objects support encoding ("auto-detect" charsets can determine the source charset when decoding, but have no way to encode). Use canEncode() to determine whether a given Charset can encode.

Charset also defines, implements, or overrides various other methods. displayName() returns a localized name for the charset, or returns the cannonical name if there is no localization. toString() returns an implementation-dependent textual representation of the charset. The equals() method compares two charsets by comparing their canonical names. Charset implements Comparable, and its compareTo() method orders charsets by their canonical name. contains() returns true if a specified charset is "contained in" this charset. That is, if every character that can be represented in the specified charset can also be represented in this charset. Note that those representations need not be the same, however. isRegistered() returns true if the charset is registered with the IANA charset registry (see *http://www.iana.org/assignments/character-sets*.)

Object — Charset ··· Comparable

```
public abstract class Charset implements Comparable<Charset> {
// Protected Constructors
   protected Charset(String canonicalName, String[] aliases);
// Public Class Methods
   public static java.util.SortedMap<String,Charset> availableCharsets();
5.0 public static Charset defaultCharset();
   public static Charset forName(String charsetName);
   public static boolean isSupported(String charsetName);
// Public Instance Methods
   public final java.util.Set<String> aliases();
   public boolean canEncode();                                              constant
   public abstract boolean contains(Charset cs);
   public final java.nio.CharBuffer decode(java.nio.ByteBuffer bb);
   public String displayName();
   public String displayName(java.util.Locale locale);
   public final java.nio.ByteBuffer encode(java.nio.CharBuffer cb);
   public final java.nio.ByteBuffer encode(String str);
   public final boolean isRegistered();
   public final String name();
   public abstract CharsetDecoder newDecoder();
   public abstract CharsetEncoder newEncoder();
// Methods Implementing Comparable
5.0 public final int compareTo(Charset that);
// Public Methods Overriding Object
   public final boolean equals(Object ob);
   public final int hashCode();
   public final String toString();
}
```

Passed To java.io.InputStreamReader.InputStreamReader(), java.io.OutputStreamWriter.OutputStreamWriter(), CharsetDecoder.CharsetDecoder(), CharsetEncoder.CharsetEncoder()

Returned By CharsetDecoder.{charset(), detectedCharset()}, CharsetEncoder.charset(), java.nio.charset.spi.CharsetProvider.charsetForName()

CharsetDecoder **Java 1.4**

java.nio.charset

A CharsetDecoder is a "decoding engine" that converts a sequence of bytes into a sequence of characters based on the encoding of some charset. Obtain a CharsetDecoder from the Charset that represents the charset to be decoded. If you have a complete sequence of bytes to be decoded in a ByteBuffer you can pass that buffer to the one-argument version of decode(). This convenience method decodes the bytes and stores the resulting characters into a newly allocated CharBuffer, resetting and flushing the decoder as necessary. It throws an exception if there are problems with the bytes to be decoded.

Typically, however, the three-argument version of decode() is used in a multistep decoding process:

1. Call the reset() method, unless this is the first time the CharsetDecoder has been used.
2. Call the three-argument version of decode() one or more times. The third argument should be true on, and only on, the last invocation of the method. The first argument to decode() is a ByteBuffer that contains bytes to be decoded. The second argument is a CharBuffer into which the resulting characters are stored. The return value of the method is a CoderResult object that specifies the state of the ongoing the decoding operation. The possible CoderResult return values are detailed below. In a typical case, however, decode() returns after it has decoded all of the bytes in the input buffer. In this case, you would then typically fill the input buffer with more bytes to be decoded, and read characters from the output buffer, calling its compact() method to make room for more. If an unexpected problem arises in the CharsetDecoder implementation, decode() throws a CoderMalfunctionError.
3. Pass the output CharBuffer to the flush() method to allow any remaining characters to be output.

The decode() method returns a CoderResult that indicates the state of the decoding operation. If the return value is CoderResult.UNDERFLOW, then it means that decode() returned because all bytes from the input buffer have been read, and more input is required. If the return value is CoderResult.OVERFLOW, then it means that decode() returned because the output CharBuffer is full, and no more characters can be decoded into it. Otherwise, the reurn value is a CoderResult whose isError() method returns true. There are two basic types of decoding errors. If isMalformed() returns true then the input included bytes that are not legal for the charset. These bytes start at the position of the input buffer, and continue for length() bytes. Otherwise, if isUnmappable() returns true, then the input bytes include a character for which there is no representation in Unicode. The relevant bytes start at the position of the input buffer and continue for length() bytes.

By default a CharsetDecoder reports all malformed input and unmappable character errors by returning a CoderResult object as described above. This behavior can be altered, however, by passing a CodingErrorAction to onMalformedInput() and onUnmappableCharacter(). (Query the current action for these types of errors with malformedInputAction() and unmappableCharacterAction().) CodingErrorAction defines three constants that represent the three possible actions. The default action is REPORT. The action IGNORE tells the CharsetDecoder to ignore (i.e. skip) malformed input and unmappable charaters. The REPLACE action tells the CharsetDecoder to replace malformed input and unmappable characters with the replacement string. This replacement string can be set with replaceWith(), and can be queried with replacement().

averageCharsPerByte() and maxCharsPerByte() return the average and maximum number of characters that are produced by this decoder per decoded byte. These values can be used to help you choose the size of the CharBuffer to allocate for decoding.

CharsetDecoder is not a thread-safe class. Only one thread should use an instance at a time.

CharsetDecoder is an abstract class. Implementors defining new charsets will need to subclass CharsetDecoder and define the abstract decodeLoop() method, which is invoked by decode().

```
public abstract class CharsetDecoder {
// Protected Constructors
   protected CharsetDecoder(Charset cs, float averageCharsPerByte, float maxCharsPerByte);
```

```
// Public Instance Methods
   public final float averageCharsPerByte();
   public final Charset charset();
   public final java.nio.CharBuffer decode(java.nio.ByteBuffer in) throws CharacterCodingException;
   public final CoderResult decode(java.nio.ByteBuffer in, java.nio.CharBuffer out, boolean endOfInput);
   public Charset detectedCharset();
   public final CoderResult flush(java.nio.CharBuffer out);
   public boolean isAutoDetecting();                                                    constant
   public boolean isCharsetDetected();
   public CodingErrorAction malformedInputAction();
   public final float maxCharsPerByte();
   public final CharsetDecoder onMalformedInput(CodingErrorAction newAction);
   public final CharsetDecoder onUnmappableCharacter(CodingErrorAction newAction);
   public final String replacement();
   public final CharsetDecoder replaceWith(String newReplacement);
   public final CharsetDecoder reset();
   public CodingErrorAction unmappableCharacterAction();
// Protected Instance Methods
   protected abstract CoderResult decodeLoop(java.nio.ByteBuffer in, java.nio.CharBuffer out);
   protected CoderResult implFlush(java.nio.CharBuffer out);
   protected void implOnMalformedInput(CodingErrorAction newAction);                     empty
   protected void implOnUnmappableCharacter(CodingErrorAction newAction);                empty
   protected void implReplaceWith(String newReplacement);                                empty
   protected void implReset();                                                           empty
}
```

Passed To java.io.InputStreamReader.InputStreamReader(), java.nio.channels.Channels.newReader()

Returned By Charset.newDecoder()

CharsetEncoder **Java 1.4**

java.nio.charset

A CharsetEncoder is an "encoding engine" that converts a sequence of characters into a sequence of bytes using some character encoding. Obtain a CharsetEncoder with the newEncoder() method of the Charset that represents the desired encoding.

A CharsetEncoder works like a CharsetDecoder in reverse. Use the encode() method to encode characters read from a CharBuffer into bytes stored in a ByteBuffer. Please see CharsetDecoder, which is documented in detail.

```
public abstract class CharsetEncoder {
// Protected Constructors
   protected CharsetEncoder(Charset cs, float averageBytesPerChar, float maxBytesPerChar);
   protected CharsetEncoder(Charset cs, float averageBytesPerChar, float maxBytesPerChar, byte[] replacement);
// Public Instance Methods
   public final float averageBytesPerChar();
   public boolean canEncode(CharSequence cs);
   public boolean canEncode(char c);
   public final Charset charset();
   public final java.nio.ByteBuffer encode(java.nio.CharBuffer in) throws CharacterCodingException;
   public final CoderResult encode(java.nio.CharBuffer in, java.nio.ByteBuffer out, boolean endOfInput);
   public final CoderResult flush(java.nio.ByteBuffer out);
   public boolean isLegalReplacement(byte[] repl);
   public CodingErrorAction malformedInputAction();
   public final float maxBytesPerChar();
```

```
    public final CharsetEncoder onMalformedInput(CodingErrorAction newAction);
    public final CharsetEncoder onUnmappableCharacter(CodingErrorAction newAction);
    public final byte[] replacement();
    public final CharsetEncoder replaceWith(byte[] newReplacement);
    public final CharsetEncoder reset();
    public CodingErrorAction unmappableCharacterAction();
// Protected Instance Methods
    protected abstract CoderResult encodeLoop(java.nio.CharBuffer in, java.nio.ByteBuffer out);
    protected CoderResult implFlush(java.nio.ByteBuffer out);
    protected void implOnMalformedInput(CodingErrorAction newAction);                empty
    protected void implOnUnmappableCharacter(CodingErrorAction newAction);           empty
    protected void implReplaceWith(byte[] newReplacement);                           empty
    protected void implReset();                                                      empty
}
```

Passed To java.io.OutputStreamWriter.OutputStreamWriter(), java.nio.channels.Channels.newWriter()

Returned By Charset.newEncoder()

CoderMalfunctionError — Java 1.4

java.nio.charset — serializable error

Signals a malfunction--typically an unknown and unrecoverable error--in a CharsetEncoder or CharsetDecoder. An error of this type is thrown by the encode() and decode() methods when the protected encodeLoop() or decodeLoop() methods upon which they are implemented throws an exception of an unexpected type.

Object — Throwable — Error — CoderMalfunctionError
(Throwable implements Serializable)

```
public class CoderMalfunctionError extends Error {
// Public Constructors
    public CoderMalfunctionError(Exception cause);
}
```

CoderResult — Java 1.4

java.nio.charset

A CoderResult object specifies the results of a call to CharsetDecoder.decode() or CharsetEncoder.encode(). There are four possible reasons why a call to the decode() or encode() would return:

- If all the bytes have been decoded or all the characters have been encoded, and the input buffer is empty, then the return value is the constant object CoderResult.UNDERFLOW, indicating that coding stopped because there was no more data to code. Calling the isUnderflow() method on the returned object returns true and calling isError() returns false. This is a normal return value.
- If there is more data to be coded, but there is no more room in the output buffer to store the coded data, then the return value is the constant object CoderResult.OVERFLOW. Calling isOverflow() on the returned object returns true, and calling isError() returns false. This is a normal return value.
- If the input data was malformed, containing characters or bytes that are not legal for the charset, and the CharsetEncoder or CharsetDecoder has not specified that malformed input should be ignored or replaced, then the returned value is a CoderResult object

whose isError() and isMalformed() methods both return true. The position of the input buffer is at the first malformed character or byte, and the length() method of the returned object specifies how many characters or bytes are malformed.

- If the input was well-formed, but contains characters or bytes that are "unmappable"--that cannot be encoded or decoded in the specified charset--and if the CharsetEncoder or CharsetDecoder has not specified that unmappable characters should be ignored or replaced, then the returned value is a CoderResult object whose isError() and isUnmappable() methods both return true. The input buffer is positioned at the first unmappable character or byte, and the length() method of the CoderResult specifies the number of unmappable characters or bytes.

```
public class CoderResult {
// No Constructor
// Public Constants
   public static final CoderResult OVERFLOW;
   public static final CoderResult UNDERFLOW;
// Public Class Methods
   public static CoderResult malformedForLength(int length);
   public static CoderResult unmappableForLength(int length);
// Public Instance Methods
   public boolean isError();
   public boolean isMalformed();
   public boolean isOverflow();
   public boolean isUnderflow();
   public boolean isUnmappable();
   public int length();
   public void throwException() throws CharacterCodingException;
// Public Methods Overriding Object
   public String toString();
}
```

Returned By CharsetDecoder.{decode(), decodeLoop(), flush(), implFlush()}, CharsetEncoder.{encode(), encodeLoop(), flush(), implFlush()}

CodingErrorAction **Java 1.4**

java.nio.charset

This class is a typesafe enumeration that defines three constants that serve as the legal argument values to the onMalformedInput() and onUnmappableCharacter() methods of CharsetDecoder and CharsetEncoder. These constants specify how malformed input and unmappable error conditions should be handled. The values are:

CodingErrorAction.REPORT

Specifies that the error should be reported. This is done by returning a CoderResult object from the three-argument version of decode() or encode() or by throwing a MalformedInputException or UnmappableCharacterException from the one-argument version of decode() or encode(). This is the default action for both error types for both CharsetDecoder and CharsetEncoder.

CodingErrorAction.IGNORE

Specifies that the malformed input or unmappable input character should simply be skipped, with no output.

CodingErrorAction.REPLACE
: Specifies that the malformed input or unmappable character should be skipped and the replacement string or replacement bytes should be appended to the output.

See CharsetDecoder for more information.

```
public class CodingErrorAction {
// No Constructor
// Public Constants
   public static final CodingErrorAction IGNORE;
   public static final CodingErrorAction REPLACE;
   public static final CodingErrorAction REPORT;
// Public Methods Overriding Object
   public String toString();
}
```

Passed To CharsetDecoder.{implOnMalformedInput(), implOnUnmappableCharacter(), onMalformedInput(), onUnmappableCharacter()}, CharsetEncoder.{implOnMalformedInput(), implOnUnmappableCharacter(), onMalformedInput(), onUnmappableCharacter()}

Returned By CharsetDecoder.{malformedInputAction(), unmappableCharacterAction()}, CharsetEncoder.{malformedInputAction(), unmappableCharacterAction()}

IllegalCharsetNameException — Java 1.4

java.nio.charset — serializable unchecked

Signals that a charset name (for example one passed to Charset.forName() or Charset.isSupported()) is not legal. Charset names may contain only the characters A–Z (in upper- and lowercase), the digits 0–9, and hyphens, underscores, colons, and periods. They must begin with a letter or a digit, not with a punctuation character.

Object — Throwable — Exception — RuntimeException — IllegalArgumentException — IllegalCharsetNameException
Throwable ⋯ Serializable

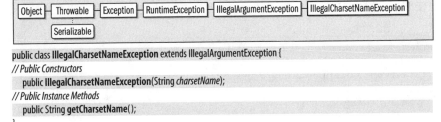

```
public class IllegalCharsetNameException extends IllegalArgumentException {
// Public Constructors
   public IllegalCharsetNameException(String charsetName);
// Public Instance Methods
   public String getCharsetName();
}
```

MalformedInputException — Java 1.4

java.nio.charset — serializable checked

Signals that input to the CharsetDecoder.decode() or CharsetEncoder.encode() method was malformed.

Object — Throwable — Exception — IOException — CharacterCodingException — MalformedInputException
Throwable ⋯ Serializable

```
public class MalformedInputException extends CharacterCodingException {
// Public Constructors
   public MalformedInputException(int inputLength);
// Public Instance Methods
   public int getInputLength();
```

```
// Public Methods Overriding Throwable
    public String getMessage();
}
```

UnmappableCharacterException

Java 1.4

java.nio.charset

serializable checked

Signals that input to the CharsetDecoder.decode() or CharsetEncoder.encode() method contained a character or byte sequence that is not mappable in the specified charset.

Object — Throwable — Exception — IOException — CharacterCodingException — UnmappableCharacterException

Serializable

```
public class UnmappableCharacterException extends CharacterCodingException {
// Public Constructors
    public UnmappableCharacterException(int inputLength);
// Public Instance Methods
    public int getInputLength();
// Public Methods Overriding Throwable
    public String getMessage();
}
```

UnsupportedCharsetException

Java 1.4

java.nio.charset

serializable unchecked

Signals that the requested charset is not supported on the current platform. This exception is thrown by Charset.forName() when no Charset object can be obtained for the named charset. See also Charset.isSupported().

Object — Throwable — Exception — RuntimeException — IllegalArgumentException — UnsupportedCharsetException

Serializable

```
public class UnsupportedCharsetException extends IllegalArgumentException {
// Public Constructors
    public UnsupportedCharsetException(String charsetName);
// Public Instance Methods
    public String getCharsetName();
}
```

Package java.nio.charset.spi

Java 1.4

This package defines a "provider" class for system developers who are defining new Charset implementations and want to make them available to the system. Application programmers never need to us this package or the class it defines.

Classes

```
public abstract class CharsetProvider;
```

CharsetProvider

Java 1.4

java.nio.charset.spi

System programmers developing new Charset implementations should implement this class to make those charsets available to the system. charsetForName() should return a

Charset instance for the given name. charsets() should return a java.util.Iterator that allows the caller to iterate through the set of Charset objects defined by the provider.

A CharsetProvider and its associated Charset implementations should be packaged in a JAR file and made available to the system in the *jre/lib/ext/* extensions directory (or some other extensions location.) The JAR file should contain a file named *META-INF/services/java.nio.charset.spi.CharsetProvider* which contains the class name of the CharsetProvider implementation.

```
public abstract class CharsetProvider {
// Protected Constructors
   protected CharsetProvider();
// Public Instance Methods
   public abstract java.nio.charset.Charset charsetForName(String charsetName);
   public abstract java.util.Iterator<java.nio.charset.Charset> charsets();
}
```

14

java.security and Subpackages

This chapter documents the java.security package and its subpackages. Those packages are:

java.security
: This large packages contains much of Java's security infrastructure, including a group of classes that provide access control through policies and permissions, and another group that provides authentication-related services such as digital signatures.

java.security.cert
: This package defines classes and interfaces for working with public key certificates, certificate revocation lists (CRLs) and, in Java 1.4 and later, certificate chains (or certificate paths). It defines classes that should work with any type of certificate, and type-specific subclasses for X.509 certificates and CRLs.

java.security.interfaces
: This package defines interfaces for algorithm-specific types of cryptographic keys. Providers that support those algorithms must implement these interfaces.

java.security.spec
: This package defines classes that define a transparent, portable representation of algorithm-specific objects such as cryptographic keys. Instances of these classes can be used with any security provider.

The java.security.acl package is part of the Java platform, but has been superseded by access-control classes in java.security. It is not documented here.

Package java.security — Java 1.1

The java.security package contains the classes and interfaces that implement the Java security architecture. These classes can be divided into two broad categories. First, there are classes that implement access control and prevent untrusted code from performing sensitive operations. Second, there are authentication classes that implement message digests and digital signatures and can authenticate Java classes and other objects.

The central access control class is AccessController; it uses the currently installed Policy object to decide whether a given class has Permission to access a given system resource. The Permissions and ProtectionDomain classes are also important pieces of the Java access control architecture.

The key classes for authentication are MessageDigest and Signature; they compute and verify cryptographic message digests and digital signatures. These classes use public-key cryptography techniques and rely on the PublicKey and PrivateKey interfaces. They also rely on an infrastructure of related classes, such as SecureRandom for producing cryptographic-strength pseudorandom numbers, KeyPairGenerator for generating pairs of public and private keys, and KeyStore for managing a collection of keys and certificates. (This package defines a Certificate interface, but it is deprecated; see the java.security.cert package for the preferred Certificate class.)

The CodeSource class unites the authentication classes with the access control classes. It represents the source of a Java class as a URL and a set of java.security.cert.Certificate objects that contain the digital signatures of the code. The AccessController and Policy classes look at the CodeSource of a class when making access control decisions.

All the cryptographic-authentication features of this package are provider-based, which means they are implemented by security provider modules that can be plugged easily into any Java 1.2 (or later) installation. Thus, in addition to defining a security API, this package also defines a service provider interface (SPI). Various classes with names that end in Spi are part of this SPI. Security provider implementations must subclass these Spi classes, but applications never need to use them. Each security provider is represented by a Provider class, and the Security class allows new providers to be dynamically installed.

The java.security package contains several useful utility classes. For example, DigestInputStream and DigestOutputStream make it easy to compute message digests. GuardedObject provides customizable access control for an individual object. SignedObject protects the integrity of an arbitrary Java object by attaching a digital signature, making it easy to detect any tampering with the object. Although the java.security package contains cryptographic classes for authentication, it does not contain classes for encryption or decryption. Instead, this functionality is part of the Java Cryptography Extension or JCE which defines the javax.crypto package and its subpackages. The JCE is part of the core platform in Java 1.4 and later, and is available as a standard extension to Java 1.2 and Java 1.3.

Interfaces

public interface **Certificate**;
public interface **DomainCombiner**;
public interface **Guard**;
public interface **Key** extends Serializable;
public interface **KeyStore.Entry**;
public interface **KeyStore.LoadStoreParameter**;
public interface **KeyStore.ProtectionParameter**;
public interface **Principal**;
public interface **PrivateKey** extends Key;
public interface **PrivilegedAction**<T>;
public interface **PrivilegedExceptionAction**<T>;
public interface **PublicKey** extends Key;

Enumerated Types

public enum **KeyRep.Type**;

Collections

public abstract class **Provider** extends java.util.Properties;
    public abstract class **AuthProvider** extends Provider;

Other Classes

public final class **AccessControlContext**;
public final class **AccessController**;
public class **AlgorithmParameterGenerator**;
public abstract class **AlgorithmParameterGeneratorSpi**;
public class **AlgorithmParameters**;
public abstract class **AlgorithmParametersSpi**;
public final class **CodeSigner** implements Serializable;
public class **CodeSource** implements Serializable;
public class **DigestInputStream** extends java.io.FilterInputStream;
public class **DigestOutputStream** extends java.io.FilterOutputStream;
public class **GuardedObject** implements Serializable;
public abstract class **Identity** implements Principal, Serializable;
    public abstract class **IdentityScope** extends Identity;
    public abstract class **Signer** extends Identity;
public class **KeyFactory**;
public abstract class **KeyFactorySpi**;
public final class **KeyPair** implements Serializable;
public abstract class **KeyPairGeneratorSpi**;
    public abstract class **KeyPairGenerator** extends KeyPairGeneratorSpi;
public class **KeyRep** implements Serializable;
public class **KeyStore**;
public abstract static class **KeyStore.Builder**;
public static class **KeyStore.CallbackHandlerProtection** implements KeyStore.ProtectionParameter;
public static class **KeyStore.PasswordProtection**
        implements javax.security.auth.Destroyable, KeyStore.ProtectionParameter;
public static final class **KeyStore.PrivateKeyEntry** implements KeyStore.Entry;
public static final class **KeyStore.SecretKeyEntry** implements KeyStore.Entry;
public static final class **KeyStore.TrustedCertificateEntry** implements KeyStore.Entry;
public abstract class **KeyStoreSpi**;
public abstract class **MessageDigestSpi**;
    public abstract class **MessageDigest** extends MessageDigestSpi;
public abstract class **Permission** implements Guard, Serializable;
    public final class **AllPermission** extends Permission;
    public abstract class **BasicPermission** extends Permission implements Serializable;
        public final class **SecurityPermission** extends BasicPermission;
    public final class **UnresolvedPermission** extends Permission implements Serializable;
public abstract class **PermissionCollection** implements Serializable;
    public final class **Permissions** extends PermissionCollection implements Serializable;
public abstract class **Policy**;
public class **ProtectionDomain**;
public static class **Provider.Service**;
public class **SecureClassLoader** extends ClassLoader;
public class **SecureRandom** extends java.util.Random;
public abstract class **SecureRandomSpi** implements Serializable;
public final class **Security**;

```
public abstract class SignatureSpi;
    public abstract class Signature extends SignatureSpi;
public final class SignedObject implements Serializable;
public final class Timestamp implements Serializable;
```

Exceptions

```
public class AccessControlException extends SecurityException;
public class GeneralSecurityException extends Exception;
    public class DigestException extends GeneralSecurityException;
    public class InvalidAlgorithmParameterException extends GeneralSecurityException;
    public class KeyException extends GeneralSecurityException;
        public class InvalidKeyException extends KeyException;
        public class KeyManagementException extends KeyException;
    public class KeyStoreException extends GeneralSecurityException;
    public class NoSuchAlgorithmException extends GeneralSecurityException;
    public class NoSuchProviderException extends GeneralSecurityException;
    public class SignatureException extends GeneralSecurityException;
    public class UnrecoverableEntryException extends GeneralSecurityException;
    public class UnrecoverableKeyException extends GeneralSecurityException;
public class InvalidParameterException extends IllegalArgumentException;
public class PrivilegedActionException extends Exception;
public class ProviderException extends RuntimeException;
```

AccessControlContext — Java 1.2

java.security

This class encapsulates the state of a call stack. The checkPermission() method can make access-control decisions based on the saved state of the call stack. Access-control checks are usually performed by the AccessController.checkPermission() method, which checks that the current call stack has the required permissions. Sometimes, however, it is necessary to make access-control decisions based on a previous state of the call stack. Call AccessController.getContext() to create an AccessControlContext for a particular call stack. In Java 1.3, this class has constructors that specify a custom context in the form of an array of ProtectionDomain objects and that associate a DomainCombiner object with an existing AccessControlContext. This class is used only by system-level code; typical applications rarely need to use it.


```
public final class AccessControlContext {
// Public Constructors
    public AccessControlContext(ProtectionDomain[] context);
1.3 public AccessControlContext(AccessControlContext acc, DomainCombiner combiner);
// Public Instance Methods
    public void checkPermission(Permission perm) throws AccessControlException;
1.3 public DomainCombiner getDomainCombiner();
// Public Methods Overriding Object
    public boolean equals(Object obj);
    public int hashCode();
}
```

Passed To AccessController.doPrivileged(), javax.security.auth.Subject.{doAsPrivileged(), getSubject()}

Returned By AccessController.getContext()

AccessControlException Java 1.2

java.security serializable unchecked

Thrown by AccessController to signal that an access request has been denied. getPermission() returns the Permission object, if any, that was involved in the denied request.

Object → Throwable → Exception → RuntimeException → SecurityException → AccessControlException

Throwable ⋯ Serializable

```
public class AccessControlException extends SecurityException {
// Public Constructors
   public AccessControlException(String s);
   public AccessControlException(String s, Permission p);
// Public Instance Methods
   public Permission getPermission();
}
```

Thrown By AccessControlContext.checkPermission(), AccessController.checkPermission()

AccessController Java 1.2

java.security

The static methods of this class implement the default access-control mechanism as of Java 1.2. checkPermission() traverses the call stack of the current thread and checks whether all classes in the call stack have the requested permission. If so, checkPermission() returns, and the operation can proceed. If not, checkPermission() throws an AccessControlException. As of Java 1.2, the checkPermission() method of the default java.lang.SecurityManager calls AccessController.checkPermission(). System-level code that needs to perform an access check should invoke the SecurityManager method rather than calling the AccessController method directly. Unless you are writing system-level code that must control access to system resources, you never need to use this class or the SecurityManager.checkPermission() method.

The various doPrivileged() methods run blocks of privileged code encapsulated in a PrivilegedAction or PrivilegedExceptionAction object. When checkPermission() is traversing the call stack of a thread, it stops if it reaches a privileged block that was executed with doPrivileged(). This means that privileged code can run with a full set of privileges, even if it was invoked by untrusted or lower-privileged code. See PrivilegedAction for more details.

The getContext() method returns an AccessControlContext that represents the current security context of the caller. Such a context might be saved and passed to a future call (perhaps a call made from a different thread). Use the two-argument version of doPrivileged() to force permission checks to check the AccessControlContext as well.

```
public final class AccessController {
// No Constructor
// Public Class Methods
   public static void checkPermission(Permission perm) throws AccessControlException;
   public static <T> T doPrivileged(PrivilegedExceptionAction<T> action) throws PrivilegedActionException;    naopdtive
   public static <T> T doPrivileged(PrivilegedAction<T> action);                                             native
   public static <T> T doPrivileged(PrivilegedExceptionAction<T> action, AccessControlContext context)       native
      throws PrivilegedActionException;
   public static <T> T doPrivileged(PrivilegedAction<T> action, AccessControlContext context);               native
   public static AccessControlContext getContext();
}
```

AlgorithmParameterGenerator Java 1.2

java.security

This class defines a generic API for generating parameters for a cryptographic algorithm, typically a Signature or a javax.crypto.Cipher. Create an AlgorithmParameterGenerator by calling one of the static getInstance() factory methods and specifying the name of the algorithm and, optionally, the name or Provider object of the desired provider. The default "SUN" provider supports the "DSA" algorithm. The "SunJCE" provider shipped with the JCE supports "DiffieHellman". Once you have obtained a generator, initialize it by calling the init() method and specifying an algorithm-independent parameter size (in bits) or an algorithm-dependent AlgorithmParameterSpec object. You may also specify a SecureRandom source of randomness when you call init(). Once you have created and initialized the AlgorithmParameterGenerator, call generateParameters() to generate an AlgorithmParameters object.

```
public class AlgorithmParameterGenerator {
// Protected Constructors
   protected AlgorithmParameterGenerator(AlgorithmParameterGeneratorSpi paramGenSpi, Provider provider,
                                         String algorithm);
// Public Class Methods
   public static AlgorithmParameterGenerator getInstance(String algorithm) throws NoSuchAlgorithmException;
1.4 public static AlgorithmParameterGenerator getInstance(String algorithm, Provider provider)
        throws NoSuchAlgorithmException;
   public static AlgorithmParameterGenerator getInstance(String algorithm, String provider)
        throws NoSuchAlgorithmException, NoSuchProviderException;
// Public Instance Methods
   public final AlgorithmParameters generateParameters();
   public final String getAlgorithm();
   public final Provider getProvider();
   public final void init(java.security.spec.AlgorithmParameterSpec genParamSpec)
        throws InvalidAlgorithmParameterException;
   public final void init(int size);
   public final void init(java.security.spec.AlgorithmParameterSpec genParamSpec, SecureRandom random)
        throws InvalidAlgorithmParameterException;
   public final void init(int size, SecureRandom random);
}
```

AlgorithmParameterGeneratorSpi Java 1.2

java.security

This abstract class defines the service-provider interface for algorithm-parameter generation. A security provider must implement a concrete subclass of this class for each algorithm it supports. Applications never need to use or subclass this class.

```
public abstract class AlgorithmParameterGeneratorSpi {
// Public Constructors
   public AlgorithmParameterGeneratorSpi();
// Protected Instance Methods
   protected abstract AlgorithmParameters engineGenerateParameters();
   protected abstract void engineInit(java.security.spec.AlgorithmParameterSpec genParamSpec, SecureRandom random)
        throws InvalidAlgorithmParameterException;
   protected abstract void engineInit(int size, SecureRandom random);
}
```

Passed To AlgorithmParameterGenerator.AlgorithmParameterGenerator()

AlgorithmParameters Java 1.2

java.security

This class is a generic, opaque representation of the parameters used by some cryptographic algorithm. You can create an instance of the class with one of the static getInstance() factory methods, specifying the desired algorithm and, optionally, the desired provider. The default "SUN" provider supports the "DSA" algorithm. The "SunJCE" provider shipped with the JCE supports "DES", "DESede", "PBE", "Blowfish", and "DiffieHellman". Once you have obtained an AlgorithmParameters object, initialize it by passing an algorithm-specific java.security.spec.AlgorithmParameterSpec object or the encoded parameter values as a byte array to the init() method. You can also create an AlgorithmParameters object with an AlgorithmParameterGenerator. getEncoded() returns the initialized algorithm parameters as a byte array, using either the algorithm-specific default encoding or the named encoding format you specified.

```
public class AlgorithmParameters {
// Protected Constructors
   protected AlgorithmParameters(AlgorithmParametersSpi paramSpi, Provider provider, String algorithm);
// Public Class Methods
   public static AlgorithmParameters getInstance(String algorithm) throws NoSuchAlgorithmException;
   public static AlgorithmParameters getInstance(String algorithm, String provider)
      throws NoSuchAlgorithmException, NoSuchProviderException;
1.4 public static AlgorithmParameters getInstance(String algorithm, Provider provider)
      throws NoSuchAlgorithmException;
// Public Instance Methods
   public final String getAlgorithm();
   public final byte[] getEncoded() throws java.io.IOException;
   public final byte[] getEncoded(String format) throws java.io.IOException;
   public final <T extends java.security.spec.AlgorithmParameterSpec> T getParameterSpec(Class<T> paramSpec)
      throws java.security.spec.InvalidParameterSpecException;
   public final Provider getProvider();
   public final void init(java.security.spec.AlgorithmParameterSpec paramSpec)
      throws java.security.spec.InvalidParameterSpecException;
   public final void init(byte[] params) throws java.io.IOException;
   public final void init(byte[] params, String format) throws java.io.IOException;
// Public Methods Overriding Object
   public final String toString();
}
```

Passed To javax.crypto.Cipher.init(), javax.crypto.CipherSpi.engineInit(), javax.crypto.EncryptedPrivateKeyInfo.EncryptedPrivateKeyInfo(), javax.crypto.ExemptionMechanism.init(), javax.crypto.ExemptionMechanismSpi.engineInit()

Returned By AlgorithmParameterGenerator.generateParameters(), AlgorithmParameterGeneratorSpi.engineGenerateParameters(), Signature.getParameters(), SignatureSpi.engineGetParameters(), javax.crypto.Cipher.getParameters(), javax.crypto.CipherSpi.engineGetParameters(), javax.crypto.EncryptedPrivateKeyInfo.getAlgParameters()

AlgorithmParametersSpi Java 1.2

java.security

This abstract class defines the service-provider interface for AlgorithmParameters. A security provider must implement a concrete subclass of this class for each cryptographic algorithm it supports. Applications never need to use or subclass this class.

```
public abstract class AlgorithmParametersSpi {
// Public Constructors
   public AlgorithmParametersSpi();
// Protected Instance Methods
   protected abstract byte[] engineGetEncoded() throws java.io.IOException;
   protected abstract byte[] engineGetEncoded(String format) throws java.io.IOException;
   protected abstract <T extends java.security.spec.AlgorithmParameterSpec>
      T engineGetParameterSpec(Class<T> paramSpec)
      throws java.security.spec.InvalidParameterSpecException;
   protected abstract void engineInit(java.security.spec.AlgorithmParameterSpec paramSpec)
      throws java.security.spec.InvalidParameterSpecException;
   protected abstract void engineInit(byte[] params) throws java.io.IOException;
   protected abstract void engineInit(byte[] params, String format) throws java.io.IOException;
   protected abstract String engineToString();
}
```

Passed To AlgorithmParameters.AlgorithmParameters()

AllPermission — Java 1.2

java.security — serializable permission

This class is a Permission subclass whose implies() method always returns true. This means that code that has been granted AllPermission is granted all other possible permissions. This class exists to provide a convenient way to grant all permissions to completely trusted code. It should be used with care. Applications typically do not need to work directly with Permission objects.

Object — Permission — AllPermission
Guard, Serializable

```
public final class AllPermission extends Permission {
// Public Constructors
   public AllPermission();
   public AllPermission(String name, String actions);
// Public Methods Overriding Permission
   public boolean equals(Object obj);
   public String getActions();                                    default:"<all actions>"
   public int hashCode();                                                        constant
   public boolean implies(Permission p);                                         constant
   public PermissionCollection newPermissionCollection();
}
```

AuthProvider — Java 5.0

java.security — cloneable serializable collection

This subclass of Provider defines methods that allow users to "log in" before using the provider's services. An implementation of the login() method should use the supplied javax.security.auth.callback.CallbackHandler class to request the user's password or other authentication credentials. If no callback handler is passed to login(), it should use the one registered with setCallbackHandler() or a default.

Object — Dictionary — Hashtable — Properties — Provider — AuthProvider
Cloneable, Map, Serializable

java.security.*

```
public abstract class AuthProvider extends Provider {
// Protected Constructors
    protected AuthProvider(String name, double version, String info);
// Public Instance Methods
    public abstract void login(javax.security.auth.Subject subject, javax.security.auth.callback.CallbackHandler handler)
        throws javax.security.auth.login.LoginException;
    public abstract void logout() throws javax.security.auth.login.LoginException;
    public abstract void setCallbackHandler(javax.security.auth.callback.CallbackHandler handler);
}
```

BasicPermission — Java 1.2

java.security — serializable permission

This Permission class is the abstract superclass for a number of simple permission types. BasicPermission is typically subclassed to implement named permissions that have a name, or target, string, but do not support actions. The implies() method of BasicPermission defines a simple wildcarding capability. The target "*" implies permission for any target. The target "x.*" implies permission for any target that begins with "x.". Applications typically do not need to work directly with Permission objects.

Object — Permission — BasicPermission
Guard, Serializable — Serializable

```
public abstract class BasicPermission extends Permission implements Serializable {
// Public Constructors
    public BasicPermission(String name);
    public BasicPermission(String name, String actions);
// Public Methods Overriding Permission
    public boolean equals(Object obj);
    public String getActions();
    public int hashCode();
    public boolean implies(Permission p);
    public PermissionCollection newPermissionCollection();
}
```

Subclasses java.io.SerializablePermission, RuntimePermission, java.lang.management.ManagementPermission, java.lang.reflect.ReflectPermission, java.net.NetPermission, SecurityPermission, java.util.PropertyPermission, java.util.logging.LoggingPermission, javax.net.ssl.SSLPermission, javax.security.auth.AuthPermission, javax.security.auth.kerberos.DelegationPermission

Certificate — Java 1.1; Deprecated in 1.2

java.security — @Deprecated

This interface was used in Java 1.1 to represent an identity certificate. It has been deprecated as of Java 1.2 in favor of the java.security.cert package (see Chapter 19). See also java.security.cert.Certificate.

```
public interface Certificate {
// Public Instance Methods
    void decode(java.io.InputStream stream) throws KeyException, java.io.IOException;
    void encode(java.io.OutputStream stream) throws KeyException, java.io.IOException;
    String getFormat();
    Principal getGuarantor();
    Principal getPrincipal();
```

```
    PublicKey getPublicKey();
    String toString(boolean detailed);
}
```

Passed To Identity.{addCertificate(), removeCertificate()}

Returned By Identity.certificates()

CodeSigner

Java 5.0

java.security — serializable

This class encapsulates the certificate path of a code signer and a signed timestamp. Instances are immutable. See CodeSource and java.util.jar.JarEntry.

Object → CodeSigner ··· Serializable

```
public final class CodeSigner implements Serializable {
// Public Constructors
    public CodeSigner(java.security.cert.CertPath signerCertPath, Timestamp timestamp);
// Public Instance Methods
    public java.security.cert.CertPath getSignerCertPath();
    public Timestamp getTimestamp();
// Public Methods Overriding Object
    public boolean equals(Object obj);
    public int hashCode();
    public String toString();
}
```

Passed To CodeSource.CodeSource()

Returned By CodeSource.getCodeSigners(), java.util.jar.JarEntry.getCodeSigners()

CodeSource

Java 1.2

java.security — serializable

This class represents the source of a Java class, as defined by the URL from which the class was loaded and the set of digital signatures attached to the class. A CodeSource object is created by specifying a java.net.URL and an array of java.security.cert.Certificate objects. In Java 5.0, the class has been generalized to accept an array of CodeSigner objects instead of Certificate objects. Only applications that create custom ClassLoader objects should ever need to use or subclass this class.

When a CodeSource represents a specific piece of Java code, it includes a fully qualified URL and the actual set of certificates used to sign the code. When a CodeSource object defines a ProtectionDomain, however, the URL may include wildcards, and the array of certificates is a minimum required set of signatures. The implies() method of such a CodeSource tests whether a particular Java class comes from a matching URL and has the required set of signatures.

Object → CodeSource ··· Serializable

```
public class CodeSource implements Serializable {
// Public Constructors
5.0 public CodeSource(java.net.URL url, CodeSigner[] signers);
    public CodeSource(java.net.URL url, java.security.cert.Certificate[] certs);
// Public Instance Methods
    public final java.security.cert.Certificate[] getCertificates();
```

java.security.*

```
5.0 public final CodeSigner[] getCodeSigners();
    public final java.net.URL getLocation();
    public boolean implies(CodeSource codesource);
// Public Methods Overriding Object
    public boolean equals(Object obj);
    public int hashCode();
    public String toString();
}
```

Passed To java.net.URLClassLoader.getPermissions(), java.security.Policy.getPermissions(), ProtectionDomain.ProtectionDomain(), SecureClassLoader.{defineClass(), getPermissions()}, javax.security.auth.Policy.getPermissions()

Returned By ProtectionDomain.getCodeSource()

DigestException — Java 1.1

java.security — serializable checked

Signals a problem creating a message digest.

Object — Throwable — Exception — GeneralSecurityException — DigestException
Serializable

```
public class DigestException extends GeneralSecurityException {
// Public Constructors
    public DigestException();
5.0 public DigestException(Throwable cause);
    public DigestException(String msg);
5.0 public DigestException(String message, Throwable cause);
}
```

Thrown By MessageDigest.digest(), MessageDigestSpi.engineDigest()

DigestInputStream — Java 1.1

java.security — closeable

This class is a byte input stream with an associated MessageDigest object. When bytes are read with any of the read() methods, those bytes are automatically passed to the update() method of the MessageDigest. When you have finished reading bytes, you can call the digest() method of the MessageDigest to obtain a message digest. If you want to compute a digest just for some of the bytes read from the stream, use on() to turn the digesting function on and off. Digesting is on by default; call on(false) to turn it off. See also DigestOutputStream and MessageDigest.

Object — InputStream — FilterInputStream — DigestInputStream
Closeable

```
public class DigestInputStream extends java.io.FilterInputStream {
// Public Constructors
    public DigestInputStream(java.io.InputStream stream, MessageDigest digest);
// Public Instance Methods
    public MessageDigest getMessageDigest();
    public void on(boolean on);
    public void setMessageDigest(MessageDigest digest);
// Public Methods Overriding FilterInputStream
```

```
    public int read() throws java.io.IOException;
    public int read(byte[] b, int off, int len) throws java.io.IOException;
// Public Methods Overriding Object
    public String toString();
// Protected Instance Fields
    protected MessageDigest digest;
}
```

DigestOutputStream — Java 1.1

java.security — closeable flushable

This class is a byte output stream with an associated MessageDigest object. When bytes are written to the stream with any of the write() methods, those bytes are automatically passed to the update() method of the MessageDigest. When you have finished writing bytes, you can call the digest() method of the MessageDigest to obtain a message digest. If you want to compute a digest just for some of the bytes written to the stream, use on() to turn the digesting function on and off. Digesting is on by default; call on(false) to turn it off. See also DigestInputStream and MessageDigest.

Object — OutputStream — FilterOutputStream — DigestOutputStream

Closeable, Flushable

```
public class DigestOutputStream extends java.io.FilterOutputStream {
// Public Constructors
    public DigestOutputStream(java.io.OutputStream stream, MessageDigest digest);
// Public Instance Methods
    public MessageDigest getMessageDigest();
    public void on(boolean on);
    public void setMessageDigest(MessageDigest digest);
// Public Methods Overriding FilterOutputStream
    public void write(int b) throws java.io.IOException;
    public void write(byte[] b, int off, int len) throws java.io.IOException;
// Public Methods Overriding Object
    public String toString();
// Protected Instance Fields
    protected MessageDigest digest;
}
```

DomainCombiner — Java 1.3

java.security

This interface defines a single combine() method that combines two arrays of ProtectionDomain objects into a single equivalent (and perhaps optimized) array. You can associate a DomainCombiner with an existing AccessControlContext by calling the two-argument AccessControlContext() constructor. Then, when the checkPermission() method of the AccessControlContext is called or when the AccessControlContext is passed to a doPrivileged() method of AccessController, the specified DomainCombiner merges the protection domains of the current stack frame with the protection domains encapsulated in the AccessControlContext. This class is used only by system-level code; typical applications rarely need to use it.

```
public interface DomainCombiner {
// Public Instance Methods
    ProtectionDomain[] combine(ProtectionDomain[] currentDomains, ProtectionDomain[] assignedDomains);
}
```

Implementations javax.security.auth.SubjectDomainCombiner

Passed To AccessControlContext.AccessControlContext()

Returned By AccessControlContext.getDomainCombiner()

GeneralSecurityException — Java 1.2

java.security — serializable checked

This class is the superclass of most of the exceptions defined by the java.security package.

Object ─ Throwable ─ Exception ─ GeneralSecurityException
Serializable

```
public class GeneralSecurityException extends Exception {
// Public Constructors
    public GeneralSecurityException();
5.0 public GeneralSecurityException(Throwable cause);
    public GeneralSecurityException(String msg);
5.0 public GeneralSecurityException(String message, Throwable cause);
}
```

Subclasses Too many classes to list.

Guard — Java 1.2

java.security

This interface guards access to an object. The checkGuard() method is passed an object to which access has been requested. If access should be granted, checkGuard() should return silently. Otherwise, if access is denied, checkGuard() should throw a java.lang.SecurityException. The Guard object is used primarily by the GuardedObject class. Note that all Permission objects implement the Guard interface.

```
public interface Guard {
// Public Instance Methods
    void checkGuard(Object object) throws SecurityException;
}
```

Implementations Permission

Passed To GuardedObject.GuardedObject()

GuardedObject — Java 1.2

java.security — serializable

This class uses a Guard object to guard against unauthorized access to an arbitrary encapsulated object. Create a GuardedObject by specifying an object and a Guard for it. The getObject() method calls the checkGuard() method of the Guard to determine whether access to the object should be allowed. If access is allowed, getObject() returns the encapsulated object. Otherwise, it throws a java.lang.SecurityException.

The Guard object used by a GuardedObject is often a Permission. In this case, access to the guarded object is granted only if the calling code is granted the specified permission by the current security policy.

Object ─ GuardedObject ··· Serializable

```
public class GuardedObject implements Serializable {
// Public Constructors
   public GuardedObject(Object object, Guard guard);
// Public Instance Methods
   public Object getObject() throws SecurityException;
}
```

Identity

Java 1.1; Deprecated in 1.2

java.security

@Deprecated serializable

This deprecated class was used in Java 1.1 to represent an entity or Principal with an associated PublicKey object. In Java 1.1, the public key for a named entity could be retrieved from the system keystore with a line like the following:

```
IdentityScope.getSystemScope().getIdentity(name).getPublicKey()
```

As of Java 1.2, the Identity class and the related IdentityScope and Signer classes have been deprecated in favor of KeyStore and java.security.cert.Certificate.

Object — Identity

Principal, Serializable

```
public abstract class Identity implements Principal, Serializable {
// Public Constructors
   public Identity(String name);
   public Identity(String name, IdentityScope scope) throws KeyManagementException;
// Protected Constructors
   protected Identity();
// Public Instance Methods
   public void addCertificate(java.security.Certificate certificate) throws KeyManagementException;
   public java.security.Certificate[] certificates();
   public String getInfo();
   public PublicKey getPublicKey();
   public final IdentityScope getScope();
   public void removeCertificate(java.security.Certificate certificate) throws KeyManagementException;
   public void setInfo(String info);
   public void setPublicKey(PublicKey key) throws KeyManagementException;
   public String toString(boolean detailed);
// Methods Implementing Principal
   public final boolean equals(Object identity);
   public final String getName();
   public int hashCode();
   public String toString();
// Protected Instance Methods
   protected boolean identityEquals(Identity identity);
}
```

Subclasses IdentityScope, Signer

Passed To IdentityScope.{addIdentity(), removeIdentity()}

Returned By IdentityScope.getIdentity()

IdentityScope

Java 1.1; Deprecated in 1.2

java.security — @Deprecated serializable

This deprecated class was used in Java 1.1 to represent a group of Identity and Signer objects and their associated PublicKey and PrivateKey objects. As of Java 1.2, it has been replaced by the KeyStore class.

Object — Identity — IdentityScope
Principal, Serializable

```
public abstract class IdentityScope extends Identity {
// Public Constructors
    public IdentityScope(String name);
    public IdentityScope(String name, IdentityScope scope) throws KeyManagementException;
// Protected Constructors
    protected IdentityScope();
// Public Class Methods
    public static IdentityScope getSystemScope();
// Protected Class Methods
    protected static void setSystemScope(IdentityScope scope);
// Public Instance Methods
    public abstract void addIdentity(Identity identity) throws KeyManagementException;
    public abstract Identity getIdentity(String name);
    public Identity getIdentity(Principal principal);
    public abstract Identity getIdentity(PublicKey key);
    public abstract java.util.Enumeration<Identity> identities();
    public abstract void removeIdentity(Identity identity) throws KeyManagementException;
    public abstract int size();
// Public Methods Overriding Identity
    public String toString();
}
```

Passed To Identity.Identity(), Signer.Signer()

Returned By Identity.getScope()

InvalidAlgorithmParameterException

Java 1.2

java.security — serializable checked

Signals that one or more algorithm parameters (usually specified by a java.security.spec.AlgorithmParameterSpec object) are not valid.

Object — Throwable — Exception — GeneralSecurityException — InvalidAlgorithmParameterException
Serializable

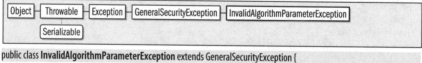

```
public class InvalidAlgorithmParameterException extends GeneralSecurityException {
// Public Constructors
    public InvalidAlgorithmParameterException();
5.0 public InvalidAlgorithmParameterException(Throwable cause);
    public InvalidAlgorithmParameterException(String msg);
5.0 public InvalidAlgorithmParameterException(String message, Throwable cause);
}
```

Thrown By Too many methods to list.

InvalidKeyException — Java 1.1

java.security — serializable checked

Signals that a Key is not valid.

Object — Throwable — Exception — GeneralSecurityException — KeyException — InvalidKeyException
Serializable

```
public class InvalidKeyException extends KeyException {
// Public Constructors
   public InvalidKeyException();
5.0 public InvalidKeyException(Throwable cause);
   public InvalidKeyException(String msg);
5.0 public InvalidKeyException(String message, Throwable cause);
}
```

Thrown By Too many methods to list.

InvalidParameterException — Java 1.1

java.security — serializable unchecked

This subclass of java.lang.IllegalArgumentException signals that a parameter passed to a security method is not valid. This exception type is not widely used.

Object — Throwable — Exception — RuntimeException — IllegalArgumentException — InvalidParameterException
Serializable

```
public class InvalidParameterException extends IllegalArgumentException {
// Public Constructors
   public InvalidParameterException();
   public InvalidParameterException(String msg);
}
```

Thrown By Signature.{getParameter(), setParameter()}, SignatureSpi.{engineGetParameter(), engineSetParameter()}, Signer.setKeyPair(), java.security.interfaces.DSAKeyPairGenerator.initialize()

Key — Java 1.1

java.security — serializable

This interface defines the high-level characteristics of all cryptographic keys. getAlgorithm() returns the name of the cryptographic algorithm (such as RSA) used with the key. getFormat() return the name of the external encoding (such as X.509) used with the key. getEncoded() returns the key as an array of bytes, encoded using the format specified by getFormat().

Serializable — Key

```
public interface Key extends Serializable {
// Public Constants
1.2 public static final long serialVersionUID;                    =6603384152749567654
// Public Instance Methods
   String getAlgorithm();
   byte[] getEncoded();
   String getFormat();
}
```

java.security.*

Implementations PrivateKey, PublicKey, javax.crypto.SecretKey

Passed To Too many methods to list.

Returned By KeyFactory.translateKey(), KeyFactorySpi.engineTranslateKey(), KeyStore.getKey(), KeyStoreSpi.engineGetKey(), javax.crypto.Cipher.unwrap(), javax.crypto.CipherSpi.engineUnwrap(), javax.crypto.KeyAgreement.doPhase(), javax.crypto.KeyAgreementSpi.engineDoPhase()

KeyException Java 1.1

java.security serializable checked

Signals that something is wrong with a key. See also the subclasses InvalidKeyException and KeyManagementException.

Object ─ Throwable ─ Exception ─ GeneralSecurityException ─ KeyException
Serializable

```
public class KeyException extends GeneralSecurityException {
// Public Constructors
    public KeyException();
5.0 public KeyException(Throwable cause);
    public KeyException(String msg);
5.0 public KeyException(String message, Throwable cause);
}
```

Subclasses InvalidKeyException, KeyManagementException

Thrown By java.security.Certificate.{decode(), encode()}, Signer.setKeyPair()

KeyFactory Java 1.2

java.security

This class translates asymmetric cryptographic keys between the two representations used by the Java Security API. java.security.Key is the opaque, algorithm-independent representation of a key used by most of the Security API. java.security.spec.KeySpec is a marker interface implemented by transparent, algorithm-specific representations of keys. KeyFactory is used with public and private keys; see javax.crypto.SecretKeyFactory if you are working with symmetric or secret keys.

To convert a Key to a KeySpec or vice versa, create a KeyFactory by calling one of the static getInstance() factory methods specifying the name of the key algorithm (e.g., DSA or RSA) and optionally specifying the name or Provider object for the desired provider. Then, use generatePublic() or generatePrivate() to create a PublicKey or PrivateKey object from a corresponding KeySpec. Or use getKeySpec() to obtain a KeySpec for a given Key. Because there can be more than one KeySpec implementation used by a particular cryptographic algorithm, you must also specify the Class of the KeySpec you desire.

If you do not need to transport keys portably between applications and/or systems, you can use a KeyStore to store and retrieve keys and certificates, avoiding KeySpec and KeyFactory altogether.

```
public class KeyFactory {
// Protected Constructors
    protected KeyFactory(KeyFactorySpi keyFacSpi, Provider provider, String algorithm);
// Public Class Methods
    public static KeyFactory getInstance(String algorithm) throws NoSuchAlgorithmException;
```

```
    public static KeyFactory getInstance(String algorithm, String provider)
        throws NoSuchAlgorithmException, NoSuchProviderException;
1.4 public static KeyFactory getInstance(String algorithm, Provider provider) throws NoSuchAlgorithmException;
// Public Instance Methods
    public final PrivateKey generatePrivate(java.security.spec.KeySpec keySpec)
        throws java.security.spec.InvalidKeySpecException;
    public final PublicKey generatePublic(java.security.spec.KeySpec keySpec)
        throws java.security.spec.InvalidKeySpecException;
    public final String getAlgorithm();
    public final <T extends java.security.spec.KeySpec> T getKeySpec(Key key, Class<T> keySpec)
        throws java.security.spec.InvalidKeySpecException;
    public final Provider getProvider();
    public final Key translateKey(Key key) throws InvalidKeyException;
}
```

KeyFactorySpi — Java 1.2

java.security

This abstract class defines the service-provider interface for KeyFactory. A security provider must implement a concrete subclass of this class for each cryptographic algorithm it supports. Applications never need to use or subclass this class.

```
public abstract class KeyFactorySpi {
// Public Constructors
    public KeyFactorySpi();
// Protected Instance Methods
    protected abstract PrivateKey engineGeneratePrivate(java.security.spec.KeySpec keySpec)
        throws java.security.spec.InvalidKeySpecException;
    protected abstract PublicKey engineGeneratePublic(java.security.spec.KeySpec keySpec)
        throws java.security.spec.InvalidKeySpecException;
    protected abstract <T extends java.security.spec.KeySpec> T engineGetKeySpec(Key key, Class<T> keySpec)
        throws java.security.spec.InvalidKeySpecException;
    protected abstract Key engineTranslateKey(Key key) throws InvalidKeyException;
}
```

Passed To KeyFactory.KeyFactory()

KeyManagementException — Java 1.1

java.security — serializable checked

Signals an exception in a key management operation. In Java 1.2, this exception is only thrown by deprecated methods.

Object — Throwable — Exception — GeneralSecurityException — KeyException — KeyManagementException
Serializable

```
public class KeyManagementException extends KeyException {
// Public Constructors
    public KeyManagementException();
5.0 public KeyManagementException(Throwable cause);
    public KeyManagementException(String msg);
5.0 public KeyManagementException(String message, Throwable cause);
}
```

Thrown By Identity.{addCertificate(), Identity(), removeCertificate(), setPublicKey()}, IdentityScope.{addIdentity(), IdentityScope(), removeIdentity()}, Signer.Signer(), javax.net.ssl.SSLContext.init(), javax.net.ssl.SSLContextSpi.engineInit()

KeyPair

Java 1.1

java.security

serializable

This class is a simple container for a PublicKey and a PrivateKey object. Because a KeyPair contains an unprotected private key, it must be used with as much caution as a PrivateKey object.

Object ─ KeyPair ··· Serializable

```
public final class KeyPair implements Serializable {
// Public Constructors
   public KeyPair(PublicKey publicKey, PrivateKey privateKey);
// Public Instance Methods
   public PrivateKey getPrivate();
   public PublicKey getPublic();
}
```

Passed To Signer.setKeyPair()

Returned By KeyPairGenerator.{generateKeyPair(), genKeyPair()}, KeyPairGeneratorSpi.generateKeyPair()

KeyPairGenerator

Java 1.1

java.security

This class generates a public/private key pair for a specified cryptographic algorithm. To create a KeyPairGenerator, call one of the static getInstance() methods, specifying the name of the algorithm and, optionally, the name or Provider object of the security provider to use. The default "SUN" provider shipped with Java 1.2 supports only the "DSA" algorithm. The "SunJCE" provider of the Java Cryptography Extension (JCE) additionally supports the "DiffieHellman" algorithm.

Once you have created a KeyPairGenerator, initialize it by calling initialize(). You can perform an algorithm-independent initialization by simply specifying the desired key size in bits. Alternatively, you can do an algorithm-dependent initialization by providing an appropriate AlgorithmParameterSpec object for the key-generation algorithm. In either case, you may optionally provide your own source of randomness in the guise of a SecureRandom object. Once you have created and initialized a KeyPairGenerator, call genKeyPair() to create a KeyPair object. Remember that the KeyPair contains a PrivateKey that *must* be kept private.

For historical reasons, KeyPairGenerator extends KeyPairGeneratorSpi. Applications should not use any methods inherited from that class.

Object ─ KeyPairGeneratorSpi ─ KeyPairGenerator

```
public abstract class KeyPairGenerator extends KeyPairGeneratorSpi {
// Protected Constructors
   protected KeyPairGenerator(String algorithm);
// Public Class Methods
   public static KeyPairGenerator getInstance(String algorithm) throws NoSuchAlgorithmException;
1.4 public static KeyPairGenerator getInstance(String algorithm, Provider provider) throws NoSuchAlgorithmException;
   public static KeyPairGenerator getInstance(String algorithm, String provider)
       throws NoSuchAlgorithmException, NoSuchProviderException;
```

```
// Public Instance Methods
1.2 public final KeyPair genKeyPair();
    public String getAlgorithm();
1.2 public final Provider getProvider();
1.2 public void initialize(java.security.spec.AlgorithmParameterSpec params) throws InvalidAlgorithmParameterException;
    public void initialize(int keysize);
// Public Methods Overriding KeyPairGeneratorSpi
    public KeyPair generateKeyPair();                                                    constant
1.2 public void initialize(java.security.spec.AlgorithmParameterSpec params, SecureRandom random)
        throws InvalidAlgorithmParameterException;                                       empty
    public void initialize(int keysize, SecureRandom random);                            empty
}
```

KeyPairGeneratorSpi — Java 1.2

java.security

This abstract class defines the service-provider interface for KeyPairGenerator. A security provider must implement a concrete subclass of this class for each cryptographic algorithm for which it can generate key pairs. Applications never need to use or subclass this class.

```
public abstract class KeyPairGeneratorSpi {
// Public Constructors
    public KeyPairGeneratorSpi();
// Public Instance Methods
    public abstract KeyPair generateKeyPair();
    public void initialize(java.security.spec.AlgorithmParameterSpec params, SecureRandom random)
        throws InvalidAlgorithmParameterException;
    public abstract void initialize(int keysize, SecureRandom random);
}
```

Subclasses KeyPairGenerator

KeyRep — Java 5.0

java.security — serializable

This class defines a serialized representation for Key implementations and is typically used only by security providers, not users of the java.security package.

Object — KeyRep ··· Serializable

```
public class KeyRep implements Serializable {
// Public Constructors
    public KeyRep(KeyRep.Type type, String algorithm, String format, byte[] encoded);
// Nested Types
    public enum Type;
// Protected Instance Methods
    protected Object readResolve() throws java.io.ObjectStreamException;
}
```

KeyRep.Type — Java 5.0

java.security — serializable comparable enum

The constants defined by this enumerated type represent the general types of cryptographic keys: public keys, private keys, and secret keys.

java.security.*

```
public enum KeyRep.Type {
// Enumerated Constants
   SECRET,
   PUBLIC,
   PRIVATE;
// Public Class Methods
   public static KeyRep.Type valueOf(String name);
   public static final KeyRep.Type[] values();
}
```

Passed To KeyRep.KeyRep()

KeyStore

Java 1.2

java.security

This class represents a mapping of names, or aliases, to Key and java.security.cert.Certificate objects. Obtain a KeyStore object by calling one of the static getInstance() methods, specifying the desired key store type and, optionally, the desired provider. Use "JKS" to specify the "Java Key Store" type defined by Sun. Because of U.S. export regulations, this default KeyStore supports only weak encryption of private keys. If you have the Java Cryptography Extension installed, use the type "JCEKS" and provider "SunJCE" to obtain a KeyStore implementation that offers much stronger password-based encryption of keys. Once you have created a KeyStore, use load() to read its contents from a stream, supplying an optional password that verifies the integrity of the stream data. Keystores are typically read from a file named *.keystore* in the user's home directory.

The KeyStore API has been substantially enhanced in Java 5.0. We describe pre-5.0 methods first, and then cover Java 5.0 enhancements below. A KeyStore may contain both public and private key entries. A public key entry is represented by a Certificate object. Use getCertificate() to look up a named public key certificate and setCertificateEntry() to add a new public key certificate to the keystore. A private key entry in the keystore contains both a password-protected Key and an array of Certificate objects that represent the certificate chain for the public key that corresponds to the private key. Use getKey() and getCertificateChain() to look up the key and certificate chain. Use setKeyEntry() to create a new private key entry. You must provide a password when reading or writing a private key from the keystore; this password encrypts the key data, and each private key entry should have a different password. If you are using the JCE, you may also store javax.crypto.SecretKey objects in a KeyStore. Secret keys are stored like private keys, except that they do not have a certificate chain associated with them. To delete an entry from a KeyStore, use deleteEntry(). If you modify the contents of a KeyStore, use store() to save the keystore to a specified stream. You may specify a password that is used to validate the integrity of the data, but it is not used to encrypt the keystore.

In Java 5.0 the KeyStore.Entry interface defines a keystore entry. Implementations include the nested types PrivateKeyEntry, SecretKeyEntry, and TrustedCertificateEntry. You can get or set an entry of any type with the new methods getEntry() and setEntry(). These methods accept a KeyStore.ProtectionParameter object, such as a password represented as a KeyStore.PasswordProtection object. Java 5.0 also defines new load() and store() methods that specify a password indirectly through a KeyStore.LoadStoreParameter.

```
public class KeyStore {
// Protected Constructors
   protected KeyStore(KeyStoreSpi keyStoreSpi, Provider provider, String type);
// Nested Types
```

```
5.0 public abstract static class Builder;
5.0 public static class CallbackHandlerProtection implements KeyStore.ProtectionParameter;
5.0 public interface Entry;
5.0 public interface LoadStoreParameter;
5.0 public static class PasswordProtection implements javax.security.auth.Destroyable, KeyStore.ProtectionParameter;
5.0 public static final class PrivateKeyEntry implements KeyStore.Entry;
5.0 public interface ProtectionParameter;
5.0 public static final class SecretKeyEntry implements KeyStore.Entry;
5.0 public static final class TrustedCertificateEntry implements KeyStore.Entry;
// Public Class Methods
    public static final String getDefaultType();
    public static KeyStore getInstance(String type) throws KeyStoreException;
    public static KeyStore getInstance(String type, String provider) throws KeyStoreException, NoSuchProviderException;
1.4 public static KeyStore getInstance(String type, Provider provider) throws KeyStoreException;
// Public Instance Methods
    public final java.util.Enumeration<String> aliases() throws KeyStoreException;
    public final boolean containsAlias(String alias) throws KeyStoreException;
    public final void deleteEntry(String alias) throws KeyStoreException;
5.0 public final boolean entryInstanceOf(String alias, Class<? extends KeyStore.Entry> entryClass)
        throws KeyStoreException;
    public final java.security.cert.Certificate getCertificate(String alias) throws KeyStoreException;
    public final String getCertificateAlias(java.security.cert.Certificate cert) throws KeyStoreException;
    public final java.security.cert.Certificate[] getCertificateChain(String alias) throws KeyStoreException;
    public final java.util.Date getCreationDate(String alias) throws KeyStoreException;
5.0 public final KeyStore.Entry getEntry(String alias, KeyStore.ProtectionParameter protParam)
        throws NoSuchAlgorithmException, UnrecoverableEntryException, KeyStoreException;
    public final Key getKey(String alias, char[] password)
        throws KeyStoreException, NoSuchAlgorithmException, UnrecoverableKeyException;
    public final Provider getProvider();
    public final String getType();
    public final boolean isCertificateEntry(String alias) throws KeyStoreException;
    public final boolean isKeyEntry(String alias) throws KeyStoreException;
5.0 public final void load(KeyStore.LoadStoreParameter param)
        throws java.io.IOException, NoSuchAlgorithmException, java.security.cert.CertificateException;
    public final void load(java.io.InputStream stream, char[] password)
        throws java.io.IOException, NoSuchAlgorithmException, java.security.cert.CertificateException;
    public final void setCertificateEntry(String alias, java.security.cert.Certificate cert) throws KeyStoreException;
5.0 public final void setEntry(String alias, KeyStore.Entry entry, KeyStore.ProtectionParameter protParam)
        throws KeyStoreException;
    public final void setKeyEntry(String alias, byte[] key, java.security.cert.Certificate[] chain) throws KeyStoreException;
    public final void setKeyEntry(String alias, Key key, char[] password, java.security.cert.Certificate[] chain)
        throws KeyStoreException;
    public final int size() throws KeyStoreException;
5.0 public final void store(KeyStore.LoadStoreParameter param)
        throws KeyStoreException, java.io.IOException, NoSuchAlgorithmException, java.security.cert.CertificateException;
    public final void store(java.io.OutputStream stream, char[] password)
        throws KeyStoreException, java.io.IOException, NoSuchAlgorithmException, java.security.cert.CertificateException;
}
```

Passed To KeyStore.Builder.newInstance(), java.security.cert.PKIXBuilderParameters.PKIXBuilderParameters(), java.security.cert.PKIXParameters.PKIXParameters(), javax.net.ssl.KeyManagerFactory.init(), javax.net.ssl.KeyManagerFactorySpi.engineInit(), javax.net.ssl.TrustManagerFactory.init(), javax.net.ssl.TrustManagerFactorySpi.engineInit()

Returned By KeyStore.Builder.getKeyStore()

KeyStore.Builder Java 5.0

java.security

An instance of this class encapsulates the parameters necessary to obtain a KeyStore object at some later time. This class is useful when you want to defer the initialization of a KeyStore (which may require the user to enter a password) until it is needed. See the javax.net.ssl.KeyStoreBuilderParameters class, for example.

```
public abstract static class KeyStore.Builder {
// Protected Constructors
    protected Builder();
// Public Class Methods
    public static KeyStore.Builder newInstance(KeyStore keyStore, KeyStore.ProtectionParameter protectionParameter);
    public static KeyStore.Builder newInstance(String type, Provider provider, KeyStore.ProtectionParameter protection);
    public static KeyStore.Builder newInstance(String type, Provider provider, java.io.File file,
                                               KeyStore.ProtectionParameter protection);
// Public Instance Methods
    public abstract KeyStore getKeyStore() throws KeyStoreException;
    public abstract KeyStore.ProtectionParameter getProtectionParameter(String alias) throws KeyStoreException;
}
```

Passed To javax.net.ssl.KeyStoreBuilderParameters.KeyStoreBuilderParameters()

KeyStore.CallbackHandlerProtection Java 5.0

java.security

This class is a KeyStore.ProtectionParameter implementation that wraps a javax.security.auth.callback.CallbackHandler for prompting the user for a password or other authentication credentials.

```
public static class KeyStore.CallbackHandlerProtection implements KeyStore.ProtectionParameter {
// Public Constructors
    public CallbackHandlerProtection(javax.security.auth.callback.CallbackHandler handler);
// Public Instance Methods
    public javax.security.auth.callback.CallbackHandler getCallbackHandler();
}
```

KeyStore.Entry Java 5.0

java.security

This marker interface represents an entry in a KeyStore.

```
public interface KeyStore.Entry {
}
```

Implementations KeyStore.PrivateKeyEntry, KeyStore.SecretKeyEntry, KeyStore.TrustedCertificateEntry

Passed To KeyStore.setEntry(), KeyStoreSpi.engineSetEntry()

Returned By KeyStore.getEntry(), KeyStoreSpi.engineGetEntry()

KeyStore.LoadStoreParameter Java 5.0

java.security

This interface represents an object passed to the load() or store() methods of KeyStore. An implementation must be able to return a KeyStore.ProtectionParameter.

```
public interface KeyStore.LoadStoreParameter {
// Public Instance Methods
   KeyStore.ProtectionParameter getProtectionParameter();
}
```

Passed To KeyStore.{load(), store()}, KeyStoreSpi.{engineLoad(), engineStore()}

KeyStore.PasswordProtection — Java 5.0

java.security

This class is a KeyStore.ProtectionParameter implementation that wraps a password specified as a char[]. Note that getPassword() returns a reference to the internal array, not a clone of it. The destroy() method zeros out this array.

```
public static class KeyStore.PasswordProtection
        implements javax.security.auth.Destroyable, KeyStore.ProtectionParameter {
// Public Constructors
   public PasswordProtection(char[] password);
// Public Instance Methods
   public char[] getPassword();                                          synchronized
// Methods Implementing Destroyable
   public void destroy() throws javax.security.auth.DestroyFailedException;  synchronized
   public boolean isDestroyed();                                         synchronized
}
```

KeyStore.PrivateKeyEntry — Java 5.0

java.security

This KeyStore.Entry implementation represents a private key. getPrivateKey() returns the key. getCertificateChain() returns the certificate chain of the corresponding public key. The first element of the returned array is the certificate of the ultimate certificate authority (CA). This "end entity" certificate is also available through the getCertificate() method.

```
public static final class KeyStore.PrivateKeyEntry implements KeyStore.Entry {
// Public Constructors
   public PrivateKeyEntry(PrivateKey privateKey, java.security.cert.Certificate[] chain);
// Public Instance Methods
   public java.security.cert.Certificate getCertificate();
   public java.security.cert.Certificate[] getCertificateChain();
   public PrivateKey getPrivateKey();
// Public Methods Overriding Object
   public String toString();
}
```

KeyStore.ProtectionParameter — Java 5.0

java.security

This marker interface should be implemented by classes that provide some form of protection for the entries in a KeyStore.

```
public interface KeyStore.ProtectionParameter {
}
```

Implementations KeyStore.CallbackHandlerProtection, KeyStore.PasswordProtection

Passed To KeyStore.{getEntry(), setEntry()}, KeyStore.Builder.newInstance(), KeyStoreSpi.{engineGetEntry(), engineSetEntry()}

Returned By KeyStore.Builder.getProtectionParameter(), KeyStore.LoadStoreParameter.getProtectionParameter()

KeyStore.SecretKeyEntry **Java 5.0**

java.security

This KeyStore.Entry implementation represents a secret key. getSecretKey() returns the key as a javax.crypto.SecretKey.

```
public static final class KeyStore.SecretKeyEntry implements KeyStore.Entry {
// Public Constructors
   public SecretKeyEntry(javax.crypto.SecretKey secretKey);
// Public Instance Methods
   public javax.crypto.SecretKey getSecretKey();
// Public Methods Overriding Object
   public String toString();
}
```

KeyStore.TrustedCertificateEntry **Java 5.0**

java.security

This implementation of KeyStore.Entry represents a certificate that contains and certifies a public key. getTrustedCertificate() returns the certificate.

```
public static final class KeyStore.TrustedCertificateEntry implements KeyStore.Entry {
// Public Constructors
   public TrustedCertificateEntry(java.security.cert.Certificate trustedCert);
// Public Instance Methods
   public java.security.cert.Certificate getTrustedCertificate();
// Public Methods Overriding Object
   public String toString();
}
```

KeyStoreException **Java 1.2**

java.security serializable checked

Signals a problem with a KeyStore.

Object — Throwable — Exception — GeneralSecurityException — KeyStoreException
Serializable

```
public class KeyStoreException extends GeneralSecurityException {
// Public Constructors
   public KeyStoreException();
5.0 public KeyStoreException(Throwable cause);
   public KeyStoreException(String msg);
5.0 public KeyStoreException(String message, Throwable cause);
}
```

Thrown By Too many methods to list.

KeyStoreSpi

Java 1.2

java.security

This abstract class defines the service-provider interface for KeyStore. A security provider must implement a concrete subclass of this class for each KeyStore type it supports. Applications never need to use or subclass this class.

```
public abstract class KeyStoreSpi {
// Public Constructors
   public KeyStoreSpi();
// Public Instance Methods
   public abstract java.util.Enumeration<String> engineAliases();
   public abstract boolean engineContainsAlias(String alias);
   public abstract void engineDeleteEntry(String alias) throws KeyStoreException;
5.0 public boolean engineEntryInstanceOf(String alias, Class<? extends KeyStore.Entry> entryClass);
   public abstract java.security.cert.Certificate engineGetCertificate(String alias);
   public abstract String engineGetCertificateAlias(java.security.cert.Certificate cert);
   public abstract java.security.cert.Certificate[] engineGetCertificateChain(String alias);
   public abstract java.util.Date engineGetCreationDate(String alias);
5.0 public KeyStore.Entry engineGetEntry(String alias, KeyStore.ProtectionParameter protParam)
      throws KeyStoreException, NoSuchAlgorithmException, UnrecoverableEntryException;
   public abstract Key engineGetKey(String alias, char[] password)
      throws NoSuchAlgorithmException, UnrecoverableKeyException;
   public abstract boolean engineIsCertificateEntry(String alias);
   public abstract boolean engineIsKeyEntry(String alias);
5.0 public void engineLoad(KeyStore.LoadStoreParameter param)
      throws java.io.IOException, NoSuchAlgorithmException, java.security.cert.CertificateException;
   public abstract void engineLoad(java.io.InputStream stream, char[] password)
      throws java.io.IOException, NoSuchAlgorithmException, java.security.cert.CertificateException;
   public abstract void engineSetCertificateEntry(String alias, java.security.cert.Certificate cert)
      throws KeyStoreException;
5.0 public void engineSetEntry(String alias, KeyStore.Entry entry, KeyStore.ProtectionParameter protParam)
      throws KeyStoreException;
   public abstract void engineSetKeyEntry(String alias, byte[] key, java.security.cert.Certificate[] chain)
      throws KeyStoreException;
   public abstract void engineSetKeyEntry(String alias, Key key, char[] password, java.security.cert.Certificate[] chain)
      throws KeyStoreException;
   public abstract int engineSize();
5.0 public void engineStore(KeyStore.LoadStoreParameter param)
      throws java.io.IOException, NoSuchAlgorithmException, java.security.cert.CertificateException;
   public abstract void engineStore(java.io.OutputStream stream, char[] password)
      throws java.io.IOException, NoSuchAlgorithmException, java.security.cert.CertificateException;
}
```

Passed To KeyStore.KeyStore()

MessageDigest

Java 1.1

java.security

This class computes a message digest (also known as a cryptographic checksum) for an arbitrary sequence of bytes. Obtain a MessageDigest object by calling one of the static getInstance() factory methods and specifying the desired algorithm (e.g., SHA or MD5) and, optionally, the desired provider. Next, specify the data to be digested by calling any of the update() methods one or more times. Prior to Java 5.0, you must pass a byte[] to update(). In Java 5.0 and later, however, you can also use a java.nio.ByteBuffer. This facilitates the computation of message digests when using the New I/O API.

After you pass data to update(), call digest(), which computes the message digest and returns it as an array of bytes. If you have only one array of bytes to be digested, you can pass it directly to digest() and skip the update() step. When you call digest(), the MessageDigest() object is reset and is then ready to compute a new digest. You can also explicitly reset a MessageDigest without computing the digest by calling reset(). To compute a digest for part of a message without resetting the MessageDigest, clone the MessageDigest and call digest() on the cloned copy. Note that not all implementations are cloneable, so the clone() method may throw an exception.

The MessageDigest class is often used in conjunction with DigestInputStream and DigestOutputStream, which automate the update() calls for you.

Object — MessageDigestSpi — MessageDigest

```
public abstract class MessageDigest extends MessageDigestSpi {
// Protected Constructors
    protected MessageDigest(String algorithm);
// Public Class Methods
    public static MessageDigest getInstance(String algorithm) throws NoSuchAlgorithmException;
    public static MessageDigest getInstance(String algorithm, String provider)
        throws NoSuchAlgorithmException, NoSuchProviderException;
1.4 public static MessageDigest getInstance(String algorithm, Provider provider)
        throws NoSuchAlgorithmException;
    public static boolean isEqual(byte[] digesta, byte[] digestb);
// Public Instance Methods
    public byte[] digest();
    public byte[] digest(byte[] input);
1.2 public int digest(byte[] buf, int offset, int len) throws DigestException;
    public final String getAlgorithm();
1.2 public final int getDigestLength();
1.2 public final Provider getProvider();
    public void reset();
    public void update(byte input);
    public void update(byte[] input);
5.0 public final void update(java.nio.ByteBuffer input);
    public void update(byte[] input, int offset, int len);
// Public Methods Overriding MessageDigestSpi
    public Object clone() throws CloneNotSupportedException;
// Public Methods Overriding Object
    public String toString();
}
```

Passed To DigestInputStream.{DigestInputStream(), setMessageDigest()}, DigestOutputStream.{DigestOutputStream(), setMessageDigest()}

Returned By DigestInputStream.getMessageDigest(), DigestOutputStream.getMessageDigest()

Type Of DigestInputStream.digest, DigestOutputStream.digest

MessageDigestSpi

Java 1.2

java.security

This abstract class defines the service-provider interface for MessageDigest. A security provider must implement a concrete subclass of this class for each message-digest algorithm it supports. Applications never need to use or subclass this class.

```
public abstract class MessageDigestSpi {
// Public Constructors
   public MessageDigestSpi();
// Public Methods Overriding Object
   public Object clone() throws CloneNotSupportedException;
// Protected Instance Methods
   protected abstract byte[] engineDigest();
   protected int engineDigest(byte[] buf, int offset, int len) throws DigestException;
   protected int engineGetDigestLength();                                    constant
   protected abstract void engineReset();
   protected abstract void engineUpdate(byte input);
5.0 protected void engineUpdate(java.nio.ByteBuffer input);
   protected abstract void engineUpdate(byte[] input, int offset, int len);
}
```

Subclasses MessageDigest

NoSuchAlgorithmException — Java 1.1

java.security — serializable checked

Signals that a requested cryptographic algorithm is not available. Thrown by getInstance() factory methods throughout the java.security package.

Object — Throwable — Exception — GeneralSecurityException — NoSuchAlgorithmException
Serializable

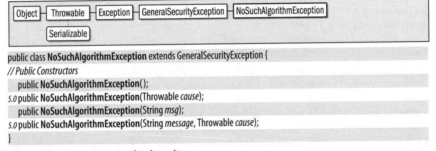

```
public class NoSuchAlgorithmException extends GeneralSecurityException {
// Public Constructors
   public NoSuchAlgorithmException();
5.0 public NoSuchAlgorithmException(Throwable cause);
   public NoSuchAlgorithmException(String msg);
5.0 public NoSuchAlgorithmException(String message, Throwable cause);
}
```

Thrown By Too many methods to list.

NoSuchProviderException — Java 1.1

java.security — serializable checked

Signals that a requested cryptographic service provider is not available. Thrown by getInstance() factory methods throughout the java.security package.

Object — Throwable — Exception — GeneralSecurityException — NoSuchProviderException
Serializable

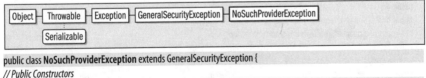

```
public class NoSuchProviderException extends GeneralSecurityException {
// Public Constructors
   public NoSuchProviderException();
   public NoSuchProviderException(String msg);
}
```

Thrown By Too many methods to list.

Permission **Java 1.2**

java.security **serializable permission**

This abstract class represents a system resource, such as a file in the filesystem, or a system capability, such as the ability to accept network connections. Concrete subclasses of Permission, such as java.io.FilePermission and java.net.SocketPermission, represent specific types of resources. Permission objects are used by system code that is requesting access to a resource. They are also used by Policy objects that grant access to resources. The AccessController.checkPermission() method considers the source of the currently running Java code, determines the set of permissions that are granted to that code by the current Policy, and then checks to see whether a specified Permission object is included in that set. As of Java 1.2, this is the fundamental Java access-control mechanism.

Each permission has a name (sometimes called the *target*) and, optionally, a comma-separated list of actions. For example, the name of a FilePermission is the name of the file or directory for which permission is being granted. The actions associated with this permission might be "read"; "write"; or "read,write". The interpretation of the name and action strings is entirely up to the implementation of Permission. A number of implementations support the use of wildcards; for example, a FilePermission can have a name of "/tmp/*", which represents access to any files in a */tmp* directory. Permission objects must be immutable, so an implementation must never define a setName() or setActions() method.

One of the most important abstract methods defined by Permission is implies(). This method must return true if this Permission implies another Permission. For example, if an application requests a FilePermission with name "/tmp/test" and action "read", and the current security Policy grants a FilePermission with name "/tmp/*" and actions "read,write", the request is granted because the requested permission is implied by the granted one.

In general, only system-level code needs to work directly with Permission and its concrete subclasses. System administrators who are configuring security policies need to understand the various Permission subclasses. Applications that want to extend the Java access-control mechanism to provide customized access control to their own resources should subclass Permission to define custom permission types.

Object — Permission
Guard, Serializable

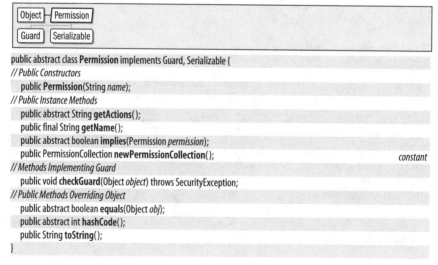

```
public abstract class Permission implements Guard, Serializable {
// Public Constructors
   public Permission(String name);
// Public Instance Methods
   public abstract String getActions();
   public final String getName();
   public abstract boolean implies(Permission permission);
   public PermissionCollection newPermissionCollection();                constant
// Methods Implementing Guard
   public void checkGuard(Object object) throws SecurityException;
// Public Methods Overriding Object
   public abstract boolean equals(Object obj);
   public abstract int hashCode();
   public String toString();
}
```

Subclasses java.io.FilePermission, java.net.SocketPermission, AllPermission, BasicPermission, UnresolvedPermission, javax.security.auth.PrivateCredentialPermission, javax.security.auth.kerberos.ServicePermission

Passed To Too many methods to list.

Returned By java.net.HttpURLConnection.getPermission(), java.net.URLConnection.getPermission(), AccessControlException.getPermission()

PermissionCollection Java 1.2

java.security — serializable

This class is used by Permissions to store a collection of Permission objects that are all the same type. Like the Permission class itself, PermissionCollection defines an implies() method that can determine whether a requested Permission is implied by any of the Permission objects in the collection. Some Permission types may require a custom PermissionCollection type in order to correctly implement the implies() method. In this case, the Permission subclass should override newPermissionCollection() to return a Permission of the appropriate type. PermissionCollection is used by system code that manages security policies. Applications rarely need to use it.

Object — PermissionCollection ··· Serializable

```
public abstract class PermissionCollection implements Serializable {
// Public Constructors
   public PermissionCollection();
// Public Instance Methods
   public abstract void add(Permission permission);
   public abstract java.util.Enumeration<Permission> elements();
   public abstract boolean implies(Permission permission);
   public boolean isReadOnly();
   public void setReadOnly();
// Public Methods Overriding Object
   public String toString();
}
```

Subclasses Permissions

Passed To ProtectionDomain.ProtectionDomain()

Returned By Too many methods to list.

Permissions Java 1.2

java.security — serializable

This class stores an arbitrary collection of Permission objects. When Permission objects are added with the add() method, they are grouped into an internal set of PermissionCollection objects that contain only a single type of Permission. Use the elements() method to obtain an Enumeration of the Permission objects in the collection. Use implies() to determine if a specified Permission is implied by any of the Permission objects in the collection. Permissions is used by system code that manages security policies. Applications rarely need to use it.

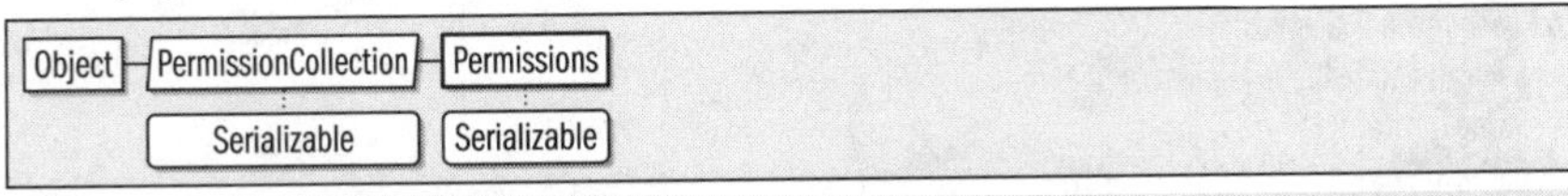


```
public final class Permissions extends PermissionCollection implements Serializable {
// Public Constructors
   public Permissions();
// Public Methods Overriding PermissionCollection
```

```
    public void add(Permission permission);
    public java.util.Enumeration<Permission> elements();
    public boolean implies(Permission permission);
}
```

Policy

Java 1.2

java.security

This class represents a security policy that determines the permissions granted to code based on its source and signers, and, in Java 1.4 and later, based on the user on whose behalf that code is running. There is only a single Policy in effect at any one time. Obtain the system policy by calling the static getPolicy() method. Code that has appropriate permissions can specify a new system policy by calling setPolicy(). The refresh() method is a request to a Policy object to update its state (for example, by rereading its configuration file). The Policy class is used primarily by system-level code. Applications should not need to use this class unless they implement some kind of custom access-control mechanism.

Prior to Java 1.4, this class provides a mapping from CodeSource objects to PermissionCollection objects. getPermissions() is the central Policy method; it evaluates the Policy for a given CodeSource and returns an appropriate PermissionCollection representing the static set of permissions available to code from that source.

As of Java 1.4, you can use a ProtectionDomain object to encapsulate a CodeSource and a set of users on whose behalf the code is running. In this release, there is a new getPermissions() method that returns a PermissionsCollection appropriate for the specified ProtectionDomain. In addition, there is a new implies() method that dynamically queries the Policy to see if the specified permission is granted to the specific ProtectionDomain.

```
public abstract class Policy {
// Public Constructors
    public Policy();
// Public Class Methods
    public static java.security.Policy getPolicy();
    public static void setPolicy(java.security.Policy p);
// Public Instance Methods
    public abstract PermissionCollection getPermissions(CodeSource codesource);
1.4 public PermissionCollection getPermissions(ProtectionDomain domain);
1.4 public boolean implies(ProtectionDomain domain, Permission permission);
    public abstract void refresh();
}
```

Principal

Java 1.1

java.security

This interface represents any entity that may serve as a principal in a cryptographic transaction of any kind. A Principal may represent an individual, a computer, or an organization, for example.

```
public interface Principal {
// Public Instance Methods
    boolean equals(Object another);
    String getName();
    int hashCode();
    String toString();
}
```

Implementations Identity, javax.security.auth.kerberos.KerberosPrincipal, javax.security.auth.x500.X500Principal

Passed To IdentityScope.getIdentity(), ProtectionDomain.ProtectionDomain(), javax.net.ssl.X509ExtendedKeyManager.{chooseEngineClientAlias(), chooseEngineServerAlias()}, javax.net.ssl.X509KeyManager.{chooseClientAlias(), chooseServerAlias(), getClientAliases(), getServerAliases()}

Returned By java.net.SecureCacheResponse.{getLocalPrincipal(), getPeerPrincipal()}, java.security.Certificate.{getGuarantor(), getPrincipal()}, ProtectionDomain.getPrincipals(), java.security.cert.X509Certificate.{getIssuerDN(), getSubjectDN()}, java.security.cert.X509CRL.getIssuerDN(), javax.net.ssl.HandshakeCompletedEvent.{getLocalPrincipal(), getPeerPrincipal()}, javax.net.ssl.HttpsURLConnection.{getLocalPrincipal(), getPeerPrincipal()}, javax.net.ssl.SSLSession.{getLocalPrincipal(), getPeerPrincipal()}

PrivateKey — Java 1.1

java.security — serializable

This interface represents a private cryptographic key. It extends the Key interface, but does not add any new methods. The interface exists in order to create a strong distinction between private and public keys. See also PublicKey.

Serializable — Key — PrivateKey

```
public interface PrivateKey extends Key {
// Public Constants
1.2 public static final long serialVersionUID;                    =6034044314589513430
}
```

Implementations java.security.interfaces.DSAPrivateKey, java.security.interfaces.ECPrivateKey, java.security.interfaces.RSAPrivateKey, javax.crypto.interfaces.DHPrivateKey

Passed To KeyPair.KeyPair(), KeyStore.PrivateKeyEntry.PrivateKeyEntry(), Signature.initSign(), SignatureSpi.engineInitSign(), SignedObject.SignedObject(), javax.security.auth.x500.X500PrivateCredential.X500PrivateCredential()

Returned By KeyFactory.generatePrivate(), KeyFactorySpi.engineGeneratePrivate(), KeyPair.getPrivate(), KeyStore.PrivateKeyEntry.getPrivateKey(), Signer.getPrivateKey(), javax.net.ssl.X509KeyManager.getPrivateKey(), javax.security.auth.x500.X500PrivateCredential.getPrivateKey()

PrivilegedAction<T> — Java 1.2

java.security

This interface defines a block of code (the run() method) that is to be executed as privileged code by the AccessController.doPrivileged() method. In Java 5.0 this interface is generic and the type variable *T* represents the return type of the run() method. When privileged code is run with the doPrivileged() method, the AccessController looks only at the permissions of the immediate caller, not the permissions of the entire call stack. The immediate caller is typically fully trusted system code that has a full set of permissions, and therefore the privileged code runs with that full set of permissions, even if the system code is invoked by untrusted code with no permissions whatsoever.

Privileged code is typically required only when you are writing a trusted system library (such as a Java extension package) that must read local files or perform other restricted actions, even when called by untrusted code. For example, a class that must call System.loadLibrary() to load native methods should make the call to loadLibrary() within the run() method of a PrivilegedAction. If your privileged code may throw a checked exception, implement it in the run() method of a PrivilegedExceptionAction instead.

Be very careful when implementing this interface. To minimize the possibility of security holes, keep the body of the run() method as short as possible.

```
public interface PrivilegedAction<T> {
// Public Instance Methods
   T run();
}
```

Passed To AccessController.doPrivileged(), java.util.concurrent.Executors.callable(), javax.security.auth.Subject.{doAs(), doAsPrivileged()}

PrivilegedActionException — Java 1.2

java.security — serializable checked

This exception class is a wrapper around an arbitrary Exception thrown by a PrivilegedExceptionAction executed by the AccessController.doPrivileged() method. Use getException() to obtain the wrapped Exception object. Or, in Java 1.4 and later, use the more general getCause() method.

Object — Throwable — Exception — PrivilegedActionException

Serializable

```
public class PrivilegedActionException extends Exception {
// Public Constructors
   public PrivilegedActionException(Exception exception);
// Public Instance Methods
   public Exception getException();
// Public Methods Overriding Throwable
1.4 public Throwable getCause();
1.3 public String toString();
}
```

Thrown By AccessController.doPrivileged(), javax.security.auth.Subject.{doAs(), doAsPrivileged()}

PrivilegedExceptionAction<T> — Java 1.2

java.security

This interface is like PrivilegedAction, except that its run() method may throw an exception. See PrivilegedAction for details.

```
public interface PrivilegedExceptionAction<T> {
// Public Instance Methods
   T run() throws Exception;
}
```

Passed To AccessController.doPrivileged(), java.util.concurrent.Executors.callable(), javax.security.auth.Subject.{doAs(), doAsPrivileged()}

ProtectionDomain — Java 1.2

java.security

This class represents a "protection domain": the set of permissions associated with code based on its source, and optionally, the identities of the users on whose behalf the code is running. Use the getProtectionDomain() of a Class object to obtain the ProtectionDomain that the class is part of.

Prior to Java 1.4, a ProtectionDomain simply associates a CodeSource with the PermissionCollection granted to code from that source by a Policy. The set of permissions is static, and the implies() method checks to see whether the specified Permission is implied by any of the permissions granted to this ProtectionDomain.

In Java 1.4 and later, a ProtectionDomain can also be created with the four-argument constructor which associates a PermissionCollection with a ClassLoader and an array of Principal objects in addition to a CodeSource. A ProtectionDomain of this sort represents permisssions granted to code loaded from a specified source, through a specified class loader, and running under the auspices of one or more specified principals. When a ProtectionDomain is instantiated with this four-argument constructor, the PermissionCollection is not static, and the implies() method calls the implies() method of the current Policy object before checking the specified collection of permissions. This allows security policies to be updated (for example to add new permissions for specific users) without having to restart long-running programs such as servers.

```
public class ProtectionDomain {
// Public Constructors
    public ProtectionDomain(CodeSource codesource, PermissionCollection permissions);
1.4 public ProtectionDomain(CodeSource codesource, PermissionCollection permissions, ClassLoader classloader,
                            Principal[] principals);
// Public Instance Methods
1.4 public final ClassLoader getClassLoader();
    public final CodeSource getCodeSource();
    public final PermissionCollection getPermissions();
1.4 public final Principal[] getPrincipals();
    public boolean implies(Permission permission);
// Public Methods Overriding Object
    public String toString();
}
```

Passed To ClassLoader.defineClass(), java.lang.instrument.ClassFileTransformer.transform(), AccessControlContext.AccessControlContext(), DomainCombiner.combine(), java.security.Policy.{getPermissions(), implies()}, javax.security.auth.SubjectDomainCombiner.combine()

Returned By Class.getProtectionDomain(), DomainCombiner.combine(), javax.security.auth.SubjectDomainCombiner.combine()

Provider — Java 1.1

java.security — cloneable serializable collection

This class represents a security provider. It specifies class names for implementations of one or more algorithms for message digests, digital signatures, key generation, key conversion, key management, secure random number generation, certificate conversion, and algorithm parameter management. The getName(), getVersion(), and getInfo() methods return information about the provider. Provider inherits from Properties and maintains a mapping of property names to property values. These name/value pairs specify the capabilities of the Provider implementation. Each property name has the form:

service_type.algorithm_name

The corresponding property value is the name of the class that implements the named algorithm. For example, say a Provider defines properties named "Signature.DSA", "MessageDigest.MD5", and "KeyStore.JKS". The values of these properties are the class names of SignatureSpi, MessageDigestSpi, and KeyStoreSpi implementations. Other properties defined by a Provider are used to provide aliases for algorithm names. For example, the property Alg.Alias.MessageDigest.SHA1 might have the value "SHA", meaning that the algorithm name "SHA1" is an alias for "SHA".

In Java 5.0, the individual services provided by a Provider are described by the nested Service class, and various methods for querying and setting the Service objects of a Provider are available.

Security providers are installed in an implementation-dependent way. For Sun's implementation, the *${java.home}/lib/security/java.security* file specifies the class names of all installed Provider implementations. An application can also install its own custom Provider with the addProvider() and insertProviderAt() methods of the Security class. Most applications do not need to use the Provider class directly. Typically, only security-provider implementors need to use the Provider class. Some applications may explicitly specify the name of a desired Provider when calling a static getInstance() factory method, however. Only applications with the most demanding cryptographic needs require custom providers.

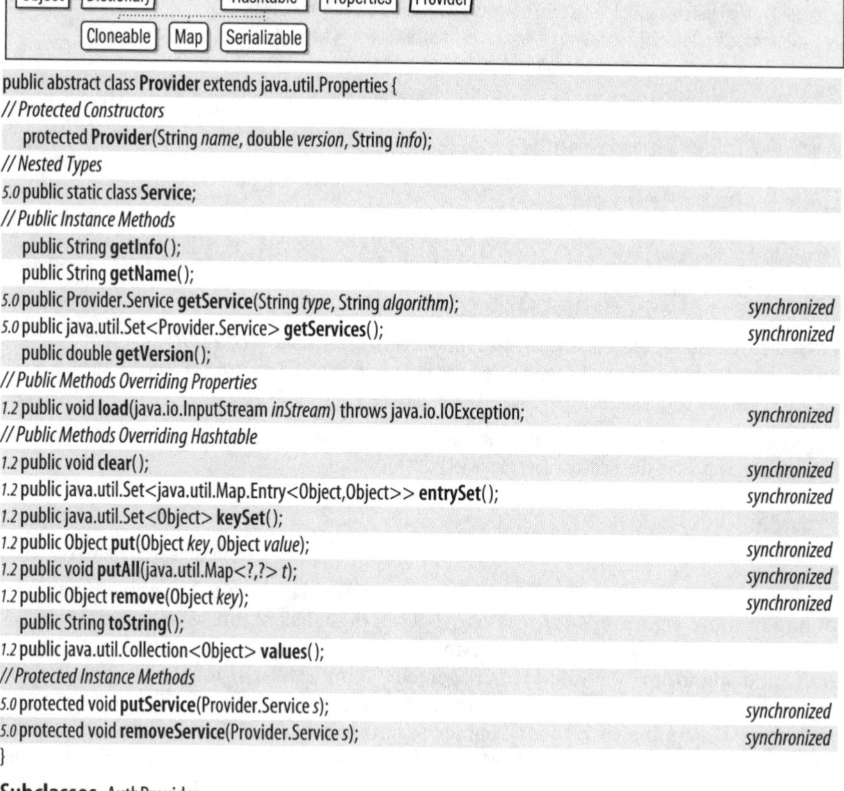


```
public abstract class Provider extends java.util.Properties {
// Protected Constructors
   protected Provider(String name, double version, String info);
// Nested Types
5.0 public static class Service;
// Public Instance Methods
   public String getInfo();
   public String getName();
5.0 public Provider.Service getService(String type, String algorithm);        synchronized
5.0 public java.util.Set<Provider.Service> getServices();                      synchronized
   public double getVersion();
// Public Methods Overriding Properties
1.2 public void load(java.io.InputStream inStream) throws java.io.IOException;  synchronized
// Public Methods Overriding Hashtable
1.2 public void clear();                                                       synchronized
1.2 public java.util.Set<java.util.Map.Entry<Object,Object>> entrySet();       synchronized
1.2 public java.util.Set<Object> keySet();
1.2 public Object put(Object key, Object value);                               synchronized
1.2 public void putAll(java.util.Map<?,?> t);                                  synchronized
1.2 public Object remove(Object key);                                          synchronized
   public String toString();
1.2 public java.util.Collection<Object> values();
// Protected Instance Methods
5.0 protected void putService(Provider.Service s);                             synchronized
5.0 protected void removeService(Provider.Service s);                          synchronized
}
```

Subclasses AuthProvider

Passed To Too many methods to list.

Returned By Too many methods to list.

Provider.Service Java 5.0

java.security

This nested class represents a single service (such as a hash algorithm) provided by a security **Provider**. The various methods return information about the service, including the name of the implementing class.

```
public static class Provider.Service {
// Public Constructors
    public Service(Provider provider, String type, String algorithm, String className, java.util.List<String> aliases,
                   java.util.Map<String,String> attributes);
// Public Instance Methods
    public final String getAlgorithm();
    public final String getAttribute(String name);
    public final String getClassName();
    public final Provider getProvider();
    public final String getType();
    public Object newInstance(Object constructorParameter) throws NoSuchAlgorithmException;
    public boolean supportsParameter(Object parameter);
// Public Methods Overriding Object
    public String toString();
}
```

Passed To Provider.{putService(), removeService()}

Returned By Provider.getService()

ProviderException Java 1.1

java.security serializable unchecked

Signals that an exception has occurred inside a cryptographic service provider. Note that **ProviderException** extends **RuntimeException** and is therefore an unchecked exception that may be thrown from any method without being declared.

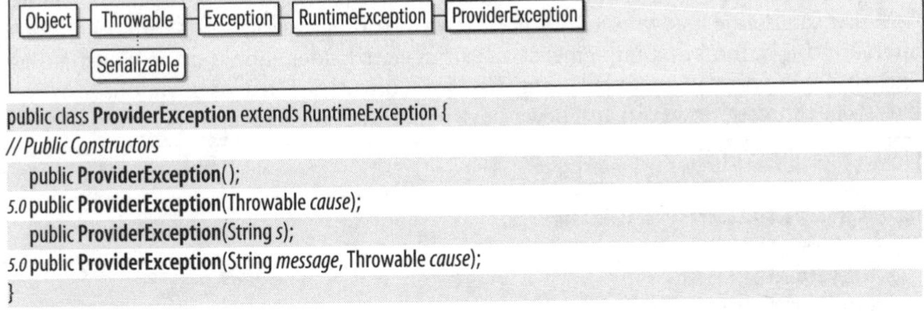


```
public class ProviderException extends RuntimeException {
// Public Constructors
    public ProviderException();
5.0 public ProviderException(Throwable cause);
    public ProviderException(String s);
5.0 public ProviderException(String message, Throwable cause);
}
```

PublicKey Java 1.1

java.security serializable

This interface represents a public cryptographic key. It extends the **Key** interface, but does not add any new methods. The interface exists in order to create a strong distinction between public and private keys. See also **PrivateKey**.

```
public interface PublicKey extends Key {
// Public Constants
1.2 public static final long serialVersionUID;                    =7187392471159151072
}
```

Implementations java.security.interfaces.DSAPublicKey, java.security.interfaces.ECPublicKey, java.security.interfaces.RSAPublicKey, javax.crypto.interfaces.DHPublicKey

Passed To Identity.setPublicKey(), IdentityScope.getIdentity(), KeyPair.KeyPair(), Signature.initVerify(), SignatureSpi.engineInitVerify(), SignedObject.verify(), java.security.cert.Certificate.verify(), java.security.cert.PKIXCertPathBuilderResult.PKIXCertPathBuilderResult(), java.security.cert.PKIXCertPathValidatorResult.PKIXCertPathValidatorResult(), java.security.cert.TrustAnchor.TrustAnchor(), java.security.cert.X509CertSelector.setSubjectPublicKey(), java.security.cert.X509CRL.verify()

Returned By java.security.Certificate.getPublicKey(), Identity.getPublicKey(), KeyFactory.generatePublic(), KeyFactorySpi.engineGeneratePublic(), KeyPair.getPublic(), java.security.cert.Certificate.getPublicKey(), java.security.cert.PKIXCertPathValidatorResult.getPublicKey(), java.security.cert.TrustAnchor.getCAPublicKey(), java.security.cert.X509CertSelector.getSubjectPublicKey()

SecureClassLoader Java 1.2

java.security

This class adds protected methods to those defined by ClassLoader. The defineClass() method is passed the bytes of a class file as a byte[] or, in Java 5.0, as a ByteBuffer and a CodeSource object that represents the source of that class. It calls the getPermissions() method to obtain a PermissionCollection for that CodeSource and then uses the CodeSource and PermissionCollection to create a ProtectionDomain, which is passed to the defineClass() method of its superclass.

The default implementation of the getPermissions() method uses the default Policy to determine the appropriate set of permissions for a given code source. The value of SecureClassLoader is that subclasses can use its defineClass() method to load classes without having to work explicitly with the ProtectionDomain and Policy classes. A subclass of SecureClassLoader can define its own security policy by overriding getPermissions(). In Java 1.2 and later, any application that implements a custom class loader should do so by extending SecureClassLoader, instead of subclassing ClassLoader directly. Most applications can use java.net.URLClassLoader, however, and never have to subclass this class.

Object — ClassLoader — SecureClassLoader

```
public class SecureClassLoader extends ClassLoader {
// Protected Constructors
   protected SecureClassLoader();
   protected SecureClassLoader(ClassLoader parent);
// Protected Instance Methods
5.0 protected final Class<?> defineClass(String name, java.nio.ByteBuffer b, CodeSource cs);
   protected final Class<?> defineClass(String name, byte[] b, int off, int len, CodeSource cs);
   protected PermissionCollection getPermissions(CodeSource codesource);
}
```

Subclasses java.net.URLClassLoader

SecureRandom **Java 1.1**

java.security **serializable**

This class generates cryptographic-quality pseudorandom bytes. Although **SecureRandom** defines public constructors, the preferred technique for obtaining a **SecureRandom** object is to call one of the static **getInstance()** factory methods, specifying the desired pseudorandom number-generation algorithm, and, optionally, the desired provider of that algorithm. Sun's implementation of Java ships with an algorithm named "SHA1PRNG" in the "SUN" provider.

Once you have obtained a **SecureRandom** object, call **nextBytes()** to fill an array with pseudorandom bytes. You can also call any of the methods defined by the **Random** superclass to obtain random numbers. The first time one of these methods is called, the **SecureRandom()** method uses its **generateSeed()** method to seed itself. If you have a source of random or very high-quality pseudorandom bytes, you may provide your own seed by calling **setSeed()**. Repeated calls to **setSeed()** augment the existing seed instead of replacing it. You can also call **generateSeed()** to generate seeds for use with other pseudorandom generators. **generateSeed()** may use a different algorithm than **nextBytes()** and may produce higher-quality randomness, usually at the expense of increased computation time.

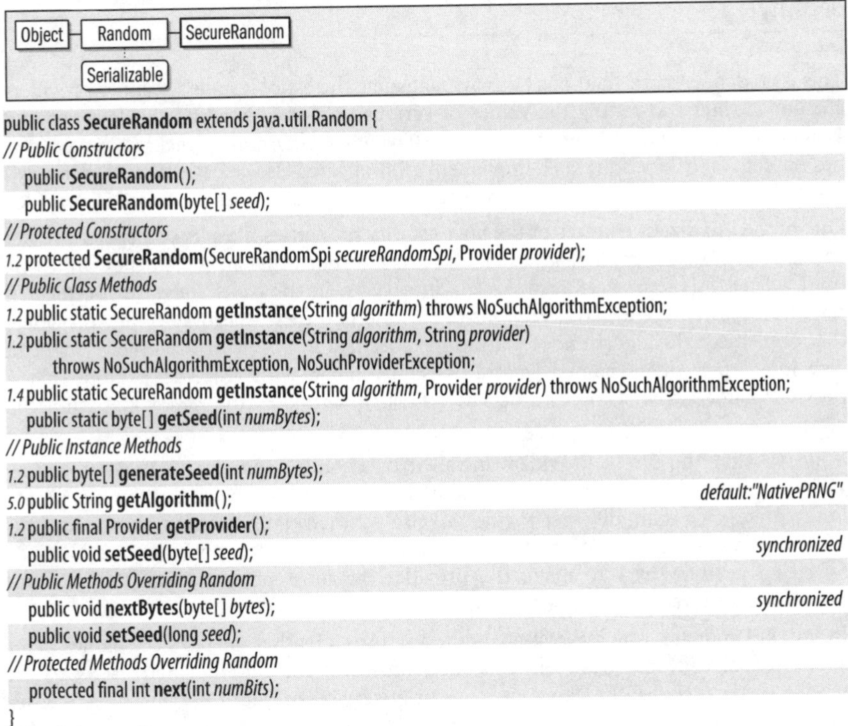


```
public class SecureRandom extends java.util.Random {
// Public Constructors
    public SecureRandom();
    public SecureRandom(byte[] seed);
// Protected Constructors
1.2 protected SecureRandom(SecureRandomSpi secureRandomSpi, Provider provider);
// Public Class Methods
1.2 public static SecureRandom getInstance(String algorithm) throws NoSuchAlgorithmException;
1.2 public static SecureRandom getInstance(String algorithm, String provider)
        throws NoSuchAlgorithmException, NoSuchProviderException;
1.4 public static SecureRandom getInstance(String algorithm, Provider provider) throws NoSuchAlgorithmException;
    public static byte[] getSeed(int numBytes);
// Public Instance Methods
1.2 public byte[] generateSeed(int numBytes);
5.0 public String getAlgorithm();                                   default:"NativePRNG"
1.2 public final Provider getProvider();
    public void setSeed(byte[] seed);                                     synchronized
// Public Methods Overriding Random
    public void nextBytes(byte[] bytes);                                  synchronized
    public void setSeed(long seed);
// Protected Methods Overriding Random
    protected final int next(int numBits);
}
```

Passed To Too many methods to list.

Type Of SignatureSpi.appRandom

SecureRandomSpi — Java 1.2

java.security — serializable

This abstract class defines the service-provider interface for SecureRandom. A security provider must implement a concrete subclass of this class for each pseudorandom number-generation algorithm it supports. Applications never need to use or subclass this class.

Object — SecureRandomSpi ··· Serializable

```
public abstract class SecureRandomSpi implements Serializable {
// Public Constructors
   public SecureRandomSpi();
// Protected Instance Methods
   protected abstract byte[] engineGenerateSeed(int numBytes);
   protected abstract void engineNextBytes(byte[] bytes);
   protected abstract void engineSetSeed(byte[] seed);
}
```

Passed To SecureRandom.SecureRandom()

Security — Java 1.1

java.security

This class defines static methods both for managing the list of installed security providers and for reading and setting the values of various properties used by the Java security system. It is essentially an interface to the *${java.home}/lib/security/java.security* properties file that is included in Sun's implementation of Java. Use getProperty() and setProperty() to query or set the value of security properties whose default values are stored in that file.

One of the important features of the *java.security* properties file is that it specifies a set of security provider implementations and a preference order in which they are to be used. getProviders() returns an array of Provider objects, in the order they are specified in the file. In Java 1.3 and later, versions of this method exist that only return providers that implement the algorithm or algorithms specified in a String or Map object. You can also look up a single named Provider object by name with getProvider(). Note that a provider name is the string returned by getName() method of the Provider class, not the classname of the Provider.

You can alter the set of providers installed by default from the java.security file. Use addProvider() to add a new Provider object to the list, placing it at the end of the list, with a lower preference than all other providers. Use insertProviderAt() to insert a provider into the list at a specified position. Note that provider preference positions are 1-based. Specify a position of 1 to make the provider the most preferred one. Finally, use removeProvider() to remove a named provider.

In Java 1.4 and later, the getAlgorithms method returns a Set that includes the names of all supported algorithms (from any installed provider) for the specified "service". A service name specifies the category of security service you are querying. It is a case-insensitive value that has the same name as one of the key service classes from this package or security-related packages—for example, "Signature", "MessageDigest", and "KeyStore" (from this package) or "Cipher" (from the javax.crypto package).

```
public final class Security {
// No Constructor
// Public Class Methods
```

```
    public static int addProvider(Provider provider);
1.4 public static java.util.Set<String> getAlgorithms(String serviceName);
    public static String getProperty(String key);
    public static Provider getProvider(String name);
    public static Provider[] getProviders();
1.3 public static Provider[] getProviders(java.util.Map<String,String> filter);
1.3 public static Provider[] getProviders(String filter);
    public static int insertProviderAt(Provider provider, int position);      synchronized
    public static void removeProvider(String name);                           synchronized
    public static void setProperty(String key, String datum);
// Deprecated Public Methods
#   public static String getAlgorithmProperty(String algName, String propName);
}
```

SecurityPermission — Java 1.2

java.security — serializable permission

This class is a **Permission** subclass that represents access to various methods of the **Policy**, **Security**, **Provider**, **Signer**, and **Identity** objects. **SecurityPermission** objects are defined by a name only; they do not use a list of actions. Important **SecurityPermission** names are "getPolicy" and "setPolicy", which represent the ability query and set the system security policy by invoking the **Policy.getPolicy()** and **Policy.setPolicy()** methods. Applications do not typically need to use this class.

```
public final class SecurityPermission extends BasicPermission {
// Public Constructors
    public SecurityPermission(String name);
    public SecurityPermission(String name, String actions);
}
```

Object — Permission — BasicPermission — SecurityPermission
Guard, Serializable (Permission); Serializable (BasicPermission)

Signature — Java 1.1

java.security

This class computes or verifies a digital signature. Obtain a **Signature** object by calling one of the static **getInstance()** factory methods and specifying the desired digital signature algorithm and, optionally, the desired provider of that algorithm. A *digital signature* is essentially a message digest encrypted by a public-key encryption algorithm. Thus, to specify a digital signature algorithm, you must specify both the digest algorithm and the encryption algorithm. The only algorithm supported by the default "SUN" provider is "SHA1withDSA".

Once you have obtained a **Signature** object, you must initialize it before you can create or verify a digital signature. To initialize a digital signature for creation, call **initSign()** and specify the private key to be used to create the signature. To initialize a signature for verification, call **initVerify()** and specify the public key of the signer. Once the **Signature** object has been initialized, call **update()** one or more times to specify the data to be signed or verified. Prior to Java 5.0, the data must be specified as an array of bytes. In Java 5.0 and later, you can also pass a **ByteBuffer** to **update()**, and this facilitates the use of the **Signature** class with the **java.nio** package.

Finally, to create a digital signature, call **sign()**, passing a byte array into which the signature is stored. Or, pass the bytes of the digital signature to **verify()**, which returns **true** if the signature is valid or **false** otherwise. After calling either **sign()** or **verify()**, the **Signature** object is reset internally and can be used to create or verify another signature.

Object — SignatureSpi — Signature

```
public abstract class Signature extends SignatureSpi {
// Protected Constructors
    protected Signature(String algorithm);
// Protected Constants
    protected static final int SIGN;                                                       =2
    protected static final int UNINITIALIZED;                                              =0
    protected static final int VERIFY;                                                     =3
// Public Class Methods
    public static Signature getInstance(String algorithm) throws NoSuchAlgorithmException;
1.4 public static Signature getInstance(String algorithm, Provider provider) throws NoSuchAlgorithmException;
    public static Signature getInstance(String algorithm, String provider)
        throws NoSuchAlgorithmException, NoSuchProviderException;
// Public Instance Methods
    public final String getAlgorithm();
1.4 public final AlgorithmParameters getParameters();
1.2 public final Provider getProvider();
    public final void initSign(PrivateKey privateKey) throws InvalidKeyException;
1.2 public final void initSign(PrivateKey privateKey, SecureRandom random) throws InvalidKeyException;
1.3 public final void initVerify(java.security.cert.Certificate certificate) throws InvalidKeyException;
    public final void initVerify(PublicKey publicKey) throws InvalidKeyException;
1.2 public final void setParameter(java.security.spec.AlgorithmParameterSpec params)
        throws InvalidAlgorithmParameterException;
    public final byte[] sign() throws SignatureException;
1.2 public final int sign(byte[] outbuf, int offset, int len) throws SignatureException;
5.0 public final void update(java.nio.ByteBuffer data) throws SignatureException;
    public final void update(byte b) throws SignatureException;
    public final void update(byte[] data) throws SignatureException;
    public final void update(byte[] data, int off, int len) throws SignatureException;
    public final boolean verify(byte[] signature) throws SignatureException;
1.4 public final boolean verify(byte[] signature, int offset, int length) throws SignatureException;
// Public Methods Overriding SignatureSpi
    public Object clone() throws CloneNotSupportedException;
// Public Methods Overriding Object
    public String toString();
// Protected Instance Fields
    protected int state;
// Deprecated Public Methods
#   public final Object getParameter(String param) throws InvalidParameterException;
#   public final void setParameter(String param, Object value) throws InvalidParameterException;
}
```

Passed To SignedObject.{SignedObject(), verify()}

SignatureException

Java 1.1

java.security

serializable checked

Signals a problem while creating or verifying a digital signature.

Object ─ Throwable ─ Exception ─ GeneralSecurityException ─ SignatureException

Serializable

```
public class SignatureException extends GeneralSecurityException {
// Public Constructors
    public SignatureException();
5.0 public SignatureException(Throwable cause);
    public SignatureException(String msg);
5.0 public SignatureException(String message, Throwable cause);
}
```

Thrown By Too many methods to list.

SignatureSpi

Java 1.2

java.security

This abstract class defines the service-provider interface for Signature. A security provider must implement a concrete subclass of this class for each digital signature algorithm it supports. Applications never need to use or subclass this class.

```
public abstract class SignatureSpi {
// Public Constructors
    public SignatureSpi();
// Public Methods Overriding Object
    public Object clone() throws CloneNotSupportedException;
// Protected Instance Methods
1.4 protected AlgorithmParameters engineGetParameters();
    protected abstract void engineInitSign(PrivateKey privateKey) throws InvalidKeyException;
    protected void engineInitSign(PrivateKey privateKey, SecureRandom random) throws InvalidKeyException;
    protected abstract void engineInitVerify(PublicKey publicKey) throws InvalidKeyException;
    protected void engineSetParameter(java.security.spec.AlgorithmParameterSpec params)
        throws InvalidAlgorithmParameterException;
    protected abstract byte[] engineSign() throws SignatureException;
    protected int engineSign(byte[] outbuf, int offset, int len) throws SignatureException;
5.0 protected void engineUpdate(java.nio.ByteBuffer input);
    protected abstract void engineUpdate(byte b) throws SignatureException;
    protected abstract void engineUpdate(byte[] b, int off, int len) throws SignatureException;
    protected abstract boolean engineVerify(byte[] sigBytes) throws SignatureException;
1.4 protected boolean engineVerify(byte[] sigBytes, int offset, int length) throws SignatureException;
// Protected Instance Fields
    protected SecureRandom appRandom;
// Deprecated Protected Methods
#   protected abstract Object engineGetParameter(String param) throws InvalidParameterException;
#   protected abstract void engineSetParameter(String param, Object value) throws InvalidParameterException;
}
```

Subclasses Signature

java.security.*

SignedObject

Java 1.2

java.security

serializable

This class applies a digital signature to any serializable Java object. Create a SignedObject by specifying the object to be signed, the PrivateKey to use for the signature, and the Signature object to create the signature. The SignedObject() constructor serializes the specified object into an array of bytes and creates a digital signature for those bytes.

After creation, a SignedObject is itself typically serialized for storage or transmission to another Java thread or process. Once the SignedObject is reconstituted, the integrity of the object it contains can be verified by calling verify() and supplying the PublicKey of the signer and a Signature that performs the verification. Whether or not verification is performed or is successful, getObject() can be called to deserialize and return the wrapped object.

Object — SignedObject ··· Serializable

```
public final class SignedObject implements Serializable {
// Public Constructors
   public SignedObject(Serializable object, PrivateKey signingKey, Signature signingEngine)
       throws java.io.IOException, InvalidKeyException, SignatureException;
// Public Instance Methods
   public String getAlgorithm();
   public Object getObject() throws java.io.IOException, ClassNotFoundException;
   public byte[] getSignature();
   public boolean verify(PublicKey verificationKey, Signature verificationEngine)
       throws InvalidKeyException, SignatureException;
}
```

Signer

Java 1.1; Deprecated in 1.2

java.security

@Deprecated serializable

This deprecated class was used in Java 1.1 to represent an entity or Principal that has an associated PrivateKey that enables it to create digital signatures. As of Java 1.2, this class and the related Identity and IdentityScope classes have been replaced by KeyStore and java.security.cert.Certificate. See also Identity.

Object — Identity — Signer

Principal Serializable

```
public abstract class Signer extends Identity {
// Public Constructors
   public Signer(String name);
   public Signer(String name, IdentityScope scope) throws KeyManagementException;
// Protected Constructors
   protected Signer();
// Public Instance Methods
   public PrivateKey getPrivateKey();
   public final void setKeyPair(KeyPair pair) throws InvalidParameterException, KeyException;
// Public Methods Overriding Identity
   public String toString();
}
```

Timestamp

Java 5.0

java.security

serializable

An instance of this class is an immutable signed timestamp. getTimestamp() returns the timestamp as a java.util.Date. getSignerCertPath() returns the certificate path of the Time-stamping Authority (TSA) that signed the object. Timestamp objects are used by the CodeSigner class.

Object ─ Timestamp ··· Serializable

```
public final class Timestamp implements Serializable {
// Public Constructors
   public Timestamp(java.util.Date timestamp, java.security.cert.CertPath signerCertPath);
// Public Instance Methods
   public java.security.cert.CertPath getSignerCertPath();
   public java.util.Date getTimestamp();
// Public Methods Overriding Object
   public boolean equals(Object obj);
   public int hashCode();
   public String toString();
}
```

Passed To CodeSigner.CodeSigner()

Returned By CodeSigner.getTimestamp()

UnrecoverableEntryException

Java 5.0

java.security

serializable checked

An exception of this type is thrown if a KeyStore.Entry cannot be recovered from a KeyStore.

Object ─ Throwable ─ Exception ─ GeneralSecurityException ─ UnrecoverableEntryException
Throwable ··· Serializable

```
public class UnrecoverableEntryException extends GeneralSecurityException {
// Public Constructors
   public UnrecoverableEntryException();
   public UnrecoverableEntryException(String msg);
}
```

Thrown By KeyStore.getEntry(), KeyStoreSpi.engineGetEntry()

UnrecoverableKeyException

Java 1.2

java.security

serializable checked

This exception is thrown if a Key cannot be retrieved from a KeyStore. This commonly occurs when an incorrect password is used.

Object ─ Throwable ─ Exception ─ GeneralSecurityException ─ UnrecoverableKeyException
Throwable ··· Serializable

```
public class UnrecoverableKeyException extends GeneralSecurityException {
// Public Constructors
   public UnrecoverableKeyException();
   public UnrecoverableKeyException(String msg);
}
```

Thrown By KeyStore.getKey(), KeyStoreSpi.engineGetKey(), javax.net.ssl.KeyManagerFactory.init(), javax.net.ssl.KeyManagerFactorySpi.engineInit()

UnresolvedPermission Java 1.2

java.security serializable permission

This class is used internally to provide a mechanism for delayed resolution of permissions (such as those whose implementation is in an external JAR file that has not been loaded yet). An UnresolvedPermission holds a representation of a Permission object that can later be used to create the actual Permission object. Java 5.0 adds methods to obtain details about the unresolved permission. Applications never need to use this class.

Object — Permission — UnresolvedPermission
Guard, Serializable, Serializable

```
public final class UnresolvedPermission extends Permission implements Serializable {
// Public Constructors
   public UnresolvedPermission(String type, String name, String actions, java.security.cert.Certificate[] certs);
// Public Instance Methods
5.0 public String getUnresolvedActions();
5.0 public java.security.cert.Certificate[] getUnresolvedCerts();
5.0 public String getUnresolvedName();
5.0 public String getUnresolvedType();
// Public Methods Overriding Permission
   public boolean equals(Object obj);
   public String getActions();
   public int hashCode();
   public boolean implies(Permission p);                                    constant
   public PermissionCollection newPermissionCollection();
   public String toString();
}
```

Package java.security.cert Java 1.2

The java.security.cert package contains classes for working with identity certificates, certificate chains (also known as certification paths) and certificate revocation lists (CRLs). It defines generic Certificate and CRL classes and also X509Certificate and X509CRL classes that provide full support for standard X.509 certificates and CRLs. The CertPath class represents a certificate chain, and CertPathValidator provides the ability to validate a certificate chain. The CertificateFactory class serves as a certificate parser, providing the ability to convert a stream of bytes (or the base64 encoding of those bytes) into a Certificate, a CertPath or a CRL object. In addition to the algorithm-independent API of CertificateFactory, this package also defines low-level algorithm-specific classes for working with certificate chains using the PKIX standards.

This package replaces the deprecated java.security.Certificate interface, and it also replaces the deprecated javax.security.cert package used by early versions of the JAAS API before javax.security.auth and its subpackages were added to the core Java platform.

Interfaces

```
public interface CertPathBuilderResult extends Cloneable;
public interface CertPathParameters extends Cloneable;
```

public interface **CertPathValidatorResult** extends Cloneable;
public interface **CertSelector** extends Cloneable;
public interface **CertStoreParameters** extends Cloneable;
public interface **CRLSelector** extends Cloneable;
public interface **PolicyNode**;
public interface **X509Extension**;

Classes

public abstract class **Certificate** implements Serializable;
  public abstract class **X509Certificate** extends Certificate implements X509Extension;
public class **CertificateFactory**;
public abstract class **CertificateFactorySpi**;
public abstract class **CertPath** implements Serializable;
public class **CertPathBuilder**;
public abstract class **CertPathBuilderSpi**;
public class **CertPathValidator**;
public abstract class **CertPathValidatorSpi**;
public class **CertStore**;
public abstract class **CertStoreSpi**;
public class **CollectionCertStoreParameters** implements CertStoreParameters;
public abstract class **CRL**;
  public abstract class **X509CRL** extends CRL implements X509Extension;
public class **LDAPCertStoreParameters** implements CertStoreParameters;
public abstract class **PKIXCertPathChecker** implements Cloneable;
public class **PKIXCertPathValidatorResult** implements CertPathValidatorResult;
  public class **PKIXCertPathBuilderResult** extends PKIXCertPathValidatorResult implements CertPathBuilderResult;
public class **PKIXParameters** implements CertPathParameters;
  public class **PKIXBuilderParameters** extends PKIXParameters;
public class **PolicyQualifierInfo**;
public class **TrustAnchor**;
public class **X509CertSelector** implements CertSelector;
public abstract class **X509CRLEntry** implements X509Extension;
public class **X509CRLSelector** implements CRLSelector;

Protected Nested Types

protected static class **Certificate.CertificateRep** implements Serializable;
protected static class **CertPath.CertPathRep** implements Serializable;

Exceptions

public class **CertificateException** extends java.security.GeneralSecurityException;
  public class **CertificateEncodingException** extends CertificateException;
  public class **CertificateExpiredException** extends CertificateException;
  public class **CertificateNotYetValidException** extends CertificateException;
  public class **CertificateParsingException** extends CertificateException;
public class **CertPathBuilderException** extends java.security.GeneralSecurityException;
public class **CertPathValidatorException** extends java.security.GeneralSecurityException;
public class **CertStoreException** extends java.security.GeneralSecurityException;
public class **CRLException** extends java.security.GeneralSecurityException;

Certificate

Java 1.2

java.security.cert

serializable

This abstract class represents an public-key (or identity) certificate. A *certificate* is an object that contains the name of an entity and a public key for that entity. Certificates are issued by, and bear the digital signature of, a (presumably trusted) third party, typically a *certificate authority* (CA). By issuing and signing the certificate, the CA is certifying that, based on their research, the entity named on the certificate really is who they say they are and that the public key in the certificate really does belong to that entity. Sometimes the signer of a certificate is not a trusted CA, and the certificate is accompanied by the signer's certificate which may be signed by a CA, or by another untrusted intermediary who provides his or her own certificate. A "chain" of such certificates is known as a "certification path". See CertPath for further details.

Use a CertificateFactory to parse a stream of bytes into a Certificate object; getEncoded() reverses this process. Use verify() to verify the digital signature of the entity that issued the certificate. If the signature cannot be verified, the certificate should not be trusted. Call getPublicKey() to obtain the java.security.PublicKey of the subject of the certificate. Note that this class does not define a method for obtaining the Principal that is associated with the PublicKey. That functionality is dependent on the type of the certificate. See X509Certificate.getSubjectDN(), for example.

Do not confuse this class with the java.security.Certificate interface that was defined in Java 1.1 and has been deprecated in Java 1.2.

Object — Certificate ··· Serializable

```
public abstract class Certificate implements Serializable {
// Protected Constructors
   protected Certificate(String type);
// Nested Types
1.3 protected static class CertificateRep implements Serializable;
// Public Instance Methods
   public abstract byte[] getEncoded() throws CertificateEncodingException;
   public abstract java.security.PublicKey getPublicKey();
   public final String getType();
   public abstract void verify(java.security.PublicKey key)
        throws CertificateException, java.security.NoSuchAlgorithmException, java.security.InvalidKeyException,
        java.security.NoSuchProviderException, java.security.SignatureException;
   public abstract void verify(java.security.PublicKey key, String sigProvider)
        throws CertificateException, java.security.NoSuchAlgorithmException, java.security.InvalidKeyException,
        java.security.NoSuchProviderException, java.security.SignatureException     ;
// Public Methods Overriding Object
   public boolean equals(Object other);
   public int hashCode();
   public abstract String toString();
// Protected Instance Methods
1.3 protected Object writeReplace() throws java.io.ObjectStreamException;
}
```

Subclasses X509Certificate

Passed To Too many methods to list.

Returned By Too many methods to list.

Certificate.CertificateRep **Java 1.3**

java.security.cert **serializable**

This protected inner class provides an alternate representation of a certificate that can be used for serialization purposes by the **writeReplace()** method of some **Certificate** implementations. Applications do not typically need this class.

```
protected static class Certificate.CertificateRep implements Serializable {
// Protected Constructors
    protected CertificateRep(String type, byte[] data);
// Protected Instance Methods
    protected Object readResolve() throws java.io.ObjectStreamException;
}
```

CertificateEncodingException **Java 1.2**

java.security.cert **serializable checked**

Signals an error while attempting to encode a certificate.

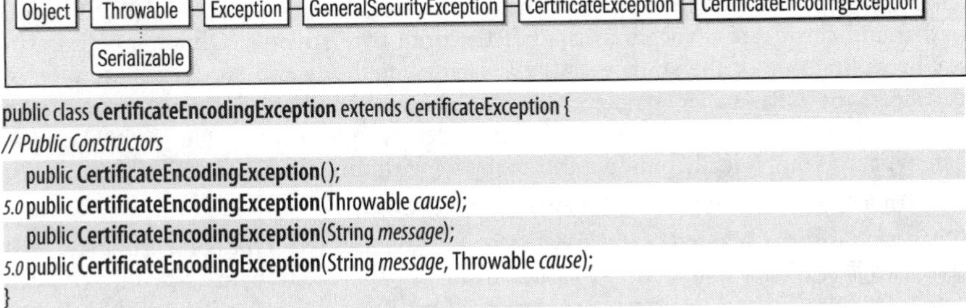


```
public class CertificateEncodingException extends CertificateException {
// Public Constructors
    public CertificateEncodingException();
5.0 public CertificateEncodingException(Throwable cause);
    public CertificateEncodingException(String message);
5.0 public CertificateEncodingException(String message, Throwable cause);
}
```

Thrown By java.security.cert.Certificate.getEncoded(), CertPath.getEncoded(), X509Certificate.getTBSCertificate()

CertificateException **Java 1.2**

java.security.cert **serializable checked**

This class is the superclass of several more specific exception types that may be thrown when working with certificates.

Object — Throwable — Exception — GeneralSecurityException — CertificateException; Serializable

```
public class CertificateException extends java.security.GeneralSecurityException {
// Public Constructors
    public CertificateException();
5.0 public CertificateException(Throwable cause);
    public CertificateException(String msg);
5.0 public CertificateException(String message, Throwable cause);
}
```

Subclasses CertificateEncodingException, CertificateExpiredException, CertificateNotYetValidException, CertificateParsingException

Thrown By Too many methods to list.

CertificateExpiredException Java 1.2

java.security.cert serializable checked

Signals that a certificate has expired or will have expired by a specified date.

Object ─ Throwable ─ Exception ─ GeneralSecurityException ─ CertificateException ─ CertificateExpiredException
Serializable

```
public class CertificateExpiredException extends CertificateException {
// Public Constructors
   public CertificateExpiredException();
   public CertificateExpiredException(String message);
}
```

Thrown By X509Certificate.checkValidity()

CertificateFactory Java 1.2

java.security.cert

This class defines methods for parsing certificates, certificate chains (certification paths) and certificate revocation lists (CRLs) from byte streams. Obtain a CertificateFactory by calling one of the static getInstance() factory methods and specifying the type of certificate or CRL to be parsed, and, optionally, the desired service provider to perform the parsing. The default "SUN" provider defines only a single "X.509" certificate type, so you typically obtain a CertificateFactory with this code:

```
CertificateFactory certFactory = CertificateFactory.getInstance("X.509");
```

Once you have obtained a CertificateFactory for the desired type of certificate, call generateCertificate() to parse a Certificate from a specified byte stream, or call generateCertificates() to parse a group of unrelated certificates (i.e. certificates that do not form a certificate chain) from a stream and return them as a Collection of Certificate objects. Similarly, call generateCRL() to parse a single CRL object from a stream, and call generateCRLs() to parse a Collection of CRL objects from the stream. These CertificateFactory methods read to the end of the specified stream. If the stream supports mark() and reset(), however, the CertificateFactory resets the stream to the position after the end of the last certificate or CRL read. If you specified a certificate type of "X.509", the Certificate and CRL objects returned by a CertificateFactory can be cast safely to X509Certificate and X509CRL. A certificate factory for X.509 certificates can parse certificates encoded in binary or printable hexadecimal form. If the certificate is in hexadecimal form, it must begin with the string "-----BEGIN CERTIFICATE-----" and end with the string "-----END CERTIFICATE-----".

The generateCertPath() methods return a CertPath object representing a certificate chain. These methods can create a CertPath object from a List of Certificate object, or by reading the chained certificates from a stream. Specify the encoding of the certificate chain by passing the name of the encoding standard to generateCertPath(). The default "SUN" provider supports the "PKCS7" and the "PkiPath" encodings. getCertPathEncoding() returns an Iterator of the encodings supported by the current provider. The first encoding returned by the iterator is the default used when no encoding is explicitly specified.

```
public class CertificateFactory {
// Protected Constructors
   protected CertificateFactory(CertificateFactorySpi certFacSpi, java.security.Provider provider, String type);
// Public Class Methods
   public static final CertificateFactory getInstance(String type) throws CertificateException;
```

```
1.4 public static final CertificateFactory getInstance(String type, java.security.Provider provider) throws CertificateException;
    public static final CertificateFactory getInstance(String type, String provider)
        throws CertificateException, java.security.NoSuchProviderException;
// Public Instance Methods
    public final java.security.cert.Certificate generateCertificate(java.io.InputStream inStream) throws CertificateException;
    public final java.util.Collection<? extends java.security.cert.Certificate>
        generateCertificates(java.io.InputStream inStream)
        throws CertificateException;
1.4 public final CertPath generateCertPath(java.util.List<? extends java.security.cert.Certificate> certificates)
        throws CertificateException;
1.4 public final CertPath generateCertPath(java.io.InputStream inStream) throws CertificateException;
1.4 public final CertPath generateCertPath(java.io.InputStream inStream, String encoding) throws CertificateException;
    public final CRL generateCRL(java.io.InputStream inStream) throws CRLException;
    public final java.util.Collection<? extends CRL> generateCRLs(java.io.InputStream inStream) throws CRLException;
1.4 public final java.util.Iterator<String> getCertPathEncodings();
    public final java.security.Provider getProvider();
    public final String getType();
}
```

CertificateFactorySpi — Java 1.2

java.security.cert

This abstract class defines the service provider interface, or SPI, for the CertificateFactory class. A security provider must implement this class for each type of certificate it wishes to support. Applications never need to use or subclass this class.

```
public abstract class CertificateFactorySpi {
// Public Constructors
    public CertificateFactorySpi();
// Public Instance Methods
    public abstract java.security.cert.Certificate engineGenerateCertificate(java.io.InputStream inStream)
        throws CertificateException;
    public abstract java.util.Collection<? extends java.security.cert.Certificate>
        engineGenerateCertificates(java.io.InputStream inStream) throws CertificateException;
1.4 public CertPath engineGenerateCertPath(java.util.List<? extends java.security.cert.Certificate> certificates)
        throws CertificateException;
1.4 public CertPath engineGenerateCertPath(java.io.InputStream inStream) throws CertificateException;
1.4 public CertPath engineGenerateCertPath(java.io.InputStream inStream, String encoding) throws CertificateException;
    public abstract CRL engineGenerateCRL(java.io.InputStream inStream) throws CRLException;
    public abstract java.util.Collection<? extends CRL> engineGenerateCRLs(java.io.InputStream inStream)
        throws CRLException;
1.4 public java.util.Iterator<String> engineGetCertPathEncodings();
}
```

Passed To CertificateFactory.CertificateFactory()

CertificateNotYetValidException — Java 1.2

java.security.cert — serializable checked

Signals that a certificate is not yet valid or will not yet be valid on a specified date.

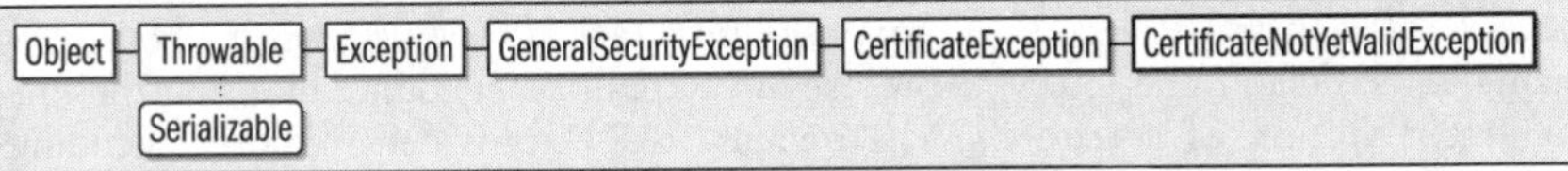

java.security.*

```
public class CertificateNotYetValidException extends CertificateException {
// Public Constructors
   public CertificateNotYetValidException();
   public CertificateNotYetValidException(String message);
}
```

Thrown By X509Certificate.checkValidity()

CertificateParsingException

Java 1.2

java.security.cert — serializable checked

Signals an error or other problem while parsing a certificate.

Object → Throwable → Exception → GeneralSecurityException → CertificateException → CertificateParsingException (Throwable implements Serializable)

```
public class CertificateParsingException extends CertificateException {
// Public Constructors
   public CertificateParsingException();
5.0 public CertificateParsingException(Throwable cause);
   public CertificateParsingException(String message);
5.0 public CertificateParsingException(String message, Throwable cause);
}
```

Thrown By X509Certificate.{getExtendedKeyUsage(), getIssuerAlternativeNames(), getSubjectAlternativeNames()}

CertPath

Java 1.4

java.security.cert — serializable

A CertPath is a immutable sequence or chain of certificates that establishes a "certification path" from an unknown "end entity" to a known and trusted Certificate Authority or "trust anchor". Use a CertPathValidator to validate a certificate chain and establish trust in the public key presented in the certificate of the end entity.

getType() returns the type of the certificates in the CertPath. For X.509 certificate chains (the only type supported by the default "SUN" provider) this method returns "X.509". getCertificates() returns a java.util.List object that contains the Certificate objects that comprise the chain. For X.509 chains, the list contains X509Certificate objects. Also, for X.509 certificate paths, the List returned by getCertificates() starts with the certificate of of the end entity, and ends with a certificate signed by the trust anchor. The signer of any certificate but the last must be the subject of the next certificate in the List. If the end entity presents a certificate that is directly signed by a trust anchor (which is a not uncommon occurrence) then the List returned by getCertificates() consists of only that single certificate. Note that the list of certificates does not include the certificate of the trust anchor. The public keys of trusted CAs must be known by the system in advance. In Sun's JDK implementation, the public-key certificates of trusted CAs are stored in the file *jre/lib/security/cacerts*.

CertPath objects can be created with a CertificateFactory, or at a lower level with a CertPathBuilder object. A CertificateFactory can parse or decode a CertPath object from a binary stream. The getEncoded() methods reverse the process and encode a CertPath into an array of bytes. getEncodings() returns the encodings supported for a CertPath. The first returned encoding name is the default one, but you can use any supported encoding by using the one-argument version of getEncoded(). The default "SUN" provider supports encodings named "PKCS7" and "PkiPath".

CertPath objects are immutable as is the List object returned by getCertificates() and the Certificate objects contained in the list. Furthermore, all CertPath methods are threadsafe.

Object — CertPath ··· Serializable

```
public abstract class CertPath implements Serializable {
// Protected Constructors
   protected CertPath(String type);
// Nested Types
   protected static class CertPathRep implements Serializable;
// Public Instance Methods
   public abstract java.util.List<? extends java.security.cert.Certificate> getCertificates();
   public abstract byte[] getEncoded() throws CertificateEncodingException;
   public abstract byte[] getEncoded(String encoding) throws CertificateEncodingException;
   public abstract java.util.Iterator<String> getEncodings();
   public String getType();
// Public Methods Overriding Object
   public boolean equals(Object other);
   public int hashCode();
   public String toString();
// Protected Instance Methods
   protected Object writeReplace() throws java.io.ObjectStreamException;
}
```

Passed To java.security.CodeSigner.CodeSigner(), java.security.Timestamp.Timestamp(), CertPathValidator.validate(), CertPathValidatorException.CertPathValidatorException(), CertPathValidatorSpi.engineValidate(), PKIXCertPathBuilderResult.PKIXCertPathBuilderResult()

Returned By java.security.CodeSigner.getSignerCertPath(), java.security.Timestamp.getSignerCertPath(), CertificateFactory.generateCertPath(), CertificateFactorySpi.engineGenerateCertPath(), CertPathBuilderResult.getCertPath(), CertPathValidatorException.getCertPath(), PKIXCertPathBuilderResult.getCertPath()

CertPath.CertPathRep — Java 1.4

java.security.cert — serializable

This protected inner class defines an implementation-independent representation of a CertPath for serialization purposes. Applications never need to use this class.

```
protected static class CertPath.CertPathRep implements Serializable {
// Protected Constructors
   protected CertPathRep(String type, byte[] data);
// Protected Instance Methods
   protected Object readResolve() throws java.io.ObjectStreamException;
}
```

CertPathBuilder — Java 1.4

java.security.cert

CertPathBuilder attempts to build a certification path from a specified certificate to a trust anchor. Unlike the CertificateFactory.generateCertPath() method, which might be used by a server to parse a certificate chain presented to it by a client, this class is used to create a new certificate chain, and might be used by a client that needs to send a certificate chain to a server. The CertPathBuilder API is provider-based, and is algorithm independent, although the use of any algorithms other than the "PKIX" standards (which work with X.509 certificate chains) require appropriate external implementations of CertPathParameters and CertPathBuilderResult.

Obtain a CertPathBuilder object by calling one of the static getInstance() methods, specifying the desired algorithm and, optionally, the desired provider. The "PKIX" algorithm is the only one supported by the default "SUN" provider, and is the only one that has the required algorithm-specific classes defined by this package. Once you have a CertPathBuilder, you create a CertPath object by passing a CertPathParameters object to the build() method. CertPathParameters is a marker interfaces that defines no method of its own, so you must use an algorithm-specific implementation such as PKIXBuilderParameters to supply the information required to build a CertPath. The build() method returns a CertPathBuilderResult object. Use the getCertPath() method of this returned object to obtain the CertPath that was built. The algorithm-specific implementation PKIXCertPathBuilderResult has additional methods that return further algorithm-specific results.

```
public class CertPathBuilder {
// Protected Constructors
   protected CertPathBuilder(CertPathBuilderSpi builderSpi, java.security.Provider provider, String algorithm);
// Public Class Methods
   public static final String getDefaultType();
   public static CertPathBuilder getInstance(String algorithm) throws java.security.NoSuchAlgorithmException;
   public static CertPathBuilder getInstance(String algorithm, String provider)
      throws java.security.NoSuchAlgorithmException, java.security.NoSuchProviderException;
   public static CertPathBuilder getInstance(String algorithm, java.security.Provider provider)
      throws java.security.NoSuchAlgorithmException;
// Public Instance Methods
   public final CertPathBuilderResult build(CertPathParameters params)
      throws CertPathBuilderException, java.security.InvalidAlgorithmParameterException;
   public final String getAlgorithm();
   public final java.security.Provider getProvider();
}
```

CertPathBuilderException — Java 1.4

java.security.cert — serializable checked

Signal a problem while building a certification path with CertPathBuilder.

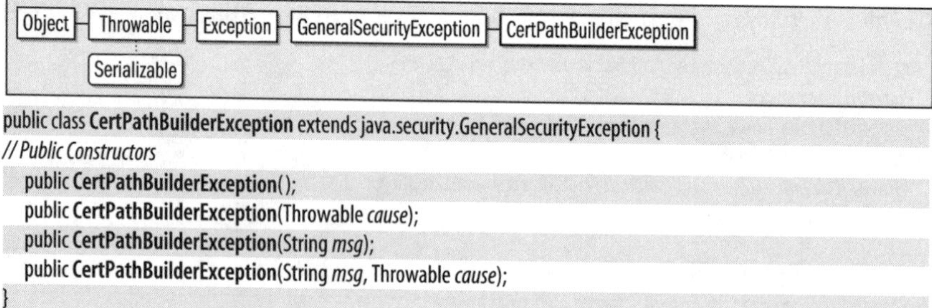


```
public class CertPathBuilderException extends java.security.GeneralSecurityException {
// Public Constructors
   public CertPathBuilderException();
   public CertPathBuilderException(Throwable cause);
   public CertPathBuilderException(String msg);
   public CertPathBuilderException(String msg, Throwable cause);
}
```

Thrown By CertPathBuilder.build(), CertPathBuilderSpi.engineBuild()

CertPathBuilderResult — Java 1.4

java.security.cert — cloneable

An object of this type is returned by the build() method of a CertPathBuilder. The getCertPath() method returns the CertPath object that was built; this method will never return null. The algorithm-specific PKIXCertPathBuilderResult implementation defines other methods to return additional information about the path that was built.

Cloneable ··· CertPathBuilderResult

```
public interface CertPathBuilderResult extends Cloneable {
// Public Instance Methods
   Object clone();
   CertPath getCertPath();
}
```

Implementations PKIXCertPathBuilderResult

Returned By CertPathBuilder.build(), CertPathBuilderSpi.engineBuild()

CertPathBuilderSpi — Java 1.4

java.security.cert

This abstract class defines the Service Provider Interface for the CertPathBuilder. Security providers must implement this interface, but applications never need to use it.

```
public abstract class CertPathBuilderSpi {
// Public Constructors
   public CertPathBuilderSpi();
// Public Instance Methods
   public abstract CertPathBuilderResult engineBuild(CertPathParameters params)
       throws CertPathBuilderException, java.security.InvalidAlgorithmParameterException;
}
```

Passed To CertPathBuilder.CertPathBuilder()

CertPathParameters — Java 1.4

java.security.cert — cloneable

CertPathParamters is a marker interface for objects that hold parameters (such as the set of trust anchors) for validating or building a certification path with CertPathValidator and CertPathBuilder. It defines no methods of its own, but requires that all implementations include a working clone() method. You must use an algorithm-specific implementation of this interface, such as PKIXParameters or PKIXBuilderParameters when validating or building a CertPath, and it is rarely useful to work with this interface directly.

Cloneable ··· CertPathParameters

```
public interface CertPathParameters extends Cloneable {
// Public Instance Methods
   Object clone();
}
```

Implementations PKIXParameters

Passed To CertPathBuilder.build(), CertPathBuilderSpi.engineBuild(), CertPathValidator.validate(), CertPathValidatorSpi.engineValidate(), javax.net.ssl.CertPathTrustManagerParameters.CertPathTrustManagerParameters()

Returned By javax.net.ssl.CertPathTrustManagerParameters.getParameters()

CertPathValidator

Java 1.4

java.security.cert

This class validates certificate chains, establishing a chain of trust from the end entity to a trust anchor, and thereby establishing the validity of the public key presented in the end entity's certificate. The CertPathValidator is provider-based and algorithm-independent. To obtain a CertPathValidator instance, call one of the static getInstance() methods specifying the name of the desired validation algorithm and, optionally, the provider to use. The "PKIX" algorithm for validating X.509 certificates is the only one supported by the default "SUN" provider.

Once you have a CertPathValidator object, you can use it to validate certificate chains by passing the CertPath object to be validated to the validate() method along with a CertPathParameters object that specifies valid trust anchors and other validation parameters. CertPathParameters is simply a marker interface, and you must use an application-specific implementation such as PKIXParameters. If validation fails, the validate() method throws a CertPathValidatorException which may include the index in the chain of the certificate that failed to validate. Otherwise, if validation is successful, the validate() method returns a CertPathValidatorResult. If you are interested in the details of the validation (such as the trust anchor that was used or the public key of the end entity), you may cast this returned value to an algorithm-specific subtype such as PKIXCertPathValidatorResult and use its methods to find out more about the result.

```
public class CertPathValidator {
// Protected Constructors
   protected CertPathValidator(CertPathValidatorSpi validatorSpi, java.security.Provider provider, String algorithm);
// Public Class Methods
   public static final String getDefaultType();
   public static CertPathValidator getInstance(String algorithm) throws java.security.NoSuchAlgorithmException;
   public static CertPathValidator getInstance(String algorithm, String provider)
       throws java.security.NoSuchAlgorithmException, java.security.NoSuchProviderException;
   public static CertPathValidator getInstance(String algorithm, java.security.Provider provider)
       throws java.security.NoSuchAlgorithmException;
// Public Instance Methods
   public final String getAlgorithm();
   public final java.security.Provider getProvider();
   public final CertPathValidatorResult validate(CertPath certPath, CertPathParameters params)
       throws CertPathValidatorException, java.security.InvalidAlgorithmParameterException;
}
```

CertPathValidatorException

Java 1.4

java.security.cert — serializable checked

Signals a problem while validating a certificate chain with a CertPathValidator. getCertPath() returns the CertPath object that was being validated, and getIndex() returns the index within the path of the certificate that caused the exception (or -1 if that information is not available).

Object — Throwable — Exception — GeneralSecurityException — CertPathValidatorException
Throwable ⋯ Serializable

```
public class CertPathValidatorException extends java.security.GeneralSecurityException {
// Public Constructors
   public CertPathValidatorException();
   public CertPathValidatorException(Throwable cause);
```

```
    public CertPathValidatorException(String msg);
    public CertPathValidatorException(String msg, Throwable cause);
    public CertPathValidatorException(String msg, Throwable cause, CertPath certPath, int index);
// Public Instance Methods
    public CertPath getCertPath();                                          default:null
    public int getIndex();                                                  default:-1
}
```

Thrown By CertPathValidator.validate(), CertPathValidatorSpi.engineValidate(), PKIXCertPathChecker.{check(), init()}

CertPathValidatorResult — Java 1.4

java.security.cert — cloneable

This marker interface defines the type of the object returned by the validate() method of a CertPathValidator, but does not define any of the contents of that object, other to specify that it must be Cloneable. If you want any details about the results of validating a CertPath, you must cast the return value of validate() to an algorithm-specific types implementation of this interface, such as PKIXCertPathValidatorResult.

Cloneable ··· CertPathValidatorResult

```
public interface CertPathValidatorResult extends Cloneable {
// Public Instance Methods
    Object clone();
}
```

Implementations PKIXCertPathValidatorResult

Returned By CertPathValidator.validate(), CertPathValidatorSpi.engineValidate()

CertPathValidatorSpi — Java 1.4

java.security.cert

This abstract class defines the Service Provider Interface for the CertPathValidator class. Security providers must implement this interface, but applications never need to use it.

```
public abstract class CertPathValidatorSpi {
// Public Constructors
    public CertPathValidatorSpi();
// Public Instance Methods
    public abstract CertPathValidatorResult engineValidate(CertPath certPath, CertPathParameters params)
        throws CertPathValidatorException, java.security.InvalidAlgorithmParameterException;
}
```

Passed To CertPathValidator.CertPathValidator()

CertSelector — Java 1.4

java.security.cert — cloneable

This interface defines an API for determining whether a Certificate meets some criteria. Implementations are used to specify critera by which a certificate or certificates should be selected from a CertStore object. The match() method should examine the Certificate it is passed and return true if it "matches" based on whatever criteria the implementation defines. See X509CertSelector for an implementation that works with X.509 certificates. See CRLSelector for a similar interface for use when selecting CRL objects from a CertStore.

Cloneable ·· CertSelector

```
public interface CertSelector extends Cloneable {
// Public Instance Methods
   Object clone();
   boolean match(java.security.cert.Certificate cert);
}
```

Implementations X509CertSelector

Passed To CertStore.getCertificates(), CertStoreSpi.engineGetCertificates(), PKIXBuilderParameters.PKIXBuilderParameters(), PKIXParameters.setTargetCertConstraints()

Returned By PKIXParameters.getTargetCertConstraints()

CertStore

Java 1.4

java.security.cert

A CertStore object is a repository for Certificate and CRL objects. You may query a CertStore for a java.util.Collection of Certificate or CRL objects that match specified criteria by passing a CertSelector or CRLSelector to getCertificates() or getCRLs(). A CertStore is conceptually similar to a java.security.KeyStore, but there are significant differences in how the two classes are intended to be used. A KeyStore is designed to store a relatively small local collection of private keys and trusted certificates. A CertStore, however, may represent a large public database (in the form of an LDAP server, for examle) of untrusted certificates.

Obtain a CertStore object by calling a getInstance() method and specifying the name of the desired CertStore type and a CertStoreParameters object that is specific to that type. Optionally, you may also specify the desired provider of your CertStore object. The default "SUN" provider defines two CertStore types, named "LDAP" and "Collection", which you should use with LDAPCertStoreParameters and CollectionCertStoreParameters objects, respectively. The "LDAP" type obtains certificates and CRLs from a network LDAP server, and the "Collection" type obtains them from a a specified Collection object.

The CertStore class may be directly useful to applications that want to query a LDAP server for certificates. It is also used by PKIXParameters.addCertStore() and PKIXParameters.setCertStores() to specify a source of certificates to by used by the CertPathBuilder and CertPathValidator classes.

All public methods of CertStore are threadsafe.

```
public class CertStore {
// Protected Constructors
   protected CertStore(CertStoreSpi storeSpi, java.security.Provider provider, String type, CertStoreParameters params);
// Public Class Methods
   public static final String getDefaultType();
   public static CertStore getInstance(String type, CertStoreParameters params)
       throws java.security.InvalidAlgorithmParameterException, java.security.NoSuchAlgorithmException;
   public static CertStore getInstance(String type, CertStoreParameters params, String provider)
       throws java.security.InvalidAlgorithmParameterException, java.security.NoSuchAlgorithmException,
       java.security.NoSuchProviderException;
   public static CertStore getInstance(String type, CertStoreParameters params, java.security.Provider provider)
       throws java.security.NoSuchAlgorithmException, java.security.InvalidAlgorithmParameterException;
// Public Instance Methods
   public final java.util.Collection<? extends java.security.cert.Certificate> getCertificates(CertSelector selector)
       throws CertStoreException;
   public final CertStoreParameters getCertStoreParameters();
   public final java.util.Collection<? extends CRL> getCRLs(CRLSelector selector) throws CertStoreException;
```

```
    public final java.security.Provider getProvider();
    public final String getType();
}
```

Passed To PKIXParameters.addCertStore()

CertStoreException

Java 1.4

java.security.cert

serializable checked

Signals a problem while querying a CertStore for certificates or CRLs.

Object — Throwable — Exception — GeneralSecurityException — CertStoreException
Serializable

```
public class CertStoreException extends java.security.GeneralSecurityException {
// Public Constructors
    public CertStoreException();
    public CertStoreException(Throwable cause);
    public CertStoreException(String msg);
    public CertStoreException(String msg, Throwable cause);
}
```

Thrown By CertStore.{getCertificates(), getCRLs()}, CertStoreSpi.{engineGetCertificates(), engineGetCRLs()}

CertStoreParameters

Java 1.4

java.security.cert

cloneable

This marker interface defines the type, but not the content, of the parameters object that is passed to the CertStore.getInstance() methods. It does not define any methods of its own and simply requires that all implementing classes be cloneable. Use one of the concrete implementations of this class for CertStore objects of type "LDAP" and "Collection".

Cloneable — CertStoreParameters

```
public interface CertStoreParameters extends Cloneable {
// Public Instance Methods
    Object clone();
}
```

Implementations CollectionCertStoreParameters, LDAPCertStoreParameters

Passed To CertStore.{CertStore(), getInstance()}, CertStoreSpi.CertStoreSpi()

Returned By CertStore.getCertStoreParameters()

CertStoreSpi

Java 1.4

java.security.cert

This abstract class defines the Service Provider Interface for the CertStore class. Security providers must implement this interface, but applications never need to use it.

```
public abstract class CertStoreSpi {
// Public Constructors
    public CertStoreSpi(CertStoreParameters params) throws java.security.InvalidAlgorithmParameterException;
// Public Instance Methods
    public abstract java.util.Collection<? extends java.security.cert.Certificate> engineGetCertificates(CertSelector selector)
        throws CertStoreException;
```

```
    public abstract java.util.Collection<? extends CRL> engineGetCRLs(CRLSelector selector) throws CertStoreException;
}
```

Passed To CertStore.CertStore()

CollectionCertStoreParameters — Java 1.4

java.security.cert — cloneable

This concrete implementation of CertStoreParameters is used when creating a CertStore object of type "Collection". Pass the Collection of Certificate and CRL objects to be searched by the CertStore to the constructor method.

Object — CollectionCertStoreParameters
Cloneable, CertStoreParameters

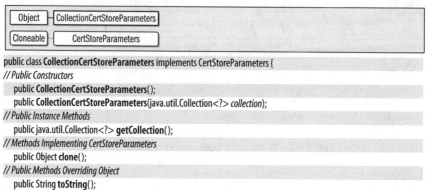

```
public class CollectionCertStoreParameters implements CertStoreParameters {
// Public Constructors
    public CollectionCertStoreParameters();
    public CollectionCertStoreParameters(java.util.Collection<?> collection);
// Public Instance Methods
    public java.util.Collection<?> getCollection();
// Methods Implementing CertStoreParameters
    public Object clone();
// Public Methods Overriding Object
    public String toString();
}
```

CRL — Java 1.2

java.security.cert

This abstract class represents a *certificate revocation list* (CRL). A CRL is an object issued by a certificate authority (or other certificate signer) that lists certificates that have been revoked, meaning that they are now invalid and should be rejected. Use a CertificateFactory to parse a CRL from a byte stream. Use the isRevoked() method to test whether a specified Certificate is listed on the CRL. Note that type-specific CRL subclasses, such as X509CRL, may provide access to substantially more information about the revocation list.

```
public abstract class CRL {
// Protected Constructors
    protected CRL(String type);
// Public Instance Methods
    public final String getType();
    public abstract boolean isRevoked(java.security.cert.Certificate cert);
// Public Methods Overriding Object
    public abstract String toString();
}
```

Subclasses X509CRL

Passed To CRLSelector.match(), X509CRLSelector.match()

Returned By CertificateFactory.generateCRL(), CertificateFactorySpi.engineGenerateCRL()

CRLException — Java 1.2

java.security.cert — serializable checked

Signals an error or other problem while working with a CRL.

Object — Throwable — Exception — GeneralSecurityException — CRLException
Serializable

```
public class CRLException extends java.security.GeneralSecurityException {
// Public Constructors
   public CRLException();
5.0 public CRLException(Throwable cause);
   public CRLException(String message);
5.0 public CRLException(String message, Throwable cause);
}
```

Thrown By CertificateFactory.{generateCRL(), generateCRLs()}, CertificateFactorySpi.{engineGenerateCRL(), engineGenerateCRLs()}, X509CRL.{getEncoded(), getTBSCertList(), verify()}, X509CRLEntry.getEncoded()

CRLSelector — Java 1.4

java.security.cert — cloneable

This interface defines an API for determining whether a CRL object meets some criteria. Implementations are used to specify critera by which a CRL objects should be selected from a CertStore. The match() method should examine the CRL it is passed and return true if it "matches" based on whatever criteria the implementation defines. See X509CRLSelector for an implementation that works with X.509 certificates. See CertSelector for a similar interface for use when selecting Certificate objects from a CertStore.

Cloneable — CRLSelector

```
public interface CRLSelector extends Cloneable {
// Public Instance Methods
   Object clone();
   boolean match(CRL crl);
}
```

Implementations X509CRLSelector

Passed To CertStore.getCRLs(), CertStoreSpi.engineGetCRLs()

LDAPCertStoreParameters — Java 1.4

java.security.cert — cloneable

This concrete implementation of CertStoreParameters is used when creating a CertStore object of type "LDAP". It specifies the hostname of the LDAP server to connect to and, optionally, the port to connect on.

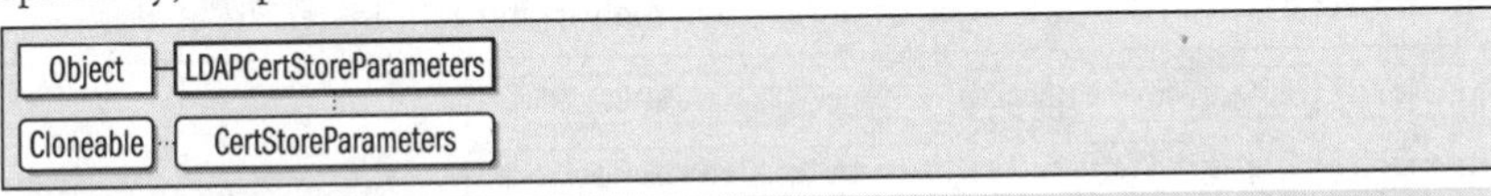


```
public class LDAPCertStoreParameters implements CertStoreParameters {
// Public Constructors
   public LDAPCertStoreParameters();
   public LDAPCertStoreParameters(String serverName);
   public LDAPCertStoreParameters(String serverName, int port);
```

```
// Public Instance Methods
    public int getPort();                                              default:389
    public String getServerName();                                     default:"localhost"
// Methods Implementing CertStoreParameters
    public Object clone();
// Public Methods Overriding Object
    public String toString();
}
```

PKIXBuilderParameters

Java 1.4

java.security.cert

cloneable

Instances of this class are used to specify parameters to the build() method of a CertPathBuilder object. These parameters must include the two mandatory ones passed to the constructors. The first is a source of trust anchors, which may be supplied as a Set of TrustAnchor objects or as a java.security.KeyStore object. The second required parameter is a CertSelector object (typically an X509CertSelector) that specifies the selection criteria for the certificate that is to have the certification path built. In addition to these parameters that are passed to the constructor, this class also inherits a number of methods for setting other parameters, and defines setMaxPathLength() for specifying the maximum length of the certificate chain that is built.

Object — PKIXParameters — PKIXBuilderParameters
Cloneable ··· CertPathParameters

```
public class PKIXBuilderParameters extends PKIXParameters {
// Public Constructors
    public PKIXBuilderParameters(java.security.KeyStore keystore, CertSelector targetConstraints)
        throws java.security.KeyStoreException, java.security.InvalidAlgorithmParameterException;
    public PKIXBuilderParameters(java.util.Set<TrustAnchor> trustAnchors, CertSelector targetConstraints)
        throws java.security.InvalidAlgorithmParameterException;
// Public Instance Methods
    public int getMaxPathLength();
    public void setMaxPathLength(int maxPathLength);
// Public Methods Overriding PKIXParameters
    public String toString();
}
```

PKIXCertPathBuilderResult

Java 1.4

java.security.cert

cloneable

An instance of this class is retured by the build() method of a CertPathBuilder created for the "PKIX" algorithm. getCertPath() returns the CertPath object that was built, and methods inherited from the superclass return additional information such as the public key of the subject of the certificate chain and the trust anchor that terminates the chain.

Object — PKIXCertPathValidatorResult — PKIXCertPathBuilderResult
Cloneable ··· CertPathValidatorResult   Cloneable ··· CertPathBuilderResult

```
public class PKIXCertPathBuilderResult extends PKIXCertPathValidatorResult implements CertPathBuilderResult {
// Public Constructors
    public PKIXCertPathBuilderResult(CertPath certPath, TrustAnchor trustAnchor, PolicyNode policyTree,
                                     java.security.PublicKey subjectPublicKey);
// Methods Implementing CertPathBuilderResult
```

```
    public CertPath getCertPath();
// Public Methods Overriding PKIXCertPathValidatorResult
    public String toString();
}
```

PKIXCertPathChecker

Java 1.4

java.security.cert

cloneable

This abstract class defines an extension mechanism for the PKIX certification path building and validation algorithms. Most applications will never need to use this class. You may pass one or more PKIXCertPathChecker objects to the setCertPathCheckers() or addCertPathChecker() methods of the PKIXParameters or PKIXBuilderParameters object that is passed to the build() or validate() methods of a CertPathBuilder or CertPathValidator. The check() method of all PKIXCertPathChecker objects registered in this way will be invoked for each certificate considered in the building or validation algorithms. check() should throw a CertPathValidatorException if a certificate does not the implemented test. The init() method is invoked to tell the checker to reset its internal state and to notify it of the direction in which certificates will be presented. Checkers are not required to support the forward direction, and should return false from isForwardCheckingSupported() if they do not.

Object — PKIXCertPathChecker ··· Cloneable

```
public abstract class PKIXCertPathChecker implements Cloneable {
// Protected Constructors
    protected PKIXCertPathChecker();
// Public Instance Methods
    public abstract void check(java.security.cert.Certificate cert, java.util.Collection<String> unresolvedCritExts)
        throws CertPathValidatorException;
    public abstract java.util.Set<String> getSupportedExtensions();
    public abstract void init(boolean forward) throws CertPathValidatorException;
    public abstract boolean isForwardCheckingSupported();
// Public Methods Overriding Object
    public Object clone();
}
```

Passed To PKIXParameters.addCertPathChecker()

PKIXCertPathValidatorResult

Java 1.4

java.security.cert

cloneable

An instance of this class is returned upon successful validation by the validate() method of a CertPathValidator created for the "PKIX" algorithm. getPublicKey() returns the validated public key of the subject of the certificate chain. getTrustAnchor() returns the TrustAnchor that anchors the chain.

Object — PKIXCertPathValidatorResult

Cloneable ··· CertPathValidatorResult

```
public class PKIXCertPathValidatorResult implements CertPathValidatorResult {
// Public Constructors
    public PKIXCertPathValidatorResult(TrustAnchor trustAnchor, PolicyNode policyTree,
                                       java.security.PublicKey subjectPublicKey);
// Public Instance Methods
    public PolicyNode getPolicyTree();
```

```
    public java.security.PublicKey getPublicKey();
    public TrustAnchor getTrustAnchor();
// Methods Implementing CertPathValidatorResult
    public Object clone();
// Public Methods Overriding Object
    public String toString();
}
```

Subclasses PKIXCertPathBuilderResult

PKIXParameters

Java 1.4

java.security.cert — cloneable

This implementation of CertPathParameters defines parameters that are passed to the validate() method of a PKIX CertPathValidator and defines a subset of the parameters that are passed to the build() method of a PKIX CertPathBuilder. A full understanding of this class requires a detailed discussion of the PKIX certification path building and validation algorithms, which is beyond the scope of this book. However, some of the more important parameters are described here.

When you create a PKIXParameters object, you must specify which trust anchors are to be used. You can do this by passing a Set of TrustAnchor objects to the constructor, or by passing a KeyStore containing trust anchor keys to the constructor. Once a PKIXParameters object is created, you can modify the set of TrustAnchor objects with setTrustAnchors(). Specify a Set of CertStore objects to be searched for certificates with setCertStores() or add a single CertStore to the set with addCertStore(). If certificate validity is to be checked for some date and time other than the current time, use setDate() to specify this date.

Object — PKIXParameters
Cloneable ··· CertPathParameters

```
public class PKIXParameters implements CertPathParameters {
// Public Constructors
    public PKIXParameters(java.security.KeyStore keystore)
        throws java.security.KeyStoreException, java.security.InvalidAlgorithmParameterException;
    public PKIXParameters(java.util.Set<TrustAnchor> trustAnchors)
        throws java.security.InvalidAlgorithmParameterException;
// Public Instance Methods
    public void addCertPathChecker(PKIXCertPathChecker checker);
    public void addCertStore(CertStore store);
    public java.util.List<PKIXCertPathChecker> getCertPathCheckers();
    public java.util.List<CertStore> getCertStores();
    public java.util.Date getDate();
    public java.util.Set<String> getInitialPolicies();
    public boolean getPolicyQualifiersRejected();
    public String getSigProvider();
    public CertSelector getTargetCertConstraints();
    public java.util.Set<TrustAnchor> getTrustAnchors();
    public boolean isAnyPolicyInhibited();
    public boolean isExplicitPolicyRequired();
    public boolean isPolicyMappingInhibited();
    public boolean isRevocationEnabled();
    public void setAnyPolicyInhibited(boolean val);
    public void setCertPathCheckers(java.util.List<PKIXCertPathChecker> checkers);
```

```
    public void setCertStores(java.util.List<CertStore> stores);
    public void setDate(java.util.Date date);
    public void setExplicitPolicyRequired(boolean val);
    public void setInitialPolicies(java.util.Set<String> initialPolicies);
    public void setPolicyMappingInhibited(boolean val);
    public void setPolicyQualifiersRejected(boolean qualifiersRejected);
    public void setRevocationEnabled(boolean val);
    public void setSigProvider(String sigProvider);
    public void setTargetCertConstraints(CertSelector selector);
    public void setTrustAnchors(java.util.Set<TrustAnchor> trustAnchors)
        throws java.security.InvalidAlgorithmParameterException;
// Methods Implementing CertPathParameters
    public Object clone();
// Public Methods Overriding Object
    public String toString();
}
```

Subclasses PKIXBuilderParameters

PolicyNode **Java 1.4**

java.security.cert

This class represents a node in the policy tree created by the PKIX certification path validation algorithm. A discussion of X.509 policy extensions and their use in the PKIX certification path algorithms is beyond the scope of this reference.

```
public interface PolicyNode {
// Public Instance Methods
    java.util.Iterator<? extends PolicyNode> getChildren();
    int getDepth();
    java.util.Set<String> getExpectedPolicies();
    PolicyNode getParent();
    java.util.Set<? extends PolicyQualifierInfo> getPolicyQualifiers();
    String getValidPolicy();
    boolean isCritical();
}
```

Passed To PKIXCertPathBuilderResult.PKIXCertPathBuilderResult(), PKIXCertPathValidatorResult.PKIXCertPathValidatorResult()

Returned By PKIXCertPathValidatorResult.getPolicyTree()

PolicyQualifierInfo **Java 1.4**

java.security.cert

This class is a low-level representation of a policy qualifier information from a X.509 certificate extension. A discussion of X.509 policy extensions and their use in the PKIX certification path algorithms is beyond the scope of this reference.

```
public class PolicyQualifierInfo {
// Public Constructors
    public PolicyQualifierInfo(byte[] encoded) throws java.io.IOException;
// Public Instance Methods
    public final byte[] getEncoded();
    public final byte[] getPolicyQualifier();
    public final String getPolicyQualifierId();
```

java.security.*

```
// Public Methods Overriding Object
   public String toString();
}
```

TrustAnchor

Java 1.4

java.security.cert

A TrustAnchor represents a certificate authority that is trusted to "anchor" a certificate chain. A TrustAnchor object includes the X.500 distinguished name of the CA and the public key of the CA. You may specify the name and key explictly or by passing an X509Certificate to the TrustAnchor() constructor. If you do not pass a certificate, you can specify the CA name as a String or as an X500Principal object from the javax.security.auth.x500 package. All forms of the TrustAnchor() constructor also allow you to specify a byte array containing a binary representation of a "Name Constraints" extension. The format and meaning of such name constraints is beyond the scope of this reference, and most applications can simply specify null for this constructor argument.

```
public class TrustAnchor {
// Public Constructors
   public TrustAnchor(X509Certificate trustedCert, byte[] nameConstraints);
5.0 public TrustAnchor(javax.security.auth.x500.X500Principal caPrincipal, java.security.PublicKey pubKey,
                        byte[] nameConstraints)
   public TrustAnchor(String caName, java.security.PublicKey pubKey, byte[] nameConstraints);
// Public Instance Methods
5.0 public final javax.security.auth.x500.X500Principal getCA();
   public final String getCAName();
   public final java.security.PublicKey getCAPublicKey();
   public final byte[] getNameConstraints();
   public final X509Certificate getTrustedCert();
// Public Methods Overriding Object
   public String toString();
}
```

Passed To PKIXCertPathBuilderResult.PKIXCertPathBuilderResult(), PKIXCertPathValidatorResult.PKIXCertPathValidatorResult()

Returned By PKIXCertPathValidatorResult.getTrustAnchor()

X509Certificate

Java 1.2

java.security.cert

serializable

This class represents an X.509 certificate. Its various methods provide complete access to the contents of the certificate. A full understanding of this class requires detailed knowledge of the X.509 standard which is beyond the scope of this reference. Some of the more important methods are described here, however. getSubjectDN() returns the Principal to whom this certificate applies, and the inherited getPublicKey() method returns the PublicKey that the certificate associates with that Principal. getIssuerDN() returns a Principal that represents the issuer of the certificate, and if you know the public key for that Principal, you can pass it to the verify() method to check the digital signature of the issuer and ensure that the certificate is not forged. checkValidity() checks whether the certificate has expired or has not yet gone into effect. Note that verify() and getPublicKey() are inherited from Certificate.

Obtain an X509Certificate object by creating a CertificateFactory for certificate type "X.509" and then using generateCertificate() to parse an X.509 certificate from a stream of bytes. Finally, cast the Certificate returned by this method to an X509Certificate.

Object — Certificate — X509Certificate
Serializable   X509Extension

```
public abstract class X509Certificate extends java.security.cert.Certificate implements X509Extension {
// Protected Constructors
   protected X509Certificate();
// Public Instance Methods
   public abstract void checkValidity() throws CertificateExpiredException, CertificateNotYetValidException;
   public abstract void checkValidity(java.util.Date date)
       throws CertificateExpiredException, CertificateNotYetValidException;
   public abstract int getBasicConstraints();
1.4 public java.util.List<String> getExtendedKeyUsage() throws CertificateParsingException;
1.4 public java.util.Collection<java.util.List<?>> getIssuerAlternativeNames() throws CertificateParsingException;
   public abstract java.security.Principal getIssuerDN();
   public abstract boolean[] getIssuerUniqueID();
1.4 public javax.security.auth.x500.X500Principal getIssuerX500Principal();
   public abstract boolean[] getKeyUsage();
   public abstract java.util.Date getNotAfter();
   public abstract java.util.Date getNotBefore();
   public abstract java.math.BigInteger getSerialNumber();
   public abstract String getSigAlgName();
   public abstract String getSigAlgOID();
   public abstract byte[] getSigAlgParams();
   public abstract byte[] getSignature();
1.4 public java.util.Collection<java.util.List<?>> getSubjectAlternativeNames() throws CertificateParsingException;
   public abstract java.security.Principal getSubjectDN();
   public abstract boolean[] getSubjectUniqueID();
1.4 public javax.security.auth.x500.X500Principal getSubjectX500Principal();
   public abstract byte[] getTBSCertificate() throws CertificateEncodingException;
   public abstract int getVersion();
}
```

Passed To TrustAnchor.TrustAnchor(), X509CertSelector.setCertificate(), X509CRL.getRevokedCertificate(), X509CRLSelector.setCertificateChecking(), javax.net.ssl.X509TrustManager.{checkClientTrusted(), checkServerTrusted()}, javax.security.auth.x500.X500PrivateCredential.X500PrivateCredential()

Returned By TrustAnchor.getTrustedCert(), X509CertSelector.getCertificate(), X509CRLSelector.getCertificateChecking(), javax.net.ssl.X509KeyManager.getCertificateChain(), javax.net.ssl.X509TrustManager.getAcceptedIssuers(), javax.security.auth.x500.X500PrivateCredential.getCertificate()

X509CertSelector — Java 1.4

java.security.cert — cloneable

This class is a CertSelector for X.509 certificates. Its various set methods allow you to specify values for various certificate fields and extensions. The match() method will only return true for certificates that have the specified values for those fields and extensions. A full understanding of this class requires detailed knowledge of the X.509 standard which is beyond the scope of this reference. Some of the more important methods are described here, however.

When you want to match exactly one specific certificate, simply pass the desired X509Certificate to setCertificate(). Constrain the subject of the certificate with setSubject(), setSubjectAlternativeNames(), of addSubjectAlternativeName(). Constrain the issuer of the certificate with setIssuer(). Constrain the public key of the certificate with setPublicKey().

Constrain the certificate to be valid on a given date with setCertificateValid(). And specify a specific issuer's serial number for the certificate with setSerialNumber().

Java 5.0 adds methods for identifying certificate subjects and issuers with javax.security.auth.x500.X500Principal objects instead of with strings.

Object — X509CertSelector
Cloneable ··· CertSelector

```
public class X509CertSelector implements CertSelector {
// Public Constructors
    public X509CertSelector();
// Public Instance Methods
    public void addPathToName(int type, String name) throws java.io.IOException;
    public void addPathToName(int type, byte[] name) throws java.io.IOException;
    public void addSubjectAlternativeName(int type, byte[] name) throws java.io.IOException;
    public void addSubjectAlternativeName(int type, String name) throws java.io.IOException;
    public byte[] getAuthorityKeyIdentifier();                                  default:null
    public int getBasicConstraints();                                           default:-1
    public X509Certificate getCertificate();                                    default:null
    public java.util.Date getCertificateValid();                                default:null
    public java.util.Set<String> getExtendedKeyUsage();                         default:null
5.0 public javax.security.auth.x500.X500Principal getIssuer();                  default:null
    public byte[] getIssuerAsBytes() throws java.io.IOException;                default:null
    public String getIssuerAsString();                                          default:null
    public boolean[] getKeyUsage();                                             default:null
    public boolean getMatchAllSubjectAltNames();                                default:true
    public byte[] getNameConstraints();                                         default:null
    public java.util.Collection<java.util.List<?>> getPathToNames();            default:null
    public java.util.Set<String> getPolicy();                                   default:null
    public java.util.Date getPrivateKeyValid();                                 default:null
    public java.math.BigInteger getSerialNumber();                              default:null
5.0 public javax.security.auth.x500.X500Principal getSubject();                 default:null
    public java.util.Collection<java.util.List<?>> getSubjectAlternativeNames(); default:null
    public byte[] getSubjectAsBytes() throws java.io.IOException;               default:null
    public String getSubjectAsString();                                         default:null
    public byte[] getSubjectKeyIdentifier();                                    default:null
    public java.security.PublicKey getSubjectPublicKey();                       default:null
    public String getSubjectPublicKeyAlgID();                                   default:null
    public void setAuthorityKeyIdentifier(byte[] authorityKeyID);
    public void setBasicConstraints(int minMaxPathLen);
    public void setCertificate(X509Certificate cert);
    public void setCertificateValid(java.util.Date certValid);
    public void setExtendedKeyUsage(java.util.Set<String> keyPurposeSet) throws java.io.IOException;
5.0 public void setIssuer(javax.security.auth.x500.X500Principal issuer);
    public void setIssuer(byte[] issuerDN) throws java.io.IOException;
    public void setIssuer(String issuerDN) throws java.io.IOException;
    public void setKeyUsage(boolean[] keyUsage);
    public void setMatchAllSubjectAltNames(boolean matchAllNames);
    public void setNameConstraints(byte[] bytes) throws java.io.IOException;
    public void setPathToNames(java.util.Collection<java.util.List<?>> names) throws java.io.IOException;
    public void setPolicy(java.util.Set<String> certPolicySet) throws java.io.IOException;
    public void setPrivateKeyValid(java.util.Date privateKeyValid);
    public void setSerialNumber(java.math.BigInteger serial);
```

```
    public void setSubject(String subjectDN) throws java.io.IOException;
5.0 public void setSubject(javax.security.auth.x500.X500Principal subject);
    public void setSubject(byte[] subjectDN) throws java.io.IOException;
    public void setSubjectAlternativeNames(java.util.Collection<java.util.List<?>> names) throws java.io.IOException;
    public void setSubjectKeyIdentifier(byte[] subjectKeyID);
    public void setSubjectPublicKey(byte[] key) throws java.io.IOException;
    public void setSubjectPublicKey(java.security.PublicKey key);
    public void setSubjectPublicKeyAlgID(String oid) throws java.io.IOException;
// Methods Implementing CertSelector
    public Object clone();
    public boolean match(java.security.cert.Certificate cert);
// Public Methods Overriding Object
    public String toString();
}
```

X509CRL — Java 1.2

java.security.cert

This class represents an X.509 CRL, which consists primarily of a set of X509CRLEntry objects. The various methods of this class provide access to the full details of the CRL, and require a complete understanding of the X.509 standard, which is beyond the scope of this reference. Use verify() to check the digital signature of the CRL to ensure that it does indeed originate from the the source it specifies. Use the inherited isRevoked() method to determine whether a given certificate has been revoked. If you are curious about the revocation date for a revoked certificate, obtain the X509CRLEntry for that certificate by calling getRevokedCertificate(). Call getThisUpdate() to obtain the date this CRL was issued. Use getNextUpdate() to find if the CRL has been superseded by a newer version. Use getRevokedCertificates() to obtain a Set of all X509CRLEntry objects from this CRL.

Obtain an X509CRL object by creating a CertificateFactory for certificate type "X.509" and then using the generateCRL() to parse an X.509 CRL from a stream of bytes. Finally, cast the CRL returned by this method to an X509CRL.

Object — CRL — X509CRL
X509Extension

```
public abstract class X509CRL extends CRL implements X509Extension {
// Protected Constructors
    protected X509CRL();
// Public Instance Methods
    public abstract byte[] getEncoded() throws CRLException;
    public abstract java.security.Principal getIssuerDN();
1.4 public javax.security.auth.x500.X500Principal getIssuerX500Principal();
    public abstract java.util.Date getNextUpdate();
5.0 public X509CRLEntry getRevokedCertificate(X509Certificate certificate);
    public abstract X509CRLEntry getRevokedCertificate(java.math.BigInteger serialNumber);
    public abstract java.util.Set<? extends X509CRLEntry> getRevokedCertificates();
    public abstract String getSigAlgName();
    public abstract String getSigAlgOID();
    public abstract byte[] getSigAlgParams();
    public abstract byte[] getSignature();
    public abstract byte[] getTBSCertList() throws CRLException;
    public abstract java.util.Date getThisUpdate();
    public abstract int getVersion();
```

```
    public abstract void verify(java.security.PublicKey key)
        throws CRLException, java.security.NoSuchAlgorithmException, java.security.InvalidKeyException,
        java.security.NoSuchProviderException, java.security.SignatureException;
    public abstract void verify(java.security.PublicKey key, String sigProvider)
        throws CRLException, java.security.NoSuchAlgorithmException, java.security.InvalidKeyException,
        java.security.NoSuchProviderException, java.security.SignatureException;
// Public Methods Overriding Object
    public boolean equals(Object other);
    public int hashCode();
}
```

X509CRLEntry Java 1.2

java.security.cert

This class represents a single entry in an X509CRL. It contains the serial number and revocation date for a revoked certificate.

Object — X509CRLEntry ··· X509Extension

```
public abstract class X509CRLEntry implements X509Extension {
// Public Constructors
    public X509CRLEntry();
// Public Instance Methods
5.0 public javax.security.auth.x500.X500Principal getCertificateIssuer();          constant
    public abstract byte[] getEncoded() throws CRLException;
    public abstract java.util.Date getRevocationDate();
    public abstract java.math.BigInteger getSerialNumber();
    public abstract boolean hasExtensions();
// Public Methods Overriding Object
    public boolean equals(Object other);
    public int hashCode();
    public abstract String toString();
}
```

Returned By X509CRL.getRevokedCertificate()

X509CRLSelector Java 1.4

java.security.cert cloneable

This class is a CRLSelector implementation for X.509 CRLs. The various set methods allow you to specify criteria that the match() method will use to accept or reject CRL objects. Use addIssuerName() to specify the distinguished name of an acceptable issuer for the CRL, or use setIssuerNames() or setIssuers() to specify a Collection of valid issuers. Use setDateAndTime() to specify a Date for which the CRL must be valid. Use setMinCRLNumber() and setMaxCRLNumber() to set bounds on the sequence number of the CRL. If you are selecting a CRL in order to check for revocation of a particular X509Certificate, pass that certificate to setCertificateChecking(). This method does not actually constrain the returned CRL objects, but it may help a CertStore optimize its search for a relevant CRL.

```
public class X509CRLSelector implements CRLSelector {
// Public Constructors
    public X509CRLSelector();
```

```
// Public Instance Methods
5.0 public void addIssuer(javax.security.auth.x500.X500Principal issuer);
    public void addIssuerName(String name) throws java.io.IOException;
    public void addIssuerName(byte[] name) throws java.io.IOException;
    public X509Certificate getCertificateChecking();                                  default:null
    public java.util.Date getDateAndTime();                                           default:null
    public java.util.Collection<Object> getIssuerNames();                             default:null
5.0 public java.util.Collection<javax.security.auth.x500.X500Principal> getIssuers(); default:null
    public java.math.BigInteger getMaxCRL();                                          default:null
    public java.math.BigInteger getMinCRL();                                          default:null
    public void setCertificateChecking(X509Certificate cert);
    public void setDateAndTime(java.util.Date dateAndTime);
    public void setIssuerNames(java.util.Collection<?> names) throws java.io.IOException;
5.0 public void setIssuers(java.util.Collection<javax.security.auth.x500.X500Principal> issuers);
    public void setMaxCRLNumber(java.math.BigInteger maxCRL);
    public void setMinCRLNumber(java.math.BigInteger minCRL);
// Methods Implementing CRLSelector
    public Object clone();
    public boolean match(CRL crl);
// Public Methods Overriding Object
    public String toString();
}
```

X509Extension — Java 1.2

java.security.cert

This interface defines methods for handling a set of extensions to X.509 certificates and CRLs. Each extension has a name, or OID (object identifier), that identifies the type of the extension. An extension may be marked critical or noncritical. Noncritical extensions whose OIDs are not recognized can safely be ignored. However, if a critical exception is not recognized, the Certificate or CRL should be rejected. Each extension in the set has a byte array of data as its value. The interpretation of these bytes depends on the OID of the extension, of course. Specific extensions are defined by the X.509 and related standards and their details are beyond the scope of this reference.

```
public interface X509Extension {
// Public Instance Methods
    java.util.Set<String> getCriticalExtensionOIDs();
    byte[] getExtensionValue(String oid);
    java.util.Set<String> getNonCriticalExtensionOIDs();
    boolean hasUnsupportedCriticalExtension();
}
```

Implementations X509Certificate, X509CRL, X509CRLEntry

Package java.security.interfaces — Java 1.1

As its name implies, the java.security.interfaces package contains only interfaces. These interfaces define methods that provide algorithm-specific information (such as key values and initialization parameter values) about DSA, RSA, and EC public and private keys. If you are using the RSA algorithm, for example, and working with a java.security.PublicKey object, you can cast that PublicKey to an RSAPublicKey object and use the RSA-specific methods defined by RSAPublicKey to query the key value directly.

The java.security.interfaces package was introduced in Java 1.1. As of Java 1.2, the java.security.spec package is the preferred way for obtaining algorithm-specific information about keys and algorithm parameters. This package remains useful in Java 1.2 and later, however, for identifying the type of a given PublicKey or PrivateKey object.

The interfaces in this package are typically of interest only to programmers who are implementing a security provider or who want to implement cryptographic algorithms themselves. Use of this package typically requires some familiarity with the mathematics underlying DSA and RSA public-key cryptography.

Interfaces

```
public interface DSAKey;
public interface DSAKeyPairGenerator;
public interface DSAParams;
public interface DSAPrivateKey extends DSAKey, java.security.PrivateKey;
public interface DSAPublicKey extends DSAKey, java.security.PublicKey;
public interface ECKey;
public interface ECPrivateKey extends ECKey, java.security.PrivateKey;
public interface ECPublicKey extends ECKey, java.security.PublicKey;
public interface RSAKey;
public interface RSAMultiPrimePrivateCrtKey extends RSAPrivateKey;
public interface RSAPrivateCrtKey extends RSAPrivateKey;
public interface RSAPrivateKey extends java.security.PrivateKey, RSAKey;
public interface RSAPublicKey extends java.security.PublicKey, RSAKey;
```

DSAKey — Java 1.1

java.security.interfaces

This interface defines a method that must be implemented by both public and private DSA keys.

```
public interface DSAKey {
// Public Instance Methods
   DSAParams getParams();
}
```

Implementations DSAPrivateKey, DSAPublicKey

DSAKeyPairGenerator — Java 1.1

java.security.interfaces

This interface defines algorithm-specific KeyPairGenerator initialization methods for DSA keys. To generate a pair of DSA keys, use the static getInstance() factory method of java.security.KeyPairGenerator and specify "DSA" as the desired algorithm name. If you wish to perform DSA-specific initialization, cast the returned KeyPairGenerator to a DSAKeyPairGenerator and call one of the initialize() methods defined by this interface. Finally, generate the keys by calling generateKeyPair() on the KeyPairGenerator.

```
public interface DSAKeyPairGenerator {
// Public Instance Methods
   void initialize(DSAParams params, java.security.SecureRandom random)
       throws java.security.InvalidParameterException;
   void initialize(int modlen, boolean genParams, java.security.SecureRandom random)
       throws java.security.InvalidParameterException;
}
```

DSAParams Java 1.1

java.security.interfaces

This interface defines methods for obtaining the DSA parameters g, p, and q. These methods are useful only if you wish to perform cryptographic computation yourself. Using these methods requires a detailed understanding of the mathematics underlying DSA public-key cryptography.

```
public interface DSAParams {
// Public Instance Methods
   java.math.BigInteger getG();
   java.math.BigInteger getP();
   java.math.BigInteger getQ();
}
```

Implementations java.security.spec.DSAParameterSpec

Passed To DSAKeyPairGenerator.initialize()

Returned By DSAKey.getParams()

DSAPrivateKey Java 1.1

java.security.interfaces serializable

This interface represents a DSA private key and provides direct access to the underlying key value. If you are working with a private key you know is a DSA key, you can cast the PrivateKey to a DSAPrivateKey.

DSAPrivateKey
DSAKey Serializable Key PrivateKey

```
public interface DSAPrivateKey extends DSAKeyjava.security.PrivateKey {
// Public Constants
1.2 public static final long serialVersionUID;                    =7776497482533790279
// Public Instance Methods
   java.math.BigInteger getX();
}
```

DSAPublicKey Java 1.1

java.security.interfaces serializable

This interface represents a DSA public key and provides direct access to the underlying key value. If you are working with a public key you know is a DSA key, you can cast the PublicKey to a DSAPublicKey.

DSAPublicKey
DSAKey Serializable Key PublicKey

```
public interface DSAPublicKey extends DSAKeyjava.security.PublicKey {
// Public Constants
1.2 public static final long serialVersionUID;                    =1234526332779022332
// Public Instance Methods
   java.math.BigInteger getY();
}
```

ECKey

Java 5.0

java.security.interfaces

This interface defines the API that must be implemented by all elliptic curve keys.

```
public interface ECKey {
// Public Instance Methods
   java.security.spec.ECParameterSpec getParams();
}
```

Implementations ECPrivateKey, ECPublicKey

ECPrivateKey

Java 5.0

java.security.interfaces

serializable

This interface defines an API that must be implemented by all elliptic curve private keys.

ECPrivateKey

ECKey Serializable Key PrivateKey

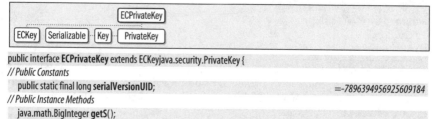

```
public interface ECPrivateKey extends ECKeyjava.security.PrivateKey {
// Public Constants
   public static final long serialVersionUID;                    =-7896394956925609184
// Public Instance Methods
   java.math.BigInteger getS();
}
```

ECPublicKey

Java 5.0

java.security.interfaces

serializable

This interface defines an API that must be implemented by all elliptic curve public keys.

```
public interface ECPublicKey extends ECKeyjava.security.PublicKey {
// Public Constants
   public static final long serialVersionUID;                    =-3314988629879632826
// Public Instance Methods
   java.security.spec.ECPoint getW();
}
```

RSAKey

Java 1.3

java.security.interfaces

This is a superinterface for RSAPublicKey and RSAPrivateKey; it defines a method shared by both classes. Prior to Java 1.3, the getModulus() method was defined independently by RSAPublicKey and RSAPrivateKey.

```
public interface RSAKey {
// Public Instance Methods
   java.math.BigInteger getModulus();
}
```

Implementations RSAPrivateKey, RSAPublicKey

RSAMultiPrimePrivateCrtKey

Java 1.4

java.security.interfaces

serializable

This interface extends RSAPrivateKey and provides a decomposition of the private key into the various numbers used to create it. This interface is very similar to RSAPrivateCrtKey, except that it is used to represent RSA private keys that are based on more than two prime factors, and implements the addition getOtherPrimeInfo() method to return information about these additional prime numbers.

Serializable — Key — PrivateKey — RSAKey — RSAPrivateKey — RSAMultiPrimePrivateCrtKey

```
public interface RSAMultiPrimePrivateCrtKey extends RSAPrivateKey {
// Public Constants
5.0 public static final long serialVersionUID;                    =618058533534628008
// Public Instance Methods
   java.math.BigInteger getCrtCoefficient();
   java.security.spec.RSAOtherPrimeInfo[] getOtherPrimeInfo();
   java.math.BigInteger getPrimeExponentP();
   java.math.BigInteger getPrimeExponentQ();
   java.math.BigInteger getPrimeP();
   java.math.BigInteger getPrimeQ();
   java.math.BigInteger getPublicExponent();
}
```

RSAPrivateCrtKey

Java 1.2

java.security.interfaces

serializable

This interface extends RSAPrivateKey and provides a decomposition (based on the Chinese remainder theorem) of the private-key value into the various pieces that comprise it. This interface is useful only if you plan to implement your own cryptographic algorithms. To use this interface, you must have a detailed understanding of the mathematics underlying RSA public-key cryptography. Given a java.security.PrivateKey object, you can use the instanceof operator to determine whether you can safely cast it to an RSAPrivateCrtKey.

Serializable — Key — PrivateKey — RSAKey — RSAPrivateKey — RSAPrivateCrtKey

```
public interface RSAPrivateCrtKey extends RSAPrivateKey {
// Public Constants
5.0 public static final long serialVersionUID;                    =-5682214253527700368
// Public Instance Methods
   java.math.BigInteger getCrtCoefficient();
   java.math.BigInteger getPrimeExponentP();
   java.math.BigInteger getPrimeExponentQ();
   java.math.BigInteger getPrimeP();
   java.math.BigInteger getPrimeQ();
   java.math.BigInteger getPublicExponent();
}
```

RSAPrivateKey

Java 1.2

java.security.interfaces

serializable

This interface represents an RSA private key and provides direct access to the underlying key values. If you are working with a private key you know is an RSA key, you can cast the PrivateKey to an RSAPrivateKey.

Serializable — Key — PrivateKey — RSAKey — RSAPrivateKey

```
public interface RSAPrivateKey extends java.security.PrivateKeyRSAKey {
// Public Constants
5.0 public static final long serialVersionUID;                    =5187144804936595022
// Public Instance Methods
   java.math.BigInteger getPrivateExponent();
}
```

Implementations RSAMultiPrimePrivateCrtKey, RSAPrivateCrtKey

RSAPublicKey

Java 1.2

java.security.interfaces

serializable

This interface represents an RSA public key and provides direct access to the underlying key values. If you are working with a public key you know is an RSA key, you can cast the PublicKey to an RSAPublicKey.

Serializable — Key — PublicKey — RSAKey — RSAPublicKey

```
public interface RSAPublicKey extends java.security.PublicKeyRSAKey {
// Public Constants
5.0 public static final long serialVersionUID;                    =-8727434096241101194
// Public Instance Methods
   java.math.BigInteger getPublicExponent();
}
```

Package java.security.spec

Java 1.2

The java.security.spec package contains classes that define transparent representations for DSA, RSA, and EC public and private keys and for X.509 and PKCS#8 encodings of those keys. It also defines a transparent representation for DSA algorithm parameters. The classes in this package are used in conjunction with java.security.KeyFactory and java.security.AlgorithmParameters for converting opaque Key and AlgorithmParameters objects to and from transparent representations.

This package is not frequently used. To make use of it, you must be somewhat familiar with the mathematics that underlies DSA and RSA public-key encryption and the encoding standards that specify how keys are encoded as byte streams.

Interfaces

```
public interface AlgorithmParameterSpec;
public interface ECField;
public interface KeySpec;
```

Classes

public class **DSAParameterSpec** implements AlgorithmParameterSpec, java.security.interfaces.DSAParams;
public class **DSAPrivateKeySpec** implements KeySpec;
public class **DSAPublicKeySpec** implements KeySpec;
public class **ECFieldF2m** implements ECField;
public class **ECFieldFp** implements ECField;
public class **ECGenParameterSpec** implements AlgorithmParameterSpec;
public class **ECParameterSpec** implements AlgorithmParameterSpec;
public class **ECPoint**;
public class **ECPrivateKeySpec** implements KeySpec;
public class **ECPublicKeySpec** implements KeySpec;
public class **EllipticCurve**;
public abstract class **EncodedKeySpec** implements KeySpec;
    public class **PKCS8EncodedKeySpec** extends EncodedKeySpec;
    public class **X509EncodedKeySpec** extends EncodedKeySpec;
public class **MGF1ParameterSpec** implements AlgorithmParameterSpec;
public class **PSSParameterSpec** implements AlgorithmParameterSpec;
public class **RSAKeyGenParameterSpec** implements AlgorithmParameterSpec;
public class **RSAOtherPrimeInfo**;
public class **RSAPrivateKeySpec** implements KeySpec;
    public class **RSAMultiPrimePrivateCrtKeySpec** extends RSAPrivateKeySpec;
    public class **RSAPrivateCrtKeySpec** extends RSAPrivateKeySpec;
public class **RSAPublicKeySpec** implements KeySpec;

Exceptions

public class **InvalidKeySpecException** extends java.security.GeneralSecurityException;
public class **InvalidParameterSpecException** extends java.security.GeneralSecurityException;

AlgorithmParameterSpec — Java 1.2

java.security.spec

This interface defines no methods; it marks classes that define a transparent representation of cryptographic parameters. You can use an AlgorithmParameterSpec object to initialize an opaque java.security.AlgorithmParameters object.

```
public interface AlgorithmParameterSpec {
}
```

Implementations DSAParameterSpec, ECGenParameterSpec, ECParameterSpec, MGF1ParameterSpec, PSSParameterSpec, RSAKeyGenParameterSpec, javax.crypto.spec.DHGenParameterSpec, javax.crypto.spec.DHParameterSpec, javax.crypto.spec.IvParameterSpec, javax.crypto.spec.OAEPParameterSpec, javax.crypto.spec.PBEParameterSpec, javax.crypto.spec.RC2ParameterSpec, javax.crypto.spec.RC5ParameterSpec

Passed To Too many methods to list.

Returned By java.security.AlgorithmParameters.getParameterSpec(), java.security.AlgorithmParametersSpi.engineGetParameterSpec(), PSSParameterSpec.getMGFParameters(), javax.crypto.Cipher.getMaxAllowedParameterSpec(), javax.crypto.spec.OAEPParameterSpec.getMGFParameters()

DSAParameterSpec — Java 1.2

java.security.spec

This class represents algorithm parameters used with DSA public-key cryptography.

Object — DSAParameterSpec ··· AlgorithmParameterSpec, DSAParams

```
public class DSAParameterSpec implements AlgorithmParameterSpec, java.security.interfaces.DSAParams {
// Public Constructors
   public DSAParameterSpec(java.math.BigInteger p, java.math.BigInteger q, java.math.BigInteger g);
// Methods Implementing DSAParams
   public java.math.BigInteger getG();
   public java.math.BigInteger getP();
   public java.math.BigInteger getQ();
}
```

DSAPrivateKeySpec — Java 1.2

java.security.spec

This class is a transparent representation of a DSA private key.

Object — DSAPrivateKeySpec ··· KeySpec

```
public class DSAPrivateKeySpec implements KeySpec {
// Public Constructors
   public DSAPrivateKeySpec(java.math.BigInteger x, java.math.BigInteger p, java.math.BigInteger q,
                            java.math.BigInteger g);
// Public Instance Methods
   public java.math.BigInteger getG();
   public java.math.BigInteger getP();
   public java.math.BigInteger getQ();
   public java.math.BigInteger getX();
}
```

DSAPublicKeySpec — Java 1.2

java.security.spec

This class is a transparent representation of a DSA public key.

Object — DSAPublicKeySpec ··· KeySpec

```
public class DSAPublicKeySpec implements KeySpec {
// Public Constructors
   public DSAPublicKeySpec(java.math.BigInteger y, java.math.BigInteger p, java.math.BigInteger q, java.math.BigInteger g);
// Public Instance Methods
   public java.math.BigInteger getG();
   public java.math.BigInteger getP();
   public java.math.BigInteger getQ();
   public java.math.BigInteger getY();
}
```

ECField — Java 5.0

java.security.spec

This interface represents a "finite field" for elliptic curve cryptography.

```
public interface ECField {
// Public Instance Methods
   int getFieldSize();
}
```

Implementations ECFieldF2m, ECFieldFp

Passed To EllipticCurve.EllipticCurve()

Returned By EllipticCurve.getField()

ECFieldF2m — Java 5.0

java.security.spec

This class defines an immutable representation of a "characteristic 2 finite field" for elliptic curve cryptography.

Object — ECFieldF2m ··· ECField

```
public class ECFieldF2m implements ECField {
// Public Constructors
   public ECFieldF2m(int m);
   public ECFieldF2m(int m, int[] ks);
   public ECFieldF2m(int m, java.math.BigInteger rp);
// Public Instance Methods
   public int getM();
   public int[] getMidTermsOfReductionPolynomial();
   public java.math.BigInteger getReductionPolynomial();
// Methods Implementing ECField
   public int getFieldSize();
// Public Methods Overriding Object
   public boolean equals(Object obj);
   public int hashCode();
}
```

ECFieldFp — Java 5.0

java.security.spec

This class defines an immutable representation of a "prime finite field" for elliptic curve cryptography.

Object — ECFieldFp ··· ECField

```
public class ECFieldFp implements ECField {
// Public Constructors
   public ECFieldFp(java.math.BigInteger p);
// Public Instance Methods
   public java.math.BigInteger getP();
// Methods Implementing ECField
   public int getFieldSize();
// Public Methods Overriding Object
   public boolean equals(Object obj);
   public int hashCode();
}
```

ECGenParameterSpec — Java 5.0

java.security.spec

This class specifies parameters for generating elliptic curve domain parameters.

Object — ECGenParameterSpec ··· AlgorithmParameterSpec

```
public class ECGenParameterSpec implements AlgorithmParameterSpec {
// Public Constructors
   public ECGenParameterSpec(String stdName);
// Public Instance Methods
   public String getName();
}
```

ECParameterSpec

Java 5.0

java.security.spec

This class defines an immutable representation for a set of parameters for elliptic curve cryptography.

Object — ECParameterSpec ··· AlgorithmParameterSpec

```
public class ECParameterSpec implements AlgorithmParameterSpec {
// Public Constructors
   public ECParameterSpec(EllipticCurve curve, ECPoint g, java.math.BigInteger n, int h);
// Public Instance Methods
   public int getCofactor();
   public EllipticCurve getCurve();
   public ECPoint getGenerator();
   public java.math.BigInteger getOrder();
}
```

Passed To ECPrivateKeySpec.ECPrivateKeySpec(), ECPublicKeySpec.ECPublicKeySpec()

Returned By java.security.interfaces.ECKey.getParams(), ECPrivateKeySpec.getParams(), ECPublicKeySpec.getParams()

ECPoint

Java 5.0

java.security.spec

This class defines an immutable representation of a point on an elliptic curve, using affine coordinates.

```
public class ECPoint {
// Public Constructors
   public ECPoint(java.math.BigInteger x, java.math.BigInteger y);
// Public Constants
   public static final ECPoint POINT_INFINITY;
// Public Instance Methods
   public java.math.BigInteger getAffineX();
   public java.math.BigInteger getAffineY();
// Public Methods Overriding Object
   public boolean equals(Object obj);
   public int hashCode();
}
```

Passed To ECParameterSpec.ECParameterSpec(), ECPublicKeySpec.ECPublicKeySpec()

Returned By java.security.interfaces.ECPublicKey.getW(), ECParameterSpec.getGenerator(), ECPublicKeySpec.getW()

ECPrivateKeySpec Java 5.0

java.security.spec

This class is an immutable representation of a private key for elliptic curve cryptography.

Object ─ ECPrivateKeySpec ··· KeySpec

```
public class ECPrivateKeySpec implements KeySpec {
// Public Constructors
   public ECPrivateKeySpec(java.math.BigInteger s, ECParameterSpec params);
// Public Instance Methods
   public ECParameterSpec getParams();
   public java.math.BigInteger getS();
}
```

ECPublicKeySpec Java 5.0

java.security.spec

This class is an immutable representation of a public key for elliptic curve cryptography.

Object ─ ECPublicKeySpec ··· KeySpec

```
public class ECPublicKeySpec implements KeySpec {
// Public Constructors
   public ECPublicKeySpec(ECPoint w, ECParameterSpec params);
// Public Instance Methods
   public ECParameterSpec getParams();
   public ECPoint getW();
}
```

EllipticCurve Java 5.0

java.security.spec

This class is an immutable representation of an elliptic curve. See ECParameterSpec.

```
public class EllipticCurve {
// Public Constructors
   public EllipticCurve(ECField field, java.math.BigInteger a, java.math.BigInteger b);
   public EllipticCurve(ECField field, java.math.BigInteger a, java.math.BigInteger b, byte[] seed);
// Public Instance Methods
   public java.math.BigInteger getA();
   public java.math.BigInteger getB();
   public ECField getField();
   public byte[] getSeed();
// Public Methods Overriding Object
   public boolean equals(Object obj);
   public int hashCode();
}
```

Passed To ECParameterSpec.ECParameterSpec()

Returned By ECParameterSpec.getCurve()

java.security.*

EncodedKeySpec

Java 1.2

java.security.spec

This abstract class represents a public or private key in an encoded format. It serves as the superclass for encoding-specific classes.

Object — EncodedKeySpec ··· KeySpec

```
public abstract class EncodedKeySpec implements KeySpec {
// Public Constructors
   public EncodedKeySpec(byte[] encodedKey);
// Public Instance Methods
   public byte[] getEncoded();
   public abstract String getFormat();
}
```

Subclasses PKCS8EncodedKeySpec, X509EncodedKeySpec

InvalidKeySpecException

Java 1.2

java.security.spec

serializable checked

Signals a problem with a KeySpec.

Object — Throwable — Exception — GeneralSecurityException — InvalidKeySpecException
Throwable ··· Serializable

```
public class InvalidKeySpecException extends java.security.GeneralSecurityException {
// Public Constructors
   public InvalidKeySpecException();
5.0 public InvalidKeySpecException(Throwable cause);
   public InvalidKeySpecException(String msg);
5.0 public InvalidKeySpecException(String message, Throwable cause);
}
```

Thrown By java.security.KeyFactory.{generatePrivate(), generatePublic(), getKeySpec()}, java.security.KeyFactorySpi.{engineGeneratePrivate(), engineGeneratePublic(), engineGetKeySpec()}, javax.crypto.EncryptedPrivateKeyInfo.getKeySpec(), javax.crypto.SecretKeyFactory.{generateSecret(), getKeySpec()}, javax.crypto.SecretKeyFactorySpi.{engineGenerateSecret(), engineGetKeySpec()}

InvalidParameterSpecException

Java 1.2

java.security.spec

serializable checked

Signals a problem with an AlgorithmParameterSpec.

Object — Throwable — Exception — GeneralSecurityException — InvalidParameterSpecException
Throwable ··· Serializable

```
public class InvalidParameterSpecException extends java.security.GeneralSecurityException {
// Public Constructors
   public InvalidParameterSpecException();
   public InvalidParameterSpecException(String msg);
}
```

Thrown By java.security.AlgorithmParameters.{getParameterSpec(), init()}, java.security.AlgorithmParametersSpi.{engineGetParameterSpec(), engineInit()}

KeySpec **Java 1.2**

java.security.spec

This interface defines no methods; it marks classes that define a transparent representation of a cryptographic key. Use a java.security.KeyFactory to convert a KeySpec to and from an opaque java.security.Key.

```
public interface KeySpec {
}
```

Implementations DSAPrivateKeySpec, DSAPublicKeySpec, ECPrivateKeySpec, ECPublicKeySpec, EncodedKeySpec, RSAPrivateKeySpec, RSAPublicKeySpec, javax.crypto.spec.DESedeKeySpec, javax.crypto.spec.DESKeySpec, javax.crypto.spec.DHPrivateKeySpec, javax.crypto.spec.DHPublicKeySpec, javax.crypto.spec.PBEKeySpec, javax.crypto.spec.SecretKeySpec

Passed To java.security.KeyFactory.{generatePrivate(), generatePublic()}, java.security.KeyFactorySpi.{engineGeneratePrivate(), engineGeneratePublic()}, javax.crypto.SecretKeyFactory.generateSecret(), javax.crypto.SecretKeyFactorySpi.engineGenerateSecret()

Returned By java.security.KeyFactory.getKeySpec(), java.security.KeyFactorySpi.engineGetKeySpec(), javax.crypto.SecretKeyFactory.getKeySpec(), javax.crypto.SecretKeyFactorySpi.engineGetKeySpec()

MGF1ParameterSpec **Java 5.0**

java.security.spec

This class represents parameters for "mask generation function" MGF1 of the OAEP Padding and RSA-PSS signature scheme, defined in the PKCS #1 standard, version 2.1. The constants represent predefined instances of the class, whose digest algorithm matches the constant name.

Object — MGF1ParameterSpec ··· AlgorithmParameterSpec

```
public class MGF1ParameterSpec implements AlgorithmParameterSpec {
// Public Constructors
    public MGF1ParameterSpec(String mdName);
// Public Constants
    public static final MGF1ParameterSpec SHA1;
    public static final MGF1ParameterSpec SHA256;
    public static final MGF1ParameterSpec SHA384;
    public static final MGF1ParameterSpec SHA512;
// Public Instance Methods
    public String getDigestAlgorithm();
}
```

PKCS8EncodedKeySpec **Java 1.2**

java.security.spec

This class represents a private key, encoded according to the PKCS#8 standard.

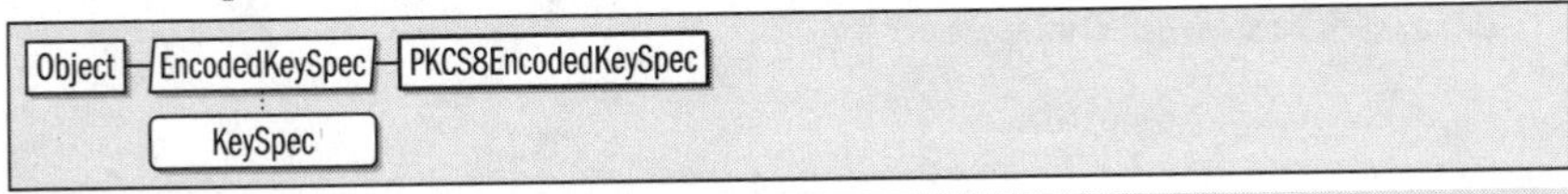


```
public class PKCS8EncodedKeySpec extends EncodedKeySpec {
// Public Constructors
    public PKCS8EncodedKeySpec(byte[] encodedKey);
// Public Methods Overriding EncodedKeySpec
```

```
    public byte[] getEncoded();
    public final String getFormat();
}
```

Returned By javax.crypto.EncryptedPrivateKeyInfo.getKeySpec()

PSSParameterSpec   Java 1.4

java.security.spec

This class represents algorithm parameters used with the RSA PSS encoding scheme, which is defined by version 2.1 of the RSA standard PKCS#1. This class has been substantially enhanced in Java 5.0.

Object — PSSParameterSpec ··· AlgorithmParameterSpec

```
public class PSSParameterSpec implements AlgorithmParameterSpec {
// Public Constructors
    public PSSParameterSpec(int saltLen);
5.0 public PSSParameterSpec(String mdName, String mgfName, AlgorithmParameterSpec mgfSpec, int saltLen,
                            int trailerField);
// Public Constants
5.0 public static final PSSParameterSpec DEFAULT;
// Public Instance Methods
5.0 public String getDigestAlgorithm();
5.0 public String getMGFAlgorithm();
5.0 public AlgorithmParameterSpec getMGFParameters();
    public int getSaltLength();
5.0 public int getTrailerField();
}
```

RSAKeyGenParameterSpec   Java 1.3

java.security.spec

This class represents parameters that generate public/private key pairs for RSA cryptography.

Object — RSAKeyGenParameterSpec ··· AlgorithmParameterSpec

```
public class RSAKeyGenParameterSpec implements AlgorithmParameterSpec {
// Public Constructors
    public RSAKeyGenParameterSpec(int keysize, java.math.BigInteger publicExponent);
// Public Constants
    public static final java.math.BigInteger F0;
    public static final java.math.BigInteger F4;
// Public Instance Methods
    public int getKeysize();
    public java.math.BigInteger getPublicExponent();
}
```

RSAMultiPrimePrivateCrtKeySpec — Java 1.4

java.security.spec

This class is a transparent representation of a multi-prime RSA private key. It is very similar to RSAPrivateCrtKeySpec, but adds an additional method for obtaining information about the other primes associated with the key.

Object — RSAPrivateKeySpec — RSAMultiPrimePrivateCrtKeySpec
KeySpec

```
public class RSAMultiPrimePrivateCrtKeySpec extends RSAPrivateKeySpec {
// Public Constructors
   public RSAMultiPrimePrivateCrtKeySpec(java.math.BigInteger modulus, java.math.BigInteger publicExponent,
                                          java.math.BigInteger privateExponent, java.math.BigInteger primeP,
                                          java.math.BigInteger primeQ, java.math.BigInteger primeExponentP,
                                          java.math.BigInteger primeExponentQ, java.math.BigInteger crtCoefficient,
                                          RSAOtherPrimeInfo[] otherPrimeInfo;)
// Public Instance Methods
   public java.math.BigInteger getCrtCoefficient();
   public RSAOtherPrimeInfo[] getOtherPrimeInfo();
   public java.math.BigInteger getPrimeExponentP();
   public java.math.BigInteger getPrimeExponentQ();
   public java.math.BigInteger getPrimeP();
   public java.math.BigInteger getPrimeQ();
   public java.math.BigInteger getPublicExponent();
}
```

RSAOtherPrimeInfo — Java 1.4

java.security.spec

This class represents the (prime, exponent, coefficient) triplet that constitues an "OtherPrimeInfo" structure that is used with RSA multi-prime private keys, as defined in version 2.1 of the PKCS#1 standard.

```
public class RSAOtherPrimeInfo {
// Public Constructors
   public RSAOtherPrimeInfo(java.math.BigInteger prime, java.math.BigInteger primeExponent,
                             java.math.BigInteger crtCoefficient);
// Public Instance Methods
   public final java.math.BigInteger getCrtCoefficient();
   public final java.math.BigInteger getExponent();
   public final java.math.BigInteger getPrime();
}
```

Passed To RSAMultiPrimePrivateCrtKeySpec.RSAMultiPrimePrivateCrtKeySpec()

Returned By java.security.interfaces.RSAMultiPrimePrivateCrtKey.getOtherPrimeInfo(), RSAMultiPrimePrivateCrtKeySpec.getOtherPrimeInfo()

RSAPrivateCrtKeySpec — Java 1.2

java.security.spec

This class is a transparent representation of an RSA private key including, for convenience, the Chinese remainder theorem values associated with the key.

Object — RSAPrivateKeySpec — RSAPrivateCrtKeySpec
KeySpec

```
public class RSAPrivateCrtKeySpec extends RSAPrivateKeySpec {
// Public Constructors
   public RSAPrivateCrtKeySpec(java.math.BigInteger modulus, java.math.BigInteger publicExponent,
                               java.math.BigInteger privateExponent, java.math.BigInteger primeP,
                               java.math.BigInteger primeQ, java.math.BigInteger primeExponentP,
                               java.math.BigInteger primeExponentQ, java.math.BigInteger crtCoefficient);
// Public Instance Methods
   public java.math.BigInteger getCrtCoefficient();
   public java.math.BigInteger getPrimeExponentP();
   public java.math.BigInteger getPrimeExponentQ();
   public java.math.BigInteger getPrimeP();
   public java.math.BigInteger getPrimeQ();
   public java.math.BigInteger getPublicExponent();
}
```

RSAPrivateKeySpec

Java 1.2

java.security.spec

This class is a transparent representation of an RSA private key.

Object — RSAPrivateKeySpec ··· KeySpec

```
public class RSAPrivateKeySpec implements KeySpec {
// Public Constructors
   public RSAPrivateKeySpec(java.math.BigInteger modulus, java.math.BigInteger privateExponent);
// Public Instance Methods
   public java.math.BigInteger getModulus();
   public java.math.BigInteger getPrivateExponent();
}
```

Subclasses RSAMultiPrimePrivateCrtKeySpec, RSAPrivateCrtKeySpec

RSAPublicKeySpec

Java 1.2

java.security.spec

This class is a transparent representation of an RSA public key.

Object — RSAPublicKeySpec ··· KeySpec

```
public class RSAPublicKeySpec implements KeySpec {
// Public Constructors
   public RSAPublicKeySpec(java.math.BigInteger modulus, java.math.BigInteger publicExponent);
// Public Instance Methods
   public java.math.BigInteger getModulus();
   public java.math.BigInteger getPublicExponent();
}
```

X509EncodedKeySpec

Java 1.2

java.security.spec

This class represents a public or private key encoded according to the X.509 standard.

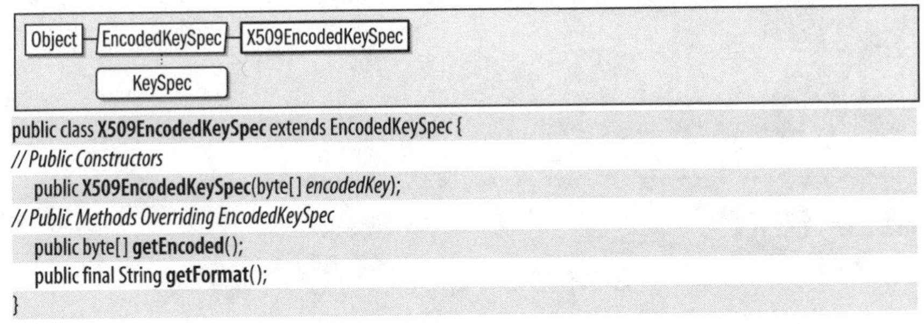


```
public class X509EncodedKeySpec extends EncodedKeySpec {
// Public Constructors
    public X509EncodedKeySpec(byte[] encodedKey);
// Public Methods Overriding EncodedKeySpec
    public byte[] getEncoded();
    public final String getFormat();
}
```

15

java.text

Package java.text

Java 1.1

The java.text package consists of classes and interfaces that are useful for writing internationalized programs that handle local customs, such as date and time formatting and string alphabetization, correctly.

The NumberFormat class formats numbers, monetary quantities, and percentages as appropriate for the default or specified locale. DateFormat formats dates and times in a locale-specific way. The concrete DecimalFormat and SimpleDateFormat subclasses of these classes can be used for customized number, date, and time formatting. MessageFormat allows substitution of dynamic values, including formatted numbers and dates, into static message strings. ChoiceFormat formats a number using an enumerated set of string values. See the Format superclass for a general description of formatting and parsing strings with these classes. Collator compares strings according to the customary sorting order for a locale. BreakIterator scans text to find word, line, and sentence boundaries following locale-specific rules. The Bidi class of Java 1.4 implements the Unicode "bidirectional" algorithm for working with languages such as Arabic and Hebrew that display text right-to-left but display numbers left-to-right.

Interfaces

```
public interface AttributedCharacterIterator extends CharacterIterator;
public interface CharacterIterator extends Cloneable;
```

Classes

```
public class Annotation;
public static class AttributedCharacterIterator.Attribute implements Serializable;
    public static class Format.Field extends AttributedCharacterIterator.Attribute;
        public static class DateFormat.Field extends Format.Field;
        public static class MessageFormat.Field extends Format.Field;
        public static class NumberFormat.Field extends Format.Field;
public class AttributedString;
```

```
public final class Bidi;
public abstract class BreakIterator implements Cloneable;
public final class CollationElementIterator;
public final class CollationKey implements Comparable<CollationKey>;
public abstract class Collator implements java.util.Comparator<Object>, Cloneable;
    public class RuleBasedCollator extends Collator;
public class DateFormatSymbols implements Cloneable, Serializable;
public final class DecimalFormatSymbols implements Cloneable, Serializable;
public class FieldPosition;
public abstract class Format implements Cloneable, Serializable;
    public abstract class DateFormat extends Format;
        public class SimpleDateFormat extends DateFormat;
    public class MessageFormat extends Format;
    public abstract class NumberFormat extends Format;
        public class ChoiceFormat extends NumberFormat;
        public class DecimalFormat extends NumberFormat;
public class ParsePosition;
public final class StringCharacterIterator implements CharacterIterator;
```

Exceptions

```
public class ParseException extends Exception;
```

Annotation Java 1.2

java.text

This class is a wrapper for a the value of a text attribute that represents an annotation. Annotations differ from other types of text attributes in two ways. First, annotations are linked to the text they are applied to, so changing the text invalidates or corrupts the meaning of the annotation. Second, annotations cannot be merged with adjacent annotations, even if they have the same value. Putting an annotation value in an Annotation wrapper serves to indicate these special characteristics. Note that two of the attribute keys defined by AttributedCharaterIterator.Attribute, READING and INPUT_METHOD_SEGMENT, must be used with Annotation objects.

```
public class Annotation {
// Public Constructors
    public Annotation(Object value);
// Public Instance Methods
    public Object getValue();
// Public Methods Overriding Object
    public String toString();
}
```

AttributedCharacterIterator Java 1.2

java.text cloneable

This interface extends CharacterIterator for working with text that is marked up with attributes in some way. It defines an inner class, AttributedCharaterIterator.Attribute, that represents attribute keys. AttributedCharacterIterator defines methods for querying the attribute keys, values, and runs for the text being iterated over. getAllAttributeKeys() returns the Set of all attribute keys that appear anywhere in the text. getAttributes() returns a Map that contains the attribute keys and values that apply to the current character. getAttribute() returns the value associated with the specified attribute key for the current character.

getRunStart() and getRunLimit() return the index of the first and last characters in a run. A *run* is a string of adjacent characters for which an attribute has the same value or is undefined (i.e., has a value of null). A run can also be defined for a set of attributes, in which case it is a set of adjacent characters for which all attributes in the set hold a constant value (which may include null). Programs that process or display attributed text must usually work with it one run at a time. The no-argument versions of getRunStart() and getRunLimit() return the start and end of the run that includes the current character and all attributes that are applied to the current character. The other versions of these methods return the start and end of the run of the specified attribute or set of attributes that includes the current character.

The AttributedString class provides a simple way to define short strings of attributed text and obtain an AttributedCharacterIterator over them. Most applications that process attributed text are working with attributed text from specialized data sources, stored in some specialized data format, so they need to define a custom implementation of AttributedCharacterIterator.

Cloneable ··· CharacterIterator ··· AttributedCharacterIterator

```
public interface AttributedCharacterIterator extends CharacterIterator {
// Nested Types
   public static class Attribute implements Serializable;
// Public Instance Methods
   java.util.Set<AttributedCharacterIterator.Attribute> getAllAttributeKeys();
   Object getAttribute(AttributedCharacterIterator.Attribute attribute);
   java.util.Map<AttributedCharacterIterator.Attribute,Object> getAttributes();
   int getRunLimit();
   int getRunLimit(java.util.Set<? extends AttributedCharacterIterator.Attribute> attributes);
   int getRunLimit(AttributedCharacterIterator.Attribute attribute);
   int getRunStart();
   int getRunStart(AttributedCharacterIterator.Attribute attribute);
   int getRunStart(java.util.Set<? extends AttributedCharacterIterator.Attribute> attributes);
}
```

Passed To AttributedString.AttributedString(), Bidi.Bidi()

Returned By AttributedString.getIterator(), DecimalFormat.formatToCharacterIterator(), Format.formatToCharacterIterator(), MessageFormat.formatToCharacterIterator(), SimpleDateFormat.formatToCharacterIterator()

AttributedCharacterIterator.Attribute Java 1.2

java.text serializable

This class defines the types of the attribute keys used with AttributedCharacterIterator and AttributedString. It defines several constant Attribute keys that are commonly used with multilingual text and input methods. The LANGUAGE key represents the language of the underlying text. The value of this key should be a Locale object. The READING key represents arbitrary reading information associated with text. The value must be an Annotation object. The INPUT_METHOD_SEGMENT key serves to define text segments (usually words) that an input method operates on. The value of this attribute should be an Annotation object that contains null. Other classes may subclass this class and define other attribute keys that are useful in other circumstances or problem domains. See, for example, java.awt.font.TextAttribute in *Java Foundation Classes in a Nutshell* (O'Reilly).

```
public static class AttributedCharacterIterator.Attribute implements Serializable {
// Protected Constructors
    protected Attribute(String name);
// Public Constants
    public static final AttributedCharacterIterator.Attribute INPUT_METHOD_SEGMENT;
    public static final AttributedCharacterIterator.Attribute LANGUAGE;
    public static final AttributedCharacterIterator.Attribute READING;
// Public Methods Overriding Object
    public final boolean equals(Object obj);
    public final int hashCode();
    public String toString();
// Protected Instance Methods
    protected String getName();
    protected Object readResolve() throws java.io.InvalidObjectException;
}
```

Subclasses Format.Field

Passed To AttributedCharacterIterator.{getAttribute(), getRunLimit(), getRunStart()}, AttributedString.{addAttribute(), AttributedString(), getIterator()}

AttributedString — Java 1.2

java.text

This class represents text and associated attributes. An AttributedString can be defined in terms of an underlying AttributedCharacterIterator or an underlying String. Additional attributes can be specified with the addAttribute() and addAttributes() methods. getIterator() returns an AttributedCharacterIterator over the AttributedString or over a specified portion of the string. Note that two of the getIterator() methods take an array of Attribute keys as an argument. These methods return an AttributedCharacterIterator that ignores all attributes that are not in the specified array. If the array argument is null, however, the returned iterator contains all attributes.

```
public class AttributedString {
// Public Constructors
    public AttributedString(String text);
    public AttributedString(AttributedCharacterIterator text);
    public AttributedString(String text, java.util.Map<? extends AttributedCharacterIterator.Attribute,?> attributes);
    public AttributedString(AttributedCharacterIterator text, int beginIndex, int endIndex);
    public AttributedString(AttributedCharacterIterator text, int beginIndex, int endIndex,
                            AttributedCharacterIterator.Attribute[] attributes);
// Public Instance Methods
    public void addAttribute(AttributedCharacterIterator.Attribute attribute, Object value);
    public void addAttribute(AttributedCharacterIterator.Attribute attribute, Object value, int beginIndex, int endIndex);
    public void addAttributes(java.util.Map<? extends AttributedCharacterIterator.Attribute,?> attributes, int beginIndex,
                              int endIndex);
    public AttributedCharacterIterator getIterator();
    public AttributedCharacterIterator getIterator(AttributedCharacterIterator.Attribute[] attributes);
    public AttributedCharacterIterator getIterator(AttributedCharacterIterator.Attribute[] attributes, int beginIndex,
                                                   int endIndex);
}
```

java.text

Bidi

Java 1.4

java.text

The Bidi class implements the "Unicode Version 3.0 Bidirectional Algorithm" for working with Arabic and Hebrew text in which letters run right-to-left and numbers run left-to-right. It is named after the first four letters of "bidirectional." A full description of the bidirectional text handling and the bidirectional algorithim is beyond the scope of this book, but the simplest use case for this class is outlined here. Create a Bidi object by passing an AttributedCharacterIterator or a String and one of the DIRECTION constants (to indicate the base direction of the text) to the Bidi() constructor. Or use createLineBidi() to return a substring of an existing Bidi object (this is usually done when formatting a paragraph of text to fit on individual lines).

Once you have a Bidi object, use isLeftToRight() and isRightToLeft() to determine whether all the text has the same direction. If both of these methods return false (which is the same as isMixed() returning true) then you cannot treat the text as a single run of uni-directional text. In this case, you must break it into two or more runs of unidirectional text. getRunCount() returns the number of distinct runs of text. For each such numbered run, getRunStart() returns the index of the first character of the run, and getRunLimit() returns the index of the first character past the end of the run. getRunLevel() returns the *level* of the text, which is an integer that represents the direction and nesting level of the text. Even levels represent left-to-right text, and odd levels represent right-to-left text. The level divided by two is the nesting level of the text. For example, left-to-right text embedded within right-to-left text has a level of 2.

```
public final class Bidi {
// Public Constructors
   public Bidi(AttributedCharacterIterator paragraph);
   public Bidi(String paragraph, int flags);
   public Bidi(char[] text, int textStart, byte[] embeddings, int embStart, int paragraphLength, int flags);
// Public Constants
   public static final int DIRECTION_DEFAULT_LEFT_TO_RIGHT;                    =-2
   public static final int DIRECTION_DEFAULT_RIGHT_TO_LEFT;                    =-1
   public static final int DIRECTION_LEFT_TO_RIGHT;                            =0
   public static final int DIRECTION_RIGHT_TO_LEFT;                            =1
// Public Class Methods
   public static void reorderVisually(byte[] levels, int levelStart, Object[] objects, int objectStart, int count);
   public static boolean requiresBidi(char[] text, int start, int limit);
// Public Instance Methods
   public boolean baseIsLeftToRight();
   public Bidi createLineBidi(int lineStart, int lineLimit);
   public int getBaseLevel();
   public int getLength();
   public int getLevelAt(int offset);
   public int getRunCount();
   public int getRunLevel(int run);
   public int getRunLimit(int run);
   public int getRunStart(int run);
   public boolean isLeftToRight();
   public boolean isMixed();
   public boolean isRightToLeft();
// Public Methods Overriding Object
   public String toString();
}
```

BreakIterator **Java 1.1**

java.text *cloneable*

This class determines character, word, sentence, and line breaks in a block of text in a way that is independent of locale and text encoding. As an abstract class, BreakIterator cannot be instantiated directly. Instead, you must use one of the class methods getCharacterInstance(), getWordInstance(), getSentenceInstance(), or getLineInstance() to return an instance of a nonabstract subclass of BreakIterator. These various factory methods return a BreakIterator object that is configured to locate the requested boundary types and is localized to work for the optionally specified locale.

Once you have obtained an appropriate BreakIterator object, use setText() to specify the text in which to locate boundaries. To locate boundaries in a Java String object, simply specify the string. To locate boundaries in text that uses some other encoding, you must specify a CharacterIterator object for that text so that the BreakIterator object can locate the individual characters of the text. Having set the text to be searched, you can determine the character positions of characters, words, sentences, or line breaks with the first(), last(), next(), previous(), current(), and following() methods, which perform the obvious functions. Note that these methods do not return text itself, but merely the position of the appropriate word, sentence, or line break.

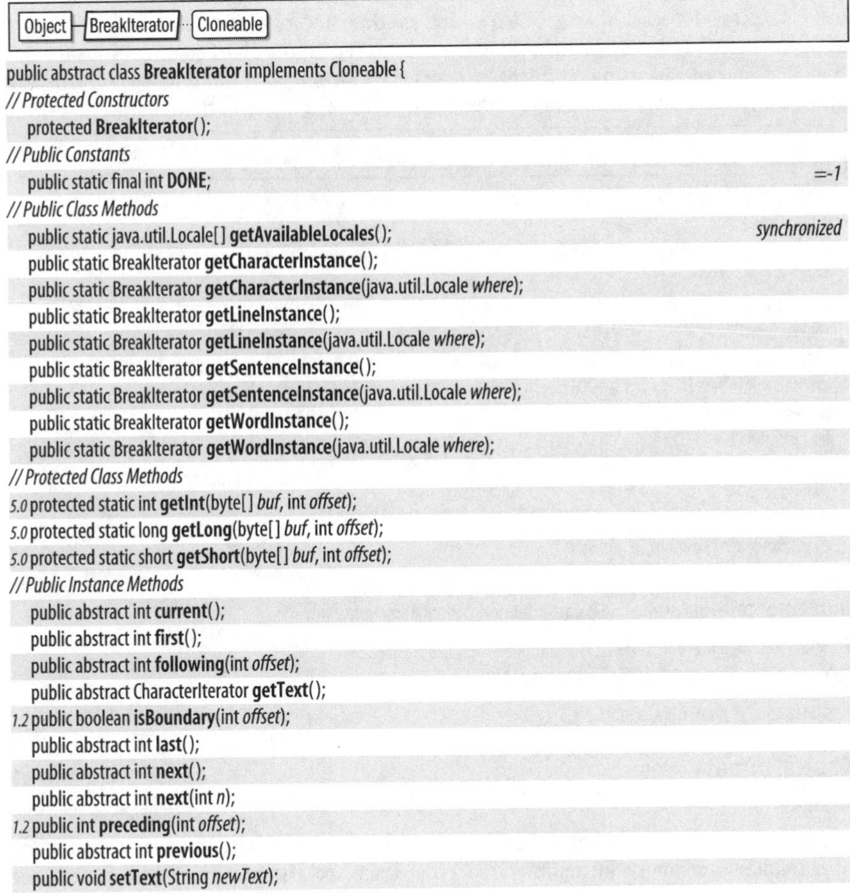


```
public abstract class BreakIterator implements Cloneable {
// Protected Constructors
   protected BreakIterator();
// Public Constants
   public static final int DONE;                                                   =-1
// Public Class Methods
   public static java.util.Locale[] getAvailableLocales();                synchronized
   public static BreakIterator getCharacterInstance();
   public static BreakIterator getCharacterInstance(java.util.Locale where);
   public static BreakIterator getLineInstance();
   public static BreakIterator getLineInstance(java.util.Locale where);
   public static BreakIterator getSentenceInstance();
   public static BreakIterator getSentenceInstance(java.util.Locale where);
   public static BreakIterator getWordInstance();
   public static BreakIterator getWordInstance(java.util.Locale where);
// Protected Class Methods
5.0 protected static int getInt(byte[] buf, int offset);
5.0 protected static long getLong(byte[] buf, int offset);
5.0 protected static short getShort(byte[] buf, int offset);
// Public Instance Methods
   public abstract int current();
   public abstract int first();
   public abstract int following(int offset);
   public abstract CharacterIterator getText();
1.2 public boolean isBoundary(int offset);
   public abstract int last();
   public abstract int next();
   public abstract int next(int n);
1.2 public int preceding(int offset);
   public abstract int previous();
   public void setText(String newText);
```

java.text

```
    public abstract void setText(CharacterIterator newText);
// Public Methods Overriding Object
    public Object clone();
}
```

CharacterIterator

Java 1.1

java.text

cloneable

This interface defines an API for portably iterating through the characters that make up a string of text, regardless of the encoding of that text. Such an API is necessary because the number of bytes per character is different for different encodings, and some encodings even use variable-width characters within the same string of text. In addition to allowing iteration, a class that implements the CharacterIterator interface for non-Unicode text also performs translation of characters from their native encoding to standard Java Unicode characters.

CharacterIterator is similar to java.util.Enumeration, but is somewhat more complex than that interface. The first() and last() methods return the first and last characters in the text, and the next() and prev() methods allow you to loop forward or backwards through the characters of the text. These methods return the DONE constant when they go beyond the first or last character in the text; a test for this constant can be used to terminate a loop. The CharacterIterator interface also allows random access to the characters in a string of text. The getBeginIndex() and getEndIndex() methods return the character positions for the start and end of the string, and setIndex() sets the current position. getIndex() returns the index of the current position, and current() returns the character at that position.

Cloneable ··· CharacterIterator

```
public interface CharacterIterator extends Cloneable {
// Public Constants
    public static final char DONE;                                  =\uFFFF
// Public Instance Methods
    Object clone();
    char current();
    char first();
    int getBeginIndex();
    int getEndIndex();
    int getIndex();
    char last();
    char next();
    char previous();
    char setIndex(int position);
}
```

Implementations AttributedCharacterIterator, StringCharacterIterator

Passed To BreakIterator.setText(), CollationElementIterator.setText(), RuleBasedCollator.getCollationElementIterator()

Returned By BreakIterator.getText()

ChoiceFormat

Java 1.1

java.text

cloneable serializable

This class is a subclass of Format that converts a number to a String in a way reminiscent of a switch statement or an enumerated type. Each ChoiceFormat object has an array of doubles known as its *limits* and an array of strings known as its *formats*. When the format() method is called to format a number x, the ChoiceFormat finds an index i such that:

```
limits[i] <= x < limits[i+1]
```

If x is less than the first element of the array, the first element is used, and if it is greater than the last, the last element is used. Once the index i has been determined, it is used as the index into the array of strings, and the indexed string is returned as the result of the format() method.

A ChoiceFormat object may also be created by encoding its limits and formats into a single string known as its *pattern*. A typical pattern looks like the one below, used to return the singular or plural form of a word based on the numeric value passed to the format() method:

```
ChoiceFormat cf = new ChoiceFormat("0#errors|1#error|2#errors");
```

A ChoiceFormat object created in this way returns the string "errors" when it formats the number 0 or any number greater than or equal to 2. It returns "error" when it formats the number 1. In the syntax shown here, note the pound sign (#) used to separate the limit number from the string that corresponds to that case and the vertical bar (|) used to separate the individual cases. You can use the applyPattern() method to change the pattern used by a ChoiceFormat object; use toPattern() to query the pattern it uses.

Object — Format — NumberFormat — ChoiceFormat
Cloneable, Serializable

```
public class ChoiceFormat extends NumberFormat {
// Public Constructors
   public ChoiceFormat(String newPattern);
   public ChoiceFormat(double[] limits, String[] formats);
// Public Class Methods
   public static final double nextDouble(double d);
   public static double nextDouble(double d, boolean positive);
   public static final double previousDouble(double d);
// Public Instance Methods
   public void applyPattern(String newPattern);
   public Object[] getFormats();
   public double[] getLimits();
   public void setChoices(double[] limits, String[] formats);
   public String toPattern();
// Public Methods Overriding NumberFormat
   public Object clone();
   public boolean equals(Object obj);
   public StringBuffer format(long number, StringBuffer toAppendTo, FieldPosition status);
   public StringBuffer format(double number, StringBuffer toAppendTo, FieldPosition status);
   public int hashCode();
   public Number parse(String text, ParsePosition status);
}
```

CollationElementIterator — Java 1.1

java.text

A CollationElementIterator object is returned by the getCollationElementIterator() method of the RuleBasedCollator object. The purpose of this class is to allow a program to iterate (with the next() method) through the characters of a string, returning ordering values for each of the collation keys in the string. Note that collation keys are not exactly the same as characters. In the traditional Spanish collation order, for example, the two-character sequence "ch" is treated as a single collation key that comes alphabetically between the letters "c" and "d." The value returned by the next() method is the collation order of the next collation key in the string. This numeric value can be directly compared to the value returned by next() for other CollationElementIterator objects. The value returned by next() can also be decomposed into primary, secondary, and tertiary ordering values with the static methods of this class. This class is used by RuleBasedCollator to implement its compare() method and to create CollationKey objects. Few applications ever need to use it directly.

```
public final class CollationElementIterator {
// No Constructor
// Public Constants
   public static final int NULLORDER;                                    =-1
// Public Class Methods
   public static final int primaryOrder(int order);
   public static final short secondaryOrder(int order);
   public static final short tertiaryOrder(int order);
// Public Instance Methods
1.2 public int getMaxExpansion(int order);
1.2 public int getOffset();
   public int next();
1.2 public int previous();
   public void reset();
1.2 public void setOffset(int newOffset);
1.2 public void setText(String source);
1.2 public void setText(CharacterIterator source);
}
```

Returned By RuleBasedCollator.getCollationElementIterator()

CollationKey — Java 1.1

java.text — comparable

CollationKey objects compare strings more quickly than is possible with Collation.compare(). Objects of this class are returned by Collation.getCollationKey(). To compare two CollationKey objects, invoke the compareTo() method of key A, passing the key B as an argument (both CollationKey objects must be created through the same Collation object). The return value of this method is less than zero if the key A is collated before the key B, equal to zero if they are equivalent for the purposes of collation, or greater than zero if the key A is collated after the key B. Use getSourceString() to obtain the string represented by a CollationKey.

Object — CollationKey ··· Comparable

```
public final class CollationKey implements Comparable<CollationKey> {
// No Constructor
// Public Instance Methods
   public int compareTo(CollationKey target);                 Implements:Comparable
   public String getSourceString();
   public byte[] toByteArray();
// Methods Implementing Comparable
   public int compareTo(CollationKey target);
```

```
// Public Methods Overriding Object
    public boolean equals(Object target);
    public int hashCode();
}
```

Returned By Collator.getCollationKey(), RuleBasedCollator.getCollationKey()

Collator **Java 1.1**

java.text *cloneable*

This class compares, orders, and sorts strings in a way appropriate for the default locale or some other specified locale. Because it is an abstract class, it cannot be instantiated directly. Instead, you must use the static getInstance() method to obtain an instance of a Collator subclass that is appropriate for the default or specified locale. You can use getAvailableLocales() to determine whether a Collator object is available for a desired locale.

Once an appropriate Collator object has been obtained, you can use the compare() method to compare strings. The possible return values of this method are –1, 0, and 1, which indicate, respectively, that the first string is collated before the second, that the two are equivalent for collation purposes, and that the first string is collated after the second. The equals() method is a convenient shortcut for testing two strings for collation equivalence.

When sorting an array of strings, each string in the array is typically compared more than once. Using the compare() method in this case is inefficient. A more efficient method for comparing strings multiple times is to use getCollationKey() for each string to create CollationKey objects. These objects can then be compared to each other more quickly than the strings themselves can be compared.

You can customize the way the Collator object performs comparisons by calling setStrength(). If you pass the constant PRIMARY to this method, the comparison looks only at primary differences in the strings; it compares letters but ignores accents and case differences. If you pass the constant SECONDARY, it ignores case differences but does not ignore accents. And if you pass TERTIARY (the default), the Collator object takes both accents and case differences into account in its comparison.

Object — Collator
Cloneable, Comparator

```
public abstract class Collator implements java.util.Comparator<Object>, Cloneable {
// Protected Constructors
    protected Collator();
// Public Constants
    public static final int CANONICAL_DECOMPOSITION;                          =1
    public static final int FULL_DECOMPOSITION;                               =2
    public static final int IDENTICAL;                                        =3
    public static final int NO_DECOMPOSITION;                                 =0
    public static final int PRIMARY;                                          =0
    public static final int SECONDARY;                                        =1
    public static final int TERTIARY;                                         =2
// Public Class Methods
    public static java.util.Locale[] getAvailableLocales();         synchronized
    public static Collator getInstance();                           synchronized
    public static Collator getInstance(java.util.Locale desiredLocale); synchronized
```

```
// Public Instance Methods
    public abstract int compare(String source, String target);
    public boolean equals(Object that);                                Implements:Comparator
    public boolean equals(String source, String target);
    public abstract CollationKey getCollationKey(String source);
    public int getDecomposition();                                     synchronized
    public int getStrength();                                          synchronized
    public void setDecomposition(int decompositionMode);               synchronized
    public void setStrength(int newStrength);                          synchronized
// Methods Implementing Comparator
1.2 public int compare(Object o1, Object o2);
    public boolean equals(Object that);
// Public Methods Overriding Object
    public Object clone();
    public abstract int hashCode();
}
```

Subclasses RuleBasedCollator

DateFormat **Java 1.1**

java.text cloneable serializable

This class formats and parses dates and times in a locale-specific way. As an abstract class, it cannot be instantiated directly, but it provides a number of static methods that return instances of a concrete subclass you can use to format dates in a variety of ways. The getDateInstance() methods return a DateFormat object suitable for formatting dates in either the default locale or a specified locale. A formatting style may also optionally be specified; the constants FULL, LONG, MEDIUM, SHORT, and DEFAULT specify this style. Similarly, the getTimeInstance() methods return a DateFormat object that formats and parses times, and the getDateTimeInstance() methods return a DateFormat object that formats both dates and times. These methods also optionally take a format style constant and a Locale. Finally, getInstance() returns a default DateFormat object that formats both dates and times in the SHORT format.

Once you have created a DateFormat object, you can use the setCalendar() and setTimeZone() methods if you want to format the date using a calendar or time zone other than the default. The various format() methods convert java.util.Date objects to strings using whatever format is encapsulated in the DateFormat object. The parse() and parseObject() methods perform the reverse operation; they parse a string formatted according to the rules of the DateFormat object and convert it into to a Date object. The DEFAULT, FULL, MEDIUM, LONG, and SHORT constants specify how verbose or compact the formatted date or time should be. The remaining constants, which all end with _FIELD, specify various fields of formatted dates and times and are used with the FieldPosition object that is optionally passed to format().

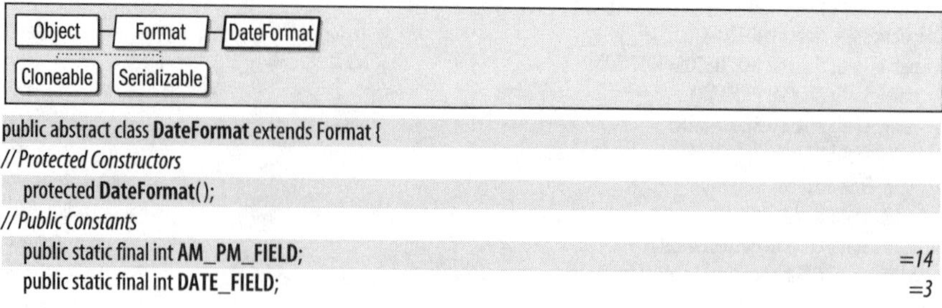


```
public abstract class DateFormat extends Format {
// Protected Constructors
    protected DateFormat();
// Public Constants
    public static final int AM_PM_FIELD;                               =14
    public static final int DATE_FIELD;                                =3
```

```
public static final int DAY_OF_WEEK_FIELD;                                        =9
public static final int DAY_OF_WEEK_IN_MONTH_FIELD;                               =11
public static final int DAY_OF_YEAR_FIELD;                                        =10
public static final int DEFAULT;                                                  =2
public static final int ERA_FIELD;                                                =0
public static final int FULL;                                                     =0
public static final int HOUR0_FIELD;                                              =16
public static final int HOUR1_FIELD;                                              =15
public static final int HOUR_OF_DAY0_FIELD;                                       =5
public static final int HOUR_OF_DAY1_FIELD;                                       =4
public static final int LONG;                                                     =1
public static final int MEDIUM;                                                   =2
public static final int MILLISECOND_FIELD;                                        =8
public static final int MINUTE_FIELD;                                             =6
public static final int MONTH_FIELD;                                              =2
public static final int SECOND_FIELD;                                             =7
public static final int SHORT;                                                    =3
public static final int TIMEZONE_FIELD;                                           =17
public static final int WEEK_OF_MONTH_FIELD;                                      =13
public static final int WEEK_OF_YEAR_FIELD;                                       =12
public static final int YEAR_FIELD;                                               =1
// Nested Types
1.4 public static class Field extends Format.Field;
// Public Class Methods
public static java.util.Locale[ ] getAvailableLocales( );
public static final DateFormat getDateInstance( );
public static final DateFormat getDateInstance(int style);
public static final DateFormat getDateInstance(int style, java.util.Locale aLocale);
public static final DateFormat getDateTimeInstance( );
public static final DateFormat getDateTimeInstance(int dateStyle, int timeStyle);
public static final DateFormat getDateTimeInstance(int dateStyle, int timeStyle, java.util.Locale aLocale);
public static final DateFormat getInstance( );
public static final DateFormat getTimeInstance( );
public static final DateFormat getTimeInstance(int style);
public static final DateFormat getTimeInstance(int style, java.util.Locale aLocale);
// Public Instance Methods
public final String format(java.util.Date date);
public abstract StringBuffer format(java.util.Date date, StringBuffer toAppendTo, FieldPosition fieldPosition);
public java.util.Calendar getCalendar( );
public NumberFormat getNumberFormat( );
public java.util.TimeZone getTimeZone( );
public boolean isLenient( );
public java.util.Date parse(String source) throws ParseException;
public abstract java.util.Date parse(String source, ParsePosition pos);
public void setCalendar(java.util.Calendar newCalendar);
public void setLenient(boolean lenient);
public void setNumberFormat(NumberFormat newNumberFormat);
public void setTimeZone(java.util.TimeZone zone);
// Public Methods Overriding Format
public Object clone( );
public final StringBuffer format(Object obj, StringBuffer toAppendTo, FieldPosition fieldPosition);
public Object parseObject(String source, ParsePosition pos);
// Public Methods Overriding Object
```

```
    public boolean equals(Object obj);
    public int hashCode();
// Protected Instance Fields
    protected java.util.Calendar calendar;
    protected NumberFormat numberFormat;
}
```

Subclasses SimpleDateFormat

DateFormat.Field — Java 1.4

java.text — serializable

This class defines a typesafe enumeration of AttributedCharacterIterator.Attribute objects that may be used by the AttributedCharacterIterator returned by the formatToCharacterIterator() inherited from Format, or that may be used when creating a FieldPosition object with which to obtain the bounds of a specific date field in formatted output. Note that the constants defined by this class correspond closely to the integer constants defined by java.util.Calendar, and that this class defines methods for converting between the two sets of constants.

```
public static class DateFormat.Field extends Format.Field {
// Protected Constructors
    protected Field(String name, int calendarField);
// Public Constants
    public static final DateFormat.Field AM_PM;
    public static final DateFormat.Field DAY_OF_MONTH;
    public static final DateFormat.Field DAY_OF_WEEK;
    public static final DateFormat.Field DAY_OF_WEEK_IN_MONTH;
    public static final DateFormat.Field DAY_OF_YEAR;
    public static final DateFormat.Field ERA;
    public static final DateFormat.Field HOUR0;
    public static final DateFormat.Field HOUR1;
    public static final DateFormat.Field HOUR_OF_DAY0;
    public static final DateFormat.Field HOUR_OF_DAY1;
    public static final DateFormat.Field MILLISECOND;
    public static final DateFormat.Field MINUTE;
    public static final DateFormat.Field MONTH;
    public static final DateFormat.Field SECOND;
    public static final DateFormat.Field TIME_ZONE;
    public static final DateFormat.Field WEEK_OF_MONTH;
    public static final DateFormat.Field WEEK_OF_YEAR;
    public static final DateFormat.Field YEAR;
// Public Class Methods
    public static DateFormat.Field ofCalendarField(int);
// Public Instance Methods
    public int getCalendarField();
// Protected Methods Overriding AttributedCharacterIterator.Attribute
    protected Object readResolve() throws java.io.InvalidObjectException;
}
```

DateFormatSymbols — Java 1.1

java.text — cloneable serializable

This class defines accessor methods for the various pieces of data, such as names of months and days, used by SimpleDateFormat to format and parse dates and times. You do not typically need to use this class unless you are formatting dates for an unsupported locale or in some highly customized way.

Object — DateFormatSymbols
Cloneable, Serializable

```
public class DateFormatSymbols implements Cloneable, Serializable {
// Public Constructors
   public DateFormatSymbols();
   public DateFormatSymbols(java.util.Locale locale);
// Public Instance Methods
   public String[] getAmPmStrings();
   public String[] getEras();
   public String getLocalPatternChars();
   public String[] getMonths();
   public String[] getShortMonths();
   public String[] getShortWeekdays();
   public String[] getWeekdays();
   public String[][] getZoneStrings();
   public void setAmPmStrings(String[] newAmpms);
   public void setEras(String[] newEras);
   public void setLocalPatternChars(String newLocalPatternChars);
   public void setMonths(String[] newMonths);
   public void setShortMonths(String[] newShortMonths);
   public void setShortWeekdays(String[] newShortWeekdays);
   public void setWeekdays(String[] newWeekdays);
   public void setZoneStrings(String[][] newZoneStrings);
// Public Methods Overriding Object
   public Object clone();
   public boolean equals(Object obj);
   public int hashCode();
}
```

Passed To SimpleDateFormat.{setDateFormatSymbols(), SimpleDateFormat()}

Returned By SimpleDateFormat.getDateFormatSymbols()

DecimalFormat — Java 1.1

java.text — cloneable serializable

This is the concrete Format class used by NumberFormat for all locales that use base 10 numbers. Most applications do not need to use this class directly; they can use the static methods of NumberFormat to obtain a default NumberFormat object for a desired locale and then perform minor locale-independent customizations on that object.

Applications that require highly customized number formatting and parsing may create custom DecimalFormat objects by passing a suitable pattern to the DecimalFormat() constructor method. The applyPattern() method can change this pattern. A pattern consists of a string of characters from the table below. For example:

```
"$#,##0.00;($#,##0.00)"
```

Character	Meaning
#	A digit; zeros show as absent.
0	A digit; zeros show as 0.
.	The locale-specific decimal separator.
,	The locale-specific grouping separator (comma).
-	The locale-specific negative prefix.
%	Shows value as a percentage.
;	Separates positive number format (on left) from optiona negative number format (on right).
'	Quotes a reserved character, so it appears literally in the output (apostrophe).
other	Appears literally in output.

A DecimalFormatSymbols object can be specified optionally when creating a DecimalFormat object. If one is not specified, a DecimalFormatSymbols object suitable for the default locale is used.

In Java 5.0, DecimalFormat can return java.math.BigDecimal values from its parse() method. Call setParseBigDecimal() to enable this feature. This is useful when working with very large numbers, very precise numbers, or financial applications that use BigDecimal to avoid rounding errors.

Object — Format — NumberFormat — DecimalFormat
Cloneable, Serializable

```
public class DecimalFormat extends NumberFormat {
// Public Constructors
   public DecimalFormat();
   public DecimalFormat(String pattern);
   public DecimalFormat(String pattern, DecimalFormatSymbols symbols);
// Public Instance Methods
   public void applyLocalizedPattern(String pattern);
   public void applyPattern(String pattern);
   public DecimalFormatSymbols getDecimalFormatSymbols();
   public int getGroupingSize();                                    default:3
   public int getMultiplier();                                      default:1
   public String getNegativePrefix();                               default:"-"
   public String getNegativeSuffix();                               default:""
   public String getPositivePrefix();                               default:""
   public String getPositiveSuffix();                               default:""
   public boolean isDecimalSeparatorAlwaysShown();                  default:false
5.0 public boolean isParseBigDecimal();                             default:false
   public void setDecimalFormatSymbols(DecimalFormatSymbols newSymbols);
   public void setDecimalSeparatorAlwaysShown(boolean newValue);
   public void setGroupingSize(int newValue);
   public void setMultiplier(int newValue);
   public void setNegativePrefix(String newValue);
   public void setNegativeSuffix(String newValue);
5.0 public void setParseBigDecimal(boolean newValue);
   public void setPositivePrefix(String newValue);
   public void setPositiveSuffix(String newValue);
   public String toLocalizedPattern();
   public String toPattern();
```

```
// Public Methods Overriding NumberFormat
    public Object clone();
    public boolean equals(Object obj);
5.0 public final StringBuffer format(Object number, StringBuffer toAppendTo, FieldPosition pos);
    public StringBuffer format(double number, StringBuffer result, FieldPosition fieldPosition);
    public StringBuffer format(long number, StringBuffer result, FieldPosition fieldPosition);
1.4 public java.util.Currency getCurrency();
5.0 public int getMaximumFractionDigits();                                    default:3
5.0 public int getMaximumIntegerDigits();                            default:2147483647
5.0 public int getMinimumFractionDigits();                                    default:0
5.0 public int getMinimumIntegerDigits();                                     default:1
    public int hashCode();
    public Number parse(String text, ParsePosition pos);
1.4 public void setCurrency(java.util.Currency currency);
1.2 public void setMaximumFractionDigits(int newValue);
1.2 public void setMaximumIntegerDigits(int newValue);
1.2 public void setMinimumFractionDigits(int newValue);
1.2 public void setMinimumIntegerDigits(int newValue);
// Public Methods Overriding Format
1.4 public AttributedCharacterIterator formatToCharacterIterator(Object obj);
}
```

DecimalFormatSymbols — Java 1.1

java.text — cloneable serializable

This class defines the various characters and strings, such as the decimal point, percent sign, and thousands separator, used by DecimalFormat when formatting numbers. You do not typically use this class directly unless you are formatting dates for an unsupported locale or in some highly customized way.

Object — DecimalFormatSymbols
Cloneable, Serializable

```
public final class DecimalFormatSymbols implements Cloneable, Serializable {
// Public Constructors
    public DecimalFormatSymbols();
    public DecimalFormatSymbols(java.util.Locale locale);
// Public Instance Methods
1.4 public java.util.Currency getCurrency();
1.2 public String getCurrencySymbol();                                  default:"$"
    public char getDecimalSeparator();                                   default:.
    public char getDigit();                                              default:#
    public char getGroupingSeparator();                                  default:,
    public String getInfinity();                                  default:"\u221E"
1.2 public String getInternationalCurrencySymbol();                   default:"USD"
    public char getMinusSign();                                          default:-
1.2 public char getMonetaryDecimalSeparator();                           default:.
    public String getNaN();                                       default:"\uFFFD"
    public char getPatternSeparator();                                   default:;
    public char getPercent();                                            default:%
    public char getPerMill();                                       default:\u2030
    public char getZeroDigit();                                          default:0
1.4 public void setCurrency(java.util.Currency currency);
```

```
1.2 public void setCurrencySymbol(String currency);
    public void setDecimalSeparator(char decimalSeparator);
    public void setDigit(char digit);
    public void setGroupingSeparator(char groupingSeparator);
    public void setInfinity(String infinity);
1.2 public void setInternationalCurrencySymbol(String currencyCode);
    public void setMinusSign(char minusSign);
1.2 public void setMonetaryDecimalSeparator(char sep);
    public void setNaN(String NaN);
    public void setPatternSeparator(char patternSeparator);
    public void setPercent(char percent);
    public void setPerMill(char perMill);
    public void setZeroDigit(char zeroDigit);
// Public Methods Overriding Object
    public Object clone();
    public boolean equals(Object obj);
    public int hashCode();
}
```

Passed To DecimalFormat.{DecimalFormat(), setDecimalFormatSymbols()}

Returned By DecimalFormat.getDecimalFormatSymbols()

FieldPosition — Java 1.1

java.text

FieldPosition objects are optionally passed to the format() methods of the Format class and its subclasses to return information about the start and end positions of a specific part or "field" of the formatted string. This kind of information is often useful for aligning formatted strings in columns—for example, aligning the decimal points in a column of numbers.

The field of interest is specified when the FieldPosition() constructor is called. The NumberFormat and DateFormat classes define integer various constants (which end with the string _FIELD) that can be used here. In Java 1.4 and later you can also construct a FieldPosition by specifying the Format.Field object that identifies the field. (For constant Field instances, see DateFormat.Field, MessageFormat.Field and NumberFormat.Field.)

After a FieldPosition has been created and passed to a format() method, use getBeginIndex() and getEndIndex() methods of this class to obtain the starting and ending character positions of the desired field of the formatted string.

```
public class FieldPosition {
// Public Constructors
1.4 public FieldPosition(Format.Field attribute);
    public FieldPosition(int field);
1.4 public FieldPosition(Format.Field attribute, int fieldID);
// Public Instance Methods
    public int getBeginIndex();
    public int getEndIndex();
    public int getField();
1.4 public Format.Field getFieldAttribute();
1.2 public void setBeginIndex(int bi);
1.2 public void setEndIndex(int ei);
// Public Methods Overriding Object
1.2 public boolean equals(Object obj);
```

```
1.2 public int hashCode();
1.2 public String toString();
}
```

Passed To ChoiceFormat.format(), DateFormat.format(), DecimalFormat.format(), Format.format(), MessageFormat.format(), NumberFormat.format(), SimpleDateFormat.format()

Format — Java 1.1

java.text — cloneable serializable

This abstract class is the base class for all number, date, and string formatting classes in the java.text package. It defines the key formatting and parsing methods that are implemented by all subclasses. format() converts an object to a string using the formatting rules encapsulated by the Format subclass and optionally appends the resulting string to an existing StringBuffer. parseObject() performs the reverse operation; it parses a formatted string and returns the corresponding object. Status information for these two operations is returned in FieldPosition and ParsePosition objects.

Java 1.4 defined a variant on the format() method. formatToCharacterIterator() performs the same formating operation as format() but returns the result as an AtttributedCharacterIterator which uses attributes to identify the various parts (such the integer part, the decimal separtator, and the fractional part of a formatted number) of the formatted string. The attribute keys are all instances of the Format.Field inner class. Each of the Format subclasses define a Field subclass that defines a set of Field constants, (such as NumberFormat.Field.DECIMAL_SEPARATOR) for use by the character iterator returned by this method. See ChoiceFormat, DateFormat, MessageFormat, and NumberFormat for subclasses that perform specific types of formatting.

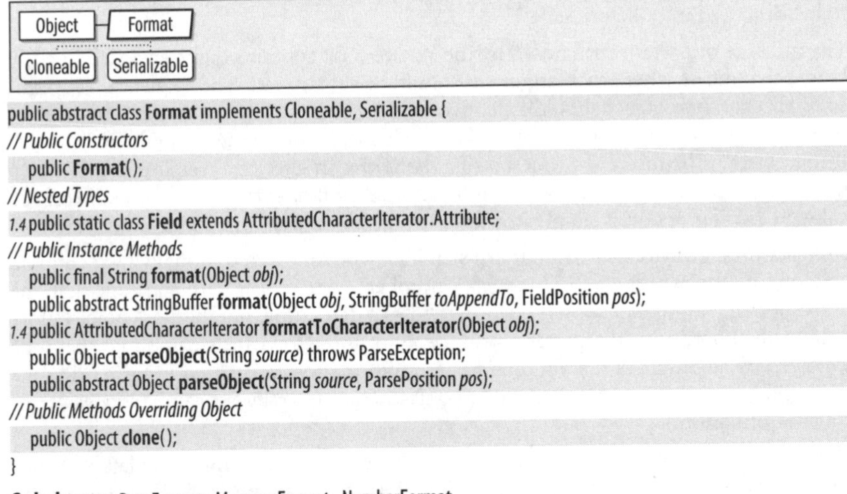


```
public abstract class Format implements Cloneable, Serializable {
// Public Constructors
   public Format();
// Nested Types
1.4 public static class Field extends AttributedCharacterIterator.Attribute;
// Public Instance Methods
   public final String format(Object obj);
   public abstract StringBuffer format(Object obj, StringBuffer toAppendTo, FieldPosition pos);
1.4 public AttributedCharacterIterator formatToCharacterIterator(Object obj);
   public Object parseObject(String source) throws ParseException;
   public abstract Object parseObject(String source, ParsePosition pos);
// Public Methods Overriding Object
   public Object clone();
}
```

Subclasses DateFormat, MessageFormat, NumberFormat

Passed To MessageFormat.{setFormat(), setFormatByArgumentIndex(), setFormats(), setFormatsByArgumentIndex()}

Returned By MessageFormat.{getFormats(), getFormatsByArgumentIndex()}

Format.Field

Java 1.4

java.text

serializable

This inner class extends AttributedCharacterIterator.Attribute and serves as the common superclass for DateFormat.Field, MessageFormat.Field, and NumberFormat.Field. See those specific subclasses for details.

```
public static class Format.Field extends AttributedCharacterIterator.Attribute {
// Protected Constructors
   protected Field(String name);
}
```

Subclasses DateFormat.Field, MessageFormat.Field, NumberFormat.Field

Passed To FieldPosition.FieldPosition()

Returned By FieldPosition.getFieldAttribute()

MessageFormat

Java 1.1

java.text

cloneable serializable

This class formats and substitutes objects into specified positions in a message string (also known as the pattern string). It provides the closest Java equivalent to the printf() function of the C programming language. If a message is to be displayed only a single time, the simplest way to use the MessageFormat class is through the static format() method. This method is passed a message or pattern string and an array of argument objects to be formatted and substituted into the string. If the message is to be displayed several times, it makes more sense to create a MessageFormat object, supplying the pattern string, and then call the format() instance method of this object, supplying the array of objects to be formatted into the message.

The message or pattern string used by the MessageFormat contains digits enclosed in curly braces to indicate where each argument should be substituted. The sequence "{0}" indicates that the first object should be converted to a string (if necessary) and inserted at that point, while the sequence "{3}" indicates that the fourth object should be inserted. If the object to be inserted is not a string, MessageFormat checks to see if it is a Date or a subclass of Number. If so, it uses a default DateFormat or NumberFormat object to convert the value to a string. If not, it simply invokes the object's toString() method to convert it.

A digit within curly braces in a pattern string may be followed optionally by a comma, and one of the words "date", "time", "number", or "choice", to indicate that the corresponding argument should be formatted as a date, time, number, or choice before being substituted into the pattern string. Any of these keywords can additionally be followed by a comma and additional pattern information to be used in formatting the date, time, number, or choice. (See SimpleDateFormat, DecimalFormat, and ChoiceFormat for more information.)

You can pass a Locale to the constructor or call setLocale() to specify a nondefault locale that the MessageFormat should use when obtaining DateFormat and NumberFormat objects to format dates, time, and numbers inserted into the pattern. You can change the Format object used at a particular position in the pattern with the setFormat() method, or change all Format objects with setFormats(). Both of these methods depend on the order of in which arguments are displayed in the pattern string. The pattern string is often subject to localization and the arguments may appear in different orders in different localizations of the pattern. Therefore, in Java 1.4 and later it is usually more convenient to use the "ByArgumentIndex" versions of the setFormat(), setFormats() methods, and getFormats() methods.

You can set a new pattern for the MessageFormat object by calling applyPattern(), and you can obtain a string that represents the current formatting pattern by calling toPattern(). MessageFormat also supports a parse() method that can parse an array of objects out of a specified string, according to the specified pattern.

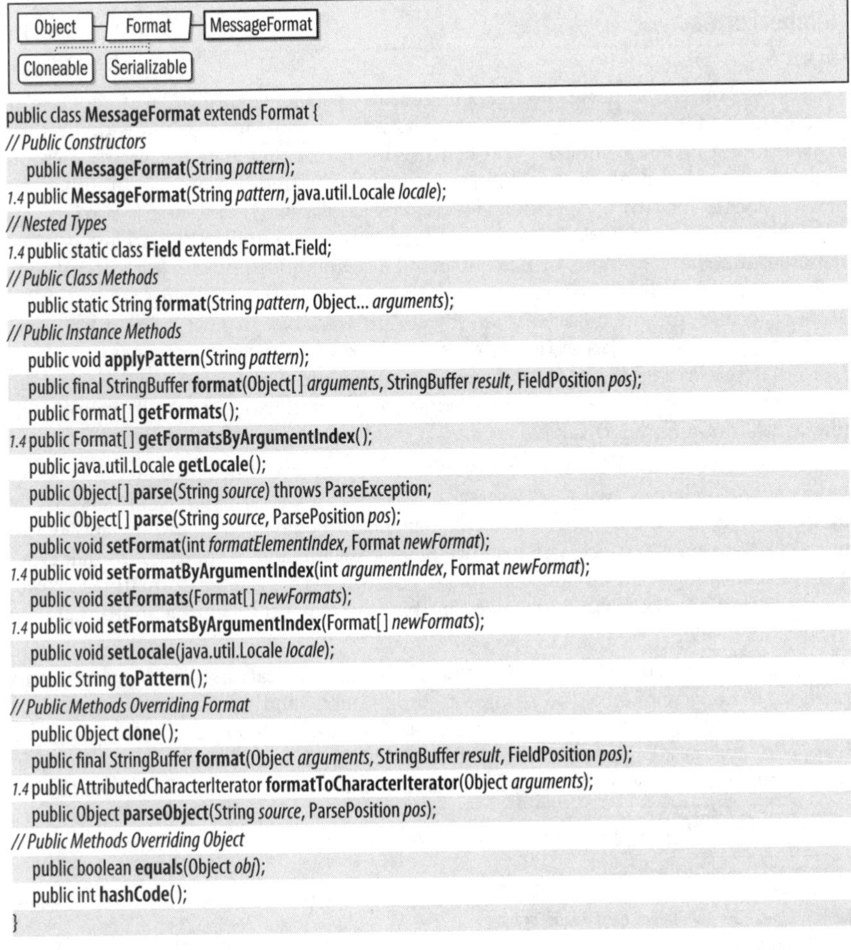


```
public class MessageFormat extends Format {
// Public Constructors
   public MessageFormat(String pattern);
1.4 public MessageFormat(String pattern, java.util.Locale locale);
// Nested Types
1.4 public static class Field extends Format.Field;
// Public Class Methods
   public static String format(String pattern, Object... arguments);
// Public Instance Methods
   public void applyPattern(String pattern);
   public final StringBuffer format(Object[ ] arguments, StringBuffer result, FieldPosition pos);
   public Format[ ] getFormats();
1.4 public Format[ ] getFormatsByArgumentIndex();
   public java.util.Locale getLocale();
   public Object[ ] parse(String source) throws ParseException;
   public Object[ ] parse(String source, ParsePosition pos);
   public void setFormat(int formatElementIndex, Format newFormat);
1.4 public void setFormatByArgumentIndex(int argumentIndex, Format newFormat);
   public void setFormats(Format[ ] newFormats);
1.4 public void setFormatsByArgumentIndex(Format[ ] newFormats);
   public void setLocale(java.util.Locale locale);
   public String toPattern();
// Public Methods Overriding Format
   public Object clone();
   public final StringBuffer format(Object arguments, StringBuffer result, FieldPosition pos);
1.4 public AttributedCharacterIterator formatToCharacterIterator(Object arguments);
   public Object parseObject(String source, ParsePosition pos);
// Public Methods Overriding Object
   public boolean equals(Object obj);
   public int hashCode();
}
```

MessageFormat.Field — Java 1.4

java.text — serializable

This class defines an ARGUMENT AttributedCharacterIterator.Attribute constant that is be used by the AttributedCharacterIterator returned by MessageFormat.formatToCharacterIterator() to identify portions of the formatted message that are derived from the arguments passed to formatToCharacterIterator(). The value associated with this ARGUMENT attribute will be an Integer specifying the argument number.

```
public static class MessageFormat.Field extends Format.Field {
// Protected Constructors
   protected Field(String name);
// Public Constants
```

```
    public static final MessageFormat.Field ARGUMENT;
// Protected Methods Overriding AttributedCharacterIterator.Attribute
    protected Object readResolve() throws java.io.InvalidObjectException;
}
```

NumberFormat **Java 1.1**

java.text **cloneable serializable**

This class formats and parses numbers in a locale-specific way. As an abstract class, it cannot be instantiated directly, but it provides a number of static methods that return instances of a concrete subclass you can use for formatting. The getInstance() method returns a NumberFormat object suitable for normal formatting of numbers in either the default locale or in a specified locale. getIntegerInstance(), getCurrencyInstance(), and getPercentInstance() return NumberFormat objects for formatting numbers that are integers, or represent monetary amounts or percentages. These methods return a NumberFormat suitable for the default locale, or for the specified Locale object. getAvailableLocales() returns an array of locales for which NumberFormat objects are available. In Java 1.4 and later, use setCurrency() to provide a java.util.Currency object for use when formating monetary values. Note that the NumberFormat class is not intended for the display of very large or very small numbers that require exponential notation, and it may not gracefully handle infinite or NaN (not-a-number) values.

Once you have created a suitable NumberFormat object, you can customize its locale-independent behavior with setMaximumFractionDigits(), setGroupingUsed(), and similar set methods. In order to customize the locale-dependent behavior, you can use instanceof to test if the NumberFormat object is an instance of DecimalFormat, and, if so, cast it to that type. The DecimalFormat class provides complete control over number formatting. Note, however, that a NumberFormat customized in this way may no longer be appropriate for the desired locale.

After creating and customizing a NumberFormat object, you can use the various format() methods to convert numbers to strings or string buffers, and you can use the parse() or parseObject() methods to convert strings to numbers. You can also use the formatToCharacterIterator() method inherited from Format (and overridden by DecimalFormat) in place of format(). The constants defined by this class are to be used by the FieldPosition object.

Object — Format — NumberFormat
Cloneable Serializable

```
public abstract class NumberFormat extends Format {
// Public Constructors
    public NumberFormat();
// Public Constants
    public static final int FRACTION_FIELD;                                    =1
    public static final int INTEGER_FIELD;                                     =0
// Nested Types
1.4 public static class Field extends Format.Field;
// Public Class Methods
    public static java.util.Locale[] getAvailableLocales();
    public static final NumberFormat getCurrencyInstance();
    public static NumberFormat getCurrencyInstance(java.util.Locale inLocale);
    public static final NumberFormat getInstance();
    public static NumberFormat getInstance(java.util.Locale inLocale);
1.4 public static final NumberFormat getIntegerInstance();
```

```
1.4 public static NumberFormat getIntegerInstance(java.util.Locale inLocale);
    public static final NumberFormat getNumberInstance();
    public static NumberFormat getNumberInstance(java.util.Locale inLocale);
    public static final NumberFormat getPercentInstance();
    public static NumberFormat getPercentInstance(java.util.Locale inLocale);
// Public Instance Methods
    public final String format(long number);
    public final String format(double number);
    public abstract StringBuffer format(long number, StringBuffer toAppendTo, FieldPosition pos);
    public abstract StringBuffer format(double number, StringBuffer toAppendTo, FieldPosition pos);
1.4 public java.util.Currency getCurrency();
    public int getMaximumFractionDigits();
    public int getMaximumIntegerDigits();
    public int getMinimumFractionDigits();
    public int getMinimumIntegerDigits();
    public boolean isGroupingUsed();
    public boolean isParseIntegerOnly();
    public Number parse(String source) throws ParseException;
    public abstract Number parse(String source, ParsePosition parsePosition);
1.4 public void setCurrency(java.util.Currency currency);
    public void setGroupingUsed(boolean newValue);
    public void setMaximumFractionDigits(int newValue);
    public void setMaximumIntegerDigits(int newValue);
    public void setMinimumFractionDigits(int newValue);
    public void setMinimumIntegerDigits(int newValue);
    public void setParseIntegerOnly(boolean value);
// Public Methods Overriding Format
    public Object clone();
    public StringBuffer format(Object number, StringBuffer toAppendTo, FieldPosition pos);
    public final Object parseObject(String source, ParsePosition pos);
// Public Methods Overriding Object
    public boolean equals(Object obj);
    public int hashCode();
}
```

Subclasses ChoiceFormat, DecimalFormat

Passed To DateFormat.setNumberFormat()

Returned By DateFormat.getNumberFormat()

Type Of DateFormat.numberFormat

NumberFormat.Field Java 1.4

java.text serializable

This class defines a typesafe enumeration of AttributedCharacterIterator.Attribute objects that may be used by the AttributedCharacterIterator returned by formatToCharacterIterator() method inherited from the Format class, or that may be used when creating a FieldPosition object to pass to format() in order to obtain the bounds of a specific number field (such as the decimal point for aligning numbers) in formatted output.

```
public static class NumberFormat.Field extends Format.Field {
// Protected Constructors
    protected Field(String name);
// Public Constants
```

```
    public static final NumberFormat.Field CURRENCY;
    public static final NumberFormat.Field DECIMAL_SEPARATOR;
    public static final NumberFormat.Field EXPONENT;
    public static final NumberFormat.Field EXPONENT_SIGN;
    public static final NumberFormat.Field EXPONENT_SYMBOL;
    public static final NumberFormat.Field FRACTION;
    public static final NumberFormat.Field GROUPING_SEPARATOR;
    public static final NumberFormat.Field INTEGER;
    public static final NumberFormat.Field PERCENT;
    public static final NumberFormat.Field PERMILLE;
    public static final NumberFormat.Field SIGN;
// Protected Methods Overriding AttributedCharacterIterator.Attribute
    protected Object readResolve() throws java.io.InvalidObjectException;
}
```

ParseException — Java 1.1

java.text — serializable checked

Signals that a string has an incorrect format and cannot be parsed. It is typically thrown by the parse() or parseObject() methods of Format and its subclasses, but is also thrown by certain methods in the java.text package that are passed patterns or other rules in string form. The getErrorOffset() method of this class returns the character position at which the parsing error occurred in the offending string.

Object — Throwable — Exception — ParseException
Serializable

```
public class ParseException extends Exception {
// Public Constructors
    public ParseException(String s, int errorOffset);
// Public Instance Methods
    public int getErrorOffset();
}
```

Thrown By DateFormat.parse(), Format.parseObject(), MessageFormat.parse(), NumberFormat.parse(), RuleBasedCollator.RuleBasedCollator()

ParsePosition — Java 1.1

java.text

ParsePosition objects are passed to the parse() and parseObject() methods of Format and its subclasses. The ParsePosition class represents the position in a string at which parsing should begin or at which parsing stopped. Before calling a parse() method, you can specify the starting position of parsing by passing the desired index to the ParsePosition() constructor or by calling the setIndex() of an existing ParsePosition object. When parse() returns, you can determine where parsing ended by calling getIndex(). When parsing multiple objects or values from a string, a single ParsePosition object can be used sequentially.

```
public class ParsePosition {
// Public Constructors
    public ParsePosition(int index);
// Public Instance Methods
1.2 public int getErrorIndex();
```

```
   public int getIndex();
1.2 public void setErrorIndex(int ei);
   public void setIndex(int index);
// Public Methods Overriding Object
1.2 public boolean equals(Object obj);
1.2 public int hashCode();
1.2 public String toString();
}
```

Passed To ChoiceFormat.parse(), DateFormat.{parse(), parseObject()}, DecimalFormat.parse(), Format.parseObject(), MessageFormat.{parse(), parseObject()}, NumberFormat.{parse(), parseObject()}, SimpleDateFormat.parse()

RuleBasedCollator — Java 1.1

java.text — cloneable

This class is a concrete subclass of the abstract Collator class. It performs collations using a table of rules that are specified in textual form. Most applications do not use this class directly; instead they call Collator.getInstance() to obtain a Collator object (typically a RuleBasedCollator object) that implements the default collation order for a specified or default locale. You should need to use this class only if you are collating strings for a locale that is not supported by default or if you need to implement a highly customized collation order.

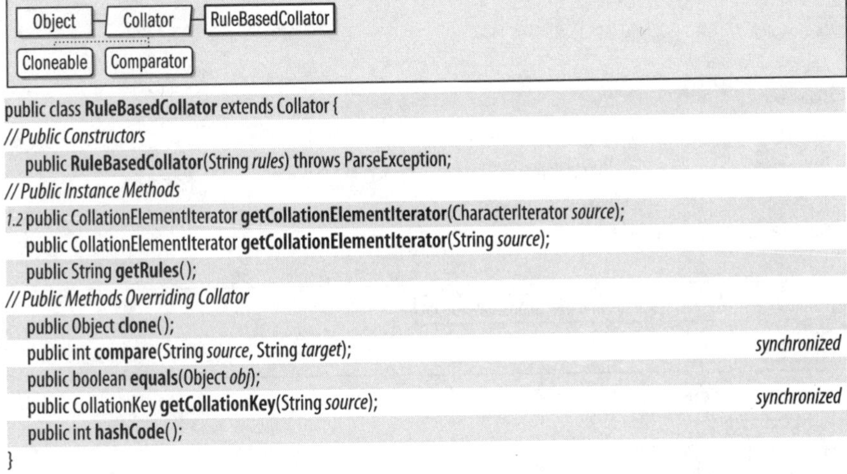


```
public class RuleBasedCollator extends Collator {
// Public Constructors
   public RuleBasedCollator(String rules) throws ParseException;
// Public Instance Methods
1.2 public CollationElementIterator getCollationElementIterator(CharacterIterator source);
   public CollationElementIterator getCollationElementIterator(String source);
   public String getRules();
// Public Methods Overriding Collator
   public Object clone();
   public int compare(String source, String target);                    synchronized
   public boolean equals(Object obj);
   public CollationKey getCollationKey(String source);                   synchronized
   public int hashCode();
}
```

SimpleDateFormat — Java 1.1

java.text — cloneable serializable

This is the concrete Format subclass used by DateFormat to handle the formatting and parsing of dates. Most applications should not use this class directly; instead, they should obtain a localized DateFormat object by calling one of the static methods of DateFormat.

SimpleDateFormat formats dates and times according to a pattern, which specifies the positions of the various fields of the date, and a DateFormatSymbols object, which specifies important auxiliary data, such as the names of months. Applications that require highly customized date or time formatting can create a custom SimpleDateFormat object by specifying the desired pattern. This creates a SimpleDateFormat object that uses the DateFormatSymbols object for the default locale. You may also specify an locale explicitly, to use the DateFormatSymbols object for that locale. You can even provide an explicit DateFormatSymbols object of your own if you need to format dates and times for an unsupported locale.

You can use the applyPattern() method of a SimpleDateFormat to change the formatting pattern used by the object. The syntax of this pattern is described in the following table. Any characters in the format string that do not appear in this table appear literally in the formatted date.

Field	Full form	Short form
Year	yyyy (4 digits)	yy (2 digits)
Month	MMM (name)	MM (2 digits), M (1 or 2 digits)
Day of week	EEEE	EE
Day of month	dd (2 digits)	d (1 or 2 digits)
Hour (1–12)	hh (2 digits)	h (1 or 2 digits)
Hour (0–23)	HH (2 digits)	H (1 or 2 digits)
Hour (0–11)	KK	K
Hour (1–24)	kk	k
Minute	mm	
Second	ss	
Millisecond	SSS	
AM/PM	a	
Time zone	zzzz	zz
Day of week in month	F (e.g., 3rd Thursday)	
Day in year	DDD (3 digits)	D (1, 2, or 3 digits)
Week in year	ww	
Era (e.g., BC/AD)	G	

Object — Format — DateFormat — SimpleDateFormat

Cloneable, Serializable

```
public class SimpleDateFormat extends DateFormat {
// Public Constructors
   public SimpleDateFormat();
   public SimpleDateFormat(String pattern);
   public SimpleDateFormat(String pattern, java.util.Locale locale);
   public SimpleDateFormat(String pattern, DateFormatSymbols formatSymbols);
// Public Instance Methods
   public void applyLocalizedPattern(String pattern);
   public void applyPattern(String pattern);
1.2 public java.util.Date get2DigitYearStart();
   public DateFormatSymbols getDateFormatSymbols();
1.2 public void set2DigitYearStart(java.util.Date startDate);
   public void setDateFormatSymbols(DateFormatSymbols newFormatSymbols);
   public String toLocalizedPattern();
   public String toPattern();
// Public Methods Overriding DateFormat
```

```
    public Object clone();
    public boolean equals(Object obj);
    public StringBuffer format(java.util.Date date, StringBuffer toAppendTo, FieldPosition pos);
    public int hashCode();
    public java.util.Date parse(String text, ParsePosition pos);
// Public Methods Overriding Format
1.4 public AttributedCharacterIterator formatToCharacterIterator(Object obj);
}
```

StringCharacterIterator

Java 1.1

java.text

cloneable

This class is a trivial implementation of the CharacterIterator interface that works for text stored in Java String objects. See CharacterIterator for details.

Object — StringCharacterIterator

Cloneable ··· CharacterIterator

```
public final class StringCharacterIterator implements CharacterIterator {
// Public Constructors
    public StringCharacterIterator(String text);
    public StringCharacterIterator(String text, int pos);
    public StringCharacterIterator(String text, int begin, int end, int pos);
// Public Instance Methods
1.2 public void setText(String text);
// Methods Implementing CharacterIterator
    public Object clone();
    public char current();
    public char first();
    public int getBeginIndex();
    public int getEndIndex();
    public int getIndex();
    public char last();
    public char next();
    public char previous();
    public char setIndex(int p);
// Public Methods Overriding Object
    public boolean equals(Object obj);
    public int hashCode();
}
```

16

java.util and Subpackages

This chapter documents the java.util package, and each of its subpackages. Those packages are:

java.util
: This package defines many important and commonly used utility classes, the most important of which are the various Collection, Set, List, and Map implementations. In Java 5.0 the collection classes and interfaces have been converted into generic types.

java.util.concurrent
: This package includes utilities for concurrent programming, including threadsafe collection classes, threadpool implementations, and synchronizer utilities.

java.util.concurrent.atomic
: This package includes classes that define atomic operations on primitive values or object references.

java.util.concurrent.locks
: This package contains low-level lock and condition utilities.

java.util.jar
: This package defines classes for reading and writing JAR (Java ARchive) files. They are based on the classes of the java.util.zip package.

java.util.logging
: This package defines a powerful and flexible logging API for Java applications.

java.util.prefs
: This package allows applications to set and query persistent values for user-specific preferences or system-wide configuration parameters.

java.util.regex
: This package defines an API for textual pattern matching using regular expressions.

java.util.zip
: This package defines classes for reading and writing ZIP files and for compressing and uncompressing data using the "gzip" format.

Package java.util **Java 1.0**

The java.util package defines a number of useful classes, primarily collections classes that are useful for working with groups of objects. This package should not be considered merely a utility package that is separate from the rest of the language; it is an integral and frequently used part of the Java platform.

The most important classes in java.util are the collections classes. Prior to Java 1.2, these were Vector, a growable list of objects, and Hashtable, a mapping between arbitrary key and value objects. Java 1.2 adds an entire collections framework consisting of the Collection, Map, Set, List, SortedMap, and SortedSet interfaces and the classes that implement them. Other important classes and interfaces of the collections framework are Comparator, Collections, Arrays, Iterator, and ListIterator. Java 1.4 extends the Collections framework with the addition of new Map and Set implementations, and a new RandomAccess marker interface used by List implementations. Java 5.0 adds a Queue collection interface and implementations. It also adds EnumSet and EnumMap which efficiently implement the Set and Map interfaces for use with enumerated types. Most importantly, Java 5.0 modifies all collection interfaces and classes to be generic types, which enable type-safe collections such as List<String>. BitSet is a related class that is not actually part of the Collections framework (and is not even a set). It provides a very compact representation of an arbitrary-size array or list of boolean values or bits. Its API was substantially enhanced in Java 1.4.

The other classes of the package are also quite useful. Date, Calendar, and TimeZone work with dates and times. Currency represents a national currency. Locale represents the language and related text formatting conventions of a country, region, or culture. ResourceBundle and its subclasses represent a bundle of localized resources that are read in by an internationalized program at runtime. Random generates and returns pseudorandom numbers in a variety of forms. StringTokenizer is a simple parser that breaks a string into tokens. In Java 1.3 and later, Timer and TimerTask provide a powerful API for scheduling code to be run by a background thread, once or repetitively, at a specified time in the future. In Java 5.0, the Formatter class enables poweful formatted text output in the style of the C programming language's printf() function. The Java 5.0 Scanner class is a text tokenizer or scanner that can also parse numbers and match tokens based on regular expressions.

Interfaces

```
public interface Collection<E> extends Iterable<E>;
public interface Comparator<T>;
public interface Enumeration<E>;
public interface EventListener;
public interface Formattable;
public interface Iterator<E>;
public interface List<E> extends Collection<E>;
```

public interface **ListIterator**<E> extends Iterator<E>;
public interface **Map**<K, V>;
public interface **Map.Entry**<K, V>;
public interface **Observer**;
public interface **Queue**<E> extends Collection<E>;
public interface **RandomAccess**;
public interface **Set**<E> extends Collection<E>;
public interface **SortedMap**<K, V> extends Map<K, V>;
public interface **SortedSet**<E> extends Set<E>;

Enumerated Types

public enum **Formatter.BigDecimalLayoutForm**;

Collections

public abstract class **AbstractCollection**<E> implements Collection<E>;
    public abstract class **AbstractList**<E> extends AbstractCollection<E> implements List<E>;
        public abstract class **AbstractSequentialList**<E> extends AbstractList<E>;
            public class **LinkedList**<E> extends AbstractSequentialList<E>
                implements List<E>, Queue<E>, Cloneable, Serializable;
        public class **ArrayList**<E> extends AbstractList<E> implements List<E>, RandomAccess, Cloneable, Serializable;
        public class **Vector**<E> extends AbstractList<E> implements List<E>, RandomAccess, Cloneable, Serializable;
            public class **Stack**<E> extends Vector<E>;
    public abstract class **AbstractQueue**<E> extends AbstractCollection<E> implements Queue<E>;
        public class **PriorityQueue**<E> extends AbstractQueue<E> implements Serializable;
    public abstract class **AbstractSet**<E> extends AbstractCollection<E> implements Set<E>;
        public abstract class **EnumSet**<E extends Enum<E>> extends AbstractSet<E> implements Cloneable, Serializable;
        public class **HashSet**<E> extends AbstractSet<E> implements Set<E>, Cloneable, Serializable;
            public class **LinkedHashSet**<E> extends HashSet<E> implements Set<E>, Cloneable, Serializable;
        public class **TreeSet**<E> extends AbstractSet<E> implements SortedSet<E>, Cloneable, Serializable;
public abstract class **AbstractMap**<K, V> implements Map<K, V>;
    public class **EnumMap**<K extends Enum<K>, V> extends AbstractMap<K, V> implements Serializable, Cloneable;
    public class **HashMap**<K, V> extends AbstractMap<K, V> implements Map<K, V>, Cloneable, Serializable;
        public class **LinkedHashMap**<K, V> extends HashMap<K, V> implements Map<K, V>;
    public class **IdentityHashMap**<K, V> extends AbstractMap<K, V> implements Map<K, V>, Serializable, Cloneable;
    public class **TreeMap**<K, V> extends AbstractMap<K, V> implements SortedMap<K, V>, Cloneable, Serializable;
    public class **WeakHashMap**<K, V> extends AbstractMap<K, V> implements Map<K, V>;
public class **Hashtable**<K, V> extends Dictionary<K, V> implements Map<K, V>, Cloneable, Serializable;
    public class **Properties** extends Hashtable<Object, Object>;

Events

public class **EventObject** implements Serializable;

Other Classes

public class **Arrays**;
public class **BitSet** implements Cloneable, Serializable;
public abstract class **Calendar** implements Serializable, Cloneable, Comparable<Calendar>;
    public class **GregorianCalendar** extends Calendar;
public class **Collections**;
public final class **Currency** implements Serializable;
public class **Date** implements Serializable, Cloneable, Comparable<Date>;
public abstract class **Dictionary**<K, V>;
public abstract class **EventListenerProxy** implements EventListener;

public class **FormattableFlags**;
public final class **Formatter** implements java.io.Closeable, java.io.Flushable;
public final class **Locale** implements Cloneable, Serializable;
public class **Observable**;
public final class **PropertyPermission** extends java.security.BasicPermission;
public class **Random** implements Serializable;
public abstract class **ResourceBundle**;
    public abstract class **ListResourceBundle** extends ResourceBundle;
    public class **PropertyResourceBundle** extends ResourceBundle;
public final class **Scanner** implements Iterator<String>;
public class **StringTokenizer** implements Enumeration<Object>;
public class **Timer**;
public abstract class **TimerTask** implements Runnable;
public abstract class **TimeZone** implements Cloneable, Serializable;
    public class **SimpleTimeZone** extends TimeZone;
public final class **UUID** implements Serializable, Comparable<UUID>;

Exceptions

public class **ConcurrentModificationException** extends RuntimeException;
public class **EmptyStackException** extends RuntimeException;
public class **FormatterClosedException** extends IllegalStateException;
public class **IllegalFormatException** extends IllegalArgumentException;
    public class **DuplicateFormatFlagsException** extends IllegalFormatException;
    public class **FormatFlagsConversionMismatchException** extends IllegalFormatException;
    public class **IllegalFormatCodePointException** extends IllegalFormatException;
    public class **IllegalFormatConversionException** extends IllegalFormatException;
    public class **IllegalFormatFlagsException** extends IllegalFormatException;
    public class **IllegalFormatPrecisionException** extends IllegalFormatException;
    public class **IllegalFormatWidthException** extends IllegalFormatException;
    public class **MissingFormatArgumentException** extends IllegalFormatException;
    public class **MissingFormatWidthException** extends IllegalFormatException;
    public class **UnknownFormatConversionException** extends IllegalFormatException;
    public class **UnknownFormatFlagsException** extends IllegalFormatException;
public class **InvalidPropertiesFormatException** extends java.io.IOException;
public class **MissingResourceException** extends RuntimeException;
public class **NoSuchElementException** extends RuntimeException;
    public class **InputMismatchException** extends NoSuchElementException;
public class **TooManyListenersException** extends Exception;

AbstractCollection<E> — Java 1.2

java.util — collection

This abstract class is a partial implementation of Collection that makes it easy to define custom Collection implementations. To create an unmodifiable collection, simply override size() and iterator(). The Iterator object returned by iterator() has to support only the hasNext() and next() methods. To define a modifiable collection, you must additionally override the add() method of AbstractCollection and make sure the Iterator returned by iterator() supports the remove() method. Some subclasses may choose to override other methods to tune performance. In addition, it is conventional that all subclasses provide two constructors: one that takes no arguments and one that accepts a Collection argument that specifies the initial contents of the collection.

Note that if you subclass **AbstractCollection** directly, you are implementing a *bag*—an unordered collection that allows duplicate elements. If your **add()** method rejects duplicate elements, you should subclass **AbstractSet** instead. See also **AbstractList**.

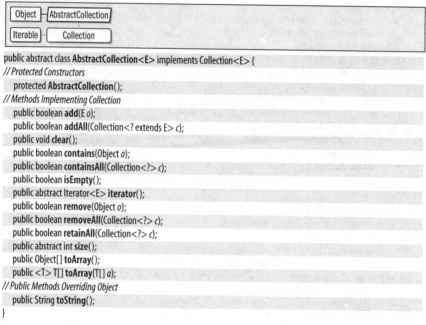

Object — AbstractCollection
Iterable ··· Collection

```
public abstract class AbstractCollection<E> implements Collection<E> {
// Protected Constructors
   protected AbstractCollection();
// Methods Implementing Collection
   public boolean add(E o);
   public boolean addAll(Collection<? extends E> c);
   public void clear();
   public boolean contains(Object o);
   public boolean containsAll(Collection<?> c);
   public boolean isEmpty();
   public abstract Iterator<E> iterator();
   public boolean remove(Object o);
   public boolean removeAll(Collection<?> c);
   public boolean retainAll(Collection<?> c);
   public abstract int size();
   public Object[] toArray();
   public <T> T[] toArray(T[] a);
// Public Methods Overriding Object
   public String toString();
}
```

Subclasses AbstractList, AbstractQueue, AbstractSet

AbstractList<E>

Java 1.2

java.util

collection

This abstract class is a partial implementation of the **List** interface that makes it easy to define custom **List** implementations based on random-access list elements (such as objects stored in an array). If you want to base a **List** implementation on a sequential-access data model (such as a linked list), subclass **AbstractSequentialList** instead.

To create an unmodifiable **List**, simply subclass **AbstractList** and override the (inherited) **size()** and **get()** methods. To create a modifiable list, you must also override **set()** and, optionally, **add()** and **remove()**. These three methods are optional, so unless you override them, they simply throw an **UnsupportedOperationException**. All other methods of the **List** interface are implemented in terms of **size()**, **get()**, **set()**, **add()**, and **remove()**. In some cases, you may want to override these other methods to improve performance. By convention, all **List** implementations should define two constructors: one that accepts no arguments and another that accepts a **Collection** of initial elements for the list.

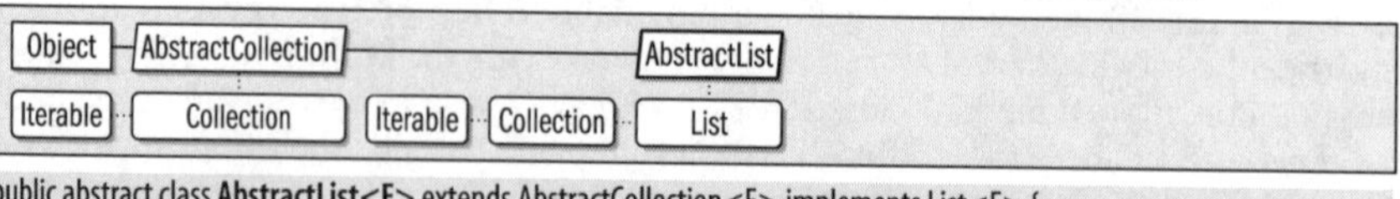


```
public abstract class AbstractList<E> extends AbstractCollection<E> implements List<E> {
// Protected Constructors
   protected AbstractList();
// Methods Implementing List
```

```
  public boolean add(E o);
  public void add(int index, E element);
  public boolean addAll(int index, Collection<? extends E> c);
  public void clear();
  public boolean equals(Object o);
  public abstract E get(int index);
  public int hashCode();
  public int indexOf(Object o);
  public Iterator<E> iterator();
  public int lastIndexOf(Object o);
  public ListIterator<E> listIterator();
  public ListIterator<E> listIterator(int index);
  public E remove(int index);
  public E set(int index, E element);
  public List<E> subList(int fromIndex, int toIndex);
// Protected Instance Methods
  protected void removeRange(int fromIndex, int toIndex);
// Protected Instance Fields
  protected transient int modCount;
}
```

Subclasses AbstractSequentialList, ArrayList, Vector

AbstractMap<K,V> — Java 1.2

java.util — collection

This abstract class is a partial implementation of the Map interface that makes it easy to define simple custom Map implementations. To define an unmodifiable map, subclass AbstractMap and override the entrySet() method so that it returns a set of Map.Entry objects. (Note that you must also implement Map.Entry, of course.) The returned set should not support add() or remove(), and its iterator should not support remove(). In order to define a modifiable Map, you must additionally override the put() method and provide support for the remove() method of the iterator returned by entrySet().iterator(). In addition, it is conventional that all Map implementations define two constructors: one that accepts no arguments and another that accepts a Map of initial mappings.

AbstractMap defines all Map methods in terms of its entrySet() and put() methods and the remove() method of the entry set iterator. Note, however, that the implementation is based on a linear search of the Set returned by entrySet() and is not efficient when the Map contains more than a handful of entries. Some subclasses may want to override additional AbstractMap methods to improve performance. HashMap and TreeMap use different algorithms are are substantially more efficient.

Object — AbstractMap ··· Map

```
public abstract class AbstractMap<K,V> implements Map<K,V> {
// Protected Constructors
  protected AbstractMap();
// Methods Implementing Map
  public void clear();
  public boolean containsKey(Object key);
  public boolean containsValue(Object value);
  public abstract Set<Map.Entry<K,V>> entrySet();
  public boolean equals(Object o);
  public V get(Object key);
```

```
    public int hashCode();
    public boolean isEmpty();
    public Set<K> keySet();
    public V put(K key, V value);
    public void putAll(Map<? extends K,? extends V> t);
    public V remove(Object key);
    public int size();
    public Collection<V> values();
// Public Methods Overriding Object
    public String toString();
// Protected Methods Overriding Object
1.4 protected Object clone() throws CloneNotSupportedException;
}
```

Subclasses EnumMap, HashMap, IdentityHashMap, TreeMap, WeakHashMap, java.util.concurrent.ConcurrentHashMap

AbstractQueue<E> — Java 5.0

java.util — collection

This abstract class provides a framework for simple Queue implementations. A concrete subclass must implement offer(), peek(), and poll() and must also implement the inherited size() and iterator() methods of the Collection interface. The Iterator returned by iterator() must support the remove() operation.

Object — AbstractCollection — AbstractQueue
Iterable ··· Collection; Iterable ··· Collection ··· Queue

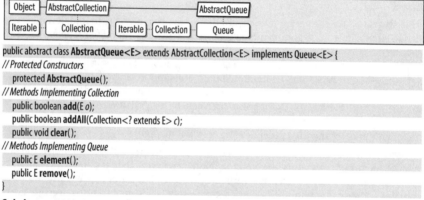

```
public abstract class AbstractQueue<E> extends AbstractCollection<E> implements Queue<E> {
// Protected Constructors
    protected AbstractQueue();
// Methods Implementing Collection
    public boolean add(E o);
    public boolean addAll(Collection<? extends E> c);
    public void clear();
// Methods Implementing Queue
    public E element();
    public E remove();
}
```

Subclasses PriorityQueue, java.util.concurrent.ArrayBlockingQueue, java.util.concurrent.ConcurrentLinkedQueue, java.util.concurrent.DelayQueue, java.util.concurrent.LinkedBlockingQueue, java.util.concurrent.PriorityBlockingQueue, java.util.concurrent.SynchronousQueue

AbstractSequentialList<E> — Java 1.2

java.util — collection

This abstract class is a partial implementation of the List interface that makes it easy to define List implementations based on a sequential-access data model, as is the case with the LinkedList subclass. To implement a List based on an array or other random-access model, subclass AbstractList instead.

To implement an unmodifiable list, subclass this class and override the size() and listIterator() methods. listIterator() must return a ListIterator that defines the hasNext(), hasPrevious(), next(), previous(), and index() methods. If you want to allow the list to be modified, the ListIterator should also support the set() method and, optionally, the add() and remove() methods. AbstractSequentialList implements all other List methods in terms of these methods. Some subclasses may want to override additional methods to improve performance. In addition, it is conventional that all List implementations define two constructors: one that accepts no arguments and another that accepts a Collection of initial elements for the list.

```
public abstract class AbstractSequentialList<E> extends AbstractList<E> {
// Protected Constructors
    protected AbstractSequentialList();
// Public Methods Overriding AbstractList
    public void add(int index, E element);
    public boolean addAll(int index, Collection<? extends E> c);
    public E get(int index);
    public Iterator<E> iterator();
    public abstract ListIterator<E> listIterator(int index);
    public E remove(int index);
    public E set(int index, E element);
}
```

Subclasses LinkedList

AbstractSet<E> Java 1.2

java.util collection

This abstract class is a partial implementation of the Set interface that makes it easy to create custom Set implementations. Since Set defines the same methods as Collection, you can subclass AbstractSet exactly as you would subclass AbstractCollection. See AbstractCollection for details. Note, however, that when subclassing AbstractSet, you should be sure that your add() method and your constructors do not allow duplicate elements to be added to the set. See also AbstractList.

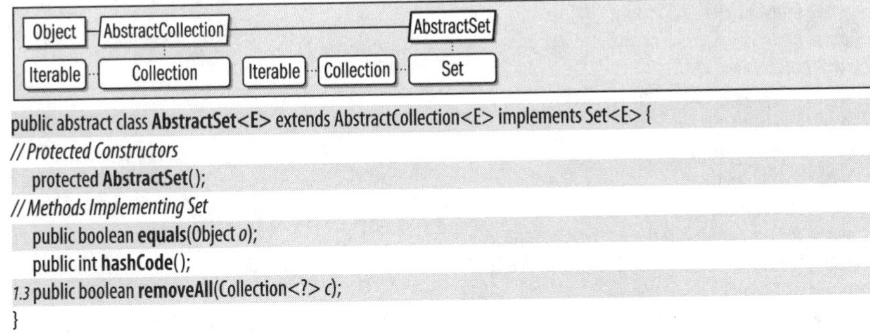


```
public abstract class AbstractSet<E> extends AbstractCollection<E> implements Set<E> {
// Protected Constructors
    protected AbstractSet();
// Methods Implementing Set
    public boolean equals(Object o);
    public int hashCode();
1.3 public boolean removeAll(Collection<?> c);
}
```

Subclasses EnumSet, HashSet, TreeSet, java.util.concurrent.CopyOnWriteArraySet

ArrayList<E> Java 1.2

java.util cloneable serializable collection

This class is a List implementation based on an array (that is recreated as necessary as the list grows or shrinks). ArrayList implements all optional List and Collection methods and allows list elements of any type (including null). Because ArrayList is based on an array, the get() and set() methods are very efficient. (This is not the case for the LinkedList implementation, for example.) ArrayList is a general-purpose implementation of List and is quite commonly used. ArrayList is very much like the Vector class, except that its methods are not synchronized. If you are using an ArrayList in a multithreaded environment, you should explicitly synchronize any modifications to the list, or wrap the list with Collections.synchronizedList(). See List and Collection for details on the methods of ArrayList. See also LinkedList.

An ArrayList has a *capacity*, which is the number of elements in the internal array that contains the elements of the list. When the number of elements exceeds the capacity, a new array, with a larger capacity, must be created. In addition to the List and Collection methods, ArrayList defines a couple of methods that help you manage this capacity. If you know in advance how many elements an ArrayList will contain, you can call ensureCapacity(), which can increase efficiency by avoiding incremental reallocation of the internal array. You can also pass an initial capacity value to the ArrayList() constructor. Finally, if an ArrayList has reached its final size and will not change in the future, you can call trimToSize() to reallocate the internal array with a capacity that matches the list size exactly. When the ArrayList will have a long lifetime, this can be a useful technique to reduce memory usage.

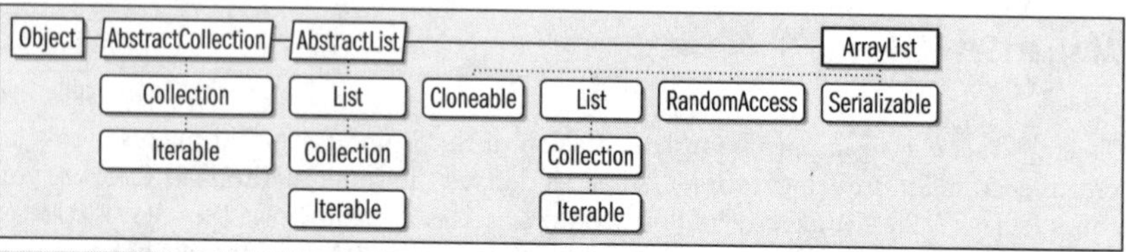


```
public class ArrayList<E> extends AbstractList<E> implements List<E>, RandomAccess, Cloneable, Serializable {
// Public Constructors
   public ArrayList();
   public ArrayList(int initialCapacity);
   public ArrayList(Collection<? extends E> c);
// Public Instance Methods
   public void ensureCapacity(int minCapacity);
   public void trimToSize();
// Methods Implementing List
   public boolean add(E o);
   public void add(int index, E element);
   public boolean addAll(Collection<? extends E> c);
   public boolean addAll(int index, Collection<? extends E> c);
   public void clear();
   public boolean contains(Object elem);
   public E get(int index);
   public int indexOf(Object elem);
   public boolean isEmpty();                                              default:true
   public int lastIndexOf(Object elem);
5.0 public boolean remove(Object o);
   public E remove(int index);
```

```
    public E set(int index, E element);
    public int size();
    public Object[] toArray();
    public <T> T[] toArray(T[] a);
// Protected Methods Overriding AbstractList
    protected void removeRange(int fromIndex, int toIndex);
// Public Methods Overriding Object
    public Object clone();
}
```

Returned By Collections.list()

Arrays — Java 1.2

java.util

This class defines static methods for sorting, searching, and performing other useful operations on arrays. It also defines the asList() method, which returns a List wrapper around a specified array of objects. Any changes made to the List are also made to the underlying array. This is a powerful method that allows any array of objects to be manipulated in any of the ways a List can be manipulated. It provides a link between arrays and the Java collections framework.

The various sort() methods sort an array (or a specified portion of an array) in place. Variants of the method are defined for arrays of each primitive type and for arrays of Object. For arrays of primitive types, the sorting is done according to the natural ordering of the type. For arrays of objects, the sorting is done according to the specified Comparator, or, if the array contains only java.lang.Comparable objects, according to the ordering defined by that interface. When sorting an array of objects, a stable sorting algorithm is used so that the relative ordering of equal objects is not disturbed. (This allows repeated sorts to order objects by key and subkey, for example.)

The binarySearch() methods perform an efficient search (in logarithmic time) of a sorted array for a specified value. If a match is found in the array, binarySearch() returns the index of the match. If no match is found, the method returns a negative number. For a negative return value r, the index -(r+1) specifies the array index at which the specified value can be inserted to maintain the sorted order of the array. When the array to be searched is an array of objects, the elements of the array must all implement java.lang.Comparable, or you must provide a Comparator object to compare them.

The equals() methods test whether two arrays are equal. Two arrays of primitive type are equal if they contain the same number of elements and if corresponding pairs of elements are equal according to the == operator. Two arrays of objects are equal if they contain the same number of elements and if corresponding pairs of elements are equal according to the equals() method defined by those objects. The fill() methods fill an array or a specified range of an array with the specified value.

Java 5.0 adds hashCode() methods that compute a hashcode for the contents of the array. These methods are compatible with the equals() methods: equal() arrays will always have the same hashCode(). Java 5.0 also adds deepEquals() and deepHashCode() methods that handle multi-dimensional arrays. Finally, the Java 5.0 toString() and deepToString() methods convert arrays to strings. The returned strings are a comma-separated list of elements enclosed in square brackets.

```
public class Arrays {
// No Constructor
// Public Class Methods
```

```
   public static <T> List<T> asList(T ... a);
   public static int binarySearch(char[ ] a, char key);
   public static int binarySearch(short[ ] a, short key);
   public static int binarySearch(long[ ] a, long key);
   public static int binarySearch(int[ ] a, int key);
   public static int binarySearch(float[ ] a, float key);
   public static int binarySearch(Object[ ] a, Object key);
   public static int binarySearch(byte[ ] a, byte key);
   public static int binarySearch(double[ ] a, double key);
   public static <T> int binarySearch(T[ ] a, T key, Comparator<? super T> c);
5.0 public static boolean deepEquals(Object[ ] a1, Object[ ] a2);
5.0 public static int deepHashCode(Object[ ] a);
5.0 public static String deepToString(Object[ ] a);
   public static boolean equals(boolean[ ] a, boolean[ ] a2);
   public static boolean equals(long[ ] a, long[ ] a2);
   public static boolean equals(float[ ] a, float[ ] a2);
   public static boolean equals(double[ ] a, double[ ] a2);
   public static boolean equals(char[ ] a, char[ ] a2);
   public static boolean equals(byte[ ] a, byte[ ] a2);
   public static boolean equals(int[ ] a, int[ ] a2);
   public static boolean equals(short[ ] a, short[ ] a2);
   public static boolean equals(Object[ ] a, Object[ ] a2);
   public static void fill(char[ ] a, char val);
   public static void fill(short[ ] a, short val);
   public static void fill(byte[ ] a, byte val);
   public static void fill(int[ ] a, int val);
   public static void fill(double[ ] a, double val);
   public static void fill(boolean[ ] a, boolean val);
   public static void fill(Object[ ] a, Object val);
   public static void fill(float[ ] a, float val);
   public static void fill(long[ ] a, long val);
   public static void fill(int[ ] a, int fromIndex, int toIndex, int val);
   public static void fill(double[ ] a, int fromIndex, int toIndex, double val);
   public static void fill(short[ ] a, int fromIndex, int toIndex, short val);
   public static void fill(char[ ] a, int fromIndex, int toIndex, char val);
   public static void fill(float[ ] a, int fromIndex, int toIndex, float val);
   public static void fill(byte[ ] a, int fromIndex, int toIndex, byte val);
   public static void fill(boolean[ ] a, int fromIndex, int toIndex, boolean val);
   public static void fill(Object[ ] a, int fromIndex, int toIndex, Object val);
   public static void fill(long[ ] a, int fromIndex, int toIndex, long val);
5.0 public static int hashCode(short[ ] a);
5.0 public static int hashCode(char[ ] a);
5.0 public static int hashCode(long[ ] a);
5.0 public static int hashCode(int[ ] a);
5.0 public static int hashCode(byte[ ] a);
5.0 public static int hashCode(double[ ] a);
5.0 public static int hashCode(Object[ ] a);
5.0 public static int hashCode(boolean[ ] a);
5.0 public static int hashCode(float[ ] a);
   public static void sort(Object[ ] a);
   public static void sort(short[ ] a);
   public static void sort(float[ ] a);
   public static void sort(double[ ] a);
   public static void sort(long[ ] a);
```

```
    public static void sort(byte[] a);
    public static void sort(char[] a);
    public static void sort(int[] a);
    public static <T> void sort(T[] a, Comparator<? super T> c);
    public static void sort(short[] a, int fromIndex, int toIndex);
    public static void sort(int[] a, int fromIndex, int toIndex);
    public static void sort(char[] a, int fromIndex, int toIndex);
    public static void sort(long[] a, int fromIndex, int toIndex);
    public static void sort(float[] a, int fromIndex, int toIndex);
    public static void sort(double[] a, int fromIndex, int toIndex);
    public static void sort(byte[] a, int fromIndex, int toIndex);
    public static void sort(Object[] a, int fromIndex, int toIndex);
    public static <T> void sort(T[] a, int fromIndex, int toIndex, Comparator<? super T> c);
5.0 public static String toString(float[] a);
5.0 public static String toString(boolean[] a);
5.0 public static String toString(Object[] a);
5.0 public static String toString(double[] a);
5.0 public static String toString(int[] a);
5.0 public static String toString(long[] a);
5.0 public static String toString(short[] a);
5.0 public static String toString(byte[] a);
5.0 public static String toString(char[] a);
}
```

BitSet — Java 1.0

java.util — cloneable serializable

This class implements an array or list of **boolean** values storing them using a very compact representation that requires only about one bit per value stored. It implements methods for setting, querying, and flipping the values stored at any given position within the list, for counting the number of **true** values stored in the list, and for finding the next **true** or **false** value in the list. It also defines a number of methods that perform bitwise boolean operations on two **BitSet** objects. Despite its name, **BitSet** does not implement the **Set** interface, and does not even have the behavior associated with a set; it is a list or vector for **boolean** values, but is not related to the **List** interface or **Vector** class. This class was introduced in Java 1.0, but was substantially enhanced in Java 1.4; note that many of the methods described below are only available in Java 1.4 and later.

Create a **BitSet** with the **BitSet()** constructor. You may optionally specify a size (the number of bits) for the **BitSet**, but this merely provides an optimization since a **BitSet** will grow as needed to accomodate any number of **boolean** values. **BitSet** does not define a precise notion of the size of a "set." The **size()** method returns the number of boolean values that can be stored before more internal storage needs to be allocated. The **length()** method returns one more than the highest index of a set bit (i.e., a **true** value). This means that a **BitSet** that contains all **false** values will have a **length()** of zero. If your code needs to remember the index of the highest value stored in a **BitSet**, regardless of whether that value was **true** or **false**, then you should maintain that length information separately from the **BitSet**.

Set values in a **BitSet** with the **set()** method. There are four versions of this method. Two set the value at a specific index, and two set values for a range of indexes. Two of the **set()** methods do not take a value argument to set: they "set" the specified bit or range of bites, which means they store the value **true**. The other two methods take a **boolean** argument, allowing you to set the specified value or range of values to **true** (a set bit) or false (a clear bit). There are also two clear() methods that "clear" (or set to false) the value at the specified index or range of indexes. The flip() methods flip, or toggle (change true to false and false to true), the value or values at the specified index or range. The set(), clear(), and flip() methods, as well as all other BitSet methods that operate on a range of values specify the range with two index values. They define the range as the values starting from, and including, the value stored at the first specified index up to, *but not including*, the value stored at the second specified index. (A number of methods of String and related classes follow the same convention for specifying a range of characters.)

To test the value stored at a specified location, use get(), which returns true if the specified bit is set, or false if it is not set. There is also a get() method that specifies a range of bits, and returns their state in the form of a BitSet: this get() method is analogous to the substring() method of a String. Because a BitSet does not define a maximum index, it is legal to pass any non-negative value to get(). If the index you specify is greater than or equal to the value returned by length(), then the returned value will always be false.

cardinality() returns the number of true values (or of set bits) stored in a BitSet. isEmpty() returns true if a BitSet has no true values stored in it (in this case, both length() and cardinality() return 0). nextSetBit() returns the first index at or after the specified index at which a true value is stored (or at which the bit is set). You can use this method in a loop to iterate through the indexes of true values. nextClearBit() is similar, but searches the BitSet for false values (clear bits) intead. The intersects() method returns true if the target BitSet and the argument BitSet intersect: that is if there is at least one index at which both BitSet objects have a true value.

BitSet defines several methods that perform bitwise Boolean operations. These methods combine the BitSet on which they are invoked (called the "target" BitSet below) with the BitSet passed as an argument, and store the result in the target BitSet. If you want to perform a Boolean operation without altering the original BitSet, you should first make a copy of the original with the clone() method and invoke the method on the copy. The and() method preforms a bitwise Boolean AND operation, much like the & does when applied to integer arguments. A value in the target BitSet will be true only if it was originally true *and* the value at the same index of argument BitSet is also true. For all false values in the argument BitSet, and() sets the corresponding value in the target BitSet to false, leaving other values unchanged. The andNot() method combines a Boolean AND operation with a Boolean NOT operation on the argument BitSet (it does not alter the contents of that argument BitSet, hoever). The result is that for all true values in the argument BitSet, the corresponding values in the target BitSet are set to false.

The or() method performs a bitwise Boolean OR operation like the | operator: a value in the BitSet will be set to true if its original value was true *or* the corresponding value in the argument BitSet was true. For all true values in the argument BitSet, the or() method sets the corresponding value in the target BitSet to true, leaving the other values unchanged. The xor() method performs an "exclusive OR" operation: sets a value in the target BitSet to true if it was originally true or if the corresponding value in the argument BitSet was true. If both values were false, or if both values were true, however, it sets the value to false.

Finally, the toString() method returns a String representation of a BitSet that consists of a list within curly braces of the indexes at which true values are stored.

The BitSet class is not threadsafe.

Object → BitSet

Cloneable, Serializable

```
public class BitSet implements Cloneable, Serializable {
// Public Constructors
    public BitSet();
    public BitSet(int nbits);
// Public Instance Methods
    public void and(BitSet set);
1.2 public void andNot(BitSet set);
1.4 public int cardinality();
1.4 public void clear();
    public void clear(int bitIndex);
1.4 public void clear(int fromIndex, int toIndex);
1.4 public void flip(int bitIndex);
1.4 public void flip(int fromIndex, int toIndex);
    public boolean get(int bitIndex);
1.4 public BitSet get(int fromIndex, int toIndex);
1.4 public boolean intersects(BitSet set);
1.4 public boolean isEmpty();                                    default:true
1.2 public int length();
1.4 public int nextClearBit(int fromIndex);
1.4 public int nextSetBit(int fromIndex);
    public void or(BitSet set);
    public void set(int bitIndex);
1.4 public void set(int bitIndex, boolean value);
1.4 public void set(int fromIndex, int toIndex);
1.4 public void set(int fromIndex, int toIndex, boolean value);
    public int size();
    public void xor(BitSet set);
// Public Methods Overriding Object
    public Object clone();
    public boolean equals(Object obj);
    public int hashCode();
    public String toString();
}
```

Calendar — Java 1.1

java.util — cloneable serializable comparable

This abstract class defines methods that perform date and time arithmetic. It also includes methods that convert dates and times to and from the machine-usable millisecond format used by the Date class and units such as minutes, hours, days, weeks, months, and years that are more useful to humans. As an abstract class, Calendar cannot be directly instantiated. Instead, it provides static getInstance() methods that return instances of a Calendar subclass suitable for use in a specified or default locale with a specified or default time zone. See also Date, DateFormat, and TimeZone.

Calendar defines a number of useful constants. Some of these are values that represent days of the week and months of the year. Other constants, such as HOUR and DAY_OF_WEEK, represent various fields of date and time information. These field constants are passed to a number of Calendar methods, such as get() and set(), in order to indicate what particular date or time field is desired.

setTime() and the various **set()** methods set the date represented by a **Calendar** object. The **add()** method adds (or subtracts) values to a calendar field, incrementing the next larger field when the field being set rolls over. **roll()** does the same, without modifying anything but the specified field. **before()** and **after()** compare two **Calendar** objects. Many of the methods of the **Calendar** class are replacements for methods of **Date** that have been deprecated as of Java 1.1. While the **Calendar** class converts a time value to its various hour, day, month, and other fields, it is not intended to present those fields in a form suitable for display to the end user. That function is performed by the **java.text.DateFormat** class, which handles internationalization issues.

Calendar implements **Comparable** in Java 5.0, but not in earlier releases.

Object — Calendar
Cloneable, Comparable, Serializable

```
public abstract class Calendar implements Serializable, Cloneable, Comparable<Calendar> {
// Protected Constructors
   protected Calendar();
   protected Calendar(TimeZone zone, Locale aLocale);
// Public Constants
   public static final int AM;                                    =0
   public static final int AM_PM;                                 =9
   public static final int APRIL;                                 =3
   public static final int AUGUST;                                =7
   public static final int DATE;                                  =5
   public static final int DAY_OF_MONTH;                          =5
   public static final int DAY_OF_WEEK;                           =7
   public static final int DAY_OF_WEEK_IN_MONTH;                  =8
   public static final int DAY_OF_YEAR;                           =6
   public static final int DECEMBER;                              =11
   public static final int DST_OFFSET;                            =16
   public static final int ERA;                                   =0
   public static final int FEBRUARY;                              =1
   public static final int FIELD_COUNT;                           =17
   public static final int FRIDAY;                                =6
   public static final int HOUR;                                  =10
   public static final int HOUR_OF_DAY;                           =11
   public static final int JANUARY;                               =0
   public static final int JULY;                                  =6
   public static final int JUNE;                                  =5
   public static final int MARCH;                                 =2
   public static final int MAY;                                   =4
   public static final int MILLISECOND;                           =14
   public static final int MINUTE;                                =12
   public static final int MONDAY;                                =2
   public static final int MONTH;                                 =2
   public static final int NOVEMBER;                              =10
   public static final int OCTOBER;                               =9
   public static final int PM;                                    =1
   public static final int SATURDAY;                              =7
   public static final int SECOND;                                =13
   public static final int SEPTEMBER;                             =8
   public static final int SUNDAY;                                =1
   public static final int THURSDAY;                              =5
```

```
public static final int TUESDAY;                                    =3
public static final int UNDECIMBER;                                 =12
public static final int WEDNESDAY;                                  =4
public static final int WEEK_OF_MONTH;                              =4
public static final int WEEK_OF_YEAR;                               =3
public static final int YEAR;                                       =1
public static final int ZONE_OFFSET;                                =15
// Public Class Methods
public static Locale[] getAvailableLocales();                       synchronized
public static Calendar getInstance();
public static Calendar getInstance(Locale aLocale);
public static Calendar getInstance(TimeZone zone);
public static Calendar getInstance(TimeZone zone, Locale aLocale);
// Public Instance Methods
public abstract void add(int field, int amount);
public boolean after(Object when);
public boolean before(Object when);
public final void clear();
public final void clear(int field);
public int get(int field);
1.2 public int getActualMaximum(int field);
1.2 public int getActualMinimum(int field);
public int getFirstDayOfWeek();
public abstract int getGreatestMinimum(int field);
public abstract int getLeastMaximum(int field);
public abstract int getMaximum(int field);
public int getMinimalDaysInFirstWeek();
public abstract int getMinimum(int field);
public final Date getTime();
public long getTimeInMillis();
public TimeZone getTimeZone();
public boolean isLenient();
public final boolean isSet(int field);
1.2 public void roll(int field, int amount);
public abstract void roll(int field, boolean up);
public void set(int field, int value);
public final void set(int year, int month, int date);
public final void set(int year, int month, int date, int hourOfDay, int minute);
public final void set(int year, int month, int date, int hourOfDay, int minute, int second);
public void setFirstDayOfWeek(int value);
public void setLenient(boolean lenient);
public void setMinimalDaysInFirstWeek(int value);
public final void setTime(Date date);
public void setTimeInMillis(long millis);
public void setTimeZone(TimeZone value);
// Methods Implementing Comparable
5.0 public int compareTo(Calendar anotherCalendar);
// Public Methods Overriding Object
public Object clone();
public boolean equals(Object obj);
1.2 public int hashCode();
public String toString();
```

java.util.*

```
// Protected Instance Methods
   protected void complete();
   protected abstract void computeFields();
   protected abstract void computeTime();
   protected final int internalGet(int field);
// Protected Instance Fields
   protected boolean areFieldsSet;
   protected int[] fields;
   protected boolean[] isSet;
   protected boolean isTimeSet;
   protected long time;
}
```

Subclasses GregorianCalendar

Passed To java.text.DateFormat.setCalendar(), javax.xml.datatype.Duration.{addTo(), getTimeInMillis(), normalizeWith()}

Returned By java.text.DateFormat.getCalendar()

Type Of java.text.DateFormat.calendar

Collection<E> Java 1.2

java.util collection

This interface represents a group, or collection, of objects. In Java 5.0 this is a generic interface and the type variable *E* represents the type of the objects in the collection. The objects may or may not be ordered, and the collection may or may not contain duplicate objects. Collection is not often implemented directly. Instead, most collection classes implement one of the more specific subinterfaces: Set, an unordered collection that does not allow duplicates, or List, an ordered collection that does allow duplicates.

The Collection type provides a general way to refer to any set, list, or other collection of objects; it defines generic methods that work with any collection. contains() and containsAll() test whether the Collection contains a specified object or all the objects in a given collection. isEmpty() returns true if the Collection has no elements, or false otherwise. size() returns the number of elements in the Collection. iterator() returns an Iterator object that allows you to iterate through the objects in the collection. toArray() returns the objects in the Collection in a new array of type Object. Another version of toArray() takes an array as an argument and stores all elements of the Collection (which must all be compatible with the array) into that array. If the array is not big enough, the method allocates a new, larger array of the same type. If the array is too big, the method stores null into the first empty element of the array. This version of toArray() returns the array that was passed in or the new array, if one was allocated.

The previous methods all query or extract the contents of a collection. The Collection interface also defines methods for modifying the contents of the collection. add() and addAll() add an object or a collection of objects to a Collection. remove() and removeAll() remove an object or collection. retainAll() is a variant that removes all objects except those in a specified Collection. clear() removes all objects from the collection. All these modification methods except clear() return true if the collection was modified as a result of the call. An interface cannot specify constructors, but it is conventional that all implementations of Collection provide at least two standard constructors: one that takes no arguments and creates an empty collection, and a copy constructor that accepts a Collection object that specifies the initial contents of the new Collection.

Implementations of Collection and its subinterfaces are not required to support all operations defined by the Collection interface. All modification methods listed above are optional; an implementation (such as an immutable Set implementation) that does not support them simply throws java.lang.UnsupportedOperationException for these methods. Furthermore, implementations are free to impose restrictions on the types of objects that can be members of a collection. Some implementations might require elements to be of a particular type, for example, and others might not allow null as an element.

See also Set, List, Map, and Collections.

Iterable ··· Collection

```
public interface Collection<E> extends Iterable<E> {
// Public Instance Methods
   boolean add(E o);
   boolean addAll(Collection<? extends E> c);
   void clear();
   boolean contains(Object o);
   boolean containsAll(Collection<?> c);
   boolean equals(Object o);
   int hashCode();
   boolean isEmpty();
   Iterator<E> iterator();
   boolean remove(Object o);
   boolean removeAll(Collection<?> c);
   boolean retainAll(Collection<?> c);
   int size();
   Object[] toArray();
   <T> T[] toArray(T[] a);
}
```

Implementations AbstractCollection, List, Queue, Set

Passed To Too many methods to list.

Returned By Too many methods to list.

Collections **Java 1.2**

java.util

This class defines static methods and constants that are useful for working with collections and maps. One of the most commonly used methods is sort(), which sorts a List in place (the list cannot be immutable, of course). The sorting algorithm is stable, which means that equal elements retain the same relative order. One version of sort() uses a specified Comparator to perform the sort; the other relies on the natural ordering of the list elements and requires all the elements to implement java.lang.Comparable. reverseOrder() returns a Comparator object that reverses the order of another Comparator or that reverse the natural ordering of Comparable objects.

A related method is binarySearch(). It efficiently (in logarithmic time) searches a sorted List for a specified object and returns the index at which a matching object is found. If no match is found, it returns a negative number. For a negative return value r, the value -(r+1) specifies the index at which the specified object can be inserted into the list to maintain the sorted order of the list. As with sort(), binarySearch() can be passed a Comparator that defines the order of the sorted list. If no Comparator is specified, the list elements must all implement Comparable, and the list is assumed to be sorted according to the natural ordering defined by this interface.

See Arrays for methods that perform sorting and searching operations on arrays instead of collections.

The various methods whose names begin with synchronized return a threadsafe collection object wrapped around the specified collection. Vector and Hashtable are the only two collection objects threadsafe by default. Use these methods to obtain a synchronized wrapper object if you are using any other type of Collection or Map in a multithreaded environment where more than one thread can modify it.

The various methods whose names begin with unmodifiable function like synchronized methods. They return a Collection or Map object wrapped around the specified collection. The returned object is unmodifiable, however, so its add(), remove(), set(), put(), etc. methods all throw java.lang.UnsupportedOperationException. In Java 5.0, the "checked" methods return wrapped collections that enforce a specified element type for the collection, so that it is not possible to add an element of the wrong type.

In addition to the "synchronized", "unmodifiable", and "checked" methods, Collections defines a number of other methods that return special-purpose collections or maps: singleton() returns an unmodifiable set that contains only the specified object. singletonList() and singletonMap() return an immutable list and an immutable map, respectively, each of which contains only a single entry. The Collections class also defines related constants, EMPTY_LIST, EMPTY_SET, and EMPTY_MAP, which are immutable List, Set, and Map objects that contain no elements or mappings. In Java 5.0, the emptySet(), emptyList(), and emptyMap() methods are preferred alternatives to these constants, because they are generic methods and return correctly parameterized empty collections. nCopies() creates a new immutable List that contains a specified number of copies of a specified object. list() returns a List object that represents the elements of the specified Enumeration object. enumeration() does the reverse: it returns an Enumeration for a Collection, which is useful when working with code that uses the old Enumeration interface instead of the newer Iterator interface.

The Collections class also defines methods that mutate a collection. These methods throw an UnsupportedOperationException if the target collection is does not allow mutation. copy() copies elements of a source list into a destination list. fill() replaces all elements of the specified list with the specified object. swap() swaps the elements at two specified indexes of a List. replaceAll() replaces all elements in a List that are equal to (using the equals() method) with another object, and returns true if any replacements were done. reverse() reverses the order of the elements in a list. rotate() "rotates" a list, adding the specified number to the index of each element, and wrapping elements from the end of the list back to the front of the list. (Specifying a negative rotation rotates the list in the other direction.) shuffle() randomizes the order of elements in a list, using either an internal source of randomness or the Random pseudorandom number generator you provide. In Java 5.0, the addAll() method adds the specified elements to the specified collection. This method is a varargs method and allows elements to be specified in an array or listed individually in the argument list.

Finally, Collections defines methods (in addition to the binarySearch() methods described above) that search the elements of a collection: min() and max() methods search an unordered Collection for the minimum and maximum elements, according either to a specified Comparator or to the natural order defined by the Comparable elements themselves. indexOfSubList() and lastIndexOfSubList() search a specified list forward or backward for a subsequence of elements that match (using `equals()`) the elements the a second specified list. They return the start index of any such matching sublist, or return -1 if no match was found. These methods are like the `indexOf()` and `lastIndexOf()` methods of `String`, and do not require the `List` to be sorted, as the `binarySearch()` methods do. In Java 5.0, `frequency()` returns the number of occurences of a specified element in a specified collection, and `disjoint()` determines whether two collections are entirely disjoint—whether they have no elements in common.

```
public class Collections {
// No Constructor
// Public Constants
    public static final List EMPTY_LIST;
1.3 public static final Map EMPTY_MAP;
    public static final Set EMPTY_SET;
// Public Class Methods
5.0 public static <T> boolean addAll(Collection<? super T> c, T ... a);
    public static <T> int binarySearch(List<? extends Comparable<? super T>> list, T key);
    public static <T> int binarySearch(List<? extends T> list, T key, Comparator<? super T> c);
5.0 public static <E> Collection<E> checkedCollection(Collection<E> c, Class<E> type);
5.0 public static <E> List<E> checkedList(List<E> list, Class<E> type);
5.0 public static <K,V> Map<K,V> checkedMap(Map<K,V> m, Class<K> keyType, Class<V> valueType);
5.0 public static <E> Set<E> checkedSet(Set<E> s, Class<E> type);
5.0 public static <K,V> SortedMap<K,V> checkedSortedMap(SortedMap<K,V> m, Class<K> keyType,
                                                      Class<V> valueType);
5.0 public static <E> SortedSet<E> checkedSortedSet(SortedSet<E> s, Class<E> type);
    public static <T> void copy(List<? super T> dest, List<? extends T> src);
5.0 public static boolean disjoint(Collection<?> c1, Collection<?> c2);
5.0 public static final <T> List<T> emptyList();
5.0 public static final <K,V> Map<K,V> emptyMap();
5.0 public static final <T> Set<T> emptySet();
    public static <T> Enumeration<T> enumeration(Collection<T> c);
    public static <T> void fill(List<? super T> list, T obj);
5.0 public static int frequency(Collection<?> c, Object o);
1.4 public static int indexOfSubList(List<?> source, List<?> target);
1.4 public static int lastIndexOfSubList(List<?> source, List<?> target);
1.4 public static <T> ArrayList<T> list(Enumeration<T> e);
    public static <T extends Object&Comparable<? super T>> T max(Collection<? extends T> coll);
    public static <T> T max(Collection<? extends T> coll, Comparator<? super T> comp);
    public static <T extends Object&Comparable<? super T>> T min(Collection<? extends T> coll);
    public static <T> T min(Collection<? extends T> coll, Comparator<? super T> comp);
    public static <T> List<T> nCopies(int n, T o);
1.4 public static <T> boolean replaceAll(List<T> list, T oldVal, T newVal);
    public static void reverse(List<?> list);
    public static <T> Comparator<T> reverseOrder();
5.0 public static <T> Comparator<T> reverseOrder(Comparator<T> cmp);
1.4 public static void rotate(List<?> list, int distance);
    public static void shuffle(List<?> list);
    public static void shuffle(List<?> list, Random rnd);
    public static <T> Set<T> singleton(T o);
1.3 public static <T> List<T> singletonList(T o);
1.3 public static <K,V> Map<K,V> singletonMap(K key, V value);
    public static <T extends Comparable<? super T>> void sort(List<T> list);
    public static <T> void sort(List<T> list, Comparator<? super T> c);
```

```
1.4 public static void swap(List<?> list, int i, int j);
    public static <T> Collection<T> synchronizedCollection(Collection<T> c);
    public static <T> List<T> synchronizedList(List<T> list);
    public static <K,V> Map<K,V> synchronizedMap(Map<K,V> m);
    public static <T> Set<T> synchronizedSet(Set<T> s);
    public static <K,V> SortedMap<K,V> synchronizedSortedMap(SortedMap<K,V> m);
    public static <T> SortedSet<T> synchronizedSortedSet(SortedSet<T> s);
    public static <T> Collection<T> unmodifiableCollection(Collection<? extends T> c);
    public static <T> List<T> unmodifiableList(List<? extends T> list);
    public static <K,V> Map<K,V> unmodifiableMap(Map<? extends K,? extends V> m);
    public static <T> Set<T> unmodifiableSet(Set<? extends T> s);
    public static <K,V> SortedMap<K,V> unmodifiableSortedMap(SortedMap<K,? extends V> m);
    public static <T> SortedSet<T> unmodifiableSortedSet(SortedSet<T> s);
}
```

Comparator<T> — Java 1.2

java.util

This interface defines a compare() method that specifies a total ordering for a set of objects, allowing those objects to be sorted. The Comparator is used when the objects to be ordered do not have a natural ordering defined by the Comparable interface, or when you want to order them using something other than their natural ordering. Comparator has been made generic in Java 5.0 and the type variable *T* represents the type of objects being compared.

The compare() method is passed two objects. If the first argument is less than the second argument or should be placed before the second argument in a sorted list, compare() should return a negative integer. If the first argument is greater than the second argument or should be placed after the second argument in a sorted list, compare() should return a positive integer. If the two objects are equivalent or if their relative position in a sorted list does not matter, compare() should return 0. Comparator implementations may assume that both Object arguments are of appropriate types and cast them as desired. If either argument is not of the expected type, the compare() method throws a ClassCastException.

Note that the magnitude of the numbers returned by compare() does not matter, only whether they are less than, equal to, or greater than zero. In most cases, you should implement a Comparator so that compare(o1,o2) returns 0 if and only if o1.equals(o2) returns true. This is particularly important when using a Comparator to impose an ordering on a TreeSet or a TreeMap.

See Collections and Arrays for various methods that use Comparator objects for sorting and searching. See also the related java.lang.Comparable interface.

```
public interface Comparator<T> {
// Public Instance Methods
   int compare(T o1, T o2);
   boolean equals(Object obj);
}
```

Implementations java.text.Collator

Passed To Arrays.{binarySearch(), sort()}, Collections.{binarySearch(), max(), min(), reverseOrder(), sort()}, PriorityQueue.PriorityQueue(), TreeMap.TreeMap(), TreeSet.TreeSet(), java.util.concurrent.PriorityBlockingQueue.PriorityBlockingQueue()

Returned By Collections.reverseOrder(), PriorityQueue.comparator(), SortedMap.comparator(), SortedSet.comparator(), TreeMap.comparator(), TreeSet.comparator(), java.util.concurrent.PriorityBlockingQueue.comparator()

Type Of String.CASE_INSENSITIVE_ORDER

ConcurrentModificationException — Java 1.2

java.util — serializable unchecked

Signals that a modification has been made to a data structure at the same time some other operation is in progress and that, as a result, the correctness of the ongoing operation cannot be guaranteed. It is typically thrown by an Iterator or ListIterator object to stop an iteration if it detects that the underlying collection has been modified while the iteration is in progress.

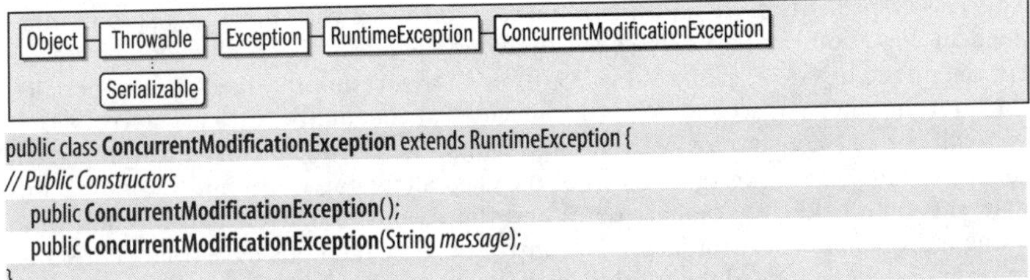


```
public class ConcurrentModificationException extends RuntimeException {
// Public Constructors
   public ConcurrentModificationException();
   public ConcurrentModificationException(String message);
}
```

Currency — Java 1.4

java.util — serializable

Instances of this class represent a currency. Obtain a Currency object by passing a "currency code" such as "USD" for U.S. Dollars or "EUR" for Euros to getInstance(). Once you have a Currency object, use getSymbol() to obtain the currency symbol (which is often different from the currency code) for the default locale or for a specified Locale. The symbol for a USD would be "$" in a U.S locale, but might be "US$" in other locales, for example. If no symbol is known, this method returns the currency code.

Use getDefaultFractionDigits() to determine how many fractional digits are conventionally used with the currency. This method returns 2 for the U.S. Dollar and other currencies that are divided into hundredths, but returns 3 for the Jordanian Dinar (JOD) and other currencies which are traditionally divided into thousandths, and returns 0 for the Japanese Yen (JPY) and other currencies that have a small unit value and are not usually divided into fractional parts at all. Currency codes are standardized by the ISO 4217 standard. For a complete list of currencies and currency codes see the website of the "maintenance agency" for this standard: *http://www.iso.org/iso/en/prods-services/popstds/currencycodeslist.html.*

Object — Currency ··· Serializable

```
public final class Currency implements Serializable {
// No Constructor
// Public Class Methods
   public static Currency getInstance(String currencyCode);
   public static Currency getInstance(Locale locale);
// Public Instance Methods
   public String getCurrencyCode();
   public int getDefaultFractionDigits();
```

```
    public String getSymbol();
    public String getSymbol(Locale locale);
// Public Methods Overriding Object
    public String toString();
}
```

Passed To java.text.DecimalFormat.setCurrency(), java.text.DecimalFormatSymbols.setCurrency(), java.text.NumberFormat.setCurrency()

Returned By java.text.DecimalFormat.getCurrency(), java.text.DecimalFormatSymbols.getCurrency(), java.text.NumberFormat.getCurrency()

Date **Java 1.0**

java.util **cloneable serializable comparable**

This class represents dates and times and lets you work with them in a system-independent way. You can create a Date by specifying the number of milliseconds from the epoch (midnight GMT, January 1st, 1970) or the year, month, date, and, optionally, the hour, minute, and second. Years are specified as the number of years since 1900. If you call the Date constructor with no arguments, the Date is initialized to the current time and date. The instance methods of the class allow you to get and set the various date and time fields, to compare dates and times, and to convert dates to and from string representations. As of Java 1.1, many of the date methods have been deprecated in favor of the methods of the Calendar class.

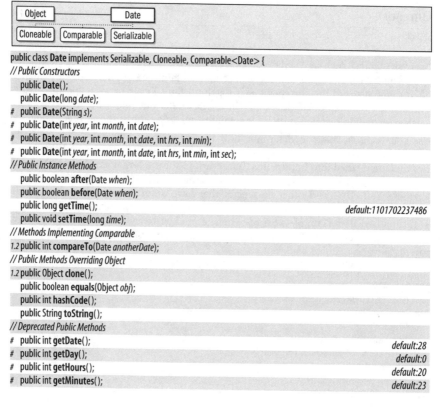

Object	—	Date
Cloneable	Comparable	Serializable

```
public class Date implements Serializable, Cloneable, Comparable<Date> {
// Public Constructors
    public Date();
    public Date(long date);
#   public Date(String s);
#   public Date(int year, int month, int date);
#   public Date(int year, int month, int date, int hrs, int min);
#   public Date(int year, int month, int date, int hrs, int min, int sec);
// Public Instance Methods
    public boolean after(Date when);
    public boolean before(Date when);
    public long getTime();                                   default:1101702237486
    public void setTime(long time);
// Methods Implementing Comparable
1.2 public int compareTo(Date anotherDate);
// Public Methods Overriding Object
1.2 public Object clone();
    public boolean equals(Object obj);
    public int hashCode();
    public String toString();
// Deprecated Public Methods
#   public int getDate();                                    default:28
#   public int getDay();                                     default:0
#   public int getHours();                                   default:20
#   public int getMinutes();                                 default:23
```

```
#  public int getMonth();                                                default:10
#  public int getSeconds();                                              default:57
#  public int getTimezoneOffset();                                       default:480
#  public int getYear();                                                 default:104
#  public static long parse(String s);
#  public void setDate(int date);
#  public void setHours(int hours);
#  public void setMinutes(int minutes);
#  public void setMonth(int month);
#  public void setSeconds(int seconds);
#  public void setYear(int year);
#  public String toGMTString();
#  public String toLocaleString();
#  public static long UTC(int year, int month, int date, int hrs, int min, int sec);
}
```

Passed To Too many methods to list.

Returned By Too many methods to list.

Dictionary<K,V> — Java 1.0

java.util

This abstract class is the superclass of Hashtable. Other hashtable-like data structures might also extend this class. See Hashtable for more information. As of Java 1.2, the Map interface replaces the functionality of this class.

```
public abstract class Dictionary<K,V> {
// Public Constructors
   public Dictionary();
// Public Instance Methods
   public abstract Enumeration<V> elements();
   public abstract V get(Object key);
   public abstract boolean isEmpty();
   public abstract Enumeration<K> keys();
   public abstract V put(K key, V value);
   public abstract V remove(Object key);
   public abstract int size();
}
```

Subclasses Hashtable

DuplicateFormatFlagsException — Java 5.0

java.util — serializable unchecked

An IllegalFormatException of this type is thrown by a Formatter when the format string contains duplicate format flags for the same conversion specifier.

```
Throwable — Exception — RuntimeException — IllegalArgumentException — IllegalFormatException — DuplicateFormatFlagsException
    :
Serializable
```

```
public class DuplicateFormatFlagsException extends IllegalFormatException {
// Public Constructors
   public DuplicateFormatFlagsException(String f);
```

java.util.*

```
// Public Instance Methods
   public String getFlags();
// Public Methods Overriding Throwable
   public String getMessage();
}
```

EmptyStackException

Java 1.0

java.util

serializable unchecked

Signals that a Stack object is empty.

Object ⊣ Throwable ⊣ Exception ⊣ RuntimeException ⊣ EmptyStackException

Serializable

```
public class EmptyStackException extends RuntimeException {
// Public Constructors
   public EmptyStackException();
}
```

Enumeration<E>

Java 1.0

java.util

This interface defines the methods necessary to enumerate, or iterate, through a set of values, such as the set of values contained in a hashtable. This interface is superseded in Java 1.2 by the Iterator inteface. In Java 5.0 this interface has been made generic and defines the type variable *E* to represent the type of the objects being enumerated.

An Enumeration is usually not instantiated directly, but instead is created by the object that is to have its values enumerated. A number of classes, such as Vector and Hashtable, have methods that return Enumeration objects.

To use an Enumeration object, you use its two methods in a loop. hasMoreElements() returns true if there are more values to be enumerated and can determine whether a loop should continue. Within a loop, a call to nextElement() returns a value from the enumeration. An Enumeration makes no guarantees about the order in which the values are returned. The values in an Enumeration can be iterated through only once; there is no way to reset it to the beginning.

```
public interface Enumeration<E> {
// Public Instance Methods
   boolean hasMoreElements();
   E nextElement();
}
```

Implementations StringTokenizer

Passed To java.io.SequenceInputStream.SequenceInputStream(), Collections.list()

Returned By Too many methods to list.

EnumMap<K extends Enum<K>,V>

Java 5.0

java.util

cloneable serializable collection

This class is a Map implementation for use with enumerated types. The key type *K* must be an enumerated type, and all keys must be enumerated constants defined by that type. null keys are not permitted. The value type *V* is unrestricted and null values are permitted.

The EnumMap implementation is based on an array of elements of type *V*. The length of this array is the same as the number of constants defined by the enumerated type *K*. All Map operations execute in constant time. The iterators of the keySet(), entrySet(), and values() collections iterate their elements in the ordinal order of the enumerated constants. EnumMap is not threadsafe, but its iterators are based on a snapshot of the underlying array and never throw ConcurrentModificationException.

Object — AbstractMap — EnumMap
Map, Cloneable, Serializable

```
public class EnumMap<K extends Enum<K>,V> extends AbstractMap<K,V> implements Serializable, Cloneable {
// Public Constructors
    public EnumMap(EnumMap<K,? extends V> m);
    public EnumMap(Class<K> keyType);
    public EnumMap(Map<K,? extends V> m);
// Public Instance Methods
    public EnumMap<K,V> clone();
    public V put(K key, V value);
// Public Methods Overriding AbstractMap
    public void clear();
    public boolean containsKey(Object key);
    public boolean containsValue(Object value);
    public Set<Map.Entry<K,V>> entrySet();
    public boolean equals(Object o);
    public V get(Object key);
    public Set<K> keySet();
    public void putAll(Map<? extends K,? extends V> m);
    public V remove(Object key);
    public int size();
    public Collection<V> values();
}
```

EnumSet<E extends Enum<E>> — Java 5.0

java.util — cloneable serializable collection

This Set implementation is specialized for use with enumerated constants. The element type *E* must be an enumerated type, and null is not allowed as a member of the set.

EnumSet does not define a constructor. Instead, it defines various static factory methods for creating sets. Use one of the of() methods for creating an EnumSet and initializing its elements. For efficiency, versions of this method that accept one through five arguments are defined. If you pass more than five arguments, the varargs version will be invoked. The allOf() and noneOf() methods define full and empty sets but require the Class of the enumerated type since they do not have any other arguments to define the element type. complementOf() returns an EnumSet that contains all enumerated constants not contained by the specified EnumSet. The range() factory creates a set that includes the two specified values and any enumerated constants that fall between them in the enumerated type declaration. (Note that this definition of a range includes both endpoints and differs from most Java methods, in which the second argument specifies the first value past the end of the range.)

The EnumSet implementation is based on a bit vector that includes one bit for each constant defined by the enumerated type *E*. Because of this compact and efficient representation, basic Set operations occur in constant time, and the Iterator returns enumerated constants in the order in which they are declared in the type *E*. EnumSet is not threadsafe, but the Iterator uses a copy of the internal bit vector and never throws ConcurrentModificationException.

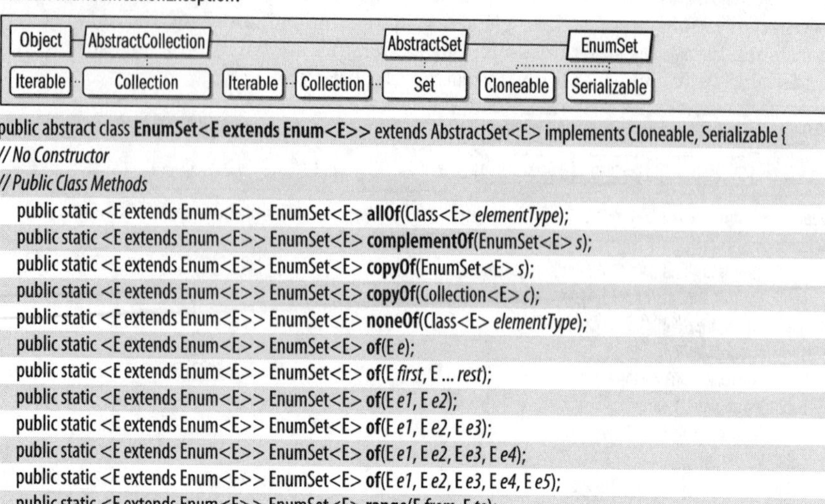


```
public abstract class EnumSet<E extends Enum<E>> extends AbstractSet<E> implements Cloneable, Serializable {
// No Constructor
// Public Class Methods
   public static <E extends Enum<E>> EnumSet<E> allOf(Class<E> elementType);
   public static <E extends Enum<E>> EnumSet<E> complementOf(EnumSet<E> s);
   public static <E extends Enum<E>> EnumSet<E> copyOf(EnumSet<E> s);
   public static <E extends Enum<E>> EnumSet<E> copyOf(Collection<E> c);
   public static <E extends Enum<E>> EnumSet<E> noneOf(Class<E> elementType);
   public static <E extends Enum<E>> EnumSet<E> of(E e);
   public static <E extends Enum<E>> EnumSet<E> of(E first, E ... rest);
   public static <E extends Enum<E>> EnumSet<E> of(E e1, E e2);
   public static <E extends Enum<E>> EnumSet<E> of(E e1, E e2, E e3);
   public static <E extends Enum<E>> EnumSet<E> of(E e1, E e2, E e3, E e4);
   public static <E extends Enum<E>> EnumSet<E> of(E e1, E e2, E e3, E e4, E e5);
   public static <E extends Enum<E>> EnumSet<E> range(E from, E to);
// Public Instance Methods
   public EnumSet<E> clone();
}
```

EventListener — Java 1.1

java.util — event listener

EventListener is a base interface for the event model that is used by AWT and Swing in Java 1.1 and later. This interface defines no methods or constants; it serves simply as a tag that identifies objects that act as event listeners. The event listener interfaces in the java.awt.event, java.beans, and javax.swing.event packages extend this interface.

```
public interface EventListener {
}
```

Implementations EventListenerProxy, java.util.prefs.NodeChangeListener, java.util.prefs.PreferenceChangeListener, javax.net.ssl.HandshakeCompletedListener, javax.net.ssl.SSLSessionBindingListener

Passed To EventListenerProxy.EventListenerProxy()

Returned By EventListenerProxy.getListener()

EventListenerProxy — Java 1.4

java.util

This abstract class serves as the superclass for event listener proxy objects. Subclasses of this class implement an event listener interface and serve as a wrapper around an event listener of that type, defining methods that provide additional information about the listener. See java.beans.PropertyChangeListenerProxy for an explanation of how event listener proxy objects are used.

Object — EventListenerProxy ··· EventListener

```
public abstract class EventListenerProxy implements EventListener {
// Public Constructors
    public EventListenerProxy(EventListener listener);
// Public Instance Methods
    public EventListener getListener();
}
```

EventObject Java 1.1

java.util serializable event

EventObject serves as the superclass for all event objects used by the event model introduced in Java 1.1 for AWT and JavaBeans and also used by Swing in Java 1.2. This class defines a generic type of event; it is extended by the more specific event classes in the java.awt, java.awt.event, java.beans, and javax.swing.event packages. The only common feature shared by all events is a source object, which is the object that, in some way, generated the event. The source object is passed to the EventObject() constructor and is returned by the getSource() method.

Object → EventObject ··· Serializable

```
public class EventObject implements Serializable {
// Public Constructors
    public EventObject(Object source);
// Public Instance Methods
    public Object getSource();
// Public Methods Overriding Object
    public String toString();
// Protected Instance Fields
    protected transient Object source;
}
```

Subclasses java.util.prefs.NodeChangeEvent, java.util.prefs.PreferenceChangeEvent, javax.net.ssl.HandshakeCompletedEvent, javax.net.ssl.SSLSessionBindingEvent

FormatFlagsConversionMismatchException Java 5.0

java.util serializable unchecked

An IllegalFormatException of this type is thrown by a Formatter when a conversion specifier and a format flag specified with it are incompatible.

··· Throwable → Exception → RuntimeException → IllegalArgumentException → IllegalFormatException → FormatFlagsConversionMismatchException
Serializable

```
public class FormatFlagsConversionMismatchException extends IllegalFormatException {
// Public Constructors
    public FormatFlagsConversionMismatchException(String f, char c);
// Public Instance Methods
    public char getConversion();
    public String getFlags();
// Public Methods Overriding Throwable
    public String getMessage();
}
```

java.util.*

Formattable Java 5.0

java.util

This interface should be implemented by classes that want to interact with the Formatter class more intimately than is possible with the toString method. When a Formattable object is the argument for a %s or %S conversion, its formatTo() method is invoked rather than its toString() method. formatTo() is responsible for formatting a textual representation of the object to the specified *formatter*, subject to the constraints imposed by the *flags*, *width*, and *precision* arguments.

The *flags* argument is a bitmask of zero or more FormattableFlags constants. Each flag provides information about the format specification that resulted in the invocation of formatTo(). FormattableFlags.ALTERNATE indicates that the # flag was used and that the Formattable should format itself using some alternate form. The interpretation of the alternate form is entirely up to the Formattable implementation. LEFT_JUSTIFY means that the - flag was used and that the Formattable should pad its output on the right, instead of on the left. UPPERCASE indicates that the %S conversion was used instead of %s and the Formattable should output uppercase characters instead of lowercase.

The *width* and *precision* arguments specify the width and precision specified along with the %s format specifier, or -1 if no width and precision are specified. The Formattable object should treat these values the same way that Formatter does. The text to be output should first be truncated to fit within *precision* characters and then padded on the left (or right if the LEFT_JUSTIFY flag is set) with spaces for a total length of *width* characters. Note that a Formattable implementation may fulfill the obligations imposed by the LEFT_JUSTIFY and UPPERCASE flags and the *width* and *precision* arguments by constructing a suitable format string to pass back to the specified Formatter.

If a Formattable implementation wants to perform locale-specific formatting, it can query the Locale of the Formatter with the locale() method. Note, however, that the returned value is the locale specified when the Formatter was created, not the Locale, if any, passed to the format() method. There is no way for a Formattable object to access that Locale.

```
public interface Formattable {
// Public Instance Methods
   void formatTo(java.util.Formatter formatter, int flags, int width, int precision);
}
```

FormattableFlags Java 5.0

java.util

This class defines three constants representing flags that may be passed as a bitmask to the Formattable.formatTo() method. See Formattable for the interpretation of these flags.

```
public class FormattableFlags {
// No Constructor
// Public Constants
   public static final int ALTERNATE;                                    =4
   public static final int LEFT_JUSTIFY;                                 =1
   public static final int UPPERCASE;                                    =2
}
```

Formatter Java 5.0

java.util closeable flushable

The Formatter class is a utility for formatting text in the style of the printf() method of the C programming language. Every Formatter has an associated java.lang.Appendable object (such as a StringBuilder or PrintWriter) that is specified when the Formatter is created. format() is a varargs method that expects a "format string" argument followed by some number of Object arguments. The format string uses a grammar, described in detail later in the entry, to specify how the arguments that follow are to be converted to strings. After the arguments are converted, they are substituted into the format string, and the resulting text is appended to the Appendable. A variant of the format() method accepts a Locale object that can affect the argument conversions.

For ease of use, a Formatter never throws a java.io.IOException, even when the underlying Appendable throws one. When using a Formatter with a stream-based Appendable object that may throw an IOException, you can use the ioException() method to obtain the most recently thrown exception, or null if no exception has been thrown by the Appendable.

Formatter implements the Closeable and Flushable interfaces of the java.io package, and its close() and flush() methods call the corresponding methods on its Appendable object, if that object itself implements Closeable or Flushable. When a Formatter sends its output to a stream or similar Appendable, remember to call close() when you are done with it. It is always safe to call close() even if the underlying Appendable is not Closeable. Note that once a Formatter has been closed, no other method except ioException() may be called.

locale() returns the Locale passed to the Formatter() constructor or null. out() returns the Appendable that this Formatter sends its output to. toString() returns the result of calling toString() on that Appendable. This is useful when the Appendable is a StringBuilder, for example, as it is when the no-argument version of the Formatter() constructor is used. If the Appendable is a stream class, however, the toString() method is not typically useful.

Note that the Java 5.0 API provides a number of convenience methods that use the Formatter class, and in many cases it is unnecessary to create a Formatter object explicitly. See the static String.format() method and the format() and printf() methods of java.io.PrintWriter and java.io.PrintStream.

If you do need to create a Formatter object explicitly, you can choose from a number of constructors. The most general case is to pass the desired Appendable or the desired Locale and Appendable objects to the constructor. The no-argument constructor is a convenience that creates a StringBuilder to append to. Obtain this StringBuilder with out() or obtain its contents as a String with toString(). If you specify a single Locale argument, the resulting Formatter uses the specified locale with a StringBuilder.

You can use a Formatter to write formatted output to a file by specifying either the File object or filename as a String. Variants of these constructors allow you to specify the name of the charset to use for character-to-byte conversion and also a Locale. Note that these methods overwrite existing files rather than appending to them. Other constructors create an Appendable object for you based on the java.io.OutputStream or java.io.PrintStream you specify. In the OutputStream case, you may optionally specify the charset to use or the charset and a Locale.

The Format String and Format Specifiers

The API for Formatter and Formatter-based convenience methods is relatively simple. The power of these formatting methods lies in the format string that is the first argument (or second argument if a Locale is specified) to the various format() and printf() methods.

The format string may contain any amount of regular text, which is printed or appended literally to the destination **Appendable** object. This plain text may be interspersed with *format specifiers* which specify how a subsequent argument is to be formatted as a string. In contrast to the simple API, the grammar for these format specifiers is surprisingly complex. Experienced C programmers will find that the grammar is largely compatible with the **printf()** format string grammar of the standard C library.

Each format specifier begins with a percent sign and ends with a one- or two-character conversion type that specifies most of the details of the conversion and formatting. In between these two are optional flags that provide additional details about how the formatting should be done. The general syntax of a format specifier is as follows. Square brackets indicate optional items:

```
%[argument][flags][width][.precision]type
```

Note that the percent sign and the *type* are the only two required portions of a format specifier. We begin, therefore, with a listing of conversion types (see Table 16-1). A discussion of *argument*, *flags*, *width*, and *precision* follows. In the table of conversion types below, if uppercase and lowercase variants of the type specifier are listed together, the uppercase variant produces the same output as the lowercase variant except that all lowercase letters are converted to uppercase. Note that **format()** never throws **NullPointerException** because of **null** arguments following the format string. A **null** argument is formatted as "null" or "NULL" for all conversion characters except **%b** and %B, which produce "false" or "FALSE".

Table 16-1. Formatter conversion types

Conversion	Description
Simple conversions	
%%	Outputs a single percent sign.This is simply an escape sequence used to embed percent signs literally in the output string. This conversion does not use an argument.
%n	Outputs the platform-specific line separator. This conversion represents the value returned by System.getProperty("line.separator"). This conversion does not use an argument.
%s, %S	Formats and outputs the argument as a string, optionally converting it to uppercase for the %S conversion. The argument may be of any type. If the argument implements Formattable, its formatTo() method is called to perform the formatting. Otherwise, its toString() method is called to convert it to a string. If the argument is null, the output string is "null" or "NULL".
%c, %C	Outputs the argument as a single character. The argument type must be Byte, Short, Character, or Integer. The argument value must represent a valid Unicode code point. (See Character.isValidCodePoint().)
%b, %B	Outputs the argument value as the string "true" or "false" (or "TRUE" or "FALSE"). The argument may be of any type and any value. If it is a Boolean argument, the output reflects the argument value. Otherwise, if the argument is null, the output is "false" or "FALSE". For any other value, the output is "true" or "TRUE". Note that this differs from normal Java conversions in which boolean values are not convertible to or from any other type.
%h, %H	Outputs the hexadecimal representation of the hashcode for the argument. Arguments of any type and value are allowed. This conversion type is useful mainly for debugging.
Numeric Conversions	
%d	Formats the argument as a base-10 integer. The argument must be a Byte, Short, Integer, Long, or BigInteger.
%o	Formats the argument as a base-8 octal integer. The allowed argument types are the same as for %d. For any argument type other than BigInteger, the value is treated as unsigned.
%x, %X	Formats the argument as a base-16 hexadecimal integer. The allowed argument types and values are the same as for %d. For any argument type other than BigInteger, the value is treated as unsigned.

Table 16-1. Formatter conversion types (continued)

Conversion	Description
%e, %E	Formats the argument as a base-10 floating-point number, using exponential notation. The output consists of a single digit, a locale-specific decimal point, and the number of fractional digits specified by the *precision* of the format specifier, or six fractional digits if no *precision* is specified. These digits are followed by the letter e or E and the exponent of the number. The argument must be a Float, Double, or BigDecimal. The values NaN and Infinity are formatted as "NaN" and "Infinity" or their uppercase equivalents.
%f	Formats the argument as a floating-point number in base-10, without using exponential notation. If the number is large, this may produce quite a few digits. Because exponential notation is never used, the output will never include a letter, and there is no uppercase variant of this conversion. Legal argument types and special-case values are as for %e.
%g, %G	Formats the argument as a base-10 floating-point number, displaying no more than the number of significant digits specified by the *precision* of the format specifier, or no more than 6 significant digits if no *precision* is specified. If the value has more than the allowed number of significant digits, it is printed using exponential notation (see %e) to limit the display to the specified number of digits. Otherwise, all digits of the value are printed explicitly as they would be with the %f conversion type. Legal argument types and special case values are as for %e.
%a, %A	Formats the argument in hexadecimal floating-point format. Legal argument types and special case values are as for %e.
Dates and Times	
%t, %T	All date and time format types are two-letter codes beginning with %t or %T. The specific format types are listed below, in alphabetical order, using %t as the prefix. For uppercase, use %T instead. Upper- and lowercase variants of the second letter of a time or date format type are sometimes completely unrelated. Other times, the lowercase conversion produces an abbreviation of the value produced by the uppercase conversion. The argument for a date or time conversion must be a Date, Calendar, or Long. In the case of Long, the value is interpreted as milliseconds since the epoch, as in System currentTimeMillis().
%tA	The locale-specific full name of the day of the week.
%ta	The locale-specific abbreviation of the day of the week.
%tB	The locale-specific name of the month. See %tm.
%tb	The locale-specific abbreviation for the month.
%tC	The century: the year divided by 100, with leading zeros if necessary to produce a value from 00 to 99
%tc	The complete date and time. Equivalent to "%ta %tb %td %tT %tZ %tY".
%tD	The date in a short numeric form used in the US locale. Equivalent to "%tm/%td/%ty".
%td	The day of the month, as a two-digit number between 01 and 31. See %te.
%tE	The date expressed as milliseconds since Midnight UTC on January 1st, 1970.
%te	The day of the month as a one- or two-digit number without leading zeros between 1 and 31. See %td.
%tF	The numeric date in ISO8601 format: %tY-%tm-%td.
%tH	Hour of the day using a 24-hour clock, formatted as two digits between 00 and 23. See %tl.
%th	The abbreviated month name. Same as %tb.
%tI	Hour of the day using a 12-hour clock, formatted as two digits between 01 and 12. See %tH and %tP.
%tj	The day of the year as three digits with leading zeros if necessary: 001-366
%tk	Hour of the day on a 24-hour clock using one or two digits without a leading zero: 0-23. See %tl.
%tL	Milliseconds within the second, expressed as three digits with leading zeros: 000-999.
%tl	Hour of the day on a 12-hour clock using one or two digits without a leading zero: 1-12.
%tM	Minute within the hour as two digits with a leading zero if necessary: 00-59.

Table 16-1. Formatter conversion types (continued)

Conversion	Description
%tm	The month of the year as a two-digit number between 01 and 12, or between 01 and 13 for lunar calendars. See %tB and %tb.
%tN	Nanosecond within the second, expressed as nine digits with leading zeros if necessary. Note that platforms are not required to able to resolve times with nanosecond precision.
%tP	The locale-specific morning or afternoon indicator (such as "am" or "pm") used with 12-hour clocks. %tP uses lowercase and %TP uses uppercase.
%tp	Like %tP but uses uppercase for both %tp and %Tp variants.
%tR	The hour and minute on a 24-hour clock. Equivalent to "%tH:%tM".
%tr	The hour, minute, and second on a 12-hour clock. Equivalent to "%tI:%tM:%tS %tP" except that the am/pm indicator %tP may be in a different locale-dependent position.
%tS	Seconds within the minute, as two digits with a leading zero if necessary. The range is normally 00-59, but a value of 60 is allowed for leap seconds.
%ts	Seconds since the beginning of the epoch. See %tE.
%tT	The time in hours, minutes, and seconds using 24-hour format. Equivalent to "%tH:%tM:%tS".
%tY	The year, using at least four digits, formatted with leading zeros, if necessary.
%ty	The last two digits of the year, 00-99
%tZ	An abbreviation for the time zone.
%tz	The time zone as numeric offset from GMT.

Argument Specifier

Every format specifier in a format string except for %% and %n requires an argument that contains the value to format. These arguments follow the format string in the call to format() or printf(). By default, a format specifier uses the next unused argument. In the following printf() call, the first and second %s format specifiers format the second and third arguments, respectively:

```
out.printf("Name: %s %s%n", first, last);
```

If a format specifier includes the character < after the %, it specifies that the argument of the previous format specifier should be reused. This allows the same object (such as a date) to be formatted more than once (yielding a formatted date and time, for example):

```
out.printf("Date: %tD%nTime: %<tr%n", System.currentTimeMillis());
```

It is an error to use < in the first format specifier of a format string.

Argument numbers may also be specified absolutely. If the % sign is followed by one or more digits and a $ sign, those digits specify an argument number. For example %1$d specifies that the first argument following the format string should be formatted as an integer. Absolute argument numbers are particularly useful for localization since the different translations of a message may need to interpolate the arguments in a different order. The following example includes a format string that might be used in a locale where a person's family name is typically printed (in uppercase) before the given name. Note that the arguments are not passed in the same order that they are formatted.

```
String name = String.format("%2$S, %1$s", firstname, lastname);
```

Neither absolute argument indexing with a number and $ character or relative argument indexing with < affect the order in which arguments are interpolated for format specifiers that use neither $ or <. The first format specifier that has neither an absolute or relative argument specification uses the first argument following the format string, regardless of what has come before. The code above could be rewritten like this, for example:

```
String name = String.format("%2$S, %s", firstname, lastname);
```

Flags

Following the optional argument specifier, a format specifier may include one or more flag characters. The defined flags, their effects, and the format types for which they are legal are specified in Table 16-2:

Table 16-2. Formatter flags

Flag	Description
-	A hyphen specifies that the formatted value should be left-justified within the specified *width*. This flag can be used with any conversion type except %n as long as the conversion specifier also includes a *width* (see below). When a width is specified without this flag, the formatted string is padded on the left to produce right-justified output.
#	The # flag specifies that output should appear in an "alternate form" that depends on the type being formatted. For %o conversions, this flag specifies that the output should include a leading 0. For %x and %X conversions, it specifies that output should include a leading 0x or 0X. For the %s and %S conversions, the # flag may be used if the argument implements Formattable. In this case, the flag is passed on to the formatTo() method of the argument, and it is up to that formatTo() method to produce its output in some alternate form.
+	This flag specifies that numeric output should always include a sign: a value that is nonnegative will have "+" added in front of it. This flag may be used with any numeric conversion that may yield a signed result. This includes %d, %e, %f, %g, %a, and their uppercase variants. It also includes %o, %x, and %X conversions applied to BigInteger arguments.
	The space character is a (hard-to-read) flag that specifies that non-negative values should be prefixed with a space. This flag may be used with the same conversion and argument types as the + flag, and is useful when aligning positive and negative numbers in a column
(	This flag specifies that negative numbers should be enclosed in parentheses, as is commonly done in financial statements, for example. This flag may be used with the same format and argument types as the + flag, except that it may not be used with %a conversions.
0	The digit zero, used as a flag, specifies that numeric values should be padded on the left (after the sign character, if any) with zeros. This flag may be used only if a width is specified, and may not be used in conjunction with the - flag.
,	This flag specifies that numbers should be formatted using the locale-specific grouping separator. In the US locale, for example, a comma would appear every three digits to separate the number into thousands, millions, and so on. This flag may be used with %d, %e, %E, %f, %g, and %G conversions only.

Width

The *width* portion of a format specifier is one or more digits that specify the minimum number of characters to be produced. If the formatted value is narrower than the specified width, (by default) it is padded on the left with spaces, producing a right-justified value. The - and 0 flags can be used to specify left-justification or padding with zeros instead.

A width may be specified with any format type except %n.

Precision

The *precision* portion of a format specifier is one or more digits following a decimal point. The meaning of this number depends on which format type it is used with:

- For %e, %E, and %f, the precision specifies the number of digits to appear after the decimal point. Zeros are appended on the right, if necessary. The default precision is 6.
- For %g and %G format types, the precision specifies the total number of significant digits to be displayed. As a corollary, it specifies the largest and smallest values that can be displayed without resorting to exponential notation. The default precision is 6. If a precision of 0 is specified, it is treated as a precision of 1.
- For %s, %h and %b format types, and their uppercase variants, the precision specifies the maximum number of characters to be output. If no precision is specified, there is no maximum. If the formatted output would exceed the *precision* of characters, it is truncated. If *precision* is smaller than *width*, the formatted value is first truncated as necessary and then padded within the specified *width*.
- Specifying a precision for any other conversion type causes an exception at runtime.

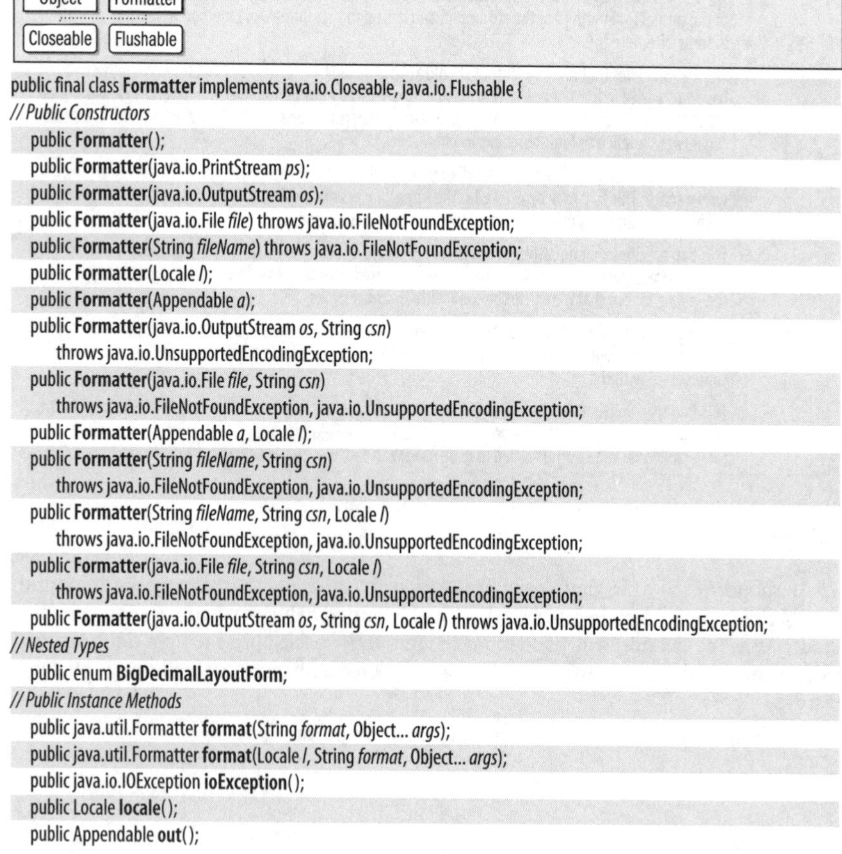


```
public final class Formatter implements java.io.Closeable, java.io.Flushable {
// Public Constructors
   public Formatter();
   public Formatter(java.io.PrintStream ps);
   public Formatter(java.io.OutputStream os);
   public Formatter(java.io.File file) throws java.io.FileNotFoundException;
   public Formatter(String fileName) throws java.io.FileNotFoundException;
   public Formatter(Locale l);
   public Formatter(Appendable a);
   public Formatter(java.io.OutputStream os, String csn)
       throws java.io.UnsupportedEncodingException;
   public Formatter(java.io.File file, String csn)
       throws java.io.FileNotFoundException, java.io.UnsupportedEncodingException;
   public Formatter(Appendable a, Locale l);
   public Formatter(String fileName, String csn)
       throws java.io.FileNotFoundException, java.io.UnsupportedEncodingException;
   public Formatter(String fileName, String csn, Locale l)
       throws java.io.FileNotFoundException, java.io.UnsupportedEncodingException;
   public Formatter(java.io.File file, String csn, Locale l)
       throws java.io.FileNotFoundException, java.io.UnsupportedEncodingException;
   public Formatter(java.io.OutputStream os, String csn, Locale l) throws java.io.UnsupportedEncodingException;
// Nested Types
   public enum BigDecimalLayoutForm;
// Public Instance Methods
   public java.util.Formatter format(String format, Object... args);
   public java.util.Formatter format(Locale l, String format, Object... args);
   public java.io.IOException ioException();
   public Locale locale();
   public Appendable out();
```

```
// Methods Implementing Closeable
    public void close();
// Methods Implementing Flushable
    public void flush();
// Public Methods Overriding Object
    public String toString();
}
```

Passed To Formattable.formatTo()

Formatter.BigDecimalLayoutForm — Java 5.0

java.util — serializable comparable enum

This enumerated type is intended for internal use by the Formatter class, but was inadvertently declared public. This type serves no useful purpose and should not be used. It will likely be removed in a future release.

```
public enum Formatter.BigDecimalLayoutForm {
// Enumerated Constants
    SCIENTIFIC,
    DECIMAL_FLOAT;
// Public Class Methods
    public static Formatter.BigDecimalLayoutForm valueOf(String name);
    public static final Formatter.BigDecimalLayoutForm[] values();
}
```

FormatterClosedException — Java 5.0

java.util — serializable unchecked

An exception of this type is thrown when an attempt is made to use a Formatter whose close() method has been called.

Object — Throwable — Exception — RuntimeException — IllegalStateException — FormatterClosedException
Serializable

```
public class FormatterClosedException extends IllegalStateException {
// Public Constructors
    public FormatterClosedException();
}
```

GregorianCalendar — Java 1.1

java.util — cloneable serializable comparable

This concrete subclass of Calendar implements the standard solar calendar with years numbered from the birth of Christ that is used is most locales throughout the world. You do not typically use this class directly, but instead obtain a Calendar object suitable for the default locale by calling Calendar.getInstance(). See Calendar for details on working with Calendar objects. There is a discontinuity in the Gregorian calendar that represents the historical switch from the Julian calendar to the Gregorian calendar. By default, GregorianCalendar assumes that this switch occurs on October 15, 1582. Most programs need not be concerned with the switch.

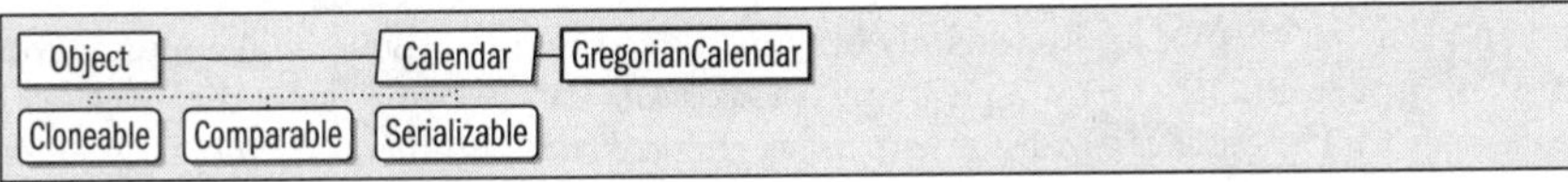

```
public class GregorianCalendar extends Calendar {
// Public Constructors
   public GregorianCalendar();
   public GregorianCalendar(Locale aLocale);
   public GregorianCalendar(TimeZone zone);
   public GregorianCalendar(TimeZone zone, Locale aLocale);
   public GregorianCalendar(int year, int month, int dayOfMonth);
   public GregorianCalendar(int year, int month, int dayOfMonth, int hourOfDay, int minute);
   public GregorianCalendar(int year, int month, int dayOfMonth, int hourOfDay, int minute, int second);
// Public Constants
   public static final int AD;                                              =1
   public static final int BC;                                              =0
// Public Instance Methods
   public final Date getGregorianChange();
   public boolean isLeapYear(int year);
   public void setGregorianChange(Date date);
// Public Methods Overriding Calendar
   public void add(int field, int amount);
5.0 public Object clone();
   public boolean equals(Object obj);
1.2 public int getActualMaximum(int field);
1.2 public int getActualMinimum(int field);
   public int getGreatestMinimum(int field);
   public int getLeastMaximum(int field);
   public int getMaximum(int field);
   public int getMinimum(int field);
5.0 public TimeZone getTimeZone();
   public int hashCode();
   public void roll(int field, boolean up);
1.2 public void roll(int field, int amount);
5.0 public void setTimeZone(TimeZone zone);
// Protected Methods Overriding Calendar
   protected void computeFields();
   protected void computeTime();
}
```

Passed To javax.xml.datatype.DatatypeFactory.newXMLGregorianCalendar()

Returned By javax.xml.datatype.XMLGregorianCalendar.toGregorianCalendar()

HashMap<K,V> — Java 1.2

java.util — cloneable serializable collection

This class implements the Map interface using an internal hashtable. It supports all optional Map methods, allows key and value objects of any types, and allows null to be used as a key or a value. Because HashMap is based on a hashtable data structure, the get() and put() methods are very efficient. HashMap is much like the Hashtable class, except that the HashMap methods are not synchronized (and are therefore faster), and HashMap allows null to be used as a key or a value. If you are working in a multithreaded environment, or if compatibility with previous versions of Java is a concern, use Hashtable. Otherwise, use HashMap.

If you know in advance approximately how many mappings a HashMap will contain, you can improve efficiency by specifying *initialCapacity* when you call the HashMap() constructor. The *initialCapacity* argument times the *loadFactor* argument should be greater than the number of mappings the HashMap will contain. A good value for *loadFactor* is 0.75; this is also the default value. See Map for details on the methods of HashMap. See also TreeMap and HashSet.

Object | AbstractMap | HashMap
Map | Cloneable | Map | Serializable

```
public class HashMap<K,V> extends AbstractMap<K,V> implements Map<K,V>, Cloneable, Serializable {
// Public Constructors
   public HashMap();
   public HashMap(int initialCapacity);
   public HashMap(Map<? extends K,? extends V> m);
   public HashMap(int initialCapacity, float loadFactor);
// Methods Implementing Map
   public void clear();
   public boolean containsKey(Object key);
   public boolean containsValue(Object value);
   public Set<Map.Entry<K,V>> entrySet();
   public V get(Object key);
   public boolean isEmpty();                                          default:true
   public Set<K> keySet();
   public V put(K key, V value);
   public void putAll(Map<? extends K,? extends V> m);
   public V remove(Object key);
   public int size();
   public Collection<V> values();
// Public Methods Overriding AbstractMap
   public Object clone();
}
```

Subclasses LinkedHashMap

HashSet<E> Java 1.2

java.util cloneable serializable collection

This class implements Set using an internal hashtable. It supports all optional Set and Collection methods and allows any type of object or null to be a member of the set. Because HashSet is based on a hashtable, the basic add(), remove(), and contains() methods are all quite efficient. HashSet makes no guarantee about the order in which the set elements are enumerated by the Iterator returned by iterator(). The methods of HashSet are not synchronized. If you are using it in a multithreaded environment, you must explicitly synchronize all code that modifies the set or obtain a synchronized wrapper for it by calling Collections.synchronizedSet().

If you know in advance approximately how many mappings a HashSet will contain, you can improve efficiency by specifying *initialCapacity* when you call the HashSet() constructor. The *initialCapacity* argument times the *loadFactor* argument should be greater than the number of mappings the HashSet will contain. A good value for *loadFactor* is 0.75; this is also the default value. See Set and Collection for details on the methods of HashSet. See also TreeSet and HashMap.

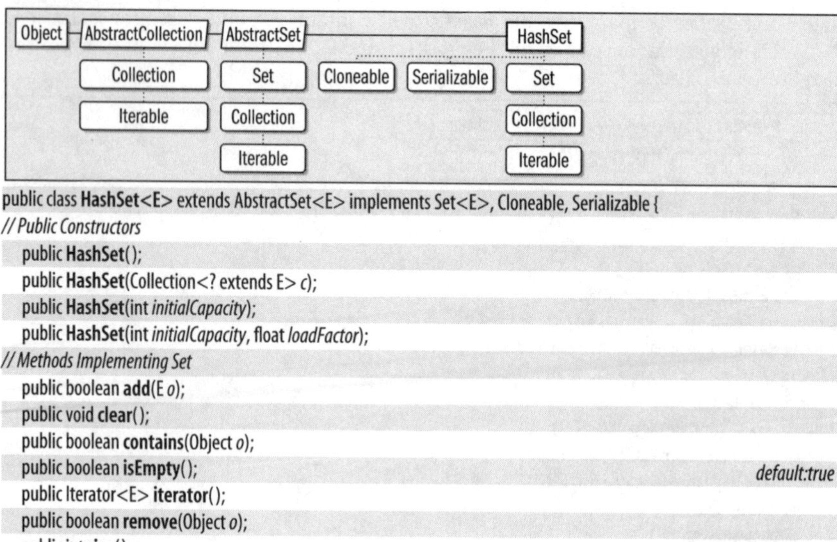


```
public class HashSet<E> extends AbstractSet<E> implements Set<E>, Cloneable, Serializable {
// Public Constructors
   public HashSet();
   public HashSet(Collection<? extends E> c);
   public HashSet(int initialCapacity);
   public HashSet(int initialCapacity, float loadFactor);
// Methods Implementing Set
   public boolean add(E o);
   public void clear();
   public boolean contains(Object o);
   public boolean isEmpty();                                              default:true
   public Iterator<E> iterator();
   public boolean remove(Object o);
   public int size();
// Public Methods Overriding Object
   public Object clone();
}
```

Subclasses LinkedHashSet

Hashtable<K,V> — Java 1.0

java.util — cloneable serializable collection

This class implements a hashtable data structure, which maps key objects to value objects and allows the efficient lookup of the value associated with a given key. In Java 1.2 and later Hashtable has been modified to impement the Map interface. The HashMap class is typically preferred over this one, although the synchronized methods of this class are useful in multi-threaded applications. (But see java.util.concurrent.ConcurrentHashMap.) In Java 5.0 this class has been made generic along with the Map interface. The type variable *K* represents the type of the hashtable keys and the type variable *V* represents the type of the hashtable values.

put() associates a value with a key in a Hashtable. get() retrieves a value for a specified key. remove() deletes a key/value association. keys() and elements() return Enumeration objects that allow you to iterate through the complete set of keys and values stored in the table. Objects used as keys in a Hashtable must have valid equals() and hashCode() methods (the versions inherited from Object are okay). null is not legal as a key or value in a Hashtable.

Object — Dictionary — Hashtable
Cloneable | Map | Serializable

```
public class Hashtable<K,V> extends Dictionary<K,V> implements Map<K,V>, Cloneable, Serializable {
// Public Constructors
   public Hashtable();
1.2 public Hashtable(Map<? extends K,? extends V> t);
   public Hashtable(int initialCapacity);
   public Hashtable(int initialCapacity, float loadFactor);
```

```
// Public Instance Methods
    public void clear();                                            Implements:Map synchronized
    public boolean contains(Object value);                                         synchronized
    public boolean containsKey(Object key);                         Implements:Map synchronized
    public V get(Object key);                                       Implements:Map synchronized
    public boolean isEmpty();                          Implements:Map synchronized default:true
    public V put(K key, V value);                                   Implements:Map synchronized
    public V remove(Object key);                                    Implements:Map synchronized
    public int size();                                              Implements:Map synchronized
// Methods Implementing Map
    public void clear();                                                           synchronized
    public boolean containsKey(Object key);                                        synchronized
1.2 public boolean containsValue(Object value);
1.2 public Set<Map.Entry<K,V>> entrySet();
1.2 public boolean equals(Object o);                                               synchronized
    public V get(Object key);                                                      synchronized
1.2 public int hashCode();                                                         synchronized
    public boolean isEmpty();                                         synchronized default:true
1.2 public Set<K> keySet();
    public V put(K key, V value);                                                  synchronized
1.2 public void putAll(Map<? extends K,? extends V> t);                            synchronized
    public V remove(Object key);                                                   synchronized
    public int size();                                                             synchronized
1.2 public Collection<V> values();
// Public Methods Overriding Dictionary
    public Enumeration<V> elements();                                              synchronized
    public Enumeration<K> keys();                                                  synchronized
// Public Methods Overriding Object
    public Object clone();                                                         synchronized
    public String toString();                                                      synchronized
// Protected Instance Methods
    protected void rehash();
}
```

Subclasses Properties

IdentityHashMap<K,V> Java 1.4

java.util cloneable serializable collection

This Map implementation has a API that is very similar to HashMap, and uses an internal hashtable, like HashMap does. However, it behaves differently from HashMap in one very important way. When testing two keys to see if they are equal, HashMap, LinkedHashMap and TreeMap use the equals() method to determine whether the two objects are indistinguishable in terms of their content or state. IdentityHashMap is different: it uses the == operator to determine whether the two key objects are identical--whether they are exactly the same object. This one difference in how key equality is tested has profound ramifications for the behavior of the Map. In most cases, the equality testing of a HashMap, LinkedHashMap or TreeMap is the appropriate behavior, and you should use one of those classes. For certain purposes, however, the identity testing of IdentityHashMap is what is required.

```
public class IdentityHashMap<K,V> extends AbstractMap<K,V> implements Map<K,V>, Serializable, Cloneable {
// Public Constructors
   public IdentityHashMap();
   public IdentityHashMap(int expectedMaxSize);
   public IdentityHashMap(Map<? extends K,? extends V> m);
// Methods Implementing Map
   public void clear();
   public boolean containsKey(Object key);
   public boolean containsValue(Object value);
   public Set<Map.Entry<K,V>> entrySet();
   public boolean equals(Object o);
   public V get(Object key);
   public int hashCode();
   public boolean isEmpty();                                    default:true
   public Set<K> keySet();
   public V put(K key, V value);
   public void putAll(Map<? extends K,? extends V> t);
   public V remove(Object key);
   public int size();
   public Collection<V> values();
// Public Methods Overriding AbstractMap
   public Object clone();
}
```

IllegalFormatCodePointException — Java 5.0

java.util — serializable unchecked

An IllegalFormatException of this type is thrown by a Formatter when an int used to represent a Unicode character is out of range.

Throwable — Exception — RuntimeException — IllegalArgumentException — IllegalFormatException — IllegalFormatCodePointException
Serializable

```
public class IllegalFormatCodePointException extends IllegalFormatException {
// Public Constructors
   public IllegalFormatCodePointException(int c);
// Public Instance Methods
   public int getCodePoint();
// Public Methods Overriding Throwable
   public String getMessage();
}
```

IllegalFormatConversionException — Java 5.0

java.util — serializable unchecked

An IllegalFormatException of this type is thrown by a Formatter when the type of the format() or printf() argument does not match the type required by the corresponding conversion specifier in the format string.

Throwable — Exception — RuntimeException — IllegalArgumentException — IllegalFormatException — IllegalFormatConversionException
Serializable

```
public class IllegalFormatConversionException extends IllegalFormatException {
// Public Constructors
    public IllegalFormatConversionException(char c, Class<?> arg);
// Public Instance Methods
    public Class<?> getArgumentClass();
    public char getConversion();
// Public Methods Overriding Throwable
    public String getMessage();
}
```

IllegalFormatException — Java 5.0

java.util — serializable unchecked

An exception of this type is thrown by a Formatter when there is problem with the format string. This package defines many subclasses of this exception type to describe particular format string problems.

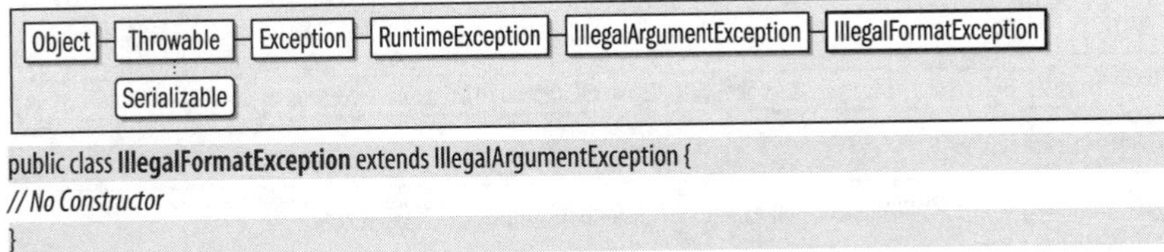


```
public class IllegalFormatException extends IllegalArgumentException {
// No Constructor
}
```

Subclasses DuplicateFormatFlagsException, FormatFlagsConversionMismatchException, IllegalFormatCodePointException, IllegalFormatConversionException, IllegalFormatFlagsException, IllegalFormatPrecisionException, IllegalFormatWidthException, MissingFormatArgumentException, MissingFormatWidthException, UnknownFormatConversionException, UnknownFormatFlagsException

IllegalFormatFlagsException — Java 5.0

java.util — serializable unchecked

An IllegalFormatException of this type is thrown by a Formatter when a format string contains an illegal combination of flags.

Throwable — Exception — RuntimeException — IllegalArgumentException — IllegalFormatException — IllegalFormatFlagsException
Serializable

```
public class IllegalFormatFlagsException extends IllegalFormatException {
// Public Constructors
    public IllegalFormatFlagsException(String f);
// Public Instance Methods
    public String getFlags();
// Public Methods Overriding Throwable
    public String getMessage();
}
```

IllegalFormatPrecisionException — Java 5.0

java.util — serializable unchecked

An IllegalFormatException of this type is thrown by a Formatter when the precision of a format string is illegal.

Throwable — Exception — RuntimeException — IllegalArgumentException — IllegalFormatException — IllegalFormatPrecisionException
Serializable

```
public class IllegalFormatPrecisionException extends IllegalFormatException {
// Public Constructors
    public IllegalFormatPrecisionException(int p);
// Public Instance Methods
    public int getPrecision();
// Public Methods Overriding Throwable
    public String getMessage();
}
```

IllegalFormatWidthException

Java 5.0

java.util

serializable unchecked

An IllegalFormatException of this type is thrown by a Formatter when the width of a format string is illegal.

Throwable — Exception — RuntimeException — IllegalArgumentException — IllegalFormatException — IllegalFormatWidthException
Serializable

```
public class IllegalFormatWidthException extends IllegalFormatException {
// Public Constructors
    public IllegalFormatWidthException(int w);
// Public Instance Methods
    public int getWidth();
// Public Methods Overriding Throwable
    public String getMessage();
}
```

InputMismatchException

Java 5.0

java.util

serializable unchecked

An exception of this type is thrown by a Scanner that is not of the expected type or is out of range. Note that the Scanner implements the Iterator interface, and this exception is a subclass of NoSuchElementException, which is thrown by Iterator.next() when no more elements are available.

Object — Throwable — Exception — RuntimeException — NoSuchElementException — InputMismatchException
Serializable

```
public class InputMismatchException extends NoSuchElementException {
// Public Constructors
    public InputMismatchException();
    public InputMismatchException(String s);
}
```

InvalidPropertiesFormatException

Java 5.0

java.util

serializable checked

An exception of this type is thrown by Properties.loadFromXML() if the specified input stream does not contain appropriate XML.

Object — Throwable — Exception — IOException — InvalidPropertiesFormatException
Serializable

```
public class InvalidPropertiesFormatException extends java.io.IOException {
// Public Constructors
    public InvalidPropertiesFormatException(String message);
    public InvalidPropertiesFormatException(Throwable cause);
}
```

Thrown By Properties.loadFromXML()

Iterator<E> Java 1.2

java.util

This interface defines methods for iterating, or enumerating, the elements of a collection. It has been made generic in Java 5.0 and the type variable *E* represents the type of the elements in the collection. The hasNext() method returns true if there are more elements to be enumerated or false if all elements have already been returned. The next() method returns the next element. These two methods make it easy to loop through an iterator with code such as the following:

```
for(Iterator i = c.iterator(); i.hasNext(); )
  processObject(i.next());
```

In Java 5.0, collections and other classes that can return an Iterator implement the java.lang.Iterable interface, which allows them to be iterated much more simply with the for/in looping statement.

The Iterator interface is much like the Enumeration interface. In Java 1.2, Iterator is preferred over Enumeration because it provides a well-defined way to safely remove elements from a collection while the iteration is in progress. The remove() method removes the object most recently returned by next() from the collection that is being iterated through. Note, however, that support for remove() is optional; if an Iterator does not support remove(), it throws a java.lang.UnsupportedOperationException when you call it. While you are iterating through a collection, you are allowed to modify the collection only by calling the remove() method of the Iterator. If the collection is modified in any other way while an iteration is ongoing, the Iterator may fail to operate correctly, or it may throw a ConcurrentModificationException.

```
public interface Iterator<E> {
// Public Instance Methods
    boolean hasNext();
    E next();
    void remove();
}
```

Implementations ListIterator, Scanner

Returned By Too many methods to list.

LinkedHashMap<K,V> Java 1.4

java.util cloneable serializable collection

This class is a Map implementation based on a hashtable, just like its superclass HashMap. It defines no new public methods, and can be used exactly as HashMap is used. What is unique about this Map is that in addition to the hashtable data structure, it also uses a doubly-linked list to connect the keys of the **Map** into an internal list which defines a predictable iteration order.

You can iterate through the keys or values of a **LinkedHashMap** by calling **entrySet()**, **keySet()**, or **values()** and then obtaining an **Iterator** for the returned collection, just as you would for a **HashMap**. When you do this, however, the keys and/or values are returned in a well-defined order rather than the essentially random order provided by a **HashMap**. The default ordering for **LinkedHashMap** is the insertion order of the key: the first key inserted into the **Map** is enumerated first (as is the value associated with it), and the last entry inserted is enumerated last. Note that this order is not affect by re-insertions. That is, if a **LinkedHashMap** contains a mapping from a key *k* to a value *v1*, and you call the **put()** method to map from *k* to a new value *v2*, this does not change the insertion order, or the iteration order of the key *k*. The iteration order of a value in the map is the iteration order of the key with which it is associated.

Insertion order is the default iteration order for this class, but if you instantiate a **LinkedHashMap** with the three-argument constructor, and pass **true** for the third argument, then the iteration order will be based on access order: the first key returned by an iterator is the one that was least-recently used in a **get()** or **put()** operation. The last key returned is the one that has been most-recently used. As with insertion order, the **values()** collection is iterated in the order defined by the keys with which those values are associated.

"Access ordering" is particularly useful for implementing "LRU" caches from which the Least-Recently Used elements are periodically purged. To facilitate this use, **LinkedHashMap** defines the protected **removeEldestEntry()** method. Each time the **put()** method is called (or for each mapping added by **putAll()**) the **LinkedHashMap** calls **removeEldestEntry()** and passes the least-recently used (or first inserted if insertion order is being used) **Map.Entry** object. If the method returns **true**, then that entry will be removed from the map. In **LinkedHashMap**, **removeEldestEntry()** always returns **false**, and old entries are never automatically removed, but you can override this behavior in a subclass. The decision to remove an old entry might be based on the content of the entry itself, or might more simply be based on the **size()** of the **LinkedHashMap**. Note that **removeEldestEntry()** need simply return **true** or **false**; it should not remove the entry itself.

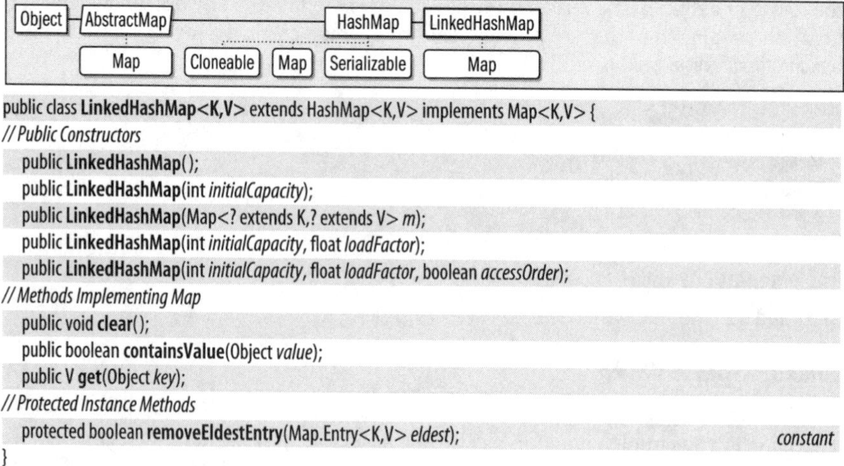


```
public class LinkedHashMap<K,V> extends HashMap<K,V> implements Map<K,V> {
// Public Constructors
   public LinkedHashMap();
   public LinkedHashMap(int initialCapacity);
   public LinkedHashMap(Map<? extends K,? extends V> m);
   public LinkedHashMap(int initialCapacity, float loadFactor);
   public LinkedHashMap(int initialCapacity, float loadFactor, boolean accessOrder);
// Methods Implementing Map
   public void clear();
   public boolean containsValue(Object value);
   public V get(Object key);
// Protected Instance Methods
   protected boolean removeEldestEntry(Map.Entry<K,V> eldest);                    constant
}
```

LinkedHashSet<E> Java 1.4

java.util cloneable serializable collection

This subclass of HashSet is a Set implementation based on a hashtable. It defines no new methods and is used just like a HashSet is used. What is unique about a LinkedHashSet is that in addition to the hashtable data structure, it also uses a doubly-linked list to connect the elements of the set into an internal list in the order in which they were inserted. This means that the Iterator returned by the inherited iterator() method always enumerates the elements of the set in the order which they were inserted. By contrast, the elements of a HashSet are enumerated in an order that is essentially random. Note that the iteration order is not affected by reinsertion of set elements. That is, if you attempt to add an element that already exists in the set, the iteration order of the set is not modified. If you delete an element and then reinsert it, the insertion order, and therefore the iteration order, does change.

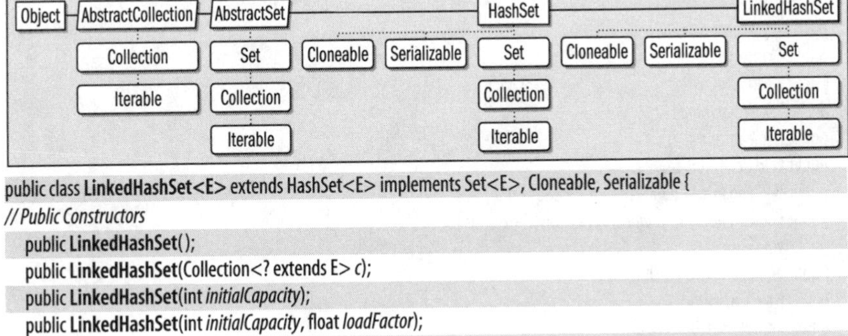


```
public class LinkedHashSet<E> extends HashSet<E> implements Set<E>, Cloneable, Serializable {
// Public Constructors
    public LinkedHashSet();
    public LinkedHashSet(Collection<? extends E> c);
    public LinkedHashSet(int initialCapacity);
    public LinkedHashSet(int initialCapacity, float loadFactor);
}
```

LinkedList<E> Java 1.2

java.util cloneable serializable collection

This class implements the List interface in terms of a doubly linked list. In Java 5.0, it also implements the Queue interface and uses its list as a first-in, first-out (FIFO) queue. LinkedList is a generic type, and the type variable *E* represents the type of the elements of the list. LinkedList supports all optional methods of List, Queue and Collection and allows list elements of any type, including null (in this it differs from most Queue implementations, which prohibit null elements).

Because LinkedList is implemented with a linked list data structure, the get() and set() methods are substantially less efficient than the same methods for an ArrayList. However, a LinkedList may be more efficient when the add() and remove() methods are used frequently. The methods of LinkedList are not synchronized. If you are using a LinkedList in a multithreaded environment, you must explicitly synchronize any code that modifies the list or obtain a synchronized wrapper object with Collections.synchronizedList().

In addition to the methods defined by the List interface, LinkedList defines methods to get the first and last elements of the list, to add an element to the beginning or end of the list, and to remove the first or last element of the list. These convenient and efficient methods make LinkedList well-suited for use as a stack or queue. See List and Collection for details on the methods of LinkedList. See also ArrayList.

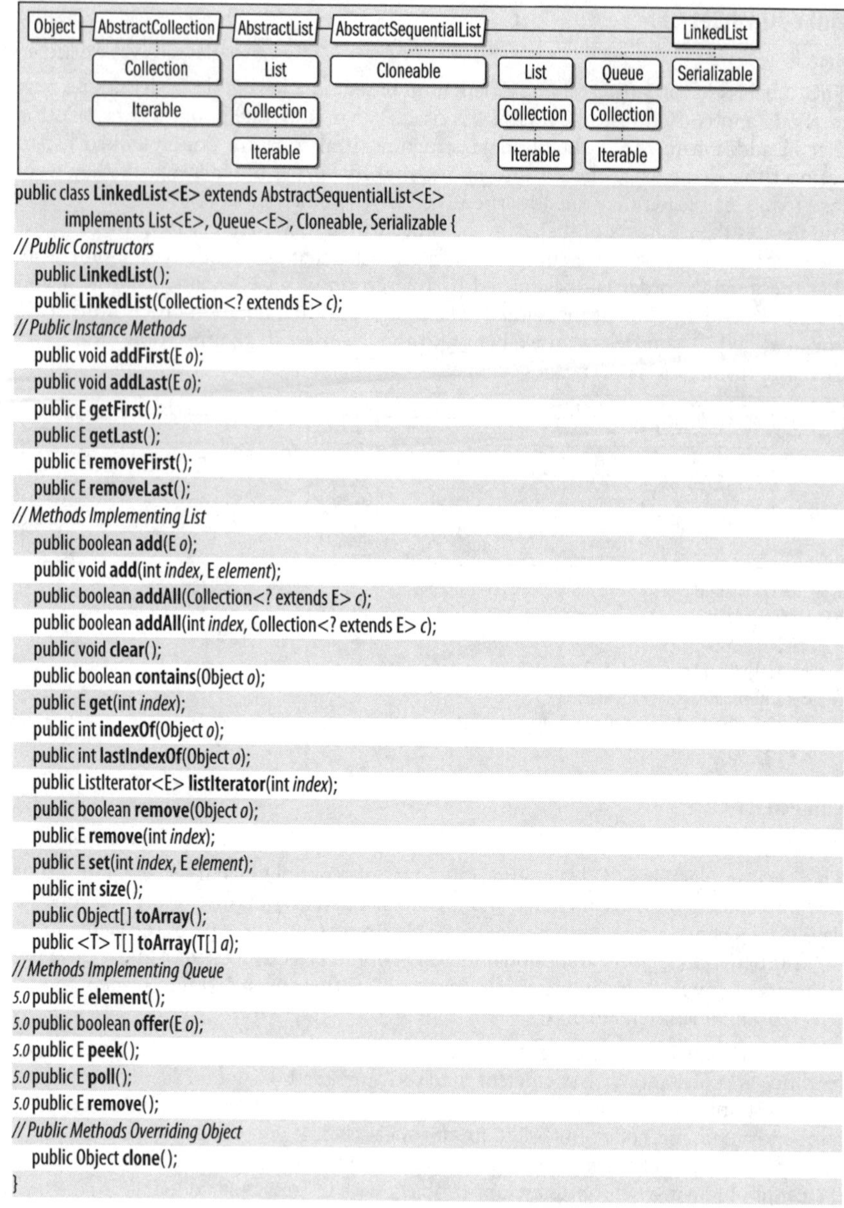


```
public class LinkedList<E> extends AbstractSequentialList<E>
        implements List<E>, Queue<E>, Cloneable, Serializable {
// Public Constructors
    public LinkedList();
    public LinkedList(Collection<? extends E> c);
// Public Instance Methods
    public void addFirst(E o);
    public void addLast(E o);
    public E getFirst();
    public E getLast();
    public E removeFirst();
    public E removeLast();
// Methods Implementing List
    public boolean add(E o);
    public void add(int index, E element);
    public boolean addAll(Collection<? extends E> c);
    public boolean addAll(int index, Collection<? extends E> c);
    public void clear();
    public boolean contains(Object o);
    public E get(int index);
    public int indexOf(Object o);
    public int lastIndexOf(Object o);
    public ListIterator<E> listIterator(int index);
    public boolean remove(Object o);
    public E remove(int index);
    public E set(int index, E element);
    public int size();
    public Object[] toArray();
    public <T> T[] toArray(T[] a);
// Methods Implementing Queue
5.0 public E element();
5.0 public boolean offer(E o);
5.0 public E peek();
5.0 public E poll();
5.0 public E remove();
// Public Methods Overriding Object
    public Object clone();
}
```

List<E> **Java 1.2**

java.util — collection

This interface represents an ordered collection of objects. In Java 5.0 List is a generic interface and the type variable *E* represents the type of the objects in the list. Each element in a List has an index, or position, in the list, and elements can be inserted, queried, and removed by index. The first element of a List has an index of 0. The last element in a list has index size()-1.

In addition to the methods defined by the superinterface, Collection, List defines a number of methods for working with its indexed elements. get() and set() query and set the object at a particular index, respectively. Versions of add() and addAll() that take an *index* argument insert an object or Collection of objects at a specified index. The versions of add() and addAll() that do not take an *index* argument insert an object or collection of objects at the end of the list. List defines a version of remove() that removes the object at a specified index.

The iterator() method is just like the iterator() method of Collection, except that the Iterator it returns is guaranteed to enumerate the elements of the List in order. listIterator() returns a ListIterator object, which is more powerful than a regular Iterator and allows the list to be modified while iteration proceeds. listIterator() can take an index argument to specify where in the list iteration should begin.

indexOf() and lastIndexOf() perform linear searches from the beginning and end, respectively, of the list, searching for a specified object. Each method returns the index of the first matching object it finds, or –1 if it does not find a match. Finally, subList() returns a List that contains only a specified contiguous range of list elements. The returned list is simply a view into the original list, so changes in the original List are visible in the returned List. This subList() method is particularly useful if you want to sort, search, clear(), or otherwise manipulate only a partial range of a larger list.

An interface cannot specify constructors, but it is conventional that all implementations of List provide at least two standard constructors: one that takes no arguments and creates an empty list, and a copy constructor that accepts an arbitrary Collection object that specifies the initial contents of the new List.

As with Collection, List methods that change the contents of the list are optional, and implementations that do not support them simply throw java.lang.UnsupportedOperationException. Different implementations of List may have significantly different efficiency characteristics. For example, the get() and set() methods of an ArrayList are much more efficient than those of a LinkedList. On the other hand, the add() and remove() methods of a LinkedList can be more efficient than those of an ArrayList. See also Collection, Set, Map, ArrayList, and LinkedList.

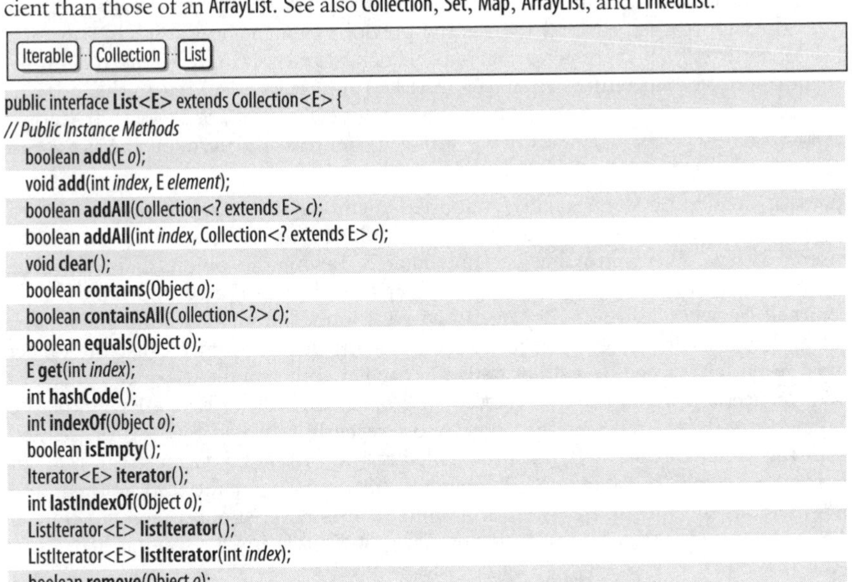

Iterable ··· Collection ··· List

```
public interface List<E> extends Collection<E> {
// Public Instance Methods
   boolean add(E o);
   void add(int index, E element);
   boolean addAll(Collection<? extends E> c);
   boolean addAll(int index, Collection<? extends E> c);
   void clear();
   boolean contains(Object o);
   boolean containsAll(Collection<?> c);
   boolean equals(Object o);
   E get(int index);
   int hashCode();
   int indexOf(Object o);
   boolean isEmpty();
   Iterator<E> iterator();
   int lastIndexOf(Object o);
   ListIterator<E> listIterator();
   ListIterator<E> listIterator(int index);
   boolean remove(Object o);
```

```
    E remove(int index);
    boolean removeAll(Collection<?> c);
    boolean retainAll(Collection<?> c);
    E set(int index, E element);
    int size();
    List<E> subList(int fromIndex, int toIndex);
    Object[] toArray();
    <T> T[] toArray(T[] a);
}
```

Implementations AbstractList, ArrayList, LinkedList, Vector, java.util.concurrent.CopyOnWriteArrayList

Passed To Too many methods to list.

Returned By Too many methods to list.

Type Of Collections.EMPTY_LIST

ListIterator<E> Java 1.2

java.util

This interface is an extension of Iterator for use with ordered collections, or lists. It defines methods to iterate forward and backward through a list, to determine the list index of the elements being iterated, and, for mutable lists, to safely insert, delete, and edit elements in the list while the iteration is in progress. For some lists, notably LinkedList, using an iterator to enumerate the list's elements may be substantially more efficient than looping through the list by index and calling get() repeatedly.

Like the Iterator interface, ListIterator has been made generic in Java 5.0. The type variable *E* represents the type of the elements on the list.

hasNext() and next() are the most commonly used methods of ListIterator; they iterate forward through the list. See Iterator for details. In addition to these two methods, however, ListIterator also defines hasPrevious() and previous() that allow you to iterate backward through the list. previous() returns the previous element on the list or throws a NoSuchElementException if there is no previous element. hasPrevious() returns true if a subsequent call to previous() returns an object. nextIndex() and previousIndex() return the index of the object that would be returned by a subsequent call to next() or previous(). If next() or previous() throw a NoSuchElementException, nextIndex() returns the size of the list, and previousIndex() returns –1.

ListIterator defines three optionally supported methods that provide a safe way to modify the contents of the underlying list while the iteration is in progress. add() inserts a new object into the list, immediately before the object that would be returned by a subsequent call to next(). Calling add() does not affect the value that is returned by next(), however. If you call previous() immediately after calling add(), the method returns the object you just added. remove() deletes from the list the object most recently returned by next() or previous(). You can only call remove() once per call to next() or previous(). If you have called add(), you must call next() or previous() again before calling remove(). set() replaces the object most recently returned by next() or previous() with the specified object. If you have called add() or remove(), you must call next() or previous() again before calling set(). Remember that support for the add(), remove(), and set() methods is optional. Iterators for immutable lists never support them, of course. An unsupported method throws a java.lang.UnsupportedOperationException when called. Also, when an iterator is in use, all modifications should be made through the iterator rather than to the list itself. If the underlying list is modified while an iteration is ongoing, the ListIterator may fail to operate correctly or may throw a ConcurrentModificationException.

Iterator ·· ListIterator

```
public interface ListIterator<E> extends Iterator<E> {
// Public Instance Methods
   void add(E o);
   boolean hasNext();
   boolean hasPrevious();
   E next();
   int nextIndex();
   E previous();
   int previousIndex();
   void remove();
   void set(E o);
}
```

Returned By AbstractList.listIterator(), AbstractSequentialList.listIterator(), LinkedList.listIterator(), List.listIterator(), java.util.concurrent.CopyOnWriteArrayList.listIterator()

ListResourceBundle **Java 1.1**

java.util

This abstract class provides a simple way to define a ResourceBundle. You may find it easier to subclass ListResourceBundle than to subclass ResourceBundle directly. ListResourceBundle provides implementations for the abstract handleGetObject() and getKeys() methods defined by ResourceBundle and adds its own abstract getContents() method a subclass must override. getContents() returns an Object[][]—an array of arrays of objects. This array can have any number of elements. Each element of this array must itself be an array with two elements: the first element of each subarray should be a String that specifies the name of a resource, and the corresponding second element should be the value of that resource; this value can be an Object of any desired type. See also ResourceBundle and PropertyResourceBundle.

Object — ResourceBundle — ListResourceBundle

```
public abstract class ListResourceBundle extends ResourceBundle {
// Public Constructors
   public ListResourceBundle();
// Public Methods Overriding ResourceBundle
   public Enumeration<String> getKeys();
   public final Object handleGetObject(String key);
// Protected Instance Methods
   protected abstract Object[][] getContents();
}
```

Locale **Java 1.1**

java.util cloneable serializable

The Locale class represents a locale: a political, geographical, or cultural region that typically has a distinct language and distinct customs and conventions for such things as formatting dates, times, and numbers. The Locale class defines a number of constants that represent commonly used locales. **Locale** also defines a static **getDefault()** method that returns the default **Locale** object, which represents a locale value inherited from the host system. **getAvailableLocales()** returns the list of all locales supported by the underlying system. If none of these methods for obtaining a **Locale** object are suitable, you can explicitly create your own **Locale** object. To do this, you must specify a language code and optionally a country code and variant string. **getISOCountries()** and **getISOLanguages()** return the list of supported country codes and language codes.

The **Locale** class does not implement any internationalization behavior itself; it merely serves as a locale identifier for those classes that can localize their behavior. Given a **Locale** object, you can invoke the various **getDisplay** methods to obtain a description of the locale suitable for display to a user. These methods may themselves take a **Locale** argument, so the names of languages and countries can be localized as appropriate.

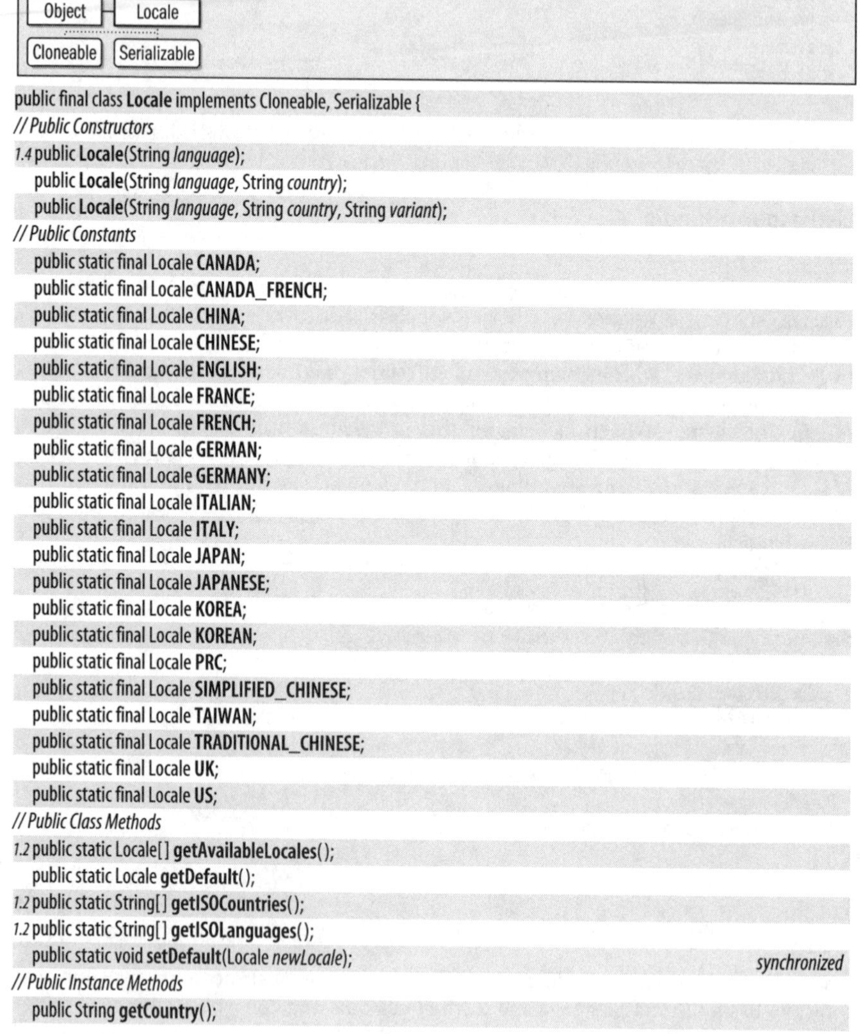


```
public final class Locale implements Cloneable, Serializable {
// Public Constructors
1.4 public Locale(String language);
    public Locale(String language, String country);
    public Locale(String language, String country, String variant);
// Public Constants
    public static final Locale CANADA;
    public static final Locale CANADA_FRENCH;
    public static final Locale CHINA;
    public static final Locale CHINESE;
    public static final Locale ENGLISH;
    public static final Locale FRANCE;
    public static final Locale FRENCH;
    public static final Locale GERMAN;
    public static final Locale GERMANY;
    public static final Locale ITALIAN;
    public static final Locale ITALY;
    public static final Locale JAPAN;
    public static final Locale JAPANESE;
    public static final Locale KOREA;
    public static final Locale KOREAN;
    public static final Locale PRC;
    public static final Locale SIMPLIFIED_CHINESE;
    public static final Locale TAIWAN;
    public static final Locale TRADITIONAL_CHINESE;
    public static final Locale UK;
    public static final Locale US;
// Public Class Methods
1.2 public static Locale[] getAvailableLocales();
    public static Locale getDefault();
1.2 public static String[] getISOCountries();
1.2 public static String[] getISOLanguages();
    public static void setDefault(Locale newLocale);                synchronized
// Public Instance Methods
    public String getCountry();
```

```
    public final String getDisplayCountry();
    public String getDisplayCountry(Locale inLocale);
    public final String getDisplayLanguage();
    public String getDisplayLanguage(Locale inLocale);
    public final String getDisplayName();
    public String getDisplayName(Locale inLocale);
    public final String getDisplayVariant();
    public String getDisplayVariant(Locale inLocale);
    public String getISO3Country() throws MissingResourceException;
    public String getISO3Language() throws MissingResourceException;
    public String getLanguage();
    public String getVariant();
// Public Methods Overriding Object
    public Object clone();
    public boolean equals(Object obj);
    public int hashCode();
    public final String toString();
}
```

Passed To Too many methods to list.

Returned By java.text.BreakIterator.getAvailableLocales(), java.text.Collator.getAvailableLocales(), java.text.DateFormat.getAvailableLocales(), java.text.MessageFormat.getLocale(), java.text.NumberFormat.getAvailableLocales(), Calendar.getAvailableLocales(), java.util.Formatter.locale(), ResourceBundle.getLocale(), Scanner.locale(), javax.security.auth.callback.LanguageCallback.getLocale()

Map<K,V> Java 1.2

java.util collection

This interface represents a collection of mappings, or associations, between key objects and value objects. Hashtables and associative arrays are examples of maps. In Java 5.0 this interface has been made generic. The type variable *K* represents the type of the keys held by the map and the type variable *V* represents the type of the values associated with those keys.

The set of key objects in a Map must not have any duplicates; the collection of value objects is under no such constraint. The key objects should usually be immutable objects, or, if they are not, care should be taken that they do not change while in use in a Map. As of Java 1.2, the Map interface replaces the abstract Dictionary class. Although a Map is not a Collection, the Map interface is still considered an integral part, along with Set, List, and others, of the Java collections framework.

You can add a key/value association to a Map with the put() method. Use putAll() to copy all mappings from one Map to another. Call get() to look up the value object associated with a specified key object. Use remove() to delete the mapping between a specified key and its value, or use clear() to delete all mappings from a Map. size() returns the number of mappings in a Map, and isEmpty() tests whether the Map contains no mappings. containsKey() tests whether a Map contains the specified key object, and containsValue() tests whether it contains the specified value. (For most implementations, containsValue() is a much more expensive operation than containsKey(), however.) keySet() returns a Set of all key objects in the Map. values() returns a Collection (not a Set, since it may contain duplicates) of all value objects in the map. entrySet() returns a Set of all mappings in a Map. The elements of this returned Set are Map.Entry objects. The collections returned by values(), keySet(), and entrySet() are based on the Map itself, so changes to the Map are reflected in the collections.

An interface cannot specify constructors, but it is conventional that all implementations of Map provide at least two standard constructors: one that takes no arguments and creates an empty map, and a copy constructor that accepts a Map object that specifies the initial contents of the new Map.

Implementations are required to support all methods that query the contents of a Map, but support for methods that modify the contents of a Map is optional. If an implementation does not support a particular method, the implementation of that method simply throws a java.lang.UnsupportedOperationException. See also Collection, Set, List, HashMap, Hashtable, WeakHashMap, SortedMap, and TreeMap.

```
public interface Map<K,V> {
// Nested Types
   public interface Entry<K,V>;
// Public Instance Methods
   void clear();
   boolean containsKey(Object key);
   boolean containsValue(Object value);
   Set<Map.Entry<K,V>> entrySet();
   boolean equals(Object o);
   V get(Object key);
   int hashCode();
   boolean isEmpty();
   Set<K> keySet();
   V put(K key, V value);
   void putAll(Map<? extends K,? extends V> t);
   V remove(Object key);
   int size();
   Collection<V> values();
}
```

Implementations AbstractMap, HashMap, Hashtable, IdentityHashMap, LinkedHashMap, SortedMap, WeakHashMap, java.util.concurrent.ConcurrentMap, java.util.jar.Attributes

Passed To Too many methods to list.

Returned By Too many methods to list.

Type Of Collections.EMPTY_MAP, java.util.jar.Attributes.map

Map.Entry<K,V> Java 1.2

java.util

This interface represents a single mapping, or association, between a key object and a value object in a Map. Like Map itself, Map.Entry has been made generic in Java 5.0 and defines the same type variables that Map does.

The entrySet() method of a Map returns a Set of Map.Entry objects that represent the set of mappings in the map. Use the iterator() method of that Set to enumerate these Map.Entry objects. Use getKey() and getValue() to obtain the key and value objects for the entry. Use the optionally supported setValue() method to change the value of an entry. This method throws a java.lang.UnsupportedOperationException if it is not supported by the implementation.

```
public interface Map.Entry<K,V> {
// Public Instance Methods
   boolean equals(Object o);
   K getKey();
   V getValue();
```

```
    int hashCode();
    V setValue(V value);
}
```

Passed To LinkedHashMap.removeEldestEntry()

MissingFormatArgumentException — Java 5.0

java.util — serializable unchecked

An IllegalFormatException of this type is thrown by a Formatter when a format() or printf() method does not have enough arguments to match the number conversion specifiers in the format string.

Throwable → Exception → RuntimeException → IllegalArgumentException → IllegalFormatException → MissingFormatArgumentException; Throwable implements Serializable

```
public class MissingFormatArgumentException extends IllegalFormatException {
// Public Constructors
    public MissingFormatArgumentException(String s);
// Public Instance Methods
    public String getFormatSpecifier();
// Public Methods Overriding Throwable
    public String getMessage();
}
```

MissingFormatWidthException — Java 5.0

java.util — serializable unchecked

An IllegalFormatException of this type is thrown by a Formatter when a format conversion requires a field width, but the width is omitted.

Throwable → Exception → RuntimeException → IllegalArgumentException → IllegalFormatException → MissingFormatWidthException; Throwable implements Serializable

```
public class MissingFormatWidthException extends IllegalFormatException {
// Public Constructors
    public MissingFormatWidthException(String s);
// Public Instance Methods
    public String getFormatSpecifier();
// Public Methods Overriding Throwable
    public String getMessage();
}
```

MissingResourceException — Java 1.1

java.util — serializable unchecked

Signals that no ResourceBundle can be located for the desired locale or that a named resource cannot be found within a given ResourceBundle. getClassName() returns the name of the ResourceBundle class in question, and getKey() returns the name of the resource that cannot be located.

Object → Throwable → Exception → RuntimeException → MissingResourceException; Throwable implements Serializable

```
public class MissingResourceException extends RuntimeException {
// Public Constructors
   public MissingResourceException(String s, String className, String key);
// Public Instance Methods
   public String getClassName();
   public String getKey();
}
```

Thrown By Locale.{getISO3Country(), getISO3Language()}

NoSuchElementException

Java 1.0

java.util

serializable unchecked

Signals that there are no elements in an object (such as a Vector) or that there are no more elements in an object (such as an Enumeration).

Object → Throwable → Exception → RuntimeException → NoSuchElementException; Throwable implements Serializable

```
public class NoSuchElementException extends RuntimeException {
// Public Constructors
   public NoSuchElementException();
   public NoSuchElementException(String s);
}
```

Subclasses InputMismatchException

Observable

Java 1.0

java.util

This class is the superclass for classes that want to provide notifications of state changes to interested Observer objects. Register an Observer to be notified by passing it to the addObserver() method of an Observable, and de-register it by passing it to the deleteObserver() method. You can delete all observers registered for an Observable with deleteObservers(), and can find out how many observers have been added with countObservers(). Note that there is not a method to enumerate the particular Observer objects that have been added.

An Observable subclass should call the protected method setChanged() when its state has changed in some way. This sets a "state changed" flag. After an operation or series of operations that may have caused the state to change, the Observable subclass should call notifyObservers(), optionally passing an arbitrary Object argument. If the state changed flag is set, this notifyObservers() calls the update() method of each registered Observer (in some arbitrary order), passing the Observable object, and the optional argument, if any. Once the update() method of each Observable has been called, notifyObservers() calls clearChanged() to clear the state changed flag. If notifyObservers() is called when the state changed flag is not set, it does not do anything. You can use hasChanged() to query the current state of the changed flag.

The Observable class and Observer interface are not commonly used. Most applications prefer the event-based notification model defined by the JavaBeans component framework and by the EventObject class and EventListener interface of this package.

```
public class Observable {
// Public Constructors
   public Observable();
```

```
// Public Instance Methods
    public void addObserver(Observer o);                       synchronized
    public int countObservers();                               synchronized
    public void deleteObserver(Observer o);                    synchronized
    public void deleteObservers();                             synchronized
    public boolean hasChanged();                               synchronized
    public void notifyObservers();
    public void notifyObservers(Object arg);
// Protected Instance Methods
    protected void clearChanged();                             synchronized
    protected void setChanged();                               synchronized
}
```

Passed To Observer.update()

Observer Java 1.0

java.util

This interface defines the update() method required for an object to observe subclasses of Observable. An Observer registers interest in an Observable object by calling the addObserver() method of Observable. Observer objects that have been registered in this way have their update() methods invoked by the Observable when that object has changed.

This interface is conceptually similar to, but less commonly used than, the EventListener interface and its various event-specific subinterfaces.

```
public interface Observer {
// Public Instance Methods
    void update(Observable o, Object arg);
}
```

Passed To Observable.{addObserver(), deleteObserver()}

PriorityQueue<E> Java 5.0

java.util serializable collection

This class is a Queue implementation that orders its elements according to a specified Comparator or orders Comparable elements according to their compareTo() methods. The head of the queue (the element removed by remove() and poll()) is the smallest element on the queue according to this ordering. The Iterator return by the iterator() method is not guaranteed to iterate the elements in their sorted order.

PriorityQueue is unbounded and prohibits null elements. It is not threadsafe.

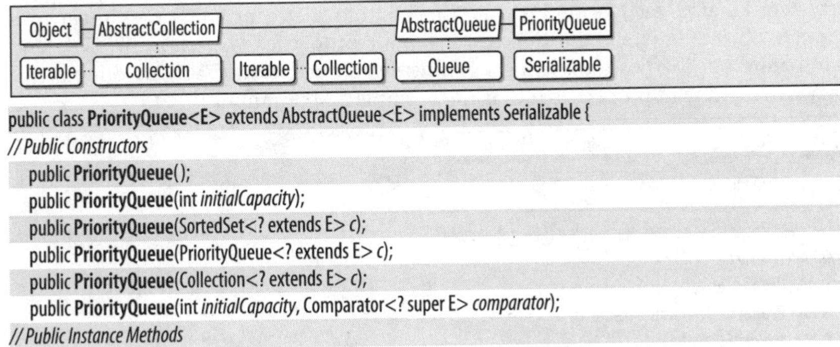


```
public class PriorityQueue<E> extends AbstractQueue<E> implements Serializable {
// Public Constructors
    public PriorityQueue();
    public PriorityQueue(int initialCapacity);
    public PriorityQueue(SortedSet<? extends E> c);
    public PriorityQueue(PriorityQueue<? extends E> c);
    public PriorityQueue(Collection<? extends E> c);
    public PriorityQueue(int initialCapacity, Comparator<? super E> comparator);
// Public Instance Methods
```

java.util.*

```
    public Comparator<? super E> comparator();
// Methods Implementing Collection
    public Iterator<E> iterator();
    public boolean remove(Object o);
    public int size();
// Methods Implementing Queue
    public boolean offer(E o);
    public E peek();
    public E poll();
// Public Methods Overriding AbstractQueue
    public boolean add(E o);
    public void clear();
}
```

Properties

Java 1.0

java.util — cloneable serializable collection

This class is an extension of Hashtable that allows key/value pairs to be read from and written to a stream. The Properties class implements the system properties list, which supports user customization by allowing programs to look up the values of named resources. Because the load() and store() methods provide an easy way to read and write properties from and to a text stream, this class provides a convenient way to implement an application configuration file.

When you create a Properties object, you may specify another Properties object that contains default values. Keys (property names) and values are associated in a Properties object with the Hashtable method put(). Values are looked up with getProperty(); if this method does not find the key in the current Properties object, it looks in the default Properties object that was passed to the constructor method. A default value can also be specified, in case the key is not found at all. Use setProperty() to add a property name/value pair to the Properties object. This Java 1.2 method is preferred over the inherited put() method because it enforces the constraint that property names and values be strings.

propertyNames() returns an enumeration of all property names (keys) stored in the Properties object and (recursively) all property names stored in the default Properties object associated with it. list() prints the properties stored in a Properties object, which can be useful for debugging. store() writes a Properties object to a stream, writing one property per line, in name=value format. As of Java 1.2, store() is preferred over the deprecated save() method, which writes properties in the same way but suppresses any I/O exceptions that may be thrown in the process. The second argument to both store() and save() is a comment that is written out at the beginning of the property file. Finally, load() reads key/value pairs from a stream and stores them in a Properties object. It is suitable for reading both properties written with store() and hand-edited properties files. In Java 5.0, storeToXML() and loadFromXML() are alternatives that write and read properties files using a simple XML grammar.

Object — Dictionary — Hashtable — Properties
Cloneable, Map, Serializable

```
public class Properties extends Hashtable<Object,Object> {
// Public Constructors
    public Properties();
    public Properties(Properties defaults);
// Public Instance Methods
```

```
    public String getProperty(String key);
    public String getProperty(String key, String defaultValue);
1.1 public void list(java.io.PrintWriter out);
    public void list(java.io.PrintStream out);
    public void load(java.io.InputStream inStream) throws java.io.IOException;          synchronized
5.0 public void loadFromXML(java.io.InputStream in)                                      synchronized
        throws java.io.IOException, InvalidPropertiesFormatException;
    public Enumeration<?> propertyNames();
1.2 public Object setProperty(String key, String value);                                  synchronized
1.2 public void store(java.io.OutputStream out, String comments) throws java.io.IOException;   synchronized
5.0 public void storeToXML(java.io.OutputStream os, String comment) throws java.io.IOException;  synchronized
5.0 public void storeToXML(java.io.OutputStream os, String comment, String encoding)     synchronized
        throws java.io.IOException;
// Protected Instance Fields
    protected Properties defaults;
// Deprecated Public Methods
#   public void save(java.io.OutputStream out, String comments);                         synchronized
}
```

Subclasses java.security.Provider

Passed To System.setProperties(), javax.xml.transform.Transformer.setOutputProperties()

Returned By System.getProperties(), javax.xml.transform.Templates.getOutputProperties(), javax.xml.transform.Transformer.getOutputProperties()

PropertyPermission — Java 1.2

java.util — serializable permission

This class is a java.security.Permission that governs read and write access to system properties with System.getProperty() and System.setProperty(). A PropertyPermission object has a name, or target, and a comma-separated list of actions. The name of the permission is the name of the property of interest. The action string can be "read" for getProperty() access, "write" for setProperty() access, or "read,write" for both types of access. PropertyPermission extends java.security.BasicPermission, so the name of the property supports simple wildcards. The name "*" represents any property name. If a name ends with ".*", it represents any property names that share the specified prefix. For example, the name "java.*" represents "java.version", "java.vendor", "java.vendor.url", and all other properties that begin with "java".

Granting access to system properties is not overtly dangerous, but caution is still necessary. Some properties, such as "user.home", reveal details about the host system that malicious code can use to mount an attack. Programmers writing system-level code and system administrators configuring security policies may need to use this class, but applications never need to use it.

Object — Permission — BasicPermission — PropertyPermission
Guard | Serializable | Serializable

```
public final class PropertyPermission extends java.security.BasicPermission {
// Public Constructors
    public PropertyPermission(String name, String actions);
// Public Methods Overriding BasicPermission
    public boolean equals(Object obj);
    public String getActions();
```

java.util.*

```
    public int hashCode();
    public boolean implies(java.security.Permission p);
    public java.security.PermissionCollection newPermissionCollection();
}
```

PropertyResourceBundle Java 1.1

java.util

This class is a concrete subclass of ResourceBundle. It reads a Properties file from a specified InputStream and implements the ResourceBundle API for looking up named resources from the resulting Properties object. A Properties file contains lines of the form:

name=value

Each such line defines a named property with the specified String value. Although you can instantiate a PropertyResourceBundle yourself, it is more common to simply define a Properties file and then allow ResourceBundle.getBundle() to look up that file and return the necessary PropertyResourceBundle object. See also Properties and ResourceBundle.

Object — ResourceBundle — PropertyResourceBundle

```
public class PropertyResourceBundle extends ResourceBundle {
// Public Constructors
    public PropertyResourceBundle(java.io.InputStream stream) throws java.io.IOException;
// Public Methods Overriding ResourceBundle
    public Enumeration<String> getKeys();
    public Object handleGetObject(String key);
}
```

Queue<E> Java 5.0

java.util collection

A Queue<E> is an ordered Collection of elements of type *E*. Unlike List, the Queue interface does not permit indexed access to its elements: elements may be inserted at the *tail* of the queue and may be removed from the *head* of the queue, but the elements in between may not be accessed by their position. Unlike Set, Queue implementations do not prohibit duplicate elements.

Queues may be manipulated through the methods of the Collection interface, including iteration via the iterator() method and the Iterator object it returns. It is more common to manipulate queues through the more specialized methods defined by the Queue interface, however. Place an element at the tail of the queue with offer(). If the queue is already full, offer() returns false. Remove an element from the head of the queue with remove() or poll(). These methods differ only in the case of an empty queue: remove() throws an unchecked NoSuchElementException and poll() returns null. (Most queue implementations prohibit null elements for this reason, but LinkedList is an exception.) Query the element at the head of a queue without removing it with element() or peek(). If the queue is empty, element() throws NoSuchElementException and peek() returns null.

Most Queue implementations order their elements in first-in, first-out (FIFO) order. Other implementations may provide other orderings. A queue Iterator is not required to traverse the queue's elements in order. A Queue implementation with a fixed size is a *bounded* queue. When a bounded queue is full, it is not possible to insert a new element until an element is first removed. Unlike the List and Set interfaces, the Queue interface does not require implementations to override the equals() method, and Queue implementations typically do not override it.

In Java 5.0, the LinkedList class has been retrofitted to implement Queue as well as List. PriorityQueue is a Queue implementation that orders elements based on the Comparable or Comparator interfaces. AbstractQueue is an abstract implementation that offers partial support for simple Queue implementations. The java.util.concurrent package defines a BlockingQueue interface that extends this implementation and includes Queue and Blocking-Queue implementations that are useful in multithreaded programming.

Iterable ··· Collection ··· Queue

```
public interface Queue<E> extends Collection<E> {
// Public Instance Methods
   E element();
   boolean offer(E o);
   E peek();
   E poll();
   E remove();
}
```

Implementations AbstractQueue, LinkedList, java.util.concurrent.BlockingQueue, java.util.concurrent.ConcurrentLinkedQueue

Random — Java 1.0

java.util — serializable

This class implements a pseudorandom number generator suitable for games and similar applications. If you need a cryptographic-strength source of pseudorandomness, see java.security.SecureRandom. nextDouble() and nextFloat() return a value between 0.0 and 1.0. nextLong() and the no-argument version of nextInt() return long and int values distributed across the range of those data types. As of Java 1.2, if you pass an argument to nextInt(), it returns a value between zero (inclusive) and the specified number (exclusive). nextGaussian() returns pseudorandom floating-point values with a Gaussian distribution; the mean of the values is 0.0 and the standard deviation is 1.0. nextBoolean() returns a pseudorandom boolean value, and nextBytes() fills in the specified byte array with pseudo-random bytes. You can use the setSeed() method or the optional constructor argument to initialize the pseudorandom number generator with some variable seed value other than the current time (the default) or with a constant to ensure a repeatable sequence of pseudorandomness.

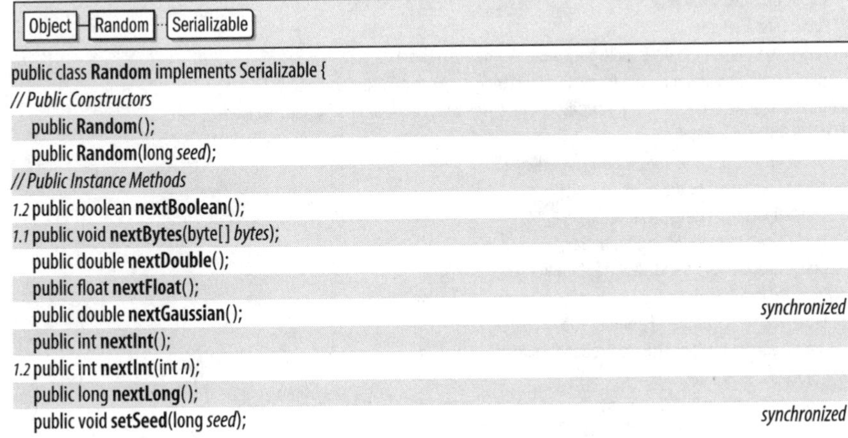

Object — Random ··· Serializable

```
public class Random implements Serializable {
// Public Constructors
   public Random();
   public Random(long seed);
// Public Instance Methods
1.2 public boolean nextBoolean();
1.1 public void nextBytes(byte[] bytes);
   public double nextDouble();
   public float nextFloat();
   public double nextGaussian();                    synchronized
   public int nextInt();
1.2 public int nextInt(int n);
   public long nextLong();
   public void setSeed(long seed);                  synchronized
```

```
// Protected Instance Methods
1.1 protected int next(int bits);
}
```

Subclasses java.security.SecureRandom

Passed To java.math.BigInteger.{BigInteger(), probablePrime()}, Collections.shuffle()

RandomAccess **Java 1.4**

java.util

This marker interface is implemented by List implementations to advertise that they provide efficient (usually constant time) random access to all list elements. ArrayList and Vector implement this interface, but LinkedList does not. Classes that manipulate generic List objects may want to test for this interface with instanceof and use different algorithms for lists that provide efficient random access than they use for lists that are most efficiently accessed sequentially.

```
public interface RandomAccess {
}
```

Implementations ArrayList, Vector, java.util.concurrent.CopyOnWriteArrayList

ResourceBundle **Java 1.1**

java.util

This abstract class allows subclasses to define sets of localized resources that can then be dynamically loaded as needed by internationalized programs. Such resources may include user-visible text and images that appear in an application, as well as more complex things such as Menu objects. Use getBundle() to load a ResourceBundle subclass that is appropriate for the default or specified locale. Use getObject(), getString(), and getStringArray() to look up a named resource in a bundle. To define a bundle, provide implementations of handleGetObject() and getKeys(). It is often easier, however, to subclass ListResourceBundle or provide a Properties file that is used by PropertyResourceBundle. The name of any localized ResourceBundle class you define should include the locale language code, and, optionally, the locale country code.

```
public abstract class ResourceBundle {
// Public Constructors
   public ResourceBundle();
// Public Class Methods
   public static final ResourceBundle getBundle(String baseName);
   public static final ResourceBundle getBundle(String baseName, Locale locale);
1.2 public static ResourceBundle getBundle(String baseName, Locale locale, ClassLoader loader);
// Public Instance Methods
   public abstract Enumeration<String> getKeys();
1.2 public Locale getLocale();
   public final Object getObject(String key);
   public final String getString(String key);
   public final String[] getStringArray(String key);
// Protected Instance Methods
   protected abstract Object handleGetObject(String key);
   protected void setParent(ResourceBundle parent);
// Protected Instance Fields
   protected ResourceBundle parent;
}
```

Subclasses ListResourceBundle, PropertyResourceBundle

Passed To java.util.logging.LogRecord.setResourceBundle()

Returned By java.util.logging.Logger.getResourceBundle(), java.util.logging.LogRecord.getResourceBundle()

Scanner **Java 5.0**

java.util

This class is a text scanner or tokenizer. It can read input from any Readable object, and convenience constructors can read text from a specified string, file, byte stream, or byte channel. The constructors for files, byte streams, and byte channels optionally allow you to specify the name of the charset to use for byte-to-character conversions.

After creating a Scanner, you can configure it. useDelimiter() specifies a regular expression (as a java.util.regex.Pattern or a String) that represents the token delimiter. The default delimiter is any run of whitespace. useLocale() specifies the Locale to use for scanning numbers: this may affect things like the character expected for decimal points and the thousands separator. useRadix() specifies the radix, or base, in which numbers should be parsed. Any value between 2 and 36 is allowed. These configuration methods may be called at any time and are not required to be called before scanning begins.

Scanner implements the Iterable<String> interface, and you can use the hasNext() and next() methods of this interface to break the input into a series of String tokens separated by whitespace or by the delimiter specified with useDelimiter(). In addition to these Iterable methods, however, Scanner defines a number of next*X* and hasNext*X* methods for various numeric types *X*. nextLine() returns the next line of input. Two variants of the next() method accept a regular expression as an argument and return the next chunk of text matching a specified regular expression. The corresponding hasNext() methods accept a regular expression and return true if the input matches it.

The skip() method ignores delimiters and skips text matching the specified regular expression. findInLine() looks ahead for text matching the specified regular expression in the current line. If a match is found, the Scanner advances past that text and returns it. Otherwise, the Scanner returns null without advancing. findWithinHorizon() is similar but looks for a match within the specified number of characters (a horizon of 0 specifies an unlimited number).

The next() methods and its next*X* variants throw a NoSuchElementException if there is no more input text. They throw an InputMismatchException (a subclass of NoSuchElementException) if the next token cannot be parsed as the specified type or does not match the specified pattern. The Readable object that the Scanner reads text from may throw a java.io.IOException, but, for ease of use, the Scanner never propagates this exception. If an IOException occurs, the Scanner assumes that no more input is available from the Readable. Call ioException() to obtain the most recent IOException, if any, thrown by the Readable.

The close() method checks whether the Readable object implements the Closeable interface and, if so, calls the close() method on that object. Once close() has been called, any attempt to read tokens from the Scanner results in an IllegalStateException.

See also StringTokenizer and java.io.StreamTokenizer.

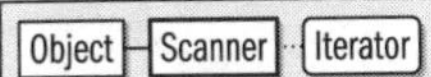


```
public final class Scanner implements Iterator<String> {
// Public Constructors
   public Scanner(Readable source);
   public Scanner(java.nio.channels.ReadableByteChannel source);
   public Scanner(java.io.InputStream source);
```

```
    public Scanner(java.io.File source) throws java.io.FileNotFoundException;
    public Scanner(String source);
    public Scanner(java.nio.channels.ReadableByteChannel source, String charsetName);
    public Scanner(java.io.InputStream source, String charsetName);
    public Scanner(java.io.File source, String charsetName) throws java.io.FileNotFoundException;
// Public Instance Methods
    public void close();
    public java.util.regex.Pattern delimiter();
    public String findInLine(String pattern);
    public String findInLine(java.util.regex.Pattern pattern);
    public String findWithinHorizon(java.util.regex.Pattern pattern, int horizon);
    public String findWithinHorizon(String pattern, int horizon);
    public boolean hasNext(java.util.regex.Pattern pattern);
    public boolean hasNext(String pattern);
    public boolean hasNextBigDecimal();
    public boolean hasNextBigInteger();
    public boolean hasNextBigInteger(int radix);
    public boolean hasNextBoolean();
    public boolean hasNextByte();
    public boolean hasNextByte(int radix);
    public boolean hasNextDouble();
    public boolean hasNextFloat();
    public boolean hasNextInt();
    public boolean hasNextInt(int radix);
    public boolean hasNextLine();
    public boolean hasNextLong();
    public boolean hasNextLong(int radix);
    public boolean hasNextShort();
    public boolean hasNextShort(int radix);
    public java.io.IOException ioException();
    public Locale locale();
    public java.util.regex.MatchResult match();
    public String next(String pattern);
    public String next(java.util.regex.Pattern pattern);
    public java.math.BigDecimal nextBigDecimal();
    public java.math.BigInteger nextBigInteger();
    public java.math.BigInteger nextBigInteger(int radix);
    public boolean nextBoolean();
    public byte nextByte();
    public byte nextByte(int radix);
    public double nextDouble();
    public float nextFloat();
    public int nextInt();
    public int nextInt(int radix);
    public String nextLine();
    public long nextLong();
    public long nextLong(int radix);
    public short nextShort();
    public short nextShort(int radix);
    public int radix();
    public Scanner skip(java.util.regex.Pattern pattern);
    public Scanner skip(String pattern);
    public Scanner useDelimiter(java.util.regex.Pattern pattern);
```

```
    public Scanner useDelimiter(String pattern);
    public Scanner useLocale(Locale locale);
    public Scanner useRadix(int radix);
// Methods Implementing Iterator
    public boolean hasNext();
    public String next();
    public void remove();
// Public Methods Overriding Object
    public String toString();
}
```

Set<E> Java 1.2

java.util collection

This interface represents an unordered Collection of objects that contains no duplicate elements. That is, a Set cannot contain two elements e1 and e2 where e1.equals(e2), and it can contain at most one null element. The Set interface defines the same methods as its superinterface, Collection. It constrains the add() and addAll() methods from adding duplicate elements to the Set. In Java 5.0 Set is a generic interface and the type variable *E* represents the type of the objects in the set.

An interface cannot specify constructors, but it is conventional that all implementations of Set provide at least two standard constructors: one that takes no arguments and creates an empty set, and a copy constructor that accepts a Collection object that specifies the initial contents of the new Set. This copy constructor must ensure that duplicate elements are not added to the Set, of course.

As with Collection, the Set methods that modify the contents of the set are optional, and implementations that do not support the methods throw java.lang.UnsupportedOperationException. See also Collection, List, Map, SortedSet, HashSet, and TreeSet.

Iterable ··· Collection ··· Set

```
public interface Set<E> extends Collection<E> {
// Public Instance Methods
    boolean add(E o);
    boolean addAll(Collection<? extends E> c);
    void clear();
    boolean contains(Object o);
    boolean containsAll(Collection<?> c);
    boolean equals(Object o);
    int hashCode();
    boolean isEmpty();
    Iterator<E> iterator();
    boolean remove(Object o);
    boolean removeAll(Collection<?> c);
    boolean retainAll(Collection<?> c);
    int size();
    Object[] toArray();
    <T> T[] toArray(T[] a);
}
```

Implementations AbstractSet, HashSet, LinkedHashSet, SortedSet

Passed To java.security.cert.PKIXBuilderParameters.PKIXBuilderParameters(), java.security.cert.PKIXParameters.{PKIXParameters(), setInitialPolicies(), setTrustAnchors()}, java.security.cert.X509CertSelector.{setExtendedKeyUsage(), setPolicy()}, java.text.AttributedCharacterIterator.{getRunLimit(), getRunStart()}, Collections.{checkedSet(), synchronizedSet(), unmodifiableSet()}, javax.security.auth.Subject.Subject()

Returned By Too many methods to list.

Type Of Collections.EMPTY_SET

SimpleTimeZone **Java 1.1**

java.util **cloneable serializable**

This concrete subclass of TimeZone is a simple implementation of that abstract class that is suitable for use in locales that use the Gregorian calendar. Programs do not normally need to instantiate this class directly; instead, they use one of the static factory methods of TimeZone to obtain a suitable TimeZone subclass. The only reason to instantiate this class directly is if you need to support a time zone with nonstandard daylight-savings-time rules. In that case, you can call setStartRule() and setEndRule() to specify the starting and ending dates of daylight-savings time for the time zone.

```
public class SimpleTimeZone extends TimeZone {
// Public Constructors
   public SimpleTimeZone(int rawOffset, String ID);
   public SimpleTimeZone(int rawOffset, String ID, int startMonth, int startDay, int startDayOfWeek, int startTime,
                         int endMonth, int endDay, int endDayOfWeek, int endTime);
1.2 public SimpleTimeZone(int rawOffset, String ID, int startMonth, int startDay, int startDayOfWeek, int startTime,
                         int endMonth, int endDay, int endDayOfWeek, int endTime, int dstSavings);
1.4 public SimpleTimeZone(int rawOffset, String ID, int startMonth, int startDay, int startDayOfWeek, int startTime,
                         int startTimeMode, int endMonth, int endDay, int endDayOfWeek, int endTime,
                         int endTimeMode, int dstSavings);
// Public Constants
1.4 public static final int STANDARD_TIME;                                                    =1
1.4 public static final int UTC_TIME;                                                         =2
1.4 public static final int WALL_TIME;                                                        =0
// Public Instance Methods
1.2 public void setDSTSavings(int millisSavedDuringDST);
1.2 public void setEndRule(int endMonth, int endDay, int endTime);
   public void setEndRule(int endMonth, int endDay, int endDayOfWeek, int endTime);
1.2 public void setEndRule(int endMonth, int endDay, int endDayOfWeek, int endTime, boolean after);
1.2 public void setStartRule(int startMonth, int startDay, int startTime);
   public void setStartRule(int startMonth, int startDay, int startDayOfWeek, int startTime);
1.2 public void setStartRule(int startMonth, int startDay, int startDayOfWeek, int startTime, boolean after);
   public void setStartYear(int year);
// Public Methods Overriding TimeZone
   public Object clone();
1.2 public int getDSTSavings();
1.4 public int getOffset(long date);
   public int getOffset(int era, int year, int month, int day, int dayOfWeek, int millis);
   public int getRawOffset();
1.2 public boolean hasSameRules(TimeZone other);
   public boolean inDaylightTime(Date date);
   public void setRawOffset(int offsetMillis);
   public boolean useDaylightTime();
```

```
// Public Methods Overriding Object
   public boolean equals(Object obj);
   public int hashCode();                                              synchronized
   public String toString();
}
```

SortedMap<K,V> Java 1.2

java.util collection

This interface represents a Map object that keeps its set of key objects in sorted order. As with Map, it is conventional that all implementations of this interface define a no-argument constructor to create an empty map and a copy constructor that accepts a Map object that specifies the initial contents of the SortedMap. Furthermore, when creating a SortedMap, there should be a way to specify a Comparator object to sort the key objects of the map. If no Comparator is specified, all key objects must implement the java.lang.Comparable interface so they can be sorted in their natural order. See also Map, TreeMap, and SortedSet.

The inherited keySet(), values(), and entrySet() methods return collections that can be iterated in the sorted order. firstKey() and lastKey() return the lowest and highest key values in the SortedMap. subMap() returns a SortedMap that contains only mappings for keys from (and including) the first specified key up to (but not including) the second specified key. headMap() returns a SortedMap that contains mappings whose keys are less than (but not equal to) the specified key. tailMap() returns a SortedMap that contains mappings whose keys are greater than or equal to the specified key. subMap(), headMap(), and tailMap() return SortedMap objects that are simply views of the original SortedMap; any changes in the original map are reflected in the returned map and vice versa.

Map ··· SortedMap

```
public interface SortedMap<K,V> extends Map<K,V> {
// Public Instance Methods
   Comparator<? super K> comparator();
   K firstKey();
   SortedMap<K,V> headMap(K toKey);
   K lastKey();
   SortedMap<K,V> subMap(K fromKey, K toKey);
   SortedMap<K,V> tailMap(K fromKey);
}
```

Implementations TreeMap

Passed To Collections.{checkedSortedMap(), synchronizedSortedMap(), unmodifiableSortedMap()}, TreeMap.TreeMap()

Returned By java.nio.charset.Charset.availableCharsets(), Collections.{checkedSortedMap(), synchronizedSortedMap(), unmodifiableSortedMap()}, TreeMap.{headMap(), subMap(), tailMap()}, java.util.jar.Pack200.Packer.properties(), java.util.jar.Pack200.Unpacker.properties()

SortedSet<E> Java 1.2

java.util collection

This interface is a Set that sorts its elements and guarantees that its iterator() method returns an Iterator that enumerates the elements of the set in sorted order. As with the Set interface, it is conventional for all implementations of SortedSet to provide a no-argument constructor that creates an empty set and a copy constructor that expects a Collection object specifying the initial (unsorted) contents of the set. Furthermore, when creating a SortedSet, there should be a way to specify a Comparator object that compares and sorts the elements of the set. If no Comparator is specified, the elements of the set must all implement java.lang.Comparable so they can be sorted in their natural order. See also Set, TreeSet, and SortedMap.

SortedSet defines a few methods in addition to those it inherits from the Set interface. first() and last() return the lowest and highest objects in the set. headSet() returns all elements from the beginning of the set up to (but not including) the specified element. tailSet() returns all elements between (and including) the specified element and the end of the set. subSet() returns all elements of the set from (and including) the first specified element up to (but excluding) the second specified element. Note that all three methods return a SortedSet that is implemented as a view onto the original SortedSet. Changes in the original set are visible through the returned set and vice versa.

Iterable · Collection · Set · SortedSet

```
public interface SortedSet<E> extends Set<E> {
// Public Instance Methods
   Comparator<? super E> comparator();
   E first();
   SortedSet<E> headSet(E toElement);
   E last();
   SortedSet<E> subSet(E fromElement, E toElement);
   SortedSet<E> tailSet(E fromElement);
}
```

Implementations TreeSet

Passed To Collections.{checkedSortedSet(), synchronizedSortedSet(), unmodifiableSortedSet()}, PriorityQueue.PriorityQueue(), TreeSet.TreeSet()

Returned By Collections.{checkedSortedSet(), synchronizedSortedSet(), unmodifiableSortedSet()}, TreeSet.{headSet(), subSet(), tailSet()}

Stack<E> **Java 1.0**

java.util — cloneable serializable collection

This class implements a last-in-first-out (LIFO) stack of objects. push() puts an object on the top of the stack. pop() removes and returns the top object from the stack. peek() returns the top object without removing it. In Java 1.2, you can instead use a LinkedList as a stack.

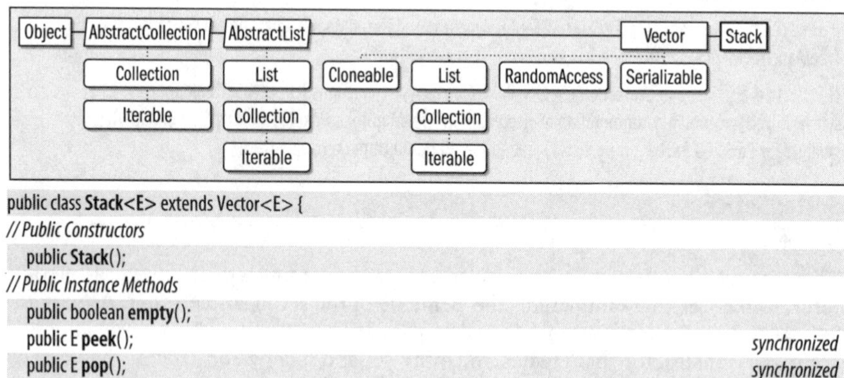


```
public class Stack<E> extends Vector<E> {
// Public Constructors
   public Stack();
// Public Instance Methods
   public boolean empty();
   public E peek();                                    synchronized
   public E pop();                                     synchronized
```

```
    public E push(E item);
    public int search(Object o);                                    synchronized
}
```

StringTokenizer Java 1.0

java.util

When a StringTokenizer is instantiated with a String, it breaks the string up into tokens separated by any of the characters in the specified string of delimiters. (For example, words separated by space and tab characters are tokens.) The hasMoreTokens() and nextToken() methods obtain the tokens in order. countTokens() returns the number of tokens in the string. StringTokenizer implements the Enumeration interface, so you may also access the tokens with the familiar hasMoreElements() and nextElement() methods. When you create a StringTokenizer, you can specify a string of delimiter characters to use for the entire string, or you can rely on the default whitespace delimiters. You can also specify whether the delimiters themselves should be returned as tokens. Finally, you can optionally specify a new string of delimiter characters when you call nextToken().

Object — StringTokenizer ··· Enumeration

```
public class StringTokenizer implements Enumeration<Object> {
// Public Constructors
    public StringTokenizer(String str);
    public StringTokenizer(String str, String delim);
    public StringTokenizer(String str, String delim, boolean returnDelims);
// Public Instance Methods
    public int countTokens();
    public boolean hasMoreTokens();
    public String nextToken();
    public String nextToken(String delim);
// Methods Implementing Enumeration
    public boolean hasMoreElements();
    public Object nextElement();
}
```

Timer Java 1.3

java.util

This class implements a timer: its methods allow you to schedule one or more runnable TimerTask objects to be executed (once or repetitively) by a background thread at a specified time in the future. You can create a timer with the Timer() constructor. The no-argument version of this constructor creates a regular non-daemon background thread, which means that the Java VM will not terminate while the timer thread is running. Pass true to the constructor if you want the background thread to be a daemon thread. In Java 5.0 you can also specify the name of the background thread when creating a Timer.

Once you have created a Timer, you can schedule TimerTask objects to be run in the future with the various schedule() and scheduleAtFixedRate() methods. To schedule a task for a single execution, use one of the two-argument schedule() methods and specify the desired execution time either as a number of milliseconds in the future or as an absolute Date. If the number of milliseconds is 0, or if the Date object represents a time already passed, the task is scheduled for immediate execution.

To schedule a repeating task, use one of the three-argument versions of schedule() or scheduleAtFixedRate(). These methods are passed an argument that specifies the time (either as a number of milliseconds or as a Date object) of the first execution of the task and another argument, *period*, that specifies the number of milliseconds between repeated executions of the task. The schedule() methods schedule the task for *fixed-interval* execution. That is, each execution is scheduled for *period* milliseconds after the previous execution *ends*. Use schedule() for tasks such as animation, where it is important to have a relatively constant interval between executions. The scheduleAtFixedRate() methods, on the other hand, schedule tasks for *fixed-rate* execution. That is, each repetition of the task is scheduled for *period* milliseconds after the previous execution *begins*. Use scheduleAtFixedRate() for tasks, such as updating a clock display, that must occur at specific absolute times rather than at fixed intervals.

A single Timer object can comfortably schedule many TimerTask objects. Note, however, that all tasks scheduled by a single Timer share a single thread. If you are scheduling many rapidly repeating tasks, or if some tasks take a long time to execute, other tasks may have their scheduled executions delayed.

When you are done with a Timer, call cancel() to stop its associated thread from running. This is particularly important when you are using a timer whose associated thread is not a daemon thread, because otherwise the timer thread can prevent the Java VM from exiting. To cancel the execution of a particular task, use the cancel() method of TimerTask.

```
public class Timer {
// Public Constructors
   public Timer();
   public Timer(boolean isDaemon);
5.0 public Timer(String name);
5.0 public Timer(String name, boolean isDaemon);
// Public Instance Methods
   public void cancel();
5.0 public int purge();
   public void schedule(TimerTask task, long delay);
   public void schedule(TimerTask task, Date time);
   public void schedule(TimerTask task, long delay, long period);
   public void schedule(TimerTask task, Date firstTime, long period);
   public void scheduleAtFixedRate(TimerTask task, long delay, long period);
   public void scheduleAtFixedRate(TimerTask task, Date firstTime, long period);
}
```

TimerTask — Java 1.3

java.util — runnable

This abstract Runnable class represents a task that is scheduled with a Timer object for one-time or repeated execution in the future. You can define a task by subclassing TimerTask and implementing the abstract run() method. Schedule the task for future execution by passing an instance of your subclass to one of the schedule() or scheduleAtFixedRate() methods of Timer. The Timer object will then invoke the run() method at the scheduled time or times.

Call cancel() to cancel the one-time or repeated execution of a TimerTask(). This method returns true if a pending execution was actually canceled. It returns false if the task has already been canceled, was never scheduled, or was scheduled for one-time execution and has already been executed. scheduledExecutionTime() returns the time in milliseconds at which the most recent execution of the TimerTask was scheduled to occur. When the host system is heavily loaded, the run() method may not be invoked exactly when scheduled. Some tasks may choose to do nothing if they are not invoked on time. The run() method can compare the return values of scheduledExecutionTime() and System.currentTimeMillis() to determine whether the current invocation is sufficiently timely.

Object — TimerTask ··· Runnable

```
public abstract class TimerTask implements Runnable {
// Protected Constructors
   protected TimerTask();
// Public Instance Methods
   public boolean cancel();
   public long scheduledExecutionTime();
// Methods Implementing Runnable
   public abstract void run();
}
```

Passed To Timer.{schedule(), scheduleAtFixedRate()}

TimeZone Java 1.1

java.util cloneable serializable

The TimeZone class represents a time zone; it is used with the Calendar and DateFormat classes. As an abstract class, TimeZone cannot be directly instantiated. Instead, you should call the static getDefault() method to obtain a TimeZone object that represents the time zone inherited from the host operating system. Or you can call the static getTimeZone() method with the name of the desired zone. You can obtain a list of the supported time-zone names by calling the static getAvailableIDs() method.

Once you have a TimeZone object, you can call inDaylightTime() to determine whether, for a given Date, daylight-savings time is in effect for that time zone. Call getID() to obtain the name of the time zone. Call getOffset() for a given date to determine the number of milliseconds to add to GMT to convert to the time zone.

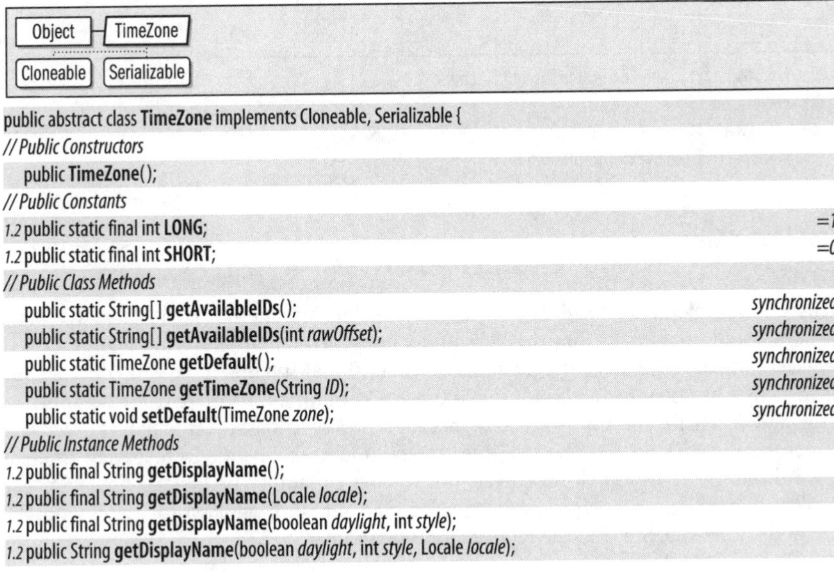

Object — TimeZone
Cloneable Serializable

```
public abstract class TimeZone implements Cloneable, Serializable {
// Public Constructors
   public TimeZone();
// Public Constants
1.2 public static final int LONG;                                    =1
1.2 public static final int SHORT;                                   =0
// Public Class Methods
   public static String[] getAvailableIDs();                         synchronized
   public static String[] getAvailableIDs(int rawOffset);            synchronized
   public static TimeZone getDefault();                              synchronized
   public static TimeZone getTimeZone(String ID);                    synchronized
   public static void setDefault(TimeZone zone);                     synchronized
// Public Instance Methods
1.2 public final String getDisplayName();
1.2 public final String getDisplayName(Locale locale);
1.2 public final String getDisplayName(boolean daylight, int style);
1.2 public String getDisplayName(boolean daylight, int style, Locale locale);
```

```
1.4 public int getDSTSavings();
    public String getID();
1.4 public int getOffset(long date);
    public abstract int getOffset(int era, int year, int month, int day, int dayOfWeek, int milliseconds);
    public abstract int getRawOffset();
1.2 public boolean hasSameRules(TimeZone other);
    public abstract boolean inDaylightTime(Date date);
    public void setID(String ID);
    public abstract void setRawOffset(int offsetMillis);
    public abstract boolean useDaylightTime();
// Public Methods Overriding Object
    public Object clone();
}
```

Subclasses SimpleTimeZone

Passed To java.text.DateFormat.setTimeZone(), Calendar.{Calendar(), getInstance(), setTimeZone()}, GregorianCalendar.{GregorianCalendar(), setTimeZone()}, SimpleTimeZone.hasSameRules(), javax.xml.datatype.XMLGregorianCalendar.toGregorianCalendar()

Returned By java.text.DateFormat.getTimeZone(), Calendar.getTimeZone(), GregorianCalendar.getTimeZone(), javax.xml.datatype.XMLGregorianCalendar.getTimeZone()

TooManyListenersException — Java 1.1

java.util — serializable checked

Signals that an AWT component, JavaBeans component, or Swing component can have only one EventListener object registered for some specific type of event. That is, it signals that a particular event is a unicast event rather than a multicast event. This exception type serves a formal purpose in the Java event model; its presence in the throws clause of an EventListener registration method (even if the method never actually throws the exception) signals that an event is a unicast event.

Object — Throwable — Exception — TooManyListenersException
Serializable

```
public class TooManyListenersException extends Exception {
// Public Constructors
    public TooManyListenersException();
    public TooManyListenersException(String s);
}
```

TreeMap<K,V> — Java 1.2

java.util — cloneable serializable collection

This class implements the SortedMap interface using an internal Red-Black tree data structure and guarantees that the keys and values of the mapping can be enumerated in ascending order of keys. TreeMap supports all optional Map methods. The objects used as keys in a TreeMap must all be mutually Comparable, or an appropriate Comparator must be provided when the TreeMap is created. Because TreeMap is based on a binary tree data structure, the get(), put(), remove(), and containsKey() methods operate in relatively efficient logarithmic time. If you do not need the sorting capability of TreeMap, however, use HashMap instead, as it is even more efficient. See Map and SortedMap for details on the methods of TreeMap. See also the related TreeSet class.

In order for a TreeMap to work correctly, the comparison method from the Comparable or Comparator interface must be consistent with the equals() method. That is, the equals() method must compare two objects as equal if and only if the comparison method also indicates those two objects are equal.

The methods of TreeMap are not synchronized. If you are working in a multithreaded environment, you must explicitly synchronize all code that modifies the TreeMap, or obtain a synchronized wrapper with Collections.synchronizedMap().

Object — AbstractMap — TreeMap
Map | Cloneable | Serializable | Map ··· SortedMap

```
public class TreeMap<K,V> extends AbstractMap<K,V> implements SortedMap<K,V>, Cloneable, Serializable {
// Public Constructors
    public TreeMap();
    public TreeMap(Comparator<? super K> c);
    public TreeMap(SortedMap<K,? extends V> m);
    public TreeMap(Map<? extends K,? extends V> m);
// Methods Implementing Map
    public void clear();
    public boolean containsKey(Object key);
    public boolean containsValue(Object value);
    public Set<Map.Entry<K,V>> entrySet();
    public V get(Object key);
    public Set<K> keySet();
    public V put(K key, V value);
    public void putAll(Map<? extends K,? extends V> map);
    public V remove(Object key);
    public int size();
    public Collection<V> values();
// Methods Implementing SortedMap
    public Comparator<? super K> comparator();
    public K firstKey();
    public SortedMap<K,V> headMap(K toKey);
    public K lastKey();
    public SortedMap<K,V> subMap(K fromKey, K toKey);
    public SortedMap<K,V> tailMap(K fromKey);
// Public Methods Overriding AbstractMap
    public Object clone();
}
```

TreeSet<E> — Java 1.2

java.util — cloneable serializable collection

This class implements SortedSet, provides support for all optional methods, and guarantees that the elements of the set can be enumerated in ascending order. In order to be sorted, the elements of the set must all be mutually Comparable objects, or they must all be compatible with a Comparator object that is specified when the TreeSet is created. TreeSet is implemented on top of a TreeMap, so its add(), remove(), and contains() methods all operate in relatively efficient logarithmic time. If you do not need the sorting capability of TreeSet, however, use HashSet instead, as it is significantly more efficient. See Set, SortedSet, and Collection for details on the methods of TreeSet.

In order for a TreeSet to operate correctly, the Comparable or Comparator comparison method must be consistent with the equals() method. That is, the equals() method must compare two objects as equal if and only if the comparison method also indicates those two objects are equal.

The methods of TreeSet are not synchronized. If you are working in a multithreaded environment, you must explicitly synchronize code that modifies the contents of the set, or obtain a synchronized wrapper with Collections.synchronizedSet().

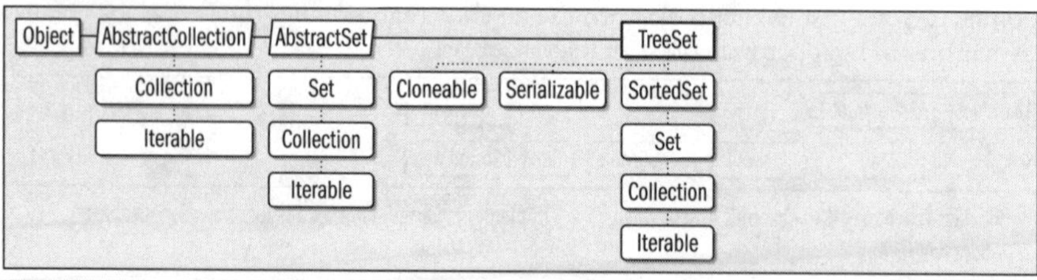


```
public class TreeSet<E> extends AbstractSet<E> implements SortedSet<E>, Cloneable, Serializable {
// Public Constructors
   public TreeSet();
   public TreeSet(Comparator<? super E> c);
   public TreeSet(SortedSet<E> s);
   public TreeSet(Collection<? extends E> c);
// Methods Implementing Set
   public boolean add(E o);
   public boolean addAll(Collection<? extends E> c);
   public void clear();
   public boolean contains(Object o);
   public boolean isEmpty();                                  default:true
   public Iterator<E> iterator();
   public boolean remove(Object o);
   public int size();
// Methods Implementing SortedSet
   public Comparator<? super E> comparator();
   public E first();
   public SortedSet<E> headSet(E toElement);
   public E last();
   public SortedSet<E> subSet(E fromElement, E toElement);
   public SortedSet<E> tailSet(E fromElement);
// Public Methods Overriding Object
   public Object clone();
}
```

UnknownFormatConversionException — Java 5.0

java.util — serializable unchecked

An IllegalFormatException of this type is thrown by a Formatter when an unknown conversion specifier is included in a format string.

Throwable — Exception — RuntimeException — IllegalArgumentException — IllegalFormatException — UnknownFormatConversionException; Serializable

```
public class UnknownFormatConversionException extends IllegalFormatException {
// Public Constructors
   public UnknownFormatConversionException(String s);
// Public Instance Methods
   public String getConversion();
```

```
// Public Methods Overriding Throwable
    public String getMessage();
}
```

UnknownFormatFlagsException

Java 5.0

java.util — serializable unchecked

An IllegalFormatException of this type is thrown by a Formatter when unknown flags are specified in a format string.

Throwable — Exception — RuntimeException — IllegalArgumentException — IllegalFormatException — UnknownFormatFlagsException

Serializable

```
public class UnknownFormatFlagsException extends IllegalFormatException {
// Public Constructors
    public UnknownFormatFlagsException(String f);
// Public Instance Methods
    public String getFlags();
// Public Methods Overriding Throwable
    public String getMessage();
}
```

UUID

Java 5.0

java.util — serializable comparable

This class is an immutable representation of 128-bit Universal Unique Identifier, or UUID, which serves as an identifier that is (with very high probability) globally unique. Create a UUID based on random bits with the randomUUID() factory method. Create a UUID based on the MD5 hash code of an array of bytes with the nameUUIDFromBytes() factory method. Or create a UUID by parsing a string with the fromString() factory method. The standard string format of a UUID is 32 hexadecimal digits, broken into five hyphen-separated groups of 8, 4, 4, 4, and 12 digits. For example:

```
7cbf3e1a-d521-40ac-87f1-e28b17530f60
```

Both lowercase and uppercase hex digits are allowed. The toString() method converts a UUID object to a string using this standard format. You can also create a UUID object by explicitly passing the 128 bits in the form of two long values to the UUID() constructor, but this option should be used only if you are intimately familiar with the relevant UUID standards.

The toString() and equals() methods define the most common operations on a UUID. The UUID class implements the Comparable interface and defines an ordering for UUID objects. Note, however, that the ordering does not represent any meaningful property, such as generation order, of the underlying bits.

Various accessor methods provide details about the bits of a UUID, but these details are rarely useful. getLeastSignificantBits() and getMostSignificantBits() return the bits of a UUID as two long values. version() and variant() return the version and variant of the UUID, which specify the type (random, name-based, time-based) and bit layout of the UUID. timestamp(), clockSequence(), and node() return values only for time-based UUIDs that have a version() of 1. Note that the UUID class does not provide a factory method for creating a time-based UUID.

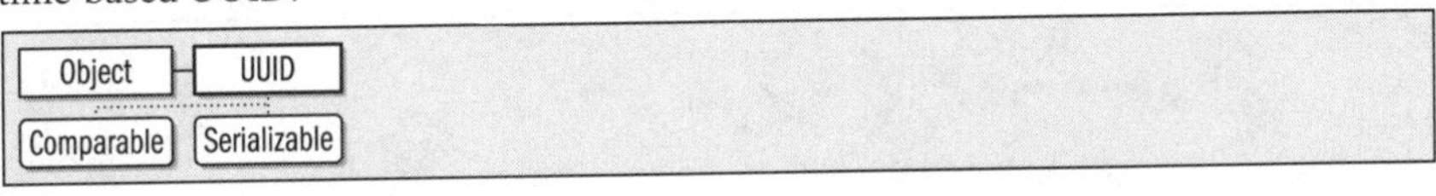

```
public final class UUID implements Serializable, Comparable<UUID> {
// Public Constructors
   public UUID(long mostSigBits, long leastSigBits);
// Public Class Methods
   public static UUID fromString(String name);
   public static UUID nameUUIDFromBytes(byte[] name);
   public static UUID randomUUID();
// Public Instance Methods
   public int clockSequence();
   public long getLeastSignificantBits();
   public long getMostSignificantBits();
   public long node();
   public long timestamp();
   public int variant();
   public int version();
// Methods Implementing Comparable
   public int compareTo(UUID val);
// Public Methods Overriding Object
   public boolean equals(Object obj);
   public int hashCode();
   public String toString();
}
```

Vector<E>

Java 1.0

java.util

cloneable serializable collection

This class implements an ordered collection—essentially an array—of objects that can grow or shrink as necessary. In Java 1.2, Vector has been modified to implement the List interface. Unless the synchronized methods of the Vector class are actually needed, ArrayList is preferred in Java 1.2 and later. In Java 5.0 this class has been made generic. The type variable *E* represents the type of the elements of the vector.

Vector is useful when you need to keep track of a number of objects, but do not know in advance how many there will be. Use setElementAt() to set the object at a given index of a Vector. Use elementAt() to retrieve the object stored at a specified index. Call add() to append an object to the end of the Vector or to insert an object at any specified position. Use removeElementAt() to delete the element at a specified index or removeElement() to remove a specified object from the vector. size() returns the number of objects currently in the Vector. elements() returns an Enumeration that allows you to iterate through those objects. capacity() is not the same as size(); it returns the maximum number of objects a Vector can hold before its internal storage must be resized. Vector automatically resizes its internal storage for you, but if you know in advance how many objects a Vector will contain, you can increase its efficiency by pre-allocating this many elements with ensureCapacity().

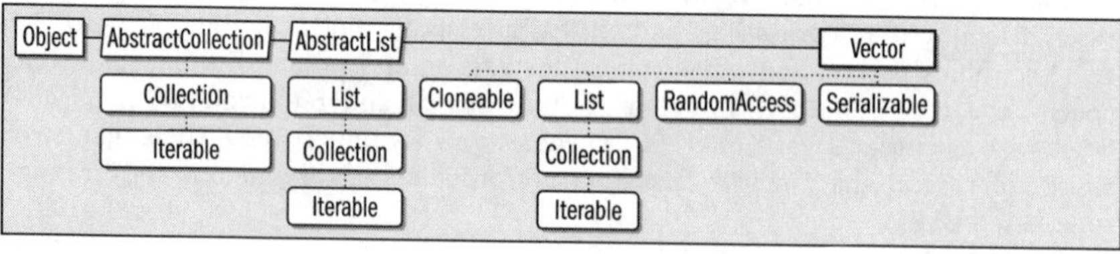

```
public class Vector<E> extends AbstractList<E> implements List<E>, RandomAccess, Cloneable, Serializable {
// Public Constructors
   public Vector();
1.2 public Vector(Collection<? extends E> c);
   public Vector(int initialCapacity);
   public Vector(int initialCapacity, int capacityIncrement);
// Public Instance Methods
   public void addElement(E obj);                                  synchronized
   public int capacity();                                          synchronized
   public boolean contains(Object elem);                           Implements:List
   public void copyInto(Object[] anArray);                         synchronized
   public E elementAt(int index);                                  synchronized
   public Enumeration<E> elements();
   public void ensureCapacity(int minCapacity);                    synchronized
   public E firstElement();                                        synchronized
   public int indexOf(Object elem);                                Implements:List
   public int indexOf(Object elem, int index);                     synchronized
   public void insertElementAt(E obj, int index);                  synchronized
   public boolean isEmpty();                                       Implements:List synchronized default:true
   public E lastElement();                                         synchronized
   public int lastIndexOf(Object elem);                            Implements:List synchronized
   public int lastIndexOf(Object elem, int index);                 synchronized
   public void removeAllElements();                                synchronized
   public boolean removeElement(Object obj);                       synchronized
   public void removeElementAt(int index);                         synchronized
   public void setElementAt(E obj, int index);                     synchronized
   public void setSize(int newSize);                               synchronized
   public int size();                                              Implements:List synchronized
   public void trimToSize();                                       synchronized
// Methods Implementing List
1.2 public boolean add(E o);                                        synchronized
1.2 public void add(int index, E element);
1.2 public boolean addAll(Collection<? extends E> c);               synchronized
1.2 public boolean addAll(int index, Collection<? extends E> c);    synchronized
1.2 public void clear();
   public boolean contains(Object elem);
1.2 public boolean containsAll(Collection<?> c);                    synchronized
1.2 public boolean equals(Object o);                                synchronized
1.2 public E get(int index);                                        synchronized
1.2 public int hashCode();                                          synchronized
   public int indexOf(Object elem);
   public boolean isEmpty();                                       synchronized default:true
   public int lastIndexOf(Object elem);                            synchronized
1.2 public boolean remove(Object o);
1.2 public E remove(int index);                                     synchronized
1.2 public boolean removeAll(Collection<?> c);                      synchronized
1.2 public boolean retainAll(Collection<?> c);                      synchronized
1.2 public E set(int index, E element);                             synchronized
   public int size();                                              synchronized
1.2 public List<E> subList(int fromIndex, int toIndex);             synchronized
1.2 public Object[] toArray();                                      synchronized
1.2 public <T> T[] toArray(T[] a);                                  synchronized
```

```
// Protected Methods Overriding AbstractList
1.2 protected void removeRange(int fromIndex, int toIndex);                synchronized
// Public Methods Overriding AbstractCollection
   public String toString();                                              synchronized
// Public Methods Overriding Object
   public Object clone();                                                 synchronized
// Protected Instance Fields
   protected int capacityIncrement;
   protected int elementCount;
   protected Object[] elementData;
}
```

Subclasses Stack

WeakHashMap<K,V> Java 1.2

java.util collection

This class implements Map using an internal hashtable. It is similar in features and performance to HashMap, except that it uses the capabilities of the java.lang.ref package, so that the key-to-value mappings it maintains do not prevent the key objects from being reclaimed by the garbage collector. When there are no more references to a key object except for the weak reference maintained by the WeakHashMap, the garbage collector reclaims the object, and the WeakHashMap deletes the mapping between the reclaimed key and its associated value. If there are no references to the value object except for the one maintained by the WeakHashMap, the value object also becomes available for garbage collection. Thus, you can use a WeakHashMap to associate an auxiliary value with an object without preventing either the object (the key) or the auxiliary value from being reclaimed. See HashMap for a discussion of the implementation features of this class. See Map for a description of the methods it defines.

WeakHashMap is primarily useful with objects whose equals() methods use the == operator for comparison. It is less useful with key objects of type String, for example, because there can be multiple String objects that are equal to one another and, even if the original key value has been reclaimed by the garbage collector, it is always possible to pass a String with the same value to the get() method.

Object — AbstractMap — WeakHashMap
Map Map

```
public class WeakHashMap<K,V> extends AbstractMap<K,V> implements Map<K,V> {
// Public Constructors
   public WeakHashMap();
   public WeakHashMap(int initialCapacity);
1.3 public WeakHashMap(Map<? extends K,? extends V> t);
   public WeakHashMap(int initialCapacity, float loadFactor);
// Methods Implementing Map
   public void clear();
   public boolean containsKey(Object key);
1.4 public boolean containsValue(Object value);
   public Set<Map.Entry<K,V>> entrySet();
   public V get(Object key);
   public boolean isEmpty();                                              default:true
1.4 public Set<K> keySet();
   public V put(K key, V value);
```

```
1.4 public void putAll(Map<? extends K,? extends V> m);
    public V remove(Object key);
    public int size();
1.4 public Collection<V> values();
}
```

Package java.util.concurrent **Java 5.0**

This package includes a number of powerful utilities for multithreaded programming. Most of these utilities fall into three main categories:

Collections

This package extends the Java Collections Framework, adding the threadsafe classes ConcurrentHashMap, CopyOnWriteArrayList, CopyOnWriteArraySet, and ConcurrentLinkedQueue. These classes achieve threadsafety without relying exclusively on synchronized methods, greatly increasing the number of threads that can safely use them concurrently. ConcurrentHashMap implements the ConcurrentMap interface, which adds important atomic methods to the base java.util.Map interface.

In addition to these Map, List, Set, and Queue implementations, this package also defines the BlockingQueue interface. Blocking queues are important in many concurrent algorithms, and this package provides a variety of useful implementations: ArrayBlockingQueue, DelayQueue, LinkedBlockingQueue, PriorityBlockingQueue, and SynchronousQueue.

Asynchronous Execution with Thread Pools

java.util.concurrent provides a robust framework for asynchronous execution of tasks defined by the existing java.lang.Runnable interface or the new Callable interface. The Executor, ExecutorService, and ScheduledExecutorService interfaces define methods for executing (or scheduling for future execution) Runnable and Callable tasks. The Future interface represents the future result of the asynchronous execution of a task. ThreadPoolExecutor and ScheduledThreadPoolExecutor are executor implementations based on highly configurable thread pools. The Executors class provides convenient factory methods for obtaining instances of these thread pool implementations.

Synchronizers

A number of classes in this package are useful for synchronizing two or more concurrent threads. See CountDownLatch, CyclicBarrier, Exchanger, and Semaphore.

Interfaces

```
public interface BlockingQueue<E> extends java.util.Queue<E>;
public interface Callable<V>;
public interface CompletionService<V>;
public interface ConcurrentMap<K, V> extends java.util.Map<K, V>;
public interface Delayed extends Comparable<Delayed>;
public interface Executor;
public interface ExecutorService extends Executor;
public interface Future<V>;
public interface RejectedExecutionHandler;
public interface ScheduledExecutorService extends ExecutorService;
public interface ScheduledFuture<V> extends Delayed, Future<V>;
public interface ThreadFactory;
```

Enumerated Types

public enum **TimeUnit**;

Collections

public class **ArrayBlockingQueue**<E> extends java.util.AbstractQueue<E> implements BlockingQueue<E>, Serializable;
public class **ConcurrentHashMap**<K, V> extends java.util.AbstractMap<K, V>
implements ConcurrentMap<K, V>
Serializable;
public class **ConcurrentLinkedQueue**<E> extends java.util.AbstractQueue<E> implements java.util.Queue<E>, Serializable;
public class **CopyOnWriteArrayList**<E> implements java.util.List<E>, java.util.RandomAccess, Cloneable, Serializable;
public class **CopyOnWriteArraySet**<E> extends java.util.AbstractSet<E> implements Serializable;
public class **DelayQueue**<E extends Delayed> extends java.util.AbstractQueue<E> implements BlockingQueue<E>;
public class **LinkedBlockingQueue**<E> extends java.util.AbstractQueue<E> implements BlockingQueue<E>, Serializable;
public class **PriorityBlockingQueue**<E> extends java.util.AbstractQueue<E> implements BlockingQueue<E>, Serializable;
public class **SynchronousQueue**<E> extends java.util.AbstractQueue<E> implements BlockingQueue<E>, Serializable;

Other Classes

public abstract class **AbstractExecutorService** implements ExecutorService;
public class **ThreadPoolExecutor** extends AbstractExecutorService;
public class **ScheduledThreadPoolExecutor** extends ThreadPoolExecutor implements ScheduledExecutorService;
public class **CountDownLatch**;
public class **CyclicBarrier**;
public class **Exchanger**<V>;
public class **ExecutorCompletionService**<V> implements CompletionService<V>;
public class **Executors**;
public class **FutureTask**<V> implements Future<V>, Runnable;
public class **Semaphore** implements Serializable;
public static class **ThreadPoolExecutor.AbortPolicy** implements RejectedExecutionHandler;
public static class **ThreadPoolExecutor.CallerRunsPolicy** implements RejectedExecutionHandler;
public static class **ThreadPoolExecutor.DiscardOldestPolicy** implements RejectedExecutionHandler;
public static class **ThreadPoolExecutor.DiscardPolicy** implements RejectedExecutionHandler;

Exceptions

public class **BrokenBarrierException** extends Exception;
public class **CancellationException** extends IllegalStateException;
public class **ExecutionException** extends Exception;
public class **RejectedExecutionException** extends RuntimeException;
public class **TimeoutException** extends Exception;

AbstractExecutorService **Java 5.0**

java.util.concurrent

This abstract class implements the submit(), invokeAll(), and invokeAny() methods of the ExecutorService interface. It does not implement the ExecutorService shutdown methods or the crucial execute() method for asynchronous execution of Runnable tasks.

The methods implemented by AbstractExecutorService wrap the submitted Callable or Runnable task in a FutureTask object. FutureTask implements Runnable and Future, which are first passed to the abstract execute() method to be run asynchronously and then returned to the caller.

See ThreadPoolExecutor for a concrete implementation, and see Executors for convenient ExecutorService factory methods.

Object — AbstractExecutorService
Executor — ExecutorService

```
public abstract class AbstractExecutorService implements ExecutorService {
// Public Constructors
    public AbstractExecutorService();
// Methods Implementing ExecutorService
    public <T> java.util.List<Future<T>> invokeAll(java.util.Collection<Callable<T>> tasks)
        throws InterruptedException;
public <T> java.util.List<Future<T>> invokeAll(java.util.Collection<Callable<T>> tasks, long timeout, TimeUnit unit)
        throws InterruptedException;
    public <T> T invokeAny(java.util.Collection<Callable<T>> tasks) throws InterruptedException, ExecutionException;
    public <T> T invokeAny(java.util.Collection<Callable<T>> tasks, long timeout, TimeUnit unit)
        throws InterruptedException, ExecutionException, TimeoutException;
    public Future<?> submit(Runnable task);
    public <T> Future<T> submit(Callable<T> task);
    public <T> Future<T> submit(Runnable task, T result);
}
```

Subclasses ThreadPoolExecutor

ArrayBlockingQueue<E> — Java 5.0

java.util.concurrent — serializable collection

This **BlockingQueue** implementation uses an array to store queue elements. The internal array has a fixed size that is specified when the queue is created, which means that this is a bounded queue and the **put()** method blocks when the queue has no more room. **ArrayBlockingQueue** orders its elements on a first-in, first-out (FIFO) basis. As with all **BlockingQueue** implementations, **null** elements are prohibited.

If you pass **true** as the second argument to the **ArrayBlockingQueue** constructor, the queue enforces a fairness policy for blocked threads: threads blocked in **put()** or **take()** are themselves queued in FIFO order, and the thread that has been waiting the longest is served first. This prevents thread starvation but may decrease overall throughput for the **ArrayBlockingQueue**.

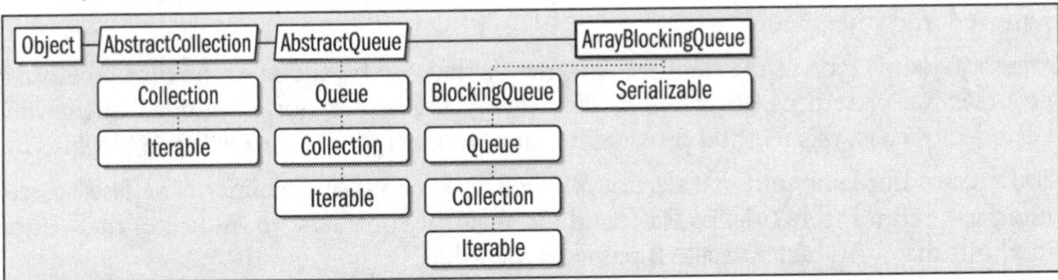


```
public class ArrayBlockingQueue<E> extends java.util.AbstractQueue<E> implements BlockingQueue<E>, Serializable {
// Public Constructors
    public ArrayBlockingQueue(int capacity);
    public ArrayBlockingQueue(int capacity, boolean fair);
    public ArrayBlockingQueue(int capacity, boolean fair, java.util.Collection<? extends E> c);
// Methods Implementing BlockingQueue
    public int drainTo(java.util.Collection<? super E> c);
    public int drainTo(java.util.Collection<? super E> c, int maxElements);
    public boolean offer(E o);
    public boolean offer(E o, long timeout, TimeUnit unit) throws InterruptedException;
```

java.util.*

```
    public E poll(long timeout, TimeUnit unit) throws InterruptedException;
    public void put(E o) throws InterruptedException;
    public int remainingCapacity();
    public E take() throws InterruptedException;
// Methods Implementing Collection
    public void clear();
    public boolean contains(Object o);
    public java.util.Iterator<E> iterator();
    public boolean remove(Object o);
    public int size();
    public Object[] toArray();
    public <T> T[] toArray(T[] a);
// Methods Implementing Queue
    public E peek();
    public E poll();
// Public Methods Overriding AbstractCollection
    public String toString();
}
```

BlockingQueue<E> Java 5.0

java.util.concurrent collection

This interface extends the java.util.Queue interface of the Java Collections Framework and adds blocking put() and take() methods. Blocking queues are useful in many concurrent algorithms in which a producer thread puts objects onto a queue and a consumer thread removes them for some kind of processing. The producer thread must block if a bounded queue fills up, and the consumer thread must block if no objects are available on the queue.

In addition to put() and take() methods that block indefinitely, BlockingQueue also defines timed versions of the Queue methods offer() and poll() that wait up to the specified time. The timeout is specified as both a long and a TimeUnit constant.

drainTo() removes all available elements from a BlockingQueue, adds them to the specified collection, and returns the number of elements removed from the queue. drainTo() does not block. A variant on this method puts an upper bound on the number of elements removed from the queue.

remainingCapacity() returns the number of elements that can be added to the queue before it becomes full or returns Integer.MAX_VALUE if the BlockingQueue is not a bounded queue. For bounded queues, this method provides a hint as to whether a call to put() will block.

BlockingQueue implementations are not allowed to accept null elements. The BlockingQueue interface refines the Collection.add() and Queue.offer() contracts to indicate that these methods throw NullPointerException if passed a null value.

Iterable ··· Collection ··· Queue ··· BlockingQueue

```
public interface BlockingQueue<E> extends java.util.Queue<E> {
// Public Instance Methods
    boolean add(E o);
    int drainTo(java.util.Collection<? super E> c);
    int drainTo(java.util.Collection<? super E> c, int maxElements);
    boolean offer(E o);
    boolean offer(E o, long timeout, TimeUnit unit) throws InterruptedException;
    E poll(long timeout, TimeUnit unit) throws InterruptedException;
```

```
    void put(E o) throws InterruptedException;
    int remainingCapacity();
    E take() throws InterruptedException;
}
```

Implementations ArrayBlockingQueue, DelayQueue, LinkedBlockingQueue, PriorityBlockingQueue, SynchronousQueue

Passed To ExecutorCompletionService.ExecutorCompletionService(), ThreadPoolExecutor.ThreadPoolExecutor()

Returned By ScheduledThreadPoolExecutor.getQueue(), ThreadPoolExecutor.getQueue()

BrokenBarrierException — Java 5.0

java.util.concurrent — serializable checked

An exception of this type is thrown when a thread calls CyclicBarrier.await() on a broken barrier, or when the barrier is broken while a thread is waiting. A CyclicBarrier enters a broken state when one of the waiting threads is interrupted or times out.

Object — Throwable — Exception — BrokenBarrierException
Serializable

```
public class BrokenBarrierException extends Exception {
// Public Constructors
    public BrokenBarrierException();
    public BrokenBarrierException(String message);
}
```

Thrown By CyclicBarrier.await()

Callable<V> — Java 5.0

java.util.concurrent

This interface is a generalized form of the java.lang.Runnable interface. Unlike the run() method of Runnable, the call() method of Callable can return a value and throw an Exception. Callable is a generic type, and the type variable *V* represents the return type of the call() method.

An ExecutorService accepts Callable objects for asynchronous execution and returns a Future object representing the future result of the call() method.

```
public interface Callable<V> {
// Public Instance Methods
    V call() throws Exception;
}
```

Passed To AbstractExecutorService.submit(), CompletionService.submit(), ExecutorCompletionService.submit(), Executors.{privilegedCallable(), privilegedCallableUsingCurrentClassLoader()}, ExecutorService.submit(), FutureTask.FutureTask(), ScheduledExecutorService.schedule(), ScheduledThreadPoolExecutor.{schedule(), submit()}

Returned By Executors.{callable(), privilegedCallable(), privilegedCallableUsingCurrentClassLoader()}

CancellationException

Java 5.0

java.util.concurrent

serializable unchecked

An exception of this type is thrown to indicate that the result of a computation cannot be retrieved because the computation was canceled. The **get()** method of the **Future** interface may throw a **CancellationException**, for example.

Object ─ Throwable ─ Exception ─ RuntimeException ─ IllegalStateException ─ CancellationException
Serializable

```
public class CancellationException extends IllegalStateException {
// Public Constructors
   public CancellationException();
   public CancellationException(String message);
}
```

CompletionService<V>

Java 5.0

java.util.concurrent

This interface combines the features of an **ExecutorService** with the features of a **BlockingQueue**. A producer thread may submit **Callable** or **Runnable** tasks for asynchronous execution. As each submitted task completes, its result, in the form of a **Future** object, becomes available to be removed from the queue by a consumer thread that calls **poll()** or **take()**.

This generic type declares a type variable *V*, which represents the result type of all tasks on the queue.

```
public interface CompletionService<V> {
// Public Instance Methods
   Future<V> poll();
   Future<V> poll(long timeout, TimeUnit unit) throws InterruptedException;
   Future<V> submit(Callable<V> task);
   Future<V> submit(Runnable task, V result);
   Future<V> take() throws InterruptedException;
}
```

Implementations ExecutorCompletionService

ConcurrentHashMap<K,V>

Java 5.0

java.util.concurrent

serializable collection

This class is a threadsafe implementation of the **java.util.Map** interface, and of the atomic operations added by the **ConcurrentMap** interface. This class is intended as a drop-in replacement for **java.util.Hashtable**. It is more efficient than that class, however, because it provides threadsafety without using **synchronized** methods that lock the entire data structure. **ConcurrentHashMap** allows any number of concurrent read operations without locking. Locking is required for updates to a **ConcurrentHashMap**, but the internal data structure is segmented so that only the segment being updated is locked, and reads and writes can proceed concurrently in other segments. You can specify the number of internal segments with the *concurrencyLevel* argument to the constructor. The default is 16. Set this to the approximate number of updater threads you expect to access the data structure. Like **Hashtable**, **ConcurrentHashMap** does not allow **null** keys or values. (Note that this differs from the behavior of **java.util.HashMap**.)

Object — AbstractMap — ConcurrentHashMap
Map | Map ··· ConcurrentMap | Serializable

```
public class ConcurrentHashMap<K,V> extends java.util.AbstractMap<K,V>
        implements ConcurrentMap<K,V>, Serializable {
// Public Constructors
    public ConcurrentHashMap();
    public ConcurrentHashMap(java.util.Map<? extends K,? extends V> t);
    public ConcurrentHashMap(int initialCapacity);
    public ConcurrentHashMap(int initialCapacity, float loadFactor, int concurrencyLevel);
// Public Instance Methods
    public boolean contains(Object value);
    public java.util.Enumeration<V> elements();
    public java.util.Enumeration<K> keys();
// Methods Implementing ConcurrentMap
    public V putIfAbsent(K key, V value);
    public boolean remove(Object key, Object value);
    public V replace(K key, V value);
    public boolean replace(K key, V oldValue, V newValue);
// Methods Implementing Map
    public void clear();
    public boolean containsKey(Object key);
    public boolean containsValue(Object value);
    public java.util.Set<java.util.Map.Entry<K,V>> entrySet();
    public V get(Object key);
    public boolean isEmpty();                                             default:true
    public java.util.Set<K> keySet();
    public V put(K key, V value);
    public void putAll(java.util.Map<? extends K,? extends V> t);
    public V remove(Object key);
    public int size();
    public java.util.Collection<V> values();
}
```

ConcurrentLinkedQueue<E> — Java 5.0

java.util.concurrent — serializable collection

This class is a threadsafe implementation of the java.util.Queue interface (but not of the BlockingQueue interface). It provides threadsafety without using synchronized methods that would lock the entire data structure. ConcurrentLinkedQueue is unbounded and orders its elements on a first-in, first-out (FIFO) basis. null elements are not allowed. This implementation uses a linked-list data structure internally. Note that the size() method must traverse the internal data structure and is therefore a relatively expensive operation for this class.

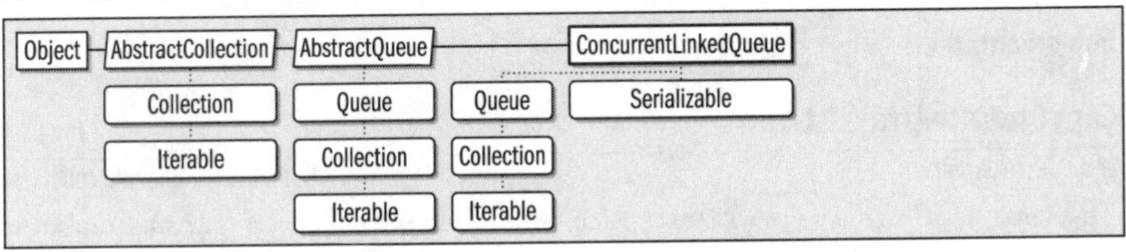

```
public class ConcurrentLinkedQueue<E> extends java.util.AbstractQueue<E>
        implements java.util.Queue<E>, Serializable {
// Public Constructors
    public ConcurrentLinkedQueue();
    public ConcurrentLinkedQueue(java.util.Collection<? extends E> c);
// Methods Implementing Collection
    public boolean add(E o);
    public boolean contains(Object o);
    public boolean isEmpty();                                           default:true
    public java.util.Iterator<E> iterator();
    public boolean remove(Object o);
    public int size();
    public Object[] toArray();
    public <T> T[] toArray(T[] a);
// Methods Implementing Queue
    public boolean offer(E o);
    public E peek();
    public E poll();
}
```

ConcurrentMap<K,V> — Java 5.0

java.util.concurrent — collection

This interface extends the java.util.Map interface to add four important atomic methods. As with the Map interface, the type variables *K* and *V* represent the types of the mapped keys and values.

putIfAbsent() atomically tests whether a key is already defined in the map, and if not, maps it to the specified value. remove() atomically removes the specified key from the map, but only if it is mapped to the specified value. It returns true if it modified the map. There are two versions of the atomic replace() method. The first checks whether the specified value is already mapped to a value. If so, it replaces the existing mapping with the specified value and returns true. Otherwise, it returns false. The three-argument version of replace() maps the specified key to the specified new value, but only if the key is currently mapped to the specified old value. It returns true if the replacement was made and false otherwise.

Map ConcurrentMap

```
public interface ConcurrentMap<K,V> extends java.util.Map<K,V> {
// Public Instance Methods
    V putIfAbsent(K key, V value);
    boolean remove(Object key, Object value);
    V replace(K key, V value);
    boolean replace(K key, V oldValue, V newValue);
}
```

Implementations ConcurrentHashMap

CopyOnWriteArrayList<E> — Java 5.0

java.util.concurrent — cloneable serializable collection

This class is a threadsafe java.util.List implementation based on an array. Any number of read operations may proceed concurrently. All update methods are synchronized and make a completely new copy of the internal array, so this class is best suited to applications in which reads greatly outnumber updates. The **Iterator** of a **CopyOnWriteArrayList** operates on the copy of the array that was current when the **iterator()** method was called: it does not see any updates that occur after the call to **iterator()** and is guaranteed never to throw **ConcurrentModificationException**. Update methods of the **Iterator** and **ListIterator** interfaces are not supported and throw **UnsupportedOperationException**.

CopyOnWriteArrayList defines a few useful methods beyond those specified by the **List** interface. **addIfAbsent()** atomically adds an element to the list, but only if the list does not already contain that element. **addAllAbsent()** adds all elements of a collection that are not already in the list. Two new **indexOf()** and **lastIndexOf()** methods are defined that specify a starting index for the search. These provide a convenient alternative to using a **subList()** view when searching for repeated matches in a list.

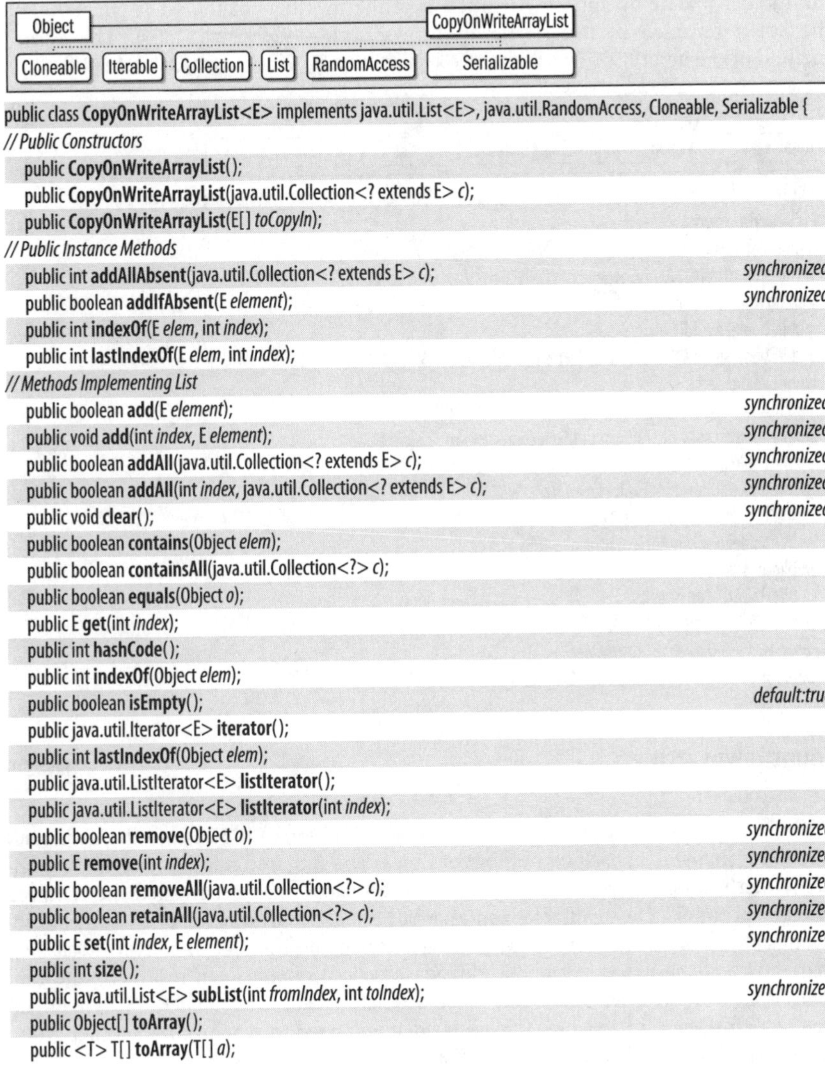


```
public class CopyOnWriteArrayList<E> implements java.util.List<E>, java.util.RandomAccess, Cloneable, Serializable {
// Public Constructors
   public CopyOnWriteArrayList();
   public CopyOnWriteArrayList(java.util.Collection<? extends E> c);
   public CopyOnWriteArrayList(E[] toCopyIn);
// Public Instance Methods
   public int addAllAbsent(java.util.Collection<? extends E> c);                    synchronized
   public boolean addIfAbsent(E element);                                          synchronized
   public int indexOf(E elem, int index);
   public int lastIndexOf(E elem, int index);
// Methods Implementing List
   public boolean add(E element);                                                  synchronized
   public void add(int index, E element);                                          synchronized
   public boolean addAll(java.util.Collection<? extends E> c);                     synchronized
   public boolean addAll(int index, java.util.Collection<? extends E> c);          synchronized
   public void clear();                                                            synchronized
   public boolean contains(Object elem);
   public boolean containsAll(java.util.Collection<?> c);
   public boolean equals(Object o);
   public E get(int index);
   public int hashCode();
   public int indexOf(Object elem);
   public boolean isEmpty();                                                       default:true
   public java.util.Iterator<E> iterator();
   public int lastIndexOf(Object elem);
   public java.util.ListIterator<E> listIterator();
   public java.util.ListIterator<E> listIterator(int index);
   public boolean remove(Object o);                                                synchronized
   public E remove(int index);                                                     synchronized
   public boolean removeAll(java.util.Collection<?> c);                            synchronized
   public boolean retainAll(java.util.Collection<?> c);                            synchronized
   public E set(int index, E element);                                             synchronized
   public int size();
   public java.util.List<E> subList(int fromIndex, int toIndex);                   synchronized
   public Object[] toArray();
   public <T> T[] toArray(T[] a);
```

java.util.*

```
// Public Methods Overriding Object
    public Object clone();
    public String toString();
}
```

CopyOnWriteArraySet<E> Java 5.0

java.util.concurrent serializable collection

This class is a threadsafe java.util.Set implementation based on the CopyOnWriteArrayList class. Because the data structure is array-based, the contains() method is O(n); this means that this class is suitable only for relatively small sets. Because the data structure uses copy-on-write, the class is best suited to cases where read operations and traversals greatly outnumber update operations. Iteration over the members of the set is efficient, and the Iterator returned by iterator() never throws ConcurrentModificationException. The remove() method of the iterator throws UnsupportedOperationException. See also CopyOnWriteArrayList.

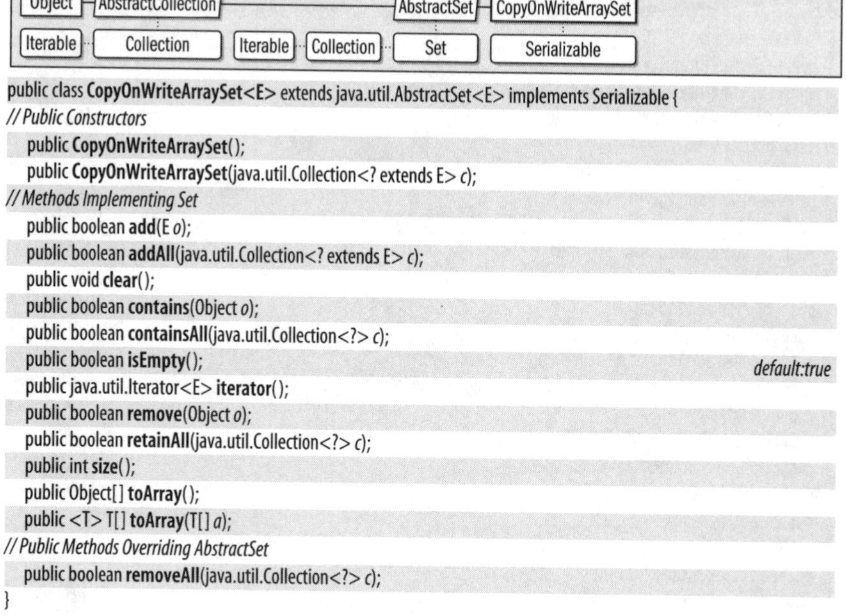


```
public class CopyOnWriteArraySet<E> extends java.util.AbstractSet<E> implements Serializable {
// Public Constructors
    public CopyOnWriteArraySet();
    public CopyOnWriteArraySet(java.util.Collection<? extends E> c);
// Methods Implementing Set
    public boolean add(E o);
    public boolean addAll(java.util.Collection<? extends E> c);
    public void clear();
    public boolean contains(Object o);
    public boolean containsAll(java.util.Collection<?> c);
    public boolean isEmpty();                                              default:true
    public java.util.Iterator<E> iterator();
    public boolean remove(Object o);
    public boolean retainAll(java.util.Collection<?> c);
    public int size();
    public Object[] toArray();
    public <T> T[] toArray(T[] a);
// Public Methods Overriding AbstractSet
    public boolean removeAll(java.util.Collection<?> c);
}
```

CountDownLatch Java 5.0

java.util.concurrent

This class synchronizes threads. All threads that call await() block until the countDown() method is invoked a specified number of times. The required number of calls is specified when the CountDownLatch is created. Once countDown() has been called the required number of times, all threads blocked in await() are allowed to resume, and any subsequent calls to await() do not block. getCount() returns the number of calls to countDown() that must still be made before the threads blocked in await() can resume. Note that there is no way to reset the count. Once a CountDownLatch has "latched," it remains in that state forever. Create a new CountDownLatch if you need to synchronize another group of threads. Contrast this class with CyclicBarrier.

```
public class CountDownLatch {
// Public Constructors
   public CountDownLatch(int count);
// Public Instance Methods
   public void await() throws InterruptedException;
   public boolean await(long timeout, TimeUnit unit) throws InterruptedException;
   public void countDown();
   public long getCount();
// Public Methods Overriding Object
   public String toString();
}
```

CyclicBarrier Java 5.0

java.util.concurrent

This class synchronizes a group of *n* threads, where *n* is specified to the CyclicBarrier() constructor. Threads call the await() method, which blocks until *n* threads are waiting. In the simple case, all *n* threads are then allowed to proceed, and the CyclicBarrier resets itself until it has another *n* threads blocked in await().

More complex behavior is possible if you pass a Runnable object to the CyclicBarrier constructor. This Runnable is a "barrier action" and when the last of the *n* threads invokes await(), that method uses the thread to invoke the run() method of the Runnable. This Runnable is typically used to perform some sort of coordinating action on the blocked threads. When the run() method returns, the CyclicBarrier allows all blocked threads to resume.

When threads resume from await(), the return value of await() is an integer that represents the order in which they called await(). This is useful if you want to be able to distinguish between otherwise identical worker threads. For example, you might have the thread that arrived first perform some special action while the remaining threads resume.

If any thread times out or is interrupted while blocked in await(), the CyclicBarrier is said to be "broken," and all waiting threads (and any threads that subsequently call await()) wake up with a BrokenBarrierException. Waiting threads also receive a BrokenBarrierException if the CyclicBarrier is reset(). The reset() method is the only way to restore a broken barrier to its initial state. This is difficult to coordinate properly, however, unless one controller thread is coded differently from the other threads at the barrier.

```
public class CyclicBarrier {
// Public Constructors
   public CyclicBarrier(int parties);
   public CyclicBarrier(int parties, Runnable barrierAction);
// Public Instance Methods
   public int await() throws InterruptedException, BrokenBarrierException;
   public int await(long timeout, TimeUnit unit) throws InterruptedException, BrokenBarrierException, TimeoutException;
   public int getNumberWaiting();
   public int getParties();
   public boolean isBroken();
   public void reset();
}
```

Delayed — Java 5.0

java.util.concurrent — comparable

An object that implements this interface has an associated delay. Typically, it is some kind of task, such as a Callable, that has been scheduled to execute at some future time. getDelay() returns the remaining time, measured in the specified TimeUnit. If no time remains, getDelay() should return zero or a negative value. See ScheduledFuture and DelayQueue.

Comparable ··· Delayed

```
public interface Delayed extends Comparable<Delayed> {
// Public Instance Methods
   long getDelay(TimeUnit unit);
}
```

Implementations ScheduledFuture

Passed To DelayQueue.{add(), offer(), put()}

Returned By DelayQueue.{peek(), poll(), take()}

DelayQueue<E extends Delayed> — Java 5.0

java.util.concurrent — collection

This BlockingQueue implementation restricts its elements to instances of some class *E* that implements the Delay interface. null elements are not allowed. Elements on the queue are ordered by the amount of delay remaining. The element whose getDelay() method returns the smallest value is the first to be removed from the queue. No element may be removed, however, until its getDelay() method returns zero or a negative number.

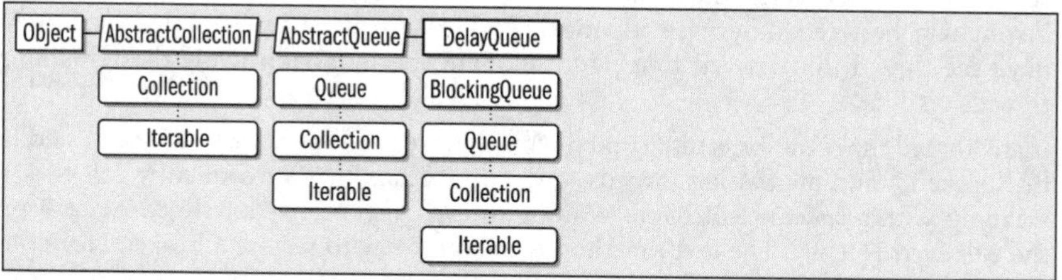


```
public class DelayQueue<E extends Delayed> extends java.util.AbstractQueue<E> implements BlockingQueue<E> {
// Public Constructors
   public DelayQueue();
   public DelayQueue(java.util.Collection<? extends E> c);
// Public Instance Methods
   public E peek();
   public E poll();
// Methods Implementing BlockingQueue
   public boolean add(E o);
   public int drainTo(java.util.Collection<? super E> c);
   public int drainTo(java.util.Collection<? super E> c, int maxElements);
   public boolean offer(E o);
   public boolean offer(E o, long timeout, TimeUnit unit);
   public E poll(long timeout, TimeUnit unit) throws InterruptedException;
   public void put(E o);
   public int remainingCapacity();
   public E take() throws InterruptedException;
```

```
// Methods Implementing Collection
    public void clear();
    public java.util.Iterator<E> iterator();
    public boolean remove(Object o);
    public int size();
    public Object[] toArray();
    public <T> T[] toArray(T[] array);
}
```

Exchanger<V> Java 5.0

java.util.concurrent

This class allows two threads to rendezvous and exchange data. This is a generic type, and the type variable *V* represents the type of data to be exchanged. Each thread should call exchange() and pass the value of type *V* that it wants to exchange. The first thread to call exchange() blocks until the second thread calls it. At that point, both threads resume. Both threads receive as their return value the object of type *V* passed by the other thread. Note that this class also defines a timed version of exchange() that throws a TimeoutException if no exchange occurs within the specified timeout interval. Unlike a CountDownLatch, which is a one-shot latch, and CyclicBarrier which can be "broken," an Exchanger may be reused for any number of exchanges.

```
public class Exchanger<V> {
// Public Constructors
    public Exchanger();
// Public Instance Methods
    public V exchange(V x) throws InterruptedException;
    public V exchange(V x, long timeout, TimeUnit unit) throws InterruptedException, TimeoutException;
}
```

ExecutionException Java 5.0

java.util.concurrent serializable checked

An exception of this type is like a checked wrapper around an arbitrary exception thrown while executing a task. The get() method of a Future object, for example, throws an ExecutionException if the call() method of a Callable throws an exception. ExecutionException may also be thrown by ExecutorService.invokeAny(). Use the Throwable.getCause() method to obtain the exception object that the ExecutionException wraps.

Object — Throwable — Exception — ExecutionException
Throwable ⋮ Serializable

```
public class ExecutionException extends Exception {
// Public Constructors
    public ExecutionException(Throwable cause);
    public ExecutionException(String message, Throwable cause);
// Protected Constructors
    protected ExecutionException();
    protected ExecutionException(String message);
}
```

Thrown By AbstractExecutorService.invokeAny(), ExecutorService.invokeAny(), Future.get(), FutureTask.get()

Executor

Java 5.0

java.util.concurrent

This interface defines a mechanism for executing **Runnable** tasks. A variety of implementations are possible for the **execute()** method. An implementation might simply synchronously invoke the **run()** method of the specified **Runnable**. Another implementation might create and start a new thread for each **Runnable** object it is passed. Another might select an existing thread from a thread pool to run the **Runnable** or queue the **Runnable** for future execution when a thread becomes available.

ExecutorService extends this interface with methods to execute **Callable** tasks and methods for canceling tasks. **ThreadPoolExecutor** is an **ExecutorService** implementation that creates a configurable thread pool. Finally, the **Executors** class defines a number of factory methods for easily obtaining **ExecutorService** instances.

```
public interface Executor {
// Public Instance Methods
   void execute(Runnable command);
}
```

Implementations ExecutorService

Passed To ExecutorCompletionService.ExecutorCompletionService()

ExecutorCompletionService<V>

Java 5.0

java.util.concurrent

This class implements the **CompletionService** interface, which uses an **Executor** object passed to its constructor for executing the tasks passed to its **submit()** method. As these tasks complete, their result (or exception) is placed, in the form of a **Future** object, on an internal queue and becomes available for removal with the blocking **take()** method or the nonblocking or timed **poll()** methods.

This class is useful when you want to execute a number of tasks concurrently and want to process their results in whatever order they complete. See **Executors** for a source of **Executor** objects to use with this class.

Object — ExecutorCompletionService ··· CompletionService

```
public class ExecutorCompletionService<V> implements CompletionService<V> {
// Public Constructors
   public ExecutorCompletionService(Executor executor);
   public ExecutorCompletionService(Executor executor, BlockingQueue<Future<V>> completionQueue);
// Methods Implementing CompletionService
   public Future<V> poll();
   public Future<V> poll(long timeout, TimeUnit unit) throws InterruptedException;
   public Future<V> submit(Callable<V> task);
   public Future<V> submit(Runnable task, V result);
   public Future<V> take() throws InterruptedException;
}
```

Executors

Java 5.0

java.util.concurrent

This utility class defines static factory methods for creating **ExecutorService** and **Scheduled-ExecutorService** objects. Each of the factory methods has a variant that allows you to explicitly specify a **ThreadFactory**. **newSingleThreadExecutor()** returns an **ExecutorService** that uses a single thread and an unbounded queue of waiting tasks. **newFixedThreadPool()** returns an

ExecutorService that uses a thread pool with the specified number of threads and an unbounded queue. newCachedThreadPool() returns an ExecutorService that does not queue tasks but instead creates as many threads as are needed. When a task terminates, its thread is cached for reuse. Cached threads are allowed to terminate if they remain unused for 60 seconds.

newSingleThreadScheduledExecutor() returns a ScheduledExecutorService that uses a single thread for running tasks. newScheduledThreadPool() returns a ScheduledExecutorService that uses a thread pool of the specified size.

The factory methods of this class typically return instances of ThreadPoolExecutor and ScheduledThreadPoolExecutor. If the returned objects are cast to these implementing types, they can be configured (to change the thread pool size, for example). If you want to prevent this from happening, use the unconfigurableExecutorService() and unconfigurableScheduledExecutorService() methods to obtain wrapper objects that implement only the ExecutorService and ScheduledExecutorService methods and do not permit configuration.

Other methods of this class include callable(), which returns a Callable object wrapped around a Runnable and an optional result, and defaultThreadFactory(), which returns a basic ThreadFactory object. Executors also define methods related to access control and the Java security system. A variant of the callable() method wraps a Callable around a java.security.PrivilegedAction. privilegedCallable() is intended to be invoked from within a PrivilegedAction being run with AccessController.doPrivileged(). When passed a Callable in this way, it returns a new Callable that can be used later to invoke the original callable in a privileged access control context, granting it permissions that it would not otherwise have.

```
public class Executors {
// No Constructor
// Public Class Methods
   public static Callable<Object> callable(java.security.PrivilegedAction action);
   public static Callable<Object> callable(Runnable task);
   public static Callable<Object> callable(java.security.PrivilegedExceptionAction action);
   public static <T> Callable<T> callable(Runnable task, T result);
   public static ThreadFactory defaultThreadFactory();
   public static ExecutorService newCachedThreadPool();
   public static ExecutorService newCachedThreadPool(ThreadFactory threadFactory);
   public static ExecutorService newFixedThreadPool(int nThreads);
   public static ExecutorService newFixedThreadPool(int nThreads, ThreadFactory threadFactory);
   public static ScheduledExecutorService newScheduledThreadPool(int corePoolSize);
   public static ScheduledExecutorService newScheduledThreadPool(int corePoolSize, ThreadFactory threadFactory);
   public static ExecutorService newSingleThreadExecutor();
   public static ExecutorService newSingleThreadExecutor(ThreadFactory threadFactory);
   public static ScheduledExecutorService newSingleThreadScheduledExecutor();
   public static ScheduledExecutorService newSingleThreadScheduledExecutor(ThreadFactory threadFactory);
   public static <T> Callable<T> privilegedCallable(Callable<T> callable);
   public static <T> Callable<T> privilegedCallableUsingCurrentClassLoader(Callable<T> callable);
   public static ThreadFactory privilegedThreadFactory();
   public static ExecutorService unconfigurableExecutorService(ExecutorService executor);
   public static ScheduledExecutorService unconfigurableScheduledExecutorService(ScheduledExecutorService executor);
}
```

ExecutorService **Java 5.0**

java.util.concurrent

This interface extends **Executor** to add methods to obtain a **Future** result of the asynchronous execution of a **Callable** task. It also adds methods for graceful termination or shutdown of an **ExecutorService**. **ThreadPoolExecutor** is a useful and highly configurable implementation of this interface. An easy way to obtain instances of this class is through the factory methods of the **Executors** utility class. Note that **ExecutorService** is not a generic type; it does not declare any type variables. It does have a number of generic methods, however, that use the type variable *T* to represent the result type of **Callable** and **Future** objects.

The **submit()** method allows you to submit a **Callable<T>** object to an **ExecutorService** for execution. Typical **ExecutorService** implementations invoke the **call()** method of the **Callable** on another thread, and the return value (of type *T*) of the method is therefore not available when the call to **submit()** returns. **submit()** therefore returns a **Future<T>** object: the promise of a return value of type *T* at some point in the future. See the **Future** interface for further details.

Two variants on the **submit()** method accept a **java.lang.Runnable** task instead of a **Callable** task. The **run()** method of a **Runnable** has no return value, so the two-argument version of **submit()** accepts a dummy return value of type *T* and returns a **Future<T>** that makes this dummy value available when the **Runnable** has completed running. The other **Runnable** variant of the **submit()** method takes no return value and returns a **Future<?>** value. The **get()** method of this **Future** object returns **null** when the **Runnable** is done.

Other **ExecutorService** methods execute **Callable** objects synchronously. **invokeAll()** is passed a **java.util.Collection** of **Callable<T>** tasks. It executes them and blocks until all have completed, or until an optionally specified timeout has elapsed. **invokeAll()** returns the results of the tasks as a **List** of **Future<T>** objects. Note that a **Callable<T>** task can complete either by returning a result of type T or by throwing an exception.

invokeAny() is also passed a **Collection** of **Callable<T>** objects. It blocks until any one of these **Callable** tasks has returned a value of type *T* and returns that value. Tasks that terminate by throwing an exception are ignored. If all tasks throw an exception, **invokeAny()** throws an **ExecutionException**. Before **invokeAny()** returns, it cancels the execution of any still-running **Callable** tasks. Like **invokeAll()**, **invokeAny()** has a variant with a timeout value.

ExecutorService defines several methods for gracefully shutting down the service. **shutdown()** puts the **ExecutorService** into a special state in which no new tasks may be submitted for execution, but all currently running tasks continue running. **isShutdown()** returns **true** if the **ExecutorService** has entered this state. **awaitTermination()** blocks until all executing tasks in an **ExecutorService** that was shut down are completed (or until a specified timeout elapses). Once this has occurred, the **isTerminated()** method returns **true**. The **shutdownNow()** method shuts down an **ExecutorService** more abruptly: it attempts to abort all currently executing tasks (typically via **Thread.interrupt()**) and returns a **List** of the tasks that have not yet started executing.

Executor ··· ExecutorService

```
public interface ExecutorService extends Executor {
// Public Instance Methods
   boolean awaitTermination(long timeout, TimeUnit unit) throws InterruptedException;
   <T> java.util.List<Future<T>> invokeAll(java.util.Collection<Callable<T>> tasks) throws InterruptedException;
   <T> java.util.List<Future<T>> invokeAll(java.util.Collection<Callable<T>> tasks, long timeout, TimeUnit unit)
       throws InterruptedException;
   <T> T invokeAny(java.util.Collection<Callable<T>> tasks) throws InterruptedException, ExecutionException;
```

```
    <T> T invokeAny(java.util.Collection<Callable<T>> tasks, long timeout, TimeUnit unit)
        throws InterruptedException, ExecutionException, TimeoutException;
    boolean isShutdown();
    boolean isTerminated();
    void shutdown();
    java.util.List<Runnable> shutdownNow();
    <T> Future<T> submit(Callable<T> task);
    Future<?> submit(Runnable task);
    <T> Future<T> submit(Runnable task, T result);
}
```

Implementations AbstractExecutorService, ScheduledExecutorService

Passed To Executors.unconfigurableExecutorService()

Returned By Executors.{newCachedThreadPool(), newFixedThreadPool(), newSingleThreadExecutor(), unconfigurableExecutorService()}

Future<V> Java 5.0

java.util.concurrent

This interface represents the result of a computation that may not be available until some time in the future. Future is a generic type, with a type variable *V*. *V* represents the type of the future value to be returned by the get() method. A Future<V> value is typically obtained by submitting a Callable<V> to an ExecutorService for asynchronous execution.

The key method of the Future interface is get(). It returns the result (of type *V*) of the computation, blocking, if necessary, until that result is ready. get() throws a CancellationException if the computation is canceled with the cancel() method before it completes. If the computation throws an exception of its own (as the Callable.call() method can), get() throws an ExecutionException wrapped around that exception. Additionally, the timed version of the get() method throws a TimeoutException if the timeout elapses before the computation completes.

As noted above, the computation represented by a Future object can be canceled by calling its cancel() method. This method returns true if the computation was canceled successfully, and false otherwise. If you pass false to cancel(), any computation that has started running is allowed to complete. In this case, only computations that have not yet started can be canceled. If you pass true to the cancel() method, running computations are interrupted with Thread.interrupt(). Note, however, that interrupting a thread does not guarantee that it will stop running.

isCancelled() returns true if a Future was canceled before it completed (either by returning a value or throwing an exception). isDone() returns true if the computation represented by a Future is finished running. This may be because it returned a value, threw an exception, or was canceled. If isDone() returns true, the get() method does not block.

```
public interface Future<V> {
// Public Instance Methods
    boolean cancel(boolean mayInterruptIfRunning);
    V get() throws InterruptedException, ExecutionException;
    V get(long timeout, TimeUnit unit) throws InterruptedException, ExecutionException, TimeoutException;
    boolean isCancelled();
    boolean isDone();
}
```

Implementations FutureTask, ScheduledFuture

Returned By Too many methods to list.

FutureTask<V> Java 5.0

java.util.concurrent runnable

This class is a Runnable wrapper around a Callable object (or around another Runnable). FutureTask is a generic type and the type variable *V* represents the return type of the wrapped Callable object. AbstractExecutorService uses FutureTask to convert Callable objects passed to the submit() method into Runnable objects it can pass to the execute() method.

FutureTask also implements the Future interface, which means that the get() method waits for the run() method to complete and provides access to the result (or exception) of the Callable's execution.

The protected methods set() and setException() are invoked when the Callable returns a value or throws an exception. done() is invoked when the Callable completes or is canceled. Subclasses can override any of these methods to insert hooks for notification, logging, and so on.

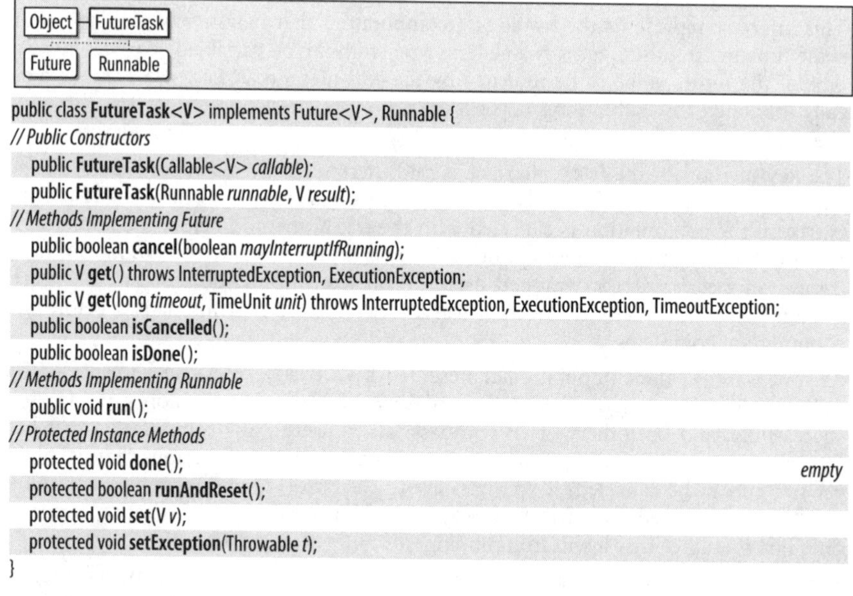


```
public class FutureTask<V> implements Future<V>, Runnable {
// Public Constructors
   public FutureTask(Callable<V> callable);
   public FutureTask(Runnable runnable, V result);
// Methods Implementing Future
   public boolean cancel(boolean mayInterruptIfRunning);
   public V get() throws InterruptedException, ExecutionException;
   public V get(long timeout, TimeUnit unit) throws InterruptedException, ExecutionException, TimeoutException;
   public boolean isCancelled();
   public boolean isDone();
// Methods Implementing Runnable
   public void run();
// Protected Instance Methods
   protected void done();                                                     empty
   protected boolean runAndReset();
   protected void set(V v);
   protected void setException(Throwable t);
}
```

LinkedBlockingQueue<E> Java 5.0

java.util.concurrent serializable collection

This threadsafe class implements the BlockingQueue interface based on a linked-list data structure. It orders elements on a first-in, first-out (FIFO) basis. You may specify a maximum queue capacity, creating a bounded queue. The default capacity is Integer.MAX_VALUE, which is effectively unbounded. null elements are not permitted.

Object — AbstractCollection — AbstractQueue — LinkedBlockingQueue
Collection — Iterable
Queue — Collection — Iterable
BlockingQueue — Queue — Collection — Iterable
Serializable

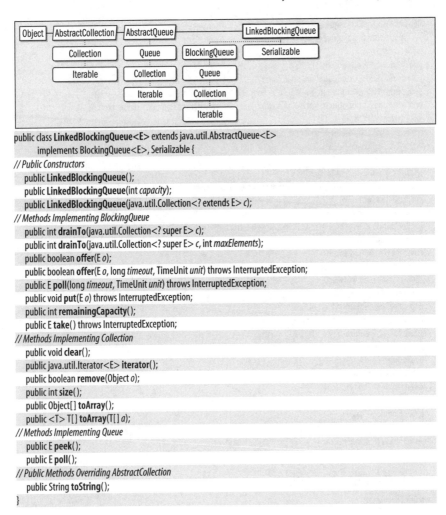

```
public class LinkedBlockingQueue<E> extends java.util.AbstractQueue<E>
        implements BlockingQueue<E>, Serializable {
// Public Constructors
    public LinkedBlockingQueue();
    public LinkedBlockingQueue(int capacity);
    public LinkedBlockingQueue(java.util.Collection<? extends E> c);
// Methods Implementing BlockingQueue
    public int drainTo(java.util.Collection<? super E> c);
    public int drainTo(java.util.Collection<? super E> c, int maxElements);
    public boolean offer(E o);
    public boolean offer(E o, long timeout, TimeUnit unit) throws InterruptedException;
    public E poll(long timeout, TimeUnit unit) throws InterruptedException;
    public void put(E o) throws InterruptedException;
    public int remainingCapacity();
    public E take() throws InterruptedException;
// Methods Implementing Collection
    public void clear();
    public java.util.Iterator<E> iterator();
    public boolean remove(Object o);
    public int size();
    public Object[] toArray();
    public <T> T[] toArray(T[] a);
// Methods Implementing Queue
    public E peek();
    public E poll();
// Public Methods Overriding AbstractCollection
    public String toString();
}
```

PriorityBlockingQueue<E> — Java 5.0

java.util.concurrent — serializable collection

This threadsafe class implements the BlockingQueue interface. It is an unbounded queue that orders its elements according to a Comparator, or, for Comparable elements, according to their compareTo() method. The head of the queue (the next element to be removed) is always the smallest element. Note that the Iterator returned by the iterator() method is not guaranteed to return elements in this order. See also java.util.PriorityQueue.

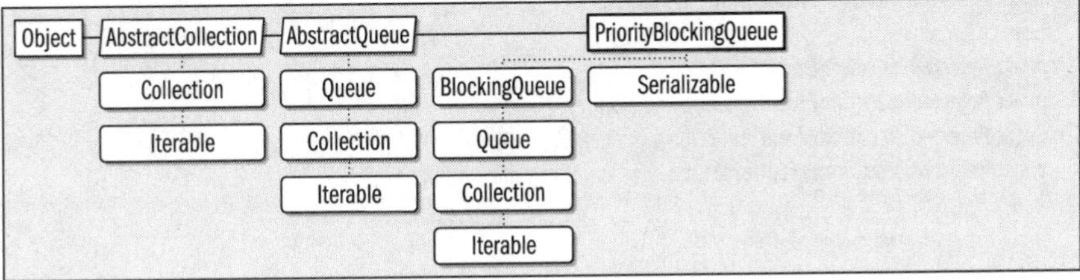

java.util.*

```
public class PriorityBlockingQueue<E> extends java.util.AbstractQueue<E>
        implements BlockingQueue<E>, Serializable {
// Public Constructors
    public PriorityBlockingQueue();
    public PriorityBlockingQueue(int initialCapacity);
    public PriorityBlockingQueue(java.util.Collection<? extends E> c);
    public PriorityBlockingQueue(int initialCapacity, java.util.Comparator<? super E> comparator);
// Public Instance Methods
    public java.util.Comparator<? super E> comparator();
// Methods Implementing BlockingQueue
    public boolean add(E o);
    public int drainTo(java.util.Collection<? super E> c);
    public int drainTo(java.util.Collection<? super E> c, int maxElements);
    public boolean offer(E o);
    public boolean offer(E o, long timeout, TimeUnit unit);
    public E poll(long timeout, TimeUnit unit) throws InterruptedException;
    public void put(E o);
    public int remainingCapacity();
    public E take() throws InterruptedException;
// Methods Implementing Collection
    public void clear();
    public boolean contains(Object o);
    public java.util.Iterator<E> iterator();
    public boolean remove(Object o);
    public int size();
    public Object[] toArray();
    public <T> T[] toArray(T[] a);
// Methods Implementing Queue
    public E peek();
    public E poll();
// Public Methods Overriding AbstractCollection
    public String toString();
}
```

RejectedExecutionException — Java 5.0

java.util.concurrent — serializable unchecked

An exception of this type is thrown by an **Executor** when it cannot accept a task for execution. When a **ThreadPoolExecutor** cannot accept a task, it attempts to invoke a **RejectedExecutionHandler**. **ThreadPoolExecutor** defines several nested implementations of that handler interface that can handle the rejected task without throwing an exception of this type.

Object — Throwable — Exception — RuntimeException — RejectedExecutionException
(Throwable implements Serializable)

```
public class RejectedExecutionException extends RuntimeException {
// Public Constructors
    public RejectedExecutionException();
    public RejectedExecutionException(Throwable cause);
    public RejectedExecutionException(String message);
    public RejectedExecutionException(String message, Throwable cause);
}
```

RejectedExecutionHandler Java 5.0

java.util.concurrent

This interface defines an API for a handler method invoked by a ThreadPoolExecutor when its execute() method cannot accept any more Runnable objects. This can occur when both the thread pool and the queue of waiting tasks is full, or when the ThreadPoolExecutor has been shut down. Register an instance of this class with the setRejectedExecutionHandler() method of ThreadPoolExecutor. ThreadPoolExecutor includes several predefined implementations of this interface as static member classes. If the rejectedExecution() method cannot arrange for the Runnable to be run and does not wish to simply discard that task, it should throw a RejectedExecutionException which propagates up to the caller that submitted the task for execution.

```
public interface RejectedExecutionHandler {
// Public Instance Methods
   void rejectedExecution(Runnable r, ThreadPoolExecutor executor);
}
```

Implementations ThreadPoolExecutor.AbortPolicy, ThreadPoolExecutor.CallerRunsPolicy, ThreadPoolExecutor.DiscardOldestPolicy, ThreadPoolExecutor.DiscardPolicy

Passed To ScheduledThreadPoolExecutor.ScheduledThreadPoolExecutor(), ThreadPoolExecutor.{setRejectedExecutionHandler(), ThreadPoolExecutor()}

Returned By ThreadPoolExecutor.getRejectedExecutionHandler()

ScheduledExecutorService Java 5.0

java.util.concurrent

This interface extends Executor and ExecutorService to add methods for scheduling Callable or Runnable tasks for future execution on a one-time basis or a repeating basis. The schedule() methods schedule a Callable or a Runnable task for one-time execution after a specified delay. The delay is specified by a long plus a TimeUnit. When a Callable<V> is scheduled, the result is a ScheduledFuture<V>. This is like a Future<V> object but also implements the Delay interface so you can call getDelay() to find out how much time remains before execution begins. If you schedule() a Runnable object, the result is a ScheduledFuture<?>. Since a Runnable has no return value, the get() method of this ScheduledFuture returns null, but the cancel(), getDelay(), and isDone() methods remain useful.

ScheduledExecutorService provides two alternatives for scheduling Runnable tasks for repeated execution. (See also java.util.Timer, which has similar methods.) scheduleAtFixedRate() begins the first execution of the Runnable after *initialDelay* time units, and begins subsequent executions at multiples of *period* time units after that. This means that the Runnable runs at a fixed rate, regardless of how long each execution takes. scheduleWithFixedDelay() also begins the first execution after *initialDelay* time units. But it waits for this first execution (and all subsequent executions) to complete before scheduling the next execution for *delay* time units in the future. Both methods return a ScheduledFuture object that you can use to cancel() the repeated execution of tasks. If the task is not canceled, the ScheduledExecutorService runs it repeatedly until the service is shut down (see ExecutorService) or the Runnable throws an exception.

Executor ··· ExecutorService ··· ScheduledExecutorService

```
public interface ScheduledExecutorService extends ExecutorService {
// Public Instance Methods
   <V> ScheduledFuture<V> schedule(Callable<V> callable, long delay, TimeUnit unit);
```

java.util.*

```
    ScheduledFuture<?> schedule(Runnable command, long delay, TimeUnit unit);
    ScheduledFuture<?> scheduleAtFixedRate(Runnable command, long initialDelay, long period, TimeUnit unit);
    ScheduledFuture<?> scheduleWithFixedDelay(Runnable command, long initialDelay, long delay, TimeUnit unit);
}
```

Implementations ScheduledThreadPoolExecutor

Passed To Executors.unconfigurableScheduledExecutorService()

Returned By Executors.{newScheduledThreadPool(), newSingleThreadScheduledExecutor(), unconfigurableScheduledExecutorService()}

ScheduledFuture<V> Java 5.0

java.util.concurrent comparable

This interface extends Future and Delayed and adds no methods of its own. A ScheduledFuture represents a computation and the future result of that computation just as Future does, but it adds a getDelay() method that returns the amount of time until the computation begins. See ScheduledExecutorService.

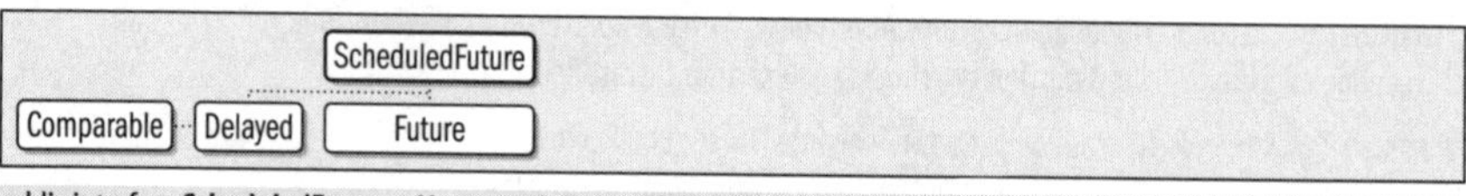


```
public interface ScheduledFuture<V> extends DelayedFuture<V> {
}
```

Returned By ScheduledExecutorService.{schedule(), scheduleAtFixedRate(), scheduleWithFixedDelay()}, ScheduledThreadPoolExecutor.{schedule(), scheduleAtFixedRate(), scheduleWithFixedDelay()}

ScheduledThreadPoolExecutor Java 5.0

java.util.concurrent

This class extends ThreadPoolExecutor to implement the methods of the ScheduledExecutorService interface to allow tasks to be submitted for execution once or repeatedly at some scheduled time in the future. Instances of this class are usually obtained through the static factory methods of the Executors utility class. You can also explicitly create one with the ScheduledThreadPoolExecutors() constructor. ScheduledThreadPoolExecutor always creates its own unbounded work queue, which means that you cannot pass a queue to the constructor. Also, there is no need to specify a *maximumPoolSize* since this configuration parameter is irrelevant with unbounded queues.

Note that tasks submitted to a ScheduledThreadPoolExecutor are not guaranteed to run at the scheduled time. That is the time at which they first become eligible to run. If all threads are busy with other tasks, however, eligible tasks may get queued up to run later.

This class provides functionality similar to java.util.Timer but adds multithreaded capability and the ability to work with Callable and Future objects.

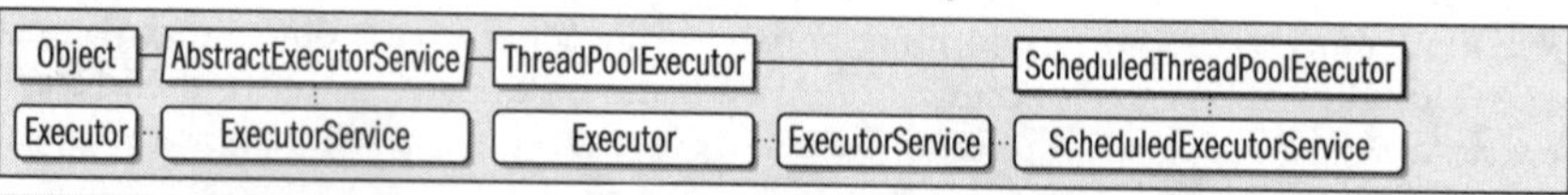


```
public class ScheduledThreadPoolExecutor extends ThreadPoolExecutor implements ScheduledExecutorService {
// Public Constructors
    public ScheduledThreadPoolExecutor(int corePoolSize);
    public ScheduledThreadPoolExecutor(int corePoolSize, ThreadFactory threadFactory);
    public ScheduledThreadPoolExecutor(int corePoolSize, RejectedExecutionHandler handler);
```

```
    public ScheduledThreadPoolExecutor(int corePoolSize, ThreadFactory threadFactory,
                                       RejectedExecutionHandler handler);
// Public Instance Methods
    public boolean getContinueExistingPeriodicTasksAfterShutdownPolicy();
    public boolean getExecuteExistingDelayedTasksAfterShutdownPolicy();
    public void setContinueExistingPeriodicTasksAfterShutdownPolicy(boolean value);
    public void setExecuteExistingDelayedTasksAfterShutdownPolicy(boolean value);
// Methods Implementing Executor
    public void execute(Runnable command);
// Methods Implementing ExecutorService
    public void shutdown();
    public java.util.List<Runnable> shutdownNow();
    public Future<?> submit(Runnable task);
    public <T> Future<T> submit(Callable<T> task);
    public <T> Future<T> submit(Runnable task, T result);
// Methods Implementing ScheduledExecutorService
    public <V> ScheduledFuture<V> schedule(Callable<V> callable, long delay, TimeUnit unit);
    public ScheduledFuture<?> schedule(Runnable command, long delay, TimeUnit unit);
    public ScheduledFuture<?> scheduleAtFixedRate(Runnable command, long initialDelay, long period, TimeUnit unit);
    public ScheduledFuture<?> scheduleWithFixedDelay(Runnable command, long initialDelay, long delay,
                                                     TimeUnit unit);
// Public Methods Overriding ThreadPoolExecutor
    public BlockingQueue<Runnable> getQueue();
    public boolean remove(Runnable task);
}
```

Semaphore — Java 5.0

java.util.concurrent — serializable

This class implements *semaphores*, a classic thread synchronization primitive that can be used to implement mutual exclusion and wait/notify-style thread synchronization. A Semaphore maintains some fixed number (specified when the Semaphore() constructor is called) of *permits*. The acquire() method blocks until a permit is available, then decrements the number of available permits and returns. The release() method does the reverse: it increments the number of permits, possibly unblocking a thread waiting in acquire().

If you pass true as the second argument to the Semaphore() constructor, the semaphore treats waiting threads fairly by placing them on a FIFO queue in the order they called acquire() and granting permits to the threads in this order. This prevents thread starvation.

Object — Semaphore ··· Serializable

```
public class Semaphore implements Serializable {
// Public Constructors
    public Semaphore(int permits);
    public Semaphore(int permits, boolean fair);
// Public Instance Methods
    public void acquire() throws InterruptedException;
    public void acquire(int permits) throws InterruptedException;
    public void acquireUninterruptibly();
    public void acquireUninterruptibly(int permits);
    public int availablePermits();
    public int drainPermits();
    public final int getQueueLength();
```

```
    public final boolean hasQueuedThreads();
    public boolean isFair();
    public void release();
    public void release(int permits);
    public boolean tryAcquire();
    public boolean tryAcquire(int permits);
    public boolean tryAcquire(long timeout, TimeUnit unit) throws InterruptedException;
    public boolean tryAcquire(int permits, long timeout, TimeUnit unit) throws InterruptedException;
// Public Methods Overriding Object
    public String toString();
// Protected Instance Methods
    protected java.util.Collection<Thread> getQueuedThreads();
    protected void reducePermits(int reduction);
}
```

SynchronousQueue<E> Java 5.0

java.util.concurrent serializable collection

This BlockingQueue implementation is the degenerate case of a bounded queue with a capacity of zero. Every call to put() blocks until a corresponding call to take(), and vice versa. You can think of this as an Exchanger that does only a one-way exchange.

The size() and remainingCapacity() methods always return 0. The peek() method always returns null. The iterator() method returns an Iterator for which the hasNext() method returns false.

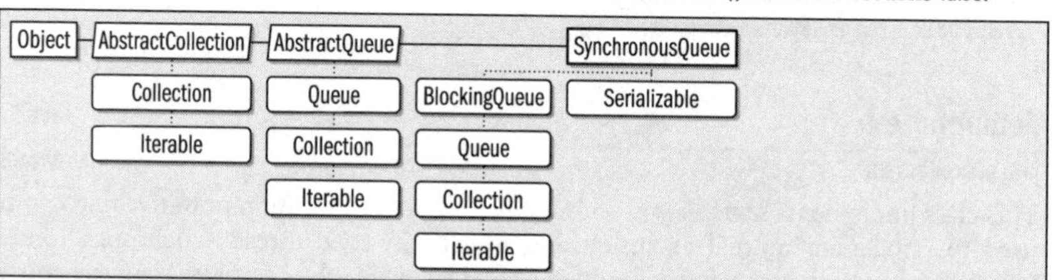


```
public class SynchronousQueue<E> extends java.util.AbstractQueue<E> implements BlockingQueue<E>, Serializable {
// Public Constructors
    public SynchronousQueue();
    public SynchronousQueue(boolean fair);
// Methods Implementing BlockingQueue
    public int drainTo(java.util.Collection<? super E> c);
    public int drainTo(java.util.Collection<? super E> c, int maxElements);
    public boolean offer(E o);
    public boolean offer(E o, long timeout, TimeUnit unit) throws InterruptedException;
    public E poll(long timeout, TimeUnit unit) throws InterruptedException;
    public void put(E o) throws InterruptedException;
    public int remainingCapacity();                                         constant
    public E take() throws InterruptedException;
// Methods Implementing Collection
    public void clear();                                                    empty
    public boolean contains(Object o);                                      constant
    public boolean containsAll(java.util.Collection<?> c);
    public boolean isEmpty();                                  constant default:true
    public java.util.Iterator<E> iterator();
    public boolean remove(Object o);                                        constant
    public boolean removeAll(java.util.Collection<?> c);                    constant
    public boolean retainAll(java.util.Collection<?> c);                    constant
```

```
    public int size();                                          constant
    public Object[] toArray();
    public <T> T[] toArray(T[] a);
// Methods Implementing Queue
    public E peek();                                            constant
    public E poll();
}
```

ThreadFactory **Java 5.0**

java.util.concurrent

An instance of this interface is an object that creates Thread objects to run Runnable objects. You might define a ThreadFactory if you want to set the priority, name, or ThreadGroup of the threads used by a ThreadPoolExecutor, for example. A number of the factory methods of the Executors utility class rely on ThreadPoolExecutor and accept a ThreadFactory argument.

```
public interface ThreadFactory {
// Public Instance Methods
    Thread newThread(Runnable r);
}
```

Passed To Executors.{newCachedThreadPool(), newFixedThreadPool(), newScheduledThreadPool(), newSingleThreadExecutor(), newSingleThreadScheduledExecutor()}, ScheduledThreadPoolExecutor.ScheduledThreadPoolExecutor(), ThreadPoolExecutor.{setThreadFactory(), ThreadPoolExecutor()}

Returned By Executors.{defaultThreadFactory(), privilegedThreadFactory()}, ThreadPoolExecutor.getThreadFactory()

ThreadPoolExecutor **Java 5.0**

java.util.concurrent

This class implements the ExecutorService interface to execute tasks using a highly configurable thread pool. The easiest way to instantiate this class is through the static factory methods of the Executors class. If you want a more highly configured thread pool, you can instantiate it directly.

Four configuration parameters must be passed to every ThreadPoolExecutor() constructor; two others are optional. Many of these parameters may also be queried and adjusted after the executor has been created through various ThreadPoolExecutor accessor methods. The most important configuration parameters specify the size of the thread pool, and the queue that the executor uses to hold tasks that it cannot currently run. *corePoolSize* is the number of threads that the pool should hold under normal usage. As tasks are submitted to the ThreadPoolExecutor, a new thread is created for each task until the total number of threads reaches this size.

If *corePoolSize* threads have already been created, newly submitted tasks are placed on the work queue. As these core threads finish the tasks they are executing, they take() a new task from the work queue. You must specify the *workQueue* when you call the ThreadPoolExecutor() constructor. It may be any BlockingQueue object and the behavior of the thread pool depends strongly on the behavior of the queue you specify. Options include an unbounded LinkedBlockingQueue, a bounded ArrayBlockingQueue with a capacity of your choosing, or even a SynchronousQueue which has a capacity of zero and cannot actually accept a task unless a thread is already waiting to execute it.

If the work queue becomes empty, it is inefficient to leave all the core threads sitting idly waiting for work. Threads are terminated if they are idle for more than the "keep alive" time. You specify this time with the *keepAliveTime* parameter and a TimeUnit constant.

If the work queue fills up, the *maximumPoolSize* parameter comes into play. ThreadPoolExecutor prefers to maintain *corePoolSize* threads but allows this number to grow up to *maximumPoolSize*. A new thread is created only when the *workQueue* is full. If you specify an unbounded work queue, *maximumPoolSize* is irrelevant because the queue never fills up. If on the other hand you specify a SynchronousQueue (which is always full), if none of the existing threads are waiting for a new task, a new thread is always created (up to the maximumPoolSize limit).

If a ThreadPoolExecutor has already created the maximum number of threads and its work queue is full, it must reject any newly submitted tasks. The default behavior is to throw a RejectedExecutionException. You can alter this behavior by specifying a RejectedExecutionHandler object to the ThreadPoolExecutor() constructor or with the setRejectedExecutionHandler() method. The four inner classes of this class are implementations of four handlers that address this case. See their individual entries for details.

The final way that you can customize a ThreadPoolExecutor is to pass ThreadFactory to the constructor or to the setThreadFactory() method. If you do not specify a factory, the ThreadPoolExecutor obtains one with Executors.defaultThreadFactory().

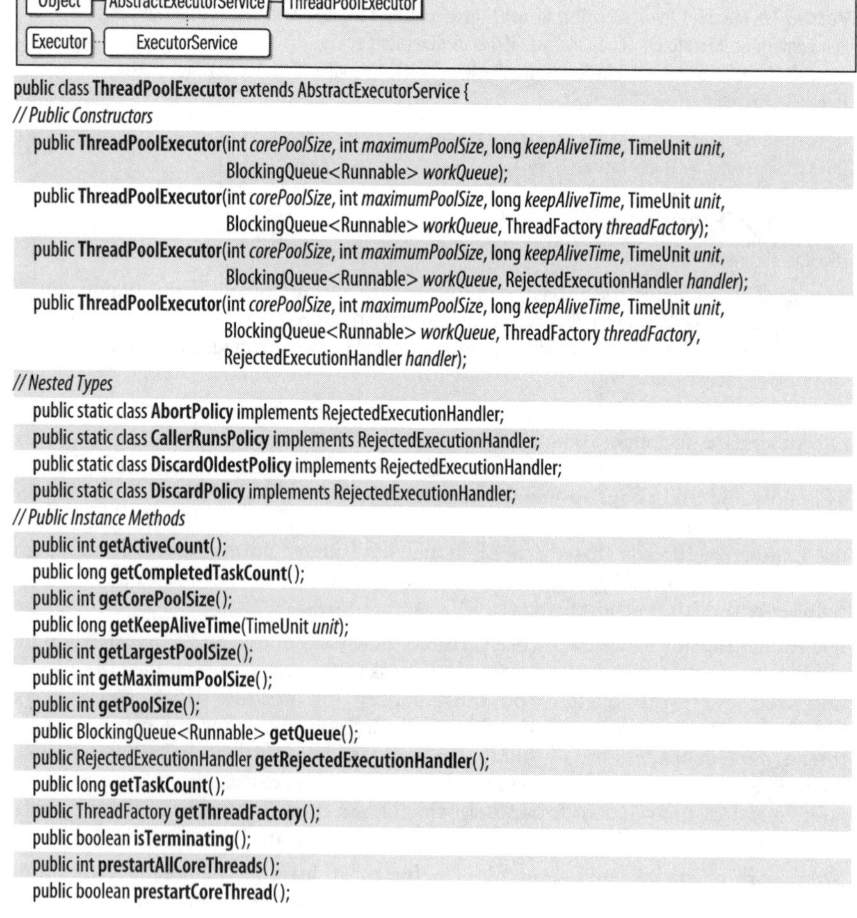


```
public class ThreadPoolExecutor extends AbstractExecutorService {
// Public Constructors
    public ThreadPoolExecutor(int corePoolSize, int maximumPoolSize, long keepAliveTime, TimeUnit unit,
                              BlockingQueue<Runnable> workQueue);
    public ThreadPoolExecutor(int corePoolSize, int maximumPoolSize, long keepAliveTime, TimeUnit unit,
                              BlockingQueue<Runnable> workQueue, ThreadFactory threadFactory);
    public ThreadPoolExecutor(int corePoolSize, int maximumPoolSize, long keepAliveTime, TimeUnit unit,
                              BlockingQueue<Runnable> workQueue, RejectedExecutionHandler handler);
    public ThreadPoolExecutor(int corePoolSize, int maximumPoolSize, long keepAliveTime, TimeUnit unit,
                              BlockingQueue<Runnable> workQueue, ThreadFactory threadFactory,
                              RejectedExecutionHandler handler);
// Nested Types
    public static class AbortPolicy implements RejectedExecutionHandler;
    public static class CallerRunsPolicy implements RejectedExecutionHandler;
    public static class DiscardOldestPolicy implements RejectedExecutionHandler;
    public static class DiscardPolicy implements RejectedExecutionHandler;
// Public Instance Methods
    public int getActiveCount();
    public long getCompletedTaskCount();
    public int getCorePoolSize();
    public long getKeepAliveTime(TimeUnit unit);
    public int getLargestPoolSize();
    public int getMaximumPoolSize();
    public int getPoolSize();
    public BlockingQueue<Runnable> getQueue();
    public RejectedExecutionHandler getRejectedExecutionHandler();
    public long getTaskCount();
    public ThreadFactory getThreadFactory();
    public boolean isTerminating();
    public int prestartAllCoreThreads();
    public boolean prestartCoreThread();
```

```
    public void purge();
    public boolean remove(Runnable task);
    public void setCorePoolSize(int corePoolSize);
    public void setKeepAliveTime(long time, TimeUnit unit);
    public void setMaximumPoolSize(int maximumPoolSize);
    public void setRejectedExecutionHandler(RejectedExecutionHandler handler);
    public void setThreadFactory(ThreadFactory threadFactory);
// Methods Implementing Executor
    public void execute(Runnable command);
// Methods Implementing ExecutorService
    public boolean awaitTermination(long timeout, TimeUnit unit) throws InterruptedException;
    public boolean isShutdown();
    public boolean isTerminated();
    public void shutdown();
    public java.util.List<Runnable> shutdownNow();
// Protected Methods Overriding Object
    protected void finalize();
// Protected Instance Methods
    protected void afterExecute(Runnable r, Throwable t);                          empty
    protected void beforeExecute(Thread t, Runnable r);                            empty
    protected void terminated();                                                   empty
}
```

Subclasses ScheduledThreadPoolExecutor

Passed To RejectedExecutionHandler.rejectedExecution(), ThreadPoolExecutor.AbortPolicy.rejectedExecution(), ThreadPoolExecutor.CallerRunsPolicy.rejectedExecution(), ThreadPoolExecutor.DiscardOldestPolicy.rejectedExecution(), ThreadPoolExecutor.DiscardPolicy.rejectedExecution()

ThreadPoolExecutor.AbortPolicy — Java 5.0

java.util.concurrent

This RejectedExecutionHandler implementation simply throws a RejectedExecutionException.

```
public static class ThreadPoolExecutor.AbortPolicy implements RejectedExecutionHandler {
// Public Constructors
    public AbortPolicy();
// Methods Implementing RejectedExecutionHandler
    public void rejectedExecution(Runnable r, ThreadPoolExecutor e);
}
```

ThreadPoolExecutor.CallerRunsPolicy — Java 5.0

java.util.concurrent

This RejectedExecutionHandler implementation runs the rejected Runnable object directly in the calling thread, causing that thread to block until the Runnable completes. If the ThreadPoolExecutor has been shut down, the Runnable is simply discarded instead of being run.

```
public static class ThreadPoolExecutor.CallerRunsPolicy implements RejectedExecutionHandler {
// Public Constructors
    public CallerRunsPolicy();
// Methods Implementing RejectedExecutionHandler
    public void rejectedExecution(Runnable r, ThreadPoolExecutor e);
}
```

ThreadPoolExecutor.DiscardOldestPolicy

Java 5.0

java.util.concurrent

This RejectedExecutionHandler implementation discards the rejected Runnable if the ThreadPoolExecutor has been shut down. Otherwise, it discards the oldest pending task that has not run and tries again to execute() the rejected task.

```
public static class ThreadPoolExecutor.DiscardOldestPolicy implements RejectedExecutionHandler {
// Public Constructors
   public DiscardOldestPolicy();
// Methods Implementing RejectedExecutionHandler
   public void rejectedExecution(Runnable r, ThreadPoolExecutor e);
}
```

ThreadPoolExecutor.DiscardPolicy

Java 5.0

java.util.concurrent

This RejectedExecutionHandler implementation silently discards the rejected Runnable.

```
public static class ThreadPoolExecutor.DiscardPolicy implements RejectedExecutionHandler {
// Public Constructors
   public DiscardPolicy();
// Methods Implementing RejectedExecutionHandler
   public void rejectedExecution(Runnable r, ThreadPoolExecutor e);                    empty
}
```

TimeoutException

Java 5.0

java.util.concurrent — serializable checked

An exception of this type is thrown by timed methods to indicate that the specified timeout has elapsed. Other timed methods are able to indicate their timeout status in a boolean or other return value.

Object — Throwable — Exception — TimeoutException
Serializable

```
public class TimeoutException extends Exception {
// Public Constructors
   public TimeoutException();
   public TimeoutException(String message);
}
```

Thrown By AbstractExecutorService.invokeAny(), CyclicBarrier.await(), Exchanger.exchange(), ExecutorService.invokeAny(), Future.get(), FutureTask.get()

TimeUnit

Java 5.0

java.util.concurrent — serializable comparable enum

The constants defined by this enumerated type represent granularities of time. Timeout and delay specifications throughout the java.util.concurrent package are specified by a long value and TimeUnit constant that specifies the interpretation of that value.

TimeUnit defines conversion methods that convert values expressed in one unit to values in another unit. More interestingly, it defines convenient alternatives to Thread.sleep(), Thread.join(), and Object.wait().

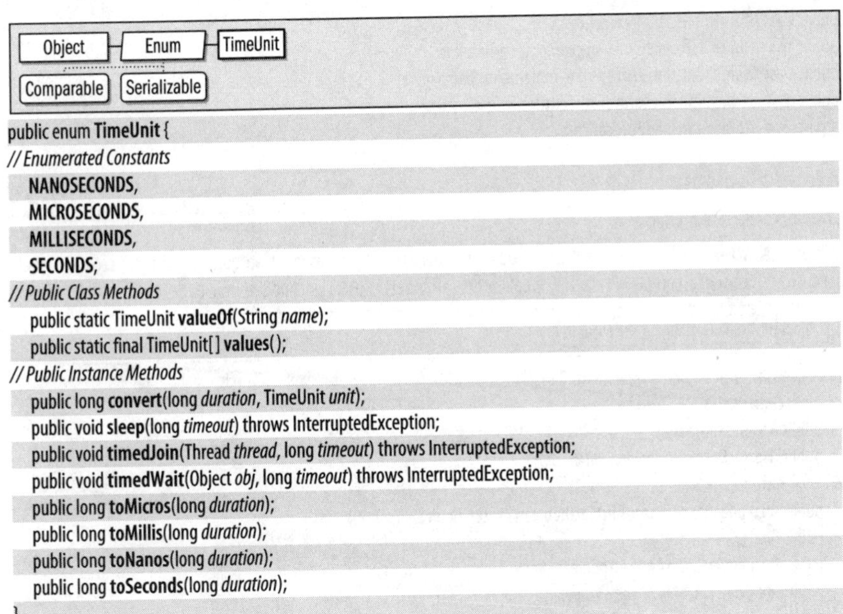


```
public enum TimeUnit {
// Enumerated Constants
    NANOSECONDS,
    MICROSECONDS,
    MILLISECONDS,
    SECONDS;
// Public Class Methods
    public static TimeUnit valueOf(String name);
    public static final TimeUnit[] values();
// Public Instance Methods
    public long convert(long duration, TimeUnit unit);
    public void sleep(long timeout) throws InterruptedException;
    public void timedJoin(Thread thread, long timeout) throws InterruptedException;
    public void timedWait(Object obj, long timeout) throws InterruptedException;
    public long toMicros(long duration);
    public long toMillis(long duration);
    public long toNanos(long duration);
    public long toSeconds(long duration);
}
```

Passed To Too many methods to list.

Package java.util.concurrent.atomic — Java 5.0

This package includes classes that provide atomic operations on boolean, integer, and reference values. Instances of the classes defined here have the properties of volatile fields but also add atomic operations like the canonical compareAndSet(), which verifies that the field holds an expected value, and, if it does, sets it to a new value. The classes also define a weakCompareAndSet() method that may be more efficient than compareAndSet() but may also fail to set the value even when the field holds the expected value.

The "Array" classes provide atomic access to arrays of values and provide volatile access semantics for array elements, which is not possible with the volatile modifier itself. The "FieldUpdater" classes use reflection to provide atomic operations on a named volatile field of an existing class. The AtomicMarkableReference class and AtomicStampedReference class maintain a reference value and an associated boolean or int value and allow the two values to be atomically manipulated together. These classes can be useful in concurrent algorithms that detect concurrent updates with version numbering, for example.

Most implementations of this package rely on low-level atomic instructions in the underlying CPU and perform atomic operations without the overhead of locking.

Classes

```
public class AtomicBoolean implements Serializable;
public class AtomicInteger extends Number implements Serializable;
public class AtomicIntegerArray implements Serializable;
public abstract class AtomicIntegerFieldUpdater<T>;
public class AtomicLong extends Number implements Serializable;
public class AtomicLongArray implements Serializable;
public abstract class AtomicLongFieldUpdater<T>;
```

```
public class AtomicMarkableReference<V>;
public class AtomicReference<V> implements Serializable;
public class AtomicReferenceArray<E> implements Serializable;
public abstract class AtomicReferenceFieldUpdater<T, V>;
public class AtomicStampedReference<V>;
```

AtomicBoolean

Java 5.0

java.util.concurrent.atomic **serializable**

This threadsafe class holds a boolean value. In addition to the get() and set() iterators, it provides atomic compareAndSet(), weakCompareAndSet(), and getAndSet() operations.

Object — AtomicBoolean ··· Serializable

```
public class AtomicBoolean implements Serializable {
// Public Constructors
   public AtomicBoolean();
   public AtomicBoolean(boolean initialValue);
// Public Instance Methods
   public final boolean compareAndSet(boolean expect, boolean update);
   public final boolean get();
   public final boolean getAndSet(boolean newValue);
   public final void set(boolean newValue);
   public boolean weakCompareAndSet(boolean expect, boolean update);
// Public Methods Overriding Object
   public String toString();
}
```

AtomicInteger

Java 5.0

java.util.concurrent.atomic **serializable**

This threadsafe class holds an int value. It extends java.lang.Number, but unlike the Integer class, it is mutable. Access the int value with the get() method and the various methods inherited from Number. You can set the value with the set() method or through various atomic methods. In addition to the basic compareAndSet() and weakCompareAndSet() methods, this class defines methods for atomic pre-increment, post-increment, pre-decrement and post-decrement operations as well as generalized addAndGet() and getAndAdd() methods. addAndGet() atomically adds the specified amount to the stored value and returns the new value. getAndAdd() atomically returns the current value and then adds the specified amount to it.

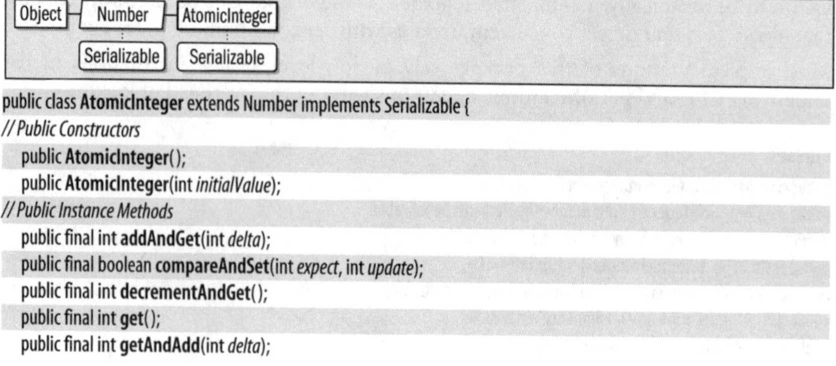


```
public class AtomicInteger extends Number implements Serializable {
// Public Constructors
   public AtomicInteger();
   public AtomicInteger(int initialValue);
// Public Instance Methods
   public final int addAndGet(int delta);
   public final boolean compareAndSet(int expect, int update);
   public final int decrementAndGet();
   public final int get();
   public final int getAndAdd(int delta);
```

```
    public final int getAndDecrement();                                    default:0
    public final int getAndIncrement();                                    default:-1
    public final int getAndSet(int newValue);
    public final int incrementAndGet();
    public final void set(int newValue);
    public final boolean weakCompareAndSet(int expect, int update);
// Public Methods Overriding Number
    public double doubleValue();
    public float floatValue();
    public int intValue();
    public long longValue();
// Public Methods Overriding Object
    public String toString();
}
```

AtomicIntegerArray

Java 5.0

java.util.concurrent.atomic — serializable

This class holds an array of int values. It provides threadsafe access to the array elements, treating each as if it was a volatile field, and defines atomic operations on them. The methods of this class are like those of AtomicInteger, except that each has an additional parameter that specifies the array index. Create an AtomicIntegerArray by specifying the desired array length or an actual int[] from which initial values can be copied.

Object — AtomicIntegerArray ··· Serializable

```
public class AtomicIntegerArray implements Serializable {
// Public Constructors
    public AtomicIntegerArray(int[] array);
    public AtomicIntegerArray(int length);
// Public Instance Methods
    public final int addAndGet(int i, int delta);
    public final boolean compareAndSet(int i, int expect, int update);
    public final int decrementAndGet(int i);
    public final int get(int i);
    public final int getAndAdd(int i, int delta);
    public final int getAndDecrement(int i);
    public final int getAndIncrement(int i);
    public final int getAndSet(int i, int newValue);
    public final int incrementAndGet(int i);
    public final int length();
    public final void set(int i, int newValue);
    public final boolean weakCompareAndSet(int i, int expect, int update);
// Public Methods Overriding Object
    public String toString();
}
```

AtomicIntegerFieldUpdater<T>

Java 5.0

java.util.concurrent.atomic

This class uses java.lang.reflect to provide atomic operations for named volatile int fields within existing types. Obtain an instance of this class with the newUpdater() factory method. Pass the name of the field (which must have been declared volatile int) to be updated and the class that it is defined within to this factory method. The instance methods of the resulting AtomicIntegerFieldUpdater object are like those of the AtomicInteger class but require you to specify the object whose field is to be manipulated. This is a generic type, and the type variable *T* represents the type whose volatile int field is being updated.

```
public abstract class AtomicIntegerFieldUpdater<T> {
// Protected Constructors
   protected AtomicIntegerFieldUpdater();
// Public Class Methods
   public static <U> AtomicIntegerFieldUpdater<U> newUpdater(Class<U> tclass, String fieldName);
// Public Instance Methods
   public int addAndGet(T obj, int delta);
   public abstract boolean compareAndSet(T obj, int expect, int update);
   public int decrementAndGet(T obj);
   public abstract int get(T obj);
   public int getAndAdd(T obj, int delta);
   public int getAndDecrement(T obj);
   public int getAndIncrement(T obj);
   public int getAndSet(T obj, int newValue);
   public int incrementAndGet(T obj);
   public abstract void set(T obj, int newValue);
   public abstract boolean weakCompareAndSet(T obj, int expect, int update);
}
```

AtomicLong

Java 5.0

java.util.concurrent.atomic

serializable

This threadsafe class holds a mutable long value and defines atomic operations on that value. It behaves just like AtomicInteger, with the substitution of long for int.

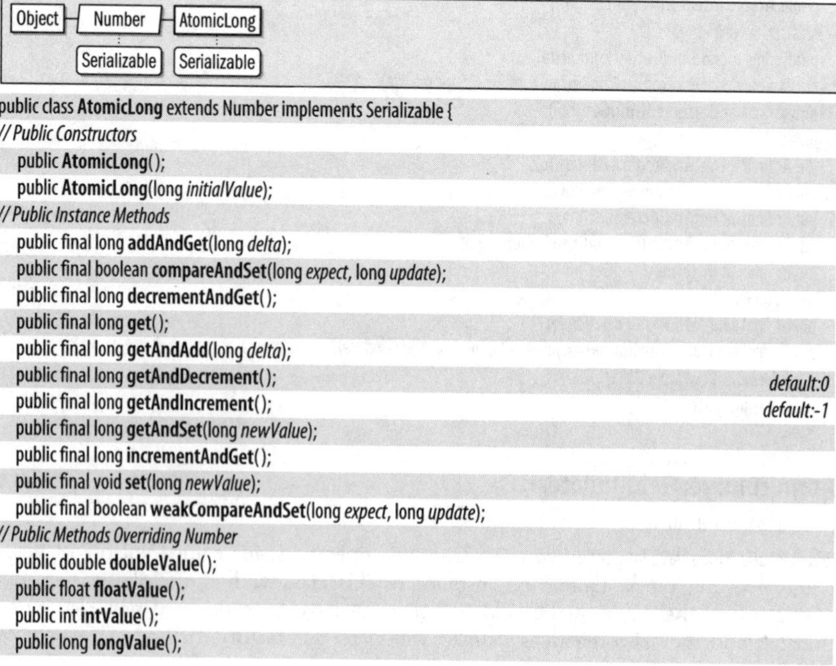


```
public class AtomicLong extends Number implements Serializable {
// Public Constructors
   public AtomicLong();
   public AtomicLong(long initialValue);
// Public Instance Methods
   public final long addAndGet(long delta);
   public final boolean compareAndSet(long expect, long update);
   public final long decrementAndGet();
   public final long get();
   public final long getAndAdd(long delta);
   public final long getAndDecrement();                                default:0
   public final long getAndIncrement();                                default:-1
   public final long getAndSet(long newValue);
   public final long incrementAndGet();
   public final void set(long newValue);
   public final boolean weakCompareAndSet(long expect, long update);
// Public Methods Overriding Number
   public double doubleValue();
   public float floatValue();
   public int intValue();
   public long longValue();
```

```
// Public Methods Overriding Object
   public String toString();
}
```

AtomicLongArray

Java 5.0

java.util.concurrent.atomic

serializable

This threadsafe class provides atomic operations for an array of long values. See AtomicIntegerArray, which offers the equivalent operations for int arrays.

Object — AtomicLongArray ··· Serializable

```
public class AtomicLongArray implements Serializable {
// Public Constructors
   public AtomicLongArray(long[] array);
   public AtomicLongArray(int length);
// Public Instance Methods
   public long addAndGet(int i, long delta);
   public final boolean compareAndSet(int i, long expect, long update);
   public final long decrementAndGet(int i);
   public final long get(int i);
   public final long getAndAdd(int i, long delta);
   public final long getAndDecrement(int i);
   public final long getAndIncrement(int i);
   public final long getAndSet(int i, long newValue);
   public final long incrementAndGet(int i);
   public final int length();
   public final void set(int i, long newValue);
   public final boolean weakCompareAndSet(int i, long expect, long update);
// Public Methods Overriding Object
   public String toString();
}
```

AtomicLongFieldUpdater<T>

Java 5.0

java.util.concurrent.atomic

This class uses java.lang.reflect to define atomic operations for named volatile long fields of a specified class. See AtomicIntegerFieldUpdater, which is very similar.

```
public abstract class AtomicLongFieldUpdater<T> {
// Protected Constructors
   protected AtomicLongFieldUpdater();
// Public Class Methods
   public static <U> AtomicLongFieldUpdater<U> newUpdater(Class<U> tclass, String fieldName);
// Public Instance Methods
   public long addAndGet(T obj, long delta);
   public abstract boolean compareAndSet(T obj, long expect, long update);
   public long decrementAndGet(T obj);
   public abstract long get(T obj);
   public long getAndAdd(T obj, long delta);
   public long getAndDecrement(T obj);
   public long getAndIncrement(T obj);
   public long getAndSet(T obj, long newValue);
   public long incrementAndGet(T obj);
```

```
    public abstract void set(T obj, long newValue);
    public abstract boolean weakCompareAndSet(T obj, long expect, long update);
}
```

AtomicMarkableReference<V> Java 5.0

java.util.concurrent.atomic

This threadsafe class holds a mutable reference to an object of type *V* and also holds a mutable boolean value or "mark." It defines atomic operations and volatile access semantics for the reference and the mark. The set() method unconditionally sets the reference and mark value. The get() method queries both, returning the reference as its return value, and storing the current value of the mark in element 0 of the specified boolean array. The reference and mark can also be queried individually (and nonatomically) with getReference() and isMarked().

The atomic compareAndSet() and weakCompareAndSet() methods take expected and new values for both the reference and the mark, and neither is set to its new value unless both match their expected values. attemptMark() atomically sets the value of the mark but only if the reference is equal to the expected value. Like weakCompareAndSet(), this method may fail spuriously, even if the reference does equal the expected value. Repeated invocation eventually succeeds, however, as long as the expected value is correct, and other threads are not continuously changing the reference value.

```
public class AtomicMarkableReference<V> {
// Public Constructors
    public AtomicMarkableReference(V initialRef, boolean initialMark);
// Public Instance Methods
    public boolean attemptMark(V expectedReference, boolean newMark);
    public boolean compareAndSet(V expectedReference, V newReference, boolean expectedMark, boolean newMark);
    public V get(boolean[] markHolder);
    public V getReference();
    public boolean isMarked();
    public void set(V newReference, boolean newMark);
    public boolean weakCompareAndSet(V expectedReference, V newReference, boolean expectedMark, boolean newMark);
}
```

AtomicReference<V> Java 5.0

java.util.concurrent.atomic serializable

This threadsafe class holds a mutable reference to an object of type *V*, provides volatile access semantics, and defines atomic operations for manipulating that value. get() and set() are ordinary accessor methods for the reference. compareAndSet(), weakCompareAndSet(), and getAndSet() perform the two named operations atomically. compareAndSet() is the canonical atomic operation: the reference is compared to an expected value, and, if it matches, is set to a new value. compareAndSet() returns true if it set the value or false otherwise. weakCompareAndSet() is similar but may fail to set the reference even if it does match the expected value (it is guaranteed to succeed eventually if the operation is repeatedly retried, however).

Object — AtomicReference ··· Serializable

```
public class AtomicReference<V> implements Serializable {
// Public Constructors
    public AtomicReference();
    public AtomicReference(V initialValue);
```

```
// Public Instance Methods
    public final boolean compareAndSet(V expect, V update);
    public final V get();
    public final V getAndSet(V newValue);
    public final void set(V newValue);
    public final boolean weakCompareAndSet(V expect, V update);
// Public Methods Overriding Object
    public String toString();
}
```

AtomicReferenceArray<E> — Java 5.0

java.util.concurrent.atomic — serializable

This threadsafe class holds an array of elements of type *E*. It provides **volatile** access semantics for these array elements and defines atomic operations for manipulating them. Its methods are like those of **AtomicReference** with the addition of a parameter that specifies the array index of the desired element.

Object — AtomicReferenceArray ··· Serializable

```
public class AtomicReferenceArray<E> implements Serializable {
// Public Constructors
    public AtomicReferenceArray(E[] array);
    public AtomicReferenceArray(int length);
// Public Instance Methods
    public final boolean compareAndSet(int i, E expect, E update);
    public final E get(int i);
    public final E getAndSet(int i, E newValue);
    public final int length();
    public final void set(int i, E newValue);
    public final boolean weakCompareAndSet(int i, E expect, E update);
// Public Methods Overriding Object
    public String toString();
}
```

AtomicReferenceFieldUpdater<T,V> — Java 5.0

java.util.concurrent.atomic

This threadsafe class uses **java.lang.reflect** to provide atomic operations for a named volatile field of type *V* within an object of type *T*. Its instance methods are like those of **AtomicReference** and the static **newUpdater()** factory method is like that of **AtomicIntegerFieldUpdater**.

```
public abstract class AtomicReferenceFieldUpdater<T,V> {
// Protected Constructors
    protected AtomicReferenceFieldUpdater();
// Public Class Methods
    public static <U,W> AtomicReferenceFieldUpdater<U,W> newUpdater(Class<U> tclass, Class<W> vclass,
        String fieldName);
// Public Instance Methods
    public abstract boolean compareAndSet(T obj, V expect, V update);
    public abstract V get(T obj);
    public V getAndSet(T obj, V newValue);
    public abstract void set(T obj, V newValue);
    public abstract boolean weakCompareAndSet(T obj, V expect, V update);
}
```

AtomicStampedReference<V> Java 5.0

java.util.concurrent.atomic

This threadsafe class holds a mutable reference to an object of type *V* and also holds a mutable int value or "stamp." It defines atomic operations and volatile access semantics for the reference and the stamp. This class works just like AtomicMarkableReference except that an int "stamp" replaces the boolean "mark." See AtomicMarkableReference for further details.

```
public class AtomicStampedReference<V> {
// Public Constructors
   public AtomicStampedReference(V initialRef, int initialStamp);
// Public Instance Methods
   public boolean attemptStamp(V expectedReference, int newStamp);
   public boolean compareAndSet(V expectedReference, V newReference, int expectedStamp, int newStamp);
   public V get(int[ ] stampHolder);
   public V getReference( );
   public int getStamp( );
   public void set(V newReference, int newStamp);
   public boolean weakCompareAndSet(V expectedReference, V newReference, int expectedStamp, int newStamp);
}
```

Package java.util.concurrent.locks Java 5.0

This package defines Lock and associated Condition interfaces as well as concrete implementations (such as ReentrantLock) that provide an alternative to locking with synchronized blocks and methods and to waiting with the wait( ), notify( ), and notifyAll( ) methods of Object.

Although Lock and Condition are somewhat more complex to use than the built-in locking, waiting, and notification mechanisms of Object, they are also more flexible. Lock, for example, does not require that locks be block-structured and enables algorithms such as "hand-over-hand locking" for traversing linked data structures. A thread waiting to acquire a Lock can time out or be interrupted, which is not possible with synchronized locking. Also, more than one Condition can be associated with a given Lock, which is simply not possible with Object-based locking and waiting.

The ReadWriteLock interface and its ReentrantReadWriteLock implementation allow multiple concurrent readers but only a single writer thread to hold the lock.

Interfaces

```
public interface Condition;
public interface Lock;
public interface ReadWriteLock;
```

Classes

```
public abstract class AbstractQueuedSynchronizer implements Serializable;
public class AbstractQueuedSynchronizer.ConditionObject implements Condition, Serializable;
public class LockSupport;
public class ReentrantLock implements Lock, Serializable;
public class ReentrantReadWriteLock implements ReadWriteLock, Serializable;
public static class ReentrantReadWriteLock.ReadLock implements Lock, Serializable;
public static class ReentrantReadWriteLock.WriteLock implements Lock, Serializable;
```

AbstractQueuedSynchronizer — Java 5.0

java.util.concurrent.locks — serializable

This abstract class is a low-level utility. A concrete subclass can be used as a helper class for implementing the Lock interface or for implementing synchronizer utilities like the CountDownLatch class of java.util.concurrent. Subclasses must define tryAcquire(), tryRelease(), tryAcquireShared(), tryReleaseShared(), and isHeldExclusively.

Object — AbstractQueuedSynchronizer ··· Serializable

```
public abstract class AbstractQueuedSynchronizer implements Serializable {
// Protected Constructors
   protected AbstractQueuedSynchronizer();
// Nested Types
   public class ConditionObject implements Condition, Serializable;
// Public Instance Methods
   public final void acquire(int arg);
   public final void acquireInterruptibly(int arg) throws InterruptedException;
   public final void acquireShared(int arg);
   public final void acquireSharedInterruptibly(int arg) throws InterruptedException;
   public final java.util.Collection<Thread> getExclusiveQueuedThreads();
   public final Thread getFirstQueuedThread();
   public final java.util.Collection<Thread> getQueuedThreads();
   public final int getQueueLength();
   public final java.util.Collection<Thread> getSharedQueuedThreads();
   public final java.util.Collection<Thread> getWaitingThreads(AbstractQueuedSynchronizer.ConditionObject condition);
   public final int getWaitQueueLength(AbstractQueuedSynchronizer.ConditionObject condition);
   public final boolean hasContended();
   public final boolean hasQueuedThreads();
   public final boolean hasWaiters(AbstractQueuedSynchronizer.ConditionObject condition);
   public final boolean isQueued(Thread thread);
   public final boolean owns(AbstractQueuedSynchronizer.ConditionObject condition);
   public final boolean release(int arg);
   public final boolean releaseShared(int arg);
   public final boolean tryAcquireNanos(int arg, long nanosTimeout) throws InterruptedException;
   public final boolean tryAcquireSharedNanos(int arg, long nanosTimeout) throws InterruptedException;
// Public Methods Overriding Object
   public String toString();
// Protected Instance Methods
   protected final boolean compareAndSetState(int expect, int update);
   protected final int getState();
   protected boolean isHeldExclusively();
   protected final void setState(int newState);
   protected boolean tryAcquire(int arg);
   protected int tryAcquireShared(int arg);
   protected boolean tryRelease(int arg);
   protected boolean tryReleaseShared(int arg);
}
```

AbstractQueuedSynchronizer.ConditionObject — Java 5.0

java.util.concurrent.locks — serializable

This class implements the Condition interface and is suitable for use with an AbstractQueuedSynchronizer.

```
public class AbstractQueuedSynchronizer.ConditionObject implements Condition, Serializable {
// Public Constructors
    public ConditionObject();
// Methods Implementing Condition
    public final void await() throws InterruptedException;
    public final boolean await(long time, java.util.concurrent.TimeUnit unit) throws InterruptedException;
    public final long awaitNanos(long nanosTimeout) throws InterruptedException;
    public final void awaitUninterruptibly();
    public final boolean awaitUntil(java.util.Date deadline) throws InterruptedException;
    public final void signal();
    public final void signalAll();
// Protected Instance Methods
    protected final java.util.Collection<Thread> getWaitingThreads();
    protected final int getWaitQueueLength();
    protected final boolean hasWaiters();
}
```

Passed To AbstractQueuedSynchronizer.{getWaitingThreads(), getWaitQueueLength(), hasWaiters(), owns()}

Condition **Java 5.0**

java.util.concurrent.locks

This interface defines an alternative to the wait(), notify(), and notifyAll() methods of java.lang.Object. Condition objects are always associated with a corresponding Lock. Obtain a Condition with the newCondition() method of Lock.

There are five choices for waiting. The no-argument version of await() is the simplest: it blocks until the thread is signaled or interrupted. awaitUninterruptibly() blocks until the thread is signaled and ignores interrupts. The other three waiting methods are timed waits: they all wait until signaled, interrupted, or until the specified time elapses. await() and awaitUntil() return true if they are signaled and false if a timeout occurs. awaitNanos() specifies the timeout in nanoseconds. It returns zero or a negative number if the timeout elapses. If it wakes up because of a signal (or because of a spurious wakeup), it returns an estimate of the time remaining in the timeout. If it turns out that the thread needs to continue waiting, this return value can be used as the new timeout value.

The signal() and signalAll() methods are just like the notify() and notifyAll() methods of Object. signal() wakes up one waiting thread, and signalAll() wakes up all waiting threads.

Locking considerations apply to the use of a Condition object just as they apply to the use of the wait() and notify() methods of Object. Before a thread can call any of the waiting or signaling methods of a Condition, it must hold the Lock associated with the condition. When the thread begins waiting, it automatically relinquishes the Lock, and when it awakes because of a signal, timeout, or interrupt, it must reacquire the lock before it can proceed. A thread is guaranteed to hold the lock when it returns from one of the waiting methods.

Threads waiting on a Condition may wake up spuriously, just as they may when waiting on an Object. Therefore, calls to wait on a Condition are typically written in the form of a loop so that the desired condition is retested when the thread wakes up.

```
public interface Condition {
// Public Instance Methods
    void await() throws InterruptedException;
    boolean await(long time, java.util.concurrent.TimeUnit unit) throws InterruptedException;
    long awaitNanos(long nanosTimeout) throws InterruptedException;
```

```
    void awaitUninterruptibly();
    boolean awaitUntil(java.util.Date deadline) throws InterruptedException;
    void signal();
    void signalAll();
}
```

Implementations AbstractQueuedSynchronizer.ConditionObject

Passed To ReentrantLock.{getWaitingThreads(), getWaitQueueLength(), hasWaiters()}, ReentrantReadWriteLock.{getWaitingThreads(), getWaitQueueLength(), hasWaiters()}

Returned By Lock.newCondition(), ReentrantLock.newCondition(), ReentrantReadWriteLock.ReadLock.newCondition(), ReentrantReadWriteLock.WriteLock.newCondition()

Lock — Java 5.0

java.util.concurrent.locks

This interface represents a flexible API for preventing thread concurrency with locking. Lock defines four methods for acquiring a lock. The simplest method is lock() which blocks indefinitely and uninterruptibly until the lock is acquired. This method is similar to entering a synchronized block. lockInterruptibly() blocks until the lock is acquired or until the thread is interrupted. The no-argument version of tryLock() acquires the lock and returns true if the lock is currently available or returns false without blocking if the lock is unavailable. The two-argument version of tryLock() is a timed method: it blocks until it acquires the lock (in which case it returns true), or until the specified timeout elapses (in which case it returns false), or until the thread is interrupted (in which case it throws InterruptedException).

Once a Lock has been acquired, no other thread can acquire it until it is released with the unlock() method. In order to ensure that locks are always released, even in the presence of unanticipated exceptions, it is typical to begin a try block immediately after acquiring the lock and to call unlock() from the associated finally clause.

Obtain a Condition object associated with a Lock by calling newCondition(). See Condition for details. See ReentrantLock for a concrete implementation of the Lock interface.

```
public interface Lock {
// Public Instance Methods
    void lock();
    void lockInterruptibly() throws InterruptedException;
    Condition newCondition();
    boolean tryLock();
    boolean tryLock(long time, java.util.concurrent.TimeUnit unit) throws InterruptedException;
    void unlock();
}
```

Implementations ReentrantLock, ReentrantReadWriteLock.ReadLock, ReentrantReadWriteLock.WriteLock

Returned By ReadWriteLock.{readLock(), writeLock()}, ReentrantReadWriteLock.{readLock(), writeLock()}

LockSupport — Java 5.0

java.util.concurrent.locks

This class provides a low-level alternative to the deprecated methods Thread.suspend() and Thread.resume(). The park(), parkNanos(), and parkUntil() methods suspend, or park, the thread until it is unparked by another thread with unpark(), or until it is interrupted by another thread, or until the specified time elapses. parkNanos() parks the thread for the specified number of nanoseconds. parkUntil() parks the thread until the specified time, using the millisecond representation of System.currentTimeMillis(). Any call to these parking methods may return spuriously, so it is important to call park() in a loop that can repark the thread if it should not have resumed.

Unpark a thread with the unpark() method. Note that while the parking methods affect the current thread, the unpark() method affects the thread you specify. If the specified thread is not parked, the next time that thread calls one of the park() methods, it returns immediately instead of blocking.

```
public class LockSupport {
// No Constructor
// Public Class Methods
   public static void park();
   public static void parkNanos(long nanos);
   public static void parkUntil(long deadline);
   public static void unpark(Thread thread);
}
```

ReadWriteLock

Java 5.0

java.util.concurrent.locks

This interface represents a pair of Lock objects with special locking behavior that is useful for concurrent algorithms in which reader threads frequently access a data structure and writer threads only infrequently modify the structure. The Lock returned by readLock() may be locked by multiple threads at the same time as long as no thread has the writeLock() locked. See ReentrantReadWriteLock for a concrete implementation with implementation-specific locking details.

```
public interface ReadWriteLock {
// Public Instance Methods
   Lock readLock();
   Lock writeLock();
}
```

Implementations ReentrantReadWriteLock

ReentrantLock

Java 5.0

java.util.concurrent.locks — serializable

This class implements the Lock interface and adds instrumentation methods to determine what thread currently holds the lock, to return the number of threads waiting to acquire the lock or waiting on an associated Condition, and to test whether a specified thread is waiting to acquire the lock.

The name of this class includes the term "reentrant" because the thread that holds the lock can call any of the locking methods again, and they return immediately without blocking. isHeldByCurrentThread() tests whether the current thread already holds the lock. getHoldCount() returns the number of times that the current thread has acquired this lock. unlock() must be called this number of times before the lock is actually relinquished.

A "fair" lock may be created by passing true to the ReentrantLock() constructor. If you do this, the lock will always be granted to the thread that has been waiting for it the longest.

Object — ReentrantLock

Lock, Serializable

```
public class ReentrantLock implements Lock, Serializable {
// Public Constructors
    public ReentrantLock();
    public ReentrantLock(boolean fair);
// Public Instance Methods
    public int getHoldCount();                                          default:0
    public final int getQueueLength();                                  default:0
    public int getWaitQueueLength(Condition condition);
    public final boolean hasQueuedThread(Thread thread);
    public final boolean hasQueuedThreads();
    public boolean hasWaiters(Condition condition);
    public final boolean isFair();                                      default:false
    public boolean isHeldByCurrentThread();                             default:false
    public boolean isLocked();                                          default:false
// Methods Implementing Lock
    public void lock();
    public void lockInterruptibly() throws InterruptedException;
    public Condition newCondition();
    public boolean tryLock();
    public boolean tryLock(long timeout, java.util.concurrent.TimeUnit unit) throws InterruptedException;
    public void unlock();
// Public Methods Overriding Object
    public String toString();
// Protected Instance Methods
    protected Thread getOwner();
    protected java.util.Collection<Thread> getQueuedThreads();
    protected java.util.Collection<Thread> getWaitingThreads(Condition condition);
}
```

ReentrantReadWriteLock — Java 5.0

java.util.concurrent.locks — serializable

This class implements the ReadWriteLock interface. The locks returned by the readLock() and writeLock() methods are instances of the inner classes ReadLock and WriteLock. ReentrantReadWriteLock defines a "fair mode" and includes instrumentation methods like ReentrantLock does.

Any number of threads can acquire the read lock as long as no thread holds or is attempting to acquire the write lock. When a thread attempts to acquire the write lock, no new read locks are granted. When all existing readers have relinquished the lock, the writer acquires the lock, and no reads are allowed until the writer has relinquished it. A thread that holds the write lock may downgrade to a read lock by acquiring the read lock and then relinquishing the write lock.

Because the read lock is not exclusive, it cannot have a Condition associated with it. The ReadLock.newCondition() method throws UnsupportedOperationException.

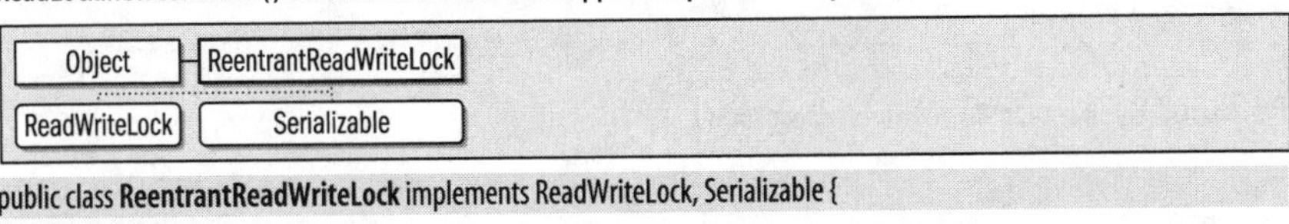


```
public class ReentrantReadWriteLock implements ReadWriteLock, Serializable {
// Public Constructors
    public ReentrantReadWriteLock();
    public ReentrantReadWriteLock(boolean fair);
```

```
// Nested Types
   public static class ReadLock implements Lock, Serializable;
   public static class WriteLock implements Lock, Serializable;
// Public Instance Methods
   public final int getQueueLength();                                        default:0
   public int getReadLockCount();                                            default:0
   public int getWaitQueueLength(Condition condition);
   public int getWriteHoldCount();                                           default:0
   public final boolean hasQueuedThread(Thread thread);
   public final boolean hasQueuedThreads();
   public boolean hasWaiters(Condition condition);
   public final boolean isFair();                                            default:false
   public boolean isWriteLocked();                                           default:false
   public boolean isWriteLockedByCurrentThread();                            default:false
   public ReentrantReadWriteLock.ReadLock readLock();
   public ReentrantReadWriteLock.WriteLock writeLock();
// Public Methods Overriding Object
   public String toString();
// Protected Instance Methods
   protected Thread getOwner();
   protected java.util.Collection<Thread> getQueuedReaderThreads();
   protected java.util.Collection<Thread> getQueuedThreads();
   protected java.util.Collection<Thread> getQueuedWriterThreads();
   protected java.util.Collection<Thread> getWaitingThreads(Condition condition);
}
```

Passed To ReentrantReadWriteLock.ReadLock.ReadLock(), ReentrantReadWriteLock.WriteLock.WriteLock()

ReentrantReadWriteLock.ReadLock **Java 5.0**

java.util.concurrent.locks serializable

A Lock implementation for reader threads. Any number of threads can acquire the lock as long as the corresponding WriteLock is not held. newCondition() throws UnsupportedOperationException.

```
public static class ReentrantReadWriteLock.ReadLock implements Lock, Serializable {
// Protected Constructors
   protected ReadLock(ReentrantReadWriteLock lock);
// Methods Implementing Lock
   public void lock();
   public void lockInterruptibly() throws InterruptedException;
   public Condition newCondition();
   public boolean tryLock();
   public boolean tryLock(long timeout, java.util.concurrent.TimeUnit unit) throws InterruptedException;
   public void unlock();
// Public Methods Overriding Object
   public String toString();
}
```

Returned By ReentrantReadWriteLock.readLock()

ReentrantReadWriteLock.WriteLock

Java 5.0

java.util.concurrent.locks

serializable

A Lock implementation for writer threads. This lock can be acquired only when all holders of the corresponding ReadLock have relinquished the locks. While this lock is held, no other thread may acquire either this lock or the corresponding ReadLock.

```
public static class ReentrantReadWriteLock.WriteLock implements Lock, Serializable {
// Protected Constructors
    protected WriteLock(ReentrantReadWriteLock lock);
// Methods Implementing Lock
    public void lock();
    public void lockInterruptibly() throws InterruptedException;
    public Condition newCondition();
    public boolean tryLock();
    public boolean tryLock(long timeout, java.util.concurrent.TimeUnit unit) throws InterruptedException;
    public void unlock();
// Public Methods Overriding Object
    public String toString();
}
```

Returned By ReentrantReadWriteLock.writeLock()

Package java.util.jar

Java 1.2

The java.util.jar package contains classes for reading and writing Java archive, or JAR, files. A JAR file is nothing more than a ZIP file whose first entry is a specially named manifest file that contains attributes and digital signatures for the ZIP file entries that follow it. Many of the classes in this package are relatively simple extensions of classes from the java.util.zip package.

The easiest way to read a JAR file is with the random-access JarFile class. This class allows you to obtain the JarEntry that describes any named file within the JAR archive. It also allows you to obtain an enumeration of all entries in the archive and an InputStream for reading the bytes of a specific JarEntry. Each JarEntry describes a single entry in the archive and allows access to the Attributes and the digital signatures associated with the entry. The JarFile also provides access to the Manifest object for the JAR archive; this object contains Attributes for all entries in the JAR file. Attributes is a mapping of attribute name/value pairs, of course, and the inner class Attributes.Name defines constants for various standard attribute names.

You can also read a JAR file with JarInputStream. This class requires to you read each entry of the file sequentially, however. JarOutputStream allows you to write out a JAR file sequentially. Finally, you can also read an entry within a JAR file and manifest attributes for that entry with a java.net.JarURLConnection object.

Interfaces

```
public interface Pack200.Packer;
public interface Pack200.Unpacker;
```

Collections

```
public class Attributes implements java.util.Map<Object, Object>, Cloneable;
```

Other Classes

public static class **Attributes.Name**;
public class **JarEntry** extends java.util.zip.ZipEntry;
public class **JarFile** extends java.util.zip.ZipFile;
public class **JarInputStream** extends java.util.zip.ZipInputStream;
public class **JarOutputStream** extends java.util.zip.ZipOutputStream;
public class **Manifest** implements Cloneable;
public abstract class **Pack200**;

Exceptions

public class **JarException** extends java.util.zip.ZipException;

Attributes — Java 1.2

java.util.jar — cloneable collection

This class is a java.util.Map that maps the attribute names of a JAR file manifest to arbitrary string values. The JAR manifest format specifies that attribute names can contain only the ASCII characters A to Z (uppercase and lowercase), the digits 0 through 9, and the hyphen and underscore characters. Thus, this class uses Attributes.Name as the type of attribute names, in addition to the more general String class. Although you can create your own Attributes objects, you more commonly obtain Attributes objects from a Manifest.

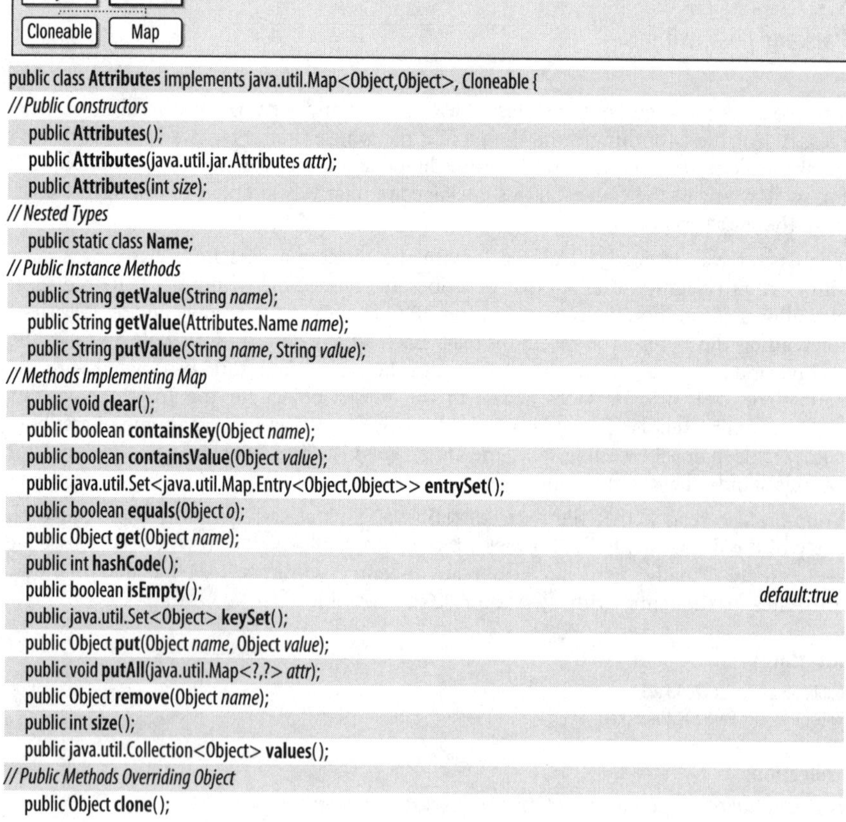


```
public class Attributes implements java.util.Map<Object,Object>, Cloneable {
// Public Constructors
   public Attributes();
   public Attributes(java.util.jar.Attributes attr);
   public Attributes(int size);
// Nested Types
   public static class Name;
// Public Instance Methods
   public String getValue(String name);
   public String getValue(Attributes.Name name);
   public String putValue(String name, String value);
// Methods Implementing Map
   public void clear();
   public boolean containsKey(Object name);
   public boolean containsValue(Object value);
   public java.util.Set<java.util.Map.Entry<Object,Object>> entrySet();
   public boolean equals(Object o);
   public Object get(Object name);
   public int hashCode();
   public boolean isEmpty();                                          default:true
   public java.util.Set<Object> keySet();
   public Object put(Object name, Object value);
   public void putAll(java.util.Map<?,?> attr);
   public Object remove(Object name);
   public int size();
   public java.util.Collection<Object> values();
// Public Methods Overriding Object
   public Object clone();
```

```
// Protected Instance Fields
   protected java.util.Map<Object,Object> map;
}
```

Returned By java.net.JarURLConnection.{getAttributes(), getMainAttributes()}, JarEntry.getAttributes(), Manifest.{getAttributes(), getMainAttributes()}

Attributes.Name — Java 1.2

java.util.jar

This class represents the name of an attribute in an Attributes object. It defines constants for the various standard attribute names used in JAR file manifests. Attribute names can contain only ASCII letters, digits, and the hyphen and underscore characters. Any other Unicode characters are illegal.

```
public static class Attributes.Name {
// Public Constructors
   public Name(String name);
// Public Constants
   public static final Attributes.Name CLASS_PATH;
   public static final Attributes.Name CONTENT_TYPE;
1.3 public static final Attributes.Name EXTENSION_INSTALLATION;
1.3 public static final Attributes.Name EXTENSION_LIST;
1.3 public static final Attributes.Name EXTENSION_NAME;
   public static final Attributes.Name IMPLEMENTATION_TITLE;
1.3 public static final Attributes.Name IMPLEMENTATION_URL;
   public static final Attributes.Name IMPLEMENTATION_VENDOR;
1.3 public static final Attributes.Name IMPLEMENTATION_VENDOR_ID;
   public static final Attributes.Name IMPLEMENTATION_VERSION;
   public static final Attributes.Name MAIN_CLASS;
   public static final Attributes.Name MANIFEST_VERSION;
   public static final Attributes.Name SEALED;
   public static final Attributes.Name SIGNATURE_VERSION;
   public static final Attributes.Name SPECIFICATION_TITLE;
   public static final Attributes.Name SPECIFICATION_VENDOR;
   public static final Attributes.Name SPECIFICATION_VERSION;
// Public Methods Overriding Object
   public boolean equals(Object o);
   public int hashCode();
   public String toString();
}
```

Passed To java.util.jar.Attributes.getValue()

JarEntry — Java 1.2

java.util.jar — cloneable

This class extends java.util.zip.ZipEntry; it represents a single file in a JAR archive and the manifest attributes and digital signatures associated with that file. JarEntry objects can be read from a JAR file with JarFile or JarInputStream, and they can be written to a JAR file with JarOutputStream. Use getAttributes() to obtain the Attributes for the entry. Use getCertificates() to obtain a java.security.cert.Certificate array that contains the certificate chains for all digital signatures associated with the file. In Java 5.0, this digital signature information may be more conveniently retrieved as an array of CodeSigner objects.

java.util.*

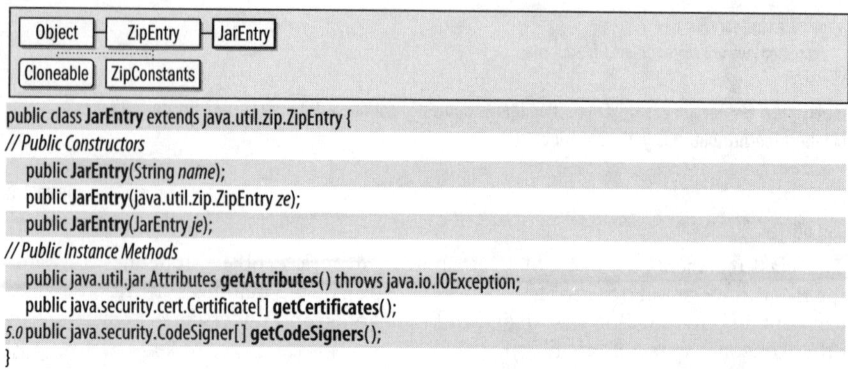


```
public class JarEntry extends java.util.zip.ZipEntry {
// Public Constructors
   public JarEntry(String name);
   public JarEntry(java.util.zip.ZipEntry ze);
   public JarEntry(JarEntry je);
// Public Instance Methods
   public java.util.jar.Attributes getAttributes() throws java.io.IOException;
   public java.security.cert.Certificate[] getCertificates();
5.0 public java.security.CodeSigner[] getCodeSigners();
}
```

Returned By java.net.JarURLConnection.getJarEntry(), JarFile.getJarEntry(), JarInputStream.getNextJarEntry()

JarException — Java 1.2

java.util.jar — serializable checked

Signals an error while reading or writing a JAR file.

Object ─ Throwable ─ Exception ─ IOException ─ ZipException ─ JarException; Serializable

```
public class JarException extends java.util.zip.ZipException {
// Public Constructors
   public JarException();
   public JarException(String s);
}
```

JarFile — Java 1.2

java.util.jar

This class represents a JAR file and allows the manifest, file list, and individual files to be read from the JAR file. It extends java.util.zip.ZipFile, and its use is similar to that of its superclass. Create a JarFile by specifying a filename or File object. If you do not want JarFile to attempt to verify any digital signatures contained in the JarFile, pass an optional boolean argument of false to the JarFile() constructor. As of Java 1.3, temporary JAR files can be automatically deleted when they are closed. To take advantage of this feature, pass ZipFile.OPEN_READ|ZipFile.OPEN_DELETE as the *mode* argument to the JarFile() constructor.

Once you have created a JarFile object, obtain the JAR Manifest with getManifest(). Obtain an enumeration of the java.util.zip.ZipEntry objects in the file with entries(). Get the JarEntry for a specified file in the JAR file with getJarEntry(). To read the contents of a specific entry in the JAR file, obtain the JarEntry or ZipEntry object that represents that entry, pass it to getInputStream(), and then read until the end of that stream. JarFile does not support the creation of new JAR files or the modification of existing files.

Object ─ ZipFile ─ JarFile; ZipConstants

```
public class JarFile extends java.util.zip.ZipFile {
// Public Constructors
   public JarFile(String name) throws java.io.IOException;
   public JarFile(java.io.File file) throws java.io.IOException;
```

```
    public JarFile(String name, boolean verify) throws java.io.IOException;
    public JarFile(java.io.File file, boolean verify) throws java.io.IOException;
1.3 public JarFile(java.io.File file, boolean verify, int mode) throws java.io.IOException;
// Public Constants
    public static final String MANIFEST_NAME;                          ="META-INF/MANIFEST.MF"
// Public Instance Methods
    public JarEntry getJarEntry(String name);
    public Manifest getManifest() throws java.io.IOException;
// Public Methods Overriding ZipFile
    public java.util.Enumeration<JarEntry> entries();
    public java.util.zip.ZipEntry getEntry(String name);
    public java.io.InputStream getInputStream(java.util.zip.ZipEntry ze) throws java.io.IOException;   synchronized
}
```

Passed To Pack200.Packer.pack()

Returned By java.net.JarURLConnection.getJarFile()

JarInputStream

Java 1.2

java.util.jar

closeable

This class allows a JAR file to be read from an input stream. It extends java.util.ZipInputStream and is used much like that class is used. To create a JarInputStream, simply specify the InputStream from which to read. If you do not want the JarInputStream to attempt to verify any digital signatures contained in the JAR file, pass false as the second argument to the JarInputStream() constructor. The JarInputStream() constructor first reads the JAR manifest entry, if one exists. The manifest must be the first entry in the JAR file. getManifest() returns the Manifest object for the JAR file.

Once you have created a JarInputStream, call getNextJarEntry() or getNextEntry() to obtain the JarEntry or java.util.zip.ZipEntry object that describes the next entry in the JAR file. Then, call a read() method (including the inherited versions) to read the contents of that entry. When the stream reaches the end of file, call getNextJarEntry() again to start reading the next entry in the file. When all entries have been read from the JAR file, getNextJarEntry() and getNextEntry() return null.

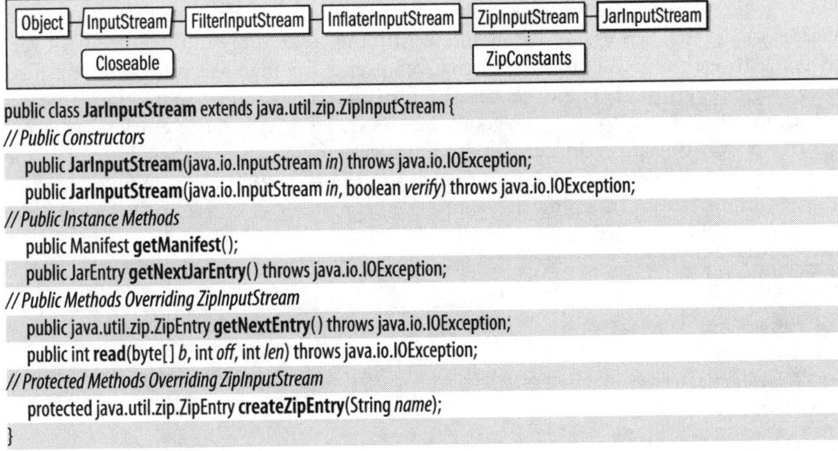


```
public class JarInputStream extends java.util.zip.ZipInputStream {
// Public Constructors
    public JarInputStream(java.io.InputStream in) throws java.io.IOException;
    public JarInputStream(java.io.InputStream in, boolean verify) throws java.io.IOException;
// Public Instance Methods
    public Manifest getManifest();
    public JarEntry getNextJarEntry() throws java.io.IOException;
// Public Methods Overriding ZipInputStream
    public java.util.zip.ZipEntry getNextEntry() throws java.io.IOException;
    public int read(byte[] b, int off, int len) throws java.io.IOException;
// Protected Methods Overriding ZipInputStream
    protected java.util.zip.ZipEntry createZipEntry(String name);
}
```

Passed To Pack200.Packer.pack()

JarOutputStream **Java 1.2**

java.util.jar **closeable flushable**

This class can write a JAR file to an arbitrary **OutputStream**. **JarOutputStream** extends **java.util.zip.ZipOutputStream** and is used much like that class is used. Create a **JarOutputStream** by specifying the stream to write to and, optionally, the **Manifest** object for the JAR file. The **JarOutputStream()** constructor starts by writing the contents of the **Manifest** object into an appropriate JAR file entry. It is the programmer's responsibility to ensure that the contents of the JAR entries written subsequently match those specified in the **Manifest** object. This class provides no explicit support for attaching digital signatures to entries in the JAR file.

After creating a **JarOutputStream**, call **putNextEntry()** to specify the **JarEntry** or **java.util.zip.ZipEntry** to be written to the stream. Then, call any of the inherited **write()** methods to write the contents of the entry to the stream. When that entry is finished, call **putNextEntry()** again to begin writing the next entry. When you have written all JAR file entries in this way, call **close()**. Before writing any entry, you may call the inherited **setMethod()** and **setLevel()** methods to specify how the entry should be compressed. See **java.util.zip.ZipOutputStream**.

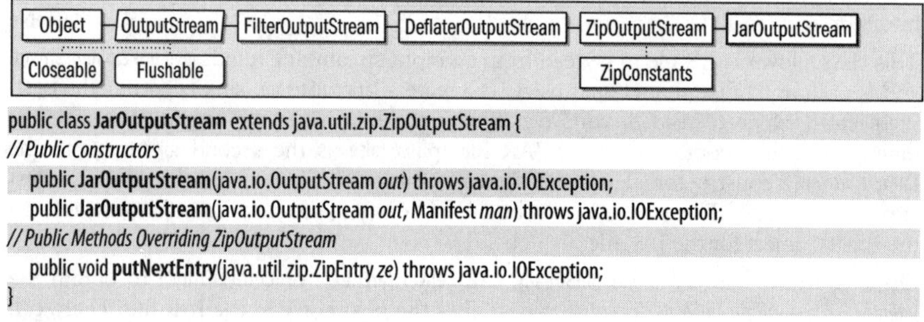


```
public class JarOutputStream extends java.util.zip.ZipOutputStream {
// Public Constructors
   public JarOutputStream(java.io.OutputStream out) throws java.io.IOException;
   public JarOutputStream(java.io.OutputStream out, Manifest man) throws java.io.IOException;
// Public Methods Overriding ZipOutputStream
   public void putNextEntry(java.util.zip.ZipEntry ze) throws java.io.IOException;
}
```

Passed To Pack200.Unpacker.unpack()

Manifest **Java 1.2**

java.util.jar **cloneable**

This class represents the manifest entry of a JAR file. **getMainAttributes()** returns an **Attributes** object that represents the manifest attributes that apply to the entire JAR file. **getAttributes()** returns an **Attributes** object that represents the manifest attributes specified for a single file in the JAR file. **getEntries()** returns a **java.util.Map** that maps the names of entries in the JAR file to the **Attributes** objects associated with those entries. **getEntries()** returns the **Map** object used internally by the **Manifest**. You can edit the contents of the **Manifest** by adding, deleting, or editing entries in the **Map**. **read()** reads manifest entries from an input stream, merging them into the current set of entries. **write()** writes the **Manifest** out to the specified output stream.

Object — Manifest ··· Cloneable

```
public class Manifest implements Cloneable {
// Public Constructors
   public Manifest();
   public Manifest(Manifest man);
   public Manifest(java.io.InputStream is) throws java.io.IOException;
// Public Instance Methods
   public void clear();
```

```
    public java.util.jar.Attributes getAttributes(String name);
    public java.util.Map<String,java.util.jar.Attributes> getEntries();          default:HashMap
    public java.util.jar.Attributes getMainAttributes();
    public void read(java.io.InputStream is) throws java.io.IOException;
    public void write(java.io.OutputStream out) throws java.io.IOException;
// Public Methods Overriding Object
    public Object clone();
    public boolean equals(Object o);
    public int hashCode();
}
```

Passed To java.net.URLClassLoader.definePackage(), JarOutputStream.JarOutputStream()

Returned By java.net.JarURLConnection.getManifest(), JarFile.getManifest(), JarInputStream.getManifest()

Pack200 — Java 5.0

java.util.jar

This class is a factory for creating Pack200.Packer and Pack200.Unpacker objects for compressing JAR files to Pack200 archives and for uncompresssing those archives back into JAR files.

```
public abstract class Pack200 {
// No Constructor
// Nested Types
    public interface Packer;
    public interface Unpacker;
// Public Class Methods
    public static Pack200.Packer newPacker();                                synchronized
    public static Pack200.Unpacker newUnpacker();
}
```

Pack200.Packer — Java 5.0

java.util.jar

This interface defines the API for an object that can convert a JAR file to an output stream in Pack200 (or gzipped Pack200) format. Obtain a Packer object with the Pack200.newPacker() factory method. Configure the packer before using it by setting properties in the Map returned by the properties() method. The constants defined by this class represent the names (and in some cases values) of properties that can be set. Pack a JAR file by passing JarFile or JarInputStream to a pack() method along with the byte output stream to which the packed representation should be written. You can monitor the progress of the packer engine by querying the PROGRESS property in the properties() map. The value is the completion percentage as an integer between 0 and 100 (or -1 to indicate a stall or error.) If you want to be notified of changes to the PROGRESS property, register a java.beans.PropertyChangeListener with addPropertyChangeListener(). See also the *pack200* command in Chapter 8.

```
public interface Pack200.Packer {
// Public Constants
    public static final String CLASS_ATTRIBUTE_PFX;                 ="pack.class.attribute."
    public static final String CODE_ATTRIBUTE_PFX;                  ="pack.code.attribute."
    public static final String DEFLATE_HINT;                        ="pack.deflate.hint"
    public static final String EFFORT;                              ="pack.effort"
    public static final String ERROR;                               ="error"
    public static final String FALSE;                               ="false"
```

java.util.*

```
    public static final String FIELD_ATTRIBUTE_PFX;                    ="pack.field.attribute."
    public static final String KEEP;                                   ="keep"
    public static final String KEEP_FILE_ORDER;                        ="pack.keep.file.order"
    public static final String LATEST;                                 ="latest"
    public static final String METHOD_ATTRIBUTE_PFX;                   ="pack.method.attribute."
    public static final String MODIFICATION_TIME;                      ="pack.modification.time"
    public static final String PASS;                                   ="pass"
    public static final String PASS_FILE_PFX;                          ="pack.pass.file."
    public static final String PROGRESS;                               ="pack.progress"
    public static final String SEGMENT_LIMIT;                          ="pack.segment.limit"
    public static final String STRIP;                                  ="strip"
    public static final String TRUE;                                   ="true"
    public static final String UNKNOWN_ATTRIBUTE;                      ="pack.unknown.attribute"
// Event Registration Methods (by event name)
    void addPropertyChangeListener(java.beans.PropertyChangeListener listener);
    void removePropertyChangeListener(java.beans.PropertyChangeListener listener);
// Public Instance Methods
    void pack(JarInputStream in, java.io.OutputStream out) throws java.io.IOException;
    void pack(JarFile in, java.io.OutputStream out) throws java.io.IOException;
    java.util.SortedMap<String,String> properties();
}
```

Returned By Pack200.newPacker()

Pack200.Unpacker **Java 5.0**

java.util.jar

This interface defines an API for converting a file or stream in Pack200 (or gzipped Pack200) format into a JAR file in the form of a JarOutputStream. Obtain an Unpacker object with the Pack200.newUnpacker() method. Before using an unpacker, you may configure it by setting properties in the Map returned by the properties() method. Unpack a JAR file with the unpack() method, specifying a File or stream of packed bytes. Monitor the progress of the unpacker by querying the PROGRESS key in the Map returned by properties(). The value should be an Integer representing a completion percentage between 0 and 100. If you want to be notified of changes to the PROGRESS property, register a java.beans.PropertyChangeListener with addPropertyChangeListener(). See also the *unpack200* command in Chapter 8.

```
public interface Pack200.Unpacker {
// Public Constants
    public static final String DEFLATE_HINT;                           ="unpack.deflate.hint"
    public static final String FALSE;                                  ="false"
    public static final String KEEP;                                   ="keep"
    public static final String PROGRESS;                               ="unpack.progress"
    public static final String TRUE;                                   ="true"
// Event Registration Methods (by event name)
    void addPropertyChangeListener(java.beans.PropertyChangeListener listener);
    void removePropertyChangeListener(java.beans.PropertyChangeListener listener);
// Public Instance Methods
    java.util.SortedMap<String,String> properties();
    void unpack(java.io.InputStream in, JarOutputStream out) throws java.io.IOException;
    void unpack(java.io.File in, JarOutputStream out) throws java.io.IOException;
}
```

Returned By Pack200.newUnpacker()

Package java.util.logging

Java 1.4

The java.util.logging package defines a sophisticated and highly-configurable logging facility that Java applications can use to emit, filter, format, and output warning, diagnostic, tracing and debugging messages. An application generates log messages by calling various methods of a Logger object. The content of a log message (with other pertinant details such as the time and sequence number) is encapsulated in a LogRecord object generated by the Logger. A Handler object represents a destination for LogRecord objects. Concrete subclasses of Handler support destinations such as files and sockets. Most Handler objects have an associated Formatter that converts a LogRecord object into the actual text that is logged. The subclasses SimpleFormatter and XMLFormatter produce simple plain-text log messages and detailed XML logs respectively.

Each log message has an associated severity level. The Level class defines a type-safe enumeration of defined levels. Logger and Handler objects both have an associated Level, and discard any log messages whose severity is less than that specified level. In addition to this level-based filtering, Logger and Handler objects may also have an associated Filter object which may be implemented to filter log messages based on any desired criteria.

Applications that desire complete control over the logs they generate can create a Logger object, along with Handler, Formatter and Filter objects that control the destination, content, and appearance of the log. Simpler applications need only to create a Logger for themselves, and can leave the rest to the LogManager class. LogManager reads a system-wide configuration file (or a configuration class) and automatically directs log messages to a standard destination (or destinations) for the system. In Java 5.0, LoggingMXBean defines an interface for monitoring and management of the logging facility through the javax.management packages (which are beyond the scope of this book).

Interfaces

public interface **Filter**;
public interface **LoggingMXBean**;

Classes

public class **ErrorManager**;
public abstract class **Formatter**;
    public class **SimpleFormatter** extends Formatter;
    public class **XMLFormatter** extends Formatter;
public abstract class **Handler**;
    public class **MemoryHandler** extends Handler;
    public class **StreamHandler** extends Handler;
        public class **ConsoleHandler** extends StreamHandler;
        public class **FileHandler** extends StreamHandler;
        public class **SocketHandler** extends StreamHandler;
public class **Level** implements Serializable;
public class **Logger**;
public final class **LoggingPermission** extends java.security.BasicPermission;
public class **LogManager**;
public class **LogRecord** implements Serializable;

ConsoleHandler Java 1.4

java.util.logging

This Handler subclass formats LogRecord objects and outputs the resulting string to the System.err output stream. When a ConsoleHandler is created, the various properties inherited from Handler are initialized using system-wide defaults obtained by querying named values with LogManager.getProperty(). The table below lists these properties, the value passed to getProperty(), and the default value used if getProperty() returns null. See Handler for further details.

Handler property	LogManager property name	Default
level	java.util.logging.ConsoleHandler.level	Level.INFO
filter	java.util.logging.ConsoleHandler.filter	null
formatter	java.util.logging.ConsoleHandler.formatter	SimpleFormatter
encoding	java.util.logging.ConsoleHandler.encoding	platform default

Object → Handler → StreamHandler → ConsoleHandler

```
public class ConsoleHandler extends StreamHandler {
// Public Constructors
   public ConsoleHandler();
// Public Methods Overriding StreamHandler
   public void close();
   public void publish(LogRecord record);
}
```

ErrorManager Java 1.4

java.util.logging

An important feature of the Logging API is that the logging methods called by applications never throw exceptions: it is not reasonable to expect programmers to nest all their logging calls within try/catch blocks, and even if they did, there is no useful way for an application to recover from an exception in the logging subsystem. Since handler classes such as FileHandler are inherently subject to I/O exceptions, the ErrorManager provides a way for a handler to report an exception instead of simply discarding it.

All Handler objects have an instance of ErrorManager associated with them. If an exception occurs in the handler, it passes the exception, along with a message and one of the error code constants defined by ErrorManager to the error() method. error() writes a message describing the exception to System.err, but does so only the first time it is called: the expectation is that a Handler that throws an exception once will continue to throw the same exception with each subsequent log message, and it is not useful to flood System.err with repeated error messages. You can of course define subclasses of ErrorManager that override error() to provide some other reporting mechanism. If you do this, register an instance of your custom ErrorManager by calling the setErrorManager() method of your Handler.

```
public class ErrorManager {
// Public Constructors
   public ErrorManager();
// Public Constants
   public static final int CLOSE_FAILURE;                                    =3
   public static final int FLUSH_FAILURE;                                    =2
```

```
    public static final int FORMAT_FAILURE;                                        =5
    public static final int GENERIC_FAILURE;                                       =0
    public static final int OPEN_FAILURE;                                          =4
    public static final int WRITE_FAILURE;                                         =1
// Public Instance Methods
    public void error(String msg, Exception ex, int code);              synchronized
}
```

Passed To Handler.setErrorManager()

Returned By Handler.getErrorManager()

FileHandler **Java 1.4**

java.util.logging

This Handler subclass formats LogRecord objects and outputs the resulting strings to a file or to a rotating set of files. Arguments passed to the FileHandler() constructor specify which file or files are used, and how they are used. The arguments are optional, and if they are not specified, defaults are obtained through LogManager.getProperty() as described below. The constructor arguments are:

pattern
: A string containing substitution characters that describes one or more files to use. The substitutions performed to convert this pattern to a filename are described below.

limit
: An approximate maximum file size for the log file, or 0 for no limit. If *count* is set to greater than one, then when a log file reaches this maximum, FileHandler closes it, renames it, and then starts a new log with the original filename.

count
: When *limit* is set to be nonzero, this arguemnt specifies the number of old log files to retain.

append
: true if the FileHandler should append to log messages already in the named file, or false if it should overwrite the file.

The *pattern* argument is the most important of these: it specifies which file or files the FileHandler will write to. FileHandler performs the following substitutions on the specified pattern to convert it to a filename:

For	Substitute
/	The directory separator character for the platform. This means that you can always use a forward slash in your patterns, even on Windows filesystems that use backward slashes.
%%	A single literal percent sign.
%h	The user's home directory: the value of the system property "user.home".
%t	The temporary directory for the system.
%u	A unique number to be used to distinguish this log file from other log files with the same pattern (this may be necessary when multiple Java programs are creating logs at the same time).
%g	The "generation number" of old log files when the *limit* argument is nonzero and the *count* argument is greater than one. FileHandler always writes log records into a file in which %g is replaced by 0. But when that file fills up, it is closed and renamed with the 0 replaced by a 1. Older files are similarly renamed, with their generation number being incremented. When the number of log files reaches the number specifed by *count*, then the oldest file is deleted to make room for the new one.

When a **FileHandler** is created, the **LogManager.getProperty()** method is used to obtain defaults for any unspecified constructor arguments, and also to obtian initial values for the various properties inherited from **Handler**. The table below lists these arguments and properties, the value passed to **getProperty()**, and the default value used if **getProperty()** returns **null**. See **Handler** for further details.

Property or argument	LogManager property name	Default
level	java.util.logging.FileHandler.level	Level.ALL
filter	java.util.logging.FileHandler.filter	null
formatter	java.util.logging.FileHandler.formatter	XMLFormatter
encoding	java.util.logging.FileHandler.encoding	platform default
pattern	java.util.logging.FileHandler.pattern	%h/java%u.log
limit	java.util.logging.FileHandler.limit	0 (no limit)
count	java.util.logging.FileHandler.count	1
append	java.util.logging.FileHandler.append	false

Object — Handler — StreamHandler — FileHandler

```
public class FileHandler extends StreamHandler {
// Public Constructors
   public FileHandler() throws java.io.IOException, SecurityException;
   public FileHandler(String pattern) throws java.io.IOException, SecurityException;
   public FileHandler(String pattern, boolean append) throws java.io.IOException, SecurityException;
   public FileHandler(String pattern, int limit, int count) throws java.io.IOException, SecurityException;
   public FileHandler(String pattern, int limit, int count, boolean append) throws java.io.IOException, SecurityException;
// Public Methods Overriding StreamHandler
   public void close() throws SecurityException;                                    synchronized
   public void publish(LogRecord record);                                           synchronized
}
```

Filter

Java 1.4

java.util.logging

This interface defines the method that a class must implement if it wants to filter log messages for a **Logger** or **Handler** class. **isLoggable()** should return **true** if the specified **LogRecord** contains information that should be logged. It should return **false** if the **LogRecord** should be filtered out not appear in any destination log. Note that both **Logger** and **Handler** provide built-in filtering based on the severity level of the **LogRecord**. This **Filter** interface exists to provide a customized filtering capability.

```
public interface Filter {
// Public Instance Methods
   boolean isLoggable(LogRecord record);
}
```

Passed To Handler.setFilter(), Logger.setFilter()

Returned By Handler.getFilter(), Logger.getFilter()

Formatter Java 1.4

java.util.logging

A Formatter object is used by a Handler to convert a LogRecord to a String prior to logging it. Most applications can simply use one one of the pre-defined concrete subclasses: SimpleFormatter or XMLFormatter. Applications requiring custom formatting of log messages will need to subclass this class and define the format() method to perform the desired conversion. Such subclasses may find the formatMessage() method useful: it performs localization using java.util.ResourceBundle and formatting using the facilities of the java.text package. getHead() and getTail() return a prefix and suffix (such as opening and closing XML tags) for a log file.

```
public abstract class Formatter {
// Protected Constructors
   protected Formatter();
// Public Instance Methods
   public abstract String format(LogRecord record);
   public String formatMessage(LogRecord record);                    synchronized
   public String getHead(Handler h);
   public String getTail(Handler h);
}
```

Subclasses SimpleFormatter, XMLFormatter

Passed To Handler.setFormatter(), StreamHandler.StreamHandler()

Returned By Handler.getFormatter()

Handler Java 1.4

java.util.logging

A Handler takes LogRecord objects from a Logger and, if their severity level is high enough, formats and publishes them to some destination (a file or socket, for example). The subclasses of this abstract class support various destinations, and implement destination-specific publish(), flush() and close() methods.

In addition to the destination-specific abstract methods, this class also defines concrete methods used by most Handler subclasses. These are property getter and setter methods to specify the severity Level of logging messages to be handled, an optional Filter, a Formatter to convert log messages from LogRecord objects to text, a text encoding for the output text, and an ErrorManager to handle any exceptions that arise during log output. Subclass-specific defaults for each of these properties are typically defined as properties of LogManager and are read from a system-wide logging configuration file.

In the simplest uses of the Logging API, a Logger sends it log messages to one or more handlers defined by the LogManager class for its "root logger". In this case there is no need for the application to ever instantiate or use a Handler directly. Applications that want custom control over the destination of their logs create and configure an instance of a Handler subclass, but never need to call its publish(), flush() or close() methods directly: that is done by the Logger.

```
public abstract class Handler {
// Protected Constructors
   protected Handler();
// Public Instance Methods
   public abstract void close() throws SecurityException;
   public abstract void flush();
```

```
    public String getEncoding();
    public ErrorManager getErrorManager();
    public Filter getFilter();
    public java.util.logging.Formatter getFormatter();
    public Level getLevel();                                                  synchronized
    public boolean isLoggable(LogRecord record);
    public abstract void publish(LogRecord record);
    public void setEncoding(String encoding) throws SecurityException, java.io.UnsupportedEncodingException;
    public void setErrorManager(ErrorManager em);
    public void setFilter(Filter newFilter) throws SecurityException;
    public void setFormatter(java.util.logging.Formatter newFormatter) throws SecurityException;
    public void setLevel(Level newLevel) throws SecurityException;            synchronized
// Protected Instance Methods
    protected void reportError(String msg, Exception ex, int code);
}
```

Subclasses MemoryHandler, StreamHandler

Passed To java.util.logging.Formatter.{getHead(), getTail()}, Logger.{addHandler(), removeHandler()}, MemoryHandler.MemoryHandler(), XMLFormatter.{getHead(), getTail()}

Returned By Logger.getHandlers()

Level — Java 1.4

java.util.logging — serializable

This class defines constants that represent the seven standard severity levels for log messages plus constants that turn logging off and enable logging at any level. When logging is enabled at one severity level, it is also enabled at all higher levels. The seven level constants, in order from most severe to least severe are: SEVERE, WARNING, INFO, CONFIG, FINE, FINER, and FINEST. The constant ALL enable logging of any message, regardless of its level. The constant OFF disables logging entirely. Note that these constants are all Level objects, rather than integers. This provides type safety.

Application code should rarely, if ever, need to use any of the methods of this class: instead they can simply use the constants it defines.

Object — Level ··· Serializable

```
public class Level implements Serializable {
// Protected Constructors
    protected Level(String name, int value);
    protected Level(String name, int value, String resourceBundleName);
// Public Constants
    public static final Level ALL;
    public static final Level CONFIG;
    public static final Level FINE;
    public static final Level FINER;
    public static final Level FINEST;
    public static final Level INFO;
    public static final Level OFF;
    public static final Level SEVERE;
    public static final Level WARNING;
// Public Class Methods
    public static Level parse(String name) throws IllegalArgumentException;   synchronized
```

```
// Public Instance Methods
    public String getLocalizedName();
    public String getName();
    public String getResourceBundleName();
    public final int intValue();
// Public Methods Overriding Object
    public boolean equals(Object ox);
    public int hashCode();
    public final String toString();
}
```

Passed To Too many methods to list.

Returned By Handler.getLevel(), Logger.getLevel(), LogRecord.getLevel(), MemoryHandler.getPushLevel()

Logger — Java 1.4

java.util.logging

A Logger object is used to emit log messages. Logger does not have a public constructor, but there are several ways to obtain a Logger object to use in your code:

- Typically, applications call the static getLogger() method to create or lookup a named Logger within a hierarchy of named loggers. Loggers have dot-separated hierarchical names, which should be based on the name of the class or package that uses them. Loggers obtained in this way inherit their logging level, resource bundle (for localization), and Handler objects from their ancestors in the hierarchy and, ultimately, from the root Logger defined by the global LogManager.
- Applets that require a Logger with no security restrictions should use the static getAnonymousLogger() method to create an unnamed Logger that is not part of the hierarchy of named Logger objects managed by the LogManager. A Logger created by this method has the LogManager root logger as its parent, and inherits the logging level and handlers of that root logger.
- Finally, the static Logger.global field refers to a pre-defined Logger named "global"; programmers may find this pre-defined Logger convenient during the early stages of application development, but it should not be used in production code.

Once a suitable Logger has been obtained, there are a variety of methods that can be used to create a log message:

- The log() methods log a specified message at the specified level, with optional parameters that can be used in message localization. These methods examine the call stack and make an attempt to determine the class and method name from which the method is emitted. Because of code optimization and just-in-time compilation techniques, however, they may not always be able to determine this information.
- The logp() ("log precise") methods are like the log() methods but allow you to explicitly specify the name of the class and method that are emitting the log message.
- The logrb() methods are like the logp() methods, but additionally take the name of a resource bundle to use for localizing the message.
- entering(), exiting(), and throwing() are convenience methods for emitting log messages that trace the execution of a program. These methods use a logging level of Level.FINER. Note that there are variants of entering() and exiting() that allow specification of method arguments and return values.

- Finally, Logger defines a set of easy-to-use convenience methods for logging a simple message at a specific logging level. These methods have the same names as the logging levels: severe(), warning(), info(), config(), fine(), finer(), finest().

A Logger has an associated logging Level, and discards any log messages with a severity lower than this. The severity level is initialized from the system configuration file, which is usually the desired behavior. You can explicitly override this setting with setLevel(). You might want to do this if you created the Logger with getAnonymousLogger() and have read the desired logging level from a configuration file of your own. If level-based filtering of log messages is not sufficient, you can associate a Filter with your Logger by calling setFilter. If you do this, any log messages rejected by the Filter will be discarded.

A Logger sends its log messages to any Handler objects that have been registered with addHandler(). Call getHandlers() to obtain an array of all registered handlers, and call removeHandler() to de-register a handler. By default, all log messages are also sent to the handlers of the parent logger and any other ancestor loggers. Since all named and anonymous loggers have the LogManager root logger as a parent or ancestor, all loggers by default send their log messages to the handlers defined in the system logging configuration file. See LogManager for details. If you do not want a Logger to use the handlers of its ancestors, pass false to setUseParentHandlers().

getLogger() and getAnonymousLogger() allow you to specify the name of a java.util.ResourceBundle for use in localizing log messages, and logrb() allows you to specify the name of a resource bundle to use to localize a specific log message. If a resource bundle is specified for the Logger or for a specific log message, then the message argument to the various logging methods is treated not as a literal message but instead as a localization key for which a localized version is to be looked up in the resource bundle. As part of the localization, any parameters, such as those specified by the *param1* and *params* arguments to the log() method are substituted into the localized message string as per java.text.MessageFormat. (Note, however that this localization and formatting is not performed by the Logger itself: instead, it simply stores the ResourceBundle and parameters in the LogRecord. It is the Formatter associated with the output Handler object that actually performs the localization.)

All the methods of this class are threadsafe and do not require external synchronization.

```
public class Logger {
// Protected Constructors
   protected Logger(String name, String resourceBundleName);
// Public Constants
   public static final Logger global;
// Public Class Methods
   public static Logger getAnonymousLogger();                                      synchronized
   public static Logger getAnonymousLogger(String resourceBundleName);             synchronized
   public static Logger getLogger(String name);                                    synchronized
   public static Logger getLogger(String name, String resourceBundleName);         synchronized
// Public Instance Methods
   public void addHandler(Handler handler) throws SecurityException;               synchronized
   public void config(String msg);
   public void entering(String sourceClass, String sourceMethod);
   public void entering(String sourceClass, String sourceMethod, Object param1);
   public void entering(String sourceClass, String sourceMethod, Object[] params);
   public void exiting(String sourceClass, String sourceMethod);
   public void exiting(String sourceClass, String sourceMethod, Object result);
```

```
    public void fine(String msg);
    public void finer(String msg);
    public void finest(String msg);
    public Filter getFilter();
    public Handler[] getHandlers();                                                    synchronized
    public Level getLevel();
    public String getName();
    public Logger getParent();
    public java.util.ResourceBundle getResourceBundle();
    public String getResourceBundleName();
    public boolean getUseParentHandlers();                                             synchronized
    public void info(String msg);
    public boolean isLoggable(Level level);
    public void log(LogRecord record);
    public void log(Level level, String msg);
    public void log(Level level, String msg, Throwable thrown);
    public void log(Level level, String msg, Object param1);
    public void log(Level level, String msg, Object[] params);
    public void logp(Level level, String sourceClass, String sourceMethod, String msg);
    public void logp(Level level, String sourceClass, String sourceMethod, String msg, Object param1);
    public void logp(Level level, String sourceClass, String sourceMethod, String msg, Object[] params);
    public void logp(Level level, String sourceClass, String sourceMethod, String msg, Throwable thrown);
    public void logrb(Level level, String sourceClass, String sourceMethod, String bundleName, String msg);
    public void logrb(Level level, String sourceClass, String sourceMethod, String bundleName, String msg, Object param1);
    public void logrb(Level level, String sourceClass, String sourceMethod, String bundleName, String msg, Throwable thrown);
    public void logrb(Level level, String sourceClass, String sourceMethod, String bundleName, String msg, Object[] params);
    public void removeHandler(Handler handler) throws SecurityException;               synchronized
    public void setFilter(Filter newFilter) throws SecurityException;
    public void setLevel(Level newLevel) throws SecurityException;
    public void setParent(Logger parent);
    public void setUseParentHandlers(boolean useParentHandlers);                       synchronized
    public void severe(String msg);
    public void throwing(String sourceClass, String sourceMethod, Throwable thrown);
    public void warning(String msg);
}
```

Passed To LogManager.addLogger()

Returned By LogManager.getLogger()

LoggingMXBean **Java 5.0**

java.util.logging

This interface defines the API for the javax.management "management bean" for the logging system. Obtain an instance with the static method LogManager.getLoggingMXBean(). The methods of this class allow the monitoring of all registered loggers and their logging level and allow management to change the logging level of any named logger.

```
public interface LoggingMXBean {
// Public Instance Methods
    String getLoggerLevel(String loggerName);
    java.util.List<String> getLoggerNames();
    String getParentLoggerName(String loggerName);
    void setLoggerLevel(String loggerName, String levelName);
}
```

Returned By LogManager.getLoggingMXBean()

LoggingPermission **Java 1.4**

java.util.logging **serializable permission**

This class is a java.security.Permission that governs the use of security-sensitive logging methods. The single defined name (or target) for LoggingPermission is "control" which represents permission to invoke various logging control methods such as Logger.setLevel() and LogManager.readConfiguration(). The methods in this package that throw SecurityException all require a LoggingPermission named "control" in order to run. Application programmers never need to use this class. System adminstrators configuring security policies may need to be familiar with it.

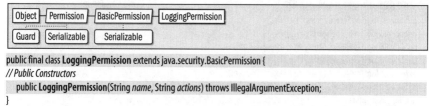

```
public final class LoggingPermission extends java.security.BasicPermission {
// Public Constructors
    public LoggingPermission(String name, String actions) throws IllegalArgumentException;
}
```

LogManager **Java 1.4**

java.util.logging

As its name implies, this class is the manager for the java.util.logging API. It has three specific purposes: (1) to read a logging configuration file and create the default Handler objects specified in that file; (2) to manage a set of Logger objects, arranging them into a tree based on their heirarchical names; and (3) to create and manage the unnamed Logger object that serves as the parent or ancestor of every other Logger. This class handles the important behind-the-scenes details that makes the Logging API work. Typical applications can make use of logging without ever having to use this class explicitly. Although its API is not commonly used by application programmers, it is still useful to understand the LogManager class, so it is described in detail here.

There is a single global instance of LogManager, which is obtained with the static getLogManager() method. By default, this global log manager object is an instance of the LogManager class itself. You may instead instantiate an instance of a subclass of LogManager by specifing the full class name of the subclass as the value of the system property java.util.logging.manager.

One of the primary purposes of the LogManager class is to read a java.util.Properties file that specifies the default logging configuration for the system. By default, this file is named *logging.properties* and is stored in the *jre/lib* directory of the Java installation. If you want to run a Java application using a different logging configuration, you can edit the default configuration file, but it is typically easier to create a new configuation file and tell the JVM about it by setting the system property java.util.logging.config.file to the name of your customized configuration file.

The most important purpose of the configuration file is to specify a set of Handler objects to which all log messages are sent. This is done by setting the handlers property in the file to a space-separated list of Handler class names. The LogManager will load the specified classes, and instantiate each one (using the default no-arg constructor), and then register those Handler objects on the root Logger, where they are inherited by all other loggers. (We'll see more about the root logger below.) Each of these Handler objects further configures itself by reading additional properties from the configuration file, as described in the documentation for each handler class.

The configuration file may also contain property name that are formed by appending ".level" to the name of a logger. The value of any such property is taken as the name of a logging Level for the named Logger. When the named logger is created and registered with the LogManager (described below) its logging level is automatically set to the specified level.

An application or any custom Handler or Formatter subclass or Filter implementation can read its own properties from the logging configuration file with the getProperty() method of LogManager. This is a useful way to provide customizability for logging-related classes.

In addition to managing the configuration file properties, a second purpose of LogManager is to maintain a tree of Logger objects organized into a hierarchy based on their dot-separated hierarchical names. The addLogger() method registers a new Logger object with the LogManager and inserts it into the tree. This method is called automatically by the Logger.getLogger() factory method, however, so you never need to call it yourself. The getLogger() method of LogManager finds and returns a named Logger object within the tree. Use getLoggerNames() to obtain an Enumeration of the names of all registered loggers.

At the root of the tree is a root logger, created by the LogManager, and initialized with default Handler objects specified in the logging configuration file as described above. This root logger has no name, and you can obtain a reference to it by passing the empty string to the getLogger() method. Except for this root logger and anonymous loggers (see Logger.getAnonymousLogger()), all loggers have names, and they are typically named after the package or class for which they provide logging. When a named logger is registered with the LogManager, the LogManager examines its name and inserts it into the tree of loggers at the appropriate place: a logger named "java.util.logging" would be inserted as the child of a logger named "java.util", if any such logger existed, or as a child of a logger named "java", or, if no logger with that name existed either, it would be inserted as a child of the root logger named "". When the LogManager determines the position of a logger within the tree of loggers, it calls the setParent() method of the newly-registered Logger to tell it who its parent is. This is important because, by default, loggers inherit their logging level and handlers from their parent. Although the Logger.setParent() method is public, it is intended for use only by the LogManager class.

Anonymous loggers created with Logger.getAnonymousLogger() do not have names, and are not part of the logger tree. When they are created, however, their parent is set to the root logger of the LogManager. For this reason, anonymous loggers inherit the default handlers specified in the logging configuration file.

The readConfiguration() methods are used to force the LogManager to re-read the system configuration file, or to read a new configuration file from the specified stream. Both versions of the method generate a java.beans.PropertyChangeEvent and use it to notify any listeners that have been registered with addPropertyChangeListener. Both methods also first invoke the reset() method which discards the properties of the current configuration file, removes and closes all handlers for all loggers, and sets the logging level of all loggers to null, except for the root logger's logging level, which it sets to Level.INFO. It is unlikely that you would ever want to invoke reset() yourself. A number of LogManager methods throw a SecurityException if the caller does not have appropriate permissions. You can use checkAccess() to test whether the current calling context has the required LoggingPermission named "control".

All LogManager methods can be safely used by multiple threads.

```
public class LogManager {
// Protected Constructors
   protected LogManager();
// Public Constants
5.0 public static final String LOGGING_MXBEAN_NAME;                    ="java.util.logging:type=Logging"
// Public Class Methods
5.0 public static LoggingMXBean getLoggingMXBean();                                     synchronized
   public static LogManager getLogManager();
// Event Registration Methods (by event name)
   public void addPropertyChangeListener(java.beans.PropertyChangeListener l) throws SecurityException;
   public void removePropertyChangeListener(java.beans.PropertyChangeListener l) throws SecurityException;
// Public Instance Methods
   public boolean addLogger(Logger logger);                                                 synchronized
   public void checkAccess() throws SecurityException;
   public Logger getLogger(String name);                                                    synchronized
   public java.util.Enumeration<String> getLoggerNames();                                   synchronized
   public String getProperty(String name);
   public void readConfiguration() throws java.io.IOException, SecurityException;
   public void readConfiguration(java.io.InputStream ins) throws java.io.IOException, SecurityException;
   public void reset() throws SecurityException;
}
```

LogRecord **Java 1.4**

java.util.logging **serializable**

Instances of this class are used to represent log messages as they are passed between Logger, Handler, Filter and Formatter objects. LogRecord defines a number of JavaBeans-type property getter and setter methods. The values of the various properties encapsulate all details of the log message. The LogRecord() constructor takes arguments for the two most important properties: the log level and the log message (or localization key). The constructor also initializes the millis property to the current time, the sequenceNumber property to a unique (within the VM) value that can be used to compare the order of two log messages, and the threadID property to a unique identifier for the current thread. All other properties of the LogRecord are left uninitialized with their default null values.

Object — LogRecord ··· Serializable

```
public class LogRecord implements Serializable {
// Public Constructors
   public LogRecord(Level level, String msg);
// Public Instance Methods
   public Level getLevel();
   public String getLoggerName();
   public String getMessage();
   public long getMillis();
   public Object[] getParameters();
   public java.util.ResourceBundle getResourceBundle();
   public String getResourceBundleName();
   public long getSequenceNumber();
   public String getSourceClassName();
   public String getSourceMethodName();
   public int getThreadID();
   public Throwable getThrown();
```

```
    public void setLevel(Level level);
    public void setLoggerName(String name);
    public void setMessage(String message);
    public void setMillis(long millis);
    public void setParameters(Object[] parameters);
    public void setResourceBundle(java.util.ResourceBundle bundle);
    public void setResourceBundleName(String name);
    public void setSequenceNumber(long seq);
    public void setSourceClassName(String sourceClassName);
    public void setSourceMethodName(String sourceMethodName);
    public void setThreadID(int threadID);
    public void setThrown(Throwable thrown);
}
```

Passed To ConsoleHandler.publish(), FileHandler.publish(), Filter.isLoggable(), java.util.logging.Formatter.{format(), formatMessage()}, Handler.{isLoggable(), publish()}, Logger.log(), MemoryHandler.{isLoggable(), publish()}, SimpleFormatter.format(), SocketHandler.publish(), StreamHandler.{isLoggable(), publish()}, XMLFormatter.format()

MemoryHandler — Java 1.4

java.util.logging

A MemoryHandler stores LogRecord objects in a fixed-sized buffer in memory. When the buffer fills up, it discards the oldest record one each time a new record arrives. It maintains a reference to another Handler object, and whenever the push() method is called, or whenver a LogRecord arrives with a level at or higher than the pushLevel threshold, it "pushes" all of buffered LogRecord objects to that other Handler object, which typically formats and outputs them to some appropriate destination. Because MemoryHandler never outputs log records itself, it does not use the formatter or encoding properties inherited from its superclass.

When you create a MemoryHandler, you can specify the target Handler object, the size of the in-memory buffer, and the value of the pushLevel property, or you can omit these constructor arguments and rely on system-wide defaults obtained with LogManager.getProperty(). MemoryHandler also uses LogManager.getProperty() to obtain initial values for the level and filter properties inherited from Handler. The table below lists these properties, as well as the *target*, *size*, and *pushLevel* constructor arguments, the value passed to getProperty(), and the default value used if getProperty() returns null. See Handler for further details.

Property or argument	LogManager property name	Default
level	java.util.logging.MemoryHandler.level	Level.ALL
filter	java.util.logging.MemoryHandler.filter	null
target	java.util.logging.MemoryHandler.target	no default
size	java.util.logging.MemoryHandler.size	1000 log records
pushLevel	java.util.logging.MemoryHandler.push	Level.SEVERE

Object — Handler — MemoryHandler

```
public class MemoryHandler extends Handler {
// Public Constructors
    public MemoryHandler();
    public MemoryHandler(Handler target, int size, Level pushLevel);
```

java.util.*

```
// Public Instance Methods
    public Level getPushLevel();                                          synchronized
    public void push();                                                   synchronized
    public void setPushLevel(Level newLevel) throws SecurityException;
// Public Methods Overriding Handler
    public void close() throws SecurityException;
    public void flush();
    public boolean isLoggable(LogRecord record);
    public void publish(LogRecord record);                                synchronized
}
```

SimpleFormatter — Java 1.4

java.util.logging

This Formatter subclass converts a LogRecord object to a human-readable log message that is typically one or two lines long. See also XMLFormatter.

Object → Formatter → SimpleFormatter

```
public class SimpleFormatter extends java.util.logging.Formatter {
// Public Constructors
    public SimpleFormatter();
// Public Methods Overriding Formatter
    public String format(LogRecord record);                               synchronized
}
```

SocketHandler — Java 1.4

java.util.logging

This Handler subclass formats LogRecord objects and outputs the resulting strings to a network socket. When you create a SocketHandler, you can pass the hostname and port of the socket to the constructor or you can rely on system-wide defaults obtained with LogManager.getProperty(). SocketHandler also uses LogManager.getProperty() to obtain initial values for the properties inherited from Handler. The table below lists these properties, as well as the host and port arguments, the value passed to getProperty(), and the default value used if getProperty() returns null. See Handler for further details.

Handler property	LogManager property name	Default
level	java.util.logging.SocketHandler.level	Level.ALL
filter	java.util.logging.SocketHandler.filter	null
formatter	java.util.logging.SocketHandler.formatter	XMLFormatter
encoding	java.util.logging.SocketHandler.encoding	platform default
hostname	java.util.logging.SocketHandler.host	no default
port	java.util.logging.SocketHandler.port	no default

Object → Handler → StreamHandler → SocketHandler

```
public class SocketHandler extends StreamHandler {
// Public Constructors
    public SocketHandler() throws java.io.IOException;
    public SocketHandler(String host, int port) throws java.io.IOException;
```

```
// Public Methods Overriding StreamHandler
   public void close() throws SecurityException;                                    synchronized
   public void publish(LogRecord record);                                           synchronized
}
```

StreamHandler

Java 1.4

java.util.logging

This **Handler** subclass sends log messages to an arbitrary **java.io.OutputStream**. It exists primarily to serve as the common superclass of **ConsoleHandler**, **FileHandler**, and **SocketHandler**.

Object — Handler — StreamHandler

```
public class StreamHandler extends Handler {
// Public Constructors
   public StreamHandler();
   public StreamHandler(java.io.OutputStream out, java.util.logging.Formatter formatter);
// Public Methods Overriding Handler
   public void close() throws SecurityException;                                    synchronized
   public void flush();                                                             synchronized
   public boolean isLoggable(LogRecord record);
   public void publish(LogRecord record);                                           synchronized
   public void setEncoding(String encoding) throws SecurityException, java.io.UnsupportedEncodingException;
// Protected Instance Methods
   protected void setOutputStream(java.io.OutputStream out) throws SecurityException;   synchronized
}
```

Subclasses ConsoleHandler, FileHandler, SocketHandler

XMLFormatter

Java 1.4

java.util.logging

This **Formatter** subclass converts a **LogRecord** to an XML-formatted string. The **format()** method returns a <record> element, which always contains <date>, <millis>, <sequence>, <level> and <message> tags, and may also contain <logger>, <class>, <method>, <thread>, <key>, <catalog>, <param>, and <exception> tags. See *http://java.sun.com/dtd/logger.dtd* for the DTD of the output document.

The **getHead()** and **getTail()** methods are overridden to return opening and closing <log> and </log> tags to surround all output <record> tags. Note however, that if an application terminates abnormally, the logging facility may be unable to terminate the log file with the closing <log> tag.

Object — Formatter — XMLFormatter

```
public class XMLFormatter extends java.util.logging.Formatter {
// Public Constructors
   public XMLFormatter();
// Public Methods Overriding Formatter
   public String format(LogRecord record);
   public String getHead(Handler h);
   public String getTail(Handler h);
}
```

Package java.util.prefs — Java 1.4

The java.util.prefs package contains classes and interfaces for managing persistant user and system-wide preferences for Java applications and classes. Most applications will use only the Preferences class itself. Some will also use the event objects and listener interfaces defined by this package, and some may need to explicitly catch the types of exceptions defined by this package. Application programmers never need to use the PreferencesFactory interface or the AbstractPreferences class, which are intended for Preferences implementors only.

To use the Preferences class, first use a static method to obtain an appropriate Preferences object or objects, and then use a get() method to query a preference value or a put() method to set a preference value. The code below shows a typical usage. See the Preferences class for details.

```
import java.util.prefs.Preferences;
public class TextEditor {
  // some constants that define default values for preferences
  public static final int WIDTH_DEFAULT = 80;
  public static final String DICTIONARY_DEFAULT = "";
  // Fields to be initialized from preference values
  public int width;              // Screen width in columns
  public String dictionary;      // Dictionary name for spell-checking
  public void initPrefs() {
    // Get Preferences objects for user and system preferences for this package
    Preferences userprefs = Preferences.userNodeForPackage(TextEditor.class);
    Preferences sysprefs = Preferences.systemNodeForPackage(TextEditor.class);
    // Look up preference values.  Note that we always pass a default value
    width = userprefs.getInt("width", WIDTH_DEFAULT);
    // Look up a user preference using a system preference as the default
    dictionary = userprefs.get("dictionary",
                               sysprefs.get("dictionary",
                                            DICTIONARY_DEFAULT));
  }
}
```

Interfaces

public interface **NodeChangeListener** extends java.util.EventListener;
public interface **PreferenceChangeListener** extends java.util.EventListener;
public interface **PreferencesFactory**;

Events

public class **NodeChangeEvent** extends java.util.EventObject;
public class **PreferenceChangeEvent** extends java.util.EventObject;

Other Classes

public abstract class **Preferences**;
    public abstract class **AbstractPreferences** extends Preferences;

Exceptions

public class **BackingStoreException** extends Exception;
public class **InvalidPreferencesFormatException** extends Exception;

AbstractPreferences **Java 1.4**

java.util.prefs

This class implements all the abstract methods of **Preferences** on top of a smaller set of abstract methods. Programmers creating a Preferences implementation (or "service provider") can subclass this class and need define only the nine methods whose names end in "Spi". Application programmers never need to use this class.

Object → Preferences → AbstractPreferences

```
public abstract class AbstractPreferences extends Preferences {
// Protected Constructors
   protected AbstractPreferences(AbstractPreferences parent, String name);
// Event Registration Methods (by event name)
   public void addNodeChangeListener(NodeChangeListener ncl);                    Overrides:Preferences
   public void removeNodeChangeListener(NodeChangeListener ncl);                 Overrides:Preferences
   public void addPreferenceChangeListener(PreferenceChangeListener pcl);        Overrides:Preferences
   public void removePreferenceChangeListener(PreferenceChangeListener pcl);     Overrides:Preferences
// Public Methods Overriding Preferences
   public String absolutePath();
   public String[] childrenNames() throws BackingStoreException;
   public void clear() throws BackingStoreException;
   public void exportNode(java.io.OutputStream os) throws java.io.IOException, BackingStoreException;
   public void exportSubtree(java.io.OutputStream os) throws java.io.IOException, BackingStoreException;
   public void flush() throws BackingStoreException;
   public String get(String key, String def);
   public boolean getBoolean(String key, boolean def);
   public byte[] getByteArray(String key, byte[] def);
   public double getDouble(String key, double def);
   public float getFloat(String key, float def);
   public int getInt(String key, int def);
   public long getLong(String key, long def);
   public boolean isUserNode();
   public String[] keys() throws BackingStoreException;
   public String name();
   public Preferences node(String path);
   public boolean nodeExists(String path) throws BackingStoreException;
   public Preferences parent();
   public void put(String key, String value);
   public void putBoolean(String key, boolean value);
   public void putByteArray(String key, byte[] value);
   public void putDouble(String key, double value);
   public void putFloat(String key, float value);
   public void putInt(String key, int value);
   public void putLong(String key, long value);
   public void remove(String key);
   public void removeNode() throws BackingStoreException;
   public void sync() throws BackingStoreException;
   public String toString();
// Protected Instance Methods
   protected final AbstractPreferences[] cachedChildren();
   protected abstract String[] childrenNamesSpi() throws BackingStoreException;
   protected abstract AbstractPreferences childSpi(String name);
   protected abstract void flushSpi() throws BackingStoreException;
```

```
    protected AbstractPreferences getChild(String nodeName) throws BackingStoreException;
    protected abstract String getSpi(String key);
    protected boolean isRemoved();
    protected abstract String[] keysSpi() throws BackingStoreException;
    protected abstract void putSpi(String key, String value);
    protected abstract void removeNodeSpi() throws BackingStoreException;
    protected abstract void removeSpi(String key);
    protected abstract void syncSpi() throws BackingStoreException;
// Protected Instance Fields
    protected final Object lock;
    protected boolean newNode;
}
```

BackingStoreException **Java 1.4**

java.util.prefs **serializable checked**

Signals that a Preferences method could not complete because of an implementation-specific problem with the preferences database. The most commonly used methods of the Preferences class do not throw this exception, and are guaranteed to succeed even if the implementation's preferences data is not available. Note that although this class inherits the Serializable interface, implementations are not actually required to be serializable.

Object — Throwable — Exception — BackingStoreException
Serializable

```
public class BackingStoreException extends Exception {
// Public Constructors
    public BackingStoreException(Throwable cause);
    public BackingStoreException(String s);
}
```

Thrown By Too many methods to list.

InvalidPreferencesFormatException **Java 1.4**

java.util.prefs **serializable checked**

Signals a syntax error in XML preference data. Note that although this class inherits the Serializable interface, implementations are not actually required to be serializable.

Object — Throwable — Exception — InvalidPreferencesFormatException
Serializable

```
public class InvalidPreferencesFormatException extends Exception {
// Public Constructors
    public InvalidPreferencesFormatException(String message);
    public InvalidPreferencesFormatException(Throwable cause);
    public InvalidPreferencesFormatException(String message, Throwable cause);
}
```

Thrown By Preferences.importPreferences()

NodeChangeEvent — Java 1.4

java.util.prefs — serializable event

A NodeChangeEvent object is passed to the methods of any NodeChangeListener objects registered on a Preferences object when a child Preferences node is added or removed. getChild() returns the Preferences object that was added or removed. getParent() returns the parent Preferences node from which the child was added or removed. This parent Preferences object is the one on which the NodeChangeListener was registered.

Although this class inherits the Serializable interface, it is not actually serializable.

Object — EventObject — NodeChangeEvent
Serializable

```
public class NodeChangeEvent extends java.util.EventObject {
// Public Constructors
   public NodeChangeEvent(Preferences parent, Preferences child);
// Public Instance Methods
   public Preferences getChild();
   public Preferences getParent();
}
```

Passed To NodeChangeListener.{childAdded(), childRemoved()}

NodeChangeListener — Java 1.4

java.util.prefs — event listener

This interface defines the methods that an object must implement if it wants to be notified when a child preferences node is added to or removed from a Preferences object. When such an addition or removal occurs, the parent Preferences object passes a NodeChangeEvent object to the appropriate method of any NodeChangeListener objects that have been registered through the Preferences.addNodeChangeListener() method.

EventListener — NodeChangeListener

```
public interface NodeChangeListener extends java.util.EventListener {
// Public Instance Methods
   void childAdded(NodeChangeEvent evt);
   void childRemoved(NodeChangeEvent evt);
}
```

Passed To AbstractPreferences.{addNodeChangeListener(), removeNodeChangeListener()}, Preferences.{addNodeChangeListener(), removeNodeChangeListener()}

PreferenceChangeEvent — Java 1.4

java.util.prefs — serializable event

A PreferenceChangeEvent object is passed to the preferenceChange() method of any PreferenceChangeListener objects registered on a Preferences object whenever a preferences value is added to, removed from, or modified in that Preferences node. getNode() returns the affected Preferences object. getKey() returns name of the modified preference. If the preference value was added or modified, getNewValue() returns that value. If a preference was deleted, getNewValue() returns null.

Although this class inherits the Serializable interface, it is not actually serializable.

Object ─ EventObject ─ PreferenceChangeEvent
Serializable

```
public class PreferenceChangeEvent extends java.util.EventObject {
// Public Constructors
   public PreferenceChangeEvent(Preferences node, String key, String newValue);
// Public Instance Methods
   public String getKey();
   public String getNewValue();
   public Preferences getNode();
}
```

Passed To PreferenceChangeListener.preferenceChange()

PreferenceChangeListener **Java 1.4**

java.util.prefs **event listener**

This interface defines the method that an object must implement if it wants to be notified when a preference key/value pair is added to, removed from, or changed in a Preferences object. After any such change, the Preferences object passes a PreferenceChangeEvent object describing the change to the preferenceChange() method of any PreferenceChangeListener objects that have been registered through the Preferences.addPreferenceChangeListener() method.

EventListener ─ PreferenceChangeListener

```
public interface PreferenceChangeListener extends java.util.EventListener {
// Public Instance Methods
   void preferenceChange(PreferenceChangeEvent evt);
}
```

Passed To AbstractPreferences.{addPreferenceChangeListener(), removePreferenceChangeListener()}, Preferences.{addPreferenceChangeListener(), removePreferenceChangeListener()}

Preferences **Java 1.4**

java.util.prefs

A Preferences object represents a mapping between preference names, which are case-sensitive strings, and corresponding preference values. get() allows you to query the string value of a named preference, and put() allows you to set a string value for a named preference. Although all preference values are stored as strings, various convenience methods whose names begin with "get" and "put" exist to convert preference values of type boolean byte[], double, float, int, and long to and from strings.

The remove() method allows you to delete a named preference altogether, and clear() deletes all preference values stored in a Preferences object. The keys() method returns an array of strings that specify the names of all preferences in the Preferences object.

Preference values are stored in some implementation-dependent back-end which may be a file, a LDAP directory server, the Windows Registry, or any other persistant "backing store". Note that all the get() methods of this class require a default value to be specified. They return this default if no value has been stored for the named preference, or if the backing store is unavailable for any reason. The Preferences class is completely independent of the underlying implementation, except that it enforces an

80-character limit for preference names and Preference node names (see below), and a 8192-character limit on preference value strings.

Preferences does not have a public construtor. To obtain a Preferences object for use in your application, you must must use one of the static methods described below. Each Preferences object is a node in a hierarchy of Preferences nodes. There are two distinct hierarchies: one stores user-specific preferences, and one stores system-wide preferences. All Preferences nodes (in either hierarchy) have a unique name and use the same naming convention that Unix filesystems use. Applications (and classes) may store their preferences in a Preferences node with any name, but the convention is to use a node name that corresponds to the package name of the application or class, with all "." characters in the package name converted to "/" characters. For example, the preferences node used by java.lang.System would be "/java/lang".

Preferences defines static methods that you can use to obtain the Preferences objects your application requires. Pass a Class object to systemNodeForPackage() and userNodeForPackage() to obtain the system and user Preferences objects that are specific to the package of that class. If you want a Preferences node specific to a single class rather than to the package, you can pass the class name to the node() method of the package-specific node returned by systemNodeForPackage() or userNodeForPackage(). If you want to navigate the entire tree of preferences nodes (which most applications never need to do) call systemRoot() and userRoot() to obtain the root node of the two hierarchies, and then use the node() method to look up child nodes of those roots.

Various Preferences methods allow you to traverse the preferences hierarchies. parent() returns the parent Preferences node. childrenNames() returns an array of the relative names of all children of a Preferences node. node() returns a named Preferences object from the hierarchy. If the specified node name begins with a slash, it is an absolute name and is interpreted relative to the root of the hierarchy. Otherwise, it is a relative name and is interpreted relative to the Preferences object on which node() was called. nodeExists() allows you to test whether a named node exists. removeNode() allows you to delete an entire Preferences node from the hierarchy (useful when uninstalling an application). name() returns the simple name of a Preferences node, relative to its parent. absoutePath() returns the full, absolute name of the node, relative to the root of the hierarchy. Finally, isUserNode() allows you to determine whether a Preferences object is part of the user or system hierarchies.

Many applications will simply read their preference values once at startup. Long-lived applications or applications that want to respond dynamically to modifications to preferences (such as applications that are tightly integrated with a graphical desktop) may use addPreferenceChangeListener() to register a PreferenceChangeListener to recieve notifications of preference changes (in the form of PreferenceChangeEvent objects). Applications that are interested in changes to the Preferences hierarchy itself can register a NodeChangeListener.

put() and the various type-specific put...() convenience methods may return asynchonously, before the new preference value is stored persistantly within the backing store. Call flush() to force any preference changes to this Preferences node (and any of its descendants in the hierarchy) to be stored persistantly. (Note that it is not necessary to call flush() before an application terminates: all preferences will eventually be made persistant.) More than one application (within more than one Java virtual machine) may set preference values in the same Preferences node at the same time. Call sync() to ensure that future calls to get() and its related convenience methods retrieve current preference values set by this or other virtual machines. Note that the flush() and sync() operations are typically much more expensive than get() and put() operations, and applications do not often need to use them.

Preferences implementations ensure that all the methods of this class are thread safe. If multiple threads or multiple VMs write store the same preferences concurrently, their values may overwrite one another, but the preference data will not be corrupted. Note that, for simplicity, Preferences does not define any way to set multiple preferences in a single atomic transaction. If you need to ensure atomicity for multiple preference values, define a data format that allows you to store all the requisite values in a single string, and set and query those values with a single call to put() or get().

The contents of a Preferences node, or of a node and all of its descendants may be exported as an XML file with exportNode() and exportSubtree(). The static importPreferences() method reads an exported XML file back into the preferences hierarchy. These methods allow backups to be made of preference data, and allow preferences to be transferred between systems or between users.

Prior to Java 1.4, application preferences were sometimes managed with the java.util.Properties object.

```
public abstract class Preferences {
// Protected Constructors
   protected Preferences();
// Public Constants
   public static final int MAX_KEY_LENGTH;                                    =80
   public static final int MAX_NAME_LENGTH;                                   =80
   public static final int MAX_VALUE_LENGTH;                                  =8192
// Public Class Methods
   public static void importPreferences(java.io.InputStream is)
      throws java.io.IOException, InvalidPreferencesFormatException;
   public static Preferences systemNodeForPackage(Class<?> c);
   public static Preferences systemRoot();
   public static Preferences userNodeForPackage(Class<?> c);
   public static Preferences userRoot();
// Event Registration Methods (by event name)
   public abstract void addNodeChangeListener(NodeChangeListener ncl);
   public abstract void removeNodeChangeListener(NodeChangeListener ncl);
   public abstract void addPreferenceChangeListener(PreferenceChangeListener pcl);
   public abstract void removePreferenceChangeListener(PreferenceChangeListener pcl);
// Public Instance Methods
   public abstract String absolutePath();
   public abstract String[] childrenNames() throws BackingStoreException;
   public abstract void clear() throws BackingStoreException;
   public abstract void exportNode(java.io.OutputStream os) throws java.io.IOException, BackingStoreException;
   public abstract void exportSubtree(java.io.OutputStream os) throws java.io.IOException, BackingStoreException;
   public abstract void flush() throws BackingStoreException;
   public abstract String get(String key, String def);
   public abstract boolean getBoolean(String key, boolean def);
   public abstract byte[] getByteArray(String key, byte[] def);
   public abstract double getDouble(String key, double def);
   public abstract float getFloat(String key, float def);
   public abstract int getInt(String key, int def);
   public abstract long getLong(String key, long def);
   public abstract boolean isUserNode();
   public abstract String[] keys() throws BackingStoreException;
   public abstract String name();
   public abstract Preferences node(String pathName);
   public abstract boolean nodeExists(String pathName) throws BackingStoreException;
```

```
    public abstract Preferences parent();
    public abstract void put(String key, String value);
    public abstract void putBoolean(String key, boolean value);
    public abstract void putByteArray(String key, byte[] value);
    public abstract void putDouble(String key, double value);
    public abstract void putFloat(String key, float value);
    public abstract void putInt(String key, int value);
    public abstract void putLong(String key, long value);
    public abstract void remove(String key);
    public abstract void removeNode() throws BackingStoreException;
    public abstract void sync() throws BackingStoreException;
// Public Methods Overriding Object
    public abstract String toString();
}
```

Subclasses AbstractPreferences

Passed To NodeChangeEvent.NodeChangeEvent(), PreferenceChangeEvent.PreferenceChangeEvent()

Returned By AbstractPreferences.{node(), parent()}, NodeChangeEvent.{getChild(), getParent()}, PreferenceChangeEvent.getNode(), PreferencesFactory.{systemRoot(), userRoot()}

PreferencesFactory — Java 1.4

java.util.prefs

The PreferencesFactory interface defines the factory methods used by the static methods of the Preferences class to obtain the root Preferences nodes for user-specific and system-wide preferences hierarchies. Application programmers never need to use this interface.

An implementation of the preferences API for a specific back-end data store must include an implementation of this interface that works with that data store. Sun's implementation of Java includes a default filesystem-based implementation, which you can override by specifying the name of a PreferencesFactory implementation as the value of the "java.util.prefs.PreferencesFactory" system property.

```
public interface PreferencesFactory {
// Public Instance Methods
    Preferences systemRoot();
    Preferences userRoot();
}
```

Package java.util.regex — Java 1.4

This small package provides a facility for textual pattern matching with regular expressions. Pattern objects represent regular expressions, which are specified using a syntax very close to the one used by the Perl programming language. The Matcher class encapsulates a Pattern and a java.lang.CharSequence of text, and defines various methods for matching the pattern to the text. In Java 5.0, the MatchResult interface represents the result of a match. Matcher implements this interface and can be queried directly.

In addition to the pattern matching methods defined in this package, the java.lang.String class has been augmented in Java 1.4 with a number of convenience methods for matching strings against regular expressions that are specified in their text form as strings, rather than in their compiled form as Pattern objects. Applications with simple pattern matching needs can use these convenience methods and may never have to directly use the Pattern or Matcher classes.

Interfaces

public interface **MatchResult**;

Classes

public final class **Matcher** implements MatchResult;
public final class **Pattern** implements Serializable;

Exceptions

public class **PatternSyntaxException** extends IllegalArgumentException;

Matcher — Java 1.4

java.util.regex

A Matcher objects encapsulate a regular expression and a string of text (a Pattern and a java.lang.CharSequence) and defines methods for matching the pattern to the text in several different ways, for obtaining details about pattern matches, and for doing search-and-replace operations on the text. Matcher has no public constructor. Obtain a Matcher by passing the character sequence to be matched to the matcher() method of the desired Pattern object. You can also reuse an existing Matcher object with a new character sequence (but the same Pattern) by passing a new CharSequence to the matcher's reset() method. In Java 5.0, you can use a new Pattern object on the current character sequence with the usePattern() method.

Once you have created or reset a Matcher, there are three types of comparisons you can perform between the regular expression and the character sequence. All three comparisons operate on the current *region* of the character sequence. By default, this region is the entire sequence. In Java 5.0, however, you can set the bound of the region with region(). The simplest type of comparison is the matches() method. It returns true if the pattern matches the complete region of the character sequence, and returns false otherwise. The lookingAt() method is similar: it returns true if the pattern matches the complete region, or if it matches some subsequence at the beginning of the region. If the pattern does not match the start of the region, lookingAt() returns false. matches() requires the pattern to match both the beginning and ending of the region, and lookingAt() requires the pattern to match the beginning. The find() method, on the other hand, has neither of these requirements: it returns true if the pattern matches any part of the region. As will be described below, find() has some special behavior that allows it to be used in a loop to find all matches in the text.

If matches(), lookingAt(), or find() return true, then several other Matcher methods can be used to obtain details about the matched text. The MatchResult interface defines the start(), end() and group() methods that return the starting position, the ending position and the text of the match, and of any matching subexpressions within the Pattern. See MatchResult for details. The MatchResult interface is new in Java 5.0, but Matcher implements all of its methods in Java 1.4 as well. Calling MatchResult methods on a Matcher returns results from the most recent match. If you want to store these results, call toMatchResult() to obtain an indepedent, immutable MatchResult object whose methods can be queried later.

The no-argument version of find() has special behavior that makes it suitable for use in a loop to find all matches of a pattern within a region. The first time find() is called after a Matcher is created or after the reset() method is called, it starts it search at the beginning of the string. If it finds a match, it stores the start and end position of the matched text. If reset() is not called in the meantime, then the next call to find() searches again but starts the search at the first character after the match: at the position returned by end().

(If the previous call to find() matched the empty string, then the next call begins at end()+1 instead.) In this way, it is possible to find all matches of a pattern within a string simply by calling find() repeatedly until it returns false indicating that no match was found. After each repeated call to find() you can use the MatchResult methods to obtain more information about the text that matched the pattern and any of its subpatterns.

Matcher also defines methods that perform search-and-replace operations. replaceFirst() searches the character sequence for the first subsequence that matches the pattern. It then returns a string that is the character sequence with the matched text replaced with the specified replacement string. replaceAll() is similar, but replaces all matching subsequences within the character sequence instead of just replacing the first. The replacement string passed to replaceFirst() and replaceAll() is not always replaced literally. If the replacement contains a dollar sign followed by an integer that is a valid group number, then the dollar sign and the number are replaced by the text that matched the numbered group. If you want to include a literal dollar sign in the replacement string, preceed it with a backslash. In Java 5.0, you can use the static quoteReplacement() method to properly quote any special characters in a replacement string so that the string will be interpreted literally.

replaceFirst() and replaceAll() are convenience methods that cover the most common search-and-replace cases. However, Matcher also defines lower-level methods that you can use to do a custom search-and-replace operation in conjunction with calls to find(), and build up a modified string in a StringBuffer. In order to understand this search-and-replace procedure, you must know that a Matcher maintains a "append position", which starts at zero when the Matcher is created, and is restored to zero by the reset() method. The appendReplacement() method is designed to be used after a successful call to find(). It copies all the text between the append position and the character before the start() position for the last match into the specified string buffer. Then it appends the specified replacement text to that string buffer (performing the same substitutions that replaceAll() does). Finally, it sets the append position to the end() of the last match, so that a subsequent call to appendReplacement() starts at a new character. appendReplacement() is intended for use after a call to find() that returns true. When find() cannot find another match and returns false, you should complete the replacement operation by calling appendTail(): this method copies all text between the end() position of the last match and the end of the character sequence into the specified StringBuffer.

The reset() method has been mentioned several times. It erases any saved information about the last match, and restores the Matcher to its initial state so that subsequent calls to find() and appendReplacement() start at the begining of the character sequence. The one-argument version of reset() also allows you to specify an entirely new character sequence to match against. It is important to understand that several other Matcher methods call reset() themselves before they perform their operation. They are: matches(), lookingAt(), the one-argument version of find(), replaceAll(), and replaceFirst().

Prior to Java 5.0, the region of the input text that a Matcher operates on is the entire character sequence. In Java 5.0, you can define a different region with the region() method, which specifies the position of the first character in the region and the position of the first character after the end of the region. regionStart() and regionEnd() return the current value of these region bounds. By default, regions are "anchoring" which means that the start and end of the region match the ^ and $ anchors. (See Pattern for regular expression grammar details.) Call useAnchoringBounds() to turn anchoring bounds on or off in Java 5.0. The bounds of a region are "opaque" by default, which means that the Matcher will not look through the bounds in an attempt to match look-ahead or look-behind assertions (see Pattern). In Java 5.0, you can make the bounds transparent with useTransparentBounds(true).

Matcher is not threadsafe, and should not be used by more than one thread concurrently.

Object ─ Matcher ··· MatchResult

```
public final class Matcher implements MatchResult {
// No Constructor
// Public Class Methods
5.0 public static String quoteReplacement(String s);
// Public Instance Methods
   public Matcher appendReplacement(StringBuffer sb, String replacement);
   public StringBuffer appendTail(StringBuffer sb);
   public int end();                                  Implements:MatchResult
   public int end(int group);                         Implements:MatchResult
   public boolean find();
   public boolean find(int start);
   public String group();                             Implements:MatchResult
   public String group(int group);                    Implements:MatchResult
   public int groupCount();                           Implements:MatchResult
5.0 public boolean hasAnchoringBounds();
5.0 public boolean hasTransparentBounds();
5.0 public boolean hitEnd();
   public boolean lookingAt();
   public boolean matches();
   public Pattern pattern();
5.0 public Matcher region(int start, int end);
5.0 public int regionEnd();
5.0 public int regionStart();
   public String replaceAll(String replacement);
   public String replaceFirst(String replacement);
5.0 public boolean requireEnd();
   public Matcher reset();
   public Matcher reset(CharSequence input);
   public int start();                                Implements:MatchResult
   public int start(int group);                       Implements:MatchResult
5.0 public MatchResult toMatchResult();
5.0 public Matcher useAnchoringBounds(boolean b);
5.0 public Matcher usePattern(Pattern newPattern);
5.0 public Matcher useTransparentBounds(boolean b);
// Methods Implementing MatchResult
   public int end();
   public int end(int group);
   public String group();
   public String group(int group);
   public int groupCount();
   public int start();
   public int start(int group);
// Public Methods Overriding Object
5.0 public String toString();
}
```

Returned By Pattern.matcher()

MatchResult **Java 5.0**

java.util.regex

This interface represents the results of a regular expression matching operation performed by a Matcher. Matcher implements this interface directly, and you can use the methods defined here to obtain the results of the most recent match performed by a Matcher. You can also save those most recent match results in a separate immutable MatchResult object by calling the toMatchResult() method of the Matcher.

The no-argument versions of the start() and end() method return the index of the first character that matched the pattern and the index of the last character that matched plus one (the index of the first character following the matched text), respectively. Some regular expressions can match the empty string. If this occurs, end() returns the same value as start(). The no-argument version of group() returns the text that matched the pattern.

If the matched Pattern includes capturing subexpressions within parentheses, the other methods of this interface provide details about the text that matched each of those subexpressions. Pass a group number to start(), end(), or group() to obtain the start, end, or text that matched the specified group. groupCount() returns the number of subexpressions. Groups are numbered from 1, however, so legal group numbers run from 1 to the value returned by groupCount(). Groups are ordered from left-to-right within the regular expression. When there are nested groups, their ordering is based on the position of the opening left parenthesis that begins the group. Group 0 represents the entire regular expression, so passing 0 to start(), end(), or group() is the same as calling the no-argument version of the method.

```
public interface MatchResult {
// Public Instance Methods
   int end();
   int end(int group);
   String group();
   String group(int group);
   int groupCount();
   int start();
   int start(int group);
}
```

Implementations Matcher

Returned By java.util.Scanner.match(), Matcher.toMatchResult()

Pattern **Java 1.4**

java.util.regex serializable

This class represents a regular expression. It has no public constructor: obtain a Pattern by calling one of the static compile() methods, passing the string representation of the regular expression, and an optional bitmask of flags that modify the behavior of the regex. pattern() and flags() return the string form of the regular expression and the bitmask that were passed to compile().

If you want to perform only a single match operation with a regular expression, and don't need to use any of the flags, you don't have to create a Pattern object: simply pass the string representation of the pattern and the CharSequence to be matched to the static matches() method: the method returns true if the specified pattern matches the complete specified text, or returns false otherwise.

Pattern represents a regular expression, but does not actually define any primitive methods for matching regular expressions to text. To do that, you must create a Matcher object that encapsulates a pattern and the text it is to be compared with. Do this by calling the matcher() method and specifying the CharSequence you want to match against. See Matcher for a description of what you can do with it.

The split() methods are the exception to the rule that you must obtain a Matcher in order to be able to do anything with a Pattern (although they create and use a Matcher internally). They take a CharSequence as input, and split it into substrings, using text that matches the regular expression as the delimiter, returning the substrings as a String[]. The two-argument version of split() takes an integer argument that specifies the maximum number of substrings to break the input into.

Pattern defines the following flags that control various aspects of how regular expression matching is performed. The flags are the following:

CANON_EQ
: The Unicode standard sometimes allows more than one way to specify the same character. If this flag is set, characters are compared by comparing their full canonical decompositions, so that characters will match even if expressed in different ways. Enabling this flag typically slows down performance. Unlike all the other flags, there is no way to temporarily enable this flag within a pattern.

CASE_INSENSITIVE
: Match letters without regard to case. By default this flag only affects the comparisons of ASCII letters. Also set the UNICODE_CASE flag if you want to ignore the case of all Unicode characters. You can enable this flag within a pattern with (?i).

COMMENTS
: If this flag is set, then whitespace and comments within a pattern are ignored. Comments are all characters between a # and end of line. You can enable this flag within a pattern with (?x)

DOTALL
: If this flag is set, then the . expression matches any character. If it is not set, then it does not match line terminator characters. This is also known as "single-line mode" and you can enable it within a pattern with (?s).

MULTILINE
: If this flag is set, then the ^ and $ anchors match not only at the beginning and end of the input string, but also at the beginning and end of any lines within that string. Within a pattern you can enable this flag with (?m).

UNICODE_CASE
: If this flag is set along with the CASE_INSENSITIVE flag, then case-insensitive comparison is done for all Unicode letters, rather than just for ASCII letters. You can enable both flags within a pattern with (?iu).

UNIX_LINES
: If this flag is set, then only the newline character is considered a line terminator for the purposes of ., ^, and $. If the flag is not set, then newlines (\n) carriage returns (\r) and carriage return newline sequences (\r\n) are all considered line terminators, as are the Unicode characters \u0085 ("next line") \u2028 ("line separator") and \u2029 ("paragraph separator"). You can turn this flag on within a pattern with (?d).

Although the API for the Pattern class is quite simple, the syntax for the text representation of regular expressions is fairly complex. A complete tutorial on regular expressions is beyond the scope of this book. The table below, is a quick-reference for regular expression syntax. It is very similar to the syntax used in Perl. Note that many of the syntax elements of a regular expression include a backslash character, such as \d to match one of the digits 0-9. Because Java strings also use the backslash character as an escape, you must double the backslashes when expressing a regular expression as a string literal: "\\d". In Java 5.0, the static quote() method quotes all special characters in a string so that you can match arbitrary text literally without worrying that punctuation in that text will be interpreted specially. For complete details on regular expressions see a book like *Programming Perl* by Larry Wall et. al., or *Mastering Regular Expressions* by Jeffrey E. F. Friedl.

Table 16-3. Java regular expression quick reference

Syntax	Matches
Single characters	
x	The character *x*, as long as *x* is not a punctuation character with special meaning in the regular expression syntax.
p	The punctuation character *p*.
\\\\	The backslash character
\n	Newline character \u000A.
\t	Tab character \u0009.
\r	Carriage return character \u000D.
\f	Form feed character \u000C.
\e	Escape character \u001B.
\a	Bell (alert) character \u0007.
\u*xxxx*	Unicode character with hexadecimal code *xxxx*.
\x*xx*	Character with hexadecimal code *xx*.
\0*n*	Character with octal code *n*.
\0*nn*	Character with octal code *nn*.
\0*nnn*	Character with octal code *nnn*, where *nnn* <= 377.
\c*x*	The control character ^*x*.
Character classes	
[...]	One of the characters between the brackets. Characters may be specified literally, and the syntax also allows the specification of character ranges, with intersection, union, and subtraction operators. See specific examples below.
[^...]	Any one character not between the brackets.
[a-z0-9]	Character range: a character between (inclusive) a and z or 0 and 9.
[0-9[a-fA-F]]	Union of classes: same as [0-9a-fA-F]
[a-z&&[aeiou]]	Intersection of classes: same as [aeiou].
[a-z&&[^aeiou]]	Subtraction: the characters a through z except for the vowels.
.	Any character except a line terminator. If the DOTALL flag is set, then it matches any character including line terminators.
\d	ASCII digit: [0-9].
\D	Anything but an ASCII digit: [^\d].
\s	ASCII whitespace: [\t\n\f\r\x0B]
\S	Anything but ASCII whitespace: [^\s].
\w	ASCII word character: [a-zA-Z0-9_].

Table 16-3. Java regular expression quick reference (continued)

<table>
<tr><th>Syntax</th><th>Matches</th></tr>
<tr><td>\W</td><td>Anything but ASCII word characters: [^\w].</td></tr>
<tr><td>\p{group}</td><td>Any character in the named group. See group names below. Many of the group names are from POSIX, which is why p is used for this character class.</td></tr>
<tr><td>\P{group}</td><td>Any character not in the named group.</td></tr>
<tr><td>\p{Lower}</td><td>ASCII lowercase letter: [a-z].</td></tr>
<tr><td>\p{Upper}</td><td>ASCII uppercase: [A-Z].</td></tr>
<tr><td>\p{ASCII}</td><td>Any ASCII character: [\x00-\x7f].</td></tr>
<tr><td>\p{Alpha}</td><td>ASCII letter: [a-zA-Z].</td></tr>
<tr><td>\p{Digit}</td><td>ASCII digit: [0-9].</td></tr>
<tr><td>\p{XDigit}</td><td>Hexadecimal digit: [0-9a-fA-F].</td></tr>
<tr><td>\p{Alnum}</td><td>ASCII letter or digit: [\p{Alpha}\p{Digit}].</td></tr>
<tr><td>\p{Punct}</td><td>ASCII punctuation: one of !"#$%& ()*+,-./:;<=>?@[\]^_{|}~].</td></tr>
<tr><td>\p{Graph}</td><td>visible ASCII character: [\p{Alnum}\p{Punct}].</td></tr>
<tr><td>\p{Print}</td><td>visible ASCII character: same as \p{Graph}.</td></tr>
<tr><td>\p{Blank}</td><td>ASCII space or tab: [\t].</td></tr>
<tr><td>\p{Space}</td><td>ASCII whitespace: [\t\n\f\r\x0b].</td></tr>
<tr><td>\p{Cntrl}</td><td>ASCII control character: [\x00-\x1f\x7f].</td></tr>
<tr><td>\p{category}</td><td>Any character in the named Unicode category. Category names are one or two letter codes defined by the Unicode standard. One letter codes include L for letter, N for number, S for symbol, Z for separator, and P for punctuation. Two letter codes represent subcategories, such as Lu for uppercase letter, Nd for decimal digit, Sc for currency symbol, Sm for math symbol, and Zs for space separator. See <code>java.lang.Character</code> for a set of constants that correspond to these subcategories; however, note that the full set of one- and two-letter codes is not documented in this book.</td></tr>
<tr><td>\p{block}</td><td>Any character in the named Unicode block. In Java regular expressions, block names begin with "In", followed by mixed-case capitalization of the Unicode block name, without spaces or underscores. For example: \p{InOgham} or \p{InMathematicalOperators}. See <code>java.lang.Character.UnicodeBlock</code> for a list of Unicode block names.</td></tr>
<tr><td colspan="2">Sequences, alternatives, groups, and references</td></tr>
<tr><td>xy</td><td>Match x followed by y.</td></tr>
<tr><td>x|y</td><td>Match x or y.</td></tr>
<tr><td>(...)</td><td>Grouping. Group subexpression within parentheses into a single unit that can be used with *, +, ?, |, and so on. Also "capture" the characters that match this group for use later.</td></tr>
<tr><td>(?:...)</td><td>Grouping only. Group subexpression as with ( ), but do not capture the text that matched.</td></tr>
<tr><td>\n</td><td>Match the same characters that were matched when capturing group number n was first matched. Be careful when n is followed by another digit: the largest number that is a valid group number will be used.</td></tr>
<tr><td colspan="2">Repetition[a]</td></tr>
<tr><td>x?</td><td>zero or one occurrence of x; i.e., x is optional.</td></tr>
<tr><td>x*</td><td>zero or more occurrences of x.</td></tr>
<tr><td>x+</td><td>one or more occurrences of x.</td></tr>
<tr><td>x{n}</td><td>exactly n occurrences of x.</td></tr>
<tr><td>x{n,}</td><td>n or more occurrences of x.</td></tr>
<tr><td>x{n,m}</td><td>at least n, and at most m occurrences of x.</td></tr>
</table>

Table 16-3. Java regular expression quick reference (continued)

Syntax	Matches
Anchors[b]	
^	The beginning of the input string, or if the MULTILINE flag is specified, the beginning of the string or of any new line.
$	The end of the input string, or if the MULTILINE flag is specified, the end of the string or of line within the string.
\b	A word boundary: a position in the string between a word and a nonword character.
\B	A position in the string that is not a word boundary.
\A	The beginning of the input string. Like ^, but never matches the beginning of a new line, regardless of what flags are set.
\Z	The end of the input string, ignoring any trailing line terminator.
\z	The end of the input string, including any line terminator.
\G	The end of the previous match.
(?=*x*)	A positive look-ahead assertion. Require that the following characters match *x*, but do not include those characters in the match.
(?!*x*)	A negative look-ahead assertion. Require that the following characters do not match the pattern *x*.
(?<=*x*)	A positive look-behind assertion. Require that the characters immediately before the position match *x*, but do not include those characters in the match. *x* must be a pattern with a fixed number of characters.
(?<!*x*)	A negative look-behind assertion. Require that the characters immediately before the position do not match *x*. *x* must be a pattern with a fixed number of characters.
Miscellaneous	
(?>*x*)	Match *x* independently of the rest of the expression, without considering whether the match causes the rest of the expression to fail to match. Useful to optimize certain complex regular expressions. A group of this form does not capture the matched text.
(?*onflags*-*offflags*)	Don t match anything, but turn on the flags specified by *onflags*, and turn off the flags specified by *offflags*. These two strings are combinations in any order of the following letters and correspond to the following Pattern constants: i (CASE_INSENSITIVE), d (UNIX_LINES), m (MULTILINE), s (DOTALL), u (UNICODE_CASE), and x (COMMENTS). Flag settings specified in this way take effect at the point that they appear in the expression and persist until the end of the expression, or until the end of the parenthesized group of which they are a part, or until overridden by another flag setting expression.
(?*onflags*-*offflags*:*x*)	Match *x*, applying the specified flags to this subexpression only. This is a noncapturing group, like (?:...), with the addition of flags.
\Q	Don't match anything, but quote all subsequent pattern text until \E. All characters within such a quoted section are interpreted as literal characters to match, and none (except \E) have special meanings.
\E	Don't match anything; terminate a quote started with \Q.
#comment	If the COMMENT flag is set, pattern text between a # and the end of the line is considered a comment and is ignored.

[a] These repetition characters are known as "greedy quantifiers," because they match as many occurrences of x as possible while still allowing the rest of the regular expression to match. If you want a "reluctant quantifier" which matches as few occurrences as possible while still allowing the rest of the regular expression to match, follow the quantifiers above with a question mark. For example, use *? instead of *, and use {2,}? instead of {2,}. Or, if you follow a quantifier with a plus sign instead of a question mark, then you specify a "possessive quantifier" which matches as many occurrences as possible, even if it means that the rest of the regular expression will not match. Possessive quantifiers can be useful when you are sure that they will not adversely affect the rest of the match, because they can be implemented more efficiently than regular "greedy quantifiers."

[b] Anchors do not match characters but instead match the zero-width positions between characters, "anchoring" the match to a position at which a specific condition holds.

Object ─ Pattern ··· Serializable

```
public final class Pattern implements Serializable {
// No Constructor
// Public Constants
    public static final int CANON_EQ;                                    =128
    public static final int CASE_INSENSITIVE;                            =2
    public static final int COMMENTS;                                    =4
    public static final int DOTALL;                                      =32
5.0 public static final int LITERAL;                                     =16
    public static final int MULTILINE;                                   =8
    public static final int UNICODE_CASE;                                =64
    public static final int UNIX_LINES;                                  =1
// Public Class Methods
    public static Pattern compile(String regex);
    public static Pattern compile(String regex, int flags);
    public static boolean matches(String regex, CharSequence input);
5.0 public static String quote(String s);
// Public Instance Methods
    public int flags();
    public Matcher matcher(CharSequence input);
    public String pattern();
    public String[] split(CharSequence input);
    public String[] split(CharSequence input, int limit);
// Public Methods Overriding Object
5.0 public String toString();
}
```

Passed To java.util.Scanner.{findInLine(), findWithinHorizon(), hasNext(), next(), skip(), useDelimiter()}, Matcher.usePattern()

Returned By java.util.Scanner.delimiter(), Matcher.pattern()

PatternSyntaxException **Java 1.4**

java.util.regex **serializable unchecked**

Signals a syntax error in the text representation of a regular expression. An exception of this type may be thrown by the Pattern.compile() and Pattern.matches() methods, and also by the String matches(), replaceFirst(), replaceAll() and split() methods which call those Pattern methods.

getPattern() returns the text that contained the syntax error, and getIndex() returns the approximate location of the error within that text, or -1, if the location is not known. getDescription() returns an error message that provides further detail about the error. The inherited getMessage() method combines the information provided by these other three methods into a single multiline message.

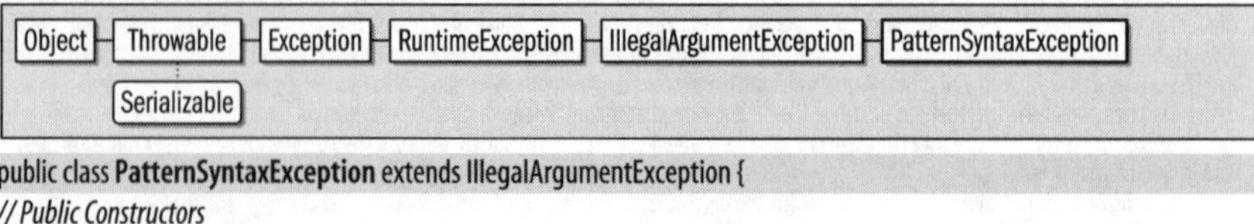


```
public class PatternSyntaxException extends IllegalArgumentException {
// Public Constructors
    public PatternSyntaxException(String desc, String regex, int index);
// Public Instance Methods
    public String getDescription();
```

```
    public int getIndex();
    public String getPattern();
// Public Methods Overriding Throwable
    public String getMessage();
}
```

Package java.util.zip — Java 1.1

The java.util.zip package contains classes for data compression and decompression. The Deflater and Inflater classes perform data compression and decompression. DeflaterOutputStream and InflaterInputStream apply that functionality to byte streams; the subclasses of these streams implement both the GZIP and ZIP compression formats. The Adler32 and CRC32 classes implement the Checksum interface and compute the checksums required for data compression.

Interfaces

```
public interface Checksum;
```

Classes

```
public class Adler32 implements Checksum;
public class CheckedInputStream extends java.io.FilterInputStream;
public class CheckedOutputStream extends java.io.FilterOutputStream;
public class CRC32 implements Checksum;
public class Deflater;
public class DeflaterOutputStream extends java.io.FilterOutputStream;
    public class GZIPOutputStream extends DeflaterOutputStream;
    public class ZipOutputStream extends DeflaterOutputStream implements ZipConstants;
public class Inflater;
public class InflaterInputStream extends java.io.FilterInputStream;
    public class GZIPInputStream extends InflaterInputStream;
    public class ZipInputStream extends InflaterInputStream implements ZipConstants;
public class ZipEntry implements Cloneable, ZipConstants;
public class ZipFile implements ZipConstants;
```

Exceptions

```
public class DataFormatException extends Exception;
public class ZipException extends java.io.IOException;
```

Adler32 — Java 1.1

java.util.zip

This class implements the Checksum interface and computes a checksum on a stream of data using the Adler-32 algorithm. This algorithm is significantly faster than the CRC-32 algorithm and is almost as reliable. The CheckedInputStream and CheckedOutputStream classes provide a higher-level interface to computing checksums on streams of data.

Object — Adler32 ··· Checksum

```
public class Adler32 implements Checksum {
// Public Constructors
    public Adler32();
// Public Instance Methods
```

java.util.*

```
    public void update(byte[] b);
// Methods Implementing Checksum
    public long getValue();                                    default:1
    public void reset();
    public void update(int b);
    public void update(byte[] b, int off, int len);
}
```

CheckedInputStream **Java 1.1**

java.util.zip **closeable**

This class is a subclass of java.io.FilterInputStream; it allows a stream to be read and a checksum computed on its contents at the same time. This is useful when you want to check the integrity of a stream of data against a published checksum value. To create a CheckedInputStream, you must specify both the stream it should read and a Checksum object, such as CRC32, that implements the particular checksum algorithm you desire. The read() and skip() methods are the same as those of other input streams. As bytes are read, they are incorporated into the checksum that is being computed. The getChecksum() method does not return the checksum value itself, but rather the Checksum object. You must call the getValue() method of this object to obtain the checksum value.

Object — InputStream — FilterInputStream — CheckedInputStream

Closeable

```
public class CheckedInputStream extends java.io.FilterInputStream {
// Public Constructors
    public CheckedInputStream(java.io.InputStream in, Checksum cksum);
// Public Instance Methods
    public Checksum getChecksum();
// Public Methods Overriding FilterInputStream
    public int read() throws java.io.IOException;
    public int read(byte[] buf, int off, int len) throws java.io.IOException;
    public long skip(long n) throws java.io.IOException;
}
```

CheckedOutputStream **Java 1.1**

java.util.zip **closeable flushable**

This class is a subclass of java.io.FilterOutputStream that allows data to be written to a stream and a checksum computed on that data at the same time. To create a CheckedOutput-Stream, you must specify both the output stream to write its data to and a Checksum object, such as an instance of Adler32, that implements the particular checksum algorithm you desire. The write() methods are similar to those of other OutputStream classes. The getChecksum() method returns the Checksum object. You must call getValue() on this object in order to obtain the actual checksum value.

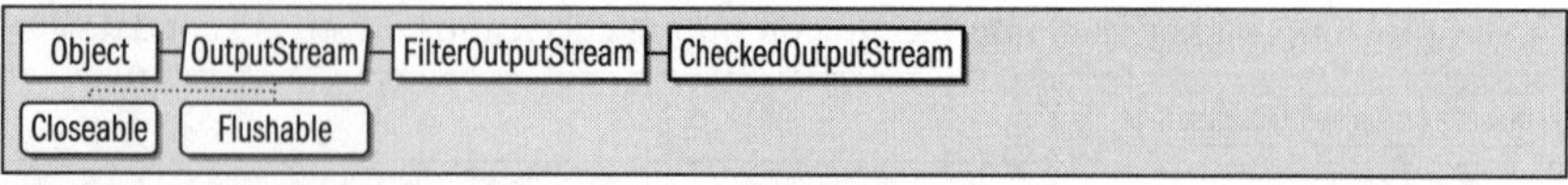


```
public class CheckedOutputStream extends java.io.FilterOutputStream {
// Public Constructors
    public CheckedOutputStream(java.io.OutputStream out, Checksum cksum);
```

```
// Public Instance Methods
    public Checksum getChecksum();
// Public Methods Overriding FilterOutputStream
    public void write(int b) throws java.io.IOException;
    public void write(byte[] b, int off, int len) throws java.io.IOException;
}
```

Checksum **Java 1.1**

java.util.zip

This interface defines the methods required to compute a checksum on a stream of data. The checksum is computed based on the bytes of data supplied by the update() methods; the current value of the checksum can be obtained at any time with the getValue() method. reset() resets the checksum to its default value; use this method before beginning a new stream of data. The checksum value computed by a Checksum object and returned through the getValue() method must fit into a long value. Therefore, this interface is not suitable for the cryptographic checksum algorithms used in cryptography and security. The classes CheckedInputStream and CheckedOutputStream provide a higher-level API for computing a checksum on a stream of data. See also java.security.MessageDigest.

```
public interface Checksum {
// Public Instance Methods
    long getValue();
    void reset();
    void update(int b);
    void update(byte[] b, int off, int len);
}
```

Implementations Adler32, CRC32

Passed To CheckedInputStream.CheckedInputStream(), CheckedOutputStream.CheckedOutputStream()

Returned By CheckedInputStream.getChecksum(), CheckedOutputStream.getChecksum()

CRC32 **Java 1.1**

java.util.zip

This class implements the Checksum interface and computes a checksum on a stream of data using the CRC-32 algorithm. The CheckedInputStream and CheckedOutputStream classes provide a higher-level interface to computing checksums on streams of data.

Object — CRC32 ··· Checksum

```
public class CRC32 implements Checksum {
// Public Constructors
    public CRC32();
// Public Instance Methods
    public void update(byte[] b);
// Methods Implementing Checksum
    public long getValue();                                    default:0
    public void reset();
    public void update(int b);
    public void update(byte[] b, int off, int len);
}
```

Type Of GZIPInputStream.crc, GZIPOutputStream.crc

DataFormatException

Java 1.1

java.util.zip — serializable checked

Signals that invalid or corrupt data has been encountered while uncompressing data.

Object — Throwable — Exception — DataFormatException
Serializable

```
public class DataFormatException extends Exception {
// Public Constructors
   public DataFormatException();
   public DataFormatException(String s);
}
```

Thrown By Inflater.inflate()

Deflater

Java 1.1

java.util.zip

This class implements the general ZLIB data-compression algorithm used by the *gzip* and *PKZip* compression programs. The constants defined by this class are used to specify the compression strategy and the compression speed/strength tradeoff level to be used. If you set the *nowrap* argument to the constructor to true, the ZLIB header and checksum data are omitted from the compressed output, which is the format both *gzip* and *PKZip* use.

The important methods of this class are setInput(), which specifies input data to be compressed, and deflate(), which compresses the data and returns the compressed output. The remaining methods exist so that Deflater can be used for stream-based compression, as it is in higher-level classes, such as GZIPOutputStream and ZipOutputStream. These stream classes are sufficient in most cases. Most applications do not need to use Deflater directly. The Inflater class uncompresses data compressed with a Deflater object.

```
public class Deflater {
// Public Constructors
   public Deflater();
   public Deflater(int level);
   public Deflater(int level, boolean nowrap);
// Public Constants
   public static final int BEST_COMPRESSION;                    =9
   public static final int BEST_SPEED;                          =1
   public static final int DEFAULT_COMPRESSION;                 =-1
   public static final int DEFAULT_STRATEGY;                    =0
   public static final int DEFLATED;                            =8
   public static final int FILTERED;                            =1
   public static final int HUFFMAN_ONLY;                        =2
   public static final int NO_COMPRESSION;                      =0
// Public Instance Methods
   public int deflate(byte[] b);
   public int deflate(byte[] b, int off, int len);              synchronized
   public void end();                                           synchronized
   public void finish();                                        synchronized
```

```
    public boolean finished();                                          synchronized
    public int getAdler();                                   synchronized default:1
5.0 public long getBytesRead();                              synchronized default:0
5.0 public long getBytesWritten();                           synchronized default:0
    public int getTotalIn();                                              default:0
    public int getTotalOut();                                             default:0
    public boolean needsInput();
    public void reset();                                                synchronized
    public void setDictionary(byte[] b);
    public void setDictionary(byte[] b, int off, int len);              synchronized
    public void setInput(byte[] b);
    public void setInput(byte[] b, int off, int len);                   synchronized
    public void setLevel(int level);                                    synchronized
    public void setStrategy(int strategy);                              synchronized
// Protected Methods Overriding Object
    protected void finalize();
}
```

Passed To DeflaterOutputStream.DeflaterOutputStream()

Type Of DeflaterOutputStream.def

DeflaterOutputStream **Java 1.1**

java.util.zip **closeable flushable**

This class is a subclass of java.io.FilterOutputStream; it filters a stream of data by compressing (deflating) it and then writing the compressed data to another output stream. To create a DeflaterOutputStream, you must specify both the stream it is to write to and a Deflater object to perform the compression. You can set various options on the Deflater object to specify just what type of compression is to be performed. Once a DeflaterOutputStream is created, its write() and close() methods are the same as those of other output streams. The InflaterInputStream class can read data written with a DeflaterOutputStream. A DeflaterOutputStream writes raw compressed data; applications often prefer one of its subclasses, GZIPOutputStream or ZipOutputStream, that wraps the raw compressed data within a standard file format.

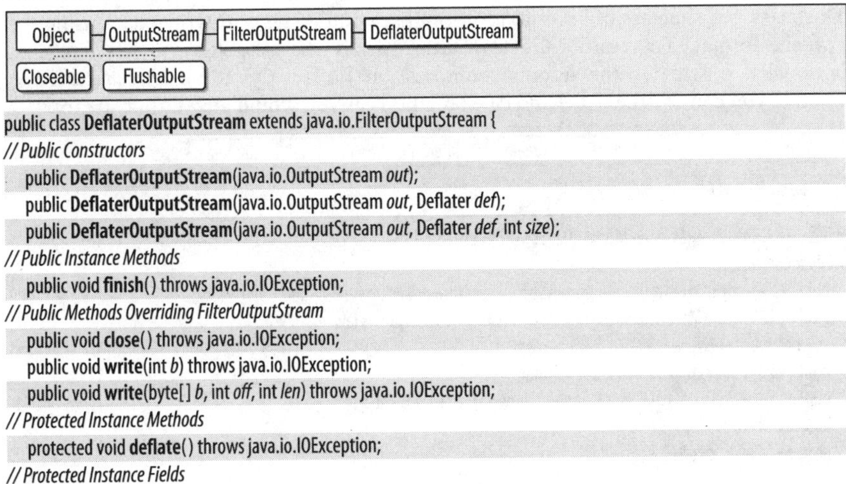


```
public class DeflaterOutputStream extends java.io.FilterOutputStream {
// Public Constructors
    public DeflaterOutputStream(java.io.OutputStream out);
    public DeflaterOutputStream(java.io.OutputStream out, Deflater def);
    public DeflaterOutputStream(java.io.OutputStream out, Deflater def, int size);
// Public Instance Methods
    public void finish() throws java.io.IOException;
// Public Methods Overriding FilterOutputStream
    public void close() throws java.io.IOException;
    public void write(int b) throws java.io.IOException;
    public void write(byte[] b, int off, int len) throws java.io.IOException;
// Protected Instance Methods
    protected void deflate() throws java.io.IOException;
// Protected Instance Fields
```

java.util.*

```
    protected byte[] buf;
    protected Deflater def;
}
```

Subclasses GZIPOutputStream, ZipOutputStream

GZIPInputStream **Java 1.1**

java.util.zip closeable

This class is a subclass of InflaterInputStream that reads and uncompresses data compressed in *gzip* format. To create a GZIPInputStream, simply specify the InputStream to read compressed data from and, optionally, a buffer size for the internal decompression buffer. Once a GZIPInputStream is created, you can use the read() and close() methods as you would with any input stream.

Object — InputStream — FilterInputStream — InflaterInputStream — GZIPInputStream
Closeable

```
public class GZIPInputStream extends InflaterInputStream {
// Public Constructors
    public GZIPInputStream(java.io.InputStream in) throws java.io.IOException;
    public GZIPInputStream(java.io.InputStream in, int size) throws java.io.IOException;
// Public Constants
    public static final int GZIP_MAGIC;                                   =35615
// Public Methods Overriding InflaterInputStream
    public void close() throws java.io.IOException;
    public int read(byte[] buf, int off, int len) throws java.io.IOException;
// Protected Instance Fields
    protected CRC32 crc;
    protected boolean eos;
}
```

GZIPOutputStream **Java 1.1**

java.util.zip closeable flushable

This class is a subclass of DeflaterOutputStream that compresses and writes data using the *gzip* file format. To create a GZIPOutputStream, specify the OutputStream to write to and, optionally, a size for the internal compression buffer. Once the GZIPOutputStream is created, you can use the write() and close() methods as you would any output stream.

Object — OutputStream — FilterOutputStream — DeflaterOutputStream — GZIPOutputStream
Closeable, Flushable

```
public class GZIPOutputStream extends DeflaterOutputStream {
// Public Constructors
    public GZIPOutputStream(java.io.OutputStream out) throws java.io.IOException;
    public GZIPOutputStream(java.io.OutputStream out, int size) throws java.io.IOException;
// Public Methods Overriding DeflaterOutputStream
    public void finish() throws java.io.IOException;
    public void write(byte[] buf, int off, int len) throws java.io.IOException;      synchronized
// Protected Instance Fields
    protected CRC32 crc;
}
```

Inflater Java 1.1

java.util.zip

This class implements the general ZLIB data-decompression algorithm used by *gzip*, *PKZip*, and other data-compression applications. It decompresses or inflates data compressed through the **Deflater** class. The important methods of this class are **setInput()**, which specifies input data to be decompressed, and **inflate()**, which decompresses the input data into an output buffer. A number of other methods exist so that this class can be used for stream-based decompression, as it is in the higher-level classes, such as **GZIPInputStream** and **ZipInputStream**. These stream-based classes are sufficient in most cases. Most applications do not need to use **Inflater** directly.

```
public class Inflater {
// Public Constructors
   public Inflater();
   public Inflater(boolean nowrap);
// Public Instance Methods
   public void end();                                                   synchronized
   public boolean finished();                                           synchronized
   public int getAdler();                                    synchronized default:1
5.0 public long getBytesRead();                              synchronized default:0
5.0 public long getBytesWritten();                           synchronized default:0
   public int getRemaining();                                synchronized default:0
   public int getTotalIn();                                               default:0
   public int getTotalOut();                                              default:0
   public int inflate(byte[] b) throws DataFormatException;
   public int inflate(byte[] b, int off, int len) throws DataFormatException;  synchronized
   public boolean needsDictionary();                                    synchronized
   public boolean needsInput();                                         synchronized
   public void reset();                                                 synchronized
   public void setDictionary(byte[] b);
   public void setDictionary(byte[] b, int off, int len);               synchronized
   public void setInput(byte[] b);
   public void setInput(byte[] b, int off, int len);                    synchronized
// Protected Methods Overriding Object
   protected void finalize();
}
```

Passed To InflaterInputStream.InflaterInputStream()

Type Of InflaterInputStream.inf

InflaterInputStream Java 1.1

java.util.zip closeable

This class is a subclass of **java.io.FilterInputStream**; it reads a specified stream of compressed input data (typically one that was written with **DeflaterOutputStream** or a subclass) and filters that data by uncompressing (inflating) it. To create an **InflaterInputStream**, specify both the input stream to read from and an **Inflater** object to perform the decompression. Once an **InflaterInputStream** is created, the **read()** and **skip()** methods are the same as those of other input streams. The **InflaterInputStream** uncompresses raw data. Applications often prefer one of its subclasses, **GZIPInputStream** or **ZipInputStream**, that work with compressed data written in the standard *gzip* and *PKZip* file formats.

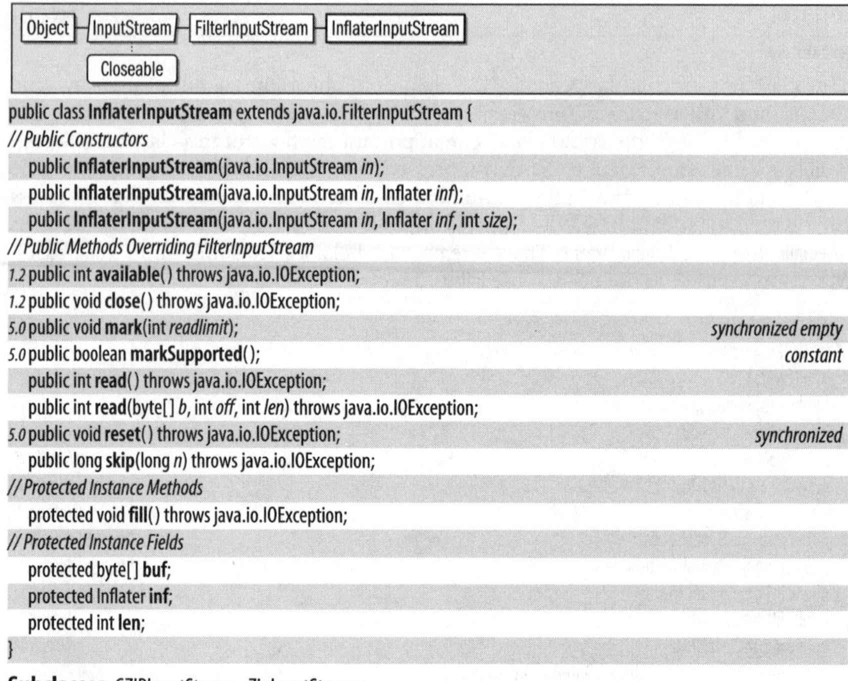


```
public class InflaterInputStream extends java.io.FilterInputStream {
// Public Constructors
    public InflaterInputStream(java.io.InputStream in);
    public InflaterInputStream(java.io.InputStream in, Inflater inf);
    public InflaterInputStream(java.io.InputStream in, Inflater inf, int size);
// Public Methods Overriding FilterInputStream
1.2 public int available() throws java.io.IOException;
1.2 public void close() throws java.io.IOException;
5.0 public void mark(int readlimit);                                    synchronized empty
5.0 public boolean markSupported();                                     constant
    public int read() throws java.io.IOException;
    public int read(byte[] b, int off, int len) throws java.io.IOException;
5.0 public void reset() throws java.io.IOException;                     synchronized
    public long skip(long n) throws java.io.IOException;
// Protected Instance Methods
    protected void fill() throws java.io.IOException;
// Protected Instance Fields
    protected byte[] buf;
    protected Inflater inf;
    protected int len;
}
```

Subclasses GZIPInputStream, ZipInputStream

ZipEntry

Java 1.1

java.util.zip | cloneable

This class describes a single entry (typically a compressed file) stored within a ZIP file. The various methods get and set various pieces of information about the entry. The **ZipEntry** class is used by **ZipFile** and **ZipInputStream**, which read ZIP files, and by **ZipOutputStream**, which writes ZIP files.

When you are reading a ZIP file, a **ZipEntry** object returned by **ZipFile** or **ZipInputStream** contains the name, size, modification time, and other information about an entry in the file. When writing a ZIP file, on the other hand, you must create your own **ZipEntry** objects and initialize them to contain the entry name and other appropriate information before writing the contents of the entry.

Object — ZipEntry; Cloneable, ZipConstants

```
public class ZipEntry implements Cloneable, ZipConstants {
// Public Constructors
    public ZipEntry(String name);
1.2 public ZipEntry(ZipEntry e);
// Public Constants
    public static final int DEFLATED;                                   =8
    public static final int STORED;                                     =0
```

```
// Public Instance Methods
   public String getComment();
   public long getCompressedSize();
   public long getCrc();
   public byte[] getExtra();
   public int getMethod();
   public String getName();
   public long getSize();
   public long getTime();
   public boolean isDirectory();
   public void setComment(String comment);
1.2 public void setCompressedSize(long csize);
   public void setCrc(long crc);
   public void setExtra(byte[] extra);
   public void setMethod(int method);
   public void setSize(long size);
   public void setTime(long time);
// Public Methods Overriding Object
1.2 public Object clone();
1.2 public int hashCode();
   public String toString();
}
```

Subclasses java.util.jar.JarEntry

Passed To java.util.jar.JarEntry.JarEntry(), java.util.jar.JarFile.getInputStream(), java.util.jar.JarOutputStream.putNextEntry(), ZipFile.getInputStream(), ZipOutputStream.putNextEntry()

Returned By java.util.jar.JarFile.getEntry(), java.util.jar.JarInputStream.{createZipEntry(), getNextEntry()}, ZipFile.getEntry(), ZipInputStream.{createZipEntry(), getNextEntry()}

ZipException — Java 1.1

java.util.zip — serializable checked

Signals that an error has occurred in reading or writing a ZIP file.

Object — Throwable — Exception — IOException — ZipException
Throwable ··· Serializable

```
public class ZipException extends java.io.IOException {
// Public Constructors
   public ZipException();
   public ZipException(String s);
}
```

Subclasses java.util.jar.JarException

Thrown By ZipFile.ZipFile()

ZipFile — Java 1.1

java.util.zip

This class reads the contents of ZIP files. It uses a random-access file internally so that the entries of the ZIP file do not have to be read sequentially, as they do with the ZipInputStream class. A ZipFile object can be created by specifying the ZIP file to be read either as a String filename or as a File object. In Java 1.3, temporary ZIP files can be marked for automatic deletion when they are closed. To take advantage of this feature, pass ZipFile.OPEN_READ|ZipFile.OPEN_DELETE as the *mode* argument to the ZipFile() constructor.

Once a ZipFile is created, the getEntry() method returns a ZipEntry object for a named entry, and the entries() method returns an Enumeration object that allows you to loop through all the ZipEntry objects for the file. To read the contents of a specific ZipEntry within the ZIP file, pass the ZipEntry to getInputStream(); this returns an InputStream object from which you can read the entry's contents.

Object | ZipFile | ZipConstants

```
public class ZipFile implements ZipConstants {
// Public Constructors
   public ZipFile(String name) throws java.io.IOException;
   public ZipFile(java.io.File file) throws ZipException, java.io.IOException;
1.3 public ZipFile(java.io.File file, int mode) throws java.io.IOException;
// Public Constants
1.3 public static final int OPEN_DELETE;                                    =4
1.3 public static final int OPEN_READ;                                      =1
// Public Instance Methods
   public void close() throws java.io.IOException;
   public java.util.Enumeration<? extends ZipEntry> entries();
   public ZipEntry getEntry(String name);
   public java.io.InputStream getInputStream(ZipEntry entry) throws java.io.IOException;
   public String getName();
1.2 public int size();
// Protected Methods Overriding Object
1.3 protected void finalize() throws java.io.IOException;
}
```

Subclasses java.util.jar.JarFile

ZipInputStream **Java 1.1**

java.util.zip closeable

This class is a subclass of InflaterInputStream that reads the entries of a ZIP file in sequential order. Create a ZipInputStream by specifying the InputStream from which it is to read the contents of the ZIP file. Once the ZipInputStream is created, you can use getNextEntry() to begin reading data from the next entry in the ZIP file. This method must be called before read() is called to begin reading the first entry. getNextEntry() returns a ZipEntry object that describes the entry being read, or null when there are no more entries to be read from the ZIP file.

The read() methods of ZipInputStream read until the end of the current entry and then return –1, indicating that there is no more data to read. To continue with the next entry in the ZIP file, you must call getNextEntry() again. Similarly, the skip() method only skips bytes within the current entry. closeEntry() can be called to skip the remaining data in the current entry, but it is usually easier simply to call getNextEntry() to begin the next entry.

```
public class ZipInputStream extends InflaterInputStream implements ZipConstants {
// Public Constructors
   public ZipInputStream(java.io.InputStream in);
// Public Instance Methods
   public void closeEntry() throws java.io.IOException;
   public ZipEntry getNextEntry() throws java.io.IOException;
// Public Methods Overriding InflaterInputStream
1.2 public int available() throws java.io.IOException;
   public void close() throws java.io.IOException;
   public int read(byte[] b, int off, int len) throws java.io.IOException;
   public long skip(long n) throws java.io.IOException;
// Protected Instance Methods
1.2 protected ZipEntry createZipEntry(String name);
}
```

Subclasses java.util.jar.JarInputStream

ZipOutputStream **Java 1.1**

java.util.zip **closeable flushable**

This class is a subclass of DeflaterOutputStream that writes data in ZIP file format to an output stream. Before writing any data to the ZipOutputStream, you must begin an entry within the ZIP file with putNextEntry(). The ZipEntry object passed to this method should specify at least a name for the entry. Once you have begun an entry with putNextEntry(), you can write the contents of that entry with the write() methods. When you reach the end of an entry, you can begin a new one by calling putNextEntry() again, you can close the current entry with closeEntry(), or you can close the stream itself with close().

Before beginning an entry with putNextEntry(), you can set the compression method and level with setMethod() and setLevel(). The constants DEFLATED and STORED are the two legal values for setMethod(). If you use STORED, the entry is stored in the ZIP file without any compression. If you use DEFLATED, you can also specify the compression speed/strength tradeoff by passing a number from 1 to 9 to setLevel(), where 9 gives the strongest and slowest level of compression. You can also use the constants Deflater.BEST_SPEED, Deflater.BEST_COMPRESSION, and Deflater.DEFAULT_COMPRESSION with the setLevel() method.

If you are storing an entry without compression, the ZIP file format requires that you specify, in advance, the entry size and CRC-32 checksum in the ZipEntry object for the entry. An exception is thrown if these values are not specified or specified incorrectly.

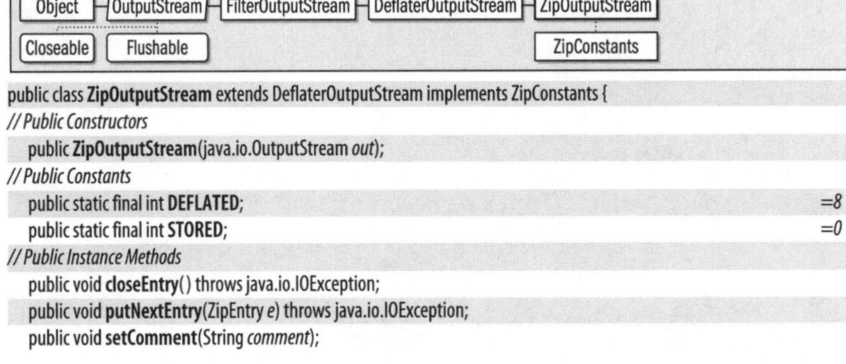


```
public class ZipOutputStream extends DeflaterOutputStream implements ZipConstants {
// Public Constructors
   public ZipOutputStream(java.io.OutputStream out);
// Public Constants
   public static final int DEFLATED;                                          =8
   public static final int STORED;                                            =0
// Public Instance Methods
   public void closeEntry() throws java.io.IOException;
   public void putNextEntry(ZipEntry e) throws java.io.IOException;
   public void setComment(String comment);
```

```
    public void setLevel(int level);
    public void setMethod(int method);
// Public Methods Overriding DeflaterOutputStream
    public void close() throws java.io.IOException;
    public void finish() throws java.io.IOException;
    public void write(byte[] b, int off, int len) throws java.io.IOException;                synchronized
}
```

Subclasses java.util.jar.JarOutputStream

17

javax.crypto and Subpackages

This chapter documents the cryptographic features (including encryption and decryption) of the javax.crypto package and its subpackages. These packages were originally part of the Java Cryptography Extension (JCE) before being integrated into Java 1.4, which is why they have the "javax" extension prefix. All of the commonly-used cryptography classes are in the javax.crypto package itself. The javax.crypto.interfaces subpackage defines algorithm-specific interfaces for certain type of cryptographic keys. The javax.crypto.spec subpackage defines classes that provide a transparent, portable, and provider-independent representation of cryptographic keys and related objects.

Package javax.crypto **Java 1.4**

The javax.crypto package defines classes and interfaces for various cryptographic operations. The central class is Cipher, which is used to encrypt and decrypt data. CipherInputStream and CipherOutputStream are utility classes that use a Cipher object to encrypt or decrypt streaming data. SealedObject is another important utility class that uses a Cipher object to encrypt an arbitrary serializable Java object.

The KeyGenerator class creates the SecretKey objects used by Cipher for encryption and decryption. SecretKeyFactory encodes and decodes SecretKey objects. The KeyAgreement class enables two or more parties to agree on a SecretKey in such a way that an eavesdropper cannot determine the key. The Mac class computes a message authentication code (MAC) that can ensure the integrity of a transmission between two parties who share a SecretKey. A MAC is akin to a digital signature, except that it is based on a secret key instead of a public/private key pair.

Like the java.security package, the javax.crypto package is provider-based, so that arbitrary cryptographic implementations may be plugged into any Java installation. Various classes in this package have names that end in Spi. These classes define a service-provider interface and must be implemented by each cryptographic provider that wishes to provide an implementation of a particular cryptographic service or algorithm.

This package was originally shipped as part of the Java Cryptography Extension (JCE), but it has been added to the core platform in Java 1.4. A version of the JCE is still available (see *http://java.sun.com/security*) as a standard extension for Java 1.2 and Java 1.3. This package is distributed with a cryptographic provider named "SunJCE" that includes a robust set of implementations for Cipher, KeyAgreement, Mac, and other classes. This provider is installed by the default java.security properties in Java 1.4 distributions.

A full tutorial on cryptography is beyond the scope of this chapter and of this book. In order to use this package, you need to have a basic understanding of cryptographic algorithms such as DES. In order to take full advantage of this package, you also need to have a detailed understanding of things like feedback modes, padding schemes, the Diffie-Hellman key-agreement protocol, and so on. For a good introduction to modern cryptography in Java, see *Java Cryptography* by Jonathan Knudsen (O'Reilly). For more in-depth coverage, not specific to Java, see *Applied Cryptography* by Bruce Schneier (Wiley).

Interfaces

public interface **SecretKey** extends java.security.Key;

Classes

public class **Cipher**;
    public class **NullCipher** extends Cipher;
public class **CipherInputStream** extends java.io.FilterInputStream;
public class **CipherOutputStream** extends java.io.FilterOutputStream;
public abstract class **CipherSpi**;
public class **EncryptedPrivateKeyInfo**;
public class **ExemptionMechanism**;
public abstract class **ExemptionMechanismSpi**;
public class **KeyAgreement**;
public abstract class **KeyAgreementSpi**;
public class **KeyGenerator**;
public abstract class **KeyGeneratorSpi**;
public class **Mac** implements Cloneable;
public abstract class **MacSpi**;
public class **SealedObject** implements Serializable;
public class **SecretKeyFactory**;
public abstract class **SecretKeyFactorySpi**;

Exceptions

public class **BadPaddingException** extends java.security.GeneralSecurityException;
public class **ExemptionMechanismException** extends java.security.GeneralSecurityException;
public class **IllegalBlockSizeException** extends java.security.GeneralSecurityException;
public class **NoSuchPaddingException** extends java.security.GeneralSecurityException;
public class **ShortBufferException** extends java.security.GeneralSecurityException;

BadPaddingException **Java 1.4**

javax.crypto serializable checked

Signals that input data to a Cipher is not padded correctly.

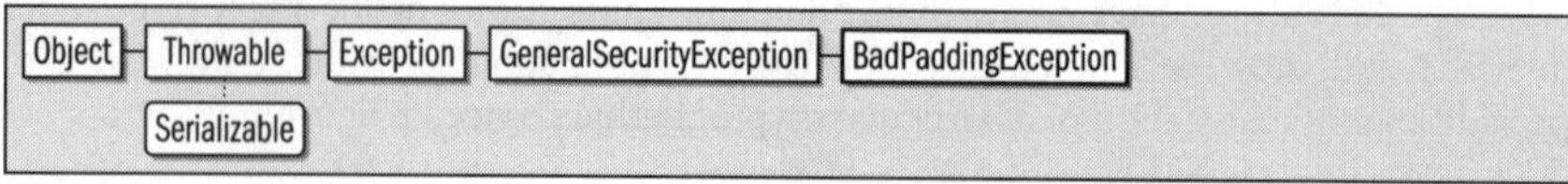

```
public class BadPaddingException extends java.security.GeneralSecurityException {
// Public Constructors
   public BadPaddingException();
   public BadPaddingException(String msg);
}
```

Thrown By Cipher.doFinal(), CipherSpi.engineDoFinal(), SealedObject.getObject()

Cipher **Java 1.4**

javax.crypto

This class performs encryption and decryption of byte arrays. Cipher is provider-based, so to obtain a Cipher object, you must call the static getInstance() factory method. The arguments to getInstance() are a string that describes the type of encryption desired and, optionally, the name of the provider whose implementation should be used. To specify the desired type of encryption, you can simply specify the name of an encryption algorithm, such as "DES". In Java 5.0, the "SunJCE" provider supports the following algorithm names:

AES	DES	RSA
AESWrap	DESede	PBEWithMD5AndDES
ARCFOUR	DESedeWrap	PBEWithMD5AndTripleDES
Blowfish	RC2	PBEWithSHA1AndRC2_40

Advanced users may specify a three-part algorithm name that includes the encryption algorithm, the algorithm operating mode, and the padding scheme. These three parts are separated by slash characters, as in "DES/CBC/PKCS5Padding". Finally, if you are requesting a block cipher algorithm in a stream mode, you can specify the number of bits to be processed at a time by following the name of the feedback mode with a number of bits. For example: "DES/CFB8/NoPadding". Details of supported operating modes and padding schemes are beyond the scope of this book. In Java 5.0, you can obtain details about the services available through the SunJCE (or any other) provider through the java.security.Provider.Services class.

Once you have obtained a Cipher object for the desired cryptographic algorithm, mode, and padding scheme, you must initialize it by calling one of the init() methods. The first argument to init() is one of the constants ENCRYPT_MODE or DECRYPT_MODE. The second argument is a java.security.Key object that performs the encryption or decryption. If you use one of the symmetric (i.e., nonpublic key) encryption algorithms supported by the "SunJCE" provider, this Key object is a SecretKey implementation. Note that some cryptographic providers restrict the maximum allowed key length based on a jurisdiction policy file. In Java 5.0 you can query the maximum allowed key length for a named encryption algorithm with getMaxAllowedKeyLength(). You can optionally pass a java.security.SecureRandom object to init() to provide a source of randomness. If you do not, the Cipher implementation provides its own pseudorandom number generator.

Some cryptographic algorithms require additional initialization parameters; these can be passed to init() as a java.security.AlgorithmParameters object or as a java.security.spec.AlgorithmParameterSpec object. When encrypting, you can omit these parameters, and the Cipher implementation uses default values or generates appropriate random parameters for you. In this case, you should call getParameters() after performing encryption to obtain the AlgorithmParameters used to encrypt. These parameters are required in order to decrypt, and must therefore be saved or transferred along with the encrypted data. Of the algorithms supported by the "SunJCE" provider, the block ciphers "DES", "DESede", and "Blowfish" all require an initialization vector when they are used in "CBC", "CFB", "OFB", or "PCBC" mode. You can represent an initialization vector with a javax.crypto.spec.IvParameterSpec object and obtain the raw bytes of the initialization vector used by a Cipher with the getIV() method. The "PBEWithMD5AndDES" algorithm requires a salt and iteration count as parameters. These can be specified with a javax.crypto.spec.PBEParameterSpec object.

Once you have obtained and initialized a Cipher object, you are ready to use it for encryption or decryption. If you have only a single array of bytes to encrypt or decrypt, pass that input array to one of the doFinal() methods. Some versions of this method return the encrypted or decrypted bytes as the return value of the function. Other versions store the encrypted or decrypted bytes to another byte array you specify. If you choose to use one of these latter methods, you should first call getOutputSize() to determine the required size of the output array. If you want to encrypt or decrypt data from a streaming source or have more than one array of data, pass the data to one of the update() methods, calling it as many times as necessary. Then pass the last array of data to one of the doFinal() methods. If you are working with streaming data, consider using the CipherInputStream and CipherOutputStream classes instead.

Java 5.0 adds versions of the update() and doFinal() that work with ByteBuffer objects, which facilitates the use of encryption and decryption with the New I/O API of java.nio.

```
public class Cipher {
// Protected Constructors
   protected Cipher(CipherSpi cipherSpi, java.security.Provider provider, String transformation);
// Public Constants
   public static final int DECRYPT_MODE;                                    =2
   public static final int ENCRYPT_MODE;                                    =1
   public static final int PRIVATE_KEY;                                     =2
   public static final int PUBLIC_KEY;                                      =1
   public static final int SECRET_KEY;                                      =3
   public static final int UNWRAP_MODE;                                     =4
   public static final int WRAP_MODE;                                       =3
// Public Class Methods
   public static final Cipher getInstance(String transformation)
      throws java.security.NoSuchAlgorithmException, NoSuchPaddingException;
   public static final Cipher getInstance(String transformation, String provider)
      throws java.security.NoSuchAlgorithmException, java.security.NoSuchProviderException, NoSuchPaddingException;
   public static final Cipher getInstance(String transformation, java.security.Provider provider)
      throws java.security.NoSuchAlgorithmException, NoSuchPaddingException;
5.0 public static final int getMaxAllowedKeyLength(String transformation)
      throws java.security.NoSuchAlgorithmException;
5.0 public static final java.security.spec.AlgorithmParameterSpec getMaxAllowedParameterSpec(String transformation)
      throws java.security.NoSuchAlgorithmException;
// Public Instance Methods
   public final byte[] doFinal() throws IllegalBlockSizeException, BadPaddingException;
   public final byte[] doFinal(byte[] input) throws IllegalBlockSizeException, BadPaddingException;
   public final int doFinal(byte[] output, int outputOffset)
      throws IllegalBlockSizeException, ShortBufferException, BadPaddingException;
5.0 public final int doFinal(java.nio.ByteBuffer input, java.nio.ByteBuffer output)
      throws ShortBufferException, IllegalBlockSizeException, BadPaddingException;
   public final byte[] doFinal(byte[] input, int inputOffset, int inputLen)
      throws IllegalBlockSizeException, BadPaddingException;
```

```
    public final int doFinal(byte[] input, int inputOffset, int inputLen, byte[] output)
        throws ShortBufferException, IllegalBlockSizeException, BadPaddingException;
    public final int doFinal(byte[] input, int inputOffset, int inputLen, byte[] output, int outputOffset)
        throws ShortBufferException, IllegalBlockSizeException, BadPaddingException;
    public final String getAlgorithm();
    public final int getBlockSize();
    public final ExemptionMechanism getExemptionMechanism();
    public final byte[] getIV();
    public final int getOutputSize(int inputLen);
    public final java.security.AlgorithmParameters getParameters();
    public final java.security.Provider getProvider();
    public final void init(int opmode, java.security.cert.Certificate certificate) throws java.security.InvalidKeyException;
    public final void init(int opmode, java.security.Key key) throws java.security.InvalidKeyException;
    public final void init(int opmode, java.security.Key key, java.security.AlgorithmParameters params)
        throws java.security.InvalidKeyException, java.security.InvalidAlgorithmParameterException;
    public final void init(int opmode, java.security.cert.Certificate certificate, java.security.SecureRandom random)
        throws java.security.InvalidKeyException;
    public final void init(int opmode, java.security.Key key, java.security.SecureRandom random)
        throws java.security.InvalidKeyException;
    public final void init(int opmode, java.security.Key key, java.security.spec.AlgorithmParameterSpec params)
        throws java.security.InvalidKeyException, java.security.InvalidAlgorithmParameterException;
    public final void init(int opmode, java.security.Key key, java.security.spec.AlgorithmParameterSpec params,
                           java.security.SecureRandom random)
        throws java.security.InvalidKeyException, java.security.InvalidAlgorithmParameterException;
    public final void init(int opmode, java.security.Key key, java.security.AlgorithmParameters params,
                           java.security.SecureRandom random)
        throws java.security.InvalidKeyException, java.security.InvalidAlgorithmParameterException;
    public final java.security.Key unwrap(byte[] wrappedKey, String wrappedKeyAlgorithm, int wrappedKeyType)
        throws java.security.InvalidKeyException, java.security.NoSuchAlgorithmException;
    public final byte[] update(byte[] input);
5.0 public final int update(java.nio.ByteBuffer input, java.nio.ByteBuffer output) throws ShortBufferException;
    public final byte[] update(byte[] input, int inputOffset, int inputLen);
    public final int update(byte[] input, int inputOffset, int inputLen, byte[] output) throws ShortBufferException;
    public final int update(byte[] input, int inputOffset, int inputLen, byte[] output, int outputOffset)
        throws ShortBufferException;
    public final byte[] wrap(java.security.Key key) throws IllegalBlockSizeException, java.security.InvalidKeyException;
}
```

Subclasses NullCipher

Passed To CipherInputStream.CipherInputStream(), CipherOutputStream.CipherOutputStream(), EncryptedPrivateKeyInfo.getKeySpec(), SealedObject.{getObject(), SealedObject()}

CipherInputStream — Java 1.4

javax.crypto — closeable

This class is an input stream that uses a Cipher object to encrypt or decrypt the bytes it reads from another stream. You must initialize the Cipher object before passing it to the CipherInputStream() constructor.

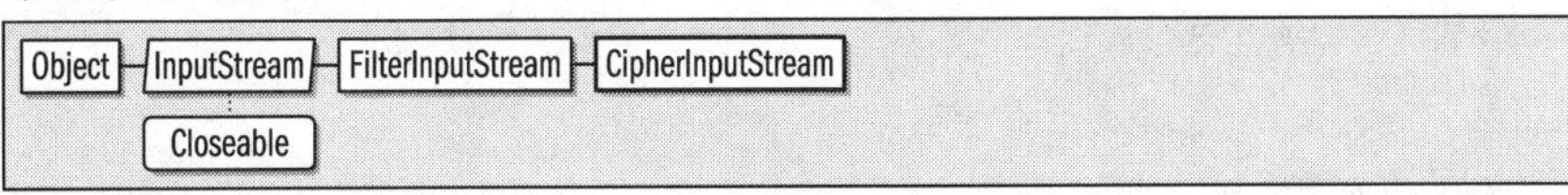


```
public class CipherInputStream extends java.io.FilterInputStream {
// Public Constructors
```


JCE

```
    public CipherInputStream(java.io.InputStream is, Cipher c);
// Protected Constructors
    protected CipherInputStream(java.io.InputStream is);
// Public Methods Overriding FilterInputStream
    public int available() throws java.io.IOException;
    public void close() throws java.io.IOException;
    public boolean markSupported();                                    constant
    public int read() throws java.io.IOException;
    public int read(byte[] b) throws java.io.IOException;
    public int read(byte[] b, int off, int len) throws java.io.IOException;
    public long skip(long n) throws java.io.IOException;
}
```

CipherOutputStream — Java 1.4

javax.crypto — closeable flushable

This class is an output stream that uses a **Cipher** object to encrypt or decrypt bytes before passing them to another output stream. You must initialize the **Cipher** object before passing it to the **CipherOutputStream()** constructor. If you are using a **Cipher** with any kind of padding, you must not call **flush()** until you are done writing all data to the stream; otherwise decryption fails.

Object — OutputStream — FilterOutputStream — CipherOutputStream
Closeable, Flushable

```
public class CipherOutputStream extends java.io.FilterOutputStream {
// Public Constructors
    public CipherOutputStream(java.io.OutputStream os, Cipher c);
// Protected Constructors
    protected CipherOutputStream(java.io.OutputStream os);
// Public Methods Overriding FilterOutputStream
    public void close() throws java.io.IOException;
    public void flush() throws java.io.IOException;
    public void write(int b) throws java.io.IOException;
    public void write(byte[] b) throws java.io.IOException;
    public void write(byte[] b, int off, int len) throws java.io.IOException;
}
```

CipherSpi — Java 1.4

javax.crypto

This abstract class defines the service-provider interface for **Cipher**. A cryptographic provider must implement a concrete subclass of this class for each encryption algorithm it supports. A provider can implement a separate class for each combination of algorithm, mode, and padding scheme it supports or implement more general classes and leave the mode and/or padding scheme to be specified in calls to **engineSetMode()** and **engineSetPadding()**. Applications never need to use or subclass this class.

```
public abstract class CipherSpi {
// Public Constructors
    public CipherSpi();
// Protected Instance Methods
5.0 protected int engineDoFinal(java.nio.ByteBuffer input, java.nio.ByteBuffer output)
        throws ShortBufferException, IllegalBlockSizeException, BadPaddingException;
```

```
    protected abstract byte[] engineDoFinal(byte[] input, int inputOffset, int inputLen)
        throws IllegalBlockSizeException, BadPaddingException;
    protected abstract int engineDoFinal(byte[] input, int inputOffset, int inputLen, byte[] output, int outputOffset)
        throws ShortBufferException, IllegalBlockSizeException, BadPaddingException;
    protected abstract int engineGetBlockSize();
    protected abstract byte[] engineGetIV();
    protected int engineGetKeySize(java.security.Key key) throws java.security.InvalidKeyException;
    protected abstract int engineGetOutputSize(int inputLen);
    protected abstract java.security.AlgorithmParameters engineGetParameters();
    protected abstract void engineInit(int opmode, java.security.Key key, java.security.SecureRandom random)
        throws java.security.InvalidKeyException;
    protected abstract void engineInit(int opmode, java.security.Key key, java.security.AlgorithmParameters params,
                                       java.security.SecureRandom random)
        throws java.security.InvalidKeyException, java.security.InvalidAlgorithmParameterException;
    protected abstract void engineInit(int opmode, java.security.Key key, java.security.spec.AlgorithmParameterSpec params,
                                       java.security.SecureRandom random)
        throws java.security.InvalidKeyException, java.security.InvalidAlgorithmParameterException;
    protected abstract void engineSetMode(String mode) throws java.security.NoSuchAlgorithmException;
    protected abstract void engineSetPadding(String padding) throws NoSuchPaddingException;
    protected java.security.Key engineUnwrap(byte[] wrappedKey, String wrappedKeyAlgorithm, int wrappedKeyType)
        throws java.security.InvalidKeyException, java.security.NoSuchAlgorithmException;
5.0 protected int engineUpdate(java.nio.ByteBuffer input, java.nio.ByteBuffer output) throws ShortBufferException;
    protected abstract byte[] engineUpdate(byte[] input, int inputOffset, int inputLen);
    protected abstract int engineUpdate(byte[] input, int inputOffset, int inputLen, byte[] output, int outputOffset)
        throws ShortBufferException;
    protected byte[] engineWrap(java.security.Key key)
        throws IllegalBlockSizeException, java.security.InvalidKeyException;
}
```

Passed To Cipher.Cipher()

EncryptedPrivateKeyInfo **Java 1.4**

javax.crypto

This class represents an encrypted private key. getEncryptedData() returns the encrypted bytes. getAlgName() and getAlgParameters() return the algorithm name and parameters used to encrypt it. Pass a Cipher object to getKeySpec() to decrypt the key.

```
public class EncryptedPrivateKeyInfo {
// Public Constructors
    public EncryptedPrivateKeyInfo(byte[] encoded) throws java.io.IOException;
    public EncryptedPrivateKeyInfo(java.security.AlgorithmParameters algParams, byte[] encryptedData)
        throws java.security.NoSuchAlgorithmException;
    public EncryptedPrivateKeyInfo(String algName, byte[] encryptedData)
        throws java.security.NoSuchAlgorithmException;
// Public Instance Methods
    public String getAlgName();
    public java.security.AlgorithmParameters getAlgParameters();
    public byte[] getEncoded() throws java.io.IOException;
    public byte[] getEncryptedData();
5.0 public java.security.spec.PKCS8EncodedKeySpec getKeySpec(java.security.Key decryptKey)
        throws java.security.NoSuchAlgorithmException, java.security.InvalidKeyException;
    public java.security.spec.PKCS8EncodedKeySpec getKeySpec(Cipher cipher)
        throws java.security.spec.InvalidKeySpecException;
```

JCE

```
5.0 public java.security.spec.PKCS8EncodedKeySpec getKeySpec(java.security.Key decryptKey,
        java.security.Provider provider)
        throws java.security.NoSuchAlgorithmException, java.security.InvalidKeyException;
5.0 public java.security.spec.PKCS8EncodedKeySpec getKeySpec(java.security.Key decryptKey, String providerName)
        throws java.security.NoSuchProviderException, java.security.NoSuchAlgorithmException,
        java.security.InvalidKeyException;
}
```

ExemptionMechanism **Java 1.4**

javax.crypto

Some countries place legal restrictions on the use of cryptographic algorithms. In some cases, a program may be exempt from these restrictions if it implements an "exemption mechanism" such as key recovery, key escrow, or key weakening. This class defines a very general API to such mechanism. This class is rarely used, and is not supported in the default implementation provided by Sun. Using this class successfully is quite complex, and is beyond the scope of this reference. For details, see the discussion "How to Make Applications 'Exempt' from Cryptographic Restrictions" in the *JCE Reference Guide* which is part of the standard bundle of documentation shipped by Sun with the JDK.

```
public class ExemptionMechanism {
// Protected Constructors
    protected ExemptionMechanism(ExemptionMechanismSpi exmechSpi, java.security.Provider provider,
        String mechanism);
// Public Class Methods
    public static final ExemptionMechanism getInstance(String algorithm) throws java.security.NoSuchAlgorithmException;
    public static final ExemptionMechanism getInstance(String algorithm, String provider)
        throws java.security.NoSuchAlgorithmException, java.security.NoSuchProviderException;
    public static final ExemptionMechanism getInstance(String algorithm, java.security.Provider provider)
        throws java.security.NoSuchAlgorithmException;
// Public Instance Methods
    public final byte[] genExemptionBlob() throws IllegalStateException, ExemptionMechanismException;
    public final int genExemptionBlob(byte[] output)
        throws IllegalStateException, ShortBufferException, ExemptionMechanismException;
    public final int genExemptionBlob(byte[] output, int outputOffset)
        throws IllegalStateException, ShortBufferException, ExemptionMechanismException;
    public final String getName();
    public final int getOutputSize(int inputLen) throws IllegalStateException;
    public final java.security.Provider getProvider();
    public final void init(java.security.Key key) throws java.security.InvalidKeyException, ExemptionMechanismException;
    public final void init(java.security.Key key, java.security.spec.AlgorithmParameterSpec params)
        throws java.security.InvalidKeyException, java.security.InvalidAlgorithmParameterException,
        ExemptionMechanismException
    public final void init(java.security.Key key, java.security.AlgorithmParameters params)
        throws java.security.InvalidKeyException, java.security.InvalidAlgorithmParameterException,
        ExemptionMechanismException;
    public final boolean isCryptoAllowed(java.security.Key key) throws ExemptionMechanismException;
// Protected Methods Overriding Object
    protected void finalize();
}
```

Returned By Cipher.getExemptionMechanism()

ExemptionMechanismException — Java 1.4

javax.crypto — serializable checked

Signals a problem in one of the ExcemptionMechanism methods.

Object — Throwable — Exception — GeneralSecurityException — ExemptionMechanismException

Serializable

```
public class ExemptionMechanismException extends java.security.GeneralSecurityException {
// Public Constructors
   public ExemptionMechanismException();
   public ExemptionMechanismException(String msg);
}
```

Thrown By ExemptionMechanism.{genExemptionBlob(), init(), isCryptoAllowed()}, ExemptionMechanismSpi.{engineGenExemptionBlob(), engineInit()}

ExemptionMechanismSpi — Java 1.4

javax.crypto

This abstract class defines the Service Provider Interface for ExemptionMechanism. Security providers may implement this interface, but applications never need to use it. Note that the default "SunJCE" provider does not provide an implementation.

```
public abstract class ExemptionMechanismSpi {
// Public Constructors
   public ExemptionMechanismSpi();
// Protected Instance Methods
   protected abstract byte[] engineGenExemptionBlob() throws ExemptionMechanismException;
   protected abstract int engineGenExemptionBlob(byte[] output, int outputOffset)
       throws ShortBufferException,  ExemptionMechanismException;
   protected abstract int engineGetOutputSize(int inputLen);
   protected abstract void engineInit(java.security.Key key)
       throws java.security.InvalidKeyException, ExemptionMechanismException;
   protected abstract void engineInit(java.security.Key key, java.security.AlgorithmParameters params)
       throws java.security.InvalidKeyException, java.security.InvalidAlgorithmParameterException,
       ExemptionMechanismException;
   protected abstract void engineInit(java.security.Key key, java.security.spec.AlgorithmParameterSpec params)
       throws java.security.InvalidKeyException, java.security.InvalidAlgorithmParameterException,
       ExemptionMechanismException;
}
```

Passed To ExemptionMechanism.ExemptionMechanism()

IllegalBlockSizeException — Java 1.4

javax.crypto — serializable checked

Signals that the length of data provided to a block cipher (as implemented, for example, by Cipher and SealedObject) does not match the block size for the cipher.

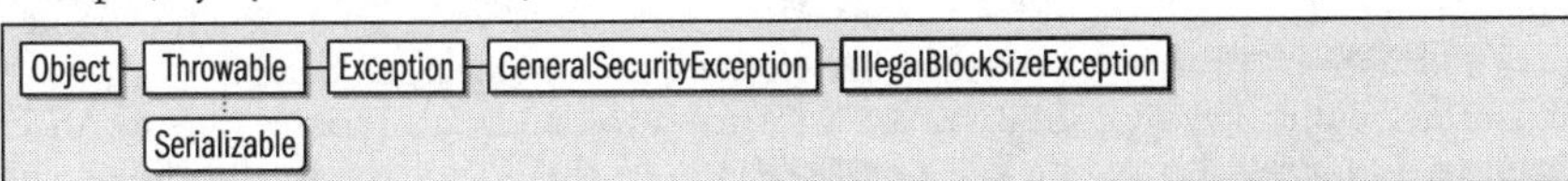

```
public class IllegalBlockSizeException extends java.security.GeneralSecurityException {
// Public Constructors
   public IllegalBlockSizeException();
   public IllegalBlockSizeException(String msg);
}
```

Thrown By Cipher.{doFinal(), wrap()}, CipherSpi.{engineDoFinal(), engineWrap()}, SealedObject.{getObject(), SealedObject()}

KeyAgreement **Java 1.4**

javax.crypto

This class provides an API to a key-agreement protocol that allows two or more parties to agree on a secret key without exchanging any secrets and in such a way that an eavesdropper listening in on the communication between those parties cannot determine the secret key. The KeyAgreement class is algorithm-independent and provider-based, so you must obtain a KeyAgreement object by calling one of the static getInstance() factory methods and specifying the name of the desired key agreement algorithm and, optionally, the name of the desired provider of that algorithm. The "SunJCE" provider implements a single key-agreement algorithm named "DiffieHellman".

To use a KeyAgreement object, each party first calls the init() method and supplies a Key object of its own. Then, each party obtains a Key object from one of the other parties to the agreement and calls doPhase(). Each party obtains an intermediate Key object as the return value of doPhase(), and these keys are again exchanged and passed to doPhase(). This process typically repeats n–1 times, where n is the number of parties, but the actual number of repetitions is algorithm-dependent. When doPhase() is called the last time, the second argument must be true to indicate that it is the last phase of the agreement. After all calls to doPhase() have been made, each party calls generateSecret() to obtain an array of bytes or a SecretKey object for a named algorithm type. All parties obtain the same bytes or SecretKey from this method. The KeyAgreement class is not responsible for the transfer of Key objects between parties or for mutual authentication among the parties. These tasks must be accomplished through some external mechanism.

The most common type of key agreement is "DiffieHellman" key agreement between two parties. It proceeds as follows. First, both parties obtain a java.security.KeyPairGenerator for the "DiffieHellman" algorithm and use it to generate a java.security.KeyPair of Diffie-Hellman public and private keys. Each party passes its private key to the init() method of its KeyAgreement object. (The init() method can be passed a java.security.spec.AlgorithmParameterSpec object, but the Diffie-Hellman protocol does not require any additional parameters.) Next, the two parties exchange public keys, typically through some kind of networking mechanism (the KeyAgreement class is not responsible for the actual exchange of keys). Each party passes the public key of the other party to the doPhase() method of its KeyAgreement object. There are only two parties to this agreement, so only one phase is required, and the second argument to doPhase() is true. At this point, both parties call generateSecret() to obtain the shared secret key.

A three-party Diffie-Hellman key agreement requires two phases and is slightly more complicated. Let's call the three parties Alice, Bob, and Carol. Each generates a key pair and uses its private key to initialize its KeyAgreement object, as before. Then Alice passes her public key to Bob, Bob passes his to Carol, and Carol passes hers to Alice. Each party passes this public key to doPhase(). Since this is not the final doPhase(), the second argument is false, and doPhase() returns an intermediate Key object. The three parties exchange these intermediate keys again in the same way: Alice to Bob, Bob to

Carol, and Carol to Alice. Now each party passes the intermediate key it has received to doPhase() a second time, passing true to indicate that this is the final phase. Finally, all three can call generateSecret() to obtain a shared key to encrypt future communication.

```
public class KeyAgreement {
// Protected Constructors
   protected KeyAgreement(KeyAgreementSpi keyAgreeSpi, java.security.Provider provider, String algorithm);
// Public Class Methods
   public static final KeyAgreement getInstance(String algorithm) throws java.security.NoSuchAlgorithmException;
   public static final KeyAgreement getInstance(String algorithm, String provider)
       throws java.security.NoSuchAlgorithmException, java.security.NoSuchProviderException;
   public static final KeyAgreement getInstance(String algorithm, java.security.Provider provider)
       throws java.security.NoSuchAlgorithmException;
// Public Instance Methods
   public final java.security.Key doPhase(java.security.Key key, boolean lastPhase)
       throws java.security.InvalidKeyException, IllegalStateException;
   public final byte[] generateSecret() throws IllegalStateException;
   public final SecretKey generateSecret(String algorithm)
       throws IllegalStateException, java.security.NoSuchAlgorithmException, java.security.InvalidKeyException;
   public final int generateSecret(byte[] sharedSecret, int offset) throws IllegalStateException, ShortBufferException;
   public final String getAlgorithm();
   public final java.security.Provider getProvider();
   public final void init(java.security.Key key) throws java.security.InvalidKeyException;
   public final void init(java.security.Key key, java.security.SecureRandom random)
       throws java.security.InvalidKeyException;
   public final void init(java.security.Key key, java.security.spec.AlgorithmParameterSpec params)
       throws java.security.InvalidKeyException, java.security.InvalidAlgorithmParameterException;
   public final void init(java.security.Key key, java.security.spec.AlgorithmParameterSpec params,
       java.security.SecureRandom random)
       throws java.security.InvalidKeyException, java.security.InvalidAlgorithmParameterException;
}
```

KeyAgreementSpi — Java 1.4

javax.crypto

This abstract class defines the service-provider interface for KeyAgreement. A cryptographic provider must implement a concrete subclass of this class for each encryption algorithm it supports. Applications never need to use or subclass this class.

```
public abstract class KeyAgreementSpi {
// Public Constructors
   public KeyAgreementSpi();
// Protected Instance Methods
   protected abstract java.security.Key engineDoPhase(java.security.Key key, boolean lastPhase)
       throws java.security.InvalidKeyException, IllegalStateException;
   protected abstract byte[] engineGenerateSecret() throws IllegalStateException;
   protected abstract SecretKey engineGenerateSecret(String algorithm)
       throws IllegalStateException, java.security.NoSuchAlgorithmException, java.security.InvalidKeyException;
   protected abstract int engineGenerateSecret(byte[] sharedSecret, int offset)
       throws IllegalStateException, ShortBufferException;
   protected abstract void engineInit(java.security.Key key, java.security.SecureRandom random)
       throws java.security.InvalidKeyException;
```

JCE

```
    protected abstract void engineInit(java.security.Key key, java.security.spec.AlgorithmParameterSpec params,
        java.security.SecureRandom random)
        throws java.security.InvalidKeyException, java.security.InvalidAlgorithmParameterException;
}
```

Passed To KeyAgreement.KeyAgreement()

KeyGenerator **Java 1.4**

javax.crypto

This class provides an API for generating secret keys for symmetric cryptography. It is similar to java.security.KeyPairGenerator, which generates public/private key pairs for asymmetric or public-key cryptography. KeyGenerator is algorithm-independent and provider-based, so you must obtain a KeyGenerator instance by calling one of the static getInstance() factory methods and specifying the name of the cryptographic algorithm for which a key is desired and, optionally, the name of the security provider whose key-generation implementation is to be used. In Java 5.0 the "SunJCE" provider includes KeyGenerator implementations algorithms with the following names:

AES	DESede	HmacSHA384
ARCFOUR	HmacMD5	HmacSHA512
Blowfish	HmacSHA1	RC2
DES	HmacSHA256	

Once you have obtained a KeyGenerator, you initialize it with the init() method. You can provide a java.security.spec.AlgorithmParameterSpec object to provide algorithm-specific initialization parameters or simply specify the desired size (in bits) of the key to be generated. In either case, you can also specify a source of randomness in the form of a SecureRandom object. If you do not specify a SecureRandom, the KeyGenerator instantiates one of its own. None of the algorithms supported by the "SunJCE" provider require algorithm-specific parameters.

After calling getInstance() to obtain a KeyGenerator and init() to initialize it, simply call generateKey() to create a new SecretKey. Remember that the SecretKey must be kept secret. Take precautions when storing or transmitting the key, so that it does not fall into the wrong hands. You may want to use a java.security.KeyStore object to store the key in a password-protected form.

```
public class KeyGenerator {
// Protected Constructors
    protected KeyGenerator(KeyGeneratorSpi keyGenSpi, java.security.Provider provider, String algorithm);
// Public Class Methods
    public static final KeyGenerator getInstance(String algorithm) throws java.security.NoSuchAlgorithmException;
    public static final KeyGenerator getInstance(String algorithm, java.security.Provider provider)
        throws java.security.NoSuchAlgorithmException;
    public static final KeyGenerator getInstance(String algorithm, String provider)
        throws java.security.NoSuchAlgorithmException, java.security.NoSuchProviderException;
// Public Instance Methods
    public final SecretKey generateKey();
    public final String getAlgorithm();
    public final java.security.Provider getProvider();
    public final void init(int keysize);
    public final void init(java.security.spec.AlgorithmParameterSpec params)
        throws java.security.InvalidAlgorithmParameterException;
```

```
    public final void init(java.security.SecureRandom random);
    public final void init(int keysize, java.security.SecureRandom random);
    public final void init(java.security.spec.AlgorithmParameterSpec params, java.security.SecureRandom random)
        throws java.security.InvalidAlgorithmParameterException;
}
```

KeyGeneratorSpi Java 1.4

javax.crypto

This abstract class defines the service-provider interface for KeyGenerator. A cryptographic provider must implement a concrete subclass of this class for each key-generation algorithm it supports. Applications never need to use or subclass this class.

```
public abstract class KeyGeneratorSpi {
// Public Constructors
    public KeyGeneratorSpi();
// Protected Instance Methods
    protected abstract SecretKey engineGenerateKey();
    protected abstract void engineInit(java.security.SecureRandom random);
    protected abstract void engineInit(int keysize, java.security.SecureRandom random);
    protected abstract void engineInit(java.security.spec.AlgorithmParameterSpec params,
                                       java.security.SecureRandom random)
        throws java.security.InvalidAlgorithmParameterException;
}
```

Passed To KeyGenerator.KeyGenerator()

Mac Java 1.4

javax.crypto cloneable

This class defines an API for computing a *message authentication code* (MAC) that can check the integrity of information transmitted between two parties that share a secret key. A MAC is similar to a digital signature, except that it is generated with a secret key rather than with a public/private key pair. The Mac class is algorithm-independent and provider-based. Obtain a Mac object by calling one of the static getInstance() factory methods and specifying the name of the desired MAC algorithm and, optionally, the name of the provider of the desired implementation. In Java 5.0 The "SunJCE" provider implement MAC algorithms with the following names:

HmacMD5	HmacSHA1	HmacSHA256
HmacSHA384	HmacSHA512	HmacPBESHA1

After obtaining a Mac object, initialize it by calling the init() method and specifying a SecretKey and, optionally, a java.security.spec.AlgorithmParameterSpec object. The "HmacMD5" and "HmacSHA1" algorithms can use any kind of SecretKey; they are not restricted to a particular cryptographic algorithm. And neither algorithm requires an AlgorithmParameterSpec object.

After obtaining and initializing a Mac object, specify the data for which the MAC is to be computed. If the data is contained in a single byte array, simply pass it to doFinal(). If the data is streaming or is stored in various locations, you can supply the data in multiple calls to update(). In Java 5.0, you can pass a ByteBuffer to update() which facilities use with the java.nio New I/O API. End the series of update() calls with a single call to doFinal(). Note that some versions of doFinal() return the MAC data as the function return value. Another version stores the MAC data in a byte array you supply. If you use this version of doFinal(), be sure to call getMacLength() to instantiate an array of the correct length.

A call to doFinal() resets the internal state of a Mac object. If you want to compute a MAC for part of your data and then proceed to compute the MAC for the full data, you should clone() the Mac object before calling doFinal(). Note, however, that Mac implementations are not required to implement Cloneable.

Object — Mac ··· Cloneable

```
public class Mac implements Cloneable {
// Protected Constructors
   protected Mac(MacSpi macSpi, java.security.Provider provider, String algorithm);
// Public Class Methods
   public static final Mac getInstance(String algorithm) throws java.security.NoSuchAlgorithmException;
   public static final Mac getInstance(String algorithm, String provider)
       throws java.security.NoSuchAlgorithmException, java.security.NoSuchProviderException;
   public static final Mac getInstance(String algorithm, java.security.Provider provider)
       throws java.security.NoSuchAlgorithmException;
// Public Instance Methods
   public final byte[] doFinal() throws IllegalStateException;
   public final byte[] doFinal(byte[] input) throws IllegalStateException;
   public final void doFinal(byte[] output, int outOffset) throws ShortBufferException, IllegalStateException;
   public final String getAlgorithm();
   public final int getMacLength();
   public final java.security.Provider getProvider();
   public final void init(java.security.Key key) throws java.security.InvalidKeyException;
   public final void init(java.security.Key key, java.security.spec.AlgorithmParameterSpec params)
       throws java.security.InvalidKeyException, java.security.InvalidAlgorithmParameterException;
   public final void reset();
   public final void update(byte input) throws IllegalStateException;
5.0 public final void update(java.nio.ByteBuffer input);
   public final void update(byte[] input) throws IllegalStateException;
   public final void update(byte[] input, int offset, int len) throws IllegalStateException;
// Public Methods Overriding Object
   public final Object clone() throws CloneNotSupportedException;
}
```

MacSpi — Java 1.4

javax.crypto

This abstract class defines the service-provider interface for Mac. A cryptographic provider must implement a concrete subclass of this class for each MAC algorithm it supports. Applications never need to use or subclass this class.

```
public abstract class MacSpi {
// Public Constructors
   public MacSpi();
// Public Methods Overriding Object
   public Object clone() throws CloneNotSupportedException;
// Protected Instance Methods
   protected abstract byte[] engineDoFinal();
   protected abstract int engineGetMacLength();
   protected abstract void engineInit(java.security.Key key, java.security.spec.AlgorithmParameterSpec params)
       throws java.security.InvalidKeyException, java.security.InvalidAlgorithmParameterException;
```

```
    protected abstract void engineReset();
5.0 protected void engineUpdate(java.nio.ByteBuffer input);
    protected abstract void engineUpdate(byte input);
    protected abstract void engineUpdate(byte[] input, int offset, int len);
}
```

Passed To Mac.Mac()

NoSuchPaddingException — Java 1.4

javax.crypto — serializable checked

Signals that no implementation of the requested padding scheme can be found.

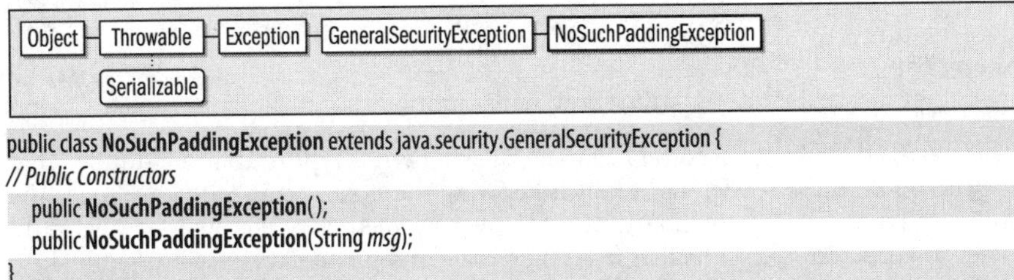


```
public class NoSuchPaddingException extends java.security.GeneralSecurityException {
// Public Constructors
    public NoSuchPaddingException();
    public NoSuchPaddingException(String msg);
}
```

Thrown By Cipher.getInstance(), CipherSpi.engineSetPadding()

NullCipher — Java 1.4

javax.crypto

This trivial subclass of Cipher implements an identity cipher that does not transform plain text in any way. Unlike Cipher objects returned by Cipher.getInstance(), a NullCipher must be created with the NullCipher() constructor.

```
public class NullCipher extends Cipher {
// Public Constructors
    public NullCipher();
}
```

SealedObject — Java 1.4

javax.crypto — serializable

This class is a wrapper around a serializable object. It serializes the object and encrypts the resulting data stream, thereby protecting the confidentiality of the object. Create a SealedObject by specifying the object to be sealed and a Cipher object to perform the encryption. Retrieve the sealed object by calling getObject() and specifying the Cipher or java.security.Key to use for decryption. The SealedObject keeps track of the encryption algorithm and parameters so that a Key object alone can decrypt the object.

```
public class SealedObject implements Serializable {
// Public Constructors
    public SealedObject(Serializable object, Cipher c) throws java.io.IOException, IllegalBlockSizeException;
// Protected Constructors
    protected SealedObject(SealedObject so);
// Public Instance Methods
```

```
    public final String getAlgorithm();
    public final Object getObject(java.security.Key key)
        throws java.io.IOException, ClassNotFoundException, java.security.NoSuchAlgorithmException,
          java.security.InvalidKeyException;
    public final Object getObject(Cipher c)
        throws java.io.IOException, ClassNotFoundException, IllegalBlockSizeException, BadPaddingException;
    public final Object getObject(java.security.Key key, String provider)
        throws java.io.IOException, ClassNotFoundException, java.security.NoSuchAlgorithmException,
          java.security.NoSuchProviderException, java.security.InvalidKeyException;
// Protected Instance Fields
    protected byte[] encodedParams;
}
```

SecretKey Java 1.4

javax.crypto serializable

This interface represents a secret key used for symmetric cryptographic algorithms that depend on both the sender and receiver knowing the same secret. SecretKey extends the java.security.Key interface, but does not add any new methods. The interface exists in order to keep secret keys distinct from the public and private keys used in public-key, or asymmetric, cryptography. See also java.security.PublicKey and java.security.PrivateKey.

A secret key is nothing more than arrays of bytes and does not require a specialized encoding format. Therefore, an implementation of this interface should return the format name "RAW" from getFormat() and should return the bytes of the key from getEncoded(). (These two methods are defined by the java.security.Key interface that SecretKey extends.)

Serializable · Key · SecretKey

```
public interface SecretKey extends java.security.Key {
// Public Constants
5.0 public static final long serialVersionUID;                    =-4795878709595146952
}
```

Implementations javax.crypto.interfaces.PBEKey, javax.crypto.spec.SecretKeySpec, javax.security.auth.kerberos.KerberosKey

Passed To java.security.KeyStore.SecretKeyEntry.SecretKeyEntry(), SecretKeyFactory.{getKeySpec(), translateKey()}, SecretKeyFactorySpi.{engineGetKeySpec(), engineTranslateKey()}

Returned By java.security.KeyStore.SecretKeyEntry.getSecretKey(), KeyAgreement.generateSecret(), KeyAgreementSpi.engineGenerateSecret(), KeyGenerator.generateKey(), KeyGeneratorSpi.engineGenerateKey(), SecretKeyFactory.{generateSecret(), translateKey()}, SecretKeyFactorySpi.{engineGenerateSecret(), engineTranslateKey()}, javax.security.auth.kerberos.KerberosTicket.getSessionKey()

SecretKeyFactory Java 1.4

javax.crypto

This class defines an API for translating a secret key between its opaque SecretKey representation and its transparent javax.crypto.SecretKeySpec representation. It is much like java.security.KeyFactory, except that it works with secret (or symmetric) keys rather than with public and private (asymmetric) keys. SecretKeyFactory is algorithm-independent and provider-based, so you must obtain a SecretKeyFactory object by calling one of the static getInstance() factory methods and specifying the name of the desired secret-key algorithm and, optionally, the name of the provider whose implementation is desired. In

Java 5.0, the "SunJCE" provider provides SecretKeyFactory implementations for algorithms with the following names:

DES	DESede	PBE
PBEWithMD5AndDES	PBEWithMD5AndTripleDES	PBEWithSHA1AndDESede
PBEWithSHA1AndRC2		

Once you have obtained a SecretKeyFactory, use generateSecret() to create a SecretKey from a java.security.spec.KeySpec (or its subclass, javax.crypto.spec.SecretKeySpec). Or call getKeySpec() to obtain a KeySpec for a Key object. Because there can be more than one suitable type of KeySpec, getKeySpec() requires a Class object to specify the type of the KeySpec to be created. See also DESKeySpec, DESedeKeySpec, and PBEKeySpec in the javax.crypto.spec package.

```
public class SecretKeyFactory {
// Protected Constructors
   protected SecretKeyFactory(SecretKeyFactorySpi keyFacSpi, java.security.Provider provider, String algorithm);
// Public Class Methods
   public static final SecretKeyFactory getInstance(String algorithm) throws java.security.NoSuchAlgorithmException;
   public static final SecretKeyFactory getInstance(String algorithm, java.security.Provider provider)
       throws java.security.NoSuchAlgorithmException;
   public static final SecretKeyFactory getInstance(String algorithm, String provider)
       throws java.security.NoSuchAlgorithmException, java.security.NoSuchProviderException;
// Public Instance Methods
   public final SecretKey generateSecret(java.security.spec.KeySpec keySpec)
       throws java.security.spec.InvalidKeySpecException;
   public final String getAlgorithm();
   public final java.security.spec.KeySpec getKeySpec(SecretKey key, Class keySpec)
       throws java.security.spec.InvalidKeySpecException;
   public final java.security.Provider getProvider();
   public final SecretKey translateKey(SecretKey key) throws java.security.InvalidKeyException;
}
```

SecretKeyFactorySpi — Java 1.4

javax.crypto

This abstract class defines the service-provider interface for SecretKeyFactory. A cryptographic provider must implement a concrete subclass of this class for each type of secret key it supports. Applications never need to use or subclass this class.

```
public abstract class SecretKeyFactorySpi {
// Public Constructors
   public SecretKeyFactorySpi();
// Protected Instance Methods
   protected abstract SecretKey engineGenerateSecret(java.security.spec.KeySpec keySpec)
       throws java.security.spec.InvalidKeySpecException;
   protected abstract java.security.spec.KeySpec engineGetKeySpec(SecretKey key, Class keySpec)
       throws java.security.spec.InvalidKeySpecException;
   protected abstract SecretKey engineTranslateKey(SecretKey key) throws java.security.InvalidKeyException;
}
```

Passed To SecretKeyFactory.SecretKeyFactory()

ShortBufferException **Java 1.4**

javax.crypto **serializable checked**

Signals that an output buffer is too short to hold the results of an operation.

Object ─ Throwable ─ Exception ─ GeneralSecurityException ─ ShortBufferException
Serializable

```
public class ShortBufferException extends java.security.GeneralSecurityException {
// Public Constructors
   public ShortBufferException();
   public ShortBufferException(String msg);
}
```

Thrown By Too many methods to list.

Package javax.crypto.interfaces **Java 1.4**

The interfaces in the javax.crypto.interfaces package define the public methods that must be supported by various types of encryption keys. The "DH" interfaces respresent Diffie-Hellman public/private key pairs used in the Diffie-Hellman key-agreement protocol. The "PBE" iterface is for Password-Based Encryption. These interfaces are typically of interest only to programmers who are implementing a cryptographic provider or who want to implement cryptographic algorithms themselves. Use of this package requires basic familiarity with the encryption algorithms and the mathematics that underlie them. Note that the javax.crypto.spec package contains classes that provide algorithm-specific details about encryption keys.

Interfaces

```
public interface DHKey;
public interface DHPrivateKey extends DHKey, java.security.PrivateKey;
public interface DHPublicKey extends DHKey, java.security.PublicKey;
public interface PBEKey extends javax.crypto.SecretKey;
```

DHKey **Java 1.4**

javax.crypto.interfaces

This interface represents a Diffie-Hellman key. The javax.crypto.spec.DHParameterSpec returned by getParams() specifies the parameters that generate the key; they define a key family. See the subinterfaces DHPublicKey and DHPrivateKey for the actual key values.

```
public interface DHKey {
// Public Instance Methods
   javax.crypto.spec.DHParameterSpec getParams();
}
```

Implementations DHPrivateKey, DHPublicKey

DHPrivateKey **Java 1.4**

javax.crypto.interfaces **serializable**

This interface represents a Diffie-Hellman private key. Note that it extends two interfaces: DHKey and java.security.PrivateKey. getX() returns the private-key value. If you are working with a PrivateKey you know is a Diffie-Hellman key, you can cast your PrivateKey to a DHPrivateKey.

```
public interface DHPrivateKey extends DHKeyjava.security.PrivateKey {
// Public Constants
5.0 public static final long serialVersionUID;                    =2211791113380396553
// Public Instance Methods
   java.math.BigInteger getX();
}
```

DHPublicKey **Java 1.4**

javax.crypto.interfaces **serializable**

This interface represents a Diffie-Hellman public key. Note that it extends two interfaces: DHKey and java.security.PublicKey. getY() returns the public-key value. If you are working with a PublicKey you know is a Diffie-Hellman key, you can cast your PublicKey to a DHPublicKey.


```
public interface DHPublicKey extends DHKey, java.security.PublicKey {
// Public Constants
5.0 public static final long serialVersionUID;                    =-6628103563352519193
// Public Instance Methods
   java.math.BigInteger getY();
}
```

PBEKey **Java 1.4**

javax.crypto.interfaces **serializable**

This interface represents a key for password-based encryption. If you are working with a SecretKey that you know is a password-based key, you can cast it to a PBEKey.


```
public interface PBEKey extends javax.crypto.SecretKey {
// Public Constants
5.0 public static final long serialVersionUID;                    =-1430015993304333921
// Public Instance Methods
   int getIterationCount();
   char[] getPassword();
   byte[] getSalt();
}
```

Package javax.crypto.spec **Java 1.4**

The javax.crypto.spec package contains classes that define transparent java.security.spec.KeySpec and java.security.spec.AlgorithmParameterSpec representations of secret keys, Diffie-Hellman public and private keys, and parameters used by various cryptographic algorithms. The classes in this package are used in conjunction with java.security.KeyFactory, javax.crypto.SecretKeyFactory and java.security.AlgorithmParameters for converting opaque Key, and

AlgorithmParameters objects to and from transparent representations. In order to make good use of this package, you must be familiar with the specifications of the various cryptographic algorithms it supports and the basic mathematics that underlie those algorithms.

Classes

```
public class DESedeKeySpec implements java.security.spec.KeySpec;
public class DESKeySpec implements java.security.spec.KeySpec;
public class DHGenParameterSpec implements java.security.spec.AlgorithmParameterSpec;
public class DHParameterSpec implements java.security.spec.AlgorithmParameterSpec;
public class DHPrivateKeySpec implements java.security.spec.KeySpec;
public class DHPublicKeySpec implements java.security.spec.KeySpec;
public class IvParameterSpec implements java.security.spec.AlgorithmParameterSpec;
public class OAEPParameterSpec implements java.security.spec.AlgorithmParameterSpec;
public class PBEKeySpec implements java.security.spec.KeySpec;
public class PBEParameterSpec implements java.security.spec.AlgorithmParameterSpec;
public class PSource;
   public static final class PSource.PSpecified extends PSource;
public class RC2ParameterSpec implements java.security.spec.AlgorithmParameterSpec;
public class RC5ParameterSpec implements java.security.spec.AlgorithmParameterSpec;
public class SecretKeySpec implements java.security.spec.KeySpec, javax.crypto.SecretKey;
```

DESedeKeySpec — Java 1.4

javax.crypto.spec

This class is a transparent representation of a DESede (triple-DES) key. The key is 24 bytes long.

Object — DESedeKeySpec ··· KeySpec

```
public class DESedeKeySpec implements java.security.spec.KeySpec {
// Public Constructors
   public DESedeKeySpec(byte[] key) throws java.security.InvalidKeyException;
   public DESedeKeySpec(byte[] key, int offset) throws java.security.InvalidKeyException;
// Public Constants
   public static final int DES_EDE_KEY_LEN;                                =24
// Public Class Methods
   public static boolean isParityAdjusted(byte[] key, int offset) throws java.security.InvalidKeyException;
// Public Instance Methods
   public byte[] getKey();
}
```

DESKeySpec — Java 1.4

javax.crypto.spec

This class is a transparent representation of a DES key. The key is eight bytes long.

Object — DESKeySpec ··· KeySpec

```
public class DESKeySpec implements java.security.spec.KeySpec {
// Public Constructors
   public DESKeySpec(byte[] key) throws java.security.InvalidKeyException;
   public DESKeySpec(byte[] key, int offset) throws java.security.InvalidKeyException;
// Public Constants
```

```
    public static final int DES_KEY_LEN;                                              =8
// Public Class Methods
    public static boolean isParityAdjusted(byte[] key, int offset) throws java.security.InvalidKeyException;
    public static boolean isWeak(byte[] key, int offset) throws java.security.InvalidKeyException;
// Public Instance Methods
    public byte[] getKey();
}
```

DHGenParameterSpec — Java 1.4

javax.crypto.spec

This class is a transparent representation of the values needed to generate a set of Diffie-Hellman parameters (see DHParameterSpec). An instance of this class can be passed to the init() method of a java.security.AlgorithmParameterGenerator that computes Diffie-Hellman parameters.

Object — DHGenParameterSpec ··· AlgorithmParameterSpec

```
public class DHGenParameterSpec implements java.security.spec.AlgorithmParameterSpec {
// Public Constructors
    public DHGenParameterSpec(int primeSize, int exponentSize);
// Public Instance Methods
    public int getExponentSize();
    public int getPrimeSize();
}
```

DHParameterSpec — Java 1.4

javax.crypto.spec

This class is a transparent representation of the set of parameters required by the Diffie-Hellman key-agreement algorithm. All parties to the key agreement must share these parameters and use them to generate a Diffie-Hellman public/private key pair.

Object — DHParameterSpec ··· AlgorithmParameterSpec

```
public class DHParameterSpec implements java.security.spec.AlgorithmParameterSpec {
// Public Constructors
    public DHParameterSpec(java.math.BigInteger p, java.math.BigInteger g);
    public DHParameterSpec(java.math.BigInteger p, java.math.BigInteger g, int l);
// Public Instance Methods
    public java.math.BigInteger getG();
    public int getL();
    public java.math.BigInteger getP();
}
```

Returned By javax.crypto.interfaces.DHKey.getParams()

DHPrivateKeySpec — Java 1.4

javax.crypto.spec

This java.security.spec.KeySpec is a transparent representation of a Diffie-Hellman private key.

Object — DHPrivateKeySpec ··· KeySpec

JCE

```
public class DHPrivateKeySpec implements java.security.spec.KeySpec {
// Public Constructors
   public DHPrivateKeySpec(java.math.BigInteger x, java.math.BigInteger p, java.math.BigInteger g);
// Public Instance Methods
   public java.math.BigInteger getG();
   public java.math.BigInteger getP();
   public java.math.BigInteger getX();
}
```

DHPublicKeySpec — Java 1.4

javax.crypto.spec

This java.security.spec.KeySpec is a transparent representation of a Diffie-Hellman public key.

Object — DHPublicKeySpec ··· KeySpec

```
public class DHPublicKeySpec implements java.security.spec.KeySpec {
// Public Constructors
   public DHPublicKeySpec(java.math.BigInteger y, java.math.BigInteger p, java.math.BigInteger g);
// Public Instance Methods
   public java.math.BigInteger getG();
   public java.math.BigInteger getP();
   public java.math.BigInteger getY();
}
```

IvParameterSpec — Java 1.4

javax.crypto.spec

This java.security.spec.AlgorithmParameterSpec is a transparent representation of an *initialization vector* or IV. An IV is required for block ciphers used in feedback mode, such as DES in CBC mode.

Object — IvParameterSpec ··· AlgorithmParameterSpec

```
public class IvParameterSpec implements java.security.spec.AlgorithmParameterSpec {
// Public Constructors
   public IvParameterSpec(byte[] iv);
   public IvParameterSpec(byte[] iv, int offset, int len);
// Public Instance Methods
   public byte[] getIV();
}
```

OAEPParameterSpec — Java 5.0

javax.crypto.spec

This class specifies parameters for OAEP padding, defined by the PKCS #1 standard.

Object — OAEPParameterSpec ··· AlgorithmParameterSpec

```
public class OAEPParameterSpec implements java.security.spec.AlgorithmParameterSpec {
// Public Constructors
   public OAEPParameterSpec(String mdName, String mgfName, java.security.spec.AlgorithmParameterSpec mgfSpec,
                            PSource pSrc);
// Public Constants
```

```
    public static final OAEPParameterSpec DEFAULT;
// Public Instance Methods
    public String getDigestAlgorithm();
    public String getMGFAlgorithm();
    public java.security.spec.AlgorithmParameterSpec getMGFParameters();
    public PSource getPSource();
}
```

PBEKeySpec Java 1.4

javax.crypto.spec

This class is a transparent representation of a password used in password-based encryption (PBE). The password is stored as a char array rather than as a String, so that the characters of the password can be overwritten when they are no longer needed (for increased security).

Object ─ PBEKeySpec ··· KeySpec

```
public class PBEKeySpec implements java.security.spec.KeySpec {
// Public Constructors
    public PBEKeySpec(char[] password);
    public PBEKeySpec(char[] password, byte[] salt, int iterationCount);
    public PBEKeySpec(char[] password, byte[] salt, int iterationCount, int keyLength);
// Public Instance Methods
    public final void clearPassword();
    public final int getIterationCount();
    public final int getKeyLength();
    public final char[] getPassword();
    public final byte[] getSalt();
}
```

PBEParameterSpec Java 1.4

javax.crypto.spec

This class is a transparent representation of the parameters used with the password-based encryption algorithm defined by PKCS#5.

Object ─ PBEParameterSpec ··· AlgorithmParameterSpec

```
public class PBEParameterSpec implements java.security.spec.AlgorithmParameterSpec {
// Public Constructors
    public PBEParameterSpec(byte[] salt, int iterationCount);
// Public Instance Methods
    public int getIterationCount();
    public byte[] getSalt();
}
```

PSource Java 5.0

javax.crypto.spec

This class is a representation of the source of "encoding input P" in OAEP padding, defined by the PKCS #1 standard.

```
public class PSource {
// Protected Constructors
```

```
    protected PSource(String pSrcName);
// Nested Types
    public static final class PSpecified extends PSource;
// Public Instance Methods
    public String getAlgorithm();
}
```

Subclasses PSource.PSpecified

Passed To OAEPParameterSpec.OAEPParameterSpec()

Returned By OAEPParameterSpec.getPSource()

PSource.PSpecified — Java 5.0

javax.crypto.spec

This class extends and is nested within PSource. It explicitly specifies the bytes of "encoding input P" for OAEP padding.

```
public static final class PSource.PSpecified extends PSource {
// Public Constructors
    public PSpecified(byte[]);
// Public Constants
    public static final PSource.PSpecified DEFAULT;
// Public Instance Methods
    public byte[] getValue();
}
```

RC2ParameterSpec — Java 1.4

javax.crypto.spec

This class is a transparent representation of the parameters used by the RC2 encryption algorithm. An object of this class initializes a Cipher object that implements RC2. Note that the "SunJCE" provider supplied by Sun does not implement RC2.

Object — RC2ParameterSpec ··· AlgorithmParameterSpec

```
public class RC2ParameterSpec implements java.security.spec.AlgorithmParameterSpec {
// Public Constructors
    public RC2ParameterSpec(int effectiveKeyBits);
    public RC2ParameterSpec(int effectiveKeyBits, byte[] iv);
    public RC2ParameterSpec(int effectiveKeyBits, byte[] iv, int offset);
// Public Instance Methods
    public int getEffectiveKeyBits();
    public byte[] getIV();
// Public Methods Overriding Object
    public boolean equals(Object obj);
    public int hashCode();
}
```

RC5ParameterSpec — Java 1.4

javax.crypto.spec

This class is a transparent representation of the parameters used by the RC5 encryption algorithm. An object of this class initializes a Cipher object that implements RC5. Note that the "SunJCE" provider supplied by Sun does not implement RC5.

```
public class RC5ParameterSpec implements java.security.spec.AlgorithmParameterSpec {
// Public Constructors
    public RC5ParameterSpec(int version, int rounds, int wordSize);
    public RC5ParameterSpec(int version, int rounds, int wordSize, byte[] iv);
    public RC5ParameterSpec(int version, int rounds, int wordSize, byte[] iv, int offset);
// Public Instance Methods
    public byte[] getIV();
    public int getRounds();
    public int getVersion();
    public int getWordSize();
// Public Methods Overriding Object
    public boolean equals(Object obj);
    public int hashCode();
}
```

SecretKeySpec — Java 1.4

javax.crypto.spec — serializable

This class is a transparent and algorithm-independent representation of a secret key. This class is useful only for encryption algorithms (such as DES and DESede) whose secret keys can be represented as arbitrary byte arrays and do not require auxiliary parameters. Note that SecretKeySpec implements the javax.crypto.SecretKey interface directly, so no algorithm-specific javax.crypto.SecretKeyFactory object is required.


```
public class SecretKeySpec implements java.security.spec.KeySpec, javax.crypto.SecretKey {
// Public Constructors
    public SecretKeySpec(byte[] key, String algorithm);
    public SecretKeySpec(byte[] key, int offset, int len, String algorithm);
// Methods Implementing Key
    public String getAlgorithm();
    public byte[] getEncoded();
    public String getFormat();
// Public Methods Overriding Object
    public boolean equals(Object obj);
    public int hashCode();
}
```

18

javax.net and javax.net.ssl

This chapter documents the javax.net package and, more importantly, its subpackage javax.net.ssl. These packages were originally defined by the Java Secure Sockets Extension (JSSE) before they were integrated into Java 1.4, which is why they have a "javax" prefix.

javax.net is a small package that simply defines abstract factory classes for creating network sockets and servers sockets. javax.net.ssl provides subclasses of these factory classes that have the specific purpose of creating sockets and server sockets that enable secure network communication through the SSL protocol and the closely-related TLS protocol.

Package javax.net Java 1.4

This small package defines factory classes for creating sockets and server sockets. These factory classes can be used to create regular java.net.Socket and java.net.ServerSocket objects. More importantly, however, these factory classes can be subclassed to serve as factories for other types of sockets such as the SSL-enabled sockets of the javax.net.ssl package.

Classes

public abstract class **ServerSocketFactory**;
public abstract class **SocketFactory**;

ServerSocketFactory Java 1.4

javax.net

This abstract class defines a factory API for creating server socket objects. Use the static getDefault() method to obtain a default ServerSocketFactory object that is suitable for creating regular java.net.ServerSocket sockets. Once you have a ServerSocketFactory object, call one of the createServerSocket() methods to create a new socket and optionally bind it to a local port and specify the allowed backlog of queued connections. See javax.net.ssl.SSLServerSocketFactory for a socket factory that can create secure javax.net.ssl.SSLServerSocket objects.

```
public abstract class ServerSocketFactory {
// Protected Constructors
   protected ServerSocketFactory();
// Public Class Methods
   public static ServerSocketFactory getDefault();
// Public Instance Methods
   public java.net.ServerSocket createServerSocket() throws java.io.IOException;
   public abstract java.net.ServerSocket createServerSocket(int port) throws java.io.IOException;
   public abstract java.net.ServerSocket createServerSocket(int port, int backlog) throws java.io.IOException;
   public abstract java.net.ServerSocket createServerSocket(int port, int backlog, java.net.InetAddress ifAddress)
      throws java.io.IOException;
}
```

Subclasses javax.net.ssl.SSLServerSocketFactory

Returned By javax.net.ssl.SSLServerSocketFactory.getDefault()

SocketFactory — Java 1.4

javax.net

This abstract class defines a factory API for creating socket objects. Use the static getDefault() method to obtain a default SocketFactory object that is suitable for creating regular java.net.Socket sockets. (This default SocketFactory is the one used by the Socket() constructor, which usually provides an easier way to create normal sockets.) Once you have a SocketFactory object, call one of the createSocket() methods to create a new socket and optionally connect it to a remote host and optionally bind it to a local address and port. See javax.net.ssl.SSLSocketFactory for a socket factory that can create secure javax.net.ssl.SSLSocket objects.

```
public abstract class SocketFactory {
// Protected Constructors
   protected SocketFactory();
// Public Class Methods
   public static SocketFactory getDefault();
// Public Instance Methods
   public java.net.Socket createSocket() throws java.io.IOException;
   public abstract java.net.Socket createSocket(String host, int port) throws java.io.IOException,
      java.net.UnknownHostException;
   public abstract java.net.Socket createSocket(java.net.InetAddress host, int port) throws java.io.IOException;
   public abstract java.net.Socket createSocket(java.net.InetAddress address, int port, java.net.InetAddress localAddress,
      int localPort)
      throws java.io.IOException;
   public abstract java.net.Socket createSocket(String host, int port, java.net.InetAddress localHost, int localPort)
      throws java.io.IOException, java.net.UnknownHostException;
}
```

Subclasses javax.net.ssl.SSLSocketFactory

Returned By javax.net.ssl.SSLSocketFactory.getDefault()

Package javax.net.ssl — Java 1.4

This package defines an API for secure network sockets using the SSL (Secure Sockets Layer) protocol, or the closely related TLS (Transport Layer Security) protocol. It defines the SSLSocket and SSLServerSocket subclasses of the java.net socket and server socket classes. And it defines SSLSocketFactory and SSLServerSocketFactory subclasses of the javax.net factory classes to create those SSL-enabled sockets and server sockets. Clients that want to perform simple SSL-enabled networking can create an SSLSocket with code like the following:

```
SSLSocketFactory factory = SSLSocketFactory.getDefault();
SSLSocket securesock = (SSLSocket)factory.getSocket(hostname,
                                                    443);     // https port
```

Once an SSLSocket has been created, it can be used just like a normal java.net.Socket. Once a connection is established over an SSLSocket, you can use the getSession() method to obtain an SSLSession object that provides information about the connection. Note that despite the name of this package and of its key classes, it supports the TLS protocol in addition to the SSL. (The default provider in Sun's implementation supports SSL 3.0 and TLS 1.0.) The TLS protocol is closely related to SSL, and we'll simply use the term SSL here.

The SSLSocket class allows you to do arbitrary networking with an SSL-enabled peer. The most common use of SSL today is with the https: protocol on the web. The addition of this package to the core Java platform enables support for https: URLs in the java.net.URL class, which allows you to securely transfer data over the web without having to directly use this package at all. When you call openConnection() on a https: URL, the URLConnection object that is returned can be cast to an HttpsURLConnection object, which defines some SSL-specific methods. See java.net.URL and java.net.URLConnection for more information about networking with URLs.

Although the code shown above to create a SSLSocket is quite simple, this package is much more complex because it exposes a lot of SSL infrastructure so that applications with advanced networking needs can configure it as needed. Also, like all security-related packages, this one is provider-based and algorithm-independent, which adds a layer of complexity. If you want to explore this package beyond the two socket classes, the two factory classes, and the HttpsURLConnection class, start with SSLContext. This class is a factory for socket factories, and as such is the central class of the API. To customize the way SSL networking is done, you create an SSLContext optionally specifing the desired provider of the implementation. Next, you initialize the SSLContext by providing a custom KeyManager as a source of authentication information to be supplied to the remote host if required, a custom TrustManager as a verifier for the authentication information (if any) presented by the remote host, and a custom java.security.SecureRandom object as a source of randomness. Once the SSLContext is initialized in this way, you can use it to create SSLSocketFactory and SSLServerSocketFactory objects that use the KeyManager and TrustManager objects you supplied.

In Java 5.0, the SSLContext can also be used to create an SSLEngine object, which performs transport-independent SSL encryption of outbound packets and SSL decryption of inbound packets. This enables the use of SSL with the nonblocking networking facilities of the java.nio.channels package, for example.

Interfaces

public interface **HandshakeCompletedListener** extends java.util.EventListener;
public interface **HostnameVerifier**;
public interface **KeyManager**;
public interface **ManagerFactoryParameters**;
public interface **SSLSession**;
public interface **SSLSessionBindingListener** extends java.util.EventListener;
public interface **SSLSessionContext**;
public interface **TrustManager**;

public interface **X509KeyManager** extends KeyManager;
public interface **X509TrustManager** extends TrustManager;

Enumerated Types

public enum **SSLEngineResult.HandshakeStatus**;
public enum **SSLEngineResult.Status**;

Events

public class **HandshakeCompletedEvent** extends java.util.EventObject;
public class **SSLSessionBindingEvent** extends java.util.EventObject;

Other Classes

public class **CertPathTrustManagerParameters** implements ManagerFactoryParameters;
public abstract class **HttpsURLConnection** extends java.net.HttpURLConnection;
public class **KeyManagerFactory**;
public abstract class **KeyManagerFactorySpi**;
public class **KeyStoreBuilderParameters** implements ManagerFactoryParameters;
public class **SSLContext**;
public abstract class **SSLContextSpi**;
public abstract class **SSLEngine**;
public class **SSLEngineResult**;
public final class **SSLPermission** extends java.security.BasicPermission;
public abstract class **SSLServerSocket** extends java.net.ServerSocket;
public abstract class **SSLServerSocketFactory** extends javax.net.ServerSocketFactory;
public abstract class **SSLSocket** extends java.net.Socket;
public abstract class **SSLSocketFactory** extends javax.net.SocketFactory;
public class **TrustManagerFactory**;
public abstract class **TrustManagerFactorySpi**;
public abstract class **X509ExtendedKeyManager** implements X509KeyManager;

Exceptions

public class **SSLException** extends java.io.IOException;
    public class **SSLHandshakeException** extends SSLException;
    public class **SSLKeyException** extends SSLException;
    public class **SSLPeerUnverifiedException** extends SSLException;
    public class **SSLProtocolException** extends SSLException;

CertPathTrustManagerParameters — Java 5.0

javax.net.ssl

This class implements the ManagerFactoryParameters interface and wraps a java.security.cert.CertPathParameters object used to initialize a TrustManager based on a certificate path. See the init() method of TrustManagerFactory.

Object — CertPathTrustManagerParameters ··· ManagerFactoryParameters

```
public class CertPathTrustManagerParameters implements ManagerFactoryParameters {
// Public Constructors
   public CertPathTrustManagerParameters(java.security.cert.CertPathParameters parameters);
// Public Instance Methods
   public java.security.cert.CertPathParameters getParameters();
}
```

HandshakeCompletedEvent **Java 1.4**

javax.net.ssl **serializable event**

An instance of this class is passed to the handshakeCompleted() method of any registered HandshakeCompletedListener objects by an SSLSocket when that socket completes the handshake phase of establishing a connection. The various methods of a HandshakeCompletedEvent return information (such as the name of the cipher suite in use and the certificate chain of the remote host) that was determined during that handshake.

Note that the getPeerCertificateChain() method returns an object from the javax.security.cert package, which is not documented in this book. The method and package exist only for backward compatibility with earlier versions of the JSSE API, and should be considered deprecated. Use getPeerCertificates(), which uses java.security.cert instead.

Object — EventObject — HandshakeCompletedEvent

Serializable

```
public class HandshakeCompletedEvent extends java.util.EventObject {
// Public Constructors
   public HandshakeCompletedEvent(SSLSocket sock, SSLSession s);
// Public Instance Methods
   public String getCipherSuite();
   public java.security.cert.Certificate[] getLocalCertificates();
5.0 public java.security.Principal getLocalPrincipal();
   public javax.security.cert.X509Certificate[] getPeerCertificateChain() throws SSLPeerUnverifiedException;
   public java.security.cert.Certificate[] getPeerCertificates() throws SSLPeerUnverifiedException;
5.0 public java.security.Principal getPeerPrincipal() throws SSLPeerUnverifiedException;
   public SSLSession getSession();
   public SSLSocket getSocket();
}
```

Passed To HandshakeCompletedListener.handshakeCompleted()

HandshakeCompletedListener **Java 1.4**

javax.net.ssl **event listener**

This interface is implemented by any class that wants to receive notifications (in the form of a call to handshakeCompleted() method) when an SSLSocket completes the SSL handshake. Register a HandshakeCompletedListener for an SSLSocket by passing it to the addHandshakeCompletedListener() method of the socket. When the socket completes the handshake phase of connection, it will call the handshakeCompleted() method of all registered listeners, passing in a HandshakeCompletedEvent object.

EventListener ··· HandshakeCompletedListener

```
public interface HandshakeCompletedListener extends java.util.EventListener {
// Public Instance Methods
   void handshakeCompleted(HandshakeCompletedEvent event);
}
```

Passed To SSLSocket.{addHandshakeCompletedListener(), removeHandshakeCompletedListener()}

HostnameVerifier Java 1.4

javax.net.ssl

An object that implements this interface may be used with an HttpsURLConnection object to handle the case in which the hostname that appears in the URL does not match the hostname obtained during the SSL handshake with the server. This occurs, for example, when a website uses the secure certificate of its parent web hosting company, for example. In this situation, the verify() method of the HostnameVerifier is called to determine whether the connection should proceed or not. verify() should return true to allow the connection to proceed, and should return false to cause the connection to fail. The *hostname* argument to verify() specifies the hostname that appeared in the URL. The *session* argument specifies the SSLSession object that was established during the handshake. Call getPeerHost() on this object to determine the hostname reported during server authentication. If no HostnameVerifier is registered with a HttpsURLConnection object, and no default verifier is registered with the HttpsURLConnection class, then hostname mismatches will always cause the connection to fail. In user-driven applications such as web browsers, a HostnameVerifier can be used to ask the user whether to proceed or not.

```
public interface HostnameVerifier {
// Public Instance Methods
    boolean verify(String hostname, SSLSession session);
}
```

Passed To HttpsURLConnection.{setDefaultHostnameVerifier(), setHostnameVerifier()}

Returned By HttpsURLConnection.{getDefaultHostnameVerifier(), getHostnameVerifier()}

Type Of HttpsURLConnection.hostnameVerifier

HttpsURLConnection Java 1.4

javax.net.ssl

This class is a java.net.URLConnection for a URL that uses the https: protocol. It extends java.net.HttpURLConnection and, in addition to inheriting the methods of its superclasses, it defines methods for specifying the SSLSocketFactory and HostnameVerifier to use when establishing the connection. Static versions of these methods allow you to specify a default factory and verifier objects for use with all HttpsURLConnection objects. After the connection has been established, several other methods exist to obtain information (such as the cipher suite and the server certificates) about the connection itself.

Obtain a HttpsURLConnection object by calling the openConnection() method of a URL that uses the https:// protocol specifier, and casting the returned value to this type. The HttpsURLConnection object is unconnected at this point, and you can call setHostnameVerifier() and setSSLSocketFactory() to customize the way the connection is made. (If you do not specify a HostnameVerifier for the instance, or a default one for the class, then hostname mismatches will always cause the connection to fail. If you do not specify an SSLSocketFactory for the instance or class, then a default one will be used.) To connect, call the inherited connect() method, and then call the inherited getContent() to retrieve the content of the URL as an object, or use the inherited getInputStream() to obtain a java.io.InputStream with which you can read the content of the URL.

Object — URLConnection — HttpURLConnection — HttpsURLConnection

```
public abstract class HttpsURLConnection extends java.net.HttpURLConnection {
// Protected Constructors
    protected HttpsURLConnection(java.net.URL url);
```

```
// Public Class Methods
   public static HostnameVerifier getDefaultHostnameVerifier();
   public static SSLSocketFactory getDefaultSSLSocketFactory();
   public static void setDefaultHostnameVerifier(HostnameVerifier v);
   public static void setDefaultSSLSocketFactory(SSLSocketFactory sf);
// Public Instance Methods
   public abstract String getCipherSuite();
   public HostnameVerifier getHostnameVerifier();
   public abstract java.security.cert.Certificate[] getLocalCertificates();
5.0 public java.security.Principal getLocalPrincipal();
5.0 public java.security.Principal getPeerPrincipal() throws SSLPeerUnverifiedException;
   public abstract java.security.cert.Certificate[] getServerCertificates() throws SSLPeerUnverifiedException;
   public SSLSocketFactory getSSLSocketFactory();
   public void setHostnameVerifier(HostnameVerifier v);
   public void setSSLSocketFactory(SSLSocketFactory sf);
// Protected Instance Fields
   protected HostnameVerifier hostnameVerifier;
}
```

KeyManager **Java 1.4**

javax.net.ssl

This is a marker interface to identify key manager objects. A key manager is responsible for obtaining and managing authentication credentials (such as a certificate chain and an associated private key) that the local host can use to authenticate itself to the remote host. It is usually used on the server-side of an SSL connection, but can be used on the client-side as well.

Use a KeyManagerFactory to obtain KeyManager objects. KeyManager objects returned by a KeyManagerFactory can always be cast to a subinterface specific to a particular type of authentication credentials. See X509KeyManager, for example.

```
public interface KeyManager {
}
```

Implementations X509KeyManager

Passed To SSLContext.init(), SSLContextSpi.engineInit()

Returned By KeyManagerFactory.getKeyManagers(), KeyManagerFactorySpi.engineGetKeyManagers()

KeyManagerFactory **Java 1.4**

javax.net.ssl

A KeyManagerFactory is responsible for creating KeyManager objects for a specific key management algorithm. Obtain a KeyManagerFactory object by calling one of the getInstance() methods and specifying the desired algorithm and, optionally, the desired provider. In Java 1.4, the "SunX509" algorithm is the only one supported by the default "SunJSSE" provider. After calling getInstance(), you initialize the factory object with init(). For the "SunX509" algorithm, you always use the two-argument version of init() passing in a KeyStore object that contains the private keys and certificates required by X509KeyManager objects, and also specifying the password used to protect the private keys in that KeyStore. Once a KeyManagerFactory has been created and initialized, use it to create a KeyManager by calling getKeyManagers(). This method returns an array of KeyManager objects because some key management algorithms may handle more than one type of key. The "SunX509" algorithm manages only X509 keys, and always returns an array with an X509KeyManager object as its single element. This returned array is typically passed to the init() method of an SSLContext object.

If a KeyStore and password are not passed to the init() method of the KeyManagerFactory for the "SunX509" algorithm, then the factory uses attempts to read a KeyStore from the file specified by the javax.net.ssl.keyStore system property using the password specified by the javax.net.ssl.keyStorePassword. The type of the keystore is specified by javax.net.ssl.keyStoreType.

```
public class KeyManagerFactory {
// Protected Constructors
   protected KeyManagerFactory(KeyManagerFactorySpi factorySpi, java.security.Provider provider, String algorithm);
// Public Class Methods
   public static final String getDefaultAlgorithm();
   public static final KeyManagerFactory getInstance(String algorithm) throws java.security.NoSuchAlgorithmException;
   public static final KeyManagerFactory getInstance(String algorithm, java.security.Provider provider)
      throws java.security.NoSuchAlgorithmException;
   public static final KeyManagerFactory getInstance(String algorithm, String provider)
      throws java.security.NoSuchAlgorithmException, java.security.NoSuchProviderException;
// Public Instance Methods
   public final String getAlgorithm();
   public final KeyManager[] getKeyManagers();
   public final java.security.Provider getProvider();
   public final void init(ManagerFactoryParameters spec) throws java.security.InvalidAlgorithmParameterException;
   public final void init(java.security.KeyStore ks, char[] password)
      throws java.security.KeyStoreException, java.security.NoSuchAlgorithmException,
      java.security.UnrecoverableKeyException;
}
```

KeyManagerFactorySpi — Java 1.4

javax.net.ssl

This abstract class defines the Service Provider Interface for KeyManagerFactory. Security providers must implement this interface, but applications never need to use it.

```
public abstract class KeyManagerFactorySpi {
// Public Constructors
   public KeyManagerFactorySpi();
// Protected Instance Methods
   protected abstract KeyManager[] engineGetKeyManagers();
   protected abstract void engineInit(ManagerFactoryParameters spec)
      throws java.security.InvalidAlgorithmParameterException;
   protected abstract void engineInit(java.security.KeyStore ks, char[] password)
      throws java.security.KeyStoreException, java.security.NoSuchAlgorithmException,
      java.security.UnrecoverableKeyException;
}
```

Passed To KeyManagerFactory.KeyManagerFactory()

KeyStoreBuilderParameters — Java 5.0

javax.net.ssl

This class implements the ManagerFactoryParameters interface and encapsulates a java.util.List of java.security.KeyStore.Builder object for use by an X509KeyManager. See the init() method of KeyManagerFactory.

Object → KeyStoreBuilderParameters ··· ManagerFactoryParameters

```
public class KeyStoreBuilderParameters implements ManagerFactoryParameters {
// Public Constructors
   public KeyStoreBuilderParameters(java.util.List parameters);
   public KeyStoreBuilderParameters(java.security.KeyStore.Builder builder);
// Public Instance Methods
   public java.util.List getParameters();
}
```

ManagerFactoryParameters Java 1.4

javax.net.ssl

This marker interface identifies objects that provide algorithm-specific or provider-specific initialization parameters for KeyManagerFactory and TrustManagerFactory objects. In the default "SunJSSE" provider shiped by Sun, the only supported type for these factory classes is "SunX509". Factories of these types need to be initialized with a KeyStore object but do not require any specialized ManagerFactoryParameters object. Therefore, the javax.net.ssl package does not define any subinterfaces of this interface, and it is never used with the default provider. Third-party or future providers may use it, however.

```
public interface ManagerFactoryParameters {
}
```

Implementations CertPathTrustManagerParameters, KeyStoreBuilderParameters

Passed To KeyManagerFactory.init(), KeyManagerFactorySpi.engineInit(), TrustManagerFactory.init(), TrustManagerFactorySpi.engineInit()

SSLContext Java 1.4

javax.net.ssl

This class is a factory for socket and server socket factories. Although most applications do not need to use this class directly, it is the central class of the javax.net.ssl package. Most applications use the default SSLSocketFactory and SSLServerSocketFactory objects returned by the static getDefault() methods of those classes. Applications that want to perform SSL networking using a security provider other than the default provider, or that want to customize key management or trust management for the SSL connection should use custom socket factories created from a custom SSLContext. In Java 5.0, this class also includes createSSLEngine() factory methods for creating SSLEngine objects.

Create an SSLContext by passing the name of the desired secure socket protocol and, optionally, the desired provider to getInstance(). The default "SunJSSE" provider supports protocol strings "SSL", "SSLv2", "SSLv3", "TLS", and "TLSv1". Once you have created an SSLContext object, call its init() method to supply the KeyManager, TrustManager, and SecureRandom objects it requires. If any of the init() arguments is null, a default value will be used. Finally, obtain a SSLSocketFactory and SSLServerSocketFactory by calling getSocketFactory() and getServerSocketFactory().

```
public class SSLContext {
// Protected Constructors
   protected SSLContext(SSLContextSpi contextSpi, java.security.Provider provider, String protocol);
// Public Class Methods
   public static SSLContext getInstance(String protocol) throws java.security.NoSuchAlgorithmException;
   public static SSLContext getInstance(String protocol, String provider)
      throws java.security.NoSuchAlgorithmException, java.security.NoSuchProviderException;
```

```
    public static SSLContext getInstance(String protocol, java.security.Provider provider)
        throws java.security.NoSuchAlgorithmException;
// Public Instance Methods
5.0 public final SSLEngine createSSLEngine();
5.0 public final SSLEngine createSSLEngine(String peerHost, int peerPort);
    public final SSLSessionContext getClientSessionContext();
    public final String getProtocol();
    public final java.security.Provider getProvider();
    public final SSLSessionContext getServerSessionContext();
    public final SSLServerSocketFactory getServerSocketFactory();
    public final SSLSocketFactory getSocketFactory();
    public final void init(KeyManager[] km, TrustManager[] tm, java.security.SecureRandom random)
        throws java.security.KeyManagementException;
}
```

SSLContextSpi — Java 1.4

javax.net.ssl

This abstract class defines the Service Provider Interface for SSLContext. Security providers must implement this interface, but applications never need to use it.

```
public abstract class SSLContextSpi {
// Public Constructors
    public SSLContextSpi();
// Protected Instance Methods
5.0 protected abstract SSLEngine engineCreateSSLEngine();
5.0 protected abstract SSLEngine engineCreateSSLEngine(String host, int port);
    protected abstract SSLSessionContext engineGetClientSessionContext();
    protected abstract SSLSessionContext engineGetServerSessionContext();
    protected abstract SSLServerSocketFactory engineGetServerSocketFactory();
    protected abstract SSLSocketFactory engineGetSocketFactory();
    protected abstract void engineInit(KeyManager[] km, TrustManager[] tm, java.security.SecureRandom sr)
        throws java.security.KeyManagementException;
}
```

Passed To SSLContext.SSLContext()

SSLEngine — Java 5.0

javax.net.ssl

This class performs SSL handshaking, encryption and decryption, but does not send or receive messages over the network. This leaves the network transport mechanism up to the user of this class, and enables SSL communication using the nonblocking I/O mechanisms of the java.nio package. The price of this flexibility is that your code must follow a relatively complex protocol to use an SSLEngine correctly.

Create an SSLEngine with SSLContext.createSSLEngine(). Next, configure it with the various setter methods to specify authentication requirements, encryption algorithms, etc. After creating and configuring an engine, you use it to encrypt outbound data from one ByteBuffer to another with wrap() and to decrypt inbound data from one byte buffer to another with unwrap(). (Note that the wrap() and unwrap() methods also come in gathering and scattering variants.) Both methods return an SSLEngineResult.

The initial call or calls to wrap() produce outbound handshaking data without consuming any of the source bytes in the buffer you provide. Initial calls to unwrap() may consume inbound handshaking data without producing any result bytes. Monitor the SSLEngine-

Result.HandshakeStatus value to ensure that handshaking is proceeding as needed. When handshaking is complete, you can call getSession() to obtain the SSLSession object that describes session details negotiated during handshaking. Remember that either peer of an SSL connection may request a new handshake at any time; this means that you must monitor the HandshakeStatus after every wrap() or unwrap() call in case a new handshake has been requested. You can request a new handshake yourself with beginHandshake().

As part of the handshaking protocol, the SSLEngine typically needs to use the KeyManager or TrustManager of the originating SSLContext object. Rather than blocking a wrap() or unwrap() method while these operations are performed, it instead returns an SSLResult.Handshake-Status, indicating that a task needs to be performed. When this happens, you must call getDelegatedTask() repeatedly, calling the run() methods of the Runnable objects it returns until it returns null to indicate that all necessary tasks have been completed. (If it returns more than one Runnable, it is safe to run them in parallel (with a java.util.concurrent.ExecutorCompletionService, for example). Once all such tasks have been run, the original call to wrap() or unwrap() should be repeated.

When you are done sending outbound data, call closeOutbound(), and then call wrap() one or more times to flush any remaining data from the engine. Call wrap() until the returned SSLEngineResult.Status indicates that the connection has closed. Similarly, if you are done reading inbound data, call closeInbound() and final calls to unwrap() until the connection is closed.

It is safe for one thread to call wrap() while another thread is calling unwrap(). It is not safe, however, for either method to be called by two threads at once.

```
public abstract class SSLEngine {
// Protected Constructors
   protected SSLEngine();
   protected SSLEngine(String peerHost, int peerPort);
// Public Instance Methods
   public abstract void beginHandshake() throws SSLException;
   public abstract void closeInbound() throws SSLException;
   public abstract void closeOutbound();
   public abstract Runnable getDelegatedTask();
   public abstract String[] getEnabledCipherSuites();
   public abstract String[] getEnabledProtocols();
   public abstract boolean getEnableSessionCreation();
   public abstract SSLEngineResult.HandshakeStatus getHandshakeStatus();
   public abstract boolean getNeedClientAuth();
   public String getPeerHost();
   public int getPeerPort();
   public abstract SSLSession getSession();
   public abstract String[] getSupportedCipherSuites();
   public abstract String[] getSupportedProtocols();
   public abstract boolean getUseClientMode();
   public abstract boolean getWantClientAuth();
   public abstract boolean isInboundDone();
   public abstract boolean isOutboundDone();
   public abstract void setEnabledCipherSuites(String[] suites);
   public abstract void setEnabledProtocols(String[] protocols);
   public abstract void setEnableSessionCreation(boolean flag);
   public abstract void setNeedClientAuth(boolean need);
   public abstract void setUseClientMode(boolean mode);
   public abstract void setWantClientAuth(boolean want);
```

```
    public SSLEngineResult unwrap(java.nio.ByteBuffer src, java.nio.ByteBuffer dst) throws SSLException;
    public SSLEngineResult unwrap(java.nio.ByteBuffer src, java.nio.ByteBuffer[] dsts) throws SSLException;
    public abstract SSLEngineResult unwrap(java.nio.ByteBuffer src, java.nio.ByteBuffer[] dsts, int offset, int length)
        throws SSLException;
    public SSLEngineResult wrap(java.nio.ByteBuffer[] srcs, java.nio.ByteBuffer dst) throws SSLException;
    public SSLEngineResult wrap(java.nio.ByteBuffer src, java.nio.ByteBuffer dst) throws SSLException;
    public abstract SSLEngineResult wrap(java.nio.ByteBuffer[] srcs, int offset, int length, java.nio.ByteBuffer dst)
        throws SSLException;
}
```

Passed To X509ExtendedKeyManager.{chooseEngineClientAlias(), chooseEngineServerAlias()}

Returned By SSLContext.createSSLEngine(), SSLContextSpi.engineCreateSSLEngine()

SSLEngineResult — Java 5.0

javax.net.ssl

An object of this type is returned by the wrap() and unwrap() methods of an SSLEngine. Use the methods of this object to determine how much data was consumed and produced and to obtain the Status of the operation and the HandshakeStatus of the connection. These two nested enumerated types return important values. Correct operation of an SSLEngine requires that your code respond correctly to the Status and HandshakeStatus results.

```
public class SSLEngineResult {
// Public Constructors
    public SSLEngineResult(SSLEngineResult.Status status, SSLEngineResult.HandshakeStatus handshakeStatus,
                           int bytesConsumed, int bytesProduced);
// Nested Types
    public enum HandshakeStatus;
    public enum Status;
// Public Instance Methods
    public final int bytesConsumed();
    public final int bytesProduced();
    public final SSLEngineResult.HandshakeStatus getHandshakeStatus();
    public final SSLEngineResult.Status getStatus();
// Public Methods Overriding Object
    public String toString();
}
```

Returned By SSLEngine.{unwrap(), wrap()}

SSLEngineResult.HandshakeStatus — Java 5.0

javax.net.ssl — serializable comparable enum

The constants defined by this enumerated type specify the handshake status of the SSLEngine and often specify the action your code must take next in order to ensure correct operation. The values are the following:

NOT_HANDSHAKING
: Handshaking is not currently in progress.

FINISHED
: Handshaking just completed as a result of the wrap() or unwrap() call that generated this value.

NEED_WRAP
: The SSLEngine needs to send more handshake data, so a call to wrap() is necessary.

NEED_UNWRAP
: The SSLEngine needs to receive more handshake data, so a call to unwrap() is necessary.

NEED_TASK
: The SSLEngine needs to perform an authentication or related task, so you must repeatedly call getDelegatedTask() and run() any Runnable objects it returns.

```
public enum SSLEngineResult.HandshakeStatus {
// Enumerated Constants
   NOT_HANDSHAKING,
   FINISHED,
   NEED_TASK,
   NEED_WRAP,
   NEED_UNWRAP;
// Public Class Methods
   public static SSLEngineResult.HandshakeStatus valueOf(String name);
   public static final SSLEngineResult.HandshakeStatus[] values();
}
```

Passed To SSLEngineResult.SSLEngineResult()

Returned By SSLEngine.getHandshakeStatus(), SSLEngineResult.getHandshakeStatus()

SSLEngineResult.Status — Java 5.0

javax.net.ssl — serializable comparable enum

The constants of this enumerated type indicate the status of a wrap() or unwrap() operation:

OK
: The operation completed normally.

CLOSED
: The most recent call to wrap() or unwrap() completed the closing handshake and closed the outbound or inbound connection. Or, that connection is already closed, and so the wrap() or unwrap() call could not proceed.

BUFFER_OVERFLOW
: There were not enough bytes in the destination buffer to hold the results. Drain the buffer and try again.

BUFFER_UNDERFLOW
: There were not enough incoming bytes in the source buffer to produce a complete output packet. Fill the buffer with more bytes from the network and call unwrap() again.

```
public enum SSLEngineResult.Status {
// Enumerated Constants
   BUFFER_UNDERFLOW,
   BUFFER_OVERFLOW,
   OK,
   CLOSED;
// Public Class Methods
   public static SSLEngineResult.Status valueOf(String name);
   public static final SSLEngineResult.Status[] values();
}
```

Passed To SSLEngineResult.SSLEngineResult()

Returned By SSLEngineResult.getStatus()

SSLException — Java 1.4

javax.net.ssl — serializable checked

Signals an SSL-related problem. This class serves as the common superclass of more specific SSL exception subclasses.

Object — Throwable — Exception — IOException — SSLException
Serializable

```
public class SSLException extends java.io.IOException {
// Public Constructors
5.0 public SSLException(Throwable cause);
    public SSLException(String reason);
5.0 public SSLException(String message, Throwable cause);
}
```

Subclasses SSLHandshakeException, SSLKeyException, SSLPeerUnverifiedException, SSLProtocolException

Thrown By SSLEngine.{beginHandshake(), closeInbound(), unwrap(), wrap()}

SSLHandshakeException — Java 1.4

javax.net.ssl — serializable checked

Signals that the SSL handshake failed for some reason other than failed authentication (see SSLPeerUnverifiedException). For example, it may be thrown because the client and server count not agree on a mutually-acceptable cipher suite. When this exception is thrown, the SSLSocket object is no longer usable.

Object — Throwable — Exception — IOException — SSLException — SSLHandshakeException
Serializable

```
public class SSLHandshakeException extends SSLException {
// Public Constructors
    public SSLHandshakeException(String reason);
}
```

SSLKeyException — Java 1.4

javax.net.ssl — serializable checked

Signals a problem with the public key certificate and private key used by a server (or client) for authentication.

Object — Throwable — Exception — IOException — SSLException — SSLKeyException
Serializable

```
public class SSLKeyException extends SSLException {
// Public Constructors
    public SSLKeyException(String reason);
}
```

SSLPeerUnverifiedException — Java 1.4

javax.net.ssl — serializable checked

Signals that authentication of the remote host was not successfully completed.

Object → Throwable → Exception → IOException → SSLException → SSLPeerUnverifiedException; Throwable implements Serializable

```
public class SSLPeerUnverifiedException extends SSLException {
// Public Constructors
   public SSLPeerUnverifiedException(String reason);
}
```

Thrown By java.net.SecureCacheResponse.{getPeerPrincipal(), getServerCertificateChain()}, HandshakeCompletedEvent.{getPeerCertificateChain(), getPeerCertificates(), getPeerPrincipal()}, HttpsURLConnection.{getPeerPrincipal(), getServerCertificates()}, SSLSession.{getPeerCertificateChain(), getPeerCertificates(), getPeerPrincipal()}

SSLPermission — Java 1.4

javax.net.ssl — serializable permission

This Permission class controls access to sensitive methods in the javax.net.ssl package. The two defined target names are "setHostnameVerifier" and "getSSLSessionContext". The first is required in order to call HttpURLConnection.setHostnameVerifier() and HttpURLConnection.setDefaultHostnameVerifier(). The second permission target is required in order to call SSLSession.getSessionContext().

Object → Permission → BasicPermission → SSLPermission; Permission implements Guard, Serializable; BasicPermission implements Serializable

```
public final class SSLPermission extends java.security.BasicPermission {
// Public Constructors
   public SSLPermission(String name);
   public SSLPermission(String name, String actions);
}
```

SSLProtocolException — Java 1.4

javax.net.ssl — serializable checked

Signals a problem at the SSL protocol level. An exception of this type usually indicates that there is a bug in the SSL implementation being used locally or on the remote host.

Object → Throwable → Exception → IOException → SSLException → SSLProtocolException; Throwable implements Serializable

```
public class SSLProtocolException extends SSLException {
// Public Constructors
   public SSLProtocolException(String reason);
}
```

SSLServerSocket **Java 1.4**

javax.net.ssl

This class is an SSL-enabled subclass of java.net.ServerSocket that is used to listen for and accept connections from clients and to create SSLSocket objects for communicating with those clients. Create an SSLServerSocket and bind it to a local port by calling one of the inherited getServerSocket() methods of an SSLServerSocketFactory. Once a SSLServerSocket is created, use it as you would a regular ServerSocket: call the inherited accept() method to wait for and accept a connection from a client, returning a Socket object. With SSLServerSocket, the Socket returned by accept() can always be cast to an instance of SSLSocket.

SSLServerSocket defines methods for setting the enabled protocols and cipher suites, and for querying the full set of supported protocols and suites. See SSLSocket, which has methods with the same names, for details. If your server desires or requires authentication by its clients, call setWantClientAuth() or setNeedClientAuth(). These methods cause the SSLSocket objects returned by accept() to be configured to request or require client authentication.

In typical SSL networking scenarios, the client requires the server to provide authentication information. When you create an SSLServerSocket using the default SSLServerSocketFactory, the authentication information required is an X.509 public key certificate and the corresponding private key. The default SSLServerSocketFactory uses an X509KeyManager to obtain this information. The default X509KeyManager attempts to read this information from the java.security.KeyStore file specified by the system property javax.net.ssl.keyStore. It uses the value of the the javax.net.ssl.keyStorePassword as the keystore password, and uses the value of the javax.net.ssl.keyStoreType system property to specify the keystore type. The key store should only contain valid keys and certificate chains that identify the server; the X509KeyManager automatically chooses a key and certificat chain that are appropriate for the client.

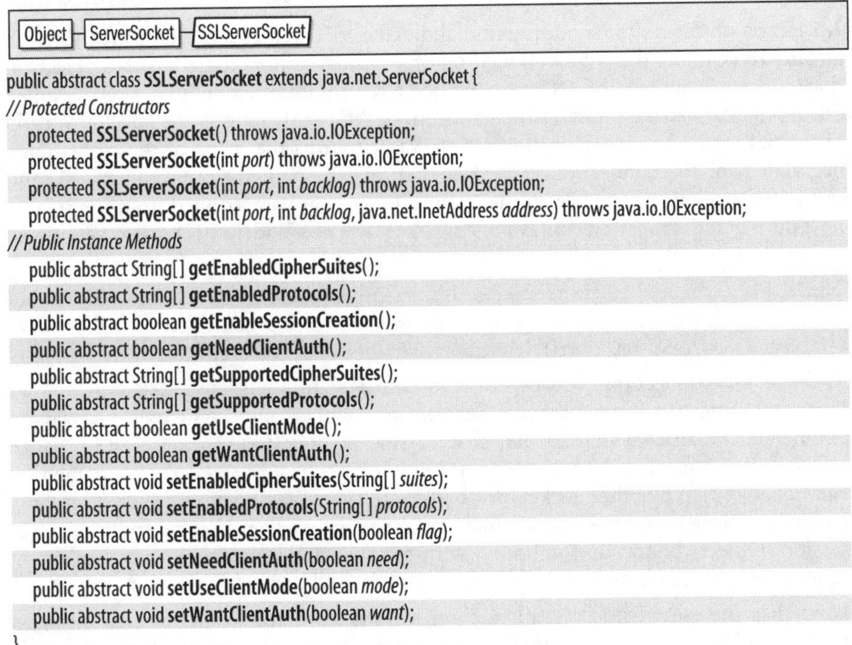


```
public abstract class SSLServerSocket extends java.net.ServerSocket {
// Protected Constructors
   protected SSLServerSocket() throws java.io.IOException;
   protected SSLServerSocket(int port) throws java.io.IOException;
   protected SSLServerSocket(int port, int backlog) throws java.io.IOException;
   protected SSLServerSocket(int port, int backlog, java.net.InetAddress address) throws java.io.IOException;
// Public Instance Methods
   public abstract String[] getEnabledCipherSuites();
   public abstract String[] getEnabledProtocols();
   public abstract boolean getEnableSessionCreation();
   public abstract boolean getNeedClientAuth();
   public abstract String[] getSupportedCipherSuites();
   public abstract String[] getSupportedProtocols();
   public abstract boolean getUseClientMode();
   public abstract boolean getWantClientAuth();
   public abstract void setEnabledCipherSuites(String[] suites);
   public abstract void setEnabledProtocols(String[] protocols);
   public abstract void setEnableSessionCreation(boolean flag);
   public abstract void setNeedClientAuth(boolean need);
   public abstract void setUseClientMode(boolean mode);
   public abstract void setWantClientAuth(boolean want);
}
```

SSLServerSocketFactory Java 1.4

javax.net.ssl

This class is a javax.net.ServerSocketFactory for creating SSLServerSocket objects. Most applications use the default SSLServerSocketFactory returned by the static getDefault() method. Once this SSLServerSocketFactory has been obtained, they use one of the inherited createServerSocket() methods to create and optionally bind a new SSLServerSocket. The return value of the createServerSocket() methods is a java.net.ServerSocket object, but you can safely cast this object to a SSLServerSocket if you need to.

Applications that need to customize the SSL configuration and cannot use the default server socket factory may obtain a custom SSLServerSocketFactory from an SSLContext, which is essentially a factory for socket factories. See SSLContext for details.

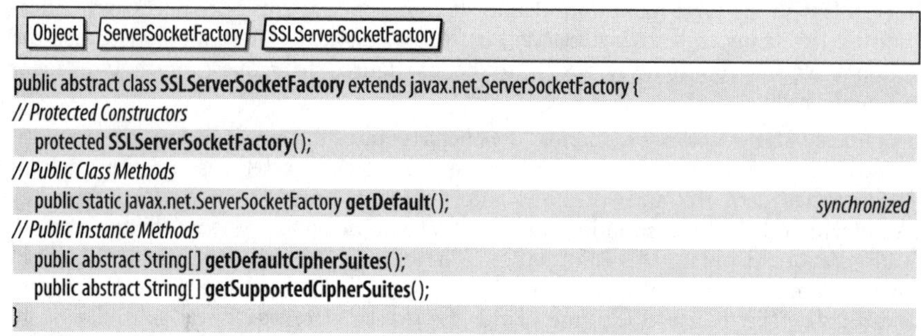


```
public abstract class SSLServerSocketFactory extends javax.net.ServerSocketFactory {
// Protected Constructors
   protected SSLServerSocketFactory();
// Public Class Methods
   public static javax.net.ServerSocketFactory getDefault();                synchronized
// Public Instance Methods
   public abstract String[] getDefaultCipherSuites();
   public abstract String[] getSupportedCipherSuites();
}
```

Returned By SSLContext.getServerSocketFactory(), SSLContextSpi.engineGetServerSocketFactory()

SSLSession Java 1.4

javax.net.ssl

A SSLSession object contains information about the SSL connection established through an SSLSocket. Use the the getSession() method of a SSLSocket to obtain the SSLSession object for that socket. Many of the SSLSession methods return information that was obtained during the handshake phase of the connection. getProtocol() returns the specific version of the SSL or TLS protocol in use. getCipherSuite() returns the name of the cipher suite negotiated for the connection. getPeerHost() returns the name of the remote host, and getPeerCertificates() returns the certificate chain, if any, that was received from the remote host during authentication. In Java 5.0 and later the peer's identity can also be queried with getPeerPrincipal()

The invalidate() method ends the session. It does not affect any current connections, but all future connections and any re-negotiations of existing connections will need to establish a new SSLSession. isValid() determines whether a session is still valid.

Multiple SSL connections between two hosts may share the same SSLSession as long as they are using the same protocol version and cipher suite. There is no way to enumerate the SSLSocket objects that share a session, but these sockets can exchange information by using putValue() to bind a shared object to some well-known name that can be looked up by other sockets with getValue(). removeValue() removes such a binding, and getValueNames() returns an array of all names that have objects bound to them in this session. Objects bound and unbound with putValue() and removeValue() may implement SSLSessionBindingListener to be notified when they are bound and unbound.

Note that the getPeerCertificateChain() method returns an object from the javax.security.cert package, which is not documented in this book. The method and package exist only for backward compatibility with earlier versions of the JSSE API, and should be considered deprecated. Use getPeerCertificates(), which uses java.security.cert instead.

```
public interface SSLSession {
// Public Instance Methods
5.0 int getApplicationBufferSize();
    String getCipherSuite();
    long getCreationTime();
    byte[] getId();
    long getLastAccessedTime();
    java.security.cert.Certificate[] getLocalCertificates();
5.0 java.security.Principal getLocalPrincipal();
5.0 int getPacketBufferSize();
    javax.security.cert.X509Certificate[] getPeerCertificateChain() throws SSLPeerUnverifiedException;
    java.security.cert.Certificate[] getPeerCertificates() throws SSLPeerUnverifiedException;
    String getPeerHost();
5.0 int getPeerPort();
5.0 java.security.Principal getPeerPrincipal() throws SSLPeerUnverifiedException;
    String getProtocol();
    SSLSessionContext getSessionContext();
    Object getValue(String name);
    String[] getValueNames();
    void invalidate();
5.0 boolean isValid();
    void putValue(String name, Object value);
    void removeValue(String name);
}
```

Passed To HandshakeCompletedEvent.HandshakeCompletedEvent(), HostnameVerifier.verify(), SSLSessionBindingEvent.SSLSessionBindingEvent()

Returned By HandshakeCompletedEvent.getSession(), SSLEngine.getSession(), SSLSessionBindingEvent.getSession(), SSLSessionContext.getSession(), SSLSocket.getSession()

SSLSessionBindingEvent — Java 1.4

javax.net.ssl — serializable event

An object of this type is passed to the valueBound() and valueUnbound() methods of and object that implements SSLSessionBindingListener when that object is bound or unbound in a SSLSession with the putValue() or removeValue() methods of SSLSession. getName() returns the name to which the object was bound or unbound, and getSession() returns the SSLSession object in which the binding was created or removed.

Object — EventObject — SSLSessionBindingEvent
Serializable

```
public class SSLSessionBindingEvent extends java.util.EventObject {
// Public Constructors
    public SSLSessionBindingEvent(SSLSession session, String name);
// Public Instance Methods
    public String getName();
    public SSLSession getSession();
}
```

Passed To SSLSessionBindingListener.{valueBound(), valueUnbound()}

SSLSessionBindingListener — Java 1.4

javax.net.ssl — event listener

This interface is implemented by an object that want to be notified when it is bound or unbound in an SSLSession object. If the object passed to the putValue() method of a SSLSession implements this interface, then its valueBound() method will be called by putValue(), and its valueUnbound() method will be called when that object is removed from the SSLSession with removeValue() or when it is replaced with a new object by putValue(). The argument to both methods of this interface is a SSLSessionBindingEvent, which specifies both the name to which the object was bound or unbound, and the SSLSession within which it was bound or unbound.

EventListener ··· SSLSessionBindingListener

```
public interface SSLSessionBindingListener extends java.util.EventListener {
// Public Instance Methods
   void valueBound(SSLSessionBindingEvent event);
   void valueUnbound(SSLSessionBindingEvent event);
}
```

SSLSessionContext — Java 1.4

javax.net.ssl

A SSLSessionContext groups and controls SSLSession objects. It is a low-level interface and is not commonly used in application code. getIds() returns an Enumeration of session IDs, and getSession() returns the SSLSession object associated with one of those IDs. setSessionCacheSize() specifies the total number of concurrent sessions allowed in the group, and setSessionTimeout() specifies the timeout length for those sessions. An SSLSessionContext can serve as a cache for SSLSession objects, facilitating reuse of those objects for multiple connections between the same two hosts.

Providers are not required to support this interface. Those that do return an implementing object from the getSessionContext() method of an SSLSession object, and also return implementing objects from the getClientSessionContext() and getServerSessionContext() methods of an SSLContext object, providing separate control over client and server SSL connections.

```
public interface SSLSessionContext {
// Public Instance Methods
   java.util.Enumeration getIds();
   SSLSession getSession(byte[] sessionId);
   int getSessionCacheSize();
   int getSessionTimeout();
   void setSessionCacheSize(int size) throws IllegalArgumentException;
   void setSessionTimeout(int seconds) throws IllegalArgumentException;
}
```

Returned By SSLContext.{getClientSessionContext(), getServerSessionContext()}, SSLContextSpi.{engineGetClientSessionContext(), engineGetServerSessionContext()}, SSLSession.getSessionContext()

SSLSocket — Java 1.4

javax.net.ssl

An SSLSocket is a "secure socket" subclass of java.net.Socket that implements the SSL or TLS protocols, which are commonly used to authenticate a server to a client and to encrypt the data transferred between the two. Create a SSLSocket for connecting to a SSL-enabled server by calling one of the createSocket() methods of a SSLSocketFactory object. See SSLSocketFactory for details. If you are writing server code, then you will obtain a SSLSocket for communicating with an SSL-enabled client from the inherited accept() method of an SSLServerSocket. See SSLServerSocket for details.

SSLSocket inherits all of the standard socket method of its superclass, and can be used for networking just like an ordinary java.net.Socket object. In addition, however, it also defines methods that control how the secure connection is established. These methods may be called before the SSL "handshake" occurs. The handshake does not occur when the socket is first created and connected, so that you can configure various SSL parameters that control how the handshake occurs. Calling startHandshake(), getSession(), or reading or writing data on the socket trigger a handshake, so you must configure the socket before doing any of these things. If you want to be notified when the handshake occurs, call addHandshakeCompletedListener() to register a listener object to receive the notification.

getSupportedProtocols() returns a list of secure socket protocols that are supported by the socket implementation. setEnabledProtocols() allows you to specify the name or names of the supported protocols that you are willing to use for this socket. getSupportedCipherSuite() returns the full set of cipher suites supported by the underlying security provider. setEnabledCipherSuites() specifies a list of one or more cipher suites that you are willing to use for the connection. Note that not all supported cipher suites are enabled by default: only suites that provide encryption and require the server to authenticate itself to the client are enabled. If you want to allow the server to remain anonymous, you can use setEnabledCipherSuites() to enable a nonauthenticating suite. Specific protocols and cipher suites are not described here because using them correctly requires a detailed understanding of cryptography, which is beyond the scope of this reference. Most applications can simply rely on the default set of enabled protocols and cipher suites.

If you are writing a server and have obtained an SSLSocket by accepting a connection on an SSLServerSocket, then you may call setWantClientAuth() to request that the client authenticate itself to you, and you may call setNeedClientAuth() to require that the client authenticate itself during the handshake. Note, however, that it is usually more efficient to request or require client authentication on the server socket than it is to call these methods on each SSLSocket it creates.

The configuration methods described above must be called before the SSL handshake occurs. Call getSession() to obtain an SSLSession object that you can query for for information about the handshake, such as the protocol and cipher suite in use, and the identity of the server. Note that a call to getSession() will cause the handshake to occur if it has not already occurred, so you can call this method at any time.

Object — Socket — SSLSocket

```
public abstract class SSLSocket extends java.net.Socket {
// Protected Constructors
   protected SSLSocket();
   protected SSLSocket(String host, int port) throws java.io.IOException, java.net.UnknownHostException;
   protected SSLSocket(java.net.InetAddress address, int port) throws java.io.IOException;
   protected SSLSocket(String host, int port, java.net.InetAddress clientAddress, int clientPort)
      throws java.io.IOException, java.net.UnknownHostException;
   protected SSLSocket(java.net.InetAddress address, int port, java.net.InetAddress clientAddress, int clientPort)
      throws java.io.IOException;
```

```
// Event Registration Methods (by event name)
   public abstract void addHandshakeCompletedListener(HandshakeCompletedListener listener);
   public abstract void removeHandshakeCompletedListener(HandshakeCompletedListener listener);
// Public Instance Methods
   public abstract String[] getEnabledCipherSuites();
   public abstract String[] getEnabledProtocols();
   public abstract boolean getEnableSessionCreation();
   public abstract boolean getNeedClientAuth();
   public abstract SSLSession getSession();
   public abstract String[] getSupportedCipherSuites();
   public abstract String[] getSupportedProtocols();
   public abstract boolean getUseClientMode();
   public abstract boolean getWantClientAuth();
   public abstract void setEnabledCipherSuites(String[] suites);
   public abstract void setEnabledProtocols(String[] protocols);
   public abstract void setEnableSessionCreation(boolean flag);
   public abstract void setNeedClientAuth(boolean need);
   public abstract void setUseClientMode(boolean mode);
   public abstract void setWantClientAuth(boolean want);
   public abstract void startHandshake() throws java.io.IOException;
}
```

Passed To HandshakeCompletedEvent.HandshakeCompletedEvent()

Returned By HandshakeCompletedEvent.getSocket()

SSLSocketFactory — Java 1.4

javax.net.ssl

This class is a javax.net.SocketFactory for creating SSLSocket objects. Most applications use the default SSLSocketFactory returned by the static getDefault() method. Once this SSLSocketFactory has been obtained, they use one of the inherited createSocket() methods to create, and optionally connect and bind, a new SSLSocket. The return value of the createSocket() methods is a java.net.Socket object, but you can safely cast this object to a SSLSocket if you need to. SSLSocketFactory defines one new version of createSocket() in addition to the ones it inherits from its superclass. This version of the method creates an SSLSocket that is layered over an existing Socket object rather than creating a new socket entirely from scratch.

Applications that need to customize the SSL configuration and cannot use the default socket factory may obtain a custom SSLSocketFactory from an SSLContext, which is essentially a factory for socket factories. See SSLContext for details.

Object — SocketFactory — SSLSocketFactory

```
public abstract class SSLSocketFactory extends javax.net.SocketFactory {
// Public Constructors
   public SSLSocketFactory();
// Public Class Methods
   public static javax.net.SocketFactory getDefault();                    synchronized
// Public Instance Methods
   public abstract java.net.Socket createSocket(java.net.Socket s, String host, int port, boolean autoClose)
       throws java.io.IOException;
   public abstract String[] getDefaultCipherSuites();
   public abstract String[] getSupportedCipherSuites();
}
```

Passed To HttpsURLConnection.{setDefaultSSLSocketFactory(), setSSLSocketFactory()}

Returned By HttpsURLConnection.{getDefaultSSLSocketFactory(), getSSLSocketFactory()}, SSLContext.getSocketFactory(), SSLContextSpi.engineGetSocketFactory()

TrustManager — Java 1.4

javax.net.ssl

This is a marker interface to identify trust manager objects. A trust manager is responsible for examining the authentication credentials (such as a certificate chain) presented by the remote host and deciding whether to trust those credentials and accept them. A TrustManager is usually used an SSL client to decide whether the SSL server is authentic, but may also be used by an SSL server when client authentication is also required.

Use a TrustManagerFactory to obtain TrustManager objects. TrustManager objects returned by a TrustManagerFactory can always be cast to a subinterface specific to a specific type of keys. See X509TrustManager, for exmaple.

```
public interface TrustManager {
}
```

Implementations X509TrustManager

Passed To SSLContext.init(), SSLContextSpi.engineInit()

Returned By TrustManagerFactory.getTrustManagers(), TrustManagerFactorySpi.engineGetTrustManagers()

TrustManagerFactory — Java 1.4

javax.net.ssl

A TrustManagerFactory is responsible for creating TrustManager objects for a specific trust management algorithm. Obtain a TrustManagerFactory object by calling one of the getInstance() methods and specifying the desired algorithm and, optionally, the desired provider. In Java 1.4, the "SunX509" algorithm is the only one supported by the default "SunJSSE" provider. After calling getInstance(), you initialize the factory object with init(). For the "SunX509" algorithm, you pass a KeyStore object to init(). This KeyStore should contain the public keys of trusted CAs (certification authorities). Once a TrustManagerFactory has been created and initialized, use it to create a TrustManager by calling getTrustManagers(). This method returns an array of TrustManager objects because some trust management algorithms may handle more than one type of key or certificate. The "SunX509" algorithm manages only X.509 keys, and always returns an array with an X509TrustManager object as its single element. This returned array is typically passed to the init() method of an SSLContext object.

If no KeyStore is passed to the init() method of the TrustManagerFactory for the "SunX509" algorithm, then the factory uses a KeyStore created from the file named by the system property javax.net.ssl.trustStore if that property is defined. (It also uses the key store type and password specified by the properties javax.net.ssl.trustStoreType and javax.net.ssl.trustStorePassword.) Otherwise, it uses the file *jre/lib/security/jssecacerts* in the Java distribution, if it exists. Otherwise it uses the file *jre/lib/security/cacerts* which is part of Sun's Java distribution. Sun ships a default *cacerts* file that contains certificates for several well-known and reputable CAs. You can use the *keytool* program to edit the *cacerts* keystore (the default password is "changeit").

```
public class TrustManagerFactory {
// Protected Constructors
    protected TrustManagerFactory(TrustManagerFactorySpi factorySpi, java.security.Provider provider, String algorithm);
```

```
// Public Class Methods
   public static final String getDefaultAlgorithm();
   public static final TrustManagerFactory getInstance(String algorithm) throws java.security.NoSuchAlgorithmException;
   public static final TrustManagerFactory getInstance(String algorithm, java.security.Provider provider)
       throws java.security.NoSuchAlgorithmException;
   public static final TrustManagerFactory getInstance(String algorithm, String provider)
       throws java.security.NoSuchAlgorithmException, java.security.NoSuchProviderException;
// Public Instance Methods
   public final String getAlgorithm();
   public final java.security.Provider getProvider();
   public final TrustManager[] getTrustManagers();
   public final void init(ManagerFactoryParameters spec) throws java.security.InvalidAlgorithmParameterException;
   public final void init(java.security.KeyStore ks) throws java.security.KeyStoreException;
}
```

TrustManagerFactorySpi — Java 1.4

javax.net.ssl

This abstract class defines the Service Provider Interface for TrustManagerFactory. Security providers must implement this interface, but applications never need to use it.

```
public abstract class TrustManagerFactorySpi {
// Public Constructors
   public TrustManagerFactorySpi();
// Protected Instance Methods
   protected abstract TrustManager[] engineGetTrustManagers();
   protected abstract void engineInit(ManagerFactoryParameters spec)
       throws java.security.InvalidAlgorithmParameterException;
   protected abstract void engineInit(java.security.KeyStore ks) throws java.security.KeyStoreException;
}
```

Passed To TrustManagerFactory.TrustManagerFactory()

X509ExtendedKeyManager — Java 5.0

javax.net.ssl

This class implements the X509KeyManager interface and extends it with two methods.

Object — X509ExtendedKeyManager
KeyManager ··· X509KeyManager

```
public abstract class X509ExtendedKeyManager implements X509KeyManager {
// Protected Constructors
   protected X509ExtendedKeyManager();
// Public Instance Methods
   public String chooseEngineClientAlias(String[] keyType, java.security.Principal[] issuers, SSLEngine engine);   constant
   public String chooseEngineServerAlias(String keyType, java.security.Principal[] issuers, SSLEngine engine);     constant
}
```

X509KeyManager — Java 1.4

javax.net.ssl

This interface is a KeyManager for working with X.509 certificates. An X509KeyManager is used during the SSL handshake by a peer that authenticates itself by providing an X.509 certificate chain to the remote host. This is usually done on the server side of the

SSL connection, and can be done on the client-side as well, although that is uncommon. Obtain an X509KeyManager object either by implementing your own or from a KeyManagerFactory created with an algorithm of "SunX509". Applications do not call the methods of an X509KeyManager themselves. Instead, they simply supply an appropriate X509KeyManager object to the SSLContext object that is responsible for setting up SSL connections. When the system needs to authenticate itself during an SSL handshake, it calls various methods of the key manager object to obtain the information in needs.

An X509KeyManager retrieves keys and certificae chains from the KeyStore object that was passed to the init() method of the KeyManagerFactory object from which it was created. getPrivateKey() and getCertificateChain() return the private key and the certificate chain for a specified alias. The other methods are called to list all aliases in the keystore or to choose one alias from the keystore that matches the specified keytype and certificate authority criteria. In this way, a X509KeyManager can choose a certificate chain (and it corresponding key) based on the types of keys and the list of certificate authorities recognized by the remote host.

KeyManager ··· X509KeyManager

```
public interface X509KeyManager extends KeyManager {
// Public Instance Methods
   String chooseClientAlias(String[] keyType, java.security.Principal[] issuers, java.net.Socket socket);
   String chooseServerAlias(String keyType, java.security.Principal[] issuers, java.net.Socket socket);
   java.security.cert.X509Certificate[] getCertificateChain(String alias);
   String[] getClientAliases(String keyType, java.security.Principal[] issuers);
   java.security.PrivateKey getPrivateKey(String alias);
   String[] getServerAliases(String keyType, java.security.Principal[] issuers);
}
```

Implementations X509ExtendedKeyManager

X509TrustManager — Java 1.4

javax.net.ssl

This interface is a TrustManager for working with X.509 certificates. Trust managers are used during the handshake phase of SSL connection to determine whether the authentication credentials presented by the remote host are trusted. This is usually done on the client-side of an SSL connection, but may also be done on the server side. Obtain an X509TrustManager either by implementing your own or from a TrustManagerFactory that was created to use the "SunX509" algorithm. Applications do call the methods of this interface themselves; instead, they simply provide an appropriate X509TrustManager object to the SSLContext object that is responsible for setting up SSL connections. When the system needs to determine whether the authentication credentials presented by the remote host are trusted, it calls the methods of the trust manager.

TrustManager ··· X509TrustManager

```
public interface X509TrustManager extends TrustManager {
// Public Instance Methods
   void checkClientTrusted(java.security.cert.X509Certificate[] chain, String authType)
       throws java.security.cert.CertificateException;
   void checkServerTrusted(java.security.cert.X509Certificate[] chain, String authType)
       throws java.security.cert.CertificateException;
   java.security.cert.X509Certificate[] getAcceptedIssuers();
}
```

19

javax.security.auth and Subpackages

This chapter documents the javax.security.auth package and its subpackages, which, together, form the Java Authentication and Authorization Service, or JAAS. Before being integrated into Java 1.4, JAAS was available as a standard extension, which is why these packages have the "javax" prefix. The individual packages are the following:

javax.security.auth
: This top-level package defines the Subject class that is central to JAAS.

javax.security.auth.callback
: This package defines a callback API to enable communication (such as the exchange of a username and password) between a low-level login module and the end-user.

javax.security.auth.kerberos
: This package contains JAAS classes related to the Kerberos network authentication protocol.

javax.security.auth.login
: This package defines the LoginContext class and related classes used by applications to perform a JAAS login.

javax.security.auth.spi
: This package defines the "service provider interface" for JAAS.

javax.security.auth.x500
: This package includes JAAS classes related to X.500 principals.

Package javax.security.auth — Java 1.4

This is the top-level package of the Java Authentication and Authorization Service (JAAS). The key class is Subject, which represents an authenticated user, and defines static methods that allow Java code be run as (i.e., using the permissions of) a specified Subject. The remaining classes and interfaces in this package are important parts of the JAAS infrastructure, but are not commonly used in application code. Applications do not create Subject objects directly, but typically obtain them from a javax.security.auth.login.LoginContext constructed with a javax.security.auth.callback.CallbackHandler.

Interfaces

public interface **Destroyable**;
public interface **Refreshable**;

Classes

public final class **AuthPermission** extends java.security.BasicPermission;
public abstract class **Policy**;
public final class **PrivateCredentialPermission** extends java.security.Permission;
public final class **Subject** implements Serializable;
public class **SubjectDomainCombiner** implements java.security.DomainCombiner;

Exceptions

public class **DestroyFailedException** extends Exception;
public class **RefreshFailedException** extends Exception;

AuthPermission — Java 1.4

javax.security.auth — serializable permission

This java.security.Permission class governs the use of various methods in this package and its subpackages. The target name of the permission specifies which methods are allowed; AuthPermission objects have no actions list. Application programmers never need to use this class directly. System implementors may need to use it, and system administrators who configure security policies may need to be familiar with the following table of target names and the permissions they represent:

Target name	Gives permission to
doAs	Invoke Subject.doAs() methods.
doAsPrivileged	Invoke Subject.doAsPriviliged() methods.
getSubject	Invoke Subject.getSubject().
getSubjectFromDomainCombiner	Invoke SubjectDomainCombiner.getSubject().
setReadOnly	Invoke Subject.setReadOnly().
modifyPrincipals	Modify the Set of principals associated with a Subject.
modifyPublicCredentials	Modify the Set of public credentials associated with a Subject.
modifyPrivateCredentials	Modify the Set of private credentials associated with a Subject.
refreshCredential	Invoke the refresh() method of a Refreshable credential class.
destroyCredential	Invoke the destroy() method of a Destroyable credential class.
createLoginContext.*name*	Instantiate a LoginContext with the specified *name*. If *name* is *, it allows a LoginContext of any name to be created.
getLoginConfiguration	Invoke the getConfiguration() method of javax.security.auth.login.Configuration.
setLoginConfiguration	Invoke the setConfiguration() method of javax.security.auth.login.Configuration.
refreshLoginConfiguration	Invoke the refresh() method of javax.security.auth.login.Configuration.

Object — Permission — BasicPermission — AuthPermission
Guard, Serializable, Serializable

```
public final class AuthPermission extends java.security.BasicPermission {
// Public Constructors
   public AuthPermission(String name);
   public AuthPermission(String name, String actions);
}
```

Destroyable Java 1.4

javax.security.auth

Classes that encapsulate sensitive information, such as security credentials, may implement this interface to provide an API that allows the sensitive information to be destroyed or erased. The destroy() method erases or clears the sensitive information. It may throw a DestroyFailedException if the information cannot be erased for any reason. It may also throw a SecurityException if the caller does not have whatever permissions are required. Once destroy() has been called on an object, the isDestroyed() method returns true. Once an object has been destroyed, any other methods it defines may throw an IllegalStateException.

```
public interface Destroyable {
// Public Instance Methods
   void destroy() throws DestroyFailedException;
   boolean isDestroyed();
}
```

Implementations java.security.KeyStore.PasswordProtection, javax.security.auth.kerberos.KerberosKey, javax.security.auth.kerberos.KerberosTicket, javax.security.auth.x500.X500PrivateCredential

DestroyFailedException Java 1.4

javax.security.auth serializable checked

Signals that the destroy() method of a Destroyable object did not succeed.

Object — Throwable — Exception — DestroyFailedException
Serializable

```
public class DestroyFailedException extends Exception {
// Public Constructors
   public DestroyFailedException();
   public DestroyFailedException(String msg);
}
```

Thrown By java.security.KeyStore.PasswordProtection.destroy(), Destroyable.destroy(), javax.security.auth.kerberos.KerberosKey.destroy(), javax.security.auth.kerberos.KerberosTicket.destroy()

Policy Java 1.4; Deprecated in 1.4

javax.security.auth @Deprecated

This deprecated class represents a Subject-based security policy. Because the JAAS API (this package and its subpackages) were introduced as an extension to the core Java platform, this class was required to augment the java.security.Policy class which, prior to Java 1.4, had no provisions for Subject-based authorization. In Java 1.4, however, java.security.Policy has been extended to represent security policies based on code origin, code signers, and subjects. Thus, this class is no longer required and has been deprecated.

```
public abstract class Policy {
// Protected Constructors
   protected Policy();
// Public Class Methods
   public static javax.security.auth.Policy getPolicy();
   public static void setPolicy(javax.security.auth.Policy policy);
// Public Instance Methods
   public abstract java.security.PermissionCollection getPermissions(Subject subject, java.security.CodeSource cs);
   public abstract void refresh();
}
```


PrivateCredentialPermission — Java 1.4

javax.security.auth — serializable permission

This Permission class protects access to private credential objects belonging to a Subject (as specified by a set of one or more Principal objects). Application programmers rarely need to use it. System programmers implementing new private credentials classes may need to use it, and system administrators configuring security policy files should be familiar with it.

The only defined action for PrivateCredentialPermssion is "read". The target name for this permission has a complex syntax and specifies the name of the credential class and a list of one or more principals. Each principal is specified as the name of the Principal class followed by the principal name in quotes. For example, a security policy file might contain a statement like the following to allow permission to read the private KerberosKey credentials of a KerberosPrincipal named "david".

```
permission javax.security.auth.PrivateCredentialPermission
    "javax.security.auth.kerberos.KerberosKey \
            javax.security.auth.kerberos.KerberosPrincipal \"david\"",
    "read";
```

The target name syntax for PrivateCredentialPermission also allows the use of the "*" wildcard in place of the credential class name or in place of the Principal class name and/or name.

Object — Permission — PrivateCredentialPermission
Guard, Serializable

```
public final class PrivateCredentialPermission extends java.security.Permission {
// Public Constructors
   public PrivateCredentialPermission(String name, String actions);
// Public Instance Methods
   public String getCredentialClass();
   public String[][] getPrincipals();
// Public Methods Overriding Permission
   public boolean equals(Object obj);
   public String getActions();
   public int hashCode();
   public boolean implies(java.security.Permission p);
   public java.security.PermissionCollection newPermissionCollection();          constant
}
```

Refreshable

Java 1.4

javax.security.auth

A class implements this interface if its instances that have a limited period of validity (as some security credentials do) and need to be periodically "refreshed" in order to remain valid. isCurrent() returns true if the object is currently valid, and false if it has expired and needs to be refreshed. refresh() attempts to revalidate or extend the validity of the object. It throws a RefreshFailedException if it does not succeed. (And may also throw a SecurityException if the caller does not have the requisite permissions.)

```
public interface Refreshable {
// Public Instance Methods
   boolean isCurrent();
   void refresh() throws RefreshFailedException;
}
```

Implementations javax.security.auth.kerberos.KerberosTicket

RefreshFailedException

Java 1.4

javax.security.auth — serializable checked

Signals that the refresh() method of a Refreshable object failed.

Object — Throwable — Exception — RefreshFailedException

Throwable ⋯ Serializable

```
public class RefreshFailedException extends Exception {
// Public Constructors
   public RefreshFailedException();
   public RefreshFailedException(String msg);
}
```

Thrown By Refreshable.refresh(), javax.security.auth.kerberos.KerberosTicket.refresh()

Subject

Java 1.4

javax.security.auth — serializable

The Subject class is the key abstraction of the JAAS API. It represents a person or other entity, and consists of:

- a java.util.Set of Principal objects that specify the identity (or identities) of the Subject.
- a Set of objects that specify the public credentials, such as the public key certificates of the Subject.
- a Set of objects that specify the private credentials, such as the private keys and Kerberos tickets of the Subject.

Subject defines methods that allow you to retreive each of these three sets, or to retreive a subset of each set that contains only objects of a specified Class. Unless the Subject is read-only, you can use the methods of java.util.Set to modify each of the three sets. Once setReadOnly() has been called, however, the sets become immutable and their contents may not be modified.

Application code does not typically create Subject objects itself. Instead, it obtains a Subject that represents the authenticated user of the application by calling the login() and getSubject() methods of a javax.security.auth.login.LoginContext object.

Once an authenticated **Subject** has been obtained from a **LoginContext**, an application can call the **doAs()** method to run code using the permissions granted to that **Subject** combined with the permissions granted to the code itself. **doAs()** runs the code defined in the **run()** method of a **PrivilegedAction** or **PrivilegedExceptionAction** object. **doAsPrivileged()** is a similar method but executes the specified **run()** method using the Subject's permissions only, unconstrained by unprivileged code in the call stack.

Note that many of the methods of this class throw a **SecurityException** if the caller has not been granted the requisite **AuthPermission**.

Object ─ Subject ··· Serializable

```
public final class Subject implements Serializable {
// Public Constructors
   public Subject();
   public Subject(boolean readOnly, java.util.Set<? extends java.security.Principal> principals, java.util.Set<?>
              pubCredentials, java.util.Set<?> privCredentials);
// Public Class Methods
   public static Object doAs(Subject subject, java.security.PrivilegedExceptionAction action)
      throws java.security.PrivilegedActionException;
   public static Object doAs(Subject subject, java.security.PrivilegedAction action);
   public static Object doAsPrivileged(Subject subject, java.security.PrivilegedExceptionAction action,
                                        java.security.AccessControlContext acc)
      throws java.security.PrivilegedActionException;
   public static Object doAsPrivileged(Subject subject, java.security.PrivilegedAction action,
                                        java.security.AccessControlContext acc);
   public static Subject getSubject(java.security.AccessControlContext acc);
// Public Instance Methods
   public java.util.Set<java.security.Principal> getPrincipals();
   public <T extends java.security.Principal> java.util.Set<T> getPrincipals(Class<T> c);
   public java.util.Set<Object> getPrivateCredentials();
   public <T> java.util.Set<T> getPrivateCredentials(Class<T> c);
   public java.util.Set<Object> getPublicCredentials();
   public <T> java.util.Set<T> getPublicCredentials(Class<T> c);
   public boolean isReadOnly();                                                      default:false
   public void setReadOnly();
// Public Methods Overriding Object
   public boolean equals(Object o);
   public int hashCode();
   public String toString();
}
```

Passed To java.security.AuthProvider.login(), javax.security.auth.Policy.getPermissions(), SubjectDomainCombiner.SubjectDomainCombiner(), javax.security.auth.login.LoginContext.LoginContext(), javax.security.auth.spi.LoginModule.initialize()

Returned By SubjectDomainCombiner.getSubject(), javax.security.auth.login.LoginContext.getSubject()

SubjectDomainCombiner — Java 1.4

javax.security.auth

This class implements the **DomainCombiner** interface. It is used to merge permissions based on code source and code signers with permissions granted to the specified **Subject**. A **SubjectDomainCombiner** is created by the **Subject.doAs()** and **Subject.doAsPrivileged()** methods for use in by the **AccessControlContext**.

Object ─ SubjectDomainCombiner ··· DomainCombiner

```
public class SubjectDomainCombiner implements java.security.DomainCombiner {
// Public Constructors
   public SubjectDomainCombiner(Subject subject);
// Public Instance Methods
   public Subject getSubject();
// Methods Implementing DomainCombiner
   public java.security.ProtectionDomain[] combine(java.security.ProtectionDomain[] currentDomains,
       java.security.ProtectionDomain[] assignedDomains);
}
```

Package javax.security.auth.callback — Java 1.4

This package defines a mechanism that allows the low-level code of a javax.security.auth.spi.LoginModule to interact with the end-user of an application to obtain a username, password, or other authentication-related information. The LoginModule sends messages and requests for information in the form of objects that implement the Callback interface. An application that wants to authenticate a user provides (via a javax.security.auth.login.LoginContext) a CallbackHandler object to convert these Callback objects into text or GUI-based interactions with the user. An application that want to provide a customized login interface must implement its own CallbackHandler. The CallbackHandler API consists of only a single method, but the implementation of that method can require a substantial amount of code. See the various Callback classes for directions on how a CallbackHandler should handle them.

Sun's J2SE SDK for Java 1.4 ships with two implementations of CallbackHandler, both in the package com.sun.security.auth.callback. Although these classes are not guaranteed to exist in all distributions, text-based applications may use the TextCallbackHandler, and GUI-based applications may use the DialogCallbackHandler. Programmers wanting to write a custom CallbackHandler may also find it useful to study the source code of these two existing handlers.

Interfaces

public interface **Callback**;
public interface **CallbackHandler**;

Classes

public class **ChoiceCallback** implements Callback, Serializable;
public class **ConfirmationCallback** implements Callback, Serializable;
public class **LanguageCallback** implements Callback, Serializable;
public class **NameCallback** implements Callback, Serializable;
public class **PasswordCallback** implements Callback, Serializable;
public class **TextInputCallback** implements Callback, Serializable;
public class **TextOutputCallback** implements Callback, Serializable;

Exceptions

public class **UnsupportedCallbackException** extends Exception;

Callback   Java 1.4

javax.security.auth.callback

This interface defines no methods but serves as a "marker interface" to identify the type of objects that can be passed to the handle() method of a CallbackHandler. All of the classes in this package, with the exception of UnsupportedCallbackException implement this interface.

```
public interface Callback {
}
```

Implementations ChoiceCallback, ConfirmationCallback, LanguageCallback, NameCallback, PasswordCallback, TextInputCallback, TextOutputCallback

Passed To CallbackHandler.handle(), UnsupportedCallbackException.UnsupportedCallbackException()

Returned By UnsupportedCallbackException.getCallback()

CallbackHandler   Java 1.4

javax.security.auth.callback

A CallbackHandler is responsible for communication between the end-user of an application and the javax.security.auth.spi.LoginModule that is performing authentication of that user on behalf of the javax.security.auth.login.LoginContext instantiated by the application. When an application needs to authenticate a user, it creates a LoginContext and specifies a CallbackHandler object for that context. The underlying LoginModule uses the CallbackHandler to communicate with the end user--for example prompting them to enter a name and password.

The LoginModule passes an array of objects that implement the Callback interface to the handle() method of CallbackHandler. The handle() method must determine the type of Callback object, and display the information and/or prompt for the input it represents. Different Callback classes have different purposes and must be handled differently. NameCallback and PasswordCallback are two of the most commonly used: they represent requests for the user's name and password. TextOutputCallback is also common: it represents a request to display a message (such as "Authentication Failed") to the user. See the descriptions of the individual Callback classes for information on how a CallbackHandler should handle them. CallbackHandler implementations are not required to support every type of Callback and my throw an UnsupportedCallbackException if passed a Callback object of a type they do not recognize or do not support.

The handle() method is passed an array of Callback objects. A CallbackHandler (such as a typical console-based handler) may choose to handle the Callback objects one at a time, prompting for and returning the user's input before moving on to the next. Or (for example in GUI-based handlers) it may choose to present all of the callbacks in a single unified "login dialog box". LoginModule implementations may, of course, call the handle() method more than once. Note, finally, that if a CallbackHandler implementation has knowledge of the user from some other source, it is allowed to handle certain callbacks automatically, such as automatically providing the user's name for a NameCallback.

Java installations may have a default CallbackHandler registered by setting the auth.login.defaultCallbackHandler security property to the name of the implementing class. No such default is defined by the default security policy that ships with Sun's distribution of Java 1.4. Sun's Java 1.4 SDK does include CallbackHandler implementations to perform text-based and GUI-based communication in the classes TextCallbackHandler and DialogCallbackHandler in the com.sun.security.auth.callback package. Note that these are part of Sun's implementation, and are not part of the specification; they are not guaranteed to exist in all releases.

```
public interface CallbackHandler {
// Public Instance Methods
   void handle(Callback[] callbacks) throws java.io.IOException, UnsupportedCallbackException;
}
```

Passed To java.security.AuthProvider.{login(), setCallbackHandler()}, java.security.KeyStore.CallbackHandlerProtection.CallbackHandlerProtection(), javax.security.auth.login.LoginContext.LoginContext(), javax.security.auth.spi.LoginModule.initialize()

Returned By java.security.KeyStore.CallbackHandlerProtection.getCallbackHandler()

ChoiceCallback **Java 1.4**

javax.security.auth.callback serializable

A Callback of this type represents a request to display set of text choices and allow the user to select one or more of them. A CallbackHandler, should display the prompt returned by getPrompt() and also the strings returned by getChoices(). If allowMultipleSelections() is true, then it should allow the user to select zero or more; otherwise, it should only allow the user to select a single one. In either case, the CallbackHandler should also call getDefaultChoice() and make the choice at the returned index the default choice. When the user has made her selection, the CallbackHandler should pass the index of a single selection to setSelectedIndex(), or the indexes of multiple selections to setSelectedIndexes().

Object — ChoiceCallback
Callback Serializable

```
public class ChoiceCallback implements Callback, Serializable {
// Public Constructors
   public ChoiceCallback(String prompt, String[] choices, int defaultChoice, boolean multipleSelectionsAllowed);
// Public Instance Methods
   public boolean allowMultipleSelections();
   public String[] getChoices();
   public int getDefaultChoice();
   public String getPrompt();
   public int[] getSelectedIndexes();
   public void setSelectedIndex(int selection);
   public void setSelectedIndexes(int[] selections);
}
```

ConfirmationCallback **Java 1.4**

javax.security.auth.callback serializable

A Callback of this type represents a request to ask the user a yes/no or multiple-choice question. A CallbackHandler should first call getPrompt() to obtain the text of the question. It should also call getMessageType() to determine the message type (INFORMATION, WARNING, or ERROR) and present the question to the user in a suitable manner based on that type.

Next, the CallbackHandler must determine the appropriate set of responses to the question. It does this by calling getOptionType(). The return values have the following meanings:

YES_NO_OPTION
: The CallbackHandler should allow the user to respond to the question with a "yes" or a "no" (or their localized equivalents).

YES_NO_CANCEL_OPTION
: The **CallbackHandler** should allow "yes", "no", and "cancel" (or their localized equivalents) responses.

OK_CANCEL_OPTION
: The **CallbackHandler** should allow "ok" and "cancel" (or their localized equivalents) responses.

UNSPECIFIED_OPTION
: The **CallbackHandler** should call **getOptions()** and use present all strings it returns as possible responses.

In each of these cases, the **CallbackHandler** should also call **getDefaultOption()** to determine which response should be presented as the default response. If **getOptionType()** returned **UNSPECIFIED_TYPE**, then **getDefaultOption()** returns an index into the array of options returned by **getOptions()**. Otherwise **getDefaultOption()** returns one of the constants **YES**, **NO**, **OK**, or **CANCEL**.

When the user has selected a response to the callback, the **CallbackHandler** should pass that response to **setSelectedIndex()**. The response value should be one of the constants **YES**, **NO**, **OK**, or **CANCEL**, or an index into the array of options returned by **getOptions()**.

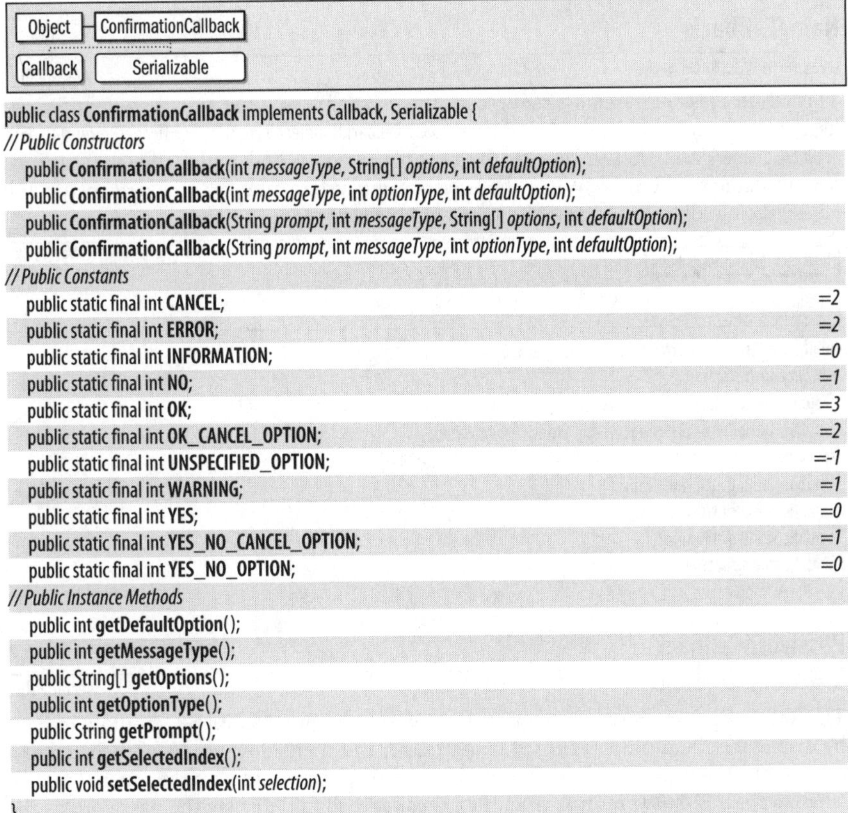


```
public class ConfirmationCallback implements Callback, Serializable {
// Public Constructors
   public ConfirmationCallback(int messageType, String[] options, int defaultOption);
   public ConfirmationCallback(int messageType, int optionType, int defaultOption);
   public ConfirmationCallback(String prompt, int messageType, String[] options, int defaultOption);
   public ConfirmationCallback(String prompt, int messageType, int optionType, int defaultOption);
// Public Constants
   public static final int CANCEL;                                    =2
   public static final int ERROR;                                     =2
   public static final int INFORMATION;                               =0
   public static final int NO;                                        =1
   public static final int OK;                                        =3
   public static final int OK_CANCEL_OPTION;                          =2
   public static final int UNSPECIFIED_OPTION;                        =-1
   public static final int WARNING;                                   =1
   public static final int YES;                                       =0
   public static final int YES_NO_CANCEL_OPTION;                      =1
   public static final int YES_NO_OPTION;                             =0
// Public Instance Methods
   public int getDefaultOption();
   public int getMessageType();
   public String[] getOptions();
   public int getOptionType();
   public String getPrompt();
   public int getSelectedIndex();
   public void setSelectedIndex(int selection);
}
```

LanguageCallback

Java 1.4

javax.security.auth.callback — serializable

This **Callback** class represents a request for the user's preferred language (as represented by a **Locale** object), which a **LoginModule** can use to localize things such as prompts and error messages in subsequent **Callback** objects. If a **CallbackHandler** already has knowledge of the user's preferred langauge, it is not required to prompt the user for this information and can simply pass an appropriate **Locale** object to **setLocale()**.

Object ─ LanguageCallback
Callback Serializable

```
public class LanguageCallback implements Callback, Serializable {
// Public Constructors
   public LanguageCallback();
// Public Instance Methods
   public java.util.Locale getLocale();                                    default:null
   public void setLocale(java.util.Locale locale);
}
```

NameCallback

Java 1.4

javax.security.auth.callback — serializable

This **Callback** class represents a request for the username or other text that identifies the user to be authenticated. An interactive **CallbackHandler** should call **getPrompt()** and **getDefaultName()** and should display the returned prompt and optionally, the returned default name to the user. When the user has entered a name (or accepted the default name) the handler should pass the user's input to **setName()**.

Object ─ NameCallback
Callback Serializable

```
public class NameCallback implements Callback, Serializable {
// Public Constructors
   public NameCallback(String prompt);
   public NameCallback(String prompt, String defaultName);
// Public Instance Methods
   public String getDefaultName();
   public String getName();
   public String getPrompt();
   public void setName(String name);
}
```

PasswordCallback

Java 1.4

javax.security.auth.callback — serializable

This **Callback** class represents a request for a password. A **CallbackHandler** should handle it by displaying the prompt returned by **getPrompt()** and then allowing the user the enter a password. When the user has entered the password, it should pass the entered text to **setPassword()**. If **isEchoOn()** returns true, then the **Handler** should display the password as the user types it.

Object → PasswordCallback; Callback, Serializable

```
public class PasswordCallback implements Callback, Serializable {
// Public Constructors
   public PasswordCallback(String prompt, boolean echoOn);
// Public Instance Methods
   public void clearPassword();
   public char[] getPassword();
   public String getPrompt();
   public boolean isEchoOn();
   public void setPassword(char[] password);
}
```


TextInputCallback — Java 1.4

javax.security.auth.callback — serializable

A Callback of this type is a request to prompt the user for text input; it is essentially a generic version of NameCallback. A CallbackHandler should call getPrompt() and should display the returned prompt text to the user. It should then allow the user to enter text, and provide the option of selecting the default text returned by getDefaultText(). When the user has entered text (or selected the default text) it should pass the user's input to setText().

Object → TextInputCallback; Callback, Serializable

```
public class TextInputCallback implements Callback, Serializable {
// Public Constructors
   public TextInputCallback(String prompt);
   public TextInputCallback(String prompt, String defaultText);
// Public Instance Methods
   public String getDefaultText();
   public String getPrompt();
   public String getText();
   public void setText(String text);
}
```

TextOutputCallback — Java 1.4

javax.security.auth.callback — serializable

A Callback of this type represents a request to display text to the user. A callback handler should call getMessage() and display the returned string to the user. It should also call getMessageType() and use the returned value (which is one of the constants defined by the class) to indicate the type or severity of the information.

Object → TextOutputCallback; Callback, Serializable

```
public class TextOutputCallback implements Callback, Serializable {
// Public Constructors
   public TextOutputCallback(int messageType, String message);
```

```
// Public Constants
   public static final int ERROR;                                    =2
   public static final int INFORMATION;                              =0
   public static final int WARNING;                                  =1
// Public Instance Methods
   public String getMessage();
   public int getMessageType();
}
```

UnsupportedCallbackException — Java 1.4

javax.security.auth.callback — serializable checked

CallbackHandler implementations may throw exceptions of this type from their handle() method if a Callback object passed to that method is of an unrecognized or unsupported type. Note that the offending Callback object must be passed to the constructor method.

Object — Throwable — Exception — UnsupportedCallbackException
Serializable

```
public class UnsupportedCallbackException extends Exception {
// Public Constructors
   public UnsupportedCallbackException(Callback callback);
   public UnsupportedCallbackException(Callback callback, String msg);
// Public Instance Methods
   public Callback getCallback();
}
```

Thrown By CallbackHandler.handle()

Package javax.security.auth.kerberos — Java 1.4

This package defines classes for use with Kerberos: a secure network authentication protocol. They are primarily of interest to system-level programmers writing Kerberos-based javax.security.auth.spi.LoginModule implementations. Developers writing Kerberos-enabled applications should use the org.ietf.jgss package. A full description of Kerberos is beyond the scope of this book; so it is assumed that the reader is familar with Kerberos authentication.

Classes

```
public final class DelegationPermission extends java.security.BasicPermission implements Serializable;
public class KerberosKey implements javax.security.auth.Destroyable, javax.crypto.SecretKey;
public final class KerberosPrincipal implements java.security.Principal, Serializable;
public class KerberosTicket implements javax.security.auth.Destroyable, javax.security.auth.Refreshable, Serializable;
public final class ServicePermission extends java.security.Permission implements Serializable;
```

DelegationPermission — Java 1.4

javax.security.auth.kerberos — serializable permission

This java.security.Permission class governs the delegation of Kerberos tickets from a Kerberos principal to a Kerberos service for use on behalf of the original principal. The target name of a DelegationPermission consists of the principal names of two Kerberos services. The first specifies the service that is being delegated to, and the second specifies the service that is to be used by the first on behalf of the original Kerberos principal.

Object — Permission — BasicPermission — DelegationPermission
Guard, Serializable, Serializable, Serializable

```
public final class DelegationPermission extends java.security.BasicPermission implements Serializable {
// Public Constructors
    public DelegationPermission(String principals);
    public DelegationPermission(String principals, String actions);
// Public Methods Overriding BasicPermission
    public boolean equals(Object obj);
    public int hashCode();
    public boolean implies(java.security.Permission p);
    public java.security.PermissionCollection newPermissionCollection();
}
```


KerberosKey — Java 1.4

javax.security.auth.kerberos — serializable

This class is a javax.crypto.SecretKey implementation that represents the secret key of a Kerberos principal. A Kerberos-based javax.security.auth.spi.LoginModule implementation instantiates a KerberosKey object and stores it in the private credential set of the authenticated Subject it creates.

Object — KerberosKey
Destroyable, Serializable, Key, SecretKey

```
public class KerberosKey implements javax.security.auth.Destroyable, javax.crypto.SecretKey {
// Public Constructors
    public KerberosKey(KerberosPrincipal principal, char[ ] password, String algorithm);
    public KerberosKey(KerberosPrincipal principal, byte[ ] keyBytes, int keyType, int versionNum);
// Public Instance Methods
    public final int getKeyType();
    public final KerberosPrincipal getPrincipal();
    public final int getVersionNumber();
// Methods Implementing Destroyable
    public void destroy() throws javax.security.auth.DestroyFailedException;
    public boolean isDestroyed();
// Methods Implementing Key
    public final String getAlgorithm();
    public final byte[ ] getEncoded();
    public final String getFormat();
// Public Methods Overriding Object
    public String toString();
}
```

KerberosPrincipal — Java 1.4

javax.security.auth.kerberos — serializable

This class represents a Kerberos principal, specified as a principal name with an optional realm. If no realm is specified in the name, the default realm (from the *krb5.conf* configuration file or from the java.security.krb5.realm system property) is used.

Object — KerberosPrincipal
Principal Serializable

```
public final class KerberosPrincipal implements java.security.Principal, Serializable {
// Public Constructors
   public KerberosPrincipal(String name);
   public KerberosPrincipal(String name, int nameType);
// Public Constants
   public static final int KRB_NT_PRINCIPAL;                    =1
   public static final int KRB_NT_SRV_HST;                      =3
   public static final int KRB_NT_SRV_INST;                     =2
   public static final int KRB_NT_SRV_XHST;                     =4
   public static final int KRB_NT_UID;                          =5
   public static final int KRB_NT_UNKNOWN;                      =0
// Public Instance Methods
   public int getNameType();
   public String getRealm();
// Methods Implementing Principal
   public boolean equals(Object other);
   public String getName();
   public int hashCode();
   public String toString();
}
```

Passed To KerberosKey.KerberosKey(), KerberosTicket.KerberosTicket()

Returned By KerberosKey.getPrincipal(), KerberosTicket.{getClient(), getServer()}

KerberosTicket — Java 1.4

javax.security.auth.kerberos — serializable

This class represents a Kerberos ticket: a credential used to authenticate a Kerberos principal to some Kerberos-enabled network service. A Kerberos-based javax.security.auth.spi.LoginModule implementation will instantiate a KerberosTicket object and store it in the private credential set of the authenticated Subject it creates.

```
public class KerberosTicket implements javax.security.auth.Destroyable, javax.security.auth.Refreshable, Serializable {
// Public Constructors
   public KerberosTicket(byte[] asn1Encoding, KerberosPrincipal client, KerberosPrincipal server, byte[] sessionKey,
                         int keyType, boolean[] flags, java.util.Date authTime, java.util.Date startTime,
                         java.util.Date endTime, java.util.Date renewTill, java.net.InetAddress[] clientAddresses);
// Public Instance Methods
   public final java.util.Date getAuthTime();
   public final KerberosPrincipal getClient();
   public final java.net.InetAddress[] getClientAddresses();
   public final byte[] getEncoded();
   public final java.util.Date getEndTime();
   public final boolean[] getFlags();
   public final java.util.Date getRenewTill();
   public final KerberosPrincipal getServer();
   public final javax.crypto.SecretKey getSessionKey();
```

```
    public final int getSessionKeyType();
    public final java.util.Date getStartTime();
    public final boolean isForwardable();
    public final boolean isForwarded();
    public final boolean isInitial();
    public final boolean isPostdated();
    public final boolean isProxiable();
    public final boolean isProxy();
    public final boolean isRenewable();
// Methods Implementing Destroyable
    public void destroy() throws javax.security.auth.DestroyFailedException;
    public boolean isDestroyed();
// Methods Implementing Refreshable
    public boolean isCurrent();
    public void refresh() throws javax.security.auth.RefreshFailedException;
// Public Methods Overriding Object
    public String toString();
}
```

ServicePermission — Java 1.4

javax.security.auth.kerberos — serializable permission

This java.security.Permission class protects access to the Kerberos tickets used to access a specified service. The target name of of a ServicePermission is the Kerberos principal name of the service. The action for the ServicePermission is either "initiate" for clients or "accept" for servers.

Object — Permission — ServicePermission
Guard — Serializable — Serializable

```
public final class ServicePermission extends java.security.Permission implements Serializable {
// Public Constructors
    public ServicePermission(String servicePrincipal, String action);
// Public Methods Overriding Permission
    public boolean equals(Object obj);
    public String getActions();
    public int hashCode();
    public boolean implies(java.security.Permission p);
    public java.security.PermissionCollection newPermissionCollection();
}
```

Package javax.security.auth.login — Java 1.4

This package defines the LoginContext class which is one of the primary JAAS classes used by application programmers. To authenticate a user, an application creates a LoginContext object, specifying the application name (used to lookup the type of authentication required for that application in the Configuration) and usually specifying a javax.security.auth.callback.CallbackHandler for communication between the user and the underlying login modules. Next, the application calls the login() method of the LoginContext to perform the actual login. If this method returns without throwing a LoginException, then the user was sucessfully authenticated, and the getSubject() method of LoginContext returns a javax.security.auth.Subject representing the user. The code might look like this:

```
import javax.security.auth.*;
import javax.security.auth.callback.*;
import javax.security.auth.login.*;
// Get a default GUI-based CallbackHandler
CallbackHandler h = new com.sun.security.auth.callback.DialogCallbackHandler();
// Try to create a LoginContext for use with this application
LoginContext context;
try {
  context = new LoginContext("MyAppName", h);
}
catch(LoginException e) {
  System.err.println("LoginContext configuration error: " + e.getMessage());
  System.exit(-1);
}
// Now use that context to authenticate the user
try {
  context.login();
}
catch(LoginException e) {
  System.err.println("Authentication failed: " + e.getMessage());
  System.exit(-1);  // Or we could allow them to try again.
}
// If we get here, authentication was successful, so get the Subject that
// represents the authenticated user.
Subject subject = context.getSubject();
```

In order to make this kind of authentication work correctly, a fair bit of configuration is required in various files in the jre/lib/security directory of the Java installation and possibly elsewhere. In particular, a login configuration file is required to specify which login modules are required to authenticate users for a particular application (some applications may require more than one). A description of how to do this is beyond the scope of this reference. See the Configuration class for a run-time representation of the login configuration information, however.

Classes

public class **AppConfigurationEntry**;
public static class **AppConfigurationEntry.LoginModuleControlFlag**;
public abstract class **Configuration**;
public class **LoginContext**;

Exceptions

public class **LoginException** extends java.security.GeneralSecurityException;
    public class **AccountException** extends LoginException;
        public class **AccountExpiredException** extends AccountException;
        public class **AccountLockedException** extends AccountException;
        public class **AccountNotFoundException** extends AccountException;
    public class **CredentialException** extends LoginException;
        public class **CredentialExpiredException** extends CredentialException;
        public class **CredentialNotFoundException** extends CredentialException;
    public class **FailedLoginException** extends LoginException;

AccountException **Java 5.0**

javax.security.auth.login **serializable checked**

A **LoginException** exception of this type signals a problem logging in to the specified account. Subclasses provide more detail.

Object ⊢ Throwable ⊢ Exception ⊢ GeneralSecurityException ⊢ LoginException ⊢ AccountException
Serializable

```
public class AccountException extends LoginException {
// Public Constructors
   public AccountException();
   public AccountException(String msg);
}
```

Subclasses AccountExpiredException, AccountLockedException, AccountNotFoundException

AccountExpiredException **Java 1.4**

javax.security.auth.login **serializable checked**

Signals that login failed because the user's account has expired. Prior to Java 5.0, this exception was a direct subclass of **LoginException**.

Object ⊢ Throwable ⊢ Exception ⊢ GeneralSecurityException ⊢ LoginException ⊢ AccountException ⊢ AccountExpiredException
Serializable

```
public class AccountExpiredException extends AccountException {
// Public Constructors
   public AccountExpiredException();
   public AccountExpiredException(String msg);
}
```

AccountLockedException **Java 5.0**

javax.security.auth.login **serializable checked**

An exception of this type indicates that the account for which login was attempted has been "locked" or otherwise made unavailable. See also **AccountExpiredException**.

Object ⊢ Throwable ⊢ Exception ⊢ GeneralSecurityException ⊢ LoginException ⊢ AccountException ⊢ AccountLockedException
Serializable

```
public class AccountLockedException extends AccountException {
// Public Constructors
   public AccountLockedException();
   public AccountLockedException(String msg);
}
```

AccountNotFoundException **Java 5.0**

javax.security.auth.login **serializable checked**

An exception of this type indicates that the account specified in a login attempt does not exist.

Object ─ Throwable ─ Exception ─ GeneralSecurityException ─ LoginException ─ AccountException ─ AccountNotFoundException

Serializable

```
public class AccountNotFoundException extends AccountException {
// Public Constructors
   public AccountNotFoundException();
   public AccountNotFoundException(String msg);
}
```

AppConfigurationEntry **Java 1.4**

javax.security.auth.login

An instance of this class represents a login module to be used for user authentication for a particular application. It encapsulates three pieces of information: the class name of the javax.security.auth.spi.LoginModule implementation that is to be used, a "control flag" that specifies whether authentication by that module is required or optional, and a java.util.Map of arbitrary string name/value pairs of options for the login module.

```
public class AppConfigurationEntry {
// Public Constructors
   public AppConfigurationEntry(String loginModuleName, AppConfigurationEntry.LoginModuleControlFlag controlFlag,
                                java.util.Map<String,?> options);
// Nested Types
   public static class LoginModuleControlFlag;
// Public Instance Methods
   public AppConfigurationEntry.LoginModuleControlFlag getControlFlag();
   public String getLoginModuleName();
   public java.util.Map<String,?> getOptions();
}
```

Returned By Configuration.getAppConfigurationEntry()

AppConfigurationEntry.LoginModuleControlFlag **Java 1.4**

javax.security.auth.login

This inner class defines a "control flag" type and four specific instances of that type. The constants defined by this class specify whether a login module is required or optional, and have the following meanings:

REQUIRED
: Authentication by this module must be successful, or the overall login process will fail. However, even if authentication fails for this module, the LoginContext continues to attempt authentication with any other modules in the list. (This can server to disguise the source of the authentication failure from an attacker)

REQUSITE
: Authentication by this module must be successful, or the overall login process will fail. If authentication fails for this module, the LoginContext does not try any further login modules.

SUFFICIENT
: Authentication by this module is not required, and the overall login process can still succeed if all REQUIRED and REQUISITE modules successfully authenticate the user. However, if authentication by this module does succeed, the LoginContext does not try any further login modules, but instead returns immediately.

OPTIONAL
: Authentication by this module is not required. Whether or not it succeeds, the LoginContext continues to with any other modules on the list.

```
public static class AppConfigurationEntry.LoginModuleControlFlag {
// No Constructor
// Public Constants
   public static final AppConfigurationEntry.LoginModuleControlFlag OPTIONAL;
   public static final AppConfigurationEntry.LoginModuleControlFlag REQUIRED;
   public static final AppConfigurationEntry.LoginModuleControlFlag REQUISITE;
   public static final AppConfigurationEntry.LoginModuleControlFlag SUFFICIENT;
// Public Methods Overriding Object
   public String toString();
}
```

Passed To AppConfigurationEntry.AppConfigurationEntry()

Returned By AppConfigurationEntry.getControlFlag()

Configuration Java 1.4

javax.security.auth.login

This abstract class is a representation of the system and user login configuration files. The static getConfiguration() method returns the global Configuration object, and the static setConfiguration() allows that global object to be replaced with some other implementation. The instance method refresh() causes a Configuration to re-read the underlying configuration files. getAppConfigurationEntry() is the key method: it returns an array of AppConfigurationEntry objects that represent the set of login modules to be used for applications with the specified name. LoginContext uses this class to determine which login modules to use to authenticate a user of the named application. Application programmers do not typically need to use this class themselves. See the documentation for your Java implementation for the syntax of the underlying login configuration files.

```
public abstract class Configuration {
// Protected Constructors
   protected Configuration();
// Public Class Methods
   public static Configuration getConfiguration();                    synchronized
   public static void setConfiguration(Configuration configuration);
// Public Instance Methods
   public abstract AppConfigurationEntry[] getAppConfigurationEntry(String name);
   public abstract void refresh();
}
```

Passed To LoginContext.LoginContext()

CredentialException Java 5.0

javax.security.auth.login serializable checked

An exception of this type indicates a problem with the credential (e.g., the password) presented during the login attempt. Subclasses provide more detail.

Object — Throwable — Exception — GeneralSecurityException — LoginException — CredentialException
Throwable ⋯ Serializable

```
public class CredentialException extends LoginException {
// Public Constructors
   public CredentialException();
   public CredentialException(String msg);
}
```

Subclasses CredentialExpiredException, CredentialNotFoundException

CredentialExpiredException — Java 1.4

javax.security.auth.login — serializable checked

Signals that a login failed because a credential (such as a password) has expired and is no longer valid. Prior to Java 5.0, this is a direct subclass of LoginException.

Object — Throwable — Exception — GeneralSecurityException — LoginException — CredentialException — CredentialExpiredException
Serializable

```
public class CredentialExpiredException extends CredentialException {
// Public Constructors
   public CredentialExpiredException();
   public CredentialExpiredException(String msg);
}
```

CredentialNotFoundException — Java 5.0

javax.security.auth.login — serializable checked

An exception of this type indicates that a credential (such as a Kerberos ticket) necessary for login could not be found. This is not the same as presenting an invalid credential, which results in a FailedLoginException.

Throwable — Exception — GeneralSecurityException — LoginException — CredentialException — CredentialNotFoundException
Serializable

```
public class CredentialNotFoundException extends CredentialException {
// Public Constructors
   public CredentialNotFoundException();
   public CredentialNotFoundException(String msg);
}
```

FailedLoginException — Java 1.4

javax.security.auth.login — serializable checked

Signals that login failed. Typically this is because an incorrect username, password, or other information was presented. Login modules that throw this exception may provide human-readable details through the getMessage() method.

Object — Throwable — Exception — GeneralSecurityException — LoginException — FailedLoginException
Serializable

```
public class FailedLoginException extends LoginException {
// Public Constructors
   public FailedLoginException();
   public FailedLoginException(String msg);
}
```

LoginContext **Java 1.4**

javax.security.auth.login

This is one of the most important classes in the JAAS API for application programmers: it defines the login() method (and the corresponding logout() method) that allows an application to authenticate a user. Create a LoginContext object using one of the public constructors. The constructor expects to be passed the name of the application, and, optionally, the javax.security.auth.Subject that is to be authenticated and a javax.security.auth.callback.CallbackHandler that is to be used for communication between the underlying login module (or modules) and the user. If no Subject is specified, then the LoginContext will instantiate a new one to represent the authenticated user. If a Subject is supplied, then the LoginContext adds new entries to its sets of principals and credentials. If no CallbackHandler is specified, then the LoginContext attempts to instantiate one using the class name specified by the auth.login.defaultCallbackHandler property in the system's security properties file.

Once a LoginContext is successfully created, you can authenticate a user simply by calling the login() method, and then calling getSubject() to obtain the Subject object that represents the authenticated user. When this Subject is no longer required, you can log them out by calling the logout() method.

```
public class LoginContext {
// Public Constructors
   public LoginContext(String name) throws LoginException;
   public LoginContext(String name, javax.security.auth.Subject subject) throws LoginException;
   public LoginContext(String name, javax.security.auth.callback.CallbackHandler callbackHandler) throws LoginException;
   public LoginContext(String name, javax.security.auth.Subject subject,
                  javax.security.auth.callback.CallbackHandler callbackHandler) throws LoginException;
5.0 public LoginContext(String name, javax.security.auth.Subject subject,
                  javax.security.auth.callback.CallbackHandler callbackHandler, Configuration config)
      throws LoginException;
// Public Instance Methods
   public javax.security.auth.Subject getSubject();
   public void login() throws LoginException;
   public void logout() throws LoginException;
}
```

LoginException **Java 1.4**

javax.security.auth.login — serializable checked

Signals that something went wrong while creating a LoginContext or during the login or logout process. The subclasses of this class represent more specific exception types.

Object — Throwable — Exception — GeneralSecurityException — LoginException
Serializable

```
public class LoginException extends java.security.GeneralSecurityException {
// Public Constructors
   public LoginException();
   public LoginException(String msg);
}
```

Subclasses AccountException, CredentialException, FailedLoginException

Thrown By java.security.AuthProvider.{login(), logout()}, LoginContext.{login(), LoginContext(), logout()}, javax.security.auth.spi.LoginModule.{abort(), commit(), login(), logout()}

Package javax.security.auth.spi — Java 1.4

This package defines the "service provider interface" for JAAS: it defines a single LoginModule interface that must be implemented by developers of login modules.

Interfaces

```
public interface LoginModule;
```

LoginModule — Java 1.4

javax.security.auth.spi

Developers of login modules to be used with the JAAS authentication API must implement this interface. Because this interface is not typically used by application developers, its methods are not documented here.

```
public interface LoginModule {
// Public Instance Methods
    boolean abort() throws javax.security.auth.login.LoginException;
    boolean commit() throws javax.security.auth.login.LoginException;
    void initialize(javax.security.auth.Subject subject, javax.security.auth.callback.CallbackHandler callbackHandler,
                java.util.Map<String,?> sharedState, java.util.Map<String,?> options);
    boolean login() throws javax.security.auth.login.LoginException;
    boolean logout() throws javax.security.auth.login.LoginException;
}
```

Package javax.security.auth.x500 — Java 1.4

This package defines classes for use with authentication schemes for on X.500 principals. Instances of these classes are designed to be stored in the principals and private credentials sets of Subject objects, and although application programmers may occasionally find the X500Principal class useful, they are primarily of interest to system-level programmers writing X.500-based javax.security.auth.spi.LoginModule implementations See also the java.security.cert package which contains a class representing an X.509 certificate.

Classes

```
public final class X500Principal implements java.security.Principal, Serializable;
public final class X500PrivateCredential implements javax.security.auth.Destroyable;
```

X500Principal — Java 1.4

javax.security.auth.x500 — serializable

This class implements the java.security.Principal interface for entities represented by X.500 distinguished names (such as "CN=David,O=davidflanagan.com,C=US"). The constructor methods can accept the distinguished name in string form or in binary encoded form. getName() returns the name in string form, using the format defined by one of the three consant values. The no-argument version of getName() (the one defined by the Principal interface) returns the distinguished name formatted as specified by RFC 2253. Finally, getEncoded() returns a binary-encoded form of the name.

Object — X500Principal
Principal, Serializable

```
public final class X500Principal implements java.security.Principal, Serializable {
// Public Constructors
   public X500Principal(java.io.InputStream is);
   public X500Principal(String name);
   public X500Principal(byte[ ] name);
// Public Constants
   public static final String CANONICAL;                                    ="CANONICAL"
   public static final String RFC1779;                                        ="RFC1779"
   public static final String RFC2253;                                        ="RFC2253"
// Public Instance Methods
   public byte[ ] getEncoded( );
   public String getName(String format);
// Methods Implementing Principal
   public boolean equals(Object o);
   public String getName( );
   public int hashCode( );
   public String toString( );
}
```

Passed To java.security.cert.TrustAnchor.TrustAnchor( ), java.security.cert.X509CertSelector.{setIssuer( ), setSubject( )}, java.security.cert.X509CRLSelector.addIssuer( )

Returned By java.security.cert.TrustAnchor.getCA( ), java.security.cert.X509Certificate.{getIssuerX500Principal( ), getSubjectX500Principal( )}, java.security.cert.X509CertSelector.{getIssuer( ), getSubject( )}, java.security.cert.X509CRL.getIssuerX500Principal( ), java.security.cert.X509CRLEntry.getCertificateIssuer( )

X500PrivateCredential — Java 1.4

javax.security.auth.x500

This class associates a java.security.cert.X509Certificate with a java.security.PrivateKey for that certificate, and, optionally, the keystore alias used to retrieve the certificate and key from a java.security.KeyStore. The class defines methods to retreive the certificate, key, and alias, and also implements the methods of the javax.security.cert.Destroyable interface.

Object — X500PrivateCredential — Destroyable

```
public final class X500PrivateCredential implements javax.security.auth.Destroyable {
// Public Constructors
   public X500PrivateCredential(java.security.cert.X509Certificate cert, java.security.PrivateKey key);
   public X500PrivateCredential(java.security.cert.X509Certificate cert, java.security.PrivateKey key, String alias);
// Public Instance Methods
   public String getAlias( );
   public java.security.cert.X509Certificate getCertificate( );
   public java.security.PrivateKey getPrivateKey( );
// Methods Implementing Destroyable
   public void destroy( );
   public boolean isDestroyed( );
}
```

20

javax.xml and Subpackages

This chapter documents javax.xml and its subpackages:

java.xml
: This simple package simply defines constants for use by its subpackages. Added in Java 5.0.

javax.xml.datatype
: This package contains Java types corresponding to types defined by XML standards such as W3C XML Schema, XQuery, and XPath.

javax.xml.namespace
: This package defines types for working with XML namespaces.

javax.xml.parsers
: This package defines parser classes that serve as a wrapper around underlying DOM and SAX XML parsers, and also defines factory classes that are used to obtain instances of those parser classes.

javax.xml.transform
: This package defines classes and interfaces for transforming the representation and content of an XML document with XSLT. It defines Source and Result interfaces to represent a source document and a result document. subpackages provide implementations of these classes that represent documents in different ways.

javax.xml.transform.dom
: This package implements the Source and Result interfaces that represent documents as DOM document trees.

javax.xml.transform.sax
: This package implements the Source and Result interfaces to represent documents as sequences of SAX parser events. It also defines other SAX-related transformation classes.

javax.xml.transform.stream
: This package implements the Source and Result interfaces that represent documents as streams of text.

javax.xml.validation
: This package contains classes for validating XML documents against a schema.

javax.xml.xpath
: This package defines types for the evaluation of XPath expressions in the context of an XML document.

Package javax.xml — Java 5.0

This package has many important subpackages but defines only a single class XMLConstants, which, as its name implies, provides symbolic names for constants defined by various XML specifications.

Classes

```
public final class XMLConstants;
```

XMLConstants — Java 5.0

javax.xml

This class is a repository for constants defined by various XML standards. Most are URIs that identify XML namespaces.

```
public final class XMLConstants {
// No Constructor
// Public Constants
   public static final String DEFAULT_NS_PREFIX;                                   =""
   public static final String FEATURE_SECURE_PROCESSING; ="http://javax.xml.XMLConstants/feature/secure-processing"
   public static final String NULL_NS_URI;                                         =""
   public static final String RELAXNG_NS_URI;                  ="http://relaxng.org/ns/structure/1.0"
   public static final String W3C_XML_SCHEMA_INSTANCE_NS_URI; ="http://www.w3.org/2001/XMLSchema-instance"
   public static final String W3C_XML_SCHEMA_NS_URI;          ="http://www.w3.org/2001/XMLSchema"
   public static final String W3C_XPATH_DATATYPE_NS_URI;      ="http://www.w3.org/2003/11/xpath-datatypes"
   public static final String XML_DTD_NS_URI;                  ="http://www.w3.org/TR/REC-xml"
   public static final String XML_NS_PREFIX;                                       ="xml"
   public static final String XML_NS_URI;                ="http://www.w3.org/XML/1998/namespace"
   public static final String XMLNS_ATTRIBUTE;                                     ="xmlns"
   public static final String XMLNS_ATTRIBUTE_NS_URI;          ="http://www.w3.org/2000/xmlns/"
}
```

Package javax.xml.datatype — Java 5.0

This package defines Java data types that correspond to certain time, date, and duration data types required by the W3C XML Schema, XQuery, and XPath standards. This package is of primary interest to those implementing schema validators and XPath evaluators and should not be required by applications that use schemas or XPath expressions.

javax.xml.datatype.DatatypeConfigurationException

Classes

```
public final class DatatypeConstants;
public static final class DatatypeConstants.Field;
public abstract class DatatypeFactory;
public abstract class Duration;
public abstract class XMLGregorianCalendar implements Cloneable;
```

Exceptions

```
public class DatatypeConfigurationException extends Exception;
```

DatatypeConfigurationException

Java 5.0

javax.xml.datatype

serializable checked

An exception of this type is thrown by DatatypeFactory.newInstance() to indicate a factory configuration error.

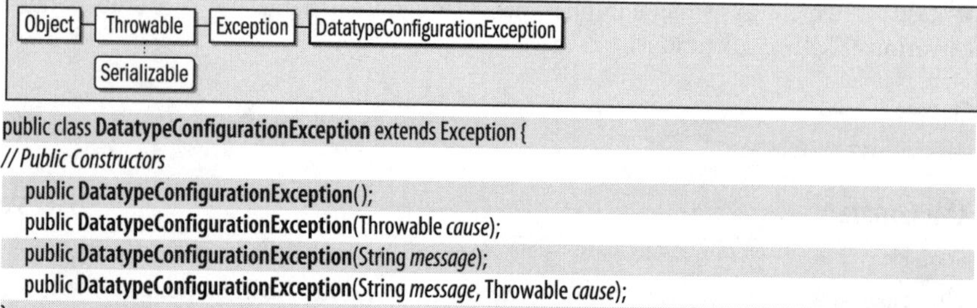


```
public class DatatypeConfigurationException extends Exception {
// Public Constructors
   public DatatypeConfigurationException();
   public DatatypeConfigurationException(Throwable cause);
   public DatatypeConfigurationException(String message);
   public DatatypeConfigurationException(String message, Throwable cause);
}
```

Thrown By DatatypeFactory.newInstance()

DatatypeConstants

Java 5.0

javax.xml.datatype

This class defines constants used in this package. Most of the constants are int values, but some are qualified names and some are instances of the DatatypeConstants.Field type.

```
public final class DatatypeConstants {
// No Constructor
// Public Constants
   public static final int APRIL;                                              =4
   public static final int AUGUST;                                             =8
   public static final javax.xml.namespace.QName DATE;
   public static final javax.xml.namespace.QName DATETIME;
   public static final DatatypeConstants.Field DAYS;
   public static final int DECEMBER;                                          =12
   public static final javax.xml.namespace.QName DURATION;
   public static final javax.xml.namespace.QName DURATION_DAYTIME;
   public static final javax.xml.namespace.QName DURATION_YEARMONTH;
   public static final int EQUAL;                                              =0
   public static final int FEBRUARY;                                           =2
   public static final int FIELD_UNDEFINED;                           =-2147483648
   public static final javax.xml.namespace.QName GDAY;
   public static final javax.xml.namespace.QName GMONTH;
   public static final javax.xml.namespace.QName GMONTHDAY;
   public static final int GREATER;                                            =1
```

```
public static final javax.xml.namespace.QName GYEAR;
public static final javax.xml.namespace.QName GYEARMONTH;
public static final DatatypeConstants.Field HOURS;
public static final int INDETERMINATE;                                    =2
public static final int JANUARY;                                          =1
public static final int JULY;                                             =7
public static final int JUNE;                                             =6
public static final int LESSER;                                           =-1
public static final int MARCH;                                            =3
public static final int MAX_TIMEZONE_OFFSET;                              =-840
public static final int MAY;                                              =5
public static final int MIN_TIMEZONE_OFFSET;                              =840
public static final DatatypeConstants.Field MINUTES;
public static final DatatypeConstants.Field MONTHS;
public static final int NOVEMBER;                                         =11
public static final int OCTOBER;                                          =10
public static final DatatypeConstants.Field SECONDS;
public static final int SEPTEMBER;                                        =9
public static final javax.xml.namespace.QName TIME;
public static final DatatypeConstants.Field YEARS;
// Nested Types
public static final class Field;
}
```

DatatypeConstants.Field — Java 5.0

javax.xml.datatype

This class defines a typesafe enumeration for some of the constants in DatatypeConstants. Note that it is a class, not a Java 5.0 enum type.

```
public static final class DatatypeConstants.Field {
// No Constructor
// Public Instance Methods
   public int getId();
// Public Methods Overriding Object
   public String toString();
}
```

Passed To Duration.{getField(), isSet()}

Type Of DatatypeConstants.{DAYS, HOURS, MINUTES, MONTHS, SECONDS, YEARS}

DatatypeFactory — Java 5.0

javax.xml.datatype

This class defines factory methods for creating Duration and XMLGregorianCalendar objects.

```
public abstract class DatatypeFactory {
// Protected Constructors
   protected DatatypeFactory();
// Public Constants
   public static final String DATATYPEFACTORY_IMPLEMENTATION_CLASS;
                  ="com.sun.org.apache.xerces.internal.jaxp.datatype.DatatypeFactoryImpl"
   public static final String DATATYPEFACTORY_PROPERTY;   ="javax.xml.datatype.DatatypeFactory"
// Public Class Methods
   public static DatatypeFactory newInstance() throws DatatypeConfigurationException;
```

```
// Public Instance Methods
    public abstract Duration newDuration(String lexicalRepresentation);
    public abstract Duration newDuration(long durationInMilliSeconds);
    public Duration newDuration(boolean isPositive, int years, int months, int days, int hours, int minutes, int seconds);
    public abstract Duration newDuration(boolean isPositive, java.math.BigInteger years, java.math.BigInteger months,
                                         java.math.BigInteger days, java.math.BigInteger hours,
                                         java.math.BigInteger minutes, java.math.BigDecimal seconds);
    public Duration newDurationDayTime(long durationInMilliseconds);
    public Duration newDurationDayTime(String lexicalRepresentation);
    public Duration newDurationDayTime(boolean isPositive, int day, int hour, int minute, int second);
    public Duration newDurationDayTime(boolean isPositive, java.math.BigInteger day, java.math.BigInteger hour,
                                       java.math.BigInteger minute, java.math.BigInteger second);
    public Duration newDurationYearMonth(long durationInMilliseconds);
    public Duration newDurationYearMonth(String lexicalRepresentation);
    public Duration newDurationYearMonth(boolean isPositive, int year, int month);
    public Duration newDurationYearMonth(boolean isPositive, java.math.BigInteger year, java.math.BigInteger month);
    public abstract XMLGregorianCalendar newXMLGregorianCalendar();
    public abstract XMLGregorianCalendar newXMLGregorianCalendar(java.util.GregorianCalendar cal);
    public abstract XMLGregorianCalendar newXMLGregorianCalendar(String lexicalRepresentation);
    public XMLGregorianCalendar newXMLGregorianCalendar(int year, int month, int day, int hour, int minute, int second,
                                                        int millisecond, int timezone);
    public abstract XMLGregorianCalendar newXMLGregorianCalendar(java.math.BigInteger year, int month, int day,
                                                                 int hour, int minute, int second,
                                                                 java.math.BigDecimal fractionalSecond,
                                                                 int timezone);
    public XMLGregorianCalendar newXMLGregorianCalendarDate(int year, int month, int day, int timezone);
    public XMLGregorianCalendar newXMLGregorianCalendarTime(int hours, int minutes, int seconds, int timezone);
    public XMLGregorianCalendar newXMLGregorianCalendarTime(int hours, int minutes, int seconds, int milliseconds,
                                                            int timezone);
    public XMLGregorianCalendar newXMLGregorianCalendarTime(int hours, int minutes, int seconds,
                                                            java.math.BigDecimal fractionalSecond, int timezone);
}
```

Duration — Java 5.0

javax.xml.datatype

An instance of this class represents a length of time. Create **Duration** objects with **DatatypeFactory**.

```
public abstract class Duration {
// Public Constructors
    public Duration();
// Public Instance Methods
    public abstract Duration add(Duration rhs);
    public abstract void addTo(java.util.Calendar calendar);
    public void addTo(java.util.Date date);
    public abstract int compare(Duration duration);
    public int getDays();
    public abstract Number getField(DatatypeConstants.Field field);
    public int getHours();
    public int getMinutes();
    public int getMonths();
    public int getSeconds();
    public abstract int getSign();
    public long getTimeInMillis(java.util.Date startInstant);
```

```
    public long getTimeInMillis(java.util.Calendar startInstant);
    public javax.xml.namespace.QName getXMLSchemaType();
    public int getYears();
    public boolean isLongerThan(Duration duration);
    public abstract boolean isSet(DatatypeConstants.Field field);
    public boolean isShorterThan(Duration duration);
    public Duration multiply(int factor);
    public abstract Duration multiply(java.math.BigDecimal factor);
    public abstract Duration negate();
    public abstract Duration normalizeWith(java.util.Calendar startTimeInstant);
    public Duration subtract(Duration rhs);
// Public Methods Overriding Object
    public boolean equals(Object duration);
    public abstract int hashCode();
    public String toString();
}
```

Passed To XMLGregorianCalendar.add()

Returned By DatatypeFactory.{newDuration(), newDurationDayTime(), newDurationYearMonth()}

XMLGregorianCalendar — Java 5.0

javax.xml.datatype — cloneable

Instances of this class represent a date or time. Create XMLGregorianCalendar objects with a DatatypeFactory.

Object → XMLGregorianCalendar ··· Cloneable

```
public abstract class XMLGregorianCalendar implements Cloneable {
// Public Constructors
    public XMLGregorianCalendar();
// Public Instance Methods
    public abstract void add(Duration duration);
    public abstract void clear();
    public abstract int compare(XMLGregorianCalendar xmlGregorianCalendar);
    public abstract int getDay();
    public abstract java.math.BigInteger getEon();
    public abstract java.math.BigInteger getEonAndYear();
    public abstract java.math.BigDecimal getFractionalSecond();
    public abstract int getHour();
    public int getMillisecond();
    public abstract int getMinute();
    public abstract int getMonth();
    public abstract int getSecond();
    public abstract int getTimezone();
    public abstract java.util.TimeZone getTimeZone(int defaultZoneoffset);
    public abstract javax.xml.namespace.QName getXMLSchemaType();
    public abstract int getYear();
    public abstract boolean isValid();
    public abstract XMLGregorianCalendar normalize();
    public abstract void reset();
    public abstract void setDay(int day);
    public abstract void setFractionalSecond(java.math.BigDecimal fractional);
    public abstract void setHour(int hour);
```

```
  public abstract void setMillisecond(int millisecond);
  public abstract void setMinute(int minute);
  public abstract void setMonth(int month);
  public abstract void setSecond(int second);
  public void setTime(int hour, int minute, int second);
  public void setTime(int hour, int minute, int second, int millisecond);
  public void setTime(int hour, int minute, int second, java.math.BigDecimal fractional);
  public abstract void setTimezone(int offset);
  public abstract void setYear(int year);
  public abstract void setYear(java.math.BigInteger year);
  public abstract java.util.GregorianCalendar toGregorianCalendar();
  public abstract java.util.GregorianCalendar toGregorianCalendar(java.util.TimeZone timezone, java.util.Locale aLocale,
                                                                  XMLGregorianCalendar defaults);
  public abstract String toXMLFormat();
// Public Methods Overriding Object
  public abstract Object clone();
  public boolean equals(Object obj);
  public int hashCode();
  public String toString();
}
```

Returned By DatatypeFactory.{newXMLGregorianCalendar(), newXMLGregorianCalendarDate(), newXMLGregorianCalendarTime()}

Package javax.xml.namespace Java 5.0

This small package defines types for working with XML namespaces. NamespaceContext represents a mapping between namespace URIs and namespace prefixes. QName represents a qualified name consisting of a local part and a namespace.

Interfaces

public interface **NamespaceContext**;

Classes

public class **QName** implements Serializable;

NamespaceContext Java 5.0

javax.xml.namespace

This interface represents a mapping between namespace URIs and the local prefixes that are bound to them. Use getNamepaceURI() to obtain the URI that a prefix is bound to. Use getPrefix() to do the reverse. More than one prefix can be bound to the same URI, and the getPrefixes() method returns an Iterator that you can use to loop through all prefixes that have been associated with a given URI.

```
public interface NamespaceContext {
// Public Instance Methods
  String getNamespaceURI(String prefix);
  String getPrefix(String namespaceURI);
  java.util.Iterator getPrefixes(String namespaceURI);
}
```

Passed To javax.xml.xpath.XPath.setNamespaceContext()

Returned By javax.xml.xpath.XPath.getNamespaceContext()

QName — Java 5.0

javax.xml.namespace — serializable

A QName represents an XML "qualified name," such as an XML element name that has both a local name and a namespace. getLocalPart() returns the unqualified local part of the name. getNamespaceURI() returns the canonical URI that formally identifies the namespace. getPrefix() returns the locally declared namespace prefix. Note that a QName does not always have a prefix and that the prefix, if it exists, is ignored for the purposes of the equals(), hashCode(), and toString() methods. The static valueOf() method parses a QName from a string in the format of toString():

{namespaceURI}localPart

Object — QName ··· Serializable

```
public class QName implements Serializable {
// Public Constructors
   public QName(String localPart);
   public QName(String namespaceURI, String localPart);
   public QName(String namespaceURI, String localPart, String prefix);
// Public Class Methods
   public static QName valueOf(String qNameAsString);
// Public Instance Methods
   public String getLocalPart();
   public String getNamespaceURI();
   public String getPrefix();
// Public Methods Overriding Object
   public final boolean equals(Object objectToTest);
   public final int hashCode();
   public String toString();
}
```

Passed To javax.xml.xpath.XPath.evaluate(), javax.xml.xpath.XPathExpression.evaluate(), javax.xml.xpath.XPathFunctionResolver.resolveFunction(), javax.xml.xpath.XPathVariableResolver.resolveVariable()

Returned By javax.xml.datatype.Duration.getXMLSchemaType(), javax.xml.datatype.XMLGregorianCalendar.getXMLSchemaType()

Type Of Too many fields to list.

Package javax.xml.parsers — Java 1.4

This package defines classes that represent XML parsers and factory classes for obtaining instances of those parser classes. DocumentBuilder is a DOM-based XML parser created from a DocumentBuilderFactory. SAXParser is a SAX-based XML parser created from a SAXParserFactory. In Java 5.0, you can configure either of the factory classes to create parsers that validate against a W3C XML Schema specified with a javax.xml.validation.Schema object. Note that this package does not include parser implementations. Instead, it is an implementation-independent layer that supports "pluggable" XML parsers. Furthermore, this package does not define a DOM or SAX API for working with XML documents. The DOM API is defined in org.w3c.dom, and the SAX API is defined in org.xml.sax and its subpackages.

Classes

```
public abstract class DocumentBuilder;
```

```
public abstract class DocumentBuilderFactory;
public abstract class SAXParser;
public abstract class SAXParserFactory;
```

Exceptions

```
public class ParserConfigurationException extends Exception;
```

Errors

```
public class FactoryConfigurationError extends Error;
```

DocumentBuilder **Java 1.4**

javax.xml.parsers

This class defines a high-level API to an underlying DOM parser implementation. Obtain a **DocumentBuilder** from a **DocumentBuilderFactory**. After obtaining a **DocumentBuilder**, you can provide **org.xml.sax.ErrorHandler** and **org.xml.sax.EntityResolver** objects, if desired. (These classes are defined by the SAX API but are useful for DOM parsers as well.) You may also want to call isNamespaceAware(), isXIncludeAware() and isValidating() to ensure that the parser is configured with the features your application requires. Finally, use one of the parse() methods to read an XML document from a stream, file, URL, or org.xml.sax.InputSource object, parse that document, and convert it into a org.w3c.dom.Document tree. Note that DocumentBuilder objects are not typically threadsafe. In Java 5.0, you can call reset() to restore the parser to its original state for reuse. Another Java 5.0 method, getSchema() returns the Schema object, if any, registered with the DocumentBuilderFactory that created this parser.

If you want to obtain an empty Document object (so that you can build the document tree from scratch, for example) call newDocument(). Or use getDOMImplementation() to obtain a the org.w3c.dom.DOMImplementation object of the underlying DOM implementation from which you can also create an empty Document.

See the org.w3c.dom package for information on what you can do with a Document object once you have used a DocumentBuilder to create it.

```
public abstract class DocumentBuilder {
// Protected Constructors
   protected DocumentBuilder();
// Public Instance Methods
   public abstract org.w3c.dom.DOMImplementation getDOMImplementation();
5.0 public javax.xml.validation.Schema getSchema();
   public abstract boolean isNamespaceAware();
   public abstract boolean isValidating();
5.0 public boolean isXIncludeAware();
   public abstract org.w3c.dom.Document newDocument();
   public org.w3c.dom.Document parse(java.io.InputStream is) throws org.xml.sax.SAXException, java.io.IOException;
   public org.w3c.dom.Document parse(String uri) throws org.xml.sax.SAXException, java.io.IOException;
   public abstract org.w3c.dom.Document parse(org.xml.sax.InputSource is)
       throws org.xml.sax.SAXException, java.io.IOException;
   public org.w3c.dom.Document parse(java.io.File f) throws org.xml.sax.SAXException, java.io.IOException;
   public org.w3c.dom.Document parse(java.io.InputStream is, String systemId)
       throws org.xml.sax.SAXException, java.io.IOException;
5.0 public void reset();
   public abstract void setEntityResolver(org.xml.sax.EntityResolver er);
   public abstract void setErrorHandler(org.xml.sax.ErrorHandler eh);
}
```

Returned By DocumentBuilderFactory.newDocumentBuilder()

DocumentBuilderFactory Java 1.4

javax.xml.parsers

A DocumentBuilderFactory is a factory class for creating DocumentBuilder objects. You can obtain a DocumentBuilderFactory by instantiating an implementation-specific subclass provided by a parser vendor, but it is much more common to simply call newInstance() to obtain an instance of the factory that has been configured as the default for the system. Once you have obtained a factory object, you can use the various set methods to configure the properties of the DocumentBuilder objects it will create. These methods allow you to specify whether the parsers created by the factory will:

- coalesce CDATA sections with adjacent text nodes;
- expand entity references or leave them unexpanded in the document tree;
- omit XML comments from the document tree;
- omit ignorable whitespace from the document tree;
- handle XML namespaces correctly; and
- validate XML documents against a DTD or other schema.

In Java 5.0, you can use setSchema() to specify the javax.xml.vaidation.Schema object against which parsers should validate their documents. And you can use setXIncludeAware() to indicate that parsers should process XInclude markup.

In addition to the various implementation-independent set methods, you can also use setAttribute() pass an implementation-dependent named attribute to the underlying parser implementation. Once you have configured the factory object as desired, simply call newDocumentBuilder() to create a DocumentBuilder object with the all of the attributes you have specified. Note that DocumentBuilderFactory objects are not typically threadsafe.

The javax.xml.parsers package allows parser implementations to be "plugged in." This pluggability is provided by the getInstance() method, which follows the following steps to determine which DocumentBuilderFactory implementation to use:

- If the javax.xml.parsers.DocumentBuilderFactory system property is defined, then the class specified by that property is used.
- Otherwise, if the *jre/lib/jaxp.properties* file exists in the Java distribution and contains a definition for the javax.xml.parsers.DocumentBuilderFactory property, then the class specified by that property is used.
- Otherwise, if any of the JAR files on the classpath includes a file named *META-INF/services/javax.xml.parsers.DocumentBuilderFactory*, then the class named in that file will be used.
- Otherwise, a default implementation provided by the Java implementation will be used.

```
public abstract class DocumentBuilderFactory {
// Protected Constructors
   protected DocumentBuilderFactory();
// Public Class Methods
   public static DocumentBuilderFactory newInstance();
// Public Instance Methods
   public abstract Object getAttribute(String name) throws IllegalArgumentException;
5.0 public abstract boolean getFeature(String name) throws ParserConfigurationException;
5.0 public javax.xml.validation.Schema getSchema();
   public boolean isCoalescing();
   public boolean isExpandEntityReferences();
```

JAXP

```
  public boolean isIgnoringComments();
  public boolean isIgnoringElementContentWhitespace();
  public boolean isNamespaceAware();
  public boolean isValidating();
5.0 public boolean isXIncludeAware();
  public abstract DocumentBuilder newDocumentBuilder() throws ParserConfigurationException;
  public abstract void setAttribute(String name, Object value) throws IllegalArgumentException;
  public void setCoalescing(boolean coalescing);
  public void setExpandEntityReferences(boolean expandEntityRef);
5.0 public abstract void setFeature(String name, boolean value) throws ParserConfigurationException;
  public void setIgnoringComments(boolean ignoreComments);
  public void setIgnoringElementContentWhitespace(boolean whitespace);
  public void setNamespaceAware(boolean awareness);
5.0 public void setSchema(javax.xml.validation.Schema schema);
  public void setValidating(boolean validating);
5.0 public void setXIncludeAware(boolean state);
}
```

FactoryConfigurationError — Java 1.4

javax.xml.parsers — serializable error

Signals a nonrecoverable problem instantiating a parser factory. This usually means that a pluggable parser implementation has been incorrectly plugged in and the getInstance() method cannot locate the specified factory implementation class.

Object — Throwable — Error — FactoryConfigurationError
Serializable

```
public class FactoryConfigurationError extends Error {
// Public Constructors
  public FactoryConfigurationError();
  public FactoryConfigurationError(Exception e);
  public FactoryConfigurationError(String msg);
  public FactoryConfigurationError(Exception e, String msg);
// Public Instance Methods
  public Exception getException();                                default:null
// Public Methods Overriding Throwable
  public String getMessage();                                     default:null
}
```

ParserConfigurationException — Java 1.4

javax.xml.parsers — serializable checked

Signals a parser configuration problem that prevents a parser factory object from creating a parser object.

Object — Throwable — Exception — ParserConfigurationException
Serializable

```
public class ParserConfigurationException extends Exception {
// Public Constructors
  public ParserConfigurationException();
  public ParserConfigurationException(String msg);
}
```

Thrown By DocumentBuilderFactory.{getFeature(), newDocumentBuilder(), setFeature()}, SAXParserFactory.{getFeature(), newSAXParser(), setFeature()}

SAXParser Java 1.4

javax.xml.parsers

The SAXParser class is a wrapper around an org.xml.sax.XMLReader class and is used to parse XML documents using the SAX version 2 API. Obtain a SAXParser from a SAXParserFactory. Call setProperty() if desired to set a property on the underlying parser. (See *www.saxproject.org* for a description of standard SAX properties and their values. Finally, call one of the parse() methods to parse an XML document from a stream, file, URL, or org.xml.sax.InputSource. The SAX API is an event-driven one. A SAX parser does not build a document tree to describe an XML document like a DOM parser does. Instead, it describes the XML document to your application by invoking methods on an object the application provides. This is the purpose of the org.xml.sax.helpers.DefaultHandler object that is passed to the parse() method: you subclass this class to implement the methods you care about, and the parser will invoke those methods at appropriate times. For example, when the parser encounters an XML tag in a document, it parses the tag, and calls the startElement() method to tell you about it. And when it finds a run of plain text, it passes that text to the characters() method. In Java 5.0, the reset() method restores a SAXParser to its original state so that it can be reused.

Instead of using one of the parse() methods of this class, you can also call getXMLReader() to obtain the underlying XMLReader object and work with it directly to parse the desired document. SAXParser objects are not typically threadsafe.

Note that the getParser() method as well as the parse() methods that take an org.xml.sax.HandlerBase object are based on the SAX version 1 API, and should be avoided.

JAXP

```
public abstract class SAXParser {
// Protected Constructors
   protected SAXParser();
// Public Instance Methods
   public abstract org.xml.sax.Parser getParser() throws org.xml.sax.SAXException;
   public abstract Object getProperty(String name)
       throws org.xml.sax.SAXNotRecognizedException, org.xml.sax.SAXNotSupportedException;
5.0 public javax.xml.validation.Schema getSchema();
   public abstract org.xml.sax.XMLReader getXMLReader() throws org.xml.sax.SAXException;
   public abstract boolean isNamespaceAware();
   public abstract boolean isValidating();
5.0 public boolean isXIncludeAware();
   public void parse(org.xml.sax.InputSource is, org.xml.sax.HandlerBase hb)
       throws org.xml.sax.SAXException, java.io.IOException;
   public void parse(org.xml.sax.InputSource is, org.xml.sax.helpers.DefaultHandler dh)
       throws org.xml.sax.SAXException, java.io.IOException;
   public void parse(java.io.File f, org.xml.sax.helpers.DefaultHandler dh)
       throws org.xml.sax.SAXException, java.io.IOException;
   public void parse(java.io.InputStream is, org.xml.sax.helpers.DefaultHandler dh)
       throws org.xml.sax.SAXException, java.io.IOException;
   public void parse(java.io.InputStream is, org.xml.sax.HandlerBase hb)
       throws org.xml.sax.SAXException, java.io.IOException;
   public void parse(String uri, org.xml.sax.HandlerBase hb) throws org.xml.sax.SAXException, java.io.IOException;
   public void parse(String uri, org.xml.sax.helpers.DefaultHandler dh)
       throws org.xml.sax.SAXException, java.io.IOException;
   public void parse(java.io.File f, org.xml.sax.HandlerBase hb) throws org.xml.sax.SAXException, java.io.IOException;
```

```
    public void parse(java.io.InputStream is, org.xml.sax.HandlerBase hb, String systemId)
        throws org.xml.sax.SAXException, java.io.IOException;
    public void parse(java.io.InputStream is, org.xml.sax.helpers.DefaultHandler dh, String systemId)
        throws org.xml.sax.SAXException, java.io.IOException;
5.0 public void reset();
    public abstract void setProperty(String name, Object value)
        throws org.xml.sax.SAXNotRecognizedException, org.xml.sax.SAXNotSupportedException;
}
```

Returned By SAXParserFactory.newSAXParser()

SAXParserFactory **Java 1.4**

javax.xml.parsers

This class is a factory for SAXParser objects. Obtain a SAXParserFactory by calling the newInstance() method which instantiates the default SAXParserFactory subclass provided with your Java implementation, or instantiates some other SAXParserFactory that has been "plugged in".

Once you have a SAXParserFactory object, you can use setValidating() and setNamespaceAware() to specify whether the parsers it creates will be validating parsers or not and whether they will know how to handle XML namespaces. You may also call setFeature() to set a feature of the underlying parser implementation. See *http://www.saxproject.org* for the names of standard parser features that can be enabled and disabled with this method. In Java 5.0, call setXIncludeAware() to specify that created parsers will recognize XInclude markup. Use setSchema() to specify a W3C XML Schema against which parsers should validate the document.

Once you have created and configured your factory object, simply call newSAXParser() to create a SAXParser object. Note that SAXParserFactory implementations are not typically threadsafe.

The javax.xml.parsers package allows parser implementations to be "plugged in". This pluggability is provided by the getInstance() method, which follows the following steps to determine which SAXBuilderFactory subclass to use:

- If the javax.xml.parsers.SAXParserFactory system property is defined, then the class specified by that property is used.
- Otherwise, if the *jre/lib/jaxp.properties* file exists in the Java distribution and contains a definition for the javax.xml.parsers.SAXParserFactory property, then the class specified by that property is used.
- Otherwise, if any of the JAR files on the classpath includes a file named *META-INF/services/javax.xml.parsers.SAXParserFactory*, then the class named in that file will be used.
- Otherwise, a default implementation provided by the Java platform will be used.

```
public abstract class SAXParserFactory {
// Protected Constructors
    protected SAXParserFactory();
// Public Class Methods
    public static SAXParserFactory newInstance();
// Public Instance Methods
    public abstract boolean getFeature(String name)
        throws ParserConfigurationException, org.xml.sax.SAXNotRecognizedException,
        org.xml.sax.SAXNotSupportedException;
```

```
5.0 public javax.xml.validation.Schema getSchema();
   public boolean isNamespaceAware();
   public boolean isValidating();
5.0 public boolean isXIncludeAware();
   public abstract SAXParser newSAXParser() throws ParserConfigurationException, org.xml.sax.SAXException;
   public abstract void setFeature(String name, boolean value)
       throws ParserConfigurationException, org.xml.sax.SAXNotRecognizedException,
       org.xml.sax.SAXNotSupportedException;
   public void setNamespaceAware(boolean awareness);
5.0 public void setSchema(javax.xml.validation.Schema schema);
   public void setValidating(boolean validating);
5.0 public void setXIncludeAware(boolean state);
}
```


Package javax.xml.transform — Java 1.4

This package defines an high-level implementation-independent API for using an XSLT engine or other document transformation system for transforming XML document content, and also for transforming XML documents from one form (such as a stream of text in a file) to anther form (such as a tree of DOM nodes). The Source interface is a very generic description of a document source. Three concrete implementations that represent documents in text form, as DOM trees, and as sequences of SAX parser events are defined in the three subpackages of this package. The Result interface is a similarly high-level description of what form the source document should be transformed into. The three subpackages define three Result implementations that represent XML documents as streams or files, as DOM trees, and as sequnces of SAX parser events.

The TransformerFactory class represents the document transformation engine. The implementation provides a default factory that represents an XSLT engine. A TransformerFactory can be used to produce Templates objects that represent compiled XSL stylesheets (or other implementation-dependent forms of transformation instructions). Documents are actually transfomed from Soruce to Result with a Transformer object, which is obtained from a Templates object, or directly from a TransformerFactory.

Interfaces

```
public interface ErrorListener;
public interface Result;
public interface Source;
public interface SourceLocator;
public interface Templates;
public interface URIResolver;
```

Classes

```
public class OutputKeys;
public abstract class Transformer;
public abstract class TransformerFactory;
```

Exceptions

```
public class TransformerException extends Exception;
   public class TransformerConfigurationException extends TransformerException;
```

Errors

```
public class TransformerFactoryConfigurationError extends Error;
```

ErrorListener Java 1.4

javax.xml.transform

This interface defines methods that Transformer and TransformerFactory use for reporting warnings, errors, and fatal errors to an application. To use an ErrorListener, an application must implement this interface and pass an implementing object to the setErrorListener() method of Transformer or TransformerFactory. The argument to each method of this interface is a TransformerException object, and the implementation of these methods can throw that exception if it chooses, or it can simply log the warning or error in some way and return. A Transformer or TransformerFactory is not required to continue processing after reporting a nonrecoverable error with an invocation of the fatalError() method.

If you are familiar with the SAX API for parsing XML documents, you'll recognize that this interface is very similar to org.xml.sax.ErrorHandler.

```
public interface ErrorListener {
// Public Instance Methods
   void error(TransformerException exception) throws TransformerException;
   void fatalError(TransformerException exception) throws TransformerException;
   void warning(TransformerException exception) throws TransformerException;
}
```

Passed To Transformer.setErrorListener(), TransformerFactory.setErrorListener()

Returned By Transformer.getErrorListener(), TransformerFactory.getErrorListener()

OutputKeys Java 1.4

javax.xml.transform

This class defines string constants that hold the names of the attributes of an <xsl:output> tag in an XSLT stylesheet. These are also legal key values for the Properties object returned by Templates.getOutputProperties() and passed to Transformer.setOutputProperties().

```
public class OutputKeys {
// No Constructor
// Public Constants
   public static final String CDATA_SECTION_ELEMENTS;          ="cdata-section-elements"
   public static final String DOCTYPE_PUBLIC;                  ="doctype-public"
   public static final String DOCTYPE_SYSTEM;                  ="doctype-system"
   public static final String ENCODING;                        ="encoding"
   public static final String INDENT;                          ="indent"
   public static final String MEDIA_TYPE;                      ="media-type"
   public static final String METHOD;                          ="method"
   public static final String OMIT_XML_DECLARATION;            ="omit-xml-declaration"
   public static final String STANDALONE;                      ="standalone"
   public static final String VERSION;                         ="version"
}
```

Result Java 1.4

javax.xml.transform

This interface represents, in a very general way, the result of an XML transformation. setSystemId() specifies a the system identifier of the result as a URL. This is useful when the result is to be written as a file, but it can also be useful for error reporting and for resolution of relative URLs even when the Result object does not represent a file. All other methods related to the result are the responsibility of the concrete implementation of this interface. See the DOMResult, SAXResult and StreamResult implementations in the three subpackages of this package.

```
public interface Result {
// Public Constants
   public static final String PI_DISABLE_OUTPUT_ESCAPING;          ="javax.xml.transform.disable-output-escaping"
   public static final String PI_ENABLE_OUTPUT_ESCAPING;           ="javax.xml.transform.enable-output-escaping"
// Public Instance Methods
   String getSystemId();
   void setSystemId(String systemId);
}
```

Implementations javax.xml.transform.dom.DOMResult, javax.xml.transform.sax.SAXResult, javax.xml.transform.stream.StreamResult

Passed To Transformer.transform(), javax.xml.transform.sax.TransformerHandler.setResult(), javax.xml.validation.Validator.validate()

Source — Java 1.4

javax.xml.transform

This interface represents, in a very general way, the source of an XML document. setSystemId() specifies a the system identifier of the document in the form of a URL. This is useful for resolving relative URLs and for error reporting even when the document is not read directly from a URL. All other methods related to the document source are the responsibility of the concrete implementation of this interface. See the DOMSource, SAXSource and StreamSource implementations in the three subpackages of this package.

```
public interface Source {
// Public Instance Methods
   String getSystemId();
   void setSystemId(String systemId);
}
```

Implementations javax.xml.transform.dom.DOMSource, javax.xml.transform.sax.SAXSource, javax.xml.transform.stream.StreamSource

Passed To Transformer.transform(), TransformerFactory.{getAssociatedStylesheet(), newTemplates(), newTransformer()}, javax.xml.transform.sax.SAXSource.sourceToInputSource(), javax.xml.transform.sax.SAXTransformerFactory.{newTransformerHandler(), newXMLFilter()}, javax.xml.validation.SchemaFactory.newSchema(), javax.xml.validation.Validator.validate()

Returned By TransformerFactory.getAssociatedStylesheet(), URIResolver.resolve()

SourceLocator — Java 1.4

javax.xml.transform

This interface defines methods that return the system and public identifiers of an XML document, and return a line number and column number within that document. SourceLocator objects are used with TransformerException and TransformerConfigurationException objects to specify the location in an XML file at which the exception occurred. Note, however that system and public identifiers are not always available for a document, and so getSystemId() and getPublicId() may return null. Also, a Tranformer is not required to track line and column numbers precisely, or at all, so getLineNumber() and getColumnNumber() may return -1 to indicate that line and column number information is not available. If they return a value other than -1, it should be considered an approximation to the actual value. Note that lines and columns within a document are numbered starting with 1, not with 0.

If you are familiar with the SAX API for parsing XML, you'll recognize this interface as a renamed version of org.xml.sax.Locator.

```
public interface SourceLocator {
// Public Instance Methods
   int getColumnNumber();
   int getLineNumber();
   String getPublicId();
   String getSystemId();
}
```

Implementations javax.xml.transform.dom.DOMLocator

Passed To TransformerConfigurationException.TransformerConfigurationException(), TransformerException.{setLocator(), TransformerException()}

Returned By TransformerException.getLocator()

Templates **Java 1.4**

javax.xml.transform

This interface represents a set of transformation instructions for transforming a Source document into a Result document. The javax.xml.transform package is nominally independent of type of transformation, but in practice, an object of this type always represents the compiled form of an XSLT stylesheet. Obtain a Templates object from a TransformerFactory object, or with a javax.xml.transform.sax.TemplatesHandler. Once you have a Templates object, you can use the newTransformer() method to create a Transformer object for applying the templates to a Source to produce a Result document.

getOutputProperties() returns a java.util.Properties object that defines name/value pairs specifying details about how a textual version of the Result document should be produced. These properties are specified in an XSLT stylesheet with the <xsl:output> element. The constants defined by the OutputKeys are legal output property names. The returned Properties object contains explicitly properties directly, and contains default values in a parent Properties object. This means that if you query a property value with getProperty(), you'll get an explicitly specified value of a default value. On the other hand, if you query a property with the get() method (inherited by Properties from its superclass) you'll get a property value if it was explictly specified in the stylesheet, or null if it was not specified. The returned Properties object is a clone of the internal value, so you can modify it (before passing it to the setOutputProperties() method of a Transformer object, for example) without affecting the Templates object.

Templates implementations are required to be threadsafe. A Templates object can be used to create any number of Transformer objects.

```
public interface Templates {
// Public Instance Methods
   java.util.Properties getOutputProperties();
   Transformer newTransformer() throws TransformerConfigurationException;
}
```

Passed To javax.xml.transform.sax.SAXTransformerFactory.{newTransformerHandler(), newXMLFilter()}

Returned By TransformerFactory.newTemplates(), javax.xml.transform.sax.TemplatesHandler.getTemplates()

Transformer Java 1.4

javax.xml.transform

Objects of this type are used to transform a **Source** document into a **Result** document. Obtain a **Transformer** object from a **TransformerFactory** object, from a **Templates** object created by a **TransformerFactory**, or from a **TransformerHandler** object created by a **SAXTransformerFactory** (these last two types are from the **javax.xml.transform.sax** package).

Once you have a **Transformer** object, you may need to configure it before using it to transform documents. **setErrorListener()** and **setURIResolver()** allow you to specify **ErrorListener** and **URLResolver** object that the **Transformer** can use. **setOutputProperty()** and **setOutputProperties()** allow you to specify name/value pairs that affect the text formatting of the **Result** document (if that document is written out in text format). **OutputKeys** defines constants that represent the set of standard output property names. The output properties you specify with these methods override any output properties specified (with an **<xsl:output>** tag) in the **Templates** object. Use **setParameter()** to supply values for any top-level parameters defined (with **<xsl:param>** tags) in the stylesheet. Note that if the name of any such parameter is a qualified name, then it appears in the stylesheet with a namespace prefix. You can't use the prefix with the **setParameter()** method, however, and you must instead specify the parameter name using the URI of the namespace within curly braces followed by the local name. If no namespace is involved, then you can just use the simple name of the parameter with no curly braces or URIs.

Once you have created and configured a **Transformer** object, use the **transform()** method to perform a document transformation. This method transforms the specified **Source** document and creates the transformed document specified by the **Result** object. In Java 5.0, you can **reset()** a **Transformer** to restore it to its original state and prepare it for reuse.

Transformer implementations are not typically threadsafe. You can reuse a **Transformer** object and call **transform()** any number of times (just not concurrently). The output properties and parameters you specify are not changed by calling the **transform()** method, and can be reused.

```
public abstract class Transformer {
// Protected Constructors
   protected Transformer();
// Public Instance Methods
   public abstract void clearParameters();
   public abstract ErrorListener getErrorListener();
   public abstract java.util.Properties getOutputProperties();
   public abstract String getOutputProperty(String name) throws IllegalArgumentException;
   public abstract Object getParameter(String name);
   public abstract URIResolver getURIResolver();
5.0 public void reset();
   public abstract void setErrorListener(ErrorListener listener) throws IllegalArgumentException;
   public abstract void setOutputProperties(java.util.Properties oformat);
   public abstract void setOutputProperty(String name, String value) throws IllegalArgumentException;
   public abstract void setParameter(String name, Object value);
   public abstract void setURIResolver(URIResolver resolver);
   public abstract void transform(Source xmlSource, Result outputTarget) throws TransformerException;
}
```

Returned By Templates.newTransformer(), TransformerFactory.newTransformer(), javax.xml.transform.sax.TransformerHandler.getTransformer()

TransformerConfigurationException — Java 1.4

javax.xml.transform — serializable checked

Signals a problem creating a **Transformer** object. This may occur, for exmaple, if there is a syntax error in the XSL stylesheet that contains the transformation instructions. Use the inherited **getLocator()** method to obtain a **SourceLocator** that describes the document location at which the exception occurred.

Object — Throwable — Exception — TransformerException — TransformerConfigurationException
Serializable

```
public class TransformerConfigurationException extends TransformerException {
// Public Constructors
   public TransformerConfigurationException();
   public TransformerConfigurationException(Throwable e);
   public TransformerConfigurationException(String msg);
   public TransformerConfigurationException(String message, SourceLocator locator);
   public TransformerConfigurationException(String msg, Throwable e);
   public TransformerConfigurationException(String message, SourceLocator locator, Throwable e);
}
```

Thrown By Templates.newTransformer(), TransformerFactory.{getAssociatedStylesheet(), newTemplates(), newTransformer(), setFeature()}, javax.xml.transform.sax.SAXTransformerFactory.{newTemplatesHandler(), newTransformerHandler(), newXMLFilter()}

TransformerException — Java 1.4

javax.xml.transform — serializable checked

Signals a problem while reading or transforming a document. Call **getLocator()** to obtain a **SourceLocator** object that describes the document location at which the exception occured.

Object — Throwable — Exception — TransformerException
Serializable

```
public class TransformerException extends Exception {
// Public Constructors
   public TransformerException(String message);
   public TransformerException(Throwable e);
   public TransformerException(String message, Throwable e);
   public TransformerException(String message, SourceLocator locator);
   public TransformerException(String message, SourceLocator locator, Throwable e);
// Public Instance Methods
   public Throwable getException();
   public String getLocationAsString();
   public SourceLocator getLocator();
   public String getMessageAndLocation();
   public void setLocator(SourceLocator location);
// Public Methods Overriding Throwable
   public Throwable getCause();
   public Throwable initCause(Throwable cause);                                      synchronized
   public void printStackTrace();
   public void printStackTrace(java.io.PrintStream s);
   public void printStackTrace(java.io.PrintWriter s);
}
```

Subclasses TransformerConfigurationException

Passed To ErrorListener.{error(), fatalError(), warning()}

Thrown By ErrorListener.{error(), fatalError(), warning()}, Transformer.transform(), URIResolver.resolve()

TransformerFactory Java 1.4

javax.xml.transform

An instance of this abstract class represents a document "transformation engine" such as an XSLT processor. A TransformerFactory is used to create Transformer objects that perform document transformations, and can also be used to process transformation instructions (such as XSLT stylesheets) into compiled Templates objects.

Obtain a TransformerFactory instance by calling the static newInstance() method. newInstance() returns an instance of the default implementation for your Java installation, or, if the system property javax.xml.transform.TransformerFactory is set, then it returns an instance of the implementation class named by that property. The default TransformerFactory implementation provided with the Java distribution transforms XML documents using XSL stylesheets.

You can configure a TransformerFactory instance by calling setErrorListener() and setURIResolver() to specify an ErrorListener object and a URIResolver object to be used by the factory when reading and parsing XSL stylesheets. The setAttribute() and getAttribute() methods can be used to set and query implementation-dependent attributes of the transformation engine. The default engine supplied by Sun does not define any attributes. The getFeature() method is used to test whether the factory supports a given feature. For uniqueness, feature names are expressed as URIs, and each of the Source and Result implementations defined in the three subpackages of this package define a FEATURE constant that specifies a URL that you can use to test whether a TransformerFactory supports that particular Source or Result type.

Once you have obtained and configured your TransformerFactory object, you can use it in several ways. If you call the newTransformer() method that takes no arguments, you'll obtain a Transformer object that transforms the format or representation of an XML document without transforming its content. For example, you could use a Transformer created in this way to transform a DOM tree (represented by a javax.xml.transform.dom.DOMSource object) to a stream of XML text stored in a file named by a javax.xml.transform.stream.StreamResult.

Another way to use a TransformerFactory is to call the newTemplates() method, passing in a Source object that represents an XSL stylesheet. This produces a Templates object, which you can use to obtain a Transformer object that applies the stylesheet to transform document content. Alternatively, if you do not plan to create more than one Transformer object from the Templates object, you can combine the two steps and simply pass the Source object representing the stylesheet to the one-argument version of newTransformer().

XML documents may include references to XSL stylesheets in the form of an xml-stylesheet processing instruction. The getAssociatedStylesheet() method reads the XML document represented by a Source object and returns a new Source object that represents the stylesheet (or the concatenation of all the stylesheets) contained in that document that match the media, title, and charset constraints defined by the other three parameters (which may be null). If you want to process an XML document using the stylesheet that it defines itself, use this method to obtain a Source object that you can pass to newTransformer() to create the Transformer object that you can use to transform the document.

TransformerFactory implementations are not typically threadsafe.

```
public abstract class TransformerFactory {
// Protected Constructors
   protected TransformerFactory();
// Public Class Methods
   public static TransformerFactory newInstance() throws TransformerFactoryConfigurationError;
// Public Instance Methods
   public abstract Source getAssociatedStylesheet(Source source, String media, String title, String charset)
       throws TransformerConfigurationException;
   public abstract Object getAttribute(String name);
   public abstract ErrorListener getErrorListener();
   public abstract boolean getFeature(String name);
   public abstract URIResolver getURIResolver();
   public abstract Templates newTemplates(Source source) throws TransformerConfigurationException;
   public abstract Transformer newTransformer() throws TransformerConfigurationException;
   public abstract Transformer newTransformer(Source source) throws TransformerConfigurationException;
   public abstract void setAttribute(String name, Object value);
   public abstract void setErrorListener(ErrorListener listener);
5.0 public abstract void setFeature(String name, boolean value) throws TransformerConfigurationException;
   public abstract void setURIResolver(URIResolver resolver);
}
```

Subclasses javax.xml.transform.sax.SAXTransformerFactory

TransformerFactoryConfigurationError — Java 1.4

javax.xml.transform — serializable error

This error class signals a fatal problem while creating a TransformerFactory. It usually signals a configuration problem, such as the system property javax.xml.transform.TransformerFactory has a value that is not a valid classname, or that the class path does not contain the specified factory implementation class.

Object — Throwable — Error — TransformerFactoryConfigurationError
Throwable ⋮ Serializable

```
public class TransformerFactoryConfigurationError extends Error {
// Public Constructors
   public TransformerFactoryConfigurationError();
   public TransformerFactoryConfigurationError(String msg);
   public TransformerFactoryConfigurationError(Exception e);
   public TransformerFactoryConfigurationError(Exception e, String msg);
// Public Instance Methods
   public Exception getException();                                    default:null
// Public Methods Overriding Throwable
   public String getMessage();                                         default:null
}
```

Thrown By TransformerFactory.newInstance()

URIResolver — Java 1.4

javax.xml.transform

This interface allows an application to tell a Transformer how to resolve the URIs that appear in an XSLT stylesheet. If you pass a URIResolver to the setURIResolver() method of a Transformer or TransformerFactory then when the Transformer or TransformerFactory encounters a

URI, it first passes that URI, along with the base URI to the resolve() method of the URIResolver. If resolve() returns a Source object, then the Transformer will use that Source. If a Transformer or TransformerFactory has no URIResolver registered, or if the resolve() method returns null, then the tranformer or factory will attempt to resolve the URI itself.

```
public interface URIResolver {
// Public Instance Methods
   Source resolve(String href, String base) throws TransformerException;
}
```

Passed To Transformer.setURIResolver(), TransformerFactory.setURIResolver()

Returned By Transformer.getURIResolver(), TransformerFactory.getURIResolver()

Package javax.xml.transform.dom — Java 1.4

This package contains Source and Result implementations that work with DOM document trees and subtrees.

Interfaces

```
public interface DOMLocator extends javax.xml.transform.SourceLocator;
```

Classes

```
public class DOMResult implements javax.xml.transform.Result;
public class DOMSource implements javax.xml.transform.Source;
```

DOMLocator — Java 1.4

javax.xml.transform.dom

This class extends SourceLocator to define a method for retrieving a DOM Node object, which is typically used to indicate the source of an error in the transformation process. See SourceLocator and TransformerException.

SourceLocator ··· DOMLocator

```
public interface DOMLocator extends javax.xml.transform.SourceLocator {
// Public Instance Methods
   org.w3c.dom.Node getOriginatingNode();
}
```

DOMResult — Java 1.4

javax.xml.transform.dom

This class is a Result implementation that writes XML content by generating a DOM tree to represent that content. If you pass an org.w3c.dom.Node to the constructor or to setNode(), the DOMResult will create the result tree as a child of the specified node (which should typically be a Document or Element node). If you do not specify a node, the DOMResult will create a new Document node when it creates the result tree. You can retrieve this Document with getNode(). In Java 5.0, you can also pass two Node objects to the constructor: these specify the parent node of the result tree and the child of that parent before which the result tree should be inserted. See also setNextSibling().

Object — DOMResult ··· Result

```
public class DOMResult implements javax.xml.transform.Result {
// Public Constructors
   public DOMResult();
   public DOMResult(org.w3c.dom.Node node);
5.0 public DOMResult(org.w3c.dom.Node node, org.w3c.dom.Node nextSibling);
   public DOMResult(org.w3c.dom.Node node, String systemId);
5.0 public DOMResult(org.w3c.dom.Node node, org.w3c.dom.Node nextSibling, String systemId);
// Public Constants
   public static final String FEATURE;            ="http://javax.xml.transform.dom.DOMResult/feature"
// Public Instance Methods
5.0 public org.w3c.dom.Node getNextSibling();                    default:null
   public org.w3c.dom.Node getNode();                            default:null
5.0 public void setNextSibling(org.w3c.dom.Node nextSibling);
   public void setNode(org.w3c.dom.Node node);
// Methods Implementing Result
   public String getSystemId();                                  default:null
   public void setSystemId(String systemId);
}
```

DOMSource — Java 1.4

javax.xml.transform.dom

This class is a Source implementation that reads an XML document from a DOM document tree or subtree. Pass the org.w3c.dom.Node object that represents the root of the tree or subtree to the constructor or to setNode(). When possible, it is also useful to provide a system id (a filename or URL) for use in error messages and for resolving relative URLs contained in the document.

Object — DOMSource ··· Source

```
public class DOMSource implements javax.xml.transform.Source {
// Public Constructors
   public DOMSource();
   public DOMSource(org.w3c.dom.Node n);
   public DOMSource(org.w3c.dom.Node node, String systemID);
// Public Constants
   public static final String FEATURE;            ="http://javax.xml.transform.dom.DOMSource/feature"
// Public Instance Methods
   public org.w3c.dom.Node getNode();                            default:null
   public void setNode(org.w3c.dom.Node node);
// Methods Implementing Source
   public String getSystemId();                                  default:null
   public void setSystemId(String systemID);
}
```

Package javax.xml.transform.sax — Java 1.4

This package defines Source and Result implementations that work with SAX events. In addition, it includes an extension to the TransformerFactory class that has additional methods for returning TemplatesHandler and TransformerHandler objects. These objects implement SAX handler interfaces and are able to work with a SAX parser object to turn a series of SAX parse events into a Templates object or into a Result document. SAXSource and SAXResult adapt the org.xml.sax framework for use in the javax.xml.transform framework. By contrast, SAXTransformerFactory, TemplatesHandler, and TransfomerHandler adapt the javax.xml.transform framework for use within the org.xml.sax parsing framework.

Interfaces

```
public interface TemplatesHandler extends org.xml.sax.ContentHandler;
public interface TransformerHandler extends org.xml.sax.ContentHandler, org.xml.sax.DTDHandler,
org.xml.sax.ext.LexicalHandler;
```

Classes

```
public class SAXResult implements javax.xml.transform.Result;
public class SAXSource implements javax.xml.transform.Source;
public abstract class SAXTransformerFactory extends javax.xml.transform.TransformerFactory;
```

JAXP

SAXResult Java 1.4

javax.xml.transform.sax

This class is a Result implementation that describes the content of a transformed document by triggering the methods of the specified ContentHandler. That is, a SAXResult acts like a org.xml.sax.SAXReader object, invoking the methods of the specified org.xml.sax.ContentHandler object as it parses the transformed document. You may also provide a org.xml.sax.ext.LexicalHandler object whose methods will be invoked by the SAXResult by calling setLexicalHandler, or by suppling a ContentHandler object that also implements the LexicalHandler interface.

Object — SAXResult ··· Result

```
public class SAXResult implements javax.xml.transform.Result {
// Public Constructors
   public SAXResult();
   public SAXResult(org.xml.sax.ContentHandler handler);
// Public Constants
   public static final String FEATURE;                    ="http://javax.xml.transform.sax.SAXResult/feature"
// Public Instance Methods
   public org.xml.sax.ContentHandler getHandler();                                           default:null
   public org.xml.sax.ext.LexicalHandler getLexicalHandler();                                default:null
   public void setHandler(org.xml.sax.ContentHandler handler);
   public void setLexicalHandler(org.xml.sax.ext.LexicalHandler handler);
// Methods Implementing Result
   public String getSystemId();                                                              default:null
   public void setSystemId(String systemId);
}
```

SAXSource Java 1.4

javax.xml.transform.sax

This class is a Source implementation that describes a document represented as a series of SAX event method calls. A SAXSource requires an org.xml.sax.InputSource object that describes the stream to parse, and may optionally specify the org.xml.sax.XMLReader or org.xml.sax.XMLFilter that generates the SAX events. (If no XMLReader or XMLFilter is specified, then the Transformer object will a default XMLReader.) Note that since an InputSource is required, a SAXSource does not behave significantly differently than a StreamSource unless an XMLFilter is used.

SAXSource also has one static method, sourceToInputSource() which returns a SAX InputSource method derived from the specified Source object, or null if the specified Source cannot be converted to an InputSource.

Object ─ SAXSource ··· Source

```
public class SAXSource implements javax.xml.transform.Source {
// Public Constructors
   public SAXSource();
   public SAXSource(org.xml.sax.InputSource inputSource);
   public SAXSource(org.xml.sax.XMLReader reader, org.xml.sax.InputSource inputSource);
// Public Constants
   public static final String FEATURE;                 ="http://javax.xml.transform.sax.SAXSource/feature"
// Public Class Methods
   public static org.xml.sax.InputSource sourceToInputSource(javax.xml.transform.Source source);
// Public Instance Methods
   public org.xml.sax.InputSource getInputSource();                                      default:null
   public org.xml.sax.XMLReader getXMLReader();                                          default:null
   public void setInputSource(org.xml.sax.InputSource inputSource);
   public void setXMLReader(org.xml.sax.XMLReader reader);
// Methods Implementing Source
   public String getSystemId();                                                          default:null
   public void setSystemId(String systemId);
}
```

SAXTransformerFactory — Java 1.4

javax.xml.transform.sax

This class extends TransformerFactory to define additional factory methods that are useful when working with documents that are represented as sequences of SAX events. Pass the FEATURE constant to the getFeature() method of your TransformerFactory object to determine whether the newTemplatesHandler() and newTransformerHandler() methods are supported and whether it is safe to cast your TransformerFactory object to a SAXTransformerFactory. Use the FEATURE_XMLFILTER constant with getFeature() to determine if the newXMLFilter() methods are also supported.

newTemplatesHandler() returns a TemplatesHandler object that you can use as an org.xml.sax.ContentHandler object to receive SAX events generated by a SAX parser and transform those events into a Templates object.

The newTransformerHandler() methods are similar: they return a TransformerHandler object that can receive SAX events and representing a source document and transform them into a Result document. The no-argument version of newTransformerHandler() creates a TransformerHandler that simply modifies the form of the document without applying a stylesheet to its content. The other two versions of newTransformerHandler() use a stylesheet specified either as a Source or Templates object.

The newXMLFilter() methods, if supported, return an org.xml.sax.XMLFilter object that can acts as both a sink and a source of SAX events and filters those events by applying the transformation instructions specified by the Templates or Source objects.

Object ─ TransformerFactory ─ SAXTransformerFactory

```
public abstract class SAXTransformerFactory extends javax.xml.transform.TransformerFactory {
// Protected Constructors
   protected SAXTransformerFactory();
```

```
// Public Constants
   public static final String FEATURE;                ="http://javax.xml.transform.sax.SAXTransformerFactory/feature"
   public static final String FEATURE_XMLFILTER;      ="http://javax.xml.transform.sax.SAXTransformerFactory/feature/
                                                                                                          xmlfilter"
// Public Instance Methods
   public abstract TemplatesHandler newTemplatesHandler()
      throws javax.xml.transform.TransformerConfigurationException;
   public abstract TransformerHandler newTransformerHandler()
      throws javax.xml.transform.TransformerConfigurationException;
   public abstract TransformerHandler newTransformerHandler(javax.xml.transform.Source src)
      throws javax.xml.transform.TransformerConfigurationException;
   public abstract TransformerHandler newTransformerHandler(javax.xml.transform.Templates templates)
      throws javax.xml.transform.TransformerConfigurationException;
   public abstract org.xml.sax.XMLFilter newXMLFilter(javax.xml.transform.Source src)
      throws javax.xml.transform.TransformerConfigurationException;
   public abstract org.xml.sax.XMLFilter newXMLFilter(javax.xml.transform.Templates templates)
      throws javax.xml.transform.TransformerConfigurationException;
}
```

JAXP

TemplatesHandler — Java 1.4

javax.xml.transform.sax

This interface extends org.xml.sax.ContentHandler and adds a getTemplates() method. An object that implements this interface can be used to receive method calls from some source of SAX events and process those events (as a XSL stylesheet) into a Templates object. Obtain a TemplatesHandler from a SAXTransformerFactory. Register it with the setContentHandler() method of an org.xml.sax.XMLReader and invoke the parse() method of the reader. When parse() returns, call the getTemplates() method to obtain the Templates object.

ContentHandler — TemplatesHandler

```
public interface TemplatesHandler extends org.xml.sax.ContentHandler {
// Public Instance Methods
   String getSystemId();
   javax.xml.transform.Templates getTemplates();
   void setSystemId(String systemID);
}
```

Returned By SAXTransformerFactory.newTemplatesHandler()

TransformerHandler — Java 1.4

javax.xml.transform.sax

This interface extends org.xml.sax.ContentHandler and related interfaces so that it can consume SAX events generated by a org.xml.sax.SAXReader or org.xml.sax.SAXFilter. Create a TransformerHandler by calling one of the newTransformerHandler() methods of a SAXTransformerFactory.

Next, call the setResult() method to specify a Result object that describes the result document you'd like the transformation to produce. You may also call getTransformer() to get the Transformer object associated with this TransformerHandler if you need to set output properties or parameter values for the transformation.

Now, register the TransformerHandler with the SAXReader or SAXFilter object by calling setContentHandler(), setDTDHandler(), and setProperty(). 'Then you use the property name "http://www.xml.org/sax/properties/lexical-handler" in the call to setProperties() to register the TransformerHandler as a org.xml.sax.ext.LexicalHandler for the parser or filter.

Finally, invoke one of the parse() methods on your XMLReader or XMLFilter object. This will cause the reader or filter to start parsing the source document and translating it into method calls on the TransformerHandler. The TransformerHandler will transform those calls as specified in the Templates or Source object (if any) that was passed to the original call to newTransformerHandler() and generate a result document as directed by the Result object that was passed to setResult().

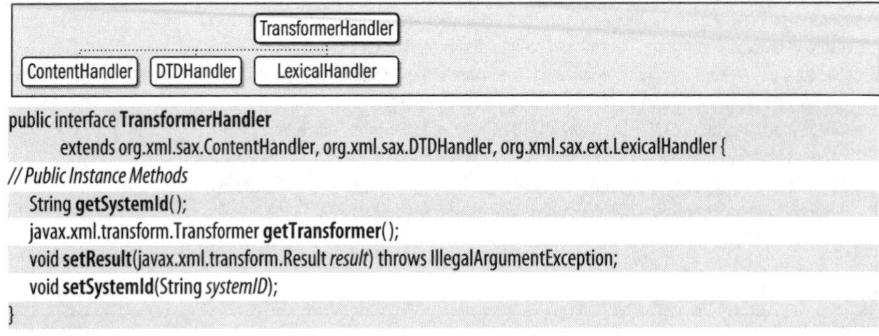


```
public interface TransformerHandler
        extends org.xml.sax.ContentHandler, org.xml.sax.DTDHandler, org.xml.sax.ext.LexicalHandler {
// Public Instance Methods
   String getSystemId();
   javax.xml.transform.Transformer getTransformer();
   void setResult(javax.xml.transform.Result result) throws IllegalArgumentException;
   void setSystemId(String systemID);
}
```

Returned By SAXTransformerFactory.newTransformerHandler()

Package javax.xml.transform.stream — Java 1.4

This package contains Source and Result implementations that work with files and streams.

Classes

```
public class StreamResult implements javax.xml.transform.Result;
public class StreamSource implements javax.xml.transform.Source;
```

StreamResult — Java 1.4

javax.xml.transform.stream

This class is a Result implementation that writes a textual representation of a transformed document to stream or file. Because XML documents define their own encoding, it is usually preferable to construct a StreamResult using a File or OutputStream instead of a character-based Writer which may use a different encoding than that specified within the document.

Object — StreamResult ··· Result

```
public class StreamResult implements javax.xml.transform.Result {
// Public Constructors
   public StreamResult();
   public StreamResult(java.io.File f);
   public StreamResult(String systemId);
   public StreamResult(java.io.Writer writer);
   public StreamResult(java.io.OutputStream outputStream);
```

```
// Public Constants
   public static final String FEATURE;                    ="http://javax.xml.transform.stream.StreamResult/feature"
// Public Instance Methods
   public java.io.OutputStream getOutputStream();                                      default:null
   public java.io.Writer getWriter();                                                  default:null
   public void setOutputStream(java.io.OutputStream outputStream);
   public void setSystemId(java.io.File f);
   public void setWriter(java.io.Writer writer);
// Methods Implementing Result
   public String getSystemId();                                                        default:null
   public void setSystemId(String systemId);
}
```

StreamSource   Java 1.4

javax.xml.transform.stream

This class is a Source implementation that reads the textual format of an XML document from a file, byte stream, or character stream. Because XML documents declare their own encoding, it is preferable to create a StreamSource object from an InputStream instead of from a Reader, so that the XML processor can correctly handle the declared encoding. When creating a StreamSource from a byte stream or character stream, you should provide the "system id" (i.e. the filename or URL) by using one of the two-argument constructors or by caling setSystemId(). The system id is required if the XML file to be processed includes relative URLs to be resolved.

Object — StreamSource ··· Source

```
public class StreamSource implements javax.xml.transform.Source {
// Public Constructors
   public StreamSource();
   public StreamSource(java.io.InputStream inputStream);
   public StreamSource(java.io.Reader reader);
   public StreamSource(java.io.File f);
   public StreamSource(String systemId);
   public StreamSource(java.io.Reader reader, String systemId);
   public StreamSource(java.io.InputStream inputStream, String systemId);
// Public Constants
   public static final String FEATURE;                    ="http://javax.xml.transform.stream.StreamSource/feature"
// Public Instance Methods
   public java.io.InputStream getInputStream();                                        default:null
   public String getPublicId();                                                        default:null
   public java.io.Reader getReader();                                                  default:null
   public void setInputStream(java.io.InputStream inputStream);
   public void setPublicId(String publicId);
   public void setReader(java.io.Reader reader);
   public void setSystemId(java.io.File f);
// Methods Implementing Source
   public String getSystemId();                                                        default:null
   public void setSystemId(String systemId);
}
```


JAXP

Package javax.xml.validation — Java 5.0

This package contains classes for validating XML documents against W3C XML Schema definitions. Implementations may also support additional schema types, such as RELAX NG. Typical usage begins with the SchemaFactory class, which parses schema specifications into immutable Schema objects. Next, the Schema object is used to create a Validator with which a document may be validated.

Classes

```
public abstract class Schema;
public abstract class SchemaFactory;
public abstract class SchemaFactoryLoader;
public abstract class TypeInfoProvider;
public abstract class Validator;
public abstract class ValidatorHandler implements org.xml.sax.ContentHandler;
```

Schema — Java 5.0

javax.xml.validation

A Schema is an immutable opaque parsed representation of a schema. Schema objects don't perform validation themselves; instead, they are factories for Validator and ValidatorHandler objects that can be used to validate individual documents.

```
public abstract class Schema {
// Protected Constructors
   protected Schema();
// Public Instance Methods
   public abstract Validator newValidator();
   public abstract ValidatorHandler newValidatorHandler();
}
```

Passed To javax.xml.parsers.DocumentBuilderFactory.setSchema(), javax.xml.parsers.SAXParserFactory.setSchema()

Returned By javax.xml.parsers.DocumentBuilder.getSchema(), javax.xml.parsers.DocumentBuilderFactory.getSchema(), javax.xml.parsers.SAXParser.getSchema(), javax.xml.parsers.SAXParserFactory.getSchema(), SchemaFactory.newSchema()

SchemaFactory — Java 5.0

javax.xml.validation

A SchemaFactory parses the textual representation of a schema into a Schema object. Obtain a SchemaFactory with the newInstance() method, passing a string that identifies the type of schema you want to parse. All implementations are required to support the W3C XML Schema language, which is identified by XMLConstants.W3C_XML_SCHEMA_NS_URL. Other schema types may also be supported, such as RELAX NG schemas, identified by XMLConstants.RELAXNG_NS_URL.

To parse a schema, call the newSchema() method, passing the File or javax.xml.transform.Source object that identifies the schema contents. For schemas in the W3C XML Schema language, you may also specify an array of Source objects that contain the schema definition. If you call newSchema() with no arguments, a special Schema object is returned that expects the document to specify the location of its own W3C XML Schema.

You can configure a SchemaFactory before calling newSchema() with setErrorHandler(), setResourceResolver(), setProperty(), and setFeature().

```
public abstract class SchemaFactory {
// Protected Constructors
   protected SchemaFactory();
// Public Class Methods
   public static final SchemaFactory newInstance(String schemaLanguage);
// Public Instance Methods
   public abstract org.xml.sax.ErrorHandler getErrorHandler();
   public boolean getFeature(String name)
       throws org.xml.sax.SAXNotRecognizedException, org.xml.sax.SAXNotSupportedException;
   public Object getProperty(String name)
       throws org.xml.sax.SAXNotRecognizedException, org.xml.sax.SAXNotSupportedException;
   public abstract org.w3c.dom.ls.LSResourceResolver getResourceResolver();
   public abstract boolean isSchemaLanguageSupported(String schemaLanguage);
   public abstract Schema newSchema() throws org.xml.sax.SAXException;
   public Schema newSchema(javax.xml.transform.Source schema) throws org.xml.sax.SAXException;
   public Schema newSchema(java.io.File schema) throws org.xml.sax.SAXException;
   public abstract Schema newSchema(javax.xml.transform.Source[] schemas) throws org.xml.sax.SAXException;
   public Schema newSchema(java.net.URL schema) throws org.xml.sax.SAXException;
   public abstract void setErrorHandler(org.xml.sax.ErrorHandler errorHandler);
   public void setFeature(String name, boolean value)
       throws org.xml.sax.SAXNotRecognizedException, org.xml.sax.SAXNotSupportedException;
   public void setProperty(String name, Object object)
       throws org.xml.sax.SAXNotRecognizedException, org.xml.sax.SAXNotSupportedException;
   public abstract void setResourceResolver(org.w3c.dom.ls.LSResourceResolver resourceResolver);
}
```

Returned By SchemaFactoryLoader.newFactory()

SchemaFactoryLoader — Java 5.0

javax.xml.validation

This class is used by implementations of the validation API to produce a SchemaFactory object for a specified schema type. Applications that use the javax.xml.validation package do not need to use this class.

```
public abstract class SchemaFactoryLoader {
// Protected Constructors
   protected SchemaFactoryLoader();
// Public Instance Methods
   public abstract SchemaFactory newFactory(String schemaLanguage);
}
```

TypeInfoProvider — Java 5.0

javax.xml.validation

A TypeInfoProvider provides information about the type of the element or attribute currently being processed by a ValidatorHandler. This type information is obtained by validating document content against a schema and may be useful to the ContentHandler to which the ValidatorHandler dispatches its method calls.

```
public abstract class TypeInfoProvider {
// Protected Constructors
   protected TypeInfoProvider();
// Public Instance Methods
   public abstract org.w3c.dom.TypeInfo getAttributeTypeInfo(int index);
   public abstract org.w3c.dom.TypeInfo getElementTypeInfo();
   public abstract boolean isIdAttribute(int index);
   public abstract boolean isSpecified(int index);
}
```

Returned By ValidatorHandler.getTypeInfoProvider()

Validator **Java 5.0**

javax.xml.validation

A Validator object validates an XML document against the Schema from which the Validator was created. The validate() method performs validation. Specify the document to be validated with a DOMSource or SAXSource object (from the javax.xml.transform.dom or javax.xml.transform.sax packages). The validate() method accepts any javax.xml.transform.Source object as an argument, but SAXSource and DOMSource are the only two supported implementations.

The document validation process can also be used to augment the source document by adding the default values of unspecified attributes. If you want to capture this augmented form of the document, pass a Result object to the two-argument version of validate(). If the source is a SAXSource, the result must be a SAXResult, and if the source is a DOMSource, the result must be a DOMResult object.

If the document is valid, the validate() method returns normally. If the document is not valid, validate() throws an org.xml.sax.SAXException. You can alter this somewhat by passing a custom org.xml.sax.ErrorHandler to setErrorHandler(). Validation exceptions are first passed to the error handler methods, which may throw the exception or handle them in some other way, such as printing a message. If the error handler does not throw an exception, the validate() method attempts to continue validation. The default error handler ignores exceptions passed to its warn() method but throws exceptions passed to its error() and fatalError() methods.

Before calling validate(), a Validator may also be configured with setResourceResolver(), setFeature(), and setProperty().

```
public abstract class Validator {
// Protected Constructors
   protected Validator();
// Public Instance Methods
   public abstract org.xml.sax.ErrorHandler getErrorHandler();
   public boolean getFeature(String name)
      throws org.xml.sax.SAXNotRecognizedException, org.xml.sax.SAXNotSupportedException;
   public Object getProperty(String name)
      throws org.xml.sax.SAXNotRecognizedException, org.xml.sax.SAXNotSupportedException;
   public abstract org.w3c.dom.ls.LSResourceResolver getResourceResolver();
   public abstract void reset();
   public abstract void setErrorHandler(org.xml.sax.ErrorHandler errorHandler);
   public void setFeature(String name, boolean value)
      throws org.xml.sax.SAXNotRecognizedException, org.xml.sax.SAXNotSupportedException;
   public void setProperty(String name, Object object)
      throws org.xml.sax.SAXNotRecognizedException, org.xml.sax.SAXNotSupportedException;
```

```
    public abstract void setResourceResolver(org.w3c.dom.ls.LSResourceResolver resourceResolver);
    public void validate(javax.xml.transform.Source source) throws org.xml.sax.SAXException, java.io.IOException;
    public abstract void validate(javax.xml.transform.Source source, javax.xml.transform.Result result)
        throws org.xml.sax.SAXException, java.io.IOException;
}
```

Returned By Schema.newValidator()

ValidatorHandler **Java 5.0**

javax.xml.validation

A ValidatorHandler is an org.xml.sax.ContentHandler that uses the streaming SAX API to validate an XML document against the Schema from which the ValidatorHandler was derived. The Validator class can be used to validate a SAXSource, but ValidatorHandler provides lower-level access to the SAX API.

If the document is not valid, one of the ContentHandler methods throws a SAXException that propagates up to your code. As with the Validator class, you can alter this by specifying a custom org.xml.sax.ErrorHandler class.

ValidatorHandler can be used as a filter for SAX parsing events. If you pass a ContentHandler to setContentHandler(), the ValidatorHandler augments the source document with attribute defaults from the schema and invokes the appropriate callback methods on the ContentHandler you supply. If you are interested in attribute and element type information provided by the schema, your ContentHandler can use the TypeInfoProvider obtained from the ValidatorHandler getTypeInfoProvider().

Object ─ ValidatorHandler ··· ContentHandler

```
public abstract class ValidatorHandler implements org.xml.sax.ContentHandler {
// Protected Constructors
    protected ValidatorHandler();
// Public Instance Methods
    public abstract org.xml.sax.ContentHandler getContentHandler();
    public abstract org.xml.sax.ErrorHandler getErrorHandler();
    public boolean getFeature(String name)
        throws org.xml.sax.SAXNotRecognizedException, org.xml.sax.SAXNotSupportedException;
    public Object getProperty(String name)
        throws org.xml.sax.SAXNotRecognizedException, org.xml.sax.SAXNotSupportedException;
    public abstract org.w3c.dom.ls.LSResourceResolver getResourceResolver();
    public abstract TypeInfoProvider getTypeInfoProvider();
    public abstract void setContentHandler(org.xml.sax.ContentHandler receiver);
    public abstract void setErrorHandler(org.xml.sax.ErrorHandler errorHandler);
    public void setFeature(String name, boolean value)
        throws org.xml.sax.SAXNotRecognizedException, org.xml.sax.SAXNotSupportedException;
    public void setProperty(String name, Object object)
        throws org.xml.sax.SAXNotRecognizedException, org.xml.sax.SAXNotSupportedException;
    public abstract void setResourceResolver(org.w3c.dom.ls.LSResourceResolver resourceResolver);
}
```

Returned By Schema.newValidatorHandler()

JAXP

Package javax.xml.xpath — Java 5.0

This package defines types for the evaluation of XPath expressions in the context of an XML document. XPath is a language for describing a "path" to a node or set of nodes within an XML document. Details of the XPath grammar are beyond the scope of this reference.

A typical use of this package begins with the XPathFactory, an instance of which is used to create an XPath object. After configuring the XPath object as desired, you can use it to evaluate XPath expressions directly or to compile XPath expressions into XPathExpression objects for later use.

Interfaces

public interface **XPath**;
public interface **XPathExpression**;
public interface **XPathFunction**;
public interface **XPathFunctionResolver**;
public interface **XPathVariableResolver**;

Classes

public class **XPathConstants**;
public abstract class **XPathFactory**;

Exceptions

public class **XPathException** extends Exception;
    public class **XPathExpressionException** extends XPathException;
        public class **XPathFunctionException** extends XPathExpressionException;
    public class **XPathFactoryConfigurationException** extends XPathException;

XPath — Java 5.0

javax.xml.xpath

An XPath object is used to compile or evaluate an XPath expression. Create an XPath object through an XPathFactory. Configuration methods of XPath allow you to specify an XPathVariableResolver and an XPathFunctionResolver to resolve variable and function references in XPath expressions. You may also specify the javax.xml.namespace.NamespaceContext with which the XPath can resolve qualified names.

After creating and configuring an XPath object, you can use the compile() method to compile an XPath expression for later evaluation, or you can use one of the evaluate() methods to compile and evaluate an expression directly. There are four versions of evaluate(). All expect a String containing an XPath expression as their first argument. The second argument is the document or portion of a document to evaluate the expression against. Two versions of evaluate() expect an org.xml.sax.InputSource for this second argument. These versions of the method first parse the document and build a DOM (or other object model) tree. The other two versions of evaluate() expect an Object as the second argument. The object passed should be a DOM (or other object model) object representing the document or some portion of it. For the org.w3c.dom object model, this might be a Document, DocumentFragment, Node, or NodeList object.

The final difference between evaluate() methods is the presence or absence of a third argument. The two-argument versions of evaluate() return the result of the expression evaluation as a String. The three-argument versions expect a third argument that specifies the desired return type and return an Object of an appropriate type. The valid types are the QName objects defined in the XPathConstants class, such as XPathConstants.NODE and XPathConstants.NODESET. With the DOM object model, evaluate() returns org.w3c.dom.Node and org.w3c.dom.NodeList objects for these types.

```
public interface XPath {
// Public Instance Methods
    XPathExpression compile(String expression) throws XPathExpressionException;
    String evaluate(String expression, Object item) throws XPathExpressionException;
    String evaluate(String expression, org.xml.sax.InputSource source) throws XPathExpressionException;
    Object evaluate(String expression, org.xml.sax.InputSource source, javax.xml.namespace.QName returnType)
        throws XPathExpressionException;
    Object evaluate(String expression, Object item, javax.xml.namespace.QName returnType)
        throws XPathExpressionException;
    javax.xml.namespace.NamespaceContext getNamespaceContext();
    XPathFunctionResolver getXPathFunctionResolver();
    XPathVariableResolver getXPathVariableResolver();
    void reset();
    void setNamespaceContext(javax.xml.namespace.NamespaceContext nsContext);
    void setXPathFunctionResolver(XPathFunctionResolver resolver);
    void setXPathVariableResolver(XPathVariableResolver resolver);
}
```

Returned By XPathFactory.newXPath()

XPathConstants Java 5.0

javax.xml.xpath

This class defines javax.xml.namespace.QName constants that represent the possible return types of the evaluate() methods of XPath and XPathExpression. It also defines the DOM_OBJECT_MODEL constant that can be passed to XPathFactory.newInstance() to specify that the resulting XPathFactory should be for the org.w3c.dom object model.

```
public class XPathConstants {
// No Constructor
// Public Constants
    public static final javax.xml.namespace.QName BOOLEAN;
    public static final String DOM_OBJECT_MODEL;                    ="http://java.sun.com/jaxp/xpath/dom"
    public static final javax.xml.namespace.QName NODE;
    public static final javax.xml.namespace.QName NODESET;
    public static final javax.xml.namespace.QName NUMBER;
    public static final javax.xml.namespace.QName STRING;
}
```

XPathException Java 5.0

javax.xml.xpath serializable checked

This is the common superclass of all XPath-related exception types.

```
Object ─ Throwable ─ Exception ─ XPathException
         Serializable
```

```
public class XPathException extends Exception {
// Public Constructors
   public XPathException(Throwable cause);
   public XPathException(String message);
// Public Methods Overriding Throwable
   public Throwable getCause();
   public void printStackTrace();
   public void printStackTrace(java.io.PrintWriter s);
   public void printStackTrace(java.io.PrintStream s);
}
```

Subclasses XPathExpressionException, XPathFactoryConfigurationException

XPathExpression Java 5.0

javax.xml.xpath

If an XPath expression is to be evaluated more than once, it is not efficient to call the XPath.evaluate() method repeatedly. Instead, compile the expression to an XPathExpression using the XPath.compile() method and then evaluate it using one of the evaluate() methods of XPathExpression. The evaluate() methods of XPathExpression behave just like the corresponding methods of XPath. See XPath for details.

```
public interface XPathExpression {
// Public Instance Methods
   String evaluate(org.xml.sax.InputSource source) throws XPathExpressionException;
   String evaluate(Object item) throws XPathExpressionException;
   Object evaluate(Object item, javax.xml.namespace.QName returnType) throws XPathExpressionException;
   Object evaluate(org.xml.sax.InputSource source, javax.xml.namespace.QName returnType)
      throws XPathExpressionException;
}
```

Returned By XPath.compile()

XPathExpressionException Java 5.0

javax.xml.xpath serializable checked

Exceptions of this type indicate an error while compiling or evaluating an XPath expression. See the compile() and evaluate() methods of XPath and XPathExpression.

Object — Throwable — Exception — XPathException — XPathExpressionException
Throwable ⋮ Serializable

```
public class XPathExpressionException extends XPathException {
// Public Constructors
   public XPathExpressionException(Throwable cause);
   public XPathExpressionException(String message);
}
```

Subclasses XPathFunctionException

Thrown By XPath.{compile(), evaluate()}, XPathExpression.evaluate()

XPathFactory Java 5.0

javax.xml.xpath

The XPathFactory class is a factory for creating XPath expression evaluators. Call the no-argument version of newInstance() to obtain an XPathFactory object that creates XPath object to work with DOM documents. The javax.xml.xpath package is nominally object-model independent, however, and you can specify the name of a different object model by calling the one-argument version of newInstance().

Once you have created an XPathFactory object, you can set default function and variable resolvers with setXPathFunctionResolver() and setXPathVariableResolver(). You can configure implementation-dependent features of an XPathFactory with setFeature(). All implementations are required to support the XMLConstants.FEATURE_SECURE_PROCESSING feature. When this feature is set to true, external functions are not allowed in XPath expressions, and the XPathFunctionResolver is not used.

After creating and configuring an XPathFactory object, use the newXPath() method to create one or more XPath objects for actually evaluating XPath expressions.


```
public abstract class XPathFactory {
// Protected Constructors
   protected XPathFactory();
// Public Constants
   public static final String DEFAULT_OBJECT_MODEL_URI;                ="http://java.sun.com/jaxp/xpath/dom"
   public static final String DEFAULT_PROPERTY_NAME;                      ="javax.xml.xpath.XPathFactory"
// Public Class Methods
   public static final XPathFactory newInstance();
   public static final XPathFactory newInstance(String uri) throws XPathFactoryConfigurationException;
// Public Instance Methods
   public abstract boolean getFeature(String name) throws XPathFactoryConfigurationException;
   public abstract boolean isObjectModelSupported(String objectModel);
   public abstract XPath newXPath();
   public abstract void setFeature(String name, boolean value) throws XPathFactoryConfigurationException;
   public abstract void setXPathFunctionResolver(XPathFunctionResolver resolver);
   public abstract void setXPathVariableResolver(XPathVariableResolver resolver);
}
```

XPathFactoryConfigurationException Java 5.0

javax.xml.xpath serializable checked

This exception is thrown by methods of XPathFactory to indicate that a specified object model or feature is not supported.

Object — Throwable — Exception — XPathException — XPathFactoryConfigurationException
Serializable

```
public class XPathFactoryConfigurationException extends XPathException {
// Public Constructors
   public XPathFactoryConfigurationException(Throwable cause);
   public XPathFactoryConfigurationException(String message);
}
```

Thrown By XPathFactory.{getFeature(), newInstance(), setFeature()}

XPathFunction Java 5.0

javax.xml.xpath

This interface defines the invocation API for user-defined XPath functions. Arguments are passed to the evaluate() method as a java.util.List and the return value should be an Object. evaluate() may throw an XPathFunctionException. See also XPathFunctionResolver.

```
public interface XPathFunction {
// Public Instance Methods
   Object evaluate(java.util.List args) throws XPathFunctionException;
}
```

Returned By XPathFunctionResolver.resolveFunction()

XPathFunctionException Java 5.0

javax.xml.xpath serializable checked

Exceptions of this type may be thrown by user-defined XPathFunction implementations. Note that this is a subclass of XPathExpressionException.

Object ─ Throwable ─ Exception ─ XPathException ─ XPathExpressionException ─ XPathFunctionException
Serializable

```
public class XPathFunctionException extends XPathExpressionException {
// Public Constructors
   public XPathFunctionException(Throwable cause);
   public XPathFunctionException(String message);
}
```

Thrown By XPathFunction.evaluate()

XPathFunctionResolver Java 5.0

javax.xml.xpath

This interface defines a single method to return the XPathFunction with the specified qualified name and specified arity (number of arguments). Objects that implement this interface may be passed to the setXPathFunctionResolver() methods of XPath or XPathFactory.

Note that the function resolvers are invoked only for functions defined in an external namespace, so they cannot be used to override the meaning of XPath's built-in functions or to add new core functions to the XPath language. Also, if the XMLConstants.FEATURE_SECURE_PROCESSING feature has been enabled on an XPathFactory, user-defined functions are not allowed in XPath expressions, and the XPathFunctionResolver is never called.

```
public interface XPathFunctionResolver {
// Public Instance Methods
   XPathFunction resolveFunction(javax.xml.namespace.QName functionName, int arity);
}
```

Passed To XPath.setXPathFunctionResolver(), XPathFactory.setXPathFunctionResolver()

Returned By XPath.getXPathFunctionResolver()

XPathVariableResolver **Java 5.0**

javax.xml.xpath

This interface defines a single method to return the Object value of a variable identified by a qualified name. The value of a named variable is allowed to change between XPath evaluations, but implementations of this interface must ensure that no variable changes *during* the evaluation of an expression. Objects that implement this interface may be passed to the setXPathVariableResolver() methods of XPath or XPathFactory.

```
public interface XPathVariableResolver {
// Public Instance Methods
    Object resolveVariable(javax.xml.namespace.QName variableName);
}
```

Passed To XPath.setXPathVariableResolver(), XPathFactory.setXPathVariableResolver()

Returned By XPath.getXPathVariableResolver()

21

org.w3c.dom

Package org.w3c.dom

Java 1.4

This package defines the Java binding to the core and XML modules of the DOM API defined by the World Wide Web Consortium (W3C). DOM stands for Document Object Model, and the DOM API defines a way to represent an XML document as a tree of nodes. Java 1.4 supports the Level 2 DOM, and Java 5.0 adds support for Level 3.

This package includes methods that allow document trees to be traversed, examined, modified, and built from scratch. Node is the central interface of the package. All nodes in a document tree implement this interface, and it defines the basic methods for traversing and modifying the tree of nodes. Most of the other interfaces in the package are extensions of Node that represent specific types of XML content. The most important and commonly used of these subinterfaces are Document, Element, and Text. A Document object serves as the root of the document tree and defines methods for searching the tree for elements with a specified tag name or ID attribute. The Element interface represents an XML element or tag and has methods for manipulating the element's attributes. The Text interface represents a run of plain text within an Element and has methods for querying or altering that text. NodeList and DOMImplementation do not extend Node but are also important interfaces.

This package is an endorsed standard, which means that it is defined outside of Sun Microsystems and the Java Community Process but has been adopted as part of the Java platform. Full documentation is available at *http://www.w3.org/TR/DOM-Level-3-Core/*. Note that Java 5.0 also adopts the bootstrap, events, and ls (load/save) subpackages. Those subpackages are not documented in this book because they are only tangentially used by the rest of the Java platform.

Interfaces

public interface **Attr** extends Node;
public interface **CDATASection** extends Text;
public interface **CharacterData** extends Node;
public interface **Comment** extends CharacterData;

public interface **Document** extends Node;
public interface **DocumentFragment** extends Node;
public interface **DocumentType** extends Node;
public interface **DOMConfiguration**;
public interface **DOMError**;
public interface **DOMErrorHandler**;
public interface **DOMImplementation**;
public interface **DOMImplementationList**;
public interface **DOMImplementationSource**;
public interface **DOMLocator**;
public interface **DOMStringList**;
public interface **Element** extends Node;
public interface **Entity** extends Node;
public interface **EntityReference** extends Node;
public interface **NamedNodeMap**;
public interface **NameList**;
public interface **Node**;
public interface **NodeList**;
public interface **Notation** extends Node;
public interface **ProcessingInstruction** extends Node;
public interface **Text** extends CharacterData;
public interface **TypeInfo**;
public interface **UserDataHandler**;

Exceptions

public class **DOMException** extends RuntimeException;

Attr — Java 1.4

org.w3c.dom

An Attr object represents an attribute of an Element node. Attr objects are associated with Element nodes, but are not directly part of the document tree: the getParentNode() method of an Attr object always returns null. Use getOwnerElement() to deterine which Element an Attr is part of. You can obtain an Attr object by calling the getAttributeNode() method of Element, or you can obtain a NamedNodeMap of all Attr objects for an element with the getAttributes() method of Node.

getName() returns the name of the attribute. getValue() returns the attribute value as a string. getSpecified() returns true if the attribute was explicitly specified in the source document through a call to setValue(), and returns false if the attribute represents a default obtained from a DTD or other schema.

XML allows attributes to contain text and entity references. The getValue() method returns the attribute value as a single string. If you want to know the precise composition of the attribute however, you can examine the children of the Attr node: they may consist of Text and/or EntityReference nodes.

In most cases the easiest way to work with attributes is with the getAttribute() and setAttribute() methods of the Element interface. These methods avoid the use of Attr nodes altogether.

Node — Attr

```
public interface Attr extends Node {
// Public Instance Methods
   String getName();
   Element getOwnerElement();
5.0 TypeInfo getSchemaTypeInfo();
   boolean getSpecified();
   String getValue();
5.0 boolean isId();
   void setValue(String value) throws DOMException;
}
```

Passed To Element.{removeAttributeNode(), setAttributeNode(), setAttributeNodeNS(), setIdAttributeNode()}

Returned By Document.{createAttribute(), createAttributeNS()}, Element.{getAttributeNode(), getAttributeNodeNS(), removeAttributeNode(), setAttributeNode(), setAttributeNodeNS()}

CDATASection Java 1.4

org.w3c.dom

This interface represents a CDATA section in an XML document. CDATASection is a subinterface of Text and does not define any methods of its own. The content of the CDATA section is available through the getNodeValue() method inherited from Node, or through the getData() method inherited from CharacterData. Although CDATASection nodes can often be treated in the same way as Text nodes, note that the Node.normalize() method does not merge adjacent CDATA sections.

Node → CharacterData → Text → CDATASection

```
public interface CDATASection extends Text {
}
```

Returned By Document.createCDATASection()

CharacterData Java 1.4

org.w3c.dom

This interface is a generic one that is extended by Text, CDATASection (which extends Text) and Comment. Any node in a document tree that implements CharacterData also implements one of these more specific types. This interface exists simply to group the string manipulation methods that these text-related node types all share.

The CharacterData interface defines a mutable string. getData() returns the "character data" as a String object, and setData() allows it to be set from a String object. getLength() returns the number of characters of character data, and substringData() returns just the specified portion of the data as a string. The appendData(), deleteData(), insertData(), and replaceData() methods mutate the data by appending a string to the end, deleting region, inserting a string at the specified location, and replacing a region with a specified string.

Node → CharacterData

```
public interface CharacterData extends Node {
// Public Instance Methods
   void appendData(String arg) throws DOMException;
   void deleteData(int offset, int count) throws DOMException;
   String getData() throws DOMException;
   int getLength();
```

```
    void insertData(int offset, String arg) throws DOMException;
    void replaceData(int offset, int count, String arg) throws DOMException;
    void setData(String data) throws DOMException;
    String substringData(int offset, int count) throws DOMException;
}
```

Implementations Comment, Text

Comment — Java 1.4

org.w3c.dom

A Comment node represents a comment in an XML document. The content of the comment (i.e. the text between <!-- and -->) is available with the getData() method inherited from CharacterData, or through the getNodeValue() method inherited from Node. This content may be manipulated using the various methods inherited from CharacterData

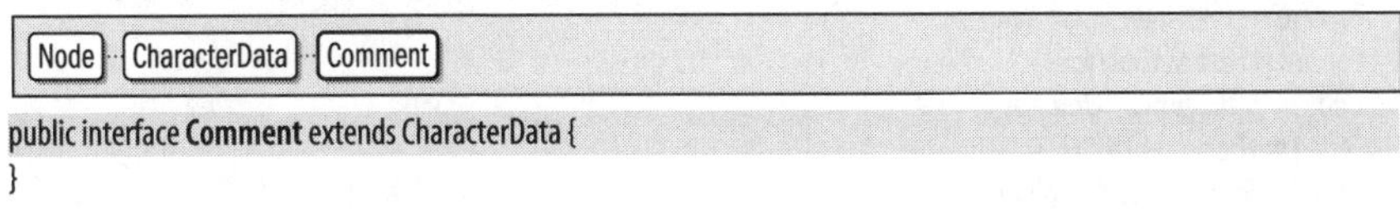


```
public interface Comment extends CharacterData {
}
```

Returned By Document.createComment()

Document — Java 1.4

org.w3c.dom

This interface represents a DOM document, and an object that implements this interface serves as the root of a DOM document tree. Most of the methods defined by the Document interface are "factory methods" that are used to create various types of nodes that can be inserted into this document. Note that there are two versions of the methods for creating attributes and elements. The methods with "NS" in their name are namespace-aware and require the attribute or element name to be specified as a combination of a namespace URI and a local name. You'll notice that throughout the DOM API, methods with "NS" in their names are namespace-aware. Other important methods include the following:

getElementsByTagName() and its namespace-aware variant getElementsByTagNameNS() search the document tree for Element nodes that have the specified tag name and return a NodeList containing those matching nodes. The Element interface defines methods by the same names that search only within the subtree defined by an Element.

getElementById() is a related method that searches the document tree for a single element with the specified unique value for an ID attribute. This is useful when you use an ID attribute to uniquely identify certain tags within an XML document. Note that this method does not search for attributes that are named "id" or "ID". It searches for attributes whose XML type (as declared in the document's DTD) is ID. Such attributes are often named "id", but this is not required.

An XML document must have a single root element. getDocumentElement() returns this Element object. Note, however that this does not mean that a Document node has only one child. It must have exactly one child that is an Element, but it can also have other children such as Comment and ProcessingInstruction nodes. The getDoctype() method returns the DocumentType object (or null if there isn't one) that represents the document's DTD. getImplementation() returns the the DOMImplementation object that represents the DOM implementation that created this document tree.

Node ··· Document

```
public interface Document extends Node {
// Public Instance Methods
5.0 Node adoptNode(Node source) throws DOMException;
    Attr createAttribute(String name) throws DOMException;
    Attr createAttributeNS(String namespaceURI, String qualifiedName) throws DOMException;
    CDATASection createCDATASection(String data) throws DOMException;
    Comment createComment(String data);
    DocumentFragment createDocumentFragment();
    Element createElement(String tagName) throws DOMException;
    Element createElementNS(String namespaceURI, String qualifiedName) throws DOMException;
    EntityReference createEntityReference(String name) throws DOMException;
    ProcessingInstruction createProcessingInstruction(String target, String data) throws DOMException;
    Text createTextNode(String data);
    DocumentType getDoctype();
    Element getDocumentElement();
5.0 String getDocumentURI();
5.0 DOMConfiguration getDomConfig();
    Element getElementById(String elementId);
    NodeList getElementsByTagName(String tagname);
    NodeList getElementsByTagNameNS(String namespaceURI, String localName);
    DOMImplementation getImplementation();
5.0 String getInputEncoding();
5.0 boolean getStrictErrorChecking();
5.0 String getXmlEncoding();
5.0 boolean getXmlStandalone();
5.0 String getXmlVersion();
    Node importNode(Node importedNode, boolean deep) throws DOMException;
5.0 void normalizeDocument();
5.0 Node renameNode(Node n, String namespaceURI, String qualifiedName) throws DOMException;
5.0 void setDocumentURI(String documentURI);
5.0 void setStrictErrorChecking(boolean strictErrorChecking);
5.0 void setXmlStandalone(boolean xmlStandalone) throws DOMException;
5.0 void setXmlVersion(String xmlVersion) throws DOMException;
}
```

Returned By javax.xml.parsers.DocumentBuilder.{newDocument(), parse()}, DOMImplementation.createDocument(), Node.getOwnerDocument()

DocumentFragment — Java 1.4

org.w3c.dom

The DocumentFragment interface represents a portion—or fragment—of a document. More specifically, it represents one or more adjacent document nodes, and all of the descendants of each. DocumentFragment nodes are never part of a document tree, and getParentNode() always returns null. Although a DocumentFragment does not have a parent, it can have children, and you can use the inherited Node methods to add child nodes (or delete or replace them) to a DocumentFragment.

DocumentFragment nodes exhibit a special behavior that makes them quite useful: when a request is made to insert a DocumentFragment into a document tree, it is not the DocumentFragment node itself that is inserted, but each of the children of the DocumentFragment instead. This makes DocumentFragment useful as a temporary placeholder for a sequence of nodes that you wish to insert, all at once, into a document.

You can create a new, empty, DocumentFragment to work with by calling the createDocumentFragment() method of the desired Document.

Node · DocumentFragment

```
public interface DocumentFragment extends Node {
}
```

Returned By Document.createDocumentFragment()

DocumentType Java 1.4

org.w3c.dom

This interface represents the Document Type Declaration, or DTD of a document. Because the DTD is not part of the document itself, a DocumentType object is not part of DOM document tree, even though it extends the Node interface. If a Document has a DTD, then you may obtain the DocumentType object that represents it by calling the getDoctype() method of the Document object.

getName(), getPublicId(), getSystemId(), and getInternalSubset() all return strings (or null) that contain the name, public identifier, system identifier, and internal subset of the document type. getEntities() returns a read-only NamedNodeMap that represents the a name-to-value mapping for all internal and external general entities declared by the DTD. You can use this NamedNodeMap to lookup an Entity object by name. Similarly, getNotations() returns a read-only NamedNodeMap that allows you to look up a Notation object declared in the DTD by name.

DocumentType does not provide access to the bulk of a DTD, which usually consists of element and attribute delcarations. Future versions of the DOM API may provide more details.

Node · DocumentType

```
public interface DocumentType extends Node {
// Public Instance Methods
   NamedNodeMap getEntities();
   String getInternalSubset();
   String getName();
   NamedNodeMap getNotations();
   String getPublicId();
   String getSystemId();
}
```

Passed To DOMImplementation.createDocument()

Returned By Document.getDoctype(), DOMImplementation.createDocumentType()

DOMConfiguration Java 5.0

org.w3c.dom

This Level 3 interface defines methods for querying and setting the values of named parameters. The DOMConfiguration object obtained with the Document.getDomConfig() method allows you to specify parameters that affect the behavior of the Document.normalizeDocument() method. You can also obtain a DOMConfiguration object from the LSParser and LSSerializer interfaces of the org.w3c.dom.ls package. Those configuration objects affect the way documents are loaded and saved, but the package is beyond the scope of this book. See the DOM specification for details on the available parameters.

DOM

```
public interface DOMConfiguration {
// Public Instance Methods
   boolean canSetParameter(String name, Object value);
   Object getParameter(String name) throws DOMException;
   DOMStringList getParameterNames();
   void setParameter(String name, Object value) throws DOMException;
}
```

Returned By Document.getDomConfig()

DOMError — Java 5.0

org.w3c.dom

This Level 3 interface describes an error that occurs while processing a document (such as when loading, saving, validating or normalizing it). An object that implements this interface is passed to the registered DOMErrorHandler, if any. The constants defined by this interface represent error severity levels.

Note that this interface is unrelated to DOMException class or to the java.lang.Error and java.lang.Exception classes.

```
public interface DOMError {
// Public Constants
   public static final short SEVERITY_ERROR;                        =2
   public static final short SEVERITY_FATAL_ERROR;                  =3
   public static final short SEVERITY_WARNING;                      =1
// Public Instance Methods
   org.w3c.dom.DOMLocator getLocation();
   String getMessage();
   Object getRelatedData();
   Object getRelatedException();
   short getSeverity();
   String getType();
}
```

Passed To DOMErrorHandler.handleError()

DOMErrorHandler — Java 5.0

org.w3c.dom

This Level 3 interface defines a handler for DOMError objects that represent errors while processing an XML document. Register an object that implements this interface by setting it as the value of the "error-handler" property through the DOMConfiguration interface.

```
public interface DOMErrorHandler {
// Public Instance Methods
   boolean handleError(DOMError error);
}
```

DOMException — Java 1.4

org.w3c.dom — serializable unchecked

An instance of this class is thrown whenever an exception is raised by the DOM API. Unlike many Java APIs, the DOM API does not define specialized subclasses to define different categories of exceptions. Instead, a more specific exception type is specified by the public field code. The value of this field will be one of the constants defined by this class, which have the following meanings:

INDEX_SIZE_ERR
: Indicates an out-of-bounds error for an array or string index.

DOMSTRING_SIZE_ERR
: Indicates that a requested text is too big to fit into a String object. Exceptions of this type are intended for DOM implementations for other languages and should not occur in Java.

HIERARCHY_REQUEST_ERR
: Indicates that an attempt was made to place a node somewhere illegal in the document tree hierarchy.

WRONG_DOCUMENT_ERR
: Indicates an attempt to use a node with a document that is different than the document that created the node.

INVALID_CHARACTER_ERR
: Indicates that an illegal character is used (in an element name, for example) .

NO_DATA_ALLOWED_ERR
: Not currently used.

NO_MODIFICATION_ALLOWED_ERR
: Indicates that an attempt was made to modify a node that is read-only and does not allow modifications. Entity, EntityReference, and Notation nodes, and all of their descendants are read-only.

NOT_FOUND_ERR
: Indicates that a node was not found where it was expected.

NOT_SUPPORTED_ERR
: Indicates that a method or property is not supported in the current DOM implementation.

INUSE_ATTRIBUTE_ERR
: Indicates that an attempt was made to associate an Attr with an Element when that Attr node was already associated with a different Element node.

INVALID_STATE_ERR
: Indicates an attempt to use an object that is not yet, or is no longer, in a state that allows such use.

SYNTAX_ERR
: Indicates that a specified string contains a syntax error. Exceptions of this type are not raised by the core module of the DOM API described here.

INVALID_MODIFICATION_ERR
: Exceptions of this type are not raised by the core module of the DOM API described here.

NAMESPACE_ERR
: Indicates an error involving element or attribute namespaces.

INVALID_ACCESS_ERR
: Indicates an attempt to access an object in a way that is not supported by the implementation.

Object — Throwable — Exception — RuntimeException — DOMException
Serializable

```
public class DOMException extends RuntimeException {
// Public Constructors
    public DOMException(short code, String message);
// Public Constants
    public static final short DOMSTRING_SIZE_ERR;                    =2
    public static final short HIERARCHY_REQUEST_ERR;                 =3
    public static final short INDEX_SIZE_ERR;                        =1
    public static final short INUSE_ATTRIBUTE_ERR;                   =10
    public static final short INVALID_ACCESS_ERR;                    =15
    public static final short INVALID_CHARACTER_ERR;                 =5
    public static final short INVALID_MODIFICATION_ERR;              =13
    public static final short INVALID_STATE_ERR;                     =11
    public static final short NAMESPACE_ERR;                         =14
    public static final short NO_DATA_ALLOWED_ERR;                   =6
    public static final short NO_MODIFICATION_ALLOWED_ERR;           =7
    public static final short NOT_FOUND_ERR;                         =8
    public static final short NOT_SUPPORTED_ERR;                     =9
    public static final short SYNTAX_ERR;                            =12
5.0 public static final short TYPE_MISMATCH_ERR;                     =17
5.0 public static final short VALIDATION_ERR;                        =16
    public static final short WRONG_DOCUMENT_ERR;                    =4
// Public Instance Fields
    public short code;
}
```

Thrown By Too many methods to list.

DOMImplementation — Java 1.4

org.w3c.dom

This interface defines methods that are global to an implementation of the DOM rather than specific to a particular Document object. Obtain a reference to the DOMImplementation object that represents your implementation by calling the getImplementation() method of any Document object. createDocument() returns a new, empty Document object which you can populate with nodes that you create using the create methods defined by the Document interface.

hasFeature() allows you to test whether your DOM implementation supports a specified version of a named feature, or module, of the DOM standard. This method should return true when you pass the feature name "core" and the verion "1.0", or when you pass the feature names "core" or "xml" and the version "2.0". The DOM standard includes a number of optional modules, but the Java platform has not adopted the subpackages of this package that define the API for those optional modules, and therefore the DOM implementation bundled with a Java implementation is not likely to support those modules.

The javax.xml.parsers.DocumentBuilder class provides another way to obtain the DOMImplementation object by calling its getDOMImplementation() object. It also defines a shortcut newDocument() method for creating empty Document objects to populate.

```
public interface DOMImplementation {
// Public Instance Methods
```

```
    Document createDocument(String namespaceURI, String qualifiedName, DocumentType doctype)
        throws DOMException;
    DocumentType createDocumentType(String qualifiedName, String publicId, String systemId) throws DOMException;
5.0 Object getFeature(String feature, String version);
    boolean hasFeature(String feature, String version);
}
```

Returned By javax.xml.parsers.DocumentBuilder.getDOMImplementation(), Document.getImplementation(), DOMImplementationList.item(), DOMImplementationSource.getDOMImplementation()

DOMImplementationList — Java 5.0

org.w3c.dom

This Level 3 interface represents a fixed-size, read-only list (or array) of DOMImplementation objects. getLength() returns the list length, and item() returns the DOMImplementation at the specified index.

```
public interface DOMImplementationList {
// Public Instance Methods
    int getLength();
    DOMImplementation item(int index);
}
```

Returned By DOMImplementationSource.getDOMImplementationList()

DOMImplementationSource — Java 5.0

org.w3c.dom

This Level 3 interface is designed for use by DOM implementors. It is also used in the org.w3c.dom.bootstrap package, which is beyond the scope of this book.

```
public interface DOMImplementationSource {
// Public Instance Methods
    DOMImplementation getDOMImplementation(String features);
    DOMImplementationList getDOMImplementationList(String features);
}
```

DOMLocator — Java 5.0

org.w3c.dom

This Level 3 interface represents the location at which a DOMError occurred. The methods return the location of the error as measured by various metrics (byte offset, line and column number, etc.) and return -1 or null if location information is not available.

```
public interface DOMLocator {
// Public Instance Methods
    int getByteOffset();
    int getColumnNumber();
    int getLineNumber();
    Node getRelatedNode();
    String getUri();
    int getUtf16Offset();
}
```

Returned By DOMError.getLocation()

DOMStringList **Java 5.0**

org.w3c.dom

This Level 3 interface represents a fixed-size, read-only list of strings. getLength() returns the length of the list, and item() returns the String at the specified index. contains() tests whether the specified String is contained in the list. An object of this type is returned by DOMConfiguration.getParameterNames().

```
public interface DOMStringList {
// Public Instance Methods
   boolean contains(String str);
   int getLength();
   String item(int index);
}
```

Returned By DOMConfiguration.getParameterNames()

Element **Java 1.4**

org.w3c.dom

This interface represents an element (or tag) in an XML document. getTagName() returns the tagname of the element, including the namespace prefix if there is one. When working with namespaces, you will probably prefer to use the namespace-aware methods defined by the Node interface. Use getNamespaceURI() to get the namespace URI of the element, and use getLocalName() to the local name of the element within that namespace. You can also use getPrefix() to query the namespace prefix, or setPrefix() to change the namespace prefix (this does not change the namespace URI).

Element defines a getElementsByTagName() method and a corresponding namespace-aware getElementsByTagNameNS() method, which behave just like the methods of the same names on the Document object, except that they search for named elements only within the subtree rooted at this Element.

The remaining methods of the Element interface are for querying and setting attribute values, testing the existence of an attribute, and removing an attribute from the Element. There are a confusing number of methods to perform these four basic attribute operations. If an attribute-related method has "NS" in its name, then it is namespace-aware. If it has "Node" in its name, then it works with Attr objects rather than with the simpler string representation of the attribute value. Attributes in XML documents may contain entity references. If your document may include entity references in attribute values, then you may need to use the Attr interface because the expansion of such an entity reference can result in a subtree of nodes beneath the Attr object. Whenver possible, however, it is much easier to work with the methods that treat attribute values as plain strings. Note also that in addition to the attribute methods defined by the Element interface you can also obtain a NamedNodeMap of Attr objects with the getAttributes() method of the Node interface.

Finally, note also that getAttribute() and related methods and hasAttribute() and related methods return the value of or test for the existance of both explicitly specified attributes, and also attributes for which a default value is specified in the document DTD. If you need to determine whether an attribute was explicitly specified in the document, obtain its Attr object, and use its getSpecified() method.

```
public interface Element extends Node {
// Public Instance Methods
    String getAttribute(String name);
    Attr getAttributeNode(String name);
    Attr getAttributeNodeNS(String namespaceURI, String localName) throws DOMException;
    String getAttributeNS(String namespaceURI, String localName) throws DOMException;
    NodeList getElementsByTagName(String name);
    NodeList getElementsByTagNameNS(String namespaceURI, String localName) throws DOMException;
5.0 TypeInfo getSchemaTypeInfo();
    String getTagName();
    boolean hasAttribute(String name);
    boolean hasAttributeNS(String namespaceURI, String localName) throws DOMException;
    void removeAttribute(String name) throws DOMException;
    Attr removeAttributeNode(Attr oldAttr) throws DOMException;
    void removeAttributeNS(String namespaceURI, String localName) throws DOMException;
    void setAttribute(String name, String value) throws DOMException;
    Attr setAttributeNode(Attr newAttr) throws DOMException;
    Attr setAttributeNodeNS(Attr newAttr) throws DOMException;
    void setAttributeNS(String namespaceURI, String qualifiedName, String value) throws DOMException;
5.0 void setIdAttribute(String name, boolean isId) throws DOMException;
5.0 void setIdAttributeNode(Attr idAttr, boolean isId) throws DOMException;
5.0 void setIdAttributeNS(String namespaceURI, String localName, boolean isId) throws DOMException;
}
```

Returned By Attr.getOwnerElement(), Document.{createElement(), createElementNS(), getDocumentElement(), getElementById()}

DOM

Entity **Java 1.4**

org.w3c.dom

This interface represents an entity defined in an XML DTD. The name of the entity is specified by the getNodeName() method inherited from the Node interface. The entity content is represented by the child nodes of the Entity node. The methods defined by this interface return the public identifier and system identifier for external entities, and the notation name for unparsed entities. Note that Entity nodes and their children are not part of the document tree (and the getParentNode() method of an Entity always returns null). Instead a document may contain one or more references to an entity: see the Entity-Reference interface.

Entities are defined in the DTD (document type definition) of a document, either as part of an external DTD file, or as part of an "internal subset" that defines local entities that are specific to the current document. The DocumentType interface has a getEntities() method that returns a NamedNodeMap mapping entity names to Entity nodes. This is the only way to obtain an Entity object: because they are part of the DTD, Entity nodes never appear within the document tree itself. Entity nodes and all descendants of an Entity node are read-only and cannot be edited or modified in any way.

Node ··· Entity

```
public interface Entity extends Node {
// Public Instance Methods
5.0 String getInputEncoding();
    String getNotationName();
    String getPublicId();
    String getSystemId();
```

```
5.0 String getXmlEncoding();
5.0 String getXmlVersion();
}
```

EntityReference **Java 1.4**

org.w3c.dom

This interface represents a reference from an XML document to an entity defined in the document's DTD. Character entities and predefined entities such as < are always expanded in XML documents and do not create EntityReference nodes. Note also that some XML parsers expand all entity references. Documents created by such parsers do not contain EntityReference nodes.

This interface defines no methods of its own. The getNodeName() method of the Node interface provides the name of the referenced entity. The getEntities() method of the DocumentType interface provides a way to look up the Entity object associated with that name. Note however, that the DocumentType may not contain an Entity with the specified name (because, for example, nonvalidating XML parsers are not required to parse the external subset of the DTD.) In this case, the EntityReference is a reference to a named entity whose content is not known, and it has no children. On the other hand, if the DocumentType does contain an Entity node with the specified name, then the child nodes of the EntityReference are a copy of the child nodes of the Entity, and represent the expansion of the entity. (The children of an EntityReference may not be an exact copy of the children of an Entity if the entity's expansion includes namespace prefixes that are not bound to namespace URIs.)

Like Entity nodes, EntityReference nodes and their descendants are read-only and cannot be edited or modified.

Node — EntityReference

```
public interface EntityReference extends Node {
}
```

Returned By Document.createEntityReference()

NamedNodeMap **Java 1.4**

org.w3c.dom

The NamedNodeMap interface defines a collection of nodes that may be looked up by name or by namespace URI and local name. It is unrelated to the java.util.Map interface. Use getNamedItem() to look for and return a node whose getNodeName() method returns the specified value. Use getNamedItemNS() to look for and return a node whose getNamespaceURI() and getLocalName() methods return the specified values. A NamedNodeMap is a mapping from names to nodes, and does not order the nodes in any particular way. Nevertheless, it does impose an arbitrary ordering on the nodes and allow them to be looked up by index. Use getLength() to find out how many nodes are contained in the NamedNodeMap, and use item() to obtain the Node object at a specified index.

If a NamedNodeMap is not read-only, you can use removeNamedItem() and removeNamedItemNS() to remove a named node from the map, and you can use setNamedItem() and setNamedItemNS() to add a node to the map, mapping to it from its name or its namespace URI and local name.

NamedNodeMap objects are "live," which means that they immediately reflect any changes to the document tree. For example, if you obtain a NamedNodeMap that represents the attributes of an element, and then add a new attribute to that element, the new attribute is automatically available through the NamedNodeMap: you do not need to obtain a new NamedNodeMap to get the modified set of attributes.

NamedNodeMap is returned only by relatively obscure methods of the DOM API. The most notable use is as the return value of the getAttributes() method of Node. It is usually easier to work with attributes through the methods of the Element interface, however. Two methods of DocumentType also return read-only NamedNodeMap objects.

```
public interface NamedNodeMap {
// Public Instance Methods
   int getLength();
   Node getNamedItem(String name);
   Node getNamedItemNS(String namespaceURI, String localName) throws DOMException;
   Node item(int index);
   Node removeNamedItem(String name) throws DOMException;
   Node removeNamedItemNS(String namespaceURI, String localName) throws DOMException;
   Node setNamedItem(Node arg) throws DOMException;
   Node setNamedItemNS(Node arg) throws DOMException;
}
```

Returned By DocumentType.{getEntities(), getNotations()}, Node.getAttributes()

DOM

NameList — Java 5.0

org.w3c.dom

This Level 3 interface represnts a fixed-size, read-only list of element or attribute names and their namespace URI. getLength() returns the length of the list. getName() and getNamespaceURI() return the name and namespace at the specified index. contains() and containsNS() test for membership in the list.

This interface is unused within the org.w3c.dom package.

```
public interface NameList {
// Public Instance Methods
   boolean contains(String str);
   boolean containsNS(String namespaceURI, String name);
   int getLength();
   String getName(int index);
   String getNamespaceURI(int index);
}
```

Node — Java 1.4

org.w3c.dom

All objects in a DOM document tree (including the Document object itself) implement the Node interface, which provides basic methods for traversing and manipulating the tree.

getParentNode() and getChildNodes() allow you to traverse up and down the document tree. You can enumerate the children of a given node by looping through the elements of the NodeList returned by getChildNodes(), or by using getFirstChild() and getNextSibling() (or getLastChild() and getPreviousSibling() to loop backwards). It is sometimes useful to call hasChildNodes() to determine whether a node has children or not. getOwnerDocument() returns the Document node of which the node is a descendant or with which it is associated. It provides a quick way to jump to the root of the document tree.

Several methods allow you to add children to a tree or alter the list of children. appendChild() adds a new child node at the end of this nodes list of children. insertChild() inserts a node into this nodes list of children, placing it immediately before a specified child node. removeChild() removes the specified node from this node's list of children. replaceChild() replaces one child node of this node with another node. For all of these methods, if the node to be appended or inserted is already part of the document tree, it is first removed from its current parent. Use cloneNode() to produce a copy of this node. Pass true if you want all descendants of this node to be cloned as well.

Every object in a document tree implements the Node interface, but also implements a more specialized subinterface, such as Element or Text. The getNodeType() method provides an easy way to determine which subinterface a node implements: the return value is one of the _NODE constants defined by this class. You might use the return value of getNodeType() in a switch statement, for exmaple, to determine how to process a node of unknown type.

getNodeName() and getNodeValue() provide additional information about a node, but the interpretation of the strings they return depends on the node type as shown in the table below. Note that subinterfaces typically define specialized methods (such as the getTagName() method of Element and the getData() method of Text) for obtaining this same information. Note also that unless a node is read-only, you can use setNodeValue() to alter the value associated with the node.

Node type	Node name	Node value
ELEMENT_NODE	The element s tag name	null
ATTRIBUTE_NODE	The attribute name	The attribute value
TEXT_NODE	#text	The text of the node
CDATA_SECTION_NODE	#cdata-section	The text of the node
ENTITY_REFERENCE_NODE	The name of the referenced entity	null
ENTITY_NODE	The entity name	null
PROCESSING_INSTRUCTION_NODE	The target of the PI	The remainder of the PI
COMMENT_NODE	#comment	The text of the comment
DOCUMENT_NODE	#document	null
DOCUMENT_TYPE_NODE	The document type name	null
DOCUMENT_FRAGMENT_NODE	#document-fragment	null
NOTATION_NODE	The notation name	null

In documents that use namespaces, the getNodeName() method of a Element or Attr node returns the qualified node name, which may include a namespace prefix. In documents that use namespaces, you may prefer to use the namespace-aware methods getNamespaceURI(), getLocalName() and getPrefix().

Element nodes may have a list of attributes, and the Element interface defines a number of methods for working with these attributes. In addition, however, Node defines the hasAttributes() method to determine if a node has any attributes. If it does, they can be retrieved with getAttributes().

Text content in an XML document is represented by Text nodes, which have methods for manipulating that textual content. The Node interface defines a normalize() method which has the specialized purpose of normalizing all descendants of a node by deleting empty Text nodes and coalescing adjacent Text nodes into a single combined node. Document trees usually start off in this normalized form, but modifications to the tree may result in non-normalized documents.

Most of the other interfaces in this package extend Node. Document, Element and Text are the most commonly used.

```
public interface Node {
// Public Constants
    public static final short ATTRIBUTE_NODE;                                   =2
    public static final short CDATA_SECTION_NODE;                               =4
    public static final short COMMENT_NODE;                                     =8
    public static final short DOCUMENT_FRAGMENT_NODE;                           =11
    public static final short DOCUMENT_NODE;                                    =9
5.0 public static final short DOCUMENT_POSITION_CONTAINED_BY;                   =16
5.0 public static final short DOCUMENT_POSITION_CONTAINS;                       =8
5.0 public static final short DOCUMENT_POSITION_DISCONNECTED;                   =1
5.0 public static final short DOCUMENT_POSITION_FOLLOWING;                      =4
5.0 public static final short DOCUMENT_POSITION_IMPLEMENTATION_SPECIFIC;        =32
5.0 public static final short DOCUMENT_POSITION_PRECEDING;                      =2
    public static final short DOCUMENT_TYPE_NODE;                               =10
    public static final short ELEMENT_NODE;                                     =1
    public static final short ENTITY_NODE;                                      =6
    public static final short ENTITY_REFERENCE_NODE;                            =5
    public static final short NOTATION_NODE;                                    =12
    public static final short PROCESSING_INSTRUCTION_NODE;                      =7
    public static final short TEXT_NODE;                                        =3
// Public Instance Methods
    Node appendChild(Node newChild) throws DOMException;
    Node cloneNode(boolean deep);
5.0 short compareDocumentPosition(Node other) throws DOMException;
    NamedNodeMap getAttributes();
5.0 String getBaseURI();
    NodeList getChildNodes();
5.0 Object getFeature(String feature, String version);
    Node getFirstChild();
    Node getLastChild();
    String getLocalName();
    String getNamespaceURI();
    Node getNextSibling();
    String getNodeName();
    short getNodeType();
    String getNodeValue() throws DOMException;
    Document getOwnerDocument();
    Node getParentNode();
    String getPrefix();
    Node getPreviousSibling();
5.0 String getTextContent() throws DOMException;
5.0 Object getUserData(String key);
    boolean hasAttributes();
    boolean hasChildNodes();
    Node insertBefore(Node newChild, Node refChild) throws DOMException;
5.0 boolean isDefaultNamespace(String namespaceURI);
5.0 boolean isEqualNode(Node arg);
5.0 boolean isSameNode(Node other);
    boolean isSupported(String feature, String version);
5.0 String lookupNamespaceURI(String prefix);
5.0 String lookupPrefix(String namespaceURI);
```

```
    void normalize();
    Node removeChild(Node oldChild) throws DOMException;
    Node replaceChild(Node newChild, Node oldChild) throws DOMException;
    void setNodeValue(String nodeValue) throws DOMException;
    void setPrefix(String prefix) throws DOMException;
5.0 void setTextContent(String textContent) throws DOMException;
5.0 Object setUserData(String key, Object data, UserDataHandler handler);
}
```

Implementations Attr, CharacterData, Document, DocumentFragment, DocumentType, Element, Entity, EntityReference, Notation, ProcessingInstruction

Passed To Too many methods to list.

Returned By Too many methods to list.

NodeList Java 1.4

org.w3c.dom

This interface represents a read-only ordered collection of nodes that can be interated through. getLength() returns the number of nodes in the list, and item() returns the Node at a specified index in the list (the index of the first node is 0). The elements of a NodeList are always valid Node objects: a NodeList never contains null elements.

Note that NodeList objects are "live"—they are not static but immediately reflect changes to the document tree. For example, if you have a NodeList that represents the children of a specific node, and you then delete one of those children, the child will be removed from your NodeList. Be careful when looping through the elements of a NodeList if the body of your loop makes changes to the document tree (such as deleting nodes) that may affect the contents of the NodeList!

```
public interface NodeList {
// Public Instance Methods
    int getLength();
    Node item(int index);
}
```

Returned By Document.{getElementsByTagName(), getElementsByTagNameNS()}, Element.{getElementsByTagName(), getElementsByTagNameNS()}, Node.getChildNodes()

Notation Java 1.4

org.w3c.dom

This interface represents a notation declared in the DTD of an XML document. In XML notations are used to specify the format of an unparsed entity or to formally declare a processing instruction target.

The getNodeName() method of the Node interface returns the name of the notation. getSystemId() and getPublicId() return the system identifier and the public identifier specified in the notation declaration. The getNotations() method of the DocumentType interface returns a NamedNodeMap of Notation objects declared in the DTD and provides a way to look up Notation objects by notation name.

Because notations appear in the DTD and not the document itself, Notation nodes are never part of the document tree, and the getParentNode() method always returns null. Similarly, since XML notation declarations never have any content, a Notation node never has children and getChildNodes() always returns null. Notation objects are read-only and cannot be modified in any way.

Node · Notation

```
public interface Notation extends Node {
// Public Instance Methods
   String getPublicId();
   String getSystemId();
}
```

ProcessingInstruction Java 1.4

org.w3c.dom

This interface represents an XML processing instruction (or PI) which specifies an arbitrary string of data to a named target processor. The getTarget() and getData() methods return the target and data portions of a PI, and these values can also be obtained using the getNodeName() and getNodeValue() methods of the Node interface. You can alter the data portion of a PI with setData() or with the setNodeValue() method of Node. ProcessingInstruction nodes never have children.

Node · ProcessingInstruction

```
public interface ProcessingInstruction extends Node {
// Public Instance Methods
   String getData();
   String getTarget();
   void setData(String data) throws DOMException;
}
```

Returned By Document.createProcessingInstruction()

Text Java 1.4

org.w3c.dom

A Text node represents a run of plain text that does not contain any XML markup. Plain text appears within XML elements and attributes, and Text nodes typically appear as children of Element and Attr nodes. Text nodes inherit from CharacterData, and the textual content of a Text node is available through the getData() method inherited from CharacterData or through the getNodeValue() method inherited from Node.

Text nodes may be manipulated using any of the methods inherited from CharacterData. The Text interface defines one method of its own: splitText() splits a Text node at the specified character position. The method changes the original node so that it contains only the text up to the specified position. Then it creates a new Text node that contains the text from the specified position on and inserts that new node into the document tree immediately after the original one. The Node.normalize() method reverses this process by deleting emty Text nodes and merging adjacent Text nodes into a single node.

Text nodes never have children.

Node · CharacterData · Text

```
public interface Text extends CharacterData {
// Public Instance Methods
5.0 String getWholeText();
5.0 boolean isElementContentWhitespace();
```

DOM

```
5.0 Text replaceWholeText(String content) throws DOMException;
    Text splitText(int offset) throws DOMException;
}
```

Implementations CDATASection

Returned By Document.createTextNode()

TypeInfo **Java 5.0**

org.w3c.dom

This Level 3 interface represents information about the type of an Element or Attr node. Obtain a TypeInfo object by calling the getSchemaTypeInfo() method of an Element or Attr. Note that TypeInfo information is only available if the document has been validated against a W3C XML Schema.

The methods of TypeInfo return the name and namespace of the element or attribute type. isDerivedFrom() determines if the type is a derivative of another named type. The constants defined by the interface specify different derivation techniques for types.

See also java.xml.validation.TypeInfoProvider.

```
public interface TypeInfo {
// Public Constants
    public static final int DERIVATION_EXTENSION;                          =2
    public static final int DERIVATION_LIST;                               =8
    public static final int DERIVATION_RESTRICTION;                        =1
    public static final int DERIVATION_UNION;                              =4
// Public Instance Methods
    String getTypeName();
    String getTypeNamespace();
    boolean isDerivedFrom(String typeNamespaceArg, String typeNameArg, int derivationMethod);
}
```

Returned By javax.xml.validation.TypeInfoProvider.{getAttributeTypeInfo(), getElementTypeInfo()}, Attr.getSchemaTypeInfo(), Element.getSchemaTypeInfo()

UserDataHandler **Java 5.0**

org.w3c.dom

This Level 3 interface defines a handler that is invoked when a node on which user-specified data has been registered is adopted, cloned, deleted, imported or renamed. Register an object that implements this interface in the call to Node.setUserData().

```
public interface UserDataHandler {
// Public Constants
    public static final short NODE_ADOPTED;                                =5
    public static final short NODE_CLONED;                                 =1
    public static final short NODE_DELETED;                                =3
    public static final short NODE_IMPORTED;                               =2
    public static final short NODE_RENAMED;                                =4
// Public Instance Methods
    void handle(short operation, String key, Object data, Node src, Node dst);
}
```

Passed To Node.setUserData()

org.xml.sax and Subpackages

This chapter documents the org.xml.sax package and its subpackages. org.xml.sax defines the Simplified API for XML, or SAX, a de facto standard for parsing XML documents. The org.xml.sax.ext package defines optional extensions to the SAX API, and the org.xml.sax.helpers package defines helper classes that are often useful with SAX.

These packages were added in Java 1.4 as "endorsed standards." This means that they are part of the Java platform, but are not defined by Sun, which is why they have the "org.xml" prefix.

Package org.xml.sax — Java 1.4

This is the core package for SAX (Simple API for XML) parsing of XML documents. SAX is an "event-driven" API: a SAX parser reads an XML document and generates a stream of "SAX events" to describe the content of the document. These "events" are actually method calls made on one or more handler objects that the application has registered with the parser. The XMLReader interface defines the API that must be implemented by a SAX parser. ContentHandler, ErrorHandler, EntityResolver, and DTDHandler are interfaces that define handler objects. An application registers objects that implement one or more of these interfaces with the XMLReader.

This package defines both the SAX1 and SAX2 interfaces. The AttributesList, DocumentHandler and Parser interfaces, as well as the HandlerBase class are part of the SAX1 API and are now deprecated in favor of Attributes, ContentHandler, XMLReader, and org.xml.sax.helpers.DefaultHandler.

Interfaces

public interface **AttributeList**;
public interface **Attributes**;
public interface **ContentHandler**;
public interface **DocumentHandler**;
public interface **DTDHandler**;
public interface **EntityResolver**;

```
public interface ErrorHandler;
public interface Locator;
public interface Parser;
public interface XMLFilter extends XMLReader;
public interface XMLReader;
```

Classes

```
public class HandlerBase implements DocumentHandler, DTDHandler, EntityResolver, ErrorHandler;
public class InputSource;
```

Exceptions

```
public class SAXException extends Exception;
    public class SAXNotRecognizedException extends SAXException;
    public class SAXNotSupportedException extends SAXException;
    public class SAXParseException extends SAXException;
```

AttributeList — Java 1.4; Deprecated in 1.4

org.xml.sax

This interface is part of the SAX1 API and has been deprecated in favor of the SAX2 **Attributes** interface, which supports XML namespaces.

```
public interface AttributeList {
// Public Instance Methods
    int getLength();
    String getName(int i);
    String getType(String name);
    String getType(int i);
    String getValue(String name);
    String getValue(int i);
}
```

Implementations org.xml.sax.helpers.AttributeListImpl

Passed To DocumentHandler.startElement(), HandlerBase.startElement(), org.xml.sax.helpers.AttributeListImpl.{AttributeListImpl(), setAttributeList()}, org.xml.sax.helpers.ParserAdapter.startElement()

Attributes — Java 1.4

org.xml.sax

This interface represents a list of attributes of an XML element and includes information about the attribute names, types, and values. If the SAX parser has read a DTD or schema for the document, this list of attributes will include attributes that are not explicitly specified in the document but which have a default value specified in the DTD or schema.

The most commonly used method is **getValue()** which returns the value of a named attribute (there is also a version of this method that returns the value of a numbered attribute; it is discussed later). If the SAX parser is not processing namespaces, you can use the one-argument version of **getValue()**. Otherwise, use the two argument version to specify the URI that uniquely identifies the namespace, and the "local name" of the desired attribute within that namespace . The **getType()** methods are similar, except that they return the type of the named attribute, rather than its value. Note that **getType()** can only return useful information if the parser has read a DTD or schema for the document and knows the type of each attribute.

In XML documents the attributes of a tag can appear in any order. **Attributes** objects make no attempt to preserve the document source order of the tags. Nevertheless, it does impose an ordering on the attributes so that you can loop through them. **getLength()** returns the number of elements in the list. There are versions of **getValue()** and **getType()** that return the value and type of the attribute at a specified position in the list. You can also query the name of the attribute at a specified position, although the way you do this depends on whether the parser handles namespaces or not. If it does not process namespaces, use **getQName()** to get the name at a specified position. Otherwise, use **getURI()** and **getLocalName()** to obtain the URI and local name pair for the numbered attribute. Note that **getQName()** may return the empty string when namespace processing is on, and **getLocalName()** may return the empty string if namespace processing is off.

```
public interface Attributes {
// Public Instance Methods
   int getIndex(String qName);
   int getIndex(String uri, String localName);
   int getLength();
   String getLocalName(int index);
   String getQName(int index);
   String getType(String qName);
   String getType(int index);
   String getType(String uri, String localName);
   String getURI(int index);
   String getValue(String qName);
   String getValue(int index);
   String getValue(String uri, String localName);
}
```

SAX

Implementations org.xml.sax.ext.Attributes2, org.xml.sax.helpers.AttributesImpl

Passed To org.xml.sax.ContentHandler.startElement(), org.xml.sax.ext.Attributes2Impl.{Attributes2Impl(), setAttributes()}, org.xml.sax.helpers.AttributesImpl.{AttributesImpl(), setAttributes()}, org.xml.sax.helpers.DefaultHandler.startElement(), org.xml.sax.helpers.XMLFilterImpl.startElement(), org.xml.sax.helpers.XMLReaderAdapter.startElement()

ContentHandler **Java 1.4**

org.xml.sax

This interface is the key one for XML parsing with the SAX API. An **XMLReader** tells your application about the content of the XML document it is parsing by invoking the various methods of the **ContentHandler** interface. In order to parse documents with SAX, you must implement this interface to define methods that take whatever actions are necessary when they are invoked by the parser. Because this interface is so critical to the SAX API, the methods are explained individually below:

setDocumentLocator()

: The parser usually calls this method (but is not required to do so) before calling any others to pass a **Locator** object to the **ContentHandler**. **Locator** defines methods that return the current line and column number of the document being parsed, and if the parser supplies a **Locator** object, it guarantees that its methods will return valid values during any other **ContentHandler** invocations that follow. A **ContentHandler** can call the methods of this object when printing error messages, for example.

startDocument(), endDocument()
: The parser calls these methods once, at the beginning and end of parsing. startDocument() is the first method called except for the optional setDocumentLocator() call, and endDocument() is always the last method call on a ContentHandler.

startElement(), endElement()
: The parser calls these methods for each start tag and end tag it encounters. Both are passed three arguments describing the name of the tag: if the parser is doing namespace processing, then the first two arguments of both methods return the URI that uniquely identifies the namespace, and the local name of the tag within that namespace. If the parser is not doing namespace parsing, then the third argument provides the full name of the tag. In addition to these tag name arguments, startElement() is also passed an Attributes object that describes the attributes of the tag.

characters()
: This method is invoked to tell the application that the parser has found a string of text in the XML document. The text is contained within the specified character array, at the specified start position, and continuing for the specified number of characters.

ignorableWhitespace()
: This method is like characters(), but parsers may use it to tell the application about "ignorable whitespace" in XML element content.

processingInstruction()
: The parser calls this method to tell the application that it has encountered an XML Processing Instruction (or PI) with the specified target and data strings.

skippedEntity()
: If the XML parser does encounters an entity in the document, but does not expand and parse its content, then it tells the application about it by passing the name of the entity to this method.

startPrefixMapping(), endPrefixMapping()
: These methods to tell the application about a namespace mapping from the specified prefix to the specified namespace URI.

DTDHandler is another interface like ContentHandler. An application can implement this interface to receive notification of DTD-related events from the parser. Similarly, the org.xml.sax.ext package defines two "extension" interfaces that can be used (if the parser supports these extensions) to obtain even more information about the document (such as comments and CDATA sections) and about the DTD (including the full set of element, attribute and entity declarations). The org.xml.sax.helpers.DefaultHandler class is a useful one. It implements ContentHandler and three other interfaces that are commonly used with the XMLReader class and provides empty implementations of all their methods. Applications can subclass DefaultHandler only need to override the methods they care about. This is usually more convenient that implementing the interfaces directly.

```
public interface ContentHandler {
// Public Instance Methods
   void characters(char[] ch, int start, int length) throws SAXException;
   void endDocument() throws SAXException;
   void endElement(String uri, String localName, String qName) throws SAXException;
   void endPrefixMapping(String prefix) throws SAXException;
   void ignorableWhitespace(char[] ch, int start, int length) throws SAXException;
   void processingInstruction(String target, String data) throws SAXException;
   void setDocumentLocator(Locator locator);
```

```
    void skippedEntity(String name) throws SAXException;
    void startDocument() throws SAXException;
    void startElement(String uri, String localName, String qName, org.xml.sax.Attributes atts) throws SAXException;
    void startPrefixMapping(String prefix, String uri) throws SAXException;
}
```

Implementations javax.xml.transform.sax.TemplatesHandler, javax.xml.transform.sax.TransformerHandler, javax.xml.validation.ValidatorHandler, org.xml.sax.helpers.DefaultHandler, org.xml.sax.helpers.XMLFilterImpl, org.xml.sax.helpers.XMLReaderAdapter

Passed To javax.xml.transform.sax.SAXResult.{SAXResult(), setHandler()}, javax.xml.validation.ValidatorHandler.setContentHandler(), XMLReader.setContentHandler(), org.xml.sax.helpers.ParserAdapter.setContentHandler(), org.xml.sax.helpers.XMLFilterImpl.setContentHandler()

Returned By javax.xml.transform.sax.SAXResult.getHandler(), javax.xml.validation.ValidatorHandler.getContentHandler(), XMLReader.getContentHandler(), org.xml.sax.helpers.ParserAdapter.getContentHandler(), org.xml.sax.helpers.XMLFilterImpl.getContentHandler()

DocumentHandler

Java 1.4; Deprecated in 1.4

org.xml.sax

This interface is part of the SAX1 API and has been deprecated in favor of the SAX2 ContentHandler interface, which supports XML namespaces.

```
public interface DocumentHandler {
// Public Instance Methods
    void characters(char[] ch, int start, int length) throws SAXException;
    void endDocument() throws SAXException;
    void endElement(String name) throws SAXException;
    void ignorableWhitespace(char[] ch, int start, int length) throws SAXException;
    void processingInstruction(String target, String data) throws SAXException;
    void setDocumentLocator(Locator locator);
    void startDocument() throws SAXException;
    void startElement(String name, AttributeList atts) throws SAXException;
}
```

Implementations HandlerBase, org.xml.sax.helpers.ParserAdapter

Passed To Parser.setDocumentHandler(), org.xml.sax.helpers.XMLReaderAdapter.setDocumentHandler()

DTDHandler

Java 1.4

org.xml.sax

This interface defines methods that an application can implement in order to receive notification from a XMLReader about notation and unparsed entity declarations in the DTD of an XML document. Notations and unparsed entities are two of the most obscure features of XML, and they (and this interface) are not frequently used. To use a DTDHandler, define a class that implements the interface, (or simply subclass the helper class org.xml.sax.helpers.DefaultHandler) and pass an instance of that class to the setDTDHandler() method of an XMLReader. Then, if the parser encounters any notation or unparsed entity declarations in the DTD of the document, it will invoke the notationDecl() or unparsedEntityDecl() method that you have supplied. Unparsed entities can appear later in a document as the value of an attribute, so if your application cares about them, it should somehow make a note of the entity name and system id for use later.

SAX

```
public interface DTDHandler {
// Public Instance Methods
   void notationDecl(String name, String publicId, String systemId) throws SAXException;
   void unparsedEntityDecl(String name, String publicId, String systemId, String notationName) throws SAXException;
}
```

Implementations javax.xml.transform.sax.TransformerHandler, HandlerBase, org.xml.sax.helpers.DefaultHandler, org.xml.sax.helpers.XMLFilterImpl

Passed To Parser.setDTDHandler(), XMLReader.setDTDHandler(), org.xml.sax.helpers.ParserAdapter.setDTDHandler(), org.xml.sax.helpers.XMLFilterImpl.setDTDHandler(), org.xml.sax.helpers.XMLReaderAdapter.setDTDHandler()

Returned By XMLReader.getDTDHandler(), org.xml.sax.helpers.ParserAdapter.getDTDHandler(), org.xml.sax.helpers.XMLFilterImpl.getDTDHandler()

EntityResolver — Java 1.4

org.xml.sax

An application can implement this interface to help the parser resolve external entities, if required. If you pass an EntityResolver instance to the setEntityResolver() method of an XMLReader, then the parser will call the resolveEntity() method whenever it needs to read an external entity. This method should use the public identifier or system identifier to return an InputSource that the parser can use to read the content of the external entity. If the external entity includes a valid system identifier, then the parser can read it directly without the need for an EntityResolver, but this interface is still useful for mapping network URLs to locally cached copies, or for mapping public identifiers to local files, for example. The helper class org.xml.sax.helpers.DefaultHandler includes a stub implementation of this interface, so if you subclass DefaultHandler you can override its resolveEntity() method.

```
public interface EntityResolver {
// Public Instance Methods
   InputSource resolveEntity(String publicId, String systemId) throws SAXException, java.io.IOException;
}
```

Implementations HandlerBase, org.xml.sax.ext.EntityResolver2, org.xml.sax.helpers.DefaultHandler, org.xml.sax.helpers.XMLFilterImpl

Passed To javax.xml.parsers.DocumentBuilder.setEntityResolver(), Parser.setEntityResolver(), XMLReader.setEntityResolver(), org.xml.sax.helpers.ParserAdapter.setEntityResolver(), org.xml.sax.helpers.XMLFilterImpl.setEntityResolver(), org.xml.sax.helpers.XMLReaderAdapter.setEntityResolver()

Returned By XMLReader.getEntityResolver(), org.xml.sax.helpers.ParserAdapter.getEntityResolver(), org.xml.sax.helpers.XMLFilterImpl.getEntityResolver()

ErrorHandler — Java 1.4

org.xml.sax

Before parsing an XML document, an application should provide an implementation of this interface to the XMLReader by calling the setErrorHandler() method of the XMLReader. If the reader needs to issue a warning or report an error or fatal error, it will call the appropriate method of the ErrorHandler object you supplied. The error() method is used to report recoverable errors, such as document validity problems. The parser continues parsing after calling error(). The fatalError() method is used to report nonrecoverable errors, such as well-formedness problems. The parser may not continue parsing after calling fatalError(). An ErrorHandler object may respond to warnings, errors, and fatal errors however it likes, and may throw exceptions from these methods.

Instead of implementing this interface directly, you may also subclass the helper class org.xml.sax.helpers.DefaultHandler and override the error reporting methods it provides. The warning() and error() methods of a DefaultHandler do nothing, and the fatalError() method throws the SAXParseException object that was passed to it.

```
public interface ErrorHandler {
// Public Instance Methods
   void error(SAXParseException exception) throws SAXException;
   void fatalError(SAXParseException exception) throws SAXException;
   void warning(SAXParseException exception) throws SAXException;
}
```

Implementations HandlerBase, org.xml.sax.helpers.DefaultHandler, org.xml.sax.helpers.XMLFilterImpl

Passed To javax.xml.parsers.DocumentBuilder.setErrorHandler(), javax.xml.validation.SchemaFactory.setErrorHandler(), javax.xml.validation.Validator.setErrorHandler(), javax.xml.validation.ValidatorHandler.setErrorHandler(), Parser.setErrorHandler(), XMLReader.setErrorHandler(), org.xml.sax.helpers.ParserAdapter.setErrorHandler(), org.xml.sax.helpers.XMLFilterImpl.setErrorHandler(), org.xml.sax.helpers.XMLReaderAdapter.setErrorHandler()

Returned By javax.xml.validation.SchemaFactory.getErrorHandler(), javax.xml.validation.Validator.getErrorHandler(), javax.xml.validation.ValidatorHandler.getErrorHandler(), XMLReader.getErrorHandler(), org.xml.sax.helpers.ParserAdapter.getErrorHandler(), org.xml.sax.helpers.XMLFilterImpl.getErrorHandler()

HandlerBase **Java 1.4; Deprecated in 1.4**

org.xml.sax

This class is part of the SAX1 API and has been deprecated in favor of the SAX2 org.xml.sax.helpers.DefaultHandler class.

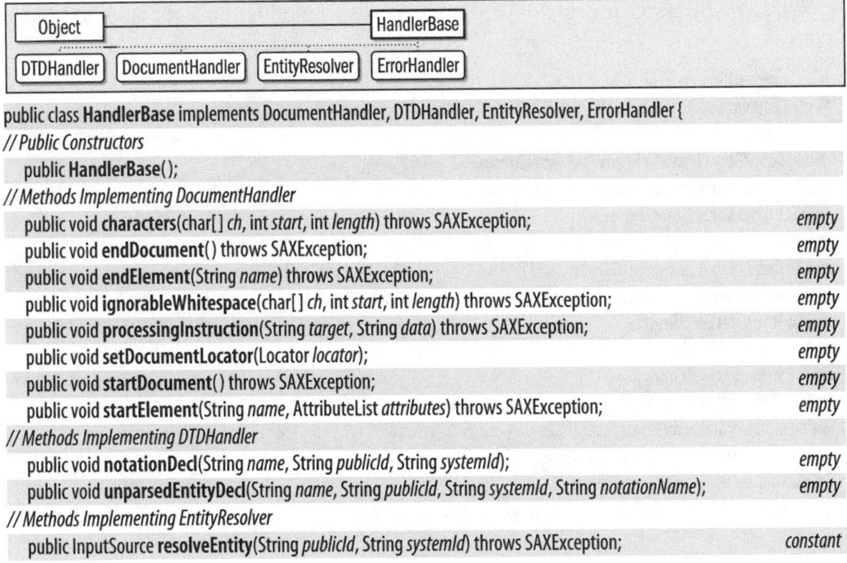


```
public class HandlerBase implements DocumentHandler, DTDHandler, EntityResolver, ErrorHandler {
// Public Constructors
   public HandlerBase();
// Methods Implementing DocumentHandler
   public void characters(char[] ch, int start, int length) throws SAXException;                  empty
   public void endDocument() throws SAXException;                                                 empty
   public void endElement(String name) throws SAXException;                                       empty
   public void ignorableWhitespace(char[] ch, int start, int length) throws SAXException;         empty
   public void processingInstruction(String target, String data) throws SAXException;             empty
   public void setDocumentLocator(Locator locator);                                               empty
   public void startDocument() throws SAXException;                                               empty
   public void startElement(String name, AttributeList attributes) throws SAXException;           empty
// Methods Implementing DTDHandler
   public void notationDecl(String name, String publicId, String systemId);                      empty
   public void unparsedEntityDecl(String name, String publicId, String systemId, String notationName);   empty
// Methods Implementing EntityResolver
   public InputSource resolveEntity(String publicId, String systemId) throws SAXException;      constant
```

```
// Methods Implementing ErrorHandler
    public void error(SAXParseException e) throws SAXException;                    empty
    public void fatalError(SAXParseException e) throws SAXException;
    public void warning(SAXParseException e) throws SAXException;                  empty
}
```

Passed To javax.xml.parsers.SAXParser.parse()

InputSource Java 1.4

org.xml.sax

This simple class describes a source of input for an XMLReader. An InputSource object can be passed to the parse() method of XMLReader, and is also the return value of the EntityResolver.resolveEntity() method.

Create an InputSource() with one of the constructor methods, specifying the system identifier (a URL) of the file to be parsed, or specifying a byte or character stream that the parser should read the document from. In addition to calling the constructor, you may also want to call setSystemId() to specify and/or setPublicId() to provide identifiers for the document being parsed. Having a filename or URL is useful if an error arises, and your ErrorHandler object needs to print an error message, for example. If you specify the document to parse as a URL or as a byte stream, you can also call setEncoding() to specify the character encoding of the document. The parser will use this encoding value if you supply it, but XML documents are supposed to describe their own encoding in the <?xml?> declaration, so the parser ought to be able to determine the encoding of the document even if you do not call setEncoding().

This class allows you to specify more than one input source. The XMLReader will first call getCharacterStream() and use the returned Reader if there is one. If that method returns false, then it calls getByteStream() and uses the InputStream it returns. Finally, if no character or byte stream is found, then the parser will call getSystemId() and will attempt to read an XML document from the returned URL.

An XMLReader will never use any of the set() methods to modify the state of an InputSource object.

```
public class InputSource {
// Public Constructors
    public InputSource();
    public InputSource(java.io.Reader characterStream);
    public InputSource(java.io.InputStream byteStream);
    public InputSource(String systemId);
// Public Instance Methods
    public java.io.InputStream getByteStream();                                default:null
    public java.io.Reader getCharacterStream();                                default:null
    public String getEncoding();                                               default:null
    public String getPublicId();                                               default:null
    public String getSystemId();                                               default:null
    public void setByteStream(java.io.InputStream byteStream);
    public void setCharacterStream(java.io.Reader characterStream);
    public void setEncoding(String encoding);
    public void setPublicId(String publicId);
    public void setSystemId(String systemId);
}
```

Passed To javax.xml.parsers.DocumentBuilder.parse(), javax.xml.parsers.SAXParser.parse(), javax.xml.transform.sax.SAXSource.{SAXSource(), setInputSource()}, javax.xml.xpath.XPath.evaluate(), javax.xml.xpath.XPathExpression.evaluate(), Parser.parse(), XMLReader.parse(), org.xml.sax.helpers.ParserAdapter.parse(), org.xml.sax.helpers.XMLFilterImpl.parse(), org.xml.sax.helpers.XMLReaderAdapter.parse()

Returned By javax.xml.transform.sax.SAXSource.{getInputSource(), sourceToInputSource()}, EntityResolver.resolveEntity(), HandlerBase.resolveEntity(), org.xml.sax.ext.DefaultHandler2.{getExternalSubset(), resolveEntity()}, org.xml.sax.ext.EntityResolver2.{getExternalSubset(), resolveEntity()}, org.xml.sax.helpers.DefaultHandler.resolveEntity(), org.xml.sax.helpers.XMLFilterImpl.resolveEntity()

Locator — Java 1.4

org.xml.sax

A XMLReader may pass an object that implements this interface to the application by calling the setDocumentLocator() method of the application's ContentHandler object before it invokes any other methods of that ContentHandler. The ContentHandler can use methods of this Locator object from within any of the other methods called by the parser in order to determine what document the parser is parsing and what line number and column number it is parsing at. This information is particularly useful when displaying error or warning messages, for example. getSystemId() and getPublicId() return the system and public identifiers of the document being parsed, if this information is available to the parser, and otherwise return null. getLineNumber() and getColumnNumber() return the line number and column number of the next character that the parser will read (line and column numbers are numbered starting at 1, not at 0). The parser is allowed to return an approximate value from these methods, or to return -1 if it does not track line and column numbers.

```
public interface Locator {
// Public Instance Methods
   int getColumnNumber();
   int getLineNumber();
   String getPublicId();
   String getSystemId();
}
```

Implementations org.xml.sax.ext.Locator2, org.xml.sax.helpers.LocatorImpl

Passed To org.xml.sax.ContentHandler.setDocumentLocator(), DocumentHandler.setDocumentLocator(), HandlerBase.setDocumentLocator(), SAXParseException.SAXParseException(), org.xml.sax.ext.Locator2Impl.Locator2Impl(), org.xml.sax.helpers.DefaultHandler.setDocumentLocator(), org.xml.sax.helpers.LocatorImpl.LocatorImpl(), org.xml.sax.helpers.ParserAdapter.setDocumentLocator(), org.xml.sax.helpers.XMLFilterImpl.setDocumentLocator(), org.xml.sax.helpers.XMLReaderAdapter.setDocumentLocator()

Parser — Java 1.4; Deprecated in 1.4

org.xml.sax

This interface is part of the SAX1 API and has been deprecated in favor of the SAX2 XMLReader interface, which supports XML namespaces.

```
public interface Parser {
// Public Instance Methods
   void parse(InputSource source) throws SAXException, java.io.IOException;
   void parse(String systemId) throws SAXException, java.io.IOException;
```

```
    void setDocumentHandler(DocumentHandler handler);
    void setDTDHandler(DTDHandler handler);
    void setEntityResolver(EntityResolver resolver);
    void setErrorHandler(ErrorHandler handler);
    void setLocale(java.util.Locale locale) throws SAXException;
}
```

Implementations org.xml.sax.helpers.XMLReaderAdapter

Passed To org.xml.sax.helpers.ParserAdapter.ParserAdapter()

Returned By javax.xml.parsers.SAXParser.getParser(), org.xml.sax.helpers.ParserFactory.makeParser()

SAXException — Java 1.4

org.xml.sax — serializable checked

Signals a problem while parsing an XML document. This class serves as the general superclass for more specific types of SAX exceptions. The parse() method of an XMLReader can throw an exception of this type. The application can also throw a SAXException from any of the handler methods (of ContentHandler and ErrorHandler for example) invoked by the parser.

Object — Throwable — Exception — SAXException
Serializable

```
public class SAXException extends Exception {
// Public Constructors
5.0 public SAXException();
    public SAXException(String message);
    public SAXException(Exception e);
    public SAXException(String message, Exception e);
// Public Instance Methods
    public Exception getException();                    default:null
// Public Methods Overriding Throwable
    public String getMessage();                         default:null
    public String toString();
}
```

Subclasses SAXNotRecognizedException, SAXNotSupportedException, SAXParseException

Thrown By Too many methods to list.

SAXNotRecognizedException — Java 1.4

org.xml.sax — serializable checked

Signals that the parser does not recognize a feature or property name. See the setFeature() and setProperty() methods of XMLReader.

Object — Throwable — Exception — SAXException — SAXNotRecognizedException
Serializable

```
public class SAXNotRecognizedException extends SAXException {
// Public Constructors
5.0 public SAXNotRecognizedException();
    public SAXNotRecognizedException(String message);
}
```

Thrown By Too many methods to list.

SAXNotSupportedException — Java 1.4

org.xml.sax — serializable checked

Signals that the parser does recognizes, but does not support a named feature or property. The property or feature may be entirely unsupported, or it may be read-only, in which case this exception will be thrown by the setFeature() or setProperty() method, but not by the corresponding getFeature() or getProperty() method of XMLReader.

Object — Throwable — Exception — SAXException — SAXNotSupportedException
Serializable

```
public class SAXNotSupportedException extends SAXException {
// Public Constructors
5.0 public SAXNotSupportedException();
    public SAXNotSupportedException(String message);
}
```

Thrown By Too many methods to list.

SAXParseException — Java 1.4

org.xml.sax — serializable checked

An exception of this type signals an XML parsing error or warning. SAXParseException includes methods to return the system and public identifiers of the document in which the error or warning occurred, as well as methods to return the approximate line number and column number at which it occurred. A parser is not required to obtain or track all of this information, and the methods may return null or -1 if the information is not available. (See Locator for more information.)

Exceptions of this type are usually thrown by the application from the methods of the ErrorHandler interface. The parser never throws a SAXParseException itself, but does pass an appropriately initialized instance of this class to each of the ErrorHandler methods. It is up to the application's ErrorHandler object to decide whether to actually throw the exception, however.

Object — Throwable — Exception — SAXException — SAXParseException
Serializable

```
public class SAXParseException extends SAXException {
// Public Constructors
    public SAXParseException(String message, Locator locator);
    public SAXParseException(String message, Locator locator, Exception e);
    public SAXParseException(String message, String publicId, String systemId, int lineNumber, int columnNumber);
    public SAXParseException(String message, String publicId, String systemId, int lineNumber, int columnNumber,
                             Exception e);
// Public Instance Methods
    public int getColumnNumber();
    public int getLineNumber();
    public String getPublicId();
    public String getSystemId();
}
```

Passed To ErrorHandler.{error(), fatalError(), warning()}, HandlerBase.{error(), fatalError(), warning()}, org.xml.sax.helpers.DefaultHandler.{error(), fatalError(), warning()}, org.xml.sax.helpers.XMLFilterImpl.{error(), fatalError(), warning()}

XMLFilter Java 1.4

org.xml.sax

An XMLFilter extends XMLReader and behaves like an XMLReader except that instead of parsing a document itself, it filters the SAX events provided by a "parent" XMLReader object. Use the setParent() method to link an XMLFilter object to the XMLReader that it is to serve as a filter for.

An XMLFilter serves as both a source of SAX events, and also as a receipient of those events, so an implementation must implement ContentHandler and related interfaces so that it can obtain events from the parent object, filter them, and then pass the filtered events on to the ContentHandler object that was registered on the filter. See the helper class org.xml.sax.helpers.XMLFilterImpl for a bare-bones implementation of an XMLFilter that implements the XMLReader interface and the ContentHandler and related handler interfaces. XMLFilterImpl does no filtering—it simply passes passes all of its method invocations through. You can subclass it and override only the methods that need filtering.

XMLReader ··· XMLFilter

```
public interface XMLFilter extends XMLReader {
// Public Instance Methods
   XMLReader getParent();
   void setParent(XMLReader parent);
}
```

Implementations org.xml.sax.helpers.XMLFilterImpl

Returned By javax.xml.transform.sax.SAXTransformerFactory.newXMLFilter()

XMLReader Java 1.4

org.xml.sax

This interface defines the methods that must be implemented by a SAX2 XML parser. Since it is an interface, XMLReader cannot define a constructor for creating an XMLReader. To obtain an XMLReader, object, you can instantiate some implementation-specific class that implements this interface. Alternatively, you can keep your code independent of any specific parser implementation by using the SAXParserFactory and SAXParser classes of the javax.xml.parsers package. See those classes for more details. Note that the XMLReader interface has no relationship to the java.io.Reader class or any other character stream classes.

Once you have obtained an XMLReader instance, you must register handler objects on it, so that it can invoke methods on those handlers to notify your application of the results of its parsing. All applications should register a ContentHandler and an ErrorHandler with setContentHandler() and setErrorHandler(). Some applications may also want to register an EntityResolver and/or a DTDHandler. Applications can also register DeclHandler and LexicalHandler objects from the org.xml.sax.ext package, if the parser implementation supports these extension handler interfaces. DeclHandler and LexicalHandler objects are registered with setProperty(), as explained below.

In addition to registering handler objects for an XMLReader, you may also want to configure the behavior of the parser using setFeature() and setProperty(). Features and properties are both name/value pairs. For uniqueness, the names of features and properties are expressed as URLs (the URLs usually do not have any web content associated with them: they are merely unique identifiers). Features have boolean values, and properties have arbitrary object values. Features and properties are an extension mechanism, allowing an application to specify implementation-specific details about how the parser should behave. But there are also several "standard" features and properties that are supported by many (or all) SAX parsers. They are listed below. If a parser does not recognize the name of a feature or property, the `setFeature()` and `setProperty()` methods (as well as the corresponding `getFeature()` and `getProperty()` query methods) throw a `SAXNotRecognizedException`. If the parser recognizes the name of a feature or property, but does not support the feature or property, the methods instead throw a `SAXNotSupportedException`. This exception is also thrown by the `set` methods when the parser allows the feature or property to be queried but not set.

The standard features are the following. Their names are all URLs that begin with the prefix "http://www.xml.org/sax/features/". For brevity, this prefix has been omitted below. Note that only two of these features must be supported by all parsers. The others may or may not be supported in any given implementation:

`namespaces`
: If `true` (the default), then the parser supports namespaces and provides the namespace URI and localname for element and attribute names. Support for this feature is required in all parser implementations .

`namespace-prefixes`
: If `true`, then the parser provides the qualified name (or "qName") that for element and attribute names. A qName consists of a namespace prefix, a colon, and the local name. The default value of this feature is `false`, and support for the feature is required in all parser implementations.

`validation`
: If `true`, then the parser will validate XML documents, and will read all external entities.

`external-general-entities`
: If `true`, then the parser handles external general entities. This is always `true` if the `validation` feature is `true`.

`external-parameter-entities`
: If `true`, then the parser handles external parameter entities. This is always `true` if the `validation` feature is `true`.

`lexical-handler/parameter-entities`
: If `true`, then the parser will report the begining and end of parameter entities to the `LexicalHandler` extension interface.

`string-interning`
: If `true`, then the parser will use the `String.intern()` method for all strings (element, attribute, entity and notation names, and namespace prefixes and URIs) it returns. If the application does the same, it can use == equality testing for these strings rather than using the more expensive `equals()` method.

The standard properties are the following. Like the features, their names are all URLs that begin with the prefix (omitted below) "http://www.xml.org/sax/properties/". Note that support for all of these properties is optional.

`declaration-handler`
: An `org.xml.sax.ext.DeclHandler` object to which the parser will report the contents of the DTD.

`lexical-handler`
: An `org.xml.sax.ext.LexicalHandler` object on which the parser will make method calls to describe the lexical structure (such as comments and CDATA sections) of the XML document.

xml-string
: This is a read-only property, and can only be queried from within a handler method invoked by the parser. The value of this property is a String that contains the document content that triggered the current handler invocation.

dom-node
: An XMLReader that "parses" a DOM tree rather than the textual form of an XML document uses the value of this property as the org.w3c.dom.Node object at which it should begin parsing.

Finally, after you have obtained an XMLReader object, have queried and configured its features and properties, and have set a ContentHandler, ErrorHandler, and any other required handler objects, you are ready to parse an XML document. Do this by calling one of the parse() methods, specifying the document to parse either as a system identifier (a URL) or as an InputSource object (which allows the use of streams as well).

```
public interface XMLReader {
// Public Instance Methods
   org.xml.sax.ContentHandler getContentHandler();
   DTDHandler getDTDHandler();
   EntityResolver getEntityResolver();
   ErrorHandler getErrorHandler();
   boolean getFeature(String name) throws SAXNotRecognizedException, SAXNotSupportedException;
   Object getProperty(String name) throws SAXNotRecognizedException, SAXNotSupportedException;
   void parse(String systemId) throws java.io.IOException, SAXException;
   void parse(InputSource input) throws java.io.IOException, SAXException;
   void setContentHandler(org.xml.sax.ContentHandler handler);
   void setDTDHandler(DTDHandler handler);
   void setEntityResolver(EntityResolver resolver);
   void setErrorHandler(ErrorHandler handler);
   void setFeature(String name, boolean value) throws SAXNotRecognizedException, SAXNotSupportedException;
   void setProperty(String name, Object value) throws SAXNotRecognizedException, SAXNotSupportedException;
}
```

Implementations XMLFilter, org.xml.sax.helpers.ParserAdapter

Passed To javax.xml.transform.sax.SAXSource.{SAXSource(), setXMLReader()}, XMLFilter.setParent(), org.xml.sax.helpers.XMLFilterImpl.{setParent(), XMLFilterImpl()}, org.xml.sax.helpers.XMLReaderAdapter.XMLReaderAdapter()

Returned By javax.xml.parsers.SAXParser.getXMLReader(), javax.xml.transform.sax.SAXSource.getXMLReader(), XMLFilter.getParent(), org.xml.sax.helpers.XMLFilterImpl.getParent(), org.xml.sax.helpers.XMLReaderFactory.createXMLReader()

Package org.xml.sax.ext — Java 1.4

This package defines extensions to the basic SAX2 API. Neither SAX parsers nor SAX applications are required to support these extensions, but when they do, the interfaces defined here provide a standard way for the parser to provide additional information about an XML document to the application. DeclHandler defines methods for reporting the content of a DTD, and LexicalHandler defines methods for reporting the lexical structure of an XML document.

In Java 5.0 adopts "SAX2 Extensions 1.1" and adds three new interfaces to this package: Attributes2, EntityResolver2, and Locator2. Each extends a similarly named interface from the core org.xml.sax package.

Interfaces

public interface **Attributes2** extends org.xml.sax.Attributes;
public interface **DeclHandler**;
public interface **EntityResolver2** extends org.xml.sax.EntityResolver;
public interface **LexicalHandler**;
public interface **Locator2** extends org.xml.sax.Locator;

Classes

public class **Attributes2Impl** extends org.xml.sax.helpers.AttributesImpl implements Attributes2;
public class **DefaultHandler2** extends org.xml.sax.helpers.DefaultHandler implements DeclHandler, EntityResolver2, LexicalHandler;
public class **Locator2Impl** extends org.xml.sax.helpers.LocatorImpl implements Locator2;

Attributes2 — Java 5.0

org.xml.sax.ext

This interface extends org.xml.sax.Attributes and adds methods for determining if an attribute was declared in the DTD and whether an attribute value was explicitly specified in the document or whether a default value from the DTD was used. If the SAX implementation supports this interface, the Attributes object passed to the startElement() method of the ContentHandler implements this interface. You can also test for support by querying the feature named "http://xml.org/sax/features/use-attributes2" with XMLReader.getFeature().

Attributes ··· Attributes2

```
public interface Attributes2 extends org.xml.sax.Attributes {
// Public Instance Methods
   boolean isDeclared(String qName);
   boolean isDeclared(int index);
   boolean isDeclared(String uri, String localName);
   boolean isSpecified(String qName);
   boolean isSpecified(int index);
   boolean isSpecified(String uri, String localName);
}
```

Implementations Attributes2Impl

Attributes2Impl — Java 5.0

org.xml.sax.ext

This extension helper class extends the org.xml.sax.helpers.AttributesImpl class to make it implement the Attributes2 interface.

Object — AttributesImpl — Attributes2Impl
Attributes (AttributesImpl) · Attributes ··· Attributes2 (Attributes2Impl)

```
public class Attributes2Impl extends org.xml.sax.helpers.AttributesImpl implements Attributes2 {
// Public Constructors
   public Attributes2Impl();
   public Attributes2Impl(org.xml.sax.Attributes atts);
// Public Instance Methods
   public void setDeclared(int index, boolean value);
   public void setSpecified(int index, boolean value);
// Methods Implementing Attributes2
```

```
    public boolean isDeclared(String qName);
    public boolean isDeclared(int index);
    public boolean isDeclared(String uri, String localName);
    public boolean isSpecified(String qName);
    public boolean isSpecified(int index);
    public boolean isSpecified(String uri, String localName);
// Public Methods Overriding AttributesImpl
    public void addAttribute(String uri, String localName, String qName, String type, String value);
    public void removeAttribute(int index);
    public void setAttributes(org.xml.sax.Attributes atts);
}
```

DeclHandler — Java 1.4

org.xml.sax.ext

This extension interface defines methods that a SAX parser can call to notify an application about element, attribute, and entity declarations in a DTD. If your application requires this information about a DTD, then pass an object that implements this interface to the setProperty() method of an XMLReader, using the property name "http://www.xml.org/sax/properties/declaration-handler". Because this is an extension handler, SAX parsers are not required to support it, and may throw a SAXNotRecognizedException or a SAXNotSupportedException when you attempt to register a DeclHandler.

```
public interface DeclHandler {
// Public Instance Methods
    void attributeDecl(String eName, String aName, String type, String mode, String value)
        throws org.xml.sax.SAXException;
    void elementDecl(String name, String model) throws org.xml.sax.SAXException;
    void externalEntityDecl(String name, String publicId, String systemId) throws org.xml.sax.SAXException;
    void internalEntityDecl(String name, String value) throws org.xml.sax.SAXException;
}
```

Implementations DefaultHandler2

DefaultHandler2 — Java 5.0

org.xml.sax.ext

This class extends org.xml.sax.helpers.DefaultHandler to add no-op methods that implement the LexicalHandler, DeclHandler, and EntityResolver2 methods. It overrides the two-argument version of resolveEntity from the core EntityResolver interface to invoke the four-argument version from the EntityResolver2 interface.

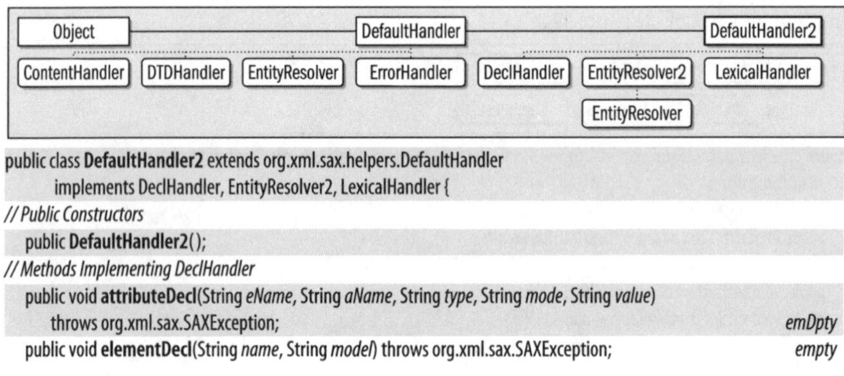


```
public class DefaultHandler2 extends org.xml.sax.helpers.DefaultHandler
        implements DeclHandler, EntityResolver2, LexicalHandler {
// Public Constructors
    public DefaultHandler2();
// Methods Implementing DeclHandler
    public void attributeDecl(String eName, String aName, String type, String mode, String value)
        throws org.xml.sax.SAXException;                                                    emDpty
    public void elementDecl(String name, String model) throws org.xml.sax.SAXException;     empty
```

```
    public void externalEntityDecl(String name, String publicId, String systemId) throws org.xml.sax.SAXException;    empty
    public void internalEntityDecl(String name, String value) throws org.xml.sax.SAXException;                      empty
// Methods Implementing EntityResolver
    public org.xml.sax.InputSource resolveEntity(String publicId, String systemId)
        throws org.xml.sax.SAXException, java.io.IOException;
// Methods Implementing EntityResolver2
    public org.xml.sax.InputSource getExternalSubset(String name, String baseURI)
        throws org.xml.sax.SAXException, java.io.IOException;                                                    constant
    public org.xml.sax.InputSource resolveEntity(String name, String publicId, String baseURI, String systemId)
        throws org.xml.sax.SAXException, java.io.IOException;                                                    constant
// Methods Implementing LexicalHandler
    public void comment(char[] ch, int start, int length) throws org.xml.sax.SAXException;                          empty
    public void endCDATA() throws org.xml.sax.SAXException;                                                        empty
    public void endDTD() throws org.xml.sax.SAXException;                                                          empty
    public void endEntity(String name) throws org.xml.sax.SAXException;                                            empty
    public void startCDATA() throws org.xml.sax.SAXException;                                                      empty
    public void startDTD(String name, String publicId, String systemId) throws org.xml.sax.SAXException;            empty
    public void startEntity(String name) throws org.xml.sax.SAXException;                                          empty
}
```

EntityResolver2 — Java 5.0

org.xml.sax.ext

This extension interface provides alternative entity resolver methods. If you register an entity resolver that implements this interface, if the SAX implementation supports this interface, and you set the feature "http://xml.org/sax/features/use-entity-resolver2" to true, then the implementation will use the methods defined by this interface instead of the method defined by the super-interface.

EntityResolver ··· EntityResolver2

```
public interface EntityResolver2 extends org.xml.sax.EntityResolver {
// Public Instance Methods
    org.xml.sax.InputSource getExternalSubset(String name, String baseURI)
        throws org.xml.sax.SAXException, java.io.IOException;
    org.xml.sax.InputSource resolveEntity(String name, String publicId, String baseURI, String systemId)
        throws org.xml.sax.SAXException, java.io.IOException;
}
```

Implementations DefaultHandler2

LexicalHandler — Java 1.4

org.xml.sax.ext

This extension interface defines methods that a SAX parser can call to notify an application about the lexical structure of an XML document. If your application requires this kind of information (for example if it wants to create a new document that has a similar structure to the one it reads), then pass an object that implements this interface to the setProperty() method of an XMLReader, using the property name "http://www.xml.org/sax/properties/lexical-handler". Because this is an extension handler, SAX parsers are not required to support it, and may throw a SAXNotRecognizedException or a SAXNotSupportedException when you attempt to register a DeclHandler.

If a LexicalHandler is successfully registered on an XMLReader, then the parser will call startDTD() and endDTD() to report the beginning and end of the document's DTD. It will call startCDATA() and endCDATA() to report the start and end of a CDATA section. The content of the CDATA section will be reported through the characters() method of the ContentHandler interface. When the parser expands an entity, it first calls startEntity() to specify the name of the entity it is about to expand, and then calls endEntity() when the entity expansion is complete. Finally, whenever the parser encounters an XML comment, it calls the comment() method.

```
public interface LexicalHandler {
// Public Instance Methods
   void comment(char[] ch, int start, int length) throws org.xml.sax.SAXException;
   void endCDATA() throws org.xml.sax.SAXException;
   void endDTD() throws org.xml.sax.SAXException;
   void endEntity(String name) throws org.xml.sax.SAXException;
   void startCDATA() throws org.xml.sax.SAXException;
   void startDTD(String name, String publicId, String systemId) throws org.xml.sax.SAXException;
   void startEntity(String name) throws org.xml.sax.SAXException;
}
```

Implementations javax.xml.transform.sax.TransformerHandler, DefaultHandler2

Passed To javax.xml.transform.sax.SAXResult.setLexicalHandler()

Returned By javax.xml.transform.sax.SAXResult.getLexicalHandler()

Locator2 — Java 5.0

org.xml.sax.ext

This interface defines an extension to the core Locator interface. If the implementation supports it, then the Locator object passed to ContentHandler.setDocumentLocator() will implement this interface. You can also test for support by querying the feature named "http://xml.org/sax/features/use-locator2".

Locator ··· Locator2

```
public interface Locator2 extends org.xml.sax.Locator {
// Public Instance Methods
   String getEncoding();
   String getXMLVersion();
}
```

Implementations Locator2Impl

Locator2Impl — Java 5.0

org.xml.sax.ext

This class extends the org.xml.sax.helpers.LocatorImpl class to make it implement the Locator2 interface.

Object — LocatorImpl — Locator2Impl

Locator | Locator ··· Locator2

```
public class Locator2Impl extends org.xml.sax.helpers.LocatorImpl implements Locator2 {
// Public Constructors
   public Locator2Impl();
   public Locator2Impl(org.xml.sax.Locator locator);
// Public Instance Methods
   public void setEncoding(String encoding);
   public void setXMLVersion(String version);
```

```
// Methods Implementing Locator2
   public String getEncoding();                                    default:null
   public String getXMLVersion();                                  default:null
}
```

Package org.xml.sax.helpers — Java 1.4

This package contains utility classes that are useful for programmers working with SAX parsers. DefaultHandler is the most commonly used: it is a default implementation of the four standard handler interfaces, suitable for easy subclassing by an application. XMLReaderFactory provides a layer implementation-independence, allowing an application to use an XMLReader implementation specified in a system property. XMLFilterImpl is a no-op implementation of the XMLFilter interface that also implements the various handler interfaces necessary to connect the filter to its "parent" XMLReader. It does no filtering of its own, but is easy to subclass to add filtering. If you need to work with legacy APIs that expect or return SAX1 Parser objects, you can use ParserAdapter to make a Parser object behave like a SAX2 XMLReader object, or use an XMLReaderAdapter to make an XMLReader behave like a Parser.

Classes

```
public class AttributeListImpl implements org.xml.sax.AttributeList;
public class AttributesImpl implements org.xml.sax.Attributes;
public class DefaultHandler implements org.xml.sax.ContentHandler, org.xml.sax.DTDHandler, org.xml.sax.EntityResolver,
org.xml.sax.ErrorHandler;
public class LocatorImpl implements org.xml.sax.Locator;
public class NamespaceSupport;
public class ParserAdapter implements org.xml.sax.DocumentHandler, org.xml.sax.XMLReader;
public class ParserFactory;
public class XMLFilterImpl implements org.xml.sax.ContentHandler, org.xml.sax.DTDHandler, org.xml.sax.EntityResolver,
org.xml.sax.ErrorHandler, org.xml.sax.XMLFilter;
public class XMLReaderAdapter implements org.xml.sax.ContentHandler, org.xml.sax.Parser;
public final class XMLReaderFactory;
```

AttributeListImpl — Java 1.4; Deprecated in 1.4

org.xml.sax.helpers

This deprecated class is an implementation of the deprecated SAX1 org.xml.sax.AttributeList interface. They have been deprecated in favor of the AttributesImpl implementation of the SAX2 org.xml.sax.Attributes interface.

Object — AttributeListImpl ··· AttributeList

```
public class AttributeListImpl implements org.xml.sax.AttributeList {
// Public Constructors
   public AttributeListImpl();
   public AttributeListImpl(org.xml.sax.AttributeList atts);
// Public Instance Methods
   public void addAttribute(String name, String type, String value);
   public void clear();
   public void removeAttribute(String name);
   public void setAttributeList(org.xml.sax.AttributeList atts);
// Methods Implementing AttributeList
   public int getLength();                                         default:0
```

SAX

```
    public String getName(int i);
    public String getType(int i);
    public String getType(String name);
    public String getValue(String name);
    public String getValue(int i);
}
```

AttributesImpl **Java 1.4**

org.xml.sax.helpers

This utility class is a general-purpose implementation of the Attributes interface. In addition to implementing all the methods of Attributes, it also defines various set methods for setting attribute names, values, and types, an addAttribute() method for adding a new attribute to the end of the list, a removeAttribute() method for removing an attribute from the list, and a clear() method for removing all attributes. Also, there is an AttributesImpl() constructor that initializes the new AttributesImpl object with a copy of a specified Attributes object. This class is useful for XMLFilter implementations that want to filter the attributes of an element, or for ContentHandler implementations that need to make and save a copy of an Attributes object for later use.

Object — AttributesImpl ··· Attributes

```
public class AttributesImpl implements org.xml.sax.Attributes {
// Public Constructors
    public AttributesImpl();
    public AttributesImpl(org.xml.sax.Attributes atts);
// Public Instance Methods
    public void addAttribute(String uri, String localName, String qName, String type, String value);
    public void clear();
    public void removeAttribute(int index);
    public void setAttribute(int index, String uri, String localName, String qName, String type, String value);
    public void setAttributes(org.xml.sax.Attributes atts);
    public void setLocalName(int index, String localName);
    public void setQName(int index, String qName);
    public void setType(int index, String type);
    public void setURI(int index, String uri);
    public void setValue(int index, String value);
// Methods Implementing Attributes
    public int getIndex(String qName);
    public int getIndex(String uri, String localName);
    public int getLength();                                                   default:0
    public String getLocalName(int index);
    public String getQName(int index);
    public String getType(String qName);
    public String getType(int index);
    public String getType(String uri, String localName);
    public String getURI(int index);
    public String getValue(int index);
    public String getValue(String qName);
    public String getValue(String uri, String localName);
}
```

Subclasses org.xml.sax.ext.Attributes2Impl

DefaultHandler **Java 1.4**

org.xml.sax.helpers

This helper class implements the four commonly-used SAX handler interfaces from the org.xml.sax package and defines stub implementations for all of their methods. It is usually easier to subclass DefaultHandler and override the desired methods than it is to implement all of the interfaces (and all of their methods) from scratch. DefaultHandler implements ContentHandler, ErrorHandler, EntityResolver and DTDHandler, so you can pass an instance of this class, (or of a subclass you define) to the setContentHandler(), setErrorHandler(), setEntityResolver(), and setDTDHandler() methods of an XMLReader. You can also pass an instance of a DefaultHandler subclass directly to one of the parse() methods of a javax.xml.parsers.SAXParser. The SAXParser will take care of calling the four relevant methods of its internal XMLReader.

All but two of the methods of DefaultHandler have empty bodies and do nothing. The exceptions are resolveEntity() which simply returns null to tell the parser to resolve the entity itself, and fatalError() which throws the SAXParseException object that is passed to it.

Object → DefaultHandler
ContentHandler | DTDHandler | EntityResolver | ErrorHandler

```
public class DefaultHandler
        implements org.xml.sax.ContentHandler, org.xml.sax.DTDHandler, org.xml.sax.EntityResolver,
        org.xml.sax.ErrorHandler{
// Public Constructors
    public DefaultHandler();
// Methods Implementing ContentHandler
    public void characters(char[] ch, int start, int length) throws org.xml.sax.SAXException;          empty
    public void endDocument() throws org.xml.sax.SAXException;                                            empty
    public void endElement(String uri, String localName, String qName) throws org.xml.sax.SAXException;  empty
    public void endPrefixMapping(String prefix) throws org.xml.sax.SAXException;                          empty
    public void ignorableWhitespace(char[] ch, int start, int length) throws org.xml.sax.SAXException;   empty
    public void processingInstruction(String target, String data) throws org.xml.sax.SAXException;       empty
    public void setDocumentLocator(org.xml.sax.Locator locator);                                          empty
    public void skippedEntity(String name) throws org.xml.sax.SAXException;                               empty
    public void startDocument() throws org.xml.sax.SAXException;                                          empty
    public void startElement(String uri, String localName, String qName, org.xml.sax.Attributes attributes)
        throws org.xml.sax.SAXException;                                                                  empty
    public void startPrefixMapping(String prefix, String uri) throws org.xml.sax.SAXException;            empty
// Methods Implementing DTDHandler
    public void notationDecl(String name, String publicId, String systemId) throws org.xml.sax.SAXException;  empty
    public void unparsedEntityDecl(String name, String publicId, String systemId, String notationName)
        throws org.xml.sax.SAXException;                                                                  empty
// Methods Implementing EntityResolver
    public org.xml.sax.InputSource resolveEntity(String publicId, String systemId)
        throws java.io.IOException, org.xml.sax.SAXException;                                             constant
// Methods Implementing ErrorHandler
    public void error(org.xml.sax.SAXParseException e) throws org.xml.sax.SAXException;                  empty
    public void fatalError(org.xml.sax.SAXParseException e) throws org.xml.sax.SAXException;
    public void warning(org.xml.sax.SAXParseException e) throws org.xml.sax.SAXException;                empty
}
```

Subclasses org.xml.sax.ext.DefaultHandler2

Passed To javax.xml.parsers.SAXParser.parse()

LocatorImpl Java 1.4

org.xml.sax.helpers

This helper class is a very simple implementation of the Locator interface. It defines a copy constructor that create a new LocatorImpl object that copies the state of a specified Locator object. This constructor is useful because it allows applications to copy the state of a Locator and save it for later use.

Object ─ LocatorImpl ··· Locator

```
public class LocatorImpl implements org.xml.sax.Locator {
// Public Constructors
   public LocatorImpl();
   public LocatorImpl(org.xml.sax.Locator locator);
// Public Instance Methods
   public void setColumnNumber(int columnNumber);
   public void setLineNumber(int lineNumber);
   public void setPublicId(String publicId);
   public void setSystemId(String systemId);
// Methods Implementing Locator
   public int getColumnNumber();                                    default:0
   public int getLineNumber();                                      default:0
   public String getPublicId();                                     default:null
   public String getSystemId();                                     default:null
}
```

Subclasses org.xml.sax.ext.Locator2Impl

NamespaceSupport Java 1.4

org.xml.sax.helpers

This utility class exists to help SAX parser implementors handle XML namespaces. It is not commonly used by SAX applications.

```
public class NamespaceSupport {
// Public Constructors
   public NamespaceSupport();
// Public Constants
5.0 public static final String NSDECL;                    ="http://www.w3.org/xmlns/2000/"
   public static final String XMLNS;            ="http://www.w3.org/XML/1998/namespace"
// Public Instance Methods
   public boolean declarePrefix(String prefix, String uri);
   public java.util.Enumeration getDeclaredPrefixes();
   public String getPrefix(String uri);
   public java.util.Enumeration getPrefixes();
   public java.util.Enumeration getPrefixes(String uri);
   public String getURI(String prefix);
5.0 public boolean isNamespaceDeclUris();                           default:false
   public void popContext();
   public String[] processName(String qName, String[] parts, boolean isAttribute);
   public void pushContext();
   public void reset();
5.0 public void setNamespaceDeclUris(boolean value);
}
```

ParserAdapter **Java 1.4**

org.xml.sax.helpers

This adapter class behaves like a SAX2 **XMLReader** object, but gets its input from the SAX1 **Parser** object that is passed to the constructor. In order to make this work, it implements the deprecated SAX1 **DocumentHandler** interface so that it can receive events from the **Parser**. **ParserAdapter** provides its own layer of namespace processing to convert a namespace-unaware **Parser** into a namespace-aware **XMLReader**. This class is useful when working you are working with a legacy API that supplies a SAX1 **Parser** object, but want to work with that parser using the SAX2 **XMLReader** API: to use it, simply pass the **Parser** object to the **ParserAdapter()** constructor and use the resulting object as you would use any other **XMLReader** object.

There is not perfect congruence between the SAX1 and SAX2 APIs, and a **Parser** cannot be perfectly adapted to a **XMLReader**. In particular, a **ParserAdapter** will never call the **skippedEntity()** handler method because the SAX1 **Parser** API does not provide notification of skipped entities. Also, it does not attempt to determine whether two namespace-prefixed attributes of an element actually resolve to the same attribute.

See also **XMLReaderAdapter**, an adapter that works in the reverse direction to make a SAX2 parser behave like a SAX1 parser.

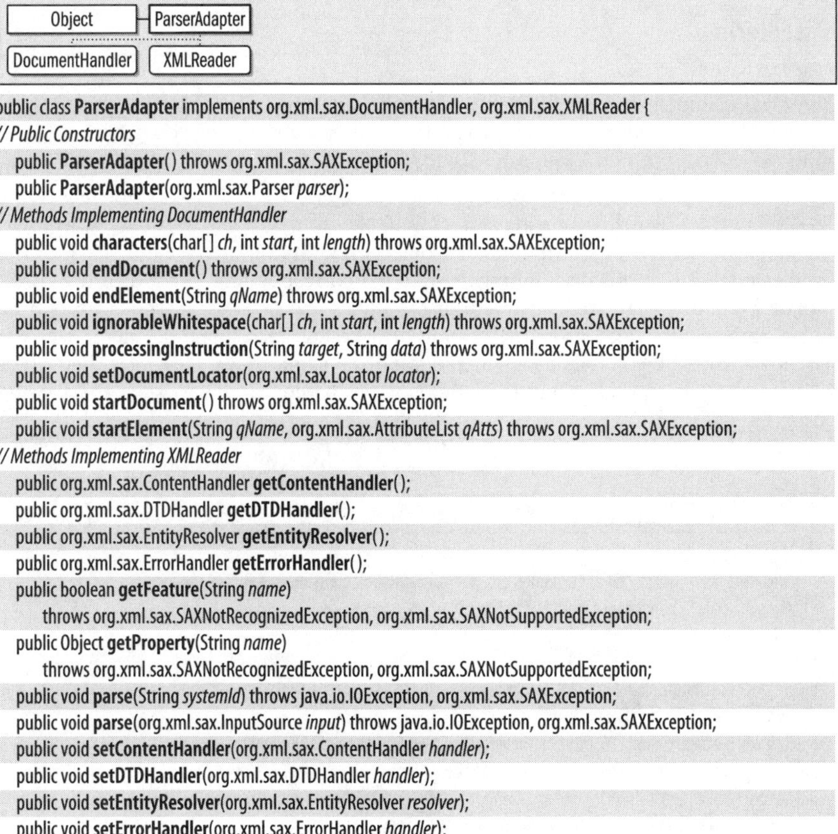


```
public class ParserAdapter implements org.xml.sax.DocumentHandler, org.xml.sax.XMLReader {
// Public Constructors
   public ParserAdapter() throws org.xml.sax.SAXException;
   public ParserAdapter(org.xml.sax.Parser parser);
// Methods Implementing DocumentHandler
   public void characters(char[] ch, int start, int length) throws org.xml.sax.SAXException;
   public void endDocument() throws org.xml.sax.SAXException;
   public void endElement(String qName) throws org.xml.sax.SAXException;
   public void ignorableWhitespace(char[] ch, int start, int length) throws org.xml.sax.SAXException;
   public void processingInstruction(String target, String data) throws org.xml.sax.SAXException;
   public void setDocumentLocator(org.xml.sax.Locator locator);
   public void startDocument() throws org.xml.sax.SAXException;
   public void startElement(String qName, org.xml.sax.AttributeList qAtts) throws org.xml.sax.SAXException;
// Methods Implementing XMLReader
   public org.xml.sax.ContentHandler getContentHandler();
   public org.xml.sax.DTDHandler getDTDHandler();
   public org.xml.sax.EntityResolver getEntityResolver();
   public org.xml.sax.ErrorHandler getErrorHandler();
   public boolean getFeature(String name)
      throws org.xml.sax.SAXNotRecognizedException, org.xml.sax.SAXNotSupportedException;
   public Object getProperty(String name)
      throws org.xml.sax.SAXNotRecognizedException, org.xml.sax.SAXNotSupportedException;
   public void parse(String systemId) throws java.io.IOException, org.xml.sax.SAXException;
   public void parse(org.xml.sax.InputSource input) throws java.io.IOException, org.xml.sax.SAXException;
   public void setContentHandler(org.xml.sax.ContentHandler handler);
   public void setDTDHandler(org.xml.sax.DTDHandler handler);
   public void setEntityResolver(org.xml.sax.EntityResolver resolver);
   public void setErrorHandler(org.xml.sax.ErrorHandler handler);
```

```
    public void setFeature(String name, boolean value)
        throws org.xml.sax.SAXNotRecognizedException, org.xml.sax.SAXNotSupportedException;
    public void setProperty(String name, Object value)
        throws org.xml.sax.SAXNotRecognizedException, org.xml.sax.SAXNotSupportedException;
}
```

ParserFactory **Java 1.4; Deprecated in 1.4**

org.xml.sax.helpers

This deprecated SAX1 class is a factory for deprecated SAX1 **Parser** objects. New applications should use the SAX2 **XMLReaderFactory** as a factory for SAX2 **XMLReader** objects.

```
public class ParserFactory {
// No Constructor
// Public Class Methods
    public static org.xml.sax.Parser makeParser()
        throws ClassNotFoundException, IllegalAccessException, InstantiationException, NullPointerException,
        ClassCastException;
    public static org.xml.sax.Parser makeParser(String className)
        throws ClassNotFoundException, IllegalAccessException, InstantiationException, ClassCastException;
}
```

XMLFilterImpl **Java 1.4**

org.xml.sax.helpers

This class is implements an **XMLFilter** that does no filtering. You can subclass it to override whatever methods are required to perform the type of filtering you desire.

XMLFilterImpl implements **ContentHandler**, **ErrorHandler**, **EntityResolver**, and **DTDHandler** so that it can receive SAX events from the "parent" **XMLReader** object. But it also implements the **XMLFilter** interface, which is an extension of **XMLReader**, so that it acts as an **XMLReader** itself, and can send SAX events to the handler objects that are registered on it. Each of the handler methods of this class simply invoke the corresponding method of the corresponding handler that was registered on the filter. The **XMLReader** methods for getting and setting features and properties simply invoke the corresponding method of the parent **XMLReader** object. The **parse()** methods do the same thing: they pass their argument to the corresponding **parse()** method of the parent reader to start the parsing process.

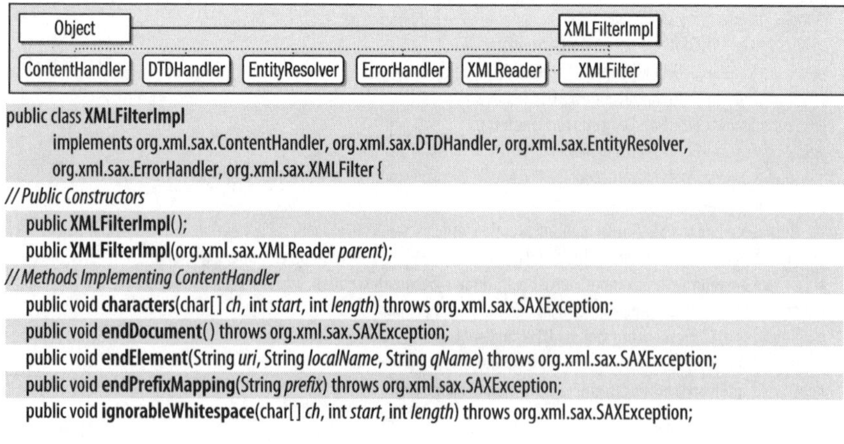


```
public class XMLFilterImpl
        implements org.xml.sax.ContentHandler, org.xml.sax.DTDHandler, org.xml.sax.EntityResolver,
        org.xml.sax.ErrorHandler, org.xml.sax.XMLFilter {
// Public Constructors
    public XMLFilterImpl();
    public XMLFilterImpl(org.xml.sax.XMLReader parent);
// Methods Implementing ContentHandler
    public void characters(char[ ] ch, int start, int length) throws org.xml.sax.SAXException;
    public void endDocument() throws org.xml.sax.SAXException;
    public void endElement(String uri, String localName, String qName) throws org.xml.sax.SAXException;
    public void endPrefixMapping(String prefix) throws org.xml.sax.SAXException;
    public void ignorableWhitespace(char[ ] ch, int start, int length) throws org.xml.sax.SAXException;
```

```
   public void processingInstruction(String target, String data) throws org.xml.sax.SAXException;
   public void setDocumentLocator(org.xml.sax.Locator locator);
   public void skippedEntity(String name) throws org.xml.sax.SAXException;
   public void startDocument() throws org.xml.sax.SAXException;
   public void startElement(String uri, String localName, String qName, org.xml.sax.Attributes atts)
       throws org.xml.sax.SAXException;
   public void startPrefixMapping(String prefix, String uri) throws org.xml.sax.SAXException;
// Methods Implementing DTDHandler
   public void notationDecl(String name, String publicId, String systemId) throws org.xml.sax.SAXException;
   public void unparsedEntityDecl(String name, String publicId, String systemId, String notationName)
       throws org.xml.sax.SAXException;
// Methods Implementing EntityResolver
   public org.xml.sax.InputSource resolveEntity(String publicId, String systemId)
       throws org.xml.sax.SAXException, java.io.IOException;
// Methods Implementing ErrorHandler
   public void error(org.xml.sax.SAXParseException e) throws org.xml.sax.SAXException;
   public void fatalError(org.xml.sax.SAXParseException e) throws org.xml.sax.SAXException;
   public void warning(org.xml.sax.SAXParseException e) throws org.xml.sax.SAXException;
// Methods Implementing XMLFilter
   public org.xml.sax.XMLReader getParent();                                          default:null
   public void setParent(org.xml.sax.XMLReader parent);
// Methods Implementing XMLReader
   public org.xml.sax.ContentHandler getContentHandler();                             default:null
   public org.xml.sax.DTDHandler getDTDHandler();                                     default:null
   public org.xml.sax.EntityResolver getEntityResolver();                             default:null
   public org.xml.sax.ErrorHandler getErrorHandler();                                 default:null
   public boolean getFeature(String name)
       throws org.xml.sax.SAXNotRecognizedException, org.xml.sax.SAXNotSupportedException;
   public Object getProperty(String name)
       throws org.xml.sax.SAXNotRecognizedException, org.xml.sax.SAXNotSupportedException;
   public void parse(String systemId) throws org.xml.sax.SAXException, java.io.IOException;
   public void parse(org.xml.sax.InputSource input) throws org.xml.sax.SAXException, java.io.IOException;
   public void setContentHandler(org.xml.sax.ContentHandler handler);
   public void setDTDHandler(org.xml.sax.DTDHandler handler);
   public void setEntityResolver(org.xml.sax.EntityResolver resolver);
   public void setErrorHandler(org.xml.sax.ErrorHandler handler);
   public void setFeature(String name, boolean value)
       throws org.xml.sax.SAXNotRecognizedException, org.xml.sax.SAXNotSupportedException;
   public void setProperty(String name, Object value)
       throws org.xml.sax.SAXNotRecognizedException, org.xml.sax.SAXNotSupportedException;
}
```

XMLReaderAdapter — Java 1.4

org.xml.sax.helpers

This adapter class wraps a SAX2 XMLReader object and makes it behave like a SAX1 Parser object. It is useful when working with a legacy API that requires a deprecated Parser object. Create an XMLReaderAdapter by passing an XMLReader to the XMLReaderAdapter() constructor. Then use the resulting object exactly as you would use any other SAX1 Parser object. This class implements ContentHandler so that it can receive SAX events from the XMLReader. But it also implements the Parser interface so that it can have a SAX1 DocumentHandler registered on it. The methods of ContentHandler are implemented to invoke the corresponding methods of the registered DocumentHandler.

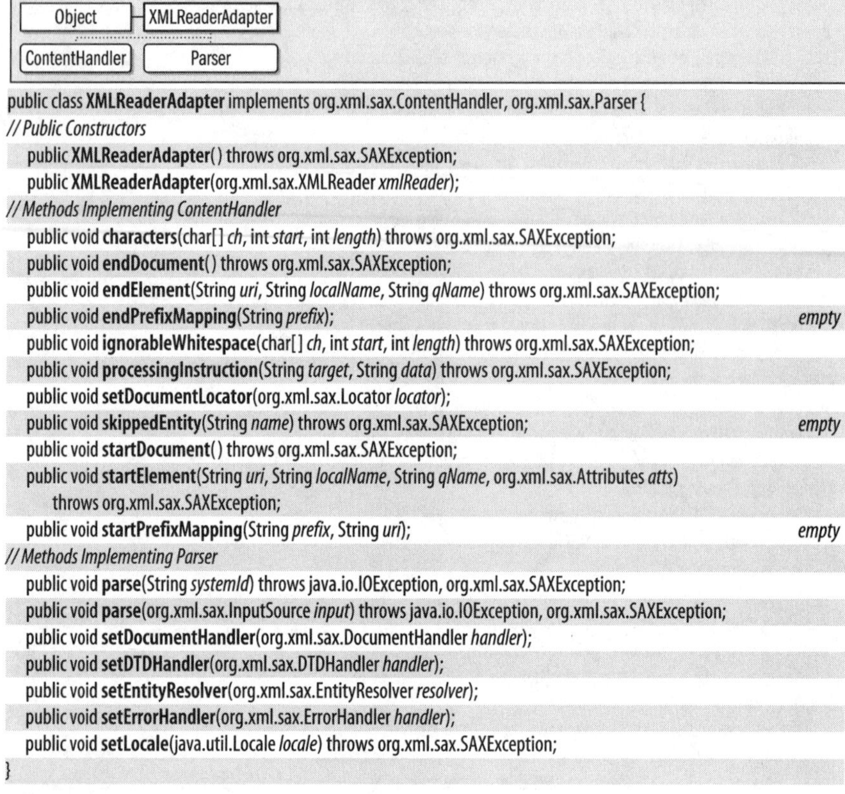


```
public class XMLReaderAdapter implements org.xml.sax.ContentHandler, org.xml.sax.Parser {
// Public Constructors
   public XMLReaderAdapter() throws org.xml.sax.SAXException;
   public XMLReaderAdapter(org.xml.sax.XMLReader xmlReader);
// Methods Implementing ContentHandler
   public void characters(char[] ch, int start, int length) throws org.xml.sax.SAXException;
   public void endDocument() throws org.xml.sax.SAXException;
   public void endElement(String uri, String localName, String qName) throws org.xml.sax.SAXException;
   public void endPrefixMapping(String prefix);                                          empty
   public void ignorableWhitespace(char[] ch, int start, int length) throws org.xml.sax.SAXException;
   public void processingInstruction(String target, String data) throws org.xml.sax.SAXException;
   public void setDocumentLocator(org.xml.sax.Locator locator);
   public void skippedEntity(String name) throws org.xml.sax.SAXException;               empty
   public void startDocument() throws org.xml.sax.SAXException;
   public void startElement(String uri, String localName, String qName, org.xml.sax.Attributes atts)
       throws org.xml.sax.SAXException;
   public void startPrefixMapping(String prefix, String uri);                            empty
// Methods Implementing Parser
   public void parse(String systemId) throws java.io.IOException, org.xml.sax.SAXException;
   public void parse(org.xml.sax.InputSource input) throws java.io.IOException, org.xml.sax.SAXException;
   public void setDocumentHandler(org.xml.sax.DocumentHandler handler);
   public void setDTDHandler(org.xml.sax.DTDHandler handler);
   public void setEntityResolver(org.xml.sax.EntityResolver resolver);
   public void setErrorHandler(org.xml.sax.ErrorHandler handler);
   public void setLocale(java.util.Locale locale) throws org.xml.sax.SAXException;
}
```

XMLReaderFactory — Java 1.4

org.xml.sax.helpers

This factory class defines two static factory methods for creating XMLReader objects. One method takes the name of a class as its argument. It dynamically loads and instantiates the class, then casts it to an XMLReader object. The second factory method takes no arguments; it reads the system property named "org.xml.sax.driver" and uses the value of that property as the name of the class XMLReader implementation class to load and instantiate. An application that instantiates its SAX parser using the no-argument method of XMLReaderFactory gains a layer of independence from the underlying parser implementation. The end user or system administrator of the system on which the application is deployed can change the parser implementation simply by setting a system property. Note that the javax.xml.parsers package provides a similar, but somewhat more useful SAXParserFactory.

```
public final class XMLReaderFactory {
// No Constructor
// Public Class Methods
   public static org.xml.sax.XMLReader createXMLReader() throws org.xml.sax.SAXException;
   public static org.xml.sax.XMLReader createXMLReader(String className) throws org.xml.sax.SAXException;
}
```

Class, Method, and Field Index

A

B

C

Class Index

Class Index

D

E

F

G

H

I

J

K

Class Index

L

M

Class Index

N

Class Index

O

P

Q

R

Class Index

S

Class Index

T

U

V

W

X

Y

Z

Index

Symbols

We'd like to hear your suggestions for improving our indexes. Send email to *index@oreilly.com*.

Numbers

A

B

C

D

E

F

G

H

I

J

K

L

M

N

O

P

S

T

U

V

W

X

Y

Z

About the Author

David Flanagan is a computer programmer who spends most of his time writing about Java and JavaScript. His other books with O'Reilly include *Java Examples in a Nutshell*, *Java Foundation Classes in a Nutshell*, and *Javascript: The Definitive Guide*. David has a degree in computer science and engineering from the Massachusetts Institute of Technology. He lives with his family in the U.S. Pacific Northwest, between the cities of Seattle, Washington and Vancouver, British Columbia.

Colophon

Our look is the result of reader comments, our own experimentation, and feedback from distribution channels. Distinctive covers complement our distinctive approach to technical topics, breathing personality and life into potentially dry subjects.

The animal on the cover of *Java in a Nutshell,* Fifth Edition is a Javan tiger, a subspecies unique to the island of Java. Although this tiger once offered unrivaled research opportunities due to its genetic isolation, these opportunities have been permanently lost due to human encroachment on the Javan tiger's habitat: in a worst-case scenario for the tiger, Java developed into the most densely populated island on earth, and awareness of the subspecies' precarious position came too late to secure the animals' survival even in captivity. The last known sighting of the tiger was in 1972, and it is now presumed extinct.

Jamie Peppard was the production editor and proofreader for *Java in a Nutshell,* Fifth Edition. Sarah Sherman, Darren Kelly, and Claire Cloutier provided quality control. Ellen Troutman Zaig wrote the index.

Edie Freedman designed the cover of this book. The cover image is a 19th-century engraving from the Dover Pictorial Archive. Emma Colby produced the cover layout with Adobe InDesign CS using Adobe's ITC Garamond font.

David Futato designed the interior layout. This book was converted by Andrew Savikas, Joe Wizda, and Ryan Grimm to FrameMaker 5.5.6 with a format conversion tool created by Erik Ray, Jason McIntosh, Neil Walls, and Mike Sierra that uses Perl and XML technologies. The text font is Linotype Birka; the heading font is Adobe Myriad Condensed; and the code font is LucasFont's TheSans Mono Condensed. The illustrations that appear in the book were produced by Robert Romano and Jessamyn Read using Macromedia FreeHand 9 and Adobe Photo-Shop 6. Jamie Peppard wrote this colophon.

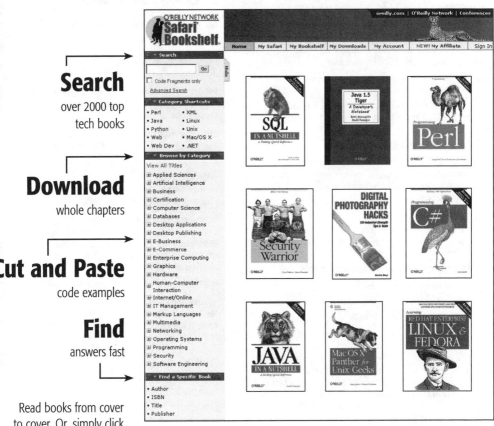

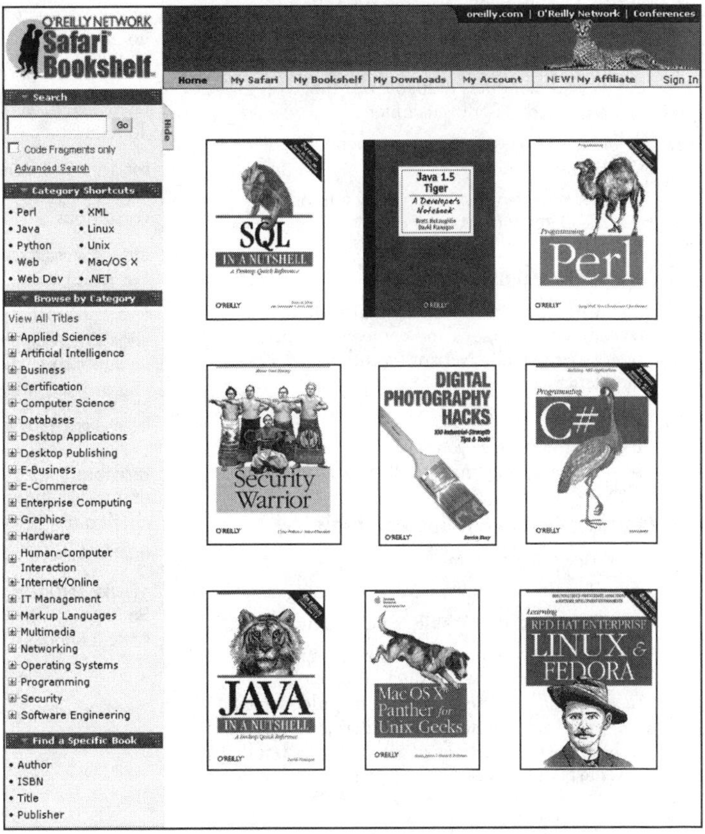

Keep in touch with O'Reilly

1. Download examples from our books

To find example files for a book, go to:

www.oreilly.com/catalog

select the book, and follow the "Examples" link.

2. Register your O'Reilly books

Register your book at *register.oreilly.com*

Why register your books? Once you've registered your O'Reilly books you can:

- Win O'Reilly books, T-shirts or discount coupons in our monthly drawing.
- Get special offers available only to registered O'Reilly customers.
- Get catalogs announcing new books (US and UK only).
- Get email notification of new editions of the O'Reilly books you own.

3. Join our email lists

Sign up to get topic-specific email announcements of new books and conferences, special offers, and O'Reilly Network technology newsletters at:

elists.oreilly.com

It's easy to customize your free elists subscription so you'll get exactly the O'Reilly news you want.

4. Get the latest news, tips, and tools

http://www.oreilly.com

- "Top 100 Sites on the Web"—PC Magazine
- CIO Magazine's Web Business 50 Awards

Our web site contains a library of comprehensive product information (including book excerpts and tables of contents), downloadable software, background articles, interviews with technology leaders, links to relevant sites, book cover art, and more.

5. Work for O'Reilly

Check out our web site for current employment opportunities:

jobs.oreilly.com

6. Contact us

O'Reilly & Associates
1005 Gravenstein Hwy North
Sebastopol, CA 95472 USA

TEL: 707-827-7000 or 800-998-9938
(6am to 5pm PST)

FAX: 707-829-0104

order@oreilly.com
For answers to problems regarding your order or our products.
To place a book order online, visit:

www.oreilly.com/order_new

catalog@oreilly.com
To request a copy of our latest catalog.

booktech@oreilly.com
For book content technical questions or corrections.

corporate@oreilly.com
For educational, library, government, and corporate sales.

proposals@oreilly.com
To submit new book proposals to our editors and product managers.

international@oreilly.com
For information about our international distributors or translation queries. For a list of our distributors outside of North America check out:

international.oreilly.com/distributors.html

adoption@oreilly.com
For information about academic use of O'Reilly books, visit:

academic.oreilly.com